The Spinning Wheel's Complete Book of Antiques

edited by

Albert Christian Revi

and the staff of
Spinning Wheel Magazine

Publishers

GROSSET & DUNLAP

New York

Published under arrangements with Ottenheimer Publishers, Inc.

Printed in the United States of America.

1977 Printing

ISBN: 0-448-01953-1

Library of Congress Catalog Card Number: 72-86565

CONTENTS

COLLECTOR PLATES

CLOCKS AND WATCHES

DOLLS

FANS AND FANCIES

FURNITURE

GLASS

GUNS AND KNIVES

JEWELRY

KITCHENWARES

LADIES CRAFTS

INTRODUCTION

In 1945, when the first edition of Spinning Wheel came off the presses in tabloid form, a standard for excellence of editorial material was established that has grown over the years. From the beginning, articles about antiques were sought from authorities in every field of collecting - well researched articles that contained new and interesting information about antique furniture, glass, ceramics, metalwares, primitives, clocks and watches, jewelry, and a host of other categories.

Many times Spinning Wheel has pioneered and fostered interest in new areas of collecting - fruit jars, bottles, ladies crafts, and country antiques of all kinds. Other antiques publications followed suit, but none of them has ever approached the quality of material offered to Spinning Wheel readers in each and every issue.

The contents of this book was very carefully selected by the editorial staff of Spinning Wheel from hundreds of articles that have appeared in our pages from 1945 to 1972. They represent the most authoritative information available in each category covered. Many of the authors of these articles went on in later years to write books based upon the initial research work done by them while writing their articles for Spinning Wheel. Such familiar names in the antiques field as Genevieve Angione, Ethel Hall Bjerkoe, Carl W. Drepperd, Lucile Henzke, Dorothy T. Rainwater, Marcia Ray, Albert Christian Revi, and Julian Harrison Toulouse, all at one time or another wrote articles for Spinning Wheel - some still do.

That Spinning Wheel is today the foremost magazine in its field is, due entirely to the diligence, dedication and foresight of its former editors - Marjorie M. Smith, Carl W. Drepperd and Marcia Ray, the latter still actively engaged in editorial work though in semi-retirement. To follow in the footsteps of these distinguished editors is a distinct privilege, and a real challenge.

Albert Christian Revi, Editor

ADVERTIQUES

A relatively new field in collecting, "Advertiques" are so broad in scope that anyone with an interest in glass, china, metalwares, woodenwares, and a host of other specialized interests, could easily include several pieces in their collection. Tin trays, china bibelots, souvenir spoons, kitchenwares, and trade cards, all fall into this category.

EARLY ADVERTISING

by KATHARINE MORRISON McCLINTON

AMERICAN business advertising had its start in the three-dimensional shop, tavern, toll, and gate signs that hung above the streets of mid-17th century towns and villages in America. The earliest tavern signs followed the design of those in England by using such names as Royal Arms, King's Head, and Queen's Head.

After the siege of Quebec, General Wolfe taverns were popular, and after the Revolution, taverns took the names of American heroes, Washington, Lafayette, Franklin, and other American historical figures. In the early 19th century, the American eagle, the American flag, the Liberty Pole, and the Goddess of Liberty were seen on signs. Other early inn signs had Biblical names, names of animals, of flowers and trees. The Indian Chief was a favorite.

One of the earliest trade signs was the "Sign of Bible" which hung over William Bradford's printing shop in New York in 1693. Watchmakers sold their wares at the Sign of the Dial; coppersmiths, brass, and tin workers used such signs as the Brass Andirons and Candlestick, the Block Tin Teapot. Iron furnaces put up the Sign of the Broad-Ax, and the Sign of the Golden Anvil and Hammer.

These signs were made of wood or metal cut in profile, painted or carved. They bore the name of the shop owner, his trade, and sometimes the date. They were held in place by iron brackets. Many well-known early American artists made a living painting these signs. Most old signs available to the collector today are of the late 19th century.

What to Look For

Newspaper and periodical advertising began a little later in the 18th century in Boston, New York, and Philadelphia. By 1726, newspapers in all three cities were carrying advertisements of goods for sale.

By the mid-18th century, broadsides which advertised articles for sale and solicited business were being distributed. Trade cards, labels, billheads, and tickets were also in use; the designs on them were engraved by the best artists of the time. Such items are of interest to the present day collector.

Each item is a part of the advertising story, and one can see that our ancestors knew the value of eye appeal, of style, quality, sentiment, and of sound. There were calendars, directories, and newspapers that carried ads; there were cards to hand out, broadsides to distribute, and novelties to give away.

From the beginning, the subject matter of advertising used themes which have lasted into the 20th century. Great names, national heroes, and sports heroes have always had a prominent place in advertising copy. The names of Washington, Franklin, Jefferson, Andrew Jackson, and Lincoln were used to popularize insurance, lotteries, steamship lines, even soaps and salves.

There was a Lafayette Insurance Company in the 19th century, and we have William Penn and Webster Cigars today. The American eagle was also tops as a trademark. Eagle Insurance was one of its earliest advertising users, but the eagle was also used in connection with ink powder, blacking, and liquor; today, although its use has diminished, we have Eagle Brand Milk and Eagle pencils.

The American Indian was introduced in early advertising to publicize inns, tobacco, patent medicines, and later clipper ships. The Indian's Panacea was advertised with a label showing an Indian medicine man offering the panacea to a sick man. The medicine man was also used in connection with other medicines, such as bitters, and also on early Lorillard tobacco labels. Indeed, so prolific is the advertising centering around the Indians that one could collect this item alone and have a never-ending hobby.

Another ageless theme is sports. Sports and figures in the sporting world have always been popular as symbols to promote sales. Old gunpowder cans bore a label with a print of the sportsman and his dog. Interest in baseball, football, golf, boxing, and even tennis has led to naming of products after champions of these sports. In the late 19th century, winners of eight-day bicycle races were similarly honored.

Early advertisers incorporated balloons in their ads. A balloon in an old Hood's Sarsparilla jig-saw puzzle ad is named Hood's Messenger. Coat's Best Six-Cord incorporated their trademark in the form of a balloon.

18th century New England inn sign. (Courtesy R. I. Historical Society)

Fan advertising Vanity Fair cigarettes. (Courtesy N. Y. Historical Society.)

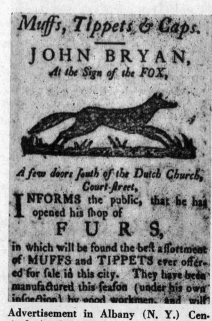

Advertisement in Albany (N. Y.) Centinel, April 5, 1803.

Advertising paperweights, 20th century. (Courtesy N. Y. Historical Society.)

Babbitt's Soap Powder also had an early ad with a package of their product up in a balloon. In the 20th century airplanes have been used in ads, and particularly the flights of Lindbergh and Amelia Earhart.

Famous Place Names

Famous places and natural wonders were also employed as advertising trademarks. Mount Shasta, Mount Hood, the geysers of the Yellowstone, the Grand Canyon, and Aurora Borealis have all been used as trade names. San Francisco's Golden Gate gives its name to a brand of coffee, Log Cabin Maple Syrup uses the log cabin of Henry Clay's day, but the early settler's log cabin was used in liquor and bitters bottles and trade names many years before. There is Pike's Peak Tobacco, Louisville Jockey Club Tobacco, and Old Oaken Bucket Tobacco. The Pilgrims and Plymouth Rock give us Pilgrim, Plymouth, and Mayflower brands.

Famous events influenced advertising trends, bringing out goods named California, Miners, Gold Rush, Golden Bear, Bonanza, Lucky Strike, Klondike.

Animals such as lions, horses, bears, camels, dogs, cats, and birds have long been favorites with the advertising world. Today we have the famous Metro-Goldwyn Mayer lion, Camel cigarettes. Dromedary Brands, Black Horse Ale, Twenty Mule Team Borax, and Humming Bird brands.

Another pictorial trend in advertising which has lasted from the 18th to the 20th century is the Oriental influence. It probably came in with tea and the tea packages originally boxed in China, but other boxes with Oriental decoration were available for ginger, cocoa, soaps, spices, and even drygoods.

In the 19th century appeared Sultana Coffee, Russian Cigars, African Coffee and Pepper, manufactured by Austin & Nichols, and an Egyptian package contained Fry's Cocoa.

An early trade card advertising Virginia tobacco shows a group of gentlemen sitting about a table smoking and drinking. The use of the distinguished gentlemen has extended down to the present day through such brand names as Planter, Kentucky Colonel, Major Grey, Admiral, Connoisseur. Newport, Beacon Hill, and Nob Hill are also trade names chosen to suggest culture and distinction.

Beautiful women have long been used in advertising. Jenny Lind, Lillian Russell, and other well known singers and actresses allowed their names to be used to advertise products. The famous Gibson Girl was a type rather than a particular woman. Women and children to represent the homely virtues, with animals or flowers were also common in pictorial advertising in the 1880s, and continue to be good attention-getters today.

The 1880s also was the heyday of verse and jingles in advertising. Songs and instrumental music as well as jingles were put out in the name of many products, including Hardman Pianos, Bixby's Stove Polish, the Uncle Sam Shoe, Bromo-Seltzer, and Peerless Stoves. Automobiles and theatres also relied on musical advertising. There were waltzes, polkas, marches, galops, two-steps, and gavottes. Within the last few decades, such items as "Socony Land," "Wrigley Eyes," "Oh You Spearmint Kiddo," and "You're a Life Saver" have been put into sheet music form, and are collector's items today.

Where to Look

Now we have scanned the field and you know what sort of material to look for, the question is where to find it. Frankly, the place to look is in attics, your own if its store is old enough, or someone else's. Sales of old houses to close estates often bring these tidbits into circulation; many antiques shops have odd boxes of such items.

To be sure, some items never come to light until they reach the rare book or old print dealer, so do not expect to casually find an 18th century broadside or a Maverick hat label; but there are still plenty of souvenirs of from fifty to one hundred years ago that can be picked up for little money.

You may want to specialize in one category. If your interest is tobacco, say, then you will want tobacco cans and boxes, cigar labels, cigarette cards, and old broadsides mentioning tobacco—or you may confine yourself to cigarette cards alone.

Medicine offers an interesting field of early American advertising, with its bottles, pill boxes, billheads, broadsides, even old account books of doctors or pharmacists which give long forgotten prescriptions.

Dry goods advertising includes old packages for shoes, collars, or pins, as well as old catalogues, billheads, posters announcing sales, and newspaper advertising.

The story of the automobile involves much more than the collecting of old cars. For those with auto interests, but small space, there are catalogues, handbills, car emblems, old license plates, souvenirs showing early automobiles, miniature toy cars which were used as ads. A folding tin cup with an old auto embossed on its cover is a collector's item, as are celluloid buttons with colored lithographs of old autos.

In the 1880s, McKesson & Robbins offered storekeepers this lithographed can free with each dozen boxes of Colgan's Taffy Tolu Chewing Gum, "suitable when empty for herbs, roots, seeds, spices."

TIN ADVERTISING TRAYS

by ART and JEWEL UMBERGER

Illustrations from the authors' collection.

Change tray advertising the non-intoxicating "Lily, A Beverage," bottled only by Rock Island Brewing Co., Rock Island, Ill.; made by American Art Works, Coshocton, O.

Left:
Tray entitled "St. Louis Levee in Early Seventies" advertised Budweiser King of Bottled Beer, 1914; made by American Can Co., Chicago.

FAST MOVING into the field of popular collectibles are tin advertising trays and signs of comparatively recent vintage — the beer, whiskey, mineral water, and soda water trays of the 1890s to the 1930s. Trays advertising shoes, foodstuffs, patent medicines, and other articles are also becoming collectors' specialties. These tin pieces of Americana, once given away as souvenirs or premiums to promote products and goodwill simultaneously, are available today in antiques shops and shows.

Colorful trays comprise an interesting collection in themselves or add depth as related items for a bottle collection. Coca Cola trays will enrich Coca Cola memorabilia, and Moxie trays or signs will enhance a collection of Moxie bottles. Both drinks were originally advertised as brain and nerve foods.

Serving trays were rectangular, round, or oval. The largest were 16 inches or more in diameter and were wall pieces or plaques used for decoration. The next smaller size, 12 to 16 inches, was probably most common. Tin art plates were 10 inches in diameter, and the miniature or "tip" size was about 4 inches. The small oval trays were approximately 4 x 6 inches.

The large trays or plaques such as Velvet Beer or Falstaff Beer are scarcer than the regular size trays. The picturesque scenes used on them add flavor to a collection and may be displayed to great advantage, although adequate space must be provided for them.

The round art plates resemble porcelain when viewed at a distance. On these plates the name of the advertiser usually appeared on the reverse; the date "1905" is frequently seen on the back, also. Anheuser-Busch, Western Coca Cola, and others used this medium in advertising. In a baroque frame the art plate with its decorative border makes an elegant wall piece.

Few trays suggest their use, but one miniature tray, put out by the Dallas Brewing Company in 1908, bore the word "Tip," printed in sizable letters.

Part of the fun of collecting trays is to trace the history of the firms who used them for advertising. The age of the trays is also exciting to a collector. Often the date is printed in an obscure corner, but it is not always this simple.

It is difficult to date a tray until a number of them have been studied and examined. New trays may have old subjects. If a tray looks new and is not dated, it could be of recent issue.

A study of clothing and hair styles may help to approximate the age of a tray. Earlier trays (1900-1910) show women with flowing Grecian hair styles, while the flapper era is documented with short bobbed hair. Hat fashions, such as the 1914 bonnet of the "Betty" Coca Cola tray and the later cloche hats of the 1920s help date the tray. The picture hat of the girl on the 1917 Coke tray is another date setter.

Other characteristics aid in determining the age. For instance, in the 1920s most of the Coke trays had green and brown borders, while the

Budweiser Beer tray, "Say When," 1915-20; maker unknown.

Wall plaque, "The Home of Fallstaff," made by Lemp, St. Louis, ca. 1905.

1930 trays had red borders.

A glass or bottle shown in a scene will sometimes indicate the date. Older Coke glasses were flared and imprinted with the 5 cent mark. Coke bottles of the 1890s had blob tops and Hutchinson stoppers; 1900-1915 bottles had straight sides; later bottles were skirted. Beer and whiskey bottles with cork-stoppered mouths were earlier than those with crown caps. Most early whiskey bottles were cylindrical; later bottles had fluted shoulders and base.

Manufacturers of early trays included: The Meek Company, American Art Works (successors to Meek Co.), and H. D. Beach Company, all of Coshocton, Ohio; Passaic Metalware Company of New Jersey; Kauffmann & Strauss of New York; Wolf & Company, Chas. W. Shonk of Chicago; and Mayer & Lavenson of New York.

In addition to the maker's name a tray may have the artist's signature on it, such as the 1912 tray of the Coca Cola Company which bears the signature of Hamilton King, a well-known artist of that day. Christian Feigenspan Brewing Company's tray of a lovely lady is signed "A. Asti." A signature will add value to a tray.

Stock designs could be obtained from manufacturers, and this economical factor helped small businesses to select a design and have their name stamped upon the trays at a nominal cost. Many different firms used the same popular design. The larger firms used original designs.

How is the desirability of a tray determined? Pictures of a bygone era such as the 1914 Budweiser tray depicting a steamboat unloading on the Mississippi or the Prohibition trays with non-alcoholic beverages add importance to a collection. Trays with

bitters advertising are a rare treat. The Lashes Bitters plaques and the Royal Pepsin Bitters tray are outstanding. The latter was silver-plated by the Homan Company between 1900-1922.

Tin pictures are more difficult to find than tin trays. Printed on a tin-like material they were washable and fairly permanent. Subjects varied, but animals were popular. A Pickwick Ale piece, an elongated tin picture, shows two large horses pulling a dray on which is strapped three huge kegs of ale. The tin was manufactured by American Art Works and directions printed on the back state: "To keep this sign clean and bright wipe the surface of it every thirty days with a damp cloth." Another tin picture, for Hanley's Peerless Ale, has only the lettering and an enormous reclining bulldog. Some of the tin pictures were framed; others, with the raw edges turned under, had cardboard backs with corks for hanging.

Large framed pictures stamped from a single piece of tin are real prizes. They measure as large as 2 by 3 feet or more. The self-frame gives added depth to the picture. The marvelous tin picture of young Theodore Roosevelt returning from a hunt is a prime collector's item. Another picture, entitled "True Fruit," advertising a soda fountain drink, is a choice item. Small advertising trays are usually inexpensive, though some of the well-advertised Western Coca Cola "topless" beauties fetch fancy prices.

Attention should be given to the condition of the tray. If the tray is just as it came from the factory it may be called "mint." With minor wear signs on rim or tiny scratches, it may be considered excellent or good, according to the degree of wear. Any marks or defacing of subject are undesirable.

Tray entitled "In Old Kentucky," artist-signed "Chs. J. Collins," advertised Stars and Stripes Bottled Beer, Willow Springs Brewing Co., Omaha, U.S.A., 1912; made by American Art Works, Coshocton, O.

Tray advertising The Geo. T. Stagg Company, Inc., Frankfort, Ky., Makers of O.F.C. Bourbon, date unknown; made by Electrical Chemical Engraving Co., New York, N.Y.

Left: Coca Cola tray, 1917, marked Stelad Signs, Passaic Metal Ware Co., Passaic, N.J. Above: Coca Cola Tray, 1925, by the American Art Works, Coshocton, O.

Portrait trays: left, Coca Cola, "Betty," 1914; top, Star Union Brewing Co.'s Pure Beers, Peru, Ill., 1905, maker unknown; right, Coca Cola, 1917; bottom, Coca Cola, 1912, artist-signed "Hamilton King." All Coca Cola trays here made by Passaic Metal Ware Co., Passaic, N.J.

Vegetable people were among the most popular gag cartoons used on trade cards.

Clark's threads suggested this means for keeping husbands home at night.

Anheuser-Busch Brewing Association issued this patriotic trade card commemorating the Columbian Exposition, in 1893.

Advertising Cards

by LEE KOVEL

The flood of "Domestic Dieties" marked a new era in advertising. The trademark made identification possible with symbolism.

THE POST-Civil War period in the United States with its population explosion and tremendous economic, industrial, and commercial growth brought a great demand for all kinds of merchandise, especially grocery and consumer goods. As long as there was a large demand and a small supply, distinguishing one manufacturer's wares from another's was relatively unimportant. But after 1865, increased production and improved transportation created keener competition. Grocery stores became diversified and offered a greater variety of products, improved goods, and better displays. Advertising became more and more important and new approaches were sought. One of the most popular in the last half of the 19th century was the advertising or trade card.

About 1870, so-called "broken record" ads were used. Magazines and newspapers discovered people did not continue to read ads that remained unchanged issue after issue, but that their attention *was* attracted by a repetitive slogan used in connection with a fresh illustration or format. The message, into which penny-pinching advertisers crowded as much information as possible, was presented in the tiniest of printed type—a magnifying glass was needed to read it. The first advertising cards were adapted from this type ads.

In the 1870s and 1880s, advertising went into a "transitional" period. New ads appeared as simple announcements, repeated as often as the manufacturer deemed practicable. Such ads proved expensive and inadequate, with results often difficult to trace. Customers would buy familiar commodities when reminded by an ad, but ignored new and unfamiliar products. Obviously a simple announcement was not enough, a fuller explanation was needed.

Just to say "Buy Akbar Coffee at Jenkins and Co." did not sell the product nearly as well as an ad containing a slogan, a promise, or a picture along with some information about the product. Trade cards with slogans, colored pictures, and some pertinent information about the product began to appear, usually passed to prospective buyers by local merchants.

In the 1890s, Charles Post, owner of the Post Cereal Company, discovered that the nutritional qualities of foods could be effectively exploited in advertising. Post advertised his Grape-Nuts as the cereal that "Makes Red Blood," and later declared that "There Are No Blotches On The Face of Beauty When Fed on Grape-Nuts." This type of medical claim for foods is found on many advertising cards of this period.

By the 1890s, advertising had be-

CUT CAREFULLY AROUND OUTLINES OF FIGURE AND ON DOTTED LINES. BEND BASE ROUND AND INSERT TAB IN SLIT.

Admiral Geo. Dewey.

During the Spanish-American War patriotic symbols, like Admiral Dewey and the American flag, were used frequently and successfully.

come big business, with writers and artists spending hours creating ads. For the most part, these men wrote and drew anonymously. Only a few artists, such as Kate Greenaway, are recognizable today.

Advertising cards by the millions were printed on light-weight cardboard, usually measuring 3 by 5 inches, and sold to retailers, department stores, manufacturers, and anyone else who could be persuaded to have his name imprinted on a few thousand cards. Lithographers and printers sometimes signed the face of the card in tiny print; these names are the best guide to the age of a card. (A list of lithographers can be found on pages 244-264 in *Know Your Antiques* by Ralph and Terry Kovel.)

Children collected the cards; boys swapped them; adults pasted them in albums. Many trade cards came in a series to be given away as purchase premiums or come-on devices. Customers would buy products just for the next installment in the story.

Advertisers longed for new ideas and gimmicks to give the advertising cards a flare of gaiety and gusto. People worked long hours and had neither time, money, nor the ability to read magazines and newspapers. If an advertisement was amusing, people would read it out loud, then save the card. Advertising men began to write rhymes and jingles about the products.

In 1896, the Spanish-American war inspired a wave of patriotism and manufacturers took advantage of it, using the American flag prolifically in

their ads. No one was more patriotic than the Sapolio soap people; "Dewey and We cleaned up with Sapolio" so shouted a trade card sailor waving a cake of soap.

Rhymes and flags were successful, but in the late 1890s the advertiser began to work to install a more permanent message through repetition by use of a slogan. The slogan did not stand alone but was coupled with an illustration, often one we would now term a "gag cartoon." Postum and Grape-Nuts used "There's a Reason"; Diamond Dyes punned, "It's Easy to Dye"; Carnation Condensed Milk came "from contented cows," while Fairy Soap asked, "Have you a little fairy in your home?"

Advertising slogans and characters were really extensions of the manufacturers' trademark, giving further assurance to the public that this was a familiar product. Although the first registered trademark in the United States was recorded October 25, 1870 (for Averil Chemical Paint Company), it was not until the end of the century that trademarks came into general use. The still familiar Underwood Devil, the paint-covered earth of Sherwin Williams, the cow from Cow Brand baking soda are just a few.

Slogans often contained puns. "Uneeda" was considered a silly name for a cracker, but after "Do You Know Uneeda Biscuit?" ads appeared (about 1900), and the National Biscuit Company was flooded with orders, the potentialities of coined trade names came under wide study. These synthetic names were often combined with a picture trademark on the advertising cards.

When identity advertising proved to be successful, artists and copywriters created a group of "domestic dieties" of animals, infants, fatherly Quakers, Pilgrims, noble Indians, young boys in raincoats, clasped hands, even a top-hatted peanut. The attractive girl who had been pictured in earlier cards was sometimes included in the trademark as in the case of the "White Rock girl."

Collecting trade cards lost its appeal about 1910. A more sophisticated public was reading magazines, and seeing colored pictures in increasing numbers; it could no longer be counted upon to save tradecards. Some of these late cards printed puzzles to appeal to children. Bookmarks with printed messages were the last important form of advertising card, but by 1914, the ad card had become obsolete.

Although the fad was over, many tradecards have survived the furnace and trash can and are still to be found at antiques shops, auctions, or hidden in books in attics. They are still plentiful, and as a collection provide a meaningful pictorial study of the dress, habits, furnishings, and common interests of the period from 1870 to 1910.

The "Heinz Boy" (above) was discontinued after the new and still used symbol, a pickle (below), was introduced.

C. D. KENNY'S COLLECTIBLE
Give-aways

All Kenny pieces shown here are from the
sizeable collection of Mr. and Mrs. Harold Mason, Baltimore, Md.

POSSIBLY no single establishment has given away more souvenirs to its customers, over a longer period of time, than the C. D. Kenny Company. Because the Kenny products were sold over such a large portion of the South and into the Midwest, would-be collectors of these advertising oddments have a wide area for search.

In 1872, young C. D. Kenny came down from Rochester, N. Y., to Baltimore, Md., and set himself up as a dealer in teas, coffees, and refined sugars. He began modestly with a single shop located at the southwest corner of Lexington and Green Streets, where he carried on his coffee roasting operations. Shortly he opened a second store in Baltimore, and 23 years later, in 1895, when his business was written up in the *Baltimore City Book of the Board of Trade*, he was noted as "the largest individual dealer in the teas, coffees, and refined sugars in the United States, being surpassed by only one or two corporations."

At that time he had 25 branch stores in 14 cities. Seven were in Baltimore, five in Washington, D.C., two in Richmond, Va., and one each in Georgetown, D. C., Norfolk, Lynchburg, Petersburg, Roanoke and Danville, Va., Wheeling, W. Va., Birmingham, Ala., Atlanta, Ga., and Knoxville and Chattanooga, Tenn. He had then over 225 employees on his payroll and according to the *Book of the Board of Trade*, "the gross annual business reached the grand total of $3,000,000 or upwards."

His business continued to expand and, by 1901, C. D. Kenny could count 50 branch stores in operation. Among new cities added to the list were Memphis, Tenn., Pittsburgh and York, Pa., Cumberland, Md., and Cleveland, Ohio, some of them having more than one store.

Mr. Kenny was a great believer in give-aways to his customers. Trade-cards, fashionable then for scrapbooks, kitchen items to please the housewife, quantities of **miniature bisque figures**

and ornaments, and lithographed tin plates of historic or holiday significance followed in succession. Though Kenny give-aways were seldom dated, the cards, at least, can be given a time sequence by the advertising on the back where the number of his stores was usually stated.

In 1934, the C. D. Kenny Company closed its retail stores—no more give-aways—to engage solely in the wholesale business. In 1940, the business was acquired by the Consolidated Grocers Corporation (now Consolidated Foods Corporation) of Chicago, and in 1952 the C. D. Kenny Division headquarters moved to that city. A distribution house still continues to operate in Baltimore.

Top Row

Tradecards: The cut-out Santa and chimney, advertising on the back "C. D. Kenny, Tea Dealer & Coffee Roaster" is one of the company's earliest. The boy saying his prayers, advertising two stores in Baltimore, is also an early one. The angel playing violin noted, "C. D. Kenny, Importer, Jobber & Retailer," with 34 branch stores; the girl with cat in hat and the little minx looking in the mirror claimed 40 stores; the angel boy with suitcase, 50. These marked advances between 1895, when he had 25 stores, and 1901.

Bottom Row

Stone bisque ornaments, in a 2-4 inch dimension, are of infinite variety. Some have their colored decoration glazed, some have the color painted on. Some are unmarked as to country of origin—likely these are before 1891, some say Germany; most say Austria. On all, "C. D. Kenny Co." is incised at the base. **Top row, left to right:** Parrot vases, blue and yellow head and wings, colors glazed, Austria; girl with watering can, green and red hat and skirt, painted, Germany; monkey on elephant, green, gray, and blue on hat, bow tie, and blanket, glazed colors, Austria. **Bottom row:** Baby with glazed gold bumblebee, red shoes, Austria; blonde equestrienne, red coat, green foliage, white horse, completely glazed, no place mark; pig bank, mottled gray and brown, top only glazed, slit for money, holes for eyes, Austria; boy on box, brown color painted, Germany; girl on sled, pink skirt, blue basket, colors glazed, no place mark. Age of these is undetermined; it is surmised the glazed color pieces are **earlier** than the painted ones.

Second Row

Tin Plates and Plaques, brightly lithographed, were supplied to the C. D. Kenny company by Kauffman & Strauss of New York, who usually put their name in small print on the rim. Advertising on these pieces was restrained, limited to "C. D. Kenny Co." or "Compliments of C. D. Kenny Co." somewhere in the design in small letters, or stamped on the back of the piece. (Full size Christmas plates are pictured in "Memo", this issue.) The little girl praying and the boy delivering a turkey are Thanksgiving greetings in a small size plate. Also small size are the coupe-shaped Washington portrait and "The Star Spangled Banner, Centennial Anniversary, 1914." The large oval teaparty plaque, made in one piece with the frame, has an overtone of Easter, and must have pleased little girls mightily. The **square** Washington portrait, "Pater Patrae," with its heavily embossed frame can be presumed, from its style, to be one of Kenny's earliest tin plaques.

Third Row

Left to right: Tin tea strainer, "C. D. Kenny Co." around sides; tin badge, "Welcome United Singers" with crossed flags waving over terrapin, crab, oysters, and duck arranged in an oyster shell; on back C. D. Kenny Teas, Coffees, Sugars, 50 branch stores. Balti. Badge & Nov. Co., Baltimore, Md. Pat. Nov 1 '01." Plated sugar shell, Lily handle, roses in bowl, "C. D. Kenny Co." is the only mark on back; heart-shaped tin box, colorful cupid decoration, "C. D. Kenny" on rim; tin spice box with blue and white sailing scene, ironstone knob, marked "C. D. Kenny Co."

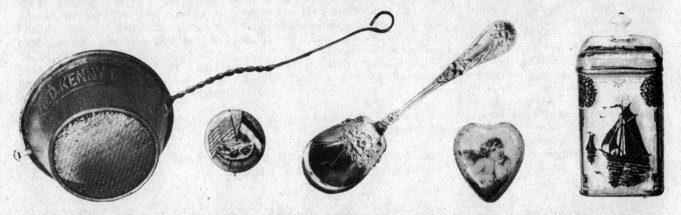

The Chiclet Zoo

by MARCIA RAY

FRANCIS PATRICK of Gaithersburg, Md., who deals in antique toys, paper goods, and advertising material, collects tin advertising pieces for himself. Rummaging in the basement of an old confectionery and ice cream parlor in Springfield, Mass., about to be torn down to make way for urban renewal, he came across a prize—a dealer's window display for a Chiclet Zoo, apparently unused.

The display consists of a brightly printed tin "Ask Your Dealer how to get this Chiclet Zoo" sign, depicting the zoo animals to be had, and individual tin cut-outs, about 9 inches high, of the 12 different animals. The pieces are pictured here, and it's easy to see what they are advertising, for each animal holds or carries in his pocket one of the American Chicle Company's products— Adams' Chiclets, Adams' Pepsin, Adams' Black Jack, or Beeman's Pepsin Gum. The background for the announcement sign is gray, and the animals on it, as in the individual pieces, are colorful in red,

blue, green, yellow, brown, and black.

The sign is dated 1914, "Patent applied for. Copyright M. B. Beach Co." The cut-out animals are dated either 1915 or 1916.

At first Mr. Patrick thought the tin animals were being offered as gum wrapper premiums. Then unexpectedly, as such things happen, he noticed a toy in a neighbor's kitchen that he might never have given a second glance if he had not seen the Chiclet Zoo. What he found, and was able to buy, was a stuffed rabbit, printed in the exact style and colors and approximately the same size as the tin cut-out—a rabbit with a Black Jack package in his pocket!

The message printed on the bottom explained the whole operation. It read:

"This is No. 9 of the Chiclet Zoo. There are 12 in all. You can get any of the others by mailing five 5 cent wrappers for either Adams' Chiclets, Adams' Pepsin, Adams' Black Jack, or Beeman's Pepsin gum and a 2 cent

stamp to American Chicle Company, Metropolitan Tower, New York City."

Evidently what you got for your five 5 cent wrappers and a 2 cent stamp was not a tin animal like those in the display, but a printed cloth replica to be cut, stuffed, and sewed at home——certainly a much safer toy for children.

All this led us to wonder about chewing gum beginnings and the American Chicle Company in particular. The Warner-Lambert Company, which acquired the American Chicle Company in 1962, and still makes Chiclets, Beeman's Pepsin gum and Adams' Black Jack, Clove, Wild Cherry, and Grape gums in its Morris Plains, N.J. plant, furnished answers. We quote from a release, which appeared in one of their publications:

A Substance Called Chicle

American Chicle was founded on a chance encounter in 1869 between a
(Please turn the page)

Tin Alligator

Tin Fox

Tin Rhinoceros

Tin Bear

Tin Tiger

Tin Elephant

Tin Squirrel

Tin Giraffe

Tin Raccoon

Tin Lion

Tin Monkey

Tin Rabbit

Stuffed Rabbit of printed cloth, what you got for five 5 cent gum wrappers and a 2 cent stamp. Stuffed and sewn at home.

New York inventor named Thomas Adams and a Mexican exile, Rudolph Napegy, secretary to General Santa Anna, ex-President of Mexico. Napegy showed Adams a rubbery fluid from certain trees growing wild in the jungles of Southern Mexico and Central America, and asked whether the American inventor might be able to find a commercial use for the Mexican product called "chicle."

Adams, without success, experimented with the chicle in hopes of formulating a synthetic rubber. Then, one day when he was in a neighborhood drugstore, he noticed a young girl purchasing paraffin chewing wax.

That evening, Adams and his son, Horatio, made a batch of what was to become the first modern chewing gum. The finished product was rolled into little round pellets and packed 200 to a box. The boxes were labeled "Adams New York Chewing Gum — Snapping and Stretching."

An inveterate tinkerer, Adams experimented with methods to flavor his tasteless gum. He tried sassafras,

then licorice which he shredded into the chicle. The results — Adams Black Jack — the oldest flavored gum still on the market.

The demand for the gum increased and by 1876 it was necessary for the young Adams enterprise to move into larger manufacturing quarters in New York City. As production machinery was perfected, the balls of gum were replaced by cylindrical pencil-like sticks, later succeeded by the familiar flat slabs of today.

Adams, however, was not to monopolize the gum field for very long. Many ambitious druggists, who had ready access to flavoring extracts, started experimenting in the hope of getting a share of the flavor gum market.

The most successful of these druggists was Dr. Edward E. Beeman. Beeman, for some time, had manufactured a pepsin compound, and one day his bookkeeper urged him to put it into gum since so many people buy pepsin for digestion and gum "for no particular reason." The suggestion resulted in Beeman's Pepsin.

The man who really revolutionized the gum market was a Cleveland popcorn salesman by the name of William J. White.

White made the critical discovery for improving the flavor in gums. Since chicle itself would not absorb flavors, White turned to sugar, which would. He found that he could obtain any flavored gum he so desired by combining flavors with corn syrup, for flavored syrup blended instantly with chicle. White decided to concentrate on peppermint flavor for his gum which he called Yucatan.

White was not only an inventor but a natural-born promoter. For instance, he went to Washington where he distributed a box of Yucatan to every Congressman in Washington. Before leaving the nation's capital, he decided to run for Congress, and returning home, won a Congressional seat in the next election.

In an attempt to broaden the market for his gum, White sailed to England and arranged to be presented to King Edward VII. It was customary for persons to speak to the king only if

spoken to. White, however, ignoring custom, promptly whipped a box of Yucatan from his pocket and walked up to the king.

"Your Majesty," he said, "I'd like to give you a box of my chewing gum. You've never tasted anything like it." King Edward, remembering White was an American Congressman, hid his amazement, and thanked him for the gift.

In 1899, The American Chicle Company, representing the largest chewing gum manufacturing company in the United States, was organized through the consolidation of most of the leading chewing gum companies of the day — Adams', White's, Beeman's, and Primley's (the first to market a fruit-flavored gum.)

[In 1916, American Chicle established a Research Department, through whose efforts it added such new products as Certs, Clorets, Sen Sen, Rolaids, Dentyne, and Trident Sugarless Gum to its product lines. Much of this expansion occurred after World War II.]

Since American Chicle's profit picture depended on marketing its products in large volume, the firm, from its earliest beginnings, relied heavily on promotion and advertising to keep its brand name products constantly before the American public.

"Sampling" was a major part of its promotion program in which pretty girls passed out sample-sized Chiclets and Dentyne at the busiest street intersections of towns and cities across the country. Advertisements appeared in magazines, newspapers, or car cards and radio, and later television. In earlier decades, the company often used testimonials from Broadway stars. One ad featured a "promising young actor" named Bob Hope, then appearing in *Roberta*.

But, alas, the present company has no information about, or remembrance of, the Chiclet Zoo. It is left to collectors to seek, and with great good luck, to find a Zoo like Mr. Patrick's. It might even be possible to assemble a set of the stuffed animals. Even one or two of the tin animals or the stuffed ones would be a fascinating find.

ARTS AND ARTISTS

Depending on an individual's taste and pocketbook, the graphic arts can be a most interesting field for collectors to indulge in. If space is limited, one can collect tiny miniatures or portfolios of colorful prints to be taken out and pored over from time to time. The rage for lithographs of the art nouveau period has made a decided impact on today's furnishings and decorations.

H. Cless, a Frenchman who worked in Paris, painted this unidentified subject in 1783 in exquisite combinations of gray, from a death-like pallor of skin where a white line separates forehead from kinky gray hair to blue gray shadows and dark gray ground.

One must recognize the hatch technique painted over a pale wash, and sharp treatment of features to know the H. Cless signature will be found in lower right corner of the ivory, almost *hidden* by frame. Back of gold locket frame has delicate ivory carving on lapis lazuli base. Urn is of mother-of-pearl and gold. *Ivory wreaths, gold thread* complete decoration.

Some Important Miniatures

and the manner of their identification

By JEANNETTE BERG STERN

A MOST important feature of any collection is the authentication of its items. Especially in the field of art should such authentication be made by experts, whose research studies and long experience have qualified them for the task. Museums of Art throughout the country are, perhaps, the best sources for exact identification.

Authentication of a miniature must be made without dependence on a signature, for miniatures were seldom signed. Even though some miniaturists did sign their work occasionally and a very few signed most of their work, the finding of a signed miniature is a rare event. Identification, then, must hinge on familiarity with the artist's style, techniques, and varying phases. Some artists deviated from the set patterns accepted as their own; others had definite color periods, or times when they employed different techniques. Yet the expert, with his background of knowledge and experience, is able to identify an important miniature as easily as he recognizes a friend's handwriting.

Left, Mr. "C.P." by Raphael Peale, American miniaturist (1744–1825), illustrates the artist's usual use of sharp detail: wiry hair, deep-set eyes, large well drawn mouth, plus a dark outline drawn from the top of the head to the chin on the far side of the face. Here is Raphael Peale's typical pastel background of blue, purple and cream, accomplished in a broad hatch or line stroke over a wash, to cause a cloud effect against the sloping shoulders of the sitter.

The etched gold frame, bearing the initials "C.P." on the reverse, has been attributed to Paul Revere.

LEFT:

This miniature of great beauty by Richard Collins, miniaturist to George III of England, depicts a young girl whose chestnut brown curls, fair complexion, white muslin dress and blue sash and scarf are done in blended brush stroke, with touches of opaque white. The background gives an iridescent effect of clouds in pale blues and tans.

RIGHT:

The reverse shows two shades of hair, probably of the young lady and her mother, in a quilted pattern. The design is held in place by tiny six pointed stars and is encased under convex glass in a gold locket.

Miniatures were painted on paper, vellum, copper, or even on old playing cards, but the most exquisite results were obtained by the use of water color on ivory. This could almost insure a luminous quality to the skin tones.

The miniatures pictured here, all on ivory, have been authenticated, and the reasons by which the artist is recognized are given in the accompanying descriptions. All miniatures pictured are from the author's collection.

Dr. George Tufton Moffatt was painted, as a lad of ten in 1846, by Thomas Sully (1783–1872), one of America's most prominent and prolific miniaturists. Little George was destined to become a founder of the Harvard University Dental School and its first Professor of Operative Dentistry. His features, loosely drawn, are painted in very short hatches with Sully's distinctive olive green background. He wears a Byronic collar and a bright red velvety shawl draped around his shoulders. The number 40755 in red on the back of the gold pin frame indicates it was exhibited in the Museum of Fine Arts in Boston, Mass. Dr. Moffatt lived on Market Street in Portsmouth, N. H. His home (the Moffatt-Ladd House) now belongs to the Colonial Dames of New Hampshire.

Lady of the English Court, set in soft paste diamonds, Samuel Cotes 1734–1814.

Portraits

in Miniature

by CLARA NISBET

MINIATURE PORTRAITS, painted on ivory, were fashionable in days gone by. Today, they are eagerly sought by collectors for their intrinsic beauty as well as for their value as works of artists of the era. It might be added that there is also a demand for them from some *nouveau riche* who are anxious to "acquire ancestors."

The miniatures shown are those of Rev. Isaac and Ann (Parker) Bird, and are the signed work of Nathaniel Rogers, an American artist who was born in 1788 at Bridgehampton, Long Island, N. Y. Young Rogers, at an early age, showed an aptitude for painting, and in 1811 was accepted as a pupil by John Wesley Jarvis, a New York artist of note. Before long, however, Rogers had his own studio at 86 Broadway, N. Y. C. where he made a name for himself as a society painter. Of him it was said that he painted all the notables of the period. He was an elected member of the National Academy. His work won him a place in history's list of American Miniature Painters.

The Birds sat for their portraits soon after their marriage in November, 1822. Isaac, a graduate of Yale in 1814, went on to Andover Theological Seminary where he received his degree in 1820. Ann, a pretty, "gently reared" young lady, had graduated from the Bradford (Mass.) Female Academy. The portraits were a farewell present to Ann's family, for the couple sailed aboard the brig "Shepherdess" on December 6, 1822, bound for the Near East and service in the field of missions. According to family legend, Ann was the first American woman missionary to set foot on the soil of the Bible Lands.

Under the stress of fourteen years there, fraught with danger and harrowing experiences, combined with bearing and raising six children in the most adverse conditions, Ann's health failed. The family returned to the States in 1836, eventually settling in Great Barrington, Mass., where they conducted a boys' school, which was carried on, first by the elder son, then by a grandson as the "old-folks" enjoyed their well-earned retirement.

A Gallery of Chapman's Paintings of Children

by GEORGIA S. CHAMBERLAIN

JOHN GADSBY CHAPMAN, born in 1808, in Alexandria, Virginia, seems best remembered for his painting, *The Baptism of Pocahontas*, in the Rotunda of the Capitol and his *American Drawing Book*, 1847, which went through so many editions. In recent years, the large body of his work, long overlooked, has come to recognition, and his originals from which engravings were made are being sought for preservation.

In the 1840's, he was one of the busiest and most popular illustrators in the country. Particularly were gift books and annuals, those "elegant ornaments of the drawing room table," enhanced by engravings of his works. Of him, Henry T. Tuckerman wrote: "Chapman was indefatigable; early and late he was at work . . . The booksellers constantly employed him in illustrating Bibles, histories, poems, and even grammars."

His landscapes were always accurately studied and pleasing; his religious and historical Illustrations, consistently dignified. His genre pieces, on the other hand, suffered from the over-sentimentality of the period. His romantic style and facility brought such excessive demand for production that the artistic merit of his work came to suffer.

In 1848, he moved to Rome where he found life easier. There he devoted himself to high art, successfully selling Italian landscapes, portraits, and ideal pieces to tourists. His paintings of children, especially in his early and late periods, are particularly charming.

16
Arts
Artists

The Snare, *then owned by E. L. Carey, was exhibited at the Pennsylvania Academy of the Fine Arts in 1838. It is full of Chapman's love of the out-of-doors and his ability to create atmosphere.*

Friar Puck, *first exhibited at the National Academy of Design, June 1838, was engraved by J. F. E. Prud'homme as frontispiece for gift book,* The Token and Atlantic Souvenir, *a Christmas and New Year's Present, 1839, published by Otis Broaders & Co., Boston.*

The Sled, *though unfortunate in its engraver, W. E. Tucker, still catches the joy of the coaster, the wintry atmosphere; typical Chapman landscape of New York City buildings in background.*

The Strawberry Girl, *with spire of Trinity Church, New York in background, appeared in New York Mirror 1837; was reprinted in the same annual as Friar Puck, 1839. More such realism might have added to Chapman's stature as genre painter.*

The Sun Fish, *engraved by J. Hinshelwood, illustrated poem in 1837 gift book* The Magnolia, *published by Bancroft & Holly, N. Y. A similar painting,* The Lazy Fisherman, *is owned by the William Rockhill Nelson Gallery of Art, Kansas City, Mo.*

The May Queen, *engraved for Godey's Lady's Book, May 1843, illustrates the formula style the busy Chapman developed for his ideal female figure: impossibly small hands, feet, and waist, face with high rounded forehead, and rather insipid air.*

American Folk Art:

Margarette Phipps Of Lancaster

by ROBERT BISHOP

WITH the current manifestation of interest in all American antiques, it is no wonder that Folk Art forms have reached the prominence they now hold.

Once, not many years ago, it was possible at a moderate cost to purchase examples of regional art and craftsmanship. No longer! Large collections of all forms of Folk Art have been assembled, eliminating many of the better pieces from the market. Consequently, to obtain a good genuine example, one must pay a premium price. This is particularly true of the Pennsylvania German Folk Art.

Figure I shows an outstanding watercolor from the late 1830s. In color it is as typically Pennsylvania German as it is in form. Burnt reds, yellows, bright blues and greens combine with good draftsmanship to make it an outstanding example of regional art. This and the other illustrations here are all works by the same nineteenth century Pennsylvania artist, Margarette Phipps.

Figure II, while again a typically German-American drawing, is not nearly as successful as *Figure I.* The execution is somewhat self-conscious and the figures unsure. Obviously the intricacy of design was just too difficult for the artist to master at this point of development.

Figure III, dated later once again, shows a strong sure artist at work. Careful observation forces one to realize how rapidly, during this period in American history, inherited traditional boundaries were being swept away in art as well as in daily living. This painting, although executed only five years after *Figure II,* retains little of the German influence and shows a definite adaptation to the oncoming Victorian period.

Other paintings, all later, are known by this same artist. They show even less German influence, and indicate a broadening of taste.

Little is known of Miss Phipps, the artist, other than that she lived in Lancaster, Pennsylvania, and worked between 1838 and 1868. It would be interesting to know more about her personal life and to be able to parallel it with her development as an artist.

**17
Arts
Artists**

FIGURE I

FIGURE II

FIGURE III

Possible Source of American Manuscript Patterns

by THORNE ROSSMAN

SOMEHOW, one of the most dangerous subjects to consider objectively is the truth about the sources of what is popularly, and erroneously, called "Pennsylvania Dutch fraktur." To begin with, many people insist that it isn't Pennsylvania Dutch but Pennsylvania German. On the other hand, the good Dr. Cornelius Weygand wants it called Pennsylvania Dutch. Personally, I am on Dr. Weygand's side of the fence.

As it happens, my own interest in antiques of this nature was sponsored under a terrific handicap. My grandfather was born and educated in Germany. Having retired from active work when I was a youngster, he took it upon himself to devote every clear, pleasant Saturday throughout the year to little journeys by trolley car to the villages and towns of Ephrata, Lititz, Manheim, and so on, in Lancaster County. Invariably there was something of historic interest he wanted to show me and tell me about. From him I learned, and it never occurred to me to question his authority, that the Hans Herr house, the oldest house in Lancaster County, was of Swiss architecture. And that the oldest house in Berks County, the Mouns Jones house, was Swedish. From him I learned that the majority of the farmhouses in Pennsylvania are based upon English architecture, and that the barns are Swiss in derivation.

The first time I ever heard the word bastard was from his lips at Ephrata, and he was not casting epithets. His name for the magnificent fracturschriften adorning the walls of the Ephrata Cloisters was "bastard Gothic." He pronounced Gothic as "Go-teek." When I was thirteen years old there were several dozen examples of this fraktur work hanging on the cloister walls. Perhaps they have been preserved. I asked him where "Bastard Gothic" came from. In fact, I liked to use the word, and perhaps used it too much around my own home. Grandfather told me that it came from the Netherlands.

At this time there was a really stout fellow in charge of the cloisters who served as minister, custodian and usher. He and my grandfather always conversed at some length at every visit, and definitely not in the lingo that is now called Pennsylvania Dutch or Pennsylvania German. They

spoke in the fluidly cadent language of Heine, yet I suspect from the guffaws that erupted from time to time the subject of the conversation was not precisely poetry.

One day my grandfather gave me a book, "The Adventures of An Illustrator" by Joseph Pennell. "This man," he said, "was at Ephrata many years ago to make pictures. I hope that someday you will learn to draw well enough to make pictures like his. But when you go to Ephrata again, do not steal from the cloisters as this man did." I wanted to know about the stealing part and was told to read the book. In it is a confession of light fingering by one of our great artists and a companion. They looted the top story of the old Brother House, way back in the 1880's. Later in life I met Mr. Pennell and asked him about Ephrata and what he ever did with the books he had purloined. He told me they went into the libraries of some very high-placed citizens, one of them a governor of the state of Pennsylvania.

What Joseph Pennell took from Ephrata is now a matter of history, perhaps obscured for all time. Certain of the books, however, were manuscript books. It has been my pleasure to examine a few of them, and most of them are in the style that is to be found in the early catalogs of Dutch typefounders under the category (you guessed it!) of "Bastard Gothic." It seems that term was used all over Europe, and that as early as the year 1500 great calligraphers were making an earnest effort to direct writing activities into

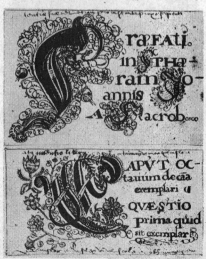

the channels of more readable text—that invented by the Latins.

The very first Pennsylvania examples of "Bastard Gothic" appear on the deeds issued by William Penn and his heirs for land in the new Province. Every individual, from no matter where, who obtained a grant of land from Penn received the most beautiful piece of "fraktur" he probably ever saw, let alone owned.

In a discussion some years ago with a noted Belgian designer, I heard all of the decorative work on the Pennsylvania art commonly called fraktur, designated as textile patterns. A study of textile pattern uses throughout continental Europe and England during the years preceding and concurrent with the settlement of colonial America, reveals the fact that hundreds of pattern books were issued, both for craftsmen in the textile trade and for women who were indulging in embroidery, cutwork, lace making, and so on. The great bibliography by Lotz on the published pattern books of Europe shows that textile pattern books were almost common in the 17th century and that they were issued in such numbers in Italy, France, Switzerland, the Netherlands and Germany that practically any man or woman could afford to own at least one, and most likely did. The designs in the various books were pirated from others, right and left.

In 1944 an American soldier in Paris found a very curious manuscript book, bound in leather over oak board. He bought it for a carton of cigarettes. He brought it home with him and, fortunately, it resided for at least a year in my possession before passing into the hands of one of America's great art libraries. Before turning over this book to its present owners I received permission to photograph certain of the pages which, written in Latin throughout, appear to be the work of a Labadist monk. The amazing thing in connection with this book is that all of the initial letters and decorations seem to point them as a possible source of Ephrata manuscript designs. It is entirely logical to assume that a book of this kind, if not this actual book, did constitute the pattern for Ephrata work.

We must remember that the man credited with all of the arts of Ephrata, Conrad Beissel, was a man who knew nothing whatever about music and nothing whatever about art. So little did he know of music that when he appointed Ludwig Blum singing master, the Sisters of the organization concocted a very pretty scheme. They told Beissel they would learn all that Blum could teach them and then they would teach Beissel, and Beissel could teach it back to them, thus maintaining his position as a master of all things.

Beissel, far from being an artist of letters, was a baker by trade. Upon arriving in the colonies he discovered that people here generally baked their own bread. When he got to Germantown, he studied weaving in order to have another and more profitable trade. Here, undoubtedly, he saw pattern books. But at Germantown he also fell under the influence of Dr. Christopher Witt, an influence we shouldn't discount. It is altogether likely that Dr. Witt found Beissel a willing vessel into which Witt poured most of the ideas that later came from Beissel. Witt was an educated gentleman of parts, a mystic, a medicus, and a mathematician. He suggested that Beissel and another young man, Van Bebber, go to the Labadist Monastery on the Elk River and study there the mystic religion established by the ex-Jesuit, Jean la Badie.

When Beissel finally established his Ephrata community he received a notable gift from Dr. Witt, a tower clock. Thus we know the friendship established at Germantown had not waned during the years Beissel worked out his ideas for Ephrata and made them come true.

The illustrations here pictured from the manuscript book carry their own Ephrata identification to any fair-minded scholar of Pennsylvania religious expressions. In fact, so well does each illustration speak for itself that captions would be superfluous.

Rex Brasher's Pen and Ink Bird Sketches

by CLARA NISBET

THE AUTOGRAPHED pen-and-ink sketch, shown here, is by Rex Brasher, naturalist and painter extraordinary. From childhood, Brasher's ambition was to study and paint birds. When he was in his teens, he risked his savings, betting on the horse named Knight of the Garter, a venture which netted him the neat sum of $12,000. This windfall enabled him to purchase a small sloop in which he sailed the Eastern Seaboard, painting its birds.

His next project was the documenting of the land birds of North America. To this end, he treked across the continent, studying and painting the different species. Brasher worked, not from collected specimens, but from life. As a result, many naturalists claim that his paintings are more realistic than those of Audubon. The late Dr. T. Gilbert, president of the National Audubon Society, is quoted as saying, "When you have seen a Brasher bird, you have seen the bird itself, life-like, in a natural attitude."

After spending 41 years afield, Rex Brasher retired to a small farm, "Chicadee Valley," near Gaylordsville, Conn. There he devoted himself to assembling the Brasher Collection of North American Birds. He was one of the fortunate ones, for during his lifetime he saw his work acclaimed by the critics. In fact, the State of Connecticut purchased the collection for $74,900.

Besides his painting, he wrote *Secrets of the Friendly Woods,* published in 1926 by the Century Company, and *Birds and Trees of North America* (12 volumes, 1934). These books and the Brasher prints now rank high on the list of collectibles. Rex Brasher died at the age of 91 in 1960.

Chinese Rice Paper Paintings

by AMELIA E. MAC SWIGGAN

RETURNING from a journey to the Far East in 1692, the German physician and world traveler, Engelbert Kampfer, author of a *History of Japan and Siam* (London, 1728), brought back a number of rice paper paintings which he had acquired in Nagasaki, Japan. From this introduction, these paintings became popular throughout most of Europe, and continued to be in demand well into the 19th century. In the 18th and 19th centuries, these beautiful works of art were brought home by European and American merchants and sea captains who traded in the Orient.

The rice-paper tree or shrub—*Tetrapanax papyrifus*—was widely cultivated in China, Japan, and Ceylon. It has large leaves with five to seven lobes, small white flowers, and stems with a whitish pith from which rice paper is made. The outer wood fiber of the stem is peeled off and lengths of the pith are put on a turning lathe against which a razor-sharp knife is held at an angle. The rice paper is peeled off in precisely the same manner wood veneers are peeled . . . the latter process deriving from the Chinese invention of rotary shaving to produce extra thin veneers.

This curly sheet from the live pith is then dried flat, under pressure, between polished stones or metal plates.

Having been trained from childhood in the manipulation of the paint brush—it was their means for writing—many Chinese painted rather well. Because painting and calligraphy are somewhat akin, practically every writer in China was an artist of sorts, and many incorporated lovely sketches and water color paintings in their writings. Their first brushes were fashioned of rabbit hair around which

the hair of sheep and deer were wrapped; the brush handles were made of twigs obtained from native mulberry trees. As writing became more complex and exacting the Chinese improved their brushes, making them of fox and rabbit hair; some brushes had elaborate handles of carved ivory or wood; being treasured possessions, they were often kept in fancy boxes.

Rice paper paintings were executed in colors which were bright and lasting. The tempera paints were molded

Chinese rice paper painting of a Mandarin and his son dressed in brilliantly colored court costumes of the mid-nineteenth century period. Size, 8 by 11 inches. (Privately owned.)

Left: Chinese rice paper painting depicting a courtroom scene. The judge presides at the table (center), two prisoners (a man and a woman) kneel in the foreground with their hands tied behind their backs; court officials stand on either side of the judge's table, and a lawyer for the defense kneels to the right of the prisoners to plead their case. Mid-nineteenth century. Size, 6 by 8½ inches. (Privately owned.) **Right:** Chinese aristocracy in colorful court costumes are depicted in this 18th century rice paper painting. (Metropolitan Museum of Art photo.)

into sticks with lovely designs on them. Powdered gold, silver, and pearl dust were used wherever the designs called for such elaboration—usually in the elegantly embroided costumes worn by the gentry. As a rule Chinese artists did not mix or dilute their colors with water beforehand. Instead, they applied the colors in their original hues, just as they were taken up on the moistened brush from the sticks of paint. This method resulted in well defined and neatly shaded pictures.

Early Chinese rice paper paintings portrayed members of the Imperial Court dressed in elegant costumes. The details of each costume were precisely and exquisitely colored in gold, silver, blue, red, yellow, green, brown, and purple. Heavy black tresses framed aristocratic oriental faces as translucent and white as alabaster. The graceful delineation of the figures made the paintings even more beautiful.

Landscapes, religious ceremonies and pageants, birds, animals, flowers, and fruits were favorite subjects for Chinese rice paper paintings. One street in Canton was once solely occupied by artists who specialized in the painting of ships in the harbor.

Historically speaking, the portrayal of Chinese artists, craftsmen, and tradesmen engaged in their various activities are of more importance then the pretty floral, fruit, and animal subjects. These paintings represent a contemporary view of life in China in the 17th, 18th, and 19th centuries, and form a nucleus for additional research into the habits and customs of the Chinese people.

Groups of rice paper paintings were sold in handsome brocade-covered books, each picture framed with a border of colored ribbon; they were also sold separately, and as sets in boxes. While rice paper paintings are not easily acquired these days, they are nevertheless avidly sought by collectors. Their rarity may be due, in part, to the ephemeral nature of the material on which they were painted.

William Robinson Leigh

"Sagebrush Rembrandt"

by CLARA NISBET

THIS ORIGINAL pen and ink sketch of a cow pony is an excellent example of the work of W. R. Leigh. To the uninitiated, it is a charming bit of art; to the artist, it shows the superb technique of the man, indicating a complete understanding of animal anatomy; the horse lover realizes that the sketch has captured the mood of this tough little animal.

William Robinson Leigh was born September 23, 1866, at Falling Waters, W. Va. At 6 years of age he was already sketching animals. At the age of 17, he went abroad to study at Munich, Germany; soon his work was winning awards there as well as in Paris.

In 1896, he returned to America where, on trips to Arizona, Wyoming, New Mexico and California, he realized his life-long dream of painting scenes of the West. In his oils and water colors he captured the vivid hues of the country and pictured the drama of its cowboys, its Indians, and its rugged little mustangs and Indian ponies. These works earned for him the title of "Sagebrush Rembrandt."

Subsequently, he worked in his New York City studio using on-the-scene sketches as a basis for his paintings. There the fortunate visitor, surrounded by Leigh paintings, as well as memorabilia of the "Great Open Spaces," sat enthralled as the artist told of his many and varied experiences. Among the books written by this gifted man is one devoted to *The Western Pony*. This is a classic. In it he paints his subjects in stark reality, stripped of all pretense of show horse beauty.

As an elected National Academician and as a member of the Grand Central Art Galleries, Leigh's work was given a prominent place in New York exhibitions. Perhaps one of his most dramatic paintings is the *Buffalo Drive*, a monumental mural alive with fury and action.

The death of William Robinson Leigh at the age of 88 in 1954, rang down the curtain on an era of great painters of the West.

Mr. Leigh and his contemporaries, Frederick Remington and Charles M. Russell, who were known as the "Big Three" of Western artists, left a rich heritage in their portrayal of that exciting period. Their works are treasured by private collectors and museums alike. Though their original oils and water colors are beyond the average pocketbook, colored prints of their works are available and are considered a choice bit of Americana.

Pen and ink sketch of a cow pony by William R. Leigh. Author's Collection. *Photo by Tassone Studios.*

How to Identify Prints

By ARTHUR T. DOBBS

THERE IS probably no field of collection which is quite so hazardous as that of collecting prints. To be able to spot the difference between a genuine valuable print and a commercially worthless reproduction demands a degree of observation bordering on true detective qualities. It is our purpose here to define a few of the fundamentals.

Every printing method ever used can be classified into one of three categories, (a) printing from a raised or relief surface; (b) printing from a plane or level surface; (c) printing from a sunken or intaglio surface. Sometimes a finished print will combine two of these basic methods, but this is unusual and beyond the scope of these general notes.

The market value of a print, or anything else, for that matter, can be said to depend upon supply and demand. In the case of prints, it is safe to assume that the skill of the artist or printmaker found public recognition which created the demand. Whenever demand exceeds supply, the field is open to the forger and the faker, and while these notes are planned to assist the collector to identify methods of reproduction, they cannot guarantee full safeguard against the skills of the deliberate counterfeiter or the vendor of his wares.

Broadly speaking, collectible prints are non-photographic in origin or production, so any evidence of camera-work can be used to eliminate photo-processed material from your portfolio of marketable prints.

The most obvious indication of photo-processed reproduction is the presence of screen-pattern, which results when the original is photographed through a ruled glass screen, not unlike a very fine window screening in appearance. This translates the picture tones into dots of varying size. A magnifying glass will reveal this dot-pattern of "half-tone" printing. Screen rulings range from 65 lines to the linear inch for coarse work, up to 400 lines for fine art reproduction.

The quality of the paper used will often indicate the age of the stock on which a print is made; new machine-made paper is an immediate

indication that the print is not old.

Printers and publishers' imprints also clearly indicate the true status of the print, though unscrupulous vendors have been known to trim off these telltale imprints, even at the sacrifice of some margin width.

Treatment of Illustration

Treatment of the illustration can be subdivided into two broad categories: (a) *Line;* (b) *Tone.* In the former, the values are interpreted by lines of varying form and thickness, while in the latter, graduating tones are used. Tone values are generally reproduced by the half-tone or screen method mentioned.

Prints using a single color are referred to as being in *monochrome;* those using two or more colors are *polychromes.* While there have long been experimental and obscure methods of pictorial reproduction, most of those generally known can be allotted to one or another of the three categories listed.

(a) *Raised or Relief Surface Printing:* wood-cuts, wood engraving, line-

St. Christopher; first wood block printed in Germany, 1423; artist unknown, exemplifies raised surface printing.

cuts, photo-engraved printing blocks on zinc, copper, etc.—all printed in the regular "letterpress" method.

(b) *Plane or Level Surface Printing:* lithography, from stone or from metal or plastic plates (either direct from the stone or plate, or indirectly from an intermediate rubber surface, called offset; collotype or photo-gelatin screenless tone reproduction; and silk-screen or serigraph (stencil) printing which can justifiably be included.

(c) *Sunken or Intaglio Surface:* where the design image is below the non-printing surface. This includes engraving, etching, drypoint, mezzotint, aquatint and gravure, sometimes known as photogravure or rotogravure.

Printing from a Raised Surface
Wood Cuts

It is claimed that wood-cut designs for playing cards were made in Europe during the 13th century. The earliest known "dated" print is the "Brussels Print", A.D. 1418.

In making a wood-cut, the desired design is drawn on the smooth surface of the block of wood, and the non-printing areas are cut away. The remaining surface is then inked, and an impression or print is taken. Usually the paper is damped evenly before printing, and the act of impressing the paper on the block results in the paper showing a slight pressure mark on the back of the sheet. Side-lighting the back of the print will often reveal this characteristic clue to printing from a relief surface.

In the Orient, Ukiyo-e prints from wood blocks were made in two colors —red and green—until Suzuki Haronubo (1725-1770) developed the Nishiki-e or "brocade pictures" involving the printing of ten or more colors.

Wood Engravings

In England, Thomas Bewick (1753-1828) adapted metal-engraving techniques to the close end-grain of boxwood and holly. His illustrations for *The History of British Birds,* and *The History of British Animals* are masterpieces of their kind. These are classified as wood engravings, as distinguished from the coarser, more elementary wood-cuts of earlier days.

In Germany, Albrecht Durer (1471-1528), painter, draughtsman, and engraver, had an illustrious career. Durer is well-documented in art reference books and encyclopaedias, which will repay study.

Wood engravings were sometimes printed on soft tissue, then mounted on to heavier paper. Fine art reproductions, especially those made in Europe during the late 19th century by the collotype or photo-gelatin process can be found in the large luxury-type art books of the period.

Woodcuts suffered the size limitation of the dimensions of the boxwood log, cut across the grain. However, in 1860, compound blocks were made by fitting uniform-sized blocks into a single large one. Such was the discipline imposed upon the engraver that as many as twenty different men could be put to work, each engraving on a different block; yet when all the pieces were bolted together, the finished picture looked as if it were the unbroken work of one man. Close examination of some of the large illustrations in magazines of the Civil War era will reveal white lines where the unit blocks have slightly "sprung."

The advent of the camera and photo-etched metal printing, with their speedier production and freedom from size limitation, sounded the death-knell of wood-engraving as a commercial process.

Printing from a Plane Surface Lithography

Printing from a plane or level surface, where the desired design is neither higher (relief) or lower (intaglio) than the non-printing area is rightly termed "planography." This category embraces more than one method, chief of which is "lithography," and its latter-day development, "offset."

Alois Serefelder, a Bavarian, is acknowledged as inventor of lithography when, in 1792, he experimented with drawing on native limestone in his efforts to find an inexpensive process for reproducing some music scores he had composed.

The merit of a fine lithographic print depends upon the texture of the stone surface drawn upon and the lithographer's artistic skill.

For graduated tones the stone surface is first "grained" with sand or other abrasives and water. The basic priciple of lithographic printing lies in the fact that grease and water will not combine. Water is repelled by the "greasy" drawing on a lithographic stone, but printer's ink, also a grease, will adhere to the drawing but not to the water-damped non-printing surface on the stone.

The years around 1820 to 1840 have been called the Golden Age of Litho-

In his Ann Arbor studio, Emile Weddige, professor of Art at University of Michigan and well-known lithographer, pulls a proof of "Child with Daisies" from an original lithographic stone, ca. 1880. The hand press is probably as old as the stone; both owned by Heritage Workshop.

graphy, and many of Europe's finest artists became practitioners of the process. Vernet, Isabey, Prout, Boys and Delacroix are but a few of the famous artists who drew on stone for the presses of Lemercier in France, Hullmandel in Germany, and Day in England. Later, Corot and Millet, Odilon Redon and Toulouse-Lautrec did distinguished work in lithography. All are extremely collectible today.

Lithography developed from single color to multi-color; then around the turn of the century, "offset" or indirect lithography, appeared. Here the design was taken from the stone on to a rubber blanket and thence transferred to the paper. Subsequent developments of thin metal plates, curved round multiple press cylinders, plus photographic plate-making methods have evolved a highly versatile and competitive process.

Collotype and Serigraphs

Collotype or photo-gelatin process printing, was first developed at Metz, Germany, about 1865. While it is a photo-mechanical process, collotype uses the natural reticulation or granular-pattern of gelatin instead of the mechanical ruled halftone screen for the interpretation of tones. Collotype is employed for the reproduction of originals containing fine detail, such as paintings, ancient documents, and anatomical charts where the mechanical screen would break up the facsimile quality of true reproduction. Because the gelatin has a limited life on the press, runs do not generally exceed 3,500 copies before a new plate is needed.

Serigraphs or silk screen prints are a development of stencil printing. Modern photo-mechanical methods of making the stencils on bolting silk permit detail not obtainable in the earlier hand-cut stencil method. It is economical for "short runs," and the use of actual paint instead of printer's ink makes for greater fidelity to an original painting. However, a critical examination will reveal a slight canvas-like patterning on solid paint areas where the silk stencil membrane has left its "footprint." While several successive "printings" can be used in a multi-color serigraph, they are usually in flat tones as distinct from subtle shadings.

Wood Engraving: *The Hermit*, by T. Bewick, after John Johnson. (1795.)

ETCHINGS—The earliest forms of etchings, it is said, were prints made by goldsmiths, silversmiths, and sword-makers as a record for themselves of the designs they had executed on metal for their clients.

In etchings, the design is eaten away by acid on a metal plate which has all of the non-printing surface protected by an acid-resisting asphaltum compound. The points of the etching needles used to trace the design and lift away the "resist" are rounded and blunt, and do not actually cut into the metal surface as is done in "engraving" proper. In order to get strength and depth and perspective, the strength of the acid bath and the length of time the plate is allowed to remain immersed play a vital role.

It was not until after Durer that etching really came to perfection; he, Rembrandt, and Whistler are reckoned among the all time "greats."

Close examination of an etching will reveal a thicker accumulation of ink in the solids and heavy lines as a result of the deeper acid-biting into the copper. A photo-gelatin reproduction of an etching (and there are many) will not have this character, but will show an ink film of uniform thickness.

AQUATINTS are a development from etching. Thomas Rowlandson, an Englishman, made good use of this process. The lines were first etched, then on top of them, the plate was again covered with a "ground"; this time, the addition of spirits of wine to the asphaltum permitted a reticulated surface, allowing the acid to etch whole areas in a uniform "tint."

ENGRAVINGS, usually made on a polished plate of copper, are done directly by hand, with a small, sharp-edged steel rod of square, triangular, or lozenge-shaped section, known as a "graver" or "burin." In 1857, the invention of steel-facing the copper plate, after engraving, made for greater life on the printing press. So-called "steel engravings" are a misnomer; actually they are steel-faced copperplate engravings.

A "Flagellation" of 1446 is the earliest dated example of line engraving on copper. Martin Schongauer of Colmar, Andrea Mantegna of Vicenza, and Jacopo de Barbari of Venice were famous 15th century engravers.

ETCHING: *Landscape with Three Gabled Cottages beside a Road, by Rembrandt.* Signed in the plate *Rembrandt f.*

MEZZOTINTS (pronounced *metzotints*) are a "tone" process of great subtlety and call for much skill and patience. A polished sheet of copper is "roughened" by hand with a rocking tool—a flat steel instrument about 2½ inches wide, with a curved cutting edge of from 50 to 200 teeth to the inch. This is rocked steadily back and forth until the plate surface has been impressed uniformly all over, and repeated from various angles. A proof from the completely "rocked" plate would print as a solid black. The artist draws directly on the prepared plate, and works from dark to light by scraping away the burr and reducing the depth of the dots.

While many mezzotints were printed in one color, it became fashionable in the 19th century for the artist to apply several colors directly to the plate, especially with portraits, and take a multi-color mezzotint print in one impression. This was, of necessity, a slow and therefore expensive process.

GRAVURE, heliogravure, photogravure, rotogravure all are terms used to describe the photo-mechanical process wherein the design is etched below the non-printing surface of the copper plate or cylinder. Known in the 1890s as the "Rembrandt Process," it is capable of excellent artistic results. After the plate or cylinder has been etched, it is immersed in a volatile liquid printing ink, the excess removed by a fine steel knife or "doctor" blade.

Goupil in Paris, in the late 19th century, produced very fine gravure reproductions; many are found in Fine Art publications of the period. Modern gravure printing was evolved from calico-printing methods, and today full-color gravure is used successfully to print popular national magazines and pictorial supplements.

Despite the fine quality of reproduction, gravure prints are not generally "collectible." Of course, a fine picture will sell for its pictorial or decorative value, but that is something quite apart from print-collecting as such.

IN SUMMARY—there is much to know about prints, their history, their evolution, and their values on today's market. Your local Public Library will have many books on the subject and exhibitions of prints at museums and art centers can act to stimulate and inform you in this fascinating field of collecting.

24
Arts
Artists

Victorian England from Court to Cottage is Meticulously and Beautifully Portrayed in Color in the Once Popular, Now Hard-to-find . . . .

Baxter Prints

by DOROTHY M. HOSKINS

SO little are Baxter prints known in America that it is quite possible to discover one of his delicate frontispieces in a pile of old sheet music for sale at some salvage or thrift shop at five or ten cents a copy, or to be offered prints for the price of the frames.

Not so in England, where Baxter prints, like Currier & Ives in this country, have for years been assiduously collected, studied, catalogued, written about—even faked!

George Baxter was born at Lewes, in Sussex, in 1804. At twenty he was illustrating books published by his father. At twenty-three, he moved to London, served a short apprenticeship with a wood engraver, and in 1827 set up his own business, specializing in color work. For several years he concentrated on book illustrations. Though his first known print, *Butterflies*, 1829, now a rarity prized by collectors, has never been found in such use, it may yet turn up in some unexplored volume.

Baxter did not invent color printing, but he combined and improved upon former methods. At first he produced his color prints with wood blocks only. Later he used a steel plate foundation in combination with wood and metal blocks, and it was on this process that he was granted a patent in 1835.

The picture, which may have been drawn by Baxter himself or by artists in his employ, was first engraved in minute detail on the steel plate. From this a print was taken in a neutral tone, on which the colors were printed, one by one, in oil inks with wood or metal blocks. This use of a separate block for each color or color variation was entirely new to the field of printing. Often twenty different blocks, each intricately cut, would be used to lay on as many different colors. Even in less important prints, as many as ten colors might be used.

Recognition as a historian came with his prints *The Coronation of Queen Victoria,* and *Opening of Her First Parliament,* both issued in 1841. In each of these 21 by 18 inch prints, more than two hundred portraits of England's nobility were accurately drawn, the exquisite colors meticulously registered. These prints were never sold cheaply, but they certainly did not cost the patriotic Britishers who bought them to frame in gold frames and hang on their walls, anything like the 125 pounds at which each was listed in 1926.

At the Great Exhibition of 1851, Baxter was the only artist with a stall. More than a half million of his prints were reported sold there. In 1853, he showed at the New York Exhibition, where his print of New York's Crystal Palace, and his popular prints of c h i l d r e n sold by the thousands.

During the 19-year lifetime of his patent, Baxter issued licenses to other printers to use his process and gave

The Bridesmaid, 1850, 15x10¾", signed, stamped mount, last catalogued at $74.50, has since increased in rarity and value. Other popular young girl prints are The Parting Look, 1858, Day Before Marriage, 1853, 1854; The Lover's Letter Box, 1856; Fruit Girl of the Alps, 1859.

**25
Arts
Artists**

instructions to those who purchased them. At least seven firms worked under his license. Eight other printers are known to have produced prints by Baxter's process after the expiration of his patent.

About 1864, in financial straits, he sold a number of his plates and blocks to Vincent Brooks of London, who republished the prints with the Baxter name. Plates and blocks were later sold to Abraham LeBlond, most successful of all printers of the Baxter process, and who had previously used it under Baxter license. LeBlond erased Baxter's signature and put his own on every plate he used, usually at the extreme bottom edge. By eliminating some of the color blocks, he cut production costs, and was more successful financially than Baxter had been.

Baxter evolved five different stamps to mark his original productions. They were, in effect, seals bearing a crown and varied phrasings. One reads "Printed in oil colors by George Baxter, inventor and patentee"; another, "Printed in oil color by George Baxter, License granted to work the process". Of prints on plain card mounts, many copies were made.

The Baxter print is always delicate, mounted on creamy-pinkish paper or very thin cardboard. The subject is invariably refined, never coarsely humorous. The registration of the color blocks, or plates, is absolutely perfect with no overlapping of colors in any part. Details of dress, furniture, flowers, or scenery are complete, never sketchy or washed in. Wherever a signature is found, on the mount, the print itself, or on the margin, it will be clearly printed. Stamped mounts have the stamp below the subject.

Left: Little Red Riding Hood, 1856, 6¼x4⅜", unsigned, on stamped mount, seldom found, high in value. Right: Jenny Lind, as used in the Julien Music Album, 1850. About 18 Baxter prints were used on music.

A. Le Ministre qui celebre LE LAVEMENT DES PIÉS B.B. Les Diaconisses
la liturgie.   qui lavent les piés.

The Foot Washing, showing the Minister celebrating the liturgy, and the deaconesses performing the foot washing rites.

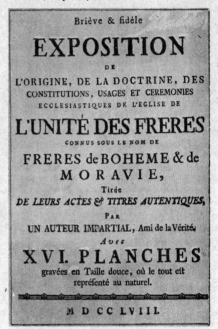

The title page of the book, printed in black and red. Bookplate is that of James Brindley, and a notation, in ink, inside front cover reads, "Bought at Zeist, near Utrecht, Septr 8, 1764."

Some Rare Moravian Prints

WHEN a true antiquarian moves into a community, purchases one of the oldest houses in town, and proceeds to restore it in every detail authentic, one may be sure that furnishings will be selected with equal reverence. So it was with the two-story stone house, built in the Moravian settlement of Lititz in Lancaster County, Pennsylvania, for the Warden of the Community in 1757-1759 (it was two-years a-building) and acquired by the late Carl W. Drepperd in 1954.

Directing his collecting interests, both documentary and objective, to antiques of the Moravians, Mr. Drepperd stripped the old house of all traces of its three modernizations, made in 1811, in 1853, and in 1906, and achieved an approximation of the original building. His furniture presented no problem; he had been a collector of Early Americana for years. But for the house to reveal on its walls, as hangings, something of the philosophy of those who built and lived in it, pictures of an authentic kind were required. It was an unchartered field; pictures of early Lititz might well be non-existent. Views of Bethlehem were known, published in the 17th century, but his interest centered in Lititz. A single water color view of Lititz Square was found at Joe Kindig's in York, Pennsylvania—then nothing.

Concerned with all historical phases of the old town, and con-vinced that *Litiz* was the original name, changed somewhere along the line to *Lititz,* Mr. Drepperd cabled colleagues in Switzerland and France for information on the European *Litiz.* Come the surprising reply: "You probably mean Lititz. Try to find a copy of *A Brief and True Exposition of the Origin and Doctrine . . . of the Church of the United Brethren, or the Brotherhood of Bohemia and Moravians, with 16 plates, Paris, 1758.* The sixteen engravings therein show Moravians in their services, personal, church, and missionary, together with a transcript of the Act of Parliament under George II, 1747, dealing with the permission and invitation of these people to migrate to the Colonies of America."

Excitedly he began a search—but not one major book dealer had ever heard of the book, much less seen it. He tucked the title far back in his mind. Then, one day, six months later, as he casually scanned a modest little booklist of McManus of Philadelphia, a source hitherto overlooked, the name of the book stared up at him. Within telephoned minutes, it was his.

The pictures shown here and on the cover are reproduced from it. All prints are 6½ inches high, more or less, and 8 inches wide, mounted on flaps for easy removal. Only one engraving is signed—J Rod(erick) Holtzhalb, Sculpsit. Their titles,

portraying the scope of Moravian religious activities are listed:

Ordination of a Moravian Bishop
Reception of New Members
Baptism of Infants
Reception of Members in a Negro Mission
Baptism of American Indians
Baptism of Greenlanders
Baptism and Prostration of Negro Members
Consecration of the Articles of Sacrament on Communion Table
Distribution of the Sacraments
Taking the Bread of the Sacrament
Prostration of the Body before God
The Ceremony of the Kiss of Peace
The Washing of Feet by Deaconesses
The Love Feast for the Young Men and Women
Allotment Marriage of Couples in the Colonies (This Month's Cover)
Commemoration for the Dead on Easter Morning (sunrise)

Mr. Drepperd did not live to enjoy much more than a year in the house on which he had worked so enthusiastically and with such detail—his joy had been in the doing. House and collections are now in other appreciative hands. But this reminiscence of his search and finding illustrates one of his precepts of research which should benefit us all: Seek diligently for information . . . ask, listen and remember . . . bear in constant mind the thing you seek. It is not coincidence that the answers—with surprising regularity—fall in the seeker's lap. Had he not asked for information, and memorized the thing to look for when he had the information, he would have skipped over what he considered one of the best buys of his collecting days.

Mourning pictured published by J. Baittie, ca. 1850.

Those Morbid, Woeful, Mourning Pictures

by EDWARD G. CORNWELL, JR.

Artist/Conservator, Rochester Museum
and Science Center, Rochester N.Y.

Mourning picture published by N. Currier, ca. 1846.

DURING THE WANING YEARS of the 18th century, called by its contemporaries the "Age of Reason," the strange fashion for mourning pictures began. This peculiar fashion was stimulated by the first birth pains of Romanticism, which were to blossom fully during the time we know as the Victorian Period.

This trend was due largely to the heroes and heroines of the newly created romantic novels. Foremost among these early efforts was *Paul and Virginia*, the tender tale of the proverbial star-crossed lovers, a wistful couple who ended their days firmly planted side by side, 'neath drooping palms and fragrant flowers on a tropic isle.

The earliest form of Mourning Picture, seldom seen in antiques shops today, was the carefully hand-painted scene on silk, paper, or velvet showing grief-stricken ladies in the high-waisted gowns of 1790 through 1820, posing beneath graceful weeping willows, with silk handkerchiefs sadly held to their dewy eyes. Occasionally, these charming dames are accompanied by slim-waisted gentlemen in dark beaver hats. Monuments, which often occupy central positions in these compositions, are duely inscribed with the name of the deceased or with an appropriately mournful poem of doubtful verse.

The potters of Staffordshire, England, during this period also produced charming statues of mournful maids in classic dress standing with downcast eyes beside Greek Urns. These figures can be found either in color or without color.

The Staffordshire potters also produced tea sets banded in black with high-collared young men weeping by the tomb of Princess Charlotte, who had been deeply loved by the English people of her time.

This preoccupation with the dearly departed may seem a strange phenomenon and a trifle morbid to modern eyes. It is necessary to remember that during this era, the average family lived with the constant threat of the early departure of loved ones to the "other life."

As the century progressed, enterprising American businessmen, capitalizing on the discovery of the lithographic process which occurred in the latter part of the 18th century, proceeded to supply the demands for "Mourning Pictures" by printing them in large quantities. The Lithographic process was discovered by Alvin Senefelder, a Bavarian. The first producers of lithographs on a large scale in this country were the brothers William and John Pendleton, of Boston. Nathaniel Currier was an apprentice with them at the age of fourteen.

Melancholy prints found a ready market. They were inexpensive, costing only a few cents each. To add to their attraction, they were colored by hand with watercolors, imitating the earlier handcrafted examples. These colors were applied at the printers by trained women and young children who worked on a production line basis, each person doing all areas of one color and passing the work on to the next. The palette for this type of print was usually limited to four colors — green, gold, blue, and black.

By the 1840s few, indeed, were the homes of the middle class which did not contain at least one of these tokens of grief. These pictures hung in solemn and soberly furnished best parlors, closed off, and seldom seen other than on formal occasions.

Although the quaint hand-painted momentoes of the early period quite often sported the neatly moulded gold leaf frame, this was soon superseded by the simple mahogany veneered and slightly beveled frame, dear to the Victorians. One quite often comes across these prints still wearing this popular frame. Usually, age has been fairly gentle with them and they suffer only the loss of some veneer.

There are a number of varieties of Mourning Prints available to the present day collectors. Among these are pictured the single female figure mourning, the single male mourning, the mother and the child mourning.

Collectible Art Nouveau Lithographs

by Albert Christian Revi

I N THE late 19th and early 20th centuries, there were revolutionary changes in decorative styles characterized by organic forms, sinuous lines, and non-geometric curves which became known as l'Art Nouveau. During this somewhat sensuous era, poster art attained a high level and many famous artists of the period were persuaded to create poster designs for a variety of commercial and artistic enterprises — foodstuffs, theatrical performances, calendars, books, beverages, etc.

These art posters appeared as advertisements in magazines and newspapers, were splashed all over cities and towns on billboards and buildings, and were passed out on street corners in the form of handbills. Literally thousands of copies were printed, but most of them ended up in the streets or were destroyed or covered over to accommodate other posters. A few artists thought enough of their works to make saleable lithographic copies. Some of these have survived the rigors of time and the inevitable changes in "art appreciation" — that elusive factor that swings back and forth like a pendulum from one extreme to the other.

Continental — and more especially French artists—were more prolific in their production of art posters than their English and American contemporaries. For this reason French lithographs are easier to find and in many instances less expensive. Unless you are collecting proofs signed by such artists as Henri de Toulouse-Lautrec, Alphonse Mucha, Henri Van de Velde, Aubrey Beardsley, and other important artists of this period, Art Nouveau prints and lithographs can be purchased for as little as $15; they can also cost several hundred dollars, depending on the subject, the artist, the condition of the lithograph, and the number of copies extant.

It would be an ambitious undertaking to attempt to enumerate all of the artists who were prominent in this area of the decorative arts, but we hope this introduction to Art Nouveau lithographs will apprise collectors of their worth and availability at a fairly nominal cost. Framed, and hung in the proper setting, they can lend a whimsical air to late Victorian furnishings and lighten an otherwise heavy atmosphere.

A Girl Gathering Flowers (Fig. 1) is typical of a style used by the Frenchman Eugene-Samuel Grasset— and others — wherein the subject is clearly defined with heavy lines and flat, subtle colors devoid of any shading; there is no attempt to make the picture three-dimensional. By declining to portray his subjects with volume and light, Grasset gave them an unreal dimension, at the same time leaving no room for conjecture or misinterpretation of any kind. Many

Figure 3. **Le Fee au Rocher,** a colored lithograph by Jules Cheret; 15½ x 11". Author's collection. (Poist's Studio photo.)

Figure 2. **Girl with Iris,** a colored lithograph by Georges Bottini; 13 x 11½". Author's collection. (Poist's Studio photo.)

Figure 1. **A Girl Gathering Flowers,** Salon des Cent; lithograph printed in colors by Eugene Grasset; 26 x 17¾". Author's collection. (Photo courtesy Parke-Bernet Galleries, Inc.)

Figure 10. **Tiger Lilies**, a colored lithograph from Walter Crane's book, **Flora's Feast**, 1889; 7¾ x 5½". Author's collection.

of Grasset's posters resemble cartoons for stained glass windows and murals, the heavy outlines having the appearance of leading. A departure from this charming, albeit saccharine style, is Grasset's *Drug Addict*, a shocking, stark portrayal of a tortured girl administering her release from reality.

George Alfred Bottini excelled in the use of gouache — a method of painting with opaque colors, ground in water and mixed with gum. This medium was particularly suitable to his hybrid Persian and Japanese style, mirroring scenes of intimate life. Bottini's *Girl with Iris (Fig. 2)* seems, at first glance, a far cry from his usual theme in which young women were depicted languishing in drug and

Figure 4. **Quinquina Dubonnet Avec Un Chat**, by Jules Cheret; a color proof before letters; 23½ x 16½". Author's collection.

The Process of Lithography

Lithography is the method of printing from flat surfaces. Originally these surfaces were of stone —hence the term "lithography" or "stone-writing." All forms of planographic printing, including lithography, are based on a printing principle first used by Aloys Senefelder, in 1796.

Senefelder reasoned that since grease and water repel each other, a lithographic plate must be so treated that the portion to be reproduced has an affinity for grease (ink) and repels water, and the balance of the plate, which is not to be reproduced, attracts water and repels the greasy ink. When the paper is applied under pressure to the lithographic stone, or plate, the inked portion will be impressed.

Later, in 1826, Senefelder invented a process for printing colored lithographs; some one hundred years after his discovery, zinc and aluminum plates replaced the old stone plates. Lithographs produced in the Art Nouveau period were usually printed from stone plates.

Figure 7. Alphonse Mucha's **Au Quartier Latin**, 1898; a lithograph proof printed from the black outline stone alone, signed with a paraphe and inscribed "Epreuve d'Artiste No. 2," with the atelier stamp at lower right; 15¾ x 11¾". (Photo courtesy Parke-Bernet Galleries, Inc.)

(Below)

Figure 6. **The Four Seasons**, by Alphonse Mucha; a proof before letters for a calendar in colors and gilt; 16¾ x 23⅜". Author's collection. (Poist's Studio photo.)

alcohol-induced melancholia. However, the lowered eyelids and relaxed attitude of the girl's face belie the danger of the serpents entwined in her auburn hair. The subject's features, somewhat reminiscent of Italian portraits of the 15th and 16th centuries, and the delicate shades of mauve, purple, yellow, green, and pink Bottini used in this lithograph require careful study to be fully appreciated.

Jean-Louis Forain, the satirical cartoonist, once described Jules Cheret (1836-1932) as the "steam-driven Watteau." Cheret's charming lithograph, *La Fee au Rocher (Fig. 3)*, would certainly confirm Forain's criticism for it easily relates to paintings by that 18th century French master, Jean Antoine Watteau. Cheret's contemporaries considered
(Please Turn the Page)

Figure 12. Poster executed for a bicycle company advertisement by William H. Bradley, ca. 1900.

Figure 14. **La Reine Wilhelmine,** a lithograph printed in yellow, grey and black, by Paul Berthon; 15⅜ x 13¾". Author's collection. (Poist's Studio photo.)

Figure 8. **The Toilette of Salome,** by Aubrey Beardsley, from Oscar Wilde's **Salome.**

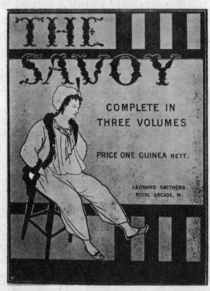

Figure 15. Cover design for **The Savoy, No. 8,** in color, by Aubrey Beardsley; initialed in the stone. (Reputed to be the only lithograph done by the artist himself.) 10¼ x 7¾". Author's collection. (Poist's Studio photo.)

Figure 9. Caricature of James Whistler; a design for the cover of The Dancing Faun, by Aubrey Beardsley.

him a better poster artist than a painter. His quick, nervous delineations of very young women, seemingly caught at the precise moment of a flirtatious affectation, reflects the gay mood of Paris at the peak of the Art Nouveau period. In *Dubonnet (Fig. 4),* a poster advertising a sweet wine, the artist's penchant for pretty faces is evident. "Very 1900" is what his mid-20th century critics say of Cheret's poster art; the graceful pose of the young woman portrayed in his *Palais de Glace* poster is unmistakably *fin de siecle.*

One of the most popular poster artists in France at the turn of the century was Alphonse Marie Mucha (1860–1939), a Czech decorative painter and illustrator. Mucha's portrayals of the "Divine Sarah" Bernhardt in some of her elaborate stage

costumes are much sought after by collectors and usually command a very high price. Some of these theatre posters are as much as 5 to 6 feet tall, and about 2 to 3 feet wide. All of the details of the costumes are laboriously reproduced in various colors, and the name of the actress and the play in which she was appearing at that time are woven into the overall design of the poster like a fine Flemish tapestry. Mucha's calendar art *(Fig. 6)* is equally important, and paintings by this famous illustrator—whenever they appear for sale—are very expensive.

Lithographs of works created by Aubrey Vincent Beardsley (1872–1898), a young English illustrator, are few and far between these days; they are rarely on the market, and always expensive. Nevertheless, in spite of

Beardsley's short working career (he died in his mid-twenties) he was very productive and "spoke" the *Esperanto* of Art Nouveau fluently. Before he became a celebrated illustrator of books—*Morte d'Arthur, Rape of the Lock, Madamoiselle de Maupin,* Oscar Wilde's *Salome,* and others—he was employed in an architect's office. In 1894, Beardsley was art director of *The Yellow Book.* His contributions to *The Studio,* another *avant garde* magazine featuring all facets of the Art Nouveau trend, were often used as models by both professional and amateur artists. At the height of the Victorian era, his risque sketches

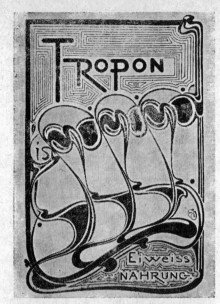

Figure 13. **Tropon,** a rare lithograph for the magazine **Pan,** Vol. IV, Number 1, by Henri Van de Velde, printed in yellow, orange, purple and black; 12¼ x 7⅞". Author's collection. (Photo courtesy Parke-Bernet Galleries, Inc.)

Figure 11. **Dancing Girls,** by William H. Bradley, 1894.

vised, and finally drawn in India ink. Beardsley's cover design for *The Savoy* (*Fig. 15*) is reputed to be the only lithograph actually drawn on the stone by the artist; the rest of his works were, for the most part, reproduced in offset, at that time a relatively new printing process.

On the Continent, Walter Crane (1845–1915) was considered the most important representative of the "English style" in Art Nouveau drawing and painting. The children's books which he illustrated are considered to be the most beautiful pictorial works for the young produced in the last half of the 19th century. Some art critics believe that Crane was imitating a fluid style of drawing initiated by William Blake, an 18th century English illustrator. In *Flora's Feast,* the flower creatures seem to be a blend of animal and human forms (*Fig. 10*), similar to some produced by Blake. As a wood engraver, Crane studied the works of Pre-Raphaelites; he was influenced by Botticelli; and with William Morris, he was a leader in the romantic movement in British decorative art.

Henri Van de Velde (1863–1957), a Belgian architect and craftsman, was a leader of a modern movement in his country at the turn of the century. While the influence of Post-Impressionism is visible in his works, he translated all this into two-dimensional, poster-like figures with concentric lines in an unnaturalistic manner. Van de Velde's *Tropon* (*Fig. 13*) is acknowledged as one of the best abstraction posters of the Art Nouveau period. Aubrey Beardsley's influence on Van de Velde's work is evidenced in the merging of the abstract decoration into a synthetic whole, a technique Beardsley employed in his

were thought much too naughty, and only a few of them were ever published for public consumption in their original state. The waspish nature of the artist is best seen in his satirical sketches, his caricature of the American artist, James Abbott McNeill Whistler, being one of the best examples (*Fig. 9*). Perhaps Beardsley's disdain for established standards of deportment—in art at least—was the reason for his continued fame as an illustrator long after his death, in 1898. With the exception of a single oil painting and a few colored drawings and lithographs, all of Beardsley's works were done in black and white. Initially, the sketches were executed in pencil, refined and re-

illustrations for Malory's *Morte d'Arthur.*

The American artist William H. Bradley (born 1868), like most of his contemporaries, used a profusion of curved lines in his art poster designs. His works were known and admired in Europe as early as 1894, and continued to be popular long after the Art Nouveau period had phased out completely. As late as 1930, Bradley was the best-paid designer in the United States, creating designs for interiors, wallpaper, and architectural structures. His style suggests a strong Japanese impetus, but his use of concentric lines and curves (*Fig. 11*) can be related to the works of Aubrey Beardsley, too.

Figure 5. **Les Montmartroises, Poesies et Chansons,** by Georges De Feure; original colored lithograph initialed in the stone; 31¾ x 12". Author's collection. (Poist's Studio photo.)

Ornamental Pen Drawing

by CARROLL HOPF, Curator

Pennsylvania Farm Museum of Landis Valley

FLOURISHING, or ornamental pen drawing, originates in the method of hand writing known as "English Round Hand." This particular technique is derived from the "Carolingian minuscule" developed in the late 14th century by Italian scholars intent upon developing a more legible handwriting for manuscripts. By the early 1700s, Round Hand technique of writing (characterized by rounded connected letters) was more universally accepted by English businessmen and scholars alike, as it was advocated by the calligraphic copybooks of the period.

English commercial enterprise then called for a round, even-flowing hand that could be executed quickly and still be neat and efficient.

Besides containing alphabets in Round Hand and examples of properly executed business transactions, copybooks often included flourished designs of animals, fish, plant forms, and human figures. *Calligraphia Latina,* published in Austria in 1756 by Johann Schwandner, contains many such delightful subjects interspersed among 300 ornamental initials forming 12 complete alphabets.

Probably the most noteworthy Eng-

lish copybook produced during the 18th century is *The Universal Penman,* engraved by George Bickman of London. Bickham began his project in 1733 and took approximately eight years for its completion. He, like Schwandner, included various designs to draw for, in his words, "Drawing is another necessary Qualification (writing is first for the educated individual) and therefore I have attempted to make the Decoration of the Work fit for the imitation of those whose Genius prompts them to the Study of that Art."

Undoubtly Bickham's work was an important source for practicing writing-masters in American seaport towns. Lesser itinerant penman, probably many of whom were self-taught, traveled throughout the New England countryside holding penmanship classes in private homes or the village school. Copybooks by American authors were being used in this country in the early 19th century.

There is in the Landis Valley Farm Museum's library a well preserved copy of *The Penman's Paradise,* published by Nathaniel Knapp and Levi Rightmyer in St. Louis, in 1848. The publishers maintained it was "designed and executed for the improvement of youth or amusement of the curious." Its 14 pages afforded the student many fine flourished examples of birds, fish, flowers, and initials. A sincere and concentrated effort was needed on the part of the student to execute in free hand the illustrated examples. Frequently the finished drawing assumed a delightfully individual touch extending into the realm of folk art, such as the lion, illustrated here.

Later penmanship authors found it more profitable to pursue the concept of "Yes, you too can create a perfect flourished specimen," for *Smith's Quick Learning Method of Penmanship,* published in 1883, and *Real Pen Work, Self Instructor in Penmanship,* published in 1881, advocated "The Tracing Process." This "plain and easy" process amounted to tracing the design pictured in the book. Traces of pencil lines may frequently be noticed where the later inked line did not completely cover on examples executed by this process.

The horse, deer, lion, and various bird forms seem to be the most popular subjects for flourish draw-

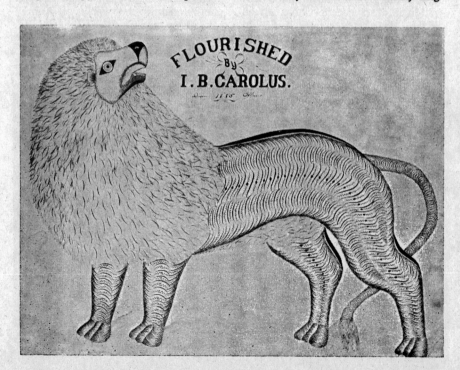

Flourished lion, executed by
I. B. Carolius of Dixon, Illinois,
in 1885, measures 27½" by 21½".
Author's collection.

Spencerian Steel Pens.

No. 1 (College). A pen similar to the Zanerian Ideal and Gillott's No. 604.
1 gross, $1.00; ¼ gross, 25c.; 1 doz., 10c.

No. 12 (Epistolaire). A small, very fine pointed pen, and probably the finest pointed pen made with which free hand writing can be executed by a skillful hand. This is really a remarkable pen for executing exceedingly fine writing, engrossing script, drawing, etc., and is wonderfully durable.
1 gross, $1.00; ¼ gross, 25c.; 1 doz., 10c.

No. 14 (Artistic). A pen much like the Zanerian Fine Writer and Gillott's Principality No. 1.
1 gross, $1.00; ¼ gross, 25c.; 1 doz. 10c.

No. 25 (Drawing Pen). A very fine pointed pen for writing and drawing.
1 gross, $1.00; ¼ gross, 25c.; 1 doz., 10c.

ing. Less frequently seen are profile views of human heads, winged cherubs, fish forms, and various types of smaller animals. Probably the majority of examples found today in antiques shops and museum collections date from the last half of the 19th century.

It is appropriate to comment here on the term "Spencerian Work," which is often applied to flourish drawings. The styles and designs Platt Rogers Spencer advocated were in use long before 1849, when his first copybook was published.

Flourished fish form executed on the first page of a Lancaster County, Pa., will dated 1771. The style and form is closely related to the fish appearing in "Calligraphia Latina." Author's collection.

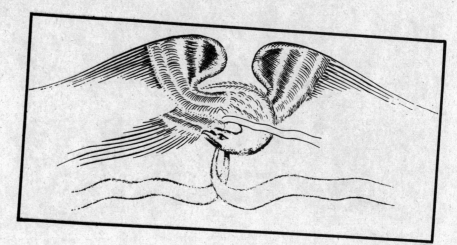

Eagle, deer, and lion flourished by J. M. Scheaffer of Farmersville, Pa., in 1883; each measures 28" by 20". The deer was probably copied from an example illustrated in "Real Pen Work, Self Instructor in Penmanship." Collection Pennsylvania Farm Museum of Landis Valley.

A rare hollow-cut profile of a young man mounted on a mirror, with protective covering of thin cardboard and carrying case covered with hand-stenciled wallpaper. "Anne Parvins glass" written in pen and ink on back of the mirror. (The subject could have been Anne's suitor.) New England, ca. 1830. 3½ x 4¾ inches. (Collection Mrs. Claudia Hopf.)

Full length silhouette of Mrs. Frank Talta-vull made on the Boardwalk at Atlantic City, N. J., in 1922. The figure was cut with a scissors freehand and slashes made with a knife to accentuate details of the costume. (Author's collection.)

Silhouettes...

"Shades" of the Past

by PHYLLIS T. BALLINGER

 FORM OF FOLK ART which well deserves our attention are those lovely little silhouettes that were so popular during the 18th and 19th century. These interesting shadow likenesses of people from the past have great charm. They were not only accurate profiles of the subject but they also give us clues to clothing and hair styling popular at the time.

Some people even thought they were helpful in studying a person's character and intelligence through the science of physiognomy. In fact, Joseph Sansom, an 18th century silhouettist who lived in Philadelphia, called his collection of silhouettes, now in the possession of the Historical Society of Pennsylvania, "Physiognomical Sketches." He did the likenesses of many famous people who visited the city during the years that it was our Nation's capital.

The word "silhouette" is taken from the name of a Frenchman, Etienne de Silhouette, who lived from 1709 to 1767. He was minister of finance during the reign of Louis XV

and had a reputation for being very tight with money. In fact, he was so much so that any object that was cheap was called "a' la Silhouette." Etienne de Silhouette also cut "shades" as a pastime. Since portraits of this type were inexpensive, they too got to be known as Silhouettes.

No one really knows who first made shadow profiles. Outline drawings executed in contrasting colors were made by early cave dwellers in Southern France, and throughout the history of art outline drawings emphasizing facial contours and shadows were used effectively and dramatically. How paper cutting as applied to shadow profiles came about is unknown, but by the 18th century it was a well developed art. Cut-out artists would snip a profile in black paper and with a few outline touches in white or gold produce a very effective likeness of the subject. Sometimes the technique was reversed and the likeness was cut leaving an open area which was put against a contrasting background. This was called "hollow-cut." The likeness could be

of just the head or the full figure. Later entire family groups appeared in one picture and the background might depict a room in their home or a stylized setting.

The artist Charles Willson Peale, progenitor of that great family of artists, used a physiognotrace as early as 1803 to make silhouettes in his museum in the State House (Independence Hall, Philadelphia). For a charge of eight cents, visitors to the museum could have their profiles traced. Then, by folding the paper twice, four copies could be cut at one time with a pair of sharp scissors. Usually they were mounted on cream colored paper, 4¼ by 5¼ inches in size. An embossed "Museum" under the image was proof of where it had been made.

Peale's physiognotrace was made by John Hawkins in 1802. It was a clever gadget mounted on a wall. The device could be raised or lowered permitting the sitter to place his cheek against a projecting rest. A pointer, which was part of the apparatus, was guided over the face and head. This

Silhouette of Thomas Ballinger, cut in Paris in 1932, "in the shadow of the Eiffel Tower." It was popular for tourists to have a profile cut as a souvenir. This was also being done on the Boardwalk at Atlantic City, N. J., and at other resorts in America and abroad. (Author's collection.)

Left: Profile of Benjamin Franklin by Joseph Sansom, ca. 1890-92. "Drawn from memory, without the use of a scale, the first stroke that conveyed a resemblance necessarily determined the size of the figure, as it was dangerous to retouch." Written by Sansom for the preface to his collection of "Physiogonomical Sketches," this description relates his method of working. **Center:** The fine detail and careful cutting of this silhouette by Charles Willson Peale gives this silhouette a particular charm. Many of Peale's silhouettes were cut at his museum in the State House, Philadelphia, by his servant, Moses Williams, who became very skilled at the art. Barely visible in the photograph is the word "Museum." Peale also used an embossed stamp of an eagle with its wings spread over the inscription "Peales Museum." **Right:** In this hollow-cut, Peale used pen and ink to add details to the hair and dress of his subject.

1930s could have their likenesses made in black and white between strolls along the Boardwalk. Travelers in Paris were doing the same in the shadow of the Eiffel Tower. Silhouettes of this vintage can be had at a fraction of the cost of earlier specimens. All of them are charming little portraits, whether "drawn from life" or "drawn from memory."

action in turn moved a second pointer which was so situated as to reduce the lines proportionately such as a pantograph will do. The end result was a diminutive "shade."

Working in Salem, No. Car., from 1816 to 1830, the Moravian clockmaker and silversmith, John Vogler, practiced the craft as a side-line. Some of his silhouettes and his ingenious Silhouette "machine" can still be seen by visitors to Old Salem, the restored Moravian town which is now a living museum.

There were a number of people who did this type of portraiture, both professional and amateur. One professional whose work is highly regarded was August Edouart. Born in France, Edouart was unsuccessful as a teacher and turned to the art of the silhouette. By 1825 he was quite successful at it. He cut a number of silhouettes in England before coming to the United States where he was particularly popular among Quaker families who were willing to accept this form of portraiture above the more ostentatious paintings in oil. William Henry Brown made a number of cuts of well-known Americans. Silhouettes produced by William King, William Bache, James Hubare and William Doyle are very much sought after these days.

Although they waned in popularity with the introduction of daguerreotypes just prior to the Civil War, ever so often there was a revival of interest in silhouette portraiture. Visitors to Atlantic City, N. J., in the 1920s and

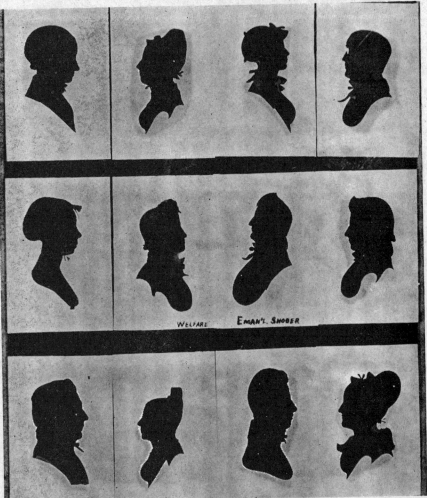

Shades showing a variety of profiles cut by the early 19th century Moravian silhouettist, John Vogler, at his clock and silversmithing shop in Salem, N. C. (Courtesy of Old Salem, Inc., Winston-Salem, N. C.)

Rubbings From Monumental Brasses

Fig. 1—Rubbing of brass memorial to Sir Simon Felbrigg reproduced on 10" card. Original rubbing measures 5' 4".

MRS. ROSEMARY HAKLISCH of Haddonfield, N. J., is English, married to an American, and most fortunate to be able to visit her family in England every spring. While in her homeland, she devotes as much time as possible to "brass rubbing"— a hobby she was introduced to in 1964. She joined the Monumental Brass Society of Great Britian (established in 1886), and in the last three years she has rubbed about 100 brasses. These memorials to the dead are of great historical value representing as they do a pictorial record of costume and heraldry during the Medieval Ages. All classes of society were commemorated—knights, ladies, civilians, tradesmen, and many ecclesiastical ranks. Mrs. Haklisch has framed several of her rubbings for wall decorations; one of them she reproduced in black, to fit on a 10" card.

Three factors favored the development of brasses: (a) the metal was a beautiful color; (b) the memorial could be set in the floor of the church, so created few problems of arrangement or space; (c) a pictorial representation, unlike sculpture, could be varied in size without distortion. Stone effig'es of equal antiquity are frequently mutilated, but brass, being a remarkedly hard metal, defies the hand of time and the penknife of the desecrator.

Brasses vary considerably in size— 13th century knights are often represented nearly life-size. A knight is shown in a recumbent position, with his hands joined in an attitude of prayer, and quite often with a lion— the symbol of strength and courage— at his feet. The legs of a few knights are crossed, and some people theorize that this was to signify that they went on the Crusades.

The oldest existing brass memorial in England, dated 1277, is a representation of Sir John D'Abernon. It's located in the village church of Stoke D'Abernon, Surrey. The oldest brass rubbed by Mrs. Haklisch depicts Sir John de Creke, and is dated 1325; it can be found in Westley Waterless, Cambridgeshire.

One church containing a wealth of brasses' is located in Felbrigg, Norfolk. The brasses in Felbrigg Church

Fig. 2—Rubbing of brass memorial to Margaret Bernard of Isleham, wife of Sir Thomas Peyton; obit, ca. 1470; length 28".

span 300 years, the most important being that of Sir Simon Felbrigg, standard bearer to King Richard II, and 92nd knight to receive the Order of the Garter; his is one of six brasses still in existence showing Knights of the Garter. Very little is known about Sir Simon's exploits during the reign of Henry IV, but he accompanied Henry V to France, and participated in the famous battle of Agincourt. (Figure 1).

Changes in fashion are beautifully illustrated on brass memorials to great ladies. In the 13th century a hideous wimple was worn around the neck, hiding the chin and sides of the face. Next came the nebule or zigzag headdress, the hair being enclosed within a net in a series of wavy lines. The horned and butterfly headdresses of the 15th century were most distinctive. In Mrs. Haklisch's collection is a rubbing of Margaret Bernard, first wife of Sir Thomas Peyton, wearing a beautiful gown and butterfly headdress (Figure 2).

The Bernard family was quite wealthy and gave their daughter Margaret a substantial dowry, so she was welcomed with open arms by the slightly impoverished Peytons. Another lady wearing a butterfly headdress is Isabel Cheyne, daughter of Sir Geoffrey Boleyn and great-aunt of Queen Anne (Boleyn), who was beheaded by her husband, King Henry VIII.

Many brasses have interesting inscriptions. That of Anne Asteley reads: "Pray for the soul of Anne Wood, second wife of Thomas Asteley, Esq. of Melton Constable, who, on the day of St. Agapetus the Martyr, brought forth twins, a boy and a girl, and after the peril of Childbirth, passed straightway to the Lord in the year of Christ the Most Gracious 1512."

Some brasses reveal the trade of the deceased by the foot rests. The export of wool was England's most lucrative trade between the 14th and 16th centuries, so quite a few brasses show merchants standing on wool sacks, rams, and sheep. A tailor named William Scors, who died in 1447, in Northleach, Gloucestshire, has a pair of scissors as his foot rest.

During the reign of Henry VIII many brass memorials were destroyed; authorities in each county in England were ordered to remove all effigies, shrines and relics which might be considered Popish. In Cromwell's time, several brasses were defaced, and a number were pried up and sold to be used in the casting of cannons.

Before a brass rubbing can be made, permission must be granted by the vicar or rector of the church in which it is located; sometimes a small fee is charged for this privilege. The memorial should be examined for protruding rivets, plate joints and other irregularities. These irregularities can present some problems when the rubbing is made. Cleaning off the brass with a duster removes any grit that might tear the paper. Strong, thin paper with a rag base—like that used by architects—is laid over the brass and fixed with masking tape to prevent slipping. The wax used to rub the brass is called "black heel ball"—a mixture of beeswax, tallow and lamp black. Hard rubbing from start to finish is necessaary to produce an even black effect. Colored waxes — either blue or brown — can also be used. Thin gold or silver wallpaper can be substituted for white paper to produce interesting backgrounds for a rubbing; however, wallpaper has a slight sheen which makes it extremely difficult to produce a nice dark rubbing.

Rubbings can be rolled up and stored in plastic or cardboard tubes until they are framed according to personal taste. Mrs. Haklisch prefers black and gold frames in a Gothic style.

A. Gandon's Sketches of
"La Vie Californienne"

PUBLISHED at Geneva, 1859, the book "Scenes de la Vie Californienne" introduced the fabulous story of California . . . and the Gold Rush . . . to the people of France and Switzerland. F. Gerstacker, a German wrote the book and the French-Swiss edition of 1859 is translated from the German by the Swiss Scholar Gustave Revilliod.

We are not, as antiquarians, concerned with either the German or the French text but we are concerned with the etchings by A. Gandon which illustrate the French edition. Why? Because they are Americana — Californiana—of intense interest and, while small in size (approximately 3¼x5") what they lack in size is more than compensated for by their quality and choice of subject.

For example, would you expect to find an engraved (and so documented) picture of a rodeo done so early as 1859? Would you see a typical Gold rush bar with dancing girls, barmaids, Chinese gamblers and every kind of adventurer pictured to perfection?

A. Gandon, the artist drew with a pen dipped in fact. His etchings, in addition to those pictured (Rodeo and Gold Rush Bar), include justice, mining, and punishment examples.

To the collectors of California we can only say, seek a copy of this antiquarian book at the shops of old book dealers and you will have the kind of pictures you will want for your California interior decor.

Fore-edge painting of Strawberry Hill, the renowned seat of Horace Walpole, 4th Earl of Orford, 1717-1797, which appears on the fore-edge of a catalog listing the contents of the house. It is completely hidden under gilt until the pages are fanned. The painting is beautifully executed showing the delicate rose pink of the buildings, greens of the lawns, and lacy cloud effects in a blue sky. This rare and beautiful book may be seen in the Metropolitan Toronto Central Library, Toronto, Canada.

Fore-Edge Paintings

by MARY CAROL WILSON

FORE-EDGE PAINTINGS in rare books provide not only delight to collectors but present them with mysteries in more ways than one.

Today there are ancient, possibly cherished, gilt-edged books or books having edges with a marbled effect which conceal paintings quite unknown to the present owners. When the pages are fanned left to right a painting is revealed. More rarely, if the pages of the same book are fanned right to left, a second picture may be found.

The custom of marking books on the fore-edge is almost as old as books themselves. It is certainly older than the rarest of printed books. Manuscript books usually were stored flat with the unbound edges visible. To save the reader taking the book down and opening it to learn its contents, the title was marked on the fore-edge. This could only be read when the book was closed.

Henry VII was the first English monarch to take an interest in books and to form a royal library. Some of his books are still to be found in the British Museum; others are in Westminster Abbey Library.

In 1509 Henry VIII appointed Thomas Berthelet as King's printer. It was Berthelet who introduced into England the art of gold tooling on leather bindings in the Italian fashion. He is said to be the first person to produce heraldic designs in color on book edges. Long before Gutenberg appeared on the scene, the practice of adorning fine books with coats of arms, famous mottoes, and royal monograms had begun.

A Bible printed in Zurich in 1543 belonged to Henry VIII and was decorated by Berthelet not only on the fore-edge, but also on the top and bottom edges. But the Berthelet designs were destroyed when the book was opened.

It is now claimed that Samuel Hearne, who was appointed royal bookbinder to Charles II from 1660 to 1683, invented what we know today as fore-edging painting. This was done in water colour with a very dry brush on the fanned pages of a book. Hearne, or one of his employees, decorated in this fashion a copy of the *Book of Common Prayer* which was printed in London in 1669.

Queen Elizabeth owned a Latin Bible published in London in 1585 and bound in red velvet. On the fore-edge is a diminutive copy of Da Vinci's "Last Supper." The artist, Joseph Fletcher, concealed the painting under gilt so that it is quite hidden until the pages are fanned. This book is now in the Huntington Library in California. It solves what was for some time an enigma since previous to its discovery, collectors took for granted that the fore-edge painting on a book always was done at the same time as the book was printed and bound. Actually, it was quite often done a hundred or more years later. John Fox's *Acts and Monuments* bears a fore-edge painting of Charles II, also signed by Fletcher.

The art of fore-edge painting was practiced almost exclusively in England. For some years after its invention it was very popular, then the art was discontinued for a while. It was revived about 1750 by William Edwards, one of six members of a family known as the Edwards of Halifax, booksellers and collectors of rare books. The Edwards father became famous by his purchase at auction of the Bedford Missal for 203 guineas.

William Edwards also revived the art of Etruscan binding. A Prayer Book which he bound in transparent vellum for Queen Charlotte bears the royal coat of arms in centre oval, with the initials "C.R." in silver. The fore-edge painting of this book is under gilt and depicts the Resurrection.

Another rare book, bearing a fore-edge painting of Mount Vesuvius in eruption, is a copy of Virgil, printed in 1766. This is in the Doheny collection, California.

Edwards of Halifax inaugurated hunting and fishing scenes in fore-edge paintings. Double fore-edge paintings were also a speciality of this firm.

A fine example of double fore-edge painting is found in More's *History of Richard III* which shows the Boar Inn, Leicester, and a portrait of Richard III when the pages are fanned left to right. When fanned in the opposite direction, a view of Gloucester and a portrait of Edward V. appear.

Another handsome example is Scott's *Lay of the Last Minstrel*, in the Colby College Library. Featherstone Castle appears in one painting while Barnard Castle at Durham is shown in the other. This book is bound in maroon leather with minstrel's harps stamped in gold on the binding.

Collectors of rare books treasure the beautiful Etruscan bindings of both Hearne and Edwards, but an additional joy is provided if a hitherto unknown fore-edge painting is discovered. Because so few of these fore-edge paintings were signed, however, the names of many of these painstaking artists still remain unsolved art mysteries.

BOTTLES AND JARS

Collecting common bottles and canning jars has grown into one of the major areas of collecting from coast to coast. Strangely enough, collectors are as far apart economically as possible and include the affluent and the lower middle class. Fortunately there is an ample supply for all, encompassing everything from the lowly soda water bottle to historical flasks, stoneware canning jars to more recent Ball Brothers fruit jars.

MOLD SEAMS

An age gauge to American Bottles

BY GRACE KENDRICK

THE COLLECTING OF BOTTLES of all shapes and descriptions has suddenly become a hobby of phenomenal popularity. Collectors from New York to San Francisco are searching for old bottles with an enthusiasm reminiscent of gold-rush days. Mine detectors are being used to find the garbage pits of our ancestors. Long-forgotten communities are being visited by collectors who hope to reclaim bottles discarded by another generation.

Searches are taking place along the mangrove swamps of Florida, the old portages of the Mississippi, in attics and cellars of old houses, and among the accumulations of local junkmen.

Alert dealers in antiques have moved their bottles into front display windows. The sale of these vessels has boomed. Yesterday's utility bottles, which have never before been considered of any great interest or value, have become unexpectedly the "hottest" antique on the market today.

There are thousands and thousands of them. To make a complete catalogue or price list of all of them would be an impossible task. Collectors and dealers are forced to become connoisseurs of old glass in order to determine the value of these now marketable receptacles.

The first consideration in deter-

mining the intrinsic worth of such bottles is age. Luckily for the casual collector, it is not too difficult to estimate the approximate age of an American-made bottle.

The mechanics of bottle-making went through a dramatic revolution during the nineteenth century. In that era, the industry advanced from the primitive practices of ancient times to the bottle-making machine which today produces billions of bottles with undeviating perfection. These advancements, made step by step, left their marks on the bottles and remain there today for us to interpret.

Pontil Marks

A pontil mark is the scar left on the bottom of a glass bottle when it was broken free from the pontil, sometimes called "punty rod", the glassblower's tool used to hold the red hot bottle during the finishing of

From the last half of the 19th century, left to right: Carter's Ink, bright blue-green; sauce bottle, pontil, sheared lip; front, rare cobalt blue sauce; rear, Avan Hoboken & Co., Rotterdam, gin; demijohn, possibly for acid; umbrella ink, cobalt blue; pepper sauce, cathedral windows; Franklin Magveagh & Co., chili sauce; Wyeth Bro. Liquid Extract of Malt; "lady's leg" neck, Bitters; shape often used for Bitters.

Digging started it.

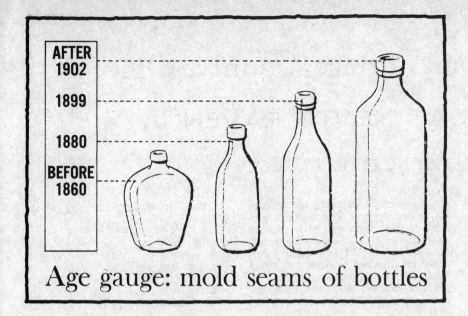

Age gauge: mold seams of bottles

AFTER 1902
1899
1880
BEFORE 1860

will show the crudeness and irregularities of being hand-formed.

As the turn of the century approaches, the mold seams rise toward the tops of the bottles, and may come within one-eighth inch of their crests. In an effort to produce a more perfect ware, a "closed mold" was used. In it, the lip of the bottle was formed in the mold. The glass was severed above the lip, leaving only the rim to be smoothed by hand.

Finally, in 1903, Michael J. Owens, an employee of Libbey Glass Company in Toledo, Ohio, perfected the first bottle-making machine. This machine reversed earlier procedure and formed the lip of the bottle first. In some cases two molds were used, one to form the lip of the bottle, the other to form its body. In all cases, the mold seams run through the very tips of the lips, and machine-made bottles can be identified by this observation.

When they fall into some specific "wanted" category, such as whiskey decanters, figure bottles or miniatures, bottles made by machinery are of interest to collectors today. Bottles blown by the power of a man's lungs (before 1900) are becoming increasingly sought—and increasingly valuable.

the neck. It usually appears as a circular depressed area with a sharp glass around the edges; it can cut you if you rub it. Such a pontil mark on an old utility-type bottle indicates a date before 1860. (Beware of recently-made "art" objects.)

Mold Seams

From about 1840, an increasing number of American-made bottles involved the use of molds. By 1860, most bottles were formed in molds. Molds are made in two or more sections which come apart to allow for the removal of the vessel. Since the sections cannot be fitted tightly enough to prevent their joints from leaving a mark, mold seams result on the finished product. They appear on all bottles except those which are free blown or turn-molded.

These mold seams can be used as an age-gauge to set an approximate date for a bottle's production. *The closer to the top the mold seam extends, the newer the bottle is.*

In the period prior to 1860, on bottles blown in the mold, the mold seam will stop somewhere on the shoulders of the bottles. The whole neck and lip were drawn out and formed "freehand." (The snapcase, replacing the punty rod, was in general use by 1850 to hold the blown mold bottle while the neck was being finished; this left no pontil mark.)

In bottles of the 1880 period, the seams will stop below the mouth of the bottle. Only the lips or mouths,

Bottles as found. Which to save?

Mrs. Kendrick with some of her ghost town bottles; she has over 5000.

Glass from Portage County, Ohio

MANTUA - KENT - RAVENNA

by DUNCAN B. WOLCOTT

REGARDING OHIO and mid-Western flasks and bottles, Helen S. McKearin once wrote: "Excepting only the finest of the Stiegel perfume or pocket bottles, the flasks and bottles produced in mid-western glasshouses operating during the first half of the 19th century have never been excelled and seldom equaled, in America or elsewhere, in colors and delicacy of molded designs. The brilliant ambers, golden yellows, and delicate shadings in greens which are rarely encountered in the products of any other glasshouses in American, England, or on the Continent, as well as the fine designs, were the rule, not the exception, of glassware blown at Mantua, Kent, and Ravenna, Ohio."

Glass from Mantua

The Mantua glass story starts December 1, 1821, when the first glass was made there. The Mantua Glass Works was located north of Mantua Village, a short distance east of the old Brick Tavern at the intersection

MANTUA GLASS PIECES—left to right: miniature amethyst decanter, extremely rare; greenish-aqua decanter with threading spiralled around neck, has long Mantua family history; greenish-aqua flask with dent "trademark" in collar made by glassmaker's tool; amber 16-rib chestnut flask, displayed at Dunham Tavern Museum in Cleveland years ago, and identified there by Harry Hall White as Mantua; recently traced family history supports this.

KENT GLASS PIECES — left to right: 20-rib broken swirl chestnut flask, variously called light amber or honey amber; aqua decanter (McKearin GII-6); aqua bar bottle (also GII-6), an amber example is at Corning Museum of Glass, Corning, N. Y.; deep amber 20-rib broken swirl chestnut flask. All glass pictured here is from the author's collection.

RAVENNA GLASS FLASKS—left to right: Aqua pint, eagle on one side, anchor and "Ravenna Glass Company" on other (GII-37); same in emerald green (comes also in 3 shades of amber and in yellow-green); aqua pint, on one side, "Ravenna Glass Works" on other side is a five-point star; same, but in yellow green.

of Route 44 and the Garrettsville road. It was first operated by David Ladd and Jonathan Tinker, who had come from Connecticut. In 1823, Ladd sold his interest and moved on to Kent. The Mantua enterprise continued, under several owners, until 1829.

In the mid-1920s, Harry Hall White, a leading authority on early glass, carried out an extensive research project at the site. His findings established certain guide lines regarding the Mantua output that make positive identification possible. (A complete report of his findings appeared in *Antiques Magazine,* for December 1934, February, July, and November 1935.)

By carefully piecing glass fragments together, he was able to prove that Mantua was one of the earliest producers, west of the Alleghenies, of the famous blown three-mold glass. His most important three-mold find-

ings were the fragments that made up a beautiful decanter. (Two known decanters, identified by this find, are considered among the top rarities in early American glass.)

Another important find was the Jackson-Masonic flask. Fragments were found, put together, and drawings made of the entire flask. Years later an actual bottle was located. One such is on exhibit at the Ohio State Historical Museum in Columbus, securely attributed to Mantua.

Evidence from fragments proved that a 16-rib dip mold was used there, and with a double insertion, a 32-rib product was achieved. One discovery that seems unique to Mantua products was that the ribs, where they converge at the base of a 16-rib flask, do not go all the way to the pontil mark, but seem to end at what is called a "terminal ring" at the base. Another so-called "trademark" of Mantua bottles was described by Mr.

White: "Occasionally the collar of a bottle will betray a pair of dents or depressions made by the points of the finisher's tool."

It was also discovered that a 15-diamond mold was used at Mantua. (A small greenish-aqua dish in this pattern, on display at the Toledo Museum in the 1920s, now in the Wolcott collection, indicates Mantua make; local family history, recently come to light, confirms the authentication.)

Though glass was manufactured at Mantua for less than nine years, many important pieces were made there, and Mantua takes a prominent place as a producer of some of our finest early glass.

Glass from Kent

There were several glasshouses at Kent, Ohio, in the years from 1824 to about 1896. The first, a very small enterprise, was started in 1824 by

RAVENNA TRAVELER'S COMPANION FLASKS — left to right: Aqua pint, "Traveler's Companion" on one side, "Ravenna Glass Co." and 8-point star on the other (also in various shades of amber, yellow-green and emerald green in Wolcott collection); aqua quart; emerald green pint (may be unique in this color); deep golden amber quart (also in yellow-green), (quart size is not shown on McKearin charts, but follows the description of pints); amber half-pint, "Traveler's Companion" on one side, 8-point star on other, generally attributed to Ravenna though "Ravenna Glass Co." does not appear on this size.

our friend from Mantua, David Ladd. Very little is known about it. His partner was Benjamin F. Hopkins, and the factory was located on the Cuyahoga River at the foot of Grant Street. The silica sand they used was obtained nearby; it has even been said they used ground-up sandstone.

The second Kent factory, called Parks, Edmunds and Parks, was started later in that same year, 1824. It was located on farmland about two and a half miles northwest of Kent, actually in Hudson township. This was, in many ways, the most notable of the Kent glass companies.

Excavation at the site by Harry Hall White has determined that a 20-rib dip mold was used here. Fragments also proved that a blown three-mold pattern was used.

Three-mold glass was a sort of "poor man's cut glass." Made to resemble cut glass, it was much cheaper. The molds used in fashioning "blown-three-mold" wares were approximately the size of the completed piece. They were made in three hinged sections, which could be opened or closed by means of a treadle or other lever. It is claimed that one way blown three-mold glass may be distinguished from pressed glass is that it has a pattern on the inside; pressed glass has none.

In later years other glass factories were started in Kent. The Franklin Glass Co., begun in 1851, later became Day and Williams, with a factory located just south of the present Erie Lackawanna depot. They made window glass. Though it was always supposed they also made off-hand pieces and hollow ware, some experts on early glass have maintained there was no proof of this whatsoever.

Recently something of proof came to hand. I had purchased some glassmaker's tools that were used in Kent, which had come from Mrs. John Jadot, widow of a Kent glassmaker. On cleaning them, I discovered that several were stamped with the glassmaker's name. One, marked "P. Deville," with a symbol, and "Val St. Lambert," especially intrigued me.

Checking with Mrs. Jadot, I learned that the tools had been brought in by workers who had come to Ohio from Namur, Belgium, where they had been employed in the Val St. Lambert glass manufactory. One was her father-in-law, Eugene Jadot. She had known Peter Deville and many of the others whose names were stamped on the tools. (The tools included dies which were used to make impressions of objects to be applied to glass

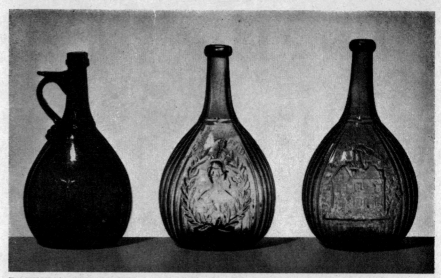

RAVENNA, UNMARKED: Deep amber handled globular calabash, 8-point star on one side, sheaf of wheat, crossed rake and pitchfork on other; "Ravenna Jeny Lind" calabash (GI-104); wreathed portrait with misspelled name on one side, glasshouse on other. Wolcott collection has examples in aqua, sapphire blue, yellow-green, light blue.

baskets at the point where the looped handle fastened to the basket itself—dies in the shape of strawberry, leaf, and conventional designs.)

She gave me a pitcher her husband had made at the Kent glasshouse in its later years.

I followed up her story, and called on her youngest Jadot brother-in-law, now living in Jeannette, Pennsylvania, who had worked at Day & Williams in Kent. In the last years of production he said, they were making crystal and white opal lamp shades, punch tumblers, and electric light bulbs. Paperweights were made, too, though not as a regular item.

Ravenna Glass

The first glass factory started in Ravenna, Ohio, in the early 1850s. It was called the Ravenna Glass Co., and many marked bottles in various colors are known. (Actually, I believe those marked "Ravenna Glass Works" may have been from an earlier factory.)

The two best known marked Ravennas are the pint and quart "Traveler's Companion" and the pint that pictures an eagle and an anchor. These bottles were made in beautiful shades of amber, and we have two in emerald green.

Many other bottles are attributed to Ravenna, but are unmarked. The most famous of these is the "Jeny Lind" calabash. Placed on the market in the 1850s, honoring the famous Swedish singer then touring the country, it is unique in that the name Jenny is misspelled. We have found four colors in this bottle, and know of one in amber—it belongs to a lady who lives in South Africa!

A characteristic that many, but not all, Ravenna bottles have is referred to as a "rusty pontil mark." McKearin explains that this black or reddish coloration at the base was caused by the method of heating punty irons and using them without dipping the end of the punty into glass. The black color, he said, was due to the oxide from the punty rod being in a low state of oxidation, and the red coloration came when the black oxide turned, through oxidation, into the ferric or red oxide. While most Ravennas do show this "rusty pontil mark," it also appears occasionally on marked bottles from other locations. It cannot be called an infallible trademark.

Books which have been particularly helpful to us in researching Portage County glass, and which we recommend to all serious collectors of glass are: *American Glass*, by George S. and Helen McKearin, a father-daughter team; *Two Hundred Years of American Blown Glass*, also by the McKearins; *Early American Bottles and Flasks*, by Stephen Van Rensselaer, out-of-print and quite hard to find; and *Early American Glass*, by Rhea Mansfield Knittle.

NATURE'S 'ART GLASS'

by GRACE KENDRICK

THE ART glasses—opaque, iridescent, frosted, opalescent, satin, crackled, and Carnival—were all inspired by what nature had done to the glasses of the ancient world.

We of the New World have never been too interested in the subject of ancient glass since the natives of the Americas never discovered the art of glassmaking. The oldest glass known to have been produced in the Western Hemisphere was made by European immigrants at Jamestown, Va., in 1608. With no ancient specimens of our own to stock local museums, we have relaxed with the comfortable illusion that glass is a transparent, durable, non-soluble substance.

In the past decade there has evolved in the United States, a fad (which may be lasting and far-reaching) of digging up glass bottles from the garbage dumps of our ancestors. For the first time we became cognizant of the effects of nature upon glass which has been buried for a long period of time. We unearth bottles which have become etched and colored in varied and breathtakingly beautiful ways. Some show a subtle glaze like an illusive mother-of-pearl lustre. Often the glass is opalescent, with a cloudy or milky look throughout, reflecting an iridescence which gives it an appearance remarkably like an opal. Some have a metallic sheen, more brilliantly colored than Carnival glass.

At times the glass is so opaque that it reflects no light at all. Often we find the surface to be permanently frosted with a delicate swirly pattern like frost on a windowpane. Some glass is rough, with a texture like moire silk and coloring more brilliant than a peacock's tail. Sometimes when we bring a bottle to the surface, we notice a multi-colored, cellophane-like layer of the glass peeling off and blowing away in the wind. Even after we wash the bottle another nacreous layer may form, and also flake away.

Early archeologists observing these textures and hues on pieces of old glass believed it to be an original decorating technique of ancient glassmakers. The scientific era in which we live demands an accurate explanation for this phenomenon. What caused this condition?

There are three ingredients in all glass, ancient and modern: sand, soda, and lime. Sand is the basic material. In order to make the sand melt, a flux must be added. The flux is an alkali, usually some form of soda. Glass which contains only sand and soda is water-soluble. Therefore, lime is added to make the glass more stable.

The percentage of sand, soda, and lime vary in glass recipes, and especially in old glass. The amounts of these basic ingredients, plus other chemicals which were put into the glass when it was made, will de-

Nature etched a swirly, iridescent pattern on this glass bottle.

Photos by
LAURA MILLS

termine how rapidly the glass will deteriorate, and what form the deterioration will take.

The soda content of the glass is mainly responsible for its deterioration. When moisture comes into contact with the glass for a long period of time, the soda content of the glass leaches out and undergoes a chemical change forming a film of sodium bicarbonate crystals. This causes a cloudy, milky look in the glass, sometimes referred to as an "alkali deposit." You may have noticed it at the water line in an old vase in which you have let water stand.

When the automatic bottle-making machine took over in 1903, greater amounts of soda were added to glass recipes. Glass bottles of a high soda content become "opaque" after being buried even less than 20 years.

In some glasses, potash was used as a flux instead of soda. When potash glass is buried, the leaching process also takes place, but there is no dry, opaque deposit on the glass. Instead, the potassium dissolves and produces

Recently excavated bottles showing the various effects of moisture damage on different glass compositions.

a shiny transparent film, like mother-of-pearl.

Glasses which have a high lime content are more durable and disintegrate slowly. Expensive lead glass, and glass which contains large amounts of iron slag, are less vulnerable to corrosion. The old "black glass," so common before 1850, can be buried for 100 years and escape the ordeal unscathed. Bottles which are noticeably resistant to decay are the European-made Gilka and Hoboken, and our own beautiful blue-green Saratoga bottles.

The weathering encrustation found on old bottles shows spectacular variations of colors, textures, and thicknesses. This corrosion takes a common course, and invariably forms thin transparent layers stacked one on another. The layers are caused by wet and dry seasons (or temperature changes, in cases where the glass stayed completely submerged in water). The moisture penetrates the surface of the glass, leaches out the

Old "black glass" bottles resist corrosion.

soluble elements, and the dissolved substance takes the form of a silica gel. In the dry season, the gel hardens into a physically separate layer. This leaching-drying process goes on and on, eventually affecting all components of the glass. A bottle can finally become a silicate skeleton, with no visual resemblance to what we think of as glass. The skeleton itself may slough away into the soil, completing the dissolution of a glass bottle.

The rainbow-like coloring of the deteriorated glass is caused by separate layers built up, one upon the other. The reflection of light on these layers produces an interference which gives off brilliant iridescent colors, like soap bubbles and oil on water.

Moisture must be present before glass will show any physical or visual change. If the moisture is a concentrated alkali solution, the attack on the glass will be very rapid. An acid or lime solution, on the other hand, would tend to protect the glass, slowing up its disintegration.

If glass is kept dry it will remain in a new-like condition for thousands of years; possibly forever.

Two American Figure Bottles

by ALBERT CHRISTIAN REVI

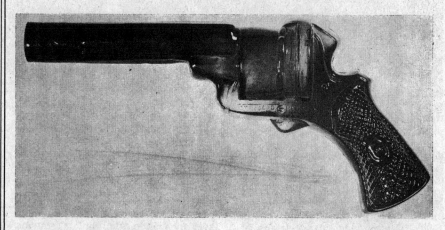

● PERFUME REVOLVER

THE version of the Revolver Bottle shown here was designed and patented by Emanuel W. Bloomingdale of New York City on November 6, 1888. It is made of a dark amber colored glass and has the patent date and legend "Standard Per'f Wk's" embossed in the glass near the trigger.

The bottle originally held perfume or cologne manufactured by the Standard Perfume Works of New York City. This bottle measures ten inches from the muzzle to the end of the gun handle. The muzzle of the gun houses the opening of the bottle which was originally fitted with a simple cork.

● MR. AND MRS. CARTER INX

ON JANUARY 6, 1914, Charles H. Henkels of Philadelphia, Pennsylvania, patented his designs for two figure bottles known to collectors as the Mr. and Mrs. Carter Inx Bottles. The designs represent the figures of a man (Mr. Carter) and a woman (Mrs. Carter), and were produced in both glass and pottery. The bottles stand about 3¾ inches tall and are realistically painted with unfired colors. In each case the head is the stopper and is fitted to the mouth of the bottles with a cork. Mrs. Carter is represented as a motherly type woman, though the rolling pin she holds in her folded hands seems to portend a menace to the rather henpecked-looking Mr. C.

According to Mr. W. T. Chapman of the sales department of the Carter's Ink Company, these bottles were used between 1914 and 1916 as a means of testing their advertising in nationally-read magazines. Each of their advertisements had a coupon which could be sent in with 25¢ for the pair of bottles, one of which held blue-black ink, the other, red ink. Some fifty thousand coupons were returned, giving adequate proof of the effectiveness of their advertising.

At first the bottles were bought in Germany and were made of pottery. When World War I broke out, the company looked for an American

source of supply and were able to get an American version so close to the German that it would have been impossible to tell them apart had it not been for the "Made in Germany" stamped on the bottles made overseas.

Figure 2.

Figure 1.

Figure 3. Mrs. Harold Holt of South Lyndeboro, N. H., holds a rare Lyndeboro glass cane.

Figures 4 and 5. Rare Lyndeboro glass globe decorated in potichomanie.

The South Lyndeboro Glass Company

by BEVERLY CHAMBERLAIN
and
VIRGINIA T. BATES

TAKING A small gather of molten glass on their blowpipes, the glass blowers of South Lyndeboro, New Hampshire, created some of the most desirable bottles and offhand pieces available to collectors today. One of their first products may have been clear window glass—still serving its purpose in many homes of the region. Tiny medicine vials, paneled and plain condiment containers, large and small demijohns, many of the Mason and, later, Lightning canning jars (embossed "PUTNAM" on the base), Lydia Pinkham containers, the familiar Moxie Nerve Tonic bottles, all were produced by the South Lyndeboro Glass Company.

Incorporated in 1866 by Joel Tarbell, Charles Eaton, George Sanborn, Luther Roby, and John Hartshorn, the glasshouse operated for a period of twenty years. In 1867, the New Hampshire Silex Company was formed and incorporated as an integral part of the glassworks. An excellent supply of white quartz, mined from nearby Putnam Hill, was ground by the Silex Company into fine sand-like particles and used as the base in making Lyndeboro glass. It would seem that this dual enterprise might have enjoyed financial success, but early records indicate the profits were meager. In 1868, fire destroyed the main glass factory, causing an additional serious setback. However, the factory was rebuilt and operated until 1886.

Many of the bottles blown at Lyndeboro are similar in shape to those attributed to the Stoddard, New Hampshire, glasshouses. Since it is known that glassblowers frequently moved from one glasshouse to another, sometimes taking their molds with them, this might be the reason for the similarities. We have been unable to discover any authenticated examples of a rough pontil on bottles blown at Lyndeboro. This seems quite understandable when one realizes that the bottles blown in the later Stoddard glasshouses also exhibited smooth bases.

Colors commonly associated with Lyndeboro glass are a lovely shade of robin's-egg blue, a light green-aqua, amber, and cobalt blue, the latter occurring most often in offhand pieces. The robin's-egg blue color is unique to Lyndeboro, and is believed to have resulted from the use of ground quartz as a base for the glass rather than the more common sand used by most New Hampshire glassworks. Blue-aqua and dark amber flasks were prominent wares and were produced in half-pint, pint, and quart sizes with "L.G.CO." embossed on many of the bases.

The largest collection of Lyndeboro glass that we have examined (pictured in *Figures 1* and *2*) is owned by Mr. W. Hannaford of South Lyndeboro, who has been a collector of bottles for over twenty years.

Figure 1 shows six demijohns in various shapes, sizes, and colors, with original wicker coverings. In the right foreground is a glass brick of deep greenish-blue color with sharp rough edges. The story is told that these bricks were made from the last of a batch of glass. Later, they would be polished and given to salesmen for use as samples or paperweights.

Figure 2 exhibits on the left a tall amber whiskey, amber demijohns, and a pint flask. In the background is a gallon fruit jar and beside it, to the front right, a half-gallon jar—both aqua and both embossed vertically with the word "RETENTIVE." These are rare examples of early Lyndeboro canning jars. The tall slim cylinder in the left foreground is a vase and was probably blown in the same mold as the cobalt rolling pin shown in *Figure 7.*

We are greatly indebted to Mrs. Harold Holt, Mrs. Adelaide Herrick, and Mr. James A. Putnam (a descendant of J. D. Putnam who was general superintendent and agent for the glassworks) for much of the information about the glassworks, and for graciously allowing us to photograph the rare end-of-day objects shown in *Figures 3* through 7.

The glass cane being displayed by Mrs. Holt in *Figure 3* is 35 inches long. It was made of aqua-colored glass and has candy stripes of red, green, and white spiraling its entire length. This delightful object has been preserved over the years by the Holt family, and displayed in their spacious front hall along with other examples of Lyndeboro glass.

Figures 4 and *5* show two views of an extremely rare glass globe measuring 26 inches in circumference. It is blown of aqua-colored glass, and enchantingly embellished with potichomanie decorations of elegant Victorian figures and phrases. (See "Potichomanie," by Lillian Baker Carlisle, SW-May '68.) Fruit and flower ornamenta-

tions, delicately designed and painted, are interspersed with endearing expressions, such as, "You charm me," "I am yours," "Forget-me-not," "With you I'll go," while a clown costumed in a yellow spotted suit frolics beside a gaily dancing Negro lad juggling tomatoes. A wagon, with a mound of hay and children atop, creates a rural scene above a snarling tiger's head baring sharp white fangs.

The globe pictured in *Figure 6* is lined with a silver-colored substance. Both globes were probably blown by Samuel Ross, a glass blower known to have been employed at South Lyndeboro. Our conjecture is that they were made as gifts for his young English bride, Sarah McMullen, and whatever useful purpose may have been intended has now been forgotten. For many years they have been in the kindly care of Mrs. Herrick, whose husband was a descendant of Samuel Ross.

In *Figure 7,* Mr. Putnam displays a rare cobalt blue rolling pin blown by an unknown worker at Lyndeboro and given as a gift to his sister who, at the time, was a very young girl. Apparently intended for utilitarian use, it has an opening at one end which would allow for filling with ice water or cracked ice. The opening would then be sealed against leakage with a cork stopper. Needless to say, this beautiful and prized possession no longer does duty in the kitchen!

Figure 8 depicts two green-aqua condiment bottles. The handsome bottle on the left probably contained ketchup, but the possibility exists that it may have been a bitters container. The short, square bottle was a horseradish bottle. Both blown in two-part molds.

Figure 9 shows a large piece of

Figure 6. Silvered glass globe made at the South Lyndeboro glassworks.

Figure 7. Mr. James A. Putnam of South Lyndeboro displaying a rare cobalt blue rolling pin.

Figure 8.

Figure 9.

Figure 10. Two quart, one quart, and pint size "Lightning" canning jars in robin's egg blue. Authors' collection.

48
Bottles
Jars

Figure 11. Left: The initials "L. C. Co." are embossed on the base of this early two-part mold flask made of robin's-egg blue glass. Right: The name "Putnam" is embossed on the base of this "Lightning" canning jar made at the South Lyndeboro glassworks.

amber glass (cullet) which was found at the site of the glassworks. The one-half gallon demijohn is amber and encased in the original wicker cover. Portions of the fifteen-paned window shown in *Figures 8* and *9* are of clear Lyndeboro glass; on one the name "Joel Tarbell" is scratched into the thin, wavy glass.

Today, there are no visible remains of the South Lyndeboro glass factory; all evidence of the buildings has been removed, leaving only a small well-cropped field with nothing to show that a glass industry ever existed. However, a trip to the base of Putnam Hill clearly indicates that the quartz once used in Lyndeboro glass is, again, being quarried. Huge sheds have been constructed to house the powdered quartz until it can be conveyed by truck and train to diverse southeastern points. Here it is combined as an aggregate in pre-cast cement panels and used to beautify the exterior of modern structures. Two fine examples are the William James Hall recently built at Harvard, and the new Federal Building in Boston.

While conducting our research in South Lyndeboro, we visited an antique shop in the vicinity of Putnam Hill. The proprietor related an interesting story concerning the many bottles she was offering for sale. Her father had been a manufacturer of extracts in the early 1900s, and when the Lyndeboro glassworks went out of business, leaving the warehouse full of bottles, he purchased as many as possible for the purpose of bottling his preparations. The bottles on sale in her shop were all that remained of her father's purchase.

Authenticated South Lyndeboro wares are, indeed, worthy of being collected; prices are constantly rising, and while the products blown in the earlier Keene and Stoddard glasshouses command premium prices, Lyndeboro glass can still be purchased at reasonable costs.

Whitall & Tatum Nursers

MRS. J. O. Ely, Newark, Delaware, asked about an Empire Nursing bottle with the embossed monogram shown. The 1896 catalog of Whitall, Tatum & Company supplied the answer. This firm manufactured glassware for druggists, chemists, and perfumers at factories in Millville, New Jersey; had offices in Philadelphia, New York, and Boston. Examples from their 1896 line, below, identify some of their un-monogramed nursers.

Left to right: *Acme*, bent neck, round bottom, graduated in fluid ounces; *Empire*, bent neck, flat bottom; *Infants*, straight neck, flat bottom; the *Millville*; the *Baltimore*. All came in both flint and green glass.

 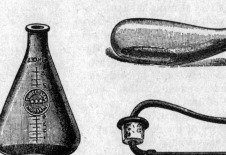

Handy Nurser, patented Feb. 24, 1891, could be lettered with customer's name in seal; *Three Star Nurser*, patented June 19, 1894; *Shoe-shaped Nurser*; all in flint glass. Typical nursing bottle fittings of black rubber, flint glass top, bone shield and connection. Other types of nipples, which attached directly to bottle were the *Home*, *Barclay*, and *Swan Bill*.

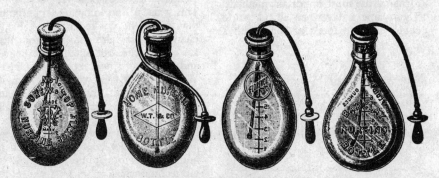

Available with fittings, packed individually with tube and bottle brushes, in flint only: *Screw-top*; *Home Nursing Bottle*; *Florence*; *Barclay*.

"W.T. & Co. Apparatus for Sterilizing Milk" consisted of tray, boiler, cup for reheating; 1 dozen 6-oz. graduated bottles, 9 combination glass and rubber stoppers, bottle brush, and 2 oz. funnel. Also offered was the *Arnold Steam Sterilizer* for sterilizing milk in bottles by application of steam rather than boiling water.

The MEN Behind the Fruit Jar

by
JULIAN HARRISON TOULOUSE

Figure 9: The Ball brothers; left to right: William C., Frank C., Lucius L. (seated), Edmund B., and George A. Illustration courtesy of Ball Brothers Company, Inc.

THERE IS A CERTAIN REFRAIN, repeated with variations by collectors and noncollectors alike, that bothers me. "Mason invented canning." "Mason invented the fruit jar." "Mason invented the screw cap." In cold reality it is these statements that could best be called inventions.

To refute them most completely is to tell the story of the development of home canning, which is in itself a true invention. At one time, people could preserve foods only by greatly altering their characteristics: by heavy salting and brining, by heavy sugar additions, by drying and by smoking—to name the most important methods. Then came a day when all the world could preserve foods at home with a new process, with the announcement of the work of Nicolas Appert in the heat-preservation of foods in sealed containers. It was a true invention, and the culmination of 14 years' study. The French Government awarded him a prize of 12,000 francs.

Appert's method also modified the character of the food—it cooked it. This was of no moment for foods that would be cooked anyway. Fruit characteristics were changed from the fresh-like taste, but all the succulence and much of the texture remained. Who could quarrel with this when it tasted like fruit, rather than dried leather, and when it was available all the year round? Appert, then, is the true inventor of canning, but a dozen men made major contributions, and a hundred or more, minor additions to the techniques.

How quickly the art of canning caught on is another story. In the second decade after the introduction of canning into the United States, the container had a common, or generic name: the fruit jar. By 1829 Thomas W. Dyott, then a glass jobber and not yet the famous glassmaker he was to become, was advertising "fruit jars." The name (fruit) probably denotes the relative ease by which fruits could be canned, as compared with the long and tedious process of canning vegetables and meats.

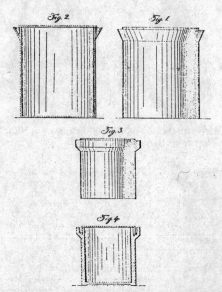

Figure 1: "Fruit Can" patented by Robert Arthur, January 2, 1855.

Figure 2 (above): "Glass Jar" patented by John L. Mason, November 30, 1858.

The new industry had its first important inventor in the person of Robert Arthur, in 1855. No doubt there were earlier inventors but they are not yet of record, and from Appert to Arthur only the expensive hand-cut cork stoppers luted into place with melted wax were used. Arthur made the art mechanical by developing a formed groove on top of the jar into which an inverted saucer-shaped tin lid could be inserted, followed by pouring the groove full of melted wax (Fig. 1). His invention also brought about a standardization needed, as in any industry, so that new sources of jars and lids could be mutually fitted. It brought about the making of wider mouthed jars than the more expensive corks made feasible. Soon an alternate cap of glass fitting the groove was developed for the GEM jar, making it the first all-glass container.

Mason made his appearance in 1858. There had been at least two screw cap devices invented before his, and the first of them hinted at an earlier one. Mason, himself, titled his patent application: *Improvement* in screw necked bottles, thus also indicating a prior use of the technique

(Fig. 2). He owed much to the fortuitous choice of his own name, calling it a Mason jar, and embellishing each jar with "Mason's Patent." The name became generic within a dozen years, since Boyd could refer to the jar, in 1869, as the "so-called Mason jar."

Its great value was its simplicity and cheapness. Only a simple, low-cost grinding operation was needed to make the annealed jar ready for use. There were two drawbacks: the jar would not vent air during the cooking process unless in the hands of an expert; and the exposure of so much zinc, not yet covered with an inner lining of opal glass (it was never porcelain as so widely advertised), that gave a metallic taste to foods. It was to deter acceptance of the jar for nearly two-thirds of its patent life—that period of greatest return to the inventor.

Mason never made any of his jars. He was a metal worker and had his

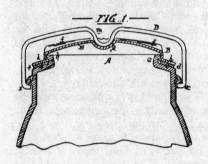

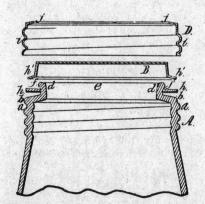

Figure 3: S. B. Rowley's "Improved Cap and Fastener for Preserve Jars," patented February 11, 1868.

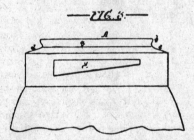

Figure 4: Rowley's patented closure for "Fruit Jars," dated December 14, 1869.

major interest in the making and selling of the zinc cap. Glass making was at first licensed to others. With the formation of the Consolidated Fruit Jar Company by a combination of companies holding licenses to make either jars or caps, most of the bottles were then made by contract, in addition to some licensed jar manufacture.

Mason's actual invention of the jar is under a cloud. It has been claimed that he obtained his idea from a mold maker to whom he applied for advice when he had been commissioned to make screw caps for a glass jar.

In the meantime the metallic taste from the zinc cap spurred efforts toward an all-glass contact with foods. Charles Imlay is credited with developing the first "over-the-top" glass lid, or cap, in 1865, but his devices, 13 in one patent, were largely inappropriate because most of them sealed on a ground surface. Salmon B. Rowley, of Hero, stepped in with the first lid that sealed on a smooth, blown surface, using a cover-all lid held by a center-perforated metal cap, generally known as a screw band (Figs. 3 and 4). Rowley was continually experimenting with glass lid designs. Both Hero and Cohansey developed usable glass lids. It was not until 1872 that Mason coined the name IMPROVED for the patent he obtained for a glass lid and metal screw band design; it was to be the last of his eight patents. In the term, IMPROVED, Mason was again lucky—the term also became one for common use and identified with him.

Boyd's great contribution, and one that "saved" the Mason jar, was in 1869, in the form of the glass liner for the zinc cap (Fig. 5). His first

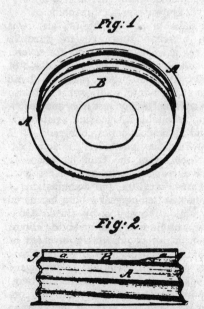

Figure 5: Patent for "Preventing Corrosion of Metallic Caps" patented by Lewis R. Boyd, March 30, 1869.

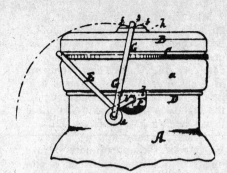

Figure 6: "Stopper For Jars, & c." patented by Henry W. Putnam, April 25, 1882.

design was in clear glass; opal glass was later adopted because its opaque character would hide the seepage of liquid between it and the cap, and mask the corrosion of the zinc. Besides, white had the appearance of cleanliness and purity. Lewis (or Louis) R. Boyd's New York Metals Company soon became a member of the Consolidated team, but not before he had licensed others, including Hero, to use the idea. It was Hero who coined the name "Porcelain Lined."

Consolidated's star waned, and about 1882 Hero seems to have acquired its assets. Mason retired from the fruit jar scene. In 1884 Hero changed its name to Hero Fruit Jar Company and placed their initials in the wings of the cross it had adopted as a trade mark about 1882.

Albert G. Smalley entered the fruit jar business about 1876, as a jobber of jars made by Consolidated. New England (Smalley did business from Boston) would have nothing of the zinc taste, so Smalley quickly swung over to glass lids held by metal screw bands (Fig. 7). When the Lightning seal was developed he adopted it, and so great was his influence that New England, Canada, and upstate New York became poor markets for the zinc-capped jars. As a result the glass lid and metal screw bands, or the Lightning, became their favorites and standards. In 1909, with the twin toggle of Smalley's partner, John Kivlan, the new firm of Smalley, Kivlan & Onthank had their own glass top.

In 1875 George Putnam bought a patent for beverage bottles called the LIGHTNING. It took seven years to develop the idea into a fruit jar seal, but it became most successful (Fig. 6). It has had more variations than almost any other seal: an old, or original style neck, a beaded neck, and an adjustable neck position, all with the lever wire secured by a tie-wire around the neck, and also a dimple, or circular depression in the neck, and a glass pivot, or stud, on either side of the neck, both eliminating the wire tie.

Matthew Brady entered the glass business as a bookkeeper for Hobbs, Brockunier Company, a fine glass maker. In 1886 he formed his own company, the Hazel Glass Company at Wellsburg, W. Va., to press opal inserts for zinc caps. About that time the Lightning jar was taking hold, but it was being badly merchandised, and the glass company making it closed. Brady seized his opportunity to take on its manufacture, and built a new factory at Washington, Pa., to make it. By the early 1890s he was commissioning Charles Blue of the Wheeling Foundry & Metals Co. to try to make a glass forming machine after the newly successful Arbogast method of pressing a hollow "blank" and then blowing it into bottle shape in a second, or finishing, mold (Fig. 11). It was successful in 1894, and within two years Brady had built the Atlas Glass Company as the first glass factory to be constructed for exclusive machine bottle making. Its initial production was the ATLAS E-Z SEAL Lightning and it firmly established Hazel and Atlas, and their later combining as Hazel-Atlas, as Lightning specialists and as food jar manufacturers.

In Buffalo, N. Y., in 1886, the five Ball brothers (Fig. 9) built the Ball Brothers Glass Manufacturing Co. in order to make gallon glass jugs for their current manufacturing business. To keep their crews busy they decided to manufacture Mason and glass topped fruit jars, since the patents had expired. A fire wiped out their factory and business the following year. In looking for a new location they received an offer from the city of

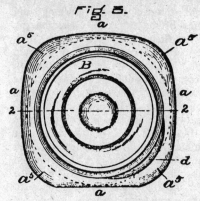

Fig. 8.

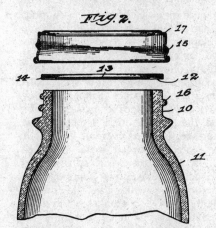

Figure 7: A. G. Smalley's patented closure for a "Fruit Jar," dated December 1, 1896.

Fig. 2.

Figure 8: Patent for a "Preserving Jar" registered by Alexander H. Kerr, August 31, 1915.

Muncie, Ind., which they accepted, and in 1888 they were again in production. When the Blue machine came out they were among the first users, but they improved upon it to patent the F. C. Ball machine in 1898 (Fig. 10), followed a few years later with the Ball-Bingham, the first semi-automatic power operated machine.

Balls' great contribution, also, was in merchandising and in research. They acted as sales agents for several small companies, but in the course of time they absorbed most of these companies into their own. Ball also established many research and teaching fellowships in leading agricultural and home economics colleges.

With Alexander Kerr the active development of the fruit jar seems to have reached a plateau. Kerr purchased, in 1903, the combination of a heat softening gasket on a lacquered metal lid, invented by Ewald Goltstein of Germany, and a spring clip to hold it during processing, invented by Julius Landsberger of Alameda, Calif. Its property of venting air during the cooking process, then hardening tightly into the sometimes erratic top contour of the jar, made home canning far more successful. In 1915 he discarded the spring clip in favor of a

Charles Blue's glass forming machine (1894).

metal screw band (Fig. 8). World War II found it responsible for half of all home canning sealing. The next 20 years brought it to about 95 percent of all home canning closures with the zinc cap almost disappearing, and with the Lightning closing the rest; even New England, Canada, and upstate New York surrendered.

This brief history touches upon the work of only a few people who made the fruit jar possible—the major few. Several hundred patents have been taken out by as many men and women inventors. The development of the fruit jar has taken a century and a half, and has been the result of a common effort.

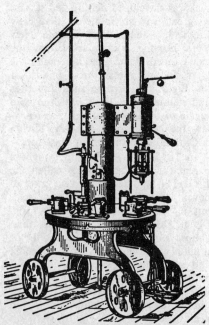

Figure 10: Glass jar machine, F. C. Ball patent N. 610515 (1898).

GEM

Ball MASON'S PATENT NOV 30TH 1858

BUTTONS

*Button collectors have more specialized interests than can
be imagined. Some collect uniform buttons, others collect
only those buttons made of glass, china, pewter or brass;
still others narrow their field to buttons made from coins,
tokens or commemorative medals. This is an area of collecting wide open to a great many interests.*

BUTTON MOLDS

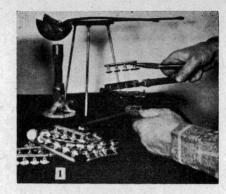

1

DURING the 18th century British artisans, world experts in the field, developed improved ways of manufacturing fine metal buttons. But their secrets were kept from outsiders — including Americans. The colonists, therefore, fell back upon the time-tested technique of casting metal in molds.

Only soft metals, such as lead and pewter, could be used. Production was a slow, tedious chore because only a few buttons could be made at a time. But, on the plus side, the equipment was simple, portable and durable. The skill required could be picked up with a little practice. The pioneers needed that same skill to make bullets and spoons. As might be expected, bullet molds are now much more plentiful than spoon molds; spoon molds far outnumber button molds, too.

Plate 1 shows a mold and a newly formed casting of buttons grasped in a pair of pliers; more castings lie in the foreground. Behind these are the torch and ladle—the only other apparatus necessary for the making of buttons. The mold is of a "classic" design and is made of brass. It has wooden handles, a base plate or die which carries the design (if any) in reverse, and a pair of arms that fold together tightly leaving only a gate or pouring hole. The arms are opened out to release the casting. Shanks for the buttons are shaped by the arms. *Plate 2* makes these details even clearer. It shows a single-handled

mold with some unusual features. For one thing, the proud maker signed it "Ts. Badman Fecit" (Thomas Badman Made It). Unlike most molds, which always make the same number of buttons each time used, this one will make from one to three buttons as wanted. The three buttons come fastened to a bar which must be cut away. All must have edges smoothed before they are finished. Of course trimmings and scraps can be remelted and used again—no metal is wasted.

Plate 3 pictures a unique mold. It makes only one button at a time, but it will produce either a plain-faced or a patterned button. The trick is that the die separates from the handle and can be put in place with either side up. Only an alert and experienced collector would recognize a matrix like this were it to turn up among odds and ends.

Owners of button molds often exchange castings (together with photographs and descriptions) of their prized possessions, most of which are one-of-a-kind. *Plate 4* suggests the variety of shapes and designs that can be found. In size, four-button castings are "regulation"; single-button ones, next. There are, however, molds that yield three, five, six, nine, ten—even twelve—buttons at a time.

(Mold shown in Plate 2 courtesy of Mr. Cornelius Vanderbilt. Plate 3 courtesy of the Metropolitan Museum of Art. Photographs by A. H. Albert.)

54
Buttons

by JANE FORD ADAMS

Ts BADMAN Fecit

2

3

4

1

2

3

4

5

6   7

8

Buttons Made From Coins

by JANE FORD ADAMS

NOVELIST Thomas Costain describes a dashing young gipsy, "He was most elaborately attired, a cluster of shilling pieces serving as buttons on his purple-braided maroon coat and pennies fairly rattling on his beige waistcoat. It was clear that he was aping the royal manner of the great gipsies, some of whom wore Spanish gold pieces for back buttons and spaded guineas and half guineas on their coats."

In sophisticated society, buttons made of ancient coins were conversation pieces; with the peasants, silver coin buttons were a display of wealth; with the Navaho Indians, silver coin buttons were gleaming jewels.

PLATE I illustrates the variety of coins that have fallen into buttonmakers' hands. These are all of the simplest possible make-up—a shank has been attached to the reverse of an otherwise unblemished coin. Nos. 1 and 4 are U. S. gold quarter eagles bearing the dates 1847 and 1843. The California gold rush inspired the fad for waistcoat, shirt and cuff buttons of this style. Nos. 2 and 3 are denarii from the Roman Republic. No. 5, dated 1868, is a silver 2½ guilder from the Netherlands; the monarch pictured is William III who reigned from 1849 to 1890.

No. 6, also silver, dates back to 1685. It was issued by the ecclesiastical prince Max Gandolf, Count of Kuenberg, Archbishop of Salzburg. The figure is St. Rupert the great Bishop of Worms who restored Christianity to the region despoiled by barbarian conquests. No. 7, dated 1712, is an 8 skilling piece from Denmark-Norway. The portrait is King Frederick IV.

PLATE II illustrates buttons that completely "transform" coins. All in the group represent a definite style, though any particular button may have been a single. No. 1 is a so-called dragon dollar of British issue. The reverse is completely covered with Chinese characters. The obverse reads TA TSING TWENTY-THIRD YEAR OF KWANG HSU/ PEI YANG ARSENAL. That sets the date as 1903. The front has been fully enamelled in shades of blue with touches of red and gold. The back is fitted with a very heavy silver shank that carries a ring, the sort of fastening appropriate for a Chinese winter coat. Coins with the picture of Queen Victoria were often enamelled.

No. 2 has in center a wine maiden garlanded with grape leaves and holding a goblet. The figure is in high relief. Originally the flat coin had the portrait of a Frederick who bore the titles Emperor of the Holy Roman Empire, Hungary, Bohemia, Dalmacia and Croatia; Archduke of Austria; Duke of Burgundy; Spanish Infante.

No. 3 is a Russian coin from 1878. Its very name, zolotnik, is now almost forgotten. The legend translates "2 zolotniks pure silver 10½ dolja." The royal eagle has been cut out in filigree; a silver stud is attached to the back. No. 4, dated 1939, is a filigreed 25 centavo piece from the Dominican Republic. It has a silver loop shank.

Nos. 5, 6 and 7 are U. S. and Canadian silver coins that have had the obverse designs completely buffed off and new designs engraved. Monograms were especially popular with Victorians who exchanged the buttons as love tokens.

No. 8 is a Navaho button made from a U. S. 50¢ piece that still shows the date 1875.

1   2   3   4

5   6   7

Left: PLATE 2   Photos by A. H. ALBERT   Above: PLATE 1

Shown From Left to Right Are Numbers One Through Seven.

Uniform Buttons From Expositions

1876-1940

by JANE FORD ADAMS and LILLIAN SMITH ALBERT

IN 1876, the Centennial International Exhibition, Philadelphia, celebrating the 100th anniversary of the signing of the Declaration of Independence, drew nearly ten million visitors who enjoyed numerous official ceremonies and viewed some 50,000 exhibits. Fairmount Park, where handsome new buildings had been erected for the event, became a veritable city with uniformed police, fire, and maintenance departments.

Button No. 1 identifies itself by the dates "1776-1876" and the initials CG, for Centennial Guard. Likewise, No. 2 is recognized as Centennial Fire Department. No. 3, with the simple word "Centennial," and No. 4, with "1876/International/Exhibition" were suitable for wear by any staff, including private ones.

The next spectacularly successful international exhibition was the Columbian World's Fair, Jackson Park, Chicago, 1893. It had been planned for the 400th anniversary of the discovery of America, but was not ready for opening until 1893. The uniformed personnel wore buttons adapted from the official exposition seal, No. 5, with a map of the Western Hemisphere replacing the dense print that covered the globe on the seal.

Buttons with a similar device were made for the Pan-American Exposition, Buffalo, 1901. In their case, however, the picture copies the exposition seal — personifications of North and South America reaching out from the continents to clasp hands, No. 6. The buttons are of unusual construction and coloring, having a silvered center and a gilt rim banded with blue enamel. They are backmarked "C.G. Penfold. Buffalo, N. Y./1900."

The Louisiana Purchase Exposition, also called the St. Louis World's Fair, produced two uniform buttons. One, No. 7, has the date 1904 and monogram LPE, it resembles the exposition seal through it is not an exact copy. The other, No. 8, has identifying caption and initials JG, for Jefferson Guard.

The dates "1607-1907" place No. 9 as belonging to the Jamestown Exposition, held at Hampton Roads, Virginia, to commemorate the establishment of the first European settlement on this continent.

The photograph below shows members of the Balboa Guard on the grounds of the Panama-California Exposition, Balboa Park, San Diego, 1915-16. These men protected property and kept order while being admired as parade escorts and ever-present guides. They were selected for height, robustness, and fine carriage. Their distinctive dress was inspired by a Spanish court uniform, and according to a contemporary newspaper, it was "a brilliant affair—sky blue coat and trousers, with gold buttons, and yellow and crimson trimmings." They

Photo From Historical Collection of Title Insurance and Trust Company, Union Title Office, San Diego, California.

Left to right, from top down: Numbers 8, 9; 10, 11; 12, 13; and 14

alone wore the official buttons, No. 10, picturing a female figure holding a ship and pointing across the continent to San Diego's place on the map; encircling caption "Panama-California Exposition/San Diego 1915." They were well equipped, however, with no less than 27 buttons per coat.

During the summer of 1915, San Francisco was also holding an exposition, titled the Panama-Pacific International Exposition, to mark the opening of the Panama Canal. The buttons worn there, No. 11, were severely plain with nothing but the initials P.P.I.E. and 1915.

World's Fairs were in a decline after World War I until the Century of Progess, Chicago, 1933-34, restored their popularity. Buttons bearing the official seal, Nos. 12 and 13, were widely distributed to liveried attendants. Note that the date was changed for the second year.

No. 14 pictures the trylon and perisphere, architectural signature of the New York World's Fair, New York City, 1939-40.

All buttons are stamped metal, two-piece construction. With the exception of Buffalo's, previously described, and New York's, part of which are silvered, all are gilt.

National Guard Uniform Buttons

by JANE FORD ADAMS and LILLIAN SMITH ALBERT

WHEN in April, 1861, President Lincoln issued a call for 75,000 volunteers, regiments of state militia, independent companies, and National Guard units responded by joining up as forces in being. Soon they appeared in Washington resplendent in uniforms designed for armory drill and parade instead of for military camp or battlefield. They came dressed like officers of the Colonial militia, or in the exotic costume of Zouaves, or with other elegant trappings.

Older and more aristocratic groups, such as the Ancient and Honorable Artillery Company of Massachusetts, founded in 1638, proudly wore insigne buttons.

As the war progressed, the showy and inconvenient garments were put aside in favor of plain Army blue. But again during the peace years, 1865-1898, when State funds were paying for three-quarters of the military training given, and the command was local, pride brought distinctive uniforms back, complete with appropriate buttons.

In several states the official guard or militia button bore the State seal, perhaps with identifying monogram. In many cases, however, single regiments had individual buttons. More than twenty-five in New York State did; nearly as many in Massachusetts; in little Rhode Island, at least ten. But again war brought change. After the Spanish-American War the U. S. government gave financial aid and equipment—including regulation uniforms—to State troops. Some units kept their own buttons; some did not.

Today under dual Federal-State control, the Guard conforms to U. S. dress regulations in every particular. Button collectors set World War I as the time when distinctive state buttons became obsolete for the military. Strictly speaking, that is misleading, since some went out of use much earlier, and a few still have special use.

Pictured here, Nos. 1-4 antedate the Civil War: No. 1 — Providence (R. I.) Horse Guards; No. 2 — New Hampshire National Blues; No. 3—Boston (Mass.) Light Dragoons; No. 4—Portland (Maine) Light Infantry.

In its long history, the Ancient and Honorable Artillery of Massachusetts has changed buttons eleven times, but usually kept either the name or the date "1638." No. 5 shows the design adopted in 1893. Incidentally, this is one of the few organizations which still has an official button.

Of the thirteen states with Naval Militia, only New York has buttons—No. 6. Logan's Rifles, Illinois, 1880s and 1890s, was named for General John A. Logan, founder of the G.A.R.—No. 7. The National Fencibles, No. 8, were disbanded in 1899.

Nos. 9-12 are National Guard buttons worn State-wide: No. 9—California; No. 10 — Kansas; No. 11—Minnesota; No. 12—Washington.

Nos. 13-16 belonged to numbered regiments of New York State.

Duryea's Zouaves, "The 5th New York Infantry Regiment," at the Battle of Big Bethel, Va., June 10, 1861, from a contemporary print. *Civil War Times* informs that this unit suffered 211 casualties before disbanding in May 1863. Uniforms of various Zouave units differed in detail, but bloomers, canvas leggings, short jackets, sashes, and Eastern headgear were common to all.

Royal Copenhagen Marks On Buttons

by JANE FORD ADAMS and LILLIAN SMITH ALBERT

NO porcelain mark is more famous than the three blue waves of "Royal Copenhagen," symbolic of Denmark's three waterways, and in continuous use since 1775. Even with articles as small as buttons, marking has been the rule, and the unmarked button is the exception.

Button making started at Copenhagen before the end of the 18th century, when a mania for porcelain swept England and the Continent. Plate I shows a few of the beautiful examples preserved in the company's museum, which the curator, Mr. Bredo L. Grandjean, dates from 1780–1800.

If it seems strange to see a Danish button with English words upon it, we have only to recall that English aristocrats who were excellent customers for made-to-order pieces from potteries as far away even as China, also had a penchant for Continental wares. Many a custom-made piece later passed into general production to become a stock item.

Of the buttons shown on Plate I, Mr. Grandjeans says: "The decoration is painted over the glaze; all painting was done freehand. No banding wheel was used, else the borders would have been more true. No stencils were employed, else the scallops around the butterfly would have been perfectly symmetrical instead of charmingly irregular. No outline transfers provided the picture, else the scene would lack its freedom. The coloring, in a higher key than usually associated with Copenhagen, is distinctive of the period. Gilt, too, is more in evidence."

Comparison of No. 7 on Plate I with No. 1, Plate II, clearly illustrates period changes in design. The first and earlier button, is elaborately painted so that the body color is almost hidden; the perforations dominate the design, but are only a part of it. The second, later

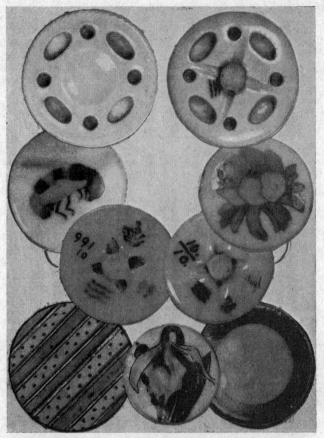

PLATE II. Courtesy National Button Society. Actual size.

button, has no trim at all. The perforations *are* the design; the gleaming white of the glaze *is* the color.

All buttons on Plate II have the blue waves mark. Nos. 2 and 3 have additional marks of significance. No. 3, which could not have been decorated before 1885 when the special technique of underglaze painting used on it was perfected at Copenhagen, shows, in addition, two blue code marks, and two scratch marks, not visible to the camera. The company explains: "The number 78 in blue indicates the paintress, Miss K. Jacobsen, who was employed in the works 1898–1908, and tells that this button was decorated at that period. The painted numbers 16./10. indicate decoration and shape, while the mark 10 incised in the mold is also indication for shape. The other incised mark is the indication for the caster, who has executed the button in question." Thus the symbol of most importance to collectors is the decorator's number.

The decorator of button No. 2, was 99, whose name unfortunately we do not have. The 10 indicates the round shape, as above, and 991 refers to the decoration. Here the crown is a new element. Although the full company trademark includes a crown, this does not form a regular part of the porcelain "signature." Arthur Hayden, writing early in the present century, says that Copenhagen artists of the time had become interested in work done a hundred years earlier and were copying it. All reproduction pieces were marked with the crown and waves, both in blue.

Though no button bearing it was available for illustration, the mark introduced in 1889 for export porcelain deserves mention. Stamped in green, this is a circle enclosing a crown with "Royal" above, "Copenhagen" below, the blue waves in accompaniment.

When
this You
for
remember
me

PLATE I. Courtesy Royal Copenhagen Porcelain Manufactory. Nos. 1-3, 17mm , actual size; Nos. 4-6, 36mm; No. 7, 37mm.

Satsuma Ware Buttons - Marked and Unmarked

by JANE FORD ADAMS and LILLIAN SMITH ALBERT

IT has become a maxim that the surest way to assemble a bad collection of Japanese pottery is to stick to the marks. It is not that discouraging, however, where Satsuma ware buttons are concerned. The worst that can be said is that the marks on them tell next to nothing; the best, that the marks are ornamental, easy to fathom, and not in the least misleading. Moreover, they are collectible for their own sake without having to be "significant".

Marks written in Japanese characters are of two kinds: proper names (presumably decorators) and expressions of sentiment. Sentimental marks are popular in the Orient. To label a button with a noble thought or a poetic word is as natural in Japan as it is for us to label it with a trademark picture. Just as a trademark gives us more confidence in a button, so does a well chosen sentiment increase its desirability in Eastern countries.

PLATE I, #1 is marked "gold brocade", "sunshine", and "mountain". To the Japanese, these words suggest elegance, comfort, and high attainment—qualities which become attached to the button by association. #2 reads "Fuji" and "sun", other words with pleasant connotations.

The mark on #3 is a proper name. Since we have no list of recognized decorators that are distinguished for superior work, none can be named. It is natural to believe, however, that signed pieces are those in which the artist took great pride.

The mark most commonly seen on Satsuma buttons is derived from the arms of the province—a cross within a ring, #4. Sometimes it is written in gold, sometimes in red, sometimes in black. The theory that the quality of the button can be determined in this sequence is as unwarranted as the notion that unmarked examples are inferior to marked ones. Some of the finest Satsumas are not marked, and while it is true that most marked ones exhibit excellent drawing and coloring, some do show mediocre work.

The cross-in-ring symbol is useless as a date reference since it has been used on them continuously from the earliest. The only mark which provides such data is the word "Japan", usually printed in gold. It indicates a very recent date; surely made since the last war.

Satsumas have not been so popular since the craze for Oriental goods reached its peak some fifty years ago. They are being imported in record quantities. This new enthusiasm has produced designs which separate current examples from earlier ones.

Classic subjects, so much admired in the 19th century are still popular. These include dragons, butterflies, peacocks, scenes, particularly Mt. Fuji, and natives in colorful dress. Today these Orientalia are augmented by pictures supplied by American customers for the Japanese to copy, hence those of obviously Occidental origin can be identified as having been made since the war.

Another post-war development has been the extensive manufacture of buttons that resemble Satsumas superficially, although they are made of other ceramic bodies. They lack the crackle glaze, and often transfer designs replace the hand drawn ones, of genuine Satsuma.

The quality of Satsuma buttons is measured by both glaze and decoration. The glaze is best when it is most finely crackled; the decoration, when the drawing and coloring are most artistic. On an unpainted background an old ivory tint is preferable to a dead white; on a painted background, a deep blue is more select.

The full name, Satsuma-Nishiki-de (meaning "enameled"), describes the kind of decorating done before World War I. Often the colored enamels and gold were laid on so heavily that they formed an encrustation. Such built-up work seems to have become obsolete.

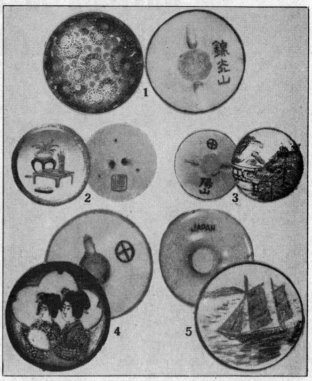

PLATE I. *Satsuma buttons with a variety of backmarks.*

PHOTOGRAPHS FROM THE NATIONAL BUTTON SOCIETY

PLATE II. *Top six Satsuma buttons are old; bottom six, modern.*

Buttons made in England for the China Trade

by JANE FORD ADAMS

Plate 1.

Photographs by A. H. Albert

BY THE MIDDLE of the 19th century, European gentlemen scarcely ever wore gilt buttons except on livery and uniforms. Hence a once highly prosperous branch of the trade found it wise to develop new markets in Asia. Neat, durable buttons with strong loop shanks suited the native dress in India, Siam and China. They proved popular in all three places, but especially in China where wearing "Made in England" buttons became a mark of distinction.

Buttons designed for export to China a hundred years ago are small or medium sized, die-struck, flat gilts. Subjects obviously chosen to please the customer include Oriental figures, the Willow pattern, foo dog, sea dragon, sampan, clipper ship and messages written in Chinese along with birds, flowers, and animals. Most are backmarked in Chinese, Chinese and English, or least often in English alone. "Treble Gilt," "Rich Treble Gilt," and other standard quality tags are in English.

The marks directed to Chinese readers have much more variety. The eight different ideagraphs found on the buttons of *Plate 1* are transcribed on *Plate 2*. Each expresses a pleasant sentiment. Ideagraph No. 1 may be in pidgin Chinese as only the first word is translatable. It means "delight." No. 2 means "prosperity in our time." No. 3 is "successful and prosperous." Note that ideagraphs No. 4, 5, 6 and 7 all begin differently, but end in the same way. The meaning in every case is "foreign merchant or company."

By law, any store owned by a non-Chinese person and also any shop that stocked imported goods was required to display a sign containing "Foreign

Merchant" as part of the name. The stores selling these particular English buttons were: 4. Unique and Original Foreign Merchant; 5. Humble and Sincere Foreign Merchant; 6. Great and Flourishing Foreign Company; 7. Lucky Omen Foreign Shop.

Literally translated ideagraph 8 reads "generous, complete, prosperous." The form, however, is that used for a proper name rather than a sentiment. It too may be a company name, legal on a buttonback without "foreign" added.

Looking again at the button fronts, we recognize the symbol "happiness" on No. 3. It is a widely used backmark also. The rotund gentleman on No. 1 wears a sash inscribed "A person with a pleasant face and a genial manner." The style of the message indicates that he is a human, not a divinity.

1. 怡夲　　5. 謀信洋行
2. 世昌　　6. 大興洋行
3. 順利　　7. 瑞記洋行
4. 元亨洋行　8. 隆全順

Plate 2.

A number of these buttons have found their way back across the ocean, some as souvenirs, some (with shanks removed) as medallions on Chinese brass boxes and trays; and some as fastenings on exquisitely embroidered Chinese garments. Those buttons were put there by the original wearers. They are not Western replacements and should not be removed.

Plate 2.

Plate 3.

Centennial Buttons

by JANE FORD ADAMS

Photographs by A. H. Albert.

Plate 1.

AT THE TIME of the Philadelphia Centennial buttons were in high favor as costume accessories. According to *Godey's Lady's Book,* they were more important to ladies of fashion than jewelry. In the words of one Godey writer, "extravagant sums" were being spent by "our *elegantes"* for "artistic buttons."

Visitors to the Exhibition had a chance to see buttons displayed by twenty-three manufacturers from seven countries. The U.S. Official Reports, published in 1880, praise them all for good quality and cheapness. (In those days "cheap" was a word of commendation.) Such phrases as "great and handsome variety," "originality and variety of design" and "fine workmanship and taste" were often used to describe these buttons.

Those shopping for souvenirs had a good choice of buttons commemo-

rating the occasion. The majority were made with stud backs, often coming in pairs suitable for wearing as cuff buttons. There were inexpensive ones, mostly stamped brass, and deluxe ones of tortoise shell inlaid with silver or mother-of-pearl. Surprisingly, glass buttons were all but non-existent. The only ones known to collectors today are of milk glass with the Liberty Bell and 1776-1876. (Plate 2.)

Other appropriate subjects included Independence Hall, the newly erected Art Gallery and Main Building, the U.S. shield and two symbolic designs of an American eagle and the British lion in confrontation. (Plate 1, extreme right.) In 1776 the eagle is frightened; in 1876 it is not. These and the pair next to them which picture the buildings, are tortoise shell inlay.

Practically every Centennial button, whatever its design, bears a date—76,

1776, 1876 or both full dates. With one exception, even the uniform buttons are dated. Plate 3 shows kinds worn by the Centennial Guard, the Centennial Fire Department, the Centennial Railroad, and personnel of other types. All of the uniform buttons are backmarked with names of uniform makers; none have a button maker's backmark.

None of the other buttons are backmarked at all. It is known, however, that the pair in the center of Plate 1 was made by Scovill Company for their own trade exhibit and not as a sales item. The beautiful pair are heavy gilt, hand engraved and chased. Scovill made for distribution copies of their famous 1824 Lafayette presentation set. Unless the buttons are still attached to the 1876 mounting card, they would not be recognized as Centennial items.

INDIAN POTTERY BUTTONS

by JANE FORD ADAMS

Zia pottery buttons in
geometric designs.
Diameter 1 1/8".
Photo by A. H. Albert.

THE ZIAS are a very small Rio Grande pueblo Indian tribe living some 40 miles north of Albuquerque, New Mexico. Since time immemorial Zia women have been skilled potters even though they have never had a potter's wheel or a good fuel for firing a kiln. In this century they have made, among other things, distinctive buttons that deserve to be better known.

Zia buttons are easy to recognize by description alone. The shape and sizes suggest that they were patted out in the palm of the hand and pierced with two holes before being smoothed off. The tops are slightly convex, the backs dished. The raw material is coarse reddish or sand-colored clay. The button backs are always covered with a red clay slip. Until about 1940 the fronts were slipped with white upon which designs were painted in soft red, black and brown. Later the white slip was tinted buff and finally it became deep tan with glaze-like brightness instead of the earlier matt finish.

The paint used to decorate was not a commercial product. The Zias made it themselves from available materials—metallic rock ground to a powder and mixed with water and the juice of the Rocky Mountain bee weed. Paint brushes were made of yucca leaves.

Zia subject matter is as limited as the palette, which is to say that traders and tourists have not persuaded these artists to "improve" their line. They draw only traditional subjects (of which birds are the great favorite) in the traditional way with solid color used dramatically and details of plumage ignored. Although no two birds are exactly alike, they can be classified as

Zia pottery buttons in bird designs from the collection of Dorothy del Castillo. Small buttons are 1 1/6" in diameter; large buttons are 1 5/8" in diameter.

belonging to three varieties—the traditional thunderbird, a conventionalized wild turkey, and a stylized road runner. Anyone who has seen the New Mexico state bird dart along the ground with the speed of flight will admire the Zia artists' genius for capturing the action. *Plate 1.*

Floral and foliate motifs, deer and frogs decorate Zia bowls and jars. But if any buttons picture them, they have eluded me. Geometric designs, both angular and curvilinear, common on larger pieces, are repeated on buttons. *Plate 2.*

The exact period during which

these buttons were made is uncertain. Perhaps it began in the 1920s and peaked in the 1940s. Production was never large and distribution seems to have been confined to the Albuquerque area.

The only buttons that could be mistakenly attributed to Zia are those decorated in multicolor with garish poster paints. They are made of the same potter's clay and have similar geometric designs. But they were made in a neighboring pueblo for sale in souvenir shops to tourists who lack appreciation of genuine Indian sensitivity to line and color.

CENTENNIAL ANTIQUES

One of the most important dates in our nation's history was the impetus for the production of a host of collectibles. There have been two great celebrations held in Philadelphia to commemorate the signing of our Declaration of Independence in 1776. The first, the 1876 Centennial, saw the erection of a host of massive buildings housing exhibitions of all kinds—arts, manufactured goods, agricultural equipment and tools, fashions, foodstuffs, and much more. Street corner hawkers sold toys, banners, broadsides and souvenirs of every description—all to the delight of present day collectors of Centennial memorabilia.

Advance Mementoes Of The 1876 Centennial

by MARCIA RAY

LONG BEFORE the 1876 Centennial celebration in Philadelphia, enterprising individuals and business firms were reaping advantage from the coming event. In 1874, the National Publishing Company (Philadelphia, Pa., Chicago, Ill., St. Louis, Mo., and Columbus, Ohio), publishers of popular Histories, Illustrated Bibles, and Biblical Works, brought out the *Centennial History of the United States from the Discovery of the American Continent to the close of the First Century of American Independence*. It was written by James D. McCabe, author of several of National's histories, and was "embellished with 442 Fine Historical Engravings and Portraits."

The brown "extra fine English cloth" cover, embossed in gold with the title and a representation of the Great Seal of the United States, surrounded by trains, steamboats, bales of cotton, sheaves of wheat, miners' picks, and agricultural implements, and in black with "The Republic Founded by the Fathers Will be Maintained by the Sons," is pictured here from the collection of Mrs. Raymond Palmer

Delano, Jr., Nottingham, Pa.

The book, 9½ by 6¼ inches wide and nearly 3 inches thick (925 pages), was sold only by house-to-house agents. The price in cloth was $3.75; with morocco back and corners, $4.50; some agents claimed to have sold as many as 30 copies a day, though 10 to 20 was a more reasonable expectation.

The contents of the book treat in absorbing detail the settlements of the

Eastern seaboard, the events leading to the Revolutionary War, and that War itself. The Civil War, then scarcely 10 years over, is covered in two short factual chapters, conveying the author's "honest effort to do justice to both sections . . . free from sectional or partisan bias." The accomplishments of each President, from Washington to Grant, are briefly chronicled.

The Appendix, a matter of 18 pages, was devoted to the coming Centennial celebration in Philadelphia. It contains liss of the members of the Centennial Commission (there were two from each state and territory except Alabama and Mississippi who had only one each); the various Acts of Congress concerned with the celebration; the President's Proclamations and his invitation to foreign countries to participate; descriptions of the five important buildings in process of construction; projected plans for other construction; and the proposed arrangements for transporting visitors by special trains and horse-railways from the city to the Exhibition grounds in Fairmount Park.

CENTENNIALS of several Revolutionary events which preceded the

Declaration of Independence to be celebrated in Philadelphia were also recognized with souvenirs. In Boston, on June 17, 1875, the *Bunker Hill Centennial* was published—an 8-page newsletter containing the history of the battle, copies of important documents and contemporary engravings. Reputedly 100,000 copies were printed and sold at 10 cents each.

On one page appeared Paul Revere's engraving of the City of Boston, made in 1768, with its deceptively tongue-in-cheek dedication: "To the Earl of Hillsborough, his majesty's sec'y of state for America. This view of the only well planned EXPEDITION formed for supporting y' dignity of Britian and chastising y' infolence of AMERICA is hum'ly subscribed." At that time the British troop under General Gage, occupying Boston, were encamped on the Common and in Faneuil Hall because the incensed people of Boston refused to supply them with quarters or food.

The newspaper pictured here belongs to Wayne Bastian, Fulton, Ill.

MARIE and Fred Meyer, Cambridge, Mass., sent this photograph of a china plate commemorating the Boston Tea Party of Dec. 16, 1773. Decorated in the center with "Philadelphia" around "1873" (not "Boston," as might be expected), it was most likely a souvenir made to be sold at the Philadelphia Centennial with an eye toward Boston trade. It carries no maker's backstamp.

Centennial Souvenirs

by MARCIA RAY

There is no maker's mark on this white bone china demi-size cup and saucer. Overglaze decoration is in a bright light blue. Both sides of the cup are shown. The seal in the center of the saucer represents early Rhode Island.

"2" />

Centennial
Antiques

CENTENNIAL SOUVENIRS of any description, local or national, are a fascination to collectors and historians alike. As 1970 ushers in a Centennial decade for the United States, the hunt is on for mementos from our first Centennial in 1876. Souvenirs in wide variety appeared in that year, many of them at the Centennial Exposition in Philadelphia, others on store shelves across the country for stay-at-homes.

Dated articles in pressed glass, made for the occasion, are quite easily found today. Gillinder & Sons set up a model glass factory on the Exposition grounds, and some of the pressed glassware made there—little slippers, small statuettes, and paperweights—were marked "Gillinder & Sons. Centennial Exhibition." Clear and colored glass canoes, toothpick holders, 3-legged kettles with wire handles, mugs, and other trinkets were often etched with the date or other identification. Since most of these pieces later went into Gillinder's regular production, only dated pieces can truly count in a Centennial collection.

Souvenirs in porcelain or pottery, by nature of their inscriptions, were one-occasion productions. They are less readily found than glass souvenirs, and are generally of greater interest. Though most of the inscriptions on china pieces were general in nature, occasionally one turns up immortalizing some minor Revolutionary event seldom recorded in present day history books.

Such a one is the cup and saucer pictured which commemorates the "First National Centennial Anniversary/1876" and the "First Blow For Freedom/Gaspee/June 10, 1772."

The *Encyclopedia Britannica* (11th edition) notes the event in one sentence: "On the 9th of June, 1772, the *Gaspee*, a British vessel which had been sent over to enforce the acts of trade and navigation, ran aground in Narragansett Bay and was burned to the water's edge by a party of men from Providence."

John Hyde Preston in his chatty *Revolution 1776*, published in 1933, gives a more elaborate account, pointing up the temper of New Englanders in the years just previous to open hostilities.

According to him, the *Gaspee*, a British coast guard schooner, Lieutenant Dudingston commanding, had been roaming the waters around Providence and Newport, seizing ships and confiscating illicit cargoes. Since smuggling (to escape unwelcome English taxes) was then, and had been for more than a hundred years, a respectable way of life for almost all the prominent seacoast families, the *Gaspee* and her hawklike master was scarcely a favorite in Providence. In fact, Rhode Islanders considered the English laws not worth obeying and the *Gaspee* no more than a pirate ship bent on depriving them of their profits.

Accordingly when a drummer, on the night of June 9, 1772, brought the news to Providence that the *Gaspee* had run aground off Namquid Point, 7 miles south, the townsmen were ripe for action. His story was that the *Gaspee*, chasing the patriot smuggling sloop *Providence Packet*, sailing close to shore because of the high tide, had grounded on her deep keel and had fired at the *Packet* until she was out of sight.

Official British records said the *Gaspee* was not chasing the *Providence Packet;* it was merely going up to Providence to meet some sailors who had come overland from Boston. The *Gaspee* had not fired any shots since they had nothing to fire at. The tide was low; she merely sailed too close to shore and stuck on a long sand bar.

Be that as it may, the men of Providence were incensed with the drummer's report. Merchants, captains, and excitable young men gathered immediately in John Sabin's tavern to mold a few bullets and load their firelocks. Getting a surgeon to join them, they all went down to Turner's Wharf, climbed into rowboats, and with muffled oars, pulled for the *Gaspee*.

Dudingston, hearing them only when they came alongside, rushed up on deck without his breeches, a big hat slapped on his head. He challenged them, and received in return a shower of bullets. One hit him in the groin and sent him sprawling, his gold laced hat skittering across the deck. (Later one of the Providence men was wearing it about town.)

The crew dashed to Dudingston's assistance, but not knowing what was going on, were quickly knocked down by the men who swarmed over the side of the ship. Also according to Preston, these somberly dressed Providence men "sat on them and cursed. Especially they cursed Dudingston and the whole breed of British agents."

While Dudingston's wound was being dressed by the surgeon, the crowd threw his clothes and personal papers into the sea, and generally smashed up the ship's furnishings. With his crew, Dudingston, wounded and almost naked, was forced into a boat and rowed to a nearby island where they were left sitting on the rocks. The *Gaspee* was fired, and burned until daylight of June 10.

A CENTENNIAL TOY

CRANDALL'S "YE HERO OF '76"

Photographs by Richard Merrill, Saugus, Mass.

CENTENNIAL REMEMBRANCES were not all for grown-ups, fragile cups and saucers and don't-touch-it glass plates. There were plenty of tokens for the children, too — little tin pails filled with peanut butter, sturdy red and white glass mugs with their names on, iron penny banks, puzzles, and toys like Crandall's "Ye Hero of '76."

The "Old Hero," an elderly but energetic gentleman in a cocked hat who could do amazing stunts, pictured here, and the instruction sheet which came with him, now belong to Mrs. Gladys H. Warren, Saugus, Mass. It had been a gift to her father when he was seven years old, and when little Gladys and her sister Pearl (Mrs. Pearl Darling, Danvers, Mass.) visited their grandmother, out of the cupboard came Papa's "Old Hero" for them to play with while their elders talked.

This flat cut-out wooden Hero came packed in a wooden box, along with a grooved platform for him to stand on, a stool, a staff, a flag, and printed suggestions for the acrobatics his jointed knees and elbows enabled him to perform. Though some of the Crandall toys of this type were merely painted wood, the Old Hero's clothing is of lithographed paper applied to the wood. The red, blue, yellow, and tan is still bright, only a bit worn at fingertips and coattail. As he approaches his second Centennial, his joints have weakened and he does not perform with the certainty of his earlier years. He is just too old and tottery now to play with children anymore. But isn't he grand to look at!

CRANDALL TOYS

Many were the Crandalls who made toys in the 19th century, and collectors delight to own even one of their products, whichever Crandall was responsible for it.

Eleven Crandalls, working from 1830 to 1929, are listed in Marshall and Inez McClintock's *Toys in America,* with their locations, specialties, and relationships to each other.

Though all of them excelled at their trade, usually combining their toys with baby carriages, Jesse A. of Brooklyn, N.Y., and Charles M. of Montrose, Pa., were the most inventive, the most prolific, and the best known. These two men, distantly related, led surprisingly similar lives. They were both born in 1833; both were working with toys by the time they were twelve years of age; and both continued profitably in the trade until their deaths, Charles in 1905, Jesse in the 1920s. Even in their own time, people confused their inventions, their toys, and their games. Collectors still do.

Their common ancestry is traced to Hopkinton, R.I., in the early 1800s. Jesse's side of the family moved to New York City in 1841 where his father had a larger baby carriage and toy factory than he had had in Hopkinton. Jesse and his brothers worked for him there, but after the Civil War, Jesse had his own shop in Brooklyn. He turned out sleds, doll carriages, rocking horses, shoo-flies (which he had previously invented and patented), velocipedes, baby carriages, go-carts and go-cart combinations. Most of these were his own inventions or incorporated some patented feature of his own.

Of his many toy inventions, his nested blocks has been the most lasting. They have never gone out of style, and are still made today. He patented his Sandometers and innumerable other toys, games, and puzzles. He also invented all sorts of things unrelated to children or toys, from a mop wringer and a silver corn spoon to a guard gate for a streetcar. Not many of his general inventions were patented.

CHARLES M. CRANDALL

Charles M. Crandall's branch of the family moved from Hopkinton, R.I., early in the 19th century, to Covington, Pa. His grandfather farmed, and his father, Asa, started a woodworking and furniture factory. Charles worked in the plant and when his father died in 1849, became the manager. He was 16 years old. He began at once to produce more toys.

By 1866 he had moved to Montrose, Pa., and was engaged in making croquet sets. The popular English game was newly introduced in this country and was creating quite a furor. Crandall seemed to have the knack of always making the right thing at the right time. His famous building blocks developed directly from his croquet boxes, and led eventually to the stand-up toys like the Old Hero. In practically every account of Charles Crandall's work, his own story of the building blocks' beginning is included:

"I was working in my small factory on the then new game of croquet and conceived the idea of locking the corners of the boxes by means of grooves and tongues instead of nailing, as had been my custom. A simple machine was constructed for the purpose, and testing it, short pieces of thin wood were used.

"My two infant boys were convalescing from scarlet fever, and I carried some of the blocks home for their amusement. A house, a bridge, fence, and other structures were built from them. In the evening, our physician called, saw and admired the blocks, and ordered a small quantity made for his own use. This was the first sale of the famous Crandall's Building Blocks."

Crandall's Building Blocks were patented Feb. 5, 1867. In the next 25 years, hundreds of thousands of sets

(Please turn the page)

HURRAH! BOYS, HURRAH!!!!!

"Lo, the Conquering Hero Comes!"

We've got him.—Mr. Crandall has dug him up, all alive:

"Ye HERO OF '76."

As Natural as Life," and Twice as Amusing!

C. M. Crandall has done it again—has made another splendid thing that will perfectly charm all the Little Folks, viz.:

The Great Centennial Toy,

a fine OLD SOLDIER, in Brilliantly Colored Uniform, with Cocked Hat, Flag, and Staff, all so ingeniously made and put together, that you can set him in a thousand different positions, and he stays there until you change him.—He is a thing of life; a real joy to all BOYS and GIRLS, (and older people too). He fits and also works well with all the ACROBATS and the MENAGERIE.

EVERY CHILD EVERYWHERE

should have " Ye Hero of '76" right away—or more than one. The Real Hero is 9 inches high, and many times larger than the greatly reduced figures on this page, which show, without the color, only a very few of the almost numberless interesting and amusing positions which the Hero will take in YOUR hands.

For Sale by

"Ye Hero" "Stands Guard."

How he meets his enemies.

He waxeth eloquent.

"Hail Columbia."

How he "tells his vote."　Hurrah for old "76."　Denounces treason.　Shows how the enemy skedaddled.　Imitates a Broadway Swell.

How to save dishonest officials.　"Shoulder Arms!"　"Yankee Doodle."　He walks "on time."　Double Quick.

"Amuse accommodations" by Rail.　He meets a Hotel Clerk.　Interviewed by Ladies.　He has seen 35 yds. silk in one dress.　Fights his battles o'er again.

Etc. Etc. Etc. Etc. Etc. Etc. THOUSANDS OF OTHER POSITIONS. Etc. Etc. Etc. Etc. Etc. Etc.

were sold; many of them went abroad. These plain basswood pieces of various shapes and sizes were notched to fit each other firmly; they were packed in a wooden box on wheels, which could be used as a pull toy. As with all of Crandall's toys, both Jesse's and Charles's, the box lid carried plenty of advertising.

Because he was too busy filling orders to attend to the selling, too, Charles made the Orange Judd Co. in New York, publishers of the *American Agriculturist,* his sales agent. They did well by him and for themselves. The blocks lent themselves to all kinds of structures, and for one of their sales gambits, the *American Agriculturist* ran contests for original designs which they published in the magazine.

These interlocking blocks led to Crandall's Acrobats where heads, arms, legs, and torsos interlocked to perform fantastic feats. This, too, was an extremely successful toy, coming at a time when the circus was at the height of its popularity. The box cover read: "CRANDALL'S GREAT SHOW . . . The ACROBATS. Full of Fun and Frolic and most Brilliant in Costume — Will exhibit at the house of the purchaser, Afternoon and Evening. No postponement on account of weather. MATINEE EVERY MORNING. Admission free. Children half price."

During the 1870s and 1880s came the Crandall toys with the flat grooved board into which flat wooden people and their accessories could be fitted to stand. The District School, Mother Goose characters, and John Gilpin were among the most favored. In 1876 came the "Centennial Toy — Ye Hero of '76."

In 1885, Charles Crandall moved to Waverly, N.Y., where he started the Waverly Toy Works with Moses Lyman who furnished capital. Here, in 1889, he brought out his greatest success of all — "Pigs in Clover," a disc-like puzzle which required dexterity to get all the so-called pigs (actually marbles) into their proper pens, or slots. It took the country by storm and stayed popular much longer than anyone expected.

Charles's son, Fred, last of the toy-making Crandalls, had his own factory in Elkland, Pa., until 1929.

—Marcia Ray

Bibliography

The following books contain more information about Crandall Toys.

McClintock, Marshall & Inez: *Toys in America*

Daiken, Leslie: *Children's Toys Throughout the Ages*

Foley, Dan: *Toys Throughout the Ages*

Hertz, Louis: *Handbook of Old American Toys; Toy Collector*

Texas Centennial Glassware

by ALBERT CHRISTIAN REVI

FOR THE Texas Centennial celebration, held in Dallas, Texas, in 1936, A. Harris & Company (now Sanger-Harris), one of "Big D's" leading department stores, ordered a limited edition of pressed crystal wares from the Imperial Glass Corporation of Bellaire, Ohio. A special design for these articles was created and patented for A. Harris & Company by the president of that firm, A. L. Kramer.

The line included goblets, pitchers, cream and sugar sets, small trays or cake plates, coasters, ash trays, cigarette boxes and possibly a few other pieces, too. A few of these pieces were marked on the base in white enamel, "Limited Edition/A. L. Kramer/Patentee." After the centennial year, no additional orders for the Texas Centennial glass were placed with the manufacturer, consequently the molds were destroyed. Since this was a limited edition, and for a special customer, there are probably not a great many pieces available in antiques shops today. Examples of this commemorative glassware have been

White enamel mark found on the base of some pieces reads, "Limited Edition/A. L. Kramer/Patentee."

found in museum collections designated "maker unknown." This need not be so any longer.

It's possible that glass souvenirs or novelties have been made commemorating the World's Fair to be held in San Angelo, Texas, April 6 through October 6, 1968, and collectors with an eye to the future value of such trifles might be wise to put aside a few pieces as an investment.

Texas Centennial cream and sugar set. The obverse side is decorated with the flags of the United States of America and the Republic of Texas and the dates "1836-1936." The reverse side has a representation of the "Alamo."

"Alamo" ash tray flanked by coasters marked "Texas Centennial/1836-1936."

CERAMICS

No matter what your interests are, whether they be for primitives, historical commemoratives, or elegant trappings, ceramics offer collectors a wide choice. To some, the simple lines and coloring of country pottery has a very warm appeal; history-minded collectors find transfer-blue historical china irresistable; and the dilletante literally melts at the sight of a superb art pottery vase. Here, again, the size of your purse will govern how much you can indulge yourself.

Pottery
of the
Galena
Area

WAYNE B. HORNEY

Top, left: bottle, 9¼″ high, 1½″ opening; mostly green with mottled orange and soft reds; probably for molasses syrup or honey; easily corked if need be. *Top right:* cream pitcher, 6½″ high, 5½″ wide; variations of beautiful greens; deep high molding for a lid. *Center left:* preserve jar, 10⅝″ high, 4½″ opening; green with orange spots; a typical Galena shape. *Center right:* footed flower pot, glazed, 6¾″ high, 6″ opening; soft greens, yellow, and orange blending colors; 2 handles with crimped tops; lovely shape with distinctive molding.

Unglazed flower pots from Mineral Point, Wisconsin

Left, 8″ high, 6⅝″ opening; spherical body over attached saucer with band of fine raised and incised lines around waist; top capped with wide 1⅛″ ruffle; a superb flower pot.

Right: 7″ high, 6¾″ opening; round flaring body with attached saucer; round top molding with under-attached ruffles; unusual straight sides on saucer; one of an exact pair.

ONE OF the native American pioneer crafts to be cherished as part of our heritage is utilitarian pottery making. Wherever a settlement sprang up, all across the country, potters appeared, and from the native clays and minerals at hand fashioned the necessary utilitarian wares for their people. Individual potters and geographic areas had their own styles and shapes and decorations and colors.

One section of the country that produced in the category of lead glazed redware in the past century is the area around Galena, Illinois. Situated in Jo Daviess County, in the extreme northwest corner of the state, Galena is just a mile or two from the Mississippi, across from Dubuque, Iowa, and close to the Wisconsin border. From about the 1830s into the 1860s, it was a very prosperous lead mining town, the cultural as well as the industrial center of the area.

Pottery made at Galena is similar to its counterpart from the New England states in some glaze coloring and some of the shapes. However, much of the Galena pottery is richly varied and unusually beautiful in its colors and markings. Also, it is well endowed with edge moundings and well turned rims.

Galena produced all the necessary utilitarian kitchenware—the basic butter jars, preserve jars, milk pans, jugs, bottles, and pitchers as well as flower pots, chimney pots, and roof and drainage tile. The flower pot category included some very large two-piece garden jardenieres about two feet high. Several dogs exist, apparently all from the same mold. Some were made as stringholders and some as doorstops. No cats have been found as yet, although it is said some were made.

The pottery was all thrown on a typical potter's kick wheel and went through the various stages of preparation to firing in the kiln.

Galena pottery is characterized by the red clay exposed on the bottom, and by the general color of the piece—either plain lead glazed redware with typical light pumpkin color, with or without yellow or cream color slip on the upper half, or as a pot that comes from the firing with accidental dark or green splotches and/or orange iron spots. Sometimes tiny brown manganese spots contained in the glaze were used.

Much of the Galena pottery is as beautiful as any made anywhere, at any time. The many collections now in existence and more being formed seems to substantiate this belief.

Left to right—Preserve jar, 12″ high, 3¾″ opening; rare Elizabeth jar with incised 2 that matches numbers found at that site; heat thinned yellow slip produced unusual color effects; slant edge molding is unique to Elizabeth pottery. Jug, 7¾″ high, 6¼″ dia.; favored by collectors for its color—about half green and half orange-red with many orange spots showing in green background; grooved neck; arched handle; tool mark at base with V-shaped end; a choice ½-gallon jug of bright light coloring and pleasing shape. Mixing bowl, 4¾″ high, 6⅝″ opening; plain red coloring; scoop molding; badly chipped inside as are most of these hard-to-find bowls.

Left to right—Rare footed pumpkin color quart jug, 5¾″ high, 5½″ wide; saucy handle, grooved neck. Milk pan, 5″ high, 10⅝″ opening; beautiful red and green coloring; holds 1 gallon; these came in several sizes, larger and smaller. Dog, 9″ high; the majority are yellow slip and dark brown splattered glaze coloring over the whole piece; this is solid brown on body; head faces straight, eyes are a round incised dot and circle.

Because of recent increased interest, many people have contributed new information. It now seems there were even more potteries in this general area than was realized. I originally had counted one at Galena (which produced the greatest amount by far since it was in continuous production for almost 50 years prior to 1895); two at Elizabeth; one south of Elizabeth; one at Mineral Point, Wisconsin; and one at Belmont, Wisconsin. Other towns in Jo Daviess County and counties adjacent are waiting to be counted and discovered as pottery-making sites. Undoubtedly, across the river at Dubuque and in other nearby Iowa towns, pottery was made with the same redware characteristics and styles.

There were so many potters all over the Midwest during the last century, it will be a long time before they have all been researched and the unique characteristics of each one revealed. It is a most fascinating and satisfying adventure to bring to light some of the history of the old potteries. By the nature of people and things, it is a continuing process of discovery and revelation. There will always be something new turning up to surprise and delight us.

Left to right—Preserve jar, 5½″ high, 3″ opening; orange redware color with cream slip inside and top half of outside. Jardeniere, 7″ high, 8″ opening; typical pumpkin red color, round molding; glazed inside and out. Preserve jar, 6″ high, 3″ opening, dark brown spot coloring applied in glaze. Jug, 9½″ high, 7½″ wide; its orange-red color with three splotches of yellow slip applied around shoulder is typical of Galena ware as is the grooved neck.

The Hyssong Potters

by MILDRED VELEY HARDCASTLE

THE NAME Hyssong, whether spelled with a "y" or an "i" is an important one in the history of Pennsylvania pottery. The following table of dates and places in which the various members of the Hyssong family worked is substantially correct, and it is safe to date marked pieces from them.

1. *Elijah Hyssong* (1827–1893?) established a pottery in Cassville, Pa., in 1847, which continued in operation until 1912.
2. *Mrs. R. E. Hissong* is shown as the owner of a pottery in Cassville on a map of that town published in 1873.
3. *Bruce Hyssong,* son of Elijah, operated at Cassville after his father's death until 1912.

Milk basin and batter jug made by Austin L. Hyssong.

4. *Austin L. Hyssong,* another son of Elijah (1851–1914), after a rather itinerant career operated his own plant in Bloomsburg, Pa., 1891–1914.
5. *Charles A. Hyssong,* son of Austin, operated the Bloomsburg pottery, 1914–1945.
6. *J. & C. Dipple,* a pottery in Lewistown, Pa., beginning date not known was operated by John Dipple until 1872, then by his widow Margaret, first alone, then for a few years from 1875 in partnership with Austin L. Hyssong before her son, Andrew G. C. Dipple, took over.
7. *Andrew G. C. Dipple,* son of John and Margaret, was operating the Lewistown pottery in 1915.

Elijah Hyssong—According to the *Columbia County History* of 1915, Elijah Hyssong was born in Franklin Co. in 1829, and was there bound out in boyhood to learn the potter's trade,

serving four years' apprenticeship. Later he went to Cassville, Huntingdon Co., where he married Rachael E. Green, a native of that county. He worked there as a journeyman, for whom it does not say. When he built his own pottery in 1849, he had to clear the location; the plant he built was carried on by Hyssongs for nearly 65 years.

Elijah was an esteemed member of his community, active in politics, public affairs, and church work. He was a Justice of the Peace for more than 20 years, a staunch Republican, and a lifelong member of the Methodist Church which he served officially for over 40 years as deacon, elder, class leader, and Sunday School Superintendent. He was also a leader of the choir. According to Mr. Glenn Hyssong of Bloomsburg, Pa., a direct descendant, it was Elijah who changed the spelling of the name from "i" to "y"; his reasons were unknown.

Charles V. Adams, Montoursville, Pa., whose father was a Methodist

Large crock made by Andrew G. C. Dipple.

minister, lived in Cassville from 1888 to 1892, and remembers Elijah well, recalling him as a potter who liked little boys enough to let them watch the fascinating business of turning pottery on a wheel. Though the *County History* lists Elijah's death as 1873, it would seem from Mr. Adams' account, that the *County History* was in error, possibly a misprint for 1893.

Elijah had a one-man operation on Main Street, making stoneware and probably redware as well. According to Mr. Adams, Elijah used local clay and sold his wares locally rather than wagoning them to other areas.

Elizah Hyssong, from a photo taken between 1888 and 1892.

In 1915, Elijah's widow was still living in Cassville. They had had 12 children. Among the 10 who reached maturity, Austin L., George, Bruce, and Russell were trained as potters. However, in 1915, only Austin and Bruce were continuing at the trade.

Mrs. R. E. Hissong—On a Cassville map of 1873, a large area between Hill and Walnut Streets is designated as "Pottery, Mrs. R. E. Hissong." Nothing further of this pottery is known at the present time, though it is of note that these could possibly be the initials of Mrs. Elijah Hyssong, who was formerly Rachael E. Green.

Handled jug made by Austin L. Hyssong.

Bruce Hyssong — After Elijah's death, his son Bruce continued the pottery in Cassville until 1912.

Austin L. Hyssong—Austin L. Hyssong remained with his father, Elijah, only until he reached his majority, then he went to Lewistown where he was located a good bit of the time in the next 20 years. From 1872–1876, he was in partnership with J. & C. Dipple there. In 1875, he married Anna Margaret Dipple, daughter of John and Margaret (Peters) Dipple. In 1877 he tried a year at Petersburg, Pa. (we have no evidence of a pottery there), then returned to Lewistown for two years (1878–1880). From 1881–1885, he did business in Huntingdon, Pa. His movings about, typical of many potters of his time, make it difficult to follow his potting year by year.

In 1891, Austin L. Hyssong purchased a pottery in Bloomsburg from John Rehm (or from Rabb & Rehm) which he operated until his death in 1914. During his ownership the plant was considerably enlarged and improved. The former owners, finding the Bloomsburg clay unsatisfactory, had been using clay from Georgia, but Austin changed to a mixture of one-half local clay and one-half clay from Woodbridge, New Jersey. He manufactured many types of pottery-crocks from 1 pint to 12 gallons, beanpots, chamber pots, dye pots, jugs, bowls and pitchers, spittoons, wine coolers and flower baskets. Most of his large pieces in my collection, such as a batter jug, 4-gallon jug, and milk basin are marked "A. L. Hyssong, Bloomsburg," incised. Smaller pieces have to be identified by their workmanship.

Five children were born to Mr. and Mrs. Austin Hyssong. Sons Charles, Walter (who died aged 24), and Irving learned and pursued the potter's trade. Irving's son Wilbur also worked at the trade until he was 20 years old, then left to work at the Navy Yard in Washington.

Charles A. Hyssong—Austin's son, Charles A. Hyssong, took over the business when his father died in 1914, and operated it until his retirement in 1945. The pottery was sold then to the Long Supply Co., and has since been torn down. It was never operated as a pottery after 1945.

While the various Hyssongs lived and worked in Pennsylvania, their jugs and crocks and other potted pieces, through the increased interstate traffic in antiques and today's particular interest in hand fashioned crocks and jugs, are as likely to be found in Texas or North Carolina as in their native state. To know a little about the makers gives them added interest.

Fig. 1

The Ack Potters of Mooresburg, Pa.

by MILDRED VELEY HARDCASTLE

THE MOORESBURG area, near Danville, Pa., was the home of many early industries whose products are being sought by today's collectors. Christopher Latham Sholes, inventor of the typewriter, lived there, as did Moses Liviticus Stecker whose home chair factory produced rockers and tables now collectible. Loom-woven carpet made by Jesse Messersmith at his home was another early local product; so was the pottery made by D. Ack and his sons, now eagerly sought by those who enjoy early hand-turned products.

Daniel Ack was born March 10, 1824, in the Reading area of Berks County. His wife was also from that locality. They moved to Mooresburg in 1854 to begin the Mooresburg Pot Shop. The clay used was obtained from nearby farms, dug by hand, and hauled by horse and wagon. A great variety of items was made, including mugs, pie pans, chimney flues, crocks, jugs, vases, flower baskets, flower urns. Redware as well as stoneware was produced.

Pictured above *(Fig. 1)* is a lovely grey stoneware batter jug, decorated with a few free-hand leaves in cobalt blue. D. ACK, MOORESBURG, PA is incised in blue at the back of the handle. It still has its original tin top and spout cover and bail with wooden handle. Also shown is a grey stoneware crock with a little more ornate cobalt decoration and the same incised signature. The small grey stoneware crock is plain, but with the same signature. Characteristic of Ack crocks is the flat-lipped rim, differing from the rounded ones used by so many potters.

Daniel had two sons, John and Clyde, who grew up to assist him in the potting business. After Daniel retired, the sons assumed operation together for at least a brief period. The grey stoneware jug below *(Fig. 2)* is incised J. F. ACK & BRO., MOORESBURG, PA. in the same blue as used by their father. This has a more elaborate cobalt decoration than the earlier pieces, with flower, leaves and blue under the strap-type handle with thumbprint.

Clyde later left the business to work in a paper factory in Maryland, and John operated the pottery by himself until 1911. We have seen plain crocks and jugs in stoneware with the marking J. F. ACK, MOORESBURG, PA. incised like the other Ack pieces. Thus Ack pottery can be dated between 1854 and 1911.

In Mooresburg, dedicated workers have transformed an old brick school-house, built in 1875 and used until 1964, into a museum, owned and maintained by the Montour County Historical Society. Among the displays is the pottery wheel of the Ack family and some of their pottery.

Mrs. Rebecca James and children of Mooresburg are direct descendants of Daniel Ack.

We are indebted to Mrs. Louise Bower of Mooresburg and Mrs. George Fornwald of Polly's Antiques in Milton, Pa., for supplying much of the information given here. Illustrations are from the author's collection.

Fig. 2

The flower pot made for Rebecca Finley Huggins and dated 1833 makes an attractive container for dried flowers. The decoration is of the sgraffito type; a coating of white clay applied to the pot which was carefully scratched away revealing the red clay body beneath. This example is thought to be from the Bucks County area of Pennsylvania. The redware dish with trailed decoration holds fresh vegetables.

Redware Pottery

by CARROLL HOPF

*Curator, Pennsylvania Farm Museum,
Lancaster, Pa.*

AT A RECENT antiques auction where several examples of slip decorated redware pottery sold for sums in three figures, I wondered what the anonymous oldtime potters who made these pieces would have thought had they witnessed this event. Little could they have imagined that collectors would ever exist who would avidly seek out the type of wares they had once so commonly made and sold so cheaply.

"Redware" generally identifies the basic raw material used in making this type of pottery. John Ramsay in his *American Potters and Pottery,* describes the clays used in making redware as "invariably shales, deposits of which are found at or near the surface of the ground." This clay burns to a soft porous body with a reddish brown color at temperatures between 1600 and 1800 degrees Fahrenheit. The rich pleasant red-brown hue is frequently

due to the presence of iron mineral compounds in the shale. Redware therefore could have been made in any area where clays of this nature existed.

The traditions of making redware pottery from red burning clays may be traced back hundreds of years on the European continent and in the British Isles, and were transplanted to this country early in the 17th century. In technique and style they remained pretty much the same for over a period of 200 years.

The potter's craft, like any other, consisted of several defined steps leading to the finished product. Clay was first dug and left to weather in heaps over the winter months. Weathering helped develop the plasticity of the clay, a trait important when clay was formed into various shapes. The clay was cleaned and ground to proper consistency by one of two methods. One process utilized a shallow circular pit, sometimes as large as 6 feet in diameter, in which stones, similar to mill stones and operated by horse power, ground the clay and water mixture to a desired fine consistency. The second method, which found favor in the early decades of the 19th century, was the "pug mill." This apparatus was comprised of a large wooden barrel in which wooden blades were attached to a vertical shaft; this in turn was fixed to a horizontal shaft to which horse power was applied. The revolving blades churned the mixture of clay and water continuously. Heavy dirt and small stones settled to the bottom while the clay in a suspended liquid

Wren house made of unglazed redware pottery. It has a small hold in the base for drainage. Birdhouses of this form have been made for many years and are still being made today.

This two-piece planter urn has floral and scroll motifs which were shaped by pressing the white clay into a mold. The motifs were afterwards applied to the sides of the redware pot. The overall clear glaze gives the white motifs a golden hue. This piece was probably made in the late 19th century.

state was drawn off and run through a sieve removing lesser debris. The clay was left to dry and "season"; then it was divided into blocks which were pounded and kneaded to remove all air pockets. At this stage the clay was ready for use.

Clay can be shaped into form in four different ways: (1) free hand, without a potter's wheel or mold; (2) pressing clay into or over a mold; (3) pouring liquid clay (slip) into a mold; or (4) forming clay on a potter's wheel.

The majority of redware was turned

or thrown on the potter's wheel. This method was employed by Egyptian potters 2500 years before Christ. The type of wheel used by American potters consisted of a flat disc made of wood or iron, mounted on top of a vertical shaft. At the base of the shaft was attached a larger heavier wheel, sometimes made of stone. The bottom wheel is referred to as the "kick wheel," since the potter revolved the total assemblage by kicking or pushing this wheel with his foot. It usually took 100 revolutions per minute for the potter to work a mass of clay into a form.

After the clay was formed into the desired shape, it was removed from the disc by passing a wire under the object to loosen it from the wheel. In the case of pitchers and crocks, lips and handles were fashioned and applied after the piece was taken off the wheel. Finished pieces were placed on shelving in the "drying area" where they remained three to four weeks. It was essential that all the ware be completely dry before being placed in the kiln. Any moisture would subject the ware to exploding in the high temperatures of the kiln.

The majority of redware, but not all of it, was formed on the wheel. Exceptions were shallow pie plates and loaf dishes, round and oval. They were shaped by rolling out a lump of clay then placing it over the mold which could be either wood or unglazed fired clay. After the number of dried-finish pieces amounted to enough for a capacity load in one kiln, they were readied for glazing and firing. Glazing was essential since redware by its nature is soft and porous and easily absorbs moisture; the glaze prevented moisture absorbtion into the clay body.

By one of two ways glazing was accomplished. A powdered lead compound might have been dusted over the body surface or a liquid glaze mixture used — the article being dipped into the liquid. The second method was probably the most utilized by potters in this country. For crocks and pans it was not necessary to glaze the exterior surface. Glaze was poured into the vessel and circulated around, covering the inside surfaces completely; excess glaze was then poured out. Lead glazes were composed of so many parts red lead to common sand and white clay, finely ground and mixed with water.

Frequently a coloring agent was added to the glaze for decorative purposes. The glaze could be a solid color covering the entire ware or splotches of color glaze could be laid over or under the clear glaze to produce a mottled appearance. Manganese dioxide was a popular coloring agent producing shades of brown. Copper salts, obtained by burning scrap copper in the kiln, gave varied hues of green that are rarely seen as solid colors on American redware pottery. Reds, oranges, and browns were derived from iron salts. Oxides of cobalt, producing blue, if used in direct contact with the unglazed redware gave a rich shiny black. In order to procure true shades of blue, redware had to be coated with a light colored slip or glaze and cobalt salts applied over this.

Another technique of decoration consisted of coating the redware with a light colored slip coating and incising a design through the slip layer with a sharp tool revealing the contrasting redware base. This method of decoration, known as "sgraffito," should not be confused with the technique of incising a design into a clay body proper without an applied slip coat.

Perhaps the most attractive and an early method of decoration was simply trailing liquid white slip clay onto the redware with a slip cup. In its most basic application slip decoration consisted of linear patterns; however the human figure, animals, birds, and various floral designs were made in this effective manner.

Firing a kiln took 30 to 36 hours and demanded a great amount of experience for there was no exact control over heat and temperature. It was indeed a skillful potter who could maintain the correct temperature approximating 1800 degrees Farenheit for the required length of time. Wood was the primary fuel for the early kilns. A potter could never be sure how his wares turned out until the kiln cooled down enough to be opened.

As many individual pieces of redware pottery are not marked, it seems apparent that this was a general procedure practiced by potters. However, occasional examples do turn up marked by incising or by means of a die pressed into the moist clay.

Fig. 1

Fig. 2

Fig. 3

Fig. 4

Fig. 5

Fig. 1: Three small items made for children — a pitcher with dark brown slip glaze coating; bowl with marblized slip decoration on the interior; and a water whistle with dark brown slip glaze coating. All three pieces date from the late 19th century. Fig. 2: Two common kitchen jars from the 19th century period. Both examples have clear glaze coatings with splotches of dark brown manganese glaze applied over the surface. This method of decorating was fast, simple, and most effective. Fig. 3: Two covered jars, the larger example is glazed with an opaque brown slip glaze while the smaller example has a clear glaze coating with mottled brown such as the examples shown in Fig. 2. Both pieces date from the 19th century. Fig. 4: These three pottery examples are purely functional in form and lack any specific attempt at embellishment. All are glazed with clear glaze, however their uncluttered forms are in themselves each a thing of beauty. Fig. 5: Two examples of pottery cups sometimes referred to as porringers. The larger example is clear glazed with streaks of dark brown manganese applied intermittently. An opaque brown glaze covers the smaller example. Both date from the late 19th century.

Far right: The red earthenware vase of Pennsylvania German origin is rare and unusual in itself; yet it is even more atypical by having only three tubes rather than the usual five. Originally some form of ornament was fixed to the bottom of the circular hollow ring. Over the red clay, white and brown slip clay was applied at random and covered with a clear glaze. Measurements are 16 inches high with a 7 3/4 inch diameter ring. The vase was probably made sometime during the last half of the 19th century. **Penna. Farm Museum Collection.**

Right: The saltglaze stoneware crock shown above was used in the process of pickling foods. Filled with cucumbers, for example, it was set into a barrel of brine water. Perforations around the lower half allowed for complete drainage when the crock was removed from the barrel. Of Southeastern Pennsylvania origin, it stands 13 1/4 inches high by 7 1/2 inches in diameter. It was probably made sometime during the last half of the 19th century. **Penna. Farm Museum Collection.**

Strainers or colanders have always had a respected place among the many utensils found in early kitchens and butteries.

The author was told that traditionally the illustrated example was primarily used to drain the whey from curds during the cheese making process. The strainer was found in Lancaster County, Pennsylvania, but it is not known if it was made and used there. A hard buff color earthenware covered with dark brown slip glaze comprises the body. It measures 12 inches high by 8 3/4 inches in diameter. **Author's Collection.**

A rare Rockingham glazed figure of a sleeping sheep on an irregularly shaped flat base. It could possibly have been made at the Bennington pottery, but other American, English and Scottish potteries made similar wares. Its history indicates that it was once used as a marker for a child's grave. Length 15". Privately owned.

Oddities in Early

L OCAL POTTERS supplied many of the basic utensils important to everyday life in early rural America. Practically every country community could boast a potter, oftentimes potter-farmer as well, who furnished his immediate neighbors with milk pans, crocks, jugs, jars, flower pots, pie plates, bowls, mugs, and cups.

Aside from these basic utensils, the potter produced articles which due to their form, function, or decoration may be considered somewhat out of the ordinary. These items were not produced in large quantity when compared to the output of ordinary pot-

That this baking dish has seen much use on the open hearth is evidenced by the grease and carbon accumulation on the unglazed exterior. Made of red earthenware, it is glazed on the interior. An interesting feature is the three legs allowing it to be placed over a bed of hot coals. The extended rim suggests it had a lid at one time. Measurements are 5 3/4 inches high by 10 1/2 inches in diameter. While its origin is unknown, it is believed to date from the first half of the 19th century. **Author's Collection.**

This unique artifact was intended for use in the spring house where it was placed on a stone ledge in the water channel. Jugs and crocks set inside were prevented from being toppled by any strong water current. The perforations allowed water to circulate freely around the jugs, keeping their liquid contents cool. Of southeastern Pennsylvania origin, this item is made of salt glaze stoneware and measures 15 inches long by 13 inches wide. It was probably made sometime during the last half of the 19th century. **Penna. Farm Museum Collection.**

Far left: Similar to the stoneware crock shown elsewhere in this article is this example with a large overhead handle. It could well have served the same purpose for pickling foods. Standing 28 inches high it is made of a buff color stoneware covered with brown slip glaze. This example was found in central New York state and probably dates from the last half of the 19th century.—A. Christian Revi Collection.

Left: Size, form and decoration relegate this jug to the catagory of unusual. Its barrel shape is akin to the pitcher and mug forms produced by the Liverpool potters during the late 18th and early 19th centuries. Particularly pleasing is the applied floral motifs which ably enhance the bold character of this piece. Formed on the potters' wheel, it stands a full 12 inches high and is made of red earthenware mottled with brown slip clay under a clear glaze. The large strap handle is vertically grooved. Of New England origin, it can be assigned to the first half of the 19th century. A. Christian Revi Collection.

American Pottery

by CARROLL HOPF

tery utensils. Because of this "curiosities" can be considered important examples of the folk material culture and individually provide us with more understanding of how our ancestor's inventiveness supplied their daily needs and desires.

Anyone interested enough to search diligently through antique and second hand shops, attend auctions and white elephant sales, may well be awarded the thrill of discovering something comparable to the examples illustrated in this article.

The pottery lamp (as a lighting device) can be traced back to the dawn of civilization. It basically consists of a reservoir for oil or grease and either a lip, spout, or wick tube to accommodate the wick.

Pottery lamps were probably in common use in this country during the 17th and 18th centuries; however, specific documentation confirming this is meager. Most existing examples today are credited to 19th century origin as is the illustrated example, yet with an artifact of such basic changeless style and form, it is almost impossible to assign a given date without any known history of it.

Probably of Pennsylvania origin, this specimen is made of red earthenware splashed with brown slip under a clear glaze. It is 8 inches high and has a 3½ inch diameter reservoir with wick tube.

Pottery lamps were still in limited use as late as 1910 in remote areas of West Virginia and Tennessee. Penna. Farm Museum Collection.

Red earthenware plates and dishes with individual's names or short inscriptions executed in white slip clay on the surface are not necessarily considered "oddities." However, this example is included since the name "Phelie" seems quite unusual. The author is assuming Phelie to be a feminine name. Am I right or wrong? This dish is 13 inches in diameter and was probably made in the first half of the 19th century, and thought to be of Connecticut origin. Author's Collection.

The earthenware roach trap, dating from the last half of the 19th century, is quite simple in principle. Water and a piece of rancid meat were placed within the glazed interior. A roach easily climbing up the unglazed and grooved exterior sides fell through the concave opening and eventually drowned. The trap was cleaned through the hole at the base. It is 5¼ inches high and 6¼ inches diameter at the base. Many of these traps were produced by local potters in southeastern Pennsylvania. Penna. Farm Museum Collection.

This unusual pottery scoop with pouring lip and applied handle was molded around a hand thrown pottery jug. The uneven turnings of the jug are in evidence on the inner surface of the scoop. Obviously two scoops could have been produced at one molding—and probably were. Glazed dark green on the outside and ochre on the inside. Origin unknown; probably dates from the last half of the 19th century. Length 9¼ inches; height to top of handle 3¼ inches. Privately owned.

Pottery pig-shaped mold with mottled green and ochre glaze. (Shown upside down.) The inner surface of the mold, showing the pig's curly tail, eyes, legs, and snout in much sharper detail, is covered with an ochre-colored glaze. Probably used to shape jellied pork dishes, such as souse. Origin unknown; probably dates from the last half of the 19th century. Length 14 inches from snout to applied handle; height 3½ inches. Privately owned.

Potters frequently expressed their sense of design and decoration when making flower pots. This example, raised on the potter's wheel, is formed in three tiers each with a fluted edge. From a distance it looks as though three pots are stacked inside each other. Made of red earthenware, it is finished in clear glaze with specks of brown throughout. It is 7 inches high and 6 inches in diameter at the top. Of Pennsylvania German origin it was probably made sometime during the last half of the 19th century. **Author's Collection.**

Below: "Of all the substances of which hives are made, and they are many, straw has been most generally preferred." The red earthenware beehive well documents this statement which appeared in **The Farmer's Guide** of 1838. Although the origin of this hive is unknown it could possibly have originated in one of our Southern states. Historically we know the Egyptians used pottery hives in their warm Mediterranean climate. This example was "raised up" on the potter's wheel and measures 15 inches high by 11¾ inches in diameter. Because the wooden box hive was generally in use by 1850, we can conclude this hive may have been a product of the first half of the 19th century. **Penna. Farm Museum Collection.**

Below: Applied relief decoration was frequently used by the Pennsylvania German potter to embellish his flower pots. Usually the relief motifs were handmade from ordinary red clay and fixed to the pot. At this point the illustrated example differs; the applied floral motifs were made of a fine white pipe clay formed in a mold. They provide strong contrast against the red clay pot. Random mottling of dark brown slip clay adds interest to the overall decoration. The pot stands 7 inches high by 8 inches in diameter. It was probably made after the middle of the 19th century. **Author's Collection.**

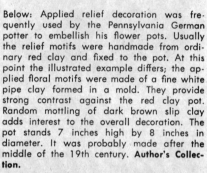

A lowly red earthenware bed pan is beautifully mottled with green and brown slip over a base of yellow slip. Dating probably from the last half of the 19th century, it is 13 inches in diameter and of Southeastern Pennsylvania origin. **Penna. Farm Museum Collection.**

Right: Red earthenware fish molds are usually associated with the products of the local Pennsylvania German potter. This example is unusual in being a completely circular form. The majority of Pennsylvania fish molds are made in a half circle form. Our example is glazed on both the interior and exterior. Dark brown spots of slip glaze are applied at random. Of Pennsylvania German origin it probably dates from the last decades of the 19th century. It is a large one, being 18 inches in diameter. **Penna. Farm Museum Collection.**

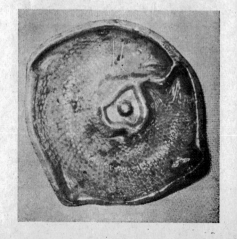

STONEWARE jugs, jars, and crocks are among the most common items to be found in antiques shops today. In 19th century America, farming progressed at rapid pace, and farm produce had to be stored. The housewife called for crocks for her pickled beef, salt pork, butter, preserved and pickled fruit and vegetables. She needed jars for cookies, cakes, and doughnuts; jugs for cider, rum, vinegar, oil, molasses, etc.

Stoneware for these utilitarian articles came into general use about 1800. It was sturdier for storage and household use than the so-called redware, which was lighter and more porous. The name "stoneware" suggests its color—usually gray but varying to shades of buff, depending upon the clay used, even in the same pottery. A salt glaze gave it lustre, and the cobalt blue decorations so often found on these wares are in pleasing contrast to the background color.

This cobalt blue decoration was mostly applied in the diluted form of zaffre, a powdered blue glaze obtained by burning cobalt ore and sand together. Zaffre was first imported from Europe, but by 1787 was said to be produced at East Haddem, Conn. The cobalt blue decorations were not affected by the high firing temperature needed for the production of stoneware.

Many a provident housewife must have been proud to have decorated pottery for use in her kitchen, her "buttr'y," and her cellar. At the time of manufacture, decorated pottery must have been more costly than undecorated wares, and collectors today gladly pay a premium price for it.

Folk Art on

Utilitarian Stoneware

by BARBARA B. CHIOLINO

FEW of the 19th century utilitarian stoneware jugs, jars, and crocks can be considered works of art. If they have more than the incised name of the maker (occasionally the name is not the maker's but perhaps a storekeeper's), place of manufacture, and the size, one generally finds a simple cobalt blue decoration, either a series of imaginative swirls or the representation of a flower.

Some happy exceptions are the delightful "spotted" deer, dogs, cows, busy fowl, flying eagles, and occasional lion or elephant that someone created at the Bennington potteries, and elsewhere, in the mid-1800s. (See Figs. 1-6.)

That these were done by the same creative workman seems evident. The simple brush strokes are similar to those used on country tin and furniture and show a facile hand. Every stroke counts in the picture, and must have been swift and sure. The color is a deep brilliant cobalt blue. The large water cooler (Fig. 2), illustrated in Richard Carter Barret's Bennington Pottery and Porcelain shows the same sort of dappled or "spotted" deer, the same little fences, similar trees and other flora which are found on less important jugs and crocks. It is evidently a masterpiece decorated by the same hand.

Surprisingly, some of these deco-

Fig. 2. Elaborately decorated stoneware water cooler made for the lobby of the Hotel Putnam, Bennington, Vermont, by J. & E. Norton, ca. 1850; decoration and ornate bandings in cobalt blue; removable cover and four holes for water spigots around base; ht. 33½". Bennington Museum Collection.

rated pieces, apparently done by the man who worked at Bennington, are found with pottery marks other than Bennington. Some are marked "West Troy," and several have been found with a Fort Edward (New York) mark (Figs. 4,5). John Spargo, in his Potters and Potteries of Bennington may account for this when he tells of the closing down (temporarily) of the Norton potteries in 1859 and the

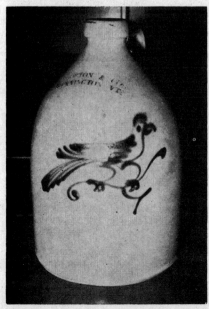

Fig. 6. Stoneware jug with bird decoration, marked "Bennington, Vt." Author's Col.

subsequent establishment of a pottery at West Troy by some skilled workers from Bennington. In a further account, he mentions Bennington workmen moving to Fort Edward, N. Y., and other places.

Consequently, one may have a stoneware crock or jar decorated by a one-time Bennington worker with identifying marks of some other location. Unfortunately, the records of the Bennington potteries do not disclose the name of the "spotted" deer decorator. Another theory, well-grounded, is that he may have been an itinerant workman. If more of his designs come to light with marks other than those mentioned, this could be the correct one.

Sometimes designs were copied. The bird design (*Fig. 6*) is frequently encountered on both Fort Edward and Bennington wares. On the other hand, the "spotted" deer, feathered eagles, and hens (*Figs. 7 and 8*) seem to be unique to Bennington wares, and each design represents an appealing example of American folk art.

Decorations representing human figures are rarely found. *Figure 9* is marked "I. Seymour, Troy Factory," and dates about 1810. Incised on this jug is an elaborately detailed full-length figure of what appears to be an Indian with feathered headdress and moccasins; it could also represent a Crusader brandishing a sword and carrying a banner with a cross on it. This rare jug may have been made for a special occasion, now forgotten; several Bennington jugs with inscriptions commemorating rare events are known.

The fish decorated jug shown in *Figure 10* was made by J. Fenton, Dorset, Vt., around 1810. (Jonathan Fenton was the father of Christopher

80
Ceramics

Fig. 1. Left to right: Rare Norton stoneware jug, 1830 period; incised decoration and owner's name, "I. Judd," partially filled with cobalt blue; ht. 17¾". Handled crock with rare umber decoration bears earliest of all Norton marks, "L. Norton"; ca. 1823-1828; ht. 9¾". Crock with deer decoration in cobalt blue, marked "J. & E. Norton"; ca. 1850-1859; ht. 13¼". All in the Bennington Museum Collection.

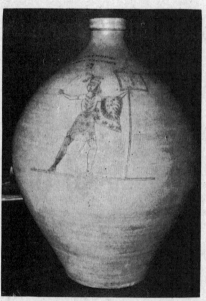

Fig. 3. Rare lion caricature in cobalt blue on "J. & E. Norton" crock; ht. 11¼". Col. Hilary Underwood.

Fig. 9. Stoneware jug with Indian or Crusader decoration, marked "I. Seymour, Troy Factory." Author's Collection.

Fig. 8. Hen decorated crock, marked "J. Norton & Co. Bennington, Vt."; ca. 1859-61. Author's Collection.

Fig. 4. Rare elephant decorated crock bearing the mark of the West Troy pottery. Col. Harry Knapp.

Fig. 5. Stoneware crock with dog decoration, marked "Fort Edward, N. Y." Author's Col.

Webber Fenton, who became famous for his work at the Bennington potteries at a later date.) The fish has been rather crudely incised in the clay and filled in with cobalt blue. A clue to Jonathan Fenton's inspiration for this decoration is suggested by the good trout fishing in the Mettowee River near his pottery. A few other jugs with fish decorations are known; one is in the Shelburne Museum.

The swan decorated jug shown in *Figure 11* could be a later piece, judging by its shape and overall appearance. The neatly drawn swan, which was obviously impressed with a die and not hand incised, is said to be the mark of its unidentified maker.

Fig. 11. Swan decorated stoneware jug; maker unknown. Author's Collection.

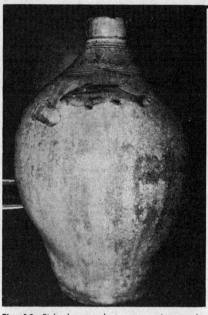

Fig. 10. Fish decorated stoneware jug made by J. Fenton, Dorset, Vt.; ca. 1810. Author's Collection.

Fig. 7. (Below) Eagle decorated crock, marked "J. & E. Norton"; ht. 13". Bennington Museum Collection.

Investing In Stoneware

by Albert Christian Revi

The Picasso-like decoration on this stoneware jug adds interest and value to an otherwise commonplace example of this ware. Signed "Ottman Bros. & Co., Fort Edward, N. Y." Height 18 inches.

STONEWARES with simple floral or leaf decorations are not difficult to find these days, and still relatively inexpensive. These less important pieces sell for anywhere from $5 to $25, depending on the size and shape of the object and what use the buyer can make of it. Jugs, jars, and small crocks can be made into attractive lamps for country-style rooms. Large, wide-mouthed crocks serve nicely as jardinieres, magazine receptacles, or waste baskets.

More elaborately decorated stonewares, especially those depicting animals, birds, fish, human figures, busy floral designs, and patriotic symbols, are not easily found; such pieces are currently commanding prices ranging from $20 to $100 or more. Why? Because collectors have suddenly decided that these decorations represent expressions of primitive American folk art.

SPATTERWARE

By ARLENE and
PAUL H. GREASER

EARLY IN nineteenth century America, there came on the ceramic scene a colorful, crudely decorated ware, now known as Spatterware. It appeared to some degree in seaport towns all along the Atlantic coast, but in the rural Pennsylvania areas, served by the Port of Philadelphia, it was imported in great quantity. Its high colors, variety of patterns, and comparatively low price appealed particularly to the Pennsylvania Dutch, who appropriated it to such an extent that Spatterware is today generally accepted as part of the Pennsylvania Dutch heritage.

While we know most Spatterware was made in the Staffordshire area of England, there is little definite infor-

FIGURE 1

mation available as to the firms who made it and which patterns they made. On maybe one piece in a hundred is there a maker's name or identification mark. It was cheap ware, made for export, and perhaps the potters took no special pride in it. No doubt some of the pieces were made in Scotland and Wales, and now and then a marked piece from France turns up. The familiar Staffordshire names of W. Adams & Sons, Mellor & Venables, Samuel Alcock & Co.,

Meigh, and Meakin, which are among the once-in-a-while marks found on Spatterware pieces, suggest that most of the well known potters, as well as a host of smaller ones, were somehow involved in its production.

Spatterware takes its name from the spattered effect used in its decoration; this may be on the border, in the center pattern or design, or over the complete object. The variety of patterns and colors to be found on Spatterware is endless. Red, yellow, blue, green, brown, and black were the colors used, but because they appear in so many different shadings, the color range seems larger. In the red family, for instance, colors will shade from a pink through lavender through dark red to maroon. There are two shades of blue, and there is an orange shade in the yellow family. Even experienced long-time collectors are continually discovering colors they have never seen before.

Spattering is accomplished by tapping a paint-laden brush against a solid object, causing the color to spatter over the object being decorated. The portion not to be spattered is previously covered with paper of the desired shape to protect it.

Sometimes spatter decoration was simulated by using a sponge. Sponges are available in many sizes, and when a sponge is an agent for the transfer of color, the sponged spatter effects may be of extremely coarse nature. Frequently the sponge was cut to form a design. This method is said to have originated in Scotland about 1845, and was introduced in Staffordshire that same year by the alert

William Adams at his Greenfield Works. Sponge decorated design spatterware is usually included in Spatterware collections.

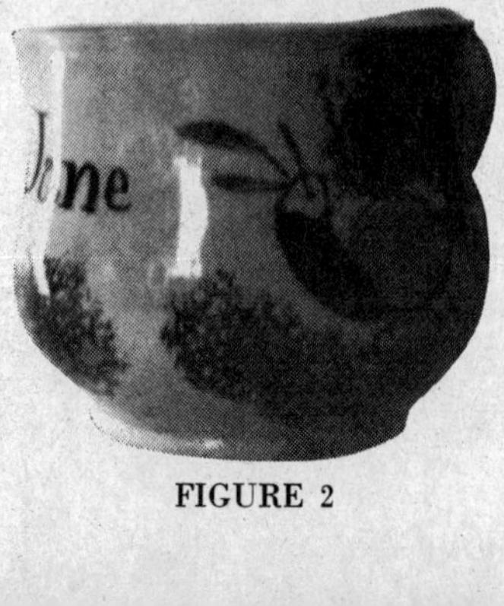

Spattering was known in England in the 18th century, and practiced on their "Delft" ware; however, these early pieces are still known among collectors and dealers as Delft. Not until the advent of Wedgwood's soft paste Pearlware in 1799 were ceramics with a spattered decoration designated as Spatterware. After 1845, the true spatter method yielded to the new sponged design spatter. The results were still very colorful. Spatter work is usually found on soft paste wares and creamwares, seldom on Ironstone.

Examples Tell The Story

Invariably when collectors consider Spatterware, they think first of the extremely popular Peafowl design (Figure 1), where the border is spattered and the design hand-painted, or of the School House design (see cover). These two patterns are the most crudely done of all Spatterware designs.

Items may be found which are personalized with a name, as the Peafowl cup, made for "Jane" (Figure 2); or with a Rose center with three-color Rainbow border (Figure 3); or completely spattered, like the cup and saucer in (Figure 4).

A spatter border may have a trans-

FIGURE 2

FIGURE 3

FIGURE 4

fer design in the center like the Eagle and Shield of *Figure 5;* or the border may form a design about a center hand-painted six-pointed star, with three colors — red, green, and blue— alternating on the point *(Figure 6);* or like *Figure 7,* the design, in sponge work, may be a poor attempt to reproduce *Figure 6.*

Items appear with different degrees of coarseness in the design, depending on the size of sponge selected to do the decorating. *Figure 8* shows a cup and saucer in the standard or conventional size, and a giant 5-inch diameter "mush cup." In each, the size of the sponge used in the decoration was proportioned to the size of the piece it decorated.

Design spatter is accomplished with a cut sponge, and Spatterware collections will include examples of this type. The star designs around the border of the cup and saucer in *Figure 9* were made by using a sponge cut to the star shape. The eagle design in *Figure 10* is made the same way, as is the daisy-like border in *Figure 11.* This last shows a return to the hand-painted center of original Spatterware.

The diversity of design spatter is apparent in *Figures 12, 13,* and in the cup and saucer on the cover. *Figure 12* shows the Rose, hand-painted in natural colors, used with a conventional spattered border; in *Figure 13,* the Rose, also hand-painted in natural colors, is framed with a design spatter border. The cup and saucer *on the cover* has a spatter border in alternating light and dark blue panels, with the Rose, hand-painted in matching two-tone shades of blue.

—Arlene and Paul H. Greaser are the authors of *Homespun Ceramics, A Study of Spatterware* (Privately printed, 1965, $4.25), a paperbound monograph which illustrates 169 pieces of Spatterware from their own collection, along with other examples for guidance and study. Information is well authenticated, and most complete. Their presumption, and the reasons for it, that the Peafowl and House decorations on Spatterware were the work of children is quite believable.

FIGURE 10

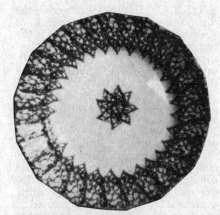

FIGURE 7

FIGURE 11

FIGURE 5

FIGURE 8

FIGURE 12

FIGURE 6

FIGURE 9

FIGURE 13

American Hand-Painted China

by Katharine Morrison McClinton

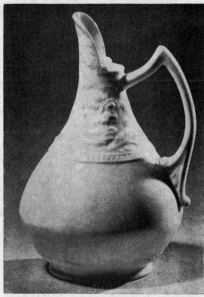

White-glazed porcelain Lotus Ware vase for amateur decorating, designed by Kenneth P. Beattie, made by Knowles, Taylor & Knowles, 1888-1898.

Shell and Cupid jug, 9½x9½″, illustrated in color — pink, white, pale green, and gold — in *The China Decorator,* March 1888, cost $12 in blank Belleek porcelain. A duplicate jug in the Newark Museum, marked "W.S.L. 1887," is said to have been designed by Walter Lenox.

CHINA PAINTING was among the fashionable accomplishments of Victorian ladies. It was a craze popular in England and the Continent from the middle of the 19th century on, but did not reach America until after the Civil War.

The first American classes in china painting, or mineral painting, as it was called, were organized in New York City by Edward Lycett, formerly of Staffordshire, England. Lycett had three sons who were also teachers of china painting in various parts of the country. But the most important influence in the spread of china painting in America was the class organized in Cincinnati in 1875 by Benn Pitman, Director of the Cincinnati School of Design. From this successful class the interest in china painting spread rapidly and in a few years there were china painting classes not only in cities throughout the country, but in young ladies seminaries and art schools.

China painting was taught at Chautauqua, and at the International Correspondence School, and articles giving instructions in china painting were printed in the *Ladies Home Journal,* the *Art Amateur,* and other magazines. In 1887, the *China Decorator,* a magazine devoted to china painting, printed designs with directions for their painting and also gave advice about china available for the china painter.

Much of the china used by the

No. 76. Size No. 1. 5 in. High
No. 77. Size No. 2. 4 in. High

amateur china painter was imported from France and other European countries, but there were also many pieces made by American potters. Among the first was A. H. Hews and Company of Cambridge, Massachusetts. In addition to machine-made flower pots, this company made a specialty of art pottery reproductions of antique Grecian, Roman, Etruscan, Phoenician, and Cypriote models. They also furnished a ware in the plain biscuit for decorators which was known as Albert and Albertine Ware.

No. 47. 7½ in. Diameter.

One of the first books published in America which included a reference to pottery decoration was *Art Recreations: A Guide to Decorative Art,* published by S. W. Tilton, Boston, 1877. This book includes designs and instructions for decorating Albert Ware using Flaxman's designs and Tilton's Colors. This, however, was pottery, not porcelain, and never gained the popularity of china painting on porcelain.

The old Jersey City Pottery, according to Edwin Atlee Barber in *Pottery and Porcelain of the United States,* engaged in making "ornamental forms in white biscuit and glazed ivory white for decorators" in the 1880s. It was this pottery that made the "Worcester" vase, decorated by Edward Lycett, which is illustrated in Barber's book. Later New Jersey pottery companies catered more to the amateur painter.

The pottery of Ott & Brewer, known as the Etruria Pottery, was

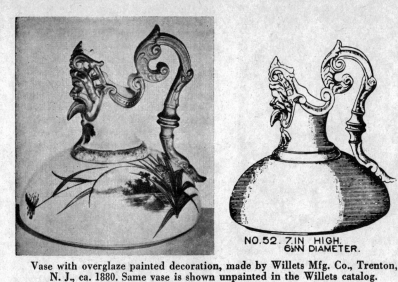

NO. 52. 7 IN HIGH.
6½ IN DIAMETER.

Vase with overglaze painted decoration, made by Willets Mfg. Co., Trenton, N. J., ca. 1880. Same vase is shown unpainted in the Willets catalog.

Cup and saucer marked Belleek/ Willets; cup is pink lined.

established about 1865 in Trenton, N. J., in the factory which had been built by Messrs. Bloor, Ott and Booth in 1863. Until 1876 the chief products of Ott & Brewer were white granite and cream-colored ware. The first Belleek was made here with the aid of William and John Bromley who came over from the Belleek factory in Ireland about 1883. The company made both useful forms, such as cups and saucers, and ornamental vases with pierced necks, feet, and handles, decorated in gold relief and chasing. This thin translucent porcelain was also made in small delicate shell and flower forms for amateur decorating. The graceful Shell and Cupid pitcher was probably designed by Walter S.

Manufacturing Company, also in Trenton, N. J., and instructed them in the process. Willets later became one of the largest potteries in the East. They carried the most varied and extensive supply of white art porcelain blanks for amateur decorators and competed successfully with Dresden, Limoges, Royal Berlin, and other foreign factories in supplying china to American china painters.

The many pages of Willets china

NO 34 6½ IN HIGH

for decoration, reproduced in *The China Decorator* in 1887 and 1888, give an excellent idea of the beauty and delicacy of the forms. One of the most important pieces was the Cupid Jug which was reproduced as a colored supplement in March 1888, together with full directions for decorating it. Another popular piece was the "soiree" plate, with matching cup. These plates were of lily-pad form about 7½ inches in diameter and had a circle into which the lily-form fluted cup fitted. In May 1888, the *Art Amateur* gives a description of other pieces made by Willets Manufacturing Company which can be identified in the illustrations of *The China Decorator*.

Although the article does not definitely state the manufacturer, it says: "One of the art potteries of Trenton, N. J., now makes vases that rival in shapes, textures, and sizes

the famous Worcester ware. They are susceptible to the same kind of decoration in mat colors, gold and bronzes. The plaques and plates are translucent. The cups, saucers, pitchers, fruit dishes and cake dishes are so shapely and delicate that one instinctively handles them with care. They are almost identical with the famous Belleek pottery of Ireland which is no longer made. There are fruit dishes something like the scollop shell in shape though larger, with a standard of coral which is charming, bread and milk bowls with an edge crimped like the azalea creamers of that delicate buff tint so pleasing in Royal Worcester, and numerous small shapes attractive for sideboard, chiffonier, or dining table."

No 71, 4½ IN LONG.

No 69 2¾ IN HIGH
3 IN DIAMETER

In 1889 the Ceramic Art Company was established in Trenton, N. J. by Jonathan Coxen, Sr., who had been superintendent of Ott & Brewer, and Walter S. Lenox, who had been head of their decorating department. One of the specialties of the Ceramics Art Company was Belleek and this was also furnished in white for decorators. In addition to vases and table pieces, such as cups and saucers, they made porcelain thimbles, ink stands, cane heads, paper knives, menu slabs, and candelabra. In the *Ceramic Monthly*, January 1897, the Ceramic Art Company illustrated a tankard design for hand painting and also stated that they had catalogues illustrating other shapes available. This company later

No 39 10 IN HIGH

Lenox when he was in charge of the decorating department at Ott & Brewer. This pitcher was later made at Willets Manufacturing Company and at the Ceramic Art Company.

The other New Jersey potteries that made Belleek stemmed from Ott & Brewer. William Bromley, Sr., went from Ott & Brewer to Willets

Nellie Bonham Foreman of Charlotte, Michigan, painted these plates, backstamped A. Haviland & Co., Limoges, France, in 1891. Design at right is "Ribbon, Cherokee Rose" pattern by Lucy Comins, illustrated in *The China Decorator*. Plates now in the Henry Ford Museum, Dearborn, Mich.

became the Lenox China Company.

The following note is from *The China Decorator*, January, 1890: "The C.A.C. china manufactured at Trenton fires remarkably well and safely. The colors take on a brilliancy superior to that produced by any other glaze and the delicate tint of the ware is extremely agreeable."

In 1891, the American Art China Works (Rittenhouse, Evans & Co.) was established in Trenton. This company also made Belleek for decorating and issued a catalogue of their designs for amateur decorators.

In 1893, Messrs. W. T. Morris and F. R. Willmore established the Columbian Art Pottery in Trenton, N. J. Both men had been connected with Belleek works in Ireland and later with Ott & Brewer. This pottery also made shapes for decorating and issued a catalogue.

China for decorating was also made at the large pottery of Knowles, Taylor and Knowles in East Liverpool, Ohio. This company had been established in 1854. In the 1880s, they

No. 95. 2½ in. High. 3 in. Diameter.

manufactured a considerable quantity of Belleek, but this was discontinued after a factory fire in 1889. It was not until the 1890s that they began to make their famous Lotus Ware, which was sold both plain and decorated. In their advertisement in the back of the 1893 edition of Barber's *Pottery and Porcelain of the United States*, the company notes of their art china: "This ware is adapted to the requirements of amateur or professional decorators and may be obtained

usually through first-class crockery dealers. It is made in artistic shapes designed for practical utility."

The Kezonta ware of the Cincinnati Art Pottery was a deep blue and white pottery made for decorators. The forms are modifications of Greek and Roman shapes and many ladies painted these for the market. The mark was "KEZONTA" impressed.

With so many American potteries manufacturing china for amateur decoration, there should be a quantity of American pieces available today even though foreign china was generally considered the most desirable. Possibly the frailty of the American china accounts for its present dearth; several people complained in the contributors' column of *The China Decorator* that pieces broke in the kiln.

There are several different methods of china painting. The majority of the pieces done by amateurs show the overglaze technique, where the painting is applied to the glazed surface that has previously been fired. The colors are then refired at a low temperature. Underglaze painting, the oil painting of the ceramic artist, is done on the biscuit china before it is glazed. Underglaze colors are applied

No. 40. Size No. 1. 4¾ in. High, 10 in. Diameter.

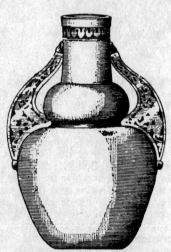

No. 92. 8½ in. High.

China painting materials used by Nellie Bonham Foreman, ca. 1890, are also at the Henry Ford Museum, the gift of her son, George F. Green.

and the surface fired with high heat.

A. H. Osgood, Director of Osgood's Art School, in *How to Apply Royal Worcester Matt Bronze, La Croix and Dresden colors to China* (1888), notes different kinds of china available for paintings. She recommends Berlin Porcelain for figure painting and French porcelain for its general excellence. "Of English ware, Copeland's (Spode) has a blue-white glaze, Minton's has a gray tone, and Doulton is creamy-good for pinks and gold. American ware is beautiful and unique in forms for table and art pieces. Trenton Ware has a creamy glaze and delicate finish." Mustache cups and rose jars of Teplitz Ware from Germany were also available to amateur china painters.

The most popular pieces for decoration by amateur china painters were plates, cups and saucers, berry sets of a bowl and twelve sauce dishes, fish sets with a dozen plates and a platter, and game sets with plates

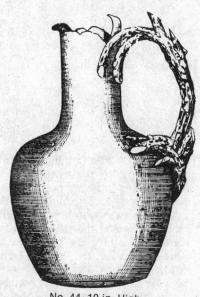

No. 44. 10 in. High.

and a platter. The fish sets had designs of various type fish and shells; the game set displayed wild birds, and the platter usually had a design with a wild turkey. A winter scene would decorate the ice cream plates; grapes were reserved for the punch bowl.

There was a set of orchid plates with different varieties of orchids on each plate. Lucy Comins, a designer and china painting teacher, furnished a set of a dozen "ribbon" plates which included sweet peas, honeysuckle, and Cherokee roses. The *Art Amateur,* 1889, contained an article on cupid designs after Boucher, and Amelia G. Austin in her series of articles in *Ladies Home Journal* says: "No branch of mineral painting is more fascinating than the painting of cupids and tiny heads." At the turn of the century the influence of Art Nouveau is seen in the conventional designs for china painting.

"She is the Subject of More Hostile Criticism" from Charles Dana Gibson's picture book *A Widow and Her Friends*, and the Royal Doulton plate on which it is reproduced. Plates and book shown, from author's collection.

Gibson Girl Plates

by MRS. GEORGE DOIL

THE Gibson Girl—tall, aristocratic, and vibrantly beautiful—the pen and ink creation of artist Charles Dana Gibson, was the feminine ideal of turn-of-the-century America. Appearing first in John Ames Mitchell's original *Life,* and later gracing many leading periodicals — Collier's once paid the artist $100,000 for one hundred sketches—she was looked-up to and emulated across the land. Her influence touched women in all walks of society.

Manufacturers produced shirt-waists with "Gibson pleats," Gibson Girl skirts, hats, riding stocks, Gibson Girl shoes, buttons, brooches, buckles, even corsets. Her patrician face appeared on wallpaper, on silver spoons, on pillow tops; it was burned by pyrography, the current craze, on wood and leather, on table tops, glove boxes, sewing boxes, and wall plaques. Dolls were made in her likeness. Songs like "Why Do They Call Me a Gibson Girl?" were written. The artist's long red picture books in which she was portrayed appeared on countless parlor tables.

In 1900–1901, the Royal Doulton Company of Lambeth, England, produced, exclusively for the American market, a set of 24–10½ inch diameter, semi-porcelain plates, decorated with a complete set of episodes from Gibson's portfolio of drawings, *A Widow and Her Friends* (see subject listing at end of this text). Doulton's American agent, William S. Pitcairn Corporation, imported them for the George F. Bassett Company. The retail price was fifty cents each.

Each plate bore a sketch with caption, date, and Gibson's signature in under-glaze black, superimposed on flower petals of bright blue. The same blue was used for the wide stylized leaf border.

The first plate of the series—each one is different—shows the widow despondent over her husband's death.

She rallies, and in the ensuing plates moves out into society, enchanting the men who flock about her to the indignation of the ladies. She is seen at a ball, a banquet, sketching, nursing the sick, riding in the country, ice skating, occasionally musing, until on plate No. 24, she has renounced the world, and appears in the habit of a nun telling stories to little boys at an orphanage.

A second set of Gibson Girls plates made by the Royal Doulton Company was in the 9-inch size. There were 12 plates in this series, each centered with a black and white sketch of a different Gibson Girl head. The heart and bow-knot border was blue.

Charles Dana Gibson was born in Roxbury, Massachusetts in 1867, his family within a few weeks moving to Flushing, Long Island. He joined the Students' Art League in New York at seventeen and within two years had sold his first sketch to *Life*. In 1895 he married the lovely Irene Langhorne of Virginia. While Mrs. Gibson often posed for her husband after their marriage, the original Gibson Girl had been a composite of various models, many of them from New York's "400." The original Gibson Man, clean-shaven, strong-jawed, and "all-American," was Richard Harding Davis, Gibson's friend and author of numerous stories illustrated by the artist.

One of the few pieces produced at the Chelsea Keramic Art Works by an "outside" artist. This redware vase, 14" tall, was executed in 1874 by G. W. Fenety, a noted Boston artist. In addition to the artist's incised initials, the full pottery mark is on the base. 14" high.

The Art Pottery Era in the United States

1870 to 1900

by PAUL F. EVANS

Illustrations from the author's collection.

With the crystallization of interest in American art pottery—pottery for primarily decorative purposes—and the marked interest in research on the subject, it becomes important to carefully define the field itself and establish the period in which it flourished.

By the mid-19th century, the first shock waves of the Industrial Revolution had swept through Europe; and across the Continent and the Atlantic a revolt began to develop against the lifeless uniformity and sterilization of expression that followed in the wake of its application to the ceramic art.

While utilitarian objects could easily be produced *en masse* to supply domestic items to a rapidly growing population, objects of art, when subjected to the techniques of mass production, were deprived of any personal creativity. What was extinguished at industrialized potteries such as those in Bennington, Vermont, was the very spirit of the artist's own life

that he had been wont to capture in his work. As the artisan was replaced by less-skilled workmen, originality and creative expression were replaced by quantity and ease of manufacture.

By 1870 there were in many parts of the world numerous craftsmen who were attempting to strike out against the inadequacy of industrial artwares and their commercial decoration. Their work marks the beginning of the era of art pottery, as distinguished from the industrial ceramics produced immediately before. Like so many movements of that age, this too was basically a revival—a revival of the traditional intimate relationship of artist and object. It could be seen in France, Denmark, and in England, where William Morris began his rebellion against the effects of industrialization by the formation of Morris, Marshall, Faulkner & Company with similarly disposed friends in 1861. His efforts and those of his followers who organized societies to promote individual artistic expression achieved fruition in the Arts and Crafts Movement of the 1880s.

The Industrial Revolution actually provided a two-pronged impetus to the art pottery movement. As observed above, it unwittingly created a rebellion by Western artisans against

industrial artwares. In a more positive vein, it provided the means and opportunity for ordinary people to acquire objects of art. In the earlier industrial artwares. In a more positive vein, it provided the means and opportunity for ordinary people to acquire objects of art. In the earlier agrarian society, utilitarian wares were all that were of any importance in the average home. With the de-

Two pieces of Stockton (California) pottery, ca. 1897. The pottery's Rekston line was an underglaze decorated brownware. Both examples bear impressed pottery and line designation. Tallest piece is 6" in height.

One of the outstanding glaze achievements of Hugh C. Robertson at Chelsea, Mass., is this pigeon feather oxblood vase made ca. 1888. Marked with C. K. A. W. cypher. 6" high.

velopment of the middle class and its purchasing power, the demand for art objects increased considerably.

It was the Centennial Exposition (Philadelphia, 1876) which gave the people of this country one of their first views of the art treasures of the world and which provided the primary stimulus for the emergence of our art pottery industry. Attending the ceramics exhibit at the Exposition were the Robertsons of Chelsea, Massachusetts, and Maria Longworth Nichols (Storer) of Cincinnati, Ohio, who were to provide the two prototypes for the development of art pottery in the United States. The Robertsons were inspired by the classical shapes and glazes, and by 1878 their Chelsea Keramic Art Works (predecessor of the Dedham Pottery) was producing superb Greek and Oriental translations. At that pottery, however, terra cotta artware had been thrown and decorated as early as 1870. Maria Nichols was stirred by the "Japanese grotesque" and the Haviland Limoges, and the resultant object of her interest—the Rookwood Pottery—was in operation by 1880.

The Robertson firm followed the traditional, old-world, family approach to the ceramic medium of artistry and its members were truly artist-potters. The person who conceived of the initial shape threw it and decorated it. This produced the integrated expression of form and decoration by an individual craftsman who was creatively involved with the piece from start to finish.

Rookwood, on the other hand, took advantage of some of the more modern industrial techniques and produced its wares through a division of labor, with the separation of the potting and decorating operations. In some instances as many as twenty-one people would be involved in the execution of a single piece of pottery before its completion. Whereas the Robertson firm achieved its integrity through the artist himself, Rookwood accomplished theirs through the cooperative union of artisan and artist. And, whereas the Robertson technique more authentically emulated the classical methods of the ceramic art, the Rookwood approach, with its various divisions of labor, offered a potentially wider scope of expression. In addition it allowed new stylistic developments or trends, such as the growing interest in art nouveau of that period, to be incorporated. For these reasons, as well as for the expanded output which was possible through the application of Rookwood's method, it was this latter approach which was taken by most of the American art potteries.

The leading influence on the shape of artware produced in the United States during this era was Oriental rather than European. While many European potters followed the over-decorative styles of the Victorian period, potters in this country turned their attention to the simple elegance of Oriental forms. In some cases the decoration reflected the Victorian tastes of the time, but the underlying shapes evidenced an attempt to return to a simplicity of form.

There were a number of significant indigenous achievements by American art potters which were manifest primarily in decorative techniques. Their application has earned world-wide respect for examples produced by the potteries involved.

The first was the revival of the high-gloss, monochrome glazes as evidenced by the work of the Robertsons at Chelsea, culminating in the rediscovery of the lost oxblood and other Oriental glaze secrets. These glazes found unique application in the whole allied art tile industry (e.g. the Low Art Tile Works of Chelsea, Massachusetts). This last-mentioned specialty was perhaps the most profitable of all the art pottery operations.

A second development was the underglaze-decorated brownware, which was successfully pursued at Rookwood. This was to be the standard Ohio-influenced pottery well into the early years of the 20th century. Its application spread across the continent from Keene, New Hampshire, as far as the Stockton Art Pottery in California, but nowhere did its expression surpass the "Standard" and iridescent "tiger-eye" glaze of the Rookwood Pottery.

Still another indigenous achievement was the commercial application of the matt glaze, which was pioneered by the Hampshire Pottery (Keene, New Hampshire) in 1892 and popularized by Grueby (Boston, Massachusetts) beginning in 1897 and Van Briggle (Colorado Springs, Colorado) beginning in 1901. Being lighter in color it provided a welcome relief from the dark glazes so common during the previous twenty years. This particular glaze technique was to be one of the decorative mainstays for the remainder of the art pottery era.

There were also numerous unique decorative achievements which resulted from the study and use of native clays. No one explored this field more thoroughly than Alexander Robertson, who was convinced that the finest clays required by an art pottery industry could be found in the United States and in particular in California. His work and that of Charles Hyten's Niloak Pottery (Benton, Arkansas), for example, give evidence of the possibilities offered when such scientific ingenuity and artistic imagination were combined.

Rookwood "Nasturtium" vase in standard brown underglaze decoration. Vase is dated 1899 and was one of the first pieces made by Howard Altman. The shape number, 583F, is also impressed in the base. 5" high.

Roblin (San Francisco, California) slip-decorated redware vase, 3¾" tall. Made and decorated from native California clays. The piece has both impressed Roblin marks and is dated 1898 and signed in slip by Linna Irelan.

The

Art Pottery Era

in the

United States

1900 to 1920

by PAUL F. EVANS

WORKING contrary to the principal ideals of the art pottery movement were the economic pressures of the Industrial Revolution, in spite of their originally having provided the market for the wares. The Robertsons' method did not offer the means for economic survival—that is, an art pottery industry in the United States could not succeed based on the classical methods of artistic expression. The Chelsea Keramic Art Works of the Robertsons failed in 1889; it was only able to reopen in 1891 when the commercial Dedham-type ware was introduced, allowing for the inclusion of the division of labor already practiced at Rookwood and elsewhere.

It was this erosion of the integrity of the ceramic art which ruptured the art pottery movement itself. The standardization of shapes and forms led in many instances to extensive casting rather than throwing and eventually to the mass production of industrial artware which gave little evidence of any originality. Thus the very thing which the art pottery movement was created to counteract, the mass production of

sterile pottery, became the only means of economic survival, as evidenced by the later pieces of Weller, Roseville, Van Briggle, and Rookwood.

By 1920, half a century after its dynamic beginning, the art pottery movement was rent by the industrial methods which it attempted to harness for its financial solvency. Once again artistic originality and creative expression were threatened with replacement by quantity of production and ease of manufacture. A few firms attempted to maintain high artistic standards and they perhaps struggled on into the Depression Decade. For the most part, however, the "art" emphasis of the movement on an industry-wide basis had succumbed by the end of the first score years of the 20th century.

What followed was, on the one hand, the voluminous production of industrial artwares. On the other, those interested in preserving the integrity of the ceramic art and the tradition of the artist's personal responsibility for the object itself, as well as its decoration, became the basis of the studio pottery movement. This movement was

basically a return to the techniques of the Robertsons, but with the lesson learned that such techniques could not provide the basis for a ceramic industry.

The hallmark characteristics of art pottery and the studioware can best be delineated by a comparative study of both. In place of the division of labor which had become a part of the art pottery industry, in studioware one person, the studio-potter himself, was responsible for a piece from beginning to end: from the pugging of the clay to the firing of the kiln and the removal of his personally thrown and decorated piece from it. Rather than working in a large pottery with its numerous gigantic kilns, the studio-potter worked in his own quarters (studio) in which his small kiln was located, or else he would affiliate with a school or university whose kilns would be at his disposal. Such affiliation reduced his financial dependence on the sale of his work, and offered the potter a greater degree of independence.

To emphasize the importance of

the potter himself, the studio worker almost always incised his pieces with his own name, whereas the art potteries rarely adopted the name of a single individual, with a few notable exceptions. In the majority of instances the names of the art potteries would be impressed with a formal cypher or mark of the pottery, sometimes with the initials of the designer or decorator added.

The ware produced by the studio-potter was most often thrown instead of cast. There were few stock designs, so one rarely finds catalogs or "stock numbers" so commonly impressed in art pottery on the studioware, which was a unique expression of the potter. Seldom did the studio-potter attain the speed or the proficiency of the specialist of the art pottery era, who gained a great degree of skill in his particular work but in few cases had the overall decorative sense of the art that the studio-potter evidenced.

Above all, the studio-potter was primarily interested in the continuation of a tradition—the tradition of the true artist-potter—rather than in the extensive production or application of a particular technique. His primary intentions were to experiment and to instruct rather than to build an industry. As a result, studio-potters often received their training in a school (art or ceramic) and learned the art there rather than by serving an apprenticeship in the art pottery plant.

As with any period or artistic technique, there is no precise line which divides the art pottery era from its successors. The movement toward the more intimate studio pottery was evident in the work of Adelaide Alsop Robineau (c. 1910) and Frederick Hurten Rhead in Santa Barbara (c. 1914) several years prior to our 1920 dating.

Then too, characteristics of both these later movements are clearly evident in the art pottery of Tiffany. While better known for his work in other media, Tiffany produced a high quality of art pottery. Making their debut at the turn of the century, the ceramics of the Tiffany Studios were incised with the L.C.T. initials of the artist, after whom the "studio" itself was named. Yet the work for the most part was subject to the mass-production techniques of extensive casting.

All periods and techniques overlap, and it is only to assist in a study and understanding of each that any attempt is made to establish particular methods and dates. What is important is to realize that such dates and techinques vary with the locale and the individuals involved.

By 1920, however, the incompatibility of creative artistic expression and commercial production was clearly evident, and the era came to an end with a precise division between the two approaches. Prior to this division, there had been a place in most art potteries for the artisan-artist. With the economic pressures which were exerted during and after World War I, these craftsmen were forced either into an industrial or institutional situation.

The distinction beween the art pottery era and its successor movements is not principally one of style, but rather one of productive techniques and responsibility. Between 1870 and 1920 what undoubtedly was to be the last attempt was made to bring together the skills of artist and artisan and combine them with the productive techniques of the age to help meet the existing demand. That it was accomplished for a time is what makes this particular era so deserving of consideration. This period is now economically beyond reproduction, a fact which further reinforces its importance in American art history.

Today's burgeoning interest in the art pottery era by antiques scholars and collectors is based on an awareness of the native artistic ingenuity which these wares evidence, and the insights they afford into the era of which they were a part. Never in so short a time, in any country of the world, did any art make more stupendous strides than was made by art pottery made in the United States between 1870 and 1920.

Low bowl with incised decoration by Rhead Pottery, Santa Barbara, California. 8¾" in diameter, 1¼" high. Primary glaze is Rhead's prized mirror black.

Rarest of Dedham-type ware. Reverse rabbit plate—of which three are known to exist—was made within a year of pottery's re-opening in 1891. 10" plate is marked with CPUS cypher of the Chelsea Pottery, U.S., successor to the Chelsea Keramic Art Works and predecessor of the Dedham Pottery.

Early dark-colored Mission ware of the Nil-oak Pottery in blues and browns. Vase is 5½" tall, with impressed registered mark.

Tiffany's pottery commands high prices today because of the Tiffany name, but it reportedly was not a commercially successful venture. This vase (3" tall), like most of the Favrile pottery, is of a white, high-fired, semi-porcelaneous body.

THE ROOKWOOD Pottery of Cincinnati, Ohio (1880-1967), was the longest-lived art pottery in the United States and, without doubt, the best known. The history of the Pottery itself has been excellently covered in Herbert Peck's *Book of Rookwood Pottery* (reviewed SW May '69). Here we concentrate on the later work of Rookwood, 1930-1967, and its attractions for collectors and admirers of decorated ceramics.

The World War I years, 1915-1919, and the boom which followed, 1920-1929, marked the peak of Rookwood's prosperity. The Pottery still posessed the status of its original Longworth connection. Its president, J. H. Gest, was from an old, socially prominent

Brilliantly colored tropical birds were used by E. T. Hurley to decorate this handsome Rookwood vase; ca. 1920. Height 14¾".

Cincinnati family; the Pottery building, atop Mount Adams, was a popular showplace, easily reached by an incline train; the nearby Cincinnati Art Museum, of which Gest was Director, proudly displayed, on loan from the Pottery, a selection of over 2,000 Rookwood pieces dating back to 1880.

In 1920, the Pottery was employing 200 people. Throughout the decade, it produced a great quantity of expensive, artist-signed items of every size and description — plaques, lamp bases, vases, and sculptures as well as inexpensive, mass-production items. The Pottery maintained its own departments to frame the underglaze-decorated plaques and to drill and assemble into lamps vases chosen by the customer.

At that period, it was commonplace to have costly Chinese and Sevres vases drilled and made into lamps, and some of Rookwood's finest vases were so treated. The early factory-mounted Rookwood lamps bore the trademark "Rookwood Pottery" stamped into the metal base. Later, when lamp mounting was done at a small specialty shop, a paper trademark sticker was applied to the base.

The introduction of "jewel porcelain" in 1915 began a series of attractive new glazes developed by Rookwood's chemist, Stanley Burt. Starting in 1920, the Pottery introduced a true flambe (a deep magenta or purplish maroon base color, obscured by patches of luminescent white haze), a classic oxblood (a crimson glaze with touches of white at rims), and an excellent ivory jewel porcelain (a translucent glaze that upon close examination reveals a myriad of imbedded bubble-like structures). The older tiger-eye crystalline glaze was revived as a shimmering green or yellow glaze. These tiger-eye glazes are formed by the crystallization of chrome oxide crystals in the glaze during the cooling process; the effect is easy to produce. Rookwood made some tiger-eye as late as 1950.

Probably the most popular artists during the 1920s were Schmidt, Hur-

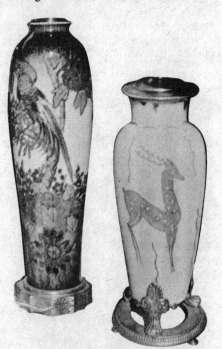

Above, left: Rookwood lamp decorated with exotic birds by Edward T. Hurley, ca. 1920. Height of lamp vase 18½".

Above, right: Gazelle decorated Rookwood lamp by E. Barrett; ca. 1944. Height of lamp vase 13".

Right: Buff and tan mat glaze accent a geometric design by Elizabeth Barrett, ca. 1930. Height 13½".

The Later Years of Rookwood Pottery

1920-1967

by CHESTER DAVIS

ley, Shirayamadani, Sax, Hentschel, McDonald, Rothenbusch, Diers, Barrett, and Jensen, although other artists had their own followings. By 1929, Rookwood had developed a thriving business in expensive decorated items for the luxury market. Pieces made during the 1920s range from decorated flambe through decorated jewel porcelain to decorated matt in styles ranging from Realistic through Impressionistic to Cubist Art.

The Great Depression of the 1930s, alas, struck Rookwood a blow from which it never fully recovered. The architectural tile business closed down completely and the depression years saw Rookwood's fortunes dependent on the sale of artistic wares at a time when competition in this field was extreme. All of the great English potteries such as Wedgwood, Doulton, and Pilkington, also abandoned or severely curtailed production of artist-decorated ware. Pilkington's "Royal Lancastrian" wares, the closest approximation to Rookwood during the 1920s, abandoned production in 1937.

After 1930, Rookwood's new superintendent, Harold Bopp, who had replaced Stanley Burt in late 1929,

Porcelain plaque depicting a Spanish galleon, by Fred Rothenbusch.

did considerable work on colorful new glazes and simple decorative techniques which are still modern and attractive. The decorating department attempted to lower costs by utilizing non-realistic decorations, such as the flowing glaze effects of Emil Decoeur. Elizabeth Barrett did some exceptional work in this style. Certain pottery-impressed wares, mostly designed by William Hentschel, were colored in relief by individual artists after their own inclinations, thereby creating individual versions of a basic pattern. The excellent glaze effects of some 1930 Rookwood resulted from such determined efforts to compete for a rapidly sinking market.

Unfortunately, the bleak economic situation of the 1930s, and the inertia displayed by an ageing, conservative management — the elderly designer, John Dee Wareham, became president in 1934 and proved a poor business-man — made improvement difficult Production of decorated ware was limited after 1934. Only a few artists

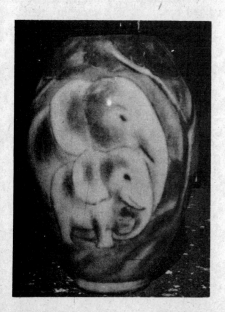

—Jensen, Hurley, Hentschel, and Shirayamadani among them — were employed on an irregular basis.

Rookwood went into receivership early in 1941, and the court-appointed trustees in bankruptcy made preparations to liquidate all assets of the Pottery. It was sold to a group headed by Walter Schott, an automobile dealer, in late 1941.

The large collection of historical Rookwood at the Cincinnati Art Museum, including pieces by the famed artist Henry Farny, was called back to the Pottery. Then it simply disappeared from sight. To this day, no public statement has ever been made as to the present whereabouts of this valuable collection or as to the method of its dispersal.

A series of liquidation sales began in December 1941 and continued throughout 1942. Early in that year, Rookwood's Harold Bopp founded the Kenton Hills Pottery in Erlanger, Kentucky, with financial backing from David Seyler, the artist, and with William Hentschel as designer. This small pottery, which turned out work similar to Rookwood's 1941 line, lasted three years, though Bopp had left in 1943 to pursue a successful career in ceramics consulting.

The Pottery was sold again late in 1942 to Sperti, Inc. Due to the insistence of Charles Williams, one of the bankruptcy trustees and a member of the Schott group, a restriction was made in the sale of the business providing that some pottery had to be made every year. To meet that restric-

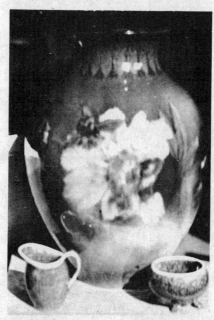

Above: Decorated flambe vase by Sara Sax; ca. 1926. Height 14½″. Oxblood cream and sugar bowl in foreground.

Left: Rookwood vase decorated with elephants by Jens Jensen, 1948. Height 11¾″.

tion Rookwood resumed production in 1943 on a small scale. A few finely modelled religious sculptures by Clotilda Zanetta of the Cincinnati Art Museum staff began to appear in 1944, and the fortunes of the Pottery improved due to the sale of these items. From 1944 to 1949, a considerable number of artist-decorated pieces came from the hands of such older decorators as Hurley, Barrett, Jensen, and McDonald, and from a number of new decorators. Some pieces were remarkably well done; many were too hastily accomplished.

Rookwood's post-World War II revival was chiefly due to the long-range planning of William Mackelfresh, Jr., a specialist in restoring ailing businesses, who had been hired by Charles Williams in late 1941. Mackelfresh himself left Rookwood in 1945 to assist the floundering Lake Geneva Porcelain Works.

The remarkable glaze quality, al-

Clotilda Zenetta's "Madonna" (1944) and "St. Francis" (1947) flank a "Jewel Porcelain" vase by Charles Jasper McLaughlin (1918). Height of Madonna, 13¾″.

ways Rookwood's major selling point, declined sharply after the loss of several experienced technicians, upon whose extensive practical experience all art potteries depend heavily. Ray Dawson, mold-maker and glazier, left in late 1946 to join Mackelfresh at Lake Geneva, and Mayo Tayler, the kiln supervisor, died about 1947.

By late 1947, much of the decorated ware began to resemble inexpensive gift shop wares. These proved difficult to sell and were closed out in 1950 by a cut-rate sale to a Cincinnati department store. The decorating staff was discontinued in 1949. Rookwood's decline accelerated. Space in the main building was rented out for offices; the salesrooms dropped from five large rooms to one small room; the working

(Please Turn the Page)

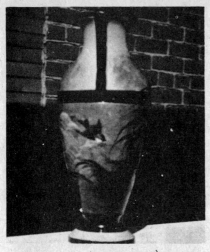

Reproduction of an early Rookwood vase marked "M.A.D." (Matthew A. Daley). Height 9"

space retreated to the area around the old beehive kilns. What was left of the Pottery Museum, stored precariously atop shelves used for stacking new production items, was sold off. As late as 1955-57, one could still buy premium quality pieces of the 1920s and 1930s there.

To fulfill production requirements under Williams' restriction, the Pottery made bisque (fired but unglazed ware) for the ceramic hobby trade. This amateur-decorated Rookwood is now coming onto the antique market; it bears the Rookwood trademark and various late 1940 and early 1950 date marks, but the glaze quality is poor. A certain amount of inexpensive glazed ware, mainly ashtrays, was sold to trading stamp firms. For 2⅓ stamp books, anyone who so desired could obtain a Rookwood ashtray. Throughout the 1950s, the Pottery made low-cost, undecorated copies of simple wares designed in the preceding decade — ashtrays, vases, paperweights, and bookends.

During the 1950s, Rookwood's prestige was so low that many finely decorated and most attractive artist-signed Rookwood items could be purchased in antique shops at far below their manufacturing cost. Interested collectors could readily buy, inexpensively, well-glazed, undecorated older Rookwood items in antiques and second-hand stores. The Pottery found itself unable to compete price-wise with its own former productions.

A local realtor, James M. Smith, purchased the pottery property in January 1956, and immediately attempted to rebuild Rookwood's reputation. The sale of bisque ware was stopped, and no further sales were made to trading stamp centers. Several co-op students were hired, and an attempt was made to expand the market. Foreign imports, however, were

cheaper than anything the Pottery could make. Though Smith was not bound by Williams' restriction, rather than close down the old pottery, he sold Rookwood in late 1959 to the Herschede Hall Clock firm, which appointed John Hoyt III as manager.

Hoyt proved a hard-working young man, determined to restore the pottery's prestige and quality. William Glass was hired as artist-designer, and the factory prepared to move to a new industrial building offered by Starksville, Mississippi. Molds on hand, too worn to be used, were destroyed, but some 1,200 molds, dating back to 1882, were shipped to Starksville. All stock on hand was liquidated by a special sale; most of the remaining museum pieces were sold off.

The new management was soon plagued by the same problems which had beset Rookwood since 1930— foreign competition, non-competitive wage scales for skilled workers, and lack of capital. Glass left in 1962, but Hoyt slowly overcame production problems. By 1963-65, he had greatly improved the glaze quality. Some nicely glazed paperweights and copies of older pieces, correctly marked with modern dates, were sold at reasonable prices. As examples of late Rookwood, some of this Starksville ware is worth collecting.

By 1966, Viet Nam inflation and foreign competition struck the pottery a deadly blow; it ceased production in 1967. (The author has been informed that there is some intention of reactivating commercial production at Starksville in 1970, if suitable demand exists.)

Collectors should bear in mind that early Rookwood is easily copied, as evidenced by the many cheap, then contemporary, copies by Weller, Roseville, Owens, and Avon. The highly-skilled, well-glazed, and well-decorated later pieces are more difficult to copy at a price to interest reproducers, who must have a high mark-up for their efforts.

It is far easier to fake pottery than most collectors realize. Any trained potter, especially in Italy and Japan, can make up a clay piece, stamp the still soft clay with the proper marks, and then decorate and glaze the piece in any desired style. Forging early Rookwood is being done; even tiger-eye glazes are now easily made. The author has seen excellent copies of such pieces, and he has in his collection a particularly well-done vase, bearing the artist's initials, "M A. D." (Matthew A. Daly), which was made in Italy.

The pottery collector should be increasingly wary of modern copies of the older Rookwood (correctly stamp-

ed), of older imitations (new decorations applied to older pieces), and of overpriced mediocre examples. In buying, the collector should obtain signed statements from the seller that the pieces he selects were *made in Cincinnati*.

A work of art has been defined as any beautiful object skillfully made. In judging Rookwood, the collector should pay more attention to the piece itself than to the artist. Rookwood was a factory product, as were the products of Sevres, Meissen, China, and Wedgwood, wherein all of the components — shape, color, glazing, decoration, and style—must be good if a piece of art pottery is to be outstanding. Unusual glazing, especially flambe, jewel porcelain, and tiger-eye, count a great deal. The collector should realize that true art pottery is an individual effort to make a functional clay object a work of art. Outstanding decoration of pottery requires more than skill, which is easily learned; it also requires imagination, originality, and judgment.

Because shape governs decoration, the most desirable decorated work is that which skillfully conforms to an attractive shape. The shape and the technical quality of the potting and glazing of a Rookwood piece add to or detract from a decoration in a definite manner. Many Rookwood vases have a "heavy" look about them because the proportions and angles are not quite right, i.e. when the shape is not geometrically sound.

Among the desirable Rookwood artists are E. T. Hurley, C. Schmidt, F. Rothenbusch, E. Diers, W. P. McDonald, E. Barrett, J. Jensen, C. Zanetta, S. Sax, and K. Shirayamadani.

Hurley was an outstanding artist; in 1949, at the age of 79, he was elected to the National Academy of Art. Barrett's work is in a class by itself, she had a true feeling for pottery decoration. Zanetta's sculptures are distinctive, though her painted work is seldom outstanding. Jensen was an outstanding artist, but his later pieces sometimes fail to reflect his real ability.

Rothenbusch was the ideal commercial artist; his work is extremely even, rarely great, but never inferior. His plaques are especially good. Schmidt's work brought top prices in its day because of his strong, showy style. Only A. H. Valentien excelled Schmidt in flower painting. Shirayamadani's work of the 1920s is good, but poor in the 1940s.

Rozane bowl-vase, shaded brown to yellow with decoration of dog with pheasant in its mouth in natural colors. Marked "RPCo." Ca. 1900; 9" high.

Rozane jug shaded dark brown to yellow with berry decoration; signed "W.H." Ca. 1905; 4" high to top of handle.

Roseville Pottery

by LUCILE HENZKE

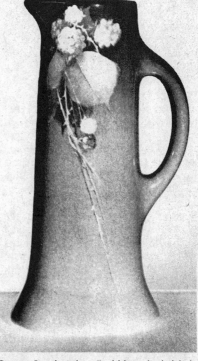

Rozane Royal pitcher. Teal-blue, shaded light to dark, with pink and yellow berries. Signed "M. Myers." Ca. 1900; 10½" high.

Rozane ewer-vase shading dark brown to yellow and decorated with yellow roses. Signed "Joseph Imlay" (a former Weller artist). Ca. 1905; 6" high.

Carnelian bowl of blue to pink. Ca. 1917; marked "R"; 9½ x 7".

Blue creamer with slip decoration in darker blue. Signed "Grace Young" and marked "RPCo." Ca. 1900; 3½" high.

THE YEAR 1890 was a depression year and the Youngs, Anna and George, were struggling desperately to get along financially. George was attempting to sell sewing machines while Anna was trying to sell millinery. In those days, one hat a season was all even wealthy ladies could afford; consequently Anna's business failed. One sewing machine in the neighborhood was more than adequate and, with neighbors being friendly the way they were, the ladies had their "sewing bees" and helped each other to make clothing and other needed articles. Most of the women had one summer and one winter outfit for Sunday and a few calico dresses for everyday needs.

George gave up the sewing machine salesman's position and decided there was more demand for pottery crocks. He tried his hand at selling stoneware for a small pottery, but this also proved unsuccessful. At this time his old friend, Sam Weller, was building a three-story factory in Zanesville, Ohio, and making a fortune in the pottery business. Hoping to get some of this business, the Youngs invested in a pottery in Roseville, Muskingum County, Ohio—just eleven miles south of Zanesville.

The clays of Muskingum Valley and a plentiful supply of gas and coal were a perfect combination of natural factors for a pottery business. Other potteries sprang up by the score in the area, and some of them grew to be quite important. One of the most productive, and perhaps the best

known, was George Young's Roseville Pottery.

On January 4, 1892, the firm was incorporated with George Young as secretary and general manager, C. F. Allison, president, J. F. Weaver, manager, and Thomas Brown, treasurer. The company prospered, and in 1895 they acquired the William and McCoy Pottery of Zanesville and the Midland Pottery of Kildow.

In 1898, the company moved to Zanesville and purchased the Clark Stoneware Company on Linden Avenue; a year later Young built his own three-story building on this site. The company continued to operate under the name Roseville.

By 1900, Young was ready to capture some of the profits claimed by other Ohio potters. Ross C. Purdy, an artist, was hired to develop an art line. He designed a line with a high glaze with under the glaze slip painting which was named "Rozane Royal." Some of these were dark and some were in pastel colors. The dark variety was very much like Weller's "Louwelsa," Rookwood's standard glaze, and Owen's "Utopian." One must look for the mark before being positive just who made it. Since the artists migrated from one pottery to another, you will find some "Rozane Royal" pieces are signed by artists whose names also appear on other Ohio pottery.

In 1902, the Roseville Company acquired a fourth plant; the Mosaic Tile Company auxiliary at Muskingum Avenue and Harrison Street in Zanesville. Cookware was made in this plant; it kept four kilns operating and employed about fifty men. By 1905, the company had 350 people on its payroll with an annual output of five hundred thousand dollars worth of merchandise.

Rozane Woodland vase. Buff colored background with dark brown flowers and stems. Ca. 1904; 6½" high.

Rozane Mongol ewer-vase in a rich oxblood color, high crystalline glaze. Ca. 1904; 6½" high.

Rozane Mara vase with blue and green designs on a red background. Ca. 1904; 5" high.

Rozane vase marked "RPCo." Brownware with nasturtiums in natural colors, signed "M. Myers." Circa 1900; 12½" high.

Rozane was popular and sold well. Every time Weller and other Ohio art potters produced a new line, Young would produce a similar one. When Weller introduced Dickensware, Young introduced not one, but three similar lines— "Rozane Woodland," "Rozane Fugi" (in 1904), and "Della Robbia" (in 1906); all of these lines are of the sgraffito type. Young also presented, in 1904, a solid red line that he named "Rozane Mongol" and a beautiful line in the Art Nouveau style with figures in white on a dark red background called "Rozane Olympic."

Partial List of Roseville Wares

For the convenience of collectors we are listing some of the earlier Roseville art wares and their descriptions. Although many different lines were produced — and it would be impossible to list them all here— it should be noted that most of the late pieces carry the obvious name of the decoration.

Dark Rozane Royal — Dark brown shading to yellow with slip painting under the glaze.

Light Rozane Royal — Pastel colors shading from dark to light with slip painting under the glaze.

Rozane Woodland—Light matt finished background with incised flowers decorated in high gloss dark glaze.

Rozane Fugi — Similar to Rozane Woodland.

Rozane Mongol—Dark red crystalline glaze with no decoration. Made in classic shapes.

Della Robbia — Incised lines with slip decoration.

Rozane Mara—Iridescent glaze in shades of deep red, purple and blue. Also a light shade with pastel pattern.

Rozane Egypto—Embossed Egyptian decorations; dark green with a matt glaze.

Pauleo — Made in Chinese shapes in two different types. The first type shades from dark brown to light red. Type two was made in two colors with a breaker between them. There is a crackled effect throughout the body of each piece, covered with a smooth glaze similar to the Sung Ko wares in Chinese porcelains.

Rozane Olympic—A rich dark red background with Art Nouveau figures in white and borders in the Roman Key design.

Mostique—Stylized flowers and arrow-shaped leaves on a rough background.

ROSEVILLE POTTERY MARKS

Early Period—1900 to 1915

During the early period the marks were not consistent. Some pieces were marked "Rozane," sometimes with the name of the line added. At times just the initials "RPCo" was used; quite often the objects have no marks at all.

Raised disc with raised letters.

Raised disc and letters with line name added.

RVPCo
ROZANE
RPC
ROZANE
67 B
RPCo

Impressed marks.

ROSEVILLE ROZANE POTTERY

Printed in dark colors.

Middle Period—1915 to 1930

During this period some of their

art lines were marked solely with paper labels. The same art line might also be marked with impressed or incised marks of this same period. The "Donatello" line bore three of the marks shown below.

Left: Impressed on some pieces. Right: Printed mark.

Left: Paper label, black on silver. Right: Incised mark. Pattern number and size in inches added.

Late Period—1930 to 1954

These marks are in high relief with "U.S.A." added; they also bear the pattern number and the size in inches.

Roseville
U.S.A.
858-8"

R USA
138 4"

Marks found on small pieces.

Roseville
USA
1 BK-8"

This mark appears on baskets.

Roseville
USA
984-10"
MOCK-ORANGE

Sometime appears with line name added.

156
raymor
by Roseville
USA

This mark used about 1952.

WELLER'S
DICKENS
WARE

by LUCILE HENZKE

(Illustrations from the author's collection.)

(*Photographs by* RAYMON ORREN, Ft. Worth, Texas.

Dickens Ware pillow-shaped vase (first line) shading from light to dark green; floral decoration in white, orange, and brown; signed "C.G." Ca. 1900; height 7 inches.

Dickens Ware vase (second line) decorated with a portrait of "Daring Fox." Shaded blue-green to chocolate-brown, matt glaze; signed "J.B." Ca. 1902; height 7½ inches.

DICKENS WARE WAS MADE in Zanesville, Ohio, where the fine rich clays of the Muskingum Valley were perfect for potting. The lads who were growing up there in the last quarter of the nineteenth century were considered shiftless, indeed, if they did not learn the art of "throwing a pot." Samuel A. Weller, who was one of these lads, grew up to become one of the most successful potters in America. He surrounded himself with some of the most talented and creative artists in ceramics. One such artist was Charles Babcock Upjohn (1866–1953). Upjohn worked for Weller for a decade, and then retired to become Professor of Art at Columbia University, a post he occupied for 25 years.

During his tenure with the Weller potteries, Upjohn created the now famous "Dickens Ware." In the late 1800s, Doulton of England was making an exquisite line of figurines, tableware and accessories which depicted characters from Charles Dickens' stories. These lines were selling well in England and also in America. Weller, being an alert businessman, decided to "hop on the bandwagon," and commissioned Upjohn to create a line called "Dickens Ware." Weller jokingly remarked, "If Dickens can create a character named Sam Weller, the least I can do is name a line after him." Upjohn immediately changed the color on the background of the Louwelsa ware, from the traditional brown to yellow, to dark green or dark blue, shading from dark to light, and christened it "Dickens Ware." The first line was made for only a brief period of time.

In a matter of months, Upjohn introduced the "second line" Dickens Ware. This line was destined to become one of the most popular and the most sought after by collectors of American Art Pottery today. Pieces

Dickens Ware mug (second line) with incised portrait of "Fox Tail." Shaded blue-green to brown, matt glaze; signed "Anna Dautherty." Ca. 1902; height 5½ inches.

that are signed by Upjohn are highly treasured.

Much of Upjohn's work was exceedingly well executed and gave the effect of being three-dimensional. This second line Dickens Ware was decorated by the sgraffito method, being incised by hand with a sharp tool, with the background sprayed or brushed and the colors blended together in beautiful shadow work. The subjects were slip-painted with natural colors, then covered with a glaze. The glazes used on the second line varied from a soft matt to a high gloss finish. The soft matt and semi-gloss are the glazes most often encountered. The pieces with the high gloss finish are indeed very rare. A dark reddish brown clay was generally used in the second line Dickens Ware; however, on occasion, a light clay was used.

The colors most often seen in the Dickens Ware line are rich chocolate browns shaded to a blue-green or turquoise. Frequently the rich brown alone was used, and then again, the blue-green or turquoise was used alone, blended from dark to light. The second line Dickens Ware was also made in other colors, such as a beautiful true royal blue, shaded from light to dark. One of the rarest shades in Dickens Ware is the pink. This is a peach-pink with shading of gray. It is quite possible that other colors were

used, though these are all this author has seen. The exact number of years the second line was made has not yet been established, but a good estimate might be a decade.

The third line introduced about 1910 or 1911, was a high glazed ware, with under-the-glaze slip painting. The background is dark, shading to light, very similar to Weller's Eocean. The obverse has a Dickens character, slip painted, under a high gloss glaze. On the reverse side is a raised disk bearing the name of the character and the story in which he appeared. The glaze on this line is clear. This is, by and large, the rarest of the Dickens Ware by Weller.

Another line created was the "Cameo," on which the head of Charles Dickens appears. This was not too popular with the public in its time; it is quite scarce and considered rare today. In the previous lines, the hand work was slow and tedious—an expensive process which entailed several separate firings. On the Cameo line the method was changed from hand work to casting in a mold.

The subjects appearing on Dickens Ware are not always taken from the Charles Dickens' tales. Some are portraits of Indians, with the Indian's name appearing on the piece, such as "Fox Tail," "Daring Fox," etc. Some are people at play, like golfers or

Dickens Ware vase (second line) shaded turquoise to brown, matt glaze; signed "I.F." The leaves of the trees have been modelled with slip in high relief. Ca. 1909; height 13 inches.

Dickens Ware pillow-shaped vase (second line) shaded turquoise, matt glaze; signed "Upjohn." Ca. 1901; height 9 inches.

Dickens Ware three-cornered vase (second line) with Monk decoration. Chocolate-brown with matt glaze; signed "Hattie Mitchell." Ca. 1902; height 6 inches.

men playing checkers, garbed in costumes of the period. Tavern scenes were also used. One of the most common subjects encountered today is the Monk, either a full-size figure or just a bust. Birds, fish, and other natural subjects can be added to this list. It was rumored that one artist, Levi Burgess, was paid one dollar for each Indian portrait he himself created on Dickens Ware pieces. Other Weller artists also created fine Indian portraits, all of them eagerly sought by collectors today.

Dickens Ware vase (second line) with rare high gloss glaze. The figure, in sgraffito, wears a long blue and brown dress; the background color is a deep cobalt-blue. Ca. 1901; height 14 inches.

The name "Dickens Ware" appears on almost all pieces of Dickens Ware; however, the third line ware is marked only "Weller." For the convenience of the collector, the marks found on this fine pottery are pictured here.

WELLER DICKENS WARE

Incised with a sharp tool; also found on some second line pieces.

DICKENS WARE WELLER

Impressed on most Dickens Ware pieces; first and second lines.

WELLER

Raised lettering inside of a raised frame. Sometimes a number appears in a duplicate frame. Found on the third line wares.

Top: A rare Dickens Ware vase (third line) decorated with full-length figure of Sam Weller, Sr., of Pickwick Papers fame, against a shaded light to dark gray background. Signed by the artist Lillie Mitchell. Ca. 1910; height 7 inches. **Below:** Reverse of vase has title disc in raised white slip.

American Art Pottery in 1904

by BRICE GARRETT

COLLECTORS of art pottery popular at the turn of the century are well acquainted with the products at Rookwood, Weller, and Dedham, and some Midwestern collectors search for examples of Pauline pottery. Examination of a catalogue of the art exhibits at the Universal Exposition at St. Louis in 1904 suggests a wider field of collecting for the student of such ceramics.

The Applied Arts division in the Art Palace at the 1904 Exposition included pottery (mostly vases and other ornamental pieces) made by the following American firms specializing in art pottery:

Gates Potteries, Terra Cotta, Ill. Trademark "Teco."

Van Briggle Pottery, Colorado Springs, Colo., established in 1901 by Artus van Briggle, and still in production.

Poillon Pottery, Woodbridge, N. J. Mark: joined "P"'s, one upside down.

Newcomb Pottery, New Orleans, La., established in 1896. Pieces frequently bear the monogram of the designer.

Grueby Faience Co., Boston, Mass., established in 1897. Marks include the name "Grueby."

Moravian Pottery and Tile Works, Doylestown, Pa., established ca. 1890 by Henry R. Mercer. The mark was the word MORAVIAN.

Merrimac Ceramic Co., Newburyport, Mass., established in 1897. The mark was the word MERRIMAC.

Among the studio potters, not connected with factories, who exhibited several pieces were: Marshal Fry, New York; Henrietta Ord Jones, St. Louis; Anna B. Leonard, New York; Lucy Fairfield Perkins, New York; Mrs. Adelaide Alsop Robineau, Syracuse, N. Y.; L. C. Tiffany, New York, (three pieces of Favrile pottery); and Charles Volkmar, New York.

In a special category were pieces submitted by the New York State School of Clay-working and Ceramics, at Alfred, New York, including several works designed by Charles F. Binns, then director of the school, and descendant of the English family that controlled the Worcester factory in the nineteenth century.

Examples from the studio potters would be quite rare today, but good examples from the factories listed should be still extant in numbers large enough to make the collector's search rewarding.

Multi-colored Hummingbirds (yellow, blue, green, orchid and black) with red flowers and green foilage. Marked "Stangl"; 9" high by 10" diameter.

STANGL AUDUBON BIRDS

by LUCILE HENZKE

THE STANGL AUDUBON BIRDS were produced by the Stangl Pottery of Trenton, New Jersey, about 1941. They are no longer being made, and today's art pottery collectors are seeking extant examples eagerly.

The Stangl Pottery began in 1805 as the Fulper Pottery, founded in Flemington, New Jersey, by the Fulper brothers. The company, continuing in the Fulper family, produced mostly drain tiles, stonewares, and simple crockery until 1910. In that year J. M. Stangl was appointed to the position of ceramic engineer. Fulper

had decided to enter the lucrative field of art pottery, and all the inherent problems of launching a new product for a rapidly expanding business were delegated to Mr. Stangl.

Through constant experimentations, many new glazes and clay bodies were developed. When imports were curtailed during World War I, Mr. Stangl created the now famous Fulper doll heads, rare today and highly prized by antique doll collectors. The heads were made of a fine translucent porcelain, of the same superb quality as was being used for Fulper art wares

such as powder boxes with figures as finials, scent lamps, birds, and the like.

From the early 1920s, the pottery grew steadily and, by 1929, two potteries were operating in Flemington and one in Trenton, New Jersey. On the morning of September 19, 1929, the main plant in Flemington was totally destroyed by fire. News of the catastrophe was broadcast by radio and newspapers throughout the United States. Great concern was registered by Flemington residents, for Fulper was one of the largest employers in the area. However, all employees were given the opportunity to transfer to the Trenton plant. There the name of the pottery was changed, almost immediately, to Stangl Pottery.

In 1941, Mr. Stangl, invariably progressive, was one of the principal American potters to introduce, in ceramics, authentic reproductions of the birds in the popular Audubon bird prints.

These bird prints were created by John James Audubon (1785-1851), an American ornithologist. He was the adopted son of Jean Audubon, a French Merchant Marine Captain, who had acquired a farm near Philadelphia during one of his sojourns in the United States. Late in 1803, John James, then age 18, arrived in this country to become manager and overseer of this farm, known as "Mill Grove."

Young Audubon had no flair for business and expended a good portion of time wandering through the woods at Mill Grove, sketching the birds and animals found there in their natural habitat, always paying particular attention to the botanical surroundings of the birds. About 1819, he resolved to publish an ornithology of America. Unable to acquire a publisher in the United States, he looked for a publisher abroad. He arrived in England on July 21, 1826, and in due course, was hailed as the "American Genius." By 1828, four volumes, titled *The Birds of America,* had been compiled and completely published. The finished works contained a total of 435 plates, showing 1065 birds of 489 different species. The original drawings for *The*

Right and left: Allen Hummingbirds in natural colors, 3½" high. Paper labels, and marked "Stangl" in script. Center: Paper label identifies this bird as an "Audubon Warbler." Blue back and head, black wings and tail; yellow flower on green foilage; 11" high. Marked "Stangl Pottery Birds" in circle.

Birds of America are now in the collection of the New York Historical Society.

Audubon prints became extremely popular, and almost everyone was familiar with them. Many artists in ceramics. especially abroad, began fashioning figures of birds in the Audubon style. Consequently many of these were imported into the United States from England, Germany, Japan, and other foreign countries.

At the beginning of World War II, with imports again curtailed, the Stangl Pottery introduced a series of authentic Audubon reproductions in ceramics. These colorful birds were done in exquisite detail and unexcelled quality. Stangl artists managed to capture the dramatic beauty of the birds in motion among the foilage, fruits, and flowers.

In addition to the regular pottery bird line, Stangl also created 12 dif-

Parrot scent lamp made of porcelain and marked "Fulper." Colored in shades of orchid, orange and green. Small holes under the Parrot's beak allowed the perfume to escape into the atmosphere; height 9".

Rooster (10" tall) and Hen (7" tall) marked "Stangl Pottery Birds." Yellow bodies, red combs, yellow and brown striped legs; green bases. Collection Mrs. Marcia Ames Ray.

ferent birds in a porcelain body. These were produced in limited amounts, numbering less than 50 of each. Both the pottery birds and the porcelain birds, neither of which are being made currently, have become objects of interest for today's art pottery collectors.

Each Stangl bird was tagged with a paper tag. On it was noted the name of the bird that appeared in the Audubon print from which it was copied. Each piece was also stamped with the Stangl company mark on the base. Often the artist's monogram was also included. However, no definite records have been kept of these names and monograms. The tags were attached to the birds by a string. Both the ink stamp and the paper tag appeared on the same bird. However, most birds will be found with the ink stamp only; most paper tags have gone the way of all paper tags.

Marks found on Stangl Audubon birds.

1. Stamped on the base in ink in various sizes.

Blue Birds marked "Stangl"; 7½" high.

STANGL

2. Found on small pieces either stamped or impressed.

3. Paper tag (obverse).

3756
Audubon Warbler
Fulper Pottery
Trenton

4. Paper tag (reverse).

Brown and white Finches marked "Stangl"; 6" high.

Brilliantly colored Cockatoo marked "Stangl" and having the artist's full signature "Jacob," too; 12" high.

Baltimore Oriole in red and black, 5" high. Marked "Stangl."

Except as noted, illustrations from the author's collection.

Fig. 1: Dark blue matt glaze vase bearing regular Marblehead mark on base. Ht. 8½". *Private collection.* Fig. 2: Midnight blue mirror glazed squat vase with design in light blue by A. E. Baggs; ca. 1926. 5½" high. *Collection Newark (N.J.) Museum.* Fig. 3: Stylized flowers on matt green glazed vase; regular Marblehead mark plus designer's cypher (A. I. Hennessey); ca. 1910. Ht. 7". *Collection Newark (N.J.) Museum.* Fig. 4: Low matt green and black bowl; regular Marblehead mark plus incised cypher of Hennessey. Ht. 4¼". Private collection. Fig. 5: Tall dark blue and ocher matt glazed vase with deer decoration; regular Marblehead mark. Ht. 11½". Fig. 6: Green vase with brown pine cone decoration, matt glaze; regular Marblehead mark and A. E. Baggs cypher. Ht. 12". *Private collection.*

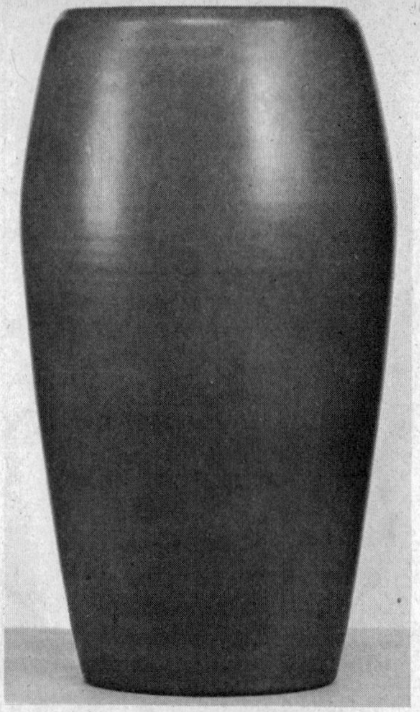

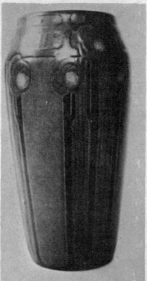

Fig. 1

The Marblehead Pottery

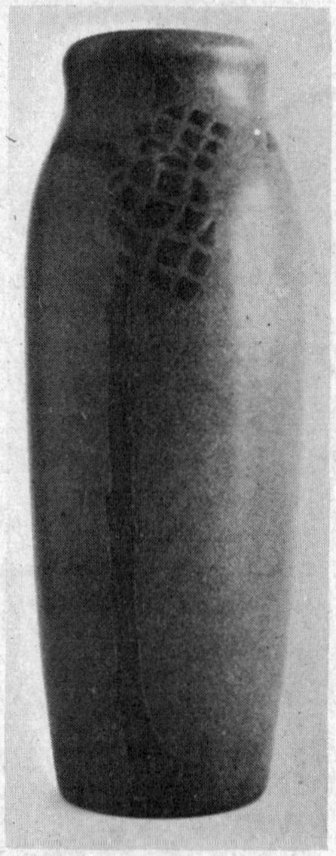

by AMELIA E. MAC SWIGGAN

ALTHOUTH 20th century products, the wares made by the Marblehead Pottery in Marblehead, Massachusetts, and marked with a sailing ship flanked by "M" and "P," have already become rare and are cherished by collectors. They are not found easily, but continued search is often well rewarded.

As a town, Marblehead was separated from Salem Village on May 2, 1649. The poet Longfellow, in 1849, called it a "Strange, old-fashioned, silent town," and through the years it has remained a delightful colonial town with historic houses and quaint crooked streets. Her rocks and sea have ever been a mecca for water and boat enthusiasts.

A tiny potting establishment, considered the nucleus of the pottery industry in this old seacoast town, was opened in 1904 by Dr. Herbert J. Hall, a local physician. Its purpose was to serve as a clinic of sorts where some of his patients might, under supervision, partake of certain occupational therapy in the form of arts and crafts. The experiments in the techniques of glazing and decorating pottery made during this early period proved so successful that it was resolved to form a commercial pottery right there, separate from the medical services. The pottery, located in the center of town, continued to operate until 1936.

Arthur E. Baggs, a well-known ceramist, and work supervisor at the pottery, became its owner in 1915. Under his aegis, experiments in clays, glazes, and designs continued, and attractive pieces were produced.

Articles from the Marblehead Pottery were in demand from the beginning—elegant vases, bowls, flower containers in many shapes, teapots, book ends, candlesticks, decorative jars, and lamps for the home. Made to order were tiles and fireplace facings in

Fig. 2

Fig. 6

Fig. 5

Fig. 3

Fig. 4

various colors and designs, as were glazed sculptured pieces.

In 1910 a small catalog was issued, listing the available goods, describing colors and designs, and including the shipping costs. Apparently the little pottery was then carrying on a mail order business. Bowls with rose and mauve colored flowers in fascinating effects, pieces decorated with sprigs of blue delphiniums, and those using blues and yellows in blooms with soft green foliage were popular.

The various motifs used for ornamentation consisted of flowers, birds, fruit, small animals and, since Marblehead was so closely associated with the sea, marine motifs, such as seashells and seaweed. Some pieces had incised outline decoration, similar to sgraffito, with the glaze cut through to a contrasting body color. Old ships had much appeal, and pictures of sailing ships painted inside medallions and placed on the sides of pitchers were most attractive. The pitchers were made in two sizes, with old fashioned handmade pulled handles.

The glaze most used was of a smooth, matt finish; some of the pieces were lined with a glossy enamel harmonizing with the outer color. Lovely semi-gloss finishes in shades of blue, yellow, and other soft tones were also used. Among their colors was an old blue, referred to as "Marblehead blue," a tobacco brown, wistaria (sic), soft yellow and green, and a warm grayish tint—all perfect backgrounds for the elegant designs placed on the articles.

Advertisements of the pottery never failed to mention that the facilities at the Marblehead Pottery were such that many odd pieces, not available elsewhere, could be fashioned there upon demand. The plant, with its skilled artists and technicians, supported a so-called "experimental department" for this very purpose.

It is gratifying to note tha pieces of Marblehead Pottery were included in several outstanding exhibitions. In 1915, it was awarded a prize for pieces displayed in an exhibit at the Art Institute of Chicago. At this time, the Marblehead Pottery was considered one of the most artistic of American art potteries.

Mark found on Marblehead Pottery

Few collectibles offer as much colorful charm as Victorian . . .

Wemyss Ware

by JOAN RANZENHOFER

ONE of the most charming of Victorian wares is the gaily decorated pottery known as Wemyss ware (pronounced *weems*). This interesting pottery, made from the 1880s to about 1905 shows none of the excesses of Victorian design, but is beautifully and simply decorated in a bold forthright style.

Wemyss ware was the product of the R. Heron & Sons Fife Pottery in Sinclairtown, Scotland. Its name derived from Wemyss Castle, an ancient landmark in the locality. The brilliant white earthenware was decorated underglaze in vivid polychrome and given a smooth and very glossy glaze. The quality of this ware is high indeed.

The distinctive decoration of Wemyss ware was inspired by the Northern Scottish countryside, and includes objects, flora, and fauna that

The bold charm of Wemyss decoration is well illustrated by this tall mug. The black hens and cockerel stand on a green sponge-ware band. Typical Wemyss deep rose is used for the comb, wattles, and rim. Courtesy Janet Patterson Collection, Huntly House Museum, Edinburgh.

were dear and familiar to the people who bought and used the wares. The Scottish national emblem, the thistle, appears on many pieces. Hens and cockerels, beehives, sloe plums, wild roses and wild strawberries are other popular themes. These basic decorative themes are found combined with deep green foliage. The same deep green was frequently used to border each piece, and to make a ribbon decoration for handles. Some pieces are found with rim or border in the typical deep Wemyss rose color.

Wemyss ware is usually found in the "useful" wares, including jam pots, honey pots (often decorated with beehives), plates, bowls, and a wide variety of mugs, ranging from small child-sized mugs to giant three-handled presentation mugs. (Mention of this ware was made in *Spinning Wheel* for May 1954, page 8, though no pictures were shown.)

Black and white photography cannot do justice to the group of charming and colorful Wemyss ware pieces, pictured above. The large mugs are 5½ inches tall and 4½ inches in diameter. The mug on the right is painted with three enormous wild roses in vivid pink tones; the one on the left, with sprays of Scottish field flowers in pink and mauve. Both have typical Wemyss greenery — leaves painted in a rich dark green and bright yellow green, with yellow enamel veining. Borders and ribbon bands on the wide handles are in the dark green. Both are incised Wemyss, with the word Wemyss also painted in green by the decorator. The plate is 6½ inches in diameter, decorated with a cluster of deep purple sloe plums. The characteristic leaves complement the dark green rim. Mark is incised R. H. & S., with Wemyss Ware in a semi-circle.

The NILOAK Pottery

by PAUL F. EVANS

SO NOVEL is the ware of the Niloak Pottery of Benton, Arkansas, that its name has become synonymous with the swirled clays which provide the decoration for its classically-shaped forms. (*An earlier attempt at this technique was made by W. F. Willard of the Gay Head Pottery on Martha's Vineyard, Mass., but pieces were baked only in the sun. The interior was not glazed and the marked wares served primarily as a souvenir of a visit to the "Vineyard."*)

This may well have been the vision of Charles Dean "Bullet" Hyten, the pottery's founder, as the name he gave it—Niloak—is simply kaolin (loosely meaning "finer pottery clay") spelled backwards. The unique treatment of the clay, however, was what distinguished Niloak from other art potteries and for which a patent was

granted by the United States Patent Office.

Charles Hyten, who succeeded his father, J. H. Hyten, as operator of the Eagle Pottery of Benton, Arkansas, began experimenting with native Arkansas clay deposits. These were primarily the natural-colored clays to be found in the hills of central Saline County. After considerable research he was convinced that from these deposits an artistic pottery could be produced.

By 1910 he had given the name "Niloak" (pronounced with a long "i": nye-loak) to the ware which resulted. It was the product of the mixing of different colored clays in layers and then letting the centrifugal force of the potter's wheel do its work. In September, 1911, the Niloak Pottery Company was formed to provide for the manufacture of this artware—originally called Niloak's Mission pottery—on a large scale. A two-story brick plant was built and equipped with all the latest material to make such production possible, and Hyten served as its superintendent.

A year later a sales force was created to market the pottery throughout the United States and Canada. Plant capacity by that time was 125 articles a day and included vases, clocks, jardinieres, smoking sets, pitchers, steins, umbrella stands, an extensive line of novelties and a bevy of new items which were constantly being added by the firm.

Even at that time prices of the ware were not inexpensive. Novelties could be purchased for as little as 50¢, but vases, depending on their size, ranged from $25–50. Yet even these prices were not commensurate for the long hours of experimentation and research, to say nothing of the time involved in securing and processing the clay as well as its careful manipulation.

All of these efforts were intermingled in the unique character of Niloak's Mission pottery, which was a product of the successful combination of Hyten's scientific ingenuity and artistic imagination. As a result

Pink high-glazed castware squirrels with molded Niloak mark in bases; 5¾" high. V. Johnson collection.

of the original process of superimposing a plurality of batches of specially treated, different colored clays in plastic condition and then rotating them on the potter's wheel, an article could possess any combination of colors desired. These ranged from deep browns to pale creams, light greens and blues to pale pinks, with the colors themselves varying in shade according to the degree of heat applied during the firing. Individual decorative effects were achieved in each article as the different colors were uniquely displaced with relation to each other. No two colors or no two pieces of the finished Mission ware were exactly alike; and, since each was thrown on the wheel, no two were identical in shape.

The principle problem faced by Hyten in his early experiments was that clays of different colors shrank to different degrees in the drying or firing, depending more or less on the silicate content or the character of the color base. To achieve the multicolored spiral pattern, with the varying colors used for the decorative process shrinking in a uniform fashion, a formula for the incorporation of the proper proportioned ingredients to control shrinkage was devised. This operation was done in the blunger mill, with the shrinkage controlling material added to the clay while it was the consistency of cream.

In some cases it was necessary to use white clay which was then artificially colored by the use of pigments, but this was done only if the natural

Mission ware vase in colors of cream, red, earth-brown, light-brown and blue; 9" tall. Collection V. Weare.

colored clays were not available. In that instance, the coloring mixture would vary according to the particular color involved, but the proportions only and not the ingredients were all that required modification to produce a composite clay mass in which the shrinkage characteristics of each of the clays was designed to be uniform throughout.

For the most part, however, only natural colored clays were used. Each would be treated separately, with each, even the white, requiring a shrinkage controlling factor. After this factor was thoroughly mixed with the clay, whether artificially or naturally colored, the creamy consistency was run through a screen of approximately 140 lines per square inch. The mixture was then placed in plaster-bottomed vats to extract the surplus water and the pasty mass was then allowed to dry for anywhere from seven to ten days depending on atmospheric conditions. At this point the clay was about the consistency of putty but somewhat more plastic.

Each separate colored clay was then kneaded well and a lump of each color desired was taken by the potter. These were placed on upon another and the whole cut into the proper sized mass for forming the particular object to be produced. The cut mass was then placed on the wheel, and between the potter's hands and the force of the wheel a unique piece took shape. This was then removed from the wheel and allowed to partly dry, whereupon it was turned on the lathe and polished until it had a smooth, fine finish. After drying completely, a glaze solution was pumped inside the piece to render it waterproof. The ware was then put in a natural gas kiln and fired about forty-eight hours

Three pieces of Niloak's Mission ware. The piece on the far left is 7" tall. F. R. Smith collection.

at approximately 2000°F.

The stoneware line of the Eagle Pottery (commercial wares consisting of jugs, jars, crocks, churns, flowerpots and the like) was continued by Hyten, as long as he remained in business, as an entirely separate operation located two miles north of Benton. It was the Niloak Pottery, however, which received his greatest interest. This continued to grow and expand, and at one time six potters including Hyten turned the ware which reached a peak annual output of 75,000 pieces. The plant itself became quite a tourist attraction and just before the onset of the Depression a new building was constructed as a showroom.

With the Depression, sales of Niloak pottery, which was relatively expensive even for those times, dwindled rapidly. To provide the income needed to maintain the operation, a line of castware was introduced which was glazed in various high gloss and semi-matt finishes in solid and drip colors. This less-expensively produced line was called "Hiwood" to distinguish it from the Mission ware. For a time a black stamp marked "Hiwood/by Niloak" was used, but eventually the castware was marked only Niloak. As Niloak becomes more collectible, care should be taken by collectors to distinguish between the two lines. The Mission ware is a unique form of pottery, carefully and artistically executed, while the mass-produced Hiwood line, for the most part, is inexpensively made and poorly glazed.

The 1929 building and the rest of the business had been heavily mortgaged during the Depression and by the mid-1930s control of the pottery had changed hands. Under the new management the Niloak name was used on all ware produced. Hyten remained with the business for a time, but primarily on the road as a salesman. The Mission ware, whose output decreased continually through the 1930s, was finally discontinued about 1942.

By 1946 the pottery had closed. All that remain today of the 1912 building are some foundations of the kilns. The 1929 building is presently in use as an apartment house, although in very poor repair. An interesting feature of this building (located in the 1200 block of Military Road, about one mile north of downtown Benton) is the fireplace and hearth inlaid with Niloak tiles. These tiles, produced during the 1920s, are also to be found in the panels on the facade and on the floor of the foyer.

Some guides are available for the dating of Niloak, although none are conclusive. A great deal of experi-

(Please Turn the Page)

Hyten at the wheel. (Courtesy of A. Rainey, the potter's daughter, to whom the author wishes to express his thanks for her generous co-operation.)

menting was done with different colors, combinations, finishes and firings before the final Mission ware technique was attained. The earlier pieces tend to be more somber in color (tan, cream and brown), and some had a clear, high glaze or a waxed finish applied. Immediately after the granting of the patent in 1928 pieces were marked with the patent number in addition to the traditional art lettering "Niloak" mark which was used continuously from September, 1910, on the Mission ware and which was a registered trademark of the pottery. The Hiwood stamp was used for a time after the castware's introduction, and items so-marked are worthwhile examples as they were the earliest and best-made cast pieces. Later cast pieces bear either an impressed NILOAK (not in art lettering) or else a raised Niloak inscription that was part of the mold and which appears under the glaze. Nearly all pieces of Niloak were marked, and in those few instances of unmarked Mission ware, attribution is fairly obvious.

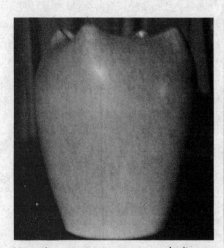

Hiwood vase, grey-green at top shading to ochre at bottom, flecked matt glaze; 7" tall. Marked with black Hiwood stamp in base. R. Blasberg collection.

Hyten left Niloak after the change in management and took a selling position with Camark Pottery in Camden, Arkansas. He continued that association until his death in 1944, a period during which he also operated a gift shop in Benton.

There have been numerous attempts to imitate the Mission ware including those by the Mineral & Sands, Pinto, and Desert Sands potteries of Boulder City, Nevada. All, however, are inferior copies in comparison to Niloak's Mission ware, which occupies a distinctive place in the art pottery movement and stands as a tribute to the creative intellect and imagination of its originator, Charles Hyten.

NEWCOMB ART POTTERY

by LUCILE HENZKE

THE NEWCOMB POTTERY was established in the art department of Sophia Newcomb College for women, New Orleans, La., in 1897. (Today Newcomb College is a part of Tulane University.) Newcomb was among the first colleges in the United States to realize that it must integrate its traditional fine arts courses with industrial courses that would benefit the community financially. At that time (1897), New Orleans was little more than a commercial port for a vast agricultural region.

The experimental pottery established at Newcomb College was never more than a studio—at no time did it ever operate on a large, factory-like scale. The artists, all Southern women educated at Newcomb, were making their living creating artistic pottery which the college undertook to sell at a profit at more than 50 widely separated agencies and outlets throughout the United States. Examples of this fine art pottery, though somewhat scarce, can be found in almost any area of this country.

A partial list of the artists working in the Newcomb studio was gleaned from the college's archives: Katherine Kopman, Sally Holt, Esther Elliot, Maria Le Blanc, Ada Lonnegan, Henrietta Bailey, Mary W. Butler, Leona Nicholson, Mary Sheerer, Martha Robinson and Sadie Irvine. Dr. Paul Cox worked at the studio as a technician from 1910 to 1915.

Among the agencies and retail outlets that sold Newcomb art pottery were: Marshall Field and William

A design of trees encircles this unusual example of Newcomb Pottery; signed by the artist, Marie LeBlanc. While the blue-green coloring is typical of this ware, the high gloss glaze is uncommon; height 5½ inches. Collection Mr. & Mrs. William Runyon.

O'Brien in Chicago; Paul Elder in San Francisco; Gustaf Stickley in New York City; and the Arts and Crafts Association in Philadelphia. There were retail outlets for Newcomb pottery in Boston, Milwaukee, Washington, D. C. and Detroit, too.

Newcomb pottery was exhibited at several international expositions, including the 1904 Louisiana Purchase

The moon shines through trees heavily laden with Spanish moss on this Newcomb Pottery vase. Though unmarked, it is thought to be the work of Sadie Irvine; height 6 inches. Author's collection.

Fig. 1

Fig. 2

Daffodils in relief decorate this handsome vase modeled by Henrietta Bailey; height 5 ½ inches. Lockerd collection.

Vase in a stylized magnolia blossom form; height 5 inches. Author's collection.

Tall pine trees decorate this handsome Newcomb Pottery vase modeled by an unidentified artist; height 11 inches. Author's collection.

Exposition at St. Louis, Mo., where it won a silver medal. They were awarded bronze medals at the World's Fair in Paris (1900) and at the Pan-American Exposition at Buffalo, N. Y. (1901). A silver medal was awarded to them at Charleston in 1902, and gold medals were won at Jamestown (1905), Knoxville (1915) and San Francisco (1915).

Newcomb pottery was completely indigenous. The rich, cream-colored clay from which it was fashioned was found in St. Tammany Parish, Louisiana, the land of orange and palm trees, the fragrant magnolia and jasmine, the bearded cypress and the noble oak. All of these local plants and trees were used as motifs for decorating the pottery — sometimes

stylized and sometimes natural. Every piece was hand thrown. The designs were drawn on the objects while they were still in a plastic condition, then incised and molded with a potter's tool. When finished, it had the effect of low relief modelling which appears to have been cast in a mold. Actually, every piece was completely hand made and a close study of the decoration reveals the fluid lines of the leaves and flowers, none of which is ever exactly the same in size or thickness.

Newcomb pottery appears to be blue in color, but it's really a combination of blue and green with designs in contrasting colors of yellow, white and pink. The various colors were brushed onto the surface of the object, one over another, before the glaze was applied. Most of the pottery was glazed with a mat finished, semi-transparent glaze which gave the designs a misty appearance. Objects with a high gloss glaze were made prior to 1910, but these are difficult to find.

Bowl-vase with begonia blossom decoration designed by Henrietta Bailey; diameter 5 ½ inches. Collection Mr. & Mrs. H. Lockerd.

Newcomb pottery's graceful, well proportioned shapes emulate those of its contemporaries, Rookwood and Weller. Every piece is marked on the bottom. The first mark (Fig. 1) was used from 1897 to 1905; the second mark (Fig. 2) was used from 1905 to the day the studio closed in 1940. (The Newcomb Guild was established in 1940, but ceased operations in 1952.) Artist's marks and monograms are also found on the base of each piece, close to the edge.

A group of Newcomb Pottery vases reproduced from an illustrated brochure issued by Newcomb College; ca. 1910.

Former Hampshire Pottery buildings on lower Main Street, Keene, New Hampshire.

Cadmon Robertson at the potter's wheel.

A portion of the private collection of Hampshire pottery of John C. Perry of Keene.

HAMPSHIRE POTTERY

by PAUL F. EVANS

KNOWN by several names, J. S. Taft & Company, Hampshire Pottery and "Keene Pottery," the wares of this important New England producer have become the objects of avid collector interest during the past few years.

Keene, New Hampshire, located in an area of rich clay deposits, has been the home of several potteries. The earliest, according to Lura Woodside Watkins in her book Early New England Potters, dates back to 1787, when utilitarian wares were produced for local use.

In 1871 James S. Taft and his uncle, James Burnap, established what was to become New Hampshire's most successful commercial pottery. After purchasing the Mile Stone Mill, which stood on the bank of the Ashuelor River, they converted it into a pottery and prepared to manufacture flower-pots. Before the first kiln could be fired, the building burned and over four thousand dollars was lost by the firm.

By that winter, however, the building had been replaced. The local paper noted that "Messrs. J. S. Taft & Co. have . . . recommenced the manufacture of earthenware. The interruption of their business by fire which destroyed their old building was only 6 weeks duration. Their new building is 160 ft. long and two stories high and has been very thoroughly and substantially built."

At first only redware was produced, but it was not long before the firm introduced stoneware items. By 1874 they acquired another Keene pottery (also begun in 1871 under the style of Starkey & Howard and later known by that of their successors, W. P. Chamberlain and E. C. Baker). This plant was then used as a redware pottery, while the original Hampshire works continued the manufacture of stoneware.

A bill headed "Main Street Works/ Deene Stone & Earthenware Manufactory" indicates that in 1876 the main Hampshire plant produced jugs, molasses jugs, butter and cake pots, covered preserve jars, pitchers, churns, water kegs and spittoons. Under the heading "Myrtle Street Works/Earthen Ware" is a list of items produced at the newly-acquired plant which included hanging vases, flowerpots, bracket pots, cuspadores (sic), florists' ware and Rockingham teapots. Watkins observes that here, as at other places, "the word 'Rockingham,' probably denotes a brown glaze on red earthenware."

Thomas Stanley came from England to join the Hampshire firm as its superintendent in 1879, and shortly thereafter a highly-glazed ware of the majolica type was introduced. Mugs, pitchers, tea sets and vases were made of a hard white body over which rich, dark glazes were applied.

This led to the firm's realization of the potential market for decorative pottery, and in 1883 a new kiln for the firing of this type of work was placed in operation. Under the direction of Wallace L. King, an artist, full scale production of a Royal Worcester-type ware was undertaken. This opaque, white-bodied ware, covered with a variety of glazes including an ivory matt finish, was to be in large part the basis of Hampshire's future success.

Souvenir items were very popular at this time (see SW aug '59, p16) and afforded a ready avenue of sales for the semi-porcelain ware. Plates, bonbon dishes, brush and comb trays, rose bowls, pitchers and other various pieces were produced at the Keene works. They were embellished with transfer-printed designs executed from copper plates made from photographs of places throughout the eastern and southern parts of the United States, and since as many as five firings would be required, the cost of production must have been considerable.

Decoration of the Worcester-type ware was not limited to souvenir pieces. An equally important facet of Hampshire's business was the production of items which were either decorated at the plant—which during this turn-of-the-century period employed about forty workers, almost half of whom were engaged in decorating—or left undecorated and sold to satisfy the home decorating craze of the era (see SW apr '67 p10).

Due to a tariff change in 1894, the potters of the United States were deprived of a protective duty of about fifty percent. The immediate effect was the closing of many marginal concerns and the forcing of others to change their product line so that items produced would not be in direct competition with those potted abroad. The Hampshire pottery stood idle for several months while Congress debated the Wilson Act.

When the result was certain, Hamp-

(Please Turn the Page)

No. 79— 4 inches high
No. 145—2½ inches high
No. 29—6½ inches high
No. 140—5½ inches high
No. 82—5½ inches high
No. 82\1—7½ inches high
No. 77—4½ inches high

Hampshire candlestick holders.

No. 51—3½ inches high
No. 15—4½ inches high
No. 97—5 inches high
No. 7—15 inches high
No. 2003—3¼ inches high
No. 108—12 inches high
No. 98—7¼ inches high
No. 55—8 inches high
No. 24—3 inches high

Some popular Hampshire pieces.

No. 202—Size 2 Cups
No. 203—Size 3 Cups

Hampshire coffee and tea sets.

shire resumed production, concentrating its effort on souvenir work, wares to be decorated either at the plant or in homes, and in the production of a full line of matt-finished art pottery.

While the first commercial production of a matt glazed ware is generally attributed to Grueby, Hampshire actually deserves the credit. The "Witch Jug," made by Hampshire for Daniel Low of Salem, Massachusetts, and which can accurately be dated as produced in 1892, was matt glazed and established the fact that Hampshire was producing pieces thus glazed at least four years before Grueby began operation.

Yet, the high point of the Hampshire works still lay ahead. In 1904, Cadmon Robertson, brother-in-law of Taft and no direct relation of the Robertson potters of Massachusetts, joined the pottery and was soon made its superintendent. A notable chemist, he introduced no fewer than nine hundred formulas and was responsible for the great variety of matt glazes from green and peacock (two-tones) blue, to old blue, gray, bronze, brown and yellow.

These colors appeared on a wide line of art pottery including vases, bowls, flowerholders, candlesticks, clocks and lamps. Originally the body of this line was an earthenware, but it gradually approached the composition of semi-porcelain. Foreign clays, especially English ball clays, were used, although for some varieties of items domestic clays from New Jersey and southern Florida were employed.

Many pieces of this art ware bear only the designation of Hampshire Pottery. Occasionally one finds items marked with an M inside an O. These were pieces designed by Robertson and the cypher was a tribute to Emmo, his wife, who assisted in the retail showroom of the pottery.

The earlier white ware is generally marked in red "Hampshire Pottery/J. S. Taft & Co.," with the Taft name in script. An artist's monogram is sometimes found on the decorated pieces, such as E. A. for Eliza Adams. The designation Keene, New Hampshire, was often included, even where the letters J. S. T. & Co. or the name J. S. Taft & Co. appeared without the Hampshire name. Examples of the art ware of the later period most commonly found today bear the impressed name Hampshire Pottery. Paper labels were also used, as is evidenced by the pieces in the Smithsonian's collection.

The retirement of King in 1908 deprived the firm of its leading artist and designer, and the death of Robertson in 1914 deprived it of its leading innovator. With the loss of both, Taft evidently found he could not continue

on his own and ceased production later that year.

In 1916 Taft sold the pottery to George Morton, who had been connected with the Grueby works. The sale included the buildings and machinery as well as the stock, process records and formulas developed by Robertson. In May of 1916 Morton fired a kiln containing over a thousand pieces of some of the most popular shapes and colors from past years as well as several new designs.

According to a catalog issued by Morton shortly after the firing, the pottery offered by mail "all the more favored of Hampshire designs in art ware" which had previously been fired there. The scope of the color line was expanded, with the Robertson glazes being applied to a far more extensive line of ware. Included in the catalog were candlesticks, pitchers, jars, tea and coffee services, clock frames and lamp stands, as well as fairy lamp bases.

"To carry in stock all our designs in each coloring," advised the brochure, "would obviously necessitate immense stock room. We aim to carry as varied a stock as our space will allow but urge that unless you can give us ample time to put through our kilns any specified piece, you should make two or three selections, and we call especially to your attention that we can often ship a much more satisfactory piece of any particular design if we are given some choice in the matter of coloring, largely owing to the fact that to portray the richness of Hampshire colorings in a catalog is well nigh impossible.

The pottery continued in operation for a year under Morton's management, but with the onset of World War I, the pottery closed in 1917 and Morton returned to Grueby. According to A. H. Kendall, in his brochure "The Story of Hampshire Pottery," Morton resumed his work at Keene after the end of the war and added machinery necessary to produce common white china for hotels and restaurants at the Hampshire plant. Later he added presses for the manufacturing of mosaic floor tile, and from 1919 to 1921 Hampshire remained busy with these lines.

Increasingly intense competition forced Hampshire to permanently close its doors in 1923. Before the year's end, the saga of the pottery for all intents and purposes was drawn to a close with the death of the firm's founder, J. S. Taft, the dismantling of equipment and the destruction or scattering of the molds responsible for the ware which had carried the name Hampshire Pottery to all corners of the country.

Bowl of leaves in a medium green matt glaze, 3" tall. Mark, "Hampshire 24" is raised, with the 24 referring to the Hampshire catalog number. Collection of Warren Zerbe.

Vase in mottled blue glaze, 8⅛" tall. Mark, "Hampshire Pottery 138" is impressed. Piece bears Robertson's MO cypher. Collection of Robert W. Blasberg.

Low bowl (2⅝" tall, 9" wide) is jade green dripped over olive matt. It bears the impressed "Hampshire Pottery" mark, the MO cypher and the catalog numbers 134 and 173.

American Art Porcelain
The Work of
Adelaide Alsop-Robineau

Adelaide Alsop-Robineau at the potter's wheel. Photo through the courtesy of her daughter, Mrs. Elisabeth Lineaweaver.

by ROBERT W. BLASBERG

"Scarab Vase" with stand and cover in pale green and ivory glaze; height 17". Everson Museum Collection.

WITH HER INHERITED wealth Adelaide Alsop-Robineau might have become a bank president or a surgeon. Instead, fate cast her in the roles of editor and master potter, and her accomplishments in that dual capacity were such that she became a key figure in the American art pottery movement.

In 1899 when Mrs. Robineau and her husband Samuel, with George Clark of Syracuse, went to that city to found *Keramic Studio* magazine, the new movement in ceramics stood at the brink of its golden age. The Robineau magazine at once took its place as the forum and bulletin board, and during the magazine's best years these men and women saw their work chronicled in its pages, and many contributed articles and reviews.

In contrast to the male-dominated European scene, American potting would soon have a full complement of women. Among this gracious group

Adelaide Alsop-Robineau became one of the best-known, and without doubt the most respected of the lady potters. Editorship alone would have raised her to prominence. But her ceramic work, though never a paying proposition, brought her the greater honor. For example, besides the medals she won, there was the added prestige of placing her work with Tiffany and Company, in 1906; and when New York's Metropolitan Museum of Art began purchasing contemporary ceramics in 1922, her work was the first to be acquired.

Mrs. Robineau's peculiar distinction as a potter lies in her several American "firsts": She made the first high-fire porcelain, both glaze and body, from wholly American ingredients. She was also the first to use colored glazes on porcelain, and the first to throw porcelain ware by hand on the wheel. This last was a well-nigh incredible feat. Even today the high-fire porcelain

Bottle-shaped vase with incised decoration about the neck; ca. 1926. Metropolitan Museum Collection.

Robineau vases (some with covers) of the type collectors are most apt to find. Illustrated in "Palette and Bench" (1910).

body is so wanting in plasticity that potters experience difficulty in raising a piece over four inches in height. As if this were not enough, she challenged the ancient Chinese masters by carving the unfired porcelain, which is so brittle that it shatters at the slightest impropriety of pressure. In some of her reticulated pieces colored light gleams through openwork spanned by a film of translucent enamel.

Being pioneers, the earliest turn-of-the-century potters had each to work his way through his own system of experiments with their attendant disappointments. But Mrs. Robineau compounded the difficulty by electing to work in a field virtually without American precedent. Had she not received assistance from Taxile Doat, who had been on the staff at Sevres, she might never have succeeded. When she sent some of her crystalline pieces (which would become her signature) to Doat he replied joyously, "You are my pupil!" and sailed for America. Considerations of assistance aside, her conceptions, though within the accepted modes of the day, were in high degree tasteful and creative, while the technical excellence of her work in porcelain has never been surpassed.

It was possibly from a blend of pride and acumen, that Mrs. Robineau, the china-painter, desired to enter the field of potting. *Keramic Studio* was the official organ of the American League of Mineral painters. But, as the art pottery movement developed, the editor realized more and more that china painting, the daubing of colors onto white china "blanks," was no more than a demi-art. Mrs. Robineau herself did not wish to make "ordinary" pottery. Then in 1903 when her husband was translating Doat's articles on high-fire porcelain for the maga-

zine, she knew at once that she must work in this medium. That summer she attended the best "quick" school in America, Dr. Binns' summer courses in ceramics at Alfred, N.Y.

The difficulty of working in porcelain is well illustrated by this anecdote: When Helen Keller visited the Panama-Pacific Exposition at San Francisco in 1915, an official took some of the Robineau porcelains out of the cases so she might enjoy them. Upon his mentioning that the wistaria lantern had required many firings, a beautiful expression came over Helen Keller's face. She tenderly ran her hand over the glazed surface and murmured, "Seven times in the fire and not found wanting."

Clays and glazes commonly behave unpredictably in the kiln, but porcelain fired at 2400F. is markedly prone to warping. True porcelain is costly because so much is ruined in both glost and biscuit firings. Once Samuel Robineau, who fired every piece of pottery his wife made, began a letter to Frederick Burten Rhead, "I never felt so discouraged and disgusted in my life. . . .every one of the new pieces warped or blistered. Anybody who is foolish enough to do cone 9 porcelain ought to be shut up in an insane asylum." With regard to these tragedies of the furnace a friend once remarked that Adelaide Robineau had the fortitude of a soldier.

That superhuman patience with which Mrs. Robineau carved the brittle clay, using fine tools like needles, must also be praised. Prime examples are the pierced lanterns like the one Helen Keller admired, the eggshell coupes of which only three survived, and ambitious projects like the Pastorale Vase and the Scarab vase.

The Scarab Vase dominates the

large collection of her work by which Syracuse, her adopted city, paid her honor. Anna W. Olmsted, formerly director of the Everson Museum, where the collection is displayed, called the Scarab Vase "the Portland Vase of modern times" because of its celebrity. Certainly Mrs. Robineau's masterpiece takes its rightful place among those older Baseball Vases and Transcontinental Cotton Oil Vases upon whose shoulders the gathering legends rest. Quite simply, Adelaide Alsop-Robineau planned this vase as a bid for immortality, and she cast it in the form of a ringing testimonial to craftsmanship. The theme, mandatory for such projects, could not be more appropriate: the scarab, whose multiple

"Crab Vase" with stand; crystalline glaze with excised and perforated decoration; height 8". Ca. 1907. Everson Museum Collection.

Robineau productions illustrated in "Palette and Bench" (1910). The reticulated Chinese Lantern vase in the center is similar to the one that so impressed Miss Helen Keller.

image forms the background to the design, represents hard work, for he is tirelessly rolling his ball of food. The title of the vase is "The Apotheosis of the Toiler." Surmounting the lid is a sphere signifying the ideal toward which labor strives.

The Scarab Vase was made in St. Louis in 1910 while the Robineaus were associated with a pretentious scheme, E. G. Lewis' American Woman's League. Taxile Doat was on the staff as well as Frederick Hurten Rhead. Rhead later said, "Many times during the carving, Mrs. Robineau would work all day, and on an otherwise clean floor there would be about enough dry porcelain dust to cover a dollar piece, and half an inch more carving on the vase." Samuel Robineau recounted the history of the proud piece in this fashion:

"It took Mrs. Robineau over one thousand hours to carve and glaze the vase, the most elaborate piece she ever made. It was done for the American Woman's League, as is marked on the base, and I did not like the idea that it would not belong to us. As I was firing it, Mr. Lewis came in the kiln room and I offered him $1000. for the vase, not knowing whether it would come

Porcelain vase, green glaze streaked with brown, with wooden stand and cover; height with stand and cover 3 3/8". Ca. 1923. Metropolitan Museum Collection.

The decoration on this large, untitled plate was influenced by Ancient Peruvian designs; diameter 15". Everson Museum Collection.

out good or bad. Mr. Lewis refused the offer. (Sharply," another account relates.) The next day we opened the kiln and to our great dismay, the precious vase was found with two or three big, gaping cracks all around the base. It appeared to be a complete failure. Mr. Doat declared there was nothing to do, the only thing was to fill the cracks with some kind of paste, color them, and keep the vase, imperfect. Mrs. Robineau never left a good piece imperfect, it always had to go in the fire again. She went to work, carefully filling the cracks with ground porcelain, reglazing the vase, and on the second firing it came out perfect as it

is today. It is impossible to detect the places which were cracked in the first firing. Fortunately this beautiful piece came back to us when the American Woman's League failed, owing us money which was secured by a mortgage on the Scarab Vase and other pieces."

The Robineaus merged their professional and private lives for thirty years. At the time of her death in 1929 Adelaide Alsop-Robineau was sixty-four and had been teaching since 1920 at Syracuse University. She was working on pieces for an exhibition of her work in England — a most grateful event inasmuch as the ceramic movement as an object of public fascination had quite run its course.

Under sedation in her final days, Mrs. Robineau believed these "green" pieces would be exhibited precisely as they were. Samuel said later that if his wife had ever realized that she would not finish her work it would have broken her heart. After her death, her husband glazed the pieces according to her specifications as best he could and fired this final group. The constancy and dedication of this couple must command our wholehearted admiration. In 1932, as a memorial to Adelaide Alsop-Robineau, the Everson Museum founded the Ceramic National Exhibition. Although discontinued after 1968, this show, like the artist herself at the turn of the century, gained world-wide recognition for its important place in the history of American ceramics.

The author is indebted to Paul F. Evans, Marion W. Quinn, and the Everson Museum for material which would otherwise have been unavailable to him.

John Ridgway & Co.'s
University

by BRICE GARRETT

THE Ridgway name is still a familiar one in the Potteries— Ridgway Potteries Ltd., **Ash Hall,** Stoke, is one of the larger contemporary firms, controlling eight potteries, and is successor to the business founded by William Ridgway. John Ridgway (1786–1860), William's older brother — they were sons of Job Ridgway, Master Potter of the Bell Bank Works, Hanley—controlled the factory and firm known in this century as Cauldon. John and William were partners in business from 1814 until 1830, controlling both their father's factory and Cauldon, founded by their uncle, George Ridgway. When the business was divided in 1830, John Ridgway took the Cauldon Place Works, on Cauldon Place, Shelton, and enjoyed a successful business and civic career until his retirement in 1859. He was appointed Potter to Queen Victoria in 1851.

We are concerned here with the period 1841–55, when the firm was styled John Ridgway & Co. The firm's productions at this time were generally marked J. R. & Co., and included bone china, transfer-printed earthenware, Parian, stoneware, and sanitary ware.

The teapot illustrated, is ironstone china, transfer-printed in blue. It is unmarked, but other pieces in this pattern are known bearing a mark consisting of a crown over an oval garter, with an attached ribbon bearing UNIVERSITY/J R & CO., printed. All examples so far recorded are blue, and indicate that dinner and toilet sets were made. The building may be an actual structure, but it has not yet been identified.

Other patterns issued by John Ridgway & Co., and marked J. R. & Co., include "Candia" (continued by the successor firm in flow blue), "Byzantium," and "Doria." The firm also produced white ironstone, elegantly styled "Porcelaine a la francais."

Collection Mrs. Mabel G. Martin

Pisgah Forest Pottery

by MARCIA RAY

THE PISGAH FOREST Pottery, at the foot of Mount Pisgah, in Arden, N. C., not far outside of Asheville, is a continuation of the Nonconnah Pottery started about 1900 by W. B. Stephen and his mother, Mrs. Andrew Stephen, in Shelby County, Tennessee, near Memphis. In 1914, both his parents then dead, Walter Stephen moved the Pottery to its present site in North Carolina.

Allen H. Eaton in *Handicrafts of the Southern Highlands*, published in 1937 by the Russell Sage Foundation, having visited the various potteries of the area, reported: "The Pisgah Forest pottery made by W. B. Stephen . . . is . . . the work of a single potter.

Sage green jasperware mug with white Covered Wagon decoration; signed "Stephen." 3" high.

Ashtray in silvery crystalline glaze; diameter 5".

. . . One of his most successful glazes is turquoise blue, a rare and beautiful color which he applies to both large and small pieces. Sometimes it crackles, either in the kiln or later, but it is always very attractive even with the crackle. [Mr. Eaton evidently did not understand that the crackle was intentional.] He has secured some por-

celain glazes that rank with the best work of this kind in our country.

"Mr. Stephen also does modeling on some of his pieces that results in a type of pottery resembling the old cameo-ware of England. . . . He is a careful experimenter, building special kilns for his work, and going to great pains to give his product an individual and beautiful appearance."

The account of Pisgah Forest Pottery which Charles R. Counts, infinitely more at home with ceramics than Mr. Eaton, published in *Ceramics Monthly* for May 1965, reads:

"Walter Stephen worked in the art-pottery tradition. His clays were of a high-fire whiteware nature, and he perfected a beautiful turquoise crackle glaze and made some excellent crystalline glazes. He is also known today for what he termed his 'free-hand cameo' technique. It is an effect similar

In "Who Knows?" (SW may '70), Mrs. Paul P. Hodon, Oakland, Calif., inquired about Pisgah Forest Pottery. Most of the responses received came from people who at some time had visited the pottery and sent us descriptive folders and price lists. For making this compilation possible, our thanks go to Mr. Melvin Reiter, East Lansing, Mich., Mrs. Onie Hildenbrandt, Greeley, Colo., Mr. Paul Evans, Mill Valley, Calif., and to Mr. and Mrs. Lawrence E. Duvall, Washington, D.C., who brought the pieces pictured here to Hanover to be photographed. They represent only a small portion of Mrs. Duvall's collection. We are also grateful to Mr. Gary G. Ledbetter of the Pisgah Pottery for filling us in on correct names and dates, and bringing us up to date on the affairs of the pottery. We should also thank Mrs. Hudon who started it all, and Marcia Ray who put the answers together.

to the Wedgwood sprigging, except that he 'slip-trailed' the light decoration over the dark body.

"Walter Stephen died about three years ago [1961, aged 86], but his shop, the Pisgah Forest Pottery, is still being run by Tommy Case, a relative, and Will Ledbetter, whom Mr. Stephen took in as an apprentice years ago."

Mr. Ledbetter, whose name, by the way, is Gary, not Will, tells us that the pottery still runs on a part time basis. Mr. Case is Mr. Stephen's step-grandson and has been connected with the pottery for about 20 years. He himself began working with Mr. Stephen in 1930, while a student at Biltmore Junior College. Both men have interests outside the pottery; Mr. Ledbetter is a dairy farmer and Mr. Case is employed at the Olin-Mathieson Chemical Corp.

Now for what the Pisgah Pottery had to say for itself in its informative descriptive folders. Though there were many editions, the material in all was practically the same, with only slight differences in wording and position of paragraphs. This fragment was taken from one on which someone had pencilled, "August 1950."

Shapes and objects from a Pisgah Forest Pottery brochure.

First there were comments on the location and Mr. Stephen's many years of experimentation, then:

"Although commercial porcelain is fired with coal, Pisgah Forest Pottery is fired with wood from the mountain forest. Its delicate colors cannot be produced with coal on account of impurities in it. The kiln must be heated to a very high temperature to make the china fire body and the soft fine colors. . . .

"The finished products are all strictly handmade articles. The shaping, turning, decorating, and glazing are all done by hand. The cameo work is strictly hand work. The figures are free hand drawings. The cameos are painted on with a brush. The creamy porcelain paste is applied layer by layer, building up the design in relief. Most American subjects are used such as the Buffalo Hunt, the Covered Wagon, etc. [The "etc.," no doubt, included Stephen's attractive pine trees in white on a sage green ground.]

"The pieces in crystalline glaze are of unusual interest. Remarkable crystal formations in multi-colored crystals form the glaze covering. This glaze is one thing that the ancients did not produce. It was first made by the Danes and exhibited at the Paris Exposition in 1900. This glaze is finely balanced chemically so that they can

Egg Plant or Wine Color (shaded turquoise to aubergine) bowl-vase, crackled glaze; 3" high. Purchased in 1948.

crystallize as the kiln cools off. It is extremely sensitive to any changes of the formula which accounts for the wide variety of color and crystal formation."

Most of the folders we examined carried "W. B. Stephen, Proprietor" on the cover; some with, below it, "Fine Handmade Pottery — Ancient Turquoise Blue, Aubergine Wine color, Free Hand Cameo, Unusual Crystalines—all in Porcelain." Later folders read: "Proprietors: G. G. Ledbetter & J. T. Case."

Though none of the folders referred to the bread-and-butter business—the

usual jugs, teapots, vases, and candlesticks that all the local potters made—these were shown on their price lists, and the Cameo and Crystaline pieces were not.

The shapes pictured in the various price lists were all alike, and offered the same range of colors: Ivory, Rose Pink, Light to Dark Jade Green, Turquoise Blue, Egg Plant or Wine Color. The prices rose a little on later lists, perhaps 25 or 50 cents an article. For instance, the "Bell-shaped Vase," marked "1" in the illustration, sold in 1950 for 75¢ for the 5" size; $2 in the 7" size, and $4 in the 9" size; in a later list, it was $1 for the 5" size, $2.25 in the 7" size, but still $4 for the 9-inchers.

The mark of the pottery is "Pisgah Forest Pottery," with or without a rough design of a potter at work. On some of the crystaline and Cameo pieces "Stephen" also appears. Those with the "Stephen" mark are the most choice and, of course, collectors' favorites.

Of current production, Mr. Ledbetter tells us that the turquoise glaze is still being made; the crystaline and cameo wares were discontinued with Mr. Stephen's death. The large woodfired kiln is still in use, supplemented with a more modern gas kiln.

Miniature covered sugar bowls and a creamer; left and center in Turquoise Blue glaze with Rose Pink lining; right in Wine Color glaze. Height to top of covers 2½".

Covered sugar bowl, teapot and creamer in light blue jasperware with white Covered Wagon decoration. All pieces signed "Stephen." Height to top of teapot 4¾". Purchased in 1952.

OHIO'S LOTUS WARE

by BRICE GARRETT

LOTUS WARE, one of the most sought American ceramics in to-day's antique market—and one of the most highly-priced—was the product of the Knowles, Taylor & Knowles Company of East Liverpool, Ohio. The dates usually given for its production are 1891 to 1898.

A bone-china body of extremely thin section and brilliantly white and translucent, Lotus Ware was the Ohio firm's second product in the category of fine china. In 1887, Isaac Watts Knowles, then senior partner in the firm, hired Joshua Poole, one of the managers at the Belleek factory in Ireland. Poole soon had a Belleek body in production for Knowles, Taylor & Knowles at East Liverpool, finely molded and very fragile. The factory's china works, however, were destroyed by fire in November 1889, and the company, very busy at the time with the production of their most successful vitreous hotel china, temporarily abandoned fine china.

About 1891 the firm came out with a new china body, basically of the bone family in composition, as translucent and as thinly potted as the earlier Belleek. It was first marketed as KTK China. By 1893, when it was shown at the World's Columbian Exposition at Chicago, it had been christened Lotus Ware. Col. John N. Taylor, then president of the company, is supposed to have selected the trade-name himself, because of the body's resemblance to the petals of the lotus blossom.

Art wares in the new body were in production before 1893. Kenneth P. Beattie was the chief modeller at the time, and some of the pieces shown at the Chicago Exposition were his work. Various decorative techniques were used on the new Lotus Ware. One of the pieces exhibited in 1893 was a 9" vase, mazarine blue under-glaze, heavily gilded, with figure-painting in a variation of the *pate-sur-pate* technique. In this case the figures were built up by the application of several layers of Limoges enamel over the glaze.

Other pieces of Lotus Ware were reticulated — pierced in frequently very elaborate designs, adding to the fragility of the product. "Jewelling" was yet another decorative device often used; it consisted of the application of slip to the biscuit to form a pattern of raised ornament, the elements of which in turn were enamelled in brilliant colors. The resulting effect suggests jewel-stones against the white body. The ewer-shaped creation illustrated is an example of the use of both forms of decoration on one piece.

The biscuit-jar shown was decorated with an applied pattern now referred to as "fish-net"—slip laid on the body to form a net-like pattern before glazing.

Above: Biscuit jar, pale blue background, ivory panels, red and blue flowers, heavy gold leaves and vines, "fish-net" applied pattern in alternate panels; Lotus mark. Left: Fine example of Lotus, paneled in pastels, blue, pink, green and gold, signed by the artist; shows both reticulation and jewelling; Lotus mark. Both from collection of Mrs. Riley Whittenberger.

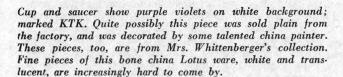

Embossed cuspidor, pale green background, pink flowers, gold trim; marked "KTK." Example of fine factory decoration.

Cup and saucer show purple violets on white background; marked KTK. Quite possibly this piece was sold plain from the factory, and was decorated by some talented china painter. These pieces, too, are from Mrs. Whittenberger's collection. Fine pieces of this bone china Lotus ware, white and translucent, are increasingly hard to come by.

Embossing, the equivalent of pattern-molding, was also used to decorate the new china body. Frequently these patterns were based on geometric figures. Other pattern-molded designs imitated natural shapes. Forms based on the shell and on the leaf were most often used.

Lotus Ware was sold from the factory both plain and decorated. The plain pieces often went into the hands of amateur china painters; Lotus was produced at the time when china painting was the rage among clubwomen. This circumstance accounts for the appearance in today's market of pieces of Lotus whose decoration is not up to the standard of quality set by the body.

Pieces painted at the factory were usually skillfully done, in a style typical of the time. The most frequent motifs for overglaze painting were flowers, landscapes, and mythological subjects.

Both useful and ornamental wares were made in the Lotus body. Among the former were tea sets, chocolate sets, *tete-a-tete* sets, and bowls of various sizes and shapes. Ornamental pieces included vases of many forms, covered jars, and other containers.

The factory mark used on Lotus Ware consisted of a circle enclosing the letters K T K Co, with a star and a crescent, above the words LOTUS WARE, usually printed overglaze in green.

The Knowles, Taylor & Knowles Company was the outgrowth of a business established at East Liverpool in 1853 by Isaac W. Knowles, for the manufacture of Rockingham and yellow-ware. The firm's first important contribution to the industry was the introduction in 1872 of the manufacture of white granite, known to modern collectors as white ironstone. It was the first factory in the Ohio district to make that type of ware, which by the end of the century was the principal product of the whole area, whose many factories produced millions of pieces for years.

More Partners

In 1870, Mr. Knowles took as partners John N. Taylor and Homer S. Knowles, thus giving the firm the style under which it is best known. Two more partners were admitted in 1888, Joseph G. Lee and Willis A. Knowles, but the firm's name remained the same. In January 1891, the company was incorporated, and Col. Taylor, then 49, became president. Isaac Knowles, the founder, then 78, was vice-president.

For a good many years in the last quarter of the nineteenth century, Knowles, Taylor & Knowles were predominant in the manufacture of vitreous hotel china, which they made in great quantities and shipped to all parts of the country. It is the KTK product most easily found today, and worth collecting. It is of course, much thicker in section, since it was destined for heavy use, but the body is true porcelain, and many pieces are quite translucent. The mark usually carried was K. T. & K./CHINA, printed, not incised.

Col. Taylor, president of the firm during the period when Lotus Ware was in production, was a veteran of the Civil War, but his military title derived from his honorary appointment to the staff of his friend, William McKinley, then Governor of Ohio, and later President of the United States.

Col. Taylor's friendship with McKinley may have brought results of more interest to the collector of American ceramics. The *Crockery and Glass Journal* for December 1, 1898, carried an item indicating that Knowles, Taylor & Knowles were producing a set of china for the White House, then occupied by the McKinleys. From the description given, one would assume that the commission was for a State service. However, James R. Ketchum, Curator of the White House, assures me that there is no record of the McKinleys ever having ordered a State Service. The reporter for the *Crockery and Glass Journal* had seen a sample for this service; it may still be in existence, even if the order for a complete service was never carried out.

Taylor owned an interest in two other potteries in East Liverpool, one of which manufactured sewer tiles; the other, various potters' supplies. He was also active in the pottery industry on a national level. He was chairman of the committee appointed by the United States Potters' Association to arrange for exhibits at the World's Columbia Exposition at Chicago in 1893.

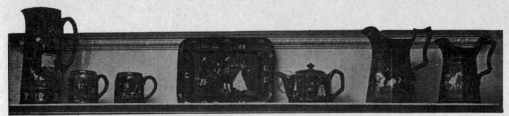

Deldare in the Author's Collection.

A Deldare Mark.

Buffalo Pottery's
Deldare Ware

by DEE ALBERT GERNERT

IT is only recently that the favor of collectors and the attention of antiques dealers has been directed to an immensely interesting line of highly decorated olive green ware known as Deldare. This distinctive semi-porcelain was made at the Buffalo Pottery in the early 1900s. The decorations are hand-painted in mineral colors under a beautiful high glaze, and most large pieces are signed with the initials or the full name of the persons who decorated them. Most pieces are also dated.

The man who originated this ware was Lewis H. Bown, a native of Trenton, New Jersey, who learned the pottery business in his home town. It was from Trenton that he was recruited to become manager of the Buffalo Pottery in Rochester, New York. (See *Spinning Wheel*, Jan.–Feb. '63)

In correspondence with the writer, Mr. Bown tells the story: "In 1908 we were making semi-porcelain at the Buffalo Pottery and I was anxious to produce a line to compete with one made by Royal Doulton in England . . . the olive green base was achieved by adding a small percentage of oxide of chrome to our regular white body." The first experimental pieces were turned out in 1908.

Since the ware was created with the definite purpose of producing an American decorative line to be associated in the public mind with famous English decorative lines such as Denholm, Deveraux, and Doulton, Mr. Bown coined the name "Deldare" which also began with a "D," and turned, quite logically to English art forms for ideas to use in decoration.

"We searched through old books," he wrote, "and found two—*The Vicar of Wakefield* and *Cranford*—which were full of old English scenes. We copied these etchings and painted them in underglaze mineral colors on a line of art ware and some dinnerware." This was the "first series," some dated 1908, others 1909.

The famous "Fallowfield Hunt" scenes were used for the second series. These are dated 1909. Then, in 1911, came the third and seemingly best series. These third-series pieces are decorated with copies of etchings from the "Tours of Dr. Syntax," done by the famous English artist, Thomas Rowlandson. Rowlandson's paintings can be identified by the beautiful greyed greens and blues which he used, and the accuracy with which these colors are reproduced on the ware gives it rare beauty and distinction.

The fourth series was named "Abino." Produced in 1912, it repre-sents an attempt at original decoration, and is hopelessly outclassed by the three preceding series which relied on the works of artists of stature.

In one letter Mr. Bown writes, "In 1912 we gave up the manufacture of semi-porcelain and also Deldare, and began the manufacture of vitrified hotel china." A second letter says: "We discontinued making this ware [Deldare] in 1916 when we were obliged to go into the production of vitrified hotel china for the government. After the First World War we resumed its production, but owing to increased cost of labor and materials, the expense of production was so high that the selling price was prohibitive."

There is no clue in the correspondence as to how much Deldare was produced after World War I. However, there were only four series or "decorations," as he calls them, and a pair of candlesticks dated 1925 and bearing the first series decorations would indicate that the pieces produced after the war duplicated the decorations of the four series.

Collectors have been searching out this art line for a very short time, but the fact that it was produced for such a short period means that the supply is limited, and accounts for Mr. Bown's observation, "It brings fabulous prices."

Deldare in the dining room of *Rita Love, Vineland, New Jersey*, antiques dealer and interior decorator, who has been collecting Deldare for her own use since 1956. The large dresser tray, second shelf, is in Heirloom pattern.

From the collection of Mrs. Lawrence E. Duvall, Washington, D. C. The 9″ pitcher, signed Hurd, 1909, shows "The Fallowfield Hunt" on one side, "The Fallowfield Hunt Breaking Cover" on the other. The 9¾″ pitcher, signed W. Foster, 1909, shows "Ye Old English Village" and "Ye Lion Inn" on opposite sides. Mrs. Duvall fell in love with Deldare fifteen years ago, and has found just about that many pieces. Her favorite is an emerald green cup and saucer, signed J. Gerhardt, 1911; on saucer is "Dr. Syntax and the Bookseller;" on the cup, "Dr. Syntax at Liverpool"—"And soon a person he addressed, whose paunch protruded from his breast"; man and spotted dog on other side.

Pieces at left, and bouillon above, from the Deldare *collection of Mr. and Mrs. W. E. Wilson, Harrisburg, Pa.* (See This Month's Cover, page 3).

Left, "Ye Lion Inn" hanging plate, 12″ diameter, dated 1909, *From Enid Wysor, Tappan Zee Heirlooms, Tarrytown, New York.*

Right, Calendar plate for 1910, in olive green, decorated with pixies, nuts, berries, chick in shell, etc. *From the collection of Mrs. Gloria Durando, Rolling Hills Estates, California.* She has also an unusual oblong shallow bowl with a Fallowfield Hunt scene.

"Dr. Syntax Sells Grizzle", large plate *from Mrs. Love's collection.*

Kenneth Carter, Laceyville, Pa. obtained this 6½″ salad plate, 1908, at the factory after Deldare production had ceased. Used perhaps as office sample or by road salesman, it is now *owned by Marcia Ray.*

"The Fallowfield Hunt, The Death" on 10″ bowl. *From Kathlene Bankert, Hanover, Pa.*

Pictures shown on these pages are from the Deldare collections of *Spinning Wheel* readers. Regrettedly, many pictures sent for this purpose could not, from lack of space, be shown. In the final selection of photographs to be used, the attempt was made to show both representative and unusual pieces, with a minimum of repetition. In addition to those whose collections are represented in picture, other Deldare collectors who contributed to the excitement of preparing this article are: Mrs. E. H. Chapman, Euclid, Ohio; Miss Elinor Waddy, Los Angeles, California, who lists among her unusuals a Colonial Dames 11x14″ tray and a hair receiver in Doctor Syntax decoration; Mrs. H. L. Kernodle, Green Bay, Wisconsin; Mabel Barber, Barber's Antiques, Plainwell, Michigan; Mrs. W. D. Wilson, Lakewood, Ohio, whose first purchase was a tobacco canister signed L. Palmer, 1909; Virginia Fitzgerald, Galena, Illinois; Frank R. Gardner, Manchester, Connecticut.

EDWARD WALLEY'S

GAUDY

IRONSTONE

by BETTY GRISSOM

Blinking (or Seeing) Eye pattern in plate, cup, and saucer; impressed circle mark, "E. Walley Niagara Shape" around edge, English Registry mark for 1856 in center; flowers are red, scallops in design, blue.

Blackberry pattern soup plate and pitcher; name of pattern impressed in a small circle with "Ironstone China/Walley" around it; colors here are deep blue, with half of the large leaves in red and yellow; shape is Niagara; blackberries are in blue dotted with gold lustre; gold lustre band around the edge. The pitcher is very lightweight, with translucent areas when held to the light.

SIMEON SHAW in his *History of the Staffordshire Potteries,* published in 1829, writes of the Burslem vicinities: "Cobridge contains a number of houses, and is in both Burslem and Stoke Parishes. The elegant mansion of W. Adams, Esq. is in the former while the neat and modest edifice belonging to J. Hales, Esq. is in the latter. At Cobridge are the manufactories of J & R Clews, N. Dillion, and some others not presently in operation. Various kinds of Pottery and Porcelain are here being manufactured in great perfection."

Shaw's commentaries appeared too soon to include the pottery of Elijah Jones, who set up his factory in Cobridge in 1831. Ten years later, in 1841, Mr. Jones took Edward Walley as his partner and the firm became Jones and Walley. From 1845 to 1856, Edward Walley continued the business by himself, operating under his own name.

About this time, Staffordshire potters had begun to copy in ironstone the fine Imari porcelains of Worcester and Derby. Though this so-called Gaudy Ironstone failed to please the home trade, it found a ready market in the Americas. It sold especially well in the Pennsylvania Dutch areas served by the Port of Philadelphia.

In his *Anglo-American China, Book I,* Sam Laidacker describes Gaudy Ironstone thus: "The opaque body is very heavy and thick, being partly pottery paste and part porcelain. The blue is under the glaze and for some reason penetrated the body and shows on the back. Most of the other colors are on top of the glaze, but some of them, in some patterns, appear to have been put on with the same firing. There is usually some gold lustre that fused with the glaze during the final firing."

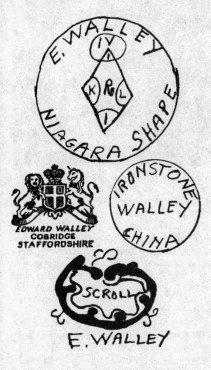

Marks found on Edward Walley's wares.

Many lovely patterns were made by Walley. *Pinwheel* was one, named after fireworks used on Guy Fawkes day in England. *Wagon Wheel,* made to appeal to the American ladies, looked just like the spokes of a wheel, striped with gold lustre and decorated on lighter bands of blue with tiny lustre leaves. *Blinking Eye* or *Seeing Eye* was an unusual pattern with scalloped blue edge and red flowers with an "eye" in the center.

Edward Walley used four different marks on his wares: an impressed small circle with "Ironstone China" around the circle edge and "Walley" in the center; a coat of arms with "Edward Walley/ Cobridge/ Staffordshire" beneath it; an impressed circle with "E. Walley/ Niagara Shape" around the edge, and an English registry mark in the center; and a printed green cartouche including the name of the pattern, "E. Walley" underneath.

The word "gaudy" as applied to various types of British pottery and porcelain has caused much confusion. There are many pieces of Staffordshire that really come under this category. If any readers find a marked Edward Walley plate in an appropriate design and color it is reassuring to know that it is Gaudy Ironstone as described so well by Mr. Laidacker.

Wagon Wheel mug.

Strawberry Pattern. At Greenfield Village, Dearborn, Mich., Luther Burbank's home has a table set with Strawberry Ironstone china. Bowl here is a variant of that design, with less blue penetrating the body, and strawberries enameled red with yellow dots.

This "Large Leaf" plate has often been pictured in books on antiques. Walley used a number of large leaf designs with variations of large and small flowers. Carnation pattern is similar to this design.

Scroll pattern handleless cup and saucer; printed green cartouche mark includes pattern name, "E. Walley" beneath; design of green scrolls and small sprays with red and purple buds, with gold lustre over the color. Possibly not a Gaudy pattern, but close.

Large leaf design with small flowers in primitive style.

Pinwheel pattern; name suggested by fireworks used on Guy Fawkes Day.

Scottish Pottery

An analysis—and a comparison with its Staffordshire parallels.

by DAVID CLARKE

SCOTLAND has never been famed for its potting as it has for building ships, and distilling whiskey; yet huge quantities of pottery and china were made there. The industry was one superimposed upon traditional Scottish crafts rather than one allowed to develop naturally.

There was, in Scotland, before the eighteenth century, a primitive pottery development parallel to that in

FIG. 1—*Competition from typical Scottish utensils made of material other than pottery—as the quaich, luggie, and cog, above—gave Scottish potters a slow start.*

the English country districts, but cruder in technique. Potters, working in isolated glens, threw their rough glazed pitchers and other household wares on the wheel, and marketed them in the immediate community.

Competition from rival materials—wood, horn, and leather—was more severe than in other parts of the British Isles. Many of the utensils which recur in various media other than pottery were peculiar to Scotland in shape and purpose. Fig. 1 shows some of the most common.

Industrial pottery, producing wares cheaply and in quantity, commenced in various centers in the second half of the eighteenth century when techniques—and many of the craftsmen—were imported from Staffordshire. Scottish potteries were never as successful, either commercially or artistically as their Staffordshire counterparts. Their products, never a true part of Scottish native life, failed to equal the invention and brilliance of the best Staffordshire.

As the population of Scotland was too small to absorb the whole production, export markets were fostered of necessity. The American colonies, and later the United States, were substantial buyers. For example, in 1791, shipments from Glasgow to Virginia and Carolina included 21,300 lbs. of coarse pottery and 45,330 lbs. of creamware. Figures on record for 1796 show marked increases for both types to 94,100 lbs. and 168,942 lbs. It is reasonable to suppose a fair proportion of this pottery has survived, though present owners may be unaware of its origin.

IN GLASGOW, the *Delftfield Pottery* achieved an important position as an exporter of a wide range of wares. Delft (tin-enamelled earthenware), brown-glazed Rockingham, black basalt, Queensware, and Derby

FIG. 3—*Jug made at Prestonpans ovars a copy of a Pratt subject and is painted in the Pratt underglaze palette of blue, ochre, brown, and green.*

porcelain were all copied. Being unmarked, the wares are extremely difficult to identify. As a general suggestion, when such wares are found and seem of less than average quality in potting and decoration, they may well be of Delftfield origin.

This pottery was built in 1748 by Laurence and Robert Dinwoodie, and continued working until 1810. In 1751, Robert was appointed Lieutenant-Governor of Virginia; from him young George Washington obtained his first surveyor's commission.

A Glasgow pottery with a considerable output of Staffordshire-type blue-printed ware was *Campbellfield* (Fig. 2). This was established in Hydepark Street, about 1837, by John McAdam. (McAdam, incidentally, was a friend of the Italian liberator, Garibaldi—another case of a Glasgow potter of international repute.) The pottery was enlarged and moved three times, first to Gallowgate; then, in 1850, to Campbellfield Street; and finally, about 1875 to Springburn. In its two early phases, the firm produced mainly brownware teapots and the like. Marks used were "C.P.Co.," "CAMPBELLFIELD," and finally "SPRINGBURN," with a thistle.

FIG. 2—*Willow ware porringer, Campbellfield, 1850.*

FIG. 4—*Pepper and salt Tobies, with printed motifs added to the usual free brush paintings, were made at both Prestopans potteries, 1830-1840.*

About the same time another pottery in Gallowgate was operated by *John Thomson,* who made transfer printed tewares. It is believed his main market was Australia. His marks were "J.T.& S.," or "J.T." over "ANNFIELD."

Between 1842 and 1881, two brothers, John and Matthew Preston Bell, operated the *Glasgow Pottery* at Port Dundas. Here, also, printed wares, including Willow pattern, were made with some success. Other patterns were the "Triumphal Car" and "Damascus," both being Scottish renderings of Eastern scenes. High quality unglazed porcelain, known as Parian, was produced for a few years, together with "Etruscan" ware, a red terra cotta, decorated with black printed pseudo-classical figures, Roman soldiers, and the like. The latter bears a strong resemblance to Wedgwood's Rosso Antico, and even more so to a series of classical vases made

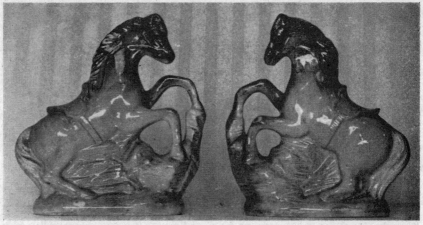

FIG. 7—*Creamware horses, grey speckled glaze, from West Lothian Pottery, Bo'ness.*

FIG. 5—*Figures attributed to Rathbone at Portobello. Similar figures were made at Sunderland.*

FIG. 6—*Plate, decorated with underglaze colors applied with quick sure brush strokes, from Bo'ness potteries, is marked only with an impressed *.*

by Dillwyn at Swansea in South Wales. The trade-mark was, of course, a bell, either impressed or printed, and sometimes in the later years, after Matthew's death in 1869, with the letters "J.B." or "B" added.

PRESTONPANS—To the collector weaned on the best Staffordshire, the most interesting and beautiful pottery from Scotland is that once made at Prestonpans, near Edinburgh. There were two potteries there in the eighteenth century, *Gordon's* and *Watson's.* In their early days they both made roofing tiles, domestic wares, and some porcelain, but it is the later under-glaze jugs and figures which are most prized today.

Until about 1830, Gordon's pottery made a series of jugs and other articles in the style of Felix Pratt (*Spinning Wheel,* August '57), full of life and color, but less carefully potted and decorated than Prattware (Fig. 3).

Watson was more inventive and produced many original figures, also with Pratt-type coloring. A large number of curious and definitely nonfunctional tobacco pipes were made, their stems resembling a plumber's nightmare in their twists, turns, and spirallings. This factory closed in 1840. In their later years, both potteries made blue-printed useful wares, and the pepper and salt tobies shown in Fig. 4.

Prestopans pots were mainly unmarked, except on the blue wares. Some of the marks are "WATSON & CO." enclosed in a rectangle, "WILLOW PATTERN" in a diamond, "SEMI/CHINA" in a diamond, "BIRD & FLY."

In the mid-nineteenth century, the town became famous for brownglazed teapots, produced by the firm of *Charles Bellfield & Sons,* who had started life by manufacturing stoneware drain pipes.

PORTOBELLO, another small town near Edinburgh, was a brickmaking center in the eighteenth century. It also supported two potteries, *Benjamin Walker's* and *Scott Bros.* Not much is known of Walker, except that he made pictorial tiles. Scott Bros. made good quality dinner and tea wares, and a small quantity of local redware, decorated in yellow slip, including animal and bird figures. Marks, when applied, were "SCOTT" over "P.B.," when impressed, "SCOTT BROS."

This pottery changed hands about 1796, Messrs. Cookson and Jardine taking over, and boasting that the business was to be run on Staffordshire lines. In 1808, Thomas Yoole took charge. Shortly after, Thomas Rathbone became a partner, having married one of Yoole's daughters. Under Rathbone's direction the company prospered, making first a series of very pleasant Scottish character figures and plaques, now rather rare, and later producing quantities of the large flat blacked figures, now usually mistaken for Staffordshire.

(Please turn the page)

FIG. 8—*Carpet bowls, frequently attributed to Staffordshire, are actually of Scottish origin. Those above were made in Bo'ness.*

Scottish Pottery
(continued)

In the writer's opinion, the Scottish potteries, including Glasgow, but Portobello in particular, were responsible for a good proportion of the mid-nineteenth century "Staffordshire" figures and spaniels. Certainly as one travels north in England, one finds a thicker distribution of these figures. The group shown in Fig. 5 is probably by Rathbone. The subject, the pale decoration, and the stylised hint of tartan are typical, and are pointers to its origin. These figures, and their Staffordshire counterparts, were very rarely marked, but some collectors assert that Rathbone's figures have the vent hole in the base pricked in the form of a rough X. This is not conclusive, but it is a useful guide. Impressed marks are sometimes seen: "T. RATHBONE" over "P," and "T.R. & Co." in a domed oval.

AT BO'NESS, on the river Forth, the potteries show much originality, liveliness, and color in their products. The principal manufacture was established there in 1784 by *Dr. John Roebuck.* The early creamwares and stonewares, although they have not been positively identified, were said to have been sent to Edinburgh market to be sold or bartered for rags!

The company changed hands many times, subsequent owners being, in turn, *McCowen, Alexander Cummings, James C. Cummings, Shaw & Sons, Jameson & Co., Redding Coal Co., John Marshall,* and *C. W. McNay.* It finally closed in 1889. Under McCowen some fine large punch bowls were made, while under Jameson the production of Staffordshire-type printed wares was a specialty. The "Bosphorous" pattern became a standby, and marked examples of dinner ware are fairly common in this pattern. In addition to the firm's name and pattern title, a small impressed * is sometimes found. This mark alone has been seen on wares decorated with underglaze colors applied with quick sure brush strokes (Fig. 6).

Another Bo'ness firm, the *West Lothian Pottery Co.,* managed by John McNay, also produced the type of colored ware as shown in Fig. 6, from about 1890. In addition they marketed a lovely range of animals and birds based on the older Bo'ness types. Spaniels and pug dogs are not uncommon in this ware. They are thinly potted, being hollow with a small round hole in the base (Fig. 7).

Carpet bowls (Fig. 8), thought by some to be of Staffordshire origin, are actually Scottish. These are solid balls, about 3 inches diameter, decorated in a variety of typical Bo'ness under-glaze colors and simple sponged and checked patterns. The game, a popular one in the border counties in the late nineteenth century, was played with six pairs and a "Jack," a plain white bowl. Bowling Clubs were formed to regulate the pastime.

Wedgwood's Stone China

by MARCIA RAY

STONE china was introduced by Josiah Spode II about 1805. It was a dense hard earthernware having china stone as an ingredient. Spode may have hoped his ware, decorated with Oriental motifs, would take the place of coarse Chinese export porcelain. But it was the ironstone china, supposed to contain pulverized slag of iron, patented in 1813 by Charles James Mason that took the public fancy and set up a popular demand for this cheap and durable ware. However, the two wares were essentially very much alike.

To compete with the popular Mason product, practically every potter in Staffordshire had soon perfected his own version of the ware, Wedgwood among them. Like everything the Wedgwood factory produced, their "Stone China" was of superior quality, and it is reasonable to surmise it was made in some quantity.

Examples of Mason's Patent Ironstone bearing his early mark, while not plentiful, are certainly not rare; a few pieces will be seen in almost any antiques show. Not so Wedgwood's Stone China. Even collectors who for years have studied intensively all aspects of Wedgwood production may never have seen a piece.

Even more surprising than the scarcity of Wedgwood's Stone China itself is the paucity of reference to it. Jewitt, in *The Wedgwoods,* wrote in 1865: "Stone China was also at one time, to some little extent, made at Etruria, examples of which are now rare. It ceased to be made about the year 1825. It was remarkably fine in body, and its decoration exceedingly good."

Mankowitz in his *Wedgwood,* 1953, says: "In 1820, stone china, a much denser and cruder body, came into manufacture, and this and the 'New Pearl Ware' displaced the finer, bone china production."

Definitive word comes from Tom Lyth, Curator of the Wedgwood Mu-

WEDGWOOD'S
STONE CHINA

seum, and Barlaston Archivist of The Wedgwood Society, who called attention to Stone China in *The Proceedings of The Wedgwood Society of London,* in 1957:

"The first experiments to make a Stone China were begun in 1819, and in the following year this type of pottery was in production in Etruria. It was termed Stone China to distinguish it from that which contained calcined bones as constituent, and has the appearance of being a much denser and non-translucent material. There is a great similarity between Stone China and porcelain produced in France.

"The composition of the body varied over the years, and as a result of study the expert is able to assess the date of manufacture with accuracy. The formula for this material in general consisted of: china stone, china clay, flint blue clay, and the addition of a stain.

"Stone China is not difficult to distinguish from other Wedgwood products. In the first instance, as previously mentioned, it is much denser and differs from Bone China because it is opaque, also it is of a greyish tone. . . . Additionally, in large type, printed in black, will be found the words WEDGWOOD'S STONE CHINA and the number of the pattern with which the piece is decorated; the numerals in almost every instance being in gold.

"The patterns used for decoration were limited in number, and these will be found always to be printed in outline with hand enameling in a variety of on-glaze colors and gilding.

"It would appear from the order sheets and other contemporary documents that for two years prior to 1861 there was a falling-off of orders. Production ceased in that year."

Mr. Lyth's information, gathered from various pottery memos and other sources in the archives of the Wedgwood Museum at Barlaston, indicates Wedgwood was making Stone China, though in limited quantity, almost up to the very year (1835) that Jewitt, who dated its cessation of manufacture as 1825, was calling it "now rare." How examples of a ware produced for sale over a span of forty-one years could almost totally disappear seems remarkable, yet Wedgwood's Stone China is as rare today in England as it is in this Country. Even the backstamp is omitted from reference books on Wedgwood marks. What has become of it all?

Back row, left to right: Longship Lighthouse, Land's End; St. Catherine's Tower, Isle of Wight; Blackpool Tower. Center row, left to right: Beachy Head Lighthouse; Norman Tower, Priory Church, Christchurch; the Look Out House, Newquay; Tenby Gate; Portland Lighthouse; Front row, left to right: Teignmouth and North Foreland Lighthouses.

The Goss China Factory   by J. R. GOFFIN

Back row, left to right: Large-sized Shakespeare, Manx, Hathaway and Robert Burns' cottages. Center row, left to right: First and Last Post Office; small-sized Shakespeare cottage; Wordsworth's birthplace, Cockermouth; small Ann Hathaway cottage; Old Maids' cottage at Lee; and Dr. Johnson's birthplace, Litchfield. Front row, left to right: Lloyd George's early home, Llanystymdwy; Ledbury Market House; and Thomas Hardy's birthplace in Dorset.

ANYBODY CONTEMPLATING entering the collecting field with only a modest capital might well consider becoming a Goss collector. As yet there is a comparatively small number of Goss enthusiasts; so prices, although rising, are still low.

When the expression "Goss china" is used, the majority of people immediately think of the small, delicate, ivory white, souvenir porcelain ornaments, decorated with a heraldic device, so popular in the British Isles during the early part of this century. Certainly it was this class of china which made the name of W. H. Goss famous, so much so that all makes of crested china—and Goss had many imitators—were erroneously referred to as "Goss china" by the general public. But there is far more to Goss than these heraldic pieces.

William Henry Goss, was born in London in 1833. As a young man he worked at the Spode china works at Stoke-on-Trent, Staffordshire, England, owned by the then Lord Mayor of London, W. T. Copeland; eventually he became chief artist and designer there.

In 1858, at the age of 25, he left Copeland's and after a few months in an unsuccessful partnership with a Mr. Peake—pieces marked "Goss & Peake" are extremely rare, the only known items being in terra-cotta—he opened his own small factory in Stoke-on-Trent. Here he produced such items as tobacco jars and milk jugs in terra-cotta, classical and other busts in Parian, and porcelain encrusted with jewels, often decorated with gold, generally referred to as "jewelled ware." The word "jewelled" is a little misleading as actually the jewels were made from enamels vitrified into imitations of precious stones.

By 1862, having just won a highly coveted award at the International Exhibition in London, he was well established. Parian and jewelled ware were manufactured in an ever-widening range of shapes and sizes from elaborate table centres to scent bottles, many items such as the jewelled ware being embellished with delicate pierced designs or with beautifully modelled flowers. Busts of contemporary British politicians and well-known personalities were popular subjects in Parian and well over 40 examples are known, many of them occurring in several different sizes. Some busts were made in both white and colored Parian as were a number of statuettes.

William Gallimore and Joseph Astley were Goss's principal modellers of these busts although Goss personally supervised many pieces. Sometimes one comes across items signed by him; in these cases he spells his name with the old-fashioned long "s." Costume jewelry, such as floral brooches and bracelets, made in plain white bisque or tinted in natural colors, also met with great success.

His egg-shell porcelain, which despite its seeming delicacy was as strong and firm as much thicker and clumsier ware, enhanced Goss's reputation still further. It is similar to Belleek; perhaps this is hardly surprising considering that the Irish factory persuaded several of Goss's best workmen, familiar with his techniques, to work for them in the formative years of their factory.

Heraldic Souvenirs

In the early 1880s, Adolphus William Henry Goss, the eldest son, joined his father in the business. Father and son shared a joint interest in heraldry and they decided to produce a range of china models of local antiquities from all over the country. Each piece was to bear the heraldic arms of the town where it was sold and the sale of such pieces was to be reserved for one agent only in each town. Adolphus travelled all around the British Isles, locating and sketching suitable antiquities and arranging with local authorities for the reproduction of their arms on the pieces chosen. It was a big enterprise but eventually hardly a town of any size did not have its sole agent selling Goss heraldic porcelain. This new type of ware had not been undertaken lightly on the part of the elder Goss. To switch much of the factory's output from highly artistic and fairly expensive wares to mass-produced low price articles represented a radical change of outlook and was a big gamble.

The venture paid off. Though the small heraldic models were mass-produced they were still made of the same superior ivory porcelain as the earlier Goss and decorated with the same high-grade enameling made from Goss's own secret recipes. Quantity production kept their price within reach of the ordinary public, and vacationers flocked to buy such attractive quality souvenirs. Happily, the introduction of these crested pieces coincided with the advent of the new cycling era; keen collectors pedalled from town to town to call on the local agents and buy each town's particular model.

At the turn of the century, Mr. J. J. Jarvis of Enfield, Middlesex, England, a Goss collector whom, it must be emphasized, had absolutely no connection with the firm of Goss whatsoever, produced a little duplicated booklet entitled *The Goss Record.* For some time collectors of Goss heraldic porcelain had been complaining about the difficulty, in sizable towns, of locating the only shop among a large number which had the sole right to sell Goss. The booklet rectified this by containing a list of all the authorized agents in the various towns throughout the country, together with the models

and arms they stocked and even their hours of opening. Within a week the little booklet was sold out; a second edition met with equal success.

Despite repeated requests, W. H. Goss had hitherto refused to associate himself with such a publication because of the tremendous amount of time and work necessary to keep it up to date. However, in view of the obvious public demand when he was again approached by Jarvis, he granted his permission to publish a properly printed edition on *The Goss Record.* This appeared in 1900 and nine different editions, plus supplements, of this invaluable handbook for Goss collectors were to appear, the last edition in 1921.

As *The Goss Record* attracted paid advertisements to its pages, it was financially able to improve its format, adding many more illustrations and a list of the various models made by Goss with details of their history. In the 5th edition (1905/6) there appeared the first mention of special Goss china display cabinets. Each of these bore a specially designed porcelain shield bearing the Goss arms. Prices ranged from 2 to 7 guineas and they could be bought by monthly installments. These cabinets ceased to be made after World War I.

The indefatigable Jarvis also started the League of Goss Collectors. This was originally formed for himself and a few friends but was eventually opened to all for a small yearly fee. By 1912 there were nearly a thousand members. The purpose of the League was to encourage the exchange of duplicate pieces among collectors, supply general information upon heraldry, and offer the opportunity to purchase special books at reduced prices. Eventually special models, bearing the arms of the League of Goss Collectors and sold only to them, became available. Four such models were issued and are greatly prized by present-day collectors.

By 1918 Goss had agents selling his china all over the world from Africa to the U. S. A.; the League was re-christened The International League of Goss Collectors, the coat of arms changed, and its membership fee doubled. As before, special models, of which there were fifteen, were issued to members only. Subsequently a few of these special models were released for general sale but *not* bearing the special League arms.

Mr. Jarvis, in the 8th edition of the *Record* noted that although there was an increase in the number of overseas agencies, that in Siam had been closed. It seems the King of Siam had seen the fine assortment of Goss china bearing the Siamese arms at the

Bangkok agent's and had bought the entire stock for himself. Not wishing to have any competition from other Siamese collectors, he then passed a law prohibiting any further imports of Goss china into the country.

Also of interest to Goss collectors are Goss postcards. These were advertised in the *Record* before the First World War. There are eight different cards, each depicting a different example of Goss heraldic ware but each of these eight pieces occurs bearing an unlimited variety of different coats of arms. The cards are in color and are numbered 1 to 8.

Parian Houses

In the 1890s, Parian models of houses, such as the cottages of Shakespeare and Ann Hathaway, had been produced in their natural colorings. They carried no crests and were exact replicas of the actual buildings. They were made in various sizes. The largest, having a hole in the back, were intended for use as nightlight burners. These houses were manufactured right up to 1929, many new models being added over the years until finally some 40 different types in various sizes, both glazed and unglazed, were available to collectors. They were a popular line throughout the 30 odd years of their production.

Of particular interest to American collectors are the models of Holden Chapel and Massachusetts Hall. Another is Sulgrave Manor of Northampton, England, where the Washington family lived and where the great-grandfather of George Washington was born.

Other models without a crest also made in natural colors of brown, grey, and white were crosses such as those of Sandbach, Iona, and St. Ives. The Iona Cross was W. H. Goss's favorite model and after his death in 1906, a full-sized replica was erected as the headstone for his grave. Models such as church fonts, gateways, and towers were made both as the usual white heraldic items and, far more attractively, in natural colors minus crests.

Not so common as the heraldic models but in my view much more interesting, are the ordinary models that bear a pictorial view in place of a crest. All types of models are to be found decorated in this manner; some of the views are multi-colored, others are in sepia, black, blue, or reddish-brown. Naturally they appear at their best on the larger pieces where the details are more easily discernible. These pieces were at the height of their popularity before 1914 but continued to be made in small numbers until 1929. Some delightful North American views are to be found.

Parian Rogers group "Courtship in Sleepy Hollow of Ichabod Crane and Katrina Van Tassel."

Parian Statuary

by CHESTER DAVIS

ALL POTTERY is a form of sculpture; but Parian statuary made of vitrified biscuit porcelain, has been the vehicle for great ceramic sculpture from its first development at Vincennes to its present use in the famous Limited Edition sculptures of Dorothy Doughty and Edward Boehm. While the average collector cannot afford to own a $15,000 pair of Doughty's decorated Parian birds or a $4500 Boehm Parian sculpture, very desirable pieces of Parian statuary are still available in the antiques field at reasonable prices.

Figure modelling in unglazed biscuit porcelain was first developed at Vincennes, France, about 1749, to compete with the white marble statuary then popular among the French nobility; but few pieces were made until the factory moved to Sevres in 1756. Production at Sevres was limited until after 1766, when the difficulties encountered in making and firing such intricate figures were overcome.

The Sevres figures came to the notice of William Duesbury of the English Chelsea-Derby factory, and he began the making of white biscuit figures about 1770. These early biscuit figures proved more expensive

Parian group of children sporting with goats, by Minton; ca. 1851.

Pair of gilt Parian statuette-candlesticks with stands in decorated porcelain, by Minton; ca. 1851.

"Reubens" in Minton parian; ca. 1850. 15" high.

"Michaelangelo" in Minton parian; ca. 1850. 14¾" high.

"St. Francis" in parian by Boehm.

than decorated pieces because only absolutely perfect figures could be sold. Flawed or speckled figures, of which there were many in those days of primitive kiln-firing conditions, were glazed, enamelled, and refired to sell at lower prices. Because of modern high labor costs, a color-decorated piece now always sells for more than white biscuit; but the collector should realize that very early Parian items have always been rarer and higher-priced than the colored versions.

Both Sevres and Derby made many fine biscuit porcelain pieces. One of the rarest Sevres groups known is Louis XVI Welcoming Ambassador Benjamin Franklin to the French Court; only six examples are known, all damaged. Other European factories made biscuit procelain figures, but production of such items gradually declined after 1810

What we now call Parian statuary was first introduced in 1842 by Copeland and Garrett (Spode) as "statue porcelain." Minton brought out its first biscuit porcelain in 1844, calling their production "Parian statuary," after the well-known statuary marble from the island of Paros. Later, Wedgwood issued a version called "Carrara porcelain." At the 1851 Crystal Palace Exposition, it was of-

ficially decided that all were modern versions of the white bisque made at Sevres and Derby.

In making Parian statuary, the original model is copied in wax or similar material; and the wax model then cut into sections from which the molds are made. Care is taken to see that the parts come from their molds with only slight seam marks (made where the molds join). Quality statuary has had the seam marks "wet-sponged" off before joining; any Parian sculpture with pronounced seam marks is not a high-grade production.

A figure might need from 5 to 35 or more molds, each making a separate part. The mold-made parts, after removal of seam marks, are allowed to dry "leather hard" and then assembled by a figure-maker, called a "repairer," into an exact copy of the original, using as an adhesive a slip (clay suspension) of the same composition. Any part of the figure liable to warp or sag during the firing is supported by a series of props made from the same clay and undergoing the same shrinkage in the kiln.

All clay-made objects contract and shrink during drying and firing; usually a 12-inch figure in the original becomes a 9-inch figure after contraction in the mold and in the firing.

After 1844 the invention of a sculpture reduction device by Benjamin Cheverton made the copying in reduced form of any original sculpture very easy; the result was a reproduction in Parian statuary of almost every well-known Victorian sculpture.

Parian statuary was most popular from 1850 to about 1880. Not only were Parian figures made but also Parian vases, pitchers, dishes (more for use as decorative wall plaques rather than for table purposes), and paperweights. In fact, almost every item made in glaze-decorated china was also made in Parian. Oddly enough, the female nude figure, such as the Venus di Milo and the Greek Slave, was extremely popular in Victorian times. The pottery at Bennington in the United States made many Parian items, most of which are still available at reasonable prices. These are usually unmarked, but most are pictured in Richard Carter Barret's *Bennington Pottery and Porcelain.*

Probably the rarest and most desirable American Victorian Parian sculptures are the Parian John Rogers groups. These remarkably well-done examples of Americana appear to have been made in England by Copeland (Spode). Two small figures by Rogers, "The Fisher Girl" and "Air Castles," were made by Copeland in

"Western Bluebirds with Wild Yellow Azaleas." Colored parian by Boehm. Limited edition, priced at $4500.

icana should look for unusual subjects and workmanship and not strive too diligently for factory-marked examples.

The more expensive Sevres bisquit porcelain figures have been copied in recent years, but as yet no copies of the Victorian Parian sculptures have appeared.

Parian "Madonna" by Boehm. 9" high.

1860. After the Civil War, beginning in 1866, three large Rogers groups, "One More Shot," "Taking the Oath," and "Courtship in Sleepy Hollow" were made by Copeland. Due to the usual clay shrinkage in drying and firing, they differ from the plaster groups in size; for example, the plaster "One More Shot" is 23½ inches high, whereas the Parian figure is 20 inches high. Later, an unknown number of other Rogers groups were reproduced in Parian by European factories. None bear a manufacturer's mark; but all of the Rogers Parian groups are signed "John Rogers, New York." All of the American porcelain manufacturers—Union Porcelain Co., Ott & Brewer, Lenox, and others—made many fine busts, figures, vases, and pitchers in Parian, many of which are unsigned.

The fad for Parian statuary never died out completely. The colored German bisque figures, sold in gift shops from 1900 to World War II, were popular and are now being collected as comic by-gones. The first revival of "art Parian" came during the Depression when Royal Worcester brought out a series of bird models by Dorothy Doughty. These intricate models were so expensive to join and color that any kiln losses suffered during a second glaze firing (when the glaze may flow or glob up) would have rendered the entire enterprise impractical.

It was decided to use mineral stains on a biscuit body; all of the colored Doughty birds are really colored Parian. The success of Worcester's Doughty bird models after World War II prompted the American sculptor, Edward M. Boehm, to manufacture similar intricate models; Boehm, also, adopted the use of a colored Parian body.

The commercial success of the Doughty and Boehm figures has lead to a marked revival of Parian statuary on a worldwide scale, and some new models rapidly go over $1800 for undecorated white bisque figures. While older Parian sculptures have increased in price in recent years, many fine examples of Spode, Minton, Wedgwood, Bennington, and other firms are still available at prices within the reach of the average purse.

As all Parian statuary is a substitute for fine sculpture in marble, bronze, or other media, it must be judged by the standards which prevail in other forms of sculpture. The Parian collector should look for quality of workmanship, fineness of detail, absence of seam marks, and overall attractiveness of the subject. Artist-signed pieces are desirable. The famous American sculptor Daniel Chester French, as a young man, designed several typical Victorian animal and child figures for Parian reproduction; these are signed "D.C. French" and bear a British registry mark. The Parian collector of Amer-

Hiram Powers' "Greek Slave" copied in parian by the Trenton Pottery Co., ca. 1869.

Mrs. Bartlett's favorite: elegant 17" square tray, beautifully detailed edges, 1850 or earlier; teapot, sugar, creamer and tea caddy, also Meissen, are of slightly later date. Tiny crossed swords at foot of tree in design show clearly on the tray.

Comparison of honest copy, plainly marked Villeroy and Boch (left), ca. 1841, and genuine Meissen Onion pattern. Bottom leaf of V & B design is slightly larger and darker; borders are darker; the whole heavier and rougher in texture.

Old or New?

Genuine or Imitation?

BLUE ONION PORCELAIN

By HELEN L. GILLUM

EVEN EXPERTS will allow there are no hard and fast rules to follow in distinguishing between Royal Meissen Onion pattern porcelain and its contemporary imitations made in other European countries. Nor is it always easy to spot pieces of more recent manufacture — M e i s s e n or otherwise — from some of the early Meissen examples.

Mrs. R. Stanley Bartlett of Long Beach, California, who has collected and studied Onion Pattern for many years, points out that the average f a n c i e r, with perseverence and thought, can develop a certain awareness and knowledgeability that will aid him greatly in determining the age and factory-make.

Her own collection of old Royal

Blue Onion pattern kitchen gadgets: left to right: sugar scoop, mixing spoon, soup ladle, large and small meat tenderizers, muddler or potato masher, tea strainer, funnel, colander, juice funnel, with holes to catch seeds, egg whip. All are Meissen.

Meissen Onion is representative of the many items made, and includes everything from a complete dinner set for twelve to Onion-handled fruit knives and forks, serving spoons, boudoir items, knicknacks, and a host of kitchen utensils.

Each piece of dinnerware bears the crossed swords mark of the Royal Meissen factory, and tiny crossed swords are found at the foot of the tree in the design. Her kitchen utensils are unmarked. Since much of the earliest Meissen was not marked, and because kitchen articles were among the first pieces made in Blue Onion pattern, absence of marks may actually be an indication of authenticity.

The Onion design was introduced at Meissen by Johann Horoldt (or Herold), who "borrowed" it from an earlier Oriental motif incorporating the Tree of Life, the pomegranate, the chrysanthemum, and a stylized peach, which could have been mistaken for an onion.

Though experiments in underglaze blue were begun about 1720, and some pieces completed, Savage, in *18th Century German Porcelain,* says it was not until 1725-30 that this glaze became practical, and that the so-called Onion pattern became popular after 1732. Mickenhagen, in *European Porcelain,* sets the date at 1740 before the underglaze blue was improved enough for its production.

Originally intended for humble kitchen use, the pattern became so well loved it was soon gracing fine dinner tables, and has remained in popular favor ever since.

Inevitably, as with most products of merit and beauty, it was copied by other European factories, and is even today being produced in limited quantities. Some of these old wares were out-and-out forgeries, right down to the crosed swords. Other factories made no secret of their reproductions, using their own marks. The Royal Copenhagen factory, for one, copied it freely, calling it the "Copenhagen" design.

Thus, although not all Onion pattern is actually the coveted, genuine Royal Meissen, or *Meissener Zwielbelmuster,* it is possible to own good Blue Onion pattern *antique* china made by other companies.

Factory marks do not always guarantee absolute authenticity, but they do furnish a starting point in the entrancing business of identification. The crossed swords of Meissen, taken from the Electoral arms of Saxony, and adopted as the official Meissen mark in 1724, underwent many variations through the years. On many of the early wares the mark was drawn or scratched on the bottom of the piece before firing and naturally differed with each handwriting or drawing. Dissimililarities in design and size are also typical of specific periods of the factory, giving clues to dates. Several, but not all, are presented here.

A good book on marks, such as

133 Ceramics

Margaret Macdonald-Taylor's recent *Dictionary of Marks,* is almost a "must" for anyone interested in Meissen. In such books, the original crosed swords mark, with its various alterations is given, along with similar, yet misleading marks used by other European factories. *German and Austrian Porcelain,* by George W. Ware, is another fine reference volume, and Cushion's recent *Pocket Book of German Ceramic Marks* is excellent.

Occasionally a piece of "tri-color" Onion is found—a red and gold or other color decoration over the glaze; this is not so avidly sought by collectors as the blue and white. There is also a diversity in the first Onion pattern design created at the Meissen factory. Slight deviations in decoration do not necessarily indicate the porcelain was not made there.

Mrs. Bartlett suggests that a dealer who handles considerable Meissen can point out to you the differences in pattern on authentic Meissen. Curators of ceramics in museums are usually willing to discuss these wares in a friendly, unbiased manner, too. If you plan on buying Blue Onion, shop near home, so that you can examine the pieces closely and at your leisure. Learn to be critically observant, and insist upon a good light when inspecting an item.

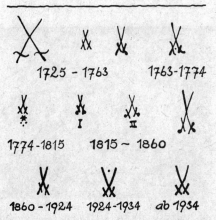

1725 - 1763   1763-1774

1774-1815   1815 ~ 1860

1860 - 1924   1924-1934   ab 1934

Pertinent Meissen marks as given in European Porcelain, by Dr. Richard Mickenhagen.

Determining the *age* of a Meissen sample presents another challenge. One authority says she can tell an old piece of Meissen Onion by the "feel"— the texture of the porcelain, the weight, glaze, and color tones. Such recognition comes only from the intelligent handling of many pieces, yet there are guidelines.

Much of the very early Meissen has a slight greenish tint when it is held to the light. This had disappeared by 1750, when the body became white and almost perfect. Translucent spots of various shapes and sizes, called "moons," noticeable when held to the light, are frequent characteristics of this early Meissen, as is an irregular texture. Old pieces most frequently found today are from the 19th century, though earlier items do come to light and should be r e c o g n i z e d. Cracks, crazing, stains, chips, and roughened edges could all be signs of age. Sometimes a bisque-like ridged surface is found on the bottom of rare pieces, another indication of age.

A single cut, or strike, across the swords mark was used on china sold in the white, to be colored in some outside atelier; it was also used, about 1760, on imperfect specimens. When two, three, or even four strikes occur, it means the piece did not come up to the high Meissen standards. Items with such multiple strikes were probably made after 1800, when Meissen began a system of grading its products.

While concentrated research such as this may not be entirely conclusive in every case, it does help to develop a better understanding of marks and wares. This, in time, results in keener perception and accuracy in judging, and the development of that "sixth sense," which is particularly necessary in identifying Meissen Onion pattern porcelain.

Royal Bayreuth Look-alikes

by DICK COLE

**134
Ceramics**

Pieces pictured are from the author's collection. Photographs by G. Vaughn.

Hanging wall pocket, 9" tall, is blue-marked Royal Bayreuth; the transfer of the Jester is signed "Noke"; words on front are "Penney in Pocket is a Merry Companion." The 10¼" plate is marked "Royal Doulton Dickens Ware/The Artful Dodger." Transfer decoration is also signed "Noke," as is the rest of the complete dinner service of which this plate is a part. (Noke was head designer for Royal Doulton from 1920 to 1936 and Art Director from 1936 to 1954.)

Covered chocolate or teapot, 9" high, is blue-marked Royal Bayreuth. The plate, 8½", is marked "J. & C., Louise, Bavaria." Grapes on the transfer on the plate are signed A. Koch. (Note similarity of grapes and style of painting on the Royal Bayreuth pot.)

WAS ROYAL Bayreuth the imitated or the imitator? To date, research has supplied no answer to this tantalizing question, much less proof. But copy or adapt, someone surely did. Similarities between almost every design and decoration used at the Royal Bayreuth manufactory and wares from other establishments, some quite illustrious, did appear, as the illustrations here will show.

Luckily for collectors, Royal Bayreuth seems always to have marked their pieces; other important potteries, proud of their work, usually marked theirs; maybe it was only the definitely copying companies who left their wares unmarked—purposely.

Perhaps the most confusing of the look-alikes, that is, the pieces whose marks you must examine before you're sure, are Royal Bayreuth's "Corinthian Ware" and Frank Beardmore's "Athenian" and "Basaltine" wares. Royal Bayreuth's "Hand Painted Old Ivory" is easily confused with that produced

Scenic Tapestry creamer, left, 4" high, decorated with goats, and the 5½" vase, right, decorated with cows, are both blue-marked Royal Bayreuth. Tapestry vase, center, 4½" high, is marked with a green shield with "G" and "H" in the center, large fancy "S" underneath (Gebruder Heubach), and "Made in Germany" in a small circle. Workmanship and quality is equal to Royal Bayreuth pieces; the figures have fine detail. The one difference is in the finish of the bottom. It has a flat semi-finished bottom while the Royal Bayreuth pieces have a slight rim and indentation on glazed bottoms.

Four pieces with the same transfer, long necked vase, cobalt blue background, has the Royal Vienna Beehive mark. The others, in varying shades of brown, are all blue-marked Royal Bayreuth pieces. The full transfer is used on the piece on the left, while only the upper part of the transfer is used on the other pieces. This same partial and complete use of transfers appears on other Royal Bayreuth pieces with other transfers.

by other makers of Old Ivory; some of their dinner services are much like other Bavarian sets, and some of their bowls cannot be distinguished from R. S. Prussia. Their Belleek types, the Flown Blues, and Noke decorated pieces may also require a look at the backstamp.

A type of Royal Bayreuth not mentioned by Virginia Salley in her book, *Royal Bayreuth China,* has a mat finished band encrusted with enamel dots forming a design around the edge of a plate or the rim of a vase. The center or lower section of these pieces is usually decorated with a typical scene or with sterling silver roses similar to those on Tapestry. The enamel dots suggest the technique so widely used on Nippon China. Mrs. Chiolino, in her article on Nippon in SW, March '70, remarks that Nippon did make wares resembling Royal Bayreuth. This may have been one of them; the figural pieces definitely were.

As a long-time collector and re-

Plate, right, 8¼", with heavy gold rim and transfer of Martha Washington is gold-marked Royal Bayreuth. Cup and saucer, center, with the transfer of George Washington and rose decorations is green-marked Royal Bayreuth. Plate, left, 9¾" with the same transfer of Martha Washington and gold and green decoration, is marked "K. T. & K. (Knowles, Taylor and Knowles, East Liverpool, Ohio) 8—V, CHINA, 3510." The Royal Bayreuth pieces are of high quality bone china; the Knowles plate is a heavy ironstone type, but the transfers of Martha are identical.

searcher of Royal Bayreuth, I would generalize that the figural-type pieces —people, animals, birds, reptiles, flowers, fish, fruit, vegetables, and the like, so often found in pitcher form— were original with Royal Bayreuth. I also understand that the Sunbonnet Babies decorated pieces were commissioned solely to them by a New York importer.

It is questionable whether their other types of wares—Old Ivory, Tapestry, and Corinthian—originated with them, though it is not beyond possibility. Their vases, dinnerwares, and bowls followed the styles of the time. Can it matter much who was "first," when all Royal Bayreuth wares were so beautifully done and of such distinguished quality? It is well, though, particularly for new collectors, to be aware of look-alikes.

Black stirrup cup, left, 3¾" tall, and the 4" black creamer, right, are decorated with white figures and white and gold Greek Key trim; both are blue-marked Royal Bayreuth "Corinthian Ware." Black stirrup cup, center, decorated with white figures and white and gold Greek Key trim, is marked Frank Beardmore & Co., Fenton, "Athenian Art Ware." (Royal Bayreuth made similar pieces in Corinthian Ware in black with colored figures and acanthus leaf trim, while Frank Beardmore & Co. made black pieces with colored figures and trim marked "Basaltine Ware.")

by JOAN SPRINGER PAPA

During the insular days of the West, prior to the establishment of regular trade routes to the East, porcelain was believed to be magical. Jewelers and silversmiths of the West mistook it for a rare kind of glass or gem stone.

In 1498 Vasco da Gama and his sea route around the Cape of Good Hope finally brought to the West a plentiful supply of this ware, and by the 17th century export trade in both Chinese and Japanese porcelains was flourishing.

The 1600s were the era of the Dutch East India Company. In 1609 the Dutch, by the efforts of one Will Adams, a shipwrecked English pilot of a Dutch ship who became the trusted adviser of the Shogun Iyeyasu, established a factory or agency for their company at Hirado. When the Japanese closed their doors to the outside world in 1638, the crafty Dutch set up residence on the nearby island of Nagasaki. From this base they and various smugglers of Siam, Sumatra, Java, India, and other countries sneaked regularly into the port of Imari to purchase gaudily colored china and other trade items.

It is reputed Japan's porcelain industry began with one Gorodayu Shonsui of Ise who returned to Japan from China in 1513 after five years of study at Ching-te-chen to establish in Hizen province a pottery. The clay for Shonsui's and other factories probably came from the mountain Izumiyama where kaolin and petuntse, premixed by nature, is found. This substance, difficult to handle as it wilted in the kiln, necessitated a light firing first, then successively higher ones.

The experts are divided on the origins of Imari painting techniques. One source asserts that in the second year of Sho-ho, about 1645, Higashi-shima Tokuzayemon learned from a Chinaman visiting Nagasaki how to paint with vitreous colors on glaze. With the assistance of another potter, Gosu Gombei, he succeeded in the use of the process.

Another source, however, although agreeing on the date (1640–1646) attributes the technique of polychrome enameling on the glaze to the potters of the Sakaida family who worked in Japan for twelve generations, beginning with the man nicknamed Kakiemon (1596–1666). This name later adhered to his descendants and the wares they produced. (Kakiemon designs differ from Imari in that they are more sparingly executed in more refined colors, omitting the huge amounts of Indian red and blue and the brocading or paneling common in Imari.)

At any rate, this underglaze and overglaze painting of Imari designs on porcelain of a very hard paste with a bluish tinge occurred in a dull underglaze blue with a muddy and/or greenish tone, a dark underglaze brown which developed first into a rusty red then a fiery crimson, and an overglaze green enamel.

The Imari designs were often set in panels. These panels were sometimes filled with the foliage and flowers of the peony and the chrysanthemum in the prevailing colors of deep blue, Indian red, and gold. Other flowers favored were the wisteria, iris, lily, hydrangea, carnation, convolvulus, and water lily. Flowers were painted in bud, full bloom, and decay.

Figure subjects, flying cranes (the emblem of longevity), the phoenix (somewhat parallel to the Chinese dragon in representing imperial dignity), and Kirin (a monster with the body and hoofs of a deer, the tail of a bull, and having a horn on its forehead) appear occasionally as motifs. Rarely, a curious lion and a sacred tortoise were employed. More commonly, fishes of the bream and carp variety were shown leaping a cascade. Quaint horses, buffaloes, oxen, dogs, and stags also appear at times. Rarest of all designs is the landscape.

One common decoration was the Ho Ho or Howo bird with its rich plumage and long tail feathers. Legend is that the Ho Ho dwells in the higher regions of the air, out of sight or knowledge of man, and descends to earth only at the birth of some great personage, like a philosopher, law-giver, or warrior. Sometimes the streaming tail is depicted as scrollwork. When two birds appear on one piece, the tails usually differ.

Trees such as the plum, fir, and palm were frequently drawn waving in the summer breeze, bending in autumn's stripping blasts, or silent with barren branches.

Unlike the Chinese potters who exported their crude wares and kept their fine china for home use, the Japanese exported the best examples of their work. The huge Imari vases, plates, and dishes found in European palaces were made especially for export and by the 18th century every good English country house contained some examples of brocaded Imari.

With growing Japanese success in Imari, the Chinese began copying this design in the early part of the 18th century. The principal differences between Chinese and Japanese Imari are:

1—The spur marks of supports used in firing are common on Japanese pieces but rare on Chinese examples.

2—Chinese porcelain is thin and dense and has a greenish tinge. Japanese wares are coarse and sandy with

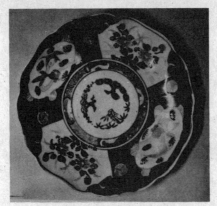

a greyish tint.

3—Chinese iron red is thin and coral colored; Japanese red is opaque, thick, dull, and Indian red.

4—Japanese yellow is greyish and lighter than the impure Ming yellows of China.

5—Japanese green is bluish compared to K'ang Hsi green.

6—Chinese black is greenish; Japanese black is brownish.

Imari was also copied all over Europe by Coalport, Derby, Bow, Chelsea, Worcester, Davenport, Mason, Delft, Meissen, Chantilly, and Spode, to name but a few. During the 17th and 18th centuries, imitation was considered a matching of skills; virtue lay in duplicating or bettering a competitor's wares.

As with other China trade items such as Canton, the demand for Imari dwindled around the second quarter of the 19th century. But about 1880 there was an upsurge of popularity of Imari and huge quantities were again imported. These later wares were made at Hizen and shipped from Nagasaki and were coarsely painted with unrefined colors. Although the early specimens of Imari found in America were most likely brought from Europe and handed down as heirlooms, these later wares were imported directly and at the time were preferred to the earlier more finely executed wares.

The older examples of Imari are rarely marked unless with a leaf painted blue, and this infrequently. More recent pieces bear numerous and unreliable marks such as Chinese date characters, or characters representing a specific potter or place of manufacture.

Indeed, to this very day the Royal Crown Derby Company has been producing copies of Imari, still referred to as "old Japan," and the market is flooded with "day old" examples. Perhaps because of its gaiety, Imari has enjoyed such enduring popularity. At any rate, a few pieces—old or new—are bound to brighten your corner.

Across the top of the page and down, from left to right:

A blue tinged late 19th century specimen, this small 4" dish has a finely executed and gilded Ho-Ho flying in its center. It is of Japanese manufacture.

The life of the silkworm is painted in the panels of this 5¾" finely executed example. The eggs, the worm, and finally the butterfly appear in various shades of orange-red. It is a late 19th century transfer-printed piece.

The familiar vase-with-flowers pattern was imitated widely by both the Chinese and the Europeans after 1700. This 7" bowl is suspect of being English as such crude painting was never done by the Japanese. Ca. 1900.

A typical 8½" plate depicting the three friends—the pine, the plum, and the bamboo in summer foliage. Two of the panels contain fish, the emblem of wealth and abundance in China. Japanese, ca. 1900.

This garden scene is bordered by chrysanthemums and the legendary Ho-Ho. The basket, artistically placed on a table beneath a weeping cherry tree, is filled with pomegranates. Size: 9¼" x 7½". Japanese, ca. 1900.

A large 11" plate featuring chrysanthemums—the Chinese symbol of autumn and emblem of fidelity and courage. Stalks of peonies alternate with a fenced garden on the rim. Fences appear frequently on Imari. Japanese, mid- to late 19th century.

An 8½" Imari porcelain plate bearing the typical double blue lines encircling the central motif. Again we see the pomegranates and mums. This is the only marked piece in these illustrations. Late 19th century.

This 10" vase displays in its quasi-ju-i head or irregular heart-shaped central motif a streaming tailed Ho-Ho. The ju-i head is a Chinese symbol of long life and good fortune, however this vase was possibly made in England early in the 20th century.

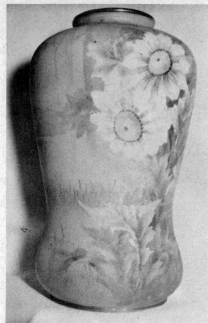

Large spectacular vase, simulating Royal Bayreuth Tapestry; Nippon blue leaf mark.

Jam jar and matching saucer in delicate blues, yellows, with deep green leaves, gold trim, could pass for hand painted Limoges china; crown mark.

Compote, photographed to show top only, is of blue jasper, simulating Wedgwood; green "M" mark.

The Diversity of Nippon China

by BARBARA B. CHIOLINO

NIPPON IS the Japanese pronunciation of the Chinese name for Japan, meaning "sun origin." Prior to World War I, the Japanese preferred that their country be called Nippon, and this was the name used on Japanese china exported to the United States from 1891, when the country of origin was required to appear on chinawares, until well into the 1900s.

Toward the end of the 17th century old Japanese wares, such as Kakiemon, Kutani, Imari, and Arita, had been introduced into wealthy Western houses through the Dutch East India Company and Chinese merchants. Once the West discovered the secret of porcelain manufacture and manufactory was established in Europe, the early patterns evolved by Japanese potters were copied at the Meissen, Chantilly, Chelsea, and Worcester potteries, and at many lesser manufactories.

Then for a space of two hundred years and more, Japan's doors were shut to international commerce. Not until trade was resumed about 1859 were Japanese chinawares seen on the Western market. The bulk of Japanese chinawares available today date from the resumption of trade and, being made especially for export, copied Western ideas. From the 1890s through the 1900s was an excessively prolific period, with Nippon producing chinawares resembling Limoges, Royal Bayreuth, Royal Worcester, Wedgwood and Spode.

There is good reason to study this late production and to appreciate its quality while there is still a quantity to be found in shops. In the past, Nippon of fine craftsmanship could

Fancy vase with plushy Victorian roses; "Royal Nippon" with "Kinran" mark.

Napkin ring with Christmas motif of holly berries and leaves on satiny bisque-like china; marked with dogwood-blossom with oriental character in center. Hatpin holder has the Royal Satsuma mark; colors are typical of this ware; Cruet, with sunset scene, shades from yellow to deep peach, satiny finish; green "M" mark.

Octagonal chocolate set, pot with 6 cups and saucers; cobalt blue border is embellished with raised gold trim; blue leaf mark.

Heart-shaped box painted in delicate lavender with early airplane as decor; green "M" mark. White pitcher with brilliant blue butterfly, rising sun mark. Bowl with shamrock decoration; red "M" mark.

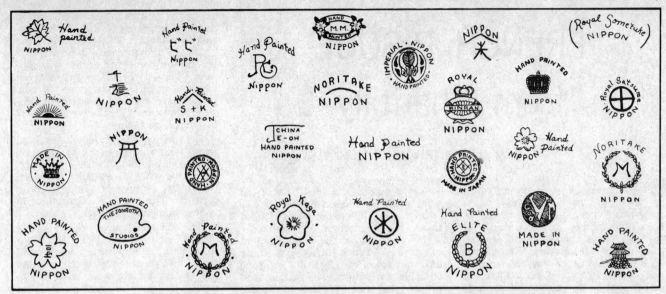

Above: Various marks found on Nippon china. Sketches by Mary Lou Robinson.

Octagonal cracker jar, in yellows, rust, and gold. Green "M" mark.

Mantel vase, one of a pair, in Japanese style; "Hand painted, Nippon" mark.

Sugar and creamer in fine translucent china, encrusted with gold and embellished with raised "turquoise-like jewels"; blue leaf Nippon mark. Heart-shaped dish, also heavily encrusted with gold, bears the green leaf mark. Knife rest, unusual in china, is marked with the green "M."

be bought cheaply; now, prices are on the rise.

Part of the beauty of Nippon is in the quality of the porcelain and the shapes produced, and part in the varied and artistic decoration. Aside from sets of dishes, such as those labelled Noritake or Sometuke, few pieces are just alike, although now and then we see some which appear to have been executed by the same hand, and the collector will be sure to find wares bearing the same mark.

About a year ago, a retired schoolteacher, Mrs. Dorotha Robinson, looking for something available and reasonable in price to collect, settled on Nippon. It was a good choice, she feels, for in a short time (she bought her first Nippon piece August 3, 1968) she has built a collection of several hundred pieces, chosen carefully for quality, beauty, and diversity. As she watches prices soar, she feels her investment is proving wise. The pieces pictured here are from her collection,

and the various marks were drawn by her daughter.

Chaffers' *Book of Marks* says that the great diversity of Japanese pottery is confusing; since Japan was a nation of potters, many of the wares were made and decorated by various family units in small home factories. We find no books in English on Nippon porcelain, but we can study the wares, enjoy the artistry, and catalog the marks. Perhaps some later researcher will interpret them for us.

After dinner coffee set, all-over bright blue, decorated with pink cherry blossoms, white swans; green "M" mark.

Colorful cider or punch set, decorated with fanciful strawberries and blossoms; marked "E-OH."

Two pieces of a 3-part desk set; humidor; and stein—all in masculine colors and style, with dull satin finish; green "M" mark.

FRENCH BISQUE
from Chantilly

by HELEN L. GILLUM

THE making of porcelain in France goes back at least to 1664, when an effort was made to establish a soft-paste factory in Paris. Artificial porcelain of a kind was also created successfully at Rouen, St. Cloud, Chantilly, and other French factories in the late 1600s and early 1700s, in an attempt to simulate the true hard-paste Oriental china.

These early French wares were exceptionally well done, and beautifully decorated. Limoges, Sevres, Vincennes, Mennecy, and Paris were among the names that would shine brightly in the story of French porcelain. It was during this period that the creation of the wonderful French biscuit ware (bisque, or unglazed porcelain), for which France was equally famous, was also developed to a fine art, in imitation of marble statuary.

One of the most important French porcelain factories was founded at Chantilly in 1725, under the aegis of the Prince de Conde, an avid collector of the colorful true porcelain from Arita, Japan. For a short period of about ten years this manufactory produced, in the opinion of many authorities, some of the most outstanding bisque figures ever made.

It closed its doors in 1800; few of the original pieces remain today.

In the late Victorian era, a great upheaval of interest in the older styles resulted in the establishment of various French firms. Especially did the town of Chantilly produce enviable earthenware, porcelain, and bisque, this time of the hard-paste type. Much of the bisque was based on original models, with some modification to suit the taste of the nineteenth century connoisseurs. Though this late Chantilly bisque often takes on a rather "pretty" style, there are other examples which closely express the spirit of eighteenth century work.

Three beautiful hard-paste bisque statuettes, shown here, are nice examples of this latter type. They are incised "Chantilly" and date to about 1880. They belong to Mrs. E. W. Lyne of Long Beach, California. While not line-for-line copies of eighteenth century Chantilly products, the workmanship is comparable to the finest of the older wares. They have the smooth, softly glowing texture characteristic of old French bisque, while emulating the charm and refinement of the eighteenth century products.

The larger, central figure portrays

a pair of young lovers engrossed in the familiar game of "She loves me—she loves me not." Torn blossoms and petals in the maiden's lap, and the beseeching demeanor of the worshipping swain as he offers her a fresh bloom, suggests that none of the petals have been plucked in the desired sequence. "Please try this one," he might be saying.

The softly-draped costumes and facial expressions of this porcelain tableau are molded with sensitivity. Even the tiny fingernails and torn petals are delicately, yet naturally formed. This central figure is 13 inches high and 14 inches wide.

Boy and girl figures on either side are 17 inches high. Here again infinite detail is manifest. The graceful form and bounteous skirts of the pretty lass impart a sense of movement and rhythm, as does the dramatic pose of the lad in flaring blue cape and gaily-flowered knee breeches, with beret perched jauntily on his flowing brown curls.

Soft pastels in blue, pink, green, and lavender are harmoniously used in the decorative patterns. Dainty flower sprigs, perfectly-molded roses, garlands, bows, ribbons, laces and ruchings enhance the Old World charm of the statuettes.

Although late nineteenth century bisque followed closely after the patterns of the older ones, later artists added a few modifications and colors of their own. These included slight variations in shape, and new shades, such as pinks and purples.

Many — but not all — of the older figures bear the original mark of the hunting horn in red or blue. These are exceedingly rare and valuable today. Most of the later pieces were incised simply "Chantilly." While infrequently the genuine early Chantilly products were not marked at all, Chantilly ware, because of its great beauty and workmanship was often copied, including the mark, by other European factories. So even the marks are not entirely conclusive. It might be added that early Chantilly designs were, in themselves, copies of many Oriental pieces. But because of the high quality of both the bisque and the glazed porcelain, they, in turn, were copied, Chantilly mark and all.

Photo by Joe Risinger

CHANTILLY MARKS

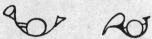

Early Chantilly, 1725-1800, a "hunting horn" in red or blue.

CHANTILLY

Late Chantilly, 1880-1900, the mark incised on the bisque figures shown. No horn appears.

COLLECTOR PLATES

Until a few years ago, Christmas plates by Bing & Grondohl and Royal Copenhagen were practically the only collector plates on the market. Now there are so many to choose from that collectors are somewhat confused about which ones will be the most desireable to invest in. Collector plates range in price from just a few dollars to several hundred dollars each. They can be had in ceramics, glass, silver, and enamel on copper. Some have been designed by famous artists—Salvador Dali, Norman Rockwell and Richard Evans Younger, to name a few. Many collector plates are limited editions, a fact that will certainly effect their value in the years to come.

Martha Washington plate.

Grant "Flower Set" plate.

Mary Todd Lincoln plate.

HAVILAND

REISSUES

OF PRESIDENTIAL CHINA

by LOIS and CLINT HERRING

OVER THE YEARS, Haviland and Company, Limoges, France, one of the world's best known manufacturers of fine porcelain, has created imposing State China Services for several of the First Ladies in the White House, contributing greatly to our American heritage.

The White House in Washington is the most famous house in the United States. It is a symbol of the character of the highest Executive office in the nation and goes beyond its historical meaning. It suggests a way of life, and its strength is a distinct mark of national pride. It is like a person living through the years. Each family that lived in the White House has left something of itself behind, reflecting the life and times of that administration for future Americans to share. One of the significant contributions is the Presidential China.

In May 1969, Haviland and Company inaugurated one of the most exciting and important collections of the

last decade. This factory is producing a series of plates commemorating the administrations of the United States Presidents who selected Haviland for the White House China Service.

This elegant Presidential series is unique in the field of collecting. Each plate is a first edition, produced in an extremely limited number. For this reason, the investment potential will be phenomenal. An added facet is the stimulation of interest for students of history, curious about our nation's first families, and to collectors of Presidential china. The White House China patterns reflect the First Ladies' personal taste and the fashion of the times in which they lived.

The first commemorative plate issued in this series is the Martha Washington. It is 8½ inches in diameter. The decoration is composed of a circular chain containing the names of the fifteen states in the Union at the time the original set was made. Vermont and Kentucky were added

to the original thirteen States in 1791 and 1792 respectively. The snake, holding its tail in its mouth, is a Chinese symbol of continuity and symbolizes the perpetuity of the Union. The interlaced letters of the monogram, M. W., in the center of the plate, are set against a sunburst of gold. The Latin motto, "Decus Et Tatamen Ab Illo," stands for "Honor and Protection Come From Him."

The original set, known as the "Martha Washington" or "States" china, was a gift to Lady Washington in 1795 from Andreas Everardus van Braam Houckgeest, a Dutchman and representative of the Dutch East India Company. The service consisted of about 45 pieces and was made in China on special order for presentation to the First Lady.

Haviland and Company was commissioned to reproduce this plate in porcelain in 1876 to celebrate the Centenary of the Signing of the Declaration of Independence of the

United States of America.

The first edition of the Mary Todd Lincoln plate was a pattern personally selected by Mrs. Lincoln and manufactured by Haviland & Co. in 1861. The center design shows an eagle with wings outstretched surmounting the national shield and coming through the dark clouds into the sunshine. The national motto, "E Pluribus Unum," floats on a pennant-like ribbon below. A wide Solferino band encircles the scalloped plate. The rim of the plate is banded in two hand-applied, entwined gold cables representing North and South united.

There has been much discussion about the symbolism of the coloring and design of the Lincoln plates. The deep purple border is said to represent the mourning for a stricken and torn country. History has now revealed that purple was Mrs. Lincoln's favorite color for clothes and room decor. It was a new and fashionable color for china and critics say that Mary Todd Lincoln enjoyed its regal implications.

Haviland's Lincoln Commemorative is numbered, inscribed and signed by Theodore Haviland II, present president of the firm, as follows: "Authentic reproduction of a plate of White House China made by Haviland at Limoges, France, in 1861 for President Abraham Lincoln and personally selected by Mary Todd Lincoln."

The extremely low mintage of these commemorative plates has already made valuable collector's items of them. The first two issues are limited to only 2500 each edition. No additional reissues will be made. They are made solely for distribution in the United States. The Martha Washington plate is priced $35 and the Lincoln $100.

The Lincoln plate Number 1 was presented to President Richard M. Nixon. Numbers 2 and 3 respectively will be displayed in the White House and the Smithsonian Institution. These plates are boxed with an illustrated copy of *White House China of the Lincoln Administration* by Margaret Brown Klapthor, Associate Curator, The Division of Political History, The Museum of History and Technology, The Smithsonian Institution, Washington, D. C. All editions are authenticated by Mrs. Klapthor as having been manufactured by Haviland.

The special French clays used in Haviland Limoges porcelain make it naturally white, extremely strong, and of a very fine degree of translucency. Pure coin gold is used in decorating and is always hand applied. The electronically controlled decorating kilns assure an evenness of color never before possible. Modern methods of manufacture have advanced the art of applying decoration efficiently through a lithographic process. Hand- or acid-etched designs are made on stones, then paper transfers are reproduced from them. The transfer design is applied to the china and the pattern remains after the paper is removed. This method gives a wide range of color and is usually used after glazing. These Presidential Commemorative plates require much time and skill to make.

The third plate produced in the series is a magnificent floral one, bearing the gold crest of the United States, made by Haviland in 1870 for the administration of President Ulysses S. Grant.

Mrs. Grant, it seems, was one of the few wives of the Presidents who were happy and enjoyed life in the White House. She was a blithe and vivacious woman and, like her husband, enjoyed entertaining. Some of their meals had as many as 29 courses "with a twenty-minute promenade and a glass of Roman Punch mid-meal to make the next session possible."

The Grant State Dinner Service is known as the "Flower Set." Almost every flower native to the United States at the time was used in decorating it. The Haviland plate selected for this Commemorative Series has a center design of a rose that entails 21 different color changes. It has a scalloped border and a quiet buff band with the Seal set into it. The price of the Grant plate is $100.

Haviland will produce eight Commemorative plates in all, bringing out one each year until the series is complete. One of these will be the china produced by the factory in 1880 for the administration of Rutherford B. Hayes. This is perhaps the most famous, and many people think that it is most beautiful of any of the White House china. To say the least, Mrs. Hayes bought china with an exuberance never seen before or after. She specified in her contract with Haviland & Co. that the artist, Mr. Theodore R. Davis, was to have exclusive supervision of the designs. He suggested if she did not have American china that she could at least have designs representing the fruits, vegetables, game, fish, and fauna indigenous to this country. A table set with this china must have had more color and vitality than any ever used in White House dining. Other plates to be reproduced in this series will be those of Presidents Andrew Johnson, Franklin Pierce, James A. Garfield, and Chester A. Arthur.

LALIQUE ANNUAL PLATES by LOIS B HERRING

AT LAST the dream of avid collectors of the beautiful Lalique crystal made in France is in the process of becoming a reality. After many requests from those who love and collect this glass, Marc Lalique, present head of Rene Lalique & Cie., Alsace, France, decided in 1965 to make an annual plate primarily aimed at the collector market.

His daughter, Marie-Claude Lalique, was chosen to design the plate as she, too, is an artist-designer at the firm along with her father. The first two plates reflect the fine creative ability and artistic achievement that has always been the tradition of the Lalique factory.

The annual plates are 8½ inches in diameter. Since these are intended to be collector's items, only a limited quantity will be produced each year, and each piece will be signed and dated. (The current signature is "Lalique, France," in script.) The mold will be destroyed and the plate never made again, creating a much sought after piece of art glass, destined to grow in value over the years.

The title of the 1965 plate is *Deux Oiseaux* (Two Birds), and the 1966 issue is entitled *Dreamrose*. Marie-Claude Lalique resorts to subjects from nature for her models, as did her famous grandfather, Rene Lalique, founder of the factory. The designs are brought to life in a skillful manner by combining transparent and etched surfaces on the glass.

At the present time no established date for the issuance of these plates has been set. The first one appeared in September, 1965; the second was issued in May, 1966. Only 2,000 were made in 1965; a somewhat larger quantity in 1966. It is Lalique's intent to limit the issues to not more than 5,000 in number. So far the annual plates are being distributed only in the United States. Established retail outlets all over the country, which handle Lalique wares, will have their share for distribution to their local customers. Currently the plates retail for $25, but these will undoubtedly find their way to collectors at a higher cost, as has been the case with Baccarat's limited editions of paperweights, and the Danish Christmas plates.

Rosenthal
GERMANY

NEW TRADEMARK

Rosenthal

R.C.
Rosenthal
GERMANY

OLD TRADEMARKS

Weinachten 1917; coupe-shaped plate decorated in blue and white. Back stamped: "Weinachten 1917"; diameter 8 ³⁄₈ inches.

Rosenthal Christmas Plates

Illustrations From the Collection of
MR. and MRS. HOWARD GIANOTTI

Weinachten 1915; coupe-shaped plate with embossed design in various shades of blue and green. Back stamped: "Jul V. Guldbrandsen" (the designer's name). Diameter 8 inches.

Weinachten 1911; coupe-shaped plate with embossed decoration in blue and white. Back stamped: "Entwurf (designed by)/Heinrich Vogeler/Warpswede." Diameter 8 inches.

Weinachten 1923; decorated blue and white. Back stamped: "Weinachsteller 1923/Entwurf von Ernest Haefer-Berlin." Diameter 8½ inches.

Weinachten 1920; decorated in blue and white; gold inner border. Back stamped: "Weinachsteller (Christmas plate) 1920/Entwurf von Dr. W. Schertel, Selb./Motiv (motif): 'Im Stalle zu Bethleham' (in the Bethlehem stable)." Diameter 8½ inches.

Ostern 1915; Rosenthal's Easter plate for the year 1915. The design has been executed in pastel shades of blue, green, brown, and white; gold inner border. The designer's name, "Jul V. Guldbrandsen," is printed on the back of the plate. Diameter 8½ inches.

Oberammergau 1922; a portrait in blue and white of Anton Lang, the actor who portrayed Jesus in the Oberammergau Passion Play, in 1922. Mr. Lang's signature appears in blue on the back of the plate. Diameter 8⅜ inches.

145
Collector Plates

IN 1895, in a hired room in an 18th century manor house, Schloss Erkersreuth, in Kronach, Bavaria, young Philip Rosenthal set up a workshop for his first porcelain factory. Much of the hard paste porcelain he produced, daintily and colorfully hand-painted in the styles of the day, came to America to brighten turn-of-the-century tea tables and china closets. The Rosenthal marks, a crown over crossed roses with "Rosenthal" beneath or a crown with " R C " arranged in crossed diagonals, became familiar wherever quality china was sold. Marshall Field's in Chicago was an important distributor. Dr. Mickenhagen in his *European Porcelain*, tells us that this was the first porcelain firm to sign its products with a full name.

Rosenthal china is still being made, still being imported. There are factories now in Selb, Selb-Plossberg, and Munchen as well as at Kronach, and a Rosenthal glassworks at Bad Soden. Recently the present Philip Rosenthal purchased the manor house in which it all began. He and his family are living in it now, but he plans, when his children are grown, to make it into a Rosenthal Museum.

While much of Rosenthal's production is tableware, their special Christmas and Easter plates, produced annually, and their Oberammergau Passion Play plates are particularly collectible. The Christmas and Easter plates are not "limited editions"; the number produced each year is determined by the firm's estimate of their anticipated sales. We have been advised by Rosenthal's New York City office that some Christmas and Easter plates from previous years can still be obtained through the various retail outlets handling their wares.—*M.R.*

Weinachten 1935; embossed decoration in light blue, light brown, and white; gold inner border. Back stamped: "Weinachten an der See (Christmas at sea)/Entwurf von Heinrich Fink." Diameter 8½ inches.

Weinachten 1939; embossed decoration in pastel shades of blue-green, blue, and white. Back stamped: " 'Schneekoppe' (snow capped)/Entwurf von Heinrich Fink." Diameter 8½ inches.

Weinachten 1936; embossed decoration in pastel blue-green, brown, yellow, and white; gold inner border. Back stamped: "Weinachtsteller 1936/Motiv: 'Lichtbote' (the candle bearer)." Diameter 8½ inches.

Weinachten 1927; embossed decoration in blue-green, brown, and white. Back stamped: "Entwurf von Professor Theo Schmuz-Baudiss." Diameter 8½ inches.

CHRISTMAS

Rorstrand trademark.

PLATES

by LOIS AND CLINT HERRING

THE RORSTRAND Porslinsfabriker is the oldest porcelain factory in all of Scandinavia and the second oldest in Europe. On June 13, 1726, an Instrument of Association was signed establishing this Swedish firm at Stora Rorstrand just outside of Stockholm. The founder was Johan Wolff.

The enterprise was a highly successful one and by 1746 was exporting its products to Russia, Germany, Holland, and Denmark. In the beginning the factory used the faience technique, earthenware decorated with opaque colored glaze, reminiscent of the styles of Delft, Berlin, and Rouen. The earliest wares were painted in cobalt blue and white only.

In 1750 a style was developed which was unmistakably Swedish. Various technical improvements were initiated resulting in the ability to obtain a greater range of colors. As early as 1771 the production of cream colored earthenware began.

During the first half of the 19th century Rorstrand was very much influenced by English techniques and designs. Transfer printing was introduced after 1850 and a number of new products like Parian ware, Ironstone, and opaque china were made. The objects of that period are highly prized by collectors today.

In 1904 Rorstrand inaugurated their first Christmas plate. Each succeeding year a limited number of plates with special Christmas motifs were made. They were blue and white in color,

round, coupe-shaped and measured approximately 8 inches in diameter. They were produced in such small quantities that one of these early plates is seldom seen outside a private collection or museum.

In 1926, exactly 200 years after the founding of Rorstrand, the factory moved from Stockholm to Lidkoping, about 110 miles northeast of Gothenburg. Because of the change in management and radical reconstruction period which followed, the Christmas plates were excluded from production. The factory at that time was concentrating on "more beautiful everyday wares."

Early this century the Swedish Society of Industrial Design was founded. It revolutionized the attitudes toward the design of standard products and helped to stimulate the preservation of traditional patterns. Out of this well of inspiration the Swedish artists have developed their ability to create in their own special style. Many objets d'art by Rorstrand are exhibited in the National Museum in Stockholm and are in the possession of His Majesty the King of Sweden at his palaces in Stockholm and Drottningholm.

Because of the increasing demand for a Rorstrand Christmas plate the factory decided in 1968 to once again make this special annual plate. The theme for this edition is "Bringing Home the Christmas Tree" (*Figure 1*). So few of this date were produced that they are extremely scarce and most difficult to obtain.

The subject for the 1969 plate is "Fisherman's Homecoming" (*Figure 2*).

The 1970 design depicts Nils Holgersson, the legendary boy who flew with the wild geese over all Sweden, from the book *The Wonderful Adventures of Nils,* by the famous Swedish author, Selma Lagerlof. The artist blends the lovely folklore of Sweden with the imaginative and fascinating account of Nils' experiences. He is pictured on this plate (*Figure 3*) at Christmastime on his father's farm amid the quaint charm of his native home in southern Sweden.

At present Rorstrand has a team of five permanently employed designers and a number of free-lance artists who create for the factory. The artist for the first three Christmas plates is Gunnar Nylund. His initials appear on the back of the plates beneath the name "Rorstrand."

The plates are of fine porcelain decorated in underglaze Scandia blue. They measure 7¾ inches and are pierced for hanging. Each edition is limited. The unusual shape of the Rorstrand plates gives them an added distinction.

In three short years collectors have quickly realized and appreciated the value of these Swedish Christmas plates. The 1968 first edition was placed on the market at $10; it is now selling between $85 and $100. The 1969 issue has also become a highly prized collector's item. The 1970 plate was placed on the market for $14.50.

Fig. 1

Fig. 2

Fig. 3

CLOCKS AND WATCHES

The ticking of a clock is both fascinating and mesmeric to a great many people. And when the clock has that special attribute of being an antique, it becomes a highly prized possession. Some collectors delight in acquiring timepieces of the most intricate kind; this is particularly true of watch collectors. The simple works used in American clocks of the 1830-1840 period appeal to collectors less knowledgeable about mechanical devices. But all collectors insist that their clocks and watches be in good running order.

Figure 1: OG by Seth Thomas, after restoration; ca. 1880.

Figure 2: Double OG by Chauncey Jerome, after restoration. Late 1850s, possibly after New Haven Clock Co. took over.

Figure 3: OG by E. N. Welch, ca. 1870.

Figure 4: Round gothic or Beehive by Jerome Mfg. Co., ca. 1853.

Figure 5: Sharp Gothic by Brewster & Ingraham, ca. 1850.

Figure 6: Sharp Gothic timepiece by E. N. Welch, ca. 1880.

Figure 7: Sharp Gothic alarm by Waterbury Clock Co. showing separate alarm movement, ca. 1870.

Figure 8: Sharp Gothic timepiece by Ansonia Clock Co. 1880s. Design on door allows pendulum to be faintly seen.

Figure 9: Sharp Gothic timepiece with dummy compensation pendulum by New Haven Clock Co., ca. 1890.

Figure 10: Pair of "cottage style" timepieces by E. N. Welch, ca. 1870. The one on the right has a patent escapement.

Figure 13: "Cottage style" alarm by E. N. Welch, 1875.

COLLECTING FACTORY MADE AMERICAN CLOCKS

by E. J. TYLER

THE THOUSANDS OF American factory-made clocks that flooded into this country (England) during the second half of the 19th century have always been held in low esteem. They never set out to be anything but cheap; most of them have been neglected during their lives and yet many are still in existence today, capable of being restored and taking their place among household timekeepers once again.

There is a feeling among clock collectors that a factory-made article is not worth collecting, but it has now been established that many of the 18th century London makers had their clocks produced for them in specialist workshops, and it is possible that this practice goes back even earlier. The interest in an American clock is not in the fine engraving on its dial nor in the fine wood of its case, but in the way that the factory that produced it worked to put on the market an article that could compete with others being sold at the time. Not only did this point have to be taken into consideration, but also the cost of production had to be kept down. The output at the beginning was very large compared with the early days of the century, but it was still small enough to involve the proprietor more directly with the product than in later years.

Factory production in America began about 1807 when Eli Terry of Plymouth, Conn., took on a contract to make 4,000 clocks in three years. He equipped a factory driven by a waterwheel and adopted the principle of producing a large number of interchangeable parts which were used for assembling the movements. The clocks were made of wood, oak for the plates, cherry for the wheels, and mountain laurel for the pinions. Terry completed his contract in time, and many other people began to imitate him. Following a national financial crisis in 1837, the wooden-wheeled clock business died out in the 1840s, but by that time cheap metal movements were being sold in their place.

Among the assistants in Terry's mass production venture were Seth Thomas and, later, Chauncey Jerome. Both were subsequently in the wooden-wheel clock business on their own, but Jerome usually gets the credit for introducing brass movements into the "cheap" trade about 1838. Brass was being rolled in Connecticut for manufacturing buttons, and provided a source of material for clock movements.

Terry's original clocks were similar to the movements of English long case clocks and were generally hung on the wall with exposed weights and pendulum. About 1814 he designed a new type of clock in which the weights had a fall of only about 18 inches and were contained inside the case, which was intended to stand on a shelf. It was at this stage that Jerome worked for Terry producing cases, while Seth Thomas, already in business on his own account, built the Terry type clock under license.

Terry had been apprenticed as a clockmaker, but Jerome and Thomas were joiners. By 1840 no more men were being apprenticed as clockmakers in U.S.A. because the factories were handling all the production far faster and cheaper than individual craftsmen could do it. The brass movement for Jerome's clock was not designed by him but by his brother, Noble Jerome. There were only three arbors in each train, and by making the barrels small and the great wheels large, the clock could run for thirty hours with something less than 18 inches of weight fall. In order to reduce the weight fall on the wooden shelf clocks, five arbors were the rule with a

limited number of teeth in each wheel. The brass wheels gave scope for large numbers of very small teeth.

The cases were of the well-known "OG" type, measuring about 26 inches by 15 inches. The type gets its name from the case moulding based on the ogive. The door was glazed with plain glass in the upper part, and the lower part would contain a picture or design painted on the rear of the glass as had been done with the Terry clocks. Two features of the latter were incorporated in the brass movement; the escapement was on the front plate between the movement and dial and the motion work for giving the 1 : 12 rotation of the hands was moved from this position to between the plates. The pendulum therefore swung near the glass door, and often a part of the glass was left clear for the swinging bob to be seen to give an indication that the clock was still going. Behind the pendulum was pasted an advertisement for the factory with "Instructions for setting the clock running." The hammer protruded below the movement to strike on a wire gong, and alarm work could be fitted without much extra trouble. Many clocks will be found with the plates already drilled to make the pivot of the alarm work. Later some cases were made with the outer moulding convex and the door moulding concave, and were known as "Double OG" or "OOG" and cost more than the normal type.

In 1842, Jerome decided to send a consignment of clocks to England. The old wooden-wheeled clocks had never been exported, and so Jerome's action was a bold one in sending clocks to the leading clock-producing country in the world. Jerome's clocks were seized by the customs as being undervalued, and he received his invoice price plus 10%. This encouraged him to send a second consignment, which was dealt with in the same way. When the third consignment arrived, the customs decided that Jerome was serious and let the clocks through to be sold in the normal way. These early OG clocks had wooden dials although the later examples had zinc dials, and the type remained in the catalogues until 1914. Other manufacturers joined in, especially Seth Thomas, and within 20 years practically all the cheaper clocks sold in Britain were of American manufacture. They completely ousted the old Black Forest wall clocks with wooden frames and exposed weights and pendulum, for the OG was more sophisticated and did not suffer from the disadvantage that the pendulum could be stopped by a strong draught, and the enclosed weights were no longer at the mercy of animals and children.

In America, the OG and similar clocks are always called "shelf clocks," and their great advantage was that they could stand instead of needing to be hung up. It is a remarkable fact that every OG that the writer has encountered has had some means of suspension fitted to enable the clock to be hung on the wall. The ideal place to stand an OG would be on the cupboards that are so often found beside the chimney breasts in Victorian terrace houses, but it seems that the wall was always the favorite position in this country.

Jerome's early clocks were produced in a factory in Bristol, Connecticut, which was burnt down in 1845. Production was then carried on at New Haven, Connecticut, until Jerome went bankrupt in the late 1850s. Although capable of organizing a factory, he was no financial wizard, and his plant was taken over by the New Haven Clock Company with Jerome's nephew Hiram Camp, as president. So far, the

Figure 11: "Cottage style" timepiece by Seth Thomas, ca. 1875.

design for alarm clocks, and even a brand new modern example was on sale in London after 1945. The "Cottage" style is very pleasing whether as a striking clock, an alarm clock or a timepiece. Here the top is square as on an OG.

Very popular were the very small clocks without strike or alarm, and many factories produced them and generally arranged for the movement to be easily adapted for an alarm if necessary. While alarm work was usually added by inserting the extra parts between the existing plates of the movement, the Waterbury Clock Company used to mount a separate little alarm movement lower down in the case. The alarm in all clocks was released by a wire riding on a brass disc which was carried with the hour hand. The disc was turned so that the hour desired came beneath the hour hand, and when this time was reached, the wire fell into a slot and allowed the hammer to sound. One does not often come across an alarm and a timepiece from the same series, but such a pair would be an interesting item for a collection. The two little timepieces by E. N. Welch shown in *Fig. 11* are the same model except that one has a patent escapement while the other has the normal type. Many American clocks have numbers of patents stamped on them in various places, be it only a patent for a special type of dial, and details of American patents are held at the Patent Office in Chancery Lane (London) and can be referred to by the public.

The OG's and early spring clocks were generally provided with cases made of cheap wood covered with veneer. The grain of the veneer often goes across the piece, especially on OG's. The tablets, or decorated pieces of glass which hide the pendulum, are often well painted on early examples, while the later ones are decorated with transfers and the work is of inferior quality. Some tablets merely have a design which allows the pendulum to be faintly seen through it, while others consist of a piece of looking-glass.

During the 'eighties, the traditional type of spring clock developed to meet German competition. Glasses generally became plainer and more decoration was applied to the woodwork in the form of mouldings or turned buttons. Some clocks, usually known as "Sidewhiskers" to American collectors, had large flat pieces of wood surrounding them, decorated with embossed patterns made while the wood was hot and damp. These clocks were usually sold wholesale in assorted lots, and it was not possible for a retailer to choose so many of a certain pattern.

The German competition previously mentioned arose as a result of the capturing of the British market by Jerome and his imitators. The makers of the old Black Forest wall clocks had to find new methods of production and new styles to keep themselves in business, so they began manufacturing clocks on the American pattern using American methods in their factories. They openly advertised their wares as American clocks, and adopted American-sounding names for their firms. In the first few years they followed American styles, producing OG's, small timepieces, Sharp Gothic, etc., but soon broke away and produced styles of their own which later induced the Americans to copy them. To distinguish between American clocks and the early German imitators is a very nice point, and it would take a complete article to deal with the subject fully. As many factories did not mark their movements and many clocks have the papers torn out of the back of the case, the task becomes increasingly difficult.

Thirty years ago, American clocks were easy to come by and prices were ridiculously low. Timepieces or alarms were about 1s. 6d. (30 cents) and striking clocks 2s. (40 cents). OG's could be had for 2s. 6d. to 5s. (50 cents to $1). Those days are gone forever. Now people are beginning to take an interest in these clocks, prices have risen and, of course, the clocks have had thirty years more of life in which to depreciate and suffer damage.

As for sources of supply, the provinces are better than London as far as prices are concerned, but the selection is not so great. The village Jumble Sale often produces an OG

writer has never seen a Jerome clock produced in Bristol, but a great number from the New Haven factory are still extant. After the New Haven Clock Company had taken over, they often used the Jerome name as goodwill, and clocks of a much later period than the 1850s are found bearing it. Some of the very late Jerome OG's are quite rough, the stamping of the wheels being done with worn dies that leave small fins of metal instead of cutting cleanly.

At the beginning of the period of export to Britain, all clocks were weight-driven. It was still not possible to produce steel springs in large quantities in America at a price that would make their use worthwhile, and so American manufacturers tried to get round the problem in the desperate attempt to compete with the weight-driven clocks. Some tried brass springs, which function quite well but tend to get weaker with use, and Joseph Ives, about whom a complete book has been written, used the "Wagon Spring." This consisted of a number of tough pieces of steel like the leaf spring of a car which exerted a great force through a small distance when put in tension, and needed extra mechanism to convert this force into a suitable one for driving a clock. Other makers used shorter steel spiral springs, but drove the clock through fusees actually mounted on the same arbor as the spring. A spring acting through a fusee does not need to be so long as one which drives the clock directly.

By the middle 1840s the problem of spring manufacture had been solved, and so these methods of getting round it had only a short life. The manufacture of steel mainsprings that could keep the clock running successfully for one to eight days immediately led to the appearance of many new designs for cases. Among the earliest was the "Round Gothic," derived from the English "Lancet" case of Regency days, and this was made for one- and eight-day movements. It is an exception to the usual rule for American clocks in that its movement is removed from the back, and cannot be lifted off after the dial has been removed. The "Round Gothic" is generally known to present day collectors as the "beehive." Another early design which lasted for a long time is the "sharp Gothic" [in America called a "Steeple" clock]. This began as a striking clock, and early examples with fusees are known, but its life was prolonged by being a favorite or Sharp Gothic for anything up to £1 ($2.60), but the clock is generally a wreck and needs a lot of attention. The main sources in London are Islington Green and Portobello Road. A dealer in the North of England specialises in American clocks and does a brisk trade with American collectors.

At an auction, an OG or a Sharp Gothic may fetch £7 to £8 ($18.20 to $20.80) as a wreck and double that amount in good condition. In shops, alarms or cottage timepieces may reach £10 to £12 ($26.00 to $31.20), and striking clocks, proportionately more.

The easiest way to add such a clock to one's collection is to buy a wreck and restore it oneself. Unfortunately, not everyone is capable of doing the necessary repairs, but restorers are still to be found who will undertake the repair of these clocks, and many amateur horologists enjoy tackling one. The ordinary watch and clock repairer does not generally wish to work on these clocks, for they are generally in a very bad condition and need a lot of experimental work and investigation until all the difficulties have been discovered and dealt with.

The amateur horologist who desires to repair American movements is advised to consult the *Horological Journal* for March 1971. The usual work that needs doing to these clocks is the replacement of a buckled pendulum suspension, rebushing and smoothing of the pallets, replacement of broken mainsprings (or weight lines in an OG) and a thorough cleaning. Apart from the movement, the case, dial and tablet will need attention, and repairs usually consist of replacing missing pieces of veneer, making good the chips in the dials and restoring the figures where necessary, replacement of cracked tablets and the restoration of the tone of the gong which usually has a most dismal sound. The labels are important, and any loose pieces should be carefully stuck in place. Not only are these labels interesting in themselves, but they often give a clue to the date of the clock from the name of the printer or other information, and a clock without its label is much decreased in value. A complete restoration of an OG should cost about £7 to £8 ($18.20 to $20.80), or more if the clock is in a very bad condition;

other types will generally cost about the same, with proportionately less for a timepiece or alarm.

Many of the manufacturers' old catalogues are now being reproduced in the U.S.A., from Jerome's of 1852 to those issued in the present century, and these are interesting reading in themselves as well as helping to identify the clocks. Many of the old catalogues have been lost, and however many of them are re-issued, there will always be clocks which cannot be identified in their pages. These reprints are obtainable from specialist booksellers such as Malcolm Gardner of Sevenoaks, Kent, and cost the equivalent of $3 to $4. They are interesting in giving the names applied to the various styles, for most American factories gave their models a title, and the practice was also copied in Germany.

There is not a great deal of literature available on the subject of American clocks. The best way to acquire a knowledge of the subject is to subscribe to the *Bulletin of the National Association of Watch and Clock Collectors of U.S.A.* which costs $12 per year and is largely concerned with American clocks. Two important books which are available in England are *The Book of American Clocks* and *Treasury of American Clocks* both by Brooks Palmer and obtainable through booksellers or the Public Library Service. The former contains a list of makers. Other books are *American Clocks and Clockmakers* by Carl W. Drepperd, and *The Old Clock Book* by N. Hudson Moore, which is now rather old-fashioned but contains a list of makers. The most complete book on the factory production of clocks in Connecticut is *The Contributions of Joseph Ives to Connecticut Clock Technology* by Kenneth D. Roberts.

Finally a list of the most usually represented makers in Britain:

Chauncey Jerome, Bristol, Conn., 1842-5; New Haven, Conn., 1845-late '50s

Jerome Manufacturing Co., New Haven, Conn., 1850s

Seth Thomas, Plymouth, Conn., later Plymouth Hollow and Thomastown. Seth Thomas Company from 1853, still in existence as part of General Time Instruments Corporation.

New Haven Clock Co., New Haven, Conn. from 1855.

E. N. Welch, Bristol and Forestville, Conn., 1856-87

E. N. Welch Manufacturing Co., Forestville, 1864-

Ansonia Clock Co., Ansonia, Conn., 1855-1880s. New York 1880s onwards.

Birge and Fuller, Bristol, Conn., 1844-7 (wagon spring clocks)

Brewster and Ingrahams, Bristol, Conn., 1844-53

Brewster, E.C. and Son, 1855-

Brewster Manufacturing Co., 1852-5

Brewster and Co., 1861-

Waterbury Clock Co., Waterbury, Conn., 1857-

William L. Gilbert, Winsted, Conn. From the wooden clock period into the present century.

(First published in the Antique Collectors' Club monthly magazine *Antique Collecting*, Clopton, Woodbridge, Suffolk, England.)

Figure 12: "Cottage style" alarm and timepiece by Seth Thomas, ca. 1875. The hands bear the letters S & T as advertisement.

Aaron Willard Clocks

WILLARD is an important name in early Massachusetts clock-making, and two families of Willards, descended from a common ancestor, contributed to make it so. Four of Benjamin and Sarah (Brooks) Willard's children were clockmakers—Benjamin, Simon, Ephraim, and Aaron. Of these, Simon had three clockmaking sons—Simon, Jr., John Mears, and Benjamin Franklin; Aaron had two—Aaron, Jr. and Henry. In the third generation, Zabadiel Adams Willard, son of Benjamin F., followed his father's footsteps.

The other Willard family contributed clockmakers Philander Jacob and Alexander Tarbell, sons of Jacob and Rhoda (Randall) Willard.

Of them all, next to his brilliant brother Simon, Aaron was the most famous. He was born in Grafton, Massachusetts, in 1757, and died in Boston in 1844. He was established as a clockmaker in Grafton before the Revolutionary War, in which he served, and some of his early clocks are marked with the Grafton place name. In 1780 he moved to Roxbury where Simon was already established, removing to 843 Washington Street, Boston, in 1792. His work was exceptionally fine and he turned out splendid tall clocks, wall and Massachusetts shelf clocks, both of which he developed, gallery clocks, and many banjo clocks, which the Willards had perfected in Grafton.

Aaron, Jr. (1783–1864), who possibly originated the lyre clock, continued the Boston factory after his father's retirement in 1823, working until 1850. Both Aarons, capable businessmen, amassed considerable fortunes.

The Aaron Willard clocks shown here were in the Joseph P. Levy collection of Americana dispersed at Parke-Bernet Galleries in December 1960. Hepplewhite inlaid mahogany tall case clock (above) ca. 1800, marked "Aaron Willard, Boston, Mass." 8 ft. high; 19 in. wide; center brass finial with spread eagle; face painted with figural lunette.

Carved mahogany lyre clock with églomisé panels, ca. 1830, with white clock face inscribed "A. Willard Jr., Boston." Leaf-carved lyre-shaped trunk and oblong plinth below are both fitted with églomisé panels painted in gold, red, and blue with foliations and the American eagle and shield. 38 in. high.

Inlaid mahogany shelf clock, ca. 1820, white-painted clock face inscribed "Aaron Willard, Boston."

The American Pocket Watch

The Badge of Man's Estate

by James W. Neilson

ANCIENT artifacts witness to a preoccupation with time and its measurement, and no doubt the invention of the mechanical clock, late in the middle ages, worked a veritable revolution in timekeeping. Only slightly less momentous was the development of the watch in the sixteenth century, not long after Peter Henlein of Nurnberg developed the spring-driven timepiece. Jewelry and timekeeping were now inexorably fused, presumably for all time.

The first watches were inaccurate by any standards, but improvements came steadily from the fertile minds of the later Renaissance. The hairspring dates to the latter half of the seventeenth century, and shortly after the eighteenth dawned, watchmakers began to use jewels in their movements. By the time our Founding Fathers reached the New World, watches were common among the well-to-do, though not within economic reach of common men.

Mass production of a variety of durable goods blurred class lines in the twentieth century by providing the people with goods once the exclusive property of the wealthy.

Democratization of the pocket watch, in the nineteenth century, came about through Aaron Lufkin Dennison. Before this time, importers supplied the American market with Swiss or English watches, expensive, handmade items all. The success of the New England clock industry failed to extend to the manufacture of watches, and it seems doubtful if American watchmakers turned out more than a few thousand before the middle of the century.

Pioneer Producer

Dennison was born in Freeport, Maine, in 1812, the son of a cobbler. As a boy he showed strong interest in things mechanical, utterly none in his father's trade. Seeing this, the senior Dennison apprenticed him to a Brunswick watchmaker. Some three years later, the 21-year old Aaron found employment in Boston as a full-fledged journeyman in his craft, and after a time he established his own shop.

Dennison failed to find contentment in repairing watches made by others. He was appalled at the quality of some of the workmanship he encountered, and he pondered the waste in producing each watch by hand.

The operation of the Springfield Armory fascinated and intrigued him; he visited it frequently, noting the efficiency of producing standardized muskets by mass production techniques. Eventually his mind encompassed a scheme by which watches could be mass-produced with standard parts fabricated by machinery. That the machine tool industry of his day was incapable of producing instruments of the precision required seems not to have occurred to him. Once he did grasp that somber fact, he began perfecting the necessary machinery.

With financial backing from Bostonian Samuel Curtis, and gifted watchmaker Edward Howard, Dennison founded the American Horologue Company, and established it in a plant at Roxbury. The sponsors soon changed the pompous-sounding name to Boston Watch Company; and determined on expanding operations to a point where mechanized mass production could be more fully utilized. Much of the machinery had proven inadequate, and Dennison set about to improve it. At last a new plant was ready at Waltham.

Success eluded Dennison. The market seemed unable to absorb the plant's output, perhaps because Dennison knew more about creating mass production than about stimulating mass demand. He was more mechanic and inventor than salesman. His company failed in the black year of 1857.

Purchased by New York interests, it became the American Watch Company in 1859, and later the Waltham Watch Company. Dennison remained as the company's superintendent until 1861. Eventually he moved to England and became an apparently successful manufacturer of watch cases in Birmingham. He died in 1895.

From such shaky beginnings, the

Author's grandfather's keywind "turnip"; Elgin National Watch Co.; silver case by Keystone Watch Case Co.; thick heavy crystal typical of 1875.

Waltham watch in Dueber gold filled case; round dial, round stem, Roman numerals on face, and relatively large size, place this about 1890.

Hamilton railroad watch, movement #524609; Philadelphia Watch Co. case; purchased in 1907 by author's father, an engineer, who used it 36 years.

Size 16 Waltham watch in a Dueber Special case; flattened bail, almost triangular stem, small size, and Arabic numbers on face date it ca. 1910.

An Illinois watch in a Keystone case of solid 10k gold; elaborately engraved; size and characteristics place it in the 1890 period.

This watch is a Hampden; case is of solid 14k gold; probably slightly older than the 1890 models shown, though not a great deal.

American watch industry developed rapidly along lines which were intensely competitive. By 1870 there were at least 37 companies devoted exclusively to watch production, while some 60 firms engaged in their manufacture. Operations tended to be small scale—the 37 firms of 1870 employed only about 1800 men. The industry was marked by new incorporations, bankruptcies, and re-organizations.

Major Manufacturers

Gradually certain firms separated themselves from the field of competition and gained a modicum of reputation and status. The pioneer producer which eventually became the Waltham Watch Company, was one.

Another was the producer generally referred to as "Elgin," the result of a union of three diversely talented men: John C. Adams, a watchmaker, Benjamin W. Raymond, a former Chicago mayor and businessman, and George B. Adams, a successful jeweler of Elgin, Illinois. The three joined forces in 1864 to organize the National Watch Company. It began to produce timepieces three years later, and in 1874 became the Elgin National Watch Company. It was, perhaps, the best managed of the watch companies; certainly it could boast it paid dividends from the beginning, and in its first six years had produced and sold 42,000 watches!

The Illinois Springfield Watch Company, organized in 1869, was the second producer of pocket watches in the Prairie State. After doubtful manoeuverings and two or three re-organizations, it became the Illinois Watch Company, and for years maintained the status of a major producer whose watches enjoyed high repute.

The Dueber-Hampden interests constituted another major producer. John C. Dueber founded a watch case business in Cincinnati in 1864, and in a few years his company held leading position in the industry. In 1886, it consolidated with the Hampden Watch Company, a Massachusetts concern organized in 1877, and the business was moved to Canton, Ohio.

A late birth characterized the final giant of the industry. This was the Hamilton Watch Company which came into existence in 1892 in Lancaster, Pennsylvania, primarily to manufacture railroad watches. Within a short time, its name was symbolic of extreme timepiece accuracy.

Watches For Everyone

While the major watch companies developed, competed, and produced high quality timekeepers, other firms tried to exploit a mass market. Despite generally declining prices, watches remained relatively expensive in an era when a dollar was a fair day's wage. The Waterbury

About the Author

James W. Neilson, Professor of History at Mayville State College, Mayville, North Dakota, not only collects pocket watches and the chains, charms, and fobs that went with them, but wears them, too. A professor, he claims, has license to be a bit different. Now that his collection contains representative examples of each type of mass-produced men's watches, he looks for unusual specimens. He's seeking particularly an octagonal-cased watch, advertised in either a Sears', or Ward's catalogue of 1889. All watches and accessories pictured here are from his collection, and were photographed by Jerry Tastad.

Watch Company, organized in 1880, began to produce inexpensive watches some ten years after its founding. Success was immediate despite mechanical inconveniences associated with the watches, best known of which was the eight or nine foot mainspring that seemingly took forever to wind.

Probably the sales policies of the company, more than any other factor, led to eventual failure. The Waterbury Company sold large numbers of its watches at low wholesale prices, and they were often given away by merchants as premiums, usually with the sale of men's or boys' suits. An image of cheap merchandise, of shoddy goods at all-wool prices, came to adhere to the Waterbury; its popularity declined. The company reorganized in 1898 as the New England Watch Company, but its best efforts could not avert failure in 1912.

It was Robert H. Ingersoll who made the "dollar watch" famous. Ingersoll was a Michigan farm boy who arrived in New York City in 1879. He established a mail order business, engaged in manufacturing gadgets he invented, and dealt in bicycles and parts. About 1893 he entered the watch business, selling the cheap watches that bore his name, first for $1.50, later for one dollar. He bought the bankrupt New England Watch Company in 1914 and utilized its facilities to produce dollar watches. Over-expansion during World War I turned out to be disasterous, and the Ingersoll company was forced to admit insolvency in the '20s.

By that date the American watch industry had been rationalized into a few major firms. The halcyon years of the pocket watch were over.

Watch Cases

Watch cases could be plain, engine-turned, or engraved. For those en-

Rather light woven chain and small charm set with diamonds (probably simulated); average, typical chain and charm c. 1900.

graved there were several favorite motifs. One was the locomotive, the monster of the steam age, generally found on cheaper watches, appealing to youths for whom the locomotive held romance and fascination.

Another, often found on the better gold-filled cases, depicted the noble woodland stag; he appeared time and again in different scenes and poses, often on the cover of hunting cases. Birds were less frequently used on watches intended for men than on ladies' timepieces where they hovered over honeysuckle, touched beaks over nests, or bore streamers of ribbons.

Most of all, engravers delighted in portraying romantic cottages in dreamy, bucolic settings. Italianate villas with towers, or sharply gabled Gothic cottages were depicted in country glades reminiscent of the work of the Hudson River artists.

The amount and quality of engraving on watch cases varied with price and material. A coin silver case was plain, or ornamented with a relatively simple picture. The technique of producing the gold-filled case limited the art which could be practised on it. Lines had to be broad and shallow; delicate engraving utilizing many fine lines was impossible.

It was on the solid gold case— usually a hunting case—that the engraver's true talent could be expended. Elaborate scroll designs could be executed, fine lines cut to produce effects of most delicate shading. Many were custom made—and a solid gold presentation piece could be truly a work of art.

The Watches Men Carried

Jewelers and mail order houses were quick to realize that different styles and price ranges appealed to various segments of watch-toters.

A farmer or workman liked a heavy, thick watch of coin silver, or silver plated with brass to resemble gold.

He referred to it as a "turnip." In the earlier period, before 1890, it was usually wound with a key rather than by a stem, and might be either open face or closed. In general, it was severely plain or engine turned, or—with a minimum of engraving. It was designed to sell at a low price and give years of service; often it kept quite accurate time.

Railroad men needed a dependable timepiece, accurate beyond the capacity of most watches, and the industry provided them "Guaranteed to pass railroad inspection." Their cases were usually gold-filled, and normally, open face. They were expensive— from $75 up, in a day when even an engineer made no more than $100 a month—and jewellers sold them on credit, so much down, so much a month.

Office workers and small business men chose watches in gold-filled cases, albeit less accurate and less costly than those carried by the railroaders. Dudes and fancy dressers preferred hunting cases on elaborate chains or fobs.

For the man of wealth, taste alone dictated the limits of elegance in a timepiece. The elder J. Pierpont Morgan is remembered to have worn a truly monumental example of the watchmaker's art, which he combined with a cable-like chain and huge bloodstone pendant.

Watches were heavy and massive not because of technological limitations, but because the market preferred them that way. Women's watches indicated very well that the industry was capable of producing small, thin watches which kept accurate time.

Watch Chains

Up to the turn of the century, most watch chains were thick and heavy. Links, either gold or gold-filled, were made in a variety of designs from

relatively simple to wondrously complex. Engraved gold fittings capped either end of the chain, and some sort of pendant was suspended from the chain proper, depending from a point near the crossbar which fitted through a vest buttonhole. For key wind watches, the pendant was likely the key itself. Legend has it that college sports first had watch keys made bearing the Greek letters of their fraternal brotherhoods.

For stem wind watches, only imagination limited what could be attached to a chain. Greek letter keys and emblems of fraternal organizations and lodges were popular. So were lockets, in a variety of shapes, engraved with the owner's initials, small compasses, plain or fancy charms from small gold amulets to carved cameos, large semi-precious stones, or of diamond-studded gold.

The dude who demanded something stunning to set off his fancy waistcoat often settled on a multi-strand chain woven from a lock of his sweetheart's hair. Properly adorned with gold or silver fittings, this "vestguard" type of chain was high style. Other snappy dressers favored fobs rather than chains. These might be as much as six inches long, and an inch and a half wide, of gold, or spangled with semi-precious stones.

Restraint in Style

But "good taste" worked a revolution in watch accessories, too. Charms became less heavy and ornate, less likely to draw attention to themselves. Some men forgot, after the turn of the century, to wear pendants at all, though occasionally a gold-plated cigar clipper was hung inconspicuously from a narrow chain. Chains now stretched entirely across a vest from pocket to pocket, and bore a small penknife at one end.

Even the fob grew genteel. It shrunk to perhaps four inches in length and three-quarters of an inch in width; it was now plain gold or of cloth, entirely unobstrusive. The whole vest front display bespoke culture and gentility. The vigorous self-assertion of the 19th century was passe. Some men even left their vests entirely unadorned, and carried their watches in small pockets in their trousers, usually on plain cloth fobs.

Watch-carrying habits of the American male were changed by World War I, when the wrist watch became increasingly popular. The young men of the '20s adopted the wrist watch as their own, and by the time of the second World War, the wrist watch had triumphed almost completely. Only a few antiquarians and men of the railroad fraternity continue to carry pocket watches now. Even the railroads, one by one, are permitting their operating employees to use wrist watches. With the pocket watch, something of the picturesque passes from the American scene.

3 A

3 B

All Photographs by
H. Ivan Rainwater

"Hawaiian Time" - Royal Fashion

by DOROTHY T. RAINWATER

THE DELIGHT OF VISITORS and the despair of hostesses with dinner waiting is the custom of observing "Hawaiian time" in Hawaii. This complete disregard for punctuality which may result in guests arriving hours late—or worse yet, hours early —is not limited to people of Polynesian background.

Lack of time consciousness, however, did not deter members of Hawaiian royalty from wearing beautifully ornamented watches. Among the treasures in Bernice P. Bishop Museum, in Honolulu, are several watches that were once the proud possessions of Hawaiian royalty.

The silver watch (1), engraved

with the British coat of arms, was given by the British Government to his Highness Mataio Kekuanaoa in 1824, when in attendance on Kamehameha II, in London. (Diamond end stone. Storr & Mortimer, Bond Street, London. Verge escapement. 2 1/8" diameter; 13/16" thick.) Worn with this watch is a watch chain (2) with two gold fobs and two silver charms. The seal fob reads "Kunanaoa," a variant spelling of the name of the man who was the father of Kamehameha IV and V.

The yellow gold watch (3) engraved with the Hawaiian coat of arms on the front outer case, was made for Princess Victoria Kaiulani,

heir-apparent of Queen Lilioukalani. Princess Kaiulani was born October 16, 1875, in Honolulu to the Hawaiian Princess Likelike and her husband, Archibald Scott Cleghorn, Collector General of Customs and later Governor of Oahu. The Princess had been educated in Scotland and England in preparation for assuming her place on the throne of Hawaii.

Engraved on the back of the watch, under the royal crown, is an uplifted arm with a tabu stick and a length of sacred *aha* cord (3A and 3B), testifying to the Princess' extremely high rank. On the dial is a photograph of Princess Kaiulani (3C), taken from one made by the Tynan Brothers firm,

3 C

6 A

41 Bath Street, Jersey. (American Watch Company, Waltham, Mass. No. 5,539,526. Diameter 1 3/8″; 3/8″ thick.)

Of particular significance is the watch (4) of yellow gold, green and black enamel, and rose diamonds. It belonged to Princess Bernice Pauahi Bishop, in whose honor Bishop Museum was founded. She was the great-granddaughter of Kamehameha I and had been adopted by Kinau and Kekuanaoa. While still a child she was betrothed to Lot Kamehameha (Kamehameha V), but this engagement was later broken to enable her to marry Charles Reed Bishop for whom she gave up her rights to the Hawaiian throne. Just before his death, in 1872, Kamehameha V asked her to succeed him on the throne. Although she again refused the crown, no one has done so much for her people. As a princess of the royal Kamehameha line, her estate consisted of all the Kamehameha lands and was used to establish the Kamehameha Schools for Hawaiian children. (Cylinder escapement. Made by Locle in Switzerland, No. 63. "TIMEKEEPER" engraved on the movement. Diameter 1 1/8″; 5/16″ thick.)

The yellow gold watch (5) decorated with rose diamonds and black enamel belonged to Princess Likelike, mother of Princess Kaiulani. (American Watch Company, Waltham, Mass. No. 1,-55,494. "RIVERSIDE" engraved on the movement. "Likelike" engraved on the dust cover. Diameter 1 5/8″; 3/8″ thick.)

Another watch (6) of yellow gold, green and black enamel and rose diamonds, was said to have belonged first to Victoria Kamamalu, the younger sister of Kamehameha IV and V. Kamamalu was *Kuhina Nui* (Premier) from January 15, 1855 to August 13, 1864. The photograph on the watch dial (6A) was identified by the writer from the original photograph in Bishop Museum files as that of A. S. Cleghorn, husband of Princess Likelike and father of Princess Kaiulani. Mr. Cleghorn's photograph is from one taken by I. W. Taber, located at No. 12 Montgomery Street, "opposite the Palace and Grand Hotels," in San Francisco.

A check with the San Francisco Public Library revealed that Mr. Taber was in business at this location from 1884 until 1906. Since Victoria Kamamalu had died in 1866, she could not possibly have been the owner of the watch. Princess Likelike is known to have worn it. It would appear that Mr. Cleghorn had watches made for his two princesses—his wife, Princess Likelike, containing his own photograph, and one for his lovely daughter, Princess Kaiulani, with her own picture on the dial. (Princess Likelike's watch made by A. Gendre, Geneva. No. 4891. Lever escapement of the Swiss type. Diameter 1 9/16″; 3/8″ thick.)

The gold watch (7) with its dial in four colors of gold, was worn by Charles Kanaina (ca. 1801–1877), the father of Lunalilo, Hawaii's first elected king. One of the finest watches in Bishop Museum's collection, it was made by L'Epine of Paris and still has the presentation case that is stamped James McCabe, London. (No. 9553. Cylinder escapement, 4 holes, dualled, jewelled. Diameter 1 3/4″; 3/8″ thick.)

Also of interest, because of its association with Hawaiian royalty, is the watch that belonged to Dr. Thomas Tisdale (8). Dr. Tisdale was personal physician to King Kalakaua in Honolulu, and later during the King's final illness and death in San Francisco, January 20, 1891. The watch is 18k yellow gold and was made by Patek, Philippe & Company, No. 76904. Stamped on the movement and also on the case is the name of the George C. Shreve & Company, of San Francisco. "1890" is engraved in elaborate script on the dust cover. "TPT," also in script, is engraved on the back of the watch. (Diameter 1 15/16″; 1/4″ thick.) The back of the gold fob opens to reveal a shallow "secret" compartment. As it does not open wide enough for a photograph to be seen, it must have been intended for some other purpose.

Left to right: Georgian shape Seth Thomas clock in mahogany, maple inlay, ca. 1890; gilt metal Waterbury clock, porcelain picture of 3 cherubs, ca. 1900; French clock, made by Marti, sold by Tiffany to Rolla Wells, former mayor of St. Louis, ca. 1890, is gold plated inside and out, on case and on works, every wheel jeweled on both ends (also shown bottom row this month's cover); Wilcox clock, ca. 1900, white marble case built like Greek temple; brass and glass Gilbert clock, ca. 1900, dome in single piece of glass; white marble clock, made in France, ca. 1890; New Haven 1-day clock, walnut case, ca. 1880.

What's O'clock?

Featuring the collection of Gordon B. Nance, Columbia, Missouri
Photographed for *Spinning Wheel* by VIVIAN HANSBROUGH

Left: The clock that started Mr. Nance's collection in 1945. Refinishing the walnut case intended as a display cabinet for trinkets, he became intrigued with putting the works in running order; has collected and repaired clocks ever since. This is an Ansonia clock, ca. 1860, with compensating pendulum, that is, when it becomes warm, the wooden rod expands down, and the brass pendulum expands up; it keeps time within 17 seconds a month of Naval Observatory time. *Right*: The type used before the invention of the pendulum in 1657. This reproduction was made to sell for $5 at the Columbian Exposition in 1893; those unsold were given away as door prizes at a N. Y. play.

Top shelf: Walnut case, glass front shows pendulum—Mr. Nance installed works from old kitchen clock; Ithaca calendar clock, ca. 1880, in walnut and ebony case, tells hour and minute in top, date of month and day of week in bottom, magnifying glass in pendulum; rosewood case intricately inlaid with boxwood—this 8-day spring clock, ca. 1850, is in demand by collectors; Seth Thomas mahogany 8-day spring clock, ca. 1870, lyre shaped movement. *Bottom shelf, left to right*: Gothic shaped walnut Seth Thomas 8-day shelf clock, ca. 1860, cornucopia painted on glass front; modern Chelsea 8-day clock, mahogany case, has balance wheel similar to a watch; Elias Ingraham 8-day clock, ca. 1875, Grecian style walnut and maple case; Mr. Nance's grandfather bought this Welch, Spring & Company 8-day clock in rosewood case in 1865.

FROM Colonial days until about 1800, American clocks were made individually by hand, with hammer, drill, and file. Brass plates and blanks for the wheels were cast in sand molds. Metals were scarce and early clockmakers frequently resorted to advertising for old metal to use in making their clock movements.

Through the 18th century, tall clocks were made, patterned on the English style. Earliest dials were metal; the cases, frequently without ornamentation, of the wood at hand; both 20-hour movements with endless chain and 8-hour movements with weights were used. Wag-on-the-wall clocks were also made; actually they were tall clock works without the case.

Of "firsts", Brooks Palmer in his *Book of American Clocks* pictures a clock made by Abel Colley of Philadelphia, who worked from 1682-1711, as perhaps the earliest American-made clock known, and one by Benjamin Bagnall, active from 1712-1740, thought to be Boston's first clockmaker. Of the Bristol, Connecticut, clockmakers, Gideon Roberts, working from 1790-1813, was the first.

After the Revolutionary War, ingenious Yankees set themselves to devise a clock that was smaller and less expensive than the tall clock. The Willards of Grafton, Massachusetts, developed their banjo clock — Simon Willard, who patented it in 1801, called it his "improved timepiece", and between 1802 and 1840, made over 4,000 of them.

Double steeple wagon-spring clock (open) is Mr. Nance's most prized item; in mint condition, and valued at $350. When clock is wound, the spring flexes, and ends pull up. Made by John Birge and Thomas Fuller between 1844 and 1848. Clockpaper is pasted inside back of case. (Also shown bottom row, on cover.)

Mr. Nance checks the walnut "grandfather" or tall clock in his living room. Made in Oakham, Mass., by William Crawford (ca. 1745), it is 7 ft. 3 in. tall.

Top shelf, left to right: Seth Thomas coach clock, ca. 1850, in walnut case is 1-day non-striking alarm spring clock, popular for carrying on stagecoach trips; Kroeber patent pendulum clock with metal gilt case, ca. 1895—pendulum swings on rod, does not get out of plumb when clock is moved; Seth Thomas brass and glass clock, ca. 1900, shows mechanism through glass sides, type of clock made by early apprentices as part of examination for journeyman clockmaker; William Gilbert clock, ca. 1890, enclosed in Royal Bonn china case, shading from purple to white—case made in Germany, works installed in this country; another walnut coach clock. *Bottom shelf, left to right:* German imported white and green china clock; Seth Thomas Westminster quarter-hour chime clock, mahogany case, ca. 1900; Royal Bonn china case in green to ivory, pink and yellow roses, Ansonia works, ca. 1890.

Waterbury wag-on-the-wall clock, ca. 1880, has 14x22" walnut case. This type clock was popular before tall case or grandfather clocks were made; sometimes bare works were hung on wall; clock peddlars carried works on horseback through the Colonies, while local cabinetmakers supplied cases to suit customers.

Bronze hunter and fisher clock, made by Ansonia, ca. 1890, top of clock pivots to swing pendulum, hunter holds goose, fisherman, 2 fish. Mr. Nance wrote 50 letters over a 5-year period to locate replacements for two missing wheels; clock now keeps reliable time.

While there was considerable experimentation with shelf clocks, credit for introducing mass production methods in their manufacture is given to Eli Terry, who in 1806, accepted an order for four thousand. Formerly clocks had been made to order, but with factory production it was possible for the first time to make the clocks first and sell them later.

Numerous companies in Connecticut and neighboring Massachusetts began turning out their own shelf clocks in quantity and selling them, like Eli Terry, through agents in large cities or through travelling peddlars in country districts. Chauncey Jerome even introduced his shelf clocks into England where they met with a profitable response. Wood was cheap, and metal still scarce; and both wood and metal works were used until about 1837, when the wood works were discontinued.

The Connecticut shelf clock remained in quantity production until the financial panic of 1857 curtailed clock-making for a time.

Around 1850, the Marine movement, with its balance wheel control, supplanted the pendulum controlled movements. From this eventually developed the round, metal cased, back-wind alarm clock, which came out about 1875. An electric clock was perfected in 1914 by Henry Warren of Ashland, Massachusetts.

The Medicine Man's Gold Watch

by MARIE C. MENEFEE

As "phony" as his medicine.

"A GOLD WATCH with every bottle purchased," was the juicy plum held out to a gullible audience by more than one 19th century hawker of patent medicines—those panaceas costing $1 a bottle that promised to cure everything from hives to poor eyesight.

To get this "prize" the customer had to promise not to open the box it came in until he got home. It seems incredible that so many people were taken in by this obvious fraud—but they were.

As the medicine man handed his customer the box containing the gold watch he lifted the lid a trifle to assure his customer that it was really inside. When the customer opened the box at home, he discovered that instead of a solid gold watch he had a piece of pressed glass, skillfully molded and gilded in the form of a watch. From a distance these fakes look exactly like the real thing, and it's not difficult to understand how the medicine man's gold watch fooled his naive clients.

Most of these "watches" were probably thrown away in disgust, but many of them were given to children for a plaything. This was the case with the person who gave me the above information. Her father gave her such a watch many years ago, and told her how he had fallen prey to the medicine man's hoax. The one illustrated was found at a rummage sale, still in its original box on which was written "From Pa Ives."

DOLLS

The late Genevieve Angione, a well-known collector and doll expert, once stated that doll collectors were fulfilling a deep-seated need to return to those "good old days" when all they had to be concerned about was getting that much-wanted doll for Christmas or some other special day in their lives. True or not, there are no more enthusiastic people in the world than doll collectors. Since dolls of the late 19th and early 20th centuries have all but priced themselves out of the reach of the average collector, dolls of the 1930s and 1940s have become more sought after than ever.

Manufacturing Wax-Covered Dolls

by LILIAN BAKER CARLISLE

Superb example of a wax-covered German doll; high-quality artificial eyes, blonde mohair braids and coiffure; 25 inches tall. Collection Shelburne Museum, Inc., Shelburne, Vermont.

STARTING WITH a kettle full of boiling dirty grey pulp and ending with a be-ringletted and beflounced, rosy-cheeked blooming doll seems almost like magic to us today. But in the latter part of the 19th century it was an everyday occurrence in the quaint, quiet little toy-making villages of Germany. Wax-covered dolls were the pride and profit of Sonneberg and neighboring towns near the northern border of Bavaria. In the final quarter of the 19th century, an incredible two million dozens of dolls were annually exported all over the world from Thuringia.

In addition to the waxen babies, countless numbers of other kinds of dolls were produced in Germany—not to mention the bisque beauties from France and the penny woodens and solid wax dolls for which England was famous. Since World War II, the Thuringen section of Germany has been under Soviet administration, and one wonders what the families who made dolls and other toys for countless generations are doing today.

Fortunately for us, *The Wonderland of Work,* by C. L. Mateaux published about 1877, captured in words and pictures the technique of producing the wax-covered dolls and illustrated the procedures with a page of wood engravings.

Would it surprise you to learn that in the German toy-maker system of division of labor, 30 pairs of hands were employed in producing an ordinary doll head? Only the head, mind you—all the rest of the doll was made by other workers.

The first pair of hands in our progression belonged to the designer—an important and artistic member of the team. His job was to model a pattern for the new doll. In large, well-lighted workrooms, seated at tall workbenches called bankers, young men spent hours at this task. Their bankers could be screwed up or down, or revolved to allow the artist to work on any part of his model. In front of him were two lumps of clay. One he used as a tool cushion, plunging his bone modeling sticks into the clay as

he finished with them. The other lump of clay, under his skilled hands, metamorphosed into a doll head. He patted and dabbed away at the soft wet clay until the shapeless grey mass assumed the form of a pretty, though expressionless face which appealed to the modeler. He marked on it a few careful lines with a piece of red chalk and turned it over to Worker Number Two, who was responsible for making an exact mold or copy of it.

After the original clay model dried and hardened, the molder would lay it, face upwards, in a dish of wet clay, carefully pressing the clay into every corner of the back of the head up to the red lines the modeler had drawn as a boundary. He then built a clay wall all around the mass, somewhat higher than the uncovered face of the model. Another worker assisted him by holding the clay walls together while he fetched a vessel full of melted sulphur or plaster-of-paris from the stove, the contents of which he poured all over the face. As soon as the sulphur or plaster was cold, the dish was turned over and the clay removed, leaving the doll's face buried in the sulphur. This procedure was repeated, building up the clay wall again, pouring sulphur or plaster-of-paris and making the mold for the back of the doll's head.

In another room, an uninviting papier-mache broth, consisting of torn scraps of paper which were once old cotton rags mixed with water, boiled away in a great cauldron, gradually cooking until it became soft and clear. A worker then squeezed and strained the dirty water out of the pulp and mixed powdered clay and a little glue in it until the whole looked like a great lump of baker's dough. The dough was rolled, banged, and beaten into long, cake-like shaped loaves. Another worker picked up the loaves, laid them on a board, and flattened them with a big rolling pin, just as a cook does with pie crust. The paste was then cut into square pieces and piled on top of one another with a little powdered clay sprinkled like flour between each square to keep them from sticking together.

The next workman removed the little pile of soft squares and pressed them into one of the hollow half-head molds. The mold was passed to another man who, with a soft wet sponge and a little bone tool, fitted the soft paste neatly into every crevice of the mold so that it would turn out an exact counterpart of its shape. He pared off the rough edges of dough with a knife, gently slipped the half-head out of the mold and laid it aside. When the face and back-of-the-head pieces were thoroughly dry, the two halves were neatly glued together.

The next workman was a rough and heartless surgeon, for his job was to set the eyes. He ran a sharp knife around each cranium and kicked the piece out with a sharp rap of a hammer. If the eyes were to be fixed or stationary, the worker with a quick twirl of his knife cut out a couple of almond-shaped holes and popped in the eyes which were slightly warmed so they would stay in place until a little melted wax could be poured into the hollow skull to seal them fast in place. If the doll's eyes opened and shut, a much longer operation was involved.

The matched pair of blown glass eyes was first firmly fastened to the ends of a long piece of curved wire, something like a fork, with a heavy ball of lead fastened in the middle of it; it was the shifting weight of the lead which drew down the sleeping part of the eyeball when the doll was laid down. The eyes, half of the eyeball covered with wax for the eyelids, were carefully placed, then the wire

fastened in place by means of plaster-of-paris and sealing wax dropped in liberally. A slice of cork or piece of sponge was glued in and so located as to prevent the hard lead support from hitting the inside of the dimpled chin every time it slipped up or down. Last of all, some chips of wood were dropped in to keep the whole set-up firm; then the sliced-off top of the head was replaced and glued on again.

Originally nearly all glass doll eyes were made in England, principally at Birmingham, but by the final quarter of the 19th century the bulk of them were being manufactured in Germany. The exact method of blowing the eyes was a closely guarded German trade secret, but it was known that each eye was blown separately, and that ordinary ones costing a few pennies the

dozen were made of white enamel—that is, of glass with an opaque white substance mixed with it. A spot of black, or more often of blue which was by far the favorite color, placed in the centre of the enamel orb represented the pupil. Hundreds of large cases filled with dolls' eyes, packed according to size, were shipped out of Germany to doll makers every year. England, however, continued its manufacture of the costly blown glass eyes used in expensive dolls. They were fashioned exactly as though they were artificial eyes for grown persons, and cost as much as a guinea a pair (equal to $5 at the time).

After the eye-setting, the doll heads passed into the hands of several young women who carefully filed away rough spots and ugly mold seams and

163
Dolls

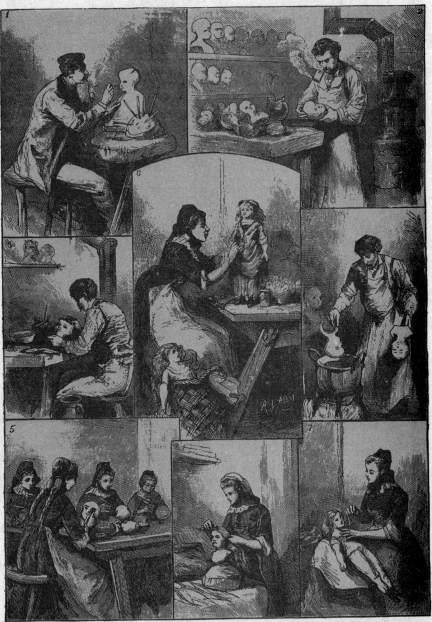

The Manufacture of German Wax Dolls: 1. Making the model. 2. Joining the head. 3. Setting the eyes. 4. Waxing the head. 5. Painting the face. 6. Hair-dressing. 7. Sewing on the head. 8. Dressing. (From "The Wonderland of Work," by C. L. Mateux. Published by Cassell, Petter, Galpin & Company, London, Paris and New York; ca. 1877.)

then splashed them all over with a fiery sort of paint, almost the color of a scraped carrot. Next they were handed over to a man standing before a huge vessel full of steaming, boiling wax, clear and white. He took each head and gave it one or more wax dips; the more dunks the better the wax doll was likely to be. The flaming red paint now shown slightly through the clear white wax and gave to the face a soft, lovely, delicate pink complexion. The expressionless heads were then dusted with sweet-scented violet powder to make their waxen skins easier to beautify further.

The dolls then journeyed to the painting room where their cheeks grew rosy and their lips reddened. Many busy people waiting to receive their batch of new heads sat along the sides of a long table running along the center of the cool, comfortable work room. One, with a stroke and a flourish, gave the doll two little bowed cherry-colored lips; his neighbor delineated the eyebrows; the head passed from hand to hand, each worker doing his or her own special task. Finally, the head with blushing cheeks and pink-lined nostrils was sent to the frau hair-dressers, whose nimble fingers effected the final transformation of the staring bold-faced doll, for it was the graceful coiffure

which gave the doll its gentle, soft, pleasant look.

The doll's hair was the costliest part of her construction, although tresses varied in texture and value. Black hair, never very popular with young customers, was really human hair. However most children wanted a doll with shining, glossy blonde curls made of a soft, silky kind of mohair. These tresses were a specialty of a house in London that did little else than manufacture this hair which was purchased by dollmakers in Germany and France, as well as England. Ready-made wigs of mohair, or of natural hair glued to a net foundation, or of raw wool braided and boiled to wave it were available for cheaper types of dolls, but for the wax-covered queens only individually rooted hair was acceptable.

When the mohair arrived from London it was tied in soft silken bundles, cut to different lengths, and ready for use. Rows of bald heads, perched on miniature hair-dressers' blocks, were lined up before the girls who were trained for this particular work. Each girl held a small bundle of hairs in her left hand, all of the same length and carefully combed out like a fringe. In her right hand, pressed to the doll's head, she held a blunted blade with which she deftly

tucked in the even roots of the hair, pushing the blade a little way down into the wax, then as dexterously switching away the bundle. This operation was continued until the tresses began to be quite thick, when she took up a little iron roller, pressed it to the doll's scalp, and rotated it gently and firmly over the surface closing up the gashes she had made with the blade. The procedure was patiently repeated until the pinky foundation was hidden and covered by soft hair. Eyelashes in the more expensive dolls were rooted in the same manner; cheaper dolls had to make do with a painted fringe of lashes.

The head was now finally finished. There still remained the hands, feet, and body. If wax hands and feet were used, they were fashioned in the same manner as the head—that is, modeled, then cast into molds. The bodies, frequently of common white calico stuffed with sawdust, were neatly made by women and children. Some of the daintier bodies were formed of pinky soft kid or snowy thin sheepskin, carefully stitched, sewn, and jointed. The home craft of doll-body making gave a livelihood to many poor people in the humble, pine-scented villages in Germany, but that is another story.

The Happifats

by GENEVIEVE ANGIONE

Photos by the Author

IN THE midst of the Kewpie madness which has been upon the land since Rose O'Neill's little figures first orbited, doll collectors have suddenly found something else to absorb attention—the little Happifats.

The Kewpie was patented in 1913; the Happifats, following in its wake, were on the scene by 1915-16. They were made of hollow bisque of widely varying quality, in two sizes and three types. The boy and girl illustrated here, quite possibly for the first time anywhere outside of trade catalog drawings, came in both 3½-and 4½-inch sizes. There was also a Happifat Baby in the 3½-inch size in a "white painted chemise."

Only the arms move, and while they are sufficiently balanced by the ballooning clothes to stand alone, the

breakage rate must have been phenomenal. This undoubtedly endeared the little creatures to their manufacturers, but parents evidently had other ideas about them for they do not now seem to exist in the quantities Kewpies still enjoy.

The little girl's dress is light blue shading into deep blue in the gathers. Her sash and shoes are pink. The boy's jacket and shoes are a pretty Hunter green and his pants

are a lively brown which also deepens in the creases. The "Mohawk" hair-dos are painted a reddish brown and divided into two back whisps on both.

Happy hunting!

The soft-bodied models with composition heads and hands, approximately 16 inches tall, seem not to have survived young mothering — or were not too popular. The same type hair-do is a sure sign of the breed, however.

INTRODUCTION

Dolls made by Philip Goldsmith are considered rare by collectors, but a large number must have been produced. They were made over a period of about 25 years, 1870–1894, and the size of the factories suggests a fairly large output. Most of these dolls have perished, but there still must remain some that have not been identified as Goldsmith dolls due to lack of information about them.

It is hoped that the information given in this article will enable collectors to identify many more Goldsmith dolls and to have a greater appreciation of them.

The excerpts from Mrs. Goldsmith's autobiography, the obituary, and notebook material, all were made available through the kindness of her son, Mr. Emil Goldsmith of Cincinnati.

PHILIP GOLDSMITH (1844-1894)

An American Dollmaker

by DOROTHY S. COLEMAN

This doll belongs to one of the great granddaughters of Philip Goldsmith. It has a red corset and red leather boots. The stockings are white with circular stripes of red. This type may be earlier than the bodies with all red stockings or it may be only a variation. The head is of untinted bisque with an unusual hairdo.
Courtesy of Minette Goldsmith Hoffheimer.

IN CINCINNATI, OHIO, and across the Ohio River in Covington, Kentucky, there was a sizeable settlement of manufacturers and distributors of dolls, toys, and games during the last half of the 19th century. One of the most famous of these was Philip Goldsmith who both made and distributed dolls and dolls' bodies. He was in this business for well over a decade before 1885 when he patented a doll's body with a corset on it.

Philip was born in 1844 in Prague, Bohemia, and come to America in 1861. He settled in Milwaukee and married Sophia Heller, a talented young lady who helped him in his business. It is thanks to her autobiography, begun in 1904, and concluded on Armistice Day, 1918, that we know so much about Philip Goldsmith, his family and their contributions to the doll world. Sophia Goldsmith always referred to Philip as "Papa" in her autobiography. Mrs. Goldsmith tells of the Goldsmith's arrival in Cincinnati, "Papa and his brother left (Chicago) for Cincinnati. One week later I received a letter to come to Cincinnati. . . . After inexperienced traveling in a sleeper I arrived at Cincinnati March 25th, 1869. . . . In the afternoon Papa took me to the store which they had rented 242 (246 W.) Fifth Street. . . . The

past few years the number has been changed to 312 West Fifth Street. He and his brother Henry were partners. $500.00 they invested together, only half of a store, about 15 feet long. It was to be a 25¢ store, no more and no less were the articles to sell. . . .

"Christmas came and we had a fine business. I must mention a marked occurence. Papa bought for cash now. There was a sale of a double wheel with a wooden man in the center, with a handle attached. It represented Weston the first pedestrian,* ("Pedestrian" was the name of an early bicycle.) as a try out in this country.

"Papa bought a few cases with a good profit for us and same was made to sell for $2.00 apiece and we sold them for 25¢. Our store could have been five times the size it was and it would not have held all the people who came to buy the toy. Finally Papa bought the entire lot about thirty-two dozen after consulting me. The bargain was so great that policemen had to be put at the entrance. A half square down the street people stood and it was just like a mob. One man became so furious because he could not get a toy he threw over the red hot stove. We thought we would all be burned to death. At 3:30 in the morning we closed our doors, with fourteen clerks behind the counters, we could not get hands enough.

First building occupied by Philip Goldsmith.

Goldsmith was employed as a clerk at 145 Walnut Street, an address made famous a few years later by Louis Amberg, a well-known doll manufacturer. Across the street at 144 Walnut Street, Strobel & Wilken carried on a toy and doll business for years. Charles Goldsmith was employed by Fechheimer who from 1881–1889 was a partner of Louis Amberg. The relationship, if any, of these other Goldsmiths to Philip is not known.

In 1875 Philip Goldsmith had a display at the Cincinnati Exhibition. Soon after that, business grew poor. About 1878 Goldsmith severed his partnership with Flechter and each of

"During that time (1869–1870) a Mr. (Wolf) Flechter, manufactured doll bodies which were much purchased for dolls' heads. Later the man manufactured baseballs. We bought from this man for years. I think all he could manufacture. Business was very satisfactory. . . . (ca. 1874) The manufacturer Flechter from Covington tried to induce Papa to become a partner in manufacturing of dolls' bodies and baseballs which he finally did."

Flechter's shop was located at 714 Madison Avenue, Covington. He made and repaired dolls for the Fall and Christmas season and made baseballs for the Spring and Summer season. The Cincinnati City Directories tell us that Philip Goldsmith kept his store at 246 West Fifth Street at least through 1875. At that time Harry

Right: All of the limbs on this doll are made in the same manner as those found on the Goldsmith corset body dolls but it does **not** have a corset. It should be noted that the laces and tassels on the boots are replacements made some time ago. The brown leather hands have the customary round sticks in each finger. The leather boots are blue and the stockings have blue circular stripes. The stockings end a short distance below the knee joint and have a simulated garter band at the top which is also a Goldsmith doll characteristic. This type of bisque head is most frequently found on lady type kid bodies and it is rarely certain that bodies and heads have always been together. However, a similar body and head have been found together in the Children's Museum of Indianapolis. Since Goldsmith dolls are rare, it probably is more than a coincidence to find the same type of head on more than one of these bodies. This type of head also is found on several of the Lacmann bodies which were patented in 1871 and 1874 and made in Philadelphia. (See illustrations 1052 and 1053 in the Coleman **Collector's Encyclopedia of Dolls**) It seems to be a logical conclusion that the doll pictured above is a Goldsmith doll made prior to his patent for a corset body. These heads all have closed mouths, applied ears and cork pates, which characterize dolls made in France. A similar type body in the Children's Museum of Indianapolis has a marked "F. G." French bisque head. Height of Doll 23 inches. Courtesy of the Western Reserve Historical Society. Photograph by Elroy Sanford.

Building occupied by Philip Goldsmith 1880–1891.

the men had their own factory where both baseballs and dolls were made.

Mrs. Goldsmith recollects these difficult times. "Business was poor, expenses large. . . . He (Papa) finally traveled for the dolls' bodies and baseball factory in Covington of which he became a partner. The factory was situated at the corner of 7th and Madison Avenue upstairs. . . . If I would be willing to help him he thought by moving to Covington we could live cheaper and I could assist him in the factory while he was on the road.

"February 15, 1878 we moved to Covington. . . . Papa had to borrow $1,000.00. . . . There was no other way of getting assistance. Papa had saved a few sewing machines which was all he had left to (re) start the business with."

Their struggles were rewarded and Mrs. Goldsmith wrote that by 1879 "Business was fine. It seemed as if all were coming our way again once more. Dear Papa worked hard and he showed it. I still kept going to the factory when I was able to do so. I had learnt to sew baseballs so as to be able to instruct the girls. After a while we dressed dolls. I made patterns for them and assisted in dressing them. . . ." (Mrs. Goldsmith had been a dressmaker at one time.)

"By this time patent dolls' heads and wax heads with hair were manufactured. Business was getting larger. . . . Dear good Papa. . . . Business was very good with him. At this time he was contemplating to rent the Alison (Elliston) House, an old hotel on Russell Street near Pike. It contained fifty two rooms. It was remodeled and the factory moved."

The Elliston Hotel, located on the northwest corner of Russell and Harvey Streets, in its day was one of the most fashionable southern hotels. It consisted of two large buildings which in 1880 were converted into the P. Goldsmith & Co. factory. A picture of the buildings shows the larger one

the corner to be five stories high. The words "P. Goldsmith & Co. Toy Manufacturers, Baseballs, Dolls Bodies & Doll Heads" were written in large letters on the building. A flag flying from the roof bore the legend, "American Toy Co."

An article published in *Playthings* Magazine in December 1908 describes the manufacturing process used in this factory as follows:

"The first doll manufactured in this Covington factory was what was styled the patent-head doll. It was a composition of flour, glue and pulp ground up. The mixture was put into a tub and worked with the feet in a truly primitive way until a dough resembling that of a pie crust, was produced. The dough was rolled out to a desired thickness and then put in a mold made of sulphur. This mold

Corset body made by Philip Goldsmith. The patent date is stamped on the upper part of the body, under the head. The corset, shoes and stockings are in red. There are two tassels, each lace which crisscrosses up the boot, ends in a tassel. There are crisscross lacings up the front of the corset and rickrack around the top of the corset. The two diagonal pieces of tape do not belong on the body. The Height of doll 18 inches. Coleman Collection.

was made in three parts; one for the back of the head and two for the face, which was cut in halves. After trimming off the dough clinging to the molds, the molds were placed on shelves in a hot room where the composition was dried.

"When the sulphur molds were removed from the hot room the now half doll heads were edged with the same composition as above described by means of a stick resembling a drumstick, and was used to stuff in the dough around the half edges, and thus connect the two halves after the stick was made wet. The heads, being connected, were thoroughly hardened again in the drying room. The rough edges were then trimmed off with a sharp knife and sandpapered. The heads were then ready for the painting.

"The first step in the process of painting was to dip the head in flesh-colored paint and then set it down to drip off. Following this, the eyes were painted in, then the hair, and finally the eyelashes and the eyebrows. A piece of cotton, dipped in a red powder, gave color to the cheeks. After the head dried it was then ready for the finishing process, which consisted of two coats of varnish to prevent the colors from wiping off.

"The doll bodies were made of muslin, which was stuffed with hair and sawdust. The upper part of the arm was made of muslin, while the lower part was made of two pieces of leather, stitched together to represent fingers. The finger stitching was guided by small sticks about the size of match sticks, which were inserted in the leather. The arms were stuffed with sawdust, and at the shoulder joints some cattle hair was used to keep the sawdust from coming out. The shoes for the doll were made of red and blue cambric."

Mrs. Goldsmith continues her story: "At this time (ca. 1880) Uncle Adolph (Goldsmith) was with Papa in business. All went well and business increased. Dolls' heads with hair, wax figures, toys, etc. were quite extensively manufactured especially show figures. Many workmen were imported from Nurnberg, business was spreading and dear Papa was looked upon as a very rich merchant. . . . He had his team of fine horses. Uncle Adolph at this time was foreman in the doll body department. . . ."

In 1882 Philip Goldsmith advertised that his company made "baseballs, doll bodies, doll heads, indestructible dolls, and novelty toys." At that time the term "indestructible" was generally applied to certain types of composition of which dolls were made.

COMPETITION with imported European dolls was growing more and more keen. In 1880 Charles Dotter of Bawo & Dotter, an international company, had patented in the U.S. a dolls' body with corsets simulated by a printed section. The china heads for these dolls were imported from Europe and it is not known whether the bodies themselves were also made in Europe. Being a resourceful man, Philip Goldsmith patented an improved type of doll's body with a corset as an integral part of the body. The article in *Playthings* of December 1908 describes his invention:

"In 1885 Mr. Goldsmith invented the corset body doll, which was the same as the ordinary stuffed doll. A piece of red or blue cambric, with rickrack on the edge, was sewed on the body. This doll became an instantaneous success, and the demand became so great that the factory was compelled to work a night turn. These dolls were shipped loose in the cases, as boxes could not be secured fast enough to meet the orders. In 1885 experiments were made in the Cincinnati potteries with bisque doll heads, but the clay continually cracked and the experiments were finally abandoned. As side line, Mr. Goldsmith began the manufacture of wax figures for window display purposes and secured skilled help from Sonneberg, Europe, for working up this branch of the business. The business grew and all kinds of show forms were manufactured."

A Montgomery Ward & Co. catalog of 1887 lists, "Patent Corset Bodies (no head), entirely new, with seat, kid arms, colored stockings, shoes with tassels, and adjustable lace corsets (105)—

Length	Each	Doz.
10 in.	$0.24	$2.50
13½ in.	.32	3.50
16½ in.	.48	5.00

The picture of this doll's body is almost the same as that shown on the 1885 patent papers.

As the business increased so did the need for leather and by 1888 Philip Goldsmith had an interest in a local tannery where his son Oscar was employed. Competition was growing at home as well as abroad. Arnoldt began to manufacture dolls in 1880 and the Klein doll factory began in 1885, both in Cincinnati. Though there were several large toy distributors in Cincinnati at this time, notably among them Strobel & Wilken and Fechheimer & Amberg, Goldsmith decided to branch out to other cities. We return to Mrs. Goldsmith's autobiography for details about this period:

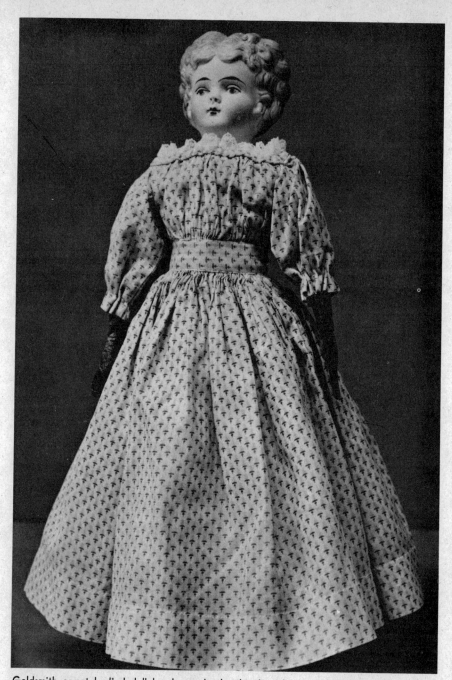

Goldsmith corset bodied doll has brown leather hands with round sticks in each finger. The boots are red leather and the stockings are red cloth to a little below the knee joint. These corsets appear to always be made in either red or blue cloth and the boots and stockings have matching colors. Sometimes the boots were made of imitation leather instead of real leather. This head is of untinted bisque. The doll wears an old blue and white cotton print dress. The lace at the neck is not old. Height of doll 14 inches. Courtesy of the Western Reserve Historical Society. Photograph by Elroy Sanford.

"Several years previous (to 1890) dear Papa brought to our home a Mr. Hensel from Pittsburgh with whom he did business. . . . Another, his name was Shueck. . . . Hensel and Shueck became partners in a toy house in Chicago. Papa was to import goods for this firm for a certain percent profit. All went well for a time. Goods were imported and shipped for this firm in Chicago. . . . Shueck would come occasionally to Cincinnati." In the 1890 Chicago Directory Schueck & Recht were located at 79 Wabash while Strobel & Wilken were located at 50–51 State Street. Both firms were described as "manufacturers" and "wholesale toy" dealers.

Mrs. Goldsmith continues, "Papa was interested at that time in Steinharter's tannery and gradually he bought it out. . . . November 26th 1890 dear Papa and Mr. Cairo left for Nurnberg, Europe. After three months trip they returned well satisfied with their enterprise. The trip was a business one. . . . Papa had bought several other business properties. Business went along successfully and we enjoyed prosperity." Philip Goldsmith's son, Emil, says that his father brought back from Nurnberg, two men who were trained in ceramic manufacturing.

The *Playthings* article of December 1908 tells us: "In 1890 Mr. Goldsmith brought a machine from Europe for making a kid leather body doll, but could not compete with the foreign trade in this line, although protected by a duty of 35 percent. The demand for the kid leather and the bisque head doll gradually began to cut into the product of P. Goldsmith Co., these foreign dolls being sold as cheap in 1891 as the cambric body with patent head made in this country.

"To maintain his ground, Mr. Goldsmith then began to make a better head. He put a coating of wax on the patent head doll, used imitation hair and put in glass eyes imported from Europe. He also commenced the manufacture of an imitation bisque head doll, which was made by the same process as the patent head, but instead of using a finish of varnish, ether was used to give a dull finish."

In 1890 Philip Goldsmith was assigned by Julius Wolf one half the right in his patent for attaching arms on a body, preferably made of papier-mache.

Tragedy descended and Mrs. Goldsmith tells of the horror of a night in April 1891:

"Our baby Emil was five weeks old, I remember the fire bells rang. From our window we could see the flames. On awakening our first thought was our factory, at the same time the door-bell rang. The private policeman was there to tell us it was our factory. How well I remember that it took less time than to explain. Edgar (one of her sons) was dressed and out of the house. Poor Papa was so stunned from it all arrangements were made to remove the factory to Hemingray's glass house which had been put into good condition for manufacturing purposes. Our building was packed for a large shipment for the next morning. It was a sad blow and an enormous loss.

"Four hours later Papa and the boys came home. Alfred and Edgar were all worn out. Our dear Papa, I can see him as if yesterday, haggard and an altered man for he well knew what loss it meant for him. He always thought it was one of the discharged foremen who took to drink and set the building on fire.

"Business in the new building was increasing yet I noticed Papa had a good many cares and many irons in the fire brought him many sleepless hours."

At this time several of his sons were working in the business of P. Goldsmith & Co. Alfred was a clerk and Oscar Goldsmith was bookkeeper. By 1892 Alfred had become manager

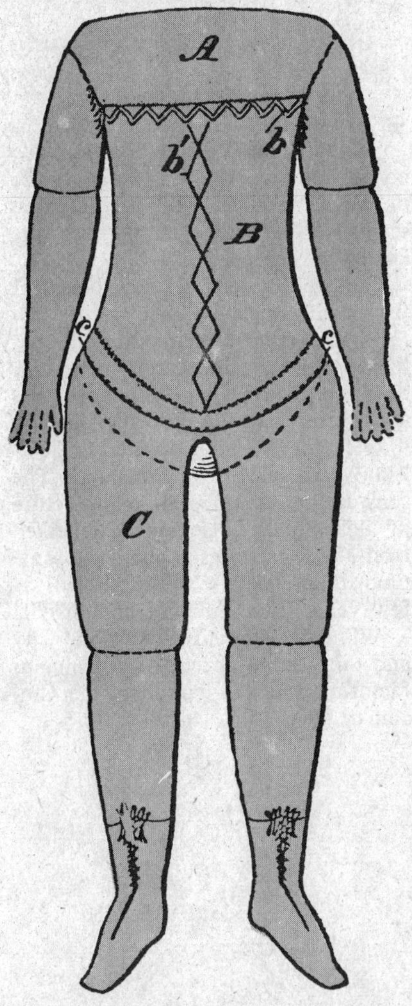

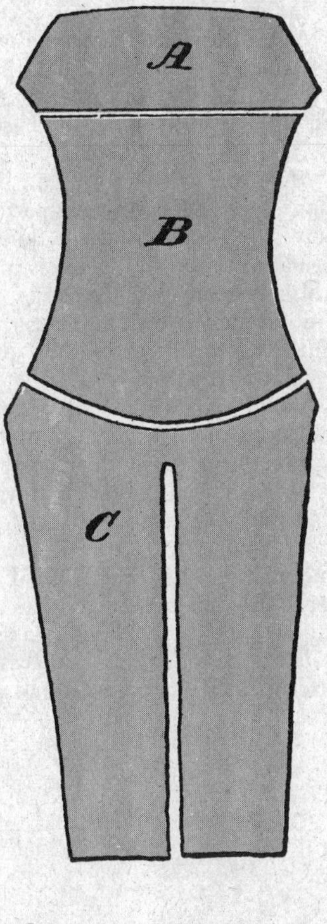

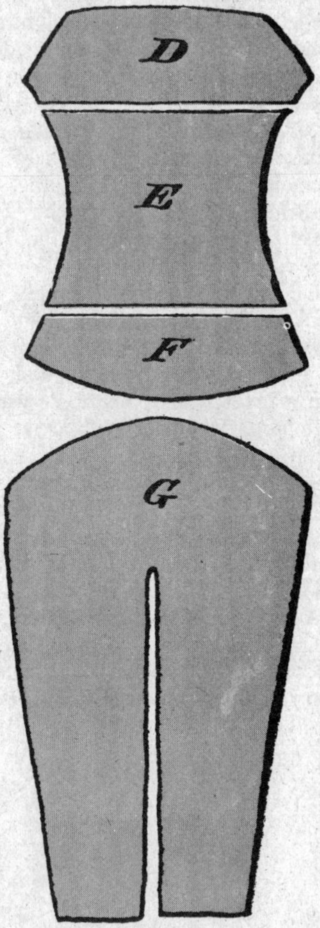

Illustrations from patent papers issued to Philip Goldsmith in 1885. At that time two years of grace were permitted before an application was made for a patent. Thus, Goldsmith could not have made corset bodied dolls earlier than 1883 and his patent would have expired in 1902. In this document, Goldsmith's given name was misspelled "Philipp." This was the fault of his attorney, for the name is spelled with only one "p" in his obituaries, and elsewhere. The patent date, "PATD. DEC.15,1885" is found on doll's bodies stamped in red or blue ink on the top of the chest where "A" is located on Fig. I in the diagram.

and Oscar was a traveling salesman for the Goldsmith Company. The new location for the factory was on the northwest corner of 2nd and Madison Streets, formerly occupied by the Hemingray glass factory.

The preceding selections from the autobiography were written in 1904 while the following excerpt was written in 1918:

"July 1894 they (Papa and two of his sons) left for Cedar Lake. . . . No room was to be had in the hotel at Cedar Lake so they lived across the lake from Cousin Ida Heller at Zimmerman's. . . . His untimely death came at Cedar Lake, Wisconsin through a terrible storm, as he could not swim."

His obituary from *The Post*, Covington, July 12, 1894 is as follows:

"DROWNED"

Fate of P. Goldsmith, the Doll Manufacturer,

While Enjoying an Outing at Cedar Lake.

He meets his death beneath the Waves.

"The family of P. Goldsmith, the toy manufacturer of Covington, was plunged into grief by a telegram received yesterday announcing his death by drowning at Cedar Lake, Wisconsin.

"Mr. Goldsmith was enjoying an outing there in company with his two youngest sons and his brother, A. Goldsmith, of the Cincinnati Freie Presse, and had been at the lakes about a week.

"The first telegram simply announced the fact without giving details. Late last night a second wire was received stating that the body had been recovered and was on its way to Covington, where it will arrive this evening.

"Mr. Goldsmith was 50 years old, and was senior partner in the firm of P. Goldsmith & Sons, manufacturers of toys and show goods at Second and Madison Avenue. He was a native of Austria, and came to this country when 17 years of age, with only a few cents in his pocket. With a letter of introduction which he brought to a

Building occupied by Philip Goldsmith after the 1891 fire.

gentleman in New York he borrowed $100 and set out for the West. He got as far as Milwaukee, where he settled down to peddling notions. In about four years Mr. Goldsmith had accumulated $1500. He married and moved to Chicago, where he went into the dry goods business.

"A few years later he came to Covington and opened the first 25-cent store in the city, and soon branched into the manufacture of baseballs, toys and wax show figures.

"Mr. Goldsmith was noted for his kindness to the poor, and performed many acts of charity in a quiet, unostentatious way. Last Christmas he furnished many of the dolls which were distributed by The Post, in Cincinnati, to the poor children of that city and Covington."

After Philip Goldsmith's death a small notebook was found among his personal belongings. This notebook contains many names and various notes, the full meaning of which elude us unfortunately. However, there are some names and notations of great interest to doll collectors. The name Amberg or L. Amberg, no doubt Louis Amberg, appears no less than thirteen times, once "stock and cases"

follows the name Amberg. The names Fechheimer, Amberg's partner, and Fahlbusch of the Cincinnati Doll Manufactory, also appear. The name Wolf appears several times and once it is next to L. W. & Co., which suggests that it could refer to Louis Wolf & Co., a famous contemporary doll manufacturer and distributor. The name Steiner appears frequently but there is no way of knowing whether this Steiner was related to any of the European Steiners who made dolls. "Bisque arms, Sample Dolls" are noted as well as just "Arms." "Red and Blue Thread" appear several times, once it is "Thread 40–." "Drill, 6 yds." and "Muslin" are noted. On a page under the heading "Corset Bodies" are found the following cryptic notations:

0/3 1/4 2/4 3/4 4/3 5/2
4 gro L 6–
1–20 dz H 125
3–12 - - 175
4–12 - - 2 –
5–12 - - 250
7–8 - - 375
1–4 gr A 350
2–2 - 550
432 -2- D 15 –
675 -2- 1350

Some of these notes are probably coded numbers and may refer to size or price or style. The first column seems to indicate quantity and the last column price.

Goldsmith's sons continued part of the business left by their father but they moved to Cincinnati and confined their products to "Baseballs, Sporting Goods" and "Show Figures and Forms" according to the signs on their factory building located at 207–211 West Pearl Street, Cincinnati. The sons did not continue the manufacture of dolls. Wolf Flechter disappeared from the Directories at about the same time that Philip Goldsmith did. A few years later, Amberg and Strobel & Wilken moved to New York City and thus ended an era of doll manufacturing and distribution in the Cincinnati area.

Late Bye-los And Bisques

by
LUCY CUNNINGHAM

At left: 15″ vinyl Bye-lo doll, 1951; original dress with label; painted eyes and hair. *Above:* Box the 15″ vinyl Bye-lo came in.

171
Dolls

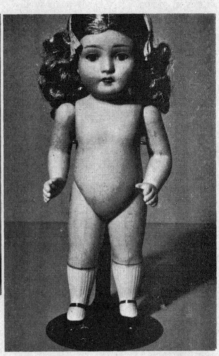

At right: 1951 all-bisque jointed doll, 7″ tall, marked on head, "83 over 125." *Above:* 6″ bisque Kewpie made in Germany, 1951.

In 1951 a quantity of Bye-lo dolls with vinyl heads was sold through the George Borgfeldt Co. of New York. As this is the company which handled the original Bye-lo Baby in 1923, there is no doubt that the dolls are authentic. They do resemble rubber in a way, but the early vinyl dolls became very sticky when stored, whereas rubber becomes hard and is apt to crack with age.

These dolls came in individual boxes labeled, "Bye-lo Baby — THE ALMOST HUMAN DOLL—Modeled and copyright in 1923 by Grace Storey Putnam. Geo. Borgfeldt Corporation, New York, N. Y."

The vinyl heads are marked "C Grace Storey Putnam." They have painted hair and eyes. The head circumference is 12″, and the complete doll 15″ tall. The cloth body is apparently cut by the original body pattern, although the hands are composition rather than celluloid. The baby wears diaper, bootees, slip, and organdy long dress and bonnet. The dress has a label of blue silk which says "Bye-lo Baby."

These dolls did not sell well because, at that time, vinyl was not considered collectible, and children did not like the faces. When I gave one to my little granddaughter, she said, "I think he looks kinda mad," and I had to replace the head before she would play with the doll.

At the same time, 1951, a factory in East Germany, not far from Bonn, was making bisque Bye-lo heads with sleeping eyes from the original molds. These dolls did not last long because production was shut down after about six months. According to Jack Fixit, who operated a doll hospital supply house in Washington, D. C. for many years, "The elderly lady who was making these dolls had to leave in the night when she learned she was going to be jailed for some reason. She has since died in Berlin."

These bisque Bye-lo heads came in five sizes and were sold without bodies. Some were of a fine, smooth bisque which compares favorably with the early dolls; others were not of high quality. The poorest were of a bright pink color which resembles a composition finish, caused by spraying the paint on after the head was fired. In time, these heads flaked, showing the uncolored bisque underneath.

All-Bisques

This short-lived factory also produced five sizes of all-bisque jointed dolls, from 5½ to 7½ inches in height. They had sleeping glass eyes and painted socks and slippers. The bisque was inferior but acceptable, and the hair was of bright synthetic material. These all-bisques were numbered in the catalog as: #25, 5½″, set eyes. #50, 5¼″, slp. eyes. #100, 5¾″. #125, 7″. #150, 7¼″. The 7-inch doll pictured here is marked on the head 83 over 125, and below that 16 0/2. The box she came in is marked "No. 83— 100 125." All these dolls were stamped "Germany" on the back in ink, which faded.

This same factory also made a line of bisque Kewpies with the little blue wings. These came in three sizes and were stamped "Germany" on the body. This marking rubbed off almost immediately, and as the bisque was of excellent quality, it is impossible to distinguish them from the original dolls.

Composition Bye-los

The composition Bye-lo dolls seem to have been made about 1926. They are shown in an old Montgomery Ward catalog, undated, but alongside a picture of a "Bubbles" doll (patented 1926), and some early composition dolls of that period. This composition doll is dressed much as the early bisque Bye-los, and the advertisement describes it as "The Genuine Bye-lo Baby Doll with hard-to-break composition head."

Black Rubber Gem

by GENEVIEVE ANGIONE

OLD RUBBER dolls come to light occasionally, but most of them are the hard, painted, shoulder-head type. Often they are chipped or even broken, and many of them are almost without paint. They are cherished nevertheless. The soft, or vulcanized, type are too often left flat on their backs in attics. They come to us without backs to their heads, with heads melted out of shape by years of high summer temperatures, and cracked open from long, cold winters.

The little 8¾-inch fellow pictured here is an exception to almost all rules. It never had any paint except the white of the eyes and the red on the lips, which is almost intact. The uniform blackness of the body would indicate that the rubber was colored before molding. The coloring material probably was carbon, better known as lamp black, used in many black rubber products. Although there is some graining of the surface texture, the doll is soft to the touch and still entirely flexible.

This is an old doll. The question is: how old? Unfortunately there are no marks of any kind to help us, so we can only know what the doll itself can tell us.

The face is the old, sweetly bland kind which was typical 100 years ago. The hair is molded in a slightly curly cap such as we find on old celluloids. Although the doll is pitch black, it is not a Negro.

The torso has wide sloping shoulders and the gourd-shaped abdomen of very old bisques, both French and

German. The arms and legs are molded with all the ridges of fat which were the signs of a healthy, happy baby in the 1800s.

All the limbs are easily moved on a full circle and will still hold many positions. The chunky little hands have molded palms. There is a small hole, similar to the pour hole in fine china and bisque figurines, on the inside surface of each arm and leg, probably air releases.

The ⅜-inch flat, scalloped squeaker button in the back is tin rather than the familiar rounded chrome metal buttons used for many years in dolls and toys. Careful manipulation discloses some sort of core of soft material in the head, which probably accounts for its wonderfully preserved shape.

Limb Attachment

One of the most interesting features of this doll is the manner in which the arms and legs are attached. Although they cannot be taken out for examination, the joints seem to be similar to those used in modern plastic dolls. Sturdy pointed thorns must have been molded on the flat upper ends of the limbs, and holes or soft spots centered in the flat hip and shoulder flanges. Once these thorns were thrust through the holes, the arrowheads kept them from being pulled out, but permitted the full circle movement on the thorn shaft.

On page 30 of *Dolls, Makers and Marks,* Elizabeth Coleman lists an interesting patent:

"HAMMOND, 1858. Thomas Rundle Hammond of Paris, a trader, was granted a French patent in 1858. His invention was for *invisible joints* on dolls, heretofore they had been visible. The dolls were to be made of *flesh colored vulcanized rubber to prevent harm from paints.*" (Italics are ours.)

This little black beauty qualifies on all three counts. The joints are invisible; black is certainly one flesh color; and the doll is vulcanized rubber. Because it could hardly be seriously considered as a French doll, the suspicion arises that some German manufacturer made use of this patent, with or without permission. Perhaps the fact that it is pitch black was the patent loophole.

At any rate, a similar doll, still in the hands of the widow of the original owner, dates the doll back approximately to 1875.

No matter what its origin, this is a fine specimen of that diminishing tribe, old rubber dolls of all kinds.

Above: *Closeup of Face and Shoulders.* Right: *Back view, showing squeaker. The doll, while black, is not Negro.*

Author's concept of invisible joints used on this old rubber doll.

THE INCOMPARABLE MRS. BLOOMER

by MARY HILLIER

Fig. 1

TO ME THE NAME OF BLOOMER had always conjured up the early days of bicycle riding and illustrations in old magazines of girls ludicrously garbed in plus-four-like suits perched stiffly up behind a high pair of handlebars.

It was left to a doll to educate me out of these misinformed ideas; a doll unique possibly in character and costume. She was bought at the 1851 Exhibition, that famous occasion when the Crystal Palace was erected in Hyde Park, London, in the hey-day of Victorian splendor.

No doubt the doll was an expensive and luxurious present since it was bought by the Duke of Northumberland for his children. When they had outgrown its charms, it was passed on to the gardener of the Estate for his young family. The family preserved it with pride and carefully kept it intact with all its possessions. The old lady who owned it, daughter of one of the gardener's children, assured me that she was never allowed to play with it and her mother kept the doll wrapped in a box lined with turpentine rags and sprinkled with pepper to keep moths at bay. (Hint for conservation!)

I doubt whether she was even allowed to lift the doll from its pretty wicker cradle with draped curtain head, for tucked away beneath the bottom mattress was a tiny card in faded handwriting which she told me she had never seen. It read: "This doll and accessories was purchased at the International Exhibition held in Hyde Park 1851. The Bloomer Costume worn by the same was introduced by Mrs. Bloomer of New York. Her name is Mary Caudle."

The doll herself is of a common type of the period. (Fig. 1.) She measures 24 inches from top to toe and, though time has added cracks to her wax face, she has a sweet expression with dark grey inset glass eyes, painted rosebud mouth, inset hair eyebrows and long ringlets of russet brown human hair.

"Mary Caudle's" Bloomer outfit consists of a shell pink skirt over long cream silk trousers, with matching jacket, waistcoat and wide brimmed hat. She has other clothes (Fig. 4) including an elegant low-cut dress, typical of the period, in narrow pink and white striped material with ribbon trimmings, dainty cambric drawers and underclothes, three pretty bonnets and two pairs of little kid shoes, one pair labelled "E. C. SPURIN, Juvenile Repository, 37 New Bond St." (a toyshop which stood nearly on the spot where Sotheby's now have their auction rooms). A wicker basket accompanying the doll in her wicker cradle, contains her Staffordshire china toilet set: jug and basin, sponge

173
Dolls

Fig. 2

Fig. 3

dish, soap dish, and foot bath, all ornamented with transfer-printed blue flower pattern and marked "DRES-DEN FLOWERS Opaque China." (Fig. 5)

In 1851 Mrs. Dexter (Amelia) Bloomer of Seneca Falls, New York, was a sensation. At 21, she had married a Quaker in 1840—the same year as Queen Victoria married. She was an ardent advocate of the temperance movement and soon joined forces with Mrs. Elizabeth Cady Stanton, the American forerunner of Mrs. Pankhurst, preaching women's suffrage. The first Women's Rights Convention was held at Seneca Falls in July 1848, and a magazine called *The Lily* (founded 1849), and edited by Mrs. Bloomer, voiced both the evils of strong liquor and the rights of women to equality.

Early in 1851, Mrs. Stanton was visited by a young cousin, Mrs. Miller, who wore an outfit she had made for use in Switzerland on her honeymoon. The long full Turkish style trousers

and a short skirt worn over the top reaching just below the knee appealed to Mrs. Stanton and Mrs. Bloomer both of whom imitated the fashion in their home town. The new-found style was described and recommended in the columns of *The Lily*. This was the beginning of a publicity and controversy which spread around the world.

Mrs. Bloomer herself was astounded and wrote: "At the outset I had no idea of fully adopting the style. No thought of setting a fashion; no thought that my action would create an excitement throughout the civilized world, and give to the style my name and the credit due to Mrs. Miller. This was all the work of the Press. I stood amazed at the furor I had unwittingly caused."

The Bloomer costume came in for both praise and ridicule. Doubtless it would have made less impact had it been just a fashion without its connection with this small band of fearless and emancipated American women. Their husbands apparently

approved though Mr. Stanton wrote amusingly:

"The worst thing about it would be, I should think, *sitting down*. These ladies will expose their legs somewhat above the knee to the delight of those genelemen who are anxious to know whether their lady friends have round and plump legs or lean and scrawny ones." (A sentiment echoed some 100 years later when mini-skirts first appeared).

In England, *Punch* lampooned the costume in the cartoons of Leech (probably the source from which our doll was designed). Long skirts, tight-lacing, and numerous undergarments were then the fashion. Floor sweepers invented for keeping floors clean at the Crystal Palace exhibitions were never used since the floors were swept clean and polished by ladies trains.

A rare little book by Watts Phillips, *"My Wife Turned Bloomer"*, published in London (Fig. 2) by Ackerman, showed ten scenes of folding pages depicting the adventures of Mrs.

Fig. 4

Fig. 5

Peregrine Perks, converted to Bloomerism by her American friend, Mrs. Colonel Nathan Sparkes.

This satire foresaw that if women wore trousers, other masculine habits would follow, such as drinking, smoking, carriage-driving and even, perish the thought, intellectual hobbies. In one scene the cook and maid have forsaken their household chores for the delights of literature and philosophy. Finally the ultimate absurdity (to the 1851 masculine mind), men were shown taking over the women's place, doing the cooking and laundry and minding the babies whilst their womenfolk are tub-thumping. (Fig. 3)

Peregrine Perks feels resistance to the movement is in vain and comforts himself with the thought that "an absurdity however Potent wears itself out in the end and leaves what is good and true to vindicate itself."

Plays on the stage, articles in the papers, musical scores, and Staffordshire china figurines, and Currier & Ives prints, spread the cult, and ladies wearing Bloomer costume even appeared in London's West End. Mrs. Bloomer herself never visited England or it might have been seen how misrepresented this serious lady was. After three years or so the American group gave up wearing the Bloomer costume as Mrs. Bloomer felt that the dress "was drawing attention from what we thought to be of far greater importance: the question of women's right to better education." She died in 1894, a pioneer in Women's Enfranchisement. By that time other dress reformers had revived the idea of Rational dress for women, and the use of the divided skirt or the old bloomer costume with modifications had become the vogue for the new cycling craze.

The name and style became imbedded in our consciousness. Only this week, in a London Bond Street window, I saw two all black Bloomer costumes. Amelia Bloomer herself would have been prouder for the recognition of her enfranchisement ideas.

With acknowledgement and thanks to Charles Neilson Gattey, author of *The Bloomer Girls* (Coward McCann, Inc., publishers), who allowed me to use facts from his book.

Webber Singing Doll

AS EARLY as 1824, bellows were used to produce sounds in dolls. Later, reeds were placed in dolls and sounds were produced by blowing on them. In 1878, Thomas Edison patented his "Phonographic Doll," but these do not appear to have been mass-produced until a decade later.

Meanwhile, William Augustus Webber of Medford, Massachusetts, was working on the invention of a doll which could sing. These dolls were patented April 25, 1882. According to the patent papers, inside the body there was a bellows, "a series of reeds and reed chambers, a raceway for a perforated music sheet, air passages leading from the raceway to the reeds, and mechanism for holding the perforated music sheet in close contact with and feeding it along the raceway."

Patents were secured for Webber's singing dolls in England, Germany, France, Belgium, and Canada as well as in the United States. Some of these patents show that Webber did not work alone. The English patent includes the names of George Bradford Kelly and Edward Lyman Rand, both of Boston, Massachusetts, and John Leslie Given of Cambridge, Massachusetts, as well as Webber.

A month after Webber obtained his U. S. patent, John Leslie Given obtained a U. S. patent for a similar doll with a perforated cylindrical drum in place of the perforated music sheet and other improvements, such as making the back of the doll rigid and activating the mechanism by pressing in the front.

Advertisements described the Webber doll in detail. The first one shown here must have appeared in 1882 or early 1883; the second one was published in the January 1884 issue of *Ladies Home Journal,* which was written before Christmas 1883.

The earlier advertisement describes the head as "finest French make," and gives the sizes as 22 inches and 30 inches. The following year the waxen (wax over papier-mache) heads are described as "best French and German make," with American-made bodies instead of the "stiff German body as in all imported dolls."

SOMETHING NEW. The picture represents the wonderful **Webber Singing Doll, just out,** and the GREATEST NOVELTY ever offered in Children's Toys. The Doll itself is of the finest French make, with Wax Head, Real Hair, and finest eyes, and is no different in appearance from the best of imported dolls; but within its body is a most ingenious machine, which when it is lightly pressed, causes the Doll to sing one of the following airs: "Home, Sweet Home," "Greenville," "I Want to be an Angel," "There is a Happy Land," "Bonnie Doon," "How Can I Leave Thee?" "A B C Song," "America," "Thou, thou reign'st" (German), "Frohe Botschaft" (German), "Tell Aunt Rhoda," "Buy a Broom," "Yankee Doodle." The singing attachment is a **perfect musical instrument,** finely made, and will not get out of order, and the doll is sold for the same price that toy dealers ask for the same quality of a doll without the singing attachment. Walking and talking dolls have been made, but at high prices, and liable to get quickly out of order, and they do not afford the little ones half the enjoyment that our wonderful Singing Doll does. We have two sizes. **No. 1**—22 inches high, wax head, real hair, fine eyes, and a very beautiful face—a strictly first-class quality French Doll. Price, complete, **$2.75. No. 1½**—Same as No. 1, but eyes close when laid down. 50¢ extra. **No. 2**—30 inches high, extra fine wax head, real hair, and finest eyes. Price $5.00. **No. 2½**—same as No. 2, but with closing eyes. 75¢ extra. These prices include boxing and packing. Sent to any address on receipt of price. An embroidered chemise, not shown in engraving, goes with each Doll . . . These prices are as low as the same quality doll is generally sold at without the Singing Attachment. It is the most beautiful present that can be made to a child, and will afford more amusement than any other toy in the market. THE TRADE SUPPLIED. Address the Massachusetts Organ Company, 57 Washington Street, Boston, Mass. U.S.A.

1882-83 Advertisement, source unknown.

Either the French origin of the doll heads was advertising fiction or French waxed heads were used on German bodies. The American body was of cloth, sewn at the joints, and the name of the song stamped on the front of the body. The later advertisement lists a choice of 14 additional songs for the doll, and 24 inches and 26 inches in height instead of the 30-inch size. The price for the 22-inch doll is the same except the chemise is 25 cents extra in the 1884 advertisement.

A Mechanical Wonder: Last year we introduced this CHARMING NOVELTY to the children of America, and it is safe to assert that no Toy ever devised attained such immediate popularity. Fully aware of its merit, we had thousands of Dolls ready for the Holiday trade, notwithstanding which the supply was exhausted early in December, and hundreds of children who came to our store were disappointed. We have been accumulating stock for the past nine months, and shall endeavor this year to fill all orders the day of receipt. **The Doll has been improved in every way since last year.** Instead of the stiff German body, as in all imported Dolls, our Doll has an AMERICAN MADE BODY with limber joints, so that it will sit easily and gracefully in any position. The arm is of Finest Kid with separate fingers. These are positively the finest bodies ever put in a Doll. They are of graceful and natural shape, and much better and more expensively made than the best imported bodies which they will outwear many times. The **Waxen Heads** with long hair are of the best French and German make, made especially for this Doll, and they are as beautiful as life, long hair, beautiful eyes, and delicately tinted cheeks. We consider them the finest Doll's Heads ever imported into this country, and that without the **Wonderful Singing Attachment,** the Doll Alone Is Worth the Entire Price.
The Singing Attachment is concealed within the body. It is one of the most ingenious inventions of the age . . . It is a perfect Musical Instrument, finely made and not liable to get out of order. [In addition to the choice of songs offered for the first doll were "Sweet Bye and Bye," "Coming Thro' the Rye," "God Bless the Prince of Wales," "Grandfather's Clock," "Child's Song," "Last Rose of Summer," "Joyful Message" (German), "Old Folks at Home," "Pop Goes the Weasel," "So many Stars" (German), "Sleep my Child" (German), "When I a Little Bird," "Cradle's Empty," "God Save the Queen."]
We can furnish 3 sizes: **No. 1,** 22 inches high, price $2.75; **No. 2,** 24 inches high, larger head, price $3.25; **No. 3,** 26 inches high, our best Doll, price $4.00. These prices include boxing. All three sizes are equally perfect and complete, but the larger the Doll, the larger the singing attachment, and better head . . . **Fine Embroidered Chemise,** 25¢ extra . . . The Massachusetts Organ Co., No. 57 Washington St., Boston, Mass. U.S.A. . . . **FINE COSTUMES** for these dolls with under clothing lace trimmed, finely made $3.00 to $5.00 extra.

Wording of 1884 advertisement from *Ladies Home Journal.*

DOLLS created by Joseph L. Kallus

by DOROTHY S. COLEMAN

Fig. 1: Mr. Joseph Kallus surrounded by Kewpies®. Courtesy of Joseph Kallus.

DOLL COLLECTORS are becoming more and more interested in the dolls that were produced between the two great wars. These are the dolls that were played with by a large portion of our present population, either as their own dolls or as their mothers' dolls. The dolls that were manufactured from 1918 through 1925 have been covered in the Coleman book, *The Collector's Encyclopedia of Dolls,* but the dolls made from 1926 through 1941 remain to be studied.

One of the outstanding doll creators of this later period was Joseph Kallus of Brooklyn, N.Y. *(Fig. 1),* President of the Cameo Doll Company of Port Allegany, Pa. He, himself, designed and made the models for many popular dolls. He also obtained numerous patents for their construction. Many of the Joseph Kallus dolls bear a decal or paper sticker with his name on it. He put his initials behind or below the ears on some of his later vinyl dolls.

The dolls of Joseph Kallus are avidly sought by knowledgeable collectors, and with a few exceptions are obtainable in good condition at two digit figures. However, they are not easy to find and this may be partially due to the fact that they are not always recognized. It is hoped that this series of articles will rectify this situation.

While not having the appeal of some of the European bisque dolls, they do have a definite charm and are among the top quality American dolls of the 20th century, both in artistry and construction. Mr. Kallus had years of training in art and the character faces which he designed and modeled have great appeal. These dolls give evidence why the American composition dolls won out in competition with the cheaply made German bisque dolls of the postwar period. *Figure 2* shows that "Margie," made by Mr. Kallus, with a wooden body and a character face, originally cost only 98 cents retail and included a one piece garment and a hair ribbon.

In the 1920s Madame Alexander made suggestions for some of the dresses worn by the Joseph Kallus dolls. It is not known which ones these were.

Joseph Kallus is most famous for working with Rose O'Neill in the modeling of the dolls which she created, especially *Kewpies®.* After Mr. Kallus assisted in this work, he became sole maker of woodpulp (composition) *Kewpies* in the U.S.A. All of the composition *Kewpies* manufactured by Mr. Kallus, doing business as the Cameo Doll Co., were distributed by Geo. Borgfeldt & Co. Joseph Kallus has continued to make Kewpies from 1916 to the present time. The changes in material and techniques during this period were consistent with the advances in technology.

Kewpies are probably one of the most popular 20th century dolls among collectors today. More want ads appear for *Kewpies* than any other type of dolls. With such a tremendous demand and a limited supply of antique Kewpies, naturally there have been many reproductions and imitations. Joseph Kallus has all of the *Kewpie* copyrights, trademarks, design and common law rights. Only firms which he licensed could produce *Kewpie* items in any form. This applies not only to graphic representations of *Kewpies* and to *Kewpie* dolls but also to *Kewpie* clothes, *Kewpie* books, *Kewpie* games etc. Through the years there have been innumerable law-suits about infringements on these *Kewpie* rights.

The *Kewpie* doll is revered in Missouri, the birthplace of Rose O'Neill, to such an extent that it was pictured in a 1963 history textbook for high schools entitled *The Heritage of Missouri*. Annually a celebration called "Kewpiesta" takes place in Missouri to honor the memory of Rose O'Neill. (See *Memo From Marcia* jun and sep '71.)

Some of the dolls made by Joseph Kallus prior to 1926 include *Babie Bundie, Bo-Fair, Dollie, Vanitie Doll, Baby Bo Kaye* and *Little Annie Rooney*.

The following is a chronological summary of most of the dolls produced by Joseph Kallus from 1926 through 1929. Some of these dolls continued in production long after 1929 and even into the Vinyl era of the 1950s and later. Other installments will describe dolls from 1930-1941.

1926

BABY BO KAYE and LITTLE ANNIE ROONEY

Some of the records on both *Baby*

Fig. 3: MARGIE undressed, showing her joints and ability to stand in a particular pose. Height 10 inches.© Coleman collection.

Bo Kaye and *Little Annie Rooney* are dated 1926 but the information on these two dolls is given in *The Collector's Encyclopedia of Dolls*.

1927

BABY BLOSSOM (Copyrighted)

This doll has the "character face of a small child," according to the copyright papers. It resembles a baby's head with eyes glancing to the side, a tiny pug nose and dimples in each fat cheek. The molded hair is short with a lock coming down over the forehead. There are composition versions and fabric versions with embossed buckram backed faces. After World War II a 16-inch composition *Baby Blossom* was made in a version with a flock spray finish. It had stencil finish decorations and shading spray for a portrait effect.

(Please turn the page)

177 Dolls

Fig. 2: MARGIE dolls in store window, New York City, 1929.© The print reads, "Over 100,000 sold— Margie 98 cents, the Doll that is Different—She balances herself in any position or poise." This picture shows two types of this doll's original clothes. A third type of original commercial clothes has been found and no doubt others exist. Courtesy of Joseph Kallus.

CANYON KIDDIES
(Copyrighted)

These *Kiddies* from Canyon Country were taken from drawings by James Swinnerton, Palo Alto, California. The children, probably a boy and a girl, had bands around their heads which held down their thick bobbed hair and bangs.

KEWPIE
(Regular patent for a cloth doll resembling a Kewpie.)

The patent for a cloth doll resembling a *Kewpie* was filed by Rose O'Neill Wilson and her sister, Calista O'Neill Schuler, of Saugatuck, Connecticut. It was later produced by Joseph Kallus. The entire doll was made of fabric and came in two versions. One had a hand-painted face with features put on with an air spray. The other version had a face that was done by a lithographic printing process. Various materials were used for the face, chief among them was sateen. This was mounted on embossed buckram or canvas to provide the contours of the features. The earliest bodies were cut in four pieces, but a 1929 improvement in this patent reduced the number of pieces in the body to two.

1928
BOZO
(Copyrighted)

This toy is in the form of a humanized dog.

SISSIE
(Copyrighted)

This doll has the head of a smiling child.

Fig. 4: MARGIE, a close-up showing the detail of her features.© Coleman collection.

1929
MARGIE
(Copyrighted and patented)

A regular patent was applied for in this year for making a doll with a separate neck piece which was a feature of *Margie*. The object of this patent is described as, "Constructing the doll necks as separate units or elements, independent of the heads or bodies, and then combining such separate necks with the heads and bodies in predetermined ways to form the completed dolls." The patent drawings show either a spring wire or a hook connecting the elements. The neck is held rigid in the body recees. The patent also states, "Up to the present time the necks of dolls . . . have always been constructed as integral parts

Fig. 5: MARGIE, an advertisement for the vinyl model.© Courtesy of Joseph Kallus.

either of the heads or bodies thereof and dolls constructed in this manner with adjustable heads are old and well known . . .

"By constructing the neck member as a separate member independently of the body or head of the doll . . . it is possible in the case of dolls having molded heads to simultaneously cast more heads per given die than has heretofore been possible; experience has shown that the number of heads which may be molded with the present construction is as much as double that which is possible under existing conditions . . . The novel construction applies with equal advantage to either soft or hard dolls, thus overcoming a disadvantage existing heretofore, which required one type of head for soft dolls and another for hard or wood turned dolls.

" . . . If the doll should be dropped either accidentally or intentionally the yielding action of the head and neck

Fig. 6: Paper tag used on dolls. This is similar but not the same as the trademark which was registered in 1930.® Courtesy of Joseph Kallus.

member within the body absorbs the impacts and thus reduces the possibility of breaking the doll to a minimum."

A soft doll has a cloth body and a hard doll has either a composition or a wooden body. Margie has a woodpulp composition head with molded hair and headband. The body is entirely of turned wood, and is composed of 18 pieces. It is articulated at the neck, shoulders, elbows, hips, knees and ankles with elastic stringing. It is the first segmented wooden doll created by Joseph Kallus. The balance is such that it will stand erect. The composition head is made in a 2-part mold. In each section of the head "an undercut recess is formed at the free edges thereof during the molding." Note the fact that the undercut was made during the molding.

The eyes are painted with large black pupils surrounded by a small circle of blue for the iris. Some glance to the right side and some to the left side. There is usually a white highlight on the left upper side of the iris. Upper eyelashes are painted on but no lower ones. *Pinkie, Joy* and other Kallus dolls have their eyes painted in the same manner. *Margie* has her mouth painted as if smiling and open with four teeth showing.

On the upper part of the torso (front or back) is a triangular heart shaped label with "MARGIE" in white letters including the quotation marks *(See Figs. 4 & 5.)* This is over two lines of smaller black letters which read, "DES. & COPYRIGHT BY JOSEPH KALLUS." It appears to be a decal label.

Margie was made in several forms of construction. The segmented wooden version was distributed all over America and England. Several hundred thousands were produced. It was made also as a soft body doll with an embossed buckram face. Recently another doll named *Margie* was made of vinyl plastic which was combined with some wooden segments *(Fig. 5)*. All of these dolls were made by Cameo. Another company which copied the wooden bodied *Margie* was eventually stopped by court order. The imitation *Margies* do not carry the label described above.

THE DOLLS created by Joseph Kallus from 1926 through 1929 were discussed in a previous issue. The dolls that Mr. Kallus and the Cameo Doll Company produced from 1930 through 1932, the depression years, are summarized here.

It should be remembered that the composition *Kewpies* and *Scootles* of Rose O'Neill and the composition *Bye-Lo Babies* of Grace Storey Putnam as well as many other dolls were produced throughout all of these periods (1926-1941) by Mr. Kallus, doing business as the Cameo Doll Company. Borgfeldt tried to get their subsidiary, K & K Toy Company, to make wood-pulp composition dolls but they were unsuccessful in their efforts and soon after 1925 Cameo took over the products formerly made by K & K Toy Company.

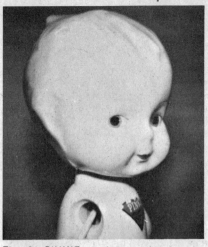

Fig. 8: PINKIE, a close-up showing the elastic stringing and the label.© Coleman collection.

1930

ADVERTISING DOLL
(Design patent)

This is an advertising doll designed by Mr. Kallus and manufactured by Cameo Doll Company. It is a R.C.A. trade figure for radiotrons, and is marked "R.C.A. Radiotrons" on its hat and on a band across its chest. (See "Who Knows," jul-aug '67, page 34 for query and pictures, and mar '68 page 37 for the answer.) It is fully jointed with complete lifelike articulation so that it can stand and hold practically any desired position. The doll has molded boots and a high hat that simulates a radio tube. It came also in a black skin version to represent Amos and Andy, a favorite radio team of the era. About 200,000 of these dolls were produced.

BABY ADELE
(Copyrighted)

This doll has a character head that represents a two-year old child.

CAMEO DOLL COMPANY
(Trademark registered)

Joseph Kallus, New York, N.Y., doing business as the Cameo Doll Co., registered a trademark bearing the profile of a child's head, with the words, "Art Quality" over the head and "Cameo Toys" under it.

KEWPIE
(patent granted)

The 1927 patent was granted for the cloth doll which resembles a *Kewpie*. Actually this patent had been superseded by a later improvement for which a patent application had been filed in 1929.

MARGIE
(Design patent)

The design patent pictures *Margie* with her smiling face, four teeth

Fig. 7: PINKIE, composition head, hands and legs, wooden torso and arms. Height 10½ inches.© Coleman collection.

showing in an open-closed mouth and around her head a ribbon is tied in a large bow over her right eye.

Regular patent application relating to limbs for dolls.

This patent was designed for a doll with a composition and wood body to enable a section of turned or carved wood to be joined to a section of plaster, papier-mache or other type of molded composition to produce a doll's limb.

PINKIE
(Copyrighted)

This is the head of a child with baby features *(Figs. 7 and 8)*. It has composition head, legs and hands. The arms, torso, and neck are wood. The same type of red triangular heart-shaped label is used as found on *Margie*, except the word *PINKIE* in white does not have quotation marks around it. *Pinkie* was made in several versions with various types of construction. It was made of segmented turned wood and/or composition parts. The eyes on *Pinkie* resemble those on *Margie* but the mouth is painted as if it were closed. *Pinkie* was also made as a fabric doll with an embossed buckram backed face. Recently another doll also named *Pinkie* was produced in vinyl *(Fig. 9)*.

1931

Regular patent application for a "Limb for a Toy Figure"

The leg as shown and described in

Fig. 9: PINKIE, vinyl version. Height 27 inches.© Courtesy of Joseph Kallus.

Fig. 10: BETTY BOOP, store display. Fleischer Studios created the movie cartoon but Mr. Kallus created the dolls.©Courtesy of Joseph Kallus.

this patent is the same as one of the types used on *Pinkie*. Previously the nail or brad which held the elastic to the limb was driven into the composition after it had hardened and become brittle which resulted in frequent breakage and loss. This was a popular method of production, although there had been others.

The patent proposes to mold the nail or metal device into the composition so that it is already there in place when the composition hardens thus eliminating possible breakage.

1932
BETTY BOOP
(Doll copyrighted by Joseph Kallus)

This doll was designed to resemble the famous movie cartoon character of the day, created by Fleischer Studios for Paramount Pictures. The head, hands, upper torso, and skirt are composition while the arms, legs, and lower torso are made of turned wood. It is fully articulated. The legs terminate in high-heeled shoes. These shoes, made from turned wood, are a masterpiece of clever designing by Joseph Kallus so that they could be made very simply but give the desired effect. *(Figs. 10 and 11)*

Betty Boop was a landmark case in the copyright office because it established the fact that a copyright on a

three-dimensional object covered a two-dimensional figure as well. This involved a lawsuit which was won by Joseph Kallus.

Betty Boop came in several versions, among them a soft body version and a version with composition legs which was dressed as a little girl *(Fig. 10)*. One of the composition and wooden versions is 12½ inches tall and has the dress, drawers, and shoes painted green. It has black eyes and long black upper eyelashes.

JOY
(Copyrighted)

This character doll represents a child. One version is fully jointed at neck, shoulders, elbows, wrists, hips, knees, and ankles. The arms, legs, and feet are wooden while the head, torso and hands are composition. Another version has composition lower legs and is not articulated at the ankles. There are still other versions. The wispy molded hair has one curl in the front on the forehead and two curls in back. *(Figs. 12, 13, and 14)* Some of the *Joy* dolls have a loop of hair on top through which a ribbon can be placed and tied into a bow. On other *Joy* dolls there is just an indentation in the curl on top of the head. The first version described above has on the upper part of the torso a red circular label with the word *"JOY"* on it. Around

the outside of the label is a gold frame with scalloped edges and on this are the words, "Des. & Copy" at the top and "J. L. Kallus" at the bottom. The lower wood extremities of the doll are shaped like shoes and painted pink or blue. It has the eyes painted like those on *Margie* and *Pinkie*. The smiling mouth is simply a curved line similar to ones found on *Kewpies*. *Joy* was made in two sizes, 11 and 15 inches, and several hundred thousand were produced.

Regular patent granted for a "Limb for a Toy Figure."

Patent application for "Jointed Toy Figures."

Mr. Kallus applied for a regular patent pertaining to "jointed toy figures having hollow bodies and other members made of collapsible material such as soft rubber." The invention provided for the construction of the rubber doll "in a manner to simulate naturally the relatively rigid and yielding parts of the original which the toy figure is intended to represent." It goes on to state, "special means is provided to prevent collapse of the doll under tension" by reinforcement with a rigid device located inside the body and vulcanized to the body. The rigid device in the body includes recesses for contact with ball joints in the rigid devices in the neck and limbs to enable the doll to have articulation. This appears to be one of the early patents for producing articulated soft skin dolls of latex. Joseph Kallus used the name "Beauty Skin" for his dolls made of latex.

POPEYE

Mr. Kallus was licensed by King Features Syndicate to make a *Popeye*

Fig. 11: BETTY BOOP close-up showing black hair and eyes. The doll wears a green dress. Height 12½ inches.© Courtesy of Dorothy Annunziato.

doll based on the Segar cartoons. After Mr. Kallus had successful experiences with *Popeye* dolls, he arranged with the King Features to license Fleischer studios and Paramount Pictures to make animated moving pictures of *Popeye*. When the moving picture cartoons were created the *Popeye* dolls were put in different poses to provide models for the Fleischer artists. The early segmented wooden *Popeye* dolls had "©//King Features//Syn. Inc.//1932" on one of their feet. Later vinyl versions were marked "Cameo K. F. S. ©" and were advertised by Sears, Roebuck & Co. in 1957-1959.

1933
MARCIA

Marcia is an all-composition doll representing a young girl *(Fig. 16)*. It is jointed at the neck, shoulders, and hips. It has molded hair and painted eyes with a wide staring look to the side. The shoes and socks are painted on the legs and feet. The doll comes in a range of sizes and wears a French-type outfit. Blanche Cromien, the chief dress designer for Mr. Kallus, designed the outfit by copying some French clothes displayed at Lord & Taylor's store.

Regular patent granted for constructing dolls like Joy.

Mr. Kallus obtained a patent which was used in the production of *Joy (Fig. 17)*. The doll shown in the patent diagram resembles the *Joy* doll shown

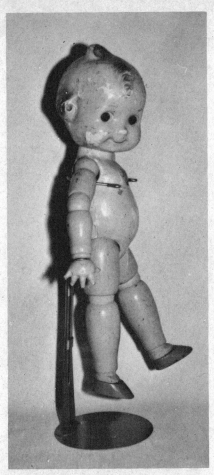

Fig. 13: JOY undressed; another version of Joy undressed will appear in the next installment. Height 15 inches.© Courtesy of Dorothy Annunziato.

181 Dolls

Fig. 14: JOY close-up showing detail of features and label.© Height 11 inches. Courtesy of Dorothy Annunziato.

in *Fig. 17*. This was a later version than the dolls with all-wooden legs. The molded wood-pulp legs had a hollow wooden core which was used for stability in stringing. The labeled *Joy* dolls shown in the previous article *(Figs. 13 and 14)* also appear to have been made in accordance with this 1933 patent.

The patent papers state: "The object of the invention is to improve the construction of the limbs or other members of the toy figure with a view to increasing the efficiency thereof and to materially reduce the cost of

Fig. 12: JOY in store display about 1932.© Joy is shown in two types of commercial outfits and a bow on its head. It is priced at 98 cents. Courtesy of Joseph Kallus.

production." In essence the invention provided for a turned wooden upper leg with "an inclined end surface" and a body that "is tapered at its lower portion having downwardly and inwardly converging external surfaces." The joint itself was produced by taking a turned wooden ball, cutting it in two and nailing the hemisphere to the "inclined end surface" of the leg to obtain a smooth rounded joint which enabled the doll to be seated without spreading its legs apart.

Regular patent for the articulated rubber doll granted.

1935
BANDMASTER (See Drum Major.)
DRUM MAJOR (Copyrighted.)

This doll was named *Drum Major* on the copyright but was later named "Bandmaster" which was soon shortened to *Bandy*. It was an advertising doll or trade figure for General Electric Company and was manufactured by Cameo Co. with the turned wooden parts made by Holgate Co. for Cameo according to the design and specifications of Joseph Kallus. Hol-

Fig. 15: KEWPIE-GAL, designed by Joseph Kallus and made in the vinyl era. It came in two sizes.© Courtesy of Joseph Kallus.

gate had the intricate wood-turning machinery which this doll required.

Printer's Ink described this doll: "He is a salesman eighteen inches tall, with a humorously cheerful painted face, a smart red and white drum major's uniform and legs and arms so limber that he assumes almost any human attitude. He was intended to be put into window displays. . . . He stopped so many doll lovers that radio shops are now going into the doll trade. They sell *Bandy* . . . to women who make doll collections, to mothers and fathers who see in him the ideal Christmas present for little Isobel, . . . And so General Electric, somewhat astonished, is in the Christmas doll business."

The body and head is of wood pulp composition and all other parts are of segmented wood. There are about 20 segments of wood which are assembled with coil springs. On the head is a high molded shako and the doll carries a baton. A molded medal around its neck bears the familiar "G. E." trademark initials.

Other trade figures designed by Mr. Kallus and made by Cameo include "Koppers Coke" and "Hotpoint." In addition Mr. Kallus designed several trade figures which Ideal Novelty and Toy Company produced. These include: Planter's, *Mr. Peanut; Conmar Major* of the Conmar Zipper Co. and a *Santa* for Shaeffer Pen Co. All of these were used as dolls and for display purposes.

Fig. 16: MARCIA, all composition doll of 1933. It wears an outfit copied from a French design.© Courtesy of Joseph Kallus.

1936-1938

No information found.

1939
BABY SNOOKS

The head for the *Baby Snooks* doll was designed by Joseph Kallus and produced by Ideal Novelty and Toy Company. From 1939-1941 Mr. Kallus designed several dolls for Ideal. *Baby Snooks* is a flexible doll which resembles Fanny Brice in her role as Baby Snooks. The head is of composition with molded hair having a loop of molded hair through which a bow or ribbon can be tied.

PINOCCHIO

Mr. Kallus designed the authentic Walt Disney *Pinocchio* doll produced by Ideal Novelty and Toy Company. This doll is 11 inches tall and has segmented wooden parts so that it can stand in any position. A colored picture of the doll shows it with a red suit trimmed with three yellow buttons and a yellow hat with a red feather. The large bow tie under its chin is white. The smiling mouth is open with lower teeth showing. In 1940 *Pinocchio* was made in three sizes, 8 inches, 11 inches, and 20 inches.

1940
CROWNIE (Copyrighted.)

This is a caricature of a king and is one of the many segmented dolls that were designed by Mr. Kallus. Note the poses which the jointed construction makes possible *(Fig. 18)*. The round ball for a hand is typical of this type of doll. Similar hands are found on *R.C.A. Radiotron, Bandy, Koppers Coke, Hotpoint,* and *Pinocchio.*

1941
COOKIE (Trademark for dolls registered by Joseph Kallus.)
Regular patent for a Toy Figure.

Application was made by Mr. Kallus for a patent relating to the joints of a doll with a body of soft rubber fabric or the like. The ball joints fit into rigid concave sleeve sections which provide stability as well as movement.

It is hoped that doll collectors have learned many things from this series of articles on the dolls created by Mr. Kallus. First of all that a doll with a given name can be found in several versions, even of the same material. *(See Figs. 13, 14 and 17 in Part Two)* If your doll has legs that differ from those on another doll with a similar named head, it does not necessarily

Fig. 18-A: CROWNIE, front view of a fully jointed character doll with a composition head and wooden body. © Courtesy of Joseph Kallus.

Fig. 18-B: Side view of Fig. 18-A.

183
Dolls

mean that there have been replacements, both types can be original. Sometimes a doll may come with molded loops in its hair and at other times it may have only an indentation in the hair. But both types are authentic and original.

The extensive use of wood in the bodies of dolls made during the late 1920s and 1930s may come as a surprise to some collectors. As collectors study composition and wooden dolls further, the patent information becomes of great importance in the dating of their construction. It must

be remembered that patent applications could not be made on products that had been on the market longer than one or two years. Thus if your doll has joints or other parts that resemble these patents, you can probably date it within a few years. However, just because the construction is similar to one of these dolls, do not jump to the conclusion that it was created by Mr. Kallus. Alas, he had many imitators. We can only be certain of a doll if it is marked or, in some cases, if it is absolutely identical with one that is marked.

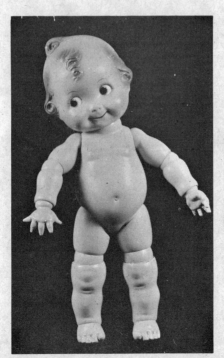
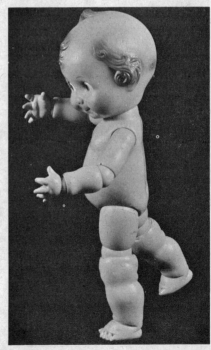

Fig. 17: JOY, front and side views showing patented hip joint. See previous installment for other pictures of Joy. © Courtesy Joseph Kallus.

Dewees Cochran and two of her *Portrait Dolls* (1960).

Dewees Cochran with her six basic *Look-Alike* heads and two complete dolls (1960).

DEWEES COCHRAN'S Dolls Are People!

by R. LANE HERRON

IN 1934, DEWEES COCHRAN arrived in New York after eight years in Europe. There she had studied Art History, given lectures, and won recognition for her own work in painting. Now that she was home again, she chose to turn to the dollmaking craft rather than continue her painting.

She took some examples of the unusual dolls she had developed to exclusive shops in New York and Philadelphia. TOPSY and TURVY and some American period dolls popularizing the pantalette era were her first sellers. Adult collectors proved the best buyers; the dolls were too cleverly wrought for children. She was told that if she intended to get into the doll business seriously, which meant designing for children, the doll should be realistic. Parents did not want their children playing with anything fantastic or grotesque that might warp their impressionable minds.

At first she was stunned. Then, if adults wanted reality, Dewees reasoned, what better than a living portrait doll of their child? She took the idea to a popular upper Madison Avenue children's shop. Her new toy would be a "Portrait Doll," meticulously sculpted and dressed, made of a durable casting compound.

Portrait Dolls (1936). Cincinnati sister and brother with plastic wood heads on Eff-An-Bee doll bodies of Dewees Cochran design.

Grow-Up Doll (Belinda Bunyan) at age 5 years and 20 years.

Within five days, orders literally rained upon her from the Madison Avenue shop—orders from their prominent patrons. Carved balsa wood and stuffed silk bodies were used for these first orders. So successful were they that *Harper's Bazaar* gave them space and started a chain of publicity which has lasted to this day.

Children, debutantes, brides, screen stars, even dignified school principals wanted a doll portrait of themselves. A well-known doll collector had her mother done from photographs taken in 1868 when she was 18 years old and just married.

Dewees soon realized the hard work entailed. Although she worked basically from photographs, eliminating tedious sittings, there were parts to buff, designs to be made of sturdy flexible joints, wigs to be brushed, combed, styled, shoes to be made that would not come unglued, costumes to be realistically fashioned, as well as the painting and finishing.

At first she did everything herself. But with the onslaught of mail orders, the work had to be shared among wig makers, special leather workers for shoes, dressmakers, and molders while she concentrated exclusively on portraiture.

To create a doll that looks "real" is not easy. There must be restraint to avoid a "dummy" appearance. If too much photographic realism is modelled into a head which is then painted, wigged, and lastly given the broken neckline to make the head swivel, the result can be a strange little "effigy" figure instead of a pleasant doll likeness.

Originally from Philadelphia where she had attended the

Portrait Dolls (the daughters of Lt. Comm. Hutton) by Dewees Cochran (1963).

186
Dolls

Academy of Fine Arts before going to Europe to live, Dewees and her husband had owned a little cottage in New Hope, Pa. On their return to American shores they rented a tiny stone house, part of an old Quaker estate, Holikong, five miles from their old home. There her doll success began.

She sold her first doll-joint patent for cloth dolls with molded faces (used on Topsy and Turvy) in 1935, and with the money obtained, moved to New York to continue doll research and develop her Portrait Dolls. A workshop and showroom was opened at 4 East 46th Street with a staff of assistants. The Silver Spoon set weren't the only ones interested in the incredible dolls. There was a considerable number of orders which definitely required financial sacrifice on the part of fond parents.

A less expensive portrait doll materialized in 1936 when Dewees, calling on her knowledge and study of physiognomy, developed six basic face shapes for American children. With these, any artist who could paint fairly well and select the correct type for a given subject could create a reasonable portrait doll.

Eff-An-Bee Doll Company contracted four of the first examples. These were manufactured briefly as "Portrait Dolls." They were an immediate success in the higher priced doll field, and were the first realistically proportioned character dolls, with the exception of baby dolls, ever mass-produced in the United States.

The *Cindy Doll* manufactured by Dewees Cochran Dolls.

In 1939, Saks Fifth Avenue featured these dolls from the angle of special order for likenesses for which they had been designed originally. *Life* gave them the April 3, 1939 cover and feature story.

All went well until that September when the war years brought doll production to a halt for Mrs. Cochran. Latex was the culprit, having been requisitioned as a strategic war material. For a while Dewees made portrait figurines in terra-cotta and unique figures and heads in plastic wood. Then she laid aside her dollmaking to go to work for the R. H. Donnelly Corp. By 1944, she was Art Director of that firm.

In 1945 she became Design Director of the School for American Craftsmen in Hanover, N.H. Two years later, when the school moved to Alfred, N.Y., Mrs. Cochran elected to remain in Norwich, Vt., across the river from Hanover, where she had been living, and established a workshop studio. Here she perfected her "Look-Alike" doll based on physiognomy types. She retained the New York studio, and formed, with an associate, a company called Dewees Cochran Dolls.

"Cindy," the modern Cinderella, was created in 1947. She was a 15-inch doll of latex made by a patented process which was owned by a New Jersey firm. This company contracted for fabrication of the dolls.

At the "Cindy" workshop at 10 East 46th Street, New York City, the doll was assembled, wigged, dressed, packed, and shipped. Dewees was gratified with the substantial first orders. However, the fabricator, with an eye to mass production, failed to keep up the first high standards. The contract was broken and Mrs. Cochran withdrew from the company. (Authentic Cindys are marked "Dewees Cochran Dolls" on the left side torso, embossed.)

Dewees Cochran's *Little Miss of 1830.* One of a series of six periods of American children (1934-1935).

In 1948 a new version of "Look-Alike" dolls was ready. Marshall Field and Co. of Chicago featured them that October, with Mrs. Cochran making a personal appearance to introduce them. The lower priced quality doll now became a reality. These were sold wholesale throughout the country as "fine handmade character dolls, no two alike."

As it was difficult to get someone to finish cast latex properly, Mrs. Cochran soon found herself doing it all in her Norwich workshop. Cast latex of top quality, she is convinced, is definitely a hand process.

In 1952 came the famous "Grow-Up" dolls. The girls grew up through ages 5, 7, 11, 16 and 20; the boys grew up through ages 5, 14, and 23. Faces, bodies and sizes developed in accordance with age. These doll children were Susan Stormalong, Angela Appleseed, Belinda Bunyan, Peter Ponsett, and Jefferson Jones.

In 1960, Dewees closed the Norwich studio and moved to California. Now at her "one-man" factory in Felton, California, she still makes dolls—portraits, Look-Alikes, and the "Grow-Up" series.

THROUGHOUT THE 19th century, the German pottery industry, especially that centered in Thuringia, turned out doll heads in such numbers and so cheaply that there was little point in English makers competing. Not until the outbreak of the 1914 War, when gradually the Continental stock in English shops was exhausted, did English potters seek to supply their own version of doll—usually a rather poor copy of German types. Staffordshire potters found it difficult to emulate the beautiful and skillful German modeling.

In my researches on English dolls, Arnold Mountford, Curator of Hanley Museum, and Mr. George Sherratt, descendent from the famous line of potters whose name he bears, have been extremely helpful.

Mr. Mountford told me that there were no locally-made dolls in the Museum, but that recently a head was presented marked "GOSS 9." I have since seen a doll made up with such a head. In his history of the Goss firm, M. J. W. Willis-Fear wrote: "Another idea tried at this time [World War I] in an attempt to help recoup the firm's fortunes was the manufacture of china dolls' legs, arms, and faces, as the chief supply for high class quality china dolls had ceased when war was declared on Germany in 1914. Apparently these Goss china dolls were just beginning to successfully capture the English toy market *despite their relatively high prices* [author's italics] when the war ended in November 1918 and the German toy industry promptly revived its former specialty, forcing the Goss factory to cease this line as the German dolls were considerably cheaper."

Mr. Mountford also passed on information on a more recent venture. The Diamond Tile Company, Ltd., of Brook St., Hanley, founded in 1933, manufactured earthenware dolls and doll heads from June 1 to September 15, 1942, copying from German baby dolls, as part of the current war effort, but in 1943, this firm was fined £ 300 "for manufacturing earthenware dolls and dolls' heads otherwise than under the authority of a license issued by the Board of Trade, contrary to article I of the Domestic Pottery Order 1942."

A contemporary press reported: "Originally the company was engaged in the manufacture of tiles and tile surround. After the outbreak of war [1939] that trade became slack, and dolls and doll heads were produced as a sideline by the defendants, Germany having previously controlled the trade." Obviously the dolls they made must be uncommonly rare.

From various correspondents came

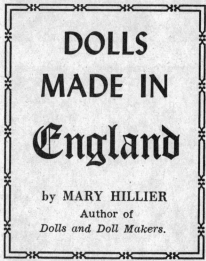

DOLLS MADE IN England

by MARY HILLIER
Author of
Dolls and Doll Makers.

Top: Melba doll dressed. Bottom: Melba doll undressed to show construction of the body.

reports that dollmaking had been carried on at the Howard Pottery, Norfolk St., Shelton, from 1925; at the Blue John Factory, Union St., Hanley, from 1939; and at the Doric China Company, China St., Fenton, before 1934 when a fire destroyed their factory. J. W. Ridgway at the Cauldon Works, Shelton, made dolls during the World War II period and perhaps it was some of these that were marked "N.T.I." and marketed in Canada and the United States by the Nottingham Toy Industry, Ltd. (*See* Dorothy Coleman's *Collector's Encyclopedia of Dolls,* 1969.)

Melba Dolls

Mr. George Sherratt, a practical potter himself, now retired, told me that there was an actual Board of Trade Instruction to Potters in the 1914-18 period to try their hands at dollmaking, and that various firms acted on that instruction. The first trial dolls were "very grotesque." He was able to give a firsthand account of actual dollmaking since Mayer & Sherratt, Clifton Works, Longton, made the doll heads marked "England," and/or "Melba."

Thinking the market for such dolls may not have been widespread, I advertised in Staffordshire papers for anyone possessing a doll head marked "England," "Melba," or both. This produced no dolls, but an informative letter came from a Mrs. Bryan, who said she was engaged in the factory at that time (1916) and that "there were different kinds of heads: baby dolls and heads that had to be cut out at the crown to have hair put on. Also dolls that had eyes that opened and shut; these also had to have crowns cut out and slits made for the eyes."

Mr. Mayer, now nearly 90 years old, recollected there were two sizes of "Melba" — an ordinary standard size and one smaller. As the mixture was a pink felspar, the finished product was called earthenware rather than bisque, which is made from china clay.

As soon as my book was published, the Melbas began to appear. Two dolls marked MELBA and CLASSIC were owned by Mrs. Tustin, of Spratton, England. The Melbas measured 16 inches, had china legs and arms on a stuffed body, rather plump dumpy faces, blue glass eyes, and fair hair. The Classic was rather sweet and pretty with blue glass eyes and black hair; she measured only 12 inches. Dr. Julia Boyd of Godalming, only ten miles from my home, produced an 18-inch Melba with blue eyes and "two left legs." (Actually all the legs seem to have been made in the same rather shapeless mold.) Her body was made of rather cheap "war-time" standard cotton. The impressed mark on her neck was

IN MELBA
4 ENGLAND.

DPC Dolls

Several collectors found small rather insignificant little dolls made up with poor style heads marked "DPC ENGLAND." Mr. Mountford thought this probably stood for Dresden Porcelain Co., Longton. One given to me was an engaging little boy in contemporary striped pajamas. The curious feature of this little chap—he measures only 8 inches — is the oddly jointed amateurish body, stuffed with coarse straw and made up rather like a Teddy Bear. The limbs are fastened on with old-fashioned "bachelors' buttons," as these metal discs were called. His blue eyes and two little white teeth are painted on; pottery is poor and matt surfaced.

Nonsuch

From Mrs. Aitken, Kingston, England, came an especially interesting discovery. Her grandfather, John Sneed, had been British representative for a firm of German Christmas card makers until the 1914 war broke out. He then teamed up with G. L. Nunn, who had been a representative in England for a German dollmaking firm and was also out of a job. Together they decided to produce dolls in Liverpool. Neither of them was a potter, but they realized dolls would be in short supply, and that they could find local talent for the technical side. They produced the NONSUCH.

Mrs. Aitken says the doll was modelled after a German doll with real hair which had been used as a hairdresser's model and then given to her mother to play with. The features and expression of the NONSUCH which Mrs. Aitken owns are curious, a little like a cariacature; obviously the head must have been made from one of the realistic type of dolls, perhaps KR or some lesser known maker, such as Wislizenus. The overlarge arms and legs are clumsy papier-mache.

Nunn's Walking Dolls

Mr. Sneed sold out his share of the business, but it seems Mr. Nunn was the inventive half of the partnership, for we find him in 1922 taking out a patent (#186,232, Nov. 15 '22) for a walking doll. This was made with spring hinges at the knee joint on legs pivoted to the body so that they could move freely. The late Queen Mary is said to have admired Nunn's Patent Walking doll when it was shown at the Wembley Exhibition in London, in 1924.

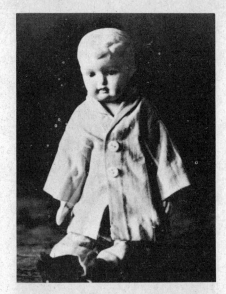

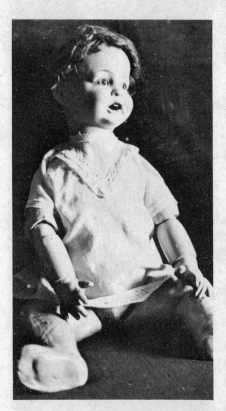

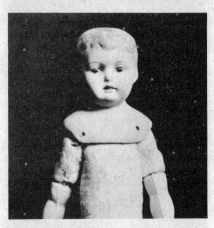

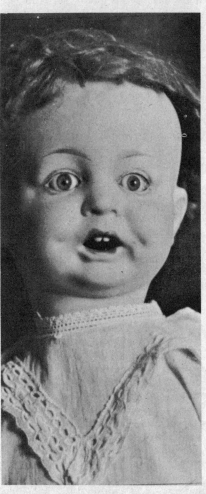

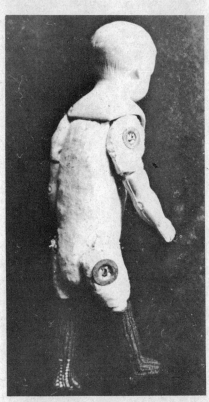

Top: DPC boy doll dressed in contemporary striped pajamas. Middle and bottom: DPC boy doll undressed to show construction. Note metal discs that fasten the joints to the body.

Top: Nonsuch doll in a seated position. Bottom: Close-up of the Nonsuch doll's curious features.

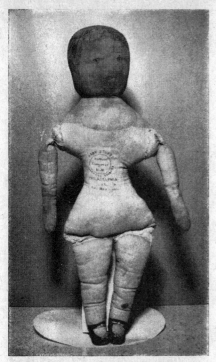

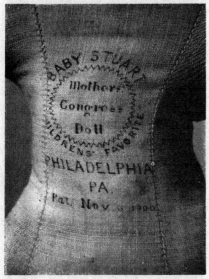

Mothers' Congress Doll

Patent Detail, Mothers' Congress

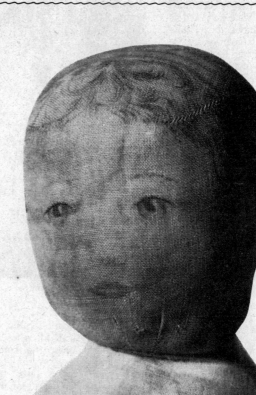

Head of Mothers' Congress Doll

PHILADELPHIA'S OWN

Rag Dolls

by Genevieve Angione

*Photographed by the author
from the collection of*
Mrs. Homer Strong, Rochester, N. Y.

NOT TOO many dolls can pinpoint their birthplace to one city with any degree of certainty but two dolls proudly hail from The City of Brotherly Love. The better known is the Sheppard or "Philadelphia Baby"; the other is the "Mothers' Congress Doll . . . Baby Stuart . . . Childrens' Favorite."

Technically both dolls classify as *cloth*, but almost without exception the old name "rag dolls," is used by both the public and collectors. Until fairly recently rag dolls did not enjoy the place in fine collections which they now hold, and always there have been comparatively few for sale.

Many battered, bursting dolls were, of course, thrown out by those apostles of neatness who settle estates, but the most surprising reason for their scarcity has always been the reluctance of families to part with existing rag dolls for the prices offered. Many rag dolls are fondly remembered by several generations, and the sentiment accumulated around these over-loved bundles of cloth and cotton is beyond price. They take no special care, cannot be further damaged, and they are just not for sale.

The Sheppard and the Chase

The Sheppard, or "Philadelphia Baby," somewhat resembles the better known Chase Stockinet Doll, and a Sheppard is pictured here with a seated Chase so that the differences can be pointed out for easier iden-

tification. Because the Sheppard seems never to have any printed trademark or evidence of a pasted label, it apparently was sold without markings or with a string-held tag which was removed. This specimen is 18 inches tall.

The picture clearly shows the funnel-like neck always found on a Sheppard, whereas the Chase neck is sufficiently play-worn to show the juncture of the neck and the shoulder. Both dolls are well painted where the body is not covered.

The two most salient differences are unmistakable. While the Chase is called "stockinet doll," it is generally covered with pink sateen, which is cleverly folded and sewed in such a way that it fits quite snugly around the shoulder plate with no evidence of any attachment. The Sheppard is actually made of a fairly coarse grade of knitted, off-white underwear material with vertical ribs like purled knitting. At the base of the neck, the heavy, painted muslin is always overcast to the body, apparently by hand.

The illustration also shows clearly the arm formations. The Sheppard has no elbow hinge because the stockinet is sewed to the painted forearm and sheathes the upperarm construction. The Chase has an elbow hinge and the painted portion extends into the upperarm.

Other differences are: Sheppards usually look like boys because their features are more rugged, their cheeks more prominent, and the ears, sometimes referred to as "bubble gum," are not as accurately formed as those of most Chases.

Clearly visible in the picture are the common stained feet of the Sheppard. Many of these dolls are found with what must be their original buttoned boots where the dyes used on the leather has bled through to the painted feet. Boots from one doll will exactly match the stains on a barefoot specimen.

The "Philadelphia Baby" is generally believed to have been made about 1900 for the J. B. Sheppard

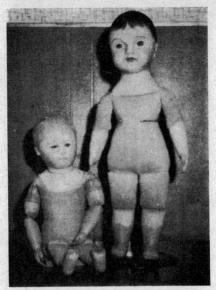

Chase, seated; Sheppard, standing

Company, a Philadelphia department store. The first identified specimens must have been the same size, 22 inches, for it was thought only one size was made. This 18-inch doll would question that conclusion.

The Mother's Congress Doll

The Mothers' Congress Doll, in-

finitely poorer in material and construction, is not so shy about its origin. Even the patent date, Nov. 6, 1900, is clearly visible in the center panel of the body.

Instead of being hand-painted over cloth, the head, shoulders, arms, and legs of this doll are printed on a thin but sturdy grade of muslin. The shoulders, arms, and legs are stippled with red to give the flesh tone. The close-up picture shows part of the seam which almost encircles the head so that it could be flattened like the Sheppard, the Chase, and others. There is also a back seam through the printed hair which leaves the face unmarred except for three darts below the mouth; these give some illusion of a chin—the only concession of any kind to sculptured features.

Although the doll is crude compared to many of the well known rag dolls, it nevertheless is factory-made. There is hand-stitching where the arms attach to the shoulder stumps, and bastings show at the leg attachment; all the rest of the sewing is machine-done with a surprisingly small stitch.

No attempt was made to indicate fingers except for printed red lines; thumbs were simply ignored. The tiny, printed Mary Jane slippers are black with white bows.

Early Imports to England of "Babies and Toyes"

by LESLEY GORDON

IN FUTURE I am resolved my conversation will be gem-studded. When I meet a neighbor on the street, no longer shall I waste my time and hers with "Beastly day!" "Yes, isn't it?" "Colder than yesterday," "Much!" and all that.

"By my taffetys," I shall greet her with a smile. "I'll lay a neganne-paut to a gorgoroon that winter is around the corner. The wind blows chill. I must away and change my nicanees."

Wearing my learning lightly, I shall charm my hosts at the next cocktail party with, "Do you prefer your inkles wrought or unwrought?" Or, mayhap, as an opening gambit, "I always feel that duretties with silk are so much more satisfactory than durance with thread, don't you?"

All this after only a few hours spent in the Library of Her Majesty's Custom and Excise.

That wasn't what I went there for, of course. I just picked it up by the

way. What I really wanted was the records of the earliest imports and exports of dolls and toys in London. And there I was rewarded, too.

The earliest mention was in a "book of Rates of Customs, being the Rates of the Custom House bothe inwarde and outwarde, the difference of measures and weyghtes and other comodities very necessarye for all marchauntes to knowe, newly corrected and imprinted, 1550. Imprinted at London by Nycolas Hyll for Thomas Petyt dwelling in Paules Churche yard at the sygne of the Maydens Head."

Here in this small brown leather-bound book, a mere three by six inches, in letters not easy to decipher, I came across "Bagges for children the groce iiis viid; Babyes for children the groce iiis & iiiid," and "Bedes in boxes the groce iis & iiiid," which proved to my satisfaction that more than four hundred years ago vessels carried dutiable goods *especially for*

children across the perilous seas.

The second Book of Rates is dated almost a hundred years later. "Subsidie Granted to the King [Charles II] of Tonnage, Poundage and other Sums of Money payable upon Merchandize exported and imported. Printed for Thomas Hewer, and Hannah Blaiklock, and are to be sold by Nicholas Bourne at the South entrance of the Royal Exchange, 1659."

Bound in with this are "The Rates of Merchandize; That is to Say The Subsidy of Poundage and The Subsidy of Woollen Clothes, or old Drapery, as they are Rated and agreed on by the Commons House of Parliament, set down and expressed in this Book, to be paid acording to the tenour of the Act of Tonnage and Poundage, from the first day of July, Anno Dom. 1642, during the continuance of the said Act. London. Printed by S. Griffin, Thomas Hewer and Hannah Blaiklock, 1657."

Here are listed "Babies, or Puppets for Children the groce, containing twelve dozen 00.13.04" and "Babies heads of earth the dozen 00.10 00."

The third of these rare little Rate books, dated 1689, is elaborately bound in red leather. This, too, is about three inches by six. The binding was restored in 1884, and again in 1964, which points to its great value. In this we find, under "Rates Inwards": "Babies or Puppets for

Children. the groce cont. 12 dozen 00.17.00," and "Babies heads of earth, the dozen 00.13.04," which shows a rise of charges, and the first appearance of toys other than dolls.

Later comes: "Babies Heads the Dozen 0¾d; Daggers for Children the dozen 00.04.00; Daggers of bone for children the dozen 00.04.00," the first mention of war toys.

From 1696 there were large volumes of handwritten records of imports and exports which contain entries such as: "Toys for Children to ye value of 004.10.0." From Germany came "179 dozen Fiddles for Children," and from Holland, "Daggers for Children, 36 dozen at 2s 6d pp. Dozen, 004.10.0," "Fidles for Children, 19 dozen at 2s 4d pp Dos. 002.17.0," and Rattles for Children, I groce and or dos. at 3d pp dos 000.5.0."

London Importations from Ladyday 1697 to Michaelmas 1697 included, from Germany: "26 Gross of Babies for Children, 40 Gross Pipes for Children, 14 Gross of Rattles without Bells, and 6 doz. Swords for Children." From Holland came "4 Gross of Bellows Birds, 3 Gross Pipes for Children, Rattles without bells, Balls," and other unspecified "Toyes."

From Christmas 1724 until Christmas 1725, toys were exported in English ships to Italy, Spain, Barbadoes, Jamaica, New England, St. Kitts, W. Indies, and Holland.

Quantities of toys from abroad came into the Out Ports, that is, ports other than London. From Germany, under the heading of Toys, came "17 Gross of Boxes Nest, 33 doz. Fiddles for Children, Pipes, Whistle Cocks, and 12 baskets of Water Span," whatever that may be. From Holland came "Children's Puppets and marbles."

Under another heading of "Toys" from Germany to London are listed "Bells for Dogs, Boxes, pills and nest, Fiddles and Pipes for Children, Sandboxes and Standishes," which latter my dictionary describes as an inkstand.

Under "Water Toys" came "Tinder boxes, Trenchers, Whistles," and other items that seem not remotely connected with either water or toys, but we must remember that a toy was once a trinket or small item, not necessarily a plaything.

The eye catches glimpses of strange cargoes, and the attention wanders. Figurines of wax from Venice; Gold and Silver Lace Counterfeit from Holland; Hair buttons; Shellpoys, Elephants' teeth; Hony, Garden seeds, and Glew. And what can "Junk Old" mean?

But I must hoard my precious cargo, my lemonees and chucklees, my buffins and mehobutbance—rare coinage to be dropped one by one into the conversation like pennies into a wishing well. Just for now, to save you the trouble of looking them up, I will tell you that *inkle* is a kind of linen tape, and *durance* and *duetto,* a stout durable cloth, eminently suited to winter nicanees.

European Creche Dolls

From The Collection of
Mrs. W. A. Wagner, Detroit, Michigan

AS FAR back as the Middle Ages, creche dolls were used at Christmas in the churches of Europe to portray the Christ Child's birth. In the scene of the Annunciation to the Shepherds, figures were shown sleeping with their herds; in Nativity scenes, the three Kings paid homage to the Baby Jesus. Many of the great artists of Italy modeled these figures for the Church. Most often they were fashioned of terra-cotta, though wax or papier-mache were sometimes used; occasionally they were carved of wood. Naples, renowned for its creche dolls, continued to make them in the time-honored manner until the early twentieth century. Now and then, as churches are remodelled, and old figures replaced with new, early creche dolls find their way into the hands of collectors, who treasure them for their age, beauty, and significance.

In addition to Holy Figures, creche scenes often included representations of everyday people who came to worship. The creche dolls pictured here show, at top, an elderly Italian couple of terra-cotta, 12" tall, ca. 1800-50; the man has no teeth, the woman a goiter.

In the second row are dolls from France and Spain. The 14" French Madonna, ca. 1730, and all original, has head, arms and upper torso of wood; the hair appears to be natural. Her gown is brocade, embroidered with roses; her blue silk cape is edged with silver braid; and her crown is of silver and pearls. The small Spanish carved wood doll with gesso finish, possibly the Christ Child, is jointed at wrist, elbows, and shoulders. His sandals are silver. He is all original, though at some time through the years the mid-section was altered and painted blue. A Spanish creche "Christ the King", ca. 1800 or earlier, is 14" tall, with head and body of wood; the eyes are glass. The green velvet garment, trimmed in gold braid, is belted with a gold cord; the robe is chartreuse satin; crown and sandals are of washed gold. These Spanish pieces came from Spain, by way of Mexico, to Boston where the present owner found them.

The figures in the bottom row are all Italian, and of terra-cotta. From left to right: a 13" figure represents an actor, ca. 1800-20, all original; woman with blue silk jacket over cotton dress, has terra-cotta hair, glass eyes, ca. 1800-30; smaller woman, also with glass eyes, has hair of undetermined material; 14" woman wears beautifully made blue silk dress, tan silk apron, vestee of fine pleated white linen with lace trim, all original. Her legs are wrapped with hemp, as are many of the terra-cotta creche dolls. The hands of all these dolls are particularly expressive.

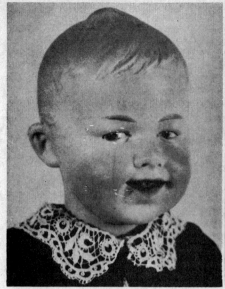

No. 1, Lenny

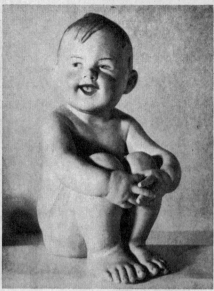

Number Two

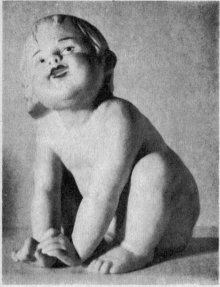

Number Three

THE BROTHERS HEUBACH

by GENEVIEVE ANGIONE

WHAT can be said in the United States about a firm established in a German hamlet in 1820? Records are understandably very sketchy and not too many people really care about it.

In *Dolls, Makers and Marks*, Elizabeth Coleman says Jean Paul and his brother, Ernest Christian Conrad Heubach, may have been "later owners" but they were young boys in 1820. The trade address was Sonneberg, but the actual factory was in Lichte, near Wallendorf, north and west of Sonneberg. Like its neighbor, Koppelsdorf, Sonneberg was close to the old Bavarian border and, presumably, to necessary transportation.

Doll collectors can thank German pride in workmanship, industrial competition, and the law for the markings which help to identify the much wanted dolls and piano babies at this late date. Apparently very little left the Gebruder Heubach factory without being marked in one or several distinctive ways, both incised and stamped.

Heubach Marks

Fig. 1 seems to be the traditional marking and the combined G H initials in the lower half of the disc is quite definite. At times this trademark is found in combination with *Fig. 2*, the Heubach square, to form an oblong which is often minute in size but unmistakable.

The peculiar lettering of "Germany" in *Fig. 3* is also unquestionably a Heubach mark. Just as clowns never copy the make-up designs which identify their fellow showmen, even though these designs are not formally copyrighted, the German dollmakers honored the markings of their com-

No. 4, Smiling Girl

No. 5, Smiling Dutch Girl

Number Six

Fig. One   **Fig. Two**

Germany

Fig. Three

petitors. Heubach incised deeply, and although some doll heads have only a size mark and this odd "Germany", countless comparisons of faces, hair molding, intaglio eyes, etc. leave no doubt about their origin.

A fourth mark, stamped on some heads and some figurines, is a small circle with MADE IN GERMANY in modern print between the two rings which form the circle. In most instances this circle is printed in the same shade of vivid green used by the workmen to mark some of the heads for piecework payments (like the red Jumeau workmen markings). There are instances, however, where the circle, printed in red, is combined with the *Fig. 1* mark. So, either green or red is authentic, combined with any of the three incised marks or with just the size figure.

To the best of available knowledge, the Gebruder Heubach firm had nothing whatsoever to do with the Heubach-Koppelsdorf porcelain works. Hearsay has it that the Heubach of Koppelsdorf was the brother-in-law of Armand Marseille. Fact or fancy, actual comparison of the workmanship of these two companies settles the argument. "A Heubach" is a Gebruder Heubach, and "a Heubach-Koppelsdorf" is just that.

Gebruder Heubach dolls are cherished by many collectors (the late Martha Thompson, for instance) because they frequently appear to be miniature portraits of real children rather than commercial dolls. Collectors have long suspected, too, that the Brothers Heubach, perhaps with a fine sense of economy peculiar to Germans, used some heads not only for figurines and piano babies but for dolls as well. Through the years rather conclusive proof of this has been accumulated.

Lenny

No. 1, Lenny — 4 inch swivel head with an 8¾ circ., incised in three lines: 5/79 Heubach square 11/ Germany. Fine grade, heavy bisque; intaglio eyes with molded highlight dot, blue iris; open mouth; one-stroke eyebrows in light brown; nicely molded hair tinted lighter brown.

No. 2 and *No. 3*—Lenny's face on an appealing piano baby boy and the same face with hair remolded for a little girl. These came in several sizes, commonly ranging from 4 to 5 inches up to 12 inches in ordinary sizes, judging from the specimens found. All had the incised disc, *Fig. 1,* sometimes augmented by a printed red or green circle to conform to the country-of-origin law.

Smiling Girl

No. 4, Smiling Girl — 5½ inch shoulder head with a 10 inch circumference above the bow, incised in two lines: the Heubach disc, Germany/ 1850. Stamped in green to the left of the incised Germany is the figure 58. Two smaller heads, 3½ inches high with 6 inch circumference, have incised figures 75 or 78 in place of the stamped green 58. Same general description as Lenny; these hair bands and bows can be either blue or pink.

The Smiling Girl is most commonly found as a shoulder head, ranging up to 6 inches or better. However, the head was also issued in a swivel neck up to tennis ball size.

Smiling Dutch Girl

No. 5, Smiling Dutch Girl—One of a pair of seated 6½ inch figurines, this face is strikingly similar to the doll above, with the head more tilted and the hair remolded at the front of the bonnet. Both the girl and her seated boy companion are incised with the disc but have no "Germany" mark, so presumably the figurines came first. They were also issued as a standing, back-to-back unit, *No. 6.*

Reference should be made to the difference in the quality of dolls and figurines or piano babies. Old timers talk about "the cry of the bisque." This is a hollow, slightly screeching sound which is produced when a finger is rubbed lightly and quickly over the bisque article. The original slip may have been the same but the figurines are a thinner shell than the doll heads. Besides being thicker, the dolls have an all-over complexion coat padded onto the smoothed outer surface, but the inside has the same texture to the touch as the figurines, a little unpleasant like very fine sandpaper.

It will be noticed that no mention has been made here about the bodies of the dolls pictured. The reason is simple: they show every indication of being replacements.

NOTHING would interest the Heubach collector and student more than some definite information about the source of Heubach doll bodies. Some of the dolls in this continuing series are on their original bodies and they are mostly a sorry lot.

It would be incorrect to call some of them "composition" bodies; they are more like compressed punk or pulp with plaster added to bind it. Hip and shoulder jointed in many instances, they are difficult to restring without a high speed drill because

they break under handboring pressure and melt if water is used to soften the plugs which hold the rubber. The body paint is poor quality, generally without a glaze; they attract dirt like magnets and wash down to the peculiar composition even when care is exercised.

The cloth bodies are not models of workmanship either. Made of sized bright pink or white muslin, they are outside-stitched with white or red machine overcasting. The hands are some form of composition; the feet are either the same material or crudely formed of cloth.

Nothing discourages a true collector, but it is amazing that while excellent workmanship and bisque characterize the Heubach heads right up to the last, few of the bodies are comparable to those of vastly inferior competitive dolls.

Another surprise is the difficulty encountered trying to find a substitute body for a Heubach swivel head. The original bodies must have been especially made because the necks of Heubach heads are longer and smaller at the base than other German heads of the same period. Seating them in the neck hole of a body from another doll is often impossible, and dozens of bodies can be tried before a satisfactory one is found — not right, just satisfactory.

It has been generally assumed that intaglio or painted eyes, closed or open-closed mouths indicated earlier dolls simply because it was thought all manufacturers followed the leaders into open-mouth, sleep-eyed production as quickly as possible. Continuous records, detailed descriptions, and relentless comparisons seem to undermine this theory. At some time in their productive life, Heubachs colored the slip pink. This simple economy eliminated the first step in the decorating procedure because no complexion coat was needed. These dolls are most accurately pinpointed by a glance inside the head or under the shoulder-plate.

This one small clue is valuable because the pink bisque was used in painted eye and sleep-eye dolls and also in closed and open mouthed heads. The most logical conclusion is that some firms continued to make the "older" type heads to beat the competition in the important item of cost. They simply had to be cheaper because they eliminated so many extra assembly steps, plus the outside cost of eyes and blinker bars. They are also lighter in weight, easier to pack and ship with less breakage.

Heubach's cunning seems to have been the appeal of the faces which resembled children rather than dolls. Eye appeal sells dolls today, whether for a collection or for a child, so when these dolls were assembled and dressed, few people examined the bodies. Once Heubach established this psychological fact, what inducement did they have to improve the bodies? None whatsoever. *(Please turn page)*

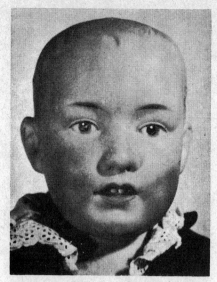

NO. 7—HERBIE

No. 7—*Herbie.* 6-inch shoulderhead of pink bisque. Deeply incised in the center back with the typical Heubach "Germany". Intaglio eyes with molded highlight dots and blue iris; open-closed mouth with two molded upper teeth; subdued, attractive coloring; single stroke brown eyebrows and lighter brown wash on the molded hair. Note the very childish, dollish nose. Substitute body.

NO. 8—WIND-UP WALKER

No. 8 — *Wind-up Walker.* 3½-inch swivel head with 8-inch circumference; incised in three lines: 3/Germany/76 Heubach disc 04. Open mouth with two molded lower teeth; intaglio eyes with molded highlight dot and blue iris; one-stroke brown eyebrows; lighter brown wash on well molded hair.

A wooden plug into the head holds it on a wood shoulder piece 1¼-inch wide and ½-inch thick, inserted and nailed in a 2-layer rolled brown cardboard chest. Gray cardboard skirt is glued at waistline with gauze, and the base is covered with 3-inch sized muslin with narrow lace, glued around

the lower edge. Two large pressed tin wheels protrude from 2½-inch slots in circular wooden base. Two ⅝-inch metal "balance" wheels are attached back and front with wire brads. Metal key in left side of skirt cannot be removed. Composition arms, mounted on extension wires in the wooden shoulder, are prebored for use on rubber and peg strung infant bodies.

This head (referred to as "Willoughby" sometimes) also came on crude-bodied walkers which, when wound up, waddled from side to side and managed to move forward.

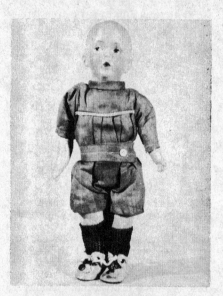

NO. 9—WHISTLER

No. 9—Whistler, all original. 2¾-inch flange-neck head with 6⅛-inch circumference. Incised in three lines: 23 8/0 / Heubach square / Germany. Pursed open mouth; intaglio eyes with molded highlight dot and blue iris; one-stroke eyebrows and blonde wash on molded hair. The composition above-elbow arms with cloth tops are attached to the stuffed pink cloth body which has boxed squeaker in front portion. Crudely pin-jointed straight cloth legs are attached on lower outer edges of body. Original blue "romper" suit is of the early 1900 period.

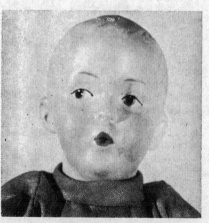

Whistler Head

Because the settlement of old estates keeps a slow but fairly constant supply of figurines coming into the open market, and because there are so many all bisque and bisque headed dolls available for study and sale, collectors are inclined to think of Heubach only as producers of bisque. This is part of our terminology problem because they were founded in the early 1820s as a Porcelain Works, which naturally implies that they also made glazed or so-called "china" objects as well. It is only by a happenstance or *era* that the market for their superb bisque objects reached a peak during the years of Heubach's greatest production.

For years the author has turned over countless large and small glazed objects looking for any of the Heubach marks; a piece finally came to light at a small antiques show on a dreary spring day in an up-state New York village. It has *Figure One* on the under side and, because the outer rim of the mark is definitely raised, it apparently was impressed on the piece rather than being incorporated in the mold.

No. 10. This small pin dish, 3¼ inches long and 2¾ inches wide, is pleasantly shaped, with an oval base. Originally there was a wide gold wash on the molded rim decoration, but most of that has worn off. The center picture of a little girl is still in perfect condition and under high magnification the small portrait looks like a handpainted fill-in on a black decal outline—just like an item in a coloring book. The painted area must have been well fired because it is not at all worn, even though the dish has been well used.

The top of the bonnet and the coat shoulder are tomato red. The round ribbon rosette and the smaller ruffle on the bonnet are yellow, the large ruffle is white, and the tied chin bow is magenta. She has brown hair, blue eyes with high pupils, and an excellent complexion. The front of her coat was painted to represent dark fur trim. The combination sounds a little outrageous but it is attractive, and typical of the period.

This marked and glazed piece proves there had to be others; Heubach was a mass production firm and this is not a worker's whimsy. The double problem is: Where are the glazed pieces and how have we, as collectors, missed them? Information about other marked and glazed Heubach items would be gratefully received.

Among the Heubach items nothing was more popular than their great variety of Piano Babies. To people who like them, these charming bisque children are irresistible; but even in

No. 10. Marked pin dish.

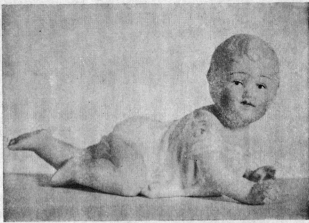

No. 12. Marked crawling child.

No. 13. Marked puppy.

their own day they were known as "dust collectors" to those who did not. Without exception, in all the years of the author's experience, the bisque in anything of this type from Heubach was the finest, whether the object was marked or unmarked. Always pure white, it is extremely fine grained and "sharp" to the touch. That is, it has a slightly metallic "cry" when rubbed with a fingertip.

No. 11. This unmarked child sits up 10½ inches high, measures 8¼ inches from the back to the toes, has a head circumference of 11 inches and is 13 inches around the body. The dress is white with a pink trim around the neck and both the neck and sleeve edges are trimmed in relief with standing dots of white, a substance which could be applied in droplets and yet in the firing hardened like the bisque.

The deep intaglio eyes have blue rims, pupils, highlight dots, and black lid linings. The open-closed mouth has a white center; the molded brows match the blonde hair in color; and the complexion is a beautiful tone, padded to an even perfection.

The arms and legs are applied to the molded head and torso—a greenware operation—and there is only a small round hole in the lower front of the dress for escaping gas to leave the hollow body during the firing.

This same child appears in several different positions—flat on its back playing with raised feet, etc., and we have no choice but to credit them to Heubach when they are carefully compared to marked pieces. No other firm used such deep intaglio eyes, or the beautifully shaped heads, hands and feet, or matched the quality and workmanship in this field.

No. 12. This crawling child has what amounts to a fifth Heubach mark. It is incised on the under side in three lines: DEP., the superimposed G over H in a raised circle, and 7285. The familiar initials in this instance fill the entire circle and the top half-daisy is missing entirely.

It is 4¾ inches long, with a 4-inch head circumference. The intaglio eyes have painted pupils and lid linings but no colored irises; and in this case the decorator did not follow the molded brow lines, but used a single blonde stroke higher on the forehead. The molded right shoulder bow is pink, and white dots in relief line the neck of the dress. The molded blonde hair and the complexion are very good.

Both arms and at least the bent leg are applied since the faint joining lines are visible on the under side; in this one the small gas hole in the base is below the number.

No. 13. The most unusual of all the Heubach pieces the author has ever found is this sad puppy. Incised on the under side with figure "1" and also stamped with the circular mark in red, he is presumably later than the other illustrated pieces. From the back to the right front paw he is 7¼ inches long, 6 inches high at the head. It is 5¼ inches across the head to the tips of his ears.

The bisque is very white and sharp;

No. 11. Unmarked Piano Baby.

the black trim shades to gray on the head, and there is some brown shading below and above the eyes. The intaglio pupils are very deep, with large white relief highlights. The eyes are brown and have both upper and lower lid linings. There is a small, round gas hole in the base under the stamped mark.

These gas holes are important, especially for novices. They are not "pour holes" from which the unset slip was poured in the original molding. Because these creations have applied parts, they have adequate pour holes from an arm or a leg opening, hence these small holes for gas to escape during firing, can be almost as small as the sew holes on some shoulder head dolls.

The quality of the bisque and the workmanship are the most important factors, but if there is a hole which accepts anything larger than the sharpened end of a pencil, be sure the piece is marked or get outside advice before making a purchase. Many types and sizes of modern pieces (this includes the past 10 or even 20 years) on the market resemble the old ones. Some of them do have small gas holes as well as painted black and red numbers which look like old German figures, or oval holes which will permit the entry of an entire cupped hand. Still others are open shells entirely without the closed bases which characterized the best of the old type. Some of these recent products enter this country with labels which are soaked off, or stamped marks which can be buffed off, so it has truly become a "buyer beware" situation.

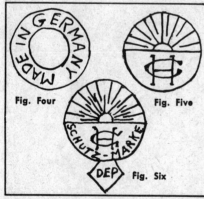

Fig. 4 is the previously described double circle which may be stamped in red or green, either alone or with some other portion of the marks. Fig. 5 may frequently have been impressed rather than incised because the surrounding circle is often depressed. Fig. 6 is stamped on some glazed pieces, impressed on others, and may have been the original pattern from which Fig. 1 was later designed because the broken straight lines would not have molded well. As the century progressed, incised numbers were more common.

Perhaps the most interesting feature about Fig. 6 is that it contains the words "Schutz Marke" which is German for "trademark." It has been suggested that the superimposed "G" and "H" might be the mark of another firm than Gebruder Heubach. This clear, old mark seems to end that controversy.

A duplicate of the author's pin dish was reported by Roslyn South. Still in mint condition, hers has the gold border intact and the same little girl with very different coloring. Constant comparison has led to the belief that the decorators were allowed great latitude in coloring to provide as wide a variety as possible in the same basic design.

A round dish, 2¾ inches in diameter, colored like the author's oval dish, was reported by Mrs. W. E. Foster.

The most beautiful piece to join the author's collection is by all odds the lovely seated lady from Mrs. Ruth L. Givens. The oval base holding the chair is 6 x 7 inches and is stamped in the center on the under, unglazed surface with Fig. 2 in dark green. The number 53 is incised above the trademark and 7527 is incised along the front of the oval underneath. She is 8 inches to the top of her hat bow; her skirt extends 1 inch beyond the base.

The coloring is soft and subtle. The hat brim, the folded scarf in her hand, the dress (especially in the deep folds), her slippers and foot pillow are tinted with a warm beige color. The sleeveless jacket and long gloves are pale blue with a hint of gray; the pillow under her elbow is sand with a deep green printed design; the chair frame is ivory; and the balance of the figure is white, including the seat of the chair.

Most importantly, she is signed. With a stylus, between the back legs

Seated Lady (front view).

of the chair, she was marked while still in the soft, greenware stage: K. Ameallor.

Front and back views of Cinderella and Doves.

From Germany came word of another delightful piece but it has not been established that it is signed. This one has a name and says on the front in German: Cinderella and the Doves.

An American wife in Germany with an officer husband, Mrs. Mabel B. Burelbach, supplied some small pictures which show a beautiful young girl, in a little printed cap, off-the-shoulder blouse and very full skirt, kneeling to feed two birds. She is flanked on the right by a large water jug and apparently is dawdling on her way to the well. She is barefooted and there is a heavy braid of blonde hair down her back. The base is like that of the very formal lady. A quote from the letter which came with the pictures:

"Heubach was a name we'd never

Seated Lady (back view).

heard until we picked up our little figurine in a shop, oh, probably almost a year ago (early 1968). We have some of the Danish figurines and on first sight we thought this might be one. The colors and quality of workmanship are quite similar. Before we had time to examine it, the dealer said, 'That's Heubach.' So, it wasn't Royal Copenhagen or Bing & Grondahl, but we liked it and brought it home.

"Meanwhile, having become Heubach conscious, we found a dog, a very typical Boxer. He is dated 1911 and has the artist's name, Fischer, impressed beside the date on the base. He sits on his haunches and leans forward, looking as belligerent as boxers do in life. He has black markings on a white background. Glazing is the same high quality as the little girl." (Author's note: Memory seems to say that white Boxers are outlawed by modern standards but 1911 is a long time ago.)

Glazed Pointer.

Miss Hupp, a well-known doll collector, also sent a picture and information about another, larger Heubach dog "which has been in our family as long as I can remember—at least over 60 years. Strange to say, I had never bothered to look for marks on either of them. It is also glazed china, white with the same soft gray underglaze markings and has an open mouth with a soft salmon-pink tongue." She sketched a complete *Fig. 1* as his marking.

"He looks like a Short-haired Pointer with a cropped tail," she continued, "and is beautifully molded with muscles and ribs showing. He crouches low in the front and has his hindquarters arched up as if barking at something. He is about 8¾ inches long and 4½ inches high. On the bottom of one foot there are four numbers, possibly 3220. People often ask if he isn't Royal Copenhagen."

As both Mrs. Burelbach and Miss Hupp suggested, most people also presume that the seated lady is Royal Danish or Royal Copenhagen.

Cobo-Alice Dolls

by
RUTH POCHMAN

THE late Mrs. George Prince of Madison, Wisconsin, recalled for me her childhood on the Isle of Guernsey, one of the Channel Islands off the coast of England and France. There, in the 1880s, she had a favorite doll, such as all the other little girls had, and all the dolls had the same name—one of two names, that is. They were called either "Cobo-Alice" or "Cobo-Judy."

The dolls originated among two families, the LeHurays and the Guilles, in the English coastal town of Cobo. The two women who owned the business were named Alice and Judy. Mrs. Prince's doll was a Cobo-Alice, and later, when she bought others for her daughters, they, too, were Cobo-Alices.

These dolls are unbreakable, being made of heavy unbleached muslin stuffed with dry hardwood sawdust. The body is easy to copy, since neither fingers nor toes are separated from the shaped hand and foot.

The head, however, has an individuality that is difficult to reproduce. Round like a ball, it is painted with ordinary household paint in flesh colors. The features are painted on in black; Mrs. Prince said a match was used for this work instead of a brush, and I am inclined to believe it, for the large oval eyes with their tiny dots for iris and pupil, the heavy brows, and the nostrils are crudely done. The mouth is outlined in red but not filled in.

Through a friend still living in Guernsey, Mrs. Price was able to get a new doll for me, but the most outstanding feature of the old primitive looking doll is missing in those made today. In the old ones the brows and nose were needle-molded before any of the painting was done—even before the head was sewed up and stuffed hard with sawdust. The new ones lack the needle-molding altogether.

To indicate hair, the heads of both the old and the new dolls have been painted a medium brown (again ordinary household paint was used); no attempt has been made to have brush marks around the hairline or comb marks in the rear. The cloth used for the heads was a wider weave than that used for the body and limbs; possibly it is part of a cotton sock. The paint used for both the face and hair extends down onto the shoulders, and there is no evidence of a seam at the joining. The hard stuffing under the dried paint makes the head heavy enough to be a lethal weapon; one wonders whether this had anything to do with the dwindling popularity of the doll in the early 20th century. No ears are sewed on or otherwise indicated. And no lashes.

The dolls were sold undressed, and clothing was made by the new owners. Mrs. Prince said people usually dressed the dolls like the women of the Islands who worked in the fields —full skirts, loose blouses, and slat bonnets. The bonnet was like those worn in our Southland by women working in cotton fields; the wide brim was stiffened by slipping reed or cardboard strips into slots sewn for this purpose, thus shading the face of the wearer from the burning sun.

Mrs. Prince's dolls are 13 and 18 inches long; the one she secured for me is 15 inches long.

Joints are at the shoulders and the hips only. The hands and forearms are painted flesh color; the feet are painted to represent flesh colored socks and black slippers.

The price 'way back in the 1880s was about 25 cents; today, it's $3.50.

Cobo-Alice doll, 1880 period.

Cobo-Alice, 1880; left: new Cobo-Alice.

Sizes and Markings on Bisque
FULPER DOLL HEADS

AMBERG DOLLS THE WORLD STANDARD MADE IN USA

COLONIAL DOLL MADE IN USA

MADE IN USA HORSMAN DOLL 19 © 10

FIG. 1   FIG. 2   FIG. 3

by RUTH RICKER

198 Dolls

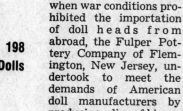

FOR a short period, from 1918 to 1921, when war conditions prohibited the importation of doll heads from abroad, the Fulper Pottery Company of Flemington, New Jersey, undertook to meet the demands of American doll manufacturers by producing a line of bisque doll heads, utilizing American clays. These doll heads were subsequently mounted on doll bodies by the doll manufacturers who purchased them.

Such doll heads were impressed with the Fulper trademark, pictured here; the factory number 2B sometimes appears above "Made in U.S.A." The doll heads made to order for Amberg dolls, Colonial dolls, and Horsman dolls carried, in addition to the Fulper mark, the impressed trademark of the specific company for which they were made. (See Figs. 1, 2, 3.)

From the additional letters and numerals which appear on Fulper doll heads can be determined the head size, style, and in specific instances, the doll manufacturer who ordered them. When doll heads are of the same circumference but facial contours differ, identifying symbols indicate a difference. For example, 11" circumference swivel-type Fulper boy heads were made in three styles, each bearing its identifying mark—16B indicates a baby boy head; 9, an older

boy head, and 13, another older boy head differing in facial contour and expression from that marked 9, but all are 11" head circumference.

The following listing of Fulper doll head sizes and corresponding markings is compiled from actual specimens of Fulper doll heads. The head circumference in inches is given first, followed by incidental information, if any, then the number always to be found on that size and type head. All markings are impressed and appear below the Fulper mark, except where noted. The eight sizes and types photographically illustrated on this page are indicated. All doll heads pictured are from the author's collection and have been mounted on bodies.

Swivel Fulper Girl Heads: head circumference 8½", closed mouth, number on head 4; 9"—1 *(illus);* 10"—2C; 10½"—7; 11"—2B; 11"—12; 12"—2A; 13½"—2AA; 14"—2 *(illus).*

Shoulder Bust Fulper Girl Heads: head circumference 8½", closed mouth, number on head S-8½; 8½"—SS-8½; 9"—No. 1 (above Fulper mark); 9"—S-9; 9½"—S-9½; 10"—S-10; 10"—H-3 (no Fulper mark); 11½"—S-11½; 13"—S-13; 14"—S-14.

Swivel Fulper Boy Heads: head circumference 10½", baby, number on head 16C; 11", baby, 16B; 11"—9; 11"—13; 11½"—A-11; 11½"—11; 12½"—10; 13"—8 *(illus);* 13½", baby—16A; 14"—A 8 *(illus);* 16"—16.

Swivel Amberg Fulper Girl Heads (see Fig. 1 for mark): head circumference 8½", number on head 40; 10½"—35; 15"—70-A *(illus);* 20", stamped *Amberg Dolls The World's Standard—*20 *(illus).*

Swivel Colonial Fulper Baby Boy Heads (see Fig. 2 for mark): head circumference 10", number on head A-15-C *(illus);* 11"—A-15-B; 14"—14"—A-8 *(illus);* 16"—16.

Swivel Horsman Fulper Girl Heads (see Fig. 3 for mark): head circumference 10", number on head H-1 *(illus);* 11"—H-2; 12"—H-3; 13"—H-4.

Colonial boy head marked A-15-C, 10" size; Horsman girl head marked H-1, 10" circumference.

Fulper swivel girl head marked 1, 9" size.

Beautiful Amberg Fulper doll head marked 70-A, 15" circumference. Largest Amberg doll head, human size, marked 20, 20" circumference, shown with Fulper swivel doll heads: girl marked 2, 14" circumference, baby boy marked 8, 13" circumference.

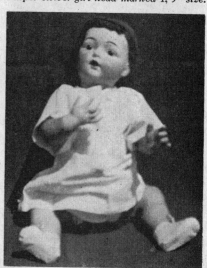

Fulper baby boy head marked A8, 14" size.

F. G. Mark on French Dolls

by LUELLA HART

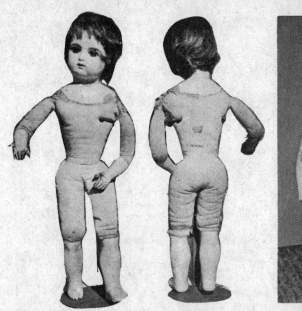

Two Gesland dolls, marked "F.G." both with swivel heads, bisque shoulders, stockinette bodies, composition legs and arms to knees and elbows, ball joints. Pierrot, also marked "Bebee Gesland", from Grimes collection; doll shown back and front, courtesy Mrs. Vincent Mosley, Tarentum, Pa.

STAMPED on the bodies of several dolls owned by Mr. and Mrs. Gordon Grimes of Corona, California, are the markings "F.G." or "F. Gesland", followed by "Brevete S.G.D.G." The Grimeses enlisted the writer's help in identification, and in the ensuing research not only was the Gesland story uncovered, but also the meaning of the S.G.D.G. mark which has long puzzled doll collectors.

According to the French Patent office, these initials stand for "without guarantee of the Government". They explained: "We make no examinations or research as to whether the idea of a patent is actually original. It is the responsibility of the applicant for a patent to do the research himself or to employ an agent. If he prefers not to take time for a patent search, he must mark his product "S.G.D.G." to protect the government and indicate that he himself is responsible for possible infringements."

As for information on the Gesland firm, the Grimeses were fortunate to find, inside the bisque head of one of their dolls, an advertising circular of the Gesland firm. Written in French, and printed on both sides, it described the company and its products.

Briefly translated, Gesland was the sole distributor of his dolls; they were sold in Paris only from his salesrooms which had been located since 1874 at 5 and 5 *bis* Rue Beranger. (The firm had been established in 1860). Salesrooms were open every day from 8 a.m. till 8 p.m. and on the day before Christmas and on New Year's from 8 a.m. to 11 p.m. The workshop was at 62 Rue d'Avron.

Gesland dolls, read the circular, were the strongest ever made. They had metal joints instead of the usual rubber, and were the only type made with feet, arms, and bust of hardened wood. They could sit, and kneel, and had long flowing hair. Prices were listed for bisque head dolls, undressed, in sizes from 12 to 31 inches; with removable satin dresses, in the same size range; and for dressed dolls, with necklaces, earrings, and ribbons, in sizes from 10 to 31 inches.

Sold separately were bisque heads, unbreakable heads, real hair wigs, Tibetan wool wigs, dolls' petticoats, shoes, dresses, coats, drawers, hats, pelisses, baptismal dresses, bonnets, pinafores, corsets, baby clothes. In addition, the firm offered talking dolls, sleeping dolls, negro dolls, and walking dolls; they produced, in all, over 200 models, ranging from 6 to 39 inches tall. They also conducted a repair service.

To substantiate the information in the circular, Mr. Alex Potter, a researcher in Paris, was called upon. He found that 5 Rue Beranger—an historic building dating from 1752—now houses an elementary school. However, in consulting the janitress, Madame Chapuis, he was in luck. Her husband, Roger Chapuis, born in

Label on body of "Mr. Bum" (Grimes collection): F Que De Bebes Gesland/ B to S.G.D.G./ Reparations en Tous Genres/ 5 & 5 bis Rue Beranger/ A L'Entresol/ Paris. Head model is 210; applied pierced ears, nose painted red, twisted mouth has hole for cigarette.

1912, had worked for the Geslands for years, and was able to supply additional facts about dolls and company.

For the doll wigs, he said, real hair was gathered from hairdressers all over France; in a period when French women wore their hair long, children's hair was utilized. The doll heads were imported from Germany and were of deluxe bisque. Hands and feet were of *paraquetine* (hardened wood), covered with a kind of cellulose paint, steeped and drained. The outstanding feature of the dolls was the body. The framework of both body and limbs was of steel covered with tin, with rivets at the joints to facilitate movement. This framework was covered with kapok, then with stockinette or fine lambskin. The dolls could be made to assume lifelike positions.

At one time, M. Chapuis, recalled, there were 50 workers on the premises and 200 outside workers who made clothing, shoes, hats, and doll accessories in their home. For holiday trade, he said he and his entire family worked long hours to fill orders for export; their dolls went to all parts of the world.

Mr. Gesland died during the First World War; Madame Gesland continued the business until her death in 1924. Though production of dolls stopped then, a Madame Proffet, who had long worked for the Geslands, continued to repair the dolls in her home at 11 Rue Beranger. She died in 1949.

NOTE: There has been much confusion over the S.F.B.J. mark and the S.G.D.G. mark. The former refers to the Societe Fabrication Bebes et Jouets, the name taken by the combine of the Jumeau, Bru, and Eden Bebe manufacturers. The S.G.D.G. mark indicates *Sans Garant du Gouvernement*. Many firms used these letters; only one was entitled to the trademark S.F.B.J.

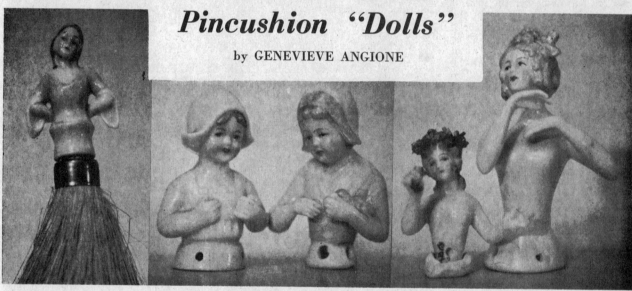

Pincushion "Dolls"
by GENEVIEVE ANGIONE

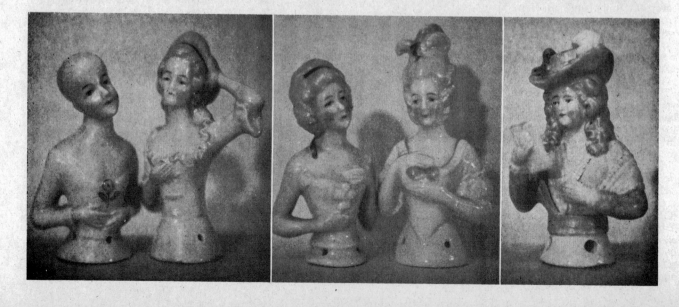

THE original appeal of the ultra-feminine china half-figures, known today as "pincushions", though many were intended for uses other than pincushion tops, must have been overwhelming. It is obvious from the variety found in present-day collections that they were made by the millions, in hundreds of types, over a rather long period of time. None classify as dolls, yet they appear in doll collections as well as collections of figurines and fine china.

The lovely Dresden and Dresden-type examples are difficult to find, but there are many attractive styles in the common types easily available at low cost. Because they require no special stands or cases, and wash like china cups, these little ladies of the past make a rewarding hobby for the collector with limited space for display, or with limited funds to invest.

The "pincushions" pictured were carefully selected to point out some of the features which make the unusual ones such prizes, and the common ones, inexpensive.

On the opposite page, the top row of illustrations shows unusually fine examples. The first, 4¾ inches, was a pincushion top, with a label on its satin cover reading "Ovington Bros., New York & Paris." Although her bosom hand is attached, she must have come from a multi-part mold, as both hands are complete and faithfully modeled. Hair is well defined; the hat has good straw marks; all ruffles, tucks, and buttons are sharp and clear. The flowers look hand-made; the tinting is excellent; the bodice is free to allow the skirt to be fitted beneath it. There is no incised mark, but inside the base is a blue-bordered paper label with the numbers 7031 in French style figures. (The 7 has a crossbar and looks like our written F.)

The second little lady, 2 inches tall, incised 5674, is a pincushion intact, 4½ inches overall. The hands are attached, but the modeling and molding are good, and her rose velvet skirt matches her painted trim. She commands double interest. First, she wears a label showing she was a 1926-27 New Year's Eve favor at a hotel party. Second, she has no incised "Germany" mark. Appearing when she did, in the midst of all the "flapper" types with their cloche hats and vivid coloring (the last manufacturing of these little boudoir items), this lack of country of origin mark suggests she may have been almost thirty-five years old when she was released, dressed for a ball.

The third, a grand lady, 8½ inches tall, holding a decorated teacup, may have been a teapot cover top. Her most obvious mark of quality is her free, occupied hands. Several molds were required to create her, but the workmanship is so fine that no mold marks show. Neck and cuff ruffles are beaded and sharp to the touch; the bodice is free for a fitted skirt; eyeballs and eyelids are beautifully

This figure, 5" tall, nude to permit a complete dress, most likely had a huge hoopskirt to hide a French cradle phone. She has all the fine points—molded eyelids; hair molded up off her forehead; two-position, free, lovely arms, with graceful hands. Besides the flowers in her hair, there is a molded ribbon in front and another, with a pretty bow, around her bun. Hair is light brown, and the entire torso has a good complection tint. The base was molded with the figure and the bottom is not closed at the waist. The mark is "4", a crown, and CW in monogram.

Undoubtedly a pincushion, this figure is 3½" tall; molding and tinting are very good. She has red eyelid lines, two-position arms with excellent hands; molded blue ribbon around her head. She is pure white with only hair, eyes, cheeks and lips tinted. The bottom is open, with a blurred incised number.

molded; lips are slightly open. The deeply molded curly hair is brown; the bodice, dark green with pink bows and white ruffles. This has a closed base without the Dresden-type drainage hole. The only mark is a blue hieroglyphic.

The second row shows examples more easily come by. The first is a brush top, 5 inches overall, with the 2-inch head somewhat smaller than expected since the body is elongated to make a solid handle. Modeling and molding are mediocre; the metal rim is not well plated; the pink brush seems to be a vegetable fibre. It is incised "Germany."

The two Dutch children, 2⅛ and 2¼ inches, are only samples of a variety of similar tops. Both are marked "Germany," but it is difficult to place their date. The one at the left has one arm molded to her body, but the free arm touches the body so lightly that the glaze seals the opening. Modeling is good, but the whole thing is pure white except for hair and face tinting. The one at the right has both arms free, but bent to the body; the fruit she holds binds one arm to the body with the help of the glaze. She is completely tinted, and coloring is very good.

The next two figures, 1¾ and 3½ inches, are both good specimens, with free hands, though the multi-mold marks are not well concealed. The flower wreath and bouquet of the small one are hand applied; the flowers and bow on the larger are molded. Both have red eyelid lines, flesh tinted bodies, and are marked "Germany." Neither base is boxed. The small one, stamped in blue, carries the size number 2; the larger is incised with style number 15278.

The bottom row shows some well done common types. The first two are 3⅛ and 3½ inches. The type requiring a wig is harder to find, indicating that fewer were made. Both are flesh tinted, and the modeling and molding is very good considering the market for which they were intended. The bald lady is marked "D R 105 Germany"; the other, "Germany 6347."

The second two, 3 and 3¾ inches, are also marked "Germany," but only the one at the right bears a number 6345. Quite obviously she was made by the same manufacturer as the doll numbered 6347. Her modeling, molding, and tinting is better than that of her companion.

For a common type, the last in this row is a nice one. With the exception of very flat hands, the molded feathers and decorations are well defined. Only the free arm holding the card was separately molded and added in the greenware state—the side ridges of a 2-part mold are faintly visible. She is marked "Germany 2871."

Not so easily found are the dresser sets in which these torso figures are completed in partly glazed bisque. There were powder, ring, and pill boxes, as well as very attractive perfume bottles.

GOO-GOOS AND PIXIES

by GENEVIEVE ANGIONE

MODERN psychiatry seems to hold with Armand Marseille, the ex-Latvian retired butcher who moved like the wind into the highly competitive field of doll making. Motivation research indicates that when adults choose dolls as gifts, they pick the ones which appeal to them and try to influence the child's choice if she is present. Adults could buy these cheap little goo-goos and pixies the year 'round without competing with the Santa Claus Christmas doll ideal. The adult appeal is still there; collectors now hunt them relentlessly.

It is difficult to establish a specific starting date for these charmers. Some women remember them from about 1910 but cannot say definitely that they were *new* then. Butler Bros. Nov. 1916 Catalogue #1443 carries a wholesale listing for dealers: *"The Happy Family:* in six styles, 9 inches, asstd boys and girls, bisque heads, asstd expressions, striped and solid color dresses and rompers, painted shoes and stockings." The accompanying small line drawings resemble some of the marked R.A.'s and Heubachs to be shown in SW next month. They have painted eyes and hair, incredibly flimsy bare cardboard bodies and the original clothing is often made of felt. They look like hastily made competition for a fad which may have already waned.

Because the bodies are in two styles, they will be described here once, and identified with the specific dolls pictured.

Most of the fat little torsos are nothing but stem-molded cardboard, with the two halves joined by wire staples at intervals down the juncture. A pasted paper strip straight down the front, under the crotch, and up the back hides the staples from busy fingers. A light wash of calcimine or a thin coat of paint completes the job. The neck holes are completely open, often with ragged edges; the arm and leg holes are roughly molded in, which accounts for the need of the center body seam.

The bent arms and fat legs are molded from an unknown mixture of papier-mache, glue, plaster, and perhaps fine sawdust. They are very pulpy and break easily; water is disastrous to them. The stringing holes in the limbs are probably bored and the whole doll is held together with two short pieces of rubber glued and pegged into these holes. Sometimes short hooks hold the head to the arm rubber; in others, a long hook at-

taches the head to the hip rubber. In most of the all-bisque heads these wires have a spiral top forced up into the neck, although some have a hole molded in the back of the neck through which the wire could be bent. The wigged dolls often have two molded holes above the ears; apparently these were never used since the wires extend up over the head in back, under the wig.

The molded composition bodies are more attractive and durable but are not common in the smaller sizes. Some of these, too, have a wash of calcimine, while others have a light coat of oil paint or a good coat of paint resembling enamel. All of which indicates a wide variety in price. The arms and legs are painted unless specifically mentioned otherwise.

Since collectors are so conscious of markings, it is interesting to note that in several instances the same face was used with a different hairdo. The bisque, incidentally, is always good and sometimes the superlative A.M. quality. The decorating is consistently good and subdued, with none of the "high" coloring associated with late German products. The painted hair on the bisque heads varies from blonde to darker honey blonde, but the wigs are another story. Some are mohair on gauze foundations but many are just mohair glued to the cardboard dome and the head. The mohair is fair to good quality, straight, waved, or pencilpoint curls in brown, brassy gold, taffy blonde, and light blonde.

ILLUSTRATIONS

No. 1—10 inches; sleep brown eyes; 8½" circ.; enameled composition body with bare feet. Marked in five lines: 253, S.B., Germany, A. O M., D.R.M.R. [German patent applied for]. The head is held with a plug; clothing appears to be original. Wig replaced.

No. 2—9½ inches; paint blue intaglio eyes; 7½" circ.; washed composition body, painted limbs, blue shoes. Marked in four lines: 253, A 5/0 M, Germany, D.R.G.M. [German patent granted] 24811 (the last two figures are not quite clear). This is the same face as No. 1 but with uncut eyes; both have "watermelon" lips.

No. 3—sits 6½ inches; paint blue intaglio eyes; 7" circ.; bent arm and leg infant body is original, painted composition with bare feet. Marked in four lines: S B 252, Germany, A 6/0 M, D.R.G.M. Watermelon mouth.

No. 4—7 inches; paint blue intaglio

eyes; 5½" circ.; washed composition body, painted limbs, blue shoes with heels. Unused stringing hole above mark in three lines: 210 A 11/0 M, Germany. Small mouth.

No. 5—7 inches; paint blue intaglio eyes; 5½" circ.; painted composition body, bare feet. Hole above mark used for stringing. Marked in three lines: 320, A 11/0 M, Germany. The "Mohawk" hair-do is well molded; watermelon lip.

No. 6—6½ inches; paint blue intaglio eyes; 5½" circ.; washed cardboard body, painted limbs, tan shoes. Spiral wire into head. Marked in three lines: 320, A 11/0 M, Germany. Watermelon lip but, without the Mohawk molded hair, it is a different doll.

No. 7—6½ inches; paint blue intaglio eyes; 5½" circ.; washed cardboard body, painted limbs, brown shoes. Spiral wire into head. Marked in three lines: 255 D R G M 2, A 11/0 M, Germany. Molded "boy" hair; watermelon lip.

No. 8 — 6½ inches; paint blue intaglio eyes; 5¾" circ.; washed cardboard body, painted limbs, brown shoes. (Also in washed composition body with bare feet.) Spiral wire into head. Marked in three lines: 322, A 11/0 M, Germany.

No. 9—10 inches; sleep blue eyes; 8" circ.; enameled composition body with slender limbs, paint black shoes. Head strung with plug; taffy mohair wig on gauze. Marked in four lines; Armand Marseille, Germany, 323, A. 4/0 M. Full goo-goo lips.

No. 10—7½ inches; sleep blue eyes; 6½" circ.; washed cardboard body, painted limbs, blue shoes. Wire over head; blonde mohair wig on gauze. Marked in four lines: Armand Marseille, Germany, 323, A 8/0 M.

No. 11—6½ inches; sleep blue eyes; 5¼" circ.; washed cardboard body, painted limbs, black shoes. Wire over top of head; mohair curls glued to dome and bisque. Marked in five lines: A 253 M, Nobbi Kid, U. S. Pat., Germany, 11/0.

No. 12—7½ inches; sleep blue eyes; 5" circ.; enameled body with slender limbs, bare feet. Wire over top of head; mohair "bob" on gauze. Original clothing is organdy. Marked in four lines: Just Me, Registered, Germany, A 310 11/0 M. Has "rosebud" mouth.

Records through the years indicate that the 253 face appeared in many types and sizes, and the 323 face, with both blue and brown sleep eyes, was the goo-goo standby in a great variety of sizes.

1   253/SB/AM—10"

2.   253/AM—9½"

3   252/SB/AM—Sits 6½"

4   210/AM—7"

5   Mohawk/320 AM—7"

6   320/AM—6½"

7   255 DRGM/AM—6½"

8   322/AM—6½"

9   323 AM—10"

10   323 AM—7½"

11   A253/Nobbi Kid—6½"

12   A310M/Just Me—7½"

COMPETITION for GOO-GOOS?

by
GENEVIEVE ANGIONE

IT IS A dangerous game to do too much guessing in doll investigating because some serious researcher may prove you wrong before your print is dry. There are times, however, when assumptions must be made simply to have some platform from which to operate.

With this thought in mind, this month's little dolls are presented for what they seem to be — competition for the tremendously popular and still numerous Armand Marseille dolls known to modern collectors as "goo-goos." The squat bodies with the fat legs and the impish faces almost invariably remind outsiders, especially comic strip buffs, of the Katzenjammer Kids.

Just as our toy counters today reflect the grinding competition for the dollars spent on children, the American dollar was vied for with great gusto by the German dollmakers. There is more than a little evidence, too, that they helped each other with heads and/or bodies to make complete dolls.

Many of the bodies on these competitive items are exactly like the bodies on the A.M. models, but so far not one has been found with a manufacturer's mark on the body. The same standards used for the A.M.'s apply to these dolls and descriptions will follow the same pattern with notes on the manufacturers of the heads.

No. 1—7 inches; sleep brown eyes; 6" circ.; washed cardboard body, painted limbs, tan shoes. Head strung with wire over the rim; blonde mohair glued to cardboard dome; redressed. Marked in four lines: 133/ S superimposed over H/ Germany/ 2.

The face of this doll looks exactly like A.M.'s model #323 (No. 10, S.W., sep '66). It also has the same good bisque, the good, well-set eyes and the slightly high pink complexion. In *Dolls, Makers and Marks,* the Colemans identify this S over H as the mark of Hermann Steiner, also shown as Herm Steiner, 1924, Sonneberg. Koppelsdorf and Sonneberg were not very far apart, in that section of Thuringia which dipped down into Bavaria. This doll seems to offer some proof that the A.M. worker quoted in the first article (S.W. March '66) was right. He said that at least during his employment there, the German Steiner heads were produced by A.M.

Numbers 2 through 5 are Heubachs, and this is the old Gebruder (brothers) Heubach firm which, besides a great variety of dolls, also produced untold thousands of the popular bisque "piano babies" and other appealing children figurines so much loved by our mothers and grandmothers around the turn of the century. On these dolls the Heubach mark is the domino-shaped oblong with HEU in the top and BACH in the bottom half. The Colemans give the business address as Sonneberg although the factory was in Lichte near Wallendorf, quite a distance away.

No. 2—6½ inches; convex molded eyes with large half-pupils and rims of gray blue; 5½" circ.; sturdy composition torso is washed, painted limbs, black shoes. Head wire strung, probably with a coil; painted blonde hair with a tiny molded curl in front. Original dress is thin felt with white cotton collar and black sateen belt; usual tacked-on gauze pants are missing. Marked in three lines: 30 6/0 11 (poorly incised)/ 95 HEU BACH 94/ Germany.

No. 3—7 inches; sleep brown eyes; 5¾" circ.; washed cardboard body with center staples, usual painted limbs, bright tan shoes. Head, strung with wire over the rim, also has two small holes above each ear and is the old type with a sloping cut and high domed forehead. Human hair wig may be replacement, but little printed dress could be original; no pants but tack holes are visible. Marked in four lines: 9573/5 over a line over 0/HEU

1 2 3 4

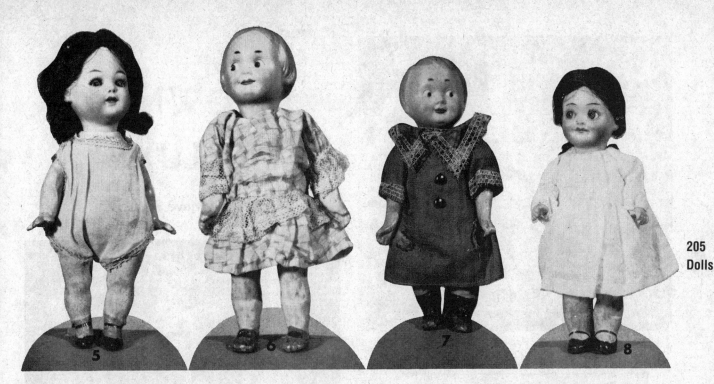

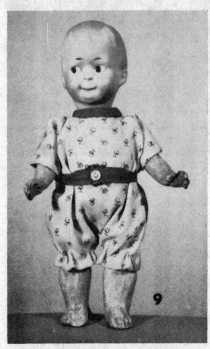

BACH/ Germany. This is one type of watermelon lip.

No. 4—7 inches; sleep gray eyes; 5¾" circ.; washed cardboard body with center staples, usual painted limbs, tan shoes. Head strung with wire over the rim; straight mohair wig glued on dome. All original. Gauze, lace-trimmed pants still tacked on; 2-piece dress and tie-on hat are white-trimmed teal blue thin felt; flowers are red and white. Marked in four lines, the name in fancy printing: Elizabeth/ 6 over a line over 0/ HEU BACH/ Germany. "Rosebud" mouth.

No. 5—7½ inches; blue sleep eyes; 5¾" circ.; entire body is enameled and composition torso is excellent; pale orange socks, bright tan shoes with

heels. Head strung with wire over the rim; two holes above ears. Human hair wig is replacement; original gauze chemise. Marked in four lines: 10542/ 4 over a line over 0/ HEU BACH/ Germany.

No. 6 — 7½ inches; intaglio blue eyes; 6" circ.; composition torso and limbs painted; blue shoes with gilded buckles. Head wire strung. Molded "bob" is light blonde with blue band across top of head. Redressed. Marked in two lines: R 46 A/ 12/0.

No. 7 — 6½ inches; blue intaglio eyes; 5⅜" circ.; unpainted stapled cardboard body; poor quality arms and legs are painted; black socks, tan shoes. Head wire strung; molded hair is light blonde; dress probably original. Marked in two lines: R 45 A/ 13/0.

This firm has not been satisfactorily identified although quite a few dolls, some of them infants with most attractive molded-on bonnets, bear this mark.

No. 8—6½ inches; blue sleep eyes; 5¼" circ.; washed composition torso, painted limbs with tan shoes. Has been restrung with neck plug; human hair wig is replacement; redressed. Marked in three lines: S superimposed over W/ in lower section of S, Germany/ 208-12.

This is the mark of Strobel & Wilken, a Cincinnati, Ohio, firm with offices in New York City (*Dolls, Makers and Marks*, pg. 71). Kammer and Reinhard and Heinrich Handwerck made dolls for them but they carried the S.W. mark.

No. 9—7½ inches; molded eyes with half-pupils only; 5¾" circ.; washed composition body, painted limbs and bare feet. Head wire strung; boy-cut molded hair is tinted blonde. True watermelon lip. Marked in three lines: Germany/ E H 27x 15/0/D.R.G.M.

This mark is **unfamiliar** and leads

to speculation because the E. I. Horseman Company of New York was very active at this time. Their 1924 infant actively competed with the Bye-Lo and it could be that the middle initial of this firm was necessarily deleted in this small head.

No. 10—6 inches; painted blue eyes; 5¼" circ.; washed composition body, poor quality painted limbs with blue shoes. Head wire strung; molded "bob" tinted reddish blonde. Dress with Dutch border print is probably original; undies missing. Marked in one line: 33 12/0.

With the exception of this last doll, which is quite ordinary, all these heads are very good German bisque and the molding and decorating is well done. In Nos. 1, 8, and 10 the color is slightly heightened, but all the others are pale and most attractive.

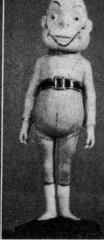

Uncle Sam   Bellhop   Indian

BROWNIES DELUXE

by Genevieve Angione

In the doll world, where the names of Rose O'Neill and her Kewpies or Grace Storey Putnam and her Bye-Lo Babies are instantly recognized by everybody, Palmer Cox and his Brownies enjoy a lesser fame. Yet they have a magic of their own both in and out of dolldom among oldsters and those who were children in the first quarter of this century.

The Dude   Chinaman   Bobbie

THE BROWNIES were born in 1883 in the twinkling imagination of bachelor Palmer Cox for a story which appeared in *St. Nicholas,* an "Illustrated Magazine for Young Folks." They were gentle, comical, little do-gooders who never sought praise, and were apparently based on some Cox combination of good fairies and gnomes. From 1887 on, Brownies roamed through all kinds of hilarious, worldwide adventures in a steady flow of books which children loved and grownups loved to read to them.

Born of Scotch immigrant parents in 1840 in Granby, Quebec, not far from the Vermont state line, Palmer Cox died in 1924 at 84, a shining example of "build a better mousetrap." He and his Brownies were known the world around.

Not many of the Brownie books survived the enthralled children for whom they were written but paper cut-outs, figurines, small printed rag dolls, souvenir cups and spoons, framed pictures, and such treasures are still to be found in those wonderful inventions of a by-gone era— attics. (SW *jul-aug '62* carried information on Brownie rag dolls; the *jul-aug '63* issue, on Napoli Glassware, showing a Brownie decorated cracker jar.)

The Brownies illustrated here are exceptional because they are beautifully molded of the finest bisque, unmarked but unquestionably German. The trim appears to be the 14-karat gold used on fine china; the colors are bright pastels; and the decorating is expertly done. They fairly scream "quality."

They vary from 7½ to 8 inches over-all. Each stands on a gold-flecked flagstone platform 2½ by 1½ inches, about ½ inch high. All have blue eyes and gray-blonde hair except the Indian; he has pitch black hair and brown eyes.

Individual Descriptions

Uncle Sam: blue-banded white topper with brush marks in the texture to indicate fur felt; blue swallowtail coat and white vest with gold bands; rose bow tie; rose-striped white pants and black shoes.

Bellhop: rose cap with yellow, gold-striped band, gold topknot and chin-strap; pink jacket with rose collar, gold buttons, gold trimmed black belt; blue pants with gold banding; white socks; black slippers.

Indian: yellow feathers, rose- and blue-tipped, with gold flecking; blue-belted yellow suit, rose and gold fringe; molded jacket decoration out-lined in gold; yellow leggings, rose and gold fringe; brown handled gold hatchet; rose moccasins.

The Dude (said to be one of the most popular c h a r a c t e r s): blue-banded white topper with gold edge; gold monocle; blue tailcoat with gold band, pink rose in lapel; white shirt, yellow bow tie; white vest, gold banded and buttoned, yellow lapels; yellow-handled brown cane; yellow gloves; pale blue g o l d - b a n d e d trousers; white spats; black shoes.

Chinaman: yellow-banded rose cap, gold knob and trim; blue smock with gold braid closures, gold-banded collar, cuffs, and edge; white under-smock; blue gold-banded pants; white socks; yellow "Dutch wooden" shoes.

London Bobbie: blue helmet, gold knob, emblem and banding; blue coat, black belt, gold buttons and all-around banding; yellow nightstick with gold bands; blue trousers with gold bands; turned-up black shoes.

As in all quality figurines, these little fellows are as perfectly detailed and decorated in back as they are in front. The paints are exactly the same shades in every one, proof that at least these six were made as a set. One cannot help but wonder if there were more—and where they are now? Anybody know?

CORNHUSK DOLLS

by ROGER L. WELSCH

ILLUSTRATION No. 3

IN THE pioneer Plains States, life centered around corn. Cornbread was a sodhouse staple; mattresses were stuffed with cornhusks; Christmas trees were decorated with strung popcorn. Foodstuffs were "stretched" with corn; toasted corn was added to coffee; cornsilk was added to tobacco.

Popcorn with sorghum molasses and milk was served for breakfast—perhaps with some fried cornmeal mush; roast ears of corn and cornbread often graced the noon table; and corncakes, dodgers, and corn soup were supper—with popcorn pudding for dessert. On Saturday nights, there might have been a bit of whiskey—from a corn mash.

The children, too, turned to corn for their amusements. Cornstalks made knightly swords and quarter-staffs. Half of a cob with two or three pheasant feathers stuck into the pith made a good game bird, or a dart. A couple of slits between stalk joints made a primitive cornstalk fiddle.

When steamed or soaked in warm water, cornhusks become flexible; dried, they remain as they have been re-formed, so the pioneer mother fashioned cornhusk dolls for her little girls. Some of these dolls were exceedingly simple; others were no less charming—and undoubtedly as much loved—as some of today's twenty-dollar automations.

The dolls were decorated in ingenious ways, reflecting the pioneer's need for improvisation. The two ladies in *Illustration No. 1*, for example, sport curly cornsilk hair. The one on the left has a cornhusk shawl and apron, while the lady on the right carries a cornhusk purse and has a bit of calico for an apron. The faces and buttons have been drawn on with ink and colored pencil.

The pixie-ish coquettes in *Illustration No. 2* have colorful sashes and caps dyed with berry juices, walnut-husk ink, and ink; their hair is also cornsilk.

ILLUSTRATION No. 1

ILLUSTRATION No. 4

Illustration No. 3 shows, on the right, a more primitive example of the cornhusk doll—the only male member of my collection. The prissy grandmother on the left is particularly interesting because her features—eyes, nose, and mouth—and her starburst brooch are made of wheat and weed seeds glued to the husk. Her shawl and bonnet, as well as her hair, brushed severely back, are bits of cornhusk. (See close-up, *Illustration No. 4*.)

Such dolls, when played with, do not last long. Some of the examples pictured are relics of the past; others are recent products fashioned in the old tradition. Old or new, these cornhusk dolls prove again that "homemade" is not synonymous with "crude," and that the products of yesterday, revived today, are no less delightful, no less clever, than they were then.

ILLUSTRATION No. 2

In *Toys in America*, Marshall and Inez McClintock tell us it's likely the cornhusk dolls so beloved by white settler's children were first made by the Indians. Pioneer children painted features on their dolls' faces; the Indians may not have done so for, in many tribes, the drawing of a face endowed the doll with a soul. In Puritan days when most play was frowned on, babies were allowed corncob dolls, and boys used discarded corncobs for blocks. By the 18th century, most girls had some sort of doll, occasionally an elaborate creation from Europe, more often one carved from wood, or made of stuffed rags, twigs, or *cornhusks*.

What Shall I Put in The Peddler's Pack?

IN THE April, 1954, issue of *Spinning Wheel,* the late Darcy, beloved of doll collectors, wrote of Mary Callinack, Hawker and Walker, and of Luella Hart's peddler doll in her likeness, made by "the mother of Miss Pease" in 1868, and of peddler dolls in general.

It was a pleasurable pastime of Victorian females to assemble these realistic little figures of the peddler women who cried their wares in London streets and through the English countryside, and outfit their baskets with all kinds of wee trinkets. Original examples are rare today, and out of reach of the average collector—some may cost as much as $400 or more. But the enjoyment long ago ladies had in outfitting them need not be confined to the past. Delight in miniatures still persists, and for those who like to collect them but are plagued with the problem of display, why not a peddler doll?

The originals were made of many materials—china, wood, or wax were usual. One in Mary Merritt's Doll Museum in Douglassville, Pennsylvania, has a bread crumb face; another is of papier-mache. The Mary Callinack, Darcy believed, was a

Miniatures, of Course!

A peddler doll is perfect to display wee trinkets and treasures. Ideas for assembling your own may be gleaned from dolls others have made—long ago, or only yesterday.

By MARCIA RAY
in collaboration with
LUELLA HART

penny wooden, carved to a portrait and stained a leathery shade.

Their hoods are traditionally black with ruffles of white, their capes red; their calico dresses may be caught up to show a black quilted petticoat. As for their stock in trade, sometimes as many as 125 fascinating objects hung from their woven baskets.

In Mary Callinack's pack, some of the objects were pinned into the cotton lining of the one-inch tall handmade basket; others were strung on black strings and pinned into the top of the pack. Ranging from one-half to two inches, these items include: 5 Frozen Charlottes; 6 penny woodens; 2 jointed bisques with hand crocheted dresses and bonnets; tiny potholders and pincushions; ivory crosses; an ivory horse; a china dog; a one-inch

silver box filled with tiny beads; a one-inch card with a dried fish on it and the handwritten words "Caught at Littlehampton"; on the back is a hand painted sea scene; a tiny coronation chair of metal; a metal locomotive; strips of handmade passementerie. *(Pictured.)*

Present Day Peddlers

Carolyn Abbott's Polly Penny came from a London antiques shop. The foundation doll has a china head and feet, kid hands. A mask, representing a witchy old woman has been fastened over the original face. Among the 25 to 30 small articles in her basket are a tiny doll, kid gloves, scissors, bag, beads, thread, charms, purse, baskets, and bookmarks. Like most Peddlers, Polly Penney has always existed under a glass dome. *(Pictured.)*

All sorts of possibilities present themselves to today's peddler doll makers. Peg Steele of Harrisburg, Pennsylvania who makes them for sale, uses apple faces and padded wire bodies. The apples—she prefers Winesaps—are pared, roughly carved, and set to dry on wood—never on metal. She dresses them appropriately and

Mary Callinack, *correctly "Kelynack,"* *1867-68. Luella Hart Collection.*

Polly Penny, *original; owned by Carolyn Abbott, Westfield, Massachusetts.*

Notion Nanny, *assembled by Fearn Brown, Oakland, California; doll is old.*

Above, left to right: rare bread crumb face peddler holds line of hot pads, ca. 1820; papier-mache, ca. 1840; leather face peddler, label on bottom, "C&H White, Milton, New Hampshire," ca. 1830. *From Mary Merritt's Doll Museum.*

fills their crocheted baskets with dried lavender flowers.

For the collector of miniatures who likes a diversified stock—and all items must be in scale — any type doll can be used. Penny woodens, either old or new are perhaps the most popular. (The gift shop in Museum of the City of New York is one place that carries new ones.)

For her Notion Nanny, Fearn Brown used an old penny wooden which Luella Hart found for her in Waldo Lanchester's Puppet Center in Stratford-on-Avon (see "Shopping for Dolls in England and France," SW May 1963). Entranced with the old Apothecary Shop in Williamsburg, Virginia, she started Nanny's pack with apothecary items. Lavender she could purchase, but rock candy, horehound, and tiny medicines she created herself. Some of her notions are present-day—the Five and Ten is a good hunting ground— but many are antiques.

Among her old pieces are a paper of small black china head veil pins from France, a small metal lantern, a one-inch square satin pillow hand painted "Bethlehem 1902", filled with sand from that ancient city, tiny doll earrings, a wee metal flatiron. For heart interest she has added a gold locket and miniature baby picture of her mother, born 1860, the tiny ½-inch wide aviator's compass her Air Force son carried on D Day as he flew across to France, and his miniature set of 1st Lieutenant's silver wings. (Pictured.)

Luella Hart made "Buy a Doll, Miss?" for her granddaughters. Her penny woodens, large and small, also came from Waldo Lanchester. The small 1½-inch size are more expensive and harder to obtain than the large ones. (Pictured.)

Ruth Russell, of Long Beach, California, who has made some fifty dolls for her own pleasure, let one of her favorites speak in verse. The recital of basket treasures is an inspiration and a goal for all miniature collectors who aspire to a "proper" peddler.

"My goods are fresh and clean and new
  Pray you, buy of me
There's cloth and lace and ribbon, too,
  And thyme and rosemary.
The little doll from Italy
  Is surely very sweet;
My remedies are made by me,

"Buy a Doll, Miss?" *Collection Marjorie & Terry Morse, Boulder, Colorado.*

My brushes keep things neat.
The spoon and fork and knife and bell
  Are used to get a meal
Of all their use I need not tell—
  I've yarns and good castile.
The rolling pin and amber beads
  Are surely worth their price;
There's everything to fill your needs—
  The pictures, too, are nice.
The casket holds so many things.
  I've goose-grease for your chest,
Some smelling salt is strong and
  sharp;
  My paregoric's best.
The shell was brought from far away
  Your whatnot to adorn;
My notions help you every day,
  The Bible, night to morn.
There's scissors small and buckles
  brave
  And books and candles, too,
A cushion for your pins to save;
  The pomander is new.
The sampler, tidies, that you see
  Are useful gifts, I trow,
So, get your pence and trade with me
  And you'll be pleased, I vow."

The Misses Marie and Grace Turner of Brighton, Massachusetts, who have been making more specialized peddlers for fun and profit for twenty years, displayed a collection of 100 at the Boston Public Library in February of this year. From 10 to 12 inches tall, with frames of pliable copper wire, padded, and with heads of ceramic, plastic, or carved wood, they bore familiar titles of fact and fiction. Not a few were famous businessmen who began their careers as peddlers—John Jacob Astor, trading furs; William Procter and James Gamble, who married sisters, peddling soap and candles; young Jim Fisk dealing in Paisley shawls; and Richard Sears of Sears-Roebuck fame, selling watches.

DOLLY'S DRESSMAKER

by BARBARA WHITTON JENDRICK

A RARE FIND today for both doll and paper doll collectors is *Dolly's Dressmaker,* a combination paper doll and real doll pattern book, published in 1896 by Raphael Tuck and Sons, Ltd., London, Paris, and New York, proud "Publishers to the Queen."

The introduction to this 7 by 10 inch book with its gaily lithographed cover reads: "This book will show you how to make new dresses for your dear Dolly, so you will have something to do on a rainy day and Dolly will always look lovely."

It contains three sheets of colored paper dolls, printed on white paper, each followed by a double page of patterns to fit a 9-inch doll, printed on a light tan stock. The patterns embrace the paper dolls' clothes, and include an apron, mantle (long cloak), skirt for blouse, blouse, cape, frock with yoke, and mantle with yoke. The colored paper dolls, like a fashion sheet, indicate variations in trimming and materials.

Because many of the patterns are printed across the centerfold of the book, the little dressmaker was supposed to trace them on a tissue paper for use. And because the directions for cutting and sewing were printed on the back of the paper doll sheets, the cutting of the paper dolls was supposed to be left until after the doll clothes were cut and sewed. Such restrictions were hard on impatient little girls who preferred paper dolls to sewing or couldn't quickly find the proper tracing paper for the patterns. Undoubtedly few books, even in their own time, remained intact. We are fortunate to have a complete book from which to show the paper doll illustrations.

Figure 1 shows a blonde doll in white underclothes with blue trim. Her brown coat and hat are trimmed with ermine; her blouse and skirt are blue with white trim, and her apron, or pinafore, is pink.

Figure 2 shows a doll with light brown hair. She wears a white chemise with a pink petticoat. Her cape is tan with a pink and blue checkered collar; her double-breasted jacket is brown; her pink dress is trimmed with white lace. The "middy" dress is blue with a white collar and dark blue trim.

Figure 3 shows a brunette in white underclothes. Her pinafore is white with pink ribbon trim; her jacket is brown; her blue dress is trimmed with white and gold lace; and her cloak is yellow with matching lining.

Figure 4 shows the cover for "Dolly's Dressmaker," published by Raphael Tuck and Sons, Ltd., in 1896.

Fig. 1

Fig. 2

Fig. 3

Fig. 4

FANS AND FANCIES

Here is an area that definitely appeals to women of all ages. The delicate, wispy fan holds a fascination many women find hard to resist. Of silk, lace or colorfully decorated paper, fans come in a wide variety to tempt the collector. Many fan collectors supplement their collections by adding fancy combs, perfume bottles and other feminine accoutrements.

Fig. 1.

AMERICA'S FIRST FAN FACTORY

by ESTHER OLDHAM

*Except as noted,
all fans are from
the author's collection.*

Fig. 10.

MANY PEOPLE ARE surprised when they learn that there was a great American fan factory in the year 1866, located in the small Massachusetts town of Weymouth Landing, near Quincy.

Its founder, Edmund Soper Hunt *(Fig. 1)*, was a man of genius whose diverse talents led him to the pinnacle of fame with his invention of The Projectile or Breeches Buoy used in life saving by the U.S. Navy and Coast Guard. His fireworks industry also won for him many gold medals and world recognition in competition with the finest displays of the famous Japanese artists of the time.

However, it is his fan manufacturing business and inventions that hold our attention here. He worked diligently and incessantly perfecting machinery for the "Improvement in Manufacturing Fans" until he finally mastered this art in 1868 when his first patent was issued *(Fig. 2)*.

This patent covered the process by which the fan sticks and fanleaf (top of the fan) were assembled in one process which also included folding or "creasing" the fanleaf, and glueing the leaf to the fan sticks at the same time under great pressure *(Fig. 3)*. Never before in the history of fan-making in Europe or America had such a feat been accomplished.

These first fans, using his patent of 1868, were made of light or dark brown linen mounted on simple wooden sticks of hornbeam, a wood which was plentiful in the Massachu-

Fig. 3.

Fig. 4.

Fig. 5.

Fig. 6.

Fig. 8.

Fig. 9.

Fig. 11.

Fig. 12.

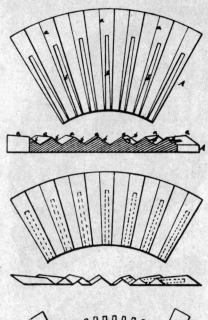

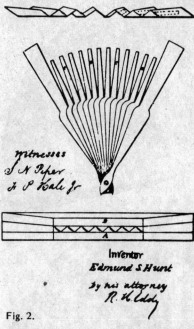

Fig. 2.

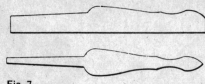

Fig. 7.

setts south shore towns at that period. This wood was especially suited for fan sticks as the hornbeam did not warp; it took a high polish; and also lent itself well to artistic "graining."

Gradually these fans became more pretentious and one finds early lace-like "punchwork" designs with crude flower paintings decorating their leaves *(Fig. 4)*. Other fans relied solely on punchwork designs of patriotic stars, popular at the close of the Civil War *(Fig. 5)*.

These linen fans were called "Summer" fans. As time passed the paintings on these fans improved in quality and the hornbeam sticks were often grained *(Fig. 6)*, the graining resembling zebra wood, marbling, tortoiseshell, etc.

In 1870, Edmund Hunt patented a "Machine for Moulding or Carving Fan Sticks" *(Fig. 7)*. Fortunately, two fans (unmounted) with these carved sticks which came directly from Hunt's fan factory have come to light *(Fig. 8)*; one shows carved wooden sticks which

are stained black; the other carved wooden sticks with gold leaf.

The figures of "Paul and Virginia," taken from a book popular in the 19th century, were often found on paper fans with scenes from the book. Such a fan is seen in *Fig. 9*. Its leaf is silver paper with a lithograph of Paul and Virginia. The carved wooden sticks are stained black like those from Hunt's fan factory.

Another great triumph of Edmund Soper Hunt was his special process o. gold-leafing (with real gold leaf) his carved wooden fan sticks. This work was beautifully executed by the women in his factory under his guidance. The gold leaf was so cleverly applied that nearly one hundred years later the fans are still in perfect condition. These fans were carried by brides and prominent ladies during the 1870s. Every bride had one or more in her trousseau reserving, however, those with leaves of white satin or silk, trimmed with gold sequins, for her wedding day.

In the beautiful portrait of Frances Pickering Adams of Quincy, Mass., *(Fig. 10)*, painted by the eminent portrait painter William Morris Hunt, ca. 1870, we see in her hand a fan with gold leaf sticks with sequins on its leaf, an example of the high esteem in which Mr. Hunt's fans were held at that time. This portrait is in the Museum of Fine Arts, Boston, Mass. A similar fan with gold leaf sticks is found in *Fig. 11*. Its leaf is royal purple satin ornamented with gilt sequins.

Mr. Hunt's talents were inexhaustible. Always seeking new challenges, he resolved to make "imitation" ivory that would "stump the experts." In this he succeeded, and to this day no one has yet solved the mystery of his "secret process." On close examination one might observe that his "ivory" appeared slightly whiter than mellowed ivory. A perfect example of this imitation ivory is found in *Fig. 12*, its pale robin's-egg blue satin leaf handsomely painted and embroidered with a lady reaching for the "Bluebird of Happiness."

During the Franco-Prussian War (1870-1871), thousands of Mr. Hunt's fans were shipped to France; the ladies of France eagerly purchased *l'eventail Americain*. Some of these fans, made in America, were later brought back to this country by the visiting tourists to become "treasured heirlooms from France."

EDMUND SOPER HUNT continued his fan-making industry until 1876 when his brother, Fred Hunt, and Frank Allen took over his factory buildings and continued the manufacture of fans.

In 1885, the factory was moved to East Braintree, Mass., and the fans made there by the Allen Fan Company were referred to as "Allen Fans." The Allen Fan Company produced quantities of unusual and interesting fans, many of which were hand painted.

The master fan painter for the factory was George Keiswetter who came from Breslau, Germany. A University graduate, he was also a fine musician and a gifted artist, a man who loved nature and beauty in all forms. *(Fig. 13)*

Keiswetter's special interest was painting birds of all sizes and varieties on fans, with incidental butterflies, bees, dragonflies, huge begonia leaves, and flowers. He had a particular gift for painting the feathers on his birds, making them look so soft and real, they almost demanded to be stroked. This effect of his was created by first "soaping" his brush before using the oil paints.

In *Fig. 14* we find an excellently painted bird on the left-hand side of the fan pecking at luscious red berries 'mid white flower branches. The wooden fan sticks are painted oyster white. Keiswetter painted this fan for his daughter, Mrs. George Oster, Braintree, Mass.

Another fan of note, owned by Mrs. Morrill R. Allen (of the Allen Fan Company family) is well painted with six swallows in soft shades of gray on a black satin leaf, with wooden sticks painted black *(Fig. 15)*.

Fig. 16 shows an exquisitely painted blue parakeet flying towards a red orchid cactus and a dainty gauze-like dragonfly. The background is goldenrod-yellow satin; its hornbeam sticks are "mahoganized."

Again showing his love for his feathered friends, Mr. Keiswetter painted a charming fanleaf with small birds, swallows and brown sparrows, eagerly chasing bees over its delicate white gauze leaf. He loved the "lowly" sparrows and liked to immortalize them on fans. *(Fig. 17)*

However, not all his fans had bird subjects. He painted Kate Greenaway-type figures on others. (In the 1880s, these quaint children were captivating the public's imagination.) Painted on a red satin leaf, a group of these colorful Kate Greenaway figures parade across the fanleaf *(Fig. 18)*. He also painted similar figures on fans made of black quill feathers with sticks of Neopolitan tortoiseshell.

Besides hand painted fans, the Allen Fan Company also produced paper fans, advertising fans, fabric fans of cretonne and crepe, gauze, brocade, silk, and satin, fans of ostrich plumes, satin fans edged with marabou feathers (sometimes dyed), and fans with machine-made lace inserted in the leaves of gauze.

Ballooning was a popular pastime in the 1880s. It was only natural to find a fan honoring that sport made by the Allen Fan Company. Its hornbeam sticks are grained and embossed in gold designs *(Fig. 19)*.

A simple souvenir fan marks the "Opening of the Bijou Theatre in Boston," December 11, 1883, with printed notice of the play "The Beggar Student." A fascinating bit of information at the bottom of the poster on the fan reads: "The Theatre is lighted by the EDISON INCANDESCENT SYSTEM" *(Fig. 20)*, an innovation in lighting at that time.

Grace E. A. Ford, later to become Mrs. George Keiswetter, was one of the most noted American women fan painters of her era as well as a prolific commercial artist *(Fig. 21)*. Loving all flowers and nature, she was a charming and suitable companion for her equally gifted husband. She had a

Fig. 13

Fig. 21

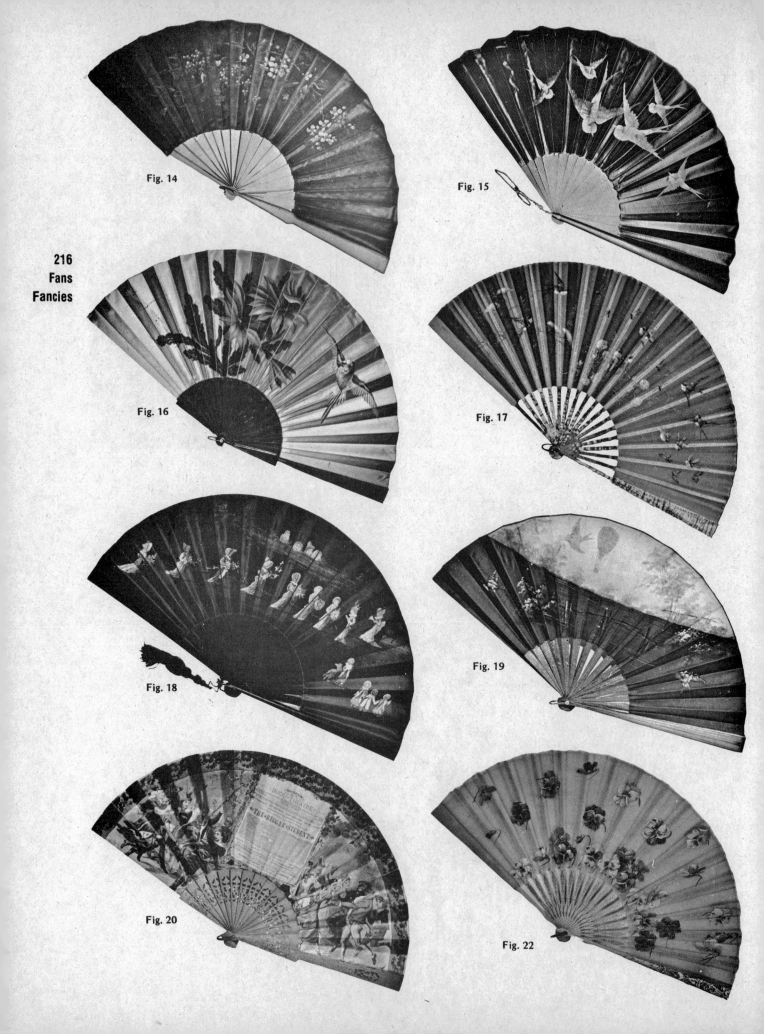

**216
Fans
Fancies**

Fig. 14

Fig. 15

Fig. 16

Fig. 17

Fig. 18

Fig. 19

Fig. 20

Fig. 22

magic touch with her brush, and flowers bloomed beautifully under her clever hand. Among her favorite flower designs were pansies, sprays of forget-me-nots, roses of all kinds, and apple blossoms.

Naturalistic and colorful pansies adorn the fan in *Fig. 22*, its white gauze leaf mounted on white painted wood sticks with gold embossing. The guard (outer) sticks are carved in a leaf design shaded with gold and silver in the manner of fans from Vienna, Austria.

Wild roses decorate the fine fan with white satin leaf shown in *Fig. 23*, the work of Grace E. A. Ford. It is a fan of the 1880s which any lady of the period would have been delighted to carry. Its charming leaf is mounted on Edmund Soper Hunt's "imitation" ivory sticks. The Allen Fan Company was privileged to use Mr. Hunt's imitation ivory process.

It would be hard to choose between the fan with the wild roses and the fan with the graceful apple blossom sprays painted by the same artist *(Fig. 24)*.

Probably there are still ladies who remember fans like the one pictured in *Fig. 25*. These were often called "Graduation" or "Debutante's" fans. This one was carried by a "Deb" at the Mardi Gras in New Orleans in 1903. It is fashioned of white gauze with inserts of machine-made lace combined with exquisite miniature painting of wild roses, forget-me-nots, and a wee brown sparrow contemplating a yellow butterfly. It represents the combined artistry of both Mr. and Mrs. George Keiswetter.

The Allen Fan company closed its doors in 1910. Today these American-made fans of Edmund Soper Hunt and the Allen Fan Company are being even more eagerly sought and cherished than when they were new.

Fig. 23

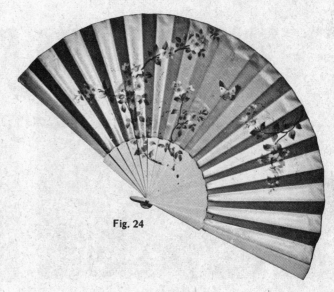

Fig. 24

Fig. 25

Commemorative and Dated Fans

by ELSA NITZCHE JAMES

PLATE 1

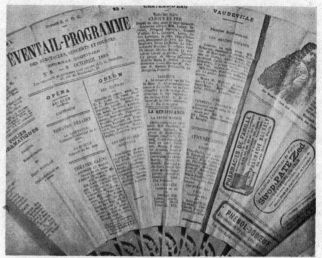

PLATE 3

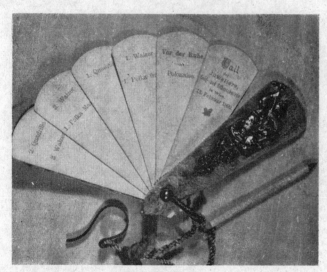

PLATE 4

PLATE 6

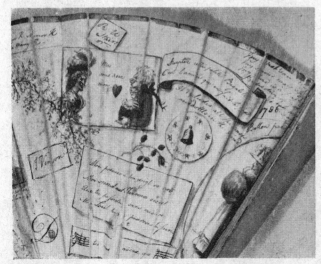

PLATE 7

PLATE 8

FASCINATING as fan collecting is, it is exasperating not to be able to give a fan an exact date. Far too often one is forced to label a collector's item with a vague "circa", "period of Louis 14th", "Victorian era", "early 18th century". Therefore, it is all the more exciting when one can definitely pin-point a fan's creation.

A fan need not necessarily be made of costly materials nor display the intricate craftsmanship of a highly trained artist to be of interest to a collector. The various cheap paper fans, printed in quantities to commemorate the Philadelphia Centennial International Exhibition in 1876, were very likely distributed as free souvenirs, yet now they make worthwhile, authentic collections.

An especially interesting group of fans from this Centennial era, are the ones which appeared in serial form. They are printed on a poor grade of paper with the backs all the same, showing an American spread eagle atop unfurled flags, with the dates 1776 and 1876, and in the center is printed "100 years". The sticks are of plain bamboo. On the right outer stick is stamped, "Registered June 8th, 1875," and on the left outer stick is "patented May 4th, 1876." The front side of each fan in the series depicts a different outstanding Centennial or historic building of Philadelphia.

A well rounded collection should include fans with Horticultural Hall, Art Gallery, better known as Memorial Hall *(Plate 1)*, Independence Hall, Main Exhibition Building, and Machinery Hall. All the fans of this series look like printed pen and ink drawings which have been hastily hand water colored, with red, white, and blue predominating. The clothing of the people and the horse-drawn vehicles add finishing touches to the authenticity of the dates.

Another cheap, and definitely crude Centennial fan shows in the sky a tremendous liberty bell with 1776 radiating like the sun over a fantastic

PLATE 2

conglomeration of boats, trains, bridges; to the right is a big balloon suspending two American flags, and on its netted surface is "1876" *(Cover)*. The whole picture is encircled with "Proclaim Liberty Throughout the Land Unto All the Inhabitants Thereof."

Enterprising advertisers also left no question as to the dates of fans. The clever wholesale milliner who distributed the fans shown in *Plate 2 and on cover*, no doubt had thousands of them made up. On cheap paper he had printed the basic, named hat styles and encircled above each, a pretty model wearing the enhanced, glorified, trimmed version. In the center of the fan is the modeled, crowning creation and under it is printed "Summer 1880." Apparently a space was left empty for each establishment to have printed its

---

As a general rule, fans are supposed by their owners or stated by dealers to be older than they really are; and to give an opinion often requires a certain amount of tact, as, for instance, when one is asked by its proud possessor to admire a specimen said to have belonged to Mary Queen of Scots, but which could not possibly have been made within a hundred years after her death.

—M. A. Flory
A Book About Fans, 1895

---

own name, for whereas *Plate 2* reads, "Plimpton Fiske and Co., Boston," an identical fan has been seen with a Rochester, N. Y. concern's name imprinted and another with that of a Baltimore fashion house.

The ingenious "Program Fan" is something which the present day summer stock theaters would do well to look into — they would prove far cheaper than modern air-conditioning, and could be financed entirely by the advertisers. In the French "Evantail-Programme" shown *(Plate 3)*, the date is distinctly, "October 8, 1880". On it are presented all the play-bills for that week in Paris. Also, there are wonderful, illustrated advertisements on how to own beautiful, long hair, how to make butter in the latest "up-to-the-minute" gadget, where to buy the best patent medicines. This program fan was some fair lady's choice souvenir of her gay week in Paris!

Another type of dated fan which no doubt brought nostalgic memories to its owner was the "dance-program" fan *(Plate 4)*. The one pictured here was made for the festive "Jeweler's Ball of gay Vienna, February 13th, 1892". The ball was organized by the gold and silversmiths of Vienna, and symbolically there is a beguiling silver and gold gnome fashioned very attractively and mounted on an end stick of blue velvet. A blue, sharpened

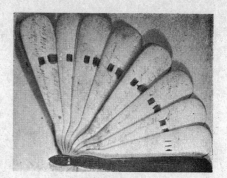

PLATE 5

pencil is attached to the loop for the convenience of eager swains who would write their names under "waltz", "polka", or "quadrille", and thus be assured a partner. The large hook secured the fan to milady's garments while she "tripped the light fantastic".

Perhaps at the same time Milady was romantically keeping a wooden "Autograph fan" on which she had each favorite "beau" write a line and sign his name. The earliest dated entry on such a fan *(Plate 5)* is November 14, 1867 by a Joseph Willing. "Girls will be girls!" isn't dated and is merely initialed "I.G. Gi. . ." Apparently, E. W. Rice, who on June 22nd, 1869, wrote "I am lonely to-night,—love without you——" caused milady to cease collecting autographs, for it is the last entry. Perhaps she chose E. W. Rice to be her lawful husband!

Turning to much earlier dates, *Plate 6* pictures the 1779 eruption of Mount Vesuvius. The Neopolitans were quick to capitalize on the catastrophic phenomena of their neighboring volcano, and eager tourists were attracted by the dramatic painted versions of Vesuvius belching great flames and molten lava. The peaceful Bay of Naples in the foreground made an interesting contrast. This fan is painted in gouache on "chicken skin" (the skin of young animals). Although many similar Vesuvius fans were painted in this late 18th century period, remarkably few exist today.

A delightfully whimsical and quaint fan is the one illustrated in *Plates 7 and 8*. It is a conglomerate collection of wit, riddles, fashions, and comic-drawings from the 18th century, executed by various lay people. Two dates appear on this paper fan; 1786 is on the front side, 1793 on the reverse side. "O Dear What Can the Matter Be?" is written directly under the 1793. Verses, beautifully penned in French predominate, but English, Latin, and German are also used. The drawings range from crude, grotesque, laughable figures of people and animals, to a rather well executed wise old owl! Written music and riddles also share space, as do various signatures. The fan as a whole leaves one with the delightful feeling that our revered ancestors also had their utterly frivolous, nonsensical moments!

* Indicates fans from the Oldham collection; others from "Facher", by George Buss. *Lockwood Studio Photos.*

German Fans

by ESTHER OLDHAM

GERMANY seems, curiously enough, to be almost forgotten among European fanmakers. Yet in 19th century Berlin, Conrad Sauerwald's Fan Shop was comparable to Alexandre's in Paris. The number and excellence of the artists who worked for him between 1875 and into the 1890s attest the importance and merit of German fan fabrication.

Fortunately for researcher and fan collector, German artists were not averse to signing their fan leaves. Most of Sauerwald's top designers signed their works—Paul Meyerheim, a superb fan painter and the pride of the studio, E. Zimmer, another favorite, E. U. Fischer-Coerlin, Max Seliger, George Schöbel, Friedrich Stahl, Anton von Werner, Hermann Götz, Gustav Schönleber, Franz Starbina, and others.

Many of them contributed fans and fan designs for the great competitive Exhibition of Fans held at Karlsruhe in 1891 under the patronage of the Grand Duke and Duchess of Baden. Ferdinand Keller took Grand Prize for his *Apotheosis of Kaiser William I*, described as "an excellent fan mount of a pretty cupid on a cloud with a medallion portrait of the Empress, and a large eagle." Max Seliger contributed a powerful painting on silk of eleven parrots and parakeets midst tropic foliage—birds were all large in size. Gustav Schönleber painted fishing boats at a pier—his boats were outsize, too.

In fact, massiveness of design was an outstanding

ILLUSTRATIONS, TOP TO BOTTOM.

Paul Meyerheim's massive Polar Bear, 1882, is exquisitely painted. Fan sticks are pearl, heavily ornamented in gold.
Also by Paul Meyerheim, tiny cupids paint large butterfly wings in gay colors on dark gray gauze. Sticks are gray pearl.
E. U. Fischer-Coerlin's "Aphrodite" flames in color and vitality, but fan lacks grace. Figures are large, scene almost too active. Rivet ends in glistening red jewel, carved ivory guard-sticks.
*Inexpensive souvenir fan printed on light gray paper, with wood sticks, honors the opening of Richard Wagner's Theatre at Bayreuth, Germany, 1876. Theatre, opera scenes, views of Bayreuth appear under portrait of the composer.
*Stunning 19th century black leather fan with gilt coat-of-arms in relief, made in Vienna for a German Baroness, shows monogram and coronet on broad-guardstick. Heavy guardsticks of simple shape are typical of Austria and Germany.

*Karl Friederich Schinkel, 1781-1841, architect and painter, died before he completed his restoration of the romantic Schloss Stolzenfels on the Rhine. Frederick William IV, in respect, ordered his unfinished projects completed according to his designs. Fan above, painted in gouache on kidskin, honors completion of the Schloss in 1842. Red shields, ivy and oak leaves separate scenes of ruins, castle, village. Feather-stitch piercing on ivory sticks and mother-of-pearl guard-sticks.

characteristic of German fans of the 19th century. The subjects, whatever they were, might have seemed almost too large had not the artists handled their designs boldly and expertly. Their coloring was correspondingly weighty and rich in tone. Roses were particularly lush.

Few such large designs were found outside of Germany. One exception is a fan leaf showing a handsome stag emerging from a forest, executed by the French artist Rosa Bonheur. Some large designs of birds, flowers, and such, were used on fans made by the Allen Fan Company of Braintree, Massachusetts, between 1880 and 1890, when their master painter was George Keiswetter, a German, who followed the heavier German and Austrian models.

German fans made a century earlier, in the 1700s, show the same love of processions, patriotic pomp, and splendor in decoration as later fans. However, figures on the printed fans of this earlier period were smaller, as they were on the printed fans of France and England. Painted fans of the first half of the 18th century in England and France often had large figures, and here, too, the Germans followed their lead in regard to size, though the German elite preferred their fans painted in rich deep colors.

In both centuries historic events and national achievements were everywhere recorded on fans; some were inexpensive for popular use, others were costly. The eminent German painter, etcher and illustrator, Daniel Nickolaus Chodowiecki, Director of the Berlin Academy of Art in 1797, designed several fans. His uncolored version of the apotheosis of Frederick William II, made in 1786, showing him borne to heaven by the Goddesses Minerva and Themis, is now in the British Museum.

About 1765 an entirely different type fan appeared in Germany, peculiar to that country, which remained in use until the end of the century. It consisted of an almost invisible square-mesh net background upon which painted paper scenes were cut out and applied to the thin net.

ILLUSTRATIONS, TOP TO BOTTOM.

E. Zimmer painted this colorful procession of ladies and gentlemen on horseback for Conrad Sauerwald's Fan Shop.

18th century printed fan leaf by Daniel Chodowiecki shows figures as small and dainty as those on French or English fans.

* *Unmounted printed fan leaf, hand painted in vivid color, shows Frederick II of Prussia riding in victory, after war of 1757. Female figures of Justice and Religion lead the way; allegory is explained on stone at right. A "news item" fan.*

Autograph fan, 1875, shows sketches and signatures of prominent artists: Ernest Zimmerman, Franz Stuck, Hermann Kaulbach, Diez, Holmberg, Lembach are among them. Autograph fans became the rage in Germany about 1875, stayed long in vogue.

* *Historic German signature fan, 1915, shows the Kaiser, center, Franz Joseph, Von Hindenburg, and other military leaders. Portraits and signatures, printed on paper, were pasted to sticks.*

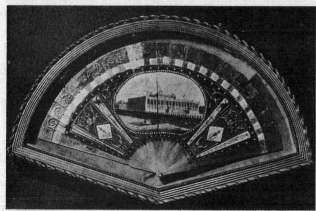

The official opening of the Royal Museum in Berlin in 1830 was also commemorated on a fan. Here, too, the architect was Schinkel, and the gouache painting of museum on fan seems to have been exactly copied from a Schinkel drawing. Sticks are of horn; blue sky harmonizes with the head of rivet—a turquoise. Side panels are painted subdued red; dividing panels, jade green; scroll work, gold. This is a small size or "minuet" fan, popular at that period and earlier.

Unmounted Fan Leaves

by ESTHER OLDHAM

WHEN A fan-shaped print or painting is found, the perplexed viewer often wonders, "Is this fan leaf merely a print, or was it actually meant to be mounted as a fan?"

During the 18th century particularly, thousands of these fan-shaped prints were issued, either in black and white, or with colors added by hand. Often they were made to celebrate important historical events, or to honor literary, dramatic, or operatic achievements; some depicted legendary and allegorical scenes.

Sometimes, too, their message was to instruct, as shown by the Botanical examples pictured here. The fan, on ivory sticks, is from the collection of Mrs. Henry W. Borntraeger, the fan leaf from the Oldham collection. They are marked, "Published as the ACT directs, July 21, 1792, by Sarah Ashton, No. 28 Little Britain (London)."

Turning to the magnificent English tome, *Fans and Fan Leaves,* describing the examples in the Lady Charlotte Schreiber Collection in the British Museum, we find this Botanical fan fully catalogued. Concerning the obverse, we read:

". . . This fan bears examples of Botanical forms, with their scientific denominations. In the center is a small bunch of flowers, jonquils, geraniums, etc. . . at the sides are some small branches, and all around are examples of various orders of seed vessels, with numerals referring to the description on the reverse. The borders contain different forms of leaves with the name of each."

The reverse of the fan gives other technical information, such as the different parts of a flower, and a list of the twenty-four orders of Botany referring to the illustrations on the obverse, with examples.

It bears, also, the lines of poetry from the II Stanza, 4 Canto, "Botanic Garden" V. I.—

Come ye soft Sylphs, who fan the Paphian Groves,
And bear on sportive wings the callow Loves;
Call with sweet whisper, in each gale that blows
The slumbering Snow-drop from her long repose;
Charm the pale Prim-rose from her clay-cold bed.
Unveil the bashful Violet's tremulous head;
While from her bud the playful Tulip breaks,
And young Carnations peep with blushing cheeks.

To our everlasting advantage, the publishers and print-sellers of the 18th century often overstocked their fan leaves which were to have been mounted on fan-sticks (brins) and sold as completed fans. When we find such treasures, mounted or unmounted, in the 20th century — and find them we occasionally do — they have as much appeal to the gardener today as to the flower enthusiast of two centuries ago. The soft yellow of the jonquils, the rose red of the geraniums, and the grassy green of the leaves make a water color flower print well worth framing.

The value and importance of all these unmounted fan leaves should not be underestimated, nor should they be given only a passing glance.

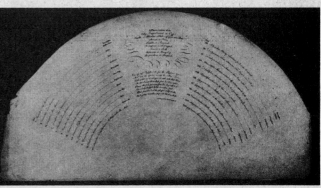

HANDCRAFTED COMBS

by CARROLL HOPF

Back Comb—a fine example illustrating an intricate hand cut design. This example probably dates from the second or third quarter of the 19th century. 5⅝" ht., 3¾" wd

Undoubtedly the two Back Combs were given equal prominence with the other fashionable attire which this charming lass proudly wears. The inscription on the back of the portrait reads: "Dolly Hackett Nov. 27, 1832," The medium is water color on paper; its dimensions are: 23¾" ht., 19" wd. From the collections of Fruitlands Museums, Prospect Hill, Harvard, Massachusetts.

THE COMBMAKER'S craft originates far back in history, for combs to manage and beautify the hair have been in consistent demand for centuries upon centuries.

Undoubtedly the skills, techniques, and tools required to make a comb were brought to colonial America by some of the 17th century settlers, though not until the first decades of the 18th century do we find combmakers advertising their products in major seaport towns like Boston. In 1759, Christopher Anger advertised, in Philadelphia, that he made and supplied "various types of combs."

Combs made by the combmaker before the processes of mechanization rang the death knell for his hand craft, can still be found on the antiques market. They make an interesting collection in themselves or can form an integral aspect of a more encompassing collection.

Comb types may be divided into two categories depending upon usage. Back Combs, Puff Combs, and Side Combs were used to hold the hair in place after it had been fashionably arranged. Dressing Combs and Folding Combs were used by both men and women to arrange the hair.

(Please turn the page)

Cattle horn, tortoiseshell, and ivory were the materials most used by comb-makers, although wood, bone, and metal were sometimes employed. Ivory and tortoiseshell were the more desirable and the costliest of materials. Cattle horn was plentiful and comparatively inexpensive.

Tanneries were usually a good source of supply for horn. The horns were collected and allowed to remain piled up long enough for the inner pith to deteriorate and rot. Then the tops and butts of the horn were sawed off and a longitudinal cut made. Soaking them in hot water for several days was usually the next step, followed by immersion in hot whale oil to make the horn pliable. After this, the horn was flattened out by pressing between heavy flat stones or iron plates, and allowed to cool.

A "guillotine," a cutting blade hinged to a wooden block beneath, was used to trim the flattened horn plates to the required size. The "crooked shave," a tool similar to a draw knife, was employed to reduce the thickness, and a "quarnet," similar to a wood rasp, was used to produce an overall uniform thickness.

The next major step involved cutting teeth into the smooth, uniform horn plate. A "gauge-leaf" or "twinning saw" was employed for this process. Comb teeth were then rounded and evened with the "bottoming saw" and "graille," another form of file. Teeth points or ends were sharpened and finished with a "topper" or "pointer" which resembles the graille but is smaller.

Polishing the combs was accomplished with "polishing balls" made of old woolen carpet or soft leather and stuffed with corn husks. These were rubbed vigorously against the comb surface with mixtures of rottenstone and vinegar, or common whiting and "coal of burnt willow."

Other steps in combmaking were clarifying the horn plates to make them more transparent, and heating and bending Back Combs over forms to produce contour shapes to fit the back of the head.

These hand processes employed in making horn combs—and they apply generally to those of tortoiseshell and ivory, too—were mechanized during the first half of the 19th century, though on better combs, partial handwork was continued into late in that century.

Decorating fashionable Back Combs could be accomplished by several methods. Gouge-carving of designs or intricate patterns cut out with a jigsaw were the more tedious methods of embellishment. Hand engraving or im-

Back Combs—The example on the left is tortoise shell; simplicity of form makes this example especially attractive. Comb on the right is horn with a floral pattern applied by utilizing the sraining process. Both date from the first half of the 19th century. Measurements are from left to right: 6⅞" ht., 6¼" wd.; 5⅛" ht., 5⅞" wd.

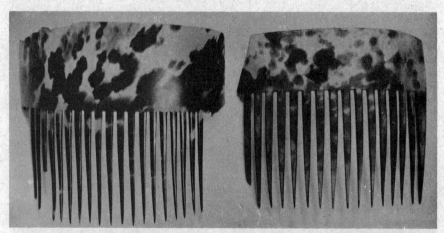

Back Combs—left example is tortoise shell, right example is horn clarified and stained to imitate tortoise shell. The stain primarily remains on the surface of the horn, whereas in real tortoise shell the dark coloration is naturally throughout the thickness of the shell. Both examples date from the first half of the 19th century. Left example is 4⅞" ht., 5½" wd.; right example is 4⅜" ht., 5⅛" wd.

pressing patterns into the horn with metal dies were among the simpler methods. Dies were also used to punch out patterns.

Because of the paucity and high cost of tortoiseshell, cattle horn was frequently dyed to resemble it. (Edward Hazen's *Popular Technology or Professions and Trades*, published in New York in 1850, states, "Eight pounds of usable shell is worth between sixty and seventy dollars.")

The formula for producing a tortoiseshell effect, as quoted below from *The American Artists' Manual*, published in Philadelphia in 1814, seems to have been standard as it appears in other 19th century publications:

"The horn to be dyed must be first pressed into a flat form, and then spread over with a paste made of two parts of quicklime and one of litharge,

Side Combs—The one on the left, stained to resemble tortoise shell, can also be termed a "Puff Comb." The one on the right is not a bit refined in regard to workmanship; both probably date from the first half of the 19th century. Right: 4½" x 1". Left: 3⅝" x 2½".

brought into a proper consistence with soap-ley. This paste must be put over all the parts of the horn, except such as are proper to be left transparent. It requires taste and judgment to dispose the paste in such a manner as to form a variety of transparent parts, of different magnitude and figures to look like nature."

Litharge (lead oxide), a reddish brown substance occurring as a natural mineral or made chemically from lead, produced the reddish color, while the soap-ley and quicklime effected the penetrating and staining qualities.

Combmakers usually established themselves in the more sizable communities. The 1843 Lancaster, Pennsylvania, City Directory, for example, lists five combmakers. A large comb-making center grew up in and around Leominster, Massachusetts.

Origins of the comb industry in Massachusetts can be traced back to early generations of the Noyes family —Enoch Noyes established a comb shop in West Newbury, Massachusetts in 1759. Noyes were still making combs in the last half of that century, and later members of the family were responsible for many of the mechanical innovations which industrialized combmaking.

With mechanization came the substitution for tortoiseshell and horn. Combs made of gutta-percha appeared before 1850. After 1870, when the pyroxyline base compound known today as celluloid began to be made into different articles, combs of this material came on the market. This, to a large degree, ruined the demand for horn, tortoiseshell, and ivory which, up to that time, had been the traditional comb material.

Excellent collections of combs and the tools with which they were made are on public exhibit at the Henry Ford Museum in Dearborn, Michigan, and the Mercer Museum in Doylestown, Pennsylvania.

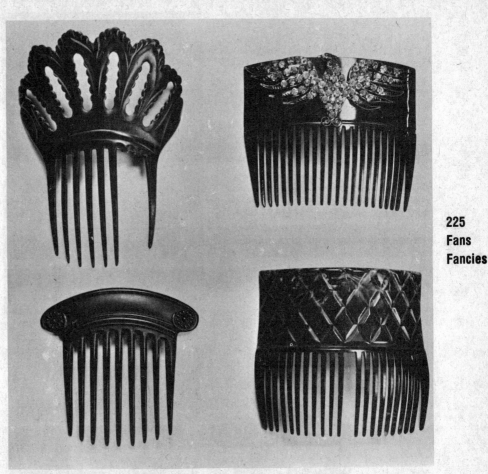

Back Combs—top left example is horn, lower left example is gutta percha and formed in a mold; two right examples are tortoise shell, top right comb maintains a patriotic theme with the eagle motif made of silver gilt wire and imitation cut diamonds; all four probably date from the first half of the 19th century. Measurements from left to right are: top—5 1/4" ht., 4" wd.; 3 1/2" ht., 4 1/4" wd.; bottom—3 5/8" ht., 3 3/4" wd.; 3 7/8" ht., 4" wd.

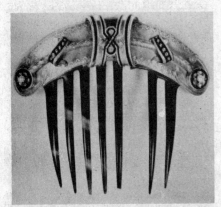

Back Comb — an elaborate example made from tortoise shell with gold mounting; dates probably from the second quarter of the 19th century; 3 1/4" ht., 3 7/8" wd.

Back Combs—three examples illustrating the use of dies to punch out repeat patterns and impress line patterns; all three are made from horn and date from the first half of the 19th century. Measurements from left to right are: 4 1/2" ht., 3 3/4" wd.; 4 1/2" ht., 4 1/2" wd.; 4 1/4" ht., 3 1/2" wd.

Top: Porcelain lavender jar; pure white, except for cover; inside frill and ribbon in lavender color; 4 in. high; Worcester, ca. 1800.

Center, left to right: Cut glass, silver-mounted Vinaigrette; below the domed top and over the sponge lies a flat disc of silver pierced with 8 pinholes; ¾ in. high; ca. 1770. Silver Vinaigrette; silver gilt grating, based on acanthus leaf, which is also engraved on top and bottom of the box; 1½ in. long; ca. 1780. Original shagreen case of this Vinaigrette; 2½ in. long. **Below:** Cut glass Attar of Roses phial, gilded; 6 in. long; Bohemia, ca. 1740.

Bottom: Perfume Pan. Ivory and brass handle 2 ft. long; brass bowl 2¼ in. in diameter; ca. 1720.

PERFUME

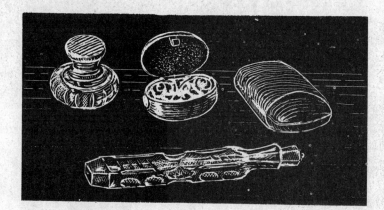

FROM THE

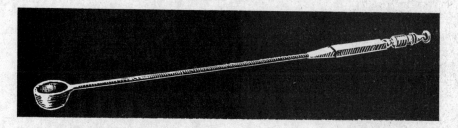

PAST

by MARGARET LOVELL RENWICK

TO REFRESH A STUFFY ROOM, Elizabethan England waved around a perfume pan, which was a two-foot ladle filled with rose-water, borage leaves, cloves, mace, and vinegar. Nor did the Georgians disdain one until the more general use of windows made to open easily allowed rooms to be thoroughly aired. As china and sashed windows came into fashion together, perfume-lovers merely changed from pans to pots.

Though Englishwomen had always dried flowers for household use, potpourri, a highly spiced mixture of dried flowers in bewildering variety, was not familiar till the mid-18th century. Earlier the words meant what they still mean in France, a spicy stew of various meats and vegetables, "pot pourri" standing for "olla Pudrida," "rotten pot," the Spaniard's gibe at his favorite dish.

When, in the 1740s, recipes for a scented potpourri reached country houses, women delightedly filled their Chinese jars or their Dutch ones painted with chinoiseries, made fashionable by Queen Mary II, 50 years before.

Then Leeds began turning out special jars in pierced creamware, and with the 19th century came the pierced top. Worcester was as practical. Dried lavender was an English speciality, and true to its flair for the homely, Worcester faithfully copied in porcelain the lavender-filled bags traditionally laid in dressing-chests and hung in wardrobes, partly to keep away moths.

Like potpourri, the vinaigrette was born in the kitchen, for originally the word meant a salad, dressed with vinegar, and in France still means a sauce. The 18th century owner felt in her reticule for her scent flask, smelling flask, or smelling bottle when, about to faint, she needed that tiny glass bottle or silver box with its morsel of sponge soaked in vinegar which had been aromatized by attars.

Modern perfume-makers, distilling herbs, nut-kernels, fruit-rinds and flower-petals, produce over 70 attars, the best-known of these fragrant oils being attar of roses, so powerful, and so costly, that nowadays it is just an ingredient in luxury soaps and toilet-creams. But aware that a drop or two of it would scent a drawerful of kerchiefs, the 18th century user sometimes indulged in a small bottle, holding perhaps 40 drops in the match-thin tube which runs down the middle of the phial.

More than 30 firms claim to own the original Italian recipe for that Kolnwasser (Cologne Water) which French officers took home in the Seven Years' War (1757–63), calling their new perfume Eau de Cologne. The claimants' scent-bottles are highly distinctive, and it has been suggested that the legitimate owner might well be the firm whose use of wickerwork is reminiscent of the straw-covered Chianti wine-flagon.

Rivalling the best French glass in sparkle and style are some 19th century scent-bottles made in the English Midlands. Unusual in form, they are square, oval, diamond-shaped, decorated with fanciful pastoral figures in painted enamel, and would do honor to any collection.

Left: Covered potpourri jar in Chinese style, decorated on a white ground in blue, reds, greens, brown, and mauve; 9¼ in. high; Holland, ca. 1725. **Right:** Potpourri jar with pierced cover; decorated on a white ground in blue with Spanish scene, probably under the influence of the Peninsular War (1808-1814); 3 in. high; Staffordshire, ca. 1810.

Left: Cut glass scent bottle, diamond-shaped, with octagonal stopper, painted with opaque white enamel in the Mary Gregory style of decoration; 6 in. high; Stourbridge, ca. 1880. **Right:** Green glass scent bottle, bound in wickerwork; 4½ in. high; Cologne, Germany, ca. 1810.

The Scraperboard Sketches used to illustrate Mrs. Renwick's article were executed by her very talented sister, Edith Lovell Andrews, an artist whose works have appeared in several prestige publications.

Umbrellas for Sale!

FEATURED AT the Libbey Glass Company's exhibit at the Columbian Exposition in Chicago in 1893, was a high-style gown, woven of spun glass threads. There was also an umbrella covered with the same material. This celebrated glass umbrella was designed by Col. James H. Sprague, and made up, "at a cost of more than $350," at the Sprague & French umbrella factory in Norwalk, Ohio. The Princess Eulalia of Spain admired this glittering ensemble at the Fair, and had a similar gown made up for her own wardrobe. The umbrella shown at the Fair was given to her to go with it.

Sprague & French, established in 1886, was at that time one of the largest, most progressive umbrella factories in the country. The firm's trade extended "from Maine to California, from Texas and Florida to Duluth and Seattle." Their patented canopies for buggies and carriages (and later for automobiles) had a wide sale in foreign countries—Mexico, Canada, Great Britain, France, Germany, and South Africa.

On April 8, 1890, the whole Sprague & French works was blown away by a cyclone. Rebuilding was swift, for in their catalog, ca. 1895–6, the new

The Celebrated Glass Dress and its Matching Umbrella. The Libbey Glass Company wove the material of spun glass threads; Sprague & French designed and made the umbrella.

factory was described in detail, giving an excellent picture, not only of their physical plant, but of the various processes embraced in umbrella manufacture in the 1890s. Exuberantly the catalog informed:

"Our factory contains about 40,000 square feet of floor room. Our Main Factory is a frame building 250 × 100 feet, two stories high, and is surmounted by a large tower, and is especially adapted to our work, and contains over eighty lathes and special machinery for doing our work. Our Covering Rooms, where all the covers are put on, is 100 × 36 feet and has a capacity for 4,000 covers per day. It is nicely furnished, and is the finest and best lighted room for covering umbrellas in the world. Our Sewing Machine Room is 40 × 36 feet, well lighted, and thirty machines of the latest improved style work on the covers, cases, ties, etc. The capacity of each machine is 200 covers per day. These machines are run by power, and make 2500 revolutions per minute. Our Finishing department is a commodious room fitted out with improved machinery for putting on umbrella heads, etc. Our Packing and Shipping Department is ample for our wants.

"In our large Stock Rooms is stored at all times over $40,000 worth of all kinds of stock for making umbrellas. Our silks are all imported for us by our New York importers direct from the large factories of Milan, Italy, and are the best in the world for umbrella covers. Our fine cotton

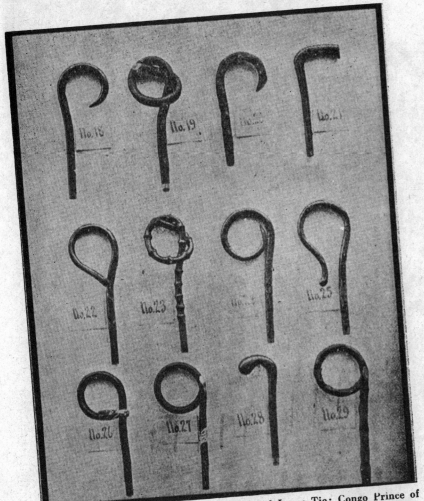

Top row, left to right: Acacia Hook; Weichsel Loose Tie; Congo Prince of Wales (also made for gent's umbrellas); Acacia Opera Hook. *Second row:* Olive Loop; Whanghi Tie; Acacia Closed Loop, Mottled; Acacia Shepherd's Crook, Mottled. *Bottom row:* Weichsel Loop, Ivory Tip; Weichsel Loop, Silver Trimmed; Acacia Bulb Crook; Congo Loop. Wholesale prices, for sticks and mounts ranged from 25¢ to $1.

goods used on Twilights and Knoxalls (a twilled Gloria material) are the product of English looms, made from selected Egyptian Cotton. Its equal does not exist, as it is fine work to tell it from silk. Our American No. 1 Cottons are the unequalled dyes of Martin, absolutely fast, never color. Our common dyes are the best available for the money.

"We make our own ribs, stretchers, frames, notches and runners, do our own brass work. In fact no other Umbrella Factory in the world does one half the work on an umbrella that we do. Our Japan Ovens, built separate from our main buildings, have a capacity of 10,000 frames at each baking, and are light and roomy, and we have a strong force of expert machinists, pattern makers, blacksmiths, etc. We make our own tools, saws, milling machinery, and all of our fine special machinery has been made in our factory by our experts."

The catalog pictured some 74 sticks and mounts which were available to their customers. These were not made at the factory but were the "choicest selections of the American and European markets." Besides those illustrated, they claimed to have "thousands of others, equally meritorious," and that they carried no old styles, for "as soon as a mount ceased to be *the thing,* it was closed out regardless of price, to make room for a novelty."

Not all their sticks and mounts were purchased elsewhere. They themselves manufactured a light high brass tube stick, lacquered in imitation of rosewood which they claimed was made by no one else. Their New Metal Point, "the finest ferrule and point ever made by anyone, light, strong, and elegant, imparting a very fine and pleasing effect to an umbrella," was also made only by Sprague & French.

Bicycle umbrellas, for both ladies and gentlemen, was one of their specialties. These made a "most complete sun protector, and could easily and firmly be attached to any bicycle. They folded neatly into a compact bag, and when strapped to the handlebar or cross-bar were entirely out of the way, yet ready to use at a moment's notice."

In addition to umbrellas, the company carried a full line of ebony canes, of all sizes, which they mounted with gold or silver mounts, and engraved if the customer desired. They also made in their own factory a fine line of aluminum canes, Prince of Wales style, finished with their patent enamel and imitation of rosewood, with silver tips. Their line of Weichsel, Congo, and Hickory Prince of Wales canes seem to have been made elsewhere.

Perhaps the company's most widely known product was wagon umbrellas. These were made of heavy buff, green, and blue drill, with 10 cast-steel giant ribs, with "a good device for fastening to any wagon or buggy."

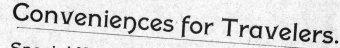
229
Fans
Fancies

The "Tourist" was made with detachable and interchangeable handles and points; any handle and point would go on any "Tourist," without regard to size. This was advertised as a "very close rolling umbrella, which had on Sprague's Patent tie"; the cases had glove button fastenings, making them cane-shaped without bulges. All had "nice suitable cases, with celluloid bands, and were elegant in shape, style, and finish." Sprague & French claimed, in the mid-1890s, they had made and sold more than 200,000 of them.

Sprague's Patent Buggy Canopy placed the pole in the rear, an innovation which left the "most desirable place, the *center* of the canopy, for the use of the occupants of the seat."

The poles were of heavy hard maple, 1⅛ to 1⅜ inches in diameter. Thousands of these were made for advertising purposes, hand-painted, not stenciled, in two bright colors. The Sprague sign painters, who worked "in the season," were so expert that they could do this work at the nominal price of $2 per dozen in dozen lots, or 25 cents each in smaller lots. However, they limited their lettering to the firm name, business, street and number. More than that was considered "unnecessary," since it could not be painted in letters large enough to read easily.

Specialty umbrellas, similarly painted, were made for "Republicans, Democrats, Populists, Prohibitionists, etc., and for all kinds of churches, societies, etc., large or small size."

Colonel Sprague

James H. Sprague, the activator and inventor of the firm, was born in Auburn, North Carolina, February 15, 1846. At fifteen, he was a sergeant of the 19th N.Y.V.G., serving in the Civil War. He was in the first battle of Bull Run, later on guard duty at the White House, then in the secret service under Secretary Stanton, then back in the ranks again as a lieutenant. Taken prisoner at Pocatelego, South Carolina, he escaped three weeks later. He was mustered out of service in Charleston, in June, 1865.

For a time after the war, he was the manager of McLean's circus. Then, in 1869, he married a Norwalk, Ohio, girl, Eliza Cunningham, and settled down in Norwalk. At first he worked as an itinerant salesman for Barney Courtright's fanning mill, F. B. Case's "Maple City Tobacco," and M. D. Osborn & Co.'s agricultural implements. Later he became manager of the Plano Harvester & Binder Co.

In 1886, with C. L. French, he established the Sprague & French Umbrella Factory in Norwalk, a successful venture from the start. At the time of his death, November 30, 1911, the company had become the Sprague Auto-Top factory. His title of Colonel was honorary, coming to him as a member of the staff of Governor J. B. Foraker.

Contemporary accounts of Colonel Sprague in *The Firelands Pioneer* and other local histories in the Norwalk Public Library, mention him as one of the largest employers of labor in the city, and his business as having done more, perhaps, than any other to give the city widespread publicity. It was noted that he was a member of most of Norwalk's secret societies, a lodge man of national repute, having held highest offices in such societies as the G.A.R., Masonic bodies, Elks, and "other organizations too numerous to mention." It was recorded that he was a gifted orator and a noted composer of popular music, and that "his genial manner and well known hustling ability made his name and features familiar to every Norwalk citizen."

UMBRELLAS ARE of Eastern origin and of great antiquity. The name itself, deriving from the Latin *umbra*, meaning shade, indicates their original use as a protection from the sun. In the hot, brilliant Asian countries, the umbrella was the insignia of royalty and rank. Among the ancient ruins of Ninevah and Egypt, carvings depict kings and lesser potentates being carried in processions, umbrellas held over their heads. Even as late as 1855, the King of Burma, addressing the Governor-General of India, termed himself, "the monarch who reigns over the great umbrella-wearing chiefs of the Eastern countries."

Umbrellas moved west through Greece and Italy, where elegant ladies carried them—they were considered too effeminate for men. Coyat, in 1611, writing of the Italians, noted: "Many of them doe carry other fine things . . . which they commonly call in the Italian tongue *umbrellaes*. These are made of leather something answerable to the forms of a little cannopy and hooped in the inside with divers little wooden hoopes that extend the umbrella in a pretty large compasse."

By mid-18th century, umbrellas were known in England, and some people owned them—the inventory of Sir R. Sutton's goods in 1732 included "Four Umbrellows"—but they were still enough of a curiosity to be mentioned in books by travelers to Persia, China, Portugal, and Spain. A Colonel Wolfe, writing in 1752, from Paris, mentioned the use of umbrellas in France and wondered why they were not introduced in England.

The umbrella in England was first thought of as a sunshade for ladies. Then Jonas Hanway, an eccentric traveler, who died in 1786, demonstrated its use against rain. He is credited with being the first Englishman who habitually carried an umbrella.

The earliest Western umbrellas, based on their Eastern prototypes, were heavy and ungainly, with long handles, ribs of whalebone or cane, stretchers of cane, and an oiled silk or cotton covering which was always sticking together in the folds. Gingham was soon substituted for the oiled cloth, and in 1834, an English market report in *Tait's Magazine* noted that "umbrella ginghams, employed for covering umbrellas, have remained steady for some time." Alpaca took over in 1848 when William Sangster patented its use as an umbrella covering material.

The greatest improvement in umbrella design came in 1852 when Samuel Fox patented his "Paragon" rib. This was formed of a thin strip of steel rolled into a U or trough section, a form which gives great strength for the weight of the metal. This is the basic umbrella rib we know today.

A story has been printed that the first umbrella in America came by merchantship to Baltimore in 1772. An adventurous soul purchased it at the dock, opened it, and started for home. At his appearance on the street, women screamed, horses bolted, children pelted him with stones. Be that as it may, by 1793 umbrellas were enough used here for John Taylor, a brass founder in Richmond, to advertise in the *Virginia Gazette* that he made and repaired "skeletons for umbrellas."

Another of Sprague's inventions was a leather carrying case to hold the "Tourist." This could be attached by its chain to any valise or travelling bag. The case could be locked to the valise and the umbrella securely locked in the case. The traveller detached the handle of the umbrella and either put it in the valise or carried it in his pocket.

MAIL ORDER FASHIONS

By VERA ELDRIDGE

Dress from National Cloak & Suit's first catalog, 1888.

BIG MAIL order houses have performed unintentionally as historians of the customs of the American people. Their catalogs over the past seven decades, known familiarly as the "Nation's Wishbook," or the "Farmer's Bible," present an accurate year-by-year account of how Americans lived. Their pages portray what people wore, the furnishings they put in their houses, the tools they used in their work, the medicine they took and, for their leisure hours, the books they read, the songs they sang, the games they played. They record inventions as they came on the market, and reflect economic booms and depressions.

Catalogs are so highly regarded as important documents, that the Library of Congress, most large city libraries, and many smaller ones have complete collections from the larger mail order houses and examples from smaller specialized firms. Hollywood uses the catalog as an indispensable source book.

While Sears-Roebuck and Montgomery Ward were the largest mail order purveyors of general merchandise—everything could be found in their catalogs from aromatic spirits of ammonia to zithers—specialized houses, with concentrated catalogs, strengthened the over-all "living" picture. National Cloak and Suit Company and Bellas-Hess, for example, filled fat catalogs with fashions for ladies (and gents), providing for today's researchers a study in depth on ready-to-wear.

The National Cloak & Suit Company was founded in 1888 by S. J. Rosenbaum in New York City, to fashion made-to-order ladies' suits, dresses, and coats. Mr. Rosenbaum's five sons, who followed him in the business, all began their careers stuffing envelopes with sales letters. The company merged with Bellas-Hess in 1926, and today the "soundless salesman" of National Bellas-Hess has a circulation of over 3 million.

The first catalog of the National Cloak and Suit Company, in 1888, emphasized the etiquette of mourning clothes, from total black, including the lining, through medium gray at the proper time, to lighter colors. In a later catalog, a listing for corsets suggested, "Our coats, dresses and suits are not made to fit your figure, but our corsets." The measurement diagram from the 1903 book allowed for a bustle in the back, a dip in the front, and for a full, curving bust.

Until the 1930s, almost all catalog illustrations were hand-drawn. Lace, embroidery, and other trimmings were sketched in fine detail. Sometimes a photographed head was superimposed on the drawing of a costume, but most models were pen-and-ink ladies, all looking alike, with luxuriant hair, round luminous eyes, and cupid's-bow mouths.

Materials have changed considerably from the cotton, wool, silk, and linen of pre-World War years. First rayon, then synthetics appeared. The current National Bellas-Hess catalog takes a page to describe 16 kinds of fabrics, their care, and what wear may be expected of them. (Fifty years from now, will anyone remember dacron?)

No. 2L25 $1.00

No. 2L26 $1.48

No. 2L27 $1.00

No. 2L28 $1.98

No. 2L29 $1.00

BELLAS HESS & CO
BROADWAY. PRINCE & CROSBY STS.
NEW YORK CITY, N.Y.

Catalog covers were made attractive with drawings by such artists as Howard Chandler Christy, hinting at high quality merchandise within. Shirtwaists from Bellas-Hess catalog, May 1, 1911.

THE "CARPET BAG"

by GRACE ROGERS COOPER
Curator, Division of Textiles, Smithsonian Institution

Fragment of Ingrain Carpeting, ca. 1840, enlarged to show weave. Geometric pattern in red on two shades of green, reversed on opposite side; fabric is a double cloth; it does not have a pile. 5½ x 6¾"

BAGS OF various descriptions, used to transport one's personal possessions when traveling, have existed for centuries. But even in the late 18th century, a traveling bag made of a carpet would seem most unlikely. Carpets were then very expensive household furnishings. Only the wealthiest homes could afford the luxury of such a rich textile on the floor — to be trampled under foot. Certainly the wear and abuse demanded of a traveling bag makes it very unlikely that such an intricate, hand-woven fabric would have been considered for a commonplace article.

Yet by the middle of the 19th century, the carpet bag was such a common household word that a new literary journal, published in 1851, chose the name "The Carpet-Bag." In their first issue the editors state:

"The name—'The Carpet-Bag'—we have adopted as expressing the miscellaneous character of a good paper, into which are crowded a variety of things necessary for comfort and happiness on the highway of life. This name, it strikes us, will 'take.' It has a familiar, everyday ring to it, that commends it to the ear at once . . ."

Carpet bag—a familiar ring in 1851, unknown fifty years earlier—how and when did it happen?

It is doubtful that a traveling bag was ever made of carpet during the period that carpeting itself was woven only by hand, whether by the slow, intricate hand-knotting technique of the Oriental or early Axminster carpets or by the use of the shuttle loom to produce the early Brussels, Wilton, or the lower class ingrain (Scotch, Kidderminster or Venetian) carpets.

It may be possible that the latter types were used; it would not have been economically unfeasible to use ingrain or Venetian carpeting in the manufacture of a carpet bag. But to date, no examples have been found. Since both types of carpets were produced throughout the 19th century, at first by hand loom, and then by power, some examples should have survived.

The earliest use of the name "carpet bag" that the author has uncovered at this writing is in the United States patent specification, No. 1620, issued May 25, 1840. The inventors report: "Be it known that we, James Sellers and Abraham L. Pennock, of the city of Philadelphia, Pennsylvania, have invented a new and improved mode of making the clasps for Mailbags, Carpet-Bags, Valises and other articles . . ."

It is quite obvious that bags made of carpets were not new, as these inventors had been granted a patent on the improvement of a clasp, and there seemed to be no need to explain the term "carpet-bag."

The English patent 3950, granted on August 11, 1815, to Richard Dixon for the "construction of trunks and portmanteaus (traveling bag) — application of materials not hitherto used," seemed to offer some promise. A review of the patent specifications revealed that no mention of carpet was proposed. In Samuel Pratt's English patent number 7250, December 9, 1836, for the "construction of portmanteaus, bags, boxes, or cases for travelers," the inventor states: "The whole of this portmanteau, knapsack, or traveling commode is constructed in the usual manner well known to trunk or traveling equipage makers, and the outside of the bag . . . covered with leather . . ."

As late as 1836, in England, we do not have carpet mentioned in use in the construction of traveling bags. Yet

in 1843, when William Thomas was granted English patent 9879 for "fastenings applicable to portmanteaus, bags, etc.," he states that certain figures in the patent drawings "represent various views of the improved fastening adapted to a carpet bag."

There were, then, carpet bags of some description produced as early as 1840, possibly a few years earlier, but probably later than 1836. Since a power loom for weaving ingrain carpets was patented in the United States in 1834 by John Haight, and it is known that some 20 or 30 looms were constructed in Paterson, New Jersey, on this principle in the year 1835, which were put into operation at Little Falls, it is equally probable that these first carpet bags were constructed of ingrain carpet (a type of double cloth with the color pattern reversing from one side to the other). Hopefully, some keen-eyed antiques collector may turn up one of these early examples.

In 1842, the first patent for the weaving of Brussels carpet by power was issued in England. This was followed by significant improvements in the mid-1840s, including those of Erastus Bigelow in the United States.

NO. THREE

Power-woven Brussels carpet is one of the more common types found in mid-19th century carpet bags. But other types of carpet, popular after the power production reduced the cost, were also used — Wilton and Tapestry. In 1856, it was reported that one power loom could weave from four to five times the amount of carpet that one hand loom could produce, requiring fewer operators and producing a better and more regularly woven fabric.

While the carpet bag was in manufacture during the 1850s and 1860s, and many inventors attempted to improve the article, as evidenced by the Patent Office records, the general popularity seems to have dwindled by the 1870s. Whether this was the result of the political feeling about "carpetbaggers," which arose during Reconstruction days following the Civil War, can be a matter for speculation only. Like other consumer products, it may have just gone out of style.

NO. FOUR

Whatever the cause, we have found no reference to its manufacture in the late 19th century, although bags of a similar style were made of a printed plush. Even today we have ladies' bags of power-woven tapestry-type fabrics and other heavy materials that closely resemble the styles and patterns of the 19th century, but the true "carpet-bag" passed into obscurity many decades ago.

ABOUT THE ILLUSTRATIONS

No. 1. *Carpet bag of Brussels carpeting, ca. 1850.* This is the most common style of the smaller-size carpet bag. It is constructed of a single width of carpet, which is 27 inches. A strip, approximately 12 inches in length, is used and folded envelope style. Narrow pieces of carpeting are set into each side. The flap edge is bound with a narrow tape, or sometimes coach lace. The rope handle is covered with the same carpeting, and the bag is lined with an inexpensive muslin. It is closed with a small brass clasp-lock. Overall dimensions of the finished bag are 11x12x1½ inches.

Brussels carpet is a looped pile construction. The pattern and color ground is produced from the worsted warp and controlled by the Jacquard attachment of the loom. Brussels carpets are described as five, four, or three frame, according to the number of sets of creel bobbins carrying the pile warp yarns. Usually all the bobbins in a given frame carry the same color. There is also a chain warp, usually of cotton, which binds the fabric, and in later power-woven Brussels, a stuffer warp to give the

NO. FIVE

carpet more body. The weft was usually of linen.

In this example the ground color of the standard carpeting used is a pale peach; the large floral pattern is off-white, outlined and centered in brown. The diamond and some figure centers are in red; other figure centers are blue. Privately owned.

No. 2. *Carpet bag, Brussels carpeting, 1850-1852.* This carpeting is 30" wide; it is not a piece of standard carpeting. The design was especially worked out for use in this style carpet bag. The bag is constructed in envelope style; it measures 14½" deep, and 12" high. Both front and back have perfectly framed motifs with a simple diamond pattern at the base. Colors are red, blue, green, and beige on an off-white ground on the front, and red, rose, white, and blue on a green ground on the back.

The cotton lining is stamped "Carpet Bags—Manufactured from—Bigelow's Brussels Carpets—by Bagley & Carleton—Clinton, Mass." Bagley & Carleton began to manufacture carpet bags in 1850. Bagley, a Boston merchant, was connected with the business for only two years. Carleton carried on alone for two years. In 1854, J. W. Caldwell managed the business. His advertisements disappeared by September 1855; it is believed that manufacture stopped at that time.

NO. SIX

No. 3—*Carpet bag, Brussels carpeting, Patent 10,484, Jan. 31, 1854.* Since patents were rarely issued in less than two months, this Brussels carpeting certainly dates from 1853. Colors are red, blue, white, beige, and shades of green. Whether or not this bag was ever manufactured for sale is not known; no other examples of this style have been found. The patentee, Frederick J. Thring, described his "new and useful manner of constructing Carpet-Bags" as follows:

"The frame serves to brace and strengthen the bag and also in connection with the metallic swinging cover admits of its being made self locking and renders it perfectly secure from the dust and rain, which generally insinuate themselves into the ordinary carpet bag."

In addition to a description of his

patent, he may also have given us a clue as to the short life span of the carpet bag. Although Mr. Thring may have solved the problems described, his method appears to be much more expensive to manufacture, which may have curtailed its success.

No. 4—*Carpet bag, Wilton carpeting, 1850s.* Wilton carpets are woven in a manner similar to Brussels carpets with this exception: In Brussels, the loops are formed over wire rods which determine the size of the loop and are removed as the looped pile is formed. In Wilton carpets the loops are formed over wire rods that have small blades at the end. As the rod is removed the blade cuts each loop leaving a cut pile.

This Wilton carpet is in a large floral and scroll pattern in tones of red, with green and brown on an off-white ground. The flap is finished with narrow coach lace in a diagonal stripe pattern in red and white. The date was determined by the carpet pattern and the coach lace.

No. 5—*Carpet bag, Tapestry Brussels carpeting, ca. 1860.* The carpeting in this bag is basically the type known as Tapestry; the Brussels is added to indicate it has a looped or uncut pile. Tapestry carpets are also produced with a cut pile, but are then referred to as Tapestry Velvet, rather than Tapestry Wilton. Although the Tapestry Brussels carpets look very much like Brussels carpets and can easily be confused by the novice, there is a considerable difference.

The principle of this type carpeting was invented by Richard Whytock of Edinburgh, Scotland, and perfected about 1852. His idea was to apply the pattern design to one set of warps in one frame in place of using multiple frames as was required in Brussels carpets. The latter consumed much more worsted yarn and was much more expensive. However, since the carpet was a pile construction, which he desired to retain, merely printing the pattern on the surface did not serve the same purpose. Mr. Whytock developed a large printing drum on which he worked out the proportion of elongation needed to print the proper section of the warp yarn so that when it was woven into a loop, the design was perfectly coordinated. Although this made Tapestry carpet weaving a two-step process, it was still less expensive than the Brussels or Wiltons.

This bag is made in the same envelope style; it has a large floral pattern in tones of rose, red, green, blue, and brown on an off-white ground. Because there was no limiting factor to the number of colors, many more are used in Tapestry carpets, and much more shading is found. The patterns are sometimes slightly fuzzy in color around the edges.

No. 6—*Carpet bag, Tapestry Brussels carpeting, ca. 1865.* Although this

NO. SEVEN

particular bag dates from the 1860s, this style bag was quite common as early as 1851. It is a larger bag and would be the type more popularly used on journeys of any extent. The overall measurements are 22" wide by 16" high. The top has two leather handles, and the bag is fastened with leather straps and buckles.

The buckles are stamped "Pat. Feb. 18—1862." This date refers to Patent 34,429, granted to George R. Kelsey for this particular style of buckle. The bottom is a type of pseudo leather; it is 5" deep. There are metal tabs on the bottom to protect the bag when it is set on the floor. The large floral pattern is in reds, pinks, yellows, blues, greens, and browns, the typical multi-color and shading of the Tapestry carpets. It is lined with an inexpensive muslin, and has a single center partition. (Privately owned.)

No. 7—*Traveling bag, printed plush,* ca. 1870. This type bag may have been called a carpet bag when it was manufactured. Since it is not constructed of a carpet fabric, we have determined that it should not be so designated. It is illustrated to show the difference and similarity between the earlier and later styles.

Plush is a cut pile fabric similar to velvet but with a deeper pile. It has a soft back and was used for upholstery, draperies, and so forth. Since it was much easier to work with, it is natural that, when suitable patterns were available, traveling bags would have been constructed of this fabric. The bag here is made of two separate pieces, with black oilcloth, machine-stitched to cardboard, set in to make the sides and bottom. Red oilcloth is used as a piping. Handles are leather covered rope and machine-stitched also. The plush is printed in red, off-white, pink (roses), blue (morning glories), and green (leaves) on a dark blue ground. The flap is bound in red velvet, and the whole is lined with cotton cambric. Overall dimensions are 13x10½x1¾ inches.

Paisley Parade

by BLANCHE BEAL LOWE

APPEARING in the street without scarf, shawl or mantle," wrote the style editor of Godey's *Lady's Book* in 1856, "is not considered ladylike, nor is it the fashion." Though hats and cloaks had then been in favor as everyday female attire for over a hundred years, church and calling costumes still demanded bonnet and shawl. Even the fur coat introduced from Vienna in 1808 failed to divert milady from the graceful shawl.

Luxurious hand-loomed and embroidered Kashmir shawls began trickling into Europe about 1786. They cost a fortune, and European textile manufacturers leaped to supply a ready-made market with a less costly garment having similar eye appeal. Handsome machine-loomed shawls called Paisley resulted. Skilled weavers in Paisley, Scotland, who outstripped competitors in producing and marketing them, provided the name.

Eighteenth century dress fashions in Europe influenced the demand for this adaptable outer garment. Only a shawl could be worn with convenience and grace over the extended, supported skirt of the day. This extreme fashion caused Addison to observe in his *Spectator* that the first woman he saw "thus blown up into a most enormous concave," he supposed to be "near her time," until he discovered "all the modish part of the sex as 'far gone' as herself."

Following the French Revolution, the classical Greek influence in fashion, and a decade of unprecedented mild winters, reduced female dress to near-nakedness. A tubular, low-bosomed muslin chemise, over tights or one thin petticoat, was the mode. Remarked a contemporary: "Caricaturists make merry over disasters of revelation consequent upon the slightest sudden shower." The dear desire of every fashionable female was that her shawl be arranged over this scant attire to display her figure like folds of drapery on a statue. The style conscious French set up schools to teach the art of drapery.

About 1820, as fashion gradually returned to wider sleeves and full stiffened skirts, the shawl continued as a pet article of dress. Grandmother agreed with *Lady's Book* that "a slight drapery about the shoulders falling to the waist or below, adds very much grace to any figure, however perfect." Not until after 1870, when she stepped out of crinolines, did she let slip from her shoulders the colorful curliques of her treasured Paisley or Kashmir shawl.

FURNITURE

Ethel Hall Bjerkoe's introductory articles on early American interiors will give collectors a firm foundation for using and identifying period furniture. The stylistic differences between early 18th century and mid-Victorian American furniture are easily explained here in words and pictures. Once again, the collector has a choice between simple country pieces and those magnificant creations by Philadelphia artisans. Your choice depends upon your taste and how much you are willing, or able, to pay.

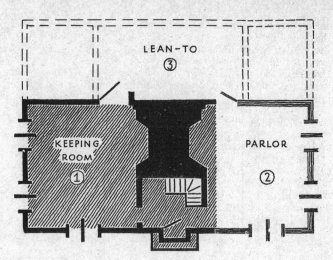

Above: when the one-unit house (1) was enlarged, a second unit (2) was added on the opposite side of chimney stack and porch. A lean-to (3) on the back provided still more room, producing the so-called salt-box house. When back was raised to same height as front, it became a central chimney house. *Left:* diagram of floor plan development.

The American Home
and How It Developed

by ETHEL HALL BJERKOE

FOR many years there was little interest in the so-called old fashioned houses and their furnishings. About 1890 a trend of interest slowly began, and today old houses and antiques are high fashion.

In America, there have been five architectural and decoration periods: *Early American,* which began soon after settlement and ended about 1720; *Colonial,* from 1720, ending directly after the Revolution; *Federal,* beginning about 1790 and ending about 1830; *Victorian,* which lasted from 1830 to 1880—overlapping the Federal and Victorian periods during 1820–1850 was the *Greek Revival;* and the *Eclectic* in which we find ourselves today, a period containing all the fads and fancies in building and furnishing since 1880, and which will doubtless develop to take its place eventually beside the others.

It is very easy to tell when a house was *not* built, since the Colonial, the Federal, the Greek Revival, and the Victorian house did not appear in America until a certain date, whereas the older type of house continued to be built long after the appearance of a new type. Each period is a growth from the one which went before, and there is always a time lag away from the centers of fashion. The Early American house being built in the Colonial period, for instance, would show some features of the new house type; furnishings, too, would show carry-overs from an earlier period.

Still being built today, though greatly modified by time, are the salt-box house, the overhang, now called "garrison" by builders, and the central chimney house of the Early American period, discussed below.

EARLY AMERICAN, CIRCA 1690–1730

No trace remains of the crude shelters built by the first settlers of Jamestown, Virginia, Plymouth or Salem, Massachusetts. Replicas of these earliest settlements may, however, be seen today. These first shelters were hastily constructed with but one thought in mind—protection. As permanent dwellings were built, the settlers constructed traditional wooden buildings similar to those in which they had lived at home. Variations in details occurred because of variations in building styles and methods in the different sections of England from which the colonists had come and because of the differ-

ences in materials available and in use in the various colonies.

Before 1680, houses were built largely from memory, but shortly after that date, manuals of architecture and building found their way to this country from England.

The houses of the simpler colonists usually consisted of a one-room house with porch and chimney stack at one end. If there was a second story, the staircase was usually in the porch, or entry as we call it today. The one-unit house was first enlarged with a second room or unit added on the opposite side of the chimney stack; then with a lean-to, or ell, generally

added in the back. This lean-to might serve as scullery, master's bedroom, the important loom room, or perhaps all three. It soon became a characteristic feature of the period, and as new houses were built, it became an integral part of the house. Thus evolved the so-called salt-box type of house. When more space was needed on the second floor, the lean-to was abandoned, and the roof at the rear raised to the same height as that in the front, making a full two-story house—the central chimney type.

An interesting feature of some early houses was the overhang. Two types were used in America. The

Early salt box type—the Major John Bradford House, Kingston, Massachusetts. Original one-unit was built in 1674; right-hand section added between 1720 and 1740, using same chimney stack for fireplaces. Diamond pane windows are in early section only. *Courtesy Bradford House Council.*

When more space was needed on the second floor, the roof of the lean-to of the salt-box house was raised to the same height as the front, making a full two-story, central chimney house. A fine example is the Secretary's House at Greenfield Village, Dearborn, Michigan.

earlier was the framed overhang like that used in England. Despite legend, these overhangs had nothing whatever to do with protection against Indians. Houses with this overhang were a definite architectural type in medieval England. At the end of the 17th century, the framed overhang in the colonies was replaced by the hewn overhang, made possible by the size of trees available for uprights.

Whether these early houses were salt-box, overhang, or central chimney, the interior was much the same. All three types had a central chimney, a small entry from which the steep stairway, hugging the chimney wall, led to the second floor. On the first floor there was the "Hall," the center of family living; on the opposite side of the entry, the "Parlor," which generally doubled as a bedroom; and at the rear, one, two, or three rooms.

The structural beams and posts always protruded on the inside of the house, and became a characteristic part of the room decoration. They were either planed smooth with chamfered edges, or covered with boards with ornamental moldings of various kinds. Sometimes there was a simple cornice of molded board with dentil-like notches at the end; occasionally these notches were painted alternately black and red.

Windows were small for protection as well as to conserve heat. At first they were of the casement type, with oiled paper or isinglass filling the rectangular or diamond-shaped panes. Many windows in the simpler homes had nothing in the panes but were furnished with wooden shutters. Soon, glass replaced these early makeshifts. Not until after 1700 did the double-hung sash come into use.

The fireplace was the center of home living. All cooking was done at it; it heated the house and furnished some of the light. Sometimes the kitchen fireplace was as much as twelve feet long. Part of this fireplace was the great oven. Before bricks came into general use, this was built of stone. Its iron door was usually three feet from the floor, and beneath was an open space for storing big kettles or oven wood. Another

feature of the early chimney was the smoke chamber. This might be either in the attic or in the cellar. In the more pretentious house, there was often a separate smoke house.

The space around fireplaces might be turned into closets, cupboards, or even a secret passage. Hearths were occasionally built of brick or cobblestones but were generally of flat stone. They varied in width from a foot and a half to two yards. Seldom were they entirely enclosed by the chimney wall.

Rooms were low-ceilinged, seldom more than seven feet high. Stone was sometimes used for flooring the first story, but oak, chestnut, and pine planks of varying widths were most common throughout the entire house. These floor boards—at times as wide as twenty-four inches—were left with a natural finish and were fastened to the joists below with wooden pins.

Interior doors were of wide vertical boards with horizontal braces at top and bottom on the reverse. Hinges and latches were of wrought iron in a great variety of design.

In the earliest houses of this period, walls were sheathed in wood. Later, there were three plastered walls, often with a dado, and one paneled or sheathed wall, the chimney wall. Until about 1700 whitewash was used for the plastered walls. Then, when color was used, Spanish brown—a deep brownish red —seems to have been favored, although a deep blue, olive green, and other more or less dark colors were popular. In this early period wallpaper was rarely used.

Furniture, if brought from England, was of oak in the Jacobean style, but soon the settlers were making simple pieces of furniture from native woods. At this time the bed was not an important piece of furniture; it consisted usually of a simple wooden frame. When a bed is spoken of in early inventories, the bed furnishings are generally meant. There were trundle beds, wooden cradles, and even the cricket bedstead, forerunner of the modern cot.

The cupboard was the most imposing piece of furniture in the more pretentious home. It was of oak,

Seventeenth century house with small diamond-shaped window panes, solid door, overhang of second story, single chimney of English inspiration.

covered with typical English or Dutch carvings of the period, and came in several types—the press, the court, and the livery cupboard. These held the serving dishes, table linen, and sometimes food. In humbler homes, various kinds of built-in cupboards and dressers answered the purposes of the expensive cupboard. In the Dutch colonies, there was the heavy wooden kas instead of the court cupboard.

The chest was probably the most important piece of furniture in these early homes, and the most common. It served the need, later filled by trunks, for transporting clothes and bedding from the mother country to the colonies, and was indispensable in the new home. The colonists also had joint stools, an occasional chair, trestle and other small tables, much coarse earthenware, woodenware (treenware), hollow ironware, and some pewter. There was an occasional loomed rug, but when a rug is mentioned in early inventories it usually refers to a table-rug. In many homes there were household linens, printed East Indian cottons, and loose cushions of damask or Turkey work for chair or stool. In every household there were spinning wheels, flax wheels, and generally the important loom. Mirrors and pictures were almost non-existent. Candles and fireplaces gave the only light.

Interior of 17th century house shows plaster walls, corner posts and beams, wide floor boards, furniture of the period. *Above and top, Courtesy Concord, Mass. Antiquarian Society.*

The "Great Hall" of the Eleazer Arnold House, Lincoln, R. I., built 1687, restored 1950–52. *Courtesy Society for the Preservation of New England Antiquities.*

(Left) NORTHERN COLONIAL INTERIOR—
*Drawing room, Jeremiah Lee Mansion.
Marblehead, Massachusetts, 1768. English
wallpaper panels, in cream through sepia
to black depict classic ruins; were custom
made for the mansion when it was built.
Courtesy Marblehead Historical Society.*

(Below) NORTHERN COLONIAL HOUSE—
*Sir William Johnson Hall, Johnstown,
New York, 1762. Note details of window
and door pediments, hip roof, two chim-
neys. Courtesy N. Y. State Education
Dept., Division of Archives and History.*

(Below) SOUTHERN COLONIAL INTERIOR—
*Palladian Room, Gunston Hall, Lorton,
Virginia, 1755-58, home of George Mason,
author of Virginia Declaration of Rights.
Carving designed and partly executed by
William Buckland, who was brought from
England under indenture to complete the
house. Woodwork, original buff color;
wall above chair rail covered with crimson silk damask. Painting over mantel is
of Mrs. Mason, a copy by Boudet of a
lost painting by John Hesselius. Courtesy
Board of Regents, Gunston Hall.*

The American Home
and How It Developed

The Colonial Period
1720 - 1790

by ETHEL HALL BJERKOE

(Right) SOUTHERN CO-
LONIAL HOUSE — *Ken-
more Mansion, Freder-
icksburg,Virginia, home
of Fielding and Betty
Washington Lewis. Con-
struction began 1752.
Note four chimneys, de-
pendencies at either
side. Courtesy Kenmore
Association.*

ABOUT 1720, in the American colonies there began a gradual change from Early American styles of architecture and decoration to the Colonial—a change influenced by various social and economic factors. Chief among them was the fact that mere survival was no longer the settler's greatest problem; he had time now to think of beauty and comfort in his home.

Communication with the mother country was constant. More and more colonial merchants were making trips to England; wealthy families sent their sons to school in Europe. Royal governors, often with suites, were assigned to the various colonies. Because they demanded more comfortable and pretentious houses than the colonists had to offer, houses, following the trend in England of the early Georgian type of Inigo Jones and Sir Christopher Wren inspiration, were constructed for them. Prosperous merchants, plantation owners, and other important colonists viewed these new structures and quickly accepted them as the latest fashion.

In the North this new house appeared first in prosperous coast towns; in the South, always a bit more sophisticated, the change occurred more quickly. The northern Colonial house was most often constructed of wood; the southern Colonial house, of brick. The use of building manuals, particularly for important houses, tended to make the style of a general type. Simpler homes, more dependent on local tradition and materials, give us representative types differing with the locality. Ordinary people continued to build their homes in the style of the earlier period.

It is doubtful whether the finest example of the Georgian house, as developed by the mid-eighteenth century in America, has been or ever will be surpassed. It reached its most glorious climax in the South in the Governor's Palace in Williamsburg, Virginia, in the plantation houses along the James River, and in such other houses as Kenmore in Alexandria. In the north there were also outstanding examples, among them the John Vassal House in Cambridge, Massachusetts; the Jumel Mansion in New York City, the Warner House in Portsmouth, New Hampshire, and the John Hancock House in Boston.

This new house differed in general from the central chimney house of the Early American period in its formality. Specifically a main difference was the chimney placement. It was taken from the center of the house, and at first placed in the middle of the dividing wall between the two rooms on either side of a central hall. Later it was placed at the ends of the house, sometimes with a chimney at either end, sometimes at each of the four corners. This change permitted a spacious transverse hall with two rooms on either side, resulting in a house more symmetrical, more formal, more convenient, and one in which all rooms could be entered from the hall.

The house usually had its length toward the street, with a central door with two windows on either side on the first floor and five windows on the second floor directly over those below. The Palladian window made its first appearance in the colonies shortly before the middle of the century. Wren had used this extensively in his English Georgian house. It consisted of a central window with a rounded top with a rectangular window on either side, each with an entablature and pilasters. This window group usually occupied the important location over the main entrance.

The roof of this new house sloped more gently than did its predecessors. Many of the important houses had a hip roof with a level cornice line on all sides. At first this gently sloping roof rose to a ridge, and this continued common in the narrow house. In the wider house, approaching the square mass of the Federal period, the roof was cut off at the top to form a deck, which was often surrounded by a balustrade. At times there was an eaves balustrade. The gambrel roof, popular in the Early American period, continued into the Colonial period as a survival of the old steep roof. Balustrades were often used on it.

Although many of the Colonial houses continued to be two stories high, houses of three stories became increasingly numerous in towns, especially those near the coast. Dormers were widely used.

The main entrance became more important and elaborate. Lights appeared in the upper panels of the main door around 1760; side lights and fanlights were not used until after the Revolution. Small windows did appear on either side of the door, but not within the door enframement.

Windows changed with regard to the number of lights. Whereas fifteen to twenty-four panes continued to be used in earlier type and simpler houses, twelve was the usual number in the later and more pretentious houses.

In important homes of this period, and to a lesser degree in simpler homes, too, there was a formal, well-organized, symmetrical interior. The stairway, when in the transverse hall, was the keynote of the entire interior. An opening string of stairs with elaborately decorated tread ends was used. Spiral and turned balusters replaced the simple ones of the earlier period. Hand rails were beautifully molded of walnut or mahogany, and the newel post became an important decorative feature. On the wall opposite the handrail, a sloping wainscoted dado was often used.

Ceilings became higher. The simplest wall treatment in any principal room consisted of a cornice, a molded strip around windows and doors, a baseboard, and a chair rail. The paneled room became less fashionable after 1750, though there were some late rooms of this type. As the fashion for wallpapers and other wall coverings increased, paneling decreased, although the dado continued popular.

As the eighteenth century advanced, doorways, window casings and cornices became more elaborate, and arched doorways were occasionally used. The fireplace, still the most important feature of any principal room, became smaller. It remained without a mantelshelf until about 1750, when a special overmantel became customary. The fireplace opening often had marble facings; by mid-century, mantelpieces entirely of marble were imported.

The colors used in the decoration of Colonial houses became softer than those of the Early American interior. Woodwork was painted a gentle gray, various shades of green, a grayed blue, primrose yellow, robin's egg blue, a golden shade of mustard, and a soft buff. Not until the Federal period did white for woodwork become popular. There was increased use of wallpapers, damask, chintz, and other fabric for wall coverings. Wallpapers were imported from France or China in scenic, floral, and architectural designs. Some houses, even important ones, retained the unpainted plastered walls with woodwork painted a beautiful rich color of the period. Wood paneling and trim were left unpainted only when of exceptionally fine quality.

There were draperies of brocatelle, chintz, velvet and similar materials. Floors, in keeping with this new elegance, were covered with Oriental and Aubusson rugs; in simpler homes, as well as in the bedrooms of many an important house, hand loomed rugs were still used.

Until mid-century, the furniture was chiefly of the Queen Anne style. Then it was slowly superseded in fashionable homes by the handsome new mahogany Chippendale. In many of the houses, even the finest, there would be some of the less comfortable furniture of the previous period, carry-overs from an earlier generation. Around 1750, the Windsor chair made its appearance.

There was much beautiful silver, china, and crystal, innumerable brass, silver, and crystal chandeliers, sidelights, and candelabra. On the walls were mirrors, paintings, portraits, color prints and mezzotints. The Colonial house glowed with brightness and color. And in this elegant and fashionable house, the men and women wore gorgeous costumes and sparkled with jewels. Both men and women wore their hair powdered, and the ladies had elaborate coiffeurs.

The Federal Period — 1790 to 1830

by ETHEL HALL BJERKOE

AMERICAN sympathy, after the Revolution, turned to France, yet in building and decoration, the new republic continued to be influenced by England. English books of building designs were still important, though they were used less and less as the number of American professional architects increased, and as American books became available. At this time, the new publications from abroad introduced the Adam style of architecture, popular in England for many years, and from the beginning of the Federal period until some years after 1800, architecture, particularly in the north, was directly influenced by this new classicism.

The older Colonial house type, based upon an English Renaissance or Jones-Wren interpretation of Palladian tradition, by no means disappeared; it remained the basis of much of the building of the early years following the Revolution. In many of the houses being built, the details alone proclaimed the coming of the new style.

In Federal New England architectural history, the two most important men were Charles Bulfinch of Boston and Samuel McIntire of Salem. Bulfinch, son of a prominent physician, graduated from Harvard in 1781 and shortly afterward went to England to study architecture. There he came under the influence of Robert Adam and his new classicism. He returned to America in 1787. In New England, Bulfinch was largely responsible for the introduction of the new style as developed by Adam, a style almost too delicate for a growing people in a new country—a style with great charm, consisting of slender columns, light cornices, chaste balustrades, fanlights and sidelights, metal traceries, and within the house, beautiful mantels and woodwork with festoons, urns, swags and classical medallions. Among the best of his buildings standing today are the State House in Boston, and several houses around Beacon, Park, and Tremont Streets in that city.

Samuel McIntire of Salem, from a family of carpenters and woodcarvers, came into prominence in 1782 as the architect and builder of the lovely Peirce-Nichols house in his home town. In the years between this first house and his last, built in 1810, McIntire confined his work almost entirely to Salem, then at the peak of its prosperity. It was he who was commissioned by the wealthy merchants and shipowners to build their mansions. When he died in 1811, he had designed and constructed some twenty, many along Chestnut Street, one of the most beautiful streets, architecturally, in America today.

McIntire not only designed these beautiful houses, but like Adam also designed furniture in the Sheraton

Dining Room. *Walls and woodwork are painted in tones of pale gray-green. It is assumed the mahogany Sheraton chairs were made by McIntire, ca. 1790; the stand at right is also attributed to him. Knife boxes are English. Portrait, by John Smibert (1688-1751) represents the three sons of Governor Daniel Oliver. Rug is Kashgar. Note alcove for sideboard, a feature of Adam's architectural designs. Here again, in the carving, are motifs characteristic of McIntire's work.*

Parlor Chamber. *Bed hangings, as well as window hangings, unseen here, are of late 18th century toile-de-Jouy, printed in red. Original colors were pale ivory woodwork, pale "King's blue" walls, "storm gray" floor. Saraband rug is ca. 1800. Oval back side chairs with Hepplewhite "Prince of Wales" feathers, probably of Philadelphia provenance ca. 1796, are examples of the painted furniture popular for chambers and parlors around 1800. Basket of fruit on door cornice is typical McIntire design.*

and Hepplewhite styles for their interiors, and he himself did much of the carving for the beautiful porticos, fireplace mantels, and interior woodwork.

This new Federal type house of Adam inspiration was usually square, and three stories tall. In New England it was commonly built of white pine, although brick was becoming more popular in the north. It had a low-pitched roof edged about with a wooden balustrade; often there was a cupola with a captain's walk atop the roof. Its most important feature was the doorway with its beautiful fanlight and sidelights, located in the center of the front facade.

Within the house the change was not too great from that of the Colonial period. There were four rooms to a floor, as the usual arrangement, with a transverse hall. Secondary stairways were common. On the upper floors, smaller rooms to be used as dressing rooms were often included as well as alcoves for beds. For the first time, the oval, round, or elliptical room made its appearance. The fireplace became smaller, but it was still an important feature.

Ceilings were high and were decorated with delicate cornices, sometimes carved, but often of "compo", a composition introduced by Adam. Windows were large, and rooms were often connected by double doorways. The interior decoration was much simplified. Paneling tended to disappear, and wall surfaces were usually of painted plaster above a simple wainscot capped by a delicate chair rail or covered with imported wallpaper or rich brocade. At times the wainscot was omitted. Wallpapers were scenic, Chinese, or of delicate

colors with a French influence. Stripes, swags, medallions or other designs popular in the French Directoire and the later French Empire were in vogue. Just as fashionable, however, were plain painted walls in shades of white, gray, buff, pale rose, or Adam green. Pure white woodwork became popular. The entire effect was one of lightness and delicacy.

No longer in fashion was the rococo Chippendale furniture. The styles of Hepplewhite and Sheraton, brought to America by means of books of furniture designs, became the rage. The entire trend in furniture was toward lighter and more cheerful woods. Although mahogany remained popular, it was often inlaid with satinwood or other light and colorful wood in a formal manner.

In Salem, Samuel McIntire and other good cabinetmakers were constructing beautiful furniture from West Indian mahogany, following the designs of Hepplewhite and Sheraton. In New York City, Duncan Phyfe was making his finest furniture, influenced by both Hepplewhite and Sheraton, and later by the Directorie styles from France. Cabinetmakers of Maryland and South Carolina came into their own. Nowhere did the art of inlay reach greater perfection than at Baltimore, and the work of such men as Thomas Elfe at Charleston was outstanding. These were but a few of the New World cabinetmakers who worked during these years.

With the declaration of war against England in 1812, a wave of patriotism swept the country. This was used to advantage by furniture makers as well as other manufacturers. The eagle of Roman and Napoleonic im-

perialism became Americanized and was used to decorate all manner of articles from clocks and mirrors to tables and chairs. Stars and stripes were used in wallpapers and fabrics and countless other decorative accessories.

Materials such as damask, brocade, satin, taffeta, velvet, printed linen and chintz were used for upholstery and hangings in these Federal houses. Satins and taffetas were striped, or dotted with medallions. New toiles-de-Jouy by Oberkampf of France were popular. Draperies were made in the formal English or French style with boxed cornices, swags, or fabric valances. Occasionally mull from India, brought home by ships in the China Trade, replaced the more opulent fabrics for window hangings.

Rugs for the highly polished or parquet floors were handsome Orientals and Aubusson and, as the period advanced, Savonnerie from France, Brussels, and English Wiltons.

Decoration in pairs, as introduced by Adam in England, was popular—a pair of sofas, a pair of mirrors, a pair of tables, et cetera. This gave balance to the room which was both useful and symmetrical.

In these beautiful houses of this Federal period, wealthy shipowners and merchants and their families lived luxuriously, surrounded by exquisite furniture and treasures from all over the world, clothed in rich fabrics, and served by innumerable servants. Yet with all this luxury, there was no central heating, no plumbing, no electricity; cooking was still done at the huge kitchen fireplace; candles and whale oil lamps were the chief sources of artificial light.

Today's Federal and Greek Revival Interiors

The decorating problems of these two closely related periods, as we interpret them today, are discussed here each as an entity.

by ETHEL HALL BJERKOE

ALTHOUGH few people today decorate and furnish a home entirely in the simple, delicate, and classical fashion inspired by Adam of England and known in America as the Federal period, those who wish to have homes in this style will not find it difficult to achieve a charming result. They should select the soft colors used in the period, funiture of Hepplewhite and Sheraton styles, supplemented with some of the less ornate Chippendale and less massive American Empire. Draperies and upholstery should be of the fabrics indicated; accessories arranged in the balanced, paired symmetry of the era—not, however, to a monotonous degree.

The Federal and Greek Revival styles of the period itself, as is also the case with the Colonial, can be followed today much more closely than is possible with either the Early American or the Victorian.

Photographs of Campbell-Whittlesey House, below, from the Society for the Preservation of Landmarks in Western New York.

CAMPBELL-WHITTLESEY HOUSE, *Rochester, New York, in Greek Revival style, was built in 1835 by Benjamin Campbell, prosperous merchant and miller. In 1852 ownership passed to the Whittlesey family who lived in it until 1937. Frederick W. Whittlesey, an occupant, was Vice-Chancellor of the N. Y. State Court of Chancery; later Justice of the State Supreme Court.*

HALL—*Though no less classic in its architectural features than the Federal hall, pictured on the opposite page, it is more robust. An unusual feature is the "splintered" entablature over door to library as it gives way to the circular sweep of the stair. Queen Anne chair in library exemplifies the carry-over of furnishings from earlier periods.*

DINING ROOM—*Indian head border is used above French wallpaper of the Second Empire; fireplace has Victorian-type grate; furniture is of American Empire style. Many pieces of furniture in this house were made in Rochester.*

DOUBLE PARLORS—*The architectural details here were inspired by Minard LeFeber's "Beauties of Modern Architecture." Note simplicity of all decoration, paired arrangement of ottomans, and inclusion of furnishings from several period styles.*

The colors to be used in a Federal interior are delicate — warm gray, beige, yellow, off-white, soft rose or other shades of pink, buff, and several shades of green. Woodwork may be painted white or to match the background color of the wall treatment. Walls may be painted or papered. Scenic wallpapers are especially effective in halls and dining rooms. Those with stripes, swags, and medallions are also indicated, but the colors should not be heavy. Today there is much use of wallpapers with eagles and other patriotic motifs.

Floor coverings appropriate for the Federal interior are Oriental, needlepoint, plain or textured broadloom. Draperies may be of satin, taffeta, brocatelle, or other formal material. Furniture should be upholstered in material of similar quality.

Today, in all period interiors, we mix furniture for interest and comfort. No one wants to live in a museum. So we add some furniture from other periods, more sturdy, perhaps, than the delicate Hepplewhite and Sheraton, but selected with care to harmonize with them. Some modern upholstered furniture will be used for comfort. All furniture, however, should have the feeling of simple elegance. Never hesitate to use mirrors; they are perhaps even more acceptable than pictures since they add spaciousness and formality.

Suggestions for a living-room in the Federal style may be helpful. The walls, for instance, could be papered with a flock paper showing a white design on a lemon-yellow background; the woodwork painted white. Draperies would be of lemon-yellow brocatelle, floor length, and with a valance. The rug would doubtless show rosy red, some blue, perhaps a bit of green, and touches of yellow, whether an Oriental or an Aubusson. Plain broadloom in a warm gray or a grayed green might also be used with success. A sofa and one chair could be upholstered in a striped material in lemon-yellow, grayed green, and cherry red; another chair, in the drapery material or in one of the colors of the striped material. Or, instead of the flock paper, a soft green wallpaper with a small gold medallion would be effective with woodwork matching the background color. With this, the room could be decorated with the same colors and materials described above. Again, the walls could be painted off-white, with matching woodwork, or lemon-yellow with white woodwork.

Against any of these backgrounds, comfortable sofas, whether of the period or modern but with the feeling of the period, Hepplewhite and Sheraton style furniture, combined with pieces from the Chippendale or American Empire periods, and formal lamps and accessories will achieve an interior which has the feeling of the Federal period, but is less delicate and more suited to today's living.

The Greek Revival house remained

Entrance Hall, Pierce Mansion, Portsmouth, New Hampshire, 1799, shows the classicism of Federal interior architecture, the simplicity of decoration, and the exquisite fanlights of the period. Small tables on either side of doorway typify the paired decoration so popular in this period. Settee is an example of Hepplewhite furniture constructed to conform to a specific space, a mode introduced by Robert Adam of England. Courtesy Art Institute of Chicago.

fashionable for a much longer period than did the chaste and classical Federal which was much too delicate for a growing people. Since it overlapped both the Federal and the Victorian periods, houses built in the early years show a tendency in furnishings toward those of the Federal period; in houses built in the later years, there was a trend toward the use of the decoration of the Victorian period. It was during the years of the Greek Revival (1820–1850) that the French influence on furniture-making, interior furnishings, and decoration became pronounced.

Today in recreating an interior in the Greek Revival style, the fashion has been to stress this French influence. More dramatic colors than the soft pastels of the Federal period or the austere simplicity of many of the Greek Revival interiors are popular. Colors are bold and contrasting. Walls should be in rich grays, greens, tones of brown, wine red, bright blues and yellows, or white. Woodwork may be white, but preferably the color of the walls. Although wallpapers were seldom used in this period, some types are excellent for today's interiors. Flock paper in designs of white on rich backgrounds, or the reverse, are effective. Broad stripes, such as gold and white, wine red and white, or green and white, with white woodwork, may be used. Papers with architectural designs in grays and blacks on white are good. In halls, French scenic paper suits well.

For today's furnishings we borrow freely from those of the French Directoire or French Empire. Many interiors are decorated and furnished completely in this French style. Homeowners who are more interested in English furnishings and decorations use those of the Regency style. Others, faithful to American crafts-

men, make use of the later work of Duncan Phyfe and his contemporaries who all showed the influence of the French styles. These are combined with some of the furniture we call American Empire and with pieces selected from the earlier styles of Victorian cabinetmakers.

Many ornaments of gold and silver, as well as ormolu and brass, were popular in this period, and can be used today to intensify formality.

Fabrics should be rich and distinctive, in strong, vivid colors, or in white to contrast with strong backgrounds. Among the most useful are satin, brocade, damask, moire, small patterned velvet, fine toiles-de-Jouy, or heavy textured modern material. Many fabrics with stripes, and some with designs symbolizing the patriotism of the new Republic or the Empire of Napoleon are available today.

Mirrors are as desirable in the Greek Revival interior as they are in the Federal house, for in both the result to be achieved is one of elegance and formality.

A suggested living room in the Greek Revival style has walls and woodwork painted an olive green, with draperies of off-white damask. A small sofa is covered in the drapery material. The rug is off-white. Two French Empire armchairs are upholstered in antique satin in olive green and white stripe; a large modern davenport is done in a rich olive green and white printed fabric in heavy textured weave. A pair of small French Empire benches on either side of the fireplace are covered in gold antique satin. Accessories are formal—tall crystal lamps with white shades, others of French or Chinese porcelain, exquisite and colorful bric-a-brac for use and color —and cherry red moire cushions on the davenport for accent.

Greek Revival Period
1820 — 1850

(Overlapping both Federal and Victorian Periods)

by ETHEL HALL BJERKOE

IN 1787, the same year Charles Bulfinch returned to Boston from England, Thomas Jefferson returned from France, filled with admiration for the classic, with little liking, as always, for the English Palladianism of Inigo Jones and Sir Christopher Wren as expressed in the American Colonial or Georgian. Shortly after his return, he designed the Virginia State Capitol, using the Maison Carrée at Nîmes, France, as his model. For the first time in America, a building was constructed using the temple-form in its Jeffersonian or Roman interpretation.

In 1796, Benjamin Henry Latrobe, born in England of American parents, arrived in America. He had studied architecture in London where he was well instructed in the Greek ideal. In 1799 he designed the Bank of Pennsylvania in Philadelphia in the form of a Greek Ionic temple, going back to Greek architecture rather than a Roman or Jeffersonian interpretation for inspiration.

Shortly after his election to the presidency in 1801, Jefferson created the position of Surveyor of Public Buildings of the United States and appointed Latrobe to fill it. Under this appointment, the temple style of architecture was used almost exclusively for new buildings constructed by the Federal government. The building of private houses in this new style quickly followed.

The effect of the temple style was less in the old settlements of New England, dominated by Bulfinch and McIntire who retained their allegiance to the Adam style, than in the newer sections of the country. But even in New England when a new town developed or an old settlement became newly prosperous, temple-like houses were built. In the new settlements growing in

Andalusia, Bensalem Township, Pennsylvania. In 1834-36, Nicholas Biddle, home from important positions in the American legations in France and England, remodeled Andalusia in the Greek Doric temple style with simple and impressive colonnade along sides as well as front. Courtesy Library of Congress.

America—in the Western Reserve, along the newly opened Erie Canal, in western New York State, in new sections of the south, and along the Mississippi River—the Greek Revival house became the fashion.

There were many reasons for the wide acceptance of this new style in architecture. This was a period of unrest in the New Republic. In 1812 there had been a second war with England and Americans were considerably irritated with the British. The sympathy of the entire country had been offered the French in their Revolution, and then the people had been repelled by the high handedness of Napoleon. In 1821, when the Greeks began their struggle for freedom, the Americans felt a close kinship with them and for their cause, and everything Greek became the fashion of the day. This Greek fad, however, was most apparent in the construction of buildings and in the naming of towns—Rome, Syracuse, Troy, Athens, Sparta, in New York State, for instance. There was no important revival in the arts, and there is no reason to believe there was any return on the part of many people to the ideals of the classic Greeks in their

Entrance Hall of Decatur House, Lafayette Square, Washington, D. C., built in 1818 by Commodore Stephen Decatur, designed by Latrobe. Though exterior is in the Adam Federal style, interior shows features in architecture, decorations, and furnishings typical of the Greek Revival style—simplicity of design, cornices, classic style of decoration, use of American Empire chairs. Decatur House pictures, courtesy National Trust for Historic Preservation

Decatur House Drawing Room furnishings show effect of Victorian period which began during last years of the Greek Revival. Note painting over fireplace instead of the usual mirror, Queen Anne side chair successfully used with Victorian furniture and lacquered end table from China, carefully designed floor. Side chair near piano from New York shop of John Henry Belter, who succeeded Phyfe as fashionable cabinetmaker. Elaborate gasolier is a much later embellishment.

Ben Hill Plantation House, *Athens, Georgia, ca. 1855, does not follow the early Temple style as does Andalusia; however, its outstandingly beautiful Corinthian colonnade also extends to the sides of the house mass, and first floor windows extend to the interior floor.* Courtesy Library of Congress.

way of thinking or in their manner of life.

Outstanding architects who helped spread this new classicism, in addition to Latrobe, were Robert Mills and Ithiel Town. Mills, born in Charleston, South Carolina, had worked under Jefferson on Monticello. He worked chiefly in Philadelphia, Baltimore, and Charleston until his appointment in 1836 by President Jackson as architect of public buildings in Washington. There he designed, among others, the Treasury Building, the Patent Office, and the Washington Monument, the last in the Greek Doric manner. Town was born in Thompson, Connecticut, and at first worked in New England. Later he formed a New York City partnership with Martin Thompson and Alex J. Davis, and became famous for his work in the Greek Revival style.

The outstanding feature of this new house type was the portico. In previous houses of the Colonial and Federal periods, a portico, when used, had been a one-story affair. Now it became freestanding, extending the height of the house with four, six, or eight columns. This projecting portico was usually from the front, but in rare instances it extended completely around the building. If, by chance, a house was built without a portico, it had at least corner pilasters or boards; the boards were never mitred as in the Colonial building.

The door was no longer confined to the center of the front facade. In the Greek Revival house, it might be at one side of it, or at the corner; it was square-headed with a triangular transom above and narrow vertical side-

lights. Clapboards or siding were joined with no overlapping. If brick was used, it was generally painted gray. Window panes became larger, and windows often extended to the floor. The roof was low-pitched, following the Greek temple ideal. Cast iron balconies, balustrades, window grilles, and various other ornaments were customary.

Greek Revival houses were of greater variety than those of the earlier periods, but called for little originality on the part of the builders as the Greek models were copied with much care.

Within the house, the change was not extreme, as the designers did not follow the Greek temple plan for their interiors. There was a new simpleness. Panelling and wall coverings were not fashionable. Walls were generally plain painted plaster in white, pale gray, or soft pastel. Woodwork was white. Ornate plaster decorations were used as cornices, to form panels, and as rosettes from which center ceiling chandeliers could be suspended. Ceilings were high, doorways wide, and principal rooms were often separated by columns. The architraves of both windows and doors were either fluted or reeded. The fireplace, no longer the important feature of a room, was much smaller in size, with marble facing and mantel, and usually carved. A gold-framed mirror, rectangular, often divided into three vertical sections, replaced the former overmantel. Sometimes an important painting would be used instead of the mirror. Mirrors, though, were popular for use through the entire house.

In many of these simple and severe houses, furniture of the Hepplewhite, Sheraton, and early Duncan Phyfe type was used, but this was often replaced by the fashionable French Directoire and French Empire and, toward the end of the period, by the more massive American Empire with its huge dressers, secretary desks, wardrobes, enormous sofas, and Gargantuan beds with four tall heavily carved posts. Toward the end of the period, the early Victorian furniture became popular.

Beautiful materials were used for upholstery and hangings, many with narrow stripes and some with designs symbolizing the patriotism of the New Republic or the Empire of Napoleon. Although much was of silk, cotton prints from both England and France were very popular, and many of these were printed with designs celebrating the independence of America.

In general, the interior furnishings of the Greek Revival house reflected the style trend of the period from the chaste and classical Sheraton and Hepplewhite through the more architectural and elaborate French Directoire and French Empire to the massive American Empire and, finally, to the American Victorian.

Drawing Room, Andalusia. *Plastered walls are painted a rich yellow with white woodwork. Deep entablature of the cornices, elliptical window bay, pilasters, absence of wainscoting, smaller marble fireplace with overmirror, flat pedimented lintels of doors are all characteristics of the Greek Revival house, as are the plaster decorations of ceiling and the rosette from which hangs a crystal chandelier. Furniture of Duncan Phyfe type in his Sheraton style. Armchairs in center show influence of the French Directoire.* Courtesy Thorne American Rooms in Miniature, Art Institute of Chicago.

Entrance Hall, The Hermitage, *near Nashville, Tennessee, 2 story colonnaded facade house with second story gallery, built by President Jackson in 1819, enlarged and elaborated in 1831, destroyed by fire in 1835, and immediately rebuilt along the same lines. Main hallway shows beautiful "flying staircase" typical of the period, scenic wallpaper with a deep blue background color. Woodwork is white. Note typical Greek Revival doorway, sperm oil chandelier. Furniture is of the American Empire style.* Courtesy Thorne American Rooms in Miniature, Art Institute of Chicago.

Webb House, Madison, Connecticut, built in 1827 as the manse for the Congregational Church is an excellent example of the mansard roof type Victorian house. Formerly the home of Captain and Mrs. Fremont Webb, now of Winter Park, Florida. Courtesy Captain and Mrs. Webb.

Sunnyside, home of Washington Irving, Tarrytown, N. Y. Irving acquired a small late 17th century stone tenant farmhouse on Philipsburg Manor in 1835, enlarged it to a Gothic Revival house "as full of nooks and corners as an old cocked hat." He added tower in 1847 after his return from Spain.

Washington Irving's study is an example of a good Victorian interior. Heavy draperies, tied back by tasseled cords separate library section; black marble fireplace with grate, large leather chair and desk oil lamp are of the period. All Sunnyside photographs courtesy Sleepy Hollow Restorations.

Dining Room at Sunnyside is Victorian, rich but restrained. Note sumptuous brocade draperies with cords and heavy tassels at tops as well as sides, lace curtains, probably from Birmingham, heavy window cornices, wall-to-wall plain carpeting, table with turned legs, chairs showing Gothic arches.

Parlor, 1850, based on that in President Theodore Roosevelt's birthplace, 28 E. 20 St., New York City, later than Sunnyside, shows patterned carpet and wallpaper, draperies of deep blue moire with fringe, rosewood furniture by Belter, "gasolier." Courtesy Thorne Miniature Rooms, Art Institute of Chicago.

Entrance Hall in fashionable home in Connecticut, ca. 1880, shows the extremes to which some Victorian homeowners went to achieve a feeling of ostentation. An amazing "clutter" was extremely fashionable late in this period. Courtesy Mrs. Arthur Taylor Gillette, Woodbury, Connecticut.

The Victorian Period — 1830-1880

by ETHEL HALL BJERKOE

IN America, classicism in architecture and decoration was followed, about 1830, by romanticism, as it was abroad. In England at this time decorative taste had slumped to a low point. The romantic mood in England had begun with Horatio (Horace) Walpole (1717–1797) and his Gothic villa, Strawberry Hill. It was furthered after 1800 by Shelley and Scott, who were true romantics. Ruskin gave it its final and greatest impetus when he returned from Italy enamored with Gothic architecture.

In America several economic factors were involved in this ready acceptance of the romantic. America had expanded enormously. Before 1850 her population had been of predominately English stock, and her economy was based largely on agriculture. By the 1850s, industry was increasing and immigrants from all over Europe poured in to fill the need for cheap labor in the growing mills and factories. After the Civil War, industry expanded at an astounding rate and, with it, a society based upon the profits of commercialism. Colonial tradition and culture were swept away. Money was being made so easily that a vast majority who came to possess it had little cultural background, little education, and little experience in handling the money they had so quickly acquired.

In spite of this new industrial development and new social group, much more agressive and individualistic than the colonists of the earlier periods, fashion in architecture and furnishing was still sought abroad; for all the protested freedom from English domination, the period, in America, has been given the name of the English ruler, Victoria.

Before 1850, there had persisted, in lessening degree as the years passed, a code of restrictions which regulated to a marked extent the lives and customs of the people. Builders and carpenters, cabinetmakers, and other artisans had followed certain precedents in their various trades. In architecture, for instance, even though builders and carpenters were not always trained in the subject, the buildings they constructed were along good architectural lines since they used as guides the many books of building designs. Workmen had been satisfied to build well without trying variations of their own.

As the Victorian period advanced, every man in America *knew* he was an individual—how better to demonstrate this than in building and furnishing his home? So, still looking to Europe for inspiration, he let his fancy roam far and wide. The country became dotted with Italian villas, Moorish cottages, Swiss chalets, the Queen Anne cottages of William Morris of England, and the sad looking little houses of Charles Locke Eastlake, also of England. Eastlake's book *Hints on Household Tastes*, which preached the "honest use of material," was popular in America.

Out of the welter of designs—imported, then changed by the desire for something different and more pretentious than what someone else had—two general types emerged: the Victorian Gothic, and that based upon the contemporary French Renaissance house with mansard roof. The English Gothic novel, the influence of Ruskin, and the publication of *Cottage Residences* by Andrew Jackson Downing, all played a part in popularizing the Victorian Gothic style with its steep roof, gables, latticed windows, and vine-clad eaves. It was given further sanction by Washington Irving who remodeled Sunnyside at Tarrytown-on-the-Hudson in this manner.

Survivals of the mansard roof building of French Renaissance inspiration may be seen in the many remaining brownstone houses of New York City and elsewhere—they were built by the thousands. Throughout the countryside, too, there are to be seen many spacious manor houses built at that time, still charming and stately.

Naturally there were some builders and homeowners during this period who did not succumb entirely to the wave of vulgarity, but they were few and far between. The average builder, whose only guide was whimsy and a desire to be different, was helped along his downward course by the industrial development of the age. The scroll saw came into use, and the homeowner ornamented his house within and without with elaborate brackets, panels, and trim of scrollwork. Rapidly growing ironworks provided him with cast iron for balconies, balustrades, trim, and ornaments, for garden seats and animals. Every lawn of any importance had its stag or barking dog!

Within the house, whether it was a rustic cottage, an Italian villa, or a brownstone front, the general effect was the same. Gone was the lightness and spaciousness of the Federal period and the rococo comfort of the Colonial. The Victorian interior had a somber, heavy feeling with its woodwork of mahogany, black walnut, or cherry. The most popular interior colors were dull brown, deep blues, strong reds and greens, and after 1859, a new color named "magenta," so-called after the great battle of that year in the Italian war.

The power loom had been developed, making carpets and rugs available to everyone. After 1850 practically every home had carpet from wall to wall, usually ingrain with large floral or geometric patterns. Stoves were now available, but a fireplace was still usual in each principal room. It was considerably smaller in size, however, and was generally of white or black marble with back and sides of cast iron, and with an iron basket-grate for burning coal.

Window draperies were elaborate and heavy, decorated with fringe and looped back by silken cords with huge tassels. Lace curtains from Birmingham, England, covered the windows.

Early in the period the massive American Empire furniture gave way to black walnut, showing the Gothic influence; chairs and sofas were upholstered with horsehair. By mid-century, those in and around New York City were able to buy the elaborately carved furniture of John Henry Belter. Other good cabinetmakers were still working in various parts of the country, but in general people everywhere were filling their houses with the mass-produced furniture pouring from the factories. There were, of course, in any house, even the most pretentious, some carry-overs from previous periods.

The Jacquard loom had been developed, and the market was flooded with much inexpensive material in complex patterns for decorative purposes. Broad stripes, large florals and huge medallions were popular. Wallpapers were heavy in design and color and often embossed to represent leather. Plumbing had been introduced and homeowners were proud of their bathrooms with huge marble washbasins and tin tubs encased in varnished wood. Ceilings were high, and the gloom of evening was but slightly lessened by flickering gaslight, even though the elaborate "gasolier" was convenient and costly.

Yet it is certain that some of the houses, particularly those of the cultured, were exceedingly beautiful; it was a period of considerably happy home life, and the houses even though cluttered, were filled with comfort; even the lowliest homes were not without charm in spite of the general trend to ugliness.

THE HOUSE, *built in 1778 by Captain Ebenezer Hayden in Essex, Connecticut, with two chimneys and hip roof, is an excellent example of Colonial architecture. It may well be the first pre-fabricated house in America, since timbers and other parts were pre-cut in Hartford and floated down the Connecticut River to Essex. It has seven fireplaces, one with beehive oven, and a large smoke oven in the attic. Fanlight in beautiful doorway shows detail of the later Federal period.*

How to Create Today's Colonial Interior

Illustrations from the Home of Mr. and Mrs. Frank Edward Irsch, Jr. Essex, Connecticut

by ETHEL HALL BJERKOE

FORMALITY marks the important difference between the Colonial and the Early American interior; the terms are not synonymous—the difference is very real. Even the so-called country Colonial interior, simpler and less formal than the elegant Colonial mansion, is much more formal than the Early American. Because more furniture is available in the styles used from 1720–1790, a Colonial interior is not difficult to recreate. The furniture of the period was in Queen Anne and Chippendale styles, with some carry-overs from earlier days. In the elegant house, carry-overs were usually relegated to bedrooms, but in simpler houses, and in isolated parts of the country, they were used more promiscuously.

In today's Colonial interior, the fireplace is still the important feature of any principal room. The chimney wall is usually paneled, with a dado, or at least a chair rail, on the other three walls. Wallpaper may be Chinese, floral, scenic, toile de Jouy type, even architectural. Plaster walls may be painted to represent old plaster, tinted a light shade of the woodwork color, or stenciled.

Colors have increased in number and are softer in quality. No longer are the pure heady colors of the earlier period used. Cream, grayed blue, primrose yellow, soft grayed green, robin's egg blue, a rosy red, a golden mustard, chamois yellow, and buff give proper backgrounds for the more formal furnishings. White for woodwork is still not used.

In the informal country Colonial, draperies will be sill length. Rugs may be handsome floral hooked rugs, braided rugs, or mellow Oriental scatter rugs. Furniture will be the less formal pieces, doubtless of cherry, maple, or other light wood, with an occasional piece of mahogany, painted or lacquered. It will be in the Queen Anne or Chippendale styles, with possibly a chest or chair of the William and Mary period, either genuinely old or a good reproduction. Hitchcock chairs, Windsors, fancy painted Sheratons, ladderback, and country Chippendale chairs suit well. An upholstered davenport and chairs, necessary for comfort, should be chosen with little, if any, wood showing. Chintz, printed linen, and similar materials are right for the windows.

In the more formal Colonial interior the draperies will generally be floor length, with or without cornices, of damask, brocatelle, chintz, or other formal fabrics. While hooked, braided, and other scatter rugs may be used in bedrooms, a room-sized rug will most likely cover the important rooms. (Avoid wall-to-wall carpeting.) Furniture may be Queen Anne, Chippendale, Hepplewhite and Sheraton styles. Mahogany first became available in America for furniture about 1725—earlier than in England.

An interior becomes more interesting when an occasional foreign piece is introduced for accent. By mid-eighteenth century, treasures were being brought to America by immigrants from various countries and, somewhat later in the century, by the American sailing ships to the Orient.

In any Colonial interior, furniture and accessories should be kept formal in arrangement and uncluttered.

LIVING ROOM woodwork is painted a deep grayed blue, the plastered walls, a cream color. The end of room not seen in photograph is entirely sheathed in wood. Draperies are floor length of chintz with design in old rose red; davenport is upholstered in blue quilted material matching woodwork paint. Furniture includes a red leather wing chair, a mahogany Martha Washington chair, a teakwood stand, a mahogany chest and tables. The rug is a palace Kirman. Lamp bases are Chinese. Many Chinese accessories are used throughout the house. Family heirlooms from Germany, France, and China have been successfully combined with American antiques. Large hallway and bedrooms are all wallpapered.

DINING ROOM woodwork is painted with Wythe House gold; the walls are tinted—one-half gold, one-half white paint mixtures; ceiling is a still lighter tint—one-quarter gold, three-quarters white. Sheraton chairs are mahogany inlaid with satinwood; table and chest of drawers in walnut are both from Virginia. Pictures over chest are Chinese stone rubbings on rice paper, framed in dull gold with inner border of red to pick up color of the window hangings. These are floor length of dark red silk damask with boxed cornices. (Window is partially seen in mirror.) The chandelier is Irish glass. Also used in the room is a walnut corner cabinet and a German tall clock. The combination of Queen Anne furniture with the later Sheraton chairs and with antiques from other countries forms a charming entity.

THE LIBRARY woodwork is Colonial red, with plaster walls painted much lighter—equal parts of red paint with white were used. Sill length draperies are of a chintz called Pot Pourri, which has a natural background with design in old red and soft old blue. Davenport is upholstered in Colonial red quilted material; small pillows are of drapery fabric. (Notice successful camouflaging of modern radiator under bookshelves.) The barometer is antique English; the teak stand, antique Chinese. The rug is sandcolored Chinese brocade — a Nicholas. Not visible in photograph is a wing chair upholstered in old blue, and a very fine French Empire secretaire. This room also has a fireplace similar to that in the dining room. Floors throughout the house are of wide boards, painted a dark brownish red.

THE KITCHEN fixtures, except stove, are like the woodwork in color— Market Square green. Walls, which do not show here, are covered with wallpaper which matches the draw curtains. One of its major colors, a soft pink, has been used for the ceiling. Floor is covered with soft green Tessara. The chandelier, a copy of an early one, is the work of a local craftsman. Oyster plates of French Limoges, displaying the same soft pink as in wallpaper, fabric, and ceiling add a decorative touch. The room also contains an antique table, chairs, and breakfast accessories.

Entrance Hall: *Boarding, retaining its old red paint, came from house in New Hampshire. Handwoven stair carpeting is old green, red, tan. Note 17th century chest.*

Library: *Paneling from a house in Vermont; fireplace with angle brick from Massachusetts. Clock made in Litchfield, Conn. Colors used are old reds and blues. Walls, as throughout entire house, are off-white plaster.*

Living room: *Feather-edge boards from Shaker settlement in Canterbury, N. H.; beams from old house in Stonington, Conn. Rug, hand braided in old colors— gold, blue, mustard, red, brown, black. Curtains and wing chair in documentary print with old blue ground.*

This reproduction of an early salt-box house with weathered clapboards, gray trim, Haddam barn red doors, designed by Norris Prentice, was built in 1952.

The Early American Interior...Today

*Photographs from the home of
the Frederick E. Bakers in Farmington, Connecticut.*

by ETHEL HALL BJERKOE

THE Early American interior of today is simple, colorful, functional, carefully avoiding quaintness. It is, of course, easier to accomplish this result if the house to be decorated has the features of the Early American period—low ceilings, small-paned windows, paneling, wide floor boards, and fireplaces; but it is entirely possible to create an Early American interior even though all these features may not be present.

Color is, perhaps, the most important factor in the creation of an interesting home. Each of the decorating periods has its own range of colors, and that of the Early American interior is good basic color—old red, deep blue, greens of several darkish tones, and mustard yellow. There is no place here for white or pastel painted woodwork.

The decorating scheme in any period style is generally built around the treatment of walls, woodwork, and floors. This is particularly true in the Early American interior as these form the background for the furnishings and accessories. In today's Early American interior, walls and woodwork may be treated in one of several ways:

(1) Plastered walls may be painted or left in their off-white, with woodwork in natural coloring. Avoid if possible knotty pine; this was never used unpainted by our early ancestors. Or woodwork may be painted a rich deep blue, some shade of green, old red, or mustard yellow.

(2) Plastered walls may be papered in a documentary small-patterned paper in colors of the period, with the woodwork either left in natural color or painted with one of the period colors to harmonize with the wallpaper. When woodwork is to be painted, select wallpaper before deciding upon woodwork color; it is much simpler to match paint to paper than paper to paint.

(3) Plastered walls may be stenciled or a wallpaper used that reproduces an old stenciled pattern, with woodwork matching a rich color in the stenciled design.

Generally in any room, all woodwork should be treated alike. It should either be all painted or all unpainted. If beams and corner posts in a room are exposed, that is, not boxed in, it is better to have all woodwork in natural finish. (Early settlers left rough-hewn beams exposed only in sheds, barns, and unimportant rooms such as the scullery.)

In an old house hinges and latches on doors may be left unpainted if they are interesting and of good workmanship. If of iron, they may need a coat of flat black paint. If they are somewhat damaged, or have been replaced by later date machine-made hardware, painting them the color of the woodwork will help conceal differences and deficiencies.

Floors, whether the house is old or a reproduction, will be of wide boards of random length. In the old house they will undoubtedly be of chestnut or pine; in the new house, of pine. They should be kept dark, not sanded and shellacked. The condition of old house floorboards may be such they can be cleaned and oiled or waxed. If there are stains that cannot be removed easily, why not paint the floors in rich colors to harmonize with the general decorating scheme? Or they may be stenciled, grained, or spattered.

The loomed rug is always good; hooked and braided rugs are most suitable. For hooked rugs, search for the more primitive designs; geometric patterns, simple scenes, crude animals, houses, etcetra. (Elaborate floral designs are better for the simple house of the next period—country Colonial.) Oriental scatter rugs may also be used if they are of the mellow, somewhat faded variety. New Oriental scatter rugs are usually too bright and the colors inappropriate. Avoid wall to wall carpeting.

Curtains may be ruffled white organdy or dotted Swiss, or sill-length draw curtains of small patterned calico, chintz, crewel embroidery, or like material, in colors appropriate to the period.

If we were recreating an exact Early American interior today, we would use furniture made before 1714, but we do not carry tradition in furnishing to that extent. There is but little of such early furniture outside of museums and private collections; and much of it is too uncomfortable and heavy for today's use. So we select available furniture that has the simplicity to fulfill the requirements of the period. Good reproductions are to be found, many of them produced from models in museums, and more or less under the guidance of such museums. We even include furniture made by country cabinetmakers as late as the mid-nineteenth century—sturdy, well constructed pieces with simple lines, of pine, cherry, maple, or other light-colored woods, even though many of the pieces were quite unknown to home-owners of the Early American years.

Furniture pieces which may be successfully and correctly used in today's Early American interior include banister-back, slat-back, Windsor, some types of early Sheraton, painted Hitchcock and Pennsylvania chairs; Boston rockers and settles; chests; blanket chests with one or two drawers; chests-on-chests; simple highboys and lowboys; butterfly, tavern, trestle, gate-leg, stretcher and drop-leaf tables; candlestands and bedside tables; dressers; dough trays and commodes; wall cabinets and shelves; slant-top and schoolmaster's desks; simple wing chairs; Windsor settees or old church benches; tall clocks, and crickets. An occasional piece of old Chinese or Queen Anne lacquered furniture in either black, green, yellow, or red, gives a charming accent. It is wise to avoid furniture made of mahogany, staying with the light woods and painted pieces such as Hitchcock chairs.

Upholstered chairs and sofas must be modern; the early American household had none. Choose those of simplest construction, keyed to the other furnishings in size, color, and quality. Handwoven materials, simple, small patterned chintz or calico, crewel embroidery or other similar material should be used. If much of the other furniture in the room is of old wood, select new pieces with as little wood showing as possible; new wood seldom resembles old. If your sofa or chair shows too much new wood, slipcover it.

Accessories are less elegant than those used in the later Colonial interior. Woven hangings and simple mirrors, as well as Chinese painted mirrors, may be used. Currier and Ives prints, though mass-products of a later century, are charming. Suitable, also, are primitive oil paintings, portraits in the same early style, framed samplers, botany prints.

Old oil lamps, electrified, may be used or a lamp made from some simple piece of pottery, pewter, brass, copper, or early wood or tin. Lamp shades should be of gingham, chintz of small design, calico, unbleached cotton dyed the wanted color, parchment, wallpaper, or Chinese tea leaf paper.

Chinese Canton, Lowestoft, pink or copper Lustre, early Staffordshire, stoneware, or even the unadorned modern pottery in rich colors fit well into this early type interior. Pewter, brass and copper are more appropriate than fine silver.

Kitchens and bathrooms allow more leeway in decorating but they should be in keeping with the rest of the house in color and feeling.

Kitchen: *Old feather-edge boards have never-been painted. Curtains of botanical print in soft old colors on white ground. Stainless steel stove; pewter-colored sink unit. Hand braided rug in green, gold, brown, red.*

Dining room: *Golds and browns are used here to complement a large collection of slipware. Walls are off-white plaster; woodwork in natural coloring.*

Bedroom: *Paneling from same house as that in library. Old crewel embroidery has much gold and mustard in coloring; bedspreads are gold; braided rugs in shades of gold and brown. Fireplace is on opposite wall.*

Drawing Room, Stanton Hall, Natchez, built 1851, one of the most elegant and formal of Mississippi mansions. Walls are painted gray, woodwork white, draperies of gold Scalamandre silk; rug outstandingly beautiful Aubusson, rosewood furniture by Belter. Courtesy of The Pilgrimage Garden Club, Natchez.

Bedroom, Stanton Hall, walls, gray; draperies, red silk taffeta; chairs, in red velvet; rug, flowered Victorian; prints on wall "Interiors of Crystal Palace, London."

Victorian In Today's Home

by ETHEL HALL BJERKOE

THE Victorian style, as achieved today, is quite different from the heavy, dull, cluttered interior of the period. Done properly, it can be elegant, charming, homey, feminine, or if you wish, whimsical. We decorate our present day Victorian-inspired interiors more to satisfy a feeling of romantic nostalgia than in entire accord with our knowledge of the period itself.

Today's Victorian interior should have the effect of genuine comfort. It is, I am sure, possible to decorate a home in this style for less money than either the Colonial or Federal. Since little Victorian furniture has entered the price brackets of Queen Anne, Chippendale, Hepplewhite, or Sheraton, it is still possible to find bargains.

A house built in the Victorian period is not essential to the creation of a Victorian interior. Naturally, it is easier if the house to be decorated is of the period, or, at least, has some of the features of the Victorian house-type—

large windows, often to the floor, high ceilings, Victorian-type fireplaces. But a homeowner, with imagination, proper use of color, careful selection of furniture and accessories, can create a home in this period style in an older house-type, or in a contemporary house or apartment.

With Victorian as a basis for the decorating scheme, it is well to dramatize the furniture and the backgrounds to create interest. This may be done in either a formal or informal manner. Color is doubtless the most important factor. During Victorian years, colors were generally sombre and deep. Today we use them in their softer and more romantic shades: rose, persimmon, watermelon pink, mauve, violet, purple, hydrangea blue, gray, orange, green, red, and yellow—but the greens and reds and yellows are quite different than those used in pre-Victorian periods. Now we use a bright green, such as emerald or Kelley; red is the orangey or lipstick hue; yellow is often lemon.

Furniture will be selected from the fast-changing fashions of the period and combined with what today has to offer to create comfort and convenience by present day needs. Highly desirable, if one is fortunate enough to secure them, are the elaborate pieces made by John Henry Belter, New York City's fashionable cabinetmaker of the mid-nineteenth century. Love seats, ladies' and gentlemen's armchairs, and side chairs in the finger-, rose-, and grape-carved black walnut or rosewood of the period are appropriate. Some of the Duncan Phyfe pieces, as well as those of the so-called American Empire, are useful, particularly the sofas, chairs, secretaries, small sideboards, tables, and chests of drawers. Pieces of English Regency, French Directoire, or French Empire also fit well into the modern Victorian scheme. In fact, many Victorian interiors are completely furnished with French Empire.

For informal homes, "spool" furniture, made for country homes around the middle of the nineteenth century, is most attractive in bedrooms. Hitchcock chairs and settees, and Boston rockers, all of which have been indicated as appropriate for the simple Early American and informal Colonial interiors, may be used. Marble-topped tables, bureaus and console tables are also popular, but in selecting them it is well to choose the earlier, more delicately designed pieces rather than later ones which were often ugly.

With these pieces from the period itself, modern sofas and chairs are used as needed for comfort. Accessories from Victorian years as well as more modern items help to create the atmosphere of the period.

Most of us own, or can secure, some of the lovely mellow

Victorian interior in contemporary house. Wallpaper in bronze colors; light fixture and off white shag rug, modern; Victorian circular table cover; chairs dramatically painted white and antiqued. Courtesy Harold de Graff.

Oriental rugs made in the eighteenth and nineteenth centuries. These are most desirable for the Victorian interior and are used in both formal and informal homes, either in room size or scatter rugs. Wall-to-wall carpeting in plain colors or in the large floral or geometric patterns of the period are also appropriate. For the informal interior, handsome floral hooked rugs are suitable.

Walls may be painted or papered. Today we generally avoid the heavy colors of the period and use one of the more dramatic shades mentioned above. Flock wallpaper, first introduced to France by Francois of Rouen in 1620—an imitation of the brocaded velvet wall hangings used by nobility and royalty—is very popular today. It is available in many colors and is used widely in modern Victorian interiors where formality is desired. Also available are many wallpapers in patterns popular during the period but in colors we like today. Floral patterns with roses, carnations, violets, and the like are charming for informal rooms. Large geometric patterns are also suitable. Woodwork is either painted white or a shade to match or harmonize with the background of the wall covering. Walls may be painted to contrast or conform to woodwork.

Drapery material for the formal house is generally satin, brocade, brocatelle, or velvet; for the informal house, blocked linen, floral or geometric prints, or linen in plain colors. Curtains may be of lace, organdie, nylon or some other modern fabric. In the formal house both draperies and curtains will extend to the floor; in the informal house, they may be either floor length or to the sill only.

The color combinations suggested below may spur you to work out color schemes for your own Victorian interiors.

DINING ROOM: a 3-inch stripe gold and white wallpaper; woodwork, white; draperies, golden-yellow satin, floor length; rug, a room-sized Oriental of the Sarouk or Kirman type; furniture, mahogany, walnut, or rosewood; chair seats, striped material in wine, green, and yellow.

LIVING ROOM: walls and woodwork painted smoke blue; floor covering, rosy-red carpeting; draperies, blue linen matching wall color, with a large white floral pattern, made with a plain blue swag; one or two large chairs upholstered in drapery material; sofa upholstered in olive green; a couple of Victorian side chairs, upholstered in blue and cranberry striped satin; cranberry glass for accents; floor length circular table cover in olive green.

FORMAL DINING ROOM: walls papered with a flock paper having a large white design on lemon yellow background; woodwork, white; hangings, heavy silk to match background of paper, over white glass curtains, both floor length; floor covering, olive green; round mahogany or walnut table; Victorian dining chairs with padded seats and backs upholstered in persimmon-colored satin.

Victorian Drawing Room in house built ca. 1830. Wallpaper is gray with white design; woodwork, white; draperies, deep rose faille with widely spaced narrow green and gold stripes; floral carpet shows pink roses on gray ground; chairs are upholstered in bright deep rose slipper satin, sofa (not shown) in bright green velvet, other pieces in black antique satin. Courtesy Miss Mary B. Danaher, Woodbury, Connecticut.

BEDROOM: wallpaper with cream background and an all-over design of large roses in shades of rose pink with mauve tinge; woodwork to match deep pink of roses; floor covering, mauve; curtains of material similar to Swiss embroidery to match woodwork color (even if they must be dyed), made very full, ruffled, floor length, looped back; bedspread, hydrangea blue linen; chaise lounge, upholstered in bedspread material; boudoir chair in mauve silk with Dresden-like flowers in blue and pink; accessories, silver and amethyst.

APARTMENT BEDROOM: walls and woodwork, oyster white; draperies, golden-yellow; rug, chocolate brown; bedspread, orange; chaise lounge or chair upholstered in a block linen showing oyster white, yellow, orange, and brown.

Views of bedroom, home of Miss Danaher. Woodwork, very light pink; wallpaper, large roses on pink ground; rug, dark wood rose; draperies and bedspread, turquoise blue striped rayon and velvet; Victorian card table serves as dressing table.

Authentic Garden Restoration

by ALDEN HOPKINS

Resident Landscape Architect, COLONIAL WILLIAMSBURG

Colonial Williamsburg Photograph

Intriguing herb garden, in the old Williamsburg tradition, in the front of the John Blair Kitchen. The Blair House, tentatively dated 1745, was occupied in days preceding the Revolution by John Blair, Jr., Justice of the U. S. Supreme Court, appointed by Pres. Washington. Many private Williamsburg Gardens will be open especially for Historic Garden Week visitors during the annual tour, April 18-25.

THE FACTORS which contribute most to the success of an authentic garden restoration are the design plan, ornamentation detail, and the correct selection and use of plant material. Of these the layout plan is fundamental, for the whole garden structure is built upon a proper basic design. Throughout recorded history of garden art, typical design patterns have evolved for each period; in Europe and America these patterns have followed closely the progress in architectural design. The periods of fashion and fads in landscape design must be understood in reconstructing any garden of the past, for landscape art is fleeting, and layout and pattern may quickly change, or disappear entirely, in a few seasons' time.

"Ornamentation" covers the overall selection of correct furnishings for the garden. Such furnishings range from the simple edging of planting beds to elaborate summer houses, and include all structural items as seats, sundials, figures, pools, railings, arbors, and outbuildings. The creation of the desired atmosphere depends upon the style and

careful use of these architectural furnishings.

Equally important for the period setting is the choice of plant material. Just as the decorator or curator rejects a Victorian object as unsuited for use in an authentic 18th century interior, so the landscape designer will discard plant materials inappropriate for the period.

Research into plant history has supplied the dates when exotic plant material from Europe, Asia, and other parts of the world were introduced into America. A plant compilation by known date of introduction can authentically determine plant materials to be used in restorations of any period. Paxton's *Botanical Dictionary,* one of the older standard publications — a "new" edition was revised and corrected by Samuel Hereman, London, in 1868— covers plants in general and their usage dates. *Gardens of Colony and State:* Vol. I and II, edited by A. G. B. Lockwood (Garden Club of America, 1934), records plant lists and style periods in America. A more contemporary publication of great

value, *Shrubs and Vines for American Gardens,* by Dr. Donald Wyman (MacMillan Company, New York, 1949), covers those two plant types but omits herbaceous materials.

In the 17th century, emphasis was placed on the individual plant and its suitability for a patterned garden. The highly prized auriculas, carnations, balsam, monkshood, Canterbury-bells, crown-imperial, hollyhock, thyme, sweet-william, ranunculus and fragrant wall flower provided an excellent background plant atmosphere for the favorite knot pattern, then so fashionable.

During the 18th century, native American plants were introduced into Europe; plants from the Far East were imported, and the great fad was for new and rare specimens. In America, along with introductions from the Continent and the exotics from the Far East, gardeners used a variety of native growth. In the north, evergreen firs, spruce, hemlock, and white pine were combined with the deciduous elm, maples, and oaks to provide background. Important native shrubs, like mountain laurel, deciduous holly, viburnums, junipers, hawthornes, and clethra were available throughout the countryside.

In the south, the broad leaved evergreen trees and shrubs gave wider variety. The great southern magnolia, liveoak, holly, loblolly pine, and common bayberry made the winter woods green, and the flowering dogwood, and redbud filled the spring with color.

The early years of the nineteenth century reflected the impact of the informal style, long popular in England and on the Continent. New exotics were introduced, with much interest placed on foliage texture and color variations. The canna again rose in popularity, vying with the newly found and developed dahlia, petunia, zinnia, and geranium. From the Orient arrived—to become immediately popular — forsythia, kerria, osmanthus, pittisporum, photinia, cotoneaster, Chinese holly, deutzia, nandina, and the wisterias. These plants were the first of many introduced during the 19th century.

Today many of these early 19th century introductions are considered "old," yet for a 17th or 18th century restoration they are not quite old enough. For an authentic restoration of any period, the selection of plant materials must be made with greatest care, for the atmosphere of authenticity depends on the correlation of correct plant furnishings with the basic design plan and ornamentation detail.

Furniture of Salem, Massachusetts

By ETHEL HALL BJERKOE

SALEM, Massachusetts, was settled in 1623 and from its earliest days had its share of joiners, as cabinetmakers were then called. The first of whom we have slight knowledge was James Symonds who was granted land in 1672; his fame, perhaps, is due to the fact that John Pease, the father of John Pease, Jr., served his apprenticeship in Symond's shop. John Pease, Jr. is known as the maker of the Hadley chest at the Museum of Fine Arts, Boston—the "Thankfull Taylor chest."

Between this early date of settlement and about 1825, we know of some 165 cabinetmakers who worked in Salem, but none reached great importance until after the Revolution.

Why Salem Prospered

During the Revolution, Salem was the only town in New England that increased in wealth and importance. This was largely owing to the fact that she had opened her warehouses and wharves to the merchants and shipowners of Boston, free of charge, when Boston Harbor had been blockaded by the British. During this period, the hammering from the shipyards was heard from early morning until late at night as all Salem helped build the fighting frigates and the little trading boats, growing wealthy in the process—and making more money as these tiny ships sailed every ocean, trading, smuggling, and privateering. By 1800, Salem was the wealthiest city of its size in the whole country. *(Please turn the page)*

Mahogany chest-on-chest, called "the masterpiece of Salem." Constructed by William Lemon, of whom little is known, and carved by Samuel McIntire; said to have been made for Elias Hasket Derby in 1796 as a wedding present for his daughter.

One of a pair of mahogany Hepplewhite-style card tables; design and carving attributed to Samuel McIntire, 1780-1800. Both table and chest-on-chest, in the M. and M. Karolik Collection, Museum of Fne Arts, Boston, Massachusetts.

Center panel of sofa-back of McIntire in Sheraton style, showing characteristic design of alternate fluting and rosette, eagle on a punch background. Right: basket of fruit carving design by Samuel McIntire.

The merchants and shipowners were the social leaders of the town; the builders and furniture makers were commissioned by them to build and furnish their mansions. It was at this time that the most beautiful houses and the finest furniture were made in Salem.

The greatest cabinetmaker of them all was Samuel McIntire. He not only designed and built beautiful houses, he also decorated the interiors with incomparable carving and designed appropriate furniture for them in the Hepplewhite and Sheraton styles.

At one time it was the fashion to attribute everything that came out of Salem to him. Again, some attempted to prove he was no cabinetmaker and even questioned his ability as a carver. The facts, however, indicate that McIntire designed furniture which was doubtless constructed in his own workshop, that he carved furniture, that he and his son, Samuel Field McIntire, were the outstanding carvers of Salem, often employed to carve the pieces made by other cabinetmakers.

The furniture designed, constructed, and carved by McIntire covers a wide field. He seems to have been fond of sofas and chairs—or else there was a special demand for them; they are in greater numbers than other pieces.

Characteristic Carving

Motifs used on furniture attributed to McIntire are closely related to those known to have been carved by him in the houses he built and decorated. These include a basket of fruit with festoons of flowers and drapery, a basket of fruit and flowers, a distinctive eagle in relief, wheat in a stack, a pendant of husks, a cluster or spray of grapes, a cornucopia spilling out its contents, an Adam-type urn with festoons of flowers and a spray of laurel. Alternating blocks of fluting and rosettes are constantly seen both in room decoration and on furniture.

While much of the furniture attributed to McIntire is of mahogany, many pieces are of a combination of woods, particularly mahogany, bird's-eye maple, and satinwood. He used inlay for a rich effect and, at times, gilding.

Sofas made by McIntire are of two general types: Hepplewhite with a curved back and Sheraton with a square back. Since Sheraton's *The Cabinet-Maker and Upholsterer's Drawing Book* did not reach the American market until 1791, any sofa of the second type was naturally not constructed until after that date.

Chairs attributed to McIntire follow the same trend as do the sofas—Hepplewhite with shield back, Sheraton with square back. The Hepplewhite shield-back chair generally had an elongated vase-shaped medial splat, flanked by curved and shaped bars. Sometimes the flanking bars have oval medallions; at other times, instead of the central vase-shaped splat, there are three bars, all with the oval medallions. Occasionally drapery swags extend across the chair back from the central splat to the others. The front legs are tapered with spade feet, the face carved with pendant flowers, husks, or grape design.

Mahogany secretary with label of Mark Pitman

The Sheraton-type chair with square back may have the top panel carved with one of several McIntire designs. An interesting eagle with outstretched wings, somewhat different from the usual McIntire eagle but evidently designed to fill the panel, appears on several chairs of a set at the Essex Institute, Salem. In addition, of course, McIntire constructed tables, double chests,

Hepplewhite sofa with carving attributed to Samuel McIntire, ca. 1795. Curved top-rail is carved with the characteristic band of fluting and rosettes, surmounted by carved cornucopias with fruit and ribbons; the rolled upholstered arms are faced in mahogany, carved with leafage and rosettes; four square tapered legs in front have carved grape design on each; from the M. and M. Karolik Collection, Museum of Fine Arts, Boston. A Sheraton sofa in the same museum has a band of fluting and rosettes surmounted by three panels, one oblong, flanked on either side by one of console type, each carved with fruit basket and leafage against punch marked field; the four front legs are turned and reed-molded.

card tables, sewing tables, and other pieces of furniture.

One of the most beautiful pieces to come from Salem is the double chest of drawers, pictured here, constructed by William Lemon and carved by McIntire. The front and sides are of crotch-mahogany veneer on pine. The band dividing the two parts of the piece is wider than usual to accommodate a row of alternate flutings and rosettes, and narrower bands are carried along the bottom and the top of the case. The center panel in the frieze has an urn of fruit. The side panels have small seated figures in relief with baskets on their heads. Cornucopias are in the lower corners, and a small basket flanked by leafage is on the skirting. Beautifully carved urns form the end finials, while a gilded figure of Justice, or Peace, is in the center.

Anyone studying the work of Samuel McIntire should visit the three McIntire rooms at the Museum of Fine Arts, Boston. These demonstrate his genius as an architect as well as cabinetmaker. Much of the furniture in them came from Salem, and was made for the first owner of Oak Hill, Elizabeth Derby West. A study of these and of the large number of pieces in the Karolik Collection at the same museum will give a comprehensive understanding of McIntire's role as cabinetmaker and carver.

Contemporaries of McIntire

Contemporaries of McIntire were Nehemiah Adams, Nathaniel Appleton, senior and junior, William Hook (Hoock), Edmund Johnson, Mark Pitman, and Elijah and Jacob Sanderson, to name the most important.

Much of the work of these men was shipped abroad. Papers at the Essex Institute show shipments of furniture by Elijah and Jacob Sanderson to Alexandria, Baltimore, Charleston, Savannah, New Orleans, the East and West Indies, and South America.

Some years ago a Hepplewhite-style secretary-bookcase was found in Cape Town, Africa, with the label of Nehemiah Adams. This is now in the Winterthur Museum, Delaware. Characteristics of Adams' work are those of the other Salem cabinetmakers of this period — elongated bulb feet and table legs with a long cylindrical neck with a pair of small beads at the top and bottom.

Some of the furniture attributed to the Appletons is not unlike that attributed to McIntire.

Hook moved to Salem in 1796 and his furniture was so much in demand that orders were placed sometimes a year in advance. Much of his work is in the Sheraton style, richly veneered and inlaid. Characteristics are carved water leaves on capitals terminating corner posts. These are slightly serrated and have an undulating outline. The concave face of each lobe is marked by four or five shallow groovings.

It is possible that Hook occasionally collaborated with Nehemiah Adams since features found on some pieces attributed to Adams are also on some furniture attributed to Hook. But all men working together in the same locality during a given period will show common features. Several pieces of documented furniture by Hook have been located, most still privately owned by descendants of those for whom they were made. There are pieces attributed to him at the Essex Institute, the Museum of Fine Arts, the Beverly Historical Society, and the Currier Gallery of Art, Manchester, New Hampshire.

Edmund Johnson was employing many carvers and apprentices in 1796, and produced furniture of a fine quality, particularly for export. He built one of the earliest of the Salem

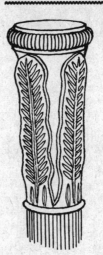

Detail showing carved water-leaves characteristic of work of William Hook, used on capitals terminating corner posts. These were slightly serrated and have an undulating outline; the concave face of each lobe is marked by four or five shallow groovings.

Sheaf-of-wheat carving design by Samuel McIntire.

Carving design of alternating fluting and rosette by Samuel McIntire.

secretaries in the Hepplewhite style. This bears his label and is now at the Henry Ford Museum, Dearborn, Michigan.

Those years from the end of the Revolution until some time after the turn of the century were the Golden Age of Salem, and its cabinetmakers made furniture which is equal in construction and beauty to any made in America at any time.

The Furniture of Newport

by ETHEL HALL BJERKOE

THE Goddards, with the Townsends—nineteen members of the two families were cabinetmakers—comprise one of the outstanding groups of cabinetmakers in America. Both families were Quakers, closely related by marriage and friendship, working and living in Newport during the eighteenth and early nineteenth centuries. The group is known variously as the Goddard-Townsend, the Newport, and the Rhode Island.

In much of their work, which must be considered on a group basis, they followed the styles current during the years in which they were active. But it was within this group that the outstanding beautiful block-front shell-carved furniture was originally made in America. No longer is it believed that John Goddard was the originator of this style; rather, that many of the group took part in its development.

Few pieces are in existence today bearing labels of individual members of the group, but many pieces have been attributed by comparison to those having labels, by some document, or by tradition. Some of their work shows characteristics not seen on furniture made elsewhere, but since these were used by several in the group, they are not in themselves sufficient to make attribution to any one man possible.

In considering the work of this group, it is apparent that in their earliest pieces they followed the Queen Anne tradition. Chairs attributed to them in this style are of choice wood and excellent design, sometimes having shell-carved knees and top rail, and flat stretchers somewhat thicker than those found on Philadelphia chairs of the same style.

Mahogany block-front, shell-carved desk-bookcase, hooded type with carved rosette in a style peculiar to Newport; attributed to John Goddard, 1760-75; one of the ten known Newport shell-carved desk-bookcases.—*Boston Museum of Fine Arts.*

Tray or silver table, 1725-50, Queen Anne style, slipper foot on cabriole leg; probably made by Job Townsend—came to Newport Historical Society from Miss Ellen Townsend, descendant.

Mahogany kneehole bureau with label of Edmund Townsend, Newport, R. I.; shows sunken central portion flanked on either side by raised block panels; outstanding for carved shells.—*Boston Museum of Fine Arts.*

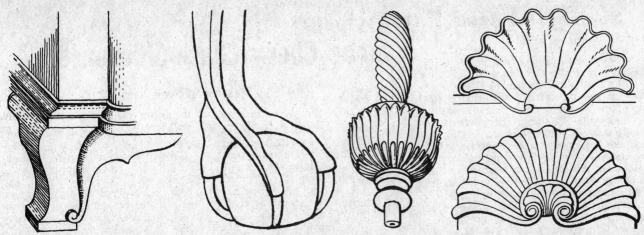

Bracket foot with scroll, found only in furniture made by Goddard-Townsend; undercut talon, attempted nowhere else in America; finial peculiar to Newport, several flutes on back always omitted; two types of carved shells used by this group.

However, the fame of the Goddard-Townsend group depends largely upon their block-front, shell-carved furniture in the Chippendale style. Although furniture of this type was made by cabinetmakers in Massachusetts, in Connecticut, and occasionally in other parts of the country, that of the Newport group is foremost in design and workmanship.

At one time all block-front shell-carved pieces were attributed to John Goddard I—his son John was a lesser cabinetmaker — but time has shown the folly of this. Undoubtedly the honor of originating and perfecting this block-front shell-carved furniture in America should be shared by John Goddard I, John Townsend, and Job and Christopher Townsend, the elders of the group. Experts set the years during which this furniture was made in Newport as 1750 to 1785.

Blocking is one of three methods used by cabinetmakers to break up the flat surface of furniture. (The other two are the serpentine and the reverse serpentine, called oxbow.) A block-front is cut in such a manner as to form a raised surface at either end with a depressed surface in the center; that is, there is a sunken central portion flanked on either side by raised block panels. Occasionally the center portion is not depressed, but blocked like the other two, giving three raised panels on a surface. It was the custom of the Newport men to cut the raised block panels on a drawer front, or door, from a single piece of wood, although they, as well as cabinetmakers in other parts of the country—a relatively small group, for most block-front furniture was made in New England—sometimes cut the blocks from separate pieces and applied them with glue so skillfully that they seldom came off.

An outstanding feature of the block-front furniture is the carved shells. At times the convex shells at the top or bottom of raised block panels were cut from the thick pieces of wood, an extremely difficult thing to do, since one slip of the carving tool could easily damage the piece beyond repair. Again they were cut from sepa-

rate pieces of wood and applied. The concave or depressed shells at the top or bottom of depressed surfaces were almost always cut from the same piece of wood and were not applied. At times the center of the shell was left plain; at others there was a combination of fluting and crosshatching.

The carving of the shell on all Goddard-Townsend furniture is so distinctive and so alike as to suggest it was done by one person. Records show that James Townsend, a son of Job, and a contemporary of John Goddard I and John and Edmund Townsend, had at the time of his death a large number of planes and many chisels. This might indicate that he was a carver rather than a joiner, and was employed by the other cabinetmakers to do their carving.

The blocking of the drawer fronts was generally carried through the heavy bottom molding, often onto the bracket feet. Quite distinctive of Goddard-Townsend furniture are feet of the ogee-bracket type. Often used with these ogee-bracket feet was a decorative scroll, another character-

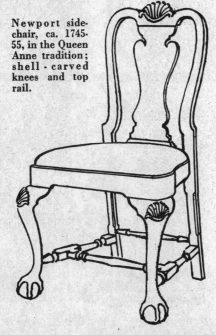

Newport side-chair, ca. 1745-55, in the Queen Anne tradition; shell-carved knees and top rail.

istic of Goddard-Townsend furniture. This consists of a narrow beading on the inside edge of the foot, ending in a scroll at the bottom of the foot. Drawers are usually flush, with a bead molding on the framework around the drawers, but not on the drawers themselves.

Although other wood was occasionally used by the Goddard-Townsend workmen, fine mahogany was their choice for their beautiful furniture. Secondary woods varied from pine to cedar and chestnut, and of the last they used a great deal. Sometimes two different woods were used in the same drawer, one for the bottom, another for the unusually thin sides. Dovetailing in all Newport furniture is of high quality and the dowels are unusually small.

It is believed that the chest of drawers was the first type of furniture to which the Newport cabinetmakers applied blocking. The greater number will be found without the shell carving. The number of drawers varies, sometimes three, again four. These are generally flush with a bead molding on the framework around the drawers. The ogee-bracket foot with tiny spiral scroll is used on the chest of drawers as on other pieces of Rhode Island block-front furniture, and is a sure sign of its origin since this feature is used nowhere else.

The base moldings are heavy and shaped to correspond with the drawer above. The chest top is generally straight, the front edge not following the line of blocking below.

Most examples of their kneehole writing or dressing tables are in the block-front form, although rare examples without blocking are known. The block-front desk constructed by the Rhode Island cabinetmakers has, as a rule, four drawers, although when shell carving is used there may be three only. A feature found on Rhode Island desks and desk-bookcases—and used by no other cabinetmakers elsewhere—is a wooden bolt on the inside of the top drawer, reached from within the desk well. This was used even by the elders of the group; it is found on the labeled

Newport Furniture

Continued

Job Townsend desk-bookcase at the Rhode Island School of Design.

The desk-bookcases made at Newport in the block-front shell-carved style are of the rich mahogany so popular with cabinetmakers everywhere during the Chippendale period, and are among the finest pieces made by the Goddard-Townsend men. The top, as is that of the chest-on-chest, is of the scroll or hooded type with a carved rosette that is somewhat geometric, in a style peculiar to Newport. Sometimes a returned molding is used at the inner edge of the scroll. The usual pediment finial is also individualistic. It consists of a shallow, rounded, fluted urn with several flutings omitted at the back and with a flame of a peculiar corkscrew type.

The lower section of the desk-bookcase usually has four drawers with block fronts ending in plain rounded corners on the topmost. Occasionally there may be three drawers only. Except in the finest examples, shell carving is not present on the lower section. The desk lid is usually blocked and shell-carved. Often the doors of the upper section are only blocked; at other times the shell carving is present. In some of the most elaborate desk-bookcases, there are three doors in the upper section instead of the customary two. When three doors are present, two are hinged, and the blocking and carving follows that of the desk lid. Pilasters of fluting or stopped fluting are the general rule on block-front desk bookcases, although on occasion fluted quarter columns will be found at the corners. On all Newport case furniture, the brasses are large and handsome. Often a large brass handle is added on either side of the desk-bookcase or chest-on-chest.

This group also constructed other pieces that differ little from furniture made by cabinetmakers elsewhere during this period. Much of this simpler furniture was made for export.

Among features peculiar to the Newport men were the paw foot used on some pieces such as screens, tea tables, and washstands, and the straight knee and turned leg with pad foot on tables with porringer top. Especially noteworthy is the undercut talon, which was attempted by no other cabinetmakers in America. This feature is a somewhat elongated webless claw, revealing openings between the inner ends of the talons and the ball, which the claw lightly grasps. The shape of both the claw and the ball may vary from piece to piece. Also used on many pieces of case furniture made at Newport is a vertical reinforcing strip on the inside of the back with chamfered reinforcing blocks. On Goddard-Townsend wall furniture, pad feet on rear legs were generally combined with claw-and-ball feet on front legs.

The Chevy Chase Sideboard

by SELETHA BROWN

THERE are over 200 Trust House Hotels, large and small, scattered throughout England, Ireland, Scotland, and Wales. Most are ancient dwellings dating from the 17th to the 19th centuries; all are subsidized by the government because of their historical significance. These Trust House Hotels provide comfortable and inviting accommodations for travellers, and many are furnished with rare antiques.

The Chevy Chase sideboard in the lounge of the Grosvenor Hotel in Shaftsbury, England, represents an outstanding example of Victorian furniture. Elaborately carved of solid oak, 10 ft. high and more than 12 ft. long, it depicts the *Ballad of Chevy Chase.*

Its six panels of three-dimensional carvings show Harry Hotspurs' departure from Alnwick Castle; his defiant morning-to-noon hunt on land claimed by his Scots rival, the Earl of Douglas; Douglas assembling his army of 2000 men for battle; the murderous conflict in which both were slain, superbly carved in the top center panel; the Earl's distraught widow; and the return of Hotspur's body to Alnwick Castle. Violence and pathos are vigorously translated in this monumental work, carved by Gerrard Robinson of New-castle-upon-Tyne, between 1857 and 1863.

Gerrard Robinson, son of a blacksmith, was early apprenticed to Thomas H. Tweedy, carver and gilder of Newcastle, under whose aegis he became an expert carver. Work was commenced on the Chevy Chase sideboard when the 4th Duke of Northumberland was restoring Alnwick Castle, but it was never delivered there. Instead, Robinson took his masterpiece to the West London Industrial Exhibition (1865) where it was awarded a first-class certificate. A year later it was sold to V. F. Benet, M.P., and taken to Pyt House, his residence in Wiltshire. In 1919, it was sold at auction to Mr. Borley, landlord of Grosvenor Hotel, for £140. Since then Borley has refused offers of up to £2000 for the sideboard, and every year hundreds of grateful sightseers flock to his hotel to marvel at it.

Robinson carved many other sideboards, statuettes, eagle lecterns for churches, and public signs. His Shakespearean sideboard was shown at the International Exhibition in London in 1862, and is now in the Saltwell Museum, Gateshead. As a sideline Robinson also illustrated several childrens' books published in England around 1870–90.

The Chevy Chase Sideboard, Grosvenor Hotel, Shaftsbury, England.

THERE ARE no records of workmen important as **furniture** makers in the Dutch colonies of New York during the last half of the seventeenth century. However, it can be assumed that many pieces of simple furniture were constructed during the period, and that they followed closely in design the pieces brought from Holland by the settlers. The imported pieces, of course, were identical to those in use in Holland; those constructed in the settlements would be similar in design, but cruder, less expertly constructed, and of native woods.

Records show that in these Dutch colonies there were stools, leather chairs similar to the Cromwellian (which had been introduced into England from Holland), cane chairs, tables, the Dutch kas (found in none but Dutch settlements), and the various other types of furniture in general use at the time.

Although the Dutch colonies fell to England in 1664, the Dutch characteristics were so firmly impressed upon the various settlements that they remained paramount until well into the eighteenth century, not only in the craftmanship of these colonies themselves but, to some extent, in the nearby coastal settlements of New Jersey.

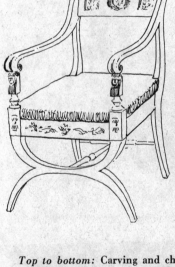

FURNITURE OF

New York

by Ethel Hall Bjerkoe

Gilbert Ash

One of the first important cabinet makers of New York City was Gilbert Ash who was listed as "freeman joiner" as early as 1748. Joseph Downs has said, "Among the earliest Chippendale chairs were those inscribed by Gilbert Ash in Wall St., where he was established in 1756 and remained active for seven years."

To Gilbert Ash is attributed, by comparison with a chair bearing his label, the handsome set of chairs constructed for Sir William Johnson. These are considered by many to be the finest chairs in the Chippendale style made by any New York craftsman; for many years they were considered of Philadelphia origin. They show an interesting scroll back with cupid's bow top rail. The front legs are of the cabriole style with elaborately carved knees and claw-and-ball feet unlike those seen on many New York chairs in that they are sinuously curved rather than blocked with square profile at knuckles. The rear legs are of the stump variety and the seat is rounded, reminiscent of the earlier Queen Anne chairs. The chair with Ash's label is almost identical except that its seat is of the usual Chippendale square style.

Ash also made much furniture for the Van Rensselaer family, and the Van Rensselaer chairs at the Metropolitan Museum of Art, New York City, are attributed to him. After 1765 Ash seems to have given up cabinetmaking. He died in 1785.

Duncan Phyfe

During the years, we know of more than one hundred cabinet- and chairmakers in New York City, but, without doubt, the name of Duncan Phyfe is the most familiar. Phyfe was the son of a Scottish cabinetmaker who came with his family to the New World in 1783 or 1784 and opened a

Top to bottom: Carving and chair leg of chair attributed to Gilbert Ash, ca. 1760; Duncan Phyfe armchairs showing, above, Sheraton influence, and below, French Empire influence. Right, mahogany sleigh bed, ormolu mounts, labels of Lannuier, New York City; one of two beds known to have been made by him. Formerly in the Van Rensssalear Manor House, Albany, now at Albany Institute of History and Art.

shop in Albany. By 1792 Duncan Phyfe (or Fife as he then spelled his name) is listed at 2 Broad St., New York City. He moved several times in the years before he opened his shop at 35 Partition St. (later Fulton). Here, before long, he was producing fine furniture and receiving orders from fashionable people not only in New York City but in Philadelphia and other parts of the country as well. He is believed to have had several agents in the South, and a relative, Lachlan Phyfe, listed at 27 Gay St., in the Baltimore Directory of 1807-9, may well have been one.

Sales were good and more room became necessary for the expanding business. In 1807, Phyfe acquired the adjoining building at 34 Partition St. and in 1811 at 33 Partition St. The house at No. 35 continued to be his home until 1815 when he bought one directly across the street from No. 34 for this purpose. Phyfe carried on the business under his own name until 1837 when it became Duncan Phyfe & Son; remaining thus until his retirement. By 1847 Phyfe had accumulated a large fortune and decided to discontinue the business. He sold the stock on hand at auction, retired, and lived in his Fulton Street house until his death in 1854.

Influences on Design

When Phyfe began his career in New York City, many published books of designs were available from which he could choose those which appealed to his own tastes and to those of his wealthy clients. He seems to have selected largely from those of Sheraton. Later he came under the influence of the more classic Directoire style, and then of the more architectural French Empire, of which he became the leading representative in America.

In the beginning of his career, Phyfe worked in the reddish mahogany which he imported from Cuba and Santo Domingo. It is said he often paid as high as one thousand dollars for a single log and himself supervised the cutting of the veneers which he used so effectively. He depended upon the choice mahogany for rich effects, seldom using contrasting wood as did many other cabinetmakers of the day; his only exceptions were the bandings of matched veneers to emphasize small panels.

Until his latest period, when much of his furniture was made of rosewood, he not only chose his wood with care, but also selected designs with consideration for proportion and line; the result is clearly shown in examples of his best work.

After 1830 the worsening fashions of the day were too strong even for him to combat and he was obliged to make furniture in the styles demanded by his clients. He himself belittled much of this later work, calling it "butcher furniture." In the decoration of his furniture he used turning, veneering, reeding, and carving.

Duncan Phyfe is the only cabinetmaker in America whose name is used as a trade name to designate a style of furniture. This includes benches, footstools, sofas, tables, sewing tables, etc.

It is safe to say that in Phyfe's earliest days in New York a great deal of the cabinetmaking in his shop was done by him personally, and it is the furniture of those years that is of the finest quality in design and workmanship. Doubtless, the great quantity made in his shop during its 55 years of existence by more than a hundred journeymen, cabinetmakers, apprentices, turners, upholsterers, and carvers was made under his supervision and from his selected designs.

The lyre was a favorite of Phyfe for chair backs, sofa and bench arms, and table bases, with strings of brass or whalebone and with a key of ebony running through the top. Among his favorite motifs for carving —and the carving on all Phyfe furniture is clearly defined and expertly executed — were acanthus leaves, somewhat flatter in style than usual with other carvers of the day, plumes, cornucopias, drapery swags, crossed branches of laurel, trumpets, and rosettes. At times the rosettes will be found on corner blocks on tables, on lyres, and at the intersection of the diagonal or curved bars in chair backs.

Reeding is found on almost every piece of Phyfe furniture, and quite

Mahogany work table-desk, 1823, with label of Michael Allison, 46-48 Vesey St., New York City.

Mahogany library table attributed to Duncan Phyfe. Both tables at the Metropolitan Museum of Art.

Right: One of a pair of carved and gilded rosewood sofas, upholstered in crimson damask, by John Henry Belter, ca. 1850. Virginia Museum of Fine Arts. *Below:* Detail of carved sofa back by Duncan Phyfe, showing use of lyre motif.

individual with him is the contraction of reeding from top to bottom of a tapered surface, such as a leg. Typical of his furniture are bulbous turnings which terminate the delicately straight reeded legs on chairs, sofas, and tables. Some of his early work shows small paw feet on the front legs of chairs, benches, and tables, so finely carved that each separate hair is plainly suggested by the use of small irregular grooves. Phyfe was fond of brass for trimming feet and for furniture mounts. Table skirtings often show a narrow border of veneer, the grain of which is at right angles to that of the rest of the wood. At times corner blocks are veneered. The Phyfe-type chairs are quite distinctive.

Although chairs, sofas, window benches, and tables were made in the Phyfe workshop in large numbers and are most characteristic of his work, he also made sideboards, piano cases, beds, and other furniture.

Michael Allison

Two contemporaries of Phyfe were Michael Allison and Charles Honoré Lannuier. Allison was working during 1800-1845. He produced work in both the Hepplewhite and Empire styles that showed him to be an excellent cabinetmaker. Several labeled pieces are in the Metropolitan Museum of Art.

Lannuier

Lannuier was born in France and arrived in New York sometime in the 1790s. It is possible that for some years after his arrival, he worked in Phyfe's shop, but in 1805 he had his own cabinetmaking establishment at 60 Broad St. Lannuier worked in the Sheraton and French Empire styles and at times his work so closely resembles that of Phyfe as to be confusing. He used two types of labels: the first, a simple printed sticker; the second, an elaborate engraved one; but both were in French and English. At times he used a steel die that stamped his name, " H. Lannuier," into the wood in the usual French method of marking. His career was a short one, however, since he died in 1819. Pieces of furniture attributed to Phyfe at one time are now known to have been made by Lannuier. Furniture made by him has found a place in many museums, as at the Metropolitan Museum of Art and Winterthur.

John Henry Belter

As the long popularity of Phyfe waned, his place in the fashionable world of New York was filled by another cabinetmaker whose name was as much a household word during the years 1844-1867 as Phyfe's had been during the previous half century. This was John Henry Belter.

Belter was born in Germany in 1804 and served his apprenticeship in Wurttemberg where he learned both cabinetmaking and carving. He appeared on the New York scene in 1844 at 40½ Chatham Square, the fashionable cabinetmaking center of the day. In 1858 he opened a large five-story factory on upper Third Avenue, where he employed as many as 40 apprentices. Many of his carvers had been trained in Alsace-Lorraine or the Black Forest of Germany. Belter died in 1863, and is known to have destroyed most of his patterns and pattern molds before his death. Although the business was continued under his name, it became bankrupt in 1867.

Much of the furniture produced by Belter was of rosewood. The curved backs so characteristic of his chairs and sofas were achieved by means of a laminated method of construction, a process developed by him to lessen shrinkage, to secure strength, and to permit carving.

The sofas and chairs made at the Belter workshop are highly individual and show his most ornate designs. The finest have the backs skillfully carved at the top in intricate lacy scrolls and floral patterns in high relief. Sometimes the elaborate carving was gilded, giving the rich appearance of carved or fashioned metal. Again, the backs were deeply carved but without pierced lacework, while those made at a later date have only flat serpentine bands to support the upholstered seats and backs. As good as a Belter label was the use of finished wood to face the backs of chairs and settees, a feature used by no other cabinetmaker.

While Belter did not overlook black walnut for his cabinetwork, it appears that he used rosewood whenever possible for his finest work. At times he stained oak and other hard wood to resemble ebony.

During the early 1960s Belter's designs changed somewhat from the rococo of his earlier years to the rectilinear of the Gothic, but they still remained ornamentally complex except in a few instances. He also made other pieces of furniture besides chairs and sofas at his factory.

Belter was an excellent cabinetmaker, carver, and craftsman. He had many competitors but none achieved the richness of carving and design shown in his work, examples of which may be seen in many museums— the Metropolitan Museum of Art; the Henry Ford Museum, Dearborn, Michigan; and the Museum of the City of New York, among them.

The cabinetmaking heritage of New York is a rich and a varied one which lasted for two full centuries.

The Furniture of Philadelphia

by ETHEL HALL BJERKOE

Detail of pediment on mahogany highboy, Chippendale style, Philadelphia, 1765-80.

IT can be said without hesitation that certain cabinetmakers, working in Philadelphia during the last half of the eighteenth century from designs in Thomas Chippendale's "The Gentleman and Cabinet-Maker's Directory," created furniture which has never been surpassed. Seldom, if ever, has it been equalled by any other group of workers in America, except, perhaps, that of the Rhode Island School of Goddard-Townsend of Newport during the same period.

Colonial Philadelphia held an important place in the New World as a city of wealth and fashion. By 1750, its cabinetmakers were coming to the fore as the makers of some of the finest furniture ever produced in America. For some years students believed that William Savery, whose work ranges from simple chairs of maple with rush seats to carved highboys, was the greatest of the Philadelphia group. Then, for a while, Benjamin Randolph, credited with the six famous "sample" chairs of unexcelled richness, was given topmost spot. In 1929, a wing chair bearing his label was sold at the Reifsnyder auction in New York City for $33,000, the highest price paid up to that time for an American chair. Later the tide of opinion placed Thomas Affect at the top.

But there were also many other men whose work is of highest quality, among them Thomas Tufft, who constructed highboys and lowboys of incomparable richness; Jonathan Gostelowe, who originated the chest-of-drawers with serpentine front and fluted corners; Adam Hains, the maker of lovely gadroon-edged breakfast tables; and James Gillingham, known for his distinctive chairs.

These Philadelphia craftsmen were of the highest order and their highboys, lowboys, secretaries, tables, chairs, and other pieces of furniture are the finest examples of design, construction, and ornamentation. The furniture is sophisticated, rococo with complicated carving, and every part of each piece is masterfully executed. Carving reached its greatest perfection in Philadelphia; it was not unusual for several cabinetmakers to employ the same professional carver to do their work.

A few of the cabinetmakers used labels, and other unlabeled pieces have been attributed to them by comparison of workmanship and design. It is usually possible for an expert to decide, even without the help of a label, whether a piece of furniture was Philadelphia-made; at times, to declare with some degree of certainty to which individual cabinetmaker it should be attributed. Generally, craftsmen in any locality worked in a similar tradition.

Walnut and mahogany were the favorite woods of the Philadelphia cabinetmakers during the Chippendale era—1760 until the Revolution. Maple was seldom used although Savery employed curly maple on occasion.

Side and arm chairs constructed by the Philadelphia cabinetmakers are

Label and Chippendale lowboy of Thomas Tufft, ca. 1770. The late Joseph Downs said of Tufft, "His carved high chests and

matching dressing tables set a standard of exquisite detail." He believed, however, that Tufft hired professional carvers. This lowboy shows knee carving similar to that used by other Philadelphia men; the elaborate brasses are used for Philadelphia pieces. *Right*, Chippendale chest of drawers, ca. 1770, with label of Jonathan Gostelowe. *Philadelphia Museum of Art*

Elaborately carved chair back of a Philadelphia Chippendale side chair, ca. 1770-80. Only in Philadelphia did chair and cabinetmakers use such elaborate carving.

Intricately carved ornament, fretwork and scroll end chest-on-frame, attributed to Thomas Affleck, ca. 1770-80.

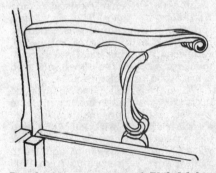

Detail of arm supports of Philadelphia Chippendale style armchair.

Carved shell detail on mahogany lowboy, Chippendale style, Philadelphia, circa 1750-80.

most skillfully designed. The backs have a delicacy and richness of carving in which the Philadelphia men excelled. Characteristic of Philadelphia chairs is a side rail extending entirely through the rear posts, its tenon wedged in. This feature is seldom found on chairs made elsewhere. The chair is generally of mahogany, the wood used so effectively for the beautiful Chippendale style furniture. Legs are cabriole for the elaborately carved chair, with either a claw-and-ball foot, carved paw, fluted drake, or French scroll. On the simpler chairs, the leg may be square, square with block foot, or square fluted. Chair arm-posts are somewhat hollowed on the inside and cut with two wide flutes which converge at the bottom, the knuckle having a characteristic roll.

Philadelphia carvers used a distinctive leafage around the outer parts of the pierced back splats of chairs and at times on crestings. On many of the well carved pieces, there are deeply carved scrolls, acanthus leaves, and vines. They also used a small, smooth attenuated nut-shaped carving surrounded by vines and scrolls, often referred to as "peanut." This is generally found on the knees of cabriole legs or on the ears of the chair top-rail. At times it was used on the center finial of a highboy, secretary, or chest-on-chest. On some of the richly carved chairs, the stiles are fluted, sometimes fluted and reeded. The center of the seat-rail is often ornamented with a shell, sometimes with a shell with streamers, with a shell at each corner extending down

Chippendale side chair, ca. 1770, attributed to Benjamin Randolph whose furniture reveals him as one of the greatest cabinetmakers and carvers of America. This is one of the famous "sample" chairs —one armchair and five side chairs were apparently made as shop samples—attributed to him by family history, the set having descended in the family of his stepson, Nathaniel Fenimore. Jefferson commissioned work by Randolph, and the table on which the Declaration of Independence was drafted is attributed to him. *Philadelphia Museum of Art.*

on the knee. The edge of the seat rail is sometimes carved in rope design.

Crestings are of many types: leafage, shell, drapery with tassels, intertwining ribbons. In the more elaborately carved chairs, the back splats are rich with ornamentation.

The most outstanding examples of Philadelphia furniture are the highboys, usually with matching lowboy. Basically these differ little from those made in other parts of the country, except of the block-front type. Philadelphia craftsmen seem not to have been interested in this block-front type so closely associated with the Rhode Island group.

The distinction of the Philadelphia pieces is not in superior design and construction—excellent as these are—but in the richly carved and applied ornamentation. The extravagance and beauty of this has never been equalled.

Their highboys are of two general types: (1) a full bonnet-top with characteristic carving; (2) an open or lattice-filled scroll top. Fewer were made of this second type. Whether scroll or bonnet-top, however, they were usually of heavy Cuban mahogany. Occasionally walnut was used; cherry or curly maple, rarely.

In the ornamentation of these highboys, the inner ends of top scrolls usually terminate in carved foliated rosettes. The center finial is often an intricately carved and pierced cartouche, sometimes a carved pot of flowers, a Cupid or other figure, an urn, or similar device. The end finials are frequently twisted flames. The Philadelphia flame did not spiral as much as the New England type.

Tea tables made by the Philadelphia workmen in the mid-eighteenth century, and for some years thereafter, are pre-eminent. Similar in design and construction to those being made in other sections of the country, they are exceedingly rich in carving. At first made with a plain or simple "dish" top, they were soon elaborated into the flamboyant "pie crust" top— one of the most popular pieces of furniture with the Philadelphia cabinetmakers. Of rich mahogany with the top of one wide board, its edge elaborately carved and scrolled, these fine tables are exceedingly beautiful. The pedestal and knees of the cabriole legs were handsomely carved. A sure sign of Philadelphia origin is the carved, "flattened" ball beneath the birdcage.

The perfection of design, careful execution, and unparalleled decoration of the furniture produced by the cabinetmakers of Philadelphia during the Chippendale period established a style known today as the "Philadelphia style." These cabinetmakers and carvers of Philadelphia used all the motifs and designs illustrated in Chippendale's "Director" to enhance the beauty and richness of their work. They did more. They gave to it an individuality that is entirely their own.

The Furniture of Baltimore

by ETHEL HALL BJERKOE

FURNITURE making began early in most of the important commercial centers of America and continued over a long period. In Baltimore, however, the making of fine furniture covered a relatively short span—from 1790 to 1820. The furniture produced during these three decades was of consummate beauty and distinction, following the designs in Hepplewhite's *The Cabinet-Maker and Upholsterer's Guide,* and Sheraton's *The Cabinet-Maker and Upholsterer's Drawing-Book,* but with a distinctive departure in details.

One may ask why fine furniture was not produced in Baltimore at an earlier date. Although a royal charter for the colony was granted to Cecil, the second Lord Baltimore, in 1632, and Leonard Calvert, his brother, came to America in 1633 with some 200 settlers, Baltimore-Town was not established until 1729 by a special act of the colonial legislature. Even then it did not become important until after the Revolution. By 1790, however, the city ranked third in volume of commerce with an annual trade export of $2,000,000. With a prosperous group of householders needing furnishings of all types, Baltimore-Town at this time attracted craftsmen of all skills. Directories, advertisements, and such show that between 1790 and 1820 there were well over 300 cabinetmakers in the city.

Since few labeled pieces of furniture have been discovered, it is difficult in most instances to assign specific items to any one man. But it is true that at any period of time, in any locality, the work of its craftsmen will show definite local characteristics. Thus, the furniture constructed in Baltimore during these years has details markedly different from that made in other parts of America.

While the inlaid spread eagle was used elsewhere as a decorative motif, it was used very early in Baltimore, and at times in a form not found elsewhere—a bird standing with its right claw outstretched, holding a rod, on the upper end of which is draped a Liberty cap. Other features peculiar to Baltimore were the so-called Baltimore balloon, latticed mullions edged with satinwood inlay for secretary doors, larger carved rosettes on arm chairs, and the use of large panels of glass showing figures in classic Roman dress done in gold leaf.

The bellflower was a favorite for inlay with the men of Baltimore as it was elsewhere in America during this period, but they used it in a unique fashion. At times these pendant bellflowers were in shades of green, inset into layers of satinwood. Only on furniture made in Baltimore will a ram's head be found above the pendant bellflowers.

Another detail peculiar to Baltimore was the use of the tear-drop panel, rounded at the top and tapering down to a point on tapered legs. Since the shape of this panel bears some resemblance to a partially inflated balloon, the design is sometimes referred to as the Baltimore balloon. Often these tear-drop panels were inlaid with satinwood bellflowers.

The inlay on furniture was also unique, aside from the motifs used. Bold oval inlays in veneer were accentuated by inlaid lines of satinwood or other light colored wood. At times, wide bands of veneer were placed on outer edges to make the straight lines of the furniture more pronounced.

The various items of furniture having distinct Baltimore characteristics are limited. They include double-topped card tables, Pembroke tables, dining tables of two or three parts,

Mahogany sideboard by John Shaw, Annapolis, 1770-1780, Sheraton style. Decoration: 3 large ovals outlined with wide crossbanding, center oval of zebra wood; fan inlays on spandrels; line inlay, rectangle with cut corners, on styles; line inlay, scalloped top, on legs. Shaw's sideboards often show each pair of forelegs close together, intervening central section unusually long. Ovoid spade feet. Baltimore Museum of Art.

arm and side chairs, benches and window seats, sideboards, secretaries and desks, and tall case clocks. Although beds and sofas, and chests-on-chests must have been constructed, none have been thus far documented with definite details characteristic of the Baltimore workmen. The wood used for their fine furniture was generally mahogany, with inlay of satinwood, tulipwood, or other light wood commonly in use at the time; imported zebra wood was also used.

While we know the names of hundreds of Baltimore men who worked at furniture making, few are associated today with specific pieces of furniture. Two with whose work we are familiar are John and Hugh Finlay, who were working from 1799 to 1833. They have been known largely as makers of painted furniture. In 1803 and 1804, however, they made sets consisting of two marble-topped corner tables, a marble-top pier table, and a pier glass. These are believed to be copies of similar pieces in the Music Salon of Fontainebleau. The Finlays also made all the furniture for the "President's House" during President Madison's administration. Practically everything was destroyed when the British burned the house in 1814. Drawings for this furniture by Benjamin Henry Latrobe, the famous architect, now in the possession of his descendants, are in the popular Greek style, and bear little relationship to that in the Hepplewhite and Sheraton manner.

Owned by the direct descendants of John B. Morris, for whom the set was made, but on indefinite loan to the Baltimore Museum of Art, is a set of ten chairs, two settees, and a pier table, all the work of the Finlays. On the back of the painted chairs and settees are depicted the homes of distinguished Baltimoreans of the period. Several of the houses still exist.

A few years ago, more than twenty labeled or documented pieces of furniture were discovered, all made by John Needles. These show him to have been an exceptionally fine worker. Records indicate that he began work in Baltimore in 1810 and retired in 1853. His earlier furniture shows a continued interest in the Hepplewhite and Sheraton styles but this was soon supplanted by the French Empire, the Grecian, and the Gothic, as shown in the design books, of Thomas Hope, George Smith, the Nicholsons, and a Baltimore designer, John Hall. Needles used many types of wood for his robust, rather architectural furniture — curly and bird's-eye maple, mahogany, walnut, and rosewood. None of his work shows the distinctive inlay used by the fine craftsmen in the earlier years of the period.

In a discussion of Baltimore cabinetmakers, John Shaw of Annapolis, one of the best known craftsmen of Maryland, should not be omitted. Shaw was English-trained, and appeared on the Annapolis scene in 1773. Since he used a label, much of his furniture has been identified. His work shows characteristics similar to those of Baltimore-made pieces.

Shaw was an importer of English furniture but he was also an expert cabinetmaker. His first documented

Mahogany cabinet-top desk from Queen Anne County, Maryland, ca. 1800; inlay of satinwood, holly, and ivory; oval glass panels with classic figures in gold leaf, a Baltimore specialty. Metropolitan Museum of Art.

Mahogany chair, Hepplewhite style, Baltimore, ca. 1790-1800, shows care Baltimore craftsmen took with details. Metropolitan Museum of Art.

piece is a rather simple pine bookcase made for the colony's Loan Office in 1775. When the new State House at Annapolis was being built, Shaw was selected to make the furniture for the House of Delegates. At the Baltimore Museum of Art there are several pieces with Shaw's label, or attributed to him.

Shaw's work is generally in a transitional style between Chippendale and Hepplewhite, but his elaborate use of inlaid panels, tapered legs, and of crossbanding and other veneers show a deepening interest in the Hepplewhite and Sheraton styles. Features commonly found on his furniture are the ovoid spade foot, used on many sideboards, hunt boards, and tables; molded top edges; and a cross-grained support at the rear of a bracket foot to give added strength, found on all his secretaries and desks.

Shaw used the finest West Indies mahogany for his work, with yellow pine, poplar, white oak, and chestnut as secondary woods. For his elaborate inlays he used the satinwood so popular with the Baltimore men, zebra wood from Africa, tulipwood from the West Indies, and the green dyes and burnt woods, also popular in Baltimore. However, Shaw did not use the bellflower, a favorite with Baltimore cabinetmakers, depending rather for his decoration upon bold medallions of conch shells, fans, eagles, acorns with leaves, and crossbandings of rare woods accentuated by line inlay.

The Furniture of CHARLESTON

by Ethel Hall Bjerkoe

Hepplewhite Card Table, mahogany with satinwood inlay, circa 1790, from Charleston, S. C. Joe Kindig says of this table, "This is the most elaborately inlaid American card table we have owned and represents the finest example of Charleston inlaid practice of actually engraving ("scratched") the surface of the satinwood, shading, etc. The treatment of the minute crossbanding inlay bordering the legs is of the highest order." The Charleston cabinetmakers not only used satinwood for their inlays but also holly, hard maple, amboyna, rosewood and tulipwood. Some few pieces were inlaid with ivory. Often the "scratches" were rubbed with lamp black for contrast.—*Courtesy The Henry Ford Museum, Dearborn, Michigan.*

Mahogany table in Chinese Chippendale style, circa 1780. Of Charleston provenance. Maker unknown. Furniture showing the Chinese influence, popular in England during the Chippendale period, was also fashionable in Charleston. In the South Carolina Gazette of December 12, 1761, a Charleston cabinetmaker by the name of Peter Hall who had arrived from London where he had apparently received his training, advertised that "gentlemen and ladies of taste may have made and be supplied with, Chinese tables of all sorts, shelves, trays, Chimney pieces, baskets, etc., being at present the most elegant and admired fashion in London."— *Courtesy The Henry Ford Museum, Dearborn, Mich.*

CHARLESTON, S. C. (Charles Town, until after the Revolution) was an important colony even before its removal to its present location in 1680. By the early 1700s, the Carolina low country was the home of a wealthy landed gentry.

In the *London Magazine* for June, 1762, Charleston was described: "Here the rich people have handsome equipages; the merchants are opulent and well bred; the people are thriving and extensive in dress and life; so that everything conspires to make the town the politest, as it is one of the richest, in America."

With all this wealth, it is certain that the city mansions and the large plantation houses were beautifully furnished. Records show that much furniture was imported from England. Communication and trade between England and the Colony were constant and there were apparently closer ties with England than with the other American colonies.

Although much furniture was imported in the early days from England, records show that between 1700 and 1825 some 250 cabinetmakers, as well as many chairmakers, carvers, gilders, and turners working with the cabinetmakers, were busily constructing furniture for the wealthy homeowners.

The first cabinetmakers — few in number—arrived in Charleston shortly after 1700; by the middle of the century this number had doubled and continued to increase until the Revolution. During the years of the Revolution, there was little activity among the cabinetmakers but by 1810 their number had reached eighty-one.

The amount of furniture produced over the years by these men must have been enormous. As of this date, however, only two labeled pieces are known—a satinwood secretary-bookcase and a clothespress, both bearing the label of Robert Walker. One other piece may be included in this small group of marked pieces, a desk-bookcase with "made by Jacob Sass, October 1794" written in ink on the side of a small drawer.

Sass was a native of Germany who arrived in Charleston in 1773 when he was twenty-three years of age. For nearly fifty years he worked in Charleston as a cabinetmaker. He must have produced a large amount of furniture but none of his account books have survived. Without doubt,

Robert Walker's Label, ca. 1815

Mahogany and satinwood secretary-cabinet (described on page 3) was made by Robert Walker, ca. 1815, and bears his label, below. This, with a clothes press in the Charleston Museum, also by Robert Walker, constitute the only two known pieces of labelled Charleston-made furniture. Walker was at 53 Church St., shown on label, between 1813 and 1819.

some of this furniture is still in existence though not yet identified as having been made by him.

Robert Walker, who came from Scotland, was established in Charleston by 1799, and was an active cabinetmaker for the next thirty years. When he died in 1833 his inventory totaled over $37,000. The two pieces of furniture bearing his label show him to have been an excellent cabinetmaker in design and construction. In thirty years he must have constructed a great deal of furniture and it is probable that other pieces will be located.

Thomas Elfe, Sr.

The other important name associated with Charleston cabinetmaking is Thomas Elfe, Sr. It is probable that he was born in 1719 in London

and there served his apprenticeship. It is not known when he arrived in Charleston, but he was there before 1747 when he advertised in the South Carolina Gazette on September 28th. It would appear that Elfe had little difficulty getting established in Charleston; he did very little advertising, yet his customers included the fashionable of South Carolina.

Elfe's account book for the years 1768-75 has been recovered and is in the archives of the Charleston Library Association. This book contains not only the names of customers, the prices they paid, and descriptions of various kinds of furniture made at the Elfe workshop, but many interesting details regarding apprentices, workmen and shop practices. During the eight years covered by the account book, some fifteen hundred pieces of furniture were made at Elfe's shop. Since the period covered by the book is a small portion of the years spent by Elfe in the cabinet-making business, the quantity of furniture made at his shop must have been tremendous. Yet not a single piece with his label has been found. This is not surprising; Elfe had received his training in England, and English cabinetmakers were not accustomed to use labels. Because of the data in the account book, however, it has been possible to trace a few pieces through family history, and other pieces have been attributed to him by comparison with these.

The book shows that Elfe made many double-chests, chests of drawers, secretary-bookcases, chairs, a few wardrobes, and a number of desks. He made simple furniture as well as elaborate. Among the latter are bedsteads of mahogany with eagle's claws, carved knees, brass caps and casters; and easy chairs with eagle's claws for feet. All furniture attributed to Elfe by family history or on stylistic grounds is of excellent design and workmanship in the Chippendale style, usually of mahogany with cypress as the secondary wood. Some beds were of tulipwood. The account book shows the purchase of much "popular plank," cedar, ash, pine, and walnut.

Distinguishing Fretwork

A feature of Elfe's work is an applied fret used so consistently as to be almost a distinguishing feature. This is found on case furniture such as bookcases, double-chests, and secretaries. Entries in the book indicate that an extra charge was made for

this detail and that Elfe also made similar frets to order for chimney pieces. He used the English type of cross brace running from front to rear in the center of large drawers. This feature is found on the work of English cabinetmakers, but Elfe used cypress for this purpose instead of the oak popular in England. Other Charleston cabinetmakers of the period also used this cross brace. Many of them also followed the English custom of using a dust board extending almost to the rear and in some cases all the way to the rear.

From the examples of furniture attributed to Charleston cabinetmakers, it appears that before the Revolution the local men followed the English styles and methods more closely than did their contemporaries in Philadelphia, New York, and New England.

Because of the short distance between Charleston and the West Indies, mahogany could be imported at a low cost, and this was the favorite wood of the Charleston men. Frequently they used beautifully crotched mahogany veneer in their mahogany pieces.

Chairs followed the imported English examples closely. Indicative of Charleston origin, however, are heavy mahogany rails and large mahogany corner blocks. Some locally-made chairs have solid brackets.

Post-War Changes

After the Revolution, the Charleston cabinetmakers constructed their furniture taller so that it would be in proportion to the higher ceilings popular at that time. Burton remarks, "The upper section of the secretary-bookcase of this period (1790-1820) is usually quite high, giving it a 'long-waisted' appearance. Frequently the lower sections are of a higher proportion than those found elsewhere."

Beds made in Charleston at this time are of greater height; nine foot bedposts were not uncommon.

Bellflowers, so popular as a decorative feature with most American cabinetmakers in the Hepplewhite period, differed in Charleston from those found elsewhere. The inlaid work was of the highest quality but the bellflowers are usually "scratched" rather than scrolled or pierced, and there is no scorching of the edges with hot sand. There are, of course, exceptions to this rule, but the great majority have "scratched" bellflowers.

The Charleston cabinetmakers apparently made no block-front furniture so popular with the Newport, R. I. cabinetmakers. Neither did they construct highboys; that place was filled by the chest-on-chest. No bombe furniture has been attributed to the Charleston men and the bonnet-top does not seem to have been used on the chest-on-chest.

Charleston has always been a cosmopolitan city, the home of a wealthy, luxury-loving people. For them the cabinetmakers produced b e a u t i f u l furniture for their mansions, more closely akin to that made in England than the furniture produced in the other colonies. To date, many cabinetmakers have been identified but since labels were not commonly used, little of their furniture has been documented. Much of the exquisite furniture has been destroyed in the many devastating fires that have swept Charleston over the years but much remains and, in the course of time, it may be possible to know who the makers were.

EARLY AMERICAN
Painted
COUNTRY FURNITURE

by CARROLL HOPF, *Curator*

Pennsylvania Farm Museum of Landis Valley

N INTERESTING facet within the study of American Decorative Art is the naive painted decoration on 19th century furniture made by local cabinetmakers in rural areas. Logically we can begin by asking: Why did people take the time to adorn their furniture with paint at all? The question can be answered partly by stating that it is an innate cultural tendency combined with man's natural love of color and form which motivates him to perform such tasks.

Occasionally one will discover a reference to painted furniture in early records and manuscripts — such as, "my blue cupboard and blue chest standing upstairs" mentioned in an 1805 Pennsylvania will. Unfortunately there is no clue as to how the paint may have been applied — whether a uniform plain surface or an overall decorative pattern.

Many utilitarian pieces of furniture were simply given a uniform coat of paint using hues of red, brown, blue,

green, ochre, or gray. The liquid base could have been skim milk, linseed oil, walnut oil, or plain water. *The Practical Farmer, Gardener and Housewife* printed in Cincinnati in 1842, provided a recipe for "paint without White lead and Oil" — two quarts skimmed milk, two ounces of fresh slaked lime and five pounds of whiting. Any coloring agent could be added to suit one's fancy.

Pigments were oftentimes a variety of locally dug and refined clays. Color could also be extracted from vegetable matter, such as blue from the indigo plant and dull reds and browns from sumac berries. An old recipe for green consisted of finely pulverized charcoal mixed with clay of a yellow ochre color.

Prussian blue, red lead, cochineal, verdigris and other commercially prepared pigments were obtainable from paint shops and merchants dealing in general merchandise. By the middle of the 19th century synthetic colors obtained from coal tars began replacing earlier coloring agents.

Aside from painting furniture simply to conceal the raw wood, or in many instances to conceal the two or more woods used in a single piece, many examples were decorated with intricate overall patterns employing such simple implements as a cork, corncob, comb, brush, textured leather, feather, sponge, and even the smoky soot of a candle or kerosene lamp.

The illustrations reveal that a strong contrast of colors make these overall patterns extremely effective. An individual sense of color and design is evident in this method of decoration whether the artist was imitating a fine wood, a variety of marble, or merely creating a delightful imaginative pattern.

There seems to be no particular regional boundaries confining these techniques of decoration, however, many pieces of painted furniture embellished in the related manners have been discovered in Northeastern United States.

Directions explaining how to pre-

Hanging Corner Cupboard—the frame of the raised panel door is combed in yellow ochre and brown imitating tiger maple, while the center panel is decorated to resemble bird's eye maple. A soft red paint covers the remainder of the cupboard. Pennsylvania origin, ca. 1800; 61" long, 29" wide. Pennsylvania Farm Museum of Landis Valley.

pare colors, mix paints and decorate furniture using these basic techniques were available to the general public during the 19th century. Subject matter of this type was often found in publications pertaining to domestic home economy, farm journals, and treatises on decorative painting and related subjects.

Regarding correct procedure for graining, A. E. Youman in his *Dictionary of Every-Day Wants* printed in 1875 stated that "in the imitations of woods and marbles, it is necessary to procure panels of bits of veneer, and copy the color and form of the

Tin Storage Hamper — a fine example of smoke decoration applied over a gray background. Pennsylvania origin, last half of the 19th century; 34" high, 22" diameter. Author's collection.

grains as near as possible." He then gave directions for imitating Black Walnut, Mahogany, Maple, Oak, Rose-Wood and various types of marble by utilizing sponges, brushes, "slender," "buckskin" and "blaze stick." The blaze stick was "made of a piece of wood shaved down thin or a paper card three inches long, one inch wide." It was used for putting in the blazes with the graining color when imitating the inner mahogany wood.

Moore's Universal Assistant printed in 1882 recommended for imitating white marble to "get up a pure white ground, then hold a lighted candle near the surface, and allow the smoke to form the shades and various tints desired."

Seldom does one find this type of painted furniture signed by the decorator. Consequently we do not usually know who was responsible for the embellishment, whether it was the cabinetmaker, a local painter or artist, or possibly the owner. A rare exception is a grained blanket chest in the Pennsylvania Farm Museum's collection signed by "L. D. Miller, Painter April 6, 1893."

The true antique and monetary value of painted furniture is in the condition of its painted decoration. Basically this decoration, now faded and mellow due to time and wear, reflects the attempts of earlier generations at making their everyday surroundings aesthetically pleasing. Consequently after discovering a good painted piece keep it that way. *Never refinish it.* If refinished furniture is desired, work on a piece devoid of paint or decoration and in such poor condition that it can't be saved. By doing so we are helping to preserve for posterity more of the simple decorative art forms produced by generations past.

Top left: Rocking Chair — decorated with smoke from a candle or kerosene lamp applied over a light green ground. Pennsylvania origin, last half of the 19th century; 34" high. Pennsylvania Farm Museum of Landis Valley.

Top right: Butter Churn — a combination of various size brushes were used to decorate this "E. H. Funk's Champion Churn, Pat'd. Sept. 1868" which was made in "Sturgis, Mich." Ground color is red with black pattern and white striping. Lettering is stenciled over the decoration; 39" high, 13 x 19" base dimension. Pennsylvania Farm Museum of Landis Valley.

Bottom of Page: Fireplace Mantel—marbleized pattern executed with different size brushes; the ground color is black with pink, white and yellow veining. Pennsylvania origin, ca. 1840; height 5½', width across the top 7½'. Courtesy Snyder's Antiques, Reinholds, Pa.

Cupboard—both corn cob and comb were used to decorate this piece. The ground color is pale red with a darker red pattern. Pennsylvania origin, ca. 1840; 7' high, 54½" wide, 20" deep. Courtesy Spear's Antiques, Robesonia, Pa.

Blanket Chest—a combination of feather and brushes was used to apply the black pattern over the reddish-orange ground color. Pennsylvania origin; 24" high, 46" long, 21" deep. Privately owned.

VICTORIAN WICKER
and
RATTAN FURNITURE

by MARGARET M. BARTLETT

SOME gay and delightful wicker and rattan furniture was made in the last half of the 19th century. In the 1850 period, wicker furniture was of simple design, but in the years following it became more ornate with embellishments of curlicues and small wooden balls. Usually this furniture is found in a natural reed color treated with clear varnish, or stained with a dark brown color.

The frames for wicker furniture were fashioned of flat reeds which were wrapped about with strands of cane. Round reed was used for the back and arms of chairs and settees and intricately woven to form links, circles and scrolls; there was usually an oval or square of spider web cane woven into the back rest. The seat frames were almost always made of maple, and were either hand caned or fitted with panels of machine woven cane.

Victorian rattan chair frames were constructed of bamboo; the seat frame, arms, and rockers were of maple. Chair arms were often piped with two bands of half inch wide bamboo strips. Round rattan was used for the curlicues which formed a pattern within the bamboo framework.

Photos by Wm. A. Shumate

Wooden balls strung on a strand of reed held the curlicues in position and were also used as a border decoration around the caned sections. When used

BELOW: Rocking chair of bamboo, rattan, and wicker construction; ca. 1885. Height 4'; width 23". Author's collection.

Wicker settee embodying characteristic design elements of the 1860 period; original Wakefield Rattan Co. paper label intact. Length 53"; height 39". Author's collection.

as a trim, the wooden balls were fastened to the bamboo framework with small wooden pegs. The inserts of woven cane for the back and seat were secured to the framework with screws.

Although rattan and wicker furniture appears to be fragile, it is actually quite sturdy. Some pieces have been found with original paper labels identifying the manufacturer. Topf, of New York City, produced rattan and wicker furniture as early as 1850. The most prolific source for this kind of furniture was the Wakefield Rattan Company of Boston and New York; they operated from 1860 to about the turn of the century. In the 1920s the unadorned, over-and-under woven reed furniture made its appearance.

* * *

Under the heading "Useful Hints to Housekeepers," the May 1908 issue of *The Modern Priscilla Embroidery Magazine* suggested that "wicker furniture coated with Mahogany, Ox-Blood Red, Malachite Green or Gloss White Jap-a-lac (a trade name for a paint product), looks better than new."

Willow furniture offered by Stickley-Brandt Furniture Co., Binghamton, N. Y., in 1903. TOP: "Small Armchair." BOTTOM: "Reclining Go-Cart with Parasol."

Rustic Art Nouveau -
OLD HICKORY FURNITURE

AS ART NOUVEAU filtered down from echelons of high-style handcrafted furnishings for the elite to mass production for the *hoi polloi*, furniture manufacturers were busily casting about for suitable designs. The Old Hickory Chair Co. of Grand Rapids, Michigan, was fortunate, both financially and artistically, in their commercial revival of the rustic hickory furniture used for years in the Southern hill country. It was sturdy and simple, and met Art Nouveau requirements in following Nature's forms.

The chairs, particularly, with their broad hand-plaited bottoms and backs, had long been familiar to hotel verandahs, and the company, in its advertising, played heavily on the thought that Andrew Jackson, "Old Hickory" himself, took comfort in the long summer days of his declining years in just such hickory chairs. Webster, Clay, Calhoun, and Benton were also credited with partiality to the hickory chair "with its broad expanse of bottom."

A catalog devoted to the Old Hickory line, put out under the imprint of the Paine Furniture Company of Boston, Massachusetts, in 1904, tied the product to the prevailing Art Nouveau style. The first page carried a single line, dignified by Old English type: "Nature unadorned is most adorned of all." Scattered throughout

Above: "Andrew Jackson" chair; height 43 inches. Price, in 1904, $2.75.

the pages were such quotes as "Nature and Wisdom never are at strife," "By forms unfashioned, fresh from Nature's hand," and "Civilized man is Nature's worst enemy."

In addition to copies of Andrew Jackson's original chairs, were offered "Settees, Tables, Tete-a-tetes, Couches, Swings, Tabourets, Lawn Vases, Lounges, Roman Stools, Beds, Dressers, Chiffoniers [labelled *tedious hand work*], Stands, Buffetts (sic), Odd Pieces [children's lawn sets, toys, umbrella stands, hat racks, footstools, etc.], and Log Cabins. One-room cabins, 12 x 14 ft., complete except for floor and chimney, sold, knocked down, as low as $110; with porches, $125.

All furniture framework was of young hickory saplings with the bark left on, chemically treated to destroy germ and insect life. Varnishing cost extra. Inner growth hickory bark, stripped from the trees only at certain seasons, was used for the hand-plaited bottoms and backs of chairs.

These pieces, inexpensive, yet in latest vogue, found acceptance nationwide. The Old Hickory Inn in Bakersfield, California, furnished its lobby with them; so did the Lake Side Club in Grand Rapids, Michigan. The historic Claremont Inn on Riverside

Right: High wing rocker, with head rest; height 51 inches. Price, in 1904, $7.

Round tea table with shelf; height 28".
Price, in 1904, $4.50.

"Old Hickory" bedroom suite. Prices in 1904: bed, $25; bureau, $35; chiffonier, $30; stand (not shown), $12.50.

Drive, New York City, overlooking Grant's Tomb, used Old Hickory tables and chairs in its terrace dining room; the First National Bank of Sewickley, Pennsylvania, in its Director's Room.

Appropriately, the Modern Woodmen Camp, 8771, Hudson, New York, furnished its hall with Old Hickory chairs and lectern. Dan Beard, celebrated artist and nature lover, supplied a handwritten testimonial, headed "Rowands, Pike Co., Pa.," which was reproduced in the Paine catalog: "The pieces of furniture most prized, most comfortable, and most appropriate to

their surroundings, which I have in my log house are a few chairs from your artistic and unique shop." Countless families, rich and poor, all over the country, used them in dens, on porches, and in garden retreats.

Though the catalog predicted that the supply of native hickory would sometime be exhausted, the fad for indoor rusticity passed first. A recently examined set of Old Hickory chairs, purchased about 1916, which has stood on a Florida porch for the past fifty years, is still sturdy, bug free, and reasonably comfortable, but the wood has weathered sadly to a

singularly dry and lifeless gray, too forlorn for resurrection.

The Old Hickory Chair Company exhibited their line in Grand Rapids, Michigan, beginning in 1896, and for several years thereafter—at least until 1914. After 1914 they gave an Indiana address. The Red Book, a reference book of the Furniture Commercial Agency Co., published in Cincinnati, Ohio, in 1899, listed them as follows: Martinsville, Morgan/Old Hickory Chr. Co. . . . Mir. Old Hickory Chrs. Rockers Tbls & Settees (Frank W. Woods, Prop. K. 1). Apparently the firm exhibited at Martinsville and Cincinnati, Ohio, and at Fort Wayne, Indiana, too.

Niagara Rustique PLANTERS

From the Notebooks of the late
CARL W. DREPPERD

THE Niagara Falls Rustique Manufacturing Company was organized in the 1840s as a by-product of woodenware, shingle and shake making. In 1868, D. M. Dewey of Rochester, New York, famed for his inimitable stencil colored prints of fruits, trees, and flowers, took on the regional representation for their rustique work planters, and began advertising them from his Arcade Hall Art Parlors in Rochester. No less than seventy-one different types were made!

"The Lulu"—was it from this came our expression "It's a Lulu?"—was priced at $6.50; the "Clarkette," a standing planter, and an oblong Window or Verandah box were each $3.50. The "Bernhardt," a tripod high planter, a later addition to the line,

The Lulu

and named for the actress, was $2.

In addition to planters, boxes, and jardinieres, the Niagara Falls Company made settees, tete-a-tetes, chairs, and benches for parks, lawns, verandahs, and gardens, all in the "Rustique" style.

BERNHARDT

Clarkette

Gothic Motifs in American Furniture

by RICHARD BURTON MARLOWE ASKEW

Carved walnut chair, one of 4, at the Hampton Baptist Church, Hampton, Virginia. These chairs, with a matching marble-topped table, were placed in the sanctuary of the Church, which was completed about 1883. Interestingly enough, both chairs and tables have turned legs in the style of the Louis XVI Revival. Courtesy of the Hampton Baptist Church.

SHORTLY AFTER the middle of the 18th century, the furniture designs of Ince and Mayhew, Thomas Chippendale, and other English designers and cabinetmakers were being recognized and appreciated by American craftsmen. In Philadelphia, Providence, Rhode Island, and other furniture centers in the Colonies, artisans were adapting English taste to suit their local clients.

English design at this time was actually a mixture of three basic elements; the "French" or rococo, the Chinese, and the "Gothick," all different, yet ingeniously combined to form one distinct style. The Gothic motifs were often overshadowed by the two former; nevertheless, these are perceptible in many articles of native furniture produced during this period. The ogee bracket foot may sometimes lend a slight Gothic flavor to a chest or desk, but it is more likely of Chinese origin. We should recall that both Chinese Art and the Art of Mediaeval Europe and in their background a strong common influence from the Near East.

It would be rare to find a lavish example of American 18th century Gothic furniture comparable to English productions; in fact, it is doubtful if such an item ever existed. Gothic design in Colonial America probably never expressed itself more fully than in a few garden pavilions and, possibly, in the famous porch of Gunston Hall in Virginia, which could also be considered Chinese. (Please turn the page)

Dining room at Lyndhurst, a Gothic Revival mansion, near Tarrytown, N. Y., now owned by the National Trust. The house was originally built in 1838 for William Paulding and his son, Philip, by the noted architect, Alexander Jackson Davis. Davis later enlarged the house for a new owner, George Merritt, and eventually it passed into the hands of the Gould family. Many pieces of furniture shown here were designed by A. J. Davis. Noteworthy are the heavy table, the richly carved chairs, and the intricate grillwork of the sideboard. The elaborate use of arches, columns, and pendants to ornament the room itself created an ideal setting for such furnishings. National Trust for Historic Preservation, photo by Sleepy Hollow Studio, 1964.

Another interior view at Lyndhurst shows several different but ornately carved chairs. The pair of "wheelback" chairs date among the earliest of the original furnishings designed by A. J. Davis in the 1830s. They were formerly in the "saloon" used as William Pouldings drawingroom. The ribbed ceiling suggests a chapel of the Middle Ages. National Trust for Historical Preservation.

Neoclassic design was the established mode during the Federal period, but occasionally among the cornucopias and festoons of chair backs one may note a slight Gothic arch; more particularly, the glazed doors of secretaries were arched in this manner. Albert Sack in his *Fine Points of Furniture, Early American*, page 168, shows an important secretary of this kind by John Seymour of Charlestown, Mass. Each door has three graceful arches, with a series of small arched motifs below.

It was really during the 19th century that the Gothic Revival achieved its most fantastic heights and came into its own in this country. As a style, it became associated with artistic circles and drew the admiring attention of painters such as Thomas Cole and architects like Alexander Jackson Davis. Furniture design followed Sheraton styling at the beginning of the 19th century, with only faint suggestions of Mediaeval picturesqueness. By the 1820s, motifs were more profuse, and during the 1830s and 1840s very often the structure of the piece was carved up into various arches, miniature rose windows, and pillars of an ecclesiastical nature.

Much of the Gothic furniture of the 19th century was designed for churches, particularly chairs and altar tables, but a wide variety of furniture for the home was also created during the Victorian era: beds, chests, sideboards, hall trees, and even such objects as chandeliers, lamps, picture and mirror frames, and daguerreotype cases. I once saw a magnificent Victorian hall tree which rose as a great mirrored pointed arch, surmounted by a number of crockets, the side wings having long turned pegs on which to hang clothing, the whole standing upon a low, carved paw-footed chest.

The Gothic style survived into the 1880s and 1890s, but most of these later furnishings were cheap mass-produced articles. They were usually harshly angular, made of the popular oak, and with little carving, only grooving or some chip carving, battlements, or pendants suspended on the underside of table tops. Pedestals for such tables might be formed of flat jigsaw cut pieces with a faint buttress outline. Marble tops were fairly common.

Many late Victorian chairs and sofas were more often a conglomeration of several styles, perhaps a Gothic back with cabriole legs, not always the most harmonious choice of elements.

White House Sideboard

IN 1887, the Women's Christian Temperance Union presented to President and Mrs. Hayes, for the White House, a handsomely carved mahogany sideboard in recognition of Mrs. Hayes's temperance work. The 2-part sideboard, over 9 feet high, was the work of William H. Fry of Cincinnati, and was a companion piece to a dining table he also made for the White House. Members of his family assisted in its carving, and Mrs. Bellamy Storer and Mrs. William Taft, then unmarried, and other ladies of the Cincinnati art group did the carved ebony inlay of the U. S. coat-of-arms in the upper section. The central lower panel, carved with an eagle, and flanking panels, with floral designs, opened on deep compartments.

When discarded White House furniture was put up at auction in 1903, this piece, to the consternation of its donors, was purchased by the owner of a Washington beer garden for use in his establishment. It is now privately owned again — this time by Mr. & Mrs. Robert E. Rose, of Waterford, Va.

Desk with bookcase, or secretary, from New England, circa. 1800. Made of mahogany with veneer of bird's-eye maple. An example of neoclassic furniture with Gothic design exemplified by the use of pointed arches in the doors. The Gothic style seems to have been much associated with learning and study and was thought particularly appropriate for library furniture. Even today, we visualize Mediaeval monks cloistered away in their cells, copying out manuscripts. The Metropolitan Museum of Art, Gift of Mrs. Russell Sage, 1909.

Carved mahogany chair, from a set of 6 in Chippendale style, circa. 1750-1785. Chairs of this general type were produced throughout England and in her Colonies. The interlaced open splat suggests the richly carved and pierced stonework found in Mediaeval windows. The ogee effect on the legs could be deemed either Gothic or Chinese. The Metropolitan Museum of Art, Gift of Mrs. Russell Sage, 1909.

EASTLAKE INFLUENCES ON AMERICAN FURNISHINGS

by FLORENCE THOMPSON HOWE

Black walnut wainscoting and door-casing in an Eastlake interior.

IN THE WORLD of antiques the swing of the pendulum is not confined to old clocks. A reversal of interest in "collectibles" follows the same pattern. Dealers, collectors, interior decorators, and students of antiques who have been catching their breath over the voluptuous curves of over-stuffed Victorian, are suddenly swung to the intellectual restraint of Charles Locke Eastlake's geometrically-felt straight lines in rosewood or solid black walnut.

Who was the Britisher Eastlake? Well, there were two of them who left their mark on the architecture, arts, and crafts of the mid-19th century. Both are recognized with increasing enthusiasm (not unprofitably) today. The elder, Sir Charles Locke Eastlake (born in Plymouth, England, in 1796), was knighted for his many contributions to British cultural life in the 19th century. He

served as Secretary of the National Commission of Fine Arts, was made Keeper of the National Gallery in 1843 and later, President of the Royal Academy.

A portrait of Sir Charles in the November '69 issue of *Spinning Wheel* ("Memo From Marcia," page 62) shows him a fastidious gentleman whose tightly pressed lips and firm chin suggest a strong opinion and relentless dedication to his crusade for good taste in the domestic environment. Marcia Ray lists him as an influential artist, critic, and patron designer who looked down his nose at the emotional Victorian decor which offended good taste, as he saw it. His more intellectual approach set him to devoting his energies to lifting the level of public taste. To do this he began, of course, with those born to the purple, yet of mediocre mold.

But it was Charles Locke Eastlake

the younger, nephew of Sir Charles, whose like beliefs and practices were most strongly felt in the United States.

Born in Plymouth, England, March 11, 1836, he too became a VIP in the cultural life of his country and his time. From 1866 to 1877 he was Secretary of the Royal Institute of British Architects, and from 1878 to 1898 Secretary of the National Gallery. He was a noted enthusiast for the Gothic style.

His impact on American cultural life is said to have stemmed largely from his book, *Hints On Household Taste*, which appeared in its sixth American edition in 1881. His wife was a writer, and even in those pre-airline days they spent much time in Italy and elsewhere abroad away from their tight little island.

With the popularity of his book in this country came an almost immediate demand for furnishing and decor in the Eastlake tradition. Records of the period (the last quarter of the 19th century) reveal that an interior done in the "Eastlake manner" was the "in" thing among the opulent families in urban America.

Eastlake did design some furniture. But it was his book which gave him wide exposure, promoted his ideas, and secured him a following both in England and the United States.

Eastlake's book emphatically reminded his readers that the simplest forms were preferable. Whereupon furniture makers discarded the fine woods he used to make his furniture both beautiful and expensive, and substituted mediocre materials. Thus they burlesqued his work—profitably. In 1877 one critic wrote:

"Mr. Eastlake has had the misfortune to have his name associated with much ugly furniture." Of all this Eastlake himself was sadly aware.

The *American Heritage* publication, *Antiques From the Civil War to World War I* gives an interesting account of Eastlake and quotes from *Hints On Household Taste*. For example:

"If a sideboard were constructed in a simple and straight-forward manner and were additionally provided with a few narrow shelves at the rear for displaying the old china vases and rare porcelain of which almost every house contains a few examples, what a picturesque appearance it might present at the end of a room." Ornamentation which did not require tedious and expensive handcarving but could be handled by machine in the straight lines of geometric designs on handsome solid woods such as rosewood or black walnut, was characteristic of Eastlake furniture. Tiles were used extensively.

Eastlake recommended tiles for flooring and even for hall wainscoting, especially tiles by Minton, Hollins & Co., the English ceramic firm.

With the tile exhibits at the Centennial (1876) a new decorating fad began. By 1881 the fad reached such porportions that an English architect suggested facetiously that impecunious ladies devoted to artistic pursuits, take up tile painting as an honorable means to gain a livelihood.

"The natural grain of such woods as oak, rosewood, walnut etc. is in itself an ornamental feature," Eastlake wrote, "if it be not obscured and clogged by artificial varnish."

A critic of the 1890s wrote with some flourish:

"In adopting the Eastlake method of furnishing, we step out of our luxurious carriage to take a bracing walk upon the firm earth!"

Harpers Bazaar was on the bandwagon, too, saying, in discussing the Eastlake trend: "Every marrying couple who could read English, consulted Eastlake's book and accepted its dictum as gospel truth." However exaggerated such reports may have been, his work obviously did create an awakening, questioning, and study of the domestic environment. The demand for Eastlake interiors indicates that some of the more privileged Americans did credit his style with a constructive principle and sincerity of purpose. Perhaps those who had "arrived" (for the woods used by Eastlake were quality and certainly not inexpensive) really did not find the voluptuous curves of the Victorian to their taste and welcomed the disciplined design and handsome woods of Eastlake. Or was it just the swing of the pendulum?

An Eastlake dining table seen through a black walnut doorway of Eastlake design.

Hall in an Eastlake interior employs Victorian Strahn wallpaper and features an Eastlake black walnut door, stair-rail and hanging finial.

A glimpse of a black walnut ceiling used in an Eastlake room. The Eastlake overmantel is inset with pale green tiles, "The Seasons," marked "Robert Minton Tile Works, Fenton near Stoke-on-Trent."

Sixteenth century Italian "trono" in the foyer of the John Ringling Residence measures roughly 8½ feet wide by 9¾ feet high by 37 inches deep.

Chest-Bench has unusual History

by JEAN H. HOUTCHENS

A "HAPPY ACCIDENT," plus some further research, has brought to light the unusual history of a large chest-bench which is part of the original furnishings in the foyer of the John Ringling Residence in Sarasota, Florida. The palatial mansion, built in 1926 at a cost of $1.5 million, and the famous John and Mable Ringling Museum of Art were bequeathed to the State of Florida by the circus magnate upon his death in 1936. Both are now owned and operated as public museums by the state, open every day of the year.

The elaborately carved, inlaid and gilded walnut seat, which resembles a double throne, was identified from the sketchy records (of his purchases) left by Ringling as an Italian piece bought through Christie's of London in 1927, and shipped to Florida to grace the foyer of "Ca 'd'Zan" (House of John in Venetian dialect). Old employees remembered his saying that it was a "sword chest," and that's as much as was known until the summer of 1971 when Kent Sobotik, assistant curator of the Ringling Museum of Art, made the lucky find which exposed its background.

Leafing through the catalog of the art collection of Sir George Holford in the Ringling Museum library, in search of information about some paintings John Ringling bought from this famous collection, Sobotik happened upon a picture and description of this selfsame piece of furniture. By means of this and other references, he was able to put together the actual story of the unique chest-bench.

History indicates that a seat of this kind was originated in the mid-15th century in Florence, Italy, and in a plain, unornamented form, was called a *cassapanca*. By the early part of the 16th century, the *cassapanca* had developed into an elaborately carved and inlaid piece called a *trono*. The *trono*

is rare, however, in comparison with the more practically-scaled *cassapanca*.

The Ringling *trono*, made in Florence in 1508, is distinguished by its association with two of the most illustrious families of the Italian Renaissance, the Medici and the Strozzi, who had feuded for generations, and were arch-rivals in banking and patronage of the arts. But now, in 1508, Clarice de'Medici and Filippo Strozzi were to be married, and this *trono* was created specifically as a wedding present to the Strozzi from the Medici.

The association of the two families dominates its decoration. The balls and crescents carved into its pilasters were heraldic symbols of the Medici and Strozzi families respectively, and the falcons used in the design represent Pope Leo X, uncle of Clarice. The broken branch with three roses was used by Piero di Lorenzo, Clarice's father, during his exile from Florence, while the house of Strozzi is represented by the lamb, symbol of Filippo Strozzi the Elder.

How the *trono* got from the Palazzo Strozzi in the Via Tornabuoni in Florence to the Exhibition of 1871 in London is not known, but that is where and when Sir George Holford acquired it and installed it in his country house, Westonbirt, in Gloucestershire, England. When the Holford collection was broken up, John Ringling bought the *trono* along with 28 paintings, some for his home and some for the Ringling Museum of Art.

History also shows that "Mr. John" was right in calling it a "sword chest," as the chests beneath the seats of the *cassapanca* or *trono* were frequently used to store the gentlemen's swords while they attended social or religious gatherings.

FRENCH EMPIRE FURNITURE

by CYRIL BRACEGIRDLE

WHEN WE SPEAK of Empire furniture it is well to bear in mind that there are two distinct varieties. There is French Empire furniture made in France between 1802 and 1815 and there is the oddly-named American Empire furniture, though nowhere in the history books will you find any reference to such an empire! This latter is really furniture made in a modified French Empire style, often by emigres who had fled across the Atlantic from the French Revolution years previously.

The original French product deserves more to be called Napoleonic. The design was on the grand Imperial scale, stamped with the personality of the Emperor and symbolizing the power of the France that he created in those years when the *Grande Armee*

An Empire ormolu clock, the case by Deniere and Matelin.

carried the tricolor from the coasts of Spain and Portugal to the streets of Moscow.

The furniture of Napoleon was, in the main, heavy and glittering with gilt-bronze mounts superbly chased and given a matt finish by the finest craftsmen in France. It was furniture for looking at rather than for sitting on—there were too many sharp corners for comfort.

The motifs were taken from Imperial Rome, and from Egypt, after Napoleon's Egyptian campaign.

The guiding lines for this furniture

of grandeur were laid down in a publication entitled *Recueil de decorations interieures* which appeared in 1801. The authors placed great stress on the designs of Rome and classical Greece and stated, "It would be vain to seek for shapes preferable to those handed down to us by the Ancients." This declaration was firmly—some might say slavishly—adhered to during the fourteen years that followed.

In 1802 there was held in the courtyard of the Louvre a "Products of French Industries" exhibition, and it was here that the new style really burst upon the world of furniture. Soon there came the full flowering of a design as grand as the Corsican's dream of a Europe united under the flag of France.

At first, a great variety of imported as well as local woods was used, but after 1806 the Continental Blockade caused the craftsmen to fall back upon French woods only. Vast quanti-

Empire satinwood "Secretaire a Abattant" by C. J. Lemarchand.

Empire giltwood "Fauteuil en Gondole" in the style of Jacob.

tics of furniture in foreign mahogany had, however, already been produced and for a while after the imposition of the Blockade a good deal was still made from stocks of Cuban mahogany and Spanish walnut, helped out no doubt by illicit cargoes which managed to reach French shores. Some of the finest Empire furniture is in several varieties of mahogany, identifiable by the grain, providing a superb ground for bronze mounts.

In the main, though, the furniture produced after 1806 makes use of woods native to France, such as maple, acacia, apple, pear, beech, and oak.

Among the famous names involved in the manufacture of Empire furniture were Percier and Fontaine, officially appointed architects to the

of a long line of such craftsmen, Desmalter refurnished part of the Grand Trianon as well as other royal palaces. At one time he employed 350 workmen and, after 'the Napoleonic wars were over, he furnished rooms in Windsor Castle for George IV.

As had been customary with royal craftsmen before them, these men signed their work so that today such pieces are easy to distinguish and rank among the most prized items in the realm of European furniture.

Clawed feet, friezes of gilt-bronze, escutcheons, mouldings, the elaborate use of Imperial motifs such as laurel wreaths, swords, shields, daggers, cornucopia and Greek dancers from the friezes of ancient temples—these are the outstanding characteristics of French Empire furniture. Neither before nor since has there been such a high peak of skill in the arts of gilding and chiselling.

There was an immense variety of items, and especially of chairs, in which the supports were heavily carved and ornamented, the ornamentation falling roughly into three groups: the human represented by caryatids, angels, cherubs; the mythological, including swans, unicorns, griffons, dragons, and examples from Egypt of winged beasts, sphinxes and scarabs; and the third group consisting of such conventional architectural symbols as ballusters and columns.

An interesting characteristic of

Empire mahogany writing and work table in the style of Jacob-Desmalter.

many chairs is that the arm supports and front legs are formed of a single piece of wood. Sometimes the backs are vertical and could hardly have provided much comfort, but others are concave with what is called the gondola back, providing a degree of comfort yet retaining a dignity of form.

Stools were also very popular, the most common form having four legs forming an "X." Some stools have a covering of intricately woven tapestry complete with tasseled border.

Couchettes were made in considerable numbers. Small, simple and con-

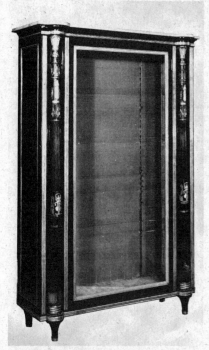

Empire ormolu-mounted mahogany "Bibliotheque" with Carrara marble top.

Emperor. They worked on the task of restoring the magnificence of royal palaces looted by revolutionary mobs.

There was Lerpscher who specialized in beds with grey, painted panels. There were the billiard tables of Pannetier, the screens of Villaume, the musical instruments of Sebastien Erard, especially his pianofortes made of the finest woods and supported on bronze caryatids or sphinxes.

The work of Pierre-Philippe Thomire (1751–1843), supreme master of the art of gilding, must also be mentioned. Thomire worked for Sevres and made use of this porcelain especially for table tops.

Giant among cabinet-makers was Jacob Desmalter (1770–1841). Born

Side table with inlaid top and gilded ornaments.

Round table with inlaid marble top and partly carved legs. Stretchers on this piece are surprisingly plain.

Upright secretaire with inlaid top.

Round table with grey marble top.

ventional, these beds had ends of equal height with legs on castors and a pediment at the end bearing a single ornamented motif.

Sofas tended to be more a triumph of the upholsterer's art with the wooden structure buried from view.

Console tables have richly ornamented friezes and were supported by caryatids, eagles, or great winged figures. Some have tops of the finest marble cut very cunningly so that the best markings are visible. An interesting trick, often used with these tables, was the provision of a mirror between the back legs. By reflecting the front legs this conveyed the illusion of greater size.

Gueridons were circular pedestal tables with the supports usually of baluster shape though there are many with three columns. Some gueridons are of a truly regal appearance with marble tops and heavily ornamented with bronze. Thomire, who made many of them, preferred tops of

Sevres porcelain. The word gueridon is believed to have been derived from a Moorish galley slave of that name.

There are numerous other items such as the *Table a Chevet*—a bedside table made usually of fruitwood and which can be rectangular or cylindrical. There were also Antheniennes— tripods used for various purposes but most commonly found acting as support for a wash-basin.

The somno was a bedside table almost square with a single decorated door at the front. Other items were cheval glasses, fire screens, bureaux and the *Table a la Tronchin,* a multipurpose table with an adjustable top so that it could serve as a reading or writing table or for toilet purposes. Commodes had two or three doors and were fitted inside with drawers or shelves.

Paris in those years was the center of fashion and taste. Haussmann had not yet driven his boulevards through the old city, but the first pavement cafes were appearing; the restaurants that were to lead to the future temples of gastronomy were being established, and Empire furniture was made to fit the grand Napoleonic concept.

When the war between America and England ended in 1814, Americans were understandably in no mood to appreciate English styles, but the French emigre craftsmen seized upon the Empire style just as the Napoleonic era was coming to an end. They adapted it to suit the needs and simpler tastes of the New World.

The Imperial motifs were left out and replaced by such symbols as the American eagle and George Washington's head. Ornamentation generally was subdued. American Empire furniture is a subject in its own right, being a distant emigrant cousin of an original ancestor.

THE BEGINNINGS OF BENTWOOD FURNITURE

by FLORENCE THOMPSON HOWE

BENTWOOD CHAIRS are in style again, equally at home in contemporary as in traditional interiors. Their origin was in Austria, and if you are fortunate, you may find a maker's name burned, painted, or glued on the inside rim of the round seat of your old Vienna Bentwood rocker, or "soda fountain" chair or table. If you are doubly lucky, it may be Thonet's mark or label for Michael Thonet (pronounced "Tonnet" as in bonnet), who lived from 1796–1871, is the acknowledged originator of the Bentwood chair.

Bentwood, the bending of wet wood, was practiced by country woodworkers, probably by wheelwrights, from earliest times. Though Thonet was a humble cabinet maker of the Rhineland, his inventiveness and skill caught the attention of Clemens von Metternich, the Austrian chancellor. In 1842, the Prince summoned Thonet to Vienna. For the next five years the gifted artisan worked on the neo-rococo interiors of the Lichtenstein Palace. Some of Thonet's work there included bent solid wood, pieces subcontracted through the important firm of Carl Leisther & Son, who were decorating the palace. By 1849, Thonet was established as the most important furniture designer of the Empire. The Emperor himself was one of his patrons.

By bending all parts of his chairs, designed so as to utilize the special strength of such parts scientifically joined together, Thonet developed a chair which he could produce rapidly. It was light, comfortable, and curvilinear, suited to both domestic and commercial use. His components, in his curvacious forms, could be inexpensively made in huge quantities by semi-skilled labor and shipped profitably to more or less distant markets. He was ready for mass production.

In 1849 Thonet closed his shop in Vienna and opened a factory in what is now Czechoslovakia. He himself designed the factory, the machines, and the conveyor belt system, and turned out his furniture in hitherto unheard-of quantities. His patent expired in 1869, but his work can be identified

Imprinted signature of J. & J. Kohn, Wsetin, Austria, on underside of the Vienna Bentwood dining chair. Photo by Robert Orwig.

Bentwood rocking chair purchased in Sanford, Florida, in the early 1900s. Collection Miss Martha Fox. (Another chair of this same design, also owned by Miss Fox, bears the inscription "J. & J. Kohn, Wsetin, Austria.") Photo by Robert Orwig.

Vienna Bentwood dining chair bearing imprinted signature "J. & J. Kohn, Wsetin, Austria." Purchased in Springfield, Mass. Early 1900s. Photo by Robert Orwig.

by his own burned in or glued-on label.

In the wake of Thonet's success, scores of German artisans, also bent on making quick fortunes, got aboard. Mass production in furniture, the pot of gold at the end of the cabinet-maker's rainbow, had been found. What better market than the affluent, ease-loving Americans? By the turn of the century, importers and jobbers in New York (and doubtless other metropolitan areas) were putting Vienna Bentwood rocking-chairs into the most remote parlors in the U.S.A. They are still rocking today—in the winter-home of the late Everett Dirksen in Florida: in a studio set pictured on a cover of *TV Guide*, with mini-skirted teenager enjoying the soothing to-and-fro.

How many of Thonet's copyists, imitators, and competitors followed his practice of branding their products with their own names is anybody's guess. Other labeled Bentwoods are beginning to turn up, and like all labeled or documented furniture, are being sought by collectors, dealers, and students in the antiques field.

The rocking chair pictured here, was purchased of a local furniture dealer in Sanford, Florida, in the early 1900s. The dealer's son, now 92 years

Bentwood table exhibited by Michael Thonet of Vienna, Austria, at the Crystal Palace Exhibition (1851). The table was entirely made of rosewood and walnut, slightly inlaid with delicate lines of brasswork. The top, which lifted to reveal a semi-spherical receptacle beneath, was elaborately inlaid with woods of various colors.

old, identified the chair and recalled the purchaser's name. "We got those chairs from Austria," he told us.

"Do you know who made them?" we asked.

He did indeed. It was J. & J. Kohn. There proved to be no identifying mark on this rocking-chair; however, "J. & J. Kohn, Wsetin, Austria," are the words stamped indelibly on the inside rim of the chair-seat on the host-chair of a dining set of Vienna Bentwoods picked up in Springfield, Massachusetts, at the turn of the century! A drawing of it appears in American Heritage's *Antiques After the Civil War to World War I* (pg. 386).

In 1851, Thonet furniture was displayed before a large public at the Crystal Palace in London. Inevitably it was soon being duplicated by American manufacturers. In 1890, remarking on its continued popularity, one of the leading decorating magazines pointed out that bentwood had obtained "a certain status owing to its neatness, finish, lightness, and great strength, although its lines seem excessively curvaceous — beyond those limits which the eye follows with pleasure."

In recognition of the historical importance of Thonet's designs, Harvard University showed a collection of his work at Carpenter Center for the Visual Arts in Cambridge, Mass., for two months, opening in December 1967.

Combination Bootjack and Towel Rack

by F. M. GOSLING

BOOT WEARERS, and there are more of them every day, as well as boot jack collectors might like to know about, and be on the lookout for, a combination Boot Jack and Towel Rack like the one pictured here.

Recently, while thumbing through Wallace Nutting's *Furniture Treasury*, we came across an illustration of this piece which was noted as being in the Monroe Tavern, Lexington, Mass. As a collector, we were intrigued, and set out to find an example. Lucky we were to locate one in less than 30 days, proof that it is not an impossible feat.

According to the paper label affixed to the back, these walnut boot jacks, made about 100 years ago, were manufactured by Clemens Darnstaedt

in Meriden, Conn. The Museum of the Meriden Historical Society, Inc., to whom we wrote, owns two, and the curator, Miss Anna B. Sands, kindly furnished information about Mr. Darnstaedt from the Meriden City Directories.

In 1873-74, he was listed as a piano key manufacturer; in 1875, as "Darnstaedt & Kraemer, Furniture and Upholstery"; in 1876, simply as a furniture dealer; and in 1878, as a picture frame and furniture dealer. By 1883, there was no record at all.

It is likely that manufacturing his Boot Jack and Towel rack was a sideline to his other businesses. How many of these useful articles he made and sold, no one knows, but it is reasonable to assume there are still a few

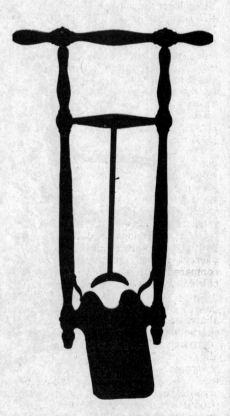

around, gathering dust in attics or barns, particularly in the northeastern United States.

The Evolution

of the Desk

by JOHN CUMMINGS

Fig. 1—(Left) Unrestored 17th century carved oak desk box, or "Bible box," perhaps English, no thorough tests have been made. Courtesy Robert Durand.
Fig. 2 — (Above) Slope-front American desk box of pine, probably early 18th century. Formerly the author's.

Fig. 3 — "Deske" or desk-on-frame, oak and pine, 17th century style. Author's collection.

Fig. 4—William and Mary desk-on-frame, cherry, done with some elegance. Privately owned.

THE FIRST settlers in this country brought with them carved oaken boxes to hold papers, writing materials, and their few books, at least, a Bible. Early collectors dubbed these "Bible boxes," and the name has stuck. Wallace Nutting wisely questioned this nomenclature, pointing out that the presence of a till, and often a lock, did not indicate a primary purpose as repository for the Good Book.

It seems quite certain that these were, in reality, desk boxes; also that those brought here were soon copied by colonial craftsmen. It is by no means easy to be sure whether a piece is of English or of local origin. Certain tests are helpful, but not infallible.

The English were accustomed to use oak throughout, whereas a colonial example usually has the bottom, sometimes the lid, and occasionally the back, of pine. Carving on an American piece is apt to be less intricate and less skillful. Finally, there is considerable difference between the English oak (a bog oak, *quercus robur*), dark and coarse as compared with the American white oak *(quercus alba)*, which has a more golden color and a finer, more figured grain. Conditions of wear, weathering, abuse, and later finishes can obscure characteristics, making an accurate "diagnosis" difficult. If doubt exists—and it might be wise on general principles — a small sample of the wood should be submitted to some organization such as the Forest Products Laboratory where microscopic examination will almost always yield a correct answer. (See *Fig*. 1.)

It was soon found that a sloping lid added greatly to convenience. The same may also be said for constructing compartments in the interior. Pine replaced oak early, and carving disappeared. These points are well illustrated by the American desk box in *Fig*. 2. While 17th century in style and construction, it was made probably during the first quarter of the 18th century.

When, or why, or how the desk box acquired a frame to support it is difficult to say. Perhaps some joiner, working on a box upon a table decided that box and table frame built as a unit would be an improvement. Possibly an owner came to the realization that since the box was usually placed upon a table, legs might be added to support it at a convenient height. There can be little doubt that this change came about in the last years of the 17th century, but that its real flowering came in the 18th century.

The new form is well shown by *Fig*. 3. Those structural members where strength is required—the legs and stretchers — are American white oak, but the flat areas of the box portion are red pine or larch. Its design and the embellishment of the understructure by chamfers have a medieval character. The lid, which opens or raises upward, is attached by dovetailed hinges (applied with hand-wrought nails), and finished with a bold, thumbnail moulding. Some nearly identical specimens are known, all found in or near Newington, Connecticut. A revival of this form in the 19th century gave us the "Schoolmaster's Desk."

The transition to a greater elegance of the style of William and Mary occurred in the first years of the 18th century, as seen in *Fig*. 4. This piece was obviously designed and constructed by a well-trained craftsman. The box and base are separate units, but the earlier pine and oak have now been replaced by cherry. The lid now hinges at the front and falls forward to be supported upon slides to serve

Fig. 5—Desk in Queen Anne style, cherry with button feet. Formerly Joseph Downs collection. Courtesy William Downs.

as a writing surface. It might have been made as early as 1710 or as late as 1740.

While we may do some violence to chronology, it is better perhaps to follow stylistic evolution. The next type is usually termed a Queen Anne button-foot, as depicted in *Fig.* 5. The development from the preceding style is fairly obvious. The chief differences lie in the changed character of turnings; also, stretchers have been dispensed, and the tops and base are a single unit. The wood is cherry and a date, ca. 1730-1750, might be safely suggested.

Shortly after 1700, a new form made its appearance, which has exerted influence upon desk design ever since. The lower portion, in essence a case of drawers, was surmounted by a slat front desk structure. The lid opened forward to be supported upon slides. Just inside there was a

or they could achieve most pleasing and interesting contours. One, of this period, termed the serpentine front, is shown in *Fig.* 7. Drawer fronts are cut from a single thick plank; thus much labor was expended as well as a considerable wastage of fine lumber. This bears some resemblance to the famous "block front" type, but is not so rare, nor nearly so costly though by no means cheaply or easily acquired. This example is cherry, of New England origin, and probably dates about mid-18th century.

The later Georgian styles were profoundly influenced by Thomas Chippendale. There has been all too little published about the Chippendale style in New York furniture but, at its best, it is fully equal to the famed Philadelphia school. It is somewhat restrained in size and embellishment. The piece shown in *Fig.* 8 is open to show the elegant interior. The pro-

Fig. 6 — Typical example of William and Mary style; figured walnut, ball feet. The Misses Downs Collection. Courtesy William Downs.

Fig. 7 — Shaped front, so popular in Georgian years, of sort called serpentine. Courtesy Mr. & Mrs. G. W. Wilson.

Fig. 8—Chippendale elegance in a New York desk. Collection Mr. John Kent.

most curious construction, located behind what would be the top drawer of the carcass of the piece. This was the well, access to which was gained by lifting a flat piece in the writing surface, and which perhaps may have been a naive concept of secrecy.

The interiors were elegantly fitted with pigeon holes and drawers, while all exterior surfaces were of beautiful walnut, chosen for its grain and color, or else veneered with this same wood. (Veneer was frequently almost ⅛-inch thick!) This use of fine walnut together with the beautiful, bold, ball feet are characteristically William and Mary style, which may have retained popular favor as late as the Georgian desks could be quite plain, 1730s. (See *Fig.* 6.)

portion, particularly the cabriole understructure is flawless, while ample interior space is provided without massiveness or bulk. The carved ornamentation leaves little to be desired. In fact this piece evoked the admiration of no less connoisseur than the late Joseph Downs. It would be safe to assign a date ca. 1760-1775.

The post-Revolutionary years denuded the desk of no little of its former grandeur. Interiors were more simple while the exteriors depended upon fine woods, with or without inlay or special veneered effects. Almost invariably these were supported upon a bracket foot or upon the so-called "French foot." The curvilinear supporting members, such as the ogee foot, were completely out-of-favor.

Fig. 9 — Country "Sherawhite" desk in butternut. Courtesy Raymond Soderburg.

The smaller or better proportioned pieces, made by skilled craftsmen in urban localities, are quite delightful, but the somewhat inept work in rural sections sometimes produced bulky or even rather crude results. (See *Fig.* 9.)

Sheraton's later designs embraced one quite different form, as shown in *Fig.* 10. It was designed for the butler to use in management of the household and gives the appearance of a hybrid between a fall front desk and sideboard. The family accounts were kept in the desk portion, which is behind the large, central upper drawer. On either side of the top were deep "bottle drawers," while the remaining drawers served for limited storage of linens, silver, *et alia.* This design never gained the widespread popularity of the slant-top, but is by no means a rarity or of important value.

Should one visit the furniture department of any store today, the styles or designs offered will undoubtedly show the influence of the Hepplewhite-Sheraton slant top desks.

Not Quite Antiques

by DOROTHEA and JAMES SHIPE

IN SPITE of the spate of books about antiques, the nation-wide movement of collecting would seem to have out-distanced the required educational program by which just anyone can know the difference between the genuine antique and its much later counterpart.

Yes, there are some very specialized tomes for the delection of the already well educated and opulent collectors. These people *know* what's what. But we speak for the general collector, the beginning collector — the people who, in this day and age, must exercise considerably more caution in their buying because there are pitfalls extant that weren't around when today's experts were tryos. We need not only to consider what is good and a sound investment, we should also know what to avoid.

When recently we fell heir to a lot of early decorating and furniture magazines, dating from 1890 to 1896, we began to notice furniture of the very sort the unwary, finding today as secondhand, would imagine to be genuine antiques. Make no mistake, please. We are not talking about *fakes.* The furniture in question was honestly made, as new goods, some sixty years ago [now seventy] to allow the then top drawer vogue of collecting antiques!

One designer of 1893 said, "Because the public soon wearies of calm refinement and good taste, the lamp of beauty must be stimulated by these sidelights of quaintness." This was said in the year of the great Chicago World's Columbian Exposition, when public taste was at so low an ebb

there was nothing for it to do but rise.

This era moved into reproduction from the antique, *with variations.* The variations were largely of Victorian and Eastlake genre. Better taste *was* expressed and, for any town or city settled after 1888, this furniture indeed may be considered an antique of the locality. But it is not an antique in fact and most certainly not to be purchased as antique — at antique prices. By all means, let it be bought by who will, but as second-hand.

If someone should compile a book of pictures of near antiques so that collectors could *know* and not wonder, speculate, and be undecided, the story might begin over a century ago with the commentary of T. Webster and Mrs. Parker in *Encyclopedia of Domestic Economy,* 1845: "It may be proper to state in what way our shops are filled with *ancient furniture* to satisfy the present demand. There are many who imagine they are obtaining genuine examples . . . . Much comes from the Continent and a great deal is taken to pieces, . . the ornamental parts preserved and made into articles . . . ." In Carl Drepperd's *Handbook of Antique Chairs,* one reads about Cummerford of New York City in the 1850s making replicas of Brewster, Carver, and Winslow chairs, from old wood!

We hope such a book may sometime appear. Meanwhile, here are some pictures we have found. Incidentally we have found some of the furniture, too, and purchased one piece of it, thinking it was real. Now you know why we *had* to write this!

289 Furniture

Fig. 10—Sheraton butler's desk, mahogany, maple interior. Collection Mrs. Henry Rowe.

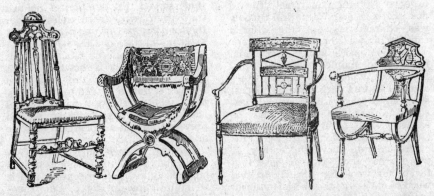

Left to right: *"King William III" style chair, as advertised in 1893; "Spanish antique" chair, as made in 1892; "Sheraton-Empire" chair of the late 1890s; "Antique Spanish" chair, 1893.*

EARLY AMERICAN CANDLESTANDS

by John Cummings

Fig. 1—17th century type stand. "X" base is oak, pinned together by dowel at bottom of boldly turned maple pedestal; top is first growth pine; considerable old paint, probably original finish, is retained. Attribution of the last years of the century seems justifiable. Formerly in the Joseph Downs Collection. Courtesy William Downs.

Fig. 2—Stand with "T" base, sometimes attributed to 17th century, but more probably early 18th.

Fig. 3—William & Mary stand, maple with pine top secured by wooden pins, believed of Massachusetts origin; double curvature at knee is considered rare, early; original paint.

CANDLESTANDS were in use in 17th century America, and all standard works on furniture illustrate pieces attributed to that era. These almost invariably have what is known as an "X" base. Two pieces, lying flat upon the floor and joined at right angles at their centers, are held together by a dowel or tenon at the lower end of the handsomely turned post. Elaborate and beautiful turning was characteristic of the Pilgrim century, as was the use of oak.

The apprentice system, poor and irregular communications, and a slowness with which newer styles were adopted caused early designs to persist long after the dates usually assigned to the pieces. Oak and ash, the earliest woods to be employed, were stubbornly retained in use by a few craftsmen into the 18th century. It was learned early that maple was a far better wood for turning, so this wood soon became the chosen material for the lathe.

Although bases and shafts were of hard wood, the tops most frequently were of native white pine (pinus

strobus), since no great strength was required. Tops were small and generally fastened to the batten with hard wood pegs, since a shortage of iron made nails a scarce commodity. The batten, in a like manner, was fastened to the top of the pedestal with wooden pins. Later, wedges inserted into cuts in the top of the shaft served this function of holding the batten (wooden crosspiece under the top) in a neater and often equally satisfactory fashion. (See Fig. 1)

Another early form, having what is termed a "T" base is shown in Fig. 2. Most students place this sort at a little later date and tend to the theory that this type base is a special adaptation. Perhaps its design was to prevent upset in a workroom or shop or tavern.

The sort termed the style of William and Mary makes appearance quite early in the 18th century and is well illustrated in Fig. 3. Fine turnery, with an early flavor, continues, but the pedestal is supported by three arched legs with a cabriole curvature. The pedestal projects downward be-

low the junction with the legs and ends in a refined bit of turnery. Legs are fastened into the pedestal with a mortise and tenon joint secured with wooden pins.

During the second quarter of the 18th century, it became the practice to secure the legs to the pedestal by wedge-shaped joints, or dovetails; with this alteration the pedestal no longer projected downward.

Stands which might be called Queen Anne-Early Georgian are characterized by light, beautiful turnings. At this time the tip-top and the shaped or "dish-top" or moulded top makes an appearance. Some of the stands from the middle colonies are of mahogany.

New England stands of this era tend to bolder turnery. (See Fig. 4). They are usually in cherry or maple, and the maple may be plain or figured. While mahogany was sometimes used in the seacoast towns, walnut seems to have been employed rarely in the northern sections.

Southern stands employed bold turnings, but of a different sort, as can be seen from *Fig. 5*. Here walnut was the favored wood, often with a bit of inlay in the top. The bases usually rose higher above the floor (from floor to bottom of pedestal) than in other sections, though this same feature occurs occasionally in stands from eastern New Hampshire. Tops are frequently octagonal, or hexagonal, with applied edge strips.

A break in the continuity of design occurred during the Revolutionary War, and some pieces produced soon after the peace show a certain mingling of pre-war and post-war styles. The new taste followed the designs of Shearer, Hepplewhite and Sheraton, which introduced a certain spareness or lightening, with less emphasis upon turning.

The full emergence of the Federal styles—those styles Holloway so aptly dubbed "Sherawhite" — does away completely with the earlier cabriole curvature. The legs exhibit continuous downward curvature, almost the arc of a circle, and are known as a "spider" leg. In better examples this leg terminates in a block which tapers downward. The term "spade foot" is used to describe this feature, usually credited to Hepplewhite, but possibly an innovation of Shearer.

These new concepts are illustrated very well in *Figs. 6* and *7*. On both, the pedestal turnings are good, but a declension may be noticed from earlier examples. Both show the spider leg with a spade foot. While mahogany was used widely, paint and/or painted decoration, as advocated by George Hepplewhite, found much favor. In addition to black, other colors were employed, a soft ivory being very popular. Of the same style and era is the mahogany tip-top stand of *Fig. 7*. Another difference is here to be noticed in the sharply oval top not seen prior to the Revolution.

At the end of the first decade of the 19th century, both design and workmanship began a rapid deterioration. Factory production was displacing the craftsman. Stands of the Empire and early Victorian modes show coarse, heavy pedestals. (See *Fig. 8*) These pedestals often project below the joint with the legs, but one should not for a moment confuse these with the superb examples of a century earlier. Crude turnings and poorly fitted mortise and tenon joints, glued in place, proclaim immediately what period the piece is.

In addition to graceless curvature, legs are usually cut from wood of insufficient thickness, hence do not give adequate support. These incorrectly designed stands are not very useful; most of them come unglued, or a leg snaps easily. It is well worth the time and effort of a prospective purchaser of candlestands to do some serious research in advance.

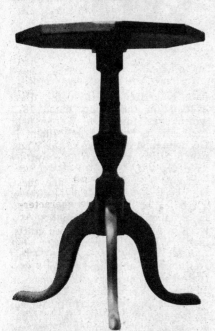

Fig. 4—Fine Georgian stand of New England origin, mid-18th century. Courtesy Mr. and Mrs. Brewer Dean.

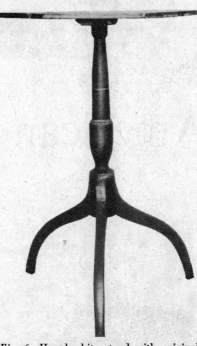

Fig. 6—Hepplewhite stand with original black paint and gold leaf decoration as done in urban centers of style—Boston, New York, Baltimore.

Fig. 5—Southern walnut stand found in Charlottesville, Virginia, made about the time of the Revolution. Height of base, elegant turnery and design of top are noteworthy.

Fig. 7—Mahogany Hepplewhite style tip-top stand; base, spade foot very fine. Courtesy Raymond Soderburg.

Fig. 8—Debased form of 19th century; note crude, heavy pedestal, graceless legs, structurally weak.

Figure 1: C. 1670-1680. Coll. The Misses Downs.

by JOHN CUMMINGS

Early American Chests

IF THE first settlers to reach our shores brought any furniture with them, it was a chest. This convenient container held their possessions during the voyage; it was equally useful for storage after their arrival, and could also double as a seat or a table.

The chest goes back almost to the dawn of civilized history; perhaps it is the primary item. It has a long religious history. According to Wallace Nutting, the Ark of the Covenant was a chest. If so, this may be the reason 16th century English joiners who wrought oak into chests were called arkwrights.

The nailed, sixboard construction, like a sea chest or a box, was not uncommon, but the paneled, oak style-and-rail product of well trained joiners, as in *Figure 1,* is most characteristic of our earliest period. It is recorded that John Alden, of the Pilgrim settlement, made oak chests, as did Kenelm Winslow, a younger brother of Edward Winslow, Governor of "Plimoth." From such early beginnings, oak paneled chests were made in many variations in Massachusetts and Connecticut until the first quarter of the 18th century.

The fine example shown in *Figure 1* depends upon applied ornaments and geometrically arranged moldings for decoration. Some are embellished with scratch carving—a shallow cutting in very low relief. Combinations of the various methods are not uncommon. The earliest "signed" piece of American furniture is the chest Nicholas Disbrowe of Hartford, Connecticut, made about 1680 for Mary Allyn, daughter of Col. John Allyn, Secretary of the Colony.

American white oak *(quercus alba)* may be difficult to distinguish from English oak, but the liberal use of pine for panels, bottoms, back, and/or

Figure 2: C. 1670-90 Author's Collection.

lids usually indicates a native example. Several sorts of pine were used—white pine *(pinus strobus),* red pine *(pinus resinos)* even pitch pine *(pinus rigida).* Occasionally larch *(larix laricina),* is found. Early panels were installed with the flat, smooth surface exposed, the bevel being inside in the true medieval fashion.

About 1670, or a few years earlier, there appeared in southern Connecticut a distinctive form of chest of pitch pine *(Figure 2).* These are board or nailed construction, quite long, and rather narrow. They depend for decoration upon elegant sheathed or "linen fold" moldings. The end boards are notched or gouged-carved and extend below the chest to form a bootjack foot. They seem to have originated in the vicinity of Long Island Sound around Saybrook, Connecticut. The example shown came from that area, as did an identical specimen, formerly in the Joseph Downs collection. The

date is arrived at from the finest example of the group, dated 1673, which was found in Wethersfield, Connecticut, by the late William B. Goodwin, and is on loan to the Wadsworth Atheneum. (Nutting *Furniture Treasury* #94.)

Figure 3 shows a rare, fine chest, with very early painted decoration, of a type called "Guilford." These striking productions were undoubtedly the work of a skilled, well-trained craftsman. While researching for her *Cabinet Makers of America,* Ethel Hall Bjerkoe uncovered evidence that these chests may have been made in Saybrook, Connecticut. The chest illustrated has been carefully studied: as far as can be determined, it has always been in Saybrook. There are no evidences that it ever had feet, unless, perhaps, they were of the loose, separate type as found on a small group of chests from the North Shore of Long Island.

There is a small group of chests (*Figure 4*), sometimes referred to as "Greenfield Chests," so-called from a piece in the collection of G. B. Dyer of that city (Nutting *Furniture Treasury* #241). Evidence strongly indicates their origin was in the Greenfield-Deerfield area of Massachusetts. Rev. C. F. Luther, author of *The Hadley Chest*, expressed opinion that these were fabricated by Hadley workers. They are completely 17th century in their concept, design, and construction, but were probably produced around 1700 or shortly thereafter. Some half-dozen are known, most of them in light-colored native woods grained in imitation of walnut. They preserve the style-and-rail construction, with the posts continued below the chest body for support, those in front being ornamentally turned.

All examples have side-run drawers as shown in the photograph, flat panels, and single arch moldings. Most have drop brasses for handles. A "poor relation" of the family, painted Indian red, with wooden knobs, appeared in the La Fountain auction at Springfield, Vermont, in 1964.

Old Sturbridge Village exhibits an unusual chest upon ball feet and with painted decoration, *Figure 5*. An early feature that perseveres is the wooden pin hinge engaging in the end battens of the lid. The painted decoration simulates panels; actually it is of nailed construction. Its date has been estimated as ca. 1700.

There are other interesting or even important variants of nailed chests with painted decoration. One should not overlook the Taunton group, with

Figure 3: Early 18th century. Privately owned.

rather nice vine and foliage decoration, bearing dates in the 1720s and 1730s. The decoration is creamy white, usually upon an iron oxide red background, though some have a black background. The turning of the feet is quite distinctive, although a few have the end boards extended in a bootjack foot. These have been attributed, with considerable certainty, to Robert Crossman. Illustrations may be found in Nutting's *Furniture Treasury* #104; Lockwood's *Colonial Furniture in America,* Vol. 1, p49, fig. 38; and Kettell's *Fine Furniture of Early New England,* p41.

Another sort, from southern Connecticut near Long Island Sound, are those Wallace Nutting christened "goose chests," a name prompted by the representation of this bird on

either end of the chest. An excellent example is on public view at The Old Stone House in Guilford, Connecticut.

Figure 6 shows a chest where Holland influence, so prevalent along the shores of Long Island Sound, is strongly evidenced both by the decoration and the owner's (?) name, *Elizabeth Klock*. However, not even among the most ultraconservative Dutch did the placing of a chest on shoes (those strips extending from front to rear to serve as feet) persist to any such relatively late date as this piece carries—1815. The shoe, as a supporting member, was decidedly out of fashion a quarter century prior to the Revolutionary War. Could it be this chest was constructed at an earlier date, then later decorated and

(Please turn the page)

Figure 5: Coll. Mr. & Mrs. Jonathan Swift.

Figure 4: Early 18th century; showing detail of side run of drawer. Wilson Coll.

Figure 6: Coll. Mr. & Mrs. Jonathan Swift.

Figure 7: Upper drawers are simulated. Author's collection.

inscribed for a daughter or grand-daughter?

The story of the chest begins with a simple chest. Almost immediately came a "chest with a draw." Such an arrangement was found so much more convenient that it became a chest with drawers, and finally a chest-of-drawers, the upper, hinged-lid, storage section having been crowded out. Toward the end, even when the upper bin section is retained, drawer fronts are simulated, as shown in *Figure 7*. Early 18th century documents very frequently refer to chests as "old."

Let no one hastily arrive at a conclusion that chests went immediately, suddenly, and completely into abandonment. They had their merits as storage space; they were easily constructed by relatively unskilled workers; and their cost was trifling. In rural regions, chests continued to be made and used into the last century. *Figure 8* shows such a survival from western Massachusetts. It is of the more simple sort, made about 1800, and grained in imitation of mahogany to give a touch of refinement.

Late chests lack the skilled design and workmanship of those of earlier date and have less attractiveness and value. These survivals may be painted iron oxide red or smalt blue or, in some instances, be "grained." A friendly word of caution — stripping these decimates their value as an antique, as a pleasing piece of furniture, and in monetary worth.

Figure 8: C. 1800. Coll. Mrs. Florence Haeberle.

Turned settee brought from Normandy to Salem, Mass., in 1685 by family of Hugue-nots. Turkey Work is well worn off today, but still discernible pattern shows strong Oriental influence.

Turkey Work by AMELIA MacSWIGGAN

MUCH can be learned of Colonial ways and days from the meticulously detailed household inventories kept by early comers to this country. Cooking utensils, furniture, clothing, linens, table appointments were included along with tools and kindred objects. Many of the items are familiar today. Others, particularly in the range of textiles and embroideries have passed into disuse, and their very names are alien to present-day vocabularies.

Such an almost forgotten term is "Turkey Work", yet from 16th century England to the 1850s in America it appeared in countless inventories, describing rugs, wall hangings, covers for chairs and sofas, and throws for tables and chests.

This work, which falls into the category of embroidery, was made in imitation of the costly Oriental carpets woven with a knotted pile in such countries as Persia and Turkey—hence, no doubt, its name. Copying the techniques of Oriental rug makers, early English and Continental needle-women tied, rather than wove, their Turkey Work patterns, drawing the wool through a foundation cloth of heavy mesh, and using the "ghiordes" knot when rugs with heavy pile were desired, or the "sehna" knot for lighter weight pieces.

Early patterns were somewhat uniform, but as workers learned to sketch their own designs, patterns showed more individuality and were seldom alike. Oriental motifs, with full black outline, were most usually adapted. Chairs covered with Turkey Work were frequently embellished with fancy gimps, fringes, and tassels.

Before imports of wool were available from Germany, Americans used mainly English lamb's wool. worsteds, and crewels from England for their embroideries. The name "worsted" derives from the town of that name in Norfolk, England, where the manufacture of woolen yarn and thread was introduced during the reign of Edward III in the 14th century. The terms "Worsted Work" and "Turkey Work", particularly in rural areas, were often used interchangeably. In city newspapers, expert workers advertised to teach the art, and furnish materials "at nominal sums".

A "Turkie rugg" was fashioned by Mollie Stark of Vermont, the wife of General John Stark of Revolutionary War fame, for their daughter Polly on her marriage in the 1770s. The foundation of this rug consisted of an old blanket, and the colored wool was pulled through the meshes by means of a simple hook. This rug may now be seen in the rooms of the Daughters of the American Revolution in Washington, D. C.

The rich colors of Oriental carpets, made of vegetable extractions by secret formula, were attempted, too, in Turkey Work, with dyes concocted from the madder plant, from dried bodies of cochineals, from indigo, saffron, and sumac plants, gall nuts and onion skins, berries, and the barks of various trees.

With the advent of the power-carpet loom, invented by Erastus Brigham in 1839, the popularity of Turkey Work and, indeed, the need for hand-made rugs yielded to manufactured carpet. Simpler hooked or braided rugs made from left-over woolens, soon became the only handmade floor coverings in the home.

Turkey Work was attractive, durable, and highly regarded by early settlers who listed it proudly among their possessions. It is an art which might happily be revived as pleasant "home work" for to-day's craftsmen.

QUEEN ANNE

American Style Chairs

By John Cummings

NO STYLE emerges fully developed, nor should it be overlooked that a considerable time lag existed between the appearance of a new style in England and its acceptance in the Colonies. Thus many of the elements that we consider Queen Anne were actually a heritage from earlier designs in Britain.

The 17th century English chair, *Figure 1*, in the style of James II, clearly shows features which foreshadowed the Queen Anne style. (1) The back posts, instead of being turned (round), are of rectangular section, and (2) they bend backward in curvilinear fashion both above and below the seat. (3) The crest or top rail is doweled on top of the styles (posts) rather than being mortised between them. (4) An upright member in the middle of the back, which separates two caned panels, might be considered the prototype of a splat. (5) The front legs are square section and are cabriole, that is, their silhouette is a graceful cyma curve.

These five elements are important parts of the Queen Anne style chair, in which the top rail assumed a graceful double "Hogarth" (cyma) curve and simulated a continuation of the back posts. By the time of the accession of Anne, in 1702, the splat (the perpendicular, urn-shaped member in the back) had achieved full development, and the Queen Anne style, quite Dutch in feeling, had evolved.

In America, the Queen Anne style may date as early as 1710. *Figure 2*,

1. Col. The Misses Downs

2. Col. Mr. & Mrs. Jonathan Swift

3. Col. Mrs. J. S. Cozzens

4. Privately owned

5. Col. Mr. & Mrs. Gerar Raipel

a very early American chair of this style, clearly illustrates the points discussed. It is maple; it came from Rhode Island, and quite possibly was made there. The back posts are finely molded, with the molding continued on to the yoke. A "saddle" at the center of the yoke is lightly carved, reminiscent of the William and Mary period. A graceful, flattened curve to the upper back (called "spooned") adds greatly to its appearance as well as to the comfort of the sitter. Cabriole front legs of the earliest type are square in section, with a bead (molding) on the exposed edges. The understructure is braced with finely turned rungs or stretchers — again a perserverance of previous work. It merits the adjectives rare, early, and desirable!

Another early variety, *Figure 3*, is quite aptly dubbed "New England Queen Anne." Above the seat it is almost identical to *Figure 2*, but its underbody is pure William and Mary. It has exterior underbracing and "block and vase" turned front legs, terminating in bold Spanish feet. A considerable number of these chairs were produced for "people of substance" from perhaps as early as 1710 until as late as 1735. They are still occasionally available, and are desirable, serviceable chairs.

Elements of design or construction on certain Queen Anne chairs have stirred controversy. One of them is the rectangular bracing of understructure at sides and back, as in *Figure 3*. Some collectors maintain this is an attempt toward more clean-lined simplicity and/or additional rigidity; others that this construction resulted from lack of knowledge or skill on the part of the maker. The writer subscribes to neither of these views, believing that this design and construction neither adds merit nor detracts from a good chair.

"Spooning" of back posts is a graceful and most desirable feature, contributing to both beauty and comfort, but it does not necessarily follow that a ramped back (one that leans toward the rear but is straight, as in *Figure 4*) is the poor product of an unskilled, unimaginative, rural craftsman. Some elderly chairmakers, knowledgeable and of no small skill, very likely held tenaciously to certain accustomed forms, even though they accepted and used elements of a newer fashion. The chair of *Figure 4* is not the work of any clumsy, country carpenter; perhaps this type of chair is early rather than unimaginative. While many collectors prefer a Spanish foot, the well turned pearshaped sort is not objectionable, and is much less common.

Armchairs exhibit the general characteristics of the side chairs. However, a new shaping of the arm appears with an emphasis on outward curvature in a horizontal plane. On many, and often the best examples, the curvature is two dimensional, producing a ram's-horn arm. This is well illustrated by the graceful arms of

6. Col. Dr. & Mrs. Earl Henne

7. Privately owned.

8. Col. Mr. & Mrs. Jonathan Swift

9. Col. Mr. & Mrs. Jonathan Swift

Figure 5, which splay outward and curve in the vertical plane as well. The upper surface is carefully molded, and there is embellishment of the roll at the forward termination.

As the period progresses further, refinements appear, as the rounding of the front cabriole leg to effect slimness. Underbracing is dispensed with to achieve a further illusion of lightness, though possibly at the expense of sturdiness. Rhode Island workers rather generally continued the use of stretchers throughout the Queen Anne and even the Georgian periods. Where it was available, walnut was the wood preferred, but maple is found frequently, and cherry, occasionally.

The elegant chair of *Figure 6* shows the fully developed Queen Anne style. It is of carefully chosen walnut, and its graceful clean lines leave nothing to be desired. Its origin is Pennsylvania, near Philadelphia, perhaps even in that city. This chair has an up-

holstered slip seat—one which may be lifted out or removed.

Sometimes when a style achieves an exceedingly high degree of excellence, search for even greater elegance or further improvements results in superficialities. Corbusier and many earlier authorities have all stressed, "It is proper to embellish construction, but meretricious to construct embellishment." Carving begins to appear on the knee of the cabriole legs and on the front of the apron; there may be a shell at the center of the yoke. A curious jog is introduced in the previously smooth line of back posts, just above the seat; and the splat outline displays ever-increasing curves or curlicues. If, in addition to the frills noted, the wood is mahogany, we must conclude that pure Queen Anne is passing and undergoing transition to Georgian styles.

By 1725, a somewhat odd and very

different form of Queen Anne or "Dutch" chair appears. Often called "fiddle back chairs" in old inventories, they were produced in the northern counties of New Jersey, in the Hudson Valley, on Long Island, and in southern Connecticut. The background is Dutch, but Holland Dutch, rather than German as Nutting inferred in his *Furniture Treasury* (#2108).

The distinctive feature is the front leg which enlarges upward as a trumpet turning. This type of leg could be produced by turning in the lathe, using a very slow speed and two separate centers at the bottom— a method necessary to produce the graceful slim ankle and the pad or "Dutch" foot, or it could be shaped by the careful use of the draw shave. The excellent example in *Figure 7* comes from New Jersey, and the cutout embellishment of the splat is highly meritorious, as well as rare. It is one of a set which has never been out of the family of the original owner.

Another specimen of the type, *Figure 8,* is from Connecticut and exhibits an attractive heart cut-out in the splat, adding to attractiveness and value. This chair has its original iron oxide red paint. Such chairs were frequently painted brown, occasionally black, and on rare occasions, finished in the natural wood. Connecticut pieces are apt to be smaller and lighter than those from Jersey or the Hudson Valley.

During the second quarter of the 18th century, a simplified, rural modification appeared which retained popularity into the post-Revolutionary period, perhaps even as late as 1800. These are frequently called "Country Queen Anne chairs," a name both appropriate and descriptive. *Figure 9.* Produced by country workers, away from urban centers of style, they relied upon turning and sawing to curved outlines as a means of decoration, no doubt the result of the craftsman's meagre equipment together with his limited skills and knowledge. These pleasing chairs are still available, excellent for dining room or "occasional" use.

How may one differentiate between an English chair and one made in the Colonies? The answer is neither simple nor easy. Our native chairs were lighter, with a leaning toward more simple, clean-cut lines, and a nice feeling of proportion. They may be more generally appealing than the elegant, embellished imported examples. Lacquering, elaborately painted decoration, much carving, and intricacies of line usually point to English rather than American origin.

For the serious student or the collector wishing to pursue the subject further, Joseph Downs's *American Furniture, Queen Anne and Chippendale,* and Luke Vincent Lockwood's *Colonial Furniture in America,* pages 55-64, is invaluable.

Rocking Chairs Before 1840

by JOHN CUMMINGS

FIGURE 1
Author's Collection

THE PRINCIPLE of the rocker was known in Europe, and applied to cradles, years before the first colonists reached America. This fact should pretty well dispose of the tale that Benjamin Franklin invented the rocker. There are, indeed, examples of rocking chairs to be discussed here which pre-date his inventive genius.

At a meeting some months ago, a highly respected dealer was heard to remark, "Rockers are hard sellers, but it doesn't help to make up fancy stories to go with them." What he was trying to bring out is that fewer than one out of five of the early chairs offered today as rockers started their existence as such. Some were converted by craftsmen, as is amply illustrated by records in daybooks and ledgers. Many, ever so many, were "improved" by some more or less handy member of the household.

How does one determine whether the chair we are looking at is a changeling or is quite authentic? This is not too difficult for the careful dealer or experienced collector; examination quickly discloses an answer.

When chair posts were turned, it was customary to mark lightly with a chisel those places where the holes were to be bored for rungs, or mortises cut for slats. This same technique was utilized, by making scoring marks, to indicate the depth to which slots were to be cut to receive the rockers. Presence of these chisel cut lines or scoring marks below the lower rungs and at the top of the rocker slots is indisputable evidence that the chair was designed and constructed with rockers.

There are some few authentic original rocking chairs which may not exhibit this valuable "sign post"— these should be examined with great care by someone with considerable experience to determine authenticity.

The earliest style chair to appear with rockers is, as one might expect, the slat back. At least one 17th century example is known, such as that which was in the collection of H. G. Buck at "Home, Sweet Home," Easthampton, Long Island, New York.

FIGURE 2
Privately Owned

FIGURE 3
Mercer Museum

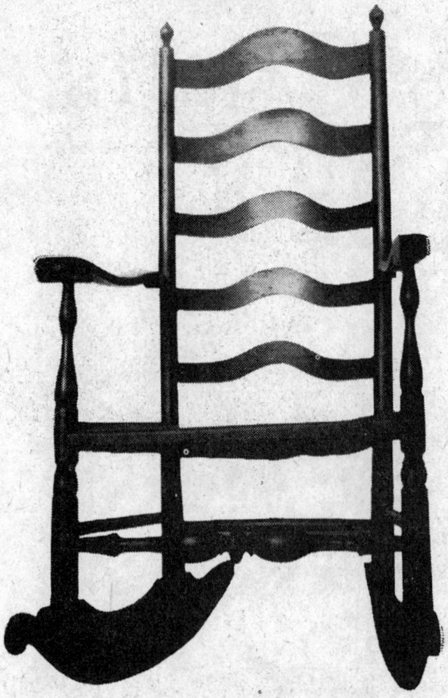

FIGURE 4
Privately Owned

FIGURE 5
Coll. Mrs. Hazel Hayes

FIGURE 6
Formerly the Author's

FIGURE 7
Formerly Jos. Downs' Coll.

FIGURE 10
Mr. & Mrs. Jonathan Swift

FIGURE 8
Coll. Mr. & Mrs. Robert Spear

FIGURE 9
Coll. Mr. & Mrs. Jonathan Swift

This is illustrated in Lockwood's *Colonial Furniture in America* (Vol. II, p 16, fig. 422). It exhibits an enlargement at the posts at the bottom to receive the rockers. Early 18th century specimens are known which show this same enlargement of the lower ends of the posts, as #1860 in Nutting's *Furniture Treasury*.

Fig. 1 shows an enitrely original slat back rocker of Connecticut origin, probably dating ca. 1720-1740. The scoring marks, indicating the depth of rocker slots, are plainly visible. Except for being re-seated, the piece has remained untouched or untampered with for more than two centuries. It is quite simple, but the turnery of arm supports and finials is well done and the graceful curvature of the arms is excellent. This short arm or double-bearing arm is an early feature which seems to have been more popular in Connecticut than in other localities. Other examples are shown in Lockwood's 3rd edition, Vol. II, p. 18, fig. 425.

Fig. 2 depicts an excellent New Jersey chair that was bequeathed as "olde grene chare" in 1749, and has always remained near Mount Holly. It still retains its original single coat of green paint. The entirely different size and symmetry of the rockers as compared with "northern" examples is worthy of note. Other details are entirely characteristic of its locality and period.

In the Mercer Museum in Doylestown, Pennsylvania, there is a fine five-slat rocker *(Fig. 3)* which epitomizes the best of its type. It is well documented, having been procured by John Dyer III for his wife in 1762. The Dyers built one of the earliest grist mills in Pennsylvania which they operated for several generations. The mill, now a restaurant, still stands in Dyerstown, a suburb of Doylestown. No chair could be in a more perfect state of preservation, with its original seat and untouched coat of reddish brown paint, doubtless the "tere de Siena" of the old advertisements.

During the early 19th century, small rocking chairs, bespeaking comfort and homeyness, were produced in rural New York State. Such a piece is shown in *Fig. 4* and, while not a rarity nor an antiquarian prize, it is pleasing and usable. A new structural feature makes appearance here—dowels are turned on the lower ends of the posts and these are inserted in holes bored in the rockers. This practice was not to have immediate widespread adoption, but as it was quicker, cheaper, and more suited to factory methods, it ultimately displaced the earlier method, as the production line was to eliminate the craftsman.

From almost their beginnings, Shaker communities were known for chair making, with perhaps the greatest emphasis on rocking chairs. At Canterbury, New Hampshire, this activity began early and was continued into the latter part of the 19th century. Quite rightly, their fine productions found widespread favor. The attractive little rocker of *Fig. 5* might very well be a product of the Canterbury Shakers, since it came from that vicinity and has the earmarks of such provenance. It is of beautifully grained "tiger" maple, with its original coat of varnish. It is light, graceful, and comfortable, and the workmanship is flawless. Instead of the more usual tape seat, this chair is rushed and its date may be the middle of the last century.

Not too many years ago the existence of an original bannister back rocker was unrecorded. Many collectors doubted the existence of one. Then the chair in *Fig. 6* appeared in an estate auction. The piece is in untouched, original condition, and shows plainly the scoring marks for the rocker slots. It is a late example (ca. 1765), toward the end of bannister back production and shows considerable Georgian influence.

Windsor chairs occur with rockers, but any of the earlier sorts are apt to be conversions. An 18th century example, the earliest known to the writer, was formerly in the collection of Joseph Downs *(Fig. 7)*. Even a glance at the illustration will demonstrate how the Windsor understructure was re-designed for the rockers, while the upper portion is the characteristic light New England comb-back.

Early in the 19th century, the late Windsors of that time, such as the double rail and the square back with comb, were not infrequently constructed as rocking chairs. An excellent example of this group is depicted in *Fig. 8*. This is the best example of the type known to the writer, and has always remained in the same family.

Windsor construction is the direct ancestor of that creation described by Wallace Nutting as "the most popular chair ever made, which people sit in, antiquarians despise, and novices seek." This is the Boston rocker *(Fig. 9)*, most of which were factory produced, literally by the thousand. They have an attractively free-hand painted decoration or a stencil on the top rail, as the illustration shows. Some confusion seems to exist between the Boston rocker and the so-called Salem rocker. The latter retains the flat Windsor seat, also a somewhat more simple but better designed top member.

At Hitchcocksville (now Riverton in the township of Barkhamstead), Connecticut, Lambert Hitchcock produced quantities of chairs by his unique combination of craft and factory methods. The operation lasted from 1826 until 1840. A few rocking chairs were produced, such as shown in *Fig. 10*, but these are rarely to be found. Decoration by the use of charming stencils is characteristic.

How Old Is The Rocking Chair?

by CARL W. DREPPERD

NUMEROUS commentaries, including some of my own, have "dated" the rocking chair as mid-18th century, say around 1750. Also, I plead guilty to the generally held habit of expressing pride that the rocking chair is an American colonial invention.

In the December issue of *Woman's Magazine*, 1949, published in London, G. Bernard Wood, Esq., comments in words and pictures on toys of long ago. One of the toys pictured is a child's rocking chair of truly Gothic quality. It was found in a London plague pit along with other shards and relics of the reign of King Charles I. S.H.Clemence, Esq. of Johannesburg, South Africa, sent a clipping with his compliments. Here, with my apology for past errors in both words and pictures about rocking chairs and their date is the only "amends" a commentator can make. All I can say is . . . I was wrong.

This plague pit rocker is a miniature, only three and a half inches high. When found at Moorfields it was treated chemically three times and then adjudged safe for handling. Amazingly, antiques found buried in plague pits (where victims of the awful plague were buried in haste by frantic officials) still bear the taint and the germ of a plague that devastated England, and especially London, three centuries ago.

Dolls, toys and other things are often found interred with child victims. Of the victims there is seldom a trace—but the toys, in most cases, are well preserved. Even the little seat cushion of this toy rocker, drawn 2/3 actual size above, was intact. This tiny toy is a new starting point in rocking chair research.

Characteristics of

EARLY SHAKER CHAIRS

by MARIUS B. PÉLADEAU

From the October-December, 1970 issue of "Historic Preservations," magazine of the National Trust for Historic Preservation. Text in italics has been added by the author since the initial publication of this article.

CHAIRS AND ROCKERS made by the Shakers reflect most perfectly the flawless grace and purity of line associated with all things Shaker. They are a distillation of that which the Shakers held most dear — the virtue of simplicity.

Because their functionalism, and cleanliness and sophistication of design make them ideally suited for decorating purposes in nearly every type of interior, Shaker chairs have become very collectible. Especially in the last decade, the interest in Shaker artifacts has become a "rage." Books on the Shakers are appearing at a great rate and collectors are, naturally, scouring antique shops and the by-ways of the countryside in an effort to find examples of Shaker craftsmanship.

As a result, occasional dealers, either because they are uninformed or for selfish pecuniary reasons, are passing off as Shaker some items which are not. This is most unfortunate and only confuses the beginning or unknowledgeable collector who trusts the seller of the article.

It is a great mistake to call every cleanly designed ladder back chair a Shaker chair. There are countless attractive, well-designed and well-made ladder back chairs which are not Shaker. The Shakers were not the only craftsmen of the 18th and 19th centuries who could make a good ladder

back and the collector must be able to distinguish what is Shaker and what is not. This knowledge comes only through study and examination of Shaker chairs and rockers with impeccable provenances.

Mother Ann Lee, early Shaker leader who with eight followers arrived from England in 1774, believed that ornamentation was unnecessary and even sinful. It distracted from the contemplation and emulation of God and prevented a meaningful relationship with the Godhead. If one's physical life and one's surroundings were cluttered with the decorative, this too impeded the giving over of the spirit to God.

Thus, ornamentation for the sake of embellishment had no rule in the Shaker faith. The mode of dress, style of architecture, design of furniture and other artifacts all reflected the beliefs of this sect that worshiped simplicity as a virtue.

Shaker chairs, combining unconscious artistic achievement with flawless craftsmanship, are admired by both artist and artisan today as yesterday. With inspiration from a faith that transcended the mere physical world, Shaker chairs illustrate a sincerity of work elevated beyond the mundane, while relating completely in the utilitarian demands of what a chair should be.

Fig. 1: This little rocker (ca. 1820) from Sabbathday Lake shows the characteristic "ball" finial found on chairs from the Maine communities. It is made of maple except for the rungs which are hickory. It is painted a deep green, called by the Shakers "Elders Green," since it was a color reserved for articles used by the Elders and Eldresses. The rockers cut off close to the front posts would allow the rocker to be pulled up close to a counter or table. The original seat is of splint. The painted pine Shaker footstool is from Enfield, Conn. (Both in collection of the author; photograph by Bluford W. Muir.)

Shaker chairs owe their basic design to the common ladder back or slat back chair found in nearly every colonial New England household during the 18th century. The ladder back was strong, functional and easily made. Since it was a well-known design, converts to the Shaker faith took the form and actual examples with them when they withdrew from the world into the Shaker communities.

Unfortunately, the best-known Shaker chairs today are those made after the mid-19th century, especially at Mt. Lebanon, N.Y., for sale to the "world." These commercial chairs, made in quantity, were advertised and sold throughout the country as late as 1935. Although solid and attractive, they were, in a way, mass produced and represent a decline in Shaker design and craftsmanship.

These commercial chairs are relatively common. It is worthwhile to have an example in one's Shaker collection, but it should be noted that because they are late in date and manufactured in number, they will never have either the aesthetic or financial value of an early, hand-crafted Shaker chair made before the Civil War.

Because these late chairs were to be made in some number, modern manufacturing methods were employed. The rockers are held in place with steel screws; the mushrooms on the arms are applied as separate pieces; the slats are glued and not pegged; the frames were often dipped in dark-colored dye; and the seat tape is machine-made rather than loomed by hand. Because they had to sell in the "world," these commercial chairs had to appeal to current public taste — which often clashed with the simple tastes of the Shakers. They are an unfortunate Shaker compromise with the "world."

The early Shaker chairs and rockers, however, made by the Shakers for their own use within their communities and not intended for the "world," possess the purity of line and perfection associated with Shaker craftsmanship.

Many of the early chairs display regional and even community characteristics allowing specific types and designs to be identified with certain communities. The two back posts of all Shaker ladder backs terminated in graceful finials. The shape of this finial, often differentiated in each community, was the feature which enabled certain chairs to be attributed to certain communities or at least to certain regions.

All Shaker communities derived their direction from the central ministry at Mt. Lebanon which grouped the communities into "bishoprics" about 1860 to facilitate administration. These bishoprics, however,

Fig. 2: This is a fine example of the very delicate chairs made at Enfield, N.H. The slenderness of the piece is emphasized by the light, airy cane seat, a characteristic of some chairs from this community. Also, a distinguishing feature are the elegant "flame" finials at the top of the back posts. They lend a feeling of height even to the smallest chair. Although this example has a wide seat its back is short in comparison to most. (Collection of the Canterbury Shakers; photograph by the author.)

merely gave formal recognition to what had long existed — a close relationship between the various geographic entities of Shakerdom. The communities at Alfred and Sabbathday Lake formed the Maine Bishopric; Canterbury and Enfield, the New Hampshire Bishopric; Harvard and Shirley, the Eastern Massachusetts Bishopric; Hancock and Tyringham, the Western Massachusetts Bishopric; and Mt. Lebanon and Watervliet, the New York Bishopric.

The communities within these geographic boundaries usually attempted to solve problems themselves before consulting Mt. Lebanon, resulting in a regional closeness of spirit. With the normal exchange of ideas between people not many miles apart, it is understandable that the chairs and other artifacts made at Alfred should resemble those of Sabbathday Lake, why those of Watervliet should reflect those of Mt. Lebanon.

Although certain similarities can be readily recognized and isolated, there are always chairs which cannot be neatly categorized. However, in a great number of instances similar characteristics will be found.

By means of illustrations these characteristics can be clearly seen. For the photographs used here, only chairs and rockers with flawless provenances to specific Shaker communities have been employed. While the text points out certain regional similarities, it is not contended that all Shaker chairs fall neatly into definite patterns. There will always turn up some chairs which are unique and fall into no pattern. This is true in all facets of collecting.

Side chairs were usually made with three slats, curved at the top, straight at the bottom. Armchairs, because of their size, normally have four slats. In the majority of cases, maple was used for the frame and slats, although in Maine and the eastern Massachusetts communities ash or hickory were often employed for the rungs. At times a chair can be found in black cherry or figured maple, and even birch and butternut were used. There were always two rungs in front and on the sides, and one in back.

The Shakers early fitted rockers to their chairs, particularly to accommodate the elderly and infirm. The earliest rockers have a short front and back and are fairly heavy. Armchairs were also distinctive. The arms were either scrolled outward, rolled downward or finished with a mushroom-shaped crest — all design features copied from colonial ladder back chairs.

Shaker chairs vary greatly in size because they were crafted to fit the individual for whom they were intended. Just as chairs were made for specific purposes — apple paring, sewing or dining — so a chair made for a small Sister would be of different dimensions than one for a robust Brother.

On the early chairs and rockers the top slat, and often the others, was pegged to the back posts. The rockers were also pegged to the posts. On the late commercial chairs, in contrast, steel screws fastened the rockers, and the slats were merely glued in place. The early chairs have narrow splint, plaited rush, cane or woven tape seats. A solid leather seat is rarely found.

Collectors are most familiar with the woven tape seats which are nearly universally found on the late Mt. Lebanon commercial chairs. If a collector is offered a Shaker chair with a tape seat it should be closely examined. These tapes are still being made commercially and many Shaker chairs (and unfortunately, non-Shaker chairs) have had the tape seats re-

placed. Naturally, a chair has less value if the seat has been replaced with modern tapes.

The tapes on the earliest chairs were hand-woven of wool or mohair. They were never placed on a seat without some sort of inner padding or lining since the weight of a person on the unsupported webbing would soon break it. The cloth lining under the webbing was usually of double calico, stuffed with a padding of wood shavings, horsehair, cloth waste, or something similar.

On the earliest chairs the splint seats are the most common, although rush seats are found with some frequency, especially in the eastern Massachusetts communities of Harvard and Shirley. By the middle of the 19th century, Canterbury and Mt. Lebanon were employing delicate cane for the seats of their chairs; they were the only communities to do so in any number.

Fig. 3: This is the finial characteristic of the chairs and rockers made at Canterbury, N.H. The chairs made at this community are extremely slender in appearance and light in weight. The shape of the finial is related to the "flame" utilized at Enfield, N.H., and Harvard, Mass., but is distinctive because of its elongated neck and slightly blunted point. This also gives it a similarity to the rounded "ball" finial found on the Shaker chairs from neighboring Maine. (Collection of the Canterbury Shakers; photograph by the author.)

The Maine Bishopric consisted of the communities at Alfred, Sabbathday Lake and Gorham, the latter merging with Sabbathday Lake in 1819. As befits their "Down East" origin, the Maine chairs are the most robust of all Shaker chairs. The finials usually terminate in a full, rounded ball. No other Shaker community made chairs with such a nearly circular finial. A number of these attractive chairs and rockers from both Alfred and Sabbathday Lake are in the museum rooms at Sabbathday Lake today.

(Please turn the page)

These rooms at Sabbathday Lake are of great importance because of the many fine documented examples of Shaker furniture and other artifacts which they contain. All the collection is excellently displayed in original Shaker rooms. Sabbathday Lake and Canterbury, the two remaining Shaker communities, are matchless locations at which to start one's search for knowledge of the Shakers. It is the

Fig. 4: This rocker from Harvard, Mass., dates from the first quarter of the 19th century. Its unusually tall five-slat back and extremely wide but low seat indicates it was made for a large Shaker brother, probably with short legs. The "flame" finial on the Harvard chairs is also found on those chairs from the Shirley, Mass., and Enfield, N.H., communities. The attractive moulded, curved and rolled arm was characteristic of Harvard armchairs. The cradle-shaped rocker and early rush seat are also noteworthy. (Collection of Fruitlands Museums, Harvard, Mass.; photograph by the author.)

best way to obtain a true "feel" for what is Shakerism, both as a religious movement and for its physical manifestations.

One noteworthy Alfred chair in the museum is fitted with the famous Shaker "ball-and-socket" device at the bottom of the rear posts. The post was cupped out and a wooden ball flattened on the bottom was fitted into it, fastened with a leather thong: when the chair was tilted back the socket in the post rotated around the ball whose flat bottom always remained in contact with the floor. This device pre-

vented the chair from slipping out from under its occupant and saved wear on carpets and floors. Although this invention was patented in metal by the Shakers in 1852, it had been employed by them in wood for years.

The chairs from Enfield, N.H., and Harvard and Shirley, Mass., are most similar. The finials from these three communities may be characterized as a flame and are perhaps the most attractive of all the Shaker finials, with smooth tapering lines lending height and dignity to the chairs they grace. Generally, the Enfield flame seems to be slimmer at the neck than the Harvard and Shirley ones. While the posts of the chairs from the two eastern Massachusetts communities are somewhat heavier than those of Enfield, the front posts of the former are more likely to end in a graceful taper at the bottom. The products of these three communities are also among the few early Shaker chairs which have cane seats.

The chairs made at Canterbury (which together with Enfield made up the New Hampshire Bishopric) are related although somewhat different. Here the Enfield flame has been slightly blunted but the neck has been elongated so that the finial nevertheless gives the feeling of height and slenderness.

As at Sabbathday Lake, the Canterbury Shakers have set aside space for museum displays of Shaker crafts, with emphasis on the two New Hampshire communities. Many fine pieces are on display, including a number of delicate Canterbury and Enfield, N.H., chairs. Canterbury possess what is undoubtedly the most beautiful location of all the Shaker societies. High atop a hill in New Hampshire's rolling countryside, it is well worth a visit. The architectural worth of its many buildings is outstanding.

The oddest of all the flame finials can be found on some Enfield, Conn., chairs and rockers. Since it was settled first, the community in Connecticut was known as "old Enfield" to distinguish it from the later "new Enfield" in New Hampshire. Being the only Shaker settlement in the Nutmeg State, Enfield was somewhat outside the Shaker mainstream. This explains why the Enfield rocker depicted here retains very early design features although it is a relatively late product (c. 1880). It is marked by five splats, heavy, solid posts, rugged rockers and extremely large mushrooms on the arms. The flame is not as graceful as others, lacking a delicacy in the transition from the post to the neck of the finial. It is, however, an extremely vigorous and brawny rocker.

Shaker scholars have always "come-a-cropper" when discussing the com-

munity at Tyringham. Small and relatively isolated, it never achieved much fame and passed out of existence fairly early. Since its remaining members and their possessions were consolidated with the societies at Enfield, Conn., and Hancock, Mass., very little furniture exists today which can, without doubt, be attributed directly to Tyringham. Because of the lack of documented examples, the author has not attempted to make any definite statements on the stylistic attributes of Tyringham chairs.

The greatest number of surviving early Shaker chairs come from Mt.

Fig. 5: This large man's rocker is from the Shaker settlement at Enfield, Conn. Although relatively late in date it retains many of the characteristics of the early Shaker products. Of special notice are the early design sled rockers, the large mushrooms on the arms, the smallness of the finials in relation to the thickness of the back posts, and the bold turnings of the front posts. It is rare to find a rocker with five slats. (One of a pair, in the collection of the Shaker Museum, Old Chatham, N.Y.; photograph by Robert F. W. Meader.)

Lebanon and Watervliet, N.Y. These two communities formed the largest and parent Shaker bishopric, and as can be expected, the chairs made by these settlements are similar. The finial is a stepped or interrupted acorn. The smooth transition from the post to the acorn-shaped finial is interrupted by a ridge or collar approximately half-way up the neck. At times the ridge is so slight as not to be seen by the eye but it can always be felt by running the fingers up the neck of the finial.

Since the Hancock, Mass., community was only a few miles removed from Mt. Lebanon, there were logical similarities in their chairs. Thus, some later Hancock chairs also have the stepped acorn finial although it is usually fatter and more rounded in appearance.

Fig. 6: This extremely early armchair rocker is from Mt. Lebanon, N.Y., and illustrates the scrolled arms and short, blunt "sled" rockers of the early period. This is a woman's size rocker, having originally been made about 1810 for Sister Molly Smith (1780-1867), and then passed on to Sister Emma Neale (1846-1943). The entire chair is of maple, the slats with a beautiful birds-eye grain, and the arms with a tiger grain. (On loan to the Smithsonian Institution; collection of the Philadelphia Museum of Art; A. J. Wyatt, staff photographer.)

Shaker chairs and rockers are a self-contained art form. Even though the design had roots outside of and antecedent to the Shakers, the form into which the chairs evolved was purely Shaker, reflecting the sect's religious spirit, as did all its other physical manifestations. Free from all vestige of ornament, the result is a product in which the beauty of pure form was stated with frankness, in which elegance and dignity were raised to a spiritual level in a physical environment.

The products of Shaker hands were designed to glorify our Creator; not to gather vain, worldly praise. Their handiwork was a religious manifestation, not an artistic one. Although the Shakers were not in any sense attempting to be artists, what they left behind we now judge to be art: an artistic expression which is unique to the Shakers. We know that the more intense, the more concentrated the inspiration, the more perfect will be the manifestation. With their deep faith as the inspiration, the Shakers gave us products we admit their worldly contemporaries could not match and which we must still admire and envy.

Fig. 7: This is a close-up of the rocker illustrated in fig. 6. It highlights the beautiful, tight birds-eye maple grain of the back slats and shows in detail the "stepped acorn" finial found on chairs made at Mt. Lebanon and Watervliet, N.Y. Notice, also, how the top slat is pegged into the back posts. The parallel score lines on the posts to mark the location of the slats are also found on nearly all Shaker chairs and rockers. They helped to emphasize the interplay of horizontal and vertical elements in the chair back. (On loan to the Smithsonian Institution; collection of the Philadelphia Museum of Art; A. J. Wyatt, staff photographer.)

Acknowledgements: For their assistance and guidance the author wishes to thank Sister R. Mildred Barker and Theodore Johnson at Sabbathday Lake; the late Eldress Marguerite Frost and Charles Thompson at Canterbury; Robert F. Meader, director of the Shaker Museum at Old Chatham, N.Y.; and William Henry Harrison, director of Fruitlands Museum at Harvard, Mass.

* * *

Mr. Péladeau, author of "The Verse of Royall Tyler" and numerous articles on American and New England history and the decorative arts is currently a Congressional Press Secretary.

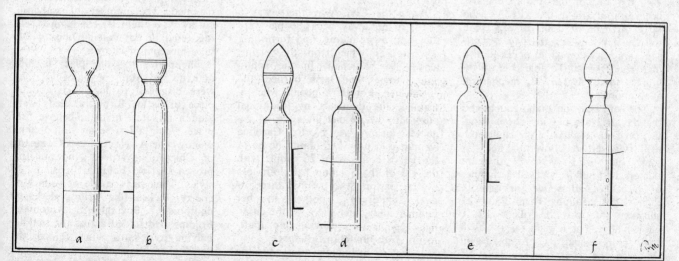

Fig. 8: This sketch illustrates the variety of Shaker chair finials, at the same time showing some of their common features. The two Maine communities at Sabbathday Lake and Alfred preferred a "ball" shaped finial (A). A variant (B) is found on some chairs and rockers from Alfred. The "flame" finial (C) is characteristic of the chairs from Enfield, N.H., and Harvard and Shirley, Mass. The other New Hampshire settlement at Canterbury varied this shape slightly (D). Enfield, Conn., developed its own version of the "flame" (E), while the two New York communities at Mount Lebanon and Watervliet evolved their own distinct "acorn" finial (F). *Sketch by Robert L. Miller.*

American walnut frame sofa, ca. 1870. The coil spring seat, hinged at the front, swings over so that the bottom of the sofa seat forms half of the bed. Presumably a feather mattress was laid over the two sections. Two iron legs swing down; one of them is marked "A. Schencke, Oliver Str." Author's collection.

Left: Ince and Mayhew sofa-bed, 1759. "A" shows the bed when folded up; "B" shows the bed as let down.

The Metamorphic Bed

by MARJORIE CONGRAM

LIKE SO MANY GOOD IDEAS, the idea of the fold-up bed has been around a long time. People who sleep on beds of quilts or hides can roll them up during the day. Americans are accustomed to a raised bed in a rigid frame. To fold this up requires some degree of mechanical adaptation.

The sofa bed, the studio couch, and the day bed are old inventions. English furniture makers of the eighteenth century advertised convertible beds for sale. Ince and Mahew, furniture makers in London, showed a number of pieces of adjustable furniture in their 1759 catalog. Their Plate 27 shows a sofa bed, described as: "A bed to appear as a soffa (sic) with a fixt canopy over it; the curtains drawn on a rod; the cheeks and seat takes off to open the bedstead . . . "

Americans of Colonial and Federal times made ready use of folding beds. Wallace Nutting's *Furniture Treasury*

(Macmillan, 1928) shows several examples.

After the Civil War there was a boom in put-away beds. People were moving west, building, and furnishing new houses which, on the plains, tended to be small. In the south, many homes had been burned and abandoned. For those people who remained, the demands of traditional hospitality were met in spite of reduced means. A North Carolina woman told how her family home of the 1870s could sleep 25 people with the aid of the open-up haircloth sofa in the parlor (two adults, three or more children), another in her father's study, and such. In the cities, more people were moving into apartments, with limitations of space.

Industrial technology nourished the new varieties of put-away beds. New machines for working and turning wood were patented, and improved steel was developed for flat and coil

springs. The nation was in a gimmicky mood; hundreds of new devices were patented. The number of stand-up, put-away, character-changing beds registered in the Patent Office would fill a museum of its own.

The parlor was one place to hide an extra bed. Many of the convertibles were disguised to look like another piece of parlor furniture. Beds were hidden in sofas, in make-believe fireplaces, in tables, even in pretend pianos. The A. H. Andrews Company of Chicago advertised Andrews Improved Parlor Folding Beds in 30 styles. Their beds, made of walnut or cherry, looked like writing desks or chiffoniers. Boyington's Automatic Folding Bed folded across the middle, halving its length. When folded, the bed looked like a chest of drawers.

The variety of sofa beds alone was enormous. The Brooklyn Furniture Company carried the Hoover Patent

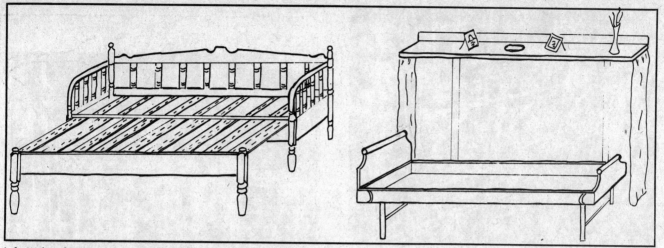

Left: Walnut frame extension lounge found in a farm house in Iowa. Two similar extension lounges were pictured in Carl. Drepperd's "Spool, Button and Ball-Turned Bedroom Furniture," SW aug '50. Right: Advertisement in **The Youth's Companion**, June 10, 1884:

"Parlor Mantel Bed. The best, cheapest and most practical Parlor Bed. Price, including best woven wire Spring Mattress, $10 and upwards. The best and cheapest invention of the age to save room. Hermon W. Ladd, 134 Richmond St., Boston."

Sofa, the Stockton Patent Bed Lounge, and the Van Cott Sofa Bed. In 1870 Henry Albee of Boston advertised a folding bed lounge called Berry's Patent Folding Spring Bed. These all had various adjustments. The sofa back could be let down, the seat could fold out to double its depth, or an extra frame could be pulled out, upon which a mattress was unrolled. The sleeper lay either parallel or perpendicular to the length of the sofa, depending on the model.

The Gunn Folding Bed made at Grand Rapids, Mich., was a whole bedroom. It combined a chest of drawers, a wardrobe closet, and a let-down bed. The three parts could be arranged with the bed on the left or right, and could be disassembled for cleaning. Their advertisement in *Harper's Bazaar* of October 3, 1891, reads:

"Going to Buy Furniture? We can save you room and money. The GUNN FOLDING BED combines everything in furniture. 13 styles. Illustrated and descriptive catalogue free."

The traveling convertible bed was still another kind perfected after the Civil War. George Pullman worked to make his Palace Car accommodations as efficient as possible. Another man created a bed which the owner could carry with him. Richard DuBois of Washington, D.C., took out a patent in 1870 for a trunk bedstead. His design had two trunks. The trunk lids made the head and footboards of the bed, and the side rails were stored inside. The unit could also be made into two short sofas. This and scores of other furniture patents were duly reported in the *Cabinetmaker*, a furniture workers' journal.

England was also enjoying a new age of travel, but there the long-distance mode was the steamship. One patent combination designed for shipboard could serve in one of Mr. Pullman's railway compartments. The English unit had a washstand, a water closet, and between them a tufted couch, opening into a bed when required. Since this model was for ocean travel, the inventor stuffed the bed with patent cork fiber to make it buoyant in water. The whole unit formed a floating surface of 50 feet "in case of danger at sea." This floating stateroom is shown in Louis Pevsner's *High Victorian Design* (1951).

As the nineteenth century flowed into the twentieth, there seemed to be no reduction of the need for collapsible beds, nor any really new variations from the old models. The "lounge," the "day bed," and the "studio couch" were household fixtures.

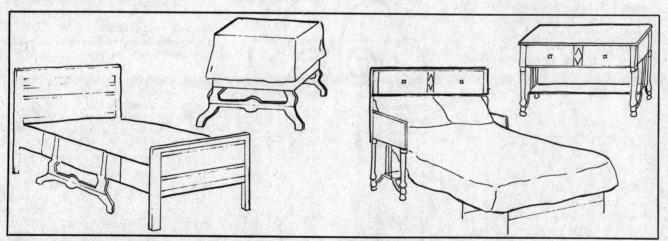

Left: Advertisement in **The Youth's Companion**, June 19, 1884: "Ask your furniture dealer for the ROSS TABLE BED. A special size for children. Eight styles from $13 to $30. A Table in day; Full Sized Bed at night. Forest City Furniture Co., Rockford, Illinois." Right: Advertisement from **Woman's Home Companion**, June 1916: "By Day . . . By Night . . . 24 hours of usefulness. Add an extra room to your home by using the Ta-Bed. An elegant, useful library table in the daytime, the Ta-Bed becomes a roomy, sanitary bed at night. Can be moved anywhere. Makes your room space do double service. Bedding, mattress, and springs fold up in drawer space. Ideal for sleeping porch or sun parlor. Made in three sizes and many beautiful designs. Write for free illustrated 'Story of the Table that Went to Bed.' Give your dealer's name. The United Table Bed Company, 3655 Morgan St., Chicago, Illinois."

Ornate wrapped brass bed; maker unknown. Headboard 48" high by 54" wide; footboard 30" high.

Ornately designed wrapped brass bed. Headboard 54" wide by 48" high; footboard 30" high.

Brass Beds Made by Foster Bros. by ITA ABER

THE BRASS BED, a status symbol of the late Victorian period and popular through the first quarter of the 20th century, is coming into its own again. Brass headboards and footboards are being featured in antiques shops and the demand for them has sent prices skyrocketing. Even so, the workmanship on the old models cannot be duplicated, for the price, on today's models.

One of the largest and best known of brass bed manufacturers was Foster Bros., who began operations in Utica, N.Y., in 1871 as "Charles Segar and Foster." The firm took over a building on West Street, just above Johnson Park, vacated by the Sweet Caporel Cigarette Company whose venture at being the first cigarette factory in the North had proved unprofitable.

Segar and Foster became Foster Bros. one year later when Segar left

and Oscar S. and William B. Foster took over, moving their bedding factory to 811 Broad Street. Their slogan, "Made in Utica for the Rest of the World," became known all over the country. Eventually they employed more than 200 people in Utica. In 1893, as their business grew, they opened a plant in St. Louis, Mo., to serve the central and western United States.

At that time, Foster Bros.' principal competitor was the Greenpoint Metallic Bed Company of Brooklyn, N.Y., now out of business. Soon other com-

panies began manufacturing brass beds, including Kimball and Chappel of Chicago and Simmons & Co., who made brass beds for Sears and Roebuck using a Sears label. These continued to appear in Sears' catalogs until 1929. Simmons & Co. made brass beds under their own label and were by far the largest manufacturers of brass beds in the country. George Gesch of Austria featured an Art Nouveau styling that was very desireable.

Most brass beds are not solid brass. They are made of iron, wrapped in brass and have a seam down each length. However, the small lengths, knobs, balls and finial trim are of solid brass. Kimball and Chappel made a few solid brass beds as did some Canadian manufacturers. In Europe, where the brass bed seems to have originated, the wrapped brass tech-

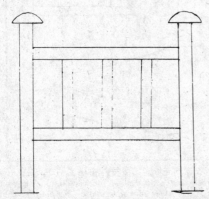

Foster single width tubular wrapped brass bed. Headboard 52" high; footboard 26" high.

Foster's scroll design in tubular wrapped brass, 63" high by 54" wide. (Courtesy *I Got A Thing About Brass Beds*, N.Y.)

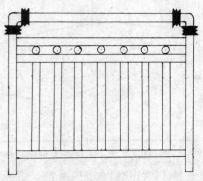

Solid squared brass headboard 60" high by 54" wide. One of a pair from Canada. Maker unknown.

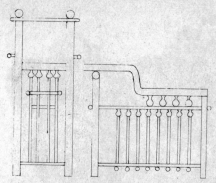

Brass cribs are difficult to find because so few were made. This one stands 7' tall at the headboard and 54" tall at the side rails. It is made of wrapped brass with solid brass knobs. The protruding knobs on the sides of the headboard (left, in the sketch above) were used to hang a curtain or mosquito netting. (Courtesy *I Got A Thing About Brass Beds, N.Y.*)

Foster tubular wrapped brass bed with eleven spokes, each 3" in diameter, balls are solid brass. Headboard 63" high; footboard 40" high.

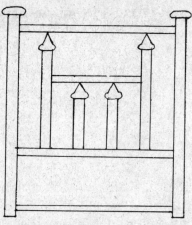

Unmarked single width tubular brass bed. Headboard 39" wide by 62" high; footboard 40" high.

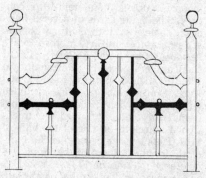

Solid brass 54" headboard can accomodate a modern Queen-size mattress. (Courtesy *Olga Antiques, N.Y.*)

nique was used in Holland, Italy, Austria, France, and Germany.

Styles and prices varied with the taste and the times. The earlier beds of the Victorian period tend to be quite ornate while the later ones, coming into the Art Nouveau period, are straighter and simpler in design.

Styles of wood-finish metal, enamel and brass combinations, and iron and brass combinations came on the scene and became very popular. Today these beds, resurrected from attic or basement or purchased at some antiques shop, are as handsome and decorative as when they were new, once the brass is polished and the iron parts painted, padded, or quilted. Combination iron and brass beds were offered in Sears and Roebuck's 1919 catalogue from $5.15 to $12.85 for a headboard and footboard with the customer specifying the color he wanted the iron painted. Today these same beds, re-

finished, sell for considerably more.

According to Mr. Ray J. Adams, present treasurer of Foster Bros., the company ceased making brass beds during World War I. During World War II, many people disposed of their brass beds as a patriotic gesture so that they could be melted down into arms and ammunition. The Europeans did not begin to dispose of theirs until the 1950s when interest in them began again here. Many of the brass beds seen in antiques shops today are from Europe.

During World War II, Foster Bros. devoted their efforts completely to the making of ship berths for the U.S. Navy LST's and hospital beds for the war zones. Over the years, Foster Bros. has made, besides brass beds, springs, mattresses, sofa sleepers, roll-away cots, studio couches and dormitory beds. In 1955, they gave up their Utica location, transferring all operations to

St. Louis. Today they concentrate on frames for sofa sleepers, bed-in-the-back chair beds, cots, bunks, box springs, and institutional bedding.

Two direct descendants of the original Fosters live in St. Louis: Mr. Townsend Foster and Mr. H. Torrey Foster. Mr. Robert Clarke, former treasurer of the firm, now retired, still lives in Utica.

HORSEHAIR UPHOLSTERY CLOTH

Haireloth sofa, ca. 1850-60.
(Author's Collection.)

HORSEHAIR upholstery cloth, or haircloth, has in the United States an English heritage. The use of haircloth on furniture comes to modern notice about mid-18th century. The trade cards of several haircloth dealers of 18th century London are reproduced in Sir Ambrose Heal's *London Furniture Makers* (1953). Chairmakers Joseph Patterson in 1730, Francis Thompson in 1750, and Alex. Wetherstone in 1760 included haircloth in their lists of household items for sale. Chippendale mentioned haircloth on one of his bills of 1767. Hepplewhite recommended haircloth in his *Cabinet-Maker and Upholsterer's Guide* of 1788.

American colonists had haircloth put on seat furniture they imported from England. Lord Botetourt of colonial Williamsburg purchased "hair bottom chairs" from the previous governor when he moved into the Governor's Palace. George Washington referred to haircloth in a letter to his agent in 1765. John Penn, grandson of William and governor of Pennsylvania, left an inventory in

which parlor chairs of haircloth are mentioned. A set of dining room chairs made by Duncan Phyfe and James Monroe are now at his home, Ash Lawn, outside of Charlottesville, Virginia. These are covered with what is said to be the original black haircloth.

There is some evidence that the Maryland Senate sat on horsehair. A shield back, saddle-seated chair at one time used in the Senate Chamber at Annapolis has black haircloth upholstered over the rail. It is now owned by the Maryland Historical Society. The first United States Assembly, meeting in Federal Hall in New York, may also have sat on horsehair. Four of the armchairs used by members of the First Congress of

by MARJORIE CONGRAM

the United States in 1789 were given by the City of New York to the New York Historical Society. Two are now on display with black haircloth upholstery.

Many artisans, including haircloth workers, followed their products across the Atlantic to set up shop in Williamsburg, Philadelphia, New York, and other colonial capitals. A Mr. Benjamin Bucktrout advertised "hair seating for chairs" in the *Virginia Gazette* of July 7, 1774. Some years later, John George came to work in Philadelphia.

In the July 1949 issue of *Antiques* is a report on John George from one of his descendants living in Oregon. George was believed to have woven haircloth in England, then migrated to the United States to pursue his trade. His wife and nine children came over later. There was some litigation in the English courts about bringing "intricate machinery" out of that country. George's descendant had one small piece of haircloth believed to be his product, a green and gold pattern brocade.

The Philadelphia city directories list John George's name as early as 1839. His shop address is given as Sixth and Cherry Streets. By 1846 he had taken a partner, G. W. Langdon, and moved to 59 Dock. George continued to be listed in the Philadelphia business directories under "hair seating and curled hair" until 1858.

In the opening years of the 19th century, haircloth was used on Federal and Duncan Phyfe settees and chairs. Its position as a long wearing fabric appropriate to fine furniture was established. By the 1850s, haircloth had more democratic associations. *Godey's Lady's Book* of November 1850 has an article on Henkels Furniture Store of Philadelphia, one of the largest of its time. The store offered "satin chairs of crimson and

Swatches of modern horsehair upholstery cloth, reproducing old patterns, in various colors, black, blue, red, green, and yellow. (David Carmel Co., and Stroheim and Romann, New York City; John Boyd & Co. Ltd., Somerset, England.)

Below: Corner commode chair; mahogany, secondary woods eastern white pine and sweet gum; haircloth seat cover; American, attributed to N. Y. City, 1760-1775. (Glen-Sanders Collection, Colonial Williamsburg.)

Footstool, 1830-1840, with embroidered picture on h a i r c l o t h cover. (Museum of the City of N. Y.) Detail of footstool embroidery is shown, *left above.*

Armchair upholstered in haircloth, 1789, used by members of the First Congress of the U.S. in Federal Hall, New York City. (N.Y. Historical Society.)

black, orange and green, . . . rose-colored and white"—this was the elegant furniture. In the plain furniture section, "mahogany and haircloth held sway." It is with the late Empire and Victorian furniture that haircloth has its popular identity.

Horsehair in upholstery fabric could well be called the hidden fiber. The plain weave of black color is well known, but is not easily identified in photographs. Haircloth was also woven in stripes, checks, and various brocade patterns in a variety of colors. A chambray effect could be had with warp of different color from the horsehair woof. Like human hair, horsehair comes in blonde, reddish, and brown colors, and can be—and was—bleached and dyed. The plain black weave was also used as a background for embroidery and petit point.

Many historic houses and museums display horsehair upholstery on their furniture, but it is often not so labeled. The colored and patterned haircloth is particularly difficult for the visitor to identify. To name a few, the Colonial Williamsburg collection includes seven black and four green patterned haircloth covered chairs; the Metropolitan Museum of Art in its American Wing has a settee of 1815, "probably Duncan Phyfe," covered in plain weave black haircloth; Abraham Lincoln's home in Springfield, Illinois, and Theodore Roosevelt's boyhood home in New York City both have haircloth covered chairs in their parlors.

Versatile and democratic haircloth covers many fine examples of chairs, stools, and sofas in furniture collections across the United States. In the future, it is hoped that this unique fabric will be restored and identified along with the fine furniture it accompanies.

Paints of the American Past

by JOHN CUMMINGS

SINCE ancient times it has been a not uncommon practice to cover the surface of wood with a finish, for its embellishment or protection. The earliest were the oils or waxes alone, or in various combinations. At some subsequent period it was discovered that various, finely ground solids could be added which would confer color or hide certain undesirable features. Thus evolved what we today term paint.

A paint consists basically of a liquid vehicle in which there is suspended a very finely divided solid material, known as the pigment. This latter confers both color and the opacity which covers or hides the underlying surfaces. There are two classes of paints we will consider—those where linseed oil is the vehicle; and those where the liquid is water with some dissolved or dispersed substance that serves as a binding and coating agent.

After the middle of the 17th century, flax culture was becoming established and the erection of oil mills was producing ever increasing amounts of linseed oil. This oil, alone or in combination with beeswax, was used to beautify and preserve the oaken Jacobean furniture. On this furniture we often find the turnings of chairs or tables, also the carvings or mouldings of chests and cupboards, picked out with black or red. What are these colors and whence did they come?

BLACKS

Black, similar to modern carbon blacks, was available in quantity from the cleaning of chimneys. Occasional "receipts" in very early day books outlined the steps in the preparation of soot to make a good, black paint. After the cleaning of a "foul chimney" the "soote" was washed or leached (much as wood ashes were leached in a perforated barrel to produce potash for soap making), ground, carefully sifted, and mixed with "oyl" (linseed oil or sometimes fish oil). We can be certain, from the impurities still detectable by analysis, that the carbon (black) came from the source suggested.

Black carried a touch of elegance, reminiscent of the rich blackwood furniture Catharine of Braganza brought with her to England as a bride. The beautiful Carolean chairs were almost always painted black, and the early bannister back chairs were often similarly finished.

REDS

A fine example of accenting carving with red is a palm-carved, oak hanging cupboard, formerly in the Joseph Downs collection, now in the Seventeenth Century Room in the H. F. duPont Winterthur Museum. A chest, probably made during the first years of the 18th Century, decorated in black and iron oxide red is shown in Fig. 1.

Naturally occurring iron oxide yields a variety of red, as well as brown and also yellow (yellow ochre). The earthy material was dug, crushed to break up lumps and ground to proper fineness; then put through a sieve, the resulting powder yielding a fine, durable pigment with excellent covering power. The range of colors is from a dark reddish brown ("Spanish Brown") through the rich maroon shades ("Indian Red") to the light, quite bright shades of red ochre ("Oker" sometimes also called "Coffin Red"). The digging, preparing and mixing were quite as apt to be done at home, as by the "joyner" or turner or housewright!

It was, and still is, a simple matter to mix the pigment with the liquid medium and to get a good paint. An economical, also durable and pleasing paint was prepared with a water base. There are innumerable "receipts" for the preparation by use of sour milk, skim milk, buttermilk, et alia. A formula from an early issue of "The Universal Receipt Book" will illustrate the modus operandi:

One pound of freshly slaked lime, which has been exposed to air, is mixed into one quart of skim milk. Then add gradually twelve ounces of linseed oil in which has been dissolved three ounces of Burgundy pitch. Now stir in three (additional) quarts of the skim milk followed by five pounds of carefully sifted red oxide of iron. It is noted that the pigment should be very finely powdered; also that it is better to have mixed the color with spirits. This paint is well nigh indestructible!

(No fewer than six excellent, authentic iron oxide reds are manufactured by C. K. Williams Co. of Easton, Pennsylvania. Also a very passable substitute for the old Spanish Brown is "Mars Brown" obtainable from E. H. & A. C. Friedericks, New York City.)

Ready mixed paint wasn't available in the early days, so the artist, the maker of furniture, or the ordinary soul wishing to embellish his possessions had to make his own.

A good paint for simulating and/or restoring old time red, sometimes referred to as "barn red", may be made as follows: Mix from 3 to 4 pounds of finely ground (250-300 mesh) red iron oxide into a gallon of raw linseed oil, then add one pint of pure gum turpentine. Since we lack the time and patience of our forebears, it is advised that three or four tablespoons of good liquid drier be added; also about a pint (one small container) of flatting compound. This last will somewhat dull the newness (gloss) giving an older, more mellow appearance, and it also assists in the final drying. (The writer has had excellent results using Sherwin Williams Gloss Modifier.)

It is perfectly proper, indeed often desirable, to repaint an old piece as a step in restoration, but new paint, no matter how carefully compounded or skillfully applied, is still new. Time alone can give the lovely, patinated surface and faded mellowness so characteristic of a truly old finish.

BLUES

Brown, reds and yellow are not the only colors conferred by iron! By a strange quirk of chemistry our deepest, strongest blue is also a compound of iron. When scrap iron and iron oxide are heated away from air with organic materials (horns, hoofs, hair, scraps of hides, etc.), potash, and traces of saltpeter and sand, the blue clinker produced is Prussian Blue. This was patented in 1704 and is often called the first artificial pigment. Easily ground and with great covering power, it immediately became popular and has never entirely gone out of favor. It is to be seen on many types of cupboards, on fine mantels and occasionally on chests.

Frequently encountered, most interesting, and perhaps the most important blue was smalt. This material has been know to potters and used by them since the 12th century. It is really a blue glass and an indirect ancestor of the modern cobalt blues. The glassy nature rendered it difficult to grind; also gave it an objectionable transparency. This last was usually overcome by the addition of pulverized chalk, which served not only as an opacifer, but also to make the expensive pigment go farther. It seems quite proper to consider the chalk added as an early use of an extender. Soft lovely blues that we admire on 18th century pieces are quite apt to be a smalt and chalk combination.

Smalt was put to a curious use by certain New England chair makers. A first coat of blue was applied, followed by a thin coat of brown, presumably umber. A number of bannister back chairs and a few slat backs have been found showing this treatment. Certain Pennsylvania clockmakers, notably Neisser and Gotschalk, first painted their softwood, tall clock cases with blue, then with a very thin finish coat of black. The inspiration or motive for such treatment is obscure.

WHITES

Chalk was sometimes mixed with oil to produce white, but the result was not entirely successful. The Dutch process for manufacturing white lead, an excellent pigment, was devised in the 16th century, but because pigments were sold by weight. the great covering power and whiteness of the material was offset by its heaviness. Transportation was slow and difficult; supply was limited, uncertain and expensive, so we find no great use of white lead in this country until just prior to the Revolutionary War.

Some of our knowledge regarding paints has been obtained by chemical analyses of scrapings, but quite as important is the information gleaned from Ships' "Bills of Lading", Store Ledgers and old advertisements. Quite a variety of colors are mentioned. Umber appears at a very early date; followed by "Terre de Siena" (burnt sienna, still much used); also red lead, white lead, vermillion and, on rare occasions, the costly ultramarine.

GRAINING

The mention of umber suggests discussion of a technique originated in the late 17th century, namely graining. Walnut had become the fashionable wood for fine furniture, so humbler or less popular light colored woods were treated to give them the more elegant appearance. To accomplish this a coat of pale brown or yellow (sometimes ochre) was first applied. When this undercoater was nearly dry, a coat of umber was laid on and immediately worked with

Fig. 1: *Early 18th century chest decorated with black and iron oxide red. From Old Sturbridge Village, Sturbridge, Mass.*

combs or other suitable tools to simulate the color and grain of the more costly walnut. Many of our ancestors would have their possessions as stylish as their more opulent neighbors! It was also done by craftsmen to keep up with the style and thus enhance the saleability and the price of their stock.

GREENS

Green often found use on furniture and there are two green pigments, both derived from copper. Terre verte produces a medium dark, soft green, occasionally found on case furniture or on beds and chairs; while verdegris, the corrosion which can be scraped from copper or brass, produces a light, bright green. This last, beloved by the Pennsylvania Deutsch, was used for trimming and, when darkened by an admixture of soot, gave a fine, deep shade such as sometimes seen on Windsor chairs. These two pigments still find use by artists and restorers, but were driven from the commercial field by the introduction of the chromes in the 19th century.

Why Paint?

The question of why our ancestors painted so much of their furniture may have many valid answers. Paint found use at an early date to emphasize ornamental features, such as carving. Fashion dictates may have played a role, as in the use of black on fine chairs or the graining of softwood (and sometimes light colored hardwood!) to simulate walnut. Some pieces contained several sorts of wood in the structure, each especially chosen to best fulfill its function, and this dissimilarity was concealed by

the application of paint. The truth may lie in something less obvious. There was little brightness or color in the lives and homes of early settlers, therefore they achieved color by brightening their furniture with paint. Then, too, it almost seems that they had an aversion for the light colored, native woods so commonly used. Soft woods were almost always painted. Maple was painted very frequently. Even the lovely cherry was often treated to a bath of iron oxide red. The only wood to escape was the aristocratic walnut and, of course, the expensive, imported mahogany.

Perhaps it might be well to take a hard look at some of the refinishing practices of the last three or four decades. The modus operandi of deeply scraping down or heavily sanding each old piece would seem the sign of little knowledge and no taste. We should try by every means in our power to retain every scrap or evidence of originality. Many years ago, Homer Eaton Keyes wrote, "We have learned to cherish the idea of age in our possessions, but have failed to learn to appreciate its charm, and its aspect or to preserve its value," while Henry F. duPont once pithily stated, "Don't pretty things up."

With apologies to Thomas Jefferson, we might properly say, "He restores best, who refinishes least." Many of the old pieces were originally painted and should be kept in such a condition. Leave the green paint on the fine old Windsor, or the red on the turned base of the stretcher table. This was their original condition and you will be surprised at how much admiration they will evoke if left in this state.

On Graining Wood Surfaces

TEN EYCK.N.Y.

ARCHITECTURE is the "father-art" of all furniture. It is the establisher of style and period. In almost every instance, the furniture styles we know, and all the variants thereof, come from architectural styles and variants which preceded them.

The graining of common woods used in 19th century architecture in order to approximate the color and appearance of richer timbers began about 1840 and lasted well into the 1900s. But such graining was known even in the 17th and 18th centuries. More of it remains in fine old houses of these centuries than is generally thought, albeit in some instances, it has required the removal of from three to six coats of later paint to get down to the graining. Rose and smoke graining is found in original homes as early as any represented in the Williamsburg restoration. Inevitably the graining of interior architectural woodwork was followed by the graining of furniture, especially case furniture.

In the nineteenth century, practically every residence, from mansion to tenement, had some grained woodwork. The painting craft had to find quick methods of doing the work. In addition to the laborious hand method, using combs and brushes and requiring considerable talent and experience on the part of the painter,

two quick methods came into general use.

One method utilized a roller called the Air Cylinder Grainer, and which would seem to constitute something, patentwise, similar to the do-it-yourself paint rollers of today. This cylinder, covered with various graining patterns, was rolled over prepared wood surfaces, impressing a grained pattern thereon. It could be used also over such protuberances as moldings. The other, a stencil method of graining, "invented" by J. J. Callow of Cleveland, Ohio, in 1870, contem-

plated the use of ten or more master metal stencils, taken from actual wood grain patterns. These, held against the surface to be grained, were stenciled through by a fine steel comb, the teeth covered with a graining cloth, or by wiping off the paint under the stencil orifices, and then graining the work with a fine comb. Both styles of paraphernalia used are pictured here.

Graining should not be regarded as a process of decoration that is passé. Rather, it must be considered a part of our heritage, and no period home after 1840 should be without it. It is not out of place even, especially in the rose and smoke tones, in an ancient salt box house of the seventeenth century, or a manor house in the Dutch style of the same period.

ADDITIONAL NOTES

IN "Footman in Powder", 1954, Helen Ashton described the graining that went into the decoration of the Marine Pavilion at Brighton, built in 1783 for George, Prince of Wales. "First . . . a couple of undercoats, then . . . you laid on a thin wood-brown coat and while it was still wet you drew a comb over it, or a goose's wing feather, to make a pattern like waves, like clouds or the grain of a tree with knots in it . . . walnut burr, dotted sycamore and satinwood."

Though C. L. Eastlake, in 1872, decried grained woodwork in his *Hints on Household Taste* as "an objectionable and pretentious deceit, which cannot be excused even on the ground of economy," Ellis Davidson, in 1877, found a ready sale for his *Practical Manual of House Painting, Graining, Marbling, and Sign Painting,* with 9 colored plates of woods and marbles, and nearly 150 wood engravings. Despite detractors, graining continued in popular use into the twentieth century. Nor is the art entirely lost. There are still to be found occasional painters who are proficient in woodwork graining, having learned the craft from old timers who flourished in a period when time was a less expensive commodity than it is today.

As for the graining of painted furniture, which present-day craftsmen sometimes use in restorations, Esther Stevens Brazer describes processes for graining in black over red, in red over black (used on many early Hitchcock chairs), and in two-toned brown "rosewood" or "walnut" finishes in her *Early American Decoration.* Ellen S. Sabine, too, in *American Antique Decoration* describes graining processes she has used. In *Furniture Decoration Made Easy,* Charles Hallet goes into considerable detail, presenting methods for rosewood graining, red hairline or feather graining, brown graining, tortoiseshell graining, and graining to imitate curly maple.

Label used by "Levi Prescott, Cabinet & Chair Maker, Boylston (Mass), 1799."

LABELS, pedigrees, and prices go hand in hand. Values on early American furniture (17th, 18th, and 19th century) are escalated substantially by reliable documentation.

Connecticut Valley cabinetmakers sometimes advertised their furniture in local newspapers of the period. A few flagged further business by gluing copies of their ads on the back or inside the drawers of their case-pieces: those chests, desks, sideboards and book-cases they made by hand, to order, for the gentry in their area. Furniture so identified is now termed "labeled," in the collector's current lingo.

WILLIAM LLOYDE of Springfield, Massachusetts, is an example. As a country cabinetmaker he courted business in this fashion. On July 6th, 1802, his advertising appearing in the *Federal Spy* is illustrated with line drawings of a serpentine front chest of drawers with cabriole legs and claw and ball feet—a la Chippendale. Also a drop-leaf table with stretcher and a lacy ladder-back chair of some elegance.

If his drawings illustrating his furniture are a bit naive, his "public" doubtless "got the message," for he must have made a quantity of beautiful furniture, some examples of which are still extant in museums and private collections.

Lloyde was born in 1779. His father was a leather-dresser, living on Ferry Lane (now Cypress Street) and presumably carrying on his business in conjunction with his homestead, as was a custom of the period. Ferry Lane was the busy street of Springfield prior to 1785. Leading, as it did, to the "Great Ferry," George Washington must have used this old thoroughfare when he crossed the Connecticut River to visit the arsenal at Springfield. William Warland, the chaisemaker, was also located on Ferry Lane. Edward Boylston, wheel-wright; Nathanel Brewer, stonecutter; and Burden the clock-maker; along with Deacon Williston, who made cocked hats, served a "generous Publick" on Ferry Lane.

Lloyde advertised making "elegant clock-cases, book-cases, desks, Bureaus, card tables, dining-tables, etc." in his shop "At the Head of the Ferry," where he lived with his wife Jerousa and fourteen children. Like many of the Colonial artisans of his ilk, he used the published design books of the great English cabinetmakers, Chippendale, Sheraton, and Hepplewhite. He must have loved beauty. But, alas, he also loved Geneva rum. It was the latter that did him in. The books of a prominent storekeeper of the period show repeated charges

Look for Labels and Documentation

ON YOUR ANTIQUE FURNITURE

by FLORENCE THOMPSON HOWE

against him for "Geneva Rum." Finally the page closing his account reads: "Account outlawed and done forever." He mortgaged and lost his property. His wife and daughters earned "a few shillings a day going out to work." He died at age 66 and is buried in lot 385, in old Springfield cemetery, on "Thistle Path."

A less melancholy story is that ERASTUS GRANT (1774-1865), a prosperous cabinetmaker of Westfield, Massachusetts, who was a consistent advertiser.

Inlaid Hepplewhite sideboard identified as the work of John Parsons, cabinetmaker of Suffield, Conn., and documented by his charge to Ebeneezer King, his client, in the Parsons account book discovered by the author.

In the *Hampshire Federalist* of Dec. 9, 1809, Grant put it this way:

E. GRANT

continues to carry on the *Cabinet Making Business* where may be had at any time, any article of *Cabinet Furniture*

100 rods East of the Meeting House

In the *Hampden Register* of May 17, 1826 (17 years later) Grant advertises thus:

CABINET FURNITURE

The subscriber has on hand and is constantly making all kinds of *Cabinetwork* which he will sell as low as can be bought at any other shop.

ALSO between three and four hundred CHAIRS from Hitchcock's Factory and elsewhere of elegant patterns and are offered very cheap.

WANTED IMMEDIATELY . . . a journeyman cabinetmaker, to whom cash will be paid at the finishing of the job.

ERASTUS GRANT

It would be interesting to know what price Grant quoted as "very cheap" on the immortal Hitchcocks. Grant's father, Alexander, was a joiner, evidently working at his Main Street home. In 1781 the town treasurer's book records having paid: "To Alexander Grant for Mr. Ballantine's coffin . . . 7-10."

Erastus Grant was a skilled craftsman as is attested by the beautiful furniture he made. He lived long and handsomely until he was 91. Evidently his advertising paid off!

Another cabinet and chairmaker of West Springfield, Mass. was a frequent advertiser in the local papers. One of

Tall clock case attributed to William Lloyde, cabinetmaker of Springfield, Mass.

his ads, found pasted on a very fine Windsor chair, is Coolidgesque in terseness. It reads:

WARRANTED CHAIRS
made and sold by
CALVIN BEDOURTHA
W. Springfield

Two of Bedourtha's "warranted" chairs, bearing his label, are of the rare 9-spindle type. He was a chairmaker of parts, no doubt.

But if you are really interested in antique furniture, this blurb in the *Hartford Courant* (June 24, 1799) will convince you that you were born just 169 years too late. This is the advertisement you missed:

JOHN I. WELLS

at his *Cabinet N Chair* shops, near the Bridge, Hartford, manufactures most kind of House Furniture such as . . .

Commode and plain sideboards, desks,

William Lloyde's advertisement in the "Federal Spy," Springfield, Mass., July 6, 1802.

bookcases, secretary, commode and plain bureaus, portable desks, dining, card, Pembroke, breakfast and stand tables . . . framed chairs of various patterns, new, neat and elegant, of mahogany and cherry tree. Highpost, field, common and creek bedsteads, soffas and rocking chairs, chamber chairs of the newest and best fashions. Windsor and common chairs of their kinds, as well as many other articles as are found at such shops, for which produce, lumber, goods, cash and credit would be accepted. Chairs repaired with flag seats.

ANSEL GOODRICH, chair-maker of Northampton, Mass., had his shop and dwelling "a few rods north of the courthouse," his advertising reveals. That would be about the site of the

present day Wiggins' Old Tavern. Although Goodrich seems to have been a good craftsman, he failed in business. His tools and household effects were eventually sold to satisfy his creditors. He and his wife Dorothy lost their baby and subsequently Dorothy lost her home; even the baby's cradle had to be sold. Ironically enough, a Windsor chair which Ansel listed at $1.50, recently brought $150 in an auction in New York, because it bore his label on the underside of the seat.

Labeled furniture is eagerly sought by students, collectors, and dealers interested in early American arts and crafts. It is desirable because it dates and places a piece and affords an example of a man's work for comparison with, and identification of, other pieces.

Although the leading urban cabinetmakers often identified their work, comparatively few country craftsmen did. Therefore the rarity. Therefore the exceptional value of a marked piece of furniture.

So, get out the flashlight. Take the drawers out of that old desk or bureau. Look for the label that might lift the mortgage. Apparently, even away back then, Yankees believed "it pays to advertise."

Labelled Windsor chair made by Ansel Goodrich, ca. 1800.

Knowledge of methods, tools, and techniques of old cabinetmakers
and of the changes time effects in wood is important in . . . .

Determining Furniture Age

by RAYMOND F. YATES

WITH the ever-growing popularity of American primitives in pine, cherry, and maple, it is important that collectors who favor such pieces of furniture learn the fundamentals of quick detection of fraud. Prospective buyers should know something about the methods and techniques used by old time cabinetmakers, and something of the changes that time effects in wood in relation to color (patina), shrinkage, and the like.

In itself, the shrinkage of old wood can offer important clues to age. In Figure 1, the circle represents the top of an old tripod table. Such old table tops are *never* perfectly round.

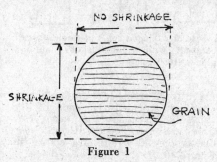

Figure 1

As a measurement of the diameter with a steel tape will quickly show, they are slightly oval in shape. Wood shrinks most at right angles to the grain. Thus, when such a top is measured across grain, the diameter will prove slightly less than when it is measured parallel with the grain. The difference will depend upon the size of the top; in large tops, it may be as great as one-half to three-quarters of an inch.

This measurement of shrinkage as a clue to age may also be applied to the round or turned legs of tables and chairs. By "turned" is meant legs made on wood lathes. Old legs of any wood will not be perfectly round, but, like table tops, slightly oval. This may be quickly detected by the use of ordinary machinist's calipers (Figure 2). The calipers are first adjusted to the diameter of a leg, then swung around 180 degrees, and another measurement taken. If the two measurements do not coincide, and the diameter of the leg is either greater or less in the new position, the leg is not truly round. In such cases, the leg is old. On the other hand, if a leg or table pedestal is found to be truly round, it may be assumed that the article of furniture is not very old.

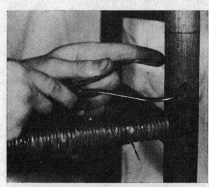

Figure 2

Today, flat wood surfaces are made by large power planers and sanders. The old cabinetmakers had no such machinery; every operation was done by hand tools. Boards were first cut with pit saws, or "gash saws" as they were sometimes called. (See Figure 3). After being sawed, they were dressed (finished) with hand tools. The so-called hollow plane—a plane with a slightly curved blade—was used to rough off the surface. The ridges left, as shown in Figure 4, were then cut with a smoothing plane. However expertly it was used, the smoothing plane still left slight undulations on the surface of a board. These may still be discovered when the tips of the fingers are swept across the surface of a board dressed in this quaint manner.

Such undulations are especially to be found in old American primitives made by country craftsmen. They will not be found in modern, machine-made boards. Nor will such crudities be found on work done by the fancy furniture makers in the larger cities of the early United States. Craftsmen working for the carriage trade received high prices for their work;

Figure 3—A, kerf marks left by circular saw; B, kerf marks left by pit or frame saws. Circular saws were not widely used in U.S. until 1830s.

they could afford to spend more time on a piece of furniture. They hand-scraped every board and used a steel straightedge to check the flatness of each board surface. Hence finger sweep or steel straightedge tests are not reliable when one examines old furniture of expensive formal type. They are valuable, however, when one is examining primitive furniture. The discovery of flat boards immediately rule out such furniture as old.

Another thing: old craftsmen rarely, if ever, used pine or other wood with knots. They invariably employed clear wood save for the back boards of chests or corner cupboards where the knots would not show. Knots in faked old furniture are fairly common.

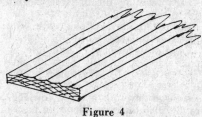

Figure 4

Modern lumber of all kinds, and especially pine, comes in standard widths and thicknesses. Old boards were cut and dressed by cabinetmakers; widths were random and thicknesses varied a great deal. (See Figure 5.) From his lumber dealer, the collector can learn the standard sizes now used for both yellow and

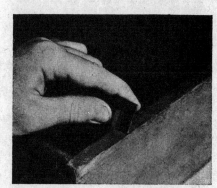

Figure 5—No two pieces of old hand-cut lumber were precisely alike.

white pine. Armed with this data— and a ruler—he can easily check boards used in any piece of pine furniture. A steel straightedge and a flashlight may also be used as a quick check for flatness of a board. These devices are used as shown in Figure

Figure 6

Figure 8—Two old methods of producing joints on chest drawers.

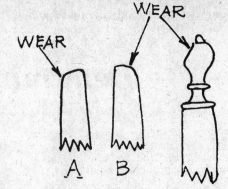

Figure 7—Large dovetail joints, usual to older drawers of chests or tables.

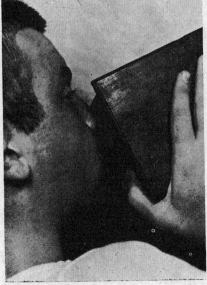

Figure 9—Beading or lips on old chest drawer fronts were cut with a molding plane; their slight undulations can be seen with the naked eye. Machine-cut beading is perfectly straight.

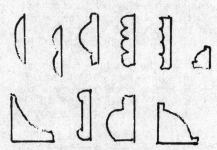

Figure 10—A and B, types of wear found on the ends of old chair legs; C, finial wear resulting from chairs in use being tilted against wall.

Figure 11—Shapes of old molding, **all hand-cut with cabinetmaker's molding planes, 1650–1800.**

6. Light coming through the bottom edge of the steel straightedge is fair proof that the board could have been dressed with hand tools.

If the drawers of a chest, table, or small stand are really old, the side pieces are usually dovetailed to the back piece. Old time cabinetmakers used large dovetails as shown in Figure 7. Early and late Victorian pieces (1837–1900) employed small dovetails cut by machine. (See also Figures 8 and 9.)

Though some methods of construction can be a clue to age, the use of wooden pegs means little or nothing. Producers of antique frauds often use wooden pegs in place of nails because so many people believe—erroneously —that pegs, or dowels as they should be called, were always used in early times. The fact is, dowels are more used in making present-day furniture than they were in olden times. The dowels old time cabinetmakers did employ were usually hand-cut and

crude. They were cut slightly bowed so that when they were driven into place in a hole, they would be sprung a bit to prevent looseness. They were more apt to be slightly oval in cross section than round. No glue was employed.

Speaking of glue, old cabinetmakers of the 18th and early 19th centuries used very little save for veneering. The legs of old chairs were made from green wood, while the rungs were cut from seasoned wood. As the

green wood of the legs gradually seasoned, it grasped the ends of the rungs tighter and tighter each year. Glue was not needed. Usual wear marks on old chairs are shown in Figure 10.

Age is more than skin deep when the color or patina of wood generated by age is considered. Wood, especially white pine, darkens in depth over the years. Furniture fakers have a difficult time providing new pine with patina. They may use all sorts of chemicals, but none provide the proper color. Nor will such treatment provide color in depth. A simple scrape with a jackknife will cut through fake finishes and show the new white pine beneath the thin surface coloring.

Hardware

by RAYMOND F. YATES

HARDWARE is a guide to dating old furniture, and the collector should learn to recognize the nails, screws, hinges, drawer pulls, and the like used on truly old pieces.

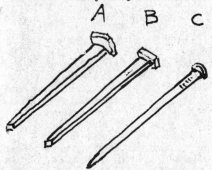

A, old crude hand-forged square nail, 1700-1800; B, machine-cut nail, 1810-1890; C, modern wire nail.

NAILS: The earliest nails used in both house and furniture construction were hand-forged, and were usually made by "nailers" who worked at home. These square nails were forged, one by one, from high purity "Russian iron," which did not rust. About 1830, nails were made by machine; these, too, were square. Since square nails were used as late as the 1880s, when the modern round nail was introduced, the sight of a square nail-head on a piece of furniture is not convincing proof that the piece is old.

Really old square nails are much cruder than the machine product. The blanks had to be heated, then shaped and headed. Hand-forged nails show hammer and anvil marks; the surfaces are rough; the heads are anything but perfectly square or oblong. They rusted very little, while machine-made nails rusted badly. If the collector carefully examines old hand-forged nails, he will quickly learn to recognize them. Such nails were used only on primitive pieces, mostly of pine. Early cabinetmakers who worked for the carriage trade did not use nails.

SCREWS: The removal of a screw and careful inspection of it by the collector—a small magnifying glass is helpful—will often help him date a piece of furniture. The crude hand-made wood screws used before 1830

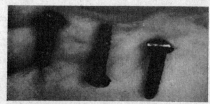

Old hand-filed screws with blunt points; some were used to 1830s.

are easily identified. The spiral threads are hand-cut with a three-cornered file; the slots on the screw heads are shallow and often badly off center; the ends are blunt instead of sharply pointed. To start the screw into the wood, a hole was made by a gimlet. The blunt-ended wood screw was inserted into it and driven home with a screw driver. Modern sharp-pointed, perfectly uniform, machine-made "gimlet screws" began to be manufactured during the 1840s by the American Screw Company. While the presence of hand-filed screws usually means a piece of furniture is a real antique, furniture fakers have been known to switch screws in an effort to fool experts.

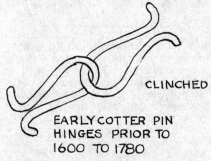

CLINCHED

EARLY COTTER PIN HINGES PRIOR TO 1600 TO 1780

HINGES: Hinges vary a great deal. The earliest forms appeared in New England on blanket chest lids. Some were no more than pieces of cowhide nailed in place. Such leather hinges are difficult to date; farmers have used them for years. Cotter pin hinges, also used on pine blanket chest lids, were made with iron wire, and can be as easily reproduced with a piece of modern iron wire as leather hinges can be replaced with an old bit of harness. Blanket chests with original cotter pin hinges are rare.

Butterfly and rattail hinges, hand-wrought by blacksmiths, were used during the eighteenth and early nineteenth centuries. Rattail hinges were usually employed on blanket chest lids. Similar hinges were manufactured from the 1840s through the 1860s, the machine-made hinges being smooth with no hammer marks. However, one must remember that modern

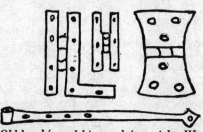

Old hand-forged hinges: left to right, HL, H, butterfly; below, rattail.

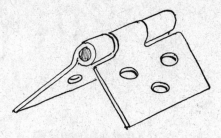

HAND-FORGED HINGES 1725-1800

hinges alone do not date a piece; worn-out hinges could have been replaced by original owners. Instances are known where an early owner had himself removed fine brass hardware to install a set of later Sandwich glass knobs.

The H and HL hinges were made in brass as well as iron. From 1760 to 1800, brass hardware was seldom used on anything but formal carriage-trade furniture. It was imported from England until the Revolution. After that, local craftsmen began to copy it for use on mahogany pieces in the Chippendale, Hepplewhite and Adams styles which they were creating from English design books.

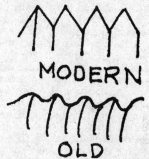

MODERN

OLD

Sharp accurate screw threads on modern machine-cut bolt; crude threads made by hand with a file, before 1830.

HAND MADE DRAW PULL POST-BRASS 1750-1820

DRAWER PULLS: Some of the earliest drawer pulls were lathe-turned wooden knobs. These cannot be classed as hardware unless they were attached with wood screws, which have their own story to tell as to date. Many wooden knobs or pulls were held to the drawer front with a dowel pin glued in place; these are usually early ones, although this is not a positive clue to dating. All screws and bolts used to hold early metal drawer pulls to drawer fronts were hand-cut. The screws with their crude threads are especially easy to recognize.

Three Hundred Years of Drawer Handles

by ETHEL BROENDEL

Sketches by HENRY BROENDEL

ALWAYS the design of drawer pulls has been of as much importance to a cabinet as the design of the cabinet itself. Over the years, pulls or handles have been made of all sorts of material—iron, brass, wood, glass, porcelain, paper—and in a wide variety of design.

Popular from time to time has been the drop pull; the earliest were in the teardrop style. These early handles were not fastened to the drawer with a bolt and nut as were those that came later, but a wire, shaped like a cotter pin, held the drop and passed through the backplate and on through a hole in the drawer front, where it was then spread open, flat against the wood. Sometimes the ends of the wire were then bent and driven into the wood to hold it more securely.

TUDOR (1485–1553)

Tudor is the earliest recognized English furniture period, and in it the pure blood of the Renaissance is evident. The lovely tracery of the Gothic period gradually gave way to the old Roman form of ornamentation, using foliage, fruit, flowers, birds, beasts, human figures, scrolls, and arabesques. At its beginning, the linen fold decoration, a form of carving which suggests the linen napkin, introduced from France, had become popular in England. It was a typical decoration of Henry the VIII's reign. The Tudor Rose, characteristic of the more ornate decoration of this period, showed the Renaissance influence, and with the linen fold, was true to the Tudor period.

Little is known of Tudor handles. Most belongings were kept in chests, but there were some Tudor tables with drawers which required pulls. Those pictured, adapted from drawings researched by the National Lock Company, show the linen fold on the backplate, *Figure 1*, and a Gothic backplate with Tudor Rose drop, *Figure 2;* both are brass.

ELIZABETHAN (1558–1603)

In Elizabeth's time, the simple linen fold gave way to bold carving in geometrical patterns, conventional flowers, fruit, and foliage cut from solid and huge turned melon-bulbs. Furniture was of oak, finished in rich, dull brown. *Figure 3* shows a grape-carved pull; *Figure 4,* a backplate of Gothic tracery with melon-bulb drop pull; these are brass.

JACOBEAN (1603–1649)

This period marked a distinct change of style. Furniture was still of oak, but wood carving was on the wane and decoration took the form of applied ornament. Jacobean furni-

IN assigning dates to the various furniture periods discussed in this study, Mrs. Broendel has used, except in instances of periods named for Royalty where dates of the reign are carried, the span of years in which the style enjoyed greatest popularity. All furniture periods overlap. Long before one period has ended, another has begun. But for the convenience of approximate dating, the core of the period, the years of highest fashion, have been bracketed.

For his sketches, Mr. Broendel has selected knobs and pulls showing what he feels the most outstanding characteristics of each period, though he admits many other designs would serve as satisfactorily—EDITOR

ture feet were sometimes egg-shaped or globular turnings, sometimes square. The globular turning was repeated in the long, turned, wooden knob, *Figure 5.* Shaped somewhat like the upper half of a bowling pin, it projected from the drawer about two and a half inches. It was either screwed into a large threaded hole, or was made without threads and pushed through the hole, with a pin driven through the shaft on the inside to secure it.

CAROLEAN (1660–1688)

In 1660, Cromwell was gone and England welcomed back the House of Stuart. The furniture of this Carolean period, so-called for Charles II, reflected the enthusiasm with which the Stuarts were received. Made of walnut, it was lighter in construction than that of Tudor days, and elaborately decorated with pierced carving. Rope turnings, the pierced carving of acanthus leaf, and large S scrolls were freely used. While the general appearance of the furniture was lightened, the square proportions of the Tudor days were not altered. *Figure 6* shows a pierced backplate made of S scrolls and "twisted rope" drop.

WILLIAM and MARY (1688–1702)

During the brief reign of William of Orange, a Hollander, and his wife Mary, the daughter of James II, the style of furniture underwent a definite change. The bulkiness of the Jacobean period turned to lighter, more graceful pieces. Furniture was made of walnut and, showing a Dutch influence, decorated with carving, inlay, lacquer, painting, and gilding, depending on the fineness of the piece. This period introduced high bedsteads, highboys and lowboys, and

further developed the gate-leg table. The legs of the furniture had pear-shaped enlargements near the top. This pear, typical of the period, is repeated in the brass drop-pull, *Figure 7.*

QUEEN ANNE (1702–1714)

The reign of Queen Anne, sister of Queen Mary, continued the strong Dutch style set by William and Mary, but with certain modifications. Formal lines were abandoned and turnings wholly omitted. Furniture, built chiefly on curved and graceful lines, achieved a subtle charm that is still intensely appealing. Bail handles appeared. They were no longer fastened on with a wire, but with a threaded rod (or bolt) and nut. The backplate in *Figure 8* shows basket of flowers; in *Figure 9,* a typical Queen Anne design is stamped in the metal to resemble engraving.

LOUIS XV (1715–1744)

The furniture which came into vogue during the reign of Louis XV of France, became extremely popular and retained some hold to the beginning of the nineteenth century. Curves, both single and double, were used extravagantly; right angles were abandoned; all angles were rounded off; volutes and curves were multiplied. From the knobs on the doors to the decorations on the walls, every line was sinuous, every surface rounded.

The individuality of Louis XV furniture lies in the irregularity of outline and complete lack of symmetry. Decorative details crowd upon each other; decorations and motifs have uneven sides; no ornament can be divided into two equal parts by a line drawn down its center. Although the two sides do not repeat one another exactly, their masses are equal in value, and balance is maintained. Handles were neither drop nor bail, but rigid, often of ormolu, or heavy gilt bronze. In *Figures 10 and 11,* gilded brass handles repeat the asymmetrical design.

CHIPPENDALE (1754–1765)

The furniture Thomas Chippendale designed from 1754–1765 was popular, and the style he created took his name. Made of mahogany and graceful in line, Chippendale furniture shows both French and Chinese influence. Outstanding characteristics are the cutting out of the solid splat in finely carved openwork designs of interlacing ribbands, and the crest, shaped like a cupid's bow and turned up at the ends, placed on the uprights. *Figure 12* shows backplate for bail handle with interlacing ribband

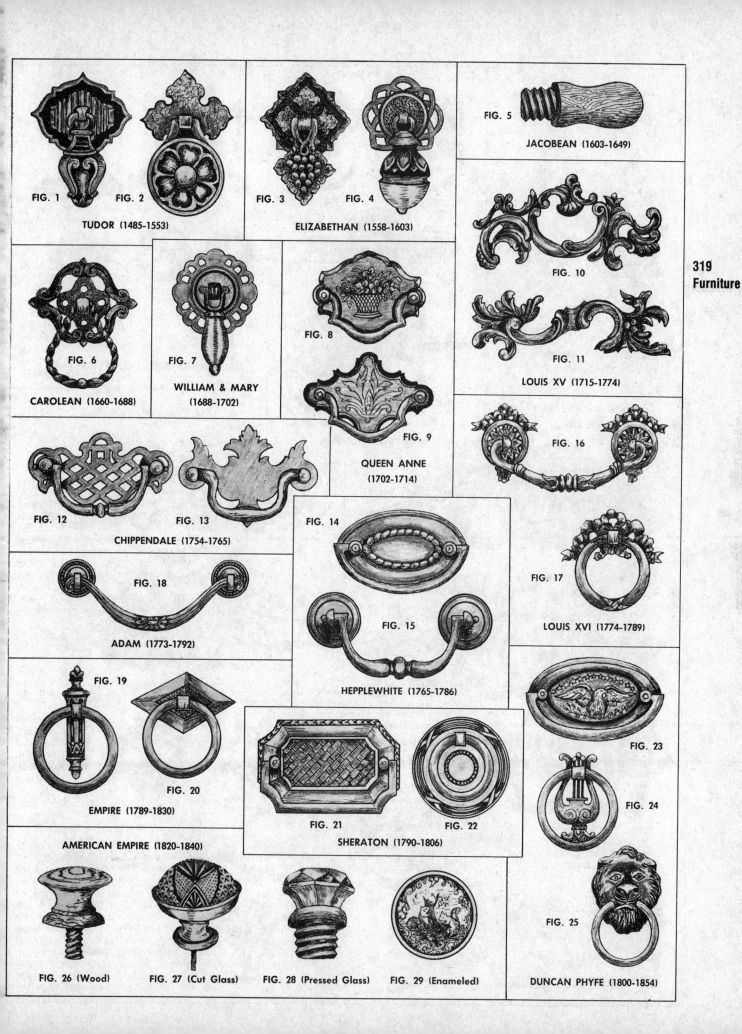

FIG. 1   FIG. 2

TUDOR (1485-1553)

FIG. 3   FIG. 4

ELIZABETHAN (1558-1603)

FIG. 5

JACOBEAN (1603-1649)

FIG. 6

CAROLEAN (1660-1688)

FIG. 7

WILLIAM & MARY
(1688-1702)

FIG. 8

FIG. 9

QUEEN ANNE
(1702-1714)

FIG. 10

FIG. 11

LOUIS XV (1715-1774)

FIG. 12   FIG. 13

CHIPPENDALE (1754-1765)

FIG. 16

FIG. 14

FIG. 15

HEPPLEWHITE (1765-1786)

FIG. 17

LOUIS XVI (1774-1789)

FIG. 18

ADAM (1773-1792)

FIG. 19

FIG. 20

EMPIRE (1789-1830)

FIG. 21   FIG. 22

SHERATON (1790-1806)

FIG. 23

FIG. 24

AMERICAN EMPIRE (1820-1840)

FIG. 26 (Wood)   FIG. 27 (Cut Glass)   FIG. 28 (Pressed Glass)   FIG. 29 (Enameled)

FIG. 25

DUNCAN PHYFE (1800-1854)

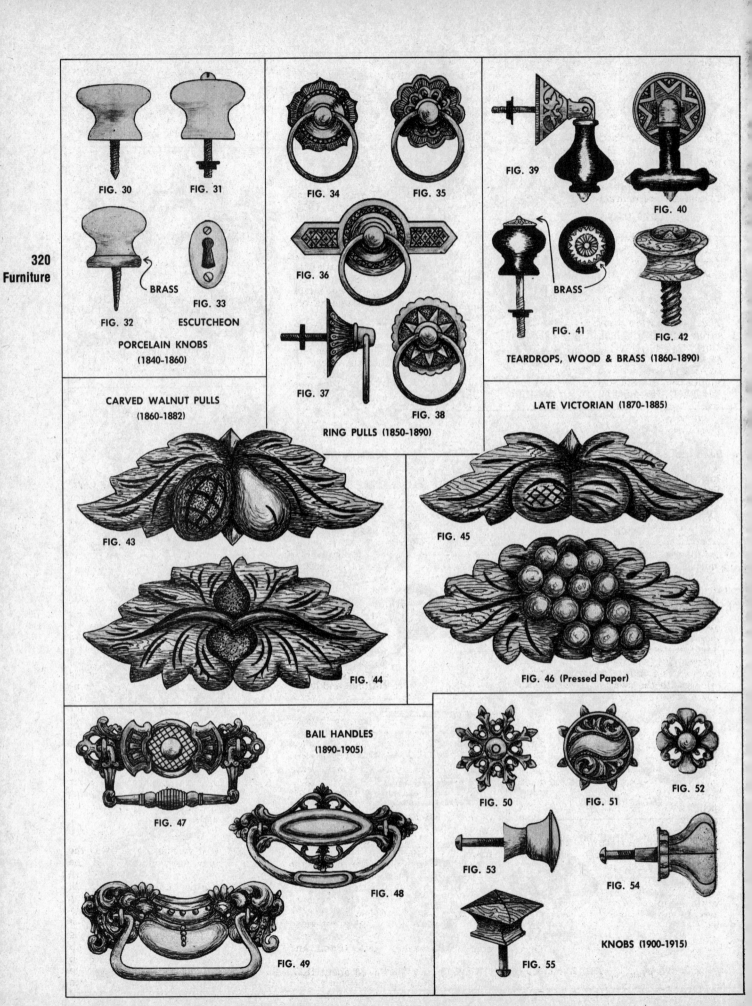

**320
Furniture**

FIG. 30

FIG. 31

FIG. 32

BRASS

FIG. 33
ESCUTCHEON

**PORCELAIN KNOBS
(1840-1860)**

FIG. 34

FIG. 35

FIG. 36

FIG. 37

FIG. 38

RING PULLS (1850-1890)

FIG. 39

FIG. 40

FIG. 41

BRASS

FIG. 42

TEARDROPS, WOOD & BRASS (1860-1890)

**CARVED WALNUT PULLS
(1860-1882)**

FIG. 43

FIG. 44

LATE VICTORIAN (1870-1885)

FIG. 45

FIG. 46 (Pressed Paper)

**BAIL HANDLES
(1890-1905)**

FIG. 47

FIG. 48

FIG. 49

FIG. 50

FIG. 51

FIG. 52

FIG. 53

FIG. 54

FIG. 55

KNOBS (1900-1915)

motif; *Figure 13,* the well known "willow" pattern.

HEPPLEWHITE (1765–1786)

In the furniture of George Hepplewhite, the influence of Adam is evident though his classicism is not as pure as Adam's. Hepplewhite confined himself almost entirely to mahogany, using lighter woods only for inlay. The two bail handles, *Figures 14 and 15,* are characteristic.

LOUIS XVI (1774–1789)

The style of furniture known now as Louis XVI was called in its own time "antique style," because it was inspired by the excavations at Pompeii. Fashion then centered on whatever was old, and all the chimerical animals used in the Middle Ages in French art were recalled to favor—often reproduced in bronze. The feature of furniture of this style is the pronounced constructional element, based on the classic order. Right angles dominated. Although at times Louis XVI resembled early Louis XIV work, a new delicacy ran through it, expressing the gay, impulsive spirit of Marie Antoinette. Garlands of roses and baskets of flowers were still used, and delicate carving, generally of scrolled ribbons or flowers, followed and accentuated the main lines. *Figures 16 and 17* show the ribbon motif.

ADAM (1773–1792)

Made of light colored woods or painted in light colors, furniture produced under the design influence of Robert Adam was based on the architectural arrangement of the classic orders and was beautiful in its simplicity and slenderness of line. Swags of leaves, flowers, and draperies, bound together with ribbons, decorate the furniture, as do husks, urns and wheat, all borrowed from Classic Rome. The husk motif is shown, along with the swag, in the bail handle in *Figure 18.*

EMPIRE (1789–1830)

Empire furniture had its beginning in Paris after the Revolution, reached its peak under the first Empire of Napoleon, 1804–1813, and lingered on for at least another decade. Napoleon, inspired by the excavations at Pompeii, wielded great influence over artistic design, preferring the bold and imposing character of Roman Art. Empire furniture is severely symmetrical, with large plane surfaces rectangular in shape, the corners sharp and square. Emblems used most frequently were the antefix, stars, Cap of Liberty, the heavy wreath with tri-colored cockade, the Fasces, and the Pike. Borrowed from the antique for decorative value were chimeras, swans, and such. These decorations were not reflected in the hardware. *Figures 19 and 20* are Roman in design, and feature the early appearance of the ring pull.

SHERATON (1790–1806)

Thomas Sheraton founded a style of furniture still popular. Its proportions were light and delicate. Inlay, carving and turning predominated in the decoration. *Figure 21* shows the typical convex end curves repeated on the backplate of the bail handle; *Figure 22,* the ring handle.

DUNCAN PHYFE (1800–1854)

In 1922, the Metropolitan Museum of Art held a loan exhibition of Duncan Phyfe's work. His name, previously little known, immediately assumed importance among American cabinetmakers. Phyfe, a Scotsman, came to this country and settled in New York in 1792. By 1800, the fine quality of his designs and workmanship was bringing him increasing orders from many cities.

Though he worked until his death in 1854, Phyfe's best work was done between 1800 and 1825, when he copied the best features of Sheraton furniture then in vogue, and also created in the Directoire and Empire styles. The finest mahogany is characteristic of his furniture, and his work is distinguished by its gracefulness and beautiful proportions. To every form he copied, he added the refinements and ornamentations of his own taste. His work appealed to cultured people of his own time—and of ours. The decorations he used, he executed delicately. Although not original with him, the lion's paw, lion's head, carved acanthus leaf, eagle, and lyre are all characteristic of his work. Motifs typical of his work are shown on his handles: *Figure 23,* eagle and stars on oval backplate for bail handle; *Figure 24,* lyre on backplate for ring handle; *Figure 25,* lion's head with ring handle in its mouth.

AMERICAN EMPIRE (1820–1840)

American Empire furniture reflected the growing independence of the new United States. People preferred to patronize national and home industries. They were buying furniture from local-cabinetmakers who, though copying the prevailing Empire style, injected their freedom of spirit in innovations which gave their work its own provincial flavor. The majority of pieces were of mahogany, lavishly veneered with crotch mahogany; some were of cherry, with or without veneer; a few pieces were of maple. Occasional turnings and the use of ogee moldings added to the decoration, and drawer handles marked a new era.

Now, the cabinetmaker needing a handle turned out a mushroom topped knob with a threaded stem (*Figure 26*) and screwed it into the threaded hole in the drawer front. For a brilliant appearance he used a cut glass knob (*Figure 27*), a lovely American confection, backed with tinfoil and set into a brass collar.

Pressed glass appeared about 1827. Soon glasshouses in Sandwich and elsewhere were making knobs for cupboards and drawers. Faceted, and with a thick, threaded base (*Figure 28*), they came in both clear and iridescent glass. An exceptionally dainty knob imitated Battersea enamel. Made of brass, the face of the knob was enameled in dainty scenic designs, like and similar to that in *Figure 29.* These knobs, and the departure by American cabinetmakers from the usual Empire pattern, mark this style American.

PORCELAIN (1840–1860)

Entering the early Victorian period, *Figures 30, 31, and 32* show three of the most popular types of porcelain knobs. Those in *Figures 30 and 32* have a fixed wood screw with which they were fastened to the drawer front, secured with a nut. Probably most of these knobs were used on cottage furniture — cupboards and such. However, *Figure 32,* with its brass base, is a nice piece of workmanship and was undoubtedly designed for better than utility use.

RING PULLS (1850–1890)

Figures 34 to 38 are typical brass ring pulls in favor from about 1850 to 1890. *Figures 34, 35, 37, and 38* have embossed rosettes which extend about an inch from the face of the drawer, as shown in *Figure 37.* These handles were fastened by a bolt and nut. These handles were used on dressers, commodes, and the like. They were also used by sewing machine companies, and often the company's name was stamped in the flat backplate.

TEARDROPS (1860–1890)

Teardrop pulls, with their pretty, graceful lines, were used extensively on mid and late Victorian furniture. A combination of brass and black-enameled maple, they were made in three different patterns. *Figure 39* shows the graceful pear-shaped drop, with embossed, cone-shaped brass backplate. *Figure 40* has the same style backplate, but the drop is shaped like an inverted T. A companion knob, *Figure 41,* also of brass and enameled wood, was made for small drawers on tops of dressers and doors of commodes. All of these fasten to the drawer by a bolt and nut, with a permanent washer attached to the nut. *Figure 42* shows a turned walnut knob, 2 inches in diameter, a popular style for over thirty years. It was fastened by the threaded wooden shaft method.

CARVED WALNUT (1860–1882)

The carved wooden handle was the most popular drawer handle of the entire Victorian period; nut and fruit designs were particularly favored. At least two dozen different patterns were carved by various cabinetmakers. *Figures 43 and 44* show two of the best. The handle in *Figure 43* is made in two pieces as most of them were. The back piece, about ⅝-inch thick, was sawed out and cut to shape with a carving chisel. The fruit was then sawed out, carved to shape, and glued onto the backplate. The one-piece handle in *Figure 44* is made, in much the same manner, from a piece of wood ⅞-inch thick, with a finger grip cut out on the lower side of the back.

LATE VICTORIAN (1870–1885)

When items first appear on the market, they are usually of excellent quality; as time goes on, cheaper copies appear. This was true of walnut drawer handles. *Figures 45 and 46* show two of the later cheaper type. The handle in *Figure 45* has the usual leaf-shaped backplate, but the glued-on part, instead of being carved, is turned on a turning lathe, split in half, glued onto the backplate, and completed with a few strokes of the veining tool. While this handle on a cabinet might seem at quick glance to look all right, closer study will reveal its inferior workmanship. *Fig-*

ure 46 is made of pressed paper as were the majority of handles in the grape design. If leaves show many fine and dainty lines, the chances are the handle is of paper. These, also, were screwed onto the drawer front from the inside.

BAIL HANDLES (1890–1905)

About 1890, the carved wooden drawer pull, the ring, and teardrop handles were out of style. The bail handle was again in favor to remain until about 1905. The style was ornate like everything of the Gay Nineties. The backplates were pierced. The best were of cast brass, with brass bails (*Figures 47 and 48*). Cheaper editions were flimsy, stamped out of thin sheet brass (*Figure 49*), the bails often of iron, brass plated. Many of these were used on the inexpensive golden oak furniture and the cheaper walnut pieces of the 1900s.

KNOBS (1900–1915)

Figures 50 to 55 show knobs popularly used on the same style of furniture as the bail handles of 1890–1905. *Figure 50* is a pierced rosette, or backplate, for the knob shown in *Figure 51*. It is dated 1899. *Figure 52* is another style of pierced knob; *Figure 53* is a lightweight, hollow brass knob. The method of fastening the knob to the drawer had now changed from the bolt and nut to the bolt that was threaded into the knob itself, to be fastened with a screw driver. In *Figure 54*, the pressed glass knob appears again in a combination of glass and brass. It is a nice knob, well made, octagonal in shape, and dated October 29, 1901. *Figure 55* shows the square wooden knob made for the square heavy Mission furniture in vogue.

REFINISHING ANTIQUE FURNITURE

by J. B. LAMBERT
Author of *Lambert's Refinishing Manual.*

Fig. 1. Although the finish is shabby, and the glue joints loose, this walnut chest of drawers is structurally sound and well worth restoring.

Fig. 2. The large drawers have been stained to show the color contrast to the sanded wood. Various portions of the upper part of the chest have been removed to be properly refinished.

Fig. 3. The chest is pulled together and squared with bar clamps. Small "C" clamps are used to hold the reglued portion of the top to the main frame. Drawer guides can be seen on inside end of chest.

FOR THE MAJORITY of novice refinishers the techniques of antique furniture restoration can be *learned* and *developed.* The only prerequisites are a sincere desire to do such work and a willingness to follow directions. The complete repair and refinishing of the Victorian period walnut chest of drawers in *Figure 1* is accomplished by carrying out seven basic restoration steps.

In its "as found" condition the chest is not suitable for use in the home. The backboard and small drawer boxes are loose, as are some of the basic glue joints. The main drawers stick and sag. A wooden knob and keyhole escutcheon are missing from one of the smaller drawers. The finish is scratched and the natural grain design and color tone of the walnut wood is hidden by coats of stain and varnish applied over the years. With all these faults the chest still remains structurally sound; no major parts are missing or broken beyond repair. The chest is well worth preserving.

Step 1 — Dismantle the piece

The restoration work can be accomplished more conveniently if certain parts of the chest, which are held in place by nails or screws, are removed from the main case (*Figure 2*). On some pieces these parts are glued in place. Do not attempt to break a glued surface in order to remove a section. Dismantle only those portions which can be taken apart and reassembled without damage to the wood or the final finished surface.

It is important that these sections be marked for identification so they can be replaced in their proper positions. Since the main drawers will often fit only one opening they also should be marked; as well as all screws and the holes in which they belong.

Step 2 — Repairing the chest

All repair work should be completed *prior* to removing the old finish. This will prevent excess glue from being smeared onto exposed raw wood causing blemishes in the final finish coat. It also prevents remover from seeping into loose joints which would make it impossible to form a solid glue bond.

Repair work is first begun on the case of the chest. Inspection indicated that a portion of the top had broken away from the main frame. In addition, some of the glue blocks inside the chest were missing and the bearing rails separating the drawer openings had pulled away from the ends of the chest causing it to wobble from side to side.

Plenty of glue was worked into the joints at each end of the bearing rails, the front of the chest pulled together with bar clamps and the corner glue blocks replaced. A framing square was used to insure that the case was being held together squarely. At the same time we were able to glue down the top with 'C' clamps (*Figure 3*). The back of the case required only a few nails to secure it in place. New caster blocks were cut from 2 x 4" lumber and glued to both the front and back corners (*Figure 4*).

Fig. 4. New castor blocks have been glued in place.

Fig. 5. A framing square is used to check the drawer before nailing bottom in place.

Fig. 6. Extreme wear shows on bottom of drawer sides. White area is a new rail strip placed on inner edge of drawer.

If the corners of the drawers are loose, glue can be worked into these areas and small brads driven into the joints. The drawer bottom should be seated securely in the grooves provided on the inside of the drawer front and sides. This will "square" the drawer and can be checked by laying a framing square in each corner before securing the bottom with nails *(Figure 5)*.

In most cases, years of use will have worn the drawer rails down to such an extent that the drawer fits loosely, tips up and down, and scrapes across the bearing rails on the front of the chest *(Figure 6)*. This fault is remedied by gluing ½ x ¾" wood strips along the inner edge of the drawer sides *(Figure 7)*. These are then planed down so as to be flush with the bottom edge of the drawer front. Adding these strips will require that new runners be placed on the inside of the chest. A wood strip ¾" x ¾" is glued to the edge of the existing runner *(Figure 8)*.

The drawer guides, attached to the inside of the case, will often need to be reglued or replaced if the drawer is to fit snug and not wiggle from side to side. Again ¾" x ¾" wood strips are used. These are positioned at right angles to the front of the case using a framing square to insure that they lie in a straight line, front to back *(Figure 9)*.

Wood blocks ¼" thick are used to replace worn stops which prevent the drawer from sliding in beyond the opening. These should be 1" wide and 1½" long. They are glued to the top or bottom of the bearing rails and located so as to stop the drawer when it is flush with the chest front *(Figure 8)*. After the refinishing work is completed, paraffin wax is rubbed on the drawer sides and rails. The new rails will then ride smoothly on the new runners.

A new wooden knob and keyhole escutcheon were acquired from a local cabinet shop. This completed the repair work.

Step 3 — Removing old finish

The removal of the old finish is accomplished by using a nonflammable, commercial solvent paint and varnish remover of semi-liquid consistency. Be fully aware of all the manufacturer's precautions pertaining to the particular remover being used.

Divide the work into sections, removing the finish from one section at a time. Begin by applying remover to the top of the chest. Do not make the coat too thin and do not re-brush the initial coat once it has been spread over an area. As the remover starts to "flat-out," apply more remover to that surface — keep the piece wet. Allow about 20 minutes for the remover to do its work. Rub the area with #2 grade steel wool and again apply a liberal coat of remover. In 10 to 15 minutes, rub the section clean with rough rags. Next, apply remover to one of the sides of the chest. Complete that section and move on to the front, finishing with the other end panel. Flush the entire piece with utility lacquer thinner or other prescribed solvent. Use a clean brush for this job making sure that all remover is eliminated from the corners, carvings, and turnings. Wipe the piece dry with clean rags and allow at least 48 hours before attempting any further work. The other parts of the chest are treated in the same manner, completing one section at a time.

Caution: Do not use the finish removal brush for any other purpose.

Step 4 — Sanding

All nail holes, cracks and gouges in the wood surface should be filled with surfacing putty prior to sanding. This is available in a variety of color tones, sets-up to the hardness of wood, and can be sanded smooth with abrasive paper. Use a small palette knife to force putty into the hole or crack. Allow a little excess putty to protrude above the level of the wood surface to compensate for any shrinkage. The

Fig. 11. "Laying-on" the finish coat.

Fig. 12. "Tipping-off" the finish coat.

Fig. 10. When filler appears "calky" it is ready for rough wiping.

Fig. 7. New rail strip glued into place.

Fig. 8. Inside of the chest, as viewed from the bottom, shows new drawer runners, glue blocks, and stops.

Fig. 9. New drawer guides are placed, and checked with a framing square.

Fig. 13. The refinished chest ready for many more years of useful service.

filled areas should dry thoroughly before sanding.

In most cases very little sanding will be necessary if the finish removal operation has been carried out correctly. Most surface smoothing that is necessary can be accomplished by using #120 (3/0) *aluminum oxide 'C' weight abrasive paper.* Purchase the open coat type. Sand *with* the grain of the wood, never against the grain or in a circular motion. Use steady pressure and even strokes, sanding all areas equally in a uniform manner. Finish by sanding with #180 (5/0) paper. No. 2 grade steel wool is used to smooth carvings, turnings, and moldings.

Step 5 — Staining

A walnut *liquid oil wood stain* is now applied to the chest. These pigmented oil stains offer the most desirable means of restoring natural color tones to antique woods *(Figure 2)*. They fade very little and are easily applied with a brush.

Apply a liberal, evenly distributed coat to the surface, starting at the top of the piece and working down to the lower sections. Make sure the stain is worked into all carvings, turnings, and corners. As the stain begins to flat-out (10 to 15 minutes) use soft rags to wipe away the excess. Wipe *with* the grain of the wood when possible until all excess stain is eliminated. Allow 24 hours to dry.

Stain the other parts of the chest in the same manner making sure that you stain the interior of the drawers as well as the outside. This will help eliminate the musty odor of age

which often accompanies antique case pieces.

Step 6 — Wood filler

Walnut, being of the variety known as "open grained" wood, requires an application of filler if the surface is to appear soft and smooth. Neutral color wood paste filler is mixed with paint thinner to the consistency of thick soup. Oil wood stain is then added to match the color of the stained wood. The filler is liberally applied brushing first *across* the grain of the wood then smoothing the coat *with* the grain. Periodically stir the mixture to keep it constant.

When the filler coat appears "calky," it is ready for rough wiping with coarse rags. Rub *across* the grain and then in a *circular* motion *(Figure 10)*. This packs the filler into the pores and grain of the wood. After all excess filler is removed, a soft rag is used to wipe *with* the grain of the wood until the surface takes on a soft sheen. Again allow 24 hours for drying.

Step 7 — The finish coats

The overall beauty and durability found in a restored piece of antique furniture will largely depend upon the type of finish used. This author believes that the modern synthetic finishes offer the best results. When selecting the proper material the craftsman must rely upon information supplied by the manufacture. This information should specify that the material (a) can be applied with a brush; (b) is a clear, self-leveling finish; (c) dries "dust free" within one hour and can be re-coated within 24 hours; (d) does not require a sealer coat when used over wood paste fillers or oil based stains.

Before applying the finish make sure that your well-lighted work area is as dust free as possible and that the temperature in the room is approximately 70 to 80 degrees F. The amount of finish required to do the immediate job at hand should be strained into a clean can and applied only with a clean brush—one that has not been used for any other purpose. The piece of furniture should be thoroughly wiped down with a "tack rag" (chemically treated to pick up

dust) which will eliminate dust and lint.

The brushing techniques employed in the application of synthetic varnish consist of two major steps — that of *laying-on* and that of *tipping-off* the varnish coat.

The laying-on should be done with smooth, even strokes, flowing the varnish over the surface rather than brushing it on like paint *(Figure 11)*. Make sure that all the surface area is covered with a liberal coating. After one complete section is covered it must be tipped-off immediately.

Tipping-off smooths out the finish coat. As much finish as possible is eliminated from the brush. This "dry" brush is then held in an almost vertical position with only the tips of the bristles touching the surface *(Figure 12)*. The tipping-off is accomplished with one continuous, gentle stroke, moving the brush with the grain of the wood across the surface from one edge to the other. This is continued until the entire surface has been "tipped."

A second coat of finish should be applied after the first coat is completely dry. Before applying this second coat it will be necessary to lightly sand the surface with #220 (6/0) abrasive paper. This light sanding will smooth off any dust nibs and scuff the surface sa as to form a "tooth" to which the second coat will adhere. The surface must then be wiped clean with the tack rag and the second coat applied in the same manner as the first.

After the piece is completely dry and surface hard (approx. 48 hours), it should be very lightly sanded with #320 (9/0) abrasive paper and wiped clean. The chest can then be reassembled and is ready for years of valuable and enjoyable service *(Figure 13)*.

All the materials used in the restoration of this walnut chest can be purchased in most local paint supply stores. Many of the better known "brand name" products on the market today are so similar in composition that one will often do just as good a job as another. For this reason the author has chosen to point out the qualities to look for when purchasing refinishing materials rather than specifying one particular brand which might not be available in all localities.

Take a Plank Bottom Chair...

by EDGAR and VERNA GUYTON

FAMILY heirlooms gathering dust in the attic? Let's take down that old plank bottom chair and fix it up for use!

If it's typical, you'll find about three to five coats of paint under its layer of dust, and there may be broken or missing parts. These should be replaced by a cabinetmaker, first of all. Then, with a pint of good quality paint remover (we use Zip Strip) and four 1-inch Red Devil scrapers, you're ready to begin.

(After many years of refinishing, we cannot hold with the theory that paint remover drives paint into the wood; the consistency of the old paint and the porosity of the wood being refinished governs the depth the paint has penetrated. We do not believe in using lye, as it bleaches the wood. So, unless the old paint is flaky and chips off so easily it can be removed with a sharp scraper, paint remover is our servant.)

Start on the Seat

Following directions on the paint remover can, start on an area of chair seat size, applying remover liberally, allowing plenty of time for it to work. If any spots are not soft after the elapsed time, scrape off old remover, and apply new.

Continue in this fashion over the rest of the chair until you have it down to bare wood. Take care to hold your scraper straight with the grain, and rigid to prevent gouge marks. Half the success in refinishing is due to the sharpness of your scrapers. We find that scrapers, put in a vise and sharpened to a wire edge with a flat file held firmly in both hands, cut work in half.

If legs and spindles have turnings, there will be paint in the cracks. Use paint remover and coarse steel wool here; scrapers will roughen the wood. Around turnings, use steel wool, rope-fashion.

Now the chair is bare of paint. Disassemble loose parts, carefully to prevent damaging the rest of the chair, and reglue with a white glue, such as Weldwood. Dig out old putty and paint in holes and cracks, and refill with a wood filler. (We like

Famowood, which comes in many colors.) Almost all seats and backs are either pine or poplar. Wood filler slightly darker than surrounding wood makes the chair look more antique.

After filler is thoroughly hardened, sand the chair completely, first with medium, then fine, production paper. This also must be done with the grain. Production paper is used because of its fast cutting action.

Since most plank bottom chairs have poplar seats and back rests, they often show a greenish color. This can be turned to a beautiful brown by brushing on oxalic acid diluted with warm water. Let it dry over night, then sand off, very lightly, with fine sandpaper. (If your piece is pine, do not use this bleach.) Oxalic acid may be obtained from your druggist, but it is highly poisonous and must be kept from children. Use it with plenty of ventilation.

Mellowness of color can be adjusted by an easy-to-make stain: one-half pint turpentine mixed with a small amount of burnt umber and a very small amount of burnt sienna. This is enough for a complete chair. Apply and allow to dry overnight. If deeper mellowness is wanted, use a second coat. Umber and burnt sienna can be bought in tubes at art or hobby shops.

If the piece is being done in pine, we find Ipp Switch Min Max gives a good antique color. The depth of coloring is governed by the length of time it's left on before wiping off.

Wax Finish

The chair is now ready for a filler coat. Using half-and-half mixture of 4 lb. cut white shellac thinner, brush this filler coat on the complete chair, and allow to dry thoroughly. Sand with fine steel wool until satin smooth, taking care not to damage the color. Repeat this procedure a total of three coats. Then apply a

good paste wax liberally. Allow an hour to dry, rub with soft cloth. *Voila,* your chair!

Varnish Finish

If you prefer a varnish finish, follow the same procedure as above, but using only one coat of shellac, followed by two coats of Valspar-Low Lustre varnish. (After many experiments, we stay now with Valspar because of its durability and non-gumming.) The secret of smoothness lies in the steel wooling between coats. When varnish is used, provide a dust-free space to work in; dust, collecting on varnish, will leave the finish rough.

Walnut

When a walnut piece that has been painted is to be refinished, we again use scrapers and paint remover. After it has been thoroughly cleaned, a walnut Famowood or plastic wood can be used to fill nail holes and cracks. Then sand it completely, using first medium, then fine, sandpaper. Here again, several coats of filler of half-and-half shellac and shellac thinner should be used, with steel woolings between each coat. Be sure each coat is thoroughly dry before sanding.

For color, use a good grade of paste wax mixed with a little burnt umber, slightly darker than the wood. This darker shade helps blend in any new wood used for repair. Mix umber well with the wax to avoid streaking, and rub with the grain. Let dry 30 minutes to an hour, and polish. Apply necessary hardware. Stand back and admire!

If you're lucky, and your walnut piece has not been painted, you will not need to use a scraper. Paint remover and light steel wool will remove the old varnish or shellac, and save the patina, too. Use clean fine steel wool to rub to satin smoothness. Here again, use three coats of half-and-half shellac, steel wooling between each coat. Apply the wax finish, leaving color out, or varnish.

Cherry

Cherry, which picks up its color as it ages, presents a little different problem. Since cherry nail hole filler is not obtainable, use redwood stick filler. This can be bought at most hardware stores or lumber companies. Using a penknife, cut off and work it into the nail holes.

Through the process of refinishing, much of the beautiful cherry color is lost, and unless the piece is at least 100 years old, it will need to be put back. By using a cherry oil stain, such as O'Brien, and following directions, your cherry will take on the color you want. Stain one area at a time, wiping off according to darkness desired. Here again, we use three coats of shellac, diluted half-and-half, followed by a good coat of paste wax, or varnish, as used on walnut.

GLASS

In ancient times, glass was considered as valuable as gold and silver. But today's collector can spend as little as a few dollars or as much as several thousand dollars acquiring a collection of glass. Pattern glass has always been a favorite, whether early lacey pressed glass made at Sandwich or late pressed wares made in the Pittsburgh and Wheeling areas. Art glass, once not so costly, has risen in value within the last twenty years to the point where only a few people can afford to acquire superb examples.

New Information on
FAMILIAR PATTERNS

The pressed glass patterns described here are not to be found in any current literature on pressed glass. The Central Glass Co., of Wheeling, W. Va., produced them all, and showed them in their catalog, ca. 1880, from which our illustrations are selected. They are attributed and listed here for the first time.

— by ALBERT CHRISTIAN REVI —

THE CENTRAL GLASS COMPANY was founded in 1863 in Wheeling, West Virginia, by a group of eight glassblowers — John Oesterling, William K. Elson, Theodore Schultz, Andrew Baggs, Peter Castle, James Leasure, John Henderson, and Roy Combs—who pooled their resources, a scanty $1,200, to start operations. Under John Oesterling as president, the firm prospered, slowly at first, then by leaps and bounds. By 1879, the home trade had reached tremendous proportions, and exports went all over the world. Shares of stock at a par value of $200 sold at $1,400; dividends in some years amounted to 63 percent. Those of the partners who held out through the lean first years became rich.

In 1887, Mr. Oesterling died, and Nathan B. Scott succeeded him as president. In 1891 Central joined the United States Glass Company, becoming "Factory O." The new owners wanted an open shop; the men refused to allow it; consequently the plant was inactive from 1893 to 1895.

In 1896, a new company was formed using the old name, with Nathan B. Scott, Peter Cassell, L. F.

No. 829 - Oesterling

4 ½" COMPORT

MOLASSES CAN SALT SHAKER SUGAR CREAM

No. 829—Oesterling

Sometime between 1876 and 1880, the Central Glass Company produced their "829 Set," which we have named "Oesterling" pattern in honor of John Oesterling, first president of this glassworks.

The pattern consists of a squat, bulbous body with a wide flaring rim made up of large flutes or panels separated by a single narrow prism, the stem and foot of each article being similarly decorated with flutes and prisms. The bulbous form of the body indicates these wares were produced by the method known as "press and blow," originated in 1865 by William Gillinder.

As with many other pressed tableware sets produced by this company, the plain portions of the objects were sometimes engraved with simple designs. (Catalog illustrations show pieces in this set decorated with Central's "Engraved #219" design.)

The *Oesterling* pattern was produced in a full line of tablewares—pitchers from creamer size to half-gallon capacity; syrup jugs; sugar bowls; spoonholders; salt and pepper shakers; covered butter dishes; compotes, covered and uncovered, in several sizes; comports in 5 different sizes; oval-shaped dishes and bowls; and salvers, from 8 to 10 inches in diameter — in crystal and possibly colored glass, though the latter is not indicated in the catalog.

Stifel, and Joseph Speidel. The works were moved to Summitville, Indiana, and by 1898 were in full production.

The depression of the 1930s closed the plant for a short time, but it reopened again in 1933, engaged in the manufacture of all kinds of bar goods. By 1939, competition from foreign wares forced the company to close for good. The Imperial Glass Company acquired their molds and machinery in 1939.

Among Centrals most important patterns were *Cabbage Rose* (1870); *Wheat in Shield* (1871), both designed by John Oesterling; *Cord and Tassel* (1872), by Andrew H. Baggs; *Log Cabin* (ca. 1875); *Silver Age*, known to collectors as *Coin*, which went on the market about the time of the merger with U. S. Glass Company and *Columbia Coin*, also 1891.

[A listing of all Central's patterns known when his book was written appears in Mr. Revi's *American Pressed Glass and Figure Bottles* (1964). Those shown here can now be added.]

No. 877 - Shell

TABLE SALT

IND. SALT

GOBLET

TUMBLER

BUTTER DISH

CREAM

No. 877—Shell

Central's "No. 877 Set," which we have named "Shell" from its resemblance to the common scallop shell, appeared in the 1880 period in a wide range of tablewares in crystal —tumblers! goblets; celery vases; compotes, covered and uncovered; pitchers, in 3 sizes; sugar bowls, in 2 sizes, with or without covers; covered butter dish; salt and pepper shakers; individual salts; table salts; nappies; various comports and syrup jugs.

The design is distinguished by prominent tapering ribs halfway up the body of each article—these are repeated on the foot of every piece in the set except the goblet — and the spiraled ribs at the base of the handles. There is a possibility collectors will encounter this pattern with engraved designs on the plain portions, or perhaps in color.

No. 810 - Tudor

6" COMPORT

SUGAR AND COVER

BONE PLATE

CREAM

ICE CREAM

ICE CREAM AND COVER

We give the name "Tudor" to the pattern the Central Glass shows as "810 Set" in their original catalog. This pattern was produced about 1880, and consisted of a wide band of diamond cut "buttons" alternating with squares in a fine-cut design. The upper portion of the objects was plain and, as evidenced by catalog illustrations, was sometimes lightly engraved in various simple patterns. There were handsomely designed stems in this set; finials or knobs resemble a Gothic Cross; and some pitchers have "shell" handles.

Our catalog showed nappies in several sizes; spoonholders; covered sugar bowls; pitchers, creamer size to half-gallon capacity; individual salt dips; salt and pepper shakers; covered butter dishes; ice cream dishes, covered and uncovered with attached saucers; pickle dishes; bone plates; tumblers; stemmed compotes, covered and uncovered; and comports in several sizes. Line was produced in crystal (possibly in colored glass, too).

No. 794 - Rope Pattern

6" LOW COV. COMPORT

CREAM

8" SALVER

4 ½" NAPPY

SUGAR SIFTER

No. 796 - Rope and Thumbprint Pattern

CELERY

4 ½" COMPORT

4 ½" NAPPY

6" COMPORT & COVER

SUGAR SIFTER

The main feature of the design of the *Rope* pattern (Central's "794 Set"), the rope-like edge around the rim of most of the pieces, is the result of the pattern being superimposed on both faces of the glass. When viewed from either side the combined effect of the inner and outer configuration has the illusion of being a twisted rope around the edge.

All pieces in this set, being rather bulbous, have a very ample capacity. Like the *Oesterling* pattern, the bulbous forms were produced by the so-called "press and blow" method. Central offered its *Rope* pattern to the trade in crystal with a choice of lightly engraved designs. A page of engraving patterns in the catalog permitted buyer's selection.

A variant of the *Rope* Pattern, Central's No. 796, we call *Rope and Thumbprint*. Here the bulbous portion of each piece has been pattern-molded with staggered rows of thumbprints; the characteristic rope-like design around most articles shows clearly in the catalog pages.

Both patterns were issued in a full line of tablewares—compotes, covered and uncovered; pitchers in various sizes, from creamer to half-gallon

capacity; salt and pepper shakers; sugar sifters; spoonholders; nappies; finger bowls; syrup jugs; sugar bowls; etc.—in crystal, and possibly in colors.

(While no current literature on pressed glass patterns has noted any

of these designs shown, Peterson's *Salt & Salt Shakers* does illustrate a salt shaker in *Rope and Thumbprint*, calling it "Thumbprint Inverted Round", but the manufacturer is not there identified.)

No. 838 - Barrel Set

PICKLE OR SUGAR

SPOONER

Among the many novelty tableware sets the Central Glass Company made, is their "No. 838 Pattern," which we dub the "Barrel Set." This 3-piece set, consisting of spoonholder, covered pickle jar (or sugar bowl), and creamer, was produced about 1880 in crystal and in colors.

The design consists of a bulbous pressed and blown body resembling a barrel and serrated arches in a scalloped formation about the rim and foot of each piece. Cover of the dual purpose pickle jar/sugar bowl is ornamented with the scalloped and serrated arches, and surmounted by a tiny replica of a barrel which serves as the knob or finial.

Though the original catalog picture was damaged, and portions of the pitcher and pickle jar are missing, enough of the distinctive pattern remains to make identification possible.

CORNER MEDALLION—In **Booklet 2**, page 12, of her **Early American Pattern Glass**, Alice Hulett Metz illustrates a pitcher in a pressed glass pattern which she named "Corner Medallion," but did not attribute to a maker.

This design is included in the Central Glass Company's catalog as their "No. 720 Set," and offered in plain and engraved crystal. The set consisted of pitchers, from creamer to half-gallon size, covered sugar bowls, spoonholders, butter dishes with drainers, covered casseroles, comports, with and without covers, comports, oval dishes, salt and pepper shakers, celery vases, syrup jugs, kerosene table lamps, hand lamps, cruet bottles to fit into metal frames, and bar bottles.

Not all the items have the elaborate lacy design from which Mrs. Metz obviously derived the pattern name. The exceptions are the salt and pepper shakers, celery vases, syrup jugs (or molasses cans), cruet bottles, bar bottles, and lamps.

Goblets, tumblers, and other articles usually included in a complete suite of tablewares were not shown in the catalog, but these may have been produced.

Handsome covered honey and butter dishes in Central's "No. 782" pattern bear striking resemblance to pieces in "Corner Medallion," and could easily have been used with it. The lacy design on "No. 782" is somewhat the same as on Corner Medallion; knobs on both are exactly alike.

(No. 782—See Text)

No. 705 - Simplicity

6" COVERED BOWL

COVERED BUTTER

4" COMPORT

WINE

SUGAR & COVER

The Central Glass Company's *Simplicity* pattern, (their "No. 705 Set") was produced about 1880 in crystal and possibly colored glass.

This rather plain design in pressed glass tablewares was often embellished with engraving as shown in the illustrations from the company catalog. The classical form of the body design is enhanced by the simple balluster stem on all pieces in the set.

This pattern was made in pitchers; spoonholders; celery vases; stemware goblets, clarets, and wine glasses; covered sugar bowls; butter dishes; comports; compotes; and nappies. There were undoubtedly other pieces in this set, but the *Simplicity* design is such that it would blend with almost any similar pattern for use.

BEAD AND CHAIN—"Bead and Chain" pattern, illustrated in **Kamm, Book 7,** pages 57 and 58, but unattributed, is now discovered in the Central Glass Company's catalog as their "No. 651 Set," plain and engraved.

Mrs. Kamm described this pattern as having a "horizontal row of large beads around the rim and down the handle and [with a] few links of chain around the base between the short feet . . . The body is six-sided with broad flat panels tapering gently from [the] rim to the waist," ending in curves at the base.

Finials on the covered pieces shown in the catalog could be described as a ring of loops or beads. Although only the creamer, half-gallon pitcher, spoonholder, covered sugar bowl, and butter dish were illustrated there, undoubtedly other pieces were made to complete the set. The distinctive character of the design would make identification of any other pieces a simple matter for collectors.

DOT AND DASH—**Kamm's Book 5,** page 11, illustrates the "Dot and Dash" pattern—Central Glass Company's "650 Set"—and describes it ably as consisting of a cylindrical body with row of beads just below a thin horizontal ring about the rim of the object, with a band of diagonal boxes, each enclosing diagonally placed dots and dashes at the base. The handles are ornamented with "rings, beading and leaves." Finials are representations of a stylized cross.

Two of the six pages illustrating this pattern in the Central Glass Company's catalog show it with various engraved designs, indicating that the set was then quite popular. Mrs. Kamm reported the cream pitcher in crystal, and stated it might well be found with engraved designs or with ruby stain on the plain portions.

Compotes, comports, bowls, nappies, celery vases, spoonholders, sugar bowls, creamers, and the large half-gallon pitcher in this pattern were shown in the catalog. It is quite possible other pieces in this set were produced to complete the suite.

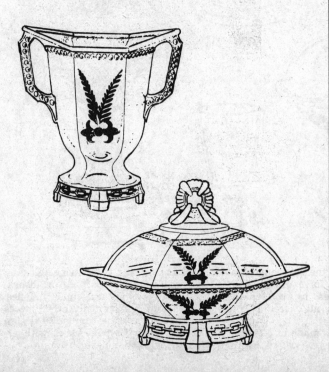

STAR GALAXY or EFFULGENT STAR—Both Mrs. Kamm and Dr. Millard noted this particular star pattern, though neither attributed it to a maker. Millard in **Goblets II,** plate 122, called it "Effulgent Star." Mrs. Kamm, in **Book 8,** page 78, referred to it as "Star Galaxy," showing a handsome salver from the collection of Mrs. Carlton Hackett of Detroit, Michigan, and suggesting other pieces might some day be discovered.

Three pages of illustrations in the Central Glass Company's catalog show 39 pieces in this set — goblets, tumblers, pitchers, syrup jugs, bowls, nappies, comports, compotes — covered and uncovered, salvers, butter dishes, sugar bowls, spooners, celery vases, finger bowls, large bread plates, ice or orange bowls, trays, salt and pepper shakers, individual table salts, toy mugs, a 5-piece water set, and the like.

The design features 6-pointed stars, all approximately the same size on each piece, rather prominently raised from the surface of the glass, and almost completely covering every piece. The sides of some of the oval dishes, trays, and the stems of the compotes are embellished with wide flutes alternated with three sharp angular prisms. Knobs on the covered pieces are handsome.

The similarity of this pattern to Gillinder's "Stippled Star" and other star designs is obvious, but collectors should have no difficulty differentiating between them.

PICTURE WINDOW—The "Picture Window" pattern was described by Mrs. Kamm in her **Book 4,** page 139, as consisting of "a large 'window' on each side [of the article] set in a mass of staggered 'bricks'." No one could have given a more succinct description of this design. It remained only to attribute this pattern to the firm that made it, and the Central Glass Company catalog does that, calling it their "No. 870" pattern. (The salt shaker in this set was illustrated by Peterson, **Salt and Salt Shakers,** page 35-K, but without attribution.)

Engraved pieces in this set were also shown in Central's illustrated catalog, and we find that the engraving (their "Eng. Pat. 221") corresponds exactly with that shown on the pitcher illustrated in Kamm. A bar bottle in this pattern, with cut stopper, produced with or without a handle, also appears in the catalog.

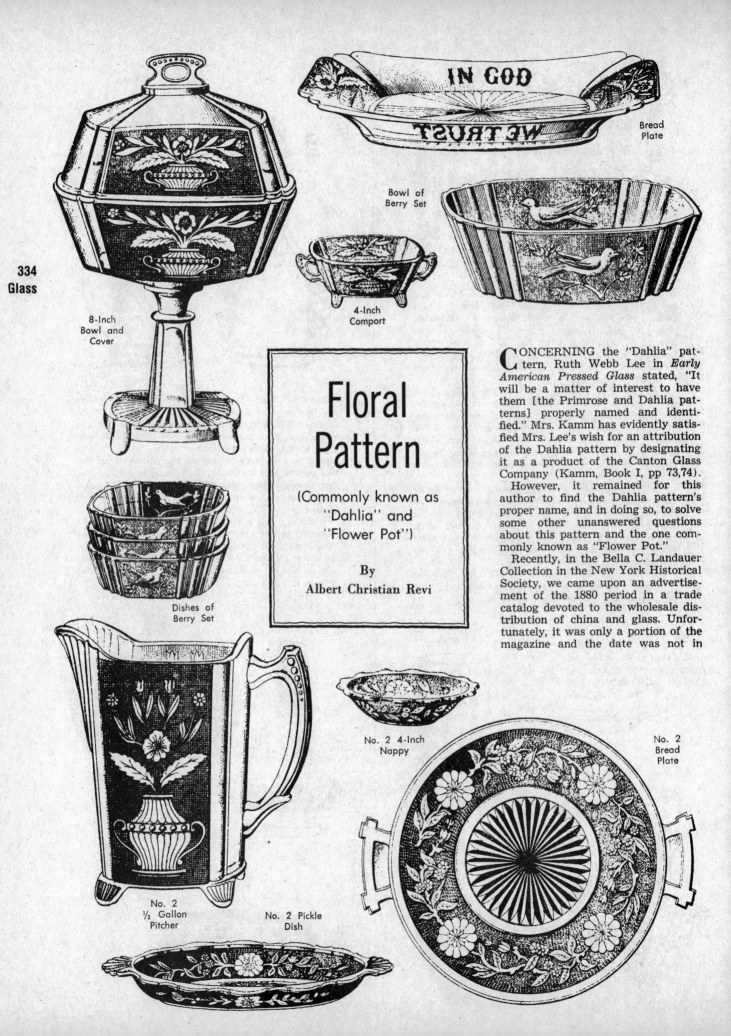

Bread
Plate

Bowl of
Berry Set

4-Inch
Comport

8-Inch
Bowl and
Cover

Dishes of
Berry Set

Floral
Pattern

(Commonly known as
"Dahlia" and
"Flower Pot")

By
Albert Christian Revi

CONCERNING the "Dahlia" pattern, Ruth Webb Lee in *Early American Pressed Glass* stated, "It will be a matter of interest to have them [the Primrose and Dahlia patterns] properly named and identified." Mrs. Kamm has evidently satisfied Mrs. Lee's wish for an attribution of the Dahlia pattern by designating it as a product of the Canton Glass Company (Kamm, Book I, pp 73,74).

However, it remained for this author to find the Dahlia pattern's proper name, and in doing so, to solve some other unanswered questions about this pattern and the one commonly known as "Flower Pot."

Recently, in the Bella C. Landauer Collection in the New York Historical Society, we came upon an advertisement of the 1880 period in a trade catalog devoted to the wholesale distribution of china and glass. Unfortunately, it was only a portion of the magazine and the date was not in

No. 2 4-Inch
Nappy

No. 2
Bread
Plate

No. 2
½ Gallon
Pitcher

No. 2 Pickle
Dish

Spoon

Cream

Sugar

evidence. Here, Young, Keiper & Company, importers and jobbers of china, glass, and Queensware, 315 & 217 North Third Street, Philadelphia, advertised the "Floral Pattern" in a full line of pressed tablewares, in crystal and colors—blue, green, canary, and amber.

All items shown on two pages of this catalog, each headed "Floral Pattern," are reproduced here, with the exception of the "qt. pitcher" and the "7 in. bowl & cov." which are the same as items in other sizes.

The goblet in this set is not pictured, but the handled bread tray, nappy, and pickle dish are readily identified as pieces in the Dahlia pattern, and the other items shown are most certainly in the Flower Pot pattern. The berry set, 12 small dishes and a large bowl, which was sold with this tableware suite is still another design — a bird perched on a leafy branch.

110-Piece Set

In a price list which accompanied Young & Keiper's advertisement, we noted that the pattern was "of recent production," and that the most expensive item in the entire set was the 10-inch cake salver. These sold at

wholesale for $6 a dozen (50¢ each); the half-gallon pitcher sold for $5.31 a dozen (37¢ each); and the round 4-inch nappies sold for 25¢ a dozen. A complete table setting in the Floral pattern, consisting of 110 pieces, sold for $11.52 wholesale.

Conspicuous by its absence from both the price list and the illustrations of the Floral pattern was stemware. Such pieces may have been added later, or they could have been produced by the Bellaire Goblet Company of Findlay, Ohio, who made many of the goblets for tableware sets produced by other glasshouses of that 1880 period.

The inability of the Lee and Metz research to certify a tumbler or goblets in the Flower Pot pattern can be explained by the fact that Dahlia and Flower Pot were one and the same pattern; therefore only one design in tumblers and stemware was needed for this set.

No. 2 Square Nappy

Pickle Jar

Butter

10-Inch Salver

Bottom in Set

FLORAL PATTERN

NO. 1 SET, of sugar, cream, spoon, butter, and "bottom in set," appear on one catalog page, along with No. 2, ½-gall. pitcher, No. 2 pickle dish, No. 2 bread plate, and No. 2, 4-in. nappy. Other pieces appear on the second catalog page, where berry set—bowl and 12 sauces—is shown with box to hold it. Both pages are headed FLORAL PATTERN.

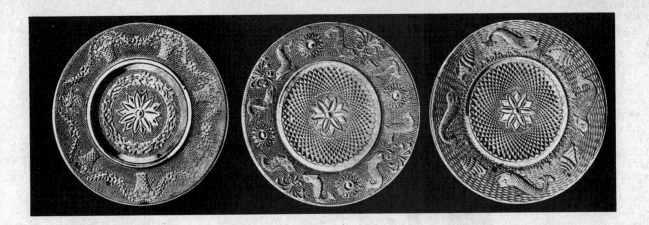

The Golden Age of Arcadia, Indiana...

A Town Full of Glassmaking Memories

by ETHEL C. LORTON

Catalogue illustrations from Mrs. Bertha Morphew, Kokomo, Indiana

IN THE FORTY years from 1893 to 1933, the little town of Arcadia, Hamilton County, Indiana, lived its chapter in the story of American glass. Now is the time, while firsthand information is available from those who participated, to set down something of Arcadia's contribution.

When the glasshouses in the east had expended the timber on which they depended for fuel, and moved west toward the coal fields, the Ohio River valley had become a great glassmaking country. With the discovery of natural gas in Indiana in the 1880s, glassmaking crossed the state line to such towns as Gas City, Portland, Greentown, Hartford, Marion, Muncie, Indianapolis, Kokomo, and Arcadia.

Railroads were built; sand was shipped in, and glass shipped out. Prosperity blanketed the area. People expected it to last forever. But by 1900, the heyday of natural gas was over—the boom had lasted less than two decades. In Arcadia, while the pressure persisted, flambeaus had burned night and day; most houses were piped for natural gas. By 1914 a worker, new in town, installed a gas burner only to have the well in his garden run dry after two weeks' use.

Arcadia's first glass factory was built in 1893, for Baker Bros., makers of window glass, based in Findlay, Ohio. John Stohan, well remembered in town, came to Arcadia in 1893 to boss construction of the factory and

Present day grandmas may still be using 8″ glass salad plates like those on this page, made between 1914-1933 by D. C. Jenkins Glass Company of Arcadia and Kokomo, Indiana.

remained as a valued man with the company. The Baker Bros. operation opened in 1894 and continued until 1902. Gas pressure was by then so low that the company moved to Oklahoma where gas wells were booming. One local farmer recalls building sheds on his farm in 1906 from lumber from their old glass sheds. Panes of glass made at the factory are still found in older residences.

Advertisements appearing in the Souvenir Program of the Dedicatory Services of the Methodist Episcopal Church, March 18, 1900, included those of "Baker Bros., Manufacturers of Window Glass, Successors to Ohio Window Glass Manufactory," and two other glass concerns in Arcadia— "Caylor and Meany, The New Lamp Chimney Factory, Watch Out for Us"; and "The American Crystal Monument Company, Samuel W. Miles, Pres. and Treas. All kinds of Lamp Chimneys, Lead and Lime Glass, and Off Hand Chimneys, Factory—Arcadia, Indiana." The last two firms seem shortlived, apparently closing in the next year or so when the gas ran out.

Despite difficulties, the town fathers worked hard to keep an established glass factory going, and sometime between 1902 and 1907, induced the Flint House Glass Company to erect a new plant near the railroad on South Street. This firm also made lamp chimneys, specializing in those decorated with hand painted flowers on a frosted band. It ran about a year at top speed, then moved away.

In 1907 the High Pressure Bottle Works built a bottle factory on the ruins of the old brickyard. In a few months it was sold to the Globe Bottle Works, and passed into receiver's hands within two weeks.

The town continued its inducements to attract industry to this small community. The labor situation was harmonious, and many men were skilled glassworkers. There was a railroad and a trolley line, and it was possible to make gas from coal. Not until 1913, when D. C. Jenkins bought the old glasshouse, were their efforts rewarded. Jenkins was an experienced glassman; he owned a busy plant in Kokomo, 20 miles distant by rail, and before that he had helped organize and run the Indiana Glass and Tumbler Company.

The *Noblesville Ledger,* the county seat newspaper, commented on February 21, 1914: "Some five years ago Arcadia people gave $58,000 for the erection of a glasshouse, but various troubles have prevented the operation . . . D. C. Jenkins of Kokomo will manufacture the same class of goods as at Kokomo. One hundred fifty or two hundred people will be employed, including thirty females. Mr. Jenkins will overhaul the factory and make it modern and safe. People feel that he means business and it will be a good thing for the town."

Later *Ledgers* gave more details—about the new blowers to manufacture gas from coal which were installed, on the lighting of the fires at 1 o'clock, May 22, 1914, on the real estate situation which disclosed no vacant houses in Arcadia.

The Busy Years

The advent of the Jenkins company heralded Arcadia's Golden Age. It was the right time for a new factory. Stockholders recall their biggest dividends came during World War I when European glassmakers had more pertinent matters on their agendas, and domestic glass was in demand. Mr. Jenkins had the "know-how" of a good glassman; he also realized the money-making possibilities in utilitarian wares. Jelly glasses, tumblers, goblets, and packers' goods rolled from his storage sheds.

Packers' goods meant containers for commodities. The prevailing fashion was to package various foodstuffs in containers which might be later used. Thus, tankard creamers held pickles, goblets were filled with jelly, spooners with mustard. Flat glass objects, not adapted to such purpose, were stocked on shelves, or given as premiums. Sometimes a coupon was placed inside the flap of a pound of coffee, entitling the holder to a specified piece of glassware—usually a nappie.

These utilitarian glasswares were pressed in molds and hand finished. Many of the skilled workmen who came from Eastern glasshouses to work in Arcadia scorned the heavy practical wares. But they kept busy.

Grocery shelves needed heavy jars in which to store Wrigley's chewing gum. Velvet Tobacco called for similar jars, with the knob hollow to hold a damp sponge and make it a humidor. The factory also turned out a fine line of glasses, goblets, sherbets, wine glasses, and beer mugs, hotel supplies and soda fountain needs. Bar ware was a flourishing item, and old timers do not recall that the 18th Amendment curtailed their manufacture. The Hoffman House beer goblets were always steady sellers. Many of their dishes were lidded, compotes and creamers as well as sugar bowls. People were becoming conscious of dust and flies.

Gold fish were a fad, and fish globes in all sizes were made, from pints to large aquariums. The factory also turned out refrigerator jars and dishes, mixing bowls, churn jars, and sanitary jars for hospitals.

Patterns

It is impossible to separate the patterns and pieces made at Arcadia from those made in Kokomo. The two factories traded molds freely, and with the Indiana Glass Company in Dunkirk and the Star Plate Glass Company in New Albany as well. Moldmakers, pressers, engravers, and elite designers, moving as the notion struck them from one plant to another, scrambled the picture further. Patterns and colors were always turning up in other factories.

But everyone agrees that the vat for making iridescent ware was at Arcadia. Glass from Kokomo would be shipped by rail to be sprayed or dipped, then returned to the Kokomo

No. 95 — Table Tumbler

No. 100 — Table Tumbler

No. 136 — Ice Tea Tumbler

No. 807 — Sugar and Cover

No. 96 — Sherbet Cup

shipping sheds. Workers from Arcadia also agree that all etching was done at Kokomo or by Kokomo workmen.

Referring to Jenkins glass, the *Kokomo Tribune* of September 9, 1962, noted: "Principal patterns were Paneled Grape, Pillow Band, Dewdrop and Raindrop." Study of the D. C. Jenkins Glass Company's catalogues for Kokomo and Arcadia wares reveal that patterns were numbered, not named, and the Tribune's listing was descriptive rather than factory named.

One design found in abundance shows a deep daisy, with a conventional daisy band, resembling "Daisy Band" in Ruth Webb Lee's *Victorian Glass*. Another design I call "Depressed Squares," both from its design, and in token of the many Arcadia residents, themselves depressed for having "got rid of all that heavy old glass."

"Arcadia Lace" might easily identify a pattern with a lacy band around vases, pitchers, celeries, nappies, and goblets. A design of cherries, pears, apples and plums, with proper leafage, encircling each article deserves the name "Fruit Salad." The "Pillow Band" has never been exactly identified. Most "colored ware" was in an all-over lattice work pattern, well adapted to the iridescent coating.

In Arcadia Cupboards

Arcadians did not prize their hometown glass highly. It was strictly for hard use and everyday wear. It didn't cost anything. Sometimes a man would try out a new mold and bring home a piece. If the lady of the house didn't care for it, it was just another piece of glass on the shelf. If she did approve, he might bring her matching pieces until she had accumulated a "set."

When a piece of glass had flaws, it was discarded for cullet. The workers felt free to take this "cull glass" home. Consequently much of the glass in Arcadia cupboards is flawed. There are "seeds" (fine sand that didn't melt), "strings" (from a cold mold), shear marks, mold marks, bubbly edges, or similar defects. Such glass was never really "finished." In the making, if a piece was found flawed, the tempering process might be skipped; when glass cools too quickly it becomes brittle. Townspeople have told me it would crack and break just sitting on the shelves. Numberless times I have heard of the worker taking home two fishbowls, who stepped into the sunshine, and had them burst like bombs.

To some collectors the flaws in Arcadia glass enhance its value—they feel it shows it was made in the days before streamlined machinery.

Many Arcadia workers made fanciful articles in off hours or with residue from the glass pots. Glass canes, decorated with a ribbon bow, hung on many a parlor wall. Tumblers, showing a fault, were easily rolled into sombreros; mugs were converted into pin dishes. Such whimsies are still to be found in Arcadia homes, in use, or as conversation pieces.

"Doped Ware"

The townspeople felt that the Jenkins Glass Company itself went whimsical when they sprayed finished articles with a tan-gold spray. This is easily distinguished from Carnival ware, and is usually termed iridescent. In Arcadia, it was simply called "doped ware." The workers remember it as a great nuisance, hard on clothes, hands, patience, and tempers.

The workers realized, as the general public might not, that the color was not "cooked in." The man who described the process to me had worked with glass compounded by Jacob Rosenthal who dropped gold pieces into each batch of ruby glass to give it sheen; he was properly critical of the artificiality of "doped ware." This "colored ware" which was evolved to compete with colored glass, seemed never to have become very popular.

End of an Era

The D. C. Jenkins Glass Co. closed its doors in June 1932, and did not reopen after the Bank Moratorium. The Golden Age was past.

There was a brief revival of glassmaking in 1945 when the Slick Glass Company of Gas City operated the old plant for about a year. Natural gas was again available, piped in by Panhandle Eastern Pipeline, but the designs the company produced were heavy and ornate. Perhaps the company bought up old molds and tried to use them. Designers must be ahead of the buying public in ideas for a successful operation. Slick Glass Company wares are common in this part of Indiana, but I was surprised to find one of their berry dishes in an antebellum home in Vicksburg, Mississippi, classified as "pre-Civil War"!

Antiques dealers have bought most of the Jenkins' glass within the last five years. A big display of it at a reunion of the workers in Kokomo in September, 1962, stirred slumbering interest. The sale of the glass was a real windfall for some of the older, retired workers who were glad to have money in return for cupboards full of "that old free glass."

No industry in Arcadia has ever taken the place of the glass factory. The younger men skilled in glass working moved on to other factories. Older men who had bought homes, remained in town, where they are still respected as "skilled workmen" although it has been many years since they "gathered" or "finished" a piece.

The glasshouse has been razed. In May 1962 workers demolished the factory. The bricks were sold for construction. Old kilns were exposed as workers cut away steel supports. Junk dealers bought the scrap. As *Tri-Town Topics* reported, "The demise of this once proud building marks the end of an era."

Local residents still own and now treasure glassware made in Arcadia. Clear glass swan, probably held mustard (courtesy Ollie Sumner); flared sundae glass (Hazel Waltz); iridescent all-over lattice work berry dish (6 matching nappies not shown) and pitcher, cut Daisy, conventional daisy band (Joe Kinder).

Display jar humidor, with hollow knob to hold damp sponge (courtesy Hazel Waltz); somewhat fancier ones in 52 oz. size were made for Liggett-Myers Tobacco Co. Bowl set, marked Sanitaire Mixing Bowl on bottom; smallest used as salt dip (author's collection); one Christmas the Jenkins company gave all of their women employees one of these bowl sets as a gift.

Northwood's "263 Ware"

by ALBERT CHRISTIAN REVI

IN 1887, Harry Northwood had severed his connections with the LaBelle Glass Works of Bridgeport, Ohio, and in October of that year, with an associate, Mr. Dunlevy, formed the Northwood Glass Company which operated the Union Glass Works of Martins Ferry, Ohio.

In 1889, the Northwood Glass Company advertised artistic glass for table and ornamental use in the "Latest Parisian Styles." Prominent among Mr. Northwood's latest presentations was his "263 Ware." This was a mold-blown ware, decorated with a pattern consisting of stylized acorns and oak leaves arranged below a representation of twisted rope or chain. The pattern shows clearly in the illustrations here, which were taken from Northwood's trade catalogs and advertisements.

"263 Ware" was produced in "Ruby" (transparent cranberry), "Rose Du Barry" (a mauve color, opaque in quality), "Rose Agate" (another opaque pink color), "Turquoise" (opaque blue), and "Topaz" (opaque amber). In most cases the colored glass was heavily coated with clear crystal before being brought to its full form by being blown into a contact mold. Some pieces of this ware can be found to be of a cased variety, lined with white glass.

The rims of all the pieces in this pattern have been ground down to a smoothness after they were knocked off the blowpipe; the exception to this rule are the pitchers, the mouths of which were reheated to shape the pouring spout, thereby fire polishing the rough edges.

Northwood's beautiful "263 Ware" was manufactured in a complete suite for the table—pitchers in at least two sizes, bowls in several sizes, a covered sugar bowl, toothpick holder, salt and pepper shakers, a spoonholder, finger bowls and plates, tumblers, and the like.

263 – 8in Bowl

263 Sugar & Cover

263 Tumbler

263 Finger Bowl

263 Ware made in Ruby, Rose Du Barry, Rose Agate, Turquoise and Topaz

263 ½ gal. Jug

263 Salt

Purple Slag

TEN years ago, Henry C. Huber, hardware dealer of Germantown, Ohio, who had been collecting antiques twice that long, began to concentrate on purple slag. He was first intrigued with the fact that no two pieces were exactly alike—and the royal color pleased him. His enthusiastic search of antiques shows and shops and mail order listings has yielded him over 630 different pieces. (His total collection numbers more than 700 examples of purple slag and some 100 in slag of other colors—green, blue, red, and brown.)

He now owns every piece pictured in Lee's *Victorian Glass,* Belknap's *Milk Glass,* and Millard's *Opaque Glass,* with two exceptions—*Opaque Glass* #222, and the rare leaf dish in *Victorian Glass,* pl. 92, lower right. None of the examples pictured here are shown in any of these references.

Among his other unusual pieces are a biscuit barrel with silver bail and cover; jam jars; Cosmos and Shell cruet, sugar, and creamer, American and very rare; watch holder; cups and saucers; reclining cow covered butter, perhaps his most expensive piece; jardinieres, one English, dated 1878; hens on nests, in both dull and shiny finish—he is uncertain of the age of these and would welcome information; a long-sought rolling pin found at Betty Gorman

Kaye's; cradle salts; and a purple slag ice cream table top, 24 x 24", ½" thick, set in a black glass base, which he found in Cincinnati.

Purple slag, or Marble Glass, a mix of white milk glass and purple glass, was originally called Mosaic. Much of it was made in England, and often bears English registry marks. In America, Challinor, Taylor & Co. of Tarentum, Pennsylvania, were the largest producers, putting out a high quality ware as, in lesser amount, did the Atterbury Company of Pittsburgh. It was also made by other companies, unidentified, and mostly in poorer quality. The English ware is slightly different in texture, and somewhat darker than American make, and can be distinguished without difficulty.

A few years ago toothpick holders in S-Repeat pattern and a medium-sized pitcher, rather poorly done, appeared in gift shops. More recently, new pieces have been made by the Imperial Glass Company of Bellaire, Ohio, including a tall three-cornered vase, an open-edge compote, a 10" cake-stand, and at least four medium-sized covered dishes with identical bases and covers, but with different knobs—one has a bee, one a dog, another a penguin, and a fourth, a squirrel. Most are marked with the IG monogram.

Profiles shown on this English pitcher are of the Marquis and Marchioness of Lorne; larger covered compote or sugar (not shown) with same profiles identifies them in words and commemorates their landing in Halifax, 1878.

[Please turn the page for more illustrations]

9" tall candleholder, beaded panel stem, 3-footed; candle also is in purple slag, 4" tall, ⅞" dia. Candles, rare, of Challinor & Taylor quality, are probably American. Mr. Huber has 7 candlesticks, 2 pair and 1 odd, with candles for all.

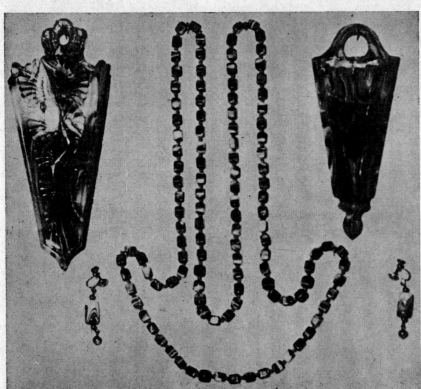

Patterned wallpockets 5" and 4" long are English, rare; string of beads about 60" long show hand work. Mr. Huber has several such strings in his collection; earrings were cut and mounted from broken pieces in his collection.

Very rare double inkwell 8½ x 5½ x 4½" high, center handle, 2 wells and caps, pattern shows some pebbled surface but on the whole is rather plain.

Most unusual trivet or plaque 9 x 12½", English, but not marked or dated; overall diamond and large hob design is on bottom, top plain.

Ring tree 2" high, 4" dia., rare; like much English slag, top is plain, design is on bottom; pattern here is of leaves; original label still in saucer.

Design on impressive English vase, one of a pair, 10¼" tall, 4¾" dia. at top, shows four wreath-encircled lions' heads in relief; one of a pair of stately tulip vases 10" tall, 6-scallop top, one was found in Vermont, one in Michigan.

"The Railway Car"

by ALBERT CHRISTIAN REVI

NAME: *Railway Car* (factory name).

MANUFACTURER: *The Bellaire Goblet Company*. This firm at Bellaire, Ohio, and Findlay, Ohio, founded in 1879 and absorbed into the United States Glass Company on July 1, 1891, produced pressed table and bar wares in considerable quantities.

DESIGNER: *Melvin L. Blackburn*, assignor to the Bellaire Goblet Company.

PATENT DATE: *October 19, 1886.*

COLOR: *Canary* (uranium yellow); possibly other transparent colors.

SIZE: 13½ by 5½ by 7 inches high. Kamm, Book 5, pg. 156 (38), listing novelty dishes, mentions a "street car, four feet long," maker and date unknown. The large size appears in error.

DESCRIPTION: The patent drawings represent a covered dish in the form of a railway car having representations of wheels at front and rear. Wheels appear imbedded in or formed integral with webs depending from the bottom of the car at the sides, and which are provided with raised figures representing the springs and bolsters of the car. Sides of the car near the base are ornamented with a raised prismatic figure. Car windows are simulated by unfigured spaces, enclosed and defined by raised panels. Doors at each end are simulated by plain portions, appearing to be made integral with the car body, and are enclosed by defining panels. The roof has a series of plain portions representing ventilating windows, and interposed panels define them.

The photograph of the actual dish, from the collection of Mr. Clyde Fahrney, Waynesboro, Pennsylvania, shows an additional Daisy and Button molded design running around the entire top of the cover below the ventilating windows. This appears the only difference between the actual article as produced by the Bellaire Goblet Company and Mr. Blackburn's patented design; all other aspects of the design check exactly with specifications.

A. H. Heisey & Company's LATE PRESSED

RECENTLY a great deal of interest has been manifested in some rather late pressed glass patterns produced by A. H. Heisey & Company of Newark, Ohio, which began operations in 1895. For the most part, these wares are beautifully designed, and sturdy enough to withstand heavy use. This latter factor made them ideal for hotel and restaurant ware, and great quantities were sold to outlets supplying such goods.

Between 1908 and 1930, several de-signs for pressed tablewares were patented for A. H. Heisey & Company by Joseph Balda, Clarence Heisey, Edgar Wilson Heisey, Thomas Clarence Heisey, Arthur J. Sanford, and Clyde S. Whipple. Sometimes two or more patents for the same design were issued on different dates (in some cases they were registered in the name of one or more of the designers listed above), but in each case, a different piece in the set was used for the patent illustration.

Most of these late patterns have the Heisey trademark — the letter "H" within a diamond-shaped figure—impressed on the inside of the bottom of the object. Whenever this was not feasible, paper labels with the trademark in white on a blue ground were placed on the glassware. This trademark was registered by A. H. Heisey & Company on August 8, 1901, and again on March 6, 1906. The trademark papers state that the Heisey company had been using this mark

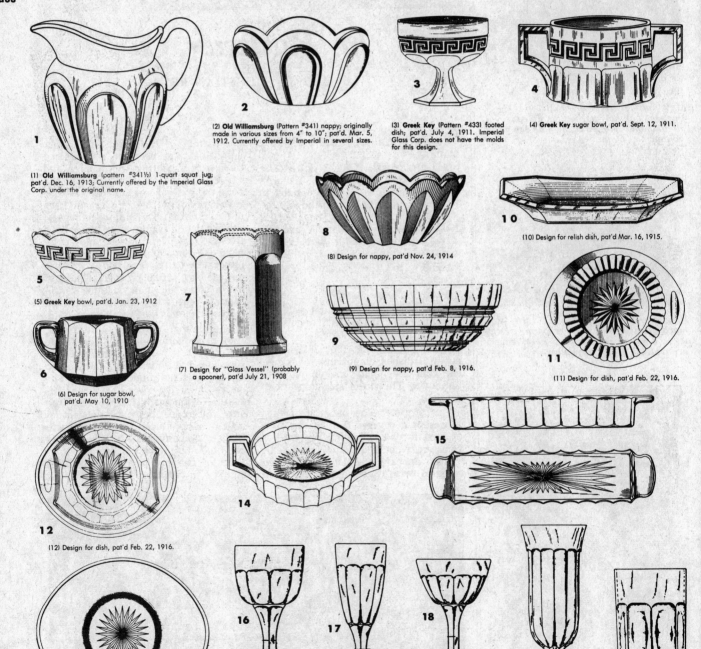

(1) **Old Williamsburg** (pattern #341½) 1-quart squat jug; pat'd. Dec. 16, 1913; Currently offered by the Imperial Glass Corp. under the original name.

(2) **Old Williamsburg** (Pattern #341) nappy; originally made in various sizes from 4" to 10"; pat'd. Mar. 5, 1912. Currently offered by Imperial in several sizes.

(3) **Greek Key** (Pattern #433) footed dish; pat'd. July 4, 1911. Imperial Glass Corp. does not have the molds for this design.

(4) **Greek Key** sugar bowl, pat'd. Sept. 12, 1911.

(5) **Greek Key** bowl, pat'd. Jan. 23, 1912.

(6) Design for sugar bowl, pat'd. May 10, 1910

(7) Design for "Glass Vessel" (probably a spooner), pat'd July 21, 1908

(8) Design for nappy, pat'd Nov. 24, 1914

(9) Design for nappy, pat'd Feb. 8, 1916.

(10) Design for relish dish, pat'd Mar. 16, 1915.

(11) Design for dish, pat'd Feb. 22, 1916.

(12) Design for dish, pat'd Feb. 22, 1916.

(13) Design for nappy, pat'd Apr. 24, 1917.

(14) Handled dish, pat'd July 2, 1912. (15) Uneeda Biscuit dish, pat'd June 2, 1914. (16, 17 and 18) Goblet designs, pat'd Aug. 25, 1914 and Nov. 10, 1914. (19) Goblet design, pat'd Dec. 8, 1914. (20) Tumbler design, pat'd Nov. 10, 1914. All of these articles appear to be of the same design, though patented by A. H. Heisey & Company at various times.

GLASS PATTERNS by Albert Christian Revi

on their pressed glasswares since November 1, 1900.

On November 23, 1909, another version of the Heisey trademark, this time, the diamond-shaped figure *without* the letter "H", was registered.

While most of Heisey's late pressed glass patterns were produced in plain crystal, they can also be found in colored glasses which they developed

and used between 1900 and 1930—"Moongleam" (a light green color), "Flamingo" (a vibrant pink), "Alexandrite (a lovely shade of orchid), "Tangerine" (orange), "Zircon" (a pale yellow color), "Sahara" (a bright canary-yellow shade produced with uranium salts), and "Ivorine Verde" (an opaque uranium-yellow glass).

Some crystal pieces have been found

with copper-wheel engraved designs of a simple character—flowers, garlands, leaves, etc. Still others were decorated with gold and silver lustre, colored stains, and enamels.

A. H. Heisey & Company went out of business in 1958. Their molds, equipment, patents, and trademarks were acquired by the Imperial Glass Corporation of Bellaire, Ohio.

(21 and 22) Designs for sugar bowl and cream pitcher, pat'd July 9, 1912.

(23) Design for footed bowl, pat'd Aug. 25, 1914

(24) Basket design, pat'd Sept. 25, 1917.

(25) Design for covered jar, pat'd Mar. 8, 1921; often found with lightly engraved decoration, or enamel and gilt decorations.

(26) Design for nappy, pat'd Mar. 24, 1925.

(27) Design for nappy, pat'd May 25, 1926.

(28) Design for stemmed compote, pat'd Oct. 5, 1926.

(29) Design for glass plate, pat'a Dec. 23, 1930.

(38) Engraved patterns for a suite of tableware, pat'd Feb. 17, 1925.

(30-33) Designs for syrup pitchers, pat'd Mar. 8, and Mar. 21, 1922.

(34-37) Tumbler designs, pat'd Mar. 11, 1913; Aug. 25, 1914; Sept. 22, 1914; and Feb. 20, 1917.

A. H. HEISEY & CO. PRESSED GLASSWARE.

A. H. HEISEY & CO. INC. PRESSED GLASSWARE.

H

(40) Heisey trade mark, registered Aug. 1, 1901 and Mar. 6, 1906. (41) Heisey trade mark, registered Nov. 23, 1909.

(39) Engraved pattern for a suite of tableware, pat'd Nov. 2, 1926.

MORE ON DEPRESSION ERA GLASSWARE

An assortment of pitchers made by Bartlett-Collins. Most came with ice tea glasses and tumblers to match.

Blown 15-oz. tumblers decorated in colors. Left to right: **Polo, Cockrell,** and **Golfer.**

Top: Card case and cover. Below: Coaster and ash tray.

THE BARTLETT - COLLINS COMPANY of Sapulpa, Oklahoma, manufactured a great deal of pressed and pressed-and-blown glassware during the depression years. Their Catalog "P", issued about 1931, illustrated many pieces of table glassware which people used to see in second hand shops and thrift stores a few years ago. Now we find these same things in antiques shops, and at much higher prices.

Most of the wares shown in Bartlett-Collins' Catalog "P" were produced in Crystal, Nu-Rose (a pale shade of rose) and Nu-Green (a light shade of apple green). Their pressed and blown pitchers and tumblers were made in a variety of optic patterns, some with simple engraved decorations. Vases 620, 630 and 640, and their 300 F Library Lamp (illustrated) were sprayed with colors in a style that today's collectors call "Goofus Glass."

H. U. Bartlett, together with five of his brothers and George F. Collins, Sr., founded the Bartlett-Collins Company about 1915. Collins left the concern about 1918, and since that time it has always been operated by members of the Bartlett family. Edward E. Bartlett, the founder's son, is presently president and treasurer of the company. His brother, Charley F. Bartlett, has been with the company for

38 years and is still quite active in its management. Harrison Irving Bartlett, the son of one of H. U. Bartlett's brothers, Chester W. Bartlett, has been with the company for the past 22 years.

The company started out as a "hand plant" with a 12-pot furnace. Later, some day tanks were added to their equipment to produce white ribbed shades, opal shades, and figured shades for lamps. This latter business was lost to an eastern concern a few years later, and from then on the company manufactured only crystal or flint glass.

In 1941, the Bartlett-Collins Company went through a labor strike that lasted two months or more. At the time the company was producing machine-made glassware, using Miller feeders and Hartford feeders. On starting up again after the strike, the production of handmade glass was discontinued.

Apparently the Bartlett-Collins Company did a considerable trade
(Please Turn the Page)

Right: **No. 300 F Library Lamp**; about 15" high. Advertised as decorated in three styles. The one shown in catalog "P" was decorated with shaded rose to green paint at the top part of the shade, and on the pedestal base. The font and lower half of the shade were of undecorated crystal glass.

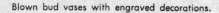

Blown bud vases with engraved decorations.

Hand-cut, handmade pressed glassware advertised to retail for 25¢ a piece. Top: **No. 91**, 8-inch plate. Below: **No. 87**, sugar and cream set. Hand blown stemware to match included goblets, high-footed sherbet, low-footed sherbet, cocktail and wine. All produced in Crystal, Nu-Green and Nu-Rose.

Bartlett-Collins' **Special 210 Assortment** were "all good sellers."

The **Puritan Line.**

with Mexico, for our copy of Catalog "P" has printed descriptions and instructions for ordering in both English and Spanish. If you're "south of the border" sometime, you may find some of the wares shown on these pages. You'll certainly find them in antiques shops throughout the United States.

Berry cream and sugar set.

Below: **No. 15** Salt shaker; **No. 200** Molasses can; and **No. 820** Ice Bucket.

Vase assortment; 9½" high. Left to right: **No. 620, Decoration A**—red rose with green leaves on shaded rose and silver background. **No. 630, Decoration B**—red flowers with yellow leaves on a shaded rose and silver background. **No. 640, Decoration C**—purple grapes with green leaves and vines on a shaded purple and silver background.

Cologne bottles.

FOSTORIA'S OPAL GLASS DRESSER SETS

by

ALBERT CHRISTIAN REVI

Rose bowls.

Puff boxes, small.

Puff boxes, large.

Candlesticks.

Hair pin boxes.

Jewel boxes.

IN THEIR CATALOG of pressed wares dated 1900, The Fostoria Glass Company of Moundsville, W. Va., offered two new lines in decorated opal glass consisting mostly of boudoir accessories—comb and brush trays, hair pin boxes, jewel boxes, pin trays, large and small puff boxes, cologne bottles, candlesticks, pen trays, rose bowls and fern dishes. These assortments were available in two different decorations—Decoration No. 1 in analine colors of green and gold and pink and gold on the raised designs. Decoration No. 2 in analine colors of green and gold and pink and gold on the raised designs with very elaborate decalcomania ornamentation of floral designs in appropriate places on each piece.

Actually, almost all of the pieces in both sets were produced in the same molds; the only difference was in the decoration. Our illustrations are arranged to show the various pieces side by side—Decoration No. 1 on the left, and Decoration No. 2 on the right.

Many of the pieces shown in our illustrations were pictured in Millard's "Opaque Glass" under various names.

Comb and brush trays.

Fern dishes.

Pen trays.

Notes on Three Fine Art Glasswares

by ALBERT CHRISTIAN REVI

• "Jewell" Glassware

ON September 6, 1866, Stevens & Williams of Brierley Hill Glass Works, Brierley Hill, England, registered their design for "Jewell" glassware. Though the design shown in the patent papers (FIG. 1) is one of vertical columns of air-blebs, the technique was manifested in other patterns as well. In many cases the registry number, 55693, was engraved in the base of the article.

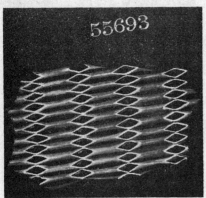

FIG. 1

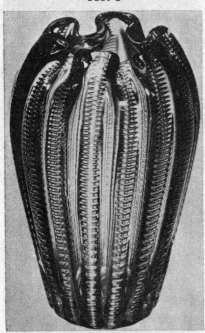

FIG. 2

FIG. 3

The method of manufacture involved several steps. First, a bulb of glass, crystal or colored, was threaded all around on a type of machine patented by William J. Hodgetts in 1876.* It was then blown into a cup of either colored or crystal glass made to receive it, and then blown into a rib mold. The last step forced the air-traps formed between the threads of glass and the outer casing of the article into vertical rows of air-blebs. The shimmering effect of the air-blebs against a colored or crystal ground does have a beautiful jewel-like appearance. The "Jewell" glass vase (FIG. 2) is of ruby colored glass with a vertical pattern of air-blebs.

A somewhat different version of Stevens & Williams' "Jewell" glass is shown in a crystal bowl-vase (FIG. 3). In this case, the last operation involved the use of John Northwood's Pull-up machine patented February 20, 1885.*

The bases of the blue finger-bowl and plate (FIG. 4) bear the etched mark of the Josephine Glass Works of Count Schaffgotsch at Josephinen-hutte, Germany. It was produced by the same method as Stevens & Williams' "Jewell" glass. After the body of the glass was blown into the rib mold, and before it had cooled and hardened, the parison was twisted slightly to produce the helically twisted pattern of air-traps seen in the finished article. This appears to be the only difference between the original design registered by Stevens & Williams and the copy made by the German factory a year or two later.

Tablewares and decorative articles of all kinds and in many colors can be found in both the English and German wares.

* Full descriptions of these machines and patents are given in A. C. Revi's *Nineteenth Century Glass.*

FIG. 4

• Metal Encased

FOR many centuries glass workers have enhanced their works of art with mountings of gold, silver, pewter, lead and other metals, the article of glass being made to the desired shape and the metal fixture or mount fashioned to fit its form.

On August 18, 1884, an easier means for producing a similar effect was patented by Fritz Heckert of Petersdorf, Germany. For this purpose, Mr. Heckert employed open metalwork ornaments formed by stamping, casting, pressing, or galvanic deposit. These he placed in a mold so as to lie close against its sides. A gather of glass was introduced into the mold and blown to fill it entirely, thereby coming into contact with the metalwork structure and adhering to it. After the article

FIG. 1

FIG. 2

lassware

was released from the mold, the "blow-over" (that part of the bulb which came above the desired height of the article) was removed and the rim fire-polished to a smooth finish.

When ornaments consisting of separate pieces of metal, porcelain, glass, mosaic, beads, precious stones, and the like were to be used, they were cemented with their faces to some material or fabric that would be destroyed by heat. The matrix was placed in a mold so as to present the back surfaces to the glass when it was blown into the mold. The ornaments were thus embedded in and, in some cases, cemented or melted onto the glass while the backing to which they were attached was either destroyed by the heat or subsequently removed by solvents.

In the patent illustrations, FIG. 1 shows the metal framework in the mold and the gather of glass already blown into it. The "blow-over" is seen extending above the mold. FIGS. 2 and 3 show other types of metalwork, used here in making tumblers. FIG. 2 is a lacy network, and FIG. 3 is somewhat like the photo illustration in that the greater portion of the outer skin of the article is encased with metal, the glass protruding through holes in the framework and forming jewel-like ornaments. FIG. 4 represents a cloth matrix on which beads of glass are being cemented in a fancy pattern. This matrix is then placed inside the mold; the glass blown into the mold picks up the design on its outer surface, FIG. 5.

After the articles were formed it was a simple task to plate base metals like copper, lead, brass, etc. with gold or silver deposit. In the case of the handsome vase pictured, a gather of deep ruby-colored glass

FIG. 4

FIG. 3   FIG. 5

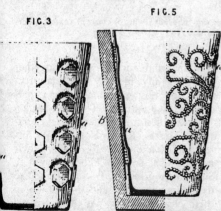

was blown into a reticulated metal casing so that the glass protruded slightly through the openings simulating odd-shaped rubies. Afterward, the copper casing was plated with 22 karat gold. The finished product appears to be of gem-encrusted gold.

On June 28, 1901, the Faulkner Bronze Company, headed by Thomas Birkett and Frederick George Faulkner, of Birmingham, England, patented their process for metal encased glassware. It more or less duplicated Mr. Heckert's method. The main feature, as outlined in their patent specifications, provided that the glass be blown into the perforated metal shell so that it projected through the

openings, to produce a very beautiful ornamental effect.

Heckert's patented method for metal encased glassware soon came into universal use. Everything from tablewares to lamp globes were made. Stevens & Williams of Brierley Hill, England, manufactured lamp globes in the Venetian style using Heckert's technique—large bulging bubbles of colored glass protruding through a simple metal framework. The Bohemian factories produced wine decanters and steins with pewter or German silver frameworks. Collectors should have no real difficulty finding splendid examples to add to their collections.

349
Glass

A Coralene Patent Glassware

A PATENT for an "Improvement in Decorating Glass Articles and Sheet Glass was issued in London, England, on July 17th, 1883, to Arthur Schierholz of Plaue, Thuringia, in the German Empire. We recognize it as the process for applying coralene decoration to glassware.

According to this invention, "ornamental and other articles of glass, whether blown, cast, or pressed, such as statuettes, vases, and the like, also plate or sheet glass, were decorated by first coating the glass with an enamel compound of a syrupy consistency, either colored or transparent, and while this was still sticky, strewing thereon small glass beads, either solid or perforated, and either colored or not, so that when the glass was subjected to heat sufficient to melt the enamel, the beads would become cemented to the surface of the glass, and thus provide it with a peculiar refracting vitreous coating that imparted great brilliancy to the colors, when such were used."

Further on in the patent papers Mr. Schierholz relates his process for preparing "Cathedral Glass." Either the entire sheet or plate was coated with a colored or colorless enamel compound, upon which glass beads, either colored or white (crystal) were strewn, or the enamel coating was only applied to part of the surface according to any desired design. The plate or sheet of glass was then placed in a kiln to frit (melt) the enamel and thereby cement the beads to the surface. The flat sheets of glass were used for decorative windows; likely the name derived from its use as ecclesiastical window ornament.

The tumbler pictured is marked "Patent" in script in the base. Its coralene decoration of yellow roses, buds and shaded green leaves is typical of all other pieces bearing the same inscription in the base, examined by the writer.

The glass used in the tumbler is a pale bottle-green with a slight opalescence near the rim, developed by

reheating. This type of coralene decorated glassware has also been examined in a transparent reddishamber color, believed a selenium-red, not a gold-ruby metal, a lovely shade of transparent electric blue, a bluish opal glass, and in an occasional opaque ivory colored glass. Most certainly other colors can and will be encountered. The coralene decorations range in variety to include fish, birds, flowers, and fruits. Some designs are accented with gold.

An extensive search of the London patent records failed to uncover any notation of assignment or license granted to English glasshouses allowing them also to manufacture coralene decorated glassware. Nor could we find a patent issued for such a decorating process here in America. However, this particular patent was in effect only a short period, and was not renewed. At the expiration of the patent, when the process was available to anyone, many factories, both in America and abroad, used it.

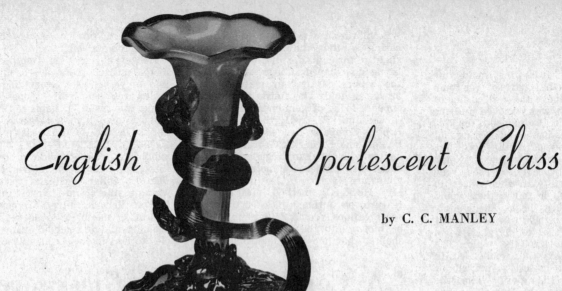

English Opalescent Glass

by C. C. MANLEY

A very unusual opalescent vase of excellent workmanship; green body with blue top. Stourbridge, ca. 1900; 5½" high.

TO ENGLISH collectors and dealers, opalescent glass is any glass which, on partially reheating, changes color.

The commonest color is very pale yellow, which when reheated, changes to a cloudy white. This color is governed to a certain extent by the amount of arsenic added to the original glass mixture.

The origin of opalescent glass in England appears to be very obscure.

But it seems highly probable that once arsenic was added to glass (as a clearing agent) that the discovery of opalescence would not long be delayed. The use of opalescence as a decoration would soon follow.

Patents for opalescent glass were taken out around 1860, but it was certainly made before the Crystal Palace Exhibition of 1851 when it was shown by Messrs. Molineaux, Webb & Co. of Manchester, England. If it wasn't invented in a Midland works it was certainly developed in that region, especially in the Stourbridge area, for some truly magnificent art glass pieces were made there before the 1880s.

The common pale yellow opalescent ware is erroneously called "vasaline" glass, a name which is often used for Thomas Webb & Sons' "Lemonescent," for this glass has a vasaline look which was obtained by adding uranium to a high content arsenic mixture. But the correct name is Lemonescent and *not vasaline*. If collectors insist on using the name vasaline glass, I feel it should be applied to free blown specimens only, for at least they were individually made.

In the hands of a good chemist, practically all colors can be made to change when reheated. The most rare is blue. This was thought for many years to be unobtainable and, when discovered, was only made at very few glassworks.

Dark blue vase with opalescent center. Stourbridge, ca. 1910; 5⅜" high.

Shape and surface taken together will generally identify the manufacturer, for most glass makers had their own surface patterns. The well-known "Horse Chestnut" pattern was exclusively Messrs. Richardsons of Wordsley until about 1936, when their moulds were sold to Thomas Webb & Sons of Stourbridge, who continued to use them, but with added uranium to their glass mixture. We therefore get

Blue ribbed opalescent vase with applied crystal feet. Stourbridge (Richardson's), ca. 1890; 5½" high.

Pressed ruby and yellow opalescent glass swan made by Burtles-Tate & Co., Manchester, ca. 1890; 4½" long.

Richardsons opalescent and Webbs Lemonescent both from the same moulds.

It is difficult to imagine a more delightful specimen of Webbs Lemonescent than their "Cascade" pattern, especially when gold ruby glass was discretely added as a decoration. Richardsons also had a cascade pattern about the same time as Webbs (1900–1910), but their glass lacked uranium and it looked rather anemic. The diamond pattern was not exclusively Webbs, but that pattern combined with their deep yellow coloring denotes its origin.

Trumpet shaped vases have always been popular with British glassmen, so it is natural to expect opalescent wares in this shape. Stevens & Williams appear to have produced a great quantity in this form, the surface patterns being ribbed to suit the design. But yellow opalescent glass was not exclusive to the larger firms, for this color was used by dozens of "Cribs" in the Midlands. Yet with close observation we can generally decide whether the product came from a crib. Very few crib products had a surface pattern, most were light in weight, and the shapes were always simple, and invariably the specimens were small.

The larger glasshouses of the Midlands produced some really fine art specimens in this glass at the turn of the century, but they were only the starting point for the more magnificent pieces. Some of these were partly or completely decorated with threads of all the colors of the rainbow. They had applied prunts, applied drops, and applied rims and feet in a variety of colors. Occasionally we find specimens with applied snakes and lizards. But of course, epergnes accounted for

more opalescent glass than all the rest of the specimens put together. Iridescence over opalescent glass was tried, but it looked ghastly.

About 1900, Thos. Webb & Sons made a very interesting type of opalescent glassware. The articles were generally plain in shape, and yellow in color. Heat was applied to the outside of the specimen only, leaving the perfect pieces with the outer surface white but with yellow inside. Unfortunately there seem to be more imperfect pieces of this type around, imperfect that is because of the patchy outer surface.

An extremely interesting situation occurs when we get away from the common yellow opalescent, for it seems that more thought and care was put into the design and production of opalescent wares of other colors. The results were some really startling spec-

The style and pattern of this yellow opalescent vase suggests it was made by Stevens & Williams, ca. 1890; it also has affinities to Tiffany opalescent wares, ca. 1925. Height 14".

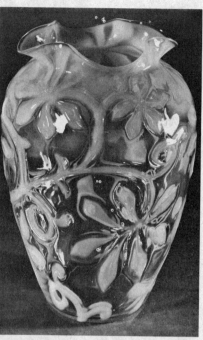

Pale "Lemonescent" vase in the Horse Chestnut pattern. Thos. Webb & Sons, Stourbridge, ca. 1936; 9" high.

imens in adventurous designs which were particularly attractive. It is with the rarer colors that we find imagination and true workmanship. Certain articles in opalescent glass were made in two or more colors. This, of course, not only improved the beauty of the product but illustrates the skills being acquired by chemists at the beginning of the 20th century.

Pontils are of great assistance in the identification of English opalescent glass. Crib work (rarely collectable) never carried a ground pontil. Thos. Webb & Sons ground and polished the pontil of at least 90% of their specimens. Richardsons of Wordsley also ground and polished the pontils, but not in such quantity. Stevens and Williams made many examples with domed bases, which being awkward to grind, were generally left rough. The rest of the glasshouses in the Midlands used bases which needed no grinding.

Continental opalescent glass is somewhat of an enigma. The glassmakers must have thoroughly understood its manufacture, yet, other than the small, cheap mantleshelf decorations, very little appears to have found its way to Britain, although undoubtedly special pieces were made. German "Annagelb" is not generally classed as opalescent glass.

(Please Turn the Page)

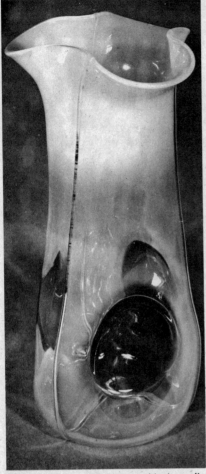

Yellow opalescent glass vase with three ribs and three bottle green indentations in base; extremely light in weight. Stourbridge (Thos. Webb & Sons), ca. 1900; 10½" high.

Webb's "Lemonescent" vase in the "cascade" pattern, the top decorated with a gold ruby lining. Ca. 1910; 8½" high.

The north of England has always produced the greatest amount of collectable pressed glass. That area probably produced the first opalescent pressed glass. Though an air of mystery surrounds English opalescent glass, pressed opalescent only adds fuel to the flames. In the late 1880s we find Davidson's of Gateshead taking out a patent for the production of pressed opalescent glass, yet ten years earlier a number of Tyne-side firms were producing it. In 1878, Sowerby's of Gateshead were in full production of crystal opalescent. Burtles-Tate & Co., Manchester, were producing both yellow and red opalescent swans in 1885. For some years after 1890, Davidson's of Gateshead made a yellowish green cheap pressed glass, with the white edges. With the scarcity of good opalescent glass this is now being sold, possibly through ignorance, for vasaline glass.

I would like to record an interesting talk I had a few years ago with an old glassmaker. We were discussing opalescent glass and the way it was made. The operation of reheating obviously came up. He told me that when he had a specimen too big to re-enter the mouth of the furnace, he knew that he could get the same effect by waving the hot glass around in cool air outside the glasshouse. This, from someone who knew his job, is an illuminating comment on the manufacture of opalescent glass.

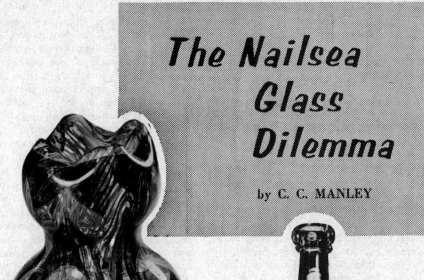

The Nailsea Glass Dilemma

by C. C. MANLEY

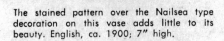

The stained pattern over the Nailsea type decoration on this vase adds little to its beauty. English, ca. 1900; 7" high.

A cased glass jug, crystal over terra-cotta, sploshed with brown—very rare Stourbridge colors. The influence of early Nailsea glass is obvious. Stourbridge, ca. 1900; 3½" high.

Bellows bottle; body stained ruby with white drag loop stripes; crystal foot and pinched and tooled decorations. Attributed to Warrington, but definitely North Country, ca. 1860; height 14½ inches.

FOR WHAT IT IS WORTH, we will agree with the widely accepted premise that the Bristol area was the origin of Nailsea glass; there seems to be no evidence of it preceding the true Bristol blue of the 1780 period. Whether or not it had its origin in Bristol, one thing is certain—Nailsea-type glass had its birth in a bottle factory. Its evolution from simple stripes on bottle glass to the elaborate and magnificent specimens of the 1900 period is easily followed, but to associate certain pieces with individual factories is difficult. Associating specimens with the districts in which they were made is much easier.

We use the word "Nailsea" to describe a type of decorated glassware—not its origin. In the early 1800s Nailsea was a splashed glass, very different from what we associate the name with today. The application of the colors resembled the sploshed decoration found on early Bristol jugs, and since these jugs had all the characteristics of Bristol manufacture, Nailsea glass could easily have been associated with Bristol. Bristol was also a center for bottle and flask manufacturing.

One remarkable feature of Nailsea glass is that throughout the 120-140 years of its so-called development,

brandy flasks were the specimens on which new or improved decorating techniques were tried. Possibly the shape of the brandy flask lent itself as a trial horse for new colors and designs.

A similar development occurred in the manufacture of salt cellars. These unobtrusive objects were made in every glasshouse throughout Great Britain, firstly, to sample the metal before using it for other things, and secondly, to try out new colors and designs. In the author's opinion flasks were used for the same purpose.

As for the evolution of Nailsea glass, it runs with dates something like this: Shortly before 1800 there was the well-known crude bottle decorated with a haphazard design of colored stripes. Examples of this decorating technique can be seen in Bristol rolling pins, too. This was followed, about 1830, by articles in clear glass with colored stripes; few of these were made of lead glass. The years 1840-1845 saw the appearance of cased glass objects with nailsea-type decorations. Nailsea was now, it seems, a definite type to be pursued. The stripes and colors were put on in a regular manner, cased in crystal, and invariably worked off the pontil rod at the furnace.

After the 1851 Exhibition, we find pinched collars and pinched decorations added to the sides of various pieces. In 1885 or 1890 commenced what is known as the pull-up pattern. The colors and patterns were usually applied to an opaque body and cased over with crystal. This type of Nailsea glass is truly beautiful to look at and

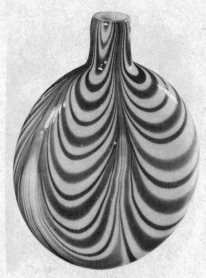

A typical Richardson Nailsea flask — red, white and blue drag loop stripes over a dense white base. (Red, white and green stripes were also used extensively.) This is not the pull-up threaded type, the colored decoration being applied by hand during manufacture. Stourbridge, ca. 1880.

it demanded all the skill of the glassmaker.

Very early Nailsea glass, using common bottle glass as a base, could have been made at any of Britain's bottle works. Since there were hundreds of bottle manufactories in Great Britain —possibly thousands of these firms— we cannot attempt a true provenance, but when the pattern is applied to clear glass, the problem of an attribution is much easier. Our research into the place of manufacture has always, without exception, led to the North of England and included Warrington and Manchester. Time and time again, when we questioned the owners of such specimens, the answer was, "We had them from Warrington-or Manchester-or Edinburgh." In some cases Robinsons of Warrington were mentioned, or Molyneaux & Webb of Manchester, or the Alloa Glasshouse in Edinburgh. The Warrington Museum has some marked examples in their collection.

In the author's opinion the earlier cased specimens came from Birmingham, because both in the Birmingham Exhibition of 1849 and the London Exhibition of 1851, at least three Birmingham firms were showing Nailsea glass. So, too, were some Stourbridge firms, but here lies a difference, for although about 1860 the problem of bonding differently colored casings of glass was tackled in earnest, as late as 1870 all of the Stourbridge glass factories were having difficulties with multi-colored casings. Well after 1900, glassmakers in the Stourbridge District thought that only certain colors would bond together. This was proved wrong, but the combination of colors thought to be compatible by the Stourbridge glass manufacturers does help us to identify wares made in this area. Even after the reproduction of the Portland Vase in 1876, there was difficulty with the bonding of two different colored glasses. This leads us to believe that Stourbridge was a little backward in their technical knowledge of cased colored glassware.

After 1880 the situation changed. At that time John Northwood of Stevens and Williams produced the threading pull-up machines, this meant that the entire operation of casing and controlling the striped decoration was well under control. So it is safe to assume that glass exhibiting the "Nailsea" technique, numerous casings of glass, and elaborate patterns in pull-up threaded decoration was made after 1885, with possibly 85 percent of it emanating from the Stourbridge District.

With Nailsea-type decorations firmly established, we find glassmakers using these as a base for more elaborate pieces. Some were externally threaded using all colors; some had applied decorations; still others had enamelled decorations.

Another attempt to elaborate on Nailsea patterns was to stain another pattern over the one incorporated in the glass itself. This type of decoration is usually well done, but can only be described as "gilding the lily." With these later decorations, such objects cannot be dated much before 1900.

Some Nailsea-type glass with pull-up decorations similar to those made under John Northwood's patent by Stevens & Williams of Brierley Hill, England, was made on the Continent. These Continental pieces, most of which were produced in the Bohemian glass district, probably date sometime after 1900.

A magnificent specimen of Stourbridge threaded glass developed from earlier Nailsea types. The lower half of the bowl is threaded with blue glass, the upper half with primrose-colored glass, all applied over a pull-up design of opal stripes; foot and welt of pinched crystal glass; ca. 1900; 4½" high, 7" diameter across top of bowl.

Colored threads of glass and swirled optic molding produce a very interesting effect in this Stourbridge flask (ca. 1890).

E. Varnish & Company's
Silvered Glassware
by ALBERT CHRISTIAN REVI

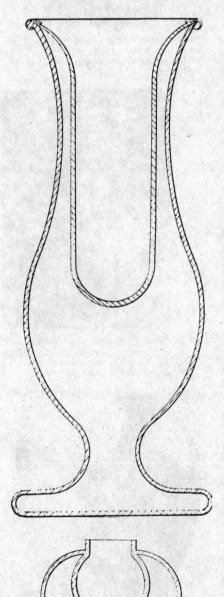

ON December 19, 1949, a process for the manufacture of the most beautiful silvered glassware ever made was patented by Frederick Hale Thomson and Edward Varnish, both of London, England. While this was not the first such patent for silvered glass issued in England or America, it was by far the most artistic accomplishment and was of the very best quality.

To produce their fine silvered glassware, Messrs. Thomson and Varnish had vessels of glass blown whose interiors were hollow (see illustrations from original patent papers, *left)*. The hollow spaces between the inner and outer walls of the vessels — goblets, mustard pots, inkwells, decanters, perfume bottles, mugs with hollow handles, flower vases, glasses, brush trays, pen trays, muffineers, smelling bottles, tea caddies, butter dishes, covers and plates, dishes, salt cellars, plateaus, wine coolers, bottle stands, cruets, etc. were silvered with a solution containing nitrate of silver, spirits of wine and saccharine. The glass articles themselves are believed to have been manufactured by James Powell & Sons of the White Friar glassworks in London.

Included in the patent papers was an interesting method for producing these hollow-walled vessels by joining together two pieces of glass—the inner and outer walls of the vessel—with a metal rim or seal which was fastened or bonded to the two pieces of glass with plaster of Paris. (See patent illustration, and vase from the Henry Ford Museum, pictured.)

Beautiful color effects were produced by plating the articles with colored glass and subsequently cutting through the colored plating to the crystal glass beneath with various kinds of designs in intaglio. For this purpose, brilliant shades of red, blue, purple, green and yellow glass were used as a plating over the crystal body glass. The dazzling effects such designs produced are far and above the usual type of silvered glass manufactured in the nineteenth century.

ILLUSTRATIONS

Above, left to right:

Silvered glass vase, blue overlaid on crystal, and cut through in a design of flowers and leaves; inner and outer sections of the vase joined together at the rim with metal seal in accordance with the method outlined in patent issued to Frederick Hale Thomson and Edward Varnish; 7⅞″ high; from the Henry Ford Museum, Dearborn, Michigan.

Silvered glass goblet, green overlay cut to silver (clear) glass, made by E. Varnish & Company; from the author's collection.

Silvered glass vase, blue overlay cut to silver (clear) glass, made by E. Varnish & Company; from the collection of Mrs. Irene Barbour.

Silvered glass scent bottle, purple overlay cut to silver (clear) glass, made by E. Varnish & Company; from the author's collection.

Left: drawings from original patent papers showing formation of hollow vessels for silvering; vase with inner and outer walls joined together by a metal rim; and an inkstand. Other patent drawings showed fingerbowl, goblet, plates.

Czech-Baroque Glass

by C. C. MANLEY

Pandora vase with threaded decoration about the neck in imitation of an ancient style in glass. Ca. 1890; 7 ¾" high.

Pandora jug-vase in an ancient style, with enamel decoration. Ca. 1890; 3 ¼" high. A larger size in this same design was also made.

Pandora jug-vase in mottled brown and rust, antique finish. Ca. 1890; 6 ½" high. Lagerberg collection.

SOME TYPES OF GLASS are associated with definite localities, but Czech-Baroque glass was made not only in old Czechoslovakia, but in various places in Germany as well. The glass does not need to be of a special mixture; the colors do not follow a pre-arranged pattern; and the way of manufacture varies, too. It is the style which gives these wares their name; and though not actually a trade name, it is one which is still commonly used throughout the Continent to describe such wares.

There are three periods to consider in discussing Czech-Baroque glass. The years 1890 to 1900 are important, for it was during this period that the manufacturing technique, if not the styles, were being developed.

After the main period, 1910 to 1930, the second World War brought all artistic glass production to an end. With peace established, the glass manufacturers again began production of art wares and it was only logical that they would resume with some of the previously successful products. This third period, 1947 to the present, saw changes in styles and in manufacturing methods.

It was during the 1890–1900 period that distinct and definite types of glass were produced. One outstanding example was a glass named "Pandora." This name was patented, and the pride felt in this glass must have been extraordinary, especially when we realize that old Czechoslovakia was the cradle of decorative glass production. Pandora glass is reminiscent of Roman glass excavated at ancient burial sites. All kinds of Roman vessels were copied in this period, but very few could be finished at the furnace. Staining and special decorations were necessary to achieve perfection, and this made the products expensive.

Subjecting the object to various mineral vapors in a muffle gave Pandora glass an azure blue surface and a slight sheen. The variegated enamel decoration is representative of the Roman epoch, even to having breaks in outline to simulate age. A pontil mark will be found on all specimens. Compared with the Roman glass originals, the Pandora pieces are, if anything, slightly heavier. They were not produced in great quantities, and therefore are scarce.

This same period witnessed the production of an iridescent glass, not with a sheen but with a true iridescent surface, blue predominating. As their technical knowledge increased, other chatoyant colors were added to the glassmaker's palette. The first shapes used for iridescent wares followed ancient and medieval vessels rather carelessly. Very soon, edges were elaborately scalloped, then applied threads and appendages of glass appeared as part of the decorations. Iridescent glass was cheap to manufacture and made a good export line.

A very great percentage of the 1910–1930 period ware was definitely a glass of its time. Colors were gaudy and used with great abandon. Shaded colors were not often used, and every operation in its manufacture was cut to the minimum. All pontil scars were left untouched; the base of the object was kicked up to allow the vessel to stand firm; and the articles were exceedingly light in weight.

The elaborately pinched handle and uninspired enamel decoration, identify this crystal jug as a rather cheap piece of Czech-Baroque glass. Ca. 1910; 12" high.

Iridescent glass vase copied from an ancient specimen found in the ruins of the Campanile in Venice, Italy. The hollow foot was formed from the original parison (blow). Ca. 1900; 8½" high.

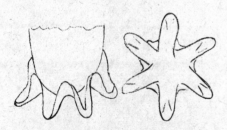

Right and left: Side and base view of an applied glass foot of a type commonly used on Czech-Baroque glass. A quantity of glass was applied to the base of an object, and from this the glassmaker pulled out as many appendages as were required.

One outstanding feature of glass of this period is its outline. This has to be seen to be believed. The waviness of the edges is incredible. Some articles, such as bowls, are of little utilitarian value because of this characteristic.

Economy was the watchword. Even the hole in a fruit bowl (into which was screwed 'a stand) was pierced by the glassblower while the glass was in a plastic state. To add a little character, the wavy edges of an object were often trimmed with glass of another color. Any form of appendage. such as feet or handles, was applied in the same elaborate style.

The application of the feet on some glass articles invariably tells us the country of origin. The process most often used was to cover the base of a vase with a quantity of glass, and from this to pull out as many feet as were required. If the glass used for the feet was crystal, the pontil can be seen through the feet. When the foot was blown as part of the article, it was always hollow.

Handles, too, tend to show the country of origin. In Czech-Baroque pieces, they were applied more for ornamentation than use. If plain, the handles are always thin; if they were thick, it was only to have enough metal for the glassblower to pinch, crimp, and distort the handle into some fantastic form.

Decorations followed the same gaudy pattern. Flowers and leaves were perfect subjects to exploit. Some of the enameled decorations of flowers and animals found on these wares do not exist in real life. Large quantities of painted and gilded glassware were made without fixing the decorations in a kiln; and quite often these decorations have worn off over a period of years.

Although the whole production of Czech-Baroque glass was intended to be cheap in every way, the cooperation of the technicians and the skilled glassblowers produced amazing results. Towards the end of the true Baroque period in the mid-1930s, certain changes began to take place. The fancy designs lingered, but the glass adopted an English appearance. The Czech manufacturers, although they had embarked on a more substantial type of glassware, continued the cheap way of production, but the glass was heavier, making it better able to compete with the finer quality English glass.

As the style of the two countries—England and Czechoslovakia—began to assimilate, the difficulty for collectors to separate one glass from the other became obvious. The first definite break from tradition came with the hand-made crystal lampshades and vases in the form of flowers and leaves. The adoption of cased glass opened the field to unlimited opportunities. All that the English glass manufacturers had done, the Czechs did cheaper—Satin glass,

Cased glass, Aventurine glass, Sploshed glass, Cased and Sploshed glass, and Marble glass—all types were imitated. But occasionally the Czechs developed something new.

Just prior to World War Two, experiments were being carried out on a type of glass which was sprayed with glass dust to form patterns and ornaments. With the coming of the war, all efforts in the European glass industry were diverted to other channels.

The war over, the glassworkers resumed experiments with this new decorating technique with great success. The result was opaque vases, sprayed with glass dust particles in varying sizes, and ranging in color from black to crystal. Flowers and leaves were the major design subjects, for these permitted great latitudes of formation. Some of the designs, after being applied, were burnt on; others were cased with crystal.

This art glass was difficult to make, but was splendid when finished. We do not think this glass was successfully copied by any other country. It may be that other artists, such as Tiffany in America, and Locke in England, had sown the seeds of this idea. Tiffany had already cased pieces of colored glass in crystal to form various designs, while Joseph Locke working for Hodgetts, Richardson & Son, had painted flowers and birds on opaque vases and cased them in crystal.

There are undoubtedly thousands of pieces of Czech-Baroque glass in many collections, their owners believing them to be English specimens. Any vase, bowl, dish, jug or decanter with any of the following characteristics is more than likely Czech—not English or American.

1. Excessive wavy edges; especially with a colored rim.
2. An elaborate form.
3. The pontil broken off and the base of the object kicked up. (Kicking up the base of the object obviates any need to polish the pontil mark; it also allows the piece to stand firm without grinding the base flat.)
4. A hollow foot formed of the original blow.
5. A vertically flattened and crimped handle.
6. Any glass with an exceptionally bright combination of colors—such as black and yellow.
7. Unnatural decorations with excessive gilt lines.
8. Feet made from one piece of glass and applied to cover the rough pontil.
9. Exceptionally light in weight in proportion to the size of the object.

All the aforementioned are the chief points to consider.

F ROM 1880, when it was established, until 1894, the Pairpoint Manufacturing Company of New Bedford, Massachusetts, was engaged only in the making of plated silver. It produced, among other items, all kinds of elaborate silver-plated holders and fittings for the art glass baskets, caster sets, condiment shakers, cracker jars, and the like, then so much in style. Much of this production was made to order for various glasshouses. Thus the Pairpoint silver mark is frequently found on holders whose glass inserts were obviously made elsewhere.

In 1894, on July 14, this flourishing company added glassware to its production when, "in consideration of one dollar and other valuable considerations," it took over the operation of the Mt. Washington Glass Works, also of New Bedford. In fact, the two plants adjoined; and the glassworks had always supplied the power for both. In 1900, the firm was reorganized as the Pairpoint Corporation and continued to manufacture both silver and glassware.

The Pairpoint Manufacturing Company, about 1896, seems also to have engaged in china importing, as indicated by the trademark, "Crown Pairpoint Ware/Limoges, France," listed for it in *Trademarks of the Jewelry and Kindred Trades* of that year.

Most likely this ware was made to Pairpoint's order in France rather than manufactured by them there. It is also quite possible they purchased the blanks in France and did the decorating themselves in this country, a practice followed by various importers with decorating facilities since import duties were lower on undecorated blanks. (Glass companies sometimes matched chinaware designs with their glassware decoration.) The 1909 edition of the same Trademarks publication again pictured the Crown Pairpoint Ware trademark, but labelled it "discontinued," giving the owner then as the Pairpoint Corporation.

by ALBERT CHRISTIAN REVI

No. 2210. Dresden Decorated Dishes. Plain, $45; Fancy Gilt, $54. (Patented Nov. 28, 1893).

No. 2342. Rich Decoration, $2.   No. 2341. Dresden Decorated, $3.

the pairpoint story

Pairpoint's Glass Production

The new owners of the glassworks continued to produce Mt. Washington's most popular wares, including the well known Crown Milano and Albertine; the condiment shakers in form of eggs, tomatoes, and figs, decorated like the Crown Milano wares; and the flower and pansy dishes, made in opalware and decorated in natural colors, whose designs had been patented in 1893 by Albert Steffin, head of Mt. Washington's decorating department. They even added somewhat to the lines of these decorative glass objects.

The Pairpoint Manufacturing Company's illustrated catalogue, issued in 1894, the year it took over the glassworks, shows many more richly decorated opal glasswares than the Mt. Washington Glass Company had put out. These were variously named. Many of the designs on the decorated opalwares show little or no difference from those on Mt. Washington pieces, though they were not always used on the exact same blank (the undecorated object). In many cases the shape, rather than the decoration, determined the designation given it in the Pairpoint catalogue. (In Mt. Washington days, the name given a ware usually referred to the type of decoration.)

It is obvious from the names the Pairpoint Manufacturing Company selected and used in this 1894 catalogue that some of their wares were made to imitate the popular porcelains of the day—such names, for example, as Decorated Porcelain, Dresden Decorated Glass, Rich Decorated Porcelain, Porcelain Decorated Glass, even Royal Worcester.

Other wares, quite similar, appeared in this same catalogue under such designations as Ivory Glass — Turquoise, Yellow, or Ruby Lined; Ivory Glass—Pink Lined, Gold Edge Glass; Pink Decorated, Velvet Finish (this was rose over white satin glass); Plush Rose, Decorated Glass (pink satin glass with an opal lining); and Rich Colonial Decorations.

This last designation—Rich Colonial Decorations—was given to a group of decorated opal glass jewel boxes with satin linings, confusingly like the decorated opal glass boxes marked "Wavecrest," "Nakara," and "Kelva," which were made by C. F. Monroe & Company of Meriden, Connecticut, during this same period. (Incidentally, Pairpoint furnished the Monroe Company with some of its blanks.)

The Ivory Glass referred to as being lined with various colors was not a pure milk white in color, but a slightly cream-colored opaque glass which looked very much like the biscuit-colored Royal Worcester porcelain of the late 1890s.

In many cases an opaque uranium yellow glass was decorated with designs similar to those used on Mt. Washington Glass Company's Crown Milano and Albertine wares. Some of

Illustrations on these pages are taken from a catalogue put out by the Pairpoint Manufacturing Company of New Bedford, Massachusetts, in 1894, soon after this firm had taken over the Mt. Washington Glass Works and commenced its own manufacture of glasswares. These pictures will serve to familiarize *Spinning Wheel* readers with the forms and types of decorations which the Pairpoint Manufacturing Company (later the Pairpoint Corporation) used on various opal glasswares.

No. 3905. Rich Decorated Glass, Silver Top, $4.

No. 535. Mushroom Flower Holder, also a good toothpick holder. Richly Decorated, $12 per doz.

No. 2586. Albertine Decorated Glass, Silver Top, $5.

No. 2263. Ivory Decorated Glass. Plain, $18.50; Fancy Gilt, $21.50.

No. 2599. Plush Rose Gold Decorated Glass, Silver Top, $5.

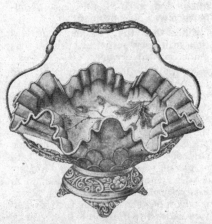

No. 4713. Pink Decorated, Velvet Finish, $8.

No. 4726. Rich Decorated Porcelain, Ruby Lined, $13.

No. 723. Decorated Porcelain Bottles, $3.25.

these pieces even bear the identifying mark "C. M." surmounted with a crown, even though the uranium yellow glass base differs from the usual bisque finish opalware of Mt. Washington's Crown Milano.

In almost every other instance a plain opal (milk white) glass was used as the blank for the richly decorated opalware which Pairpoint produced.

The colored enamels used to decorate their articles were the same as were used on Crown Milano Albertine, and Royal Flemish — wares which Pairpoint continued to make and which they illustrated in this same catalogue.

To conclude the Pairpoint glass history, the Pairpoint Corporation was soon concentrating on the production of cut glass in which Mt. Washington glassworks had excelled. Pairpoint itself originated some excellent designs. In 1900, the company was employing 350 glass cutters and 100 men in the glass blowing room. By 1918, only two furnaces were operating, and in 1938, all glass manufacture was discontinued.

Since then the Pairpoint Corporation, still very active in business, has made only silverware.

As for the glass factory itself, the Pairpoint Corporation sold it in 1939 to J. & B. Kenner, Inc., a salvage company, who in turn sold it to Robert Gundersen, who operated as the Gundersen Glass Works. When Mr. Gundersen died in 1952, it became part of the National Pairpoint Company and was known as the Gundersen-Pairpoint Works. It ended up in East Wareham, Massachusetts, where it was moved in 1957, as a small factory called the Pairpoint Glass Works. It closed in 1958.

No. 1719. (Patent Cut-off) Rich Decorated Porcelain, $3.50.

No. 705. Decorated Porcelain Bottles, $4.

No. 761. Royal Worcester, $4.

No. 4609. Glass Jewel Box, Rich Colonial Decorations, Satin Lined, $5.

The Mt. Washington Glass Company's...
Napoli Glassware

by ALBERT CHRISTIAN REVI

ON May 22, 1894, Albert Steffin, head of the Mt. Washington Glass Company's decorating department, patented a new means for decorating glassware which the firm named "Napoli."

"The invention," states Mr. Steffin in his patent specifications, "consists in forming upon one side or face of the glass article to be decorated an outline of the figure or design to be produced, and forming upon the opposite side or face of such article the complete figure or design, whereby the outline thus formed upon one side will, by reason of the transparency of the glass, combine with the main body of the decoration upon the opposite side, and produce a novel and peculiar effect."

Mr. Steffin stated also in his patent papers that the decoration should first be outlined on one side of the article to serve as a guide for producing the main body of the design upon the opposite side. This method was especially recommended in decorating hollow glassware — vases, bowls, jars, etc. Owing to the shape of such articles of hollow glassware, access to the interior is more or less difficult, and in many cases it is almost impossible to produce decorations upon the interior with any degree of accuracy. The outline of the designs on the exterior served as a guide in forming the main body of the decoration in colored enamels on the interior of the hollow vessel. In all cases, the effect of depth or solidity in the decoration produced by this method was due to the fact that the outline is upon one side of the glass and the main body of the design upon the opposite side. The result was a striking and novel effect, one that could not be produced by applying the entire decoration upon one side only of the glass.

A great practical advantage resulted from Mr. Steffin's new method for decorating glassware, since by it both the colored and the metallic gold or silver decoration could be fired at one firing. Heretofore, when both metallic and colored decorations had been employed in the production of a given design, both being applied to the same side of the glass and in contact with each other, it had been impossible to fire the article at a single firing, for either the metallic decorations would be absorbed by the colors, or would be so affected by the fumes arising from the colored enamel decoration in the process of fusing as to lose their proper color and brightness, and thus be practically spoiled. Consequently it was necessary to subject the article to two firings, applying the colored designs first and fixing them in the kiln before the gold or silver outline decorations could be added and fired at a much lower temperature. Readers familiar with the techniques of firing hand painted china will well understand the difficulties.

The covered jar shown in our illustrations is a fine example of Napoli glass. The design upon it portrays three Brownie figures, then at the zenith of their popularity. All of these figures are painted on the inside of the jar with colored enamels and in an exaggerated style. The costumes are in bright shades of blue, brown, green, red, and black; the stockings are a bright orange. On the outside of the jar, the outline of the figures has been done in gold tracery. In addition there is a network of interlacing gold lines decorating the entire surface of the jar. The silver-plated cover has a turtle finial and is marked on the under side "M.W." (for Mt. Washington). The name "Napoli" is painted on the base of the jar in black enamel lettering.

Mr. Steffin's patented technique for decorating glassware with enamels and gold does have an ancient origin in the so-called "reverse paintings on glass." Perhaps the most famous piece of ancient reverse picture painting on glass is the Paris plate, attributed to Antioch or Syria about 200 A.D. In the late 18th and early 19th centuries the technique reappeared in China where a brisk business in such wares was done with American and European merchants in the China Trade. Manifestations of the art can be found in European and American decorated mirrors and clock cases of the 18th and early 19th centuries.

It should be pointed out, however, that Steffin's added innovation (the outlining of the figures on the opposite face of the glass) does change the whole character of the decoration, making Napoli glassware different from its predecessors.

Palmer Cox's popular Brownies popped up everywhere in the 1890s, even on this fine Napoli glass covered jar! Collection of Mrs. J. M. Miller.

William T. Gillinder's

AMERICAN CAMEO GLASS

by ALBERT CHRISTIAN REVI

IN THE 1880s, William T. Gillinder produced a limited amount of cameo glass after the style of English cameo glass productions of this same period. While it has been reported that such wares were made by Gillinder (R. W. Lee's *Nineteenth Century Art Glass,* and A. C. Revi's *Nineteenth Century Glass*), the physical characteristics of these productions have never before been shown to collectors.

A few years ago we were fortunate in discovering an old color transparency of a group of cameo glass vases made by Gillinder at his works in Philadelphia. All the pieces shown in this color slide were in the possession of various members of the Gillinder family and had been handed down through the years from one to another. Indeed, they are all still owned by members of the Gillinder family.

Only a Few Pieces

Because cameo glass was so costly to make, only a very few pieces were produced. According to J. Fletcher Gillinder, the family archives indicate that these vases were made from cased colored blanks with a white overlay on ruby, on blue, and on canary; also a few pieces were made with a layer of ruby glass between canary and white glass.

Close examination of the vases shown in the color transparency reveals that most of the cameo relief was etched away from the body glass, leaving the white glass in shallow relief against a colored ground. Some engraving, possibly with a wheel, had been done on the pieces, but there is little to indicate that any hand work of any kind had been used.

Six Different Vases

The photograph we were able to make from the colored slide shows six vases of various sizes and different forms.

From right to left, they represent a small yellow vase with white cameo relief design of flowers and leaves on a branch or twig; a blue vase with white cameo relief designs of ferns and swamp plants, the top of the vase being decorated with plain bands and laurel leaves; a large poppy-red vase, with cameo designs in white of maple leaves on a branch and the collar of the vase decorated with stylized lotus flowers, separated by pyramid-shaped darts.

In the center of the photograph is a Wedgwood jasperware replica of the Portland vase.

The tallest vase in the group has a cameo relief design of leaves and ferns in white on a deep ruby body; the next vase has a decoration of maple leaves in white on a canary colored ground. The last vase is obviously the mate to the one on the far left of the illustration and appears to be decorated with leaves and flowers in white glass on a canary ground.

Gillinder cameo glass resembles the English productions of the late period, ca. 1885, and collectors would have difficulty determining whether their pieces were made here in America by Gillinder or abroad.

No Pieces Marked

We have been told by members of the family that none of the Gillinder cameo glass pieces were marked, and it would appear that this would hold true for some of the objects that were sold from the Gillinder factory at the time they were making cameo glass.

It would be reasonable to assume, though, that vases resembling those in our illustration, in form, color, and decoration, were made by Gillinder & Sons.

Gillinder Cameo Glass: (left to right) White on yellow; white on blue; white on poppy-red; the Portland vase is Wedgwood jasper; white on deep ruby; white on lemon yellow; and white on yellow. From a color transparency loaned to the author by J. Fletcher Gillinder.

"GLASS OF CLASS"

by ALBERT CHRISTIAN REVI

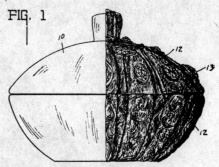

FIG. 1

Patent illustration showing "jewels" set into the applied decoration.

363 Glass

ON NOVEMBER 20, 1928, Harper J. Ransburg patented a process for decorating blown or pressed glass blanks (undecorated wares) with colorful raised designs, which he marketed at that time as "Glass of Class."

Mr. Ransburg's patented decorating technique provided that the surface of the glass object be prepared for his decorations by treating it with an application of benzol. This not only cleaned the glass, but roughened it somewhat, allowing his applied decoration to adhere more readily to the surface of the glass. The decoration was applied either by hand (with a brush), or was molded and then affixed to the object.

In his patent enumerations, Mr. Ransburg stated that the composition he used for this raised decoration was a mixture of lithopone, zinc oxide, whiting, superspectra black, lamp black, and incorporating oils. When the decoration had dried and contracted, it was more or less permanently attached to the surface of the glass. It was then painted with colors and gilded as the designs required.

Another means for producing decorative effects on his glassware was described by Ransburg in his patent. Small, colored glass "jewels" were imbedded into the composition while it was still in a plastic state; when the applied decoration hardened, these "jewels" appeared to have been set into the surface of the object in a most pleasing manner.

After more than thirty years of use, articles decorated in accordance with this patented technique show signs of wear. Often portions of the design have broken away from the surface of the glass, especially in those areas where much handling or use has taken its toll. All of the objects shown in illustration here attest to this fact. Missing are portions of the applied decoration on the rim of the covered candy dish, on the foot and rim of the fan-shaped base, and on the decorated "Sad Hound" or "Crying Dog" bottle.

The Harper J. Ransburg Company was established in Toledo, Ohio, in 1908. At that time glass-cutting and high quality tablewares were their principal output. This was discontinued about 1924, and the firm started producing the line of decorated glass described here, along with decorated candles, hand-painted kitchenware, painted bathroom accessories, and wire goods — floor stands, wall brackets, table stands, etc.

In 1912, Ransburg moved his business to Indianapolis, Indiana, where it occupied several locations before finally settling in a factory at 1234 Barth Avenue, corner of Sanders. Presently the firm manufactures pantryware and bathroom accessories which are sold at leading department stores throughout the United States and Canada.

"Glass of Class" decorated "Sad Hound" (or "Crying Dog") bottle with original matching stopper-shot glass beside it. Light green glass with raised decoration in black and gold. Height including stopper, 8¾". Collection: Mr. & Mrs. Victor Buck, Upland, California.

Fan-shaped vase decorated with green, blue, yellow, red, lavender and black on dark blue background, gold touches. Height 5½", width 5¾". Original paper labels: round, ½", "Pat'd.11-30-26"; oblong, in green, embossed gold letters, "Glass of Class. Ransburg, Indianapolis." Buck Collection.

"Glass of Class" covered candy box; pressed glass with drapery effect, heavily decorated with pink, rose, and yellow roses, green leaves; gilded decorations on legs and other portions. Height 5"; diameter 9". Original price tag label reads "Covered Candy Box." Author's Collection.

(Figure 2)
Thick yellowish glass bottle with "basket" decoration. Persia, 5th-7th cent. A.D., or later. Corning Museum of Glass.

(Figure 3)
Cage cup blue lustre glass. Ht. 3¼". Marked: "L.C. Tiffany-Favrile-6938 D." Author's collection.

Ancient Techniques in American

by ALBERT CHRISTIAN REVI

(Figure 1)
Favrile *Cypriote* glass vase in ancient form; ht. 4½". Ca. 1900. Author's collection.

(Figure 5)
Quezal footed sherbet. Opal glass with inlaid decoration of green, white, and gold lustre; ht. 4". Author's collection.

(Figure 4)
Vase, XVIII Dynasty (ca. 1450-1350 B.C.), Egyptian; ht. 3 7/16". Corning Museum of Glass.

(Figure 9)
Gold lustre vase with pinched decoration. Tiffany Furnaces; ca. 1900. Ht. 3½". Collection Mrs. Claranell M. Lewis.

ART NOUVEAU GLASS

(Figure 6)
Above: Jar, possibly 4th or 5th century A.D. (Near East); ht. 3". Corning Museum of Glass.

(Figure 7)
Right: Kew Blas vase with pulled threaded decoration of green and gold lustre on opal ground; Union Glass Works, Somerville, Mass.; ca. 1900. Ht. 4½". L. A. Randolph collection.

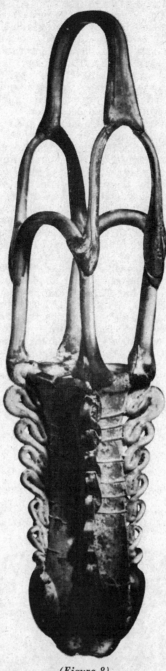

(Figure 8)
Balsamarium or saddle flask. Roman Empire, possibly Syria; ca. 3rd-4th century, A.D. Ht. 12⅝". Corning Museum of Glass.

MANY CHANGES in glass-decorating techniques were manifested at the beginning of the 20th century—for the most part—borrowed from the ancient world (Egypt, Syria, Persia and Venice). These were incorporated with Art Nouveau designs for decorative glassware by such American firms as the Tiffany Furnaces of Corona, Long Island; the Quezal Art Glass & Decorating Company, Brooklyn, New York; Steuben of Corning, New York; Victor Durand's Vineland Flint Glass Works in Vineland, New Jersey; the Union Glass Works of Somerville, Massachusetts; and a few others.

Lustred Glass

The most obvious, and most widely used decorating technique found in a preponderance of the glassware made during the Art Nouveau period was an imitation of the nacreous surface deterioration found on many pieces of ancient glass. This was manifested in lustred effects which sometimes covered the entire object, or was utilized as a part of the overall design in the form of threads and patches pulled into fantastic forms with the glassmaker's tools. In at least one instance this reproduction of the iridescent effects found on ancient specimens of glass was carried to the ultimate when Tiffany produced his "Cypriote" glass (*Fig. 1*)—an exact duplicate of the iridescent and pitted surface of badly decomposed glass.

The free standing "cage" or "basket" decoration composed of heavy zigzag threads of glass attached to a glass object, such as the ancient Persian bottle (*Fig. 2*), which made its appearance in Pre-Islamic and Islamic glass of about 6–8 A.D. was reintroduced at the Tiffany glass works. Small vases and cups of this description were made in their blue and gold lustred glass (*Fig. 3*).

Inlaid threaded designs appeared in ancient Egyptian glass of the 18th Dynasty (1546–1350 B.C.). Usually the threads of glass were "combed" into wavy or feathery designs while the object was still in a plastic condition, and then rolled on a marver to firmly embed the applied decoration into the surface of the glass. We find a decided relationship between the footed vase attributed to ancient Egypt during the 18th Dynasty (*Fig. 4*), and a footed sherbet glass produced by the Quezal Art Glass & Decorating Company about 1910 (*Fig. 5*). In the latter instance the leaf-shaped decoration on the cup and foot of the article was produced by pulling applied threads of green glass into these patterns.

We call your attention to a vase (*Fig. 6*) attributed to Syria during the Post-Roman period, about 5th century A.D., with embedded dragged threads of glass decorating its surface, and its very near counterpart (*Fig. 7*), a small Kew Blas vase with lustrous dragged decoration, produced about 1910 at the Union Glass Works.

(Figure 17)
Above: Vitro di Trina sherbet glass with lustred surface. Tiffany Furnaces, ca. 1900; ht. 3⅝". Author's collection. *Below (Figure 10):* Bottle, 1st century B.C. Ht. 4⅛". Corning Museum of Glass.

Also, the ancient multiple balsamaria *(Fig. 8)* made in Syria during the 3rd and 4th centuries A.D., and the gold lustre vase with pinched decoration *(Fig. 9)* made by the Tiffany glass works around 1910. These objects, though separated by more than a thousand years, are most definitely related in form and decoration.

Imitating striated stones, such as chalcedony, agate, and jasper was a technique practiced by ancient Roman glassmakers about the 1st century A.D. *(Fig. 10)*. This kind of glass was revived by the Venetians in the late 15th century, and references are made to the manufacture of "jasper," "chalcedony," and "Schmelzglas" in many 16th and 17th century glass recipes. In the early 19th century Friederich Eggerman of Bohemia produced a similar ware which he called "Lithyalinglas." The same kind of glass was made by the Tiffany Furnaces and the Quezal Art Glass & Decorating Company prior to, and shortly after, the year 1900. In the former factory such wares were designated "Laminated" and "Agate" glass *(Fig. 11)*, and it was very likely known by similar names at the Quezal factory.

Many people still believe that millefiori glass was a Venetian invention; actually such wares date back to ancient Alexandria during the Roman occupation—1st century B.C. to 1st

century A.D. *(Fig. 13)*. This beautiful and interesting example of the glass arts is found in many specimens of 19th century glass, but rarely do we find an object of the Art Nouveau period *(Fig. 14)* composed entirely of cross-section disks of millefiori. In most instances cross-section disks from millefiori rods were used to represent flowers *(Fig. 15)*. Paperweights and vases with heavy paperweight bases were produced at the Tiffany glass works in which sections of millefiori rods were incorporated, emulating coral formations, sea urchins, polyps, and sea anemone. The under-the-sea illusion was heightened by adding trailing threads of green glass in imitation of seaweed, and incorporating the whole set-up in a matrix of light green glass the color of sea water.

The Vitro di Trina footed sherbet glass *(Fig. 17)*, made at the Tiffany glass works was identified in A. E. Saunder's notes and papers as "a copy of the Diaper Pattern plates made by the Murano Glass Company, Venice, Italy." Mr. Saunders was a former gaffer at the Corona glass works and, if we are to accept his notes as factual, only two such specimens of this ware made by Tiffany are now in existence in this country. The Vitro di Trina technique dates back to 16th century Venice, but even this comparatively recent innovation in glass decorating has its genesis in ancient Egypt.

(Figure 13)
Below: Millefiori bowl; Roman Empire, possibly Alexandria, 100 B.C.-100 A.D.; ht. 1 7/16". Corning Museum of Glass.

(Figure 11)
Above: Favrile *Laminated* glass vase. Tiffany Glass & Decorating Co. ca. 1893. *(Figure 14) right:* Favrile gold lustre vase with millefiori decoration and inlaid decoration of green leaves and tendrils. Tiffany Furnaces; ca. 1900. Ht. 3¾".

(Figure 15)
Favrile millefiori vase made entirely of cross-sections disks of brown, tan, and black glass. Tiffany Furnaces, ca. 1900; ht. 8⅝". Author's collection.

INTARSIA GLASS

Condensed from The Glass Industry, November 1961

by ALBERT CHRISTIAN REVI

FROM 1916 to 1923 Frederick Carder, co-founder of the Steuben Glass Works at Corning, N. Y., produced artistic-glassware emulating those decorative designs created by inlaying wood in a background of wood and known as "intarsia." To make his intarsia glasses, Carder formed a small bulb of glass on the end of an iron and coated it with any desired color. The colored casing was then etched into a pattern. Thereafter, the bulb was reheated slowly, picked up on the blow iron, and blown out larger. It was then blown into a cup of crystal glass made to receive it, and the two, cohering, were blown out to the shape and size required. The stem or foot was attached and the article annealed.

In 1917 the Orrefors Glassworks of Orrefors, Sweden, featured a display of Simon Gates' Graal glass at Nordiska Kompaniet, a department store in Stockholm. The Graal glass consisted of several thin layers of colored glass, cleverly etched into pleasing designs and plated with a skin of crystal glass to leave a smooth exterior. In the 1930's Vicke Lindstrand and Edward Hald of Orrefors revamped the Graal technique, applying a thick layer of colored glass, the decorative pattern being reflected in a striking play of colors.

At an exhibition in Paris in 1937, Edvin Ohrstrom's Ariel glass made its appearance. The new Ariel glass resembled the Graal technique, but differed in its use of patterns of bubbles as part of the decoration. Interesting figure and flower composi-tions, rich in color, were combined with the silvery gleam of air bubbles to give a scintilating texture.

During the nineteenth century several patents were issued covering similar decorative productions in glass. On May 25, 1850, Edward Pettitt of Birmingham, England, registered his method for rolling plates of window glass with ornamental designs sandwiched between two layers of glass. Pieces of colored glass which had been previously stamped, cast, or cut into ornamental forms were applied to a sheet of glass and thereafter another sheet of glass was either cast or rolled over the ornamental design. Pettitt suggested in his enumerations that (1) the colored pattern could be applied to a background of opaque white or colored glass, or (2) a pattern could be drawn on a plate of glass with plumbago and connected to a galvanic battery for the purpose of depositing a metallic design which would afterward be covered with another layer of glass.

On April 6, 1853, "a communication from abroad" was registered at the Patent Offices in London by William Johnson of Glasgow, Scotland. (Mr. Johnson acted as agent only, and a careful search of the patent records offers no clue to the actual patentee). The invention related to the production of ornamental surfaces by incrustation or "inlaid work (intarsia)." Two pieces of different colored glass, laid one upon the other, were united by heat; they were then softened in an enamelling furnace, and a design of any kind impressed on their surfaces. By this means the upper colored piece was squeezed into, and partially penetrated, the lower one according to the design on the impressing die. The entire surface was then ground flat and the superfluous glass cut away, leaving the actual design imbedded in the lower piece of glass.

In another method, the die employed was simply a punch corresponding in outline to the contour of the design. A number of plates of glass of uniform thickness, but of different colors, were perforated by this punch, and the pieces so cut out were exchanged and inserted into corresponding holes in the different plates. Thus, a piece cut from a blue plate was inserted into an opening in a red plate, while the piece from the red plate was inserted into the corresponding opening of the blue plate, and so on throughout the series, with different colored glasses being inlaid together to form varied and colorful designs. The intarsia techniques registered by William Johnson

Intarsia vase by Frederick Carder. Collection of the author.

Graal glass vase of Edward Hald. Collection Orrefors Glass Works.

represent a rare and interesting development in pressed glass.

Achille Lemaire of Paris, France, registered his means for producing intarsia glass July 14, 1879. The patent received only provisional protection at the London Patent Offices. Etching an applied colored layer of glass prior to applying a second skin of glass, as Carder has done, was one of his suggestions.

On November 8, 1883, Lewis John Murray of the Soho and Vesta Glass Works, Birmingham, England, registered a means for producing intarsia glass closely resembling the procedure used by Frederick Carder and Simon Gates. Murray etched, engraved, or sand-blasted the design on a blow, plated with colored glass, before blowing it into a cup of glass, thereby entrapping the colored design between two layers of clear crystal glass. He registered his patent in America on December 23, 1884.

There are relatively few factories in operation today that can boast such intricate productions as intarsia, Graal, and Ariel glass. Consequently, the entire industry views with pride the artistic contributions of such twentieth century craftsmen as Carder, Gates, Lindstrand, Hald, and Ohrstrom.

Ariel glass vase by Edvin Ohrstrom. Collection Orrefors Glass Works.

The Art Glass

OF

LOUIS COMFORT TIFFANY

by J. JONATHAN JOSEPH, A.I.D.

LOUIS COMFORT Tiffany was born in 1848, the son of Charles Tiffany, one of the founders of Tiffany & Co. From childhood he showed remarkable concern with color, and inevitably he turned to art rather than to his father's business.

Greatly influenced by the color work of George Inness, the American painter, young Louis began to study painting seriously at the age of eighteen. Born to great wealth, at a time when the Grand Tour of Europe was a "must," and consequent "drifting" was fashionable, he pursued his studies abroad with a passion and direction which amazed his masters. Painting in both oil and water color, he was at last able to translate his exotic feeling for color into something tangible. This quality is expressed strongly in his paintings of North Africa and Southern Europe.

In 1870, at the age of twenty-two, he was elected to membership in the Century Club; in 1871, he became an Associate Member of the National Academy of Design; and in 1880, he was made a full Academician.

While exhibiting his paintings at the Philadelphia Centennial Exposition in 1876, he became intensely aware of the work of decorative artists, and inspired by stained glass

Above, *left*: Nasturtium "paperweight" vase, magnificent example of this difficult technique; flowers are pale orange, floating amongst leaves of deep bottle green and dark blue; only inner surface is iridized; inscribed: L. C. Tiffany-Favrile #3595N. *Right*: Miniature gold "tear bottle" in most unusual Cypriote technique, a replica of buried, ancient glass; H. 3¾"; inscribed: L. C. Tiffany-Favrile.

Left: Pale blue iridescent vase with famous "peacock eye" decoration, a very rare technique, not to be confused with the simpler feather decoration; "eyes" are deeper blue with black iridescent centers; H. 5¾"; inscribed: L. C. Tiffany-Favrile #V228. Black iridescent miniature vase with blue iridescent applied glass vines and leaves; H. 2½"; early signature; inscribed: "T.G.C." (Tiffany Glass Co.)

Left: left to right — Mandarin yellow opalescent vase, red *art nouveau* swirl decoration; inner surface iridized in gold; H. 5½"; inscribed: L. C. Tiffany-Favrile #7797A. Claret red vase with apple green paperweight flowers and leaves; iridescent inner surface; H.10¾"; inscribed: L. C. Tiffany-Favrile #8824L. Black iridescent bowl vase with amber iridescent leaves and vines; H. 3¼"; inscribed: L.C.T. #Q585.

Below: Yellow agate glass vase with cut panels and carved fish; H. 3¾"; inscribed: 103A-Coll. L. C. Tiffany-Favrile. Extremely rare carved glass vase; brilliant lemon yellow background with pale green Iris leaf pattern; H. 5½"; inscribed: L. C. Tiffany-Favrile #5504M. Exhibition Piece.

windows he had seen in Europe, he began to experiment with the actual making of stained glass.

Eventually he developed a glass that could be manipulated to imitate the form and draping of fabrics without further external painting or "shading" on the glass. In 1878, he set up his own glasshouse and engaged a Venetian glassblower, Andrea Boldini, to supervise the furnaces. Though both this and a subsequently-built factory burned down, he continued experiments and production at the Heidt glasshouse in Brooklyn, New York, from 1880 to 1893.

The Philadelphia Centennial had also renewed public interest in Candace Wheeler's Society of Decorative Art, a group which encouraged women possessing artistic talent to market their work. Mr. Tiffany collaborated with this society until 1879. Then, manifesting his desire to lead rather than follow, he formed his own company with Samuel Coleman, Lockwood DeForrest, and Mrs. Wheeler, who was persuaded to join him. This he called "Louis C. Tiffany Co., Associated Artists."

Sophisticated New Yorkers were enchanted with Tiffany's new style of decorating, and for the next four years he devoted himself feverishly to the complete interior decoration of fashionable homes and public institutions. He used his beloved stained glass wherever possible, and introduced glass mosaics and tiles in fireplaces and decorative screens. Rugs, tapestries, upholstery fabrics, embroideries, wallpapers, and furniture were all designed and produced by his firm of talented artists.

Mrs. Wheeler left the organization in 1883, taking with her the department of needlework and her original name, "Associated Artists." Mr. Tiffany then formed the "Tiffany Glass

Co.," concentrating on stained glass windows for interiors and churches.

In 1892, he again reorganized and expanded. The firm became the "Tiffany Glass and Decorating Co.," and construction was started on a glass factory in Corona, Long Island.

Beginnings of Favrile

It has been said Louis Tiffany developed his Favrile glass ornamental wares because of the tremendous amount of waste glass which accumulated during the making of his windows. This is plausible, but mere practicality seems strangely out-of-scale with the pattern of Tiffany's life. It would, in my opinion, seem entirely logical that he preferred to adorn his houses and interiors with objects and art born of his own talent rather than draw upon the style of others. The name he coined derived from the root word *faber,* meaning "handmade," softened first to *Fabrile,* then to *Favrile.*

The new Tiffany furnaces were in operation by the end of 1893, and Arthur J. Nash, a glass manufacturer from Stourbridge, England, was engaged to supervise the glass-blowing division. Mr. Tiffany *personally overseered all beginning production,* and after introducing the various craftsmen to his style and color preferences, would then allow them to develop the object to their interpretation of his original concept. He was a relentless taskmaster, however, and so asserted his personality that each piece, though often interpreted by many craftsmen, bears his distinct mark.

Since profit was not his prime concern, he encouraged experimenting, advising his glassblowers to work and rework a piece in the hope that an accidental effect would produce that little bit of magic he so earnestly

desired. His earliest pieces, therefore, are of a tremendous variety of shapes, and bear little resemblance to what the non-collector recognizes as Tiffany glass.

Shapes, in the beginning, were generally based on Islamic and Oriental forms or on the "nature and growth" principle of the *art nouveau* movement then in full vogue. Thus it would seem that no pieces of early Tiffany could be alike.

Contrary to what has been said, few, if any, of these earlier pieces were signed. Some were simply inscribed with an "x" or "o," followed by a number. This is a type most sought by advanced collectors today.

Intrigued by the iridescent quality of ancient, excavated glass, he experimented with chemicals to reproduce its effect. The final result was achieved by a chemical spray which emitted fumes on the hot glass when it was taken from the furnace. The resulting iridescence fused with the glass and became an integral part of it. The exact formula for this technique was kept secret.

Collectors are most familiar with the iridized glass, and it is this type which has become almost synonymous with the name Tiffany. Though hues of gold or blue were most profusely produced, almost every color was made and iridized during some phase of production.

Tiffany Signatures

Not until about 1900 was the glass consistently signed, and pieces produced which could be matched and remade in quantity. Tableware, for example, was then given pattern names, as advertised in Tiffany & Co.'s *Blue Books*. We can be certain that by 1904 every piece was supposed to have been signed, for the *Blue Book* for that year reads: "As this unique glass is being imitated and inferior products are represented as 'Favrile Glass' or 'Tiffany Glass,' patrons are cautioned to look for the distinguishing mark on every piece of Tiffany Favrile Glass, *Louis C. Tiffany* or *L.C.T.*"

The signature is often preceded or followed by a number, with a letter in front or after it. The exact meaning of letters and numbers is not yet known; collectors and museum curators are still conducting research. A signature does not in any way indicate the quality or rarity of the glass; a simple piece of gold tableware may have the full signature while a very rare paperweight vase could be signed merely "L.C.T."

Tiffany Techniques

Exact formulas for Tiffany glass are lost to us, since all processes were held in absolute secrecy. Techniques are numberless; variety and originality were rules rather than exceptions. No single formula could embrace such wide variations as the mundane gold iridescent salt dish and the supreme "flower-form," whose technique drew upon no other culture or era of glassmaking.

Carved or cameo glass was also produced, the subject matter of design being mostly floral. Paperweight glass was made with flowers, leaves, or vines "growing" between layers of glass, occasionally with the inner surface of the vase iridized. "Aquamarine" paperweight vases were blown of heavy clear glass with undersea motifs, fish, and lily pads, trapped in the solid mass of glass. These are generally completely uniridized, as are many vases in the more dynamic hues of red, yellow, brown, etc.

There is never any external decoration of Tiffany glass other than the glass itself; the flowers, carving, swirling, or iridescence are all homogeneous. Though some Tiffany glass has been found with external decoration or silver mountings, it is safe to assume that this was done by other firms after the object had been sold.

The exception is seen in the silver-mounted perfume bottles and small wares with silver caps which were sold through Tiffany & Co. The silver, however, is *always* marked "Tiffany & Co." (Tiffany & Co., the silver and jewelry store, was never associated with Louis Tiffany's enterprises ex-cept as an additional outlet for the sale of his glass.)

In 1900, Tiffany Glass and Decorating Co. reorganized as "Tiffany Studios," to lead the field in the production of electric lamps with leaded and stained glass shades. Though best known for Favrile, The Studios also designed and produced pottery, enamels, bronzes, and jewelry.

As the vogue for Tiffany glass spread, rival companies began to imitate it, especially the gold and blue iridescent types; none achieved the artistry of the originator. When less desirable imitations began to flood the market, Mr. Tiffany withdrew his support from the Studios. Mr. Nash continued to operate the furnaces, but he lacked the necessary funds, and the quality of the glass steadily declined.

Louis Comfort Tiffany died January 17, 1933, having devoted his long lifetime to the arts.

Lava vase in deep brown and earth greens; design melts away in some places to "window" the middle layer and sometimes shows the iridescent inner surface; H. 6½"; inscribed: 51A-Coll. L. C. Tiffany-Favrile.

Left, *left to right:* Extremely rare red opalescent vase with gunmetal striping, white casing; H. 12¼"; inscribed: L. C. Tiffany-Favrile #5593E. Red gourd-shaped vase, raisin brown design, white inner casing; H. 6¾"; inscribed: L. C. Tiffany-Favrile #551K. Red paperweight vase with brown leaves and vines; entire inner surface iridized in red; H. 7¾"; inscribed: L. C. Tiffany-Favrile #9452H.

BLACK SATIN GLASSWARE

by
ALBERT
CHRISTIAN
REVI

PRESSED AND BLOWN black satin glass was made at the Tiffin, Ohio, and Pittsburgh, Pennsylvania, plants owned by the United States Glass Company from 1924 to about 1940. Roy A. Williams, formerly the foreman of the blow room at the Tiffin factory, reported that the Tiffin plant manufactured vases, bowls, compotes, lamps, DeVilbiss perfume atomizers, ashtrays and combination coaster and ashtrays, stemware, bases for fancy bowls and vases, and a line of hotel stemware with crystal bowls and stems and black feet. Somewhat the same wares were produced in the United States Glass Company's Pittsburgh factory, but on a very much larger scale to meet domestic needs and those of their overseas outlet in England.

While it appears to be jet black, the glass is actually a very deep amethyst color. The satin finish, produced by dipping the objects in an acid bath, added a touch of elegance that was hard to resist. Large flat plates with wide rims, deep dishes on low or high feet, also with wide rims, and handsome vases were among the most popular pieces produced by the United States Glass Company.

Sixteen years of more or less continuous production would indicate that black satin glass was a very popular line, and that the United States Glass Company's distribution at home and abroad was widespread. Add to this the procution of other American firms that made a line of decorative black glass, and the possibilities of finding some attractive pieces for the home seems unlimited. However, black satin glass appears rather infrequently in antiques shops these days.

Bowls and compotes in black satin glass lend themselves well to artistic arrangements of fruits and flowers. Matching candlesticks, if you're lucky enough to find them, can add greatly to your decorating efforts.

Schneider ART GLASS

by JOHN W. GRAVES

Photographs by
McCORMICK ARMSTRONG CO.

*All illustrations from
the author's collection.*

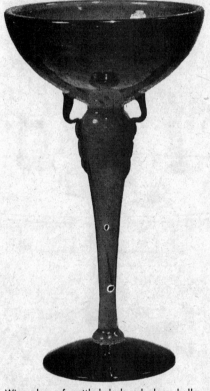

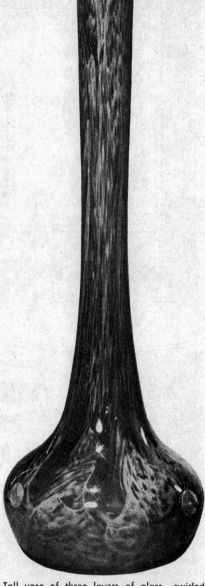

Vase of cloudy yellow glass with mauve-colored pull-up design in base, cranberry-red lining; applied pinched decorations in orange-colored glass at sides; height 6 inches.

Wine glass of mottled dark red glass, hollow red stem; foot and applied decorations of amethyst-colored glass; height 8 inches.

Tall vase of three layers of glass—swirled cranberry-red, crystal, and swirled yellow; three applied yellow prunts around base. Height 22 inches.

THE Cristallerie Schneider was established in 1903 by two brothers, Charles and Ernest Schneider, at Epinay-sur-Seine, in the Department of Seine, about seven miles from Paris, France. The glassworks operated at this location until 1962 when it was moved to the small town of Lorris, in the Department of Loiert, near Orleans, France. The factory moved to avail itself of the natural gas fuel which is distributed at Lorris but not in the area of Paris. The Schneider works is still in operation today.

Art glass was made by the Schneider firm from 1903 to 1930. Between 1930 and 1945, the firm made glass of very light and transparent colors, such as smoked and amber shades, in addition to clear crystal wares. Since 1945 only clear crystal has been produced.

Charles Schneider was the art di-rector and supervisor of the art glass department during the entire period it was active. He made many of the beautiful pieces himself. Most of their art glass wares were made by men who were taught by Charles Schneider, and they followed his designs and instructions to the letter.

Charles Schneider was born in Nancy, in the Department of Muerthe and Moselle, in 1881. He studied under Emile Gallé at the school of fine arts in Nancy. During this period he also worked at the Gallé factory, and for a time he was a designer for the Daum brothers of Nancy, France. Later, Schneider studied at *l'Ecole des Beaux Arts* in Paris. He was a member of the jury, and therefore a non-competitor, at the International Exposition of Decorative Arts in 1925, where Lalique, Marinot, and Orrefors had important glass exhibits. Because of his many accomplishments in the

fields of art and glassmaking he was honored as a *Chevalier de la Legion D'Honneur*—a French order of merit instituted by Napoleon Bonaparte in 1802. This honor is conferred upon both men and women, Frenchman or foreigner, for outstanding achievements in military or civilian life. Charles Schneider lived in the family's long-time residence at 87 Av. Jean-Jaures, in Epinay-sur-Seine. He died in 1962.

Ernest Schneider, who was two years older than his brother, was the business manager and administrator of the firm. Their father, who was a railroad official, died when Charles and Ernest were only four and six years old.

In 1944, the art direction for the firm was taken over by Charles Schneider's son, Robert Schneider, who was born in 1917. He, too, had studied at *l'Ecole des Beaux Arts* in

countries in Western Europe, as well as in Mexico, Japan, and Australia.

During the German occupation of World War II, the glassworks at Epinay-sur-Seine was used by the German army as a warehouse, and all literature and catalogs pertaining to the art glass products made by Schneider disappeared.

All of the glass made by this firm bears its signature—the name "Schneider" in script or block letters. The engraved signature in script was used prior to 1925; thereafter only the finest pieces of their glass were so marked. About 1925 or 1926, the name Schneider, in large, printed letters, was used; this signature was produced by roughing the glass with a jet of sand over a stencil.

by Schneider. Generally these wares are found in the form of vases, bowls, compotes, pitchers, candleholders, wine glasses, etc., and in vivid colors —usually a combination of two or more colors. Various shades of red, orange, yellow, blue, green, purple, and brown were used. The beautiful effects which were obtained with the mixing of contrasting colors were said to have been inspired by the French Impressionists. The French called this mottled glass *Intercalaires*. Charles Schneider had a penchant for beautiful colors, but the one most frequently found today is an orange shade which was very popular about 1926. This color, which Schneider called "Tango," was one of the most difficult to produce.

The cloudy effect of Schneider's mottled glass is often called "Cluthra," but this is not correct as most of these wares have very few bubbles in the glass—a factor that is a prerequisite for the Cluthra wares made by Steuben and others. Some of the most interesting pieces of Schneider's mottled glass have applied glass feet, stems, handles, knobs, or some other decorations in a different color than the body glass. At times these applied decorations are made of transparent colored glass, mottled, or cloudy glass.

Between 1924 and 1930, Charles Schneider often combined ironwork with his art glass productions. Compotes with wrought iron bases, and vases with an iron framework into which the plastic glass was blown, are among the items collectors can encounter. These represent some of the most interesting Schneider pieces.

Not all Schneider art glass is opaque or mottled. The writer's collection includes a tall amethyst vase with cut back geometric design; a transparent dark amber vase with splashes of red; a dark amber decanter of bubbly glass with an applied orange trim; a large vaseline-colored bowl; a French blue planter, quite bubbly, with clear applied handles; and a red-orange vase in crackle glass.

Charles Schneider also made many pieces of cameo glass, using both acid etching and hand cutting, and enamelled decoration. The writer also owns a flaming red opaque iridescent vase which very nearly approximates the rare Rouge Flambé color made by Frederick Carder at Steuben.

It is difficult to describe Schneider glass in a way that does justice to its beauty. Translucence is an important part of its charm, and it is most exciting when strong sunlight shines through it. The imagination of the artist was expressed in a variety of colors, shapes, and sizes. There seems never to have been any hesitation to experiment with unconventional combinations of color. Perhaps that explains why, though the glass was conceived in the Art Nouveau period, it fits so well in a contemporary setting.

Compote of mottled pink glass with amethyst-colored knop stem; wrought iron base decorated with orange-colored fruits mottled with blue.

Vase of mottled colors blown into a wrought iron framework—purple at base with orange spatter, shading into blue and purple, upper portion pale blue.

Paris, and was a winner of the *Prix de Rome*—an award given annually by the French government to students of the fine arts. Robert Schneider is still in charge of all design and production at the Schneider glassworks. Except for Robert Schneider, only one of the men trained by Charles Schneider remains in an active position at the factory; this man has been with the firm for 60 years.

Art glass constituted about 75 percent of Schneider's production up to 1925; from 1925 to 1930, it represented only 40 percent of the factory's output. The manufacture of art glass became unprofitable and was soon discontinued. Schneider glass was distributed in the United States through importers; they did not maintain a showroom or shop of their own in America. The clear crystal ware currently produced by this firm is being distributed in France and other

The script signature can be found in four variations: "Schneider;" "Schneider" preceded by a representation of a vase; "Schneider, France"; and "Schneider, France" preceded by a representation of a vase.

The block letter signature has been found in only two variations: "Schneider"; and "Schneider, France."

The signature in script is sometimes filled in with gold or red, and possibly in other colors, too. The writer has pieces of Schneider glass with an additional engraved signature in script—"Ovington," or "Ovington, New York." These pieces were distributed by the firm of Ovington Brothers which operated an elegant retail china and glass establishment on Fifth Avenue in New York City, and a summer store at Bar Harbor, Maine.

Most collectors of art glass are familiar with the mottled glass made

Pate de verre lamp by
Gabriel Argy-Rousseau.

The Lost Art
of
Pate de Verre

by ITA ABER

THE PROCESS of making pate de verre was known to the ancient Egyptians and Romans and to Italian glassmakers of medieval times. It was "discovered" again near the close of the 19th century by several great French artists who wanted to create a kind of sculpture with glass that would revive this lost art of the ancient craftsmen.

Pate de verre, literally translated into English, means "paste of glass." It was called "pasta vestrosa" by the Italians and "frittensmassen" by the Germans. A plastic or molded glass form, pate de verre has been described variously as a halfway step toward pottery and ceramic, and a soft enamel paste somewhere between fine enamel and glass. Varieties include *pate de riz* (rice) which is usually quite delicate and light in weight; *pate d'email* (enamel) which was made on a mold but baked without the mold; and the heavier *pate de cristal* (crystal) which is often polished like stone or marble.

Pate de verre was fabricated from glass made in many colors which was ground down into very fine powder. Clear, colored, opaque, or translucent glass was used; once ground it was mixed into a thick paste. No paint was ever used. If the artist wanted a pebbly texture called "frite" he would use small fragments of glass rather than powder. An adhesive flux of "water-glass" — a 2 or 3 per cent solution of sodium silicate — was dissolved in water to form a viscous paste which left no trace when evaporated by heat.

The next step was application of the glass paste by brushing, stamping, or pouring it into heat resistant earth or fire-clay molds that had been made from a model. This technique was favored by Gabriele Argy-Rousseau, Henri Isadore Cros, and Aleric Walter. The application was built up layer upon layer and color upon color to assume the thickness, color scheme, and design desired by the artist. The glass was then baked in a charcoal oven to fuse the work and was allowed to cool there. This process sometimes took as long as four days. Hopefully the mold would then crumble away and the pattern remain intact for affixing onto a fine glass container.

The artist usually prepared his ideas in advance and sculpted or carved a model for the mold. These models were made of wood, metal, clay, beeswax, or plaster-of-Paris. Francois Decorchement began in 1904. He preferred using plastic or rubbery-type molds that were his own secret process. He was born in 1880 and his father, Louis-Emile, was his teacher with whom he worked to revive the art of pate de verre. His work is included in the Sevres Museum collection as well as in many others. He is still living near Paris and is called the Grand Master of Pate de Verre.

Some artists allowed their work to dry naturally and then subjected the glass-containing mold to the indirect dry heat of a special oven. As the glass remelted, the mold hopefully would become powdery and crumble away. The glass piece was then removed from the oven; it hardened and fused as it cooled. In some cases additional shaping and carving were done freehand on a wheel. Sometimes opaline metals were added to produce delicate tints; or other forms of decoration would be applied.

Some experts claim that another type of pate de verre was created by fusing the cold glass under pressure into a mold, as done by Rene Lalique. But regardless, the fabrication of a piece of pate de verre was an ex-

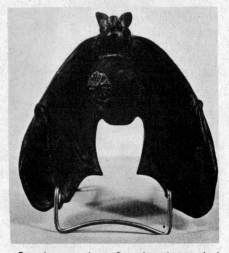

Pate de verre ashtray featuring a bat perched on a poppy capsule by Aleric Walter.

Pate de verre pieces. Left to right: Frog paperweight by Francois Decorchement; birds, bookend and beetle paperweight by Aleric Walter.

Placque of woman's head in pate de verre by Henry Cros.

"Apple Lady," a vase in pate de verre by Gabriel Argy-Rousseau.

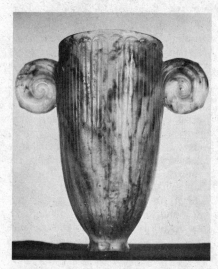

Pate de verre vase by Francois Decorchement.

ceptionally difficult and painstaking process. Often the glass would boil over the mold, or the colors would mix or run or, as also happened unless the heating temperatures were just right, the colors would be off.

The "father" of French pate de verre was the famous sculptor, painter, and potter, Henri Isidore Cros (1840-1907). Cros was a ceramist at the Sevres factory and about 1884 began experimenting there in the glass medium. The Cros Atelier in Paris was later established. Here he tried to reproduce the ancient glass which had always enthralled him. Together with his son Jean and daughter Marie, both fine artists in their own right, he produced custom made works to order and some small pieces. The three were known chiefly for their great decorative bas reliefs, plaques, heads, and works akin to sculpture. They won many awards including a gold medal at the International Exposition in 1900. Most of Cros' work was acquired by the Government of France, the Sevres Museum, and the Victor Hugo Museum.

Next came the great sculptor, ceramist Albert Dammouse, a student of Joffroy, who first exhibited in 1869. He was also an artist at Sevres who worked in, what was really fine enamel paste, described as "light as a multi-colored gauze — the epitome of delicacy." His works are to be found in the Gallery Museum and Museum of Decorative Arts in Paris, the Luxembourg Museum, Sevres and Limoges Museums as well as in museums in Germany.

Aleric Walter and an artist named Levy made some pieces in 1900. Walter worked for Daum from 1905 to 1908 and some of his pieces are signed "Daum." These were industrially made. By 1919 Walter had his own atelier. His molds and his ovens were used only once for a specific piece. He

"painted in" the colors into the mold with bent brushes.

George Despret created unusual pieces at the turn of the century in France and his pieces were exhibited as late as 1934 in Paris.

Gabriel Argy-Rosseau worked in the manner of Aleric Walter after World War I. His pieces are signed G. Argy-Rousseau. Little is known of this great artist except that he was born in 1885 and last exhibited in Paris in 1934. His works are by far the most colorful and sophisticated examples of pate de verre and are most sought after by collectors.

Decorchement did not produce industrially. He literally "built" each individual piece in the mold by hand. He had been a very successful potter and painter when he gave it all up to work in "plastic glass."

In Holland, after World War I, Lucienne Block produced a few pieces, and in the United States Frederick Carder, of the original Steuben Glass Company, made pate de verre by using the lost wax casting method. In the 1920s he produced a few pieces that were more like sculpture, but only in the very technical sense could they be called pate de verre.

While Rene Lalique is said to have made pate de verre from 1910 to 1918, he did in fact pour molten glass into molds — a highly different method of handling the material.

Modern Daum at Nancy, France, is making pate de verre in limited editions from designs of famous artists. The sculptured figures are in solid color because the art of application is now lost.

French pate de verre was produced in the form of plaques, jewelry and seals, tableware, covered boxes and other boudoir items as well as bas reliefs, busts, lamps, chandeliers, wall light fixtures, ashtrays, heavy paperweights, bowls, and vases.

Some examples seem strikingly crude and primitive but this was the deliberate effect desired by the artist. Some are sculptures in glass while others are breathtaking harmonies of color, evoking the aspect of semiprecious stones. Some pate de verre rings like crystal but this is not usual. Color, form, and motif are infinite in variety, design, and execution. Motifs often feature classical or art nouveau themes. Walter is known for subject matter frequently tending toward the bizarre and morbid.

No one really knows how much pate de verre was produced by this handful of great French glassmakers. We may safely say that even the most ordinary example is a rarity. It is difficult to find pieces of this glass in France today, except in museums and in the hands of discriminating collectors. Very little is to be found in the United States. Many people, including antique dealers, have never even heard of pate de verre and think you are speaking of pate sur pate which, of course, is porcelain and bears no relationship whatsoever. It should also be made very clear that other famous French glassmakers like Galle, LeGras, Muller Freres and Daum made cameo glass — not pate de verre.

My thanks to Minna Rosenblatt, New York antique dealer, who has brought this great glassmaking artistry to light, and to her husband, Sid Ross, roving correspondent for Parade Magazine, who assisted in the research and provided photographs for this article.

MONART and VASART
GLASS

by
C. C. MANLEY

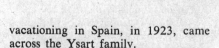

Monart footed bowl, lemon-yellow body with orange scrolls about the bottom, aventurine flecked deep purple rim and scrolls at top; diameter 9¾". Author's collection.

THE firm of John Moncrief, Ltd., North British Glass Works, Perth, Scotland, was founded by John Moncrief in 1865. For 15 years Mr. Moncrief had made glass in the Perth factory of that brilliant Scottish glass-maker Enoch Tomey, where he made steam gauge tubing and bottles. It seems extraordinary, but at this stage in his career Moncrief showed no interest in making table and decorative glassware. However, by the turn of the century, he had taken over Tomey & Son, which firm, now John Moncrief Ltd., in the early twenties, was desperately short of work to keep its employees regularly employed. It was pure chance that Mr. Moncrief, while vacationing in Spain, in 1923, came across the Ysart family.

In that year, Sebastian Ysart and his four sons, working in Spain, had discovered a way to make Aventurine glass. This type of decorative glass had been made hundreds of years earlier by the Venetians who had simply suspended chrome oxide crystals in a glass matrix. But Ysart and his sons had discovered something new—a means for controlling enamels suspended in glass. This had never before been accomplished.

Ysart's success was quickly realized by John Moncrief, and by 1924 Ysart and his sons were installed at Perth, producing and perfecting their brainchild. They dubbed their new art glass line "Monart"—the name being made from the surnames of Moncrief and Ysart. Some of their work is considered to be the finest art glass developed in England since the first World War. Unfortunately for English collectors, most of it was exported to collectors and dealers in America.

Although it was unintentional, the manufacturers of Monart developed two kinds of glass. The first type we will call "ordinary commercial." Here we get enamels being used, but with no specific design. If a single color is used, artistry is achieved by varying the density of the enamels; if two or three colors are used, the harmonizing effect is obtained by positioning the colors. Gold dust or aventurine is invariably added around the neck of the object. The effect obtained always represents a cirrocumulus (mackerel) sky. All colors are incorporated in a crystal background. The shapes are always simple in outline, and the glass is rather heavy in weight. The pontil scar is ground off leaving a projected impression at least one inch in diameter.

The second type are definitely art specimens. Here we get various colored enamels added to form designs of scrolls, feathers, etc., in both the single and multi-colored vessels. It is these added designs which make this glass unique. The shapes of these specimens remain simple (as with the commercial type), but the mackerel sky effect is generally omitted. These pieces, too, are heavy in weight.

The pontil mark of this latter type of Monart glass is totally different. About ¼" or so from the edge of the pontil mark are four equally spaced indentations; these are the marks left by an extension on the pontil iron. As will be sensed, the rotary motion of the glass during production must be stopped in certain positions to allow

Monart vase, sky-blue ground with a mixture of purples and aventurine flecks about the top; 8" high. Author's collection.

the gaffer to add enamels. If he were working off an ordinary pontil iron the stopping action would cause the glass to distort, but the added diameter support of the special pontil rod allowed more time to apply his colored enamels. The only official mark of identification on both types of Monart glass is a paper disc 1⅛ inch in diameter, gold with black lettering.

A catalog issued during this Monart period—1924 to 1957—stated that "there is no type of flower that has not here its ideal receptacle, in colors ranging from the greens and bronzes of Spring, along the whole gamut of purples, pinks and blues, to the flaming Autumn reds and oranges." At least 250 Monart designs were illustrated, all very simple in form. Only one example of a vase with a square top, which is 8″ high, is shown; two are shown with a square base. Several vases with handles were made, but only two jug designs. One style of basket was made in three sizes, 9½, 8½ or 6¾ inches high. A rather large number of round and square bottles, with and without stoppers, were made. One bottle, a ship's decanter, stood 8½ inches tall. The coloring of some of these bottles is not unlike Venetian latticinio work. Tumblers came in three sizes; these have very little coloring. A very handsome scent-spray, 4½ inches high, was also produced. Posy-bowls were offered in great profusion in all sizes to 17 inches in diameter with plain and wavy tops in various colors—but never crimped. Collectors of lampshades will be delighted with the exquisitely colored productions made at the Moncrief glassworks.

Paperweights, also made in the Monart period, rank with some of the finest produced in the last half of the 19th century. Their millefiori scent bottle with stopper, 5¼ inches high, is very beautiful. Paul Ysart, one of Sebastian Ysart's sons, is now making superb paperweights; all are signed "P. Y."; already they are being sold in better auction rooms at very high prices.

Although the life of Monart is from 1924 to 1957, there was no production during the war years—1939 to 1945. Efforts were made to start production again in 1950 but two difficulties were encountered: labor had been disbanded during the war, and colored enamels were difficult to come by. As these troubles could not be overcome easily, the firm had to cease its Monart production in 1957.

Vasart Art Glass

The Strathearn Glass Co., Ltd., Crieff, Scotland, was established originally as Vasart Ltd., The Shore, Perth, Scotland, by a member of the Ysart family. The company obviously ran into difficulties from the start by not being able to obtain the correct enamels for their wares. For this reason, and this reason alone, the colors in their productions are much less brilliant than Monart. Although the Vasart specimens do not equal Monart, some of their decorative glass is first class. Colored specimens, especially those designed and donated to charity, would be very difficult to equal.

In comparison with Monart, the Vasart coloring is very dull. Where designs have been attempted, the colors are quite similar to the background, browns being in common use. The background glass is not strictly crystal as there appears to be a little milkiness mixed with it. The shapes, as with Monart, are simple and effective. The mackerel cloud effect so skillfully employed in Monart is missing entirely from Vasart. Air bubbles are also more plentiful in Vasart wares. Size for size, Vasart is much lighter in weight. Pontil marks are similar to those found on the commercial type of Monart. Most of their pieces have the name "Vasart" clumsily engraved in large script on the base of their objects, this being done with a rough stone. We should also add that both Monart and Vasart wares are always glossy—never matte; neither type was ever molded.

Collectors must keep an open mind about Vasart for it is quite possible that many pieces were not marked—although the author has never seen any without their marking. We must remember, too, that Vasart is still being produced.

Vasart bowl of mottled white and brown glass with dark brown scrolls; diameter 8¼″. Author's collection.

Monart footed bowl, lemon-yellow ground with pink added about the rim; pattern formed with dark lemon-yellow enamel; diameter 7″.

The "Fourth" French Paperweight Factory

by Albert Christian Revi

COLLECTORS of antique French paperweights have known for many years of three glass factories in France—Baccarat, Clichy, and St. Louis — that produced paperweights during the last half of the 19th century. Only a few were aware of a possible "fourth factory." Persisting rumors of its existence placed it variously in the north of France, the south of France, and near Paris.

We believe, at long last, we have found this fourth French manufacturer of paperweights. Here follows a resume of our research, initially presented at the convention meeting of the Paperweight Collectors Association at Sturbridge Village, Massachusetts, in June 1965.

Since then, thanks to Paul Jokelson, president of that association, we have located, in the collection of paperweights willed to the New York Historical Society by Jennie H. Sinclair several paperweights we feel quite certain were produced by that "fourth factory" — Messrs. Monot, Pere et Fils, et Stumpf. Some of these examples are pictured here.

When these paperweights were made, ca. 1878, Messrs. Monot, Pere et Fils, et Stumpf, were operating the Cristallerie de Pantin. Pantin, at that time, was "near Paris," but is now within Paris city limits.

History of the Glassworks

In 1850, E. S. Monot established a glassworks at La Villette, near Paris, at No. 3 rue de Lille, under the style of Monot & Company. (Today, La Villette is also part of the city of Paris.) By 1853, the glassworks had moved to No. 4 rue de Thionville in La Villette, and in 1854, the company opened a showroom in Paris at No. 4 rue d'Hauteville. In 1859, the Cristallerie de La Villette was transferred to Pantin, and located there at No. 84 rue de Paris. Their showroom in Paris was moved to No. 66 rue d'Hauteville.

E. S. Monot was joined by Mr. F. Stumpf in 1868, and as Monot & Stumpf they opened an additional showroom in Paris at No. 33 rue Aumaire. Monot's son joined the business in 1873, and the title of the firm was changed to Monot, Pere et Fils, et Stumpf. Their Paris showrooms, located at No. 4 rue Aumaire, were closed after 1876 and replaced by one at No. 25 rue Notre Dame de Nazareth.

In 1881, E. S. Monot was a candidate (unsuccessful) in the Municipal elections in Pantin. He was listed as a "Republican Democrat," and the *Journal de Pantin,* for January 9, 1881, said of him:

"Mr. Monot, well-known industrialist, started as a worker and made his way up, thanks to his diligence, his intelligence, and his spirit of organizing. He gave to his town of Pantin a factory which can compete with Baccarat. Who does not recall the richness and perfection of his products at the Universal Exposition [1878] where they were admired by everybody? Socialist, Mr. Monot has always tried to improve the position of the working class . . . and is above all, an honest citizen and a working man."

Shortly after 1894, the name of Monot, Pere et Fils, disappeared from the listings of this firm in trade journals and business recording; thereafter it was known as Stumpf, Touvier, Violette & Company, successors to Monot & Stumpf. Mr. Stumpf continued with the firm for some years, but by the beginning of the 20th century, the name of the company had again been changed, and the Cristallerie de Pantin was being operated by Saint-Hilaire, Touvier, de Varreux & Company.

The Pantin glassworks produced glass tubes and chemical wares of all kinds for many years, and for the greater part of its existence also made some of the finest fancy wares produced in France — table glasses, tumblers, richly cut and decorated flasks, perfume bottles, chandeliers and articles of bronze for chandelier fittings, reflectors, colored enamels used by jewelers for decorating fine metalwares, engraved art crystal, opaline in a variety of lovely colors, both cut and engraved and pattern-molded, and a patented iridescent glass called "Chine Metallique," in plain and craquelled effects. (This was patented in 1878 and first shown at the Paris Universal Exposition of that year.) Pantin's artistic wares were favorably compared to those of the Cristallerie de Clichy.

Pantin Paperweights

The paperweights, with which we are principally concerned, were reported as being exhibited by Monot, Pere et Fils, et Stumpf, at the Paris Universal Exposition in 1878. At that time, the United States Congress sent over a group of able men to study and report on the industrial products and natural resources being exhibited by other nations.

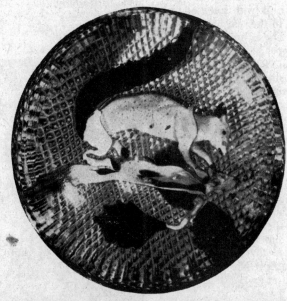

Pantin squirrel paperweight; orange and tan body; tail, ears, and tips of paws in dark green, resting on branch of transparent green glass leaves; pink and white filigree twist surround, grid-cut base. Dia. 3¼". Sinclair Collection, New York Historical Society.

Pantin Parrot paperweight; pink body, with deeper pink rings; beak and eyes dark purple; blue bands on body; wings are red, green, and blue; tail feathers, green; basket-work (latticinio) ground, shaded green leaves with air bubbles (dewdrops) throughout. Dia. 2¾". Sinclair Collection.

Charles Colne, assistant secretary of the U. S. Commissioners representing the interests of the United States, made a detailed and comprehensive report of the glass articles shown. (The fact that Colne was born in France and spoke the language fluently was a great asset.) Included among the French glassmakers in his report were such greats as Baccarat, Clichy, and Pantin.

Commissioner William P. Blake, commenting in his own report on Colne's ability, stated that Charles Colne had "long been practically familiar with the manufacture of glass." Previously, with John P. Colne of New York City, he had patented a machine for engraving and cutting designs on fine crystal wares. His scientific paper on fused quartz and quartz glass, which appeared some years later is still of recognized value to the present day glass industry.

With such a well-founded background in the glass trade, there can be no doubt but the objects he reported seeing among the glass exhibitions at the Paris Exposition were accurately evaluated and described. Excerpts from his enumeration of Pantin's wares, follow:

"Paperweights of solid glass, containing glass snakes, lizards, squirrels and flowers . . . air bubbles are distributed in the mass, looking like pearl drops . . . paperweights in millefiori of roses, leaves and fruit, embedded in lumps of clear glass . . . a paperweight containing a lizard of colored glass, which had been cut in several parts before being enclosed in the glass."

Unfortunately, as Colne pointed out in his report, French glass manufacturers seemed reluctant to have their wares pictured abroad, consequently there are no illustrations of French glass in his published report, though glass manufactured in England, Belgium, Germany, Austria, and Italy was generously represented in fine engraved illustrations.

This leaves us somewhat in the dark as to the physical aspects of the Pantin weights, but enough of their characteristics were reported by Colne to give us reason to believe they resemble paperweights given to the New York Historical Society by Mrs. Sinclair, some of which, in the past, have been attributed to Baccarat, Clichy, and St. Louis.

We are almost certain that the squirrel weight pictured is a Pantin production since no other factory (in France, at least) has been reported to have made such a subject in this medium. The three Sinclair paperweights with various birds represented in exotic colors, because of their similarity in workmanship, color of glass, weight, etc., have also been designated as products of the Pantin factory.

A very colorful parrot weight, whose workmanship is closely related to the squirrel and bird weights we have now attributed to the Pantin glassworks, was sold at Sotheby's a few years ago for $2,500. It was illus-

Pantin bird paperweight; white body with blue wings, dashes of red on tail; black crest; resting on branch of transparent green glass leaves; pink and blue filigree surround; grid-cut base. Dia. 3". Sinclair Collection.

trated in color in the June, 1964, issue of the *Paperweight Collector's Bulletin,* where it was reported to have been "definitely attributed to St. Louis."

A somewhat similar bird weight in the Frances Clemson Cross Collection was sold in White Plains, N. Y., by O. Rundle Gilbert, Auctioneer, which was identified in the sale catalog as "Clichy." It brought $1,500. (It was formerly in the Applewhaite collection, and has recently been sold for over $8,000.)

Pantin's flower weights, with bubbles distributed through the design like "pearl drops," may have close affinity to those attributed to both French and American manufacturers. The ones illustrated in Paul Jokelson's *Antique French Paperweights* as "Weights of Undetermined through French Origin" may be Pantin productions. One in the author's

collection, showing a large pink and white striped camellia on a green stem, with six green leaves, as well as some now attributed to the Mt. Washington Glass Company of New Bedford, Massachusetts, could also be paperweights produced by the Cristallerie de Pantin, even though the workmanship is quite different from the squirrel and bird weights which we can, with greater degree of certainty, attribute to Pantin. (We can find no concrete reason for the attribution of flower weights of any description to the New Bedford concern.)

Colne's reference to flower and fruit paperweights without any corresponding illustrations to help identify them is unfortunate. However, we believe they must bear some resemblance to those usually attributed to Baccarat, St. Louis, Clichy, and the Mt. Washington and Sandwich glassworks in America.

Colne's mention of "paperweights in millefiori of roses, leaves and fruits, embedded in lumps of clear glass" is at first confusing. Certainly Mr. Colne was not referring to anything like the Clichy Rose; therefore, he must be referring to something else— probably roses and fruits of the type made by lampworkers and subsequently encased in crystal. Such flower and fruit weights would approach in appearance those illustrated in Jokelson's book as B-3, 4, and 7, and UN 346 to 349.

Pantin weights of this kind could have been further embellished with opal filigree, known to most collectors as "latticinio" or "lace work," and aventurine, since Colne stated in his report that Pantin was "celebrated for the beauty of its aventurine glass," and that they produced "articles in opal filigree, well done." This gives rise to the premise that flower and fruit weights with a background or "basket" of filigree work beneath the fruits and flowers were probably made at the Cristallerie de Pantin, despite the fact that weights of this description have usually been attributed to other French or American paperweight makers.

White lily-like flower with pink stripes on petals, green leaves, and stem; illustrated in *Antique French Paperweights,* and designated as Unknown No. 346.

C. DORFLINGER & SONS
Fine Cut Glassware

by Paul J. Fitzpatrick, Ph.D.

A 75-horsepower engine turned the 100 wheels in the cutting room (top picture) at Dorflinger & Sons, White Mills, Pennsylvania. This sketch, and that of the Glass Blowing Department, above, appeared in Matthew's History of Wayne, Pike and Monroe Counties, 1886. (Collections of the Library of Congress.)

THE 1963 demise of the nationally-known cut glass firm, T. G. Hawkes & Co., Corning, New York, reported in the September 1963 issue of *Spinning Wheel* and elsewhere, recalled the passing of another outstanding manufacturer of fine cut glassware, C. Dorflinger & Sons, White Mills, Pennsylvania, in 1921— over forty years ago.

The two enterprises had much in common. Both were outstanding manufacturers of fine cut glassware in the United States, making many exquisite patterns in a variety of items. Both supplied cut glass ware for the White House, and both made cut and other fine glass wares for national and international notables, including the Prince of Wales.

Christian Dorflinger, founder of this famous glassworks, was born March 16, 1828 at Rosteig in the Canton de Bitsche, Alsace, France, the son of Francis and Charlotte (Clemens) Dorflinger. He was the oldest of five children. At the age of ten, he went to live with an uncle, a glassworker, just over the line in the Province of Lorraine, in the City of St. Louis, to learn the art of glass-making.

During his eight years there, he became a master craftsman; his particular interest was in the various methods of glass decoration—engraving, etching, enameling, and gold decorating. To improve his opportunities in his art, he decided to go to the United States, and in 1846, the year after his father died, he persuaded his mother and other members of the family to leave with him.

His mother and sisters went to live with friends in Oldenberg, Indiana, while he and his younger brother, Edward, went to Camden, New Jersey, to work in a glass factory manufacturing druggist's ware and prescription bottles.

On trips to New York City, Dorflinger stayed at the Pacific Hotel, at 162 Greenwich Street, near the waterfront, and became good friends with the proprietor, Captain Aaron Flower, a former North River pilot. On one of these trips, too, he met Miss Elizabeth Hagen of Brooklyn, his future wife and the mother of his ten children.

Kerosene oil had been recently discovered and found to be adaptable for use in lamps. Captain Flower, with associates, astutely established a glass plant in Brooklyn to manufacture lamp chimneys and shades. Dorflinger, was chosen to manage it.

Long Island Flint Glass Works

In 1852, the 24-year old Dorflinger moved to Brooklyn to take charge of this new enterprise—the Long Island Flint Glass Works. It was a small plant with one five-pot furnace, on Concord Street. The capacity of the plant soon increased to seven-pot. A $30,000 business was developed in 1853, increasing to $50,000 by the end of 1854.

By 1858, Dorflinger had purchased the glassworks from Flower and associates and had built an addition, a larger glassworks. Soon the enlarged plant was doing an annual business of $300,000.

The Green Point Flint Glass Works

In 1860, to take care of his rapidly expanding business, Dorflinger established the Green Point Flint Glass Works, at a cost of $75,000, located on Commercial Street, Brooklyn, fronting the North River and Newton Creek. It had important wharf facilities and contained sufficient land to construct houses for his more important craftsmen.

With the two glasshouses, and particularly in this newer larger plant, Dorflinger was able to manufacture the cut and engraved glasswares in which he was most interested as well as plain and colored glassware.

The exquisitely cut and engraved glassware which Mrs. Lincoln selected in 1861 to be used for state occasions at the White House was made by Dorflinger at his Green Point Flint Glass Works. This pattern was used by subsequent Presidents until Grover Cleveland, in 1886, chose the newer Russian pattern, designed by Philip McDonald, and made by the T. J. Hawkes & Co., of Corning New York.

In 1890, President Harrison purchased more of the Russian pattern for the White House—a set of 520 pieces, for which $6,000 was paid. This Harrison set was made by Dorflinger, and from Presidents Harrison to Wilson, Dorflinger continued to make some of the replacements and additions for the White House in this pattern. (The author's study "White House Glassware" appeared in *Spinning Wheel* July-August 1962.)

The Wayne County Glass Works

Dorflinger, who had set out to become the best manufacturer of fine cut and engraved glass tableware in this country, became so deeply

Dorflinger made this cut and engraved glassware which was purchased by Mrs. Lincoln for the White House in 1861.

dedicated to his art that his health broke. In 1863, his physician advised him to retire from business, and to live elsewhere.

Dorflinger sold his Long Island Flint Glass Works to J. S. Hibber and Company, and entrusted the Green Point Flint Glass Works to his capable employees, John B. Dobelmann and Nathaniel Bailey. His friend, Captain Flower, invited him to rest for the summer at his farm in Wayne County, Pennsylvania, near the village of White Mills.

The Dorflinger family enjoyed country life, and Dorflinger soon purchased the property from Flower. Located on the east bank of the Lackawaxen River, it consisted of 300 acres of pasture and timberland a house, and several farm buildings.

Two years later, his health improved, Dorflinger, now thirty-seven, decided to re-enter the glass business at his country site, and to develop very fine clear and colored glassware.

In the spring of 1865, he started construction on a five-pot furnace at White Mills, near the Delaware and Hudson canal. By fall he was employing a small force of men, and in the following year he was bringing highly skilled men, trained in Europe, from his Green Point Flint Glass Works in Brooklyn to train local workers. The new firm was called The Wayne County Glass Works.

By 1867, his plant consisted of a glasshouse and a two-story building. Decided on fine glass cutting, he erected a two-room cutting shop for that purpose. So successful was this operation that in a few years, a three-story wing was added; a one-story building for making clay pots was also erected.

He built a three-story mansard-roofed hotel, of native stone, called the St. Charles, which opened in 1869. It was used to entertain friends from New York and other cities. As business expanded, he erected over 75

homes for his workers at nominal rentals; he also assisted other workers in financing their homes.

The Dorflingers at first spent the winter months in Brooklyn, but in 1868 the Brooklyn house was sold. The family lived year-round at the White Mills farmhouse until, in 1873, a wing was added to the hotel for more spacious living quarters. This the family occupied until 1931.

Finding visits to the Brooklyn plant ardous and with the expanding Wayne County Glass Works claiming more personal attention, Dorflinger, in 1873, leased the Green Point Flint Glass Works to Dobelmann and Bailey, who had managed it so capably. In 1882, the Green Point works were sold to Elliott P. Gleason Company.

1876 Centennial Set

Dorflinger achieved international prestige at the 1876 Centennial Exhibition in Philadelphia when his cut and engraved Centennial set—a decanter and 38 glasses, symbolic of the national government and the 38 states then in the Union—won the highest award. This honor was widely reported. The *Boston Journal of Commerce* stated it was "a commercial victory, worth hundreds of thousands of dollars." Pieces from this set, now

Cut glass on this page in Russian Pattern, first made for the White House by T. G. Hawkes & Co., later by Dorflinger.

at the Philadelphia Museum of Art, are pictured in Daniel's *Cut and Engraved Glass, 1771-1905.*

C. Dorflinger & Sons

In 1881, Dorflinger's three sons, William, Louis J., and Charles, entered into partnership with him, and the name of the business was changed to C. Dorflinger & Sons, a title kept until the firm dissolved in 1921.

William, as the New York City representative, presided over two stores maintained in the city for many years. One, for retail trade, first located at 915 Broadway, near West 23rd Street, was later removed to a 3-5 West 19th Street. The second store, for wholesale and display purposes, occupied three floors at 36 Murray Street, further downtown.

Louis J. and Charles remained at White Mills, Louis in charge of financial affairs, Charles assisting his father in the actual operations of the glassworks.

Around 1900, Dorflinger's grandsons, Dwight and Charles, sons of Louis J., entered the firm and held supervisory positions.

A man of progressive ideas, Dorflinger was constantly making improvements to his products and techniques as well as enlarging the capacity of his glassworks until it became the largest of its kind in this country. No time or expense was spared to obtain the best basic ingredients to make the clearest possible cut glassware. His laboratory carefully analyzed each basic ingredient and the correct proportion to employ. Red lead, sand, and potash were imported from several regions of Europe. Special fire bricks for the construction of furnaces came from England. The glass he produced became famous

over the world for the consistency of its quality as well as its beauty and excellence of design.

During the operations at White Mills, Dorflinger saw his original 300 acres expand to 1,150 acres. By 1878 he had a monthly payroll of $10,000, and over 300 workers. By 1903, at the height of its operation, over 650 persons were employed; the plant embraced 27 buildings. Not only did Dorflinger produce glass blanks for cutting at his own shop, but supplied them to other cutting shops in the area—at one time there were 22 in Wayne County.

Dorflinger made a wide variety of cut glass pieces of beautiful designs— ice cream sets, salad bowl sets, lamps with domes, decanters, trays, glasses, water bottles, jugs, vases, candlesticks, bonbon and other fancy dishes,

cologne bottles, punch bowls with handled punch cups to match, candy jars, stemware, huge druggist window bottles and so on. He also made beautiful colored engraved and etched glass; sapphire and light ruby were his favorite colors.

Leading Dorflinger Craftsmen

Dorflinger, alert for the best craftsmen, brought to White Mills experienced workers from this country and from abroad. Nicholas Lutz, who came from St. Louis, in Dorflinger's home province of Lorraine, and who later left Dorflinger to work for the Boston and Sandwich Glass Company, became famous for his Venetian-type striped glass.

In his brochure, *Christian Dorflinger, 1828-1915,* Suydam (Dorflinger's grandson) gives a long list of craftsmen, including Ralph Barber, who developed the famous "open rose" at White Mills, Nicholas Lutz, Oscar Levine, Charles Northwood, John Johnson, Louis Aug, Alvin Falk, the Larsen and the Lilequist brothers.

One of Dorflinger's outstanding cutters was John S. O'Connor, Jr., a

veteran of the famous New York 69th Regiment who had served his apprenticeship at the glass firm of Turner and Lance in New York City. He came to White Mills in 1867. As foreman of the Dorflinger cutting shop he designed several leading cut glass patterns—Parisian, Lorraine, and the prototype of the Russian pattern, all of which were widely imitated. He invented new types of cutting machines and perfected a number of processes.

In 1892, he left Dorflinger to establish his own cutting shop, costing $80,000, in Hawley, Pennsylvania, near White Mills. McAndrews, in his brochure, *History of Hawley, Pennsylvania,* reports that O'Connor's three-story building of native bluestone, was handsome and substantial, 60 by 200 feet, containing about 200 frames; more than 200 men and boys were employed there.

Another fine craftsman was Carl F. Prosch, formerly of Vienna, an expert designer, who was the New York City representative of the Austrian wholesale glass agency, Bawo and Dotter, which had factories in Bohemia. Dorflinger had been sending his glass to New York City for gold decorating or gilding, but as the volume of this work increased, he preferred to have it done nearer White Mills. In 1900 he offered to set Prosch up in the gold decorating business: he would build a factory— the Honesdale Decorating Company— at Seelyville, Pennsylvania, a suburb of Honesdale, provided Prosch would decorate Dorflinger glass exclusively. Prosch accepted and this arrangement continued until 1915 when he bought out Dorflinger's interest.

Dorflinger Closes

Christian Dorflinger died August 11, 1915, in his 87th year, and was buried in Glenwood Cemetery, Brooklyn, beside his wife.

His sons carried on the business until 1921, but circumstances worked against them. World War I made it difficult to obtain ingredients from abroad so necessary in the making of excellent clear glassware, one very important item being German potash. The problem of changing the formula presented the possibility of a glass inferior to Dorflinger standards; the sons would rather close the plant.

Then, too, the wealthy, their best customers, began to feel the effects of the new income and other war taxes. With Prohibition, sale of drinking glasses and other tableware declined. Finally, the vogue for cut glass was on the wane.

When Dorflinger doors closed in 1921, its skilled workers scattered to obtain employment elsewhere; some went to Corning, New York with T. G. Hawkes & Co., or with the Corning Glass Company. A few older workers, preferring to stay in the area, opened small cutting shops. The writer visited those still in operation, in 1953.

William T. Gillinder's Contributions to Glassmaking

by PAUL J. FITZPATRICK, Ph.D.

THOUGH William T. Gillinder is well known as a manufacturer of pressed glass, his versatility in other fields of glass production, especially in the area of cut glass, and his considerable influence in glassmaking, in England as well as in this country, has been rather perfunctorily recognized by glass authorities.

In researching for his study on "White House Glassware" (SW jul-aug '62), this writer was himself somewhat surprised to find that Gillinder had made fine cut glass for White House use—a fact completely overlooked by other serious students of glassware. The ensuing difficulty in finding even minor references to the early Gillinder and his Franklin Flint Glass Works was likewise astonishing.

The fame of Gillinder & Sons was firmly established by the glassworks it erected at the 1876 Centennial in Philadelphia (SW jul-aug '65), and its artistic ability was pointed out by Albert C. Revi in his informative "American Cameo Glass".

However, both these accomplishments, while continuing the tradition of fine glassware he had transmitted to his sons, came about after William Gillinder's death in 1871.

His cut glass, briefly mentioned in Daniel's *Cut and Engraved Glass,* and in Revi's *American Cut and Engraved Glass,* was of high quality in his own time, as witnessed by the excellent cut decanter pictured here. This was in White House use in the Grant administration or earlier; the exact date of purchase is undetermined. It is the only Gillinder piece so far identified by either the White House or the National Park Service in the White House Collection.

William Thynne Gillinder was born in England in 1823, at Gateshead in the Newcastle-on-Tyne area. This section is claimed by Elville in *The Collector's Dictionary of Glass* to have had a much greater influence on English glassmaking than is generally supposed. "Indeed," he wrote, "during the first half of the 18th century, the Newcastle area led the country in glass production of all types, with no fewer than twenty-two glasshouses, one-third of which were producing flint glass."

William Gillinder, who had gone to work in the glass factory at Mexborough when he was seven years old, was talented both in glassmaking and in organizing. According to Daniel, in *Cut and Engraved Glass,* he was head of the British Friendly Society, a labor organization; and Angus-But-

terworth, in *British Table and Ornamental Glass,* hails him as the prime mover in the reorganization of the National Flint Glassmakers' Society, a landmark in British glass history. Gillinder served as General Secretary of this organization from 1850 until 1854 when he left for America. In this period, too, his *Treatise on the Art of Glassmaking, Containing 272 Practical Receipts,* was published in Birmingham (1854), a book apparently better known in England than in America.

With such accomplishments behind him, at the age of 31, William Gillinder came with his wife and five children to Cambridge, Massachusetts, to become superintendent of the New England Glass Company. The job there did not match his expectations, and after a short time he moved westward, stopping a while in the Pittsburgh area, then on to St. Louis where he was employed at the bottle works of George W. Scolley.

By 1860, he was back East again, his wanderings over, and in that year he established his own factory in Philadelphia. This he called The Franklin Flint Glass Works. He concentrated at first on hand blown glassware, with lamp chimneys an important part of his production.

In 1863, Edwin Bennett, one of the Bennett brothers who had pioneered potting in East Liverpool, Ohio, joined him as partner, and the company became Gillinder and Bennett. With Bennett's fresh capital, the company expanded, beginning their pressed glassware production, and developing the cut glass production in which Gillinder was well grounded.

When Bennett retired from the business in 1867 to devote his full attention to his pottery in Baltimore, the Gillinder sons, James and Frederick, purchased his interest, and the firm became Gillinder & Sons.

According to Daniel, Gillinder did not approve of the new-fangled curved split, hobstar, and rosette motifs, so at his Franklin works he

cut the old fashioned solid field of hobnail, strawberry-diamond, and single star and block he had known in England. In the 1860s, yielding to competition, he began to introduce some of the more modern designs.

The firm had always specialized in lamps, lampshades and chandeliers, often with elaborate decoration, and continued to do so after "Old Gillinder's" death. Their well known sandblast decoration was not used until after 1876, when that technique was invented.

One of William Gillinder's greatest services to the glass industry was his invention, patented in 1865, of a combination plunger, blow-pipe, and snap clamp. It was an important tool in his own century, and later the germ of his idea was applied to quantity-producing machinery.

William Gillinder passed away in 1871, and his sons continued the business through a period of great pressed glass expansion, carrying on the Gillinder tradition of quality. Westward Ho! was one of the famous patterns in pressed glass which originated with them, as did Liberty Bell, Mellor, and Classic. Stippled Star, beloved of many collectors, was designed and patented by William Gillinder himself in 1870, the year before he died.

The later history of his firm has been covered by Albert C. Revi in his *American Pressed Glass for Figure Bottles,* and his recent *American Cut and Engraved Glass.*

Gillinder Decanter in the White House Collection

EMPIRE 13"
Fruit Bowl

The Irving

Cut Glass Company

of Honesdale, Pennsylvania

by ALBERT CHRISTIAN REVI

HARVARD 8" Rd. Bowl

IN 1900, six men, all first class glass cutters, formed the Irving Glass Company, Incorporated, of Honesdale, Pennsylvania. The corporation consisted of George H. Reichenbacher, president; Eugene V. Coleman, John Gogard, William H. Hawken, George Roedine, and William H. Seitz. When Mr. Reichenbacher died in 1910, his son, Royal, then the firm's bookkeeper, managed the business office for a number of years. Mr. Coleman was secretary in 1910 and William H. Seitz, treasurer.

The firm started in an old one-story wooden building located on the south side of West 13th Street, between West Street and Spring (now Westside Avenue). In the beginning the partners did all the cutting themselves as the company was not financially able to hire glass cutters. It was a struggle to keep the business alive and the owner-operators paid themselves the small sum of $6 each a week for almost two years. For those with families to support these were not the easiest months of their lives.

Soon the business began to prosper; larger quarters were needed, and additional helpers. A plot of ground at the foot of Irving Cliff on the east side of Park Street, near the Armory and along the Dyberry River was purchased. Here a two-story brick building, 200 feet long and 40 feet wide, was erected. It was built by Kreitner Brothers, a local contracting firm still in business in Honesdale.

The Irving Cut Glass Company occupied these quarters until they closed the factory in 1933.

George H. Reichenbacher was born at Cherry Ridge, Pa., February 10, 1869, the son of Johannes and Elizabeth Reichenbacher. He married Mary A. Staengle, who bore him two sons, Royal L. and Charles. He died February 28, 1910. In 1919, his sons, Royal and Charles Reichenbacher purchased the Clinton Cut Glass Company in Aldenville, Pa., and renamed it the Elite Cut Glass Manufacturing Company.

Eugene V. Coleman was born in Uniondale, Susquehanna County, Pa., April 27, 1872, one of five brothers and two sisters. He attended public school in Uniondale and in nearby Forest City. After working a while in Forest City, he moved to Honesdale where he learned the trade of glass cutting at T. B. Clarke & Company.

With the outbreak of the Spanish-American War, Mr. Coleman enlisted in Company "E", 13th Pennsylvania Infantry, and served with that group until March 11, 1899. After he was

ZELLA 8" Rd. Bowl

mustered out, he resumed his trade at the T. B. Clark factory. On September 12, 1901, he married Margaret M. Evans. They had three children—Eugene L., Jessie M., and Gerald D. Mr. Coleman was president of the Irving Cut Glass Company from about 1916 until the factory closed in 1933. He died November 14, 1934.

William H. Hawken was the designer of all the cut glass patterns produced at the Irving Cut Glass works. An interview with his daughter, Mrs. Homer Smith, revealed that he had worked in the trade since he was 19 years old and

*"Carnation" engraved crystal pitcher, 9";
Col: Mrs. Homer Smith, (daughter of
William H. Hawken).*

that he had "blown" glass and "cut and designed glass," indicating he was well founded in every aspect of the industry.

Mr. Hawken was born in England in 1876, and was just six months old when his parents brought him to America. He had only seven years of schooling before he had to quit school and go to work. He learned his glass cutting trade at "the University"—T. B. Clark's factory in Seelyville, Pa. (The Hussco Shopping Center now occupies the site.) Hawken first learned to blow glass, then to cut and design it. His daughter said that his designing "came as a God-given talent," for he had no formal training for this sort of work at all. William Hawken died in March, 1942.

William H. Seitz was born in Honesdale, Pa., on August 4, 1870, and died in Larchmont, N. Y., March 9, 1947. He, too, had learned his trade with T. B. Clark & Company, and was so proficient in the cutting and engraving of glass that he was chosen as one of the men from the Honesdale area to demonstrate the manufacture

of richly cut glass at the World's Fair in Chicago in 1893. When he returned to Honesdale, he worked with the firm of Gibbs, Kelley & Company until he left to join the formation of the Irving Cut Glass Company. For many years he was treasurer of this company.

The Irving Cut Glass Company advertised "American Rich Cut Glass, Colored and Gold Decorated Glass," and sold their wares all over the United States and as far abroad as Johannesburg, South Africa, Spain, China, and Japan. When orders for their glassware came from China, the clerk of the company would take them to the local Chinese laundryman to have them deciphered. Gerald D. Coleman, son of Eugene Coleman, told the author that when orders came from Japan they were always accompanied by some small gift—an urn, vase, or bowl—which his father brought home to the family; their last large order came from Japan.

William H. O'Neil, bookkeeper and export manager for this concern for more than ten years, told us that they

sold great quantities of rich cut glass to an importer in London, England.

A catalogue of the Irving Cut Glass Company's wares illustrated patterns bearing the following names: C.B.C. Daisy (Chair Bottom Combination and the plainer Daisy pattern), Daisy, Doris, Elk, Empire, Eureka, Harvard, Helen, Iowa, Juliette, June, Keystone, May, Norwood, Panama, Pinwheel (patented by William H. Hawken, May 13, 1913), Rose Combination, Victrola, White Rose (patented by William Hawken, Jan. 11, 1916), and Zella. This listing by no means includes a complete compilation of their patterns in cut glass, for the firm operated for about 33 years.

Some articles made by this company were signed with the name "Irving" in script, etched lightly into the glass in a conspicuous place.

Much of their finer wares were cut on Dorflinger blanks, but in the late period they worked on figured blanks purchased from the H. C. Fry Glass Company and the Libbey Glass Company; the workers called these pressed blanks "pig iron."

Happily for collectors, the Irving Cut Glass Company gave names to the patterns it produced, and used them in catalogue pages.

The Lackawanna Cut Glass Company

Rosebud sugar bowl; 2¼" high, 5½" wide. Collection Mr. & Mrs. Jack Walker.

by ALBERT CHRISTIAN REVI

Seneca champagne.

THE Lackawanna Cut Glass Company, located at 1220 North Washington Street, Scranton, Pennsylvania, was incorporated on March 25, 1903. The principal stockholders were Wesley M. Gardner, Thomas E. Finnerty (secretary of the firm), Thomas A. Baker, Matthew D. Freer, and Roswell H. Patterson. Scranton business directories listed this company until 1905; after that date we were unable to find any record of The Lackawanna Cut Glass Company, and presumably it was no longer active. In spite of an apparently short career, the company's wares are not difficult to find, indicating a rather prolific production and a wide distribution. Their trademark, the letter "L" within a diamond-shaped lozenge, was lightly etched on most pieces emanating from this factory.

The Lackawanna Cut Glass Company sold their product direct to the consumer. "We shall not sell one dollar's worth of it to any retailer in the country," was one of several assurances they gave their customers. Order blanks accompanied each of their catalogs; these could be used to order glass for one's own use or to be sent, as selected gifts, direct from the

factory to friends and family. Safe packing and arrival at destination with the sender's card or note enclosed was warranted by a money-back guarantee should the purchaser or recipient be dissatisfied in any way with the goods. "Wherever the mail penetrates, wherever express or freight deliveries are made, there our service extends, and we can serve you as well as if you made your selections in person."

More than 90 different patterns were listed in just one of the catalogs we examined; still they claimed this was by no means their complete line. Among the articles offered were: bonbons; bowls for every use; butter dishes in several sizes; butter tubs; "Butterettes" (small dishes for individual servings or pats of butter); candlesticks; carafes; "Center Vases"; celery trays; covered cheese dishes; comports in various forms and sizes; cologne bottles; ice cream sets; ice tubs; jars for cigars, tobacco, marmalade, and "invalid use" (we presume the latter was a personal article for use in the sick room—it was not illustrated in their catalogs); jugs for champagne, claret, water, and whiskey; loving cup vases; mustard pots; nappies in many different sizes, with or without handles; "cabarets" (the proper name for sectioned nappies with two handles); punch sets consisting of a two-part punch bowl, matching cups, ladle, and a mirrored plateau; salt-

cellars; spoon holders; tumblers; and vases in every shape imaginable.

Complete suites of stemware were available, but only in the following patterns: Colonial; Marion; Seneca; Thin (known as "light ware" in the trade); Plain; and Gold Decorated (plain ware with gold decorations).

The following named patterns were illustrated in the catalogs we examined; some of the names appear to be misspelled, but they are listed exactly as they appeared:

Adair; Alachua; Alameda; Alpena; Ashland; Azalia; Belmont; Bourbon; Brittania; Catawba; Chester; Chippewa; Chrysanthemum; Clarendon; Clayton; Colfax; Colonial; Concordia; Corinth; Dekalb; Delmar; Delta; Dendron; De Sota; Dolores; Eldorado; Elmore; Elwood; Emerald; Essex; Fairfax; Fayette; Fern; Genesee; Gold Decorated; Girardian; Guadalope; Hanover; Iredel; Isabelle; Ivy; Jasper; Laramie; Lamoille; Lamone; La Peer; La Porte; Lasalle; Leflere; Lonoke; Marano; Marathon; Maimette; Marion; Marquette; Mercer; Mohawk; Monroe; Monterey; Necosta;

Seneca goblet.

Trademark used by the Lackawana.

Newbury; Oakland; Ocala; Olive; Ozark; Panola; Penobscott; Plain Ware; Rosebud; St. Clair; St. Croix; Salano; Saloma; Sanilac; Seneca; Sommerset; Sunburst; Sussex; Thin; Thistle; Touraine; Wild Rose; Windemere; York; and Yucatan.

Two engraved patterns were shown in their catalogs. No. 3038 consisted of a wreath of flowers placed around the top of each piece in a suite of tablewares. No. 3039 was a simple band of arrow-shaped pendants all around the rim of each article.

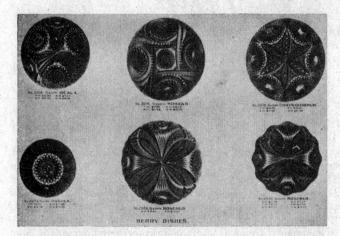

BERRY DISHES.

Pages from an original
Lackawana Cut Glass Company catalog.

PUNCH SET.

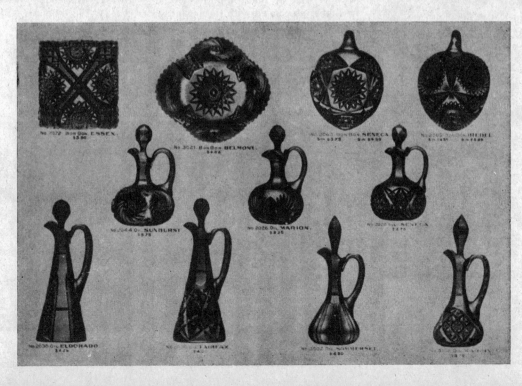

The Laurel Cut Glass Company

by ALBERT CHRISTIAN REVI

THE Laurel Cut Glass Company of Jermyn, Pa., was originally incorporated as The German Cut Glass Company, January 30, 1903, with Homer D. Carey, president and secretary; Thomas Durfee, vice president; and August F. Gebhardt, treasurer. The factory was located in a two-story brick building near the Ontario & Western Railroad station on the east side of Jermyn, and was equipped with 102 cutting frames. Messrs. Carey, Durfee, and Gebhardt were the principal stockholders, each owning 5000 shares of stock. Charles S. Burger held 800 shares of stock, but he was not active in the business.

On December 10, 1906, the style of the firm was changed to the Kohinur Cut Glass Company, with Homer D. Carey, president, and August F. Gebhardt, secretary. No mention of Messrs. Durfee and Burger was found in the new corporation papers and it's possible that at that time they were no longer associated with the business.

Finally, on April 26, 1907, the name of the corporation was again changed to the Laurel Cut Glass Company. This time M. L. (Mrs. Homer D.) Carey appeared as one of the principal stockholders in the company.

Shortly before the Laurel Cut Glass Company went out of business, in 1920, they were associated with the Cut Glass Corporation of America (also known as the Quaker Cut Glass Company) of Philadelphia.

Two former employees of the Laurel Cut Glass Company, Mr. Patrick Meehan and Mr. Harold D. Carey (a distant relative of Homer D. Carey) compiled a partial list of the Jermyn cutting shop's employees: Harold D. Carey, Melvin Dunlap, Arthur Gessler, Harold Green, William Haffner (Hafner), Thomas Hogarth, Herman Kahl, Edward Loughney, Daniel Meehan, Patrick Meehan, William McLaughlin, Leo Patridge, and James Penrose.

Women were employed as polishers by this firm and, later, Harold Carey taught some of them to cut simple designs. The Meehan-Carey list of women employees included the following: Gertrude Fitzsimmons, Lita (Leta) Fitzsimmons, Florence Gebhardt, Ida Maynes, Lena Smallacombe, and Cora (Cara) Stevens.

A rare cut glass door panel made by the Laurel Cut Glass Company was the subject of an article which appeared in SW nov '68.

Decanter and matching glasses in the "Sharon" Pattern. Height of decanter 10 inches.

Rose vase in a combination of floral and brilliant cut designs. Pattern name unknown by Mr. Harold Carey. Height 7 inches.

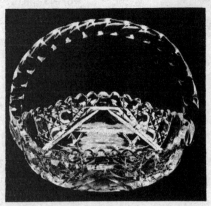

Large tray combining floral and brilliant cutting in an unidentified pattern. Diameter 14 inches.

Basket with "rope" handle in combination pattern of flowers and "Chair Bottom" (also known as "Harvard"). Diameter 6 inches.

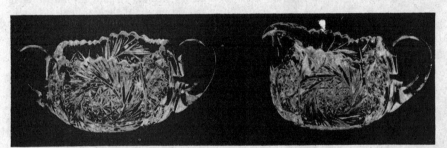

Sugar and cream set in the "Omar" pattern. Height of cream pitcher 3 inches.

Small bowl cut in a pattern of alternating "Pinwheels" and brilliant "Rosettes." Diameter 6 inches.

Tall stemmed compote in an unidentified pattern. Height 7 inches.

Pitcher in a pattern derived mainly from the "Omar" pattern combined with other motifs. Height 11 inches.

Prior to the publication of his book *American Cut and Engraved Glass*, Mr. Revi's efforts to research material on the Laurel Cut Glass Company were somewhat disappointing—to him, at least. Since that time he has collected the information contained in this article. The cut glass pieces illustrated in this article are from the collection of Mr. Harold D. Carey of Jermyn, Pa., a former employee of the Laurel Cut Glass Company.

Rose vase in No. 300 pattern; 9" high.

Left: Wine glass in pattern No. 310; 3½" high. Right: Puff box in "Brilliant" pattern; 4" high.

The Halter Cut Glass Company

by ALBERT CHRISTIAN REVI

JOSEPH HALTER, SR. was an Aide de Camp to a French Marshall during the Franco-Prussian War (1870). He was captured by the Germans, but subsequently freed because his knowledge of languages was useful to them. Halter journeyed partway across the Sahara Desert before coming to the United States where he apprenticed himself to the Dorflinger Glass Company in White Mills, Pa. Shortly afterwards he moved to Honesdale, Pa., with his wife, Magdelene Lang Halter, and their five sons — Joseph, Jr., William, John, Charles and Louis. While in Honesdale he became an expert stopper maker. (At that time all stoppers were made by hand.)

At this point there is a gap in the family records and we cannot be certain where Mr. Halter learned the glass cutting trade. The family moved to Brooklyn, N.Y., where Joseph Halter, Jr. was apprenticed, at age 12, to a Brooklyn cutting shop.

Joseph Halter, Jr. married Elizabeth Kiefer in 1898, and at this time his father established a cutting shop known as the Halter Cut Glass Company. Joseph, Jr. and John Halter joined their father in this business. A cousin, who's name no living member of the Halter family could recall, also worked for the senior Mr. Halter.

Nine months after their opening, and while they were packing their first large order for shipment, the whole factory burned to the ground. There was no insurance to cover the loss. Tragedy struck again a few months later when John Halter and his cousin drowned in a fishing accident.

Very soon thereafter the firm was started up again, this time with Joseph Halter, Jr. as the principle owner. The newly formed company grew rapidly, and soon they were employing about 60 men. Victor Brisbois, later of Becker & Brisbois, was foreman of the cutting shop. Halter supplied cut glass products to Stern Brothers (New York City), Marshall Fields (Chicago), Losser's (Brooklyn), and several other retail shops about the country.

Joseph Halter, Jr. was identified as a "glasscutter" in the 1905 edition of the "Brooklyn Directory." In 1909, the directories listed J. Halter & Company as glass cutters located at 850 DeKalb Avenue, Brooklyn. From 1910 to 1913, the "Brooklyn Directory" reported that J. Halter & Company was located at 68 West Broadway; the Halter Cut Glass Company, Inc., at that time, was located at 963-965 Kent Avenue, Brooklyn. Obviously, Halter maintained a showroom at the West Broadway address and a cutting shop at the Kent Avenue location.

Meantime, Mr. Halter's in-laws, the Kiefers, joined him in the cut glass business. The senior Mr. Kiefer invested money in the company; his sons, Charles and Edward, learned the cut glass trade from Joseph Halter, Jr.; William Kiefer supervised the bookkeeping department, and his sister Marguerite (then just 18 years old) kept the books.

The Kiefers decided to go into the cut glass business for themselves, and about 1912 the Kiefer Brothers Cut Glass Company was established. It is currently operating as The E. J. K. Company, 104-132 Montgomery Street, Brooklyn, N.Y.

In 1920/21; "The Pottery and Glass Directory" listed The Halter Cut Glass Company at 489 DeKalb Avenue; after that date no mention of the company could be found in any directories.

The author is grateful to Mrs. Lilian Halter Walburg for the information she supplied for this article. Our sincere thanks to Mr. Edward J. Kiefer for identifying the cut glass patterns by name and number. For a further study of The Halter Cut Glass Company and The Kiefer Cut Glass Company, see pages 127 and 135 in "American Cut and Engraved Glass," by Albert Christian Revi.

Covered jar in pattern No. 301; 6" high.

Cologne bottle in "Russian Diamond" (No. 315) pattern; 6" high.

Decanter in No. 305 pattern; 12" high.

Footed bowl in No. 275 pattern; 10" high.

American Cut Glass Patterns

H. P. Sinclaire & Co.

by ALBERT CHRISTIAN REVI

Wreath & Flower, from patent papers, May 4, 1909.

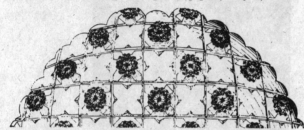

Bird-in-a-cage, from patent papers, August 3, 1909.

Greek Key & Laurel, from patent papers, April 5, 1910.

Holly, from patent papers dated February 28, 1911.

Sinclaire's *Palm-leaf and Rosettes*, in 7″ dia. relish dish.
Collection of Lee Schreiber.

THE first recording of H. P. Sinclaire & Company appears in Hanford's Corning City Directory for 1905, but it is quite possible the company was established as a cutting shop a year or two earlier, perhaps in 1903. In 1905, the officers of the company were Henry P. Sinclaire, Jr., president, and Marvin Olcott, vice-president. The business operated under the same name until 1929 with little change in its principals.

The names of Henry P. Sinclaire, Sr., Henry P. Sinclaire, Jr., and William Sinclaire appear here and there in records at Corning, New York, from 1893 to 1912. H. P. Sinclaire, Sr. was the secretary of the Corning Glass Works from 1893 until his death, sometime prior to 1903. The approximate time of his passing is determined by a listing of his widow, Anne Sinclaire, in the 1903 edition of the Corning City Directory. Henry P. Sinclaire, Jr. was the secretary of T. G. Hawkes & Company of cut glass fame from 1893 to 1903, presumably leaving that firm to establish his own cutting shop. William Sinclaire is listed as a "glassmaker" from 1893 to 1899. In 1899, he was elected assistant secretary of the Corning Glass Works, and from 1905 to 1912 served as secretary. Marvin Olcott's association with H. P. Sinclaire & Co. can be documented from 1905 to 1911, and his signature appears on all patents issued to the firm from 1909 to 1911.

H. P. Sinclaire & Company purchased their blanks for cutting from the Corning Glass Works as did many other cutting shops in the area, and the marked similarity in the shapes of their wares to other shops in the vicinity is at once apparent. The standard cuts indigenous to most American cut glass manufacturers are found in many Sinclair designs—Strawberry Diamond & Fan, Rosettes, and variations of the popular Russian (Daisy & Button). But some of their designs deviate from usual patterns as shown in several patents for cut glass designs registered in Washington, D. C., by Henry P. Sinclaire, Jr., from 1909 to 1911.

On May 4, 1909, Henry P. Sinclaire, Jr. patented his "Wreath & Flower" pattern. The design consists of a wreath of laurel leaves tastefully interlaced at equal distances with a flower and leaf motif.

Sinclaire's "Bird-in-a-cage" pattern was patented by Henry P. Sinclaire, Jr. on August 3, 1909. The close pattern of brilliant rosettes is evenly spaced in a checkered design of crosses within a square, as shown in patent drawings. Its resemblance to the "Harvard" pattern produced by The Pairpoint Corporation, T. G. Hawkes Glass Company, and others is obvious, yet this design has certain features all its own.

By 1910, cut glass patterns were leaning more toward simpler designs. Following this trend, Mr. Sinclaire registered his design patent for "Greek Key & Laurel" pattern on April 5, 1910. A vine or wreath of laurel leaves and berries overcut with a Greek Key motif is the basic idea for the design, but variations of the pattern, as applied to the several pieces in this suite of glassware, take their cue from the flat panel cutting and the simple laurel wreath shown in the patent specifications. A pitcher in this pattern is illustrated in Daniel's *Cut and Engraved Glass, 1771–1905*, plate 5. On page 143, she credits this late pattern to the "Middle Period . . . probably about 1850," and indicates it was possibly a product of the O'Hara Glass Works of James B. Lyon & Company of Pittsburgh.

On February 29, 1911, Mr. Sinclaire patented the firm's "Holly" pattern. The design reverts somewhat to the more elaborate cutting of a previous era, but with a bit more restraint in overall effect, produced by a balanced application of simple cutting combined with a brilliant pattern. Its name derives from the wreath of holly leaves and berries which surround the border of the plate used in their patent illustration. A variation of their "Bird-in-a-cage" pattern is used for a brilliant and effective center.

In 1930, the Corning Bakery Company bought the Sinclaire plant and rebuilt it into a bakery.

GUNS AND KNIVES

Definitely a man's area of collecting, guns and knives of early vintage are difficult to find these days. Kentucky rifles, once purchased for a nominal sum, are now priced in the thousands of dollars. Pistols bearing the name "Colt" are never sold for less than several hundred dollars. Perhaps this is the reason gun collectors have included early pocket knives in their field of interest. Though less costly, early pocket knives are not found in any great quantity. Most of those found have been unrecognized by the seller as being of late 18th or early 19th century vintage.

VINTAGE AIR GUNS

by LES BEITZ

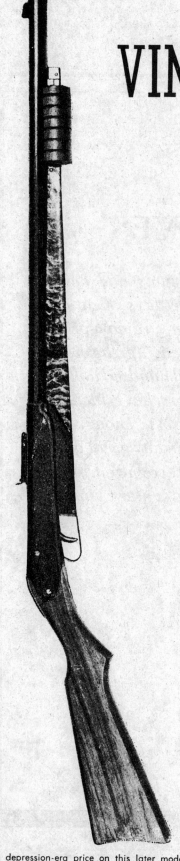

The depression-era price on this later model Daisy Repeater (ca. 1933) was $3.95. It was an exceptionally high quality product, equipped with a precision sight and genuine American walnut gunstock.

SOME ADVANCED GUN COLLECTORS (and this includes a good many sporting enthusiasts, too) are on the prowl these days in quest of a rather special breed of cat. They're hot after vintage air arms. In a sort of sly manner, these buffs are poking around at auctions, antique fairs, flea markets, junk and second-hand outlets, every place where offbeat Americana might possibly be lurking, hoping to locate early model air rifles or pistols. The going is rough. These gents just aren't coming off with what one might term "good pickin's."

This is a real switch from the situation a scant half-dozen years ago. Then, most fine old American BB guns and other early pneumatic-operated firearms were pretty much classed as dinky kid stuff. Little or no attention was afforded them because there were still some good Sharps, Winchesters, Spencers and similarly esteemed old weapons to be had. Air guns simply weren't in the swim. This is understandable to a degree, because the Civil War Centennial years had focused a strong beam of interest on military muskets and repeaters of that era; in consequence, a good bit of desirable material in the vintage air gun line had been bypassed — went begging. "Big Stuff" had been center stage, and held the spotlight.

Not so today. Looking at it realistically though, the emergence of vintage air arms as a keen area of collector interest is not too surprising. It was bound to happen when a realization of the lore and background of these unique little weapons is taken into account. The idea of compressed air forcing a springed plunger to send a projectile on its way has been around for a long, long time. Matter of fact, air guns had been developed and were in use as early as the 16th century!

Let's get back to the current state of affairs and zero in on some of the fascinating antique air guns that are still knocking about and can be picked up by vigilant browsers who have something of a fix as to what these little air guns actually amount to.

Along about the turn of the century, some twenty-odd concerns were putting out air arms of sorts. One by one, most of these outfits went "bust" —chiefly on two counts. First of all, the making of a good pneumatic valve system is extremely complex, calling for exacting tolerance and a lot of manufacturing care. Few firms have ever made the grade, including established makers of cartridge model firearms. So faulty design and poor workmanship spelled *finis* to many early endeavors in the field.

Secondly, a lot of shops that got involved in this craft, even though they came up with a commendable product, were financially unstable. They hadn't enough capital to merchandise their wares successfully. So, one way or another, they lost out at the marketplace.

Of these outfits, Apache, along with Plainsman and Kessler, stood their ground for awhile, then folded. Because of their limited output it can readily be reasoned that surviving specimens from these defunct firms are pretty difficult to come by. Then, too, some of these models were a nightmare of intricate mechanism in the way of operating principle, so over the years kids had buffetted them around to such an extent that they were junkers relatively early in the game. Finding one in decent shape today is really something to write home about.

The late Walter Benjamin had begun making air rifles around 1882. Because he had both a fine design and sufficient working capital, he acquired a nice toe-hold and was able to weather economic gales incident to the air gun market through several decades. Crosman and Sheridan are present-day survivors of the depression years, as well. Early examples of models put out by these firms are, of course, highly collectible. But, as mentioned, the real guns are ones that emanated from the workbenches of shops that fell by the wayside, and a few "classics" — odd-ball types that have

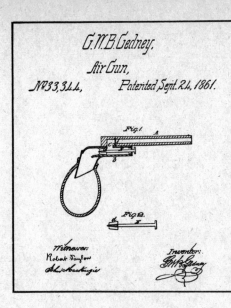

G.W.B. Gedney,
Air Gun,
Nº33,344, Patented Sept. 24, 1861.

Fig. 1

Fig. 2

Witnesses:
Robert Dunfore
Jnh. Schesslingie

Inventor:
G.W.B. Gedney

Left: Patent illustration for G. W. B. Gedney's air gun. Here's how it worked: Using the index finger, the shooter pushed back on the plunger to block the air passage. A projectile was then dropped into the barrel. A quick squeeze compressed the bulb-handle and the air within caused the plug to pop out. The air surged through the passage blowing out the projectile.

Montgomery Ward in 1904 at 90¢; an *economy* model of the same sold for less than 75¢! Any one of these vintage air rifles found in good shape today will bring upwards of $25—or roughly 30 times their original price tags. So when we're inclined to growl about the high cost of living in respect to early Colts, Winchesters, and the like, it goes without saying that early BB guns are in a class by themselves. Although they're quite high priced in relation to their original cost, I honestly believe they're worth every dime being asked for them . . . and will be worth much, much more in the months and years ahead.

Why? Simply because they're fewer and farther between than most folks realize, and as the true scarcity of some of the earliest types becomes recognized prices are bound to sky-rocket.

If you play it right, you shouldn't have too much trouble ferreting out an early Daisy, Benjamin, or Quackenbush model. If you're lucky, you're mighty apt to come up with that wonderful Webley air pistol — their circa 1929 job. And if you've parted your hair *just right,* it's entirely possible you'll hit real pay dirt and bring home the fabulous 1937 model EM GEE!

So what it all shapes up to, really, is that vintage air rifles are very, very much in the swim these days.

filtered down through the years from absolute "no name" makers. Take old Gedney's contraption, for example.

The gun that Mr. Gedney patented in 1861 is a doozie. Study the patent sketch reproduced here. If you should stumble upon one somewhere along the line, you'd do well to snatch it off the open market in a hurry because those rascals are practically extinct. They're rarer than whooping cranes. I seriously doubt if a dozen Gedneys —any condition — could be rounded up on a thorough search from Maine to California. In the lore of American air arms, they're about in the same class as a Colt Paterson, of cap-and-ball pistol fame. I'm advised that a Gedney, even in poor shape, is likely to be dickered for with an offer starting at something like fifty or sixty dollars!

The Daisy Air Rifle got its start through a rather circuitous route. In the 1880s Clarence J. Hamilton, a watch and clock repairman, teamed up with a group of businessmen in Plymouth, Mich., to produce an all-metal farm windmill he'd designed. As a sort of shirt-tail enterprise, Hamilton fiddled around with other gadgetry and eventually came up with an all-metal air rifle which he patented in 1888. His firm, the Plymouth Iron Windmill Company, integrated the air gun into their fabricating set-up and marketed it under the name "Daisy."

As frequently happens in the topsy-turvy world of economic trends and flip-flops, the windmill end of it started to fizzle out—but the Daisy had caught on. Before long the company dropped the sagging windmill line of goods and devoted all their resources and attention to the manufacture of air rifles. The name of the concern was changed to Daisy Manufacturing Company.

Now a word or two about values— and here we get into something kind of wierd. In order to establish a motif

for the pattern, suppose we take a Colt .45 six-shooter, the famed and legendary "Peacemaker" of the Old West.

In early 1874 when that wonderful firearm was first made available to the general public, it sold for $17. Today, one in tolerably decent condition (original and sound throughout) will bring anywhere from $150 to $200—roughly 10 times its original cost.

The Daisy "Take-Down" repeater illustrated here was supplied through

Air Rifles

Do not expect to get the same results from an Air Rifle that can be obtained from a Cartridge Rifle. They are but a toy, yet dangerous.

Daisy Air Rifle. D 840-42

Daisy "Take-Down" Repeater.

D 884—Daisy Repeater. Magazine holds 48 Air Rifle shot. Repeating attachment extremely simple. Both the magazine and shooting barrel can be easily removed. Length, 31 in. Weight, 1 lb. 14 oz. Price, each .... $ .90
Price per dozen 10.00

20th Century "Take-Down" Daisy.

D 886—Same as Repeater without the magazine. Shooting barrel so arranged that either Air Rifle shot or darts can be used. Can be easily taken apart and packed in small space. Length, 31 in. Weight, 1 lb. 13 oz. Price, each .... $.70
Price per dozen 8.00

1,000 Shot Daisy Repeater.

D 888—1,000 shot Daisy. A magazine gun with Winchester action. Magazine holds 1,000 BB shot and loads automatically. Working parts made of steel and brass and so arranged that any one can take the gun apart and put it together. Stock of black walnut, highly polished. Shoots accurately and with great force. The most gun-like air rifle on the market. Length, 36 in.; weight, 3 lb. Net $1.25

500 Shot Daisy.

D 890—Same as 1000 Shot Daisy except that barrel is four inches shorter and the magazine holds but 500 BB shot. Weight 2 lbs. 10 oz $1.05

Daisy Air Rifles advertised in a 1904 Montgomery Ward catalog. Because of its "Winchester" design, Model D888 (shown above) has a special collector interest and brings up to $35 in the current market.

A Miniature Pin-Fire Revolver

by CLARA NISBET

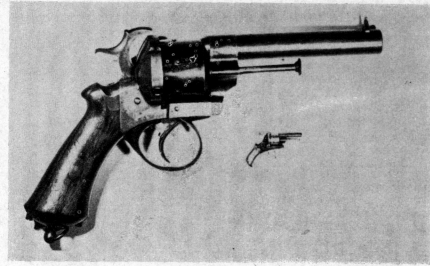

FIGURE ONE

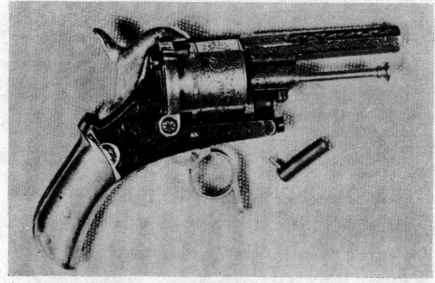

FIGURE TWO

COLLECTING MINIATURE rifles and handguns appeals to many masculine hobbyists. These miniatures are to be found in a variety of types, some having been made up for use as watch fobs.

The miniature pin-fire revolver shown here (Fig. 1) was photographed alongside a standard Lefaucheux pin-fire revolver, the better to emphasize its diminutive size, a mere 2 inches in length. The close-up (Fig. 2) shows the superb workmanship of the little revolver. It is really a gem; its trigger guard, cylinder, and hammer, the ejector and the pistol grips are all gold-filled, while the whole gun is beautifully chased. In spite of its size, the single action mechanism functions smoothly and efficiently, actually firing the pin-fire cartridge (also shown in Fig. 2) which is loaded with a tiny lead ball.

This specimen is thought to be of French or Belgian make, and is probably about 100 years old. One would think that the craftsman who produced such a work of art would have at least initialed his masterpiece, but no mark of identification can be found. It has been suggested that the workmanship itself may have been a trademark.

The pin-fire ignition system was a European development. It was invented by the two Frenchman, Lefaucheux and Houllier. In 1835, Lefaucheux first came out with a shotgun which fired a shell equipped with a projecting firing pin. His son Eugene went on to perfect a revolver of this type. This handgun is listed as a 12 mm—a large bore which approximates the 44 caliber of American guns. It is claimed that a few of these early guns are still in use.

Actually, the miniature does not copy the Lefaucheux model with which it is pictured. This standard size revolver bears the serial number LF 6629 and the mark, "Lefaucheuz a Paris" stamped on the barrel—identifications which show it to be the product of the parent plant rather than, as sometimes happened, a farmed-out job. The miniature revolver with finger spur on its trigger guard seems instead to have been patterned after a later model of the Lefaucheux—a type with serial numbers starting in the 25,000s—a model which was used by armies of both the North and the South in our own Civil War. If this is so, the miniature has the added significance of coming under the classification of "martial arms."

Carvings on
Pennsylvania Long Rifles

by **VERNON GUNNION**

*Curator, Pennsylvania
Farm Museum of
Landis Valley.*

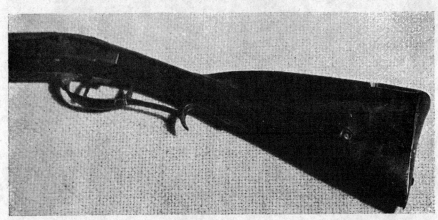

The flat butt plate, the thickness of the butt, and the very simple relief carving on this curly maple stock all indicate that this rifle was probably made ca. 1750. Collection Hermann Goring.

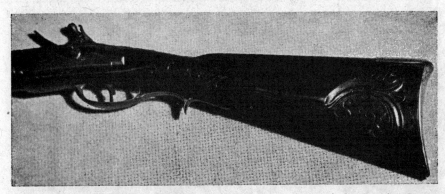

Stock of curly maple; barrel marked "J. P. Beck," a gunsmith who worked in Dauphin County, Pa., in the latter part of the 18th century. The relief carving is typical of Beck's workmanship and style. Collection Hermann Goring.

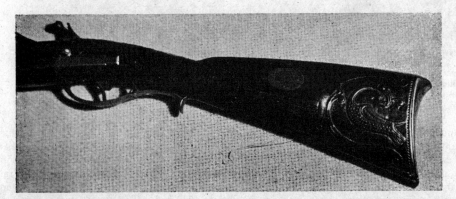

Barrel marked "N. Beyer," who probably worked in Dauphin County, Pa., near the end of the 18th century. The fine relief carved bird on the curly maple stock rates Beyer as one of the better gunsmiths of this period. Guns of this quality are extremely rare. Privately owned.

R AISED-CARVED, relief-carved, bas-relief are names given to the carving on the cheek piece side of the early 18th century Pennsylvania long rifle commonly called the Kentucky Rifle. Muzzle-loading shooters attest to the accuracy of this gun, made possible by the rifling in the barrel; gun collectors point to the curly maple stocks, brass mountings, silver inlays, and carving on the stocks.

Today's antique gun enthusiast who collects Kentucky rifles usually favors examples with carved stocks. The earliest flintlock rifles that were raised-carved in Pennsylvania generally had a simple scroll type design on the cheek piece side of the stock. After the Revolutionary War, gunsmiths started to embellish their rifle stocks with more elaborate raised-carving, mostly in the shape of scrolls. Examples are known with lions and birds carved in relief, but these are rare.

In the early part of the 19th century, incised-carved guns, easier to execute and faster to carve, started to appear, and relief-carved stocks were more and more infrequently made. However, the Kentucky rifles produced in Bedford County, Pa., continued to show relief carving as well as incised carving.

When a gunsmith carved a gun and signed his name on the barrel, it is sometimes possible to attribute an unsigned gun to the same maker, for his designs were usually similar.

Some horn powder flasks were made by flattening the horn after it was soaked in hot water, so they would fit easily in a hunter's pocket or pouch.

by PHYLLIS T. BALLINGER

POWDER HORNS AND FLASKS OF HORN

All pictures courtesy of the Pennsylvania Historical and Museum Commission, Harrisburg, Pa.

Powder horns in the collection of the Pennsylvania Farm Museum at Landis Valley show a great variation in size. The larger horns were to hold coarse powder that was placed inside the barrel of the gun. Small horns held fine grained powder used for priming the pan.

BY 1825, metal powder horns and flasks had begun to supplant those made of horn, yet that earlier type had certain advantages and it was never completely abandoned by the American hunter and military until breechloading guns made such accoutrements obsolete.

Horn was light, strong, and tough. If dropped, it was apt to bounce. It was safe in a shower of sparks and would melt before it burned. It was waterproof, and light enough to float if dropped in water, making it easy to recover. It softened in hot water and could be shaped as desired. It

could also be carved. And it was durable. One, dated 1799, and now in a private collection, bears the inscription, "Thos Ward is my name, If I fall bury me. When my bones [are] rotten, this horn shall make me not forgotten." Since right and left horns curve in opposite directions, the owner had a choice of a right or left-handed powder horn.

The ox, the common beast of burden in the American colonies, supplied the horn inexpensively. The Red Devon, with horns over 20 inches long, was the leading breed. Their large, upright, beautifully curved horns were so white that when used for powder flasks, they often had to be toned down with butternut or oak bark stain lest they be too conspicuous in the field.

During the colonial era, the Bird family of Dorchester, Mass., who were dealers in leather and had their own tannery, made it their custom to give horns free with the purchase of hides. They also sold horns, retailing them at 4 pence in the rough, 6 pence trimmed and bored. The account books of John Pynchon, a merchant of Hadley, Mass., between 1652 and 1680, showed that he sold powder flasks at 5 shillings and powder horns at 8 pence.

Soldiers were given horns in the rough and whiled away off-duty hours working on them; powder horns became something of a military scrimshaw. Many hunters and pioneers also fashioned their own horn flasks.

To make a powder horn, both ends of the horn were cut. The small end, which would be the nozzle, was bored from the top to the chamber. This had to be carefully done for if the opening, or orifice, was too big, it would be difficult to control the flow of powder into the charger. The interior had to be cleared and smoothed. The outside was also smoothed with a rasp, drawshave, or knife. A cap, which often had screw turnings, had to be fitted to the nozzle end, or a soft wood stopper without threads whittled to make a fine tight fitting plug; caps made by professional makers were sometimes fashioned in silver and pewter. A wooden base plug was then fitted and secured with wooden pins; the crevices were sealed with tallow or beeswax to make it watertight. If it was not to be decorated on the outside, the surface would be polished with pumice and oil rubbed into it with the palm of the hand. Vegetable oil from cooking or oil procured by squeezing nuts was preferred over animal fat for polishing. The vegetable oil hardened in a short time but the animal fat remained soft.

If the horn was decorated, the design was often traced on and then incised with a knife. Professional powder horn carvers often used a burin, an engraving tool. Birds, trees, animals, geometric designs, Masonic symbols—the full gambit of conventional motifs were used. The incised horn was colored with ink, grease, soot, or homemade dyes. Green came from the verdigris of the copper camp kettle. The pith of sumac gave a yellow. Brown came from alder bark or husks of butternuts or walnuts. Red coloring came from chokecherries or raspberries.

Map horns are particularly interesting, even when inaccurately done, for their historic significance and documentation of dress and equipment. Frequently military officers had horns engraved with maps showing waterways, location of harbors, forts, and settlements, and other pertinent information. Some were important contributions to cartography. New York map horns dating from the French and Indian Wars (1755–1763) seem to have been common in their time although they are rarities today. Such are now mostly in museums or private collections. Horns engraved with heraldic devices were believed to have been owned by British officers. Many horns record the name, company, and regiment of a soldier, giving credence to the unconfirmed rule that ". . . each horn be marked with a name in order to secure its prompt return after being refilled at the powder wagon." This avoided disputes as to ownership.

The date incised on a powder horn is usually considered to be the date when it was finished. Many men who decorated their own did so over a long period, filling the open areas as time and whim dictated. Experts agree it is next to impossible to date a horn accurately.

Professional powder horn carvers were often gunsmiths, silversmiths, and block cutters. As their source of design they used contemporary maps and engravings. One frequently served as a model for others. Collectors find it of interest that the carving or beading around the end is often similar to the wirework of New York silversmiths.

Any difference between a hunter's powder horn and one for military use is superficial. Almost every settler was a hunter. He carried his powder horn suspended by straps of cowhide or deerskin from his shoulder. Gut, eelskin, or twine were also used as straps. If he used a flintlock, he would carry two powder horns. The larger, about 8 inches in length would hold coarse powder for the charge. The small horn (about 3 inches) held fine-grained, high flash powder used for priming the pan. Frequently this type was slightly flattened so that it could be carried in the pocket or pouch and had a very tiny nozzle opening. All of them got a patina from long years of rubbing against buckskin and wool.

Powder horn decorated with the bust of Robert Fulton, probably made by a professional carver and sold to commemorate the successful voyage of Fulton's steam-powered ship "Katherine of Clermont." The Clermont presaged the age of steamboats when she sailed the Hudson River in record time on her trial run, August 1807.

Powder horns of this type are very common. They are impossible to date accurately and were sold in stores less than 100 years ago as regular sales items. This shows how the strap was tied to the horn for carrying over the shoulder.

Powder horn with incised decoration in geometric designs.

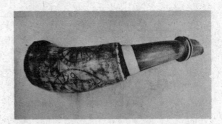

Powder horn showing wide range of decorative elements done in cameo technique by an untrained carver. The horn was cut away leaving the design in high relief.

Decorated powder horn depicting soldier in uniform, possibly dates from the Mexican War (1846).

Rare "Colt Patent" eagle flask made in England.

U.S. Eagle and Horn flask made by Robert Dingee, New York City, ca. 1830.

Zinc Dog and Hunter flask.

Dog and Bird flask made by the American Flask Co.

Bag-shaped flask decorated with oak leaves; make by G. & J. W. Hawksley, Sheffield, England.

Die - Stamped

MASS PRODUCTION of die-stamped metal powder flasks began in the United States about 1830. These replaced flasks made of horn, ivory, tortoise-shell, mother-of-pearl, engraved brass and copper and pewter. The production of stamped metal flasks continued through the Civil War period—even after Daniel Wesson, of Smith and Wesson, patented his metal cartridge, in 1857.

Actually, powder flasks were used a lot longer than most people realize. The last patent issued for a stamped metal flask was registered by D. Wright of St. Louis, Missouri, in December 1891. At this late date most powder flasks were made of copper and/or brass, tin, zinc, German silver, and Britannia metal; rarely were they made of pewter, Sheffield plate, or sterling silver. Silver flasks were usually made to order for presentation gifts.

Die-stamped flasks can be classified into three general categories: pocket pistol flasks, military flasks, and sporting flasks. Their capacities ranged from one-ounce flasks for pocket pistols, to 24-ounce flasks for sporting guns and fowling pieces. Larger flasks were fitted with cord rings for carrying; pocket flasks were made without rings. Four types of tops (pouring spouts) were made to fit the bore of a gun's muzzle or cylinder chamber—common, screw, patent, and outside patent.

Brass flask with cartouches showing birds and flowers.

Scarce copper flask marked "Dixon"; High relief design of dog and tree.

Brass flask with repousse design of dead game. American Flask Co.

Handsomely decorated brass flask made by G. & J. W. Hawksley.

Unmarked flask in a plain fluted design.

Fluted brass flask marked G. & J. W. Hawksley, Sheffield, England.

Brass Shell and Bush flask with carrying rings set off center; English.

Elegantly shaped and decorated flask. These are sometimes found with cased Colt revolvers.

Rare one-ounce Dixon pistol flask, fluted and beaded design, ca. 1858.

Elaborately shaped flask with all-over design of vines, birds, and animals.

Powder Flasks   *by EMMA STILES*

Several shapes were used for die-stamped metal flasks between 1830 and 1890, but most are bottle-shaped and fitted with long or short tops. The variety of decorative motifs embossed on these flasks seems almost limitless, and collectors will undoubtedly discover many more than we are able to illustrate here. No two shapes were ever made with exactly the same decoration.

Prices were governed by the type of pouring spout, the size of the flask, and the decoration. In 1864, the American Flask Company of Waterbury, Connecticut, wholesaled flasks with common tops at $3 less per dozen than identical flasks with outside patent tops. On the other hand, one-ounce

pistol flasks sold for $10 less per dozen than 16-ounce flasks. Decorated flasks sold for as much as $6.50 more per dozen than plain flasks.

Similar die-stamped flasks were produced in England and these are frequently more elaborately decorated than American-made flasks; English flasks are now quite rare.

At first, die-stamped flasks were rather plain, but as competition increased manufacturers employed artist-designers to decorate their wares to attract the trade. After 1850 decorations became more and more elaborate. Allegorical designs were very popular, and humorous subjects were frequently used.

Decorated brass flask marked "Birmingham."

An Indian buffalo hunter and a deerhead decorate this American Arms Company flask.

Dixon flask decorated with medallions showing a dog and rising pheasant.

Deer and tree decorated zinc flask; American Flask Co.

Rare Dixon (English) flask of pinkish brass with elaborate decoration.

ARTILLERY SHELL ART WORK

by DENNIS C. MAHR

C AN an instrument of destruction be converted into an object of beauty and peaceful usefulness? Hans Lindemann, owner of the Museum of American Treasures in National City, California, says, "Yes indeed," and he has 250 pieces of evidence to back him up.

For years homesick soldiers and sailors have taken artillery shells and hand-hammered intricate designs and thoughts of home into their cold brass surfaces. They have shaped them into pitchers, cups, candlesticks, lamp bases, vases, cuspidors, umbrella stands, and gongs.

They have written names of loved ones like "Laura—1936" in a field of flowers; stamped exotic names of foreign cities and embedded coins from foreign countries in their surfaces. The most popular subject is the Statue of Liberty.

Many of the transformed artillery shells are as recent as World War II; some date back to 1809. Some are as small as 20 millimeters; others are as large as 175 millimeters. A few are

quite crude, but most show a great deal of artistic talent and many weeks of work.

Almost all are easy to identify, for the month and year of manufacture, the name of the manufacturer, and the size are stamped into the base of each shell. Only in a few instances has this information been obliterated by the craftsman.

To prepare the shells for hammering, the serviceman had to fill them with lead or wood to provide a solid surface to hammer against. This padding was removed upon completion. It must have been quite a load for him to pack in his duffle bag as he moved from one combat area to another!

Lindemann finds a few of his decorated shells in antiques shops; more are found at swap meets; the majority come from scrap metal yards. People clean out their garages and attics and sell the oxidized shells for scrap brass. Scrap dealers in the area save the shells for Lindemann and sell them to him at the going price for scrap brass. He polishes them up and, *voilà*, an art treasure!

Mr. Lindemann considers these hand-hammered shells true American folk art and, indeed, they seem to steal the show in his 12,000-piece museum of Americana.

An umbrella stand made by the crew of the U.S.S. New Orleans in 1898 and presented to the Captain. The inscription reads: "To Spain my compliments were sent/With shell and war time ill intent/In altered shape. In friendship's name/A better fate brings higher fame."

Below: A group of artillery shell vases and trophies in various designs.

Above: Pitcher and mugs made in 1944 by a U.S. Air Force flight crew; pitcher from a 105mm shell, cups from 75mm shells. **Below:** Artillery shell vases, candlesticks with Filipino coins, and a kangaroo-handled mug.

Fig. 1

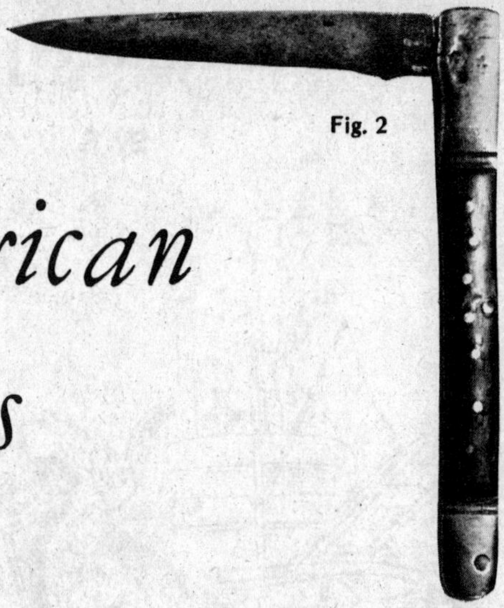

Fig. 2

Some Early American
Pocket Knives

by MADISON GRANT

(Illustrations from the author's collection.)

403
Guns
Knives

SINCE THE SCARCITY of antique gun material has encouraged many gun collectors to turn to related items which are available, the pocket knife has emerged as a highly desirable collectible.

From earliest times man has utilized an instrument to supplement the dexterity of the human hand. Such devices have ranged from a single stone or club to more complicated physical arrangements, from crude bows and arrows to elaborate guns. Yet no matter how sophisticated his surroundings became, he ever remained partial to the blade, with its almost limitless possibilities as both weapon and tool. In generations past, the knife, the most universal of all mechanisms, was man's constant companion. Nor has modern living eliminated its fascination.

The development of the clasp, pocket, or folding knife as we know it has been centuries in the process, but its great impetus arrived with the phenomenon of mass production, about 1835. Using this date as a bench mark, let us consider the previous 75

years and the following 100 years as encompassing two distinct periods which produced knives that are still available to the collector.

The first period (1760-1835) concerns the hand constructed, highly personalized knives of the folk art type. The second period (1835-1935) deals with the mass-produced stylized knives commonly found today. There seems little connection between them in either esthetic or monetary value.

As a point of reference, the American Revolutionary period is a good starting place for collectors of early American knives. At that time most articles of wood, metal, or bone were made by hand and were largely the result of personal attitudes and wishes. This permitted the tremendous variety of self-expression that is the basis of collecting delight today. In this period, too, we had ceased to be a colonial appendage to England. The Continental call to arms included one of the earliest references to the subject when recruiting posters admonished each man to bring with him "his own rifle and Barlow knife."

The era of the handmade knife in the United States was relatively short. This, coupled with the Industrial Revolution, opened the floodgates of production. Demand, ingenuity, and competition soon placed a knife into the hands of every urchin, farmer, and city dweller.

A future article will discuss modern knives still available, including the English pocket knives that have no peer for craftsmanship.

Illustrated are four knives of the first period about whose origin and character there can be no doubt. Only from back country America could such pieces have come into being.

Fig. 1. A combination blade and fork, made of bog iron with horn grips, this knife is reputed to have been used by one of the Green Mountain Boys. Length, closed, 4 7/8 inches.

Fig. 2. This single spear point blade knife is from central Pennsylvania. Its long bolsters give it added strength. Horn grips with metal studs were for decoration. Length, closed, 4¾ inches.

Fig. 3. From the Valley of Virginia came this patch or hunting knife of bog iron. It has horn grips with fishtail terminal and a central fin for protection. Length, closed, 4½ inches.

Fig. 4. This single blade, with long bolsters and central panel of bone, is typical of many knives found at Revolutionary War campsites and battlefields. This almost exclusive association pretty well authenticates its attribution to the 18th century. Length, closed, 3 7/8 inches.

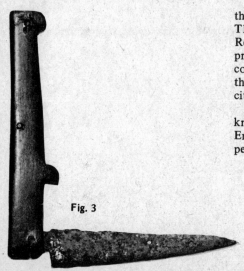

Fig. 3

Fig. 4

The Philadelphia Deringer

By R. O. Ackerman

R ºAckerman

these "Deringers" were barely 3¾ inches long! Calibers ranged from .36 to .54. Lethal, yet compact, they gained immediate popularity with Mississippi River gamblers, with ladies, and with law officers as extra "hideout" weapons.

In those days the pocket pistols were sold only in pairs, at a set price of $22.50 a pair. A fine single specimen now is usually worth around $75.00.

Several points of historical importance enhance the value. An original Deringer was used by Henry Clay in a famous duel, and, much later, Abraham Lincoln was assassinated with one.

There were many copies made of the Deringer. In order to capitalize upon the popularity of the name, these were called "derringers", and the term is still used for any pistol of that type. To the serious collector, any original by Henry Deringer is a "Deringer", while the other spelling and lack of a capital designates a similar weapon of another maker.

Best known of this latter category is the Remington double-barreled derringer. A .41 rimfire breechloader, this was only discontinued in 1937!

Our drawing will aid in identification. The standard original Deringer shown has a selected walnut stock with hand-checkered grip. The blue steel of barrel and lock contrasts sharply with the engraved German silver of other parts. A tiny receptacle in the butt carries spare percussion caps.

On many examples, a band of sterling silver was inlaid about the rear of the barrel, and the front sight was of German silver. Its beauty alone would make this a desirable item!

Our illustration also shows the lead ball and copper percussion cap, drawn to exact scale.

This, then, is the story of the pistol and of the man—the only American ever to give his own name to an entire class of weapons!

FOR the first antique firearm to be described in this new department, the Philadelphia Deringer is especially appropriate. It is one of the few purely American developments in weapons history.

Henry Deringer established his gun shop at 612 North Front Street, Phila-delphia, in 1806. At first he held government contracts to supply flintlock weapons. Around the 1840s, he developed the small pocket pistol with large bore for which he is best remembered.

Among the first civilian firearms to use the percussion system, some of

JEWELRY

Jewelry holds a fascination for both men and women. The elegant productions of the Victorian period are especially appealing to women and are more readily found than the simpler pieces of the late 18th century. Americans couldn't afford elaborate jewels in the early years of our nation. But when we became an industrial giant, sometime after 1850, women indulged themselves with baubles and bangles created at home and abroad. Men, too, acquired a taste for heavy gold chains for their watches, and handsome fobs often dangled at one end of that chain. Cufflinks and stickpins of gold set with a variety of colorful jewels became fashionable in the Victorian era.

PRE-VICTORIAN
JEWELRY
1770 to 1830

by
ELIZABETH
SCHIFFMAN

*Except as noted,
all illustrations from
the author's collection.*

OUTSIDE MUSEUMS, little remains today of important 18th century jewelry. Revolutions, changes in fashion, and the introduction of new cuts for gems took a heavy toll. However, for the purpose of the private collector, we are mainly interested in those incidental pieces that can still be found and worn and enjoyed.

America is not a rich source for jewelry of the pre-Victorian period. There were few 18th century jewelers in America and none are regarded today as outstanding or original in artistry. Silversmiths like Paul Revere worked in gold as well; and although Revere himself reported that "my chief dependence is on my Goldsmith's Business, for the expenses of my Family," his records indicate a preponderance of silver work with occasional mention of "Death's head Rings, gold," lockets, seals, bracelets, beads, buckles and buttons.

His fame as an artisan rests on his work as a silversmith. Some of his gold and silver work was done for the jewelers of the day, among whom the Boston jeweler, Josiah Flagg, a neighbor and friend, appears in Revere's journals as a purchaser both of finished goods and precious metals. Records also show that Revere did engraving on rings for Flagg.

However, little has come down to the present day in the way of jewelry that is distinctive to American colonial design. There are the usual "death's head" mourning rings, presented to family and close friends at funerals, and other *memento mori,* but these were mainly based on English designs which were introduced in the last third of the 18th century. Watch fobs, seals, beads, and other jewelry made in America may have been somewhat distinctive by virtue of simple design, but they were not outstanding. The

A miniature painting of Mrs. Michael Taney by Charles Willson Peale. Miniatures by Charles and James Peale were painted on thin ovals of ivory and framed under glass. They were usually worn as pictured here—at the end of a cord or chain, tucked into the bosom of the dress. Collection of The Metropolitan Museum of Art, Harris Brisbane Dick Fund, 1938.

style was mainly copied, rather than adapted, from English and French jewelry.

Unlike American furniture, glassware, pottery, and the many other antique articles of distinctive background and style that characterize them as 17th, 18th, or 19th century American, jewelry was a comparative latecomer. In England and on the Continent there was a long history and tradition of fine work in silver and gold. The French had formed a guild of jewelers and goldsmiths in the 13th century under their patron saint Eligius, a monk of the 6th century who was medallist to four succeeding French kings.

Strict French government standards have been in existence for a long time; Diderot, in his *Encyclopedie ou Dictionaire Raisonne . . . (1777-1779),*

reports that the marks for silver and gold were established by government decree in 1681. Not only was the maker's name and the area mark required on gold articles, but the government also specified that two crossed bars (+) appear to guarantee that the jewelry was not less than 20 karats. The present 18-karat control mark of an eagle's head was instituted in Paris, in 1798.

In England, gold and silver standards preceded those of France. From the end of the 12th century, silversmiths and goldsmiths were formed into guilds, and it was not until 1854 that England lowered its 22- and 18-karat standards to include 15, 12 and 9 karats. The first English assay mark on gold was a leopard's head. It was used between 1300 and 1544, when the lion passant replaced it. Gold standards ranged from 18 to 22 karats in this period.

Strictly controlled quality standards for gold objects did not exist in America until as late as 1938, when the manufacturers themselves adopted a recommended commercial standard which was accepted and approved for promulgation by the U. S. Department of Commerce through the National Bureau of Standards. The minimum standard for gold was set at 10 karats, and the term "solid gold," which had often been loosely used to cover any grade of gold, was specifically defined as fine gold, that is, pure gold of 24-karat quality. A leeway of 1 karat was allowed on soldered jewelry, which meant that manufacturers might mark a 9-karat soldered piece as 10 karats. However, manufacturers of quality jewelry today do not usually take advantage of this leeway.

(With this background in mind, the collector must remember that some old American jewelry may not be what it appears to be, and that the most reliable method for determining quality is to have the piece tested.)

The idea of elaborate collections of jewels, a tradition with upper class families abroad, was not consistent with either the Puritan background or the thrifty temperament of colonial Americans. That strict moral disciplinarian of colonial America, the Reverend Cotton Mather, set the tone of his time and place with this admonition: "Possessor of *Gold!* Beware lest the Observation be verified in the *unhealthy* Influences of thy *Gold* upon thy *Mind;* and lest the *love* of it betray thee into many *foolish and hurtful Lusts,* which will drown thee in *Destruction and Perdition.*"

One has only to examine the great collections of portraits painted by artists of the pre- and post-Revolutionary period—Copley, the Peales, Stuart —to find that admonitions by Mather and other Puritans still had a strong hold. Among Tory and Revolutionary family portraits alike, the most that could be boasted in the way of personal decoration—or perhaps the most that could be displayed with taste— was a simple ring or two and a "dog-collar" of several strands of small beads or pearls. This was at the time when French army officers were loading their uniforms with gold and even plaiting the manes and tails of their horses with gold braid!

In England and France the ladies of the court were portrayed with a profusion of the most elaborate jewels. In America, fashionable ladies of the pre- and post-revolutionary period wore a long, thin black cord or ribbon tied high on the neck with a framed miniature or locket at the end usually tucked into the bosom of the dress. The contrasts in the two kinds of life were noted by the painter John S. Copley who wrote from France in 1774 that "It is a very genteel company one meets with and no other, as there is a subordination of People in this Country unknown in America."

In America the artists recorded a wider range of people — artisans, farmers, lawyers, businessmen, landed gentry, and all their families. Sometimes it is difficult to guess the background of the person portrayed on an American canvas, for there is a general simplicity in pose and dress and no marked contrasts in personal adornment between the artisan's wife and the governor's wife.

With the establishment of the Republic this simplicity in dress and manner continued, for it was a difficult time for Americans. Internal strife, ongoing wars, and the need to solidify the shaky young country allowed for few luxuries and few radical changes in style. Among gems, pearls were favored — woven into the hair, used as dogcollars or necklaces, bracelets, and for decorating gold jewelry. But the owners of these ornaments were few. Even those men and women who could afford to have their portraits painted could, more often than not, claim only the head in the picture as their own. Bodies, clothing, and ornaments were often painted in by fancy, or by borrowed elegance

Early 19th century French shell cameo brooch with fine rope-edged gold frame.

copied from mezzotints or engravings done from paintings of the more fashionable English or French.

An outstanding example of "borrowing" is that of our cover illustration, Gilbert Stuart's portrait of *Mathilde de Jaudenes y Nebot,* American wife of the Spanish Commissioner at Philadelphia. In 1794, sixteen-year-old Mrs. Jaudenes sat for a painting of her head. From that point on she was no longer needed. Stuart then turned for his inspiration (perhaps a little maliciously, since Spain and her representatives were highly unpopular in America at the time) to an engraving of a Vigee-Lebrun portrait of a French actress for the

Top, left to right. Georgian memorial pins, center glass panes cover plaited hair: Kidney-shaped with gold frame; black enamel on gold; flat-cut garnets in gold; deeply engraved yellow gold. **Bottom, left to right.** Pearl-outlined gold Georgian jewelry: Fanciful serpents with deep-set pearls, flat-cut garnet center stone, tiny glass circle holds strands of hair; memorial pin with deep-set pearls; ring is two separate bands of deep-set pearls with single band shank. (Author's collection.) Late 19th century copy of 18th century wedding band. (Collection Agnes Robinson.)

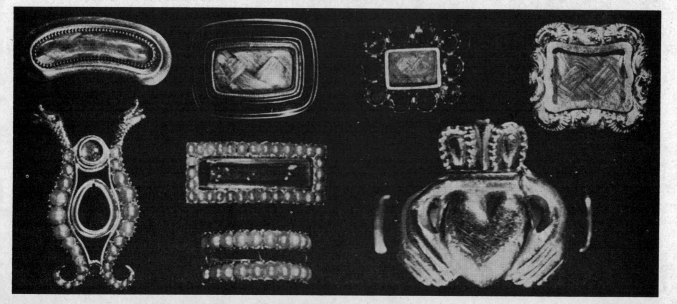

PRE-VICTORIAN JEWELRY

voluptuous body, and to a portrait of Marie Antoinette by the same painter for the jewels and headgear!

Jewels like these had never been made—nor probably even been seen—in America. On the other hand, the heavy chains, pendants, large enameled or jeweled bracelets, chatelaines, brooches, earrings, neckpieces, hair ornaments and bejeweled plumes were *de rigeur* for the aristocracy in the pre-revolutionary courts of France. Although the French Revolution temporarily put such extravagance out of fashion at home and abroad, it was not long before even more elaborate styles returned with the growth of the French bourgeoisie, and France again became the source for design inspiration in the world of fashion.

Thus, it can be said that among jewels most favored in America from the 1770s to the 1830s were the incidental pieces. Among these pieces, the miniature — in pendant, brooch, locket or bracelet form — was most highly regarded of all. These were of highly sentimental value and not designed to impress the beholder as an extravagance or luxury. Bracelet miniatures traditionally held two likenesses—that of the husband worn on the right wrist, the other a likeness of the father worn on the left wrist.

Charles Willson Peale, in a portrait of Mrs. Walter Stewart painted in 1782, shows her wearing a pair of pearl bracelets with clasps made of

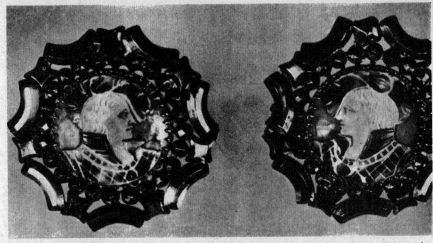

Cut steel and shell cameo cloak buckles, late 18th century, converted into pins. During this period the first factories to mass produce jewelry in England were established and turned out incidental jewelry of cut steel and cameos, crystal, and paste gems.

framed miniatures—these also painted most likely by Peale. Unlike the imaginary pearls depicted in so many portraits, one can feel most certain of the actual existence of the miniatures worn by the ladies, since if one could afford a portrait it was most likely that one could afford a miniature and both might be done at the same family sitting. Often both Charles Willson Peale and James Peale, his brother, worked together — Charles preparing the portrait, James the miniature.

Miniatures were painted on thin ovals of ivory, covered with glass, and framed with gold or gilded metal. A number of pendants contained double miniatures, one on each side, and many others displayed intricate hair work on the reverse side in the form of flowers or plumes made from the

hair of the person portrayed. Frames were usually narrow, sometimes only a bezel, but occasionally they were embossed or engraved. Chain, ribbon, or cord was passed through a loop or ring at the top of the miniature. Some pendant settings seem to have been altered by the addition of a pin.

In 1772, Peale painted the Cadwalader family, showing Mrs. Cadwalader wearing amethyst and seed-pearl pendant earrings and a necklace of small beads or pearls with a coral cross. In another portrait, painted in 1789, Peale depicts Mrs. Francis M. Charlton with an elaborate watch hanging on a short waist fob. Real or imaginary, the style of all these pieces is English or French.

The period under discussion, from about 1770 to the 1830s, showed little creative development of jewelry in America for the reasons already mentioned. France remained the center for artistic taste throughout this time, and what was fashionable in Paris soon became fashionable in London—and to a lesser degree in America. Under Louis XV and Louis XVI, the court was accustomed to elaborate surroundings, furniture covered with ormolu, lace on necks and wrists, powdered hair, ribbons, silks, tapestries, and rich rugs. It was natural for jewelers to follow these elaborate decorations as patterns for their jewelry. The ornate, the glistening and the complex design were the rule.

Paintings on enamel were set into furniture as well as into gold jewelry, and in England the Battersea works began production of copper objects overlaid with enamel that were used in the same way as the French enamels. It is quite possible that French artisans were brought to England to help develop the enameling industry, since documents show that French

Early 19th century classical style painting on enamel. The background on many enamels of this period is white. Both sides are decorated, the obverse showing a field of grain with two female figures, a child, and a remarkably docile lion. The reverse is decorated with flowers and leaves around the French word "Ete"—summer. Possibly part of a series. The gold rope frame and bale are contemporary.

artisans "were commonly employed in London" to produce all kinds of artistic objects, including jewelry. The influx into England of many finely-trained artisans was especially heavy during the period of the French Revolution.

Other styles that prevailed on the Continent and in England were the use of marcasites and cut steel with cameos, paste gems, and large crystals, and the use of silver as a setting for diamonds and other gems. Matthew Boulton played an important role during the last few decades of the 18th century in setting up the mass production of costume jewelry in Birmingham, England. Birmingham to this day is an important center for the manufacture of jewelry.

The introduction in Europe of large chandeliers towards the close of the 18th century brought more light into drawing rooms, and the new brilliant cut, offering more facets to reflect light, brought more sparkle into the diamond. Before the French Revolution of 1789, the use of diamonds was profuse. Settings became less and less conspicuous until they finally almost disappeared under the masses of stones.

Revolutions in America and France created a sobering atmosphere tending to discourage artistic elaboration in jewelry as well as in the other arts. The simpler lines of Georgian architecture, furniture and metal work directly influenced the style of jewelry in England. Bead engraving, used to ornament silver, seems to have been repeated in jewelry by the use of deeply-set pearls or gems to outline brooches and rings.

Madame Pompadour's brother and others traveling to Italy towards the close of the 18th century were enchanted with the art styles found in the Pompeian ruins; soon the more severe lines of mosaics and the classic cameos of Italy were decorating the ladies of Paris and England.

In the Paris Exposition of 1801, under Napoleon, diamonds were banned in jewelry as being associated with the former aristocracy, but many simple styles of jewelry were shown with the current simple classical dress. Classicism in jewelry for this period also included Egyptian styles as they were under the Caesars. At one point, simplicity and classic dress in France reached the height of absurdity when women wore nothing but thin Grecian or Roman draped dresses with girdles under the bosom. To accent the sheerness of their costumes, women sometimes drenched themselves in water, contracted high fevers, and died.

Cameos were a special favorite in the early 19th century, and a contemporaneous issue of the *Journal des Dames* reported that "a lady of fashion wears cameos in her belt, on her necklace, on each of her bracelets, in her tiara . . ." For a short period during this classical mania, rings on toes were revived to go with Roman sandals, and since the mixing of salads was done with fingers, it was important to show rings on several fingers.

In a more moderate form, the simplicity of the classical fashions appealed to American tastes. There is no doubt that once ships brought the much-yearned-for silks and trinkets to luxury-starved American women, there must have been cameos and pearl-outlined brooches and earrings for those who could afford them.

With expanding trade for Americans in the 1830s came prosperity and a burgeoning taste for luxuries. Industrialism was forging ahead spectacularly in England with its numerous colonies, and there was a rapidly growing, prosperous bourgeoisie in France. In America, the great middle class was developing quickly, too. The Victorian Era, with all its innovations, was about to be born. By 1836, Godey's *Lady's Book* mourned the passing of the age of simplicity in a column headed "Philadelphia Fashions":

"When the arts of sculpture and painting, in their fine specimens from the chisels of Greece and the pencils of Italy, were brought into this country [It is most probable that this article was taken from an English journal, since America was in no position to import sculpture or painting from Greece and Italy], taste began to mould the dress of our female youth after their most graceful fashion . . . But a strange caprice

An 18th century silver pendant with marcasites; center, round amethyst; pear-shaped peridot dangle. The introduction of large chandeliers at the end of the 18th century encouraged the manufacture of jewels that sparkled. Marcasites were widely used for shoe buckles as well.

seems now to have dislodged these [Graces] . . . We see immodesty on one side, unveiling the too redundant bosom; on the other, deformity, once more drawing the steeled bodice upon the bruised ribs. Here stands affectation distorting the forms into a thousand unnatural shapes; and there ill taste, loading it with grotesque ornaments, gathered (and mingled confusedly) from Grecian and Roman models, from Egypt, China, Turkey and Hindustan. All nations are ransacked to equip a modern fine lady; and, after all, she may perhaps strike a contemporary *beau* as a fine lady, but no son of nature could, at a glance, possibly find out that she meant to represent an elegant woman."

Indeed the end of one era, and the beginning of another that would bring the most bewildering assortment of fashions in clothing and in jewelry!

Chatelaine made to accommodate a watch of any size. Various "necessaires" were hung from the ends of the chains. Made by Martin, Baskett & Martin, Cheltenham, England, ca. 1850.

Victorian Jewelry
in America
1830 to 1850

by ELIZABETH SCHIFFMAN

UNDER THE ADMINISTRATION of Andrew Jackson, 1829 to 1837, American industry zoomed. After suffering through years of war, internal upheaval, economic setbacks, and piracy at sea, the United States could at last improve the situation of its people at home and expand its contacts and trade abroad. Manufactures grew at a prodigious rate, reaching one billion dollars by 1850. Among the rapidly expanding industries was the manufacture of jewelry.

Before the 1830s, little jewelry was made in the United States (See "Pre-Victorian Jewelry," *Spinning Wheel,* September 1968). *Hunt's Merchants Magazine* reported on the new development in 1839 enthusiastically:

"Scarcely any branch of manufacture has advanced more rapidly and steadily in this country, during the last twenty years, than jewelry. In 1820, it might be said with almost literal truth that nothing of the kind was manufactured in the United States. But now, much the larger part of all the more rich and solid articles are made in this country. There are very good and extensive assortments in the stores, where not a single specimen of foreign jewelry is to be found. Articles of English manufacture are entirely superseded by the superior skill and taste of our workmen; but there are some sorts of work done by the French jewelers which cannot be equalled here."

One must, of course, take this statement with more than a grain of salt. It was a time for flexing cramped muscles, for the oversized legends of Johnny Appleseed and Paul Bunyan, and the rise of the common man. Americans, as pointed out by the English geologist Charles Lyell, were not so much concerned with the past and present as with future achievements.

The larger centers for making jewelry in the 1830s were Philadelphia, New York, Boston, Providence, Newport and Newark. Most of the finest pieces of jewelry were still imported from England and France, or were made by skilled American artisans trained in the European tradition and influenced by European styles. However, the revolutionary mass production of jewelry that had brought prosperity to the industrial city of Birmingham, England, now began to reach these shores. As in textiles earlier, English immigrants and entrepreneurs brought new techniques to America.

Fragile earrings as lacey as snowflakes-minute river pearls sewn with white horsehair onto a backing of cut-out mother-of-pearl and centered with a tiny garnet. English-made sets of river-pearl jewelry were fashionable in the 1840s and 1850s.

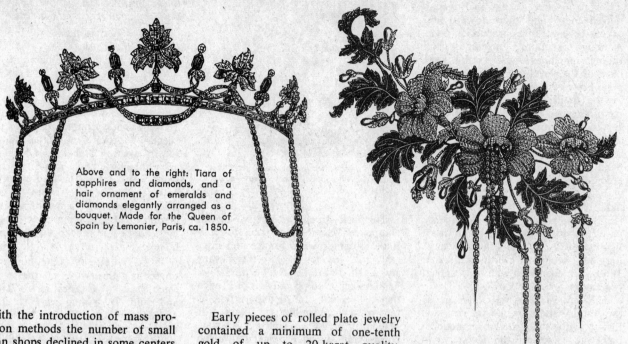

Above and to the right: Tiara of sapphires and diamonds, and a hair ornament of emeralds and diamonds elegantly arranged as a bouquet. Made for the Queen of Spain by Lemonier, Paris, ca. 1850.

With the introduction of mass production methods the number of small artisan shops declined in some centers like Philadelphia, but the manufacture by machine of inexpensive jewelry thrived in Providence, Newark, and in other centers.

Some of the old artisans turned to making new products. In Providence, Jabez Gorham, founder of the Gorham Manufacturing Company, started his trade as jeweler in 1813, and in 1831, turned to the manufacture of silver spoons when Henry L. Webster, a journeyman silversmith, arrived in Providence. Other Providence firms are reported to have grown and prospered in the years from 1825 to 1857. Many men who had started business with just their hands and ingenuity, owned large shops, imposing homes, and substantial bank accounts.

Not only was trade prosperous for owners, but for employees as well. A report from Providence in 1850 states that "no mechanical industry paid as high wages as the jewelry business. Five dollars a day for a skilled workman was not unusual, and some who worked by the piece made as much as ten dollars."

Among the outstanding Poor Richard success stories is that of Thomas H. Lowe, who from the age of nine worked on jewelry in Birmingham, England, where he learned the manufacture of rolled, or "sweat" plate. In 1848, Mr. Lowe arrived in Providence, and in a short time headed a thriving business in rolled plate jewelry. In this ingenious process, a bar of gold with silver alloy was clamped on a heavier bar of composition metal. Intense heat was applied, which "sweated" out the silver in the gold alloy, and with the addition of borax, fused the two metal bars, which were then rolled down to any thickness desired.

Early pieces of rolled plate jewelry contained a minimum of one-tenth gold of up to 20-karat quality. (Twenty-four karat gold is "fine," or pure gold; 20-karat equals 20/24ths of fine gold; 14-karat, the most commonly used in the United States is 14/24ths fine gold.) Toward the latter part of the nineteenth century, with quantity taking precedence over quality, the average rolled plate was about one-thirtieth gold and the quality of gold had worked down to 10-karat and even lower.

By 1860 electrometallurgy was introduced which opened up an even greater market for mass-producing jewelry. It enabled manufacturers to turn out ornaments with a thin coating of gold, priced within the reach of almost everyone.

The tendency of the jewelry indus-

(Please turn the page)

Serpent brooch of 18-karat gold and cobalt-blue enamel. French, ca. 1840. The serpent theme, ever-recurring as a jewelry design from ancient times, was especially popular in the mid-19th century after Prince Albert presented Queen Victoria a serpent ring as a wedding band. Collection Rita Benson.

A superb demi-parure of carved coral (ca. 1840). The soaring angel brooch has an attached swinging wreath of roses, buds and leaves. The earring stubs are the heads of angels. Coral jewelry was in fashion longer than any other kind of jewelry in the 19th century. Most of the carvings came from Italy. Collection Mrs. Raymond E. Dietz.

try, both in America and in England, moved more and more towards inexpensive and mass-produced goods. Although stamping machines and rolling machines were taking over most of the jewelry work, even rolled plate brooches, which were turned out by the thousands each day in some factories, were hand-engraved. A number of these, among them the hollow shell brooches, can be found today, some with a bit of enamel, others with hand-faceted imitation or semiprecious stones, and most of them with lovely swirls and whorls of hand chasing.

The growth of the Providence jewelry industry is reflected in these figures: 1832, 27 establishments turning out products worth $228,253; 1860, 86 factories with an annual production of $3,006,678.

The key year in the expansion of the jewelry industry in America was linked with that stirring announcement that swept the country in 1849—the discovery of gold in California. Before that time, little gold had been mined in the United States. The total annual production in 1841 was only $529,605; most of the ore coming from North Carolina and Georgia; the United States Mint was dependent on foreign coins for half its gold coinage. Just nine years later, the first year after the gold discovery, production jumped to $14,000,000, and in 1850 reached $50,000,000.

Despite the availability of gold to spur the jewelry industry, there was little originality of design in America, as pointed out in *Godey's Lady's Book* in 1848. Under the title, "The Arts of Design and Their Influence on the Mechanic Arts of this Country," Beaumont called for an improvement of American design in all manufactures, including jewelry, and pointed out that both in England and France schools of design were supported by the government. He urged that "such a course might be imitated with benefit, either by the government of the United States or by the Smithsonian Institution," and chided Americans for boasting about progress while there remained "so many matters of general utility we know little or nothing of."

Even *Hunt's Merchants Magazine* which had sanguinely reported in 1839 the vast superiority of American jewelry over most imports, felt compelled to confess, by 1853, that American gold articles were nearly worthless in Paris. In an article quoting the *New York Times*, the magazine cautioned readers that unless a government mint imprint on gold articles was instituted in the United States, as practiced in France, people should beware, since "all is not gold that glitters."

Rose pin with leaves of pave flat, or table-cut diamonds, and coral bud. Made in France, ca. 1850.

The lack of native creative design compelled American women to continue looking toward France and England for fine jewelry in the newest styles. In 1844, *La Revue des Deux Mondes* reported proudly from France that a "regular annual exportation of ten or twelve millions (francs) of goldsmith's work, trinkets, jewelry, corals, and plated articles, shows the esteem which foreigners have for our work." A substantial portion of these articles found their way to the United States and Mexico.

Fashion plates in *Godey's* and other women's magazines almost unanimously mentioned Paris as their source, and *Godey's* prided itself on adapting these fashions to American life and tastes. However, European fascination with radical change in style was often contagious, and articles of clothing, accessories, and jewels that were more suitable to the regal courts and palaces of London and Paris found their way into the modest drawing rooms of Boston and Philadelphia through the pages of *Godey's*.

The European rage for *feronnieres* was reflected in that magazine's fashion plate for November, 1842. This unlikely jewel was a cord or chain worn around the head which suspended a jewel in the center of the forehead. The ubiquitous chatelaine, a ring attached to the watch chain from which dangled all sorts of trifles, was another trinket from abroad that somehow suited the romantic mood of American women in this period, if it did not suit their surroundings.

Starting in the 1840s, *Godey's* reported on the elegance of Victoria's court, where ladies wore tiaras of sapphires and diamonds, rubies, and emeralds. For home consumption, however, a columnist, in a more practical mood, cautioned readers that "on the matter of jewelry, we have seen those who ought to know better, wear a 'pin'—as American ladies say, or *brooch*, as it should be called—of one description and bracelets of another. For instance, a cameo brooch, one of the pink ones and

topaz bracelets of yellow or purple. Nothing could be in worse taste."

In 1849, perhaps under the influence of the Gold Rush, *Godey's* predicted that shoe buckles of "diamonds, turquoise, and real pearls, will soon be sparkling on the pretty little feet for which Philadelphia ladies are so distinguished." *Sartain's Magazine*, in 1850, was less ebullient in noting the "renewed prevalence of the old fashion of wearing bracelets of black velvet ribbands, and bracelets of red wool, knit so as to be an imitation of coral." These were worn fastened with a clasp of steel or marcasite, "from which two long ends depend." No doubt, a cheap imitation of tassels!

In 1837, Tiffany's, the house synonymous with jewelry in America, was established by Charles Lewis Tiffany and John B. Young as a stationery and "fancy goods" store. In 1841, a new partner, Mr. J. L. Ellis, inaugurated the jewelry department as a result of a trip to Europe. At first, the jewelry sold was imitation, but in 1844 the firm started its investment in gold jewelry. In 1848-49 Tiffany, Young & Ellis were listed in the *Mercantile Register* as manufacturers of jewelry and silverware.

Although the growing American middle class had more money to spend than ever before, there were still vestiges of traditional puritanical restraint. The jewels and gems most popular among American women of the 1840s were the following:

Turquoise and diamonds were much in demand; however, the latter were relegated mainly to elderly ladies "whose husbands are retired from business."

The chatelaine, which dangled seals, miniature fans, shoes, coral heads, ivory and coral hands, etc. Complete sets of ornaments—parures—consisting of necklace, earrings, bracelet, ring, brooch, and sometimes a tiny watch.

The distinctly British jewels of river pearls, minute pearls, sewn with white horsehair onto a backing of cut-out mother-of-pearl, forming beautiful, fragile designs.

Antique carved corals and cameos. Both corals and cameos remained fashionable for long periods in the nineteenth century.

Smaller watches were much in favor, and long chains were out.

Buckles for belts, enamelled or chased, in silver or gold, were in universal use.

In this period, first mention was made of American cameos, fashioned by "Mr. Peabody" in Philadelphia who was producing "excellent likenesses of Philadelphia gentlemen."

Mosaic demi-parure in the style made popular by
Castellani, ca. 1850. Pieces of suitable shaded
colored marble were inlaid in black onyx to form
the design. Note the Etruscan type filigree on the
gold frames. Collection Forestine Marcia Heath.

Victorian Jewelry in America
1850 to 1865

by ELIZABETH SCHIFFMAN

BY THE 1850s, American restraint
in taste started to give ground to
the overwhelmingly diverse styles
being made in great quantities in Victorian England. For the more cau-
tious, the omnipresent cameo remained in full favor, especially those
made of coral surrounded by pearls.
For ball costume wear, diadems and
necklaces were formed of small coral
cameos, but the most costly were the
onyx cameos surrounded by diamonds.

The shape of many jewels in the
mid-century departed from the simpler balanced designs of former
periods, and resembled in many ways
the intricate swirls of hand-engraving.

Flower jewels of all kinds came
into widespread use. In the fine jewel
category, flowers were made with
precious and semi-precious gems:
daisies of sapphire and diamonds,
heart's-ease in amethyst and diamonds, roses of coral and diamonds.

Buttons assumed jewel status with
materials of carved lava, turquoise
and gold, jet and gold, coral and
mosaics. Most astonishing was a set
of buttons composed of beads formed
by woven balls of human hair clus-
tered around a center of diamonds

and mounted in gold.

For mourning, the oval hair brooch
usually surrounded by small jets or
pearls was the only ornament displayed "as a principle of good taste,"
Godey cautioned.

To help those subscribers too far
from centers where they could obtain
the lovely fashions described by
Godey's, a mail-order service was instituted in the 1850s that offered
jewelry among other items such as
bonnets, corsets, and gold pens.
Jewelry came from Warden's or Caldwell's in Philadelphia, and the choice
of the item remained with Godey's
agent.

Combs were important in the
1860s, since all women wore their
hair long and hair ornamentation was
in many respects the most notable
part of an elaborate toilet. After the
feronniere had outlived its popularity,
the French paper Moniteur observed
that "Headdresses are nearly always
round . . . a mixture of velvet, gold
and silver ribbon, pearls, and even diamonds. We have seen some . . .
with gold buckles, long plats of velvet
intermixed with chainettes, crescents,
and gold stars, which are scattered

about the hair in a thousand different
manners. . . ."

In 1861 Godey's noted the wide
selection of combs available in this
country: "Gold combs are . . . very
fashionable this winter. . . . Some of
the newest have tops either plain or
set with pearls; others are ornamented
with Byzantine and Greek design in
burnished gold on a dead ground.
Combs have also been made in coral,
diamonds, and pearls, with dendelo-
ques attached."

No event in the nineteenth century
did more to influence the design of
jewelry than the uncovering of vast
treasures in Pompeii, southern Italy,
between 1806 and 1814. First to employ these magnificent old designs
were the imaginative French jewelers,
who turned out fine mosaics in imitation of the ancient craftsmen. Taking
their cue from the French, Italian
craftsmen revived their ancient art
with vigor. From 1814 to 1851, For-
tunato Pio Castellani of Rome produced his outstanding examples of fine
jewelry, including mosaic inlay and
Etruscan filigree.

The outstanding characteristic of
Ancient Etruscan gold work was the

**414
Jewelry**

use of minute granules of gold on a smooth gold base to form lacy filigree patterns. From at least the Fourth Century B.C., Etruscans of west-central Italy were widely known for their skill in metalwork, but the secret of how they fused gold granules to the face of their jewelry without melting the granules had been lost to modern times. Castellani, after much unsuccessful experimentation, heard that there were still some workmen in a mountainous and remote Umbrian village in central Italy who had retained the art. He searched until he found them and brought them to Rome to teach his own artisans this lost skill. Travelers who visited Rome from all over the world purchased these lovely pieces from Castellani or from the many other shops that sprang up. Today, these brooches, earrings, and bracelets can occasionally be found in America, exquisite souvenirs of a long-past European tour.

Romantic interest in the Middle Ages and the Renaissance was another strong influence on jewelry design of the 1830s to the 1860s. The popularity of the romantic novels of Sir Walter Scott in England and Victor Hugo in France heightened antiquarian forms and values. In England, public buildings were erected during the 1830s in the earlier Tudor Gothic style (e.g., the Houses of Parliament), and it was natural that jewelry, too, took on antique romantic forms. Madame de Barrera, writing in Paris, recalled that in France "the Middle Age put the Greek and Roman style to flight . . . Nothing was seen but chevalieres (signet rings) and chatelaines. . . ." In England, women added to this list of appurtenances the *cordeliere* (a long beaded girdle from which the chatelaine was often suspended) and the *ferronniere.*

The French jeweler Froment-Meurice (1820–1855), thought to be the first to utilize medieval themes and designs, was acclaimed in England as well as in France. A pioneer of new and free expression in design, he might be called the precursor of the arts and crafts movement in England and the art nouveau movement in France. People, animals, buildings, foliage—all were grist for this artist's mill. Victor Hugo became so entranced with Froment-Meurice's work that he dedicated a typically romantic poem to him:

> *We are brothers: the flower
> Fashioned by two arts,
> The poet is sculptor;
> The sculptor is poet.*
>
> *On arms and neck
> You make of your dreams
> Statues of jewels,
> Palaces of gems.*

Although most new designs were born in Paris, great credit should be given English jewelers of this period. Many of the English interpretations of French designs were impeccably executed in an even finer finish than the original. England also produced a greater variety in improvisation on French themes and a considerably greater quantity of jewels than did France, largely because English coffers were full and its empire expanding while France was still plagued by political uncertainty and an impoverished treasury. Furthermore, the discovery of gold in Australia in 1851, just two years after the California discovery, brought sufficient quantities of materials for the burgeoning jewelry industry. Between the time of The Great London Exposition of 1851 and the close of the century, all British arts were spurred to new heights, placing that country among the leaders in the world in fine design and excellence of execution of jewelry.

Queen Victoria has come to symbolize all manner of articles produced during her reign from 1837 to 1901; indeed, she symbolizes a whole style of life. From her marriage to Prince Albert in 1839, when he presented her a wedding band in the form of a serpent, through her lengthy widowhood of forty years, and her use of jet and onyx during that period, the world watched and emulated this monumental little woman. From elegant drawing rooms in London to far-away American farms, serpent rings, and jet and onyx brooches appeared on fingers and bosoms, Albert chains took their place on men's vests, and nearly a whole century of jewelry of the most varied forms was given the name Victorian.

Second only to Queen Victoria in influence was the Empress Eugenie of France. The last of the women to set elaborate court styles in that country, Eugenie fashions were copied by the French and English and American women. In the 1860s, after she and her husband, Napoleon III, hoped to create a popular image of themselves by instituting a more liberal rule, Eugenie reflected the political change by a turn to simplicity in dress.

Godey's, then with a special social and fashion reporter in France, re-

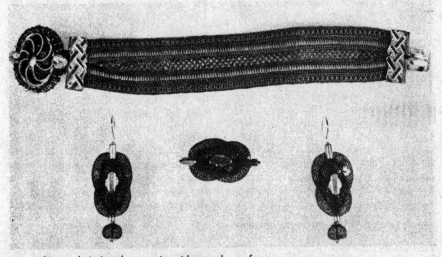

Woven human hair jewelry was in widespread use from the 1840s through the Civil War. Much of the weaving was "do-it-yourself." Above: Bracelet with unusually intricate weave and gold clasp; brooch and earrings of twisted hair tubes and gold. American, ca. 1850.

layed the news directly from Paris in 1863 that the Empress' last soiree of the season saw her dressed unostentatiously in "a simple dress of white muslin . . . without other trimming than the long floating ends of a wide pale blue sash; her sole ornament consisted of eight rows of magnificent orient pearls. . . . Instead of the gorgeous parures . . . flowers most suited to the season are now the sole ornaments admitted; and if a few sparkling diamonds do venture to show themselves, they must do so merely as adjuncts to the more simple imitations of nature. . . ."

The most sobering effect on American tastes came with the outbreak of the Civil War. The use of hair jewelry, perhaps better classified as both folk art and jewelry, received great impetus as wives, sweethearts, and friends in parting left with each other a lock of their hair made into various ornaments. *Godey's* had advertised the sale of hair jewelry for many years, and so popular had it become, that as early as 1850 detailed instructions were given on do-it-yourself methods. Advertisements for the sale

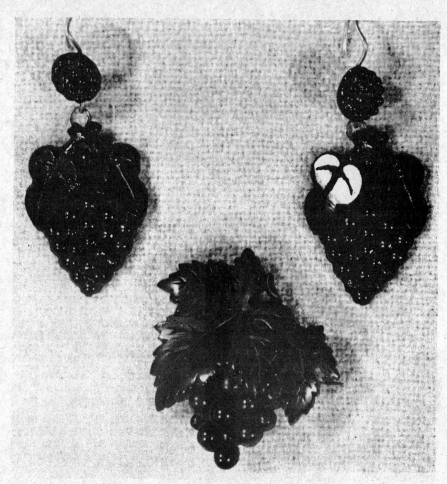

Jet earrings and composition brooch in the popular grape motif. American, ca. 1870. Black jewelry was widely used for costume wear as well as for mourning from the 1850s until the close of the Victorian period.

of hair jewelry directly from *Godey's* continued throughout the Civil War, with breastpins, earrings, bracelets, and a variety of other ornaments priced from $1.50 to $15. Hair for these was supplied by the customer. (See Hair Work Jewelry, SW apr '65.)

The most notable effect of the Civil War on jewelry styles was the increased use of black jewelry—jet, enamel, French glass, onyx, and composition materials—not only for brooches, combs and earrings, but also for elaborate dress trimmings. This somber mood coincided with the fashionable black jewelry being widely used in England in sympathy with Queen Victoria's widowhood.

With the end of the Civil War came release from the mood of mourning and from the few old remnants of puritanical simplicity. What at one time would have been scorned by *Godey's* as lacking in taste because of the too profuse use of jewels is, in this early post-war description of an English reception, praised:

"The display of precious stones seems to become (in) each Drawing Room more remarkable for the extent and costliness. The wearers are no longer satisfied with a few simple decorations, but shower upon themselves Danae fashion, a very rain of jewels. . . . Lady Edith Abney Hastings wore, in addition to a very tasteful and gorgeous display of jewels, the graceful novelty of diamond epaulettes. . . ."

Rolled plate, machine-made stamped shell brooches. Top brooch with enamelled leaves. Although machine-made in great quantities, each brooch was finished with hand engraving.

Gold repousse brooch, white and cobalt-blue enamel, large off-center garnet with oriental pearls. American, ca. 1850. The shape of much jewelry in the 1850s departed from the precisely balanced forms of the pre-Victorian period and resembled in many ways the swirls and whorls of fanciful engravings.

HAIR WORK JEWELRY

by LILLIAN BAKER CARLISLE

IN THE 1850s and 1860s, hair jewelry was the darling of fashion. Not only was it considered suitable for young ladies as "first" jewelry, but hair bracelets, with gold and black enamel clasps, and matching brooches, enclosing a braid of hair, were allowable as "second mourning" jewelry.

In the 18th and early 19th centuries, after a funeral, mourning rings were often presented to the immediate family and dearest friends of the deceased. These were frequently fashioned of plaited hair of the departed, or were of gold with a ringlet of hair enclosed in a little locket-type setting. Mourning pins, composed of hair mounted on ivory in designs featuring weeping willows, tombs, trees, etc., were also very fashionable. Even as late as 1856, a Madame L. Kampmann of Philadelphia advertised in Godey's that she would furnish such breastpins for $12 each.

Now that dresses are cut away from the throat more than for many years past, necklaces are once more in vogue. Hair necklaces are made in transparent globules or beads and united in a continuous chain, or separated by a gold bead, either plain or chased with a handsome gold clasp. Pendants of hair are almost necessary to this style of necklace. One of the most effective, and apparently most simple, is a cross woven of hair . . . suspended on a narrow black velvet ribbon, a band which always enhances the purity of a white throat and neck. –"Fashion Chit Chat," Godey's *Lady's Book,* 1855.

Hair ornaments and mourning jewelry were equally popular in Europe and England. The 1855 London Directory listed 3 merchants who

Brooch of hair work mounted on ivory, under glass; the 5 plumes represent the 5 daughters of Caroline and Samuel Newman, professor at Bowdoin College, 1820-1839; youngest daughter born 1834. *Nat'l Society DAR Museum.*

were large importers of hair from the Continent; 17 hair manufacturers; and 24 artistes or workers in hair (termed hair jewellers or device-workers) who elaborated the hair of deceased friends and relatives into memento mori such as rings, brooches, earrings, chains, and other ornaments.

Godey's *Lady's Book* endorsed the fashion of hair jewelry and made it easy to acquire. In 1855, the fashion editress offered to accommodate any lady wishing hair made up into jewelry upon receipt of the hair and the price for making. The charges listed as: Breastpins from $4 to $12; earrings from $4.50 to $10; bracelets from $5 to $15; rings from $1 to $2.

Later that year, "Faith, Hope and Charity" charms, appended to ladies' hair fob-chains, were introduced; necklaces ($4.50 to $7) and fob-chains ($4 to $8) were added; and more elaborate rings, costing $3, and necklaces, costing as much as $15, were advertised.

Orders for hair work poured into the Philadelphia office. To notify subscribers that their orders had been forwarded, the fashion editress each month listed the things she had dispatched the previous month. A tally of the hair ornament shipments during the years 1855 through the 1860s proves how enormously popular this type of jewelry was.

Beginning in January 1861, to meet the demand for novelties, Godey's published monthly engravings featuring three or four new designs in hair work jewelry that could be ordered through their office. Prices also went up; fob chains were now listed at $6 to $14. During this time, hair studs, ($5.50 to $11 the set) and sleeve

Hair Jewelry at Sheldon Museum, Middlebury, Vermont: Handsome full-sized bracelets such as Nos. 1 and 2, above, required hair 20" to 24" in length. For bracelets worked in pieces, united by slides or caps linked together, No. 3, hair 12" long would suffice. "Snake" bracelets, No. 4, required hair 30" long; plait for this was formed over tube 1¾" diameter. Nos. 5, 6, 7, 8 were watch fob chains; No. 8 has been doubled in length by using chased gold slide to join two shorter lengths. Watch fob, No. 9, shows plait of hair inside glass-topped locket; hair shorter than 3-4" was used in this manner. (Joining hair was tedious and unsatisfactory; each hair had to be separately fastened to the one it was destined to lengthen and knots ruined the smooth appearance of hair work.) Brooch, No. 10, required 8" hair. Necklace, No. 11, of "bubble" beads separated by tiny gold slides and ornamented with hair cross was one of the most expensive illustrated in Godey's; cost $15 to have made up in 1861.

buttons ($6.50 to $11 the set) were added to the inventory.

The hairwork jewelry sold through Godey's was described as a superior product, graceful in design and durable in quality. The gold in the mountings was of a warm reddish tone which contrasted beautifully with the intricate twists and plaits of the hair. Exquisite and incredibly fine chasing was used to decorate the gold mountings.

One had to take on faith that the hair sent in was the same hair used in making up the device. After Godey's began accepting orders for hair jewelry, the subject was never discussed in their mail order column, but no doubt it nagged at the minds of many of the wearers of this jewelry. Perhaps this is one of the reasons why, beginning in February 1859, Godey's commenced a series on "The Art of Ornamental Hair-Work."

Made at Home

The first two articles were devoted to the apparatus, and those following covered directions for working up 17 different braids or plaits. The series was introduced with this paragraph:

"The objects which can be made in hair are more numerous than is generally supposed. An ingenious hair-worker will think of many little domestic articles which could be either made of hair or ornamented with it. The following list contains some of its commonest applications and may suggest other applications of it: Bracelets, brooches, earrings, rings, chains, necklaces, shawl-pins, cravat,pins, purses, bags, book-markers, pencil-cases, studs, stud-chains, scent-bottles, walking-sticks, and riding whips."

The series was well illustrated with engravings showing the apparatus and the methods of lining up the strands of hair to form the different plaits. Essentially, the apparatus consisted of a small work table; thread; scissors, knitting needles, cedar pencil, or brass tubes; lead bobbins; and the hair itself.

The work table could be made from a bandbox turned upside down or even the top part of a man's high hat. The knitting needles, brass tubes or pencils were the molds around which the work was woven; the diameter of the mold setting the size of the finished plait. The hair, laid across the work table in pre-arranged patterns and hooked through the center of the table, was held in even tension by the weight of the bobbins throughout the actual braiding of the plaits.

A sketch of the bobbin was included in case the hair worker decided to cast her own lead weights; alternatives were also given — little calico bags filled with shot or a penny, or even lead bullets drilled with holes to accommodate the thread binding the tress of hair.

By alternating, crossing, and intertwining the strands of hair in a regular pattern, the braided network was

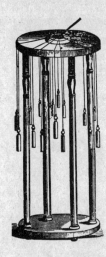

Hair work table (Lady's Book, Dec. 1850) shows individual strands of hair lying across table, held in tension by lead weights attached to them by pack thread. Bobbins weigh between ½ to ¾ oz. each; hair work plait formed over brass tube projecting from center of table.

formed around the brass tube or knitting needle mold. With the hair work fastened off, but still on the mold, it was boiled for 15 minutes, then dried before the fire. Afterwards the mold was withdrawn, and the finished work turned over to a jeweller for mounting.

The 1859 series was not the first material published by Godey on hair work. In 1850 and 1851, Lady Book carried three articles on this subject with directions for chains, bracelets, rings, and earrings. In the case of earrings, it was pointed out that it was necessary to form these over wooden molds. Three types of earring molds were illustrated and it was suggested a paper or cardboard pattern be made of them. The pattern could then be turned over to a wood-turner who could quickly produce the molds from the cardboard models.

In introducing the 1850 article, Godey's came to grips with the problem of "whose hair are you

wearing" by pointing out that by acquiring a knowledge of the art of hair work, ladies could themselves manufacture the hair of beloved friends and relatives into various devices, and thus insure that they were actually wearing the memento they prized, and not a fabric substituted for it, "as we fear has sometimes been the case."

These articles also included a do-it-yourself plan for finishing off the work. This was accomplished by covering the ends of the hair work with enough cement to fill the hollow in the fastening of gold work prepared to receive it, and inserting the finished hair plait while the cement was hot and melting. The cement, half yellow wax and half shellac, melted together and well amalgamated, was rolled into sticks to cool, and when needed, the sticks were warmed again. The little gold clasps, snaps, slides, and other things requisite for finishing were ordered from jewellers.

It is not surprising that hair work was one of the more popular art recreations of the era. As Lady Book pointed out: "Of the various employments for the fingers lately introduced among our countrywomen, none is, perhaps, more interesting than hair work—a recent importation from Germany, where it is very fashionable. Hitherto almost exclusively confined to professed manufacturers of hair tinkets, this work has now become a drawing-room occupation, as elegant and as free from all annoyances and objections of litter, dirt, or unpleasant smells, as the much-practiced knitting, netting, and crochet can be, while a small handkerchief will at any time cover the apparatus and materials in use."

Photos by Horace Eldred.

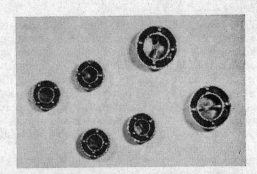

Hair Work Memento Mori—Glass-covered locket contains hair of "Janet Young Warren 1799-1839," according to engraving on back; at Sheldon Museum. Gold-cased stud set, made by Charlotte Sever for her brother, the Rev. Winslow W. Sever, of their father's hair; one stud is engraved "C.M. to W.W.S.," another "J.W.S. died May 21, 1863"; hair braid is slipped under minute gold bridges and cemented in place; collection Mabel Brownell. *Below:* Bookmark, beige moire ribbon with decoration of elaborately tied hair braid sewed under salmon ribbon bows; also at Sheldon Museum.

ANTIQUE STICKPINS

by ELIZABETH SCHIFFMAN

THE ELEGANT Edwardian man has reappeared with his lengthened jacket, nipped waist, muttonchop sideburns, long locks and, at his sparkling best, with a stickpin in his wide tie. Perhaps he wears a ruby-eyed lion biting a pearl, or a diamond-eyed ferocious dog, or the ubiquitous loveknot centered with an opal or pearl. The Edwardian period, between 1901 and 1910, brought welcome color to the drably-dressed men of the Victorian era, and raised stickpins to the peak of fashion.

The origin of stickpins goes back some centuries. During the early 17th century Englishmen and American colonial men occasionally decorated their ruffs and bands with rosettes of ribbon and even with an occasional jewel. Later, the cravat—great grandaddy of our modern tie—came into custom, but was replaced by the stock. Both the cravat and stock were used intermittently over long periods of time until the middle of the 19th century.

For a period around the turn of the 17th century the Steinkirk came into use. Named after the Battle of Steinkirk, in 1692, it clearly marks the inception of more frequent use of jewels on men's neckwear. During the Battle of Steinkirk, French officers, accustomed to an elaborate toilet, were forced to dress quickly to meet their enemy; they wrapped their

A handsome pin designed by Mr. A. William Ball and made by Miss Emma di Lauro from a keepsake brooch, family stickpins and rings. Rings were used with their shanks as stems for the two lower pieces on each side. Gems include pearls, turquoise, diamonds, opals, rubies, amethyst and moonstone. Collection Mrs. A. William Ball.

cravats hurriedly around their neck and pulled the ends through a buttonhole or brooch. The original Steinkirk brooches were, no doubt, buckles that had lost their tongues, but this function of a tie clasp was so serviceable that special Steinkirk brooches were soon made in quantity. These brooches, which can occasionally be found, are usually an oval band with a single bar attached from end to end. They were often embossed, or decorated with flat garnets, pearls, topaz, crystals, or marcasites.

By the 18th century, American men frequently wore small brooches on their stocks. It was not easy for men to undertake the delicate task of fastening a brooch, so the development of a brooch on a simple straight vertical pin was the obvious answer to this dilemma. A miniature of the 1820s shows a finely-dressed gentleman wearing in his stock a small memorial brooch mounted on a straight pin to form what appears to be a stickpin. Some French jewelry collections show stickpins that date back to the 18th century, but these were worn mainly by women to fasten scarfs. During the mid-19th century and into the 20th century, men and women wore stickpins on their hunting stocks, many in the shape of the pursued fox or the pursuing dog.

Even the drably-dressed Victorian man used a simple pearl stickpin on

A trio of insect stickpins. Left to right: Coral fly on coral branch; fine garnet and oriental pearl fly; an actual beetle set in 18-karat engraved gold setting. Author's collection.

A magnificent stickpin of opal on matrix, the matrix forming the face, neck, shoulders and necklace, and the opal carved into an elaborate hairdo. Touches of opal show through the matrix on the necklace. Collection Mrs. George Rearick.

adulation for nature were the stickpins and other jewelry made with hard-bodied beetles set in gold. (See illustration.)

Some collectors today seek a theme: cameos made of shell, stone or coral; reverse paintings on glass; glass-enclosed hair designs; Art Nouveau enamelled flowers; sulfides; dogs; serpents; and hundreds of other available motifs. Some women collect stickpins to make unique brooches, clips or bracelets. (See illustration.)

Unfortunately, there also exist imitation stickpins and recent reproductions. Imitations can often be detected by examining the reverse side to see if the long pin is connected to a round patch soldered to an old button, odd cuff link or stud. Although many of these imitations are handsome and made of materials possessing sufficient antique interest, they cannot qualify as true stickpins. Recent copies are more difficult to detect

since the use of karat marking was fairly common on stickpins during the early part of the 20th century—which is rather surprising for a period when karat markings were not frequently used.

Intricate workmanship, the once-popular gems with cabachon top and brilliant undercut, the pinstem with an additional pointed section on top of the stem (a primitive form of safety catch), interchangeable threaded stickpin heads (found mainly among English stickpins), fine mosaics (usually Italian or French), deeply cut classical cameos, and glass-covered human hair designs, are all some of the distinct characteristics of early stickpins.

Fortunately, many genuine stickpins are still available in a wide range of prices from less than a dollar for some common brass or metal ones, to several hundred dollars or more for those with sizeable precious gems.

A green enamel frog with red enamel spots is flanked on either side by two Art Nouveau stickpins of gold and pearls. Collection Mrs. J. Edward Clouse.

his dark tie, but it is essentially from the 1890s into the 1920s that a wealth of imagination and design created stickpins that are a collector's delight. Art Nouveau pins abounded—some as abstract forms of flowing lines, others as the perennial woman's face surrounded with flowing tresses. Flowers, insects, animals, birds, reptiles—all of nature lent itself to the designs as well as to the materials. Gold, silver, wood, bronze, enamel, hair, shell, glass, and all the gems imaginable, contributed to these delightful miniature works of art. There was also, of course, the Diamond Jim Brady type of man who favored huge diamonds and other stones for the sake of the gems themselves.

Among the oddities of the middle to late 19th century are the signed, and often dated, enamel portraits of dogs and foxes made by English artists, some of whom were painters of stature. Dogs "sat" for portraits, and foxes, too—the latter, we hope, safely stuffed for their pose! Typical also of the 19th-century's romantic

A pair of bracelets made with stickpin heads. Gems include diamonds, turquoise, pearls, garnets, rubies, topaz and sapphires. Note baroque pearl "roadrunner" and the dangling turquoise parrot. Private collection.

Photographs courtesy Dickinson College Department of Art.

LOOKING THROUGH old family albums of photographs taken in the 19th century, one sometimes notices a splendidly attired ancestor sporting an outstanding example of mosaic jewelry.

Mosaics date back to the 12th Egyptian Dynasty, around 1900 B.C., but the use of mosaics as miniatures in jewelry did not become popular until the beginning of the 19th century.

In ancient times mosaics were made of pebbles, light and dark stones forming the patterns. Later, marble, semiprecious stones, shells, glass, terra cotta, mother-of-pearl or enamels, were cut into proper shapes, called

tessarae, and attached to a background with cement or putty to form decorative floors, ceilings, and walls. This art form was especially valuable for its permanence of color and durability.

The earliest mention of mosaic artisans dates to the 4th century A.D. in an edict from Diocletiān mentioning the wages of "lapidarious structor" and other mosaic craftsmen, but Italy had already been the chief center for mosaic production for five centuries. It was not until the Grand Tours of the late 18th century that mosaics appeared in miniature form, first serving as small decorative plaques in furniture. Some of the early miniature

designs were inspired by mosaics produced by ancient artisans such as Sosos, a master artist who worked in Pergamon, the Hellenistic center of culture from the 3rd to the 2nd century B.C. Sosos was connected with an important school of mosaic craftsmen who have left behind some magnificent examples of workmanship and artistry. Most familiar of his designs are doves drinking from a fountain, a theme used on many a Victorian mosaic or painted brooch.

It is possible that the idea for using miniature mosaics as jewelry was originated by French jewelry craftsmen inspired by early French excavations at Pompeii. A demi-parure of mosaics, dating back to the early part of the 19th century, was made in a manner distinctly different from most Italian pieces *(see Figure 1)*. Unlike the tesserae used in most Italian-made jewelry, each background segment in this set is of uniform, miniscule, square shape, different from the commonly used doubly large and somewhat elongated segments. The subject matter, rather than relating to ancient architectural, floral, or animal forms, which characterize Italian mosaics, is composed of plaques with romantic scenes popularized by the novels of Sir Walter Scott, which were widely read in France. Each of the scenes shows the ruined castles, waterfalls, and shady glens prevalent in Scott's novels. Scott's stories played an important role in the early part of the 19th century in influencing the design of clothing, furniture and buildings, as well as jewelry.

Although some mosaic jewelry was made in England by Italian craftsmen *(see Figure 2)*, Italy was without question the leader in making and selling mosaic jewelry. Europeans and Americans on Grand Tours from the late 18th century to the end of the 19th century, delighted with the minutely detailed jewelry, often wore a piece as a proud souvenir of a visit to Rome or Florence. These brooches, earrings, bracelets, necklaces, cuffbuttons, studs, and tiepins carried detailed pictures of flowers, birds, insects, animals, buildings, and complete panoramic scenes, banded in jet, slate, onyx or glass and framed in gold, silver or gilt *(see Figures 3 and 4)*.

Mosaic beads, sometimes called *millefiori*, (a thousand flowers) since the design was almost always floral, were another curiosity for the traveler. The principle behind the making of beads and other mosaic jewelry was the same—use of separate bits of color in small pieces to create the design. The beads, however, were fused with heat into one entity and polished to create a smooth surface. An American publication, *Merchants Magazine*, of January 1843, describes the distressing circumstances of labor under which these beads were made:

"We saw sheaves of glass waving like . . . [wheat] in the laps of women who sat assorting the vitreous harvest according to size. In another stage a number of men were clipping the long threads into very small bits, the elements of the beads. . . . A very distressing part of the operation was to be seen below, where stood a number of poor wretches . . . [employed] to receive the bits of sifted glass, melt them into beads by means of charcoal and sand, in the midst of dreadful fire-blasts, which they were constantly

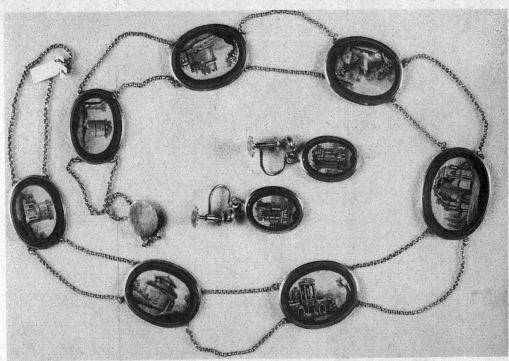

Fig. 1: An unusually fine demi-parure, necklace and earrings, possibly French, ca. 1820. Eartops, originally for pierced ears, were converted in recent years to French backs. The background tesserae in this set are unusually tiny and of uniformly square pieces rather than the usual slightly elongated pieces. The scenes are of the romantic type made popular by the novels of Sir Walter Scott which were widely read in France. Center plaque 1" wide. *Author's collection.*

Fig. 2: Doves—drinking from fountains, fluttering (as above), standing—were a favorite theme for Italian craftsmen making fine mosaic jewelry. This handsome demi-parure of brooch-pendant (the bale detaches when worn as a brooch) and earrings is a fine example of a set that was possibly made in England by Italian craftsmen. The use of 15-karat gold, in which these tesserae are set, is characteristic of England. Brooch 2½" long. *Collection Forestine Marcia Heath.*

Fig. 3: A few outstanding examples of tesserae mosaic workmanship showing examples of Roman architecture and ruins. Top: Mosaic bracelet set in onyx and framed in silver gilt; 7¼" long. Bottom, left to right: A Roman triumphal arch in onyx and gold; a panoramic view of Roman ruins; the Colesium. Center brooch 2¼" wide. *Author's collection.*

Fig. 5: Two superb mosaic bracelets. Top: Florentine, or pietra dura mosaic with inlays of agate, marble, turquoise and carnelian, each plaque set in onyx and framed in granulated gold; 8" long. Bottom: Nosegays of colorful roses are formed with finely inlaid glass tesserae banded in onyx and framed in gold; 7½" long. *Collections Mrs. Edward Clouse and the author.*

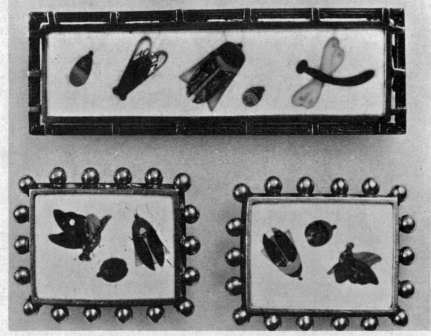

Fig. 7: One might take these as the very examples of the "high-toned bugs" described by Mark Twain. Malachite, lapis lazuli, carnelian, agates and crystal (the transparent wings of the fly), inlaid in white onyx. Top, a barpin, 2" wide; bottom, a pair of cuffbuttons, 1" wide. *Author's collection.*

feeding, and within three feet of which they stood, steaming at every pore." Conditions such as these were typical in many industries in the early days of the industrial revolution and it is in Charles Dickens' novels that one finds the awareness expressed in the description above.

Aside from beads, two kinds of mosaic jewelry were produced in Italy during the 19th century: the aforementioned more or less uniform glass tesserae, and *pietra dura* (hard stone), or Florentine mosaic *(see Figure 5).* This latter type of mosaic jewelry was made popular by Castellani of Rome. As in champleve, the design was cut out and replaced with another substance: in champleve the background was metal and the filler enamel; in *pietra dura* the background was of black onyx, slate, jet or other colored stones, or glass. The filler for Florentine mosaic was small pieces of carnelian, lapis lazuli, malachite, marble, turquoise, or other semi-precious stones, which were cut to fit perfectly into the base material. The pieces of stone were chosen for their varied tints to represent the shading in a petal or the subtle varieties of color in a leaf *(see Figure 6).*

Fig. 6: A beautifully executed Florentine mosaic brooch framed in granulated gold. Note that pieces of marble were carefully cut to fit into place and were selected to show shading of flower petals and leaves; 2¼" wide. *Collection Mrs. Edward Clouse.*

Mark Twain in *Innocents Abroad,* published in 1869, praised the wonderful ability of Florentine mosaic craftsmen: "These artists will take particles no larger than a mustard seed, and piece them together on a sleeve button or a shirt stud, so smoothly and with such nice adjustment of the delicate shades of colour the pieces bear, as to form a pigmy rose with stem, thorn, leaves, petals complete, and all so softly and as truthfully tinted as though Nature had builded it herself. They will counterfeit a fly, or a high-toned bug *(see Figure 7),* or the ruined Coliseum *(see Figure 3),* within the cramped circle of a breastpin, and do

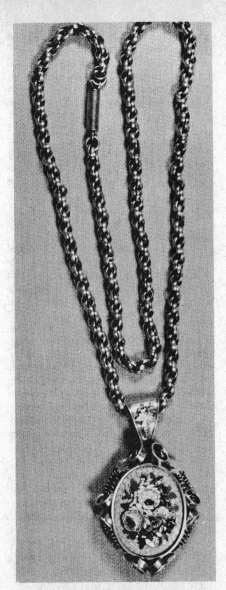

Fig. 4: Flowers were favorite themes for both Florentine and tesserae mosaics. Here, a late Victorian floral pendant in tesserae framed in baroque silver strapwork with a glass locket on the reverse side. Pendant 1½" long. *Collection Mrs. Edward Clouse.*

it so deftly and so neatly that many might think a master painted it." Twain was especially impressed with a table in the school at Florence where the art of mosaic was taught. The top

was made of "some sort of precious polished stone, and in the stone was inlaid the figure of a flute, with bell-mouth and mazy complication of keys. No painting in the world could have been softer or richer; no shading out of one tint into another could have been more perfect." At that time, 1869, the table was priced at $35,000 and required ten years labor on the part of one man. Tables of this superb workmanship can be seen today in the Prado Museum in Madrid and the Louvre in Paris.

Fine pieces of mosaic jewelry are also displayed today in several of the world's leading museums as outstanding examples of 19th century jewelry craftsmanship. With luck, the collector can still discover good quality old necklaces, brooches, earrings, pendants, bracelets, and stickpins of both the tesserae and *pietra dura* variety, but the price has risen substantially in the past several years. Coarser pieces, set in brass and held in place by wire cloisons, are more plentiful and less expensive. These are often a combination of tesserae and sliced flower rods, similar to the rods used in making mosaic beads. Although they were turned out in quantity from the turn of the century to World War II as inexpensive mementos, many were fashioned with considerable artistry and are finer than the brass-backed pieces made and sold in Italy today.

Aside from *millefiori* beads, some of which are still made by the high standards of the past, artistic workmanship on mosaics has suffered a decline. Requiring skill and artistry, the work today is deemed tedious, confining, and poorly paid, so that few people reach the level of expertise attained in the 19th century. Thus, another art of the past is becoming extinct, along with granulation on jewelry, finely painted miniatures for ivory or porcelain brooches, and the making of intricate hair jewelry. This unfortunate situation makes the 19th century tourist's souvenir an increasingly precious collector's item.

Jeweled Butterflies

THE butterfly has long been a popular motif in jewelry design. The mariposa brooch pictured is an early one, with documentary papers from Peru dating it circa 1787. About five inches wide, it is of 18 karat gold, set with twelve old mine diamonds totalling about a karat and a quarter. It was probably worn in the hair as well as for a brooch.

By the mid-1830s, the butterfly motif was found frequently in gold pins set with colored gems, and on pendants in seed pearls, jewels, or gold. In the late 1860s when "insect jewelry" was the vogue, and fashionable ladies were wearing jeweled grasshoppers, dragon flies, beetles, bees and such, butterflies maintained their popularity. Flora and fauna were in the mode then, too — lions, dogs, doves, and snakes, pansies, roses, and violets were among popular motifs for bracelets, necklaces, and earrings, on lockets, bracelet pendants, and bonnet pins.

Margaret Flower in *Victorian Jewelry* reports such extreme 1860–70 novelties as coal scuttles, tongs, hammers, ladders, trowels, even locomotives. Horseshoes, along with miniature saddles and bridles, whips, bits, spurs and stirrups were favored by the sporting set. A fashion reporter in 1880 wrote of such jewelry fancies as a "Delft plate with a gold spoon in it", and a "pea pod half-opened disclosing pearls as peas".

A novelty brooch of 1867 was a gold butterfly fashioned with a tube beneath to hold a flower so that the butterfly appeared poised on it. In the 1880s, safety pins of gold set with jeweled butterflies were something new. Large and elaborate diamond butterflies were particularly enjoyed as shoulder knots, or as ornaments for the elborate chignons, and as late as 1900 were still being used as formal dress hair ornaments.

Claddagh ring by Andrew Robinson.

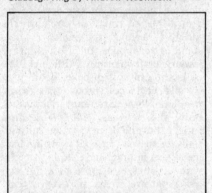

Claddagh ring bearing Dublin Assay Office marks.

The triple Claddagh ring as it is worn. The letter "M" would be the owner's initial.

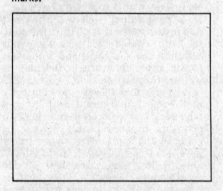

A triple Claddagh ring showing the three sections opened out. When closed the clasped hands meet over the heart engraved with the letter "M."

Irish 19th Century Claddagh Rings

by CYRIL BRACEGIRDLE

AMONG THE VARIED and little known aspects of 19th century Irish metalwork are the Claddagh rings which were made and worn in the Galway region of western Ireland. They were used in the main as wedding rings by the peasantry and were in the form of two hands holding between them a heart surmounted by a crown.

They seem to have come into fashion early in the 19th century but their real origin is lost in the mists of Irish antiquity. In fact, there is a strong argument for the belief that the design came to Ireland from Spain, Galway having a large and prosperous trade with that country throughout most of the 18th century.

A Mr. W. Dillon, in a report to the Galway Archaeological and Historical Society in 1905, mentions a Lieutenant of the British Royal Navy who showed a Claddagh ring to a Spanish jeweller who immediately recognized it as being similar to designs used in Spain.

Old records also mention a similar type of ring called the Munster; but it is suspected that the Munsters were actually made in Birmingham, England, in imitation of the Claddagh.

There was even a similar ring in use among the peasants of Brittany, but this still does not rule out a common origin.

The first designer of Claddagh rings of whom there is any mention, and one of the best known, is George Robinson, a goldsmith who probably came from England and who registered at the Goldsmiths' Hall, Dublin, in 1784. He seems to have begun turning out Claddagh rings just after the turn of the century, stamping them inside the shank with the letters GR. Sometimes there would be other initials also, engraved, not stamped; these would be the initials of the owner.

After the famine years of 1846 and 1847 hundreds of these rings were pawned by the people of Claddagh who needed the money to emigrate to the United States. Many such rings, being unredeemed, were cast into the melting pot by the pawnbrokers and sold for the value of their gold.

In 1873 a silver ring was discovered in Galway. The shank was ornamented but otherwise it bore a strong resemblance to the gold Claddagh ring. Possibly this was an example of a foreign ring which Robinson may well have found and copied.

After George Robinson the next best-known designer was Andrew Robinson who made rings out of melted down gold guineas.

No rings have been found prior to the activities of the two Robinsons, but this does not necessarily mean that there were none, although they might not have been made of gold. It is improbable that the country people of Galway, tenacious as peasants are in adhering to old customs and traditions, should have suddenly and universally adopted a new fashion set by an English goldsmith. It is very likely that the earlier rings were of base metal and were discarded or destroyed when George Robinson came along and set the fashion for wearing rings of gold only.

In 1890 there was found during excavations in Galway a bronze Claddagh ring made roughly from an old coin, some of the lettering of which was still visible. It almost certainly predated the gold ones of George Robinson.

The Claddagh rings became known outside Ireland towards the middle of the 19th century, especially when one was made for Queen Victoria, an incident which brought the charm of the design to outsiders.

The limits of the area over which the ring was worn were, roughly, from the Aran Islands on the east and all through Connemara and Joyce's Country to Galway, and then eastward and southward for not more than 12 miles at the most. The whole district, it should be noted, is one served by Galway as the trade center.

The desire of even the poorest peasant to have the orthodox gold ring for marriage was remarked upon during the latter half of the century. People were willing to stint themselves and save in many ways in order to buy a Claddagh ring.

It is safe to say that 99 percent of Claddagh rings still in existence will bear the five marks in use at the Dublin Assay Office from 1807 to 1890. These are: (1) A crowned harp; (2) Maker's mark; (3) Date-letter; (4) Figure of Hibernia; (5) Head of British sovereign.

Sir Charles Jackson, in his monumental work *English Goldsmiths and their Marks*, has listed approximately 150 goldsmiths at work in this period as having their work assayed at Dublin. Jackson also seems to have made what is almost certainly the most accurate list of the date-letters which seem to be the subject of many errors by other authorities.

The shape of the shield or stamp in which Hibernia appears is a useful guide to dates in the 19th century on account of a number of alterations which were made.

From 1794 to 1810 Hibernia appears in an upright parallelogram with rounded corners. From 1810 to 1821 the shield has an engrailed top and from 1821 to 1827 it is oval. Then followed a rather confusing variation of shapes until 1846 after which it has parallel sides, a straight base with the lower corners hollowed and an invected top. Thereafter the octagonal shape was introduced until 1890, the latest date with which we need be concerned.

MOURNING RINGS

by CLARENCE T. HUBBARD

THE DISTRIBUTION of mourning rings to family and friends of the deceased was a custom practiced by families who could afford to do so in the 16th century, through the 17th, most of the 18th, and revived for a brief period in the mid-19th.

Early wills often show a sum of money set aside for commemorative rings to be distributed to as many mourners as the provisions would allow. Wealthy families might give out several hundred such mementos.

Though most mourning rings were plain gold bands, simply inscribed within the loop with the name of the deceased and the date, some were quite ornate. Creative jewelers often found in them the opportunity to fashion the unusual, even bizarre.

Sometimes a likeness of the one being mourned was inserted, either a cameo type, or in miniature painting. Some rings were enameled in violet, a color associated with funerals. Some showed great ingenuity in symbolization, like one decorated with a skeleton in gold against a black ground. Others had crystals cut to resemble a skull, with a hair of the deceased placed thereunder. Gold threads were often added, and fine filigree gold art work showed up on many.

In the 16th century, mourning rings ran to black enamel and niello, with colored stones, though pearls and diamonds were also included.

The 17th century found mourning rings still in high favor and much more fanciful. The practice of including hair of the deceased came into general use. Usually the hair was set inside a glass case, or in the bezel or center of the ring, glass covered.

In the 18th century, tiny black and white paintings of the deceased began to be used on mourning rings. Either these were made in advance of death or they came to the mourners months later. Sometimes these rings bore verses or inscriptions such as "Death Parts United Hearts."

In contrast to the many macabre themes, a plain gold band, similar to a wedding ring, was discovered in

Mourning rings at Museum of Fine Arts, Boston: American, miniature set in gold, 1788; English ?, gold, vase set in diamonds, 1782. *Below:* American, attrib. to John Ramage; American, gold, 1837; Transylvanian, gold with porcelain.

Connecticut, inscribed inside, "H. Loomis. Obt. April 16, 1742, age 13." This was distributed in memory of Hannah Loomis of Windsor. Of particular interest were the initials, "E. B." which also appeared on the ring, representing Ebenezer Balch, a silversmith in Hartford around 1744.

This mourning ring, and a gold necklace clasp made by John Garner of New London, constitute the only two known pieces of gold jewelry ever made in colonial Connecticut. Both are now on display at the old historical State House in Hartford.

Mourning rings made by noted silversmiths are known, as the one made by Myer Myers, memorializing A. Maria Panet in 1764, and one made by John Burt Lyng of New York, for Mary Marston in 1766.

As late as 1783, a large number of mourning rings was distributed at a funeral in Boston, Massachusetts, and at an earlier funeral there, in 1730, it is recorded that 200 mourning rings were given away. These were gold rings, properly inscribed, devoid of any outlines of palms, skulls, or coffins.

In the revival of the mourning ring custom in the mid-1800s, hair jewelry became especially popular. This seems to have been made for close family rather than for general distribution. Besides rings, hairwork earrings, bracelets, and brooches were made for lady mourners; cuff links and watch fobs for gentlemen.

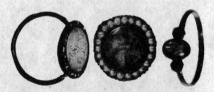

From the Metropolitan Museum, New York: American, gold and enamel, 1762; gold, set with miniature and pearls, 18th-early 19th century; gold, set with glass jewel over hair, and jet.

Mid-Victorian Jewelry
For the Gentleman

by ADA DARLING

Moss agate cuff buttons, Ascot tie pin.

Gold toothpick, shown open.

Gold cigar cutter.

Open face, engraved gold watch.

Silver matchsafe.

THE Victorian gentleman wore black — black suits, overcoats, gaiters, and hats, reserving colored or white vests for formal events. He lightened this decorous choice by the use of rich and elaborate accessories.

The self-respecting head of a household carried a cane, frequently gold-headed, as he strolled to his office. Canes were usually ebony sticks; handles were straight, square crooks, round crooks, or pear heads. Those of gold, or gold plate, were handsomely engraved; pear heads were elaborately embossed. If space in the design permitted, the owner's name was engraved in it.

Men's rings were large and impressive—perhaps an initial outlined in diamonds on a black onyx stone, or a cameo of the tiger-eye variety.

Vest chains were heavy, consisting of two long chains fastened together by a ring which held a short chain with a bar at the end. This bar slipped into a buttonhole in the vest, and the long chains, watch on one end, accessories on the other, were worn across the front to a pocket on each side.

Vest chain accessories were many and varied. For the man who smoked there were gold cigar cutters. There were also gold toothpicks. The one pictured here screws into the handle and can be completely enclosed. Gold pencils and silver pens were often used. Charms hung from a short chain were popular. Sometimes the charm indicated the profession or avocation of its wearer — a horseman might choose a stirrup; a seaman, a "reliable compass." Fraternal emblems were in demand. For those who could afford them, there were large lockets of gold or platinum, finely engraved, flashing with diamonds. No one can deny that the man of the 1860s and 1870s did not put up an impressive front!

Silver match boxes made convenient pocket pieces. There were also tobacco boxes, quite similar to the match box pictured, but a little larger, and opening from the side.

Necessary collar buttons, shirt studs, and cuff buttons became important. Some buttons had solid posts; others separated by pressing on the little buttons on each side. The moss agate cuff buttons shown here are of the latter type. Studs in solid gold or plate, or of diamonds, vied in importance with the watch chain. A close second was the tie pin. The conventional gentleman might select a large but simple Ascot pin like the one pictured; his sportier fellows liked a tie pin as flashing as their studs. All kinds of designs were used--stars, crescents, birds, and wishbones--all jeweled.

Watches for men were thick and heavy, and flippantly called "turnips." Here the engraver did his finest work. Landscape, floral, and conventional designs were equally popular. Many cases were contemporarily listed as "18-K or plump quality."

KITCHENWARES

While usually associated with women's work, early kitchenwares made of wood or metal appeal to men as well as women. There's a warmth about the feel of a burl bowl or wooden spoon that few people can resist. Pewter spoons and plates vie with painted tinwares to capture the attention of kitchenware collectors. Even the late gadgets of the early 20th century are being snatched up by collectors at antiques shops, flea markets and antiques shows. Of late, converting old cast iron kitchen stoves into usable modern ranges has become more widespread.

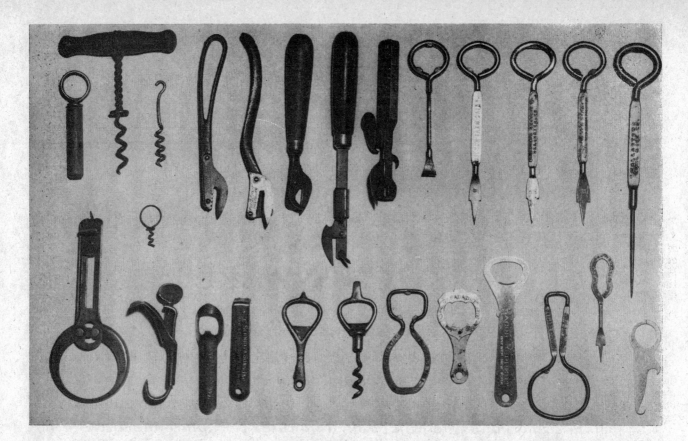

Can and Bottle Openers

by LOUISE K. LANTZ

A DIFFERENT, interesting, and inexpensive hobby is the collecting of bottle and can openers, the older the better. Their shapes and sizes are myriad. A whole collection could be made of just advertising openers. Advertisers range from grocers, pharmacies, and dairies to restaurant suppliers, hotels, green stamp, foodstuffs and ice companies. Patent dated openers are of particular interest because they can be placed in time. Some of the openers are combined with such oddities as spatulas, buttonhooks, pancake turners, spoons, and ice picks.

ILLUSTRATIONS

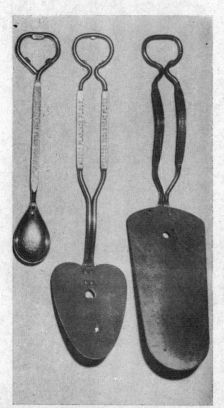

Left to right, top row: ring-handled corkscrew, protected in wood cylinder, advertises a grocer; wooden grip-handled, also grocer's advertisement; simple corkscrew, curved end handy for removing broken cork, also as buttonhook; iron "Peerless," patented Feb. 11, 1890; "Delmonico," blade also patented Feb. 11, 1890, but with thicker, heavier handle differently placed; 19th century opener, bulbous wood handle; modern-looking opener, sold in Sears, Roebuck's 1905 catalog for 9¢, has steel blade, varnished wood handle; multi-opener, patented June 4, 1929, opens round cans, square cans, friction cans, and cork stoppers, has thumb guard; Albert W. Rhine, Inc., Paints-Varnishes-Lacquers give-away, one end to open turpentine bottles, the other, paint cans; the next three have the same patent date, Jan. 26, 1912; one reads "S & H Green Stamps, Your Earned Discount," and "S & H Premiums Always Valuable"; another "Wilton Farm Dairy"; the third, "Neubauer's Grocery and Delicatessen, Portland, Oregon," pointed end was for lifting cardboard lids; heavy cast iron ice pick-bottle opener combination, "Dallastown Coal & Ice Co."

Bottom row: jar opener, "J. C. Forster & Son, Pittsburgh, Pa.," patented Sept. 13, 1910, called "4 in 1"; jar opener with thumbscrew, marked "Victory"; simple opener, "Royal Crown Cola, Best by Taste Test"; common type opener, marked "C. Schmidt & Sons, Inc. Brewers in Philadelphia since 1860"; next two are crude cast iron, one with hole for hanging, one with corkscrew end; hourglass-shaped opener from Star Brewery Company, Vancouver, Washington; fancy little iron opener, "Canada Dry, Champagne of Ginger Ales," in script; ornately embossed aluminum opener, "Jacob Ruppert, Brewer, New York"; type popular with dairies, from Fairfield Western Maryland Dairy; dainty lifter for cardboard lids from York Sanitary Milk Co.; "Handy Pocket Companion," patented Nov. 28, 1905, boasts 2-inch ruler on one side, curved tip serves as buttonhook, too.

Left: Opener-stirrer, "Heathman Hotels for Hospitality," one of many similar examples; heart-shaped flipper, heart cut-out, handle reads "Albers Flapjack Flour and Peacock Buckwheat Flour"; broad turner, patented Nov. 24, 1914, opener handle advertises McLarty's Pharmacy, Old York Road and Franklin Terrace.

Old Mashers and Beaters

by LOUISE K. LANTZ

NO OLDTIME American kitchen was complete without a variety of mashers and at least one good eggbeater and cream whipper. Mashers have been around for centuries, while the crank-style eggbeater is a more modern kitchen tool.

The old American kitchen had huge mashers for making sauerkraut, smaller ones for potatoes and vegetables, and very small ones for mashing, grinding, and powdering spices. They were made of common maple, lovely grained bird's-eye and curly maple, deep brown walnut, or the magnificent red lignum vitae, a hard, heavy wood.

Mashers Pictured—Top Row

The first masher pictured is a common turn-of-the-century wooden-handled wire potato masher. It has a heavy retinned wire twisted shank and a hardwood handle. It was advertised as "the best kitchen utensil ever used," and sold for about 5¢.

The next two mashers are sturdy iron with circular cut-out heads. The first has the added feature of a bottle opener handle, but the handle of the second is much more comfortable to hold. Similar heads were also mounted on wooden handles.

The smallest masher is a spice and vegetable masher. It was especially suited to small portions of vegetables for a young child. Its shape is both attractive and efficient.

The four medium-size mashers are the common wooden type. All are of hardwood showing the marks of years and years of good hard usage. The second one has a companion of a wooden meat tenderizer with the same pattern handle. The third one is often called a Shaker masher, its simple, utilitarian shape being similar to the bold, plain lines of all Shaker furnishings. It is possible to build a sizable collection of wooden mashers of this size without repeating a single design. Some of these had a smaller masher on the handle end, making it of dual purpose.

The giant masher is almost two feet long and was used for tamping cabbage in the barrel when making sauerkraut. It is quite old and is still in use by the author for its original purpose.

Beaters Pictured—Bottom Row

Before the invention of the crank eggbeater, eggs were beaten with the two or three tined fork, a wire whisk, or a miniature splintered birch broom.

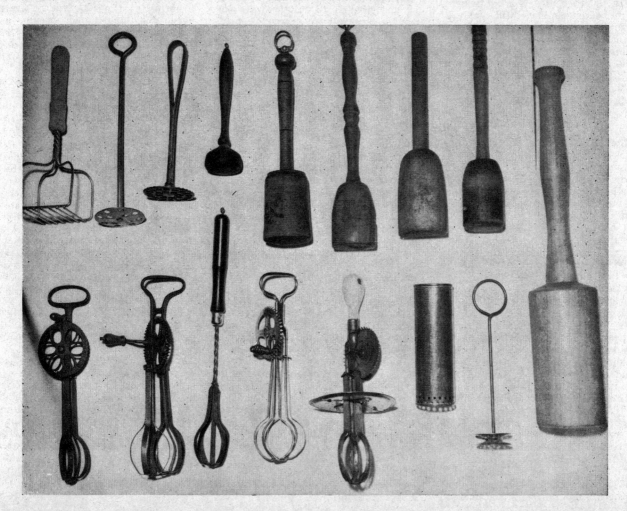

A collection of old metal crank eggbeaters is interesting to anyone fascinated with old kitchenware.

There are many models of old patent-dated rotary crank eggbeaters. A primitive tin and iron one, called the Dover eggbeater, first in the bottom row, was patented in 1878. The Taplin, second in the row, along with the similar "Cyclone", and Holt models (not pictured), were all patented between 1901-1908. The Cyclone had the unique feature of perforated blades.

All of these patented eggbeaters were well advertised. Holt's beater was touted as "guaranteed to whip a pint of cream fine in 2 or 3 minutes and to beat eggs in 20 seconds. We guarantee it to beat eggs or whip cream in 1/3rd the time of the best Dover beater. It is larger and stronger than the best Dover beater and has improved flaring dashers." It came in a 10½-inch family size and a 12½-inch hotel size. These early eggbeaters all had heavy iron cranks and handles and tinned blades. The various attractive designs on the crankwheels, in the shapes of hearts, flowers, and other motifs, are interesting in themselves.

The third shown is a push-handle whipper of 1900. It is a one-handle model apt to lead to a tipped bowl. Modern ones almost identical to this original are still made and used.

The fourth beater is a lightweight all tin beater, similar to the first two pictured. It was patented in 1926 and is much the same as its modern counterpart. The one beside it is the same patent fitted with its own bowl (not shown) and tin cover to prevent spattering on an energetic high-speed whipper.

Beater-Whipper

The last beater is the oldest one here—a combination eggbeater-cream whipper, consisting of two parts. It is made of heavy tinplate with an iron handle and is one of several slightly different ones in this author's collection. One is marked, "Patented 1868," and another is stamped, "Lightning Cream Whip and Egg Beater." Whip churns such as these were recommended by Fannie Merritt Farmer in her 1896 edition of *The Boston Cooking School Cook Book* for whipping thin cream and heavy cream diluted with milk.

The procedure for using a whip churn was to place the cylinder on the bottom of the bowl of eggs or cream. Holding the cylinder still with one hand, the user whipped the rod section up and down with the other hand, a tiresome job but eventually effective. A similar looking closed tin container with a loose rod and wheels inside was shaken much as a cocktail shaker, and the loose mechanism inside hastened the whipping process.

The ingenuity and progress of the early Americans are evidenced even in their humble mashers and beaters.

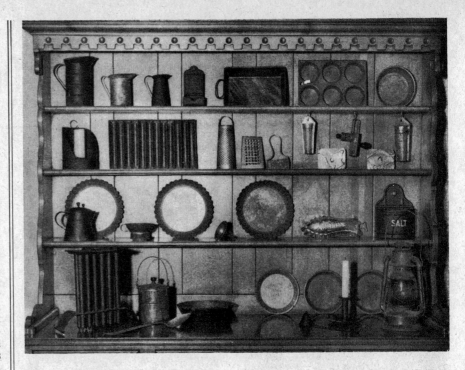

Kitchen Tinware

by LOUISE LANTZ

THE early nineteenth century cook, accustomed to kitchenware of cumbersome iron and heavy pottery, welcomed the advent of the tin-plated iron or steel called tinware. Quite literally, it lightened her work; today's thin weight products were beyond imagining. The tinware pictured here, from the author's collection, embraces a time span of nearly a hundred years, from hand-crafted pieces of the early 1800s to patented gadgets of 1911.

First on the top shelf are three sizes of measures, handmade, probably by the master of the house. The hanging wall match safe, so convenient to hold the many matches needed for oil lamps and coal or wood stoves, is factory made. These were produced in quantity and in wide variety of designs. Next are a heavy single-handled early bread pan, a muffin tin patented in 1874, and a small deep pie pan.

On the second shelf is a shielded candleholder, home-crafted, to be hung by its brass ring, or set solidly on its wide base. The breadstick pan makes 12 sticks; others may make 6, 8, or 10. The handled round vegetable grater is hand-punched, probably early nineteenth century; the factory-made grater beside it is of the same period. The handled chopper with corrugated blade is one of six different shapes in the author's collection. The three hanging graters are nutmeg graters. The center one, with wood knobs, was patented in 1896 and guaranteed not to "clog, tear the fingers, nor drop the nutmeg." (The

nutmeg is held tight to the grater by a spring on the side, and is grated very fine, distributed evenly and entirely, leaving no waste.) The backed cookie cutters, in shape of duck and fish, are handmade. Many other intriguing shapes are to be found, with a hole or two for poking out the cut cookie.

The third shelf boasts three fluted-rim cake pans; a small coffee pot with heavy copper bottom; a funnel for filling canning jars; a smaller funnel advertising C. D. Kenny Co. (an old Maryland grocer); a fish-shaped aspic mold; and a hanging salt box.

Bottom Shelf

On the bottom shelf is a graceful 12-hole candlemold, from the collection of Mary Keefer. Next come a covered, bail-handled lard pail, and a deep heavy cake pan with tapering sides, sometimes called a corn pone pan. A well used stirring spoon is in front. The first of the three pie pans advertises the Baltimore Pie Bakery, last listed in City directories in 1911. In front is a tin candleholder, with an extinguisher near by, and a Dietz lantern. The lantern, commonly used outdoors and in the barn, was often handily hung by the kitchen door.

Other interesting old tin-plated kitchen articles to be found without great difficulty are tart and patty pans, tube cake pans, japanned bread boxes, rotary flour sifters, egg beaters, dippers, colanders, scoops, serrated-edge bread knives, spatulas, drip pans, doughnut cutters, fruit and vegetable presses, even dustpans!

Pie Crimpers

and

Pastry Jaggers

by LOUISE K. LANTZ

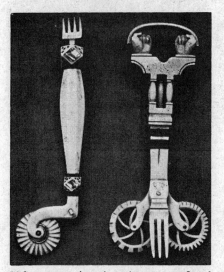

18th century American jaggers, made of walrus ivory. Metropolitan Museum of Art.

THE pie crimper is a simple device for cutting pastry, pie strips, and cookies, and for fluting pie edges and sealing two pie crusts together. It is also sometimes called a pastry jagger, pie trimmer, or pie sealer. Early nineteenth century cookbooks often refer to this gadget as a gigling iron. Olden day menus were rich with pies, not just the usual apple, peach, or pumpkin pie, but plum, dried apple, green gage, cranberry, and rhubarb, whortleberry, gooseberry, green grape, and squash. So the crimpers saw much use.

Some pie crimpers had a fluted wheel on one end for the dual purpose of fluting and cutting. Others consisted of a wheel on one end and a curved serrated jagger on the other. Rarer ones had points for pricking air holes in the pie crusts.

The earliest crimpers were of all wood, cast brass, iron, or whalebone, or a combination of these materials.

There were also wooden-handled ones with porcelain wheels. Later ones were tinplated, and in the early 1900s, some were patented with aluminum wheels.

The early bone or walrus ivory crimpers were often elaborately carved on the homeward voyages of a whaling vessel. Old wrought iron ones were sometimes most attractively designed and decorated with hand chasing. One wrought iron one in the Metropolitan Museum of Art has a quaint cut-out silhouette of a bird on one end. Other hand wrought iron ones have the initials of their creators on them. Some of these were presented by the makers to their sweethearts.

There is a great variety in the design and material of pie crimpers, and it is possible to accumulate an interesting diversified collection of this kitchen tool which is seldom used today.

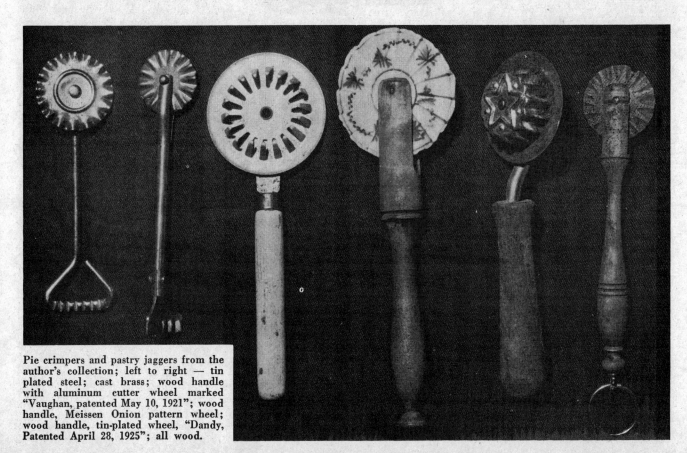

Pie crimpers and pastry jaggers from the author's collection; left to right — tin plated steel; cast brass; wood handle with aluminum cutter wheel marked "Vaughan, patented May 10, 1921"; wood handle, Meissen Onion pattern wheel; wood handle, tin-plated wheel, "Dandy, Patented April 28, 1925"; all wood.

Old Lemon Juicers

by LOUISE K. LANTZ

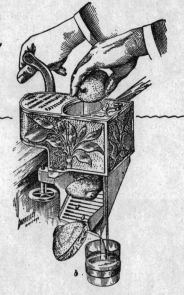

The "Mosteller" Automatic Lemon Squeezer cut, squeezed, and discarded rind all in one operation.

THE LEMON seems to have been unknown to the ancient Greeks and Romans; however, it was widely used in Europe from the year 1200 A.D., and mechanical means for extracting its tangy juice were probably first contrived in this period. The lemon was considered an essential foodstuff on merchant ships during the 1860s as a preventive against scurvy. The earliest lemon juice extractors were probably of the reamer type — resembling a small potato masher with a corrugated head. In early New England the reamer-juicer was commonly made of maple and beech; finer ones had wooden handles and china heads.

The manual reamer-juicer gradually developed into a more sophisticated mechanical extractor consisting of two hinged sections made of wood, and later of iron. The head and cup of the wooden models were sometimes also of wood. Lignum vitae was considered the best wood to use for this part of the juicer. Tin, cast white metal, or white ironstone heads were used later. Sometimes this simple wooden juicer was elevated on a wooden stand allowing for better leverage; the bowl or tumbler for catching the juices was placed underneath the stand. In the 1880s, a similar lemon squeezer on a stand, marked "Acme," was available in iron. During this same period, there was a very robust iron clamp-on-the-table model with a cast aluminum cup marked "Quick and Easy."

The Victorian era witnessed the development of many patented extractors. During this period there were numerous varieties of hinged juicers made completely of tinned cast iron.

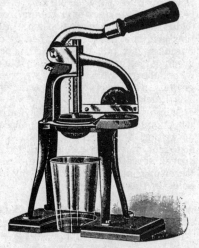

The "Acme" Lemon Squeezer cut and squeezed the fruit all in one operation.

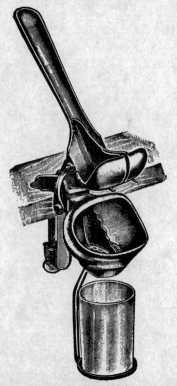

"Barth" Lemon Squeezer cut and squeezed the fruit in one swift motion.

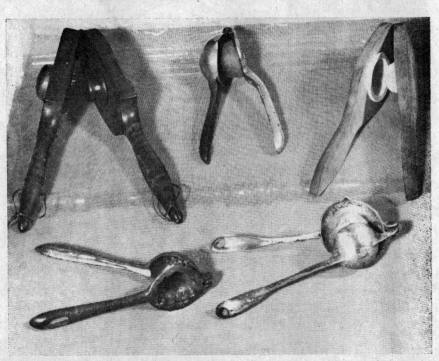

Top, left to right: Hinged wood, lignum vitae head; iron with wooden presser, marked "Pearl;" hinged wood with ironstone head. **Bottom, left to right:** Tinned iron with corrugated head; cast iron with plain head.

Top, left to right: Hinged iron frame, white metal cup parts, marked "Yankee Lidon"; hinged cast iron, marked "Williams," glass insert, ca. 1898. Bottom, left to right: Glass juicer, marked "Easley's patent, 1900"; glass juicer, marked "Easley's patent, July 10, 1888."

An Ingenious Tin Oddity

by BARBARA B. CHIOLINO

Some had plain cups; other had fluted ones. A patented model marked "Williams" had a hinged japanned cast iron frame and a glass head. There is also a cast iron one marked "Pearl," having a hardwood head. Easley's patent of July 10, 1888, and his later patent of 1900, covered glass juicers similar to today's inexpensive manual extractors where the hand is the main working part. Elegant old porcelain two-part lemon squeezers are most likely of European manufacture— probably the majority are French. Some of these are delicately and artistically hand-painted.

A polytypic collection of old lemon

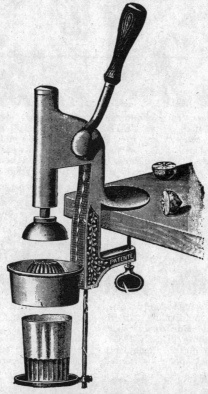

The "Rapid" Lemon Squeezer extracted juice with a rotary plunger.

The "Quick and Easy" Lemon Squeezer combined a squeezing and rotary movement to extract juice.

juicers would include iron, wood, glass, and china items in the reamer and hinged types. The rare elevated and clamp-on designs would be necessary to call the collection really complete.

THIS HOMELY little piece of tin-ware (6" tall, 3½" at its widest diameter) is more than it appears to be at first glance. In fact, you wonder exactly what to call it!

Since tinsmiths were known to do such things, perhaps it was designed as a *tour de force*. It was artistically conceived and executed — scalloped, fluted, pierced, and serrated. (The blob of solder at the base of the handle is a later repair.)

More than likely, it was an offering or gift to someone the tinsmith could well appreciate—a good cook. Though it is pictured as a candlestick, its uses are mainly in the cooking area, where it serves many functions:

1 — a candlestick; 2 — a funnel (turned over); 3—a scalloped cookie cutter (using the larger end); 4—a a doughnut cutter (using both ends); 5—an apple corer (using the smaller end); 6—a nutmeg grater, using the pierced side of the handle; 7—a shredder, using the serrated edge of the handle.

Perhaps there are even more uses that we have overlooked. Had this item been patented and offered for sale, it might not have been the unique kitchen tool it seems to be today.

Flower and pineapple stamps, left and right; center, unusual rectangular mold with hand-carved wheat design.

Of Butter Molds and Prints

THE collector searching for butter molds and prints will hear many intriguing stories of their origin and evolution. If he is serious in his interest — whether he owns one butter mold or two hundred—it is well for him to examine some of these mistaken "statements of fact," and put a quietus to them.

More than ocasionally he will be told, often by a dealer with prints to sell, that the butter mold is an American innovation, originated with the Pennsylvania Dutch. An appealing thought, but quite untrue!

Butter printing was common in England and Continental Europe by the end of the seventeenth century, and

Rectangular and square molds, *left to right:* crude handmade initialed cedar mold; open-sided mold, often called "Early American," (all old molds made in this country are in the Early American category); open-sided mold with brass top and handle; closed shell with designed stamp; plain square and plain rectangular molds.

Left to right: ornate square mold, shell cut from one piece of wood; barrel mold of walnut staves, pewter hoops, removable designed end plate—pestle was used to tamp the butter; hinged mold with removable end plates, design on bottom; collapsible mold held together with brass hooks, design on bottom; open-ended rectangular mold hinged on one side.

Round molds, *left to right:* conventional wooden mold; glass mold which proved impractical; aluminum mold, made by T. R. Hall, Burlington, N. C., and according to the Burlington Chamber of Commerce, sold through Sears, Roebuck in early 1900s; china or pottery mold. Information is sought on this. Presumably the outer shell was packed with butter, the inner cone rotated

into it, and lifted out as a smoothly molded cup of butter; proof is lacking that it was actually used for butter.

Fruit designs, *above,* show painstaking detail in carving; individual wheat design in one-piece square mold; stamps with pear, cherry, acorn; individual mold with acorn.

Left to right: cow and sheep designs; swans in round and one-piece square shells; flower design (this was Mrs. Knudson's grandmother's mold which sparked the collection); geometric design.
Photographs from the author's collection

immigrants to the new land, bringing their traditions, their manners and customs with them, included the practice. No doubt the Pennsylvania settlers, particularly the Swiss and Germans among them, adept at carving and fond of decoration, greatly furthered the craft in this country. English colonists of the same period—some hundred and fifty years after the Pilgrims landed—brought butter molds to New England. The Pennsylvania designs were compact and symmetrical; New Englanders favored a more open and free style of carving. Many of the designs used in Pennsylvania and New England were sold by wandering traders and copied by early wood-carvers in other parts of the country. So, though a design may be categorized *by type,* it is seldom possible, unless it is signed, to allocate it to a definite area.

As the selling of butter became an important source of income, butter molds reached full development. The first designs were whittled by hand, likely for trademark purposes, but almost immediately housewives were using them to decorate butter for the home table. Very soon molds were being produced commercially. Several in the collection pictured here bear patent dates of 1859. From that time on, most designs were machine cut. By 1872, commercial production was in full swing, with seven mold print patents then on file at the U. S. Patent Office.

Another popular story, open to question, is that the first designs were carved on one-piece stamps (or presses), followed by the round three-piece (shell, stamp, and handle) molds, and lastly, by those of rectangular shape.

This arbitrary method of setting the age for a butter mold is at variance with facts exemplified by actual molds. If such evolution of shapes were true, hand-cut designs would be found only in the stamps and perhaps a few of the round molds, and none at all in the rectangular and square ones. Study of the author's collection in its entirety reveals more hand-carved designs among the rectangular molds than among either of the other two common shapes.

Nor does such an evolution theory account for the making of molds in other shapes and designs as shown in the first picture opposite. Instead of a marked evolution of shapes, the molds themselves indicate that all types appeared at an early date as the pioneers ingeniously experimented. Commercial experimentation is most marked in the round and rectangular plunger types.

A third story which bears scrutiny is that all designs were made by steaming wooden blocks and then stamping them under high pressure with metal patterns. While this may be true of some commercially made molds, all those examined by the author, indicate some cutting in the finished product.

Ice Cream Freezers

by LOUISE K. LANTZ

ICE CREAM, as we know it, was concocted in Europe over 300 years ago. It was often called frozen milk, cream ice, and ice milk. In early America, Dolly Madison served ice cream in the White House, and wealthy families, including George Washington's, enjoyed ice cream desserts in their homes. By 1850, it was being produced commercially at 180 Exeter Street, Baltimore, Md., by Jacob Fussell, and its manufacture proved a highly successful business.

Despite the ease of obtaining commercially made ice cream, the Victorian housewife dearly loved to make this dessert at home. The variety of ice cream freezers available in the 1800s and early 1900s abetted her.

Many different companies produced a variety of ice cream freezers, each professing to be better than the other. Competition was keen. The Gooch Freezer Co. of Cincinnati, Ohio, claimed its freezer used very little of the then precious ice. The White Mountain Freezer Co. of Nashua, N.H., boasted its freezer was warranted to freeze cream in one-half the time of any other freezer in existence. With great confidence, the Shepard's Lightning Freezer made at the Mammoth Foundry in Buffalo, N. Y., stated that its freezer made "the lightest, purest and best ice cream that can be made."

The Lightning Freezer made by the North Brothers Manufacturing Co. of Philadelphia, Pa., lured customers with a free booklet, *Freezers and Freezing,* by Mrs. S. T. Rorer. The White Mountain Freezer Co. countered with a book of "practical receipts compiled by Mrs. Lincoln of cook book fame." Their guarantee of "no danger from zinc poisoning" must also have boosted sales.

The advent of the ice cream cone at the St. Louis World's Fair in 1904 increased use of commercial ice cream, but did not dim the housewife's enthusiasm for making it at home. The *Delineator* for August, 1906, gave detailed directions in a column called "The Progress of a Housewife."

Below: Advertisements for ice cream freezers: White Mountain in "Century," 1888; Gooch, in "Century," 1889; Shepard's Lightning, in "Harper's," 1892.

Fig. 1: Unmarked wooden parer, only slightly different from the model patented by Reuben and Amos Mosher, in 1829. On display at Huntington (N.Y.) Historical Society.

Fig. 2: Improved Apple Paring and Slicing Machine, 1856.

Fig. 3: Browne's Apple Paring Machine, 1855.

Fig. 4: Alcott's Apple Corer, 1859.

Fig. 5: Manufactured by Goodell Co., Antrim, N.H.; patented March 18, 1884.

Fig. 6: Also manufactured by Goodell Co., patented March 24, 1898, marked "White Mountain APE"; designated as the "Turntable '98" model.

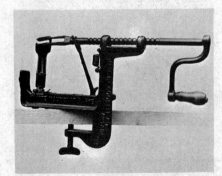

Fig. 7: Manufactured by Goodell Co., Antrim, N.H.; no patent date appears on it.

Fig. 8: Unmarked; possibly a copy of one of the Goodell patents.

APPLE complex

by ALAN ANDERSON

APPLES WERE a staple commodity in early 19th century New England and other settled localities in America. They were pressed into cider, dried, strung, made into apple butter and apple sauce. They were fried, stewed, baked, cooked into pies and other pastries, like dumplings and Brown Bettys. Since so many of these edibles required that the apple be peeled, ingenious Yankees were quick to invent and put into use mechanical apple parers.

The earliest American parer now known is a wooden one designed and built around 1750. Until about 1849, when cast metal parers appeared, apple parers were made of wood, except for the metal knives.

The first recorded U.S. patent for a parer was granted to Moses Coates, Downing Fields, Pa., in February 1803. In the next 35 years, several other patents for wooden parers were issued. They went to S. Crittenden, Connecticut, Aug. 1809; Willard Badger, Massachusetts, Feb. 16, 1809; Cyrus Gates, Rutland, Vt., Dec. 15, 1810; Reuben and Amos Mosher, Saratoga County, N.Y., Dec. 28, 1829; A. Glendenning, Loudon County, Va., Sept. 9, 1823; Cyprian C. Pratt, Paris, Me., Dec. 28, 1833; Daniel Davis II, Tolland County, Conn., March 14, 1834; Robert W. Mitchell, Martins Hill, Ohio, April 13, 1838; and J. W. Hatcher, Bedford County, Va., Feb. 3, 1836.

Most of these parers operated on the same principle, but all had variations acceptable for patent rulings. Skilled home craftsmen, copying patented models on their own lathes, produced many personal variations. Yet the parers all achieved the same end. The apple was impaled on a fork and by simple or complicated means, was skinned by the rotation of the parer with a knife blade held against it. Some parers operated by direct drive; some by belt drive; others had a coupling of a large wooden wheel with rachets engaging a small wheel carrying the apple fork; still others employed multiple gears to speed up the apple and the paring operation.

The *Scientific American* for December 1, 1849, carried an illustrated ac-

PARERS

& simple

nd WILLIAM THOMAS

count of what appears to be the first patented metal parer. Juliu(s) Weed of Painesville, Ohio, was the holder of the patent, dated July 31, 1849. (Fig. 13) Though partially constructed of wood, the principal mechanisms were of metal. Its special feature was that it not only pared, but also cored and sliced the apple.

In the August 11, 1855 issue, *Scientific American* showed Browne's Apple Paring Machine. (Fig. 3), invented by J. D. Browne of Cincinnati, Ohio, who called it "a very compact and simple machine for paring apples and other fruit."

Alcott's Apple Corer (Fig. 4) was shown in the April 2, 1859 issue of *Scientific American*. The article accompanying the diagram stated, in part: "This machine may also be made into a parer by placing the three pronged holder, J, over I, and placing the apple upon it, it can be pared very quickly by hand."

The only other parer illustrated in *Scientific American* appeared March 22, 1856, and was listed as the Improved Apple Paring and Slicing Machine. (Fig. 2) The accompanying description shows clearly the operation of this model and all others similar to it:

"The machine is small nearly all its parts being of cast-iron the whole weighing only 2 lb. 10 oz. The contrivance is secured to the table by means of the clamp, A, and to this is attached the standard, B, by means of the strong joint at B, which permits the careening of the machine both right and left. E is the driving wheel, motion being given by means of the crank to all the parts. Upon the face of the driving wheel E, is an inclined scroll, R, upon which one end of the rack bar, G, glides; this rack connects with, and gives motion to, the loop gear H, which supports and guides the spring rod, I, upon which is affixed the paring knife, J.

"The machine being careened, as shown in the cut, an apple is placed upon the fork, K, when by rotation of the crank the driving wheel, E, gives motion to the pinion, E, and thence to the fork and apple, while the scroll, F, acting through the rack bar, G, upon

Fig. 9: No manufacturer's name on this, but the patent dates of May 5, 1858, June 7, 1870, and March 26, 1872, appear.

Fig. 10: Patented by H. Keyes, June 17 and Dec. 16, 1856.

Fig. 11: No markings; possibly a metal variation of Julius Weed's wooden parer and slicer.

Fig. 12: Known as the Turntable Apple Parer, this bears the same patent dates, June 17 and Dec. 16, 1856, as the Keyes model, but also carries the name of Lockley and Howland.

NW APPLE PARING, CORING AND SLICING MACHINE.
Figure 1.

his machine is the invention of Juliu not easily seen, but is fixed on a small head, d of Painesville, Ohio, and patented by him with an opening in it through which the pa

Fig. 13: Julius Weed's invention, patented July 31, 1849.

Fig. 14: No markings; possibly a variation of the Goodell Co. parer.

Fig. 15: Manufactured by C. E. Hudson, Leominster, Mass.; patented Jan. 24, 1889.

Fig. 16: "Made only by the Reading Hardware Co., Reading, Pa.; patents dated May 5, 1868, May 3, 1875, Oct. 19, 1875, Nov. 14, 1875, May 22, 1877.

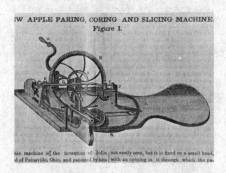

the loop gear, H, the paring knife, J, is thereby passed, during the rotation of the apple, from its base around to its outer end, and effectively pares the apple, when the outer circuit of the scroll, F, having passed the end of the rack bar, G, the coiled spring attached to the other and lower end of the rack bar, contracts, and returns the rack bar, loop gear, spring rod, and paring knife to their original positions in readiness to repeat the operation of paring.

"Without removing the apple from the fork the machine is now careened in an opposite direction, when the pin, L, which secures the loop gear, H, within its socket, comes in contact with the tripping post, M, causing the partial revolution of the loop gear, and thereby withdrawing the end of the rack bar, G, from the scroll, F, thus permitting the backward rotation of

the crank and driving wheel, together with the fork and apple. The slicing arm, N, which is the one hinged to the standard, B, and sustains the slicing knife, O, is now swung by the left hand and pressed lightly against the apple, which is thereby cut into one continuous slice or ribbon, leaving only the core, in cylindrical form upon the fork.

"The careening of the machine perfectly accomplishes the separation of the slices from the parings, while the parabolic curvature of the slicing knife produces such a formation of slices that they do not pack closely together while drying and yet are not in the least objectionable for immediate cooking. This is a novel contrivance; that it works well we know from actual experiment. More information may be obtained, by letter, of the proprietors, Maxam and Smith, Shelburne Falls, Mass."

The rest of the parers illustrated are from the collection of Elsa Anderson of Huntington, N.Y. They give a fine display of the varieties of metal parers available. Only the advent of cast iron made this variety and large production possible. Notice in this assemblage of parers the useless complexity of some, and the utter simplicity of others. All had one single purpose, the paring of apples as quickly as possible.

Unless otherwise noted, all photographed apple parers are from the collection of Elsa Anderson, Huntington, N.Y. Photos by Alan Anderson.

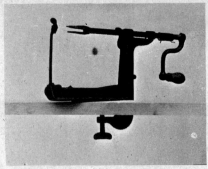

Fig. 18: Similar to the Goodell parers, but unmarked.

Fig. 17: Patented Oct. 6, 1863; no other markings.

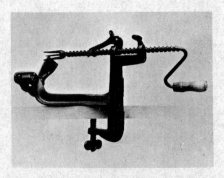

Fig. 19: Similar to the Goodell parers, but unmarked.

by F. M. GOSLING

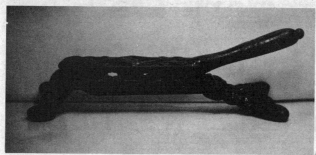

FIG. 1

A GOOD BIT OF information about old bottles has appeared in print in recent years as the bottle collecting hobby has attracted more and more adherents. Even the collecting of corkscrews has gained considerable interest. But it seems that not much thought has been given to the procedure of sealing the necks of bottles with corks, and until the advent of the screw cap, ca. 1850, all bottles were stoppered.

When putting a cork into a bottle, it was the usual practice to soak the cork in water, then compress it, then insert it into the neck of the bottle.

Figs. 1 and 2 show hinged-type presses, each having four holes of different sizes to accommodate different size corks to be compressed. (This is the type pictured with Mrs. Day's query, SW Jun '70.) *Fig. 3* pictures a wheel-type compressor. The handle is lifted and the cork rolled under the wheel as the handle is brought down. Both these types usually come from old drug stores where they were used in bottling medicine before the screw cap bottle appeared.

Fig. 4 is a larger version of the same type compressor, probably used in wineries and places where most of the bottles took larger corks. The opening on the left is rubber-lined. Though we have not been able to learn the use for this opening, it may have been used to place lead foil around the neck after the bottle has been corked.

The two objects shown in *Fig. 5*, one hinged and one not, are known as bottle corkers. They are made of wood and contain tapered metal linings. To operate, the plunger, which has a metal tip, is raised and the cork placed in the opening. The corker is then placed on top of the bottle and the plunger driven down, causing the cork to be compressed and forced into the bottle neck. Corkers similar to the one at the right still can be purchased new; they are made in West Germany.

**439
Kitchen-
ware**

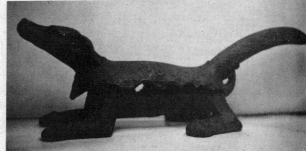

FIG. 2

FIG. 3

how the
corks got in the
bottles

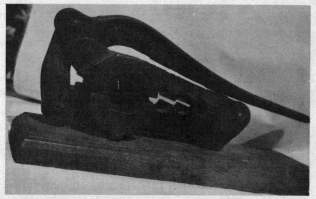

FIG. 4

FIG. 5

Kitchenware Gadgets from the "Roaring Twenties"

by LOUISE K. LANTZ

Author of "Old American Kitchenware—1725 to 1925," and "Price Guide to Old Kitchenwares."

DESPITE THE frivolity of the "Roaring 'Twenties," the kitchens of that era were practical, orderly, and ultra clean. White floors, walls, ceilings, and cabinets were the norm. A lack of frills and of decorative accessories contributed to the aseptic look. A reliable clock on a clock shelf and a set of canisters decorated in Bavarian style were often the only kitchen adornments.

Pots and pans were made of graniteware, tin, cast iron, copper, brass, and the newly popular aluminum. Coal stoves, gas ranges, and the less common combination coal-gas ranges were used. The combination ranges burned natural or fuel gas and coal or wood. The expensive electric range was gaining in favor with the housewife because of its cleanliness and ease of care.

Many kitchen gadgets and cooking accoutrements were patented in the 1920s. An aluminum cookie and doughnut cutter, patented July 4, 1922, is often an object of mysterious purpose to the modern collector. When it is pushed by its handle on a sheet of dough the head revolves and cuts continuous perfect circles of cookies or doughnuts. A grapefruit corer, patented November 29, 1927, has a sharp-edged cutting head with side perforations. The handles are squeezed together as the cutter is pushed and rotated into the core of a halved grapefruit; then the handles are spread and the core lifted out as the juices are released through the perforations. This tinned-steel item came with all metal grips or painted wooden handles.

Pastry blenders for mixing and blending pastry dough were marked "Androck" and "patented 11-12-29." Several springy steel wires bent into a U shape and attached to a wooden or Bakelite handle blended a light and tender pastry. "Bakelite" is a trade name for a synthetic resin with properties similar to modern plastics. It is a molded, hard, rigid, and strong material.

A tinned eggbeater patented October 9, 1923, came fitted with a glass bowl and an attached tin cover to prevent spattering. It is ideal for whipping cream.

A pot lid with a hook-end handle was made in graniteware. It was claimed in an advertisement in the *Ladies Home Journal*, August 1920, that eight of these lids could be hung on one nail.

The idea of the right tool for each job is as good for the cook as for the carpenter. Double forks were made for handling hot baked potatoes and other foods. A clamp handle moved small hot custard cups and baking dishes. A broad lifter removed hot pies from the oven.

A collection of kitchenware from the 1920s, although modern in appearance, seem curious and antiquated to us today.

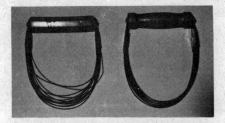

Two pastry blenders marked "Androck" and "Patented 11-12-29." Left with Bakelite handle; right with wooden handle.

Eggbeater marked "A & J" and "Pat. Oct. 9, 1923."

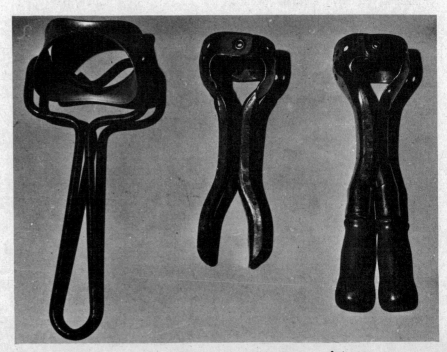

Left: Revolving cookie cutter. Center and right: Two grapefruit corers.

Collecting

ROLLING PINS

by GLADYS REID HOLTON, *Curator of History,*
Rochester Museum of Arts and Sciences, Rochester, N. Y.

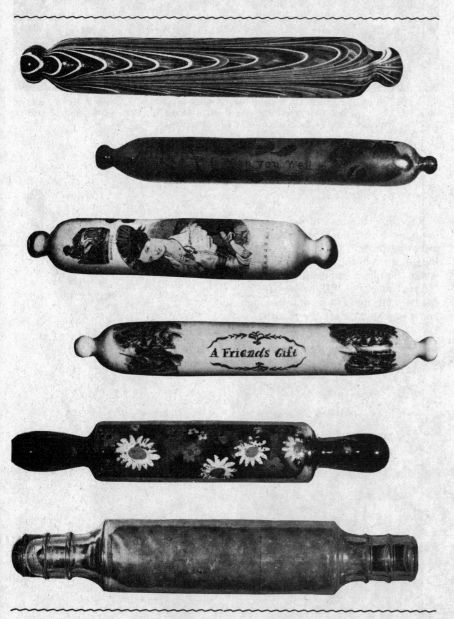

Glass rolling pins from the collection of Mrs. Homer Strong. Top to Bottom: Nailsea-type, pink with drag loop decoration of opal glass; mid-19th century; 16" long. Dark blue glass with darker blue enamel decoration and the inscription "I Wish You Well"; mid-19th century; 14" long. Potichomanie decorated; mid-19th century; 13" long. Milk glass decorated with sailing ships and the legends "A Friend's Gift" and "The Duke of Wellington/Success to the Baltic Fleet"; England, ca. 1814; 14" long. Green glass with painted decoration of large daisies; late 19th century; 16" long. Blue-green glass with open end (stopper missing); ca. 1830; 17" long.

A ROLLING PIN is an implement used to flatten dough into smooth, even sheets for the preparation of cookies, biscuits, and pie crust. Over the years from ancient times, these kitchen utensils have been made of stone, wood, glass, pottery, and metal. Most early civilizations used a primitive roller and a flat stone to crush their grain into a coarse flour or meal. In ancient Mexican and Indian cultures, the roller was called a "mano" and the grinding stone a "metate." Stone rollers and grinding stones are still being made and used in undeveloped parts of the world.

Most of the rolling pins found by collectors today are made of wood; the older ones are more commonly of maple or sycamore. A dense wood that would not absorb fats or oils was preferred, and to please the lady of the house pieces with a nice grain or color were chosen for this purpose. The simplest of all the rolling pins is the French type—a plain wooden rod tapered so that the middle was thicker than the ends. These were especially adapted for the making of fancy pastries. They are very popular in today's antique market, but their traditional shape makes them difficult to date with a degree of accuracy.

Probably the most popular of the wooden rolling pins are those with handles—either stationary or of the type that allowed the roller to rotate freely while being pushed back and forth across the dough. The wide variety of wooden rolling pins can be seen in our illustrations: some are handsomely decorated with vari-colored woods or inlaid with designs in bone or ivory. Wooden rolling pins with a series of intaglio designs on the working surface were used to make fancy cookies called "Springerle."

Most rolling pins made during and prior to the 19th century were made by individuals for members of their families, or for their friends. There is an old mill at Williamsville, N. Y., where people from the surrounding communities brought their grain to be made into flour. On the floor below the mill there is a lathe, powered by a shaft emanating from the millstone above, on which chair legs (and quite likely rolling pins) were fashioned.

In researching this field of collecting, we found two rather late advertisements for rolling pins. One, dated 1916, offered a "Solid Maple Rolling Pin, 18 inches long, and weighing one and one-half pounds," for 8¢. The other, dated 1926, offered a "Polished Solid Maple Rolling Pin," 18 inches long, for only 26¢.

Glass rolling pins, sometimes hollow and fitted with glass or cork stoppers, were popular in the early 19th century. The hollow glass rolling pins were filled with cracked ice or ice water to chill the dough and keep it at a working temperature. Many glass rolling pins were decorated; some with inscriptions or poems to remind the recipient of a friend, sweetheart, or close relative.

Delft and Meissen pottery rolling pins with typical Dutch and German decorations are also popular with collectors. Very often these pins were part of a complete set of pottery kitchenwares, all decorated to match.

Rolling pins came in several sizes, usually ranging from 9 to 18 inches long. A very large one, 8 inches in diameter and 20 inches long, has been found; this was not for pastry rolling but was used to squeeze moisture out of heavy household linens.

Regarding the care of wooden rolling pins: Never wash one with water; just wipe it clean with a cloth and let the oil or fat in the dough preserve the wood. Southern superstition advises: "If you put water on, the biscuits will not be light, the cookies will be tough, and you just can't eat the piecrust."

Rolling pin of lignum vitae with whale ivory handles, brought home from one of his voyages by Capt. Eli H. White for his wife, Phoebe Halsey White, ca. 1850. Capt. White was master of the "Tuscarora," a whaling vessel operating out of Cold Spring Harbor, N. Y., from 1841 to 1856. Length 16". Collection Mrs. Keith Spencer.

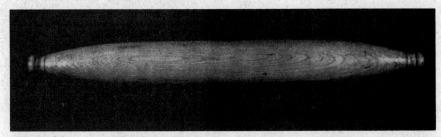

Applewood rolling pin made by Richard Dearborn for his bride, Elizabeth Hutchins (married April 12, 1793). At that time, the Dearborns lived in Biddeford, Maine; later, they moved to Buckfield, Maine. Length 14". Collection Miss Alice Hutchinson.

Meissen porcelain rolling pin in the popular blue and white Onion pattern; possibly late 19th century, though the design has been in use since 1740; 15" long. Collection Mrs. Homer Strong.

Delft faience rolling pins; late 19th century; 18, 16 and 14 inches long. Collection Mrs. Homer Strong.

ALUMINUM

A NEW DEPARTURE IN COOKING UTENSILS

LIGHTNESS
DURABILITY
PURITY

Left: An advertisement used by The Aluminum Cooking Utensil Co., Pittsburgh, Pa., ca. 1925.

An article on **OLD ALUMINUM KITCHENWARE,** *by* **LOUISE K. LANTZ**
author of "Old American Kitchenware 1725–1925."

HOUSEWIVES WERE SLOW to accept the advantages of aluminum kitchenwares when they first became available, around the turn of the century. However, aluminum's light weight and its ability to transfer heat quickly and evenly soon convinced them that it was ideal material for cooking utensils.

The earliest ware was made by pouring molten aluminum into molds, thereby shaping it into thick-walled vessels with a pebbled texture; these wares were known as "cast aluminum." Aluminum wares were also fabricated from thin sheets of the metal by means of huge stamping machines; objects made by this method were called "stamped aluminum." Stamped aluminum wares heated quickly, but they did not retain the heat as well as cast aluminum wares. After the turn of the century, pots, pans, coffee pots, kettles, double boilers, colanders, egg separators, egg scales, eggbeaters, revolving cookie cutters, and pastry jaggers were being made of aluminum.

During the 1920s the Aluminum Goods Manufacturing Company, with its general offices in Manitowic, Wisconsin, called itself the "world's largest manufacturer of aluminum ware." Its products bore the trademark "VIKO." This company later became the Mirro Aluminum Company.

"Alcoa," The Aluminum Company of America, introduced its line of aluminum cooking pots in 1901. Their first kitchenware ad appeared in *The Ladies Home Journal*, March 1902. They used the trade name "WearEver."

The Wagner Manufacturing Company, best known for their cast iron cookware, made utensils of cast aluminum, also. Their original Wagner design tea kettles with pattern names such as "Priscilla" and "Colonial" are most attractive. Wagner's heavy, seamless, rivetless, virtually unbreakable cast aluminum was very popular. Their old pieces are handsome and finely finished.

"A businesslike preserving outfit" in VIKO brand aluminum, ca. 1924.

Wagner cast aluminum tea kettles—"Grand Prize," "Sidney," "Priscilla."

"Oven" andirons; hollow, with slides for baking potatoes inside

PRE-STOVE COOKING

by EDWIN C. WHITTEMORE

BACK THERE in the 1600s and the 1700s, how did your Great-great-great-great-grandmother Hepzibah and your Great-great-great-aunt Piety do the cooking? What were the conditions they had to work under? What were the big differences from today?

First of all, there was no semblance of a constant, steady, even heat. Stoves were not used until the early 1800s, and then only by a few. They were not at all common until the middle of the century. So the source of heat for cooking was the fireplace, roaring hot one minute, ashen and cool a little later. A fundamental problem in cooking was constant re-adjustment to varying cooking temperatures.

Secondly, there may not have been fire there when you wanted it. There were no electric switches, no gas spigots, not even matches. Lighting a fire with flint and steel by means of the family tinder box was both tricky and tedious, and often took more than a half hour to do. Therefore, fires were, so far as possible, made perpetual by constant feeding with fuel, skillful banking at night and when not in active use.

Thirdly, there was no refrigeration. The cool depths of the dug well and

the corner of the backyard brook helped, but in a limited way.

Fourth, there was no running water. Very occasionally an ingenious home-owner would draw water from a hillside spring to his kitchen by gravity, but this was rare. Water had to be dipped, pumped, lifted and carried—carried in endless repetition.

How in simple terms did those industrious early housewives actually perform the cooking processes, prior to the arrival of the cook stove?

There were really two distinct periods, not definable so much by date as describable in terms of the living habits and facilities that created two separate eras. Here are the distinctive marks of the two:

A. The period of: Wooden chimneys, clay lined—Hearths with limited capacity — Wooden lug poles — Dutch Oven baking.

B. The period of: Brick chimneys—Hearths with huge capacity—Iron lug poles—Built-in-chimney baking.

Wooden lard press with leather hinge; pierced tin grater with wooden back; temse or sieve with wooden rim and woven horsehair mesh; herb grinder of burl wood.

Because of primitive conditions, strictly local sources for the materials, and limited labor supplies, the early years were shy of building materials such as brick. Great wide boards, 30 inches wide and wider, were sawed by hand in the pit, fashioned into chimney form and lined with clay which baked hard, dry, and fire resistant.

Across over head would be a long, freshly cut pole, often of swamp maple which, being green and moist, would last for months before drying out and burning. This lug pole, so-called, was usually about five feet above the floor of the fireplace, the hearth. From it hung all manner of "S" hooks, trammel hooks, either ratchet or tongued, and on them in turn were the various kettles and pots in all manner of shape and size.

On the hearth itself was another series of utensils, all on legs, most with pad feet, ready to be moved forward and back, to and fro, amid the hot coals and the warm ashes to get more or less heat as needed.

Baking in this early period was most often done in a tightly lidded heavy iron pot. Most authorities agree this is the true "Dutch oven," though the name has often been used for other devices also. This Dutch oven had legs and, most important, a lid so strong and nicely fitted that not only could the oven be set in among the hot coals, but hot coals could also be heaped upon the lid. All kind of baking was done in it.

The second period presents the same theories and practices, but slightly more refined. Brick, made locally or imported as ship's ballast, was used to construct fine big solid fireplaces and chimneys. Iron was being "worked" in the colonies, so the perishable wooden lug poles give way to various types of iron lug poles and back bars, firmly and permanently implanted along the upper reaches of the fireplace.

In place of the Dutch oven, built-in bricked ovens handled the baking. These were large and small; often in a domed beehive shape, at one side, at both sides, or to the rear of the fireplace. They were connected to the

Top to bottom: large iron skimmer or strainer; pothook with wooden handle; average-size skimmer; wooden toddy ladle.

chimney with an independent flue.

Of course, neither Dutch ovens nor built-in ovens were always used. It would not be uncommon to push a bed of hot coals and ash to one side of the hearth and bury potatoes directly in it to bake. Andirons were there to hold up the burning logs, and one ingenious person fashioned hollow "box" andirons. The front ends slid forward revealing attached interior trays. Potatoes were put upon them and the trays slid back within the andirons for baking.

Cooking Processes

The actual processes of cooking fell into the same categories as they do today:

Roasting. In the earliest times the bird or piece of meat was simply suspended from the front edge of the fireplace and made to revolve. Sometimes a child was assigned to this task. Sometimes the busy housewife twisted the suspending cord at handy intervals, letting it "unwind" itself in the opposite direction. Later, revolving spits were used, operated by a descending weight as in a grandfather's clock. There were also mechanical key-wound spring-driven "jacks" for the purpose and, on more occasions that one first realizes, a spit operated by a treadmill on which a dog ran.

Proper capture of the maximum amount of heat and the increased availability of tin produced the re-

flector oven, or tin kitchen, or hearth kitchen, as it is called. Sitting on short legs, a giant hood with curved back and open front faced the fire. Across it ran a wrought iron spit or skewer which was manually turned a little at a time as necessary. Suitable holes in the tin sidewall, and a properly placed hook or position-setter beside the spit, made many positions possible. To conserve heat there was a hinged "peep hole" in the curved back wall. Through this, the cook could observe how the roast was doing without turning the whole reflector oven. These reflector ovens came in various sizes from about twelve to twenty-four inches.

Baking was chiefly accomplished in the Dutch oven, the built-in-brick chimney oven, and reflector ovens.

Toasting is a form of roasting. There were many toasters. some of them exceptional examples of the fine work that a blacksmith could do in decoration with iron. As a group they were characterized by the various methods of turning or flipping the carrying unit (the toast holder, etc.) so that each side could be exposed to the heat without changing the position of the toaster handle which naturally was kept where it would not get too hot to manipulate.

Broiling, where the meat, fowl, or fish to be cooked was brought close to the heat, is the method where the juices are of great volume, and to the colonists these juices were of great importance. Consequently, every effort was made to catch and save them. A broiler may have been stationary or revolving, and it was often made with grooved arms leading to a reservoir area. The revolving feature, as in the toaster, placed the material near to the flame without having the handle get too close; it also provided an adjustment for greater or less heat, the ever-constant problem with an uneven heat supply.

Boiling and *Stewing* call for the same procedures, but with more or less heat. A variety of pots and kettles were used, often of iron, also of copper and brass. Portable, they could be used anywhere within the fireplace.

It should be pointed out that the huge 8 foot, 10 foot, and larger fireplaces were rarely used for one huge enormous fire. Actually, the sides and

Small tin reflector oven with spit adjustable to many fixed positions; wire potato boiler or basket.

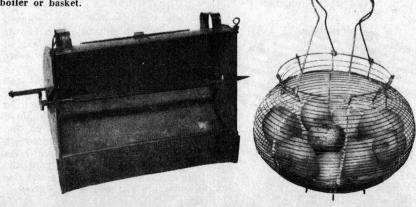

corners of the hearth were often used for a bench or small settle so that members of the family could really sit within the chimney for warmth. It would also be a common experience to find two or more fires within the same fireplace at the same time—a medium sized one in the center, perhaps, while a low burning heap of red coals might be performing another cooking process to one side. So there were big pots, little pots, covered pots, open pots, pots with bails, pots with side handles, almost always on legs.

Frying has changed little over the years. In the early days the problem, as in the other methods of cooking, was in the varying degrees of heat available, and in the practical problem of handling the hot pans over an open fire. One s o l u t i o n was the long-handled wrought-iron frying pan, a common item. More rare and more interesting were the revolving frying pans on legs, with a handle. Actually, there were a great many kinds, sizes, and styles of fry pans in the equipment of early kitchens. Interesting note — there were almost never any small ones.

Comes the Crane

The crane which replaced the lug pole, and which became such an important central unit of hearth or fireplace cooking, is said to have been an American invention, but that is questionable. The crane is the horizontal arm suspended from the side wall of the fireplace and swinging out as desired into any one of many positions. It gradually replaced the lug pole, often was supplementary to it.

The manner in which a large heavy duty crane was installed in a fireplace explains why the original suspending rings or pintel units are rarely rescued from old houses even though the cranes are. There were usually five thicknesses of brick to the wall of the fireplace. The pintel pins not only went through these five layers but also had right angle terminals. The stock was heavy iron bar stock. They could not have been removed without tearing down the chimney!

In some homes there was another built-in cooking unit — an iron kettle set into brick, much as the oven was built. With a fire and flue of its own, or taking its heat from the chimney which it abutted, the built-in or "set" kettle was used primarily

as a source of hot water, for "scalding" pigs, and for other tasks calling for a large container of hot liquid.

Food and Equipment

There was romance, variety, and ingenuity connected with products accessory to the cooking processes. Salt was done without, was made from sea water, even imported, until sources of salt were developed in this country. Spices were obtainable through import, being compact and of high value, and were used even more than they are today. Sugar was scarce, came in heavy cones and was cut into chunks with special sugar cutters, then pulverized in crushers. Only city folk had it. Those in the country depended on honey, molasses and maple syrup.

There was variety and ingenuity, too, in the tools or equipment of the cooking area, crude as they may have been. There were all sorts of ladles, strainers, and dippers; there were herb drying racks and herb grinders. There were sieves with wood frames and lovely plaid-design woven horse-hair mesh. There were graters, large and small, simple and complex. There were rotary apple parers and potato parers. There were lard presses, food choppers, countless different sizes and shapes in mortars and pestles. There were large and small pot hooks of iron, or wood and iron, with which hot containers could be handled. Wood and iron were the usual materials but brass and copper were also used.

"Mixture" dishes were the order of the day — porridges, stews, broths, mush, and hash. A big kettle was kept simmering over the fire almost continuously, and a newly-shot rabbit or squirrel would be dressed and popped into it. Because potatoes disintegrated if cooked too long, they were often placed in a globe-like potato basket of wire, and set down into the simmering kettle, being removed when done, as the whole simmered on. Similar contrivances were used for foods such as eggs. There was considerable of this cooking-within-cooking.

To accompany the meal, the beverage was very often beer or hard cider, both of which were normally preferred to water. The table was extreme simplicity. There were wood and horn spoons, no forks, few knives, much eating from the fingers.

Baking in a Bricked Oven

by Edwin C. Whittemore

JUST AS the frontiersman dug a "bean hole," kept a fire going in it, removed the fire, placed his pot where it had been . . . just as the fisherman has his clam bakes by heating rocks all day under a fire, then removes the fire and puts the food to be cooked on the hot rocks— so was the built-in chimney oven used.

A hot fire was built, often by burning small twigs and pieces of hard wood which give a very hot fire. After it had been kept going vigorously for several hours, it was shoveled out, ashes and all, with an iron peel. The ashes were saved, often in a built-in ash pit below, for making soap. The breads, cakes, and pies to be cooked were then inserted into the oven, the door closed tight, and the baking took place.

Getting the right amount of heat into the oven was a problem. An old book reads, "A smart fire for one hour and a half is a general rule for common sized family ovens, provided brown bread and beans are to be baked. An hour is long enough to heat an oven for flour bread. Pies bear about as much heat as flour bread; pumpkin pies will bear more."

Some Tricks

There were tricks to the trade. Some folks measured the heat of the oven by tossing into it a little flour, then closing the door for one minute. If, on inspection, the flour was nicely brown, the oven heat was good; if scorched black, "the heat was too furious."

Ovens that were too hot were cooled by wetting a broom two or three times and turning it around and around near the top of the oven until it dried. If, however, the oven had not been hot enough during the baking process and the crust of a pie was not nicely brown, then a salamander was used. A salamander was a huge heavy thick iron device like a short peel. It was heated almost red hot, then "waved" like a magic wand close over the pale pie crust to give it a quick tan!

Once the fire had been removed from a built-in chimney oven, it was very dark within. Various methods of examining the baking process were used. One of the most unique was a type of torch. A sturdy wrought iron candleholder on the end of a long pole had also a heavy rigid hook at its extremity. When it was lighted and inserted into the oven area, the housewife could see how things were doing, and by using the strong hook end, she could pull or push pans and pots around to suit her; she could also draw a pan to the door for examination.

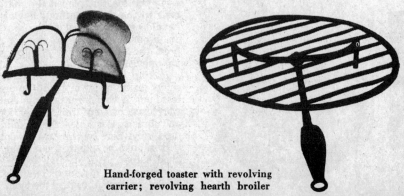

Hand-forged toaster with revolving carrier; revolving hearth broiler

Salt Shaker Agitators

by ARTHUR G. PETERSON

(author of *Salt and Salt Shakers*)

SALT has been intimately associated with culture and folklore; as an essential food, it has been the most universal item of commerce throughout history. Yet until a century ago, little, if anything, was done to improve table salt or the mechanics for its application on food to suit individual tastes.

Technology began to have a major impact on the pattern of living about a century ago. By the 1860s this was even reflected in attempts to develop a convenient and practical dispenser of salt to replace the unsatisfactory salt dish. In 1858, John Mason invented his famous jar whereby screw threads were molded in the glass, on the neck, so as to provide an airtight fit with a one-piece top. This innovation revolutionized the preservation of perishable foods; it also set the stage for the modern salt shaker.

Salt, a hundred years ago, was largely crude sea salt, or the equivalent, with about 18 percent impurities, most of which were highly moisture absorbent. Hence salt became sticky and caked, and could not readily be dispensed through a perforated top. (Today, table salt is highly purified and each crystal is coated.) What seemed to be needed was some mechanical device in the dispenser to keep the salt from caking or to pulverize it. To that end, over 350 mechanical devices have been patented in the United States since 1863; some within the last year. One group of these devices consists of agitators, five of which are pictured below.

The first patent on a mechanical device in a salt shaker, in 1863, was for a stationary agitator, which proved of little value. The first agitator to meet with some success bears a Dec. 3, 1867 patent date (FIG. 1), and is not too difficult to find today, although it is seldom found in an original container. Like most of the many and varied salt agitators patented since 1863, it is of metal. It is an unattached agitator, patented by George Richardson of Boston, who described it as "the first movable pulverizer, provided with points or projections—having a piece of cork, or equivalent, placed in the bottom of the bottle."

The glass body of the Richardson shaker was made in several sizes, shapes, and designs. On or near the bottom, rather faintly at times, can be detected: "Pat. Dec. 3. 67," although the patent applied to the agitator.

Rotary agitators were the most numerous and serviceable of salt-shaker agitators. The most common of these was patented on Dec. 25, 1877, by Hiram J. White of Boston and assigned to Dana K. Alden & Co., Boston, Massachusetts. The patent was issued on a Tuesday, as all patents are, but it happened that Tuesday was Christmas, and the glass containers in which the agitators were used came to be called "Christmas Salts." The agitator patent (FIG. 2) was illustrated in a small container with concave sides, whereas the common types of containers actually used have either convex sides, as in the "Christmas Barrel," or straight sides, as in the taller shakers. The Christmas date did much to popularize the little barrel shaker, despite its lack of any pattern except for a rayed base. It was made in various colors; the vaseline or canary ones contain a little uranium and will fluoresce in ultraviolet light.

When used in taller shakers, such as the "Christmas Panel", the agitator was supplied with a longer stem. These tall shakers have a wider top on which was stamped "Dana K. Alden's World Renowned Rotary Salt Agitator. Boston. Pat. Dec. 25, 1877", whereas the tops on the barrel shakers had room for only "Dana K. Alden. Boston. Pat. Dec. 25, 1877." The manufacturer of these agitators and perforated tops apparently supplied a large number—perhaps his total production—of the short type and a large proportion of the tall type to the Boston and Sandwich Glass Company.

Hiram White had patented another rotary agitator earlier in 1877. This he described as "a cheap, simple, and efficient pulverizer." It consisted of projections from a pendant rod which was affixed to the perforated metal top (FIG. 3). Turning the top provided a rotary as well as a limited longitudinal action. This device apparently could not compete with his celebrated "Dana K. Alden" agitator which appeared a few months later.

An unusual agitator, patented in 1879, by John Putnam of Pittsburgh, (FIG. 4), consisted of a bar resting in a slot at the base, having lateral arms, and extending through the top, with a handle knob for rotating it.

A rather elaborate agitator was the frame-like device patented in 1891 by Frank Heyer of Philadelphia (FIG. 5). Here a rotary agitator was affixed to an "independent bottom" and extended through the perforated tops. A handle knob was used to rotate the entire device, including the bottom. However, when the salt caked around this extensive device, the rotating of the salt-imprisoned framework or the surrounding cylinder failed to solve the problem. It still challenges inventors.

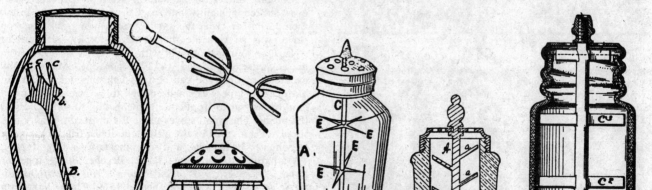

FIG. 1   FIG. 2   FIG. 3   FIG. 4   FIG. 5

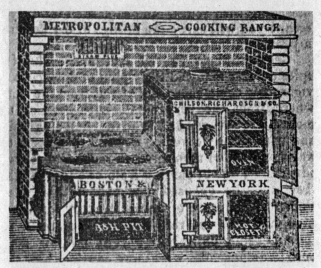

Figure 1. The Metropolitan Cooking Range was advertised in the Manchester, N. H., "American & Messinger," March 25, 1854.

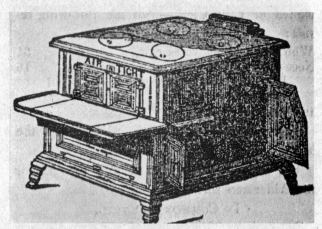

Figure 2. North Star Cooking Stove advertised in the Manchester, N. H., "American & Messinger," March 25, 1854.

Figure 3. Model cooking stove with accessories was illustrated in "The American Woman's Home: Principles of Domestic Science," 1869.

At Home With The Old Kitchen Range

by MARJORIE CONGRAM

MANY PEOPLE furnishing with antiques want a period flavor in their kitchens. The appliances are a challenge. Modern stoves look new and incongruous with antique cupboards and other old kitchen furniture. Few modern women want to go back to fireplace cooking, however authentic. A growing number have found a satisfactory solution with an old black nickel-trimmed range. The decorative detail, the weighty image of stability, and the weathered look of the old cooking stoves are making them popular today as usable antiques.

A variety of wood- and coal-burning stoves were manufactured in the 19th century. One kind used in the 1850s was part brick and part cast iron (Figure 1). The bottom and back of the stove were brick, and were built into the wall. The general shape of the stove suggests that it was built into an existing fireplace. The Metropolitan Cooking Range was advertised in 1854, and claimed to fulfill all major functions of the kitchen stove. It cooked with "simplicity and convenience," and had a "quick and even" baking oven plus a "complete arrangement" for roasting and broiling. The Metropolitan also heated water for bathing and washing. Its "hot closet" under the oven kept the prepared dishes warm. It heated the kitchen, and probably the room above it, with either coal or wood as fuel. An improvement on this paragon would seem hard to achieve.

Cooking ranges of the built-in Metropolitan type, however, lacked flexibility and needed a bricklayer to install them. Another type, the small, free-standing, all cast iron stove, was so versatile that it never totally went out of style. One four-plate model with small oven is shown from an advertisement dated 1853 (Figure 2). Many, many examples of this type can be found throughout the United States. This type was small enough to be transported overland by wagon to frontier settlements and to sod houses of the plains. The small stoves made the most of a scanty fuel supply. Their small ovens were doubtless a trial to the cook who had to bake bread and roast meats for a large family.

Catharine Beecher and Harriet Beecher Stowe together wrote *The American Woman's Home, Principles of Domestic Science* which was published in 1869. Their chapter on kitchens has an interesting example of a stove (Figure 3). This stove is one of the smaller cast iron types with sheet metal accessories added. Later, when the roaster, baking cover, and reservoir were built into the main body, the stove, naturally, became much larger.

Mr. and Mrs. Joseph Lyman published their manual, *Philosophy of Housekeeping,* in 1869. In it they comment on the objectives of the patent stoves of their day:

"What a multitude of curious cast-iron contrivances

have we seen, the object of which is to make three little sticks of wood, or half a peck of coal, cook for a whole family, and at the same time warm them all!"

The Beecher sisters in their book discussed efficient working arrangements in the kitchen. Miss Parloa, predecessor of Fannie Farmer in the famous Boston Cooking School, also considered the problem. In her 1887 cookbook, *Miss Parloa's Kitchen Companion, A Guide for All Who Would Be Good Housekeepers*, she shows a model stove in a model kitchen (Figure 4). She discusses the merits of "set" versus "portable" ranges, and decides that she prefers the portable.

The high-back iron cooking range is the kind most often seen today. The virtues of this type are manifold. The fuel was whatever was convenient, sometimes corncobs or brushwood. The stove baked the bread, roasted the meat, and warmed the dinner plates. The "reservoir" held and heated a supply of water for washing. The towel-rack utilized the heat of the stove to dry the dishtowels and small hand-washed items. A special plate heated sadirons, and another shelf held them to cool. Like the Metropolitan, the high-back iron range heated the kitchen and the room above it. The range also served as a dispose-all for small dry refuse such as private letters and deceased pet birds. Lizzie Borden is reported to have burned up her murder-day dress in the kitchen range before it could be examined for bloodstains. To do all of these things, the cooking range had to be large, and it was.

By the 1880s, the range made of all cast iron was being challenged in popularity by a range made partially of sheet steel. The sheet steel range developed along with central heating of houses. When the kitchen was heated by hot air from the cellar furnace, the heat radiated by a cast iron stove was not wanted. In the summertime, a cast iron range was so uncomfortably hot that often a second stove, burning kerosene, was used instead. A stove made of sheet steel did not throw the heat into the room because it had layers of insulating asbestos in its walls. The range advertised by the Boynton Furnace Company in 1884 is a good example of a sheet steel stove (Figure 5).

By the 1890s, gadgets were all over the kitchen range. A housewife could get as many levers, dampers, foot pedals, lids, receptacles, flues, and shelves on her stove as she was willing to pay for. The Sears, Roebuck catalog of 1897 shows nine types of "Sunshine" cooking stoves, each in several models. Their weight varied from 295 to 708 pounds. Four hundred pounds of cookstove could be had for twenty-five dollars. Both cast iron and sheet steel stoves were offered by Sears, the sheet steel being more expensive.

Putting some of these stoves of yesterday to use in modern homes has become increasingly popular. The smaller two- and four-plate stoves are used in summer homes, guest cottages, and the like where room heating is desired. The larger cooking ranges are being fitted into modern kitchens. Many homemakers enjoy the substantial charm of an old range without wanting to build and keep a fire in it. To have the best of both old and new, the ranges are converted to electricity or gas.

Mrs. Robert Haines of Pluckemin, New Jersey, had a deluxe model of a full-function range in her kitchen (Figure 6). Her "Gem" has a reservoir, warming oven, sadiron shelf, and two round flip-up shelves in addition to six stove-plates and a large oven. The stove has been converted to gas, with gas rings fitted under the stoveplates and in the oven. The burner controls are placed in front, above the oven door. When the stoveplates are in position, the conversion to gas is not apparent.

Mrs. Frederick Best of Berkeley Heights, New Jersey, has installed a wood-burning range in her 1760 kitchen. The room-warming qualities of the range are wanted since the kitchen has five windows and two outside doors. A gas

Figure 4. Sketch of an ideal kitchen in "Miss Parloa's Kitchen Companion, A Guide for All Who Would Be Good Housekeepers"; Boston, Mass., 1887.

Figure 5. Boynton's Duplex Range manufactured by the Boynton Furnace Co., N.Y.C., and advertised in "Century Magazine," December 1884.

Figure 6. The Haines "Gem" cooking range.

burner unit has been installed in the firebox section (Figures 7 and 8). Further adaptations of this stove, perhaps electrical, are being considered.

Those who seek a usable style of the past in their kitchens may consider the available old ranges. A nickel-trim black iron range conveys feelings of tradition, warmth, and stability. The stove's many shelves and warming ovens can still serve their functions efficiently. A six-plate stove top has a generously large cooking and working area.

Perhaps one day the built-in brick and iron range will also have a revival. Brick has become a popular material all through the house. A brick stove base could be equipped with electric or gas burner units if so desired. It could include a small, table-height open fireplace. Modern variations on a brick range like the Metropolitan would serve beauty, utility, and tradition.

Figure 8. Inside of the firebox of the Best's range showing the gas burner unit.

Figure 7. The Best's "South Bend Malleable" range with ash box removed, showing adaptations for gas burner.

LADIES' CRAFTS

"Busy hands make happy hearts," said one Victorian wit. With so little outside amusements to entertain them, the ladies of earlier centuries found delight in needlework, painting, and modelling a variety of decorative objects. Today, these expressions of talented amateurs are sought after by a great many collectors to accent period furnishings. Wax flower arrangements, paintings on velvet, samplers, simple water colors and elaborate arrangements made of human hair, add colorful accents in a great many contemporary homes.

Potichomanie

by LILIAN BAKER CARLISLE

POTICHOMANIE was the name given to the home craft of decorating the interior of glass vases or other forms with paper cut-outs pasted flat against the inner wall of the vessel, and then coating the interior with paint. The 1880 edition of Merriam-Webster's unabridged dictionary says that the word derives from *potiche*—a French word meaning porcelain vase.

Godey's *Ladies' Book* for January 1855 was the first to publish directions for this new mode of ornamenting. The article introducing this work pointed out that potichomanie had just made its appearance in Paris and from the rage it had there, it was also expected to become a craze with American ladies.

To the practitioners themselves, potichomanie ranked with the fine arts. In addition to being an elegant accomplishment, its practice produced results of real value—articles of ornament and domestic utility in perfect imitation "of the most beautiful examples of ceramic art—of Chinese and Japanese porcelains, of Sèvres and Dresden China."

Still other advantages were detailed for the ladies. The process was simple and easily acquired; it was a pleasing and interesting employment requiring no previous knowledge of drawing, yet affording abundant space for the exercise of the most exquisite taste; the time employed was "richly repaid with an inexhaustible and inexpensive source of useful and elegant presents which were carefully preserved by the recipients as tokens of friendship, and as proof of the fastidious taste and talent of the giver." With so many appealing reasons for practicing the art it is no wonder that potichomanie flourished and remained a favorite home craft for nearly 20 years.

Directions for executing potichomanie were included in household encyclopedias as late as 1873. Articles necessary for its accomplishment included: (1) glass vases in shapes suitable to the different orders of Chinese, Japanese, Etruscan and French porcelain; cups, saucers, plates and so forth of Sèvres and Dresden design; (2) sheets of colored drawings or prints representative of the designs or decorations suitable to each kind of porcelain or china; (3) bottles of liquid gum and varnish; (4) three or four hog-hair brushes; (5) fine pointed scissors for cutting out the designs; and (6) an assortment of paints for the foundation, in bottles, together with a glass vessel for mixing and diluting the colors, and a small packet of gold powder for decorating borders.

The directions given in all the ladies' magazines and home encyclopedias were essentially the same. The instructions quoted here are from *Inquire Within, or Over 3,700 Facts Worth Knowing,* a book published by Garrett, Dick and Fitzgerald of New York in 1857.

"We will suppose the object selected for imitation to be a Chinese vase. After providing yourself with a plain glass vase, of the proper shape, you take your sheets of colored prints on which are depicted subjects characteristic of that peculiar style. From these sheets you can select a great variety of designs, of the most varied character, on the arrangement and grouping of which you will exercise your own taste.

"After you have fully decided upon the arrangement of your drawings, cut them out accurately with a pair of scissors, then apply some liquid gum carefully over the colored side of the drawings, and stick them on the inside of the vase, according to your own previous arrangement—pressing them down till they adhere closely, without any bubbles of air appearing between the glass and the drawings.

"When the drawings have had sufficient time to dry, take a fine brush

and cover every part of them (without touching the glass) with a coat of parchment size or liquid gum, which prevents the oil color (which is next applied) from sinking into or becoming absorbed by the paper.

"When the interior of the vase is perfectly dry, and any particles of gum size that may have been left on the glass, have been removed, your vase is ready for the final and most important process. You have now to tint the whole of the vase with a proper color to give it the appearance of porcelain, for up to this time, you will recollect it is but a glass vase, with a few colored prints stuck thereon.

"Select from your stock of prepared colors, in bottles, the tint most appropriate to the kind of china you are imitating. As we are now supposed to be making a Chinese vase, it will be of a greenish hue. Mix fully sufficient color in a glass vessel, then pour the whole into the vase. Take now your vase in both hands and turn it round continually in the same direction, until the color is equally spread over the whole of the interior; when this is satisfactorily accomplished, pour back the remainder. If the prepared color is too thick, add a little varnish to the mixture before applying it. If preferred, the color may be laid on with a soft brush. Should the vase be intended to hold water, the interior must be well varnished after the above operation, or lined with zinc or tin foil.

"If the Potichomanist wishes to decorate the mouth of her vase with a gold border, she can do so by mixing some gold powder in a few drops of the essence of lavender and some varnish, applying it on the vase with a fine brush, or she can purchase gold bands, already prepared for application, in varied sheets, suitable to the potichomanie designs."

The June 1855 issue of Godey's described another type of potichomanie. Old earthenware vases were used instead of glass. The vessels were carefully colored with oil paint on the outside and then the designs were pasted on top of the painted surface. Afterwards the vase was glazed over with a varnish laid on sufficiently thick to make the unornamented parts of the vase on a level with those where the flowers or figures had been glued. The finished vase was supposed to resemble stone china.

Judging from the comments in Godey's, about a year passed before potichomanie really caught on with their readers. However, by 1856 there were frequent mentions in the mail order department column of the shipment to correspondents of sheets of figures or flowers for potichomanie. At first the ladies purchased the glass vases in whatever shape was at hand, but by 1857, an enterprising Philadelphia firm, W. P. Walter, was advertising for sale "potichomanie jars" made by the Philadelphia Glass Company, "in the correct shapes for making imitation china vases."

Potichomanie was used also to ornament panels of glass which were then mounted in four-sided wooden frames and used as free-standing flower pedestals. The August 1859 Godey's featured a pair of these flower stands, and included instructions for the carpenter work as well as the potichomanie patterns for the glass inserts.

The following year, Mrs. Jane Weaver published an article in *Peterson's Magazine* with directions for ornamenting vases, flower-pot covers, plates, jugs, wine-coolers and panes of glass for hall doors in the potichomanie manner. In the same issue a full page of potichomanie figure engravings was included. Mrs. Weaver suggested that these designs be traced on paper, painted with oil colors, cut out, and used inside the vases, thus saving the cost of decorations. However, should the ladies prefer to purchase their materials, Mrs. Hollingsworth of Philadelphia was recommended. This lady sold all sorts of materials for different types of fancy work.

By the latter part of the 19th century, potichomanie had gone out of fashion as one of the parlor recreations for artistic ladies. However, a new variant had come upon the scene. Glass jars or bottles were now packed with layers of vari-colored sands in pre-arranged designs. This craft attracted expert practitioners, especially the handicapped, and some really adept and facile representations of portraits, landscapes and even Biblical subjects, such as the Lord's Prayer, were built up inside the jars, grain by grain. In homey kitchens, on top of wooden work-cabinets, one could find these rock sand examples or some other innovation—romantic pictures glued inside wide-mouthed glass canning jars, which were filled with flour or salt and planted with fronds of asparagus fern.

Potichomanie vases and ornaments illustrated in "Peterson's Magazine," June 1860.

DECOUPAGE

The REVIVAL
of an ART

by CONNIE GOING

WEALTHY Europeans of the mid-18th century were enamoured of the lacquered furniture being brought from the Orient. They adored its delicate designs and patterns, often in colors, so intricately executed by the finest Oriental artists and craftsmen, and paid huge sums for it. Since only the very rich could afford this imported lacquer work, it was inevitable that it should be imitated; a new art form, called decoupage, was created to resemble it.

Decoupage (pronounced day-co-podge) originated in Italy, but gained its popularity in France. Ladies of the French court, including Marie Antoninette, took up the art as an elegant pursuit, making small pictures and boxes. The execution of these delicate compositions on larger pieces of furniture was left to professionals. At first these artist-craftsmen sought to achieve works of art equalling Oriental lacquerwork. They took infinite pains in creating even the smallest detail in decoration. But as the demand for decoupage increased, greedy fast-working artisans flooded the market with poorly-done pieces, and the popularity of the art declined even before the century was ended.

In the Victorian era, decoupage was revived, more or less as a parlor pastime. Now it is being revived again as a "modern" art form. Though today's materials necessarily differ, the method of production is similar. A complete boxed outfit of decoupage materials, dated 1855, containing pictures, paints, paint bowls and the like, was recently found in Houston, Texas. The accompanying directions, which are in French, could be followed today.

The word "decoupage" means to "cut out," and the art of decoupage is the making of patterns or designs with paper cut-outs and applying them to furniture, wood, slate, or other surfaces. (Present day artists sometimes use driftwood and board.) The pictures and decorations are permanently applied, with glue, and the surfaces are then brought up flush with the paper paste-ons by the application of coat after coat of varnish or lacquer. The more coats of lacquer, the more depth to the design and the greater its protection.

Decoupage should not be confused with collage, which is a composite of materials and objects of various textures glued to a surface to form a pattern or design. Materials and objects used in collages range from string, wire, fabric, and wood fragments to watch dials and such. Neither is decoupage the pasting of seashells or black beans and the like in high relief on boxes or plaques. Nor is it a collection of unrelated objects assembled to form a flower or a basket.

Decoupage is not "artsy-craftsy," but rather a delicate and colorful composition applied with good taste, technique and creativity to permanently decorate and enhance the beauty of an object. The extent of surfaces one may use in this art form is almost unlimited. Wooden moldings in rooms, screens, trays, mirrors, all sorts of things, even grand pianos, have been decorated in this fashion. Decoupage is a flexible art, and each piece can be unique.

Directions for Decoupage

If you want to try your hand at decoupage, you will learn faster and be more satisfied with the results if you experiment with some small piece, perhaps a tray, a wastebasket, or a wood panel. For paste-on pictures, prints with flowers or figures are the easiest to start with, or old maps, from books. You will need matching

Decoupage kit found in Houston, Tex., by Mrs. Morgan Fellers. The delicately designed box has the word "Decalcomanie" embossed on the lid; the sides are decorated with gold embossed scrolls on a rich blue ground. The kit, dated Paris, 1855, contains colored pictures for cut-outs, paints, decorated china dishes for holding paints, a pair of scissors, and an instruction book written in French. (Fellers collection.)

or complimentary borders and other decorations compatible to the main picture. Old maps can be effectively trimmed with compasses, small boats, and blowing winds; other suitable trimming designs may take more searching. You may use either colored cut-outs, or black and whites. In the latter case, you can color them yourself, using Derwent oil pencils.

These paper paste-ons should be of the same thickness. You may find that some of the paste-ons you want to combine are thicker than the others. In such cases, you can soak the thicker pieces in water, then peel off the back in layers until they match the thinnest you are using.

For the cutting-out use a good pair of curved cuticle scissors, practising first on throw-away material. Cut your center portion first—this is the most important part of your design—then the borders and the trim. The edges must be cut to fit tight against each other rather than to overlap. Overlapping will cause a heavier build-up and require many more coats of varnish to bring up the surface to the desired height.

The object to which the decoupage is to be applied should be clean and dry. If you are using raw wood, seal the piece with a good sealer, and allow it to dry thoroughly. Arrange the cutouts on the object to create the most pleasing design. Strive for balance and proportion. Only when you know exactly where you want each piece to

go, and that each one is properly cut to fit against its neighbors, is it time for pasting.

Cover the back of the cut-outs, working with one at a time, with a water-soluble white glue. Place them, piece by piece, on the surface, pressing down from the center toward the outer edges, and clean off any excess glue. As you fit each piece into the planned design, be sure there are no lumps or bubbles. A small paint roller can be used for tightening and smoothing as you go along. When the design is pasted down and the glue is dry, brush the surface and the cut-outs with a solution of one-half alcohol and one-half shellac. Allow a 10 to 12 hour drying period, then rub with 0000 steel wool.

You are ready now for the final step — the longest and slowest — the laying on of the lacquer or varnish, either of which may be used. A flat varnish is easier to work with, but it

should be of good quality. Using a clean brush, flow the varnish across the surface. Allow it 24 hours to dry, then varnish again. When the second coat has dried the prescribed 24 hours, you can glaze the surface if you wish. Glazing the surface will give the appearance of age to the design. A prepared glaze is available in paint stores or you can mix your own by using two-thirds cup of turpentine, one-third cup of varnish, one tablespoon of boiled linseed oil, and a very small dash of raw umber *or* black oil paint.

Apply at least 10 more coats of varnish, one at a time, drying thoroughly between each application. After the 10th coat, sand it down lightly with a fine sandpaper, clean the surface, and rub with 0000 steel wool, then clean the surface again. Sanding and rubbing down will give the piece a finished and professional look. From then on, you can apply as many more coats of varnish as you wish. Some artists use as many as 20 coats in all. After the final coat is applied and dried, rub it again with 0000 steel wool, wipe clean, apply a colorless furniture wax, and buff to a soft, lustrous finish.

With plenty of time, careful planning, good technique, and a lot of luck, you can create a thing of beauty! Several pieces of modern decoupage have been placed in museums. As this art form grows in popularity here in the United States, more "new" examples of this 18th century art will become heirlooms of the future.

Victorian decoupage picture of black and white cut-outs from contemporary magazines. (Shelburne Museum collection.) Can you match the figures surrounding our title with those in the picture? They were taken from another decoupage picture of the same period, ca. 1880.

Still Life—Oil on tea-dyed cotton velveteen in antique frame. Painted by the author in 1969.

Velvet Painting

by CLAUDIA HOPF

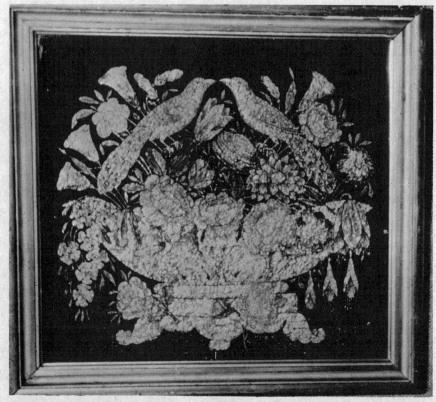

Oriental Tinting—Known also as "Tinsel" or "Reverse Painting on Glass" today. Colors were applied to back of glass in a thin gouche or tint allowing the lead foil backing to reflect through the glass. Author's Collection.

THE TERM Velvet Painting is a generalization defining a number of methods of applying paint to a fabric. A few of the more popular terms include: Poonah, Oriental Tinting, Chinese Painting, and Theorem.

In the early 1790s, the Chinese painted on material that had the texture of velvet, made from wood pulp pounded paper thin, giving a soft, velvety appearance.

The Oriental paintings became popular in Europe after their exposure through trade. As early as 1800 Poonah, Oriental Tinting, and Theorem Painting were being taught in English schools. The first known publication explaining the subject was J. W. Alston's *Hints to Young Practisioners In The Study Of Landscape Painting,* Edinburgh 1804. The following year *The Art of Painting on Velvet* was added, which included the following directions for color preparation:

1. Gum Water—dissolve gum astragant (or dragon) in water to consistency of oil.
2. Yellow—boil French berries in pint of water; add alum.
3. Green—boil verdigris and cream of tartar in quart of water.
4. Crisom—carmine boiled in water and sal ammoniac added.
5. Rose colours—saffron flowers prepared in saucers and called saucer colour. Moisten with lemon juice.
6. Bright blue—1 pound indigo, 3 ounces oil of vitriol and water. Pale by adding water.
7. Dark blue—Prussian and water and salt.
8. Black—take common ink.
9. Paler black—genuine India ink.
10. Orange—saffron in water.
11. Purple—logwood chips, water and alum. Add gum dragon to prevent from running.

By the first half of the 18th century, the American colonies were enjoying more leisure and needlework was the popular accomplishment for ladies of the time. By the end of the century needlework pictures were displaying painted faces and figures, some executed by theorem. These were usually worked and painted on "bolting cloth" (a thin pure silk) or satin. In the early 1800s, painting had taken over the surface completely. The silk or satin had to be sized with a solution of alum diluted with water and combined with gum arabic to prevent color running. If the work was done on muslin, the cloth required a thin coating of isinglass (gelatin).

The Chinese paintings, which were done on dark velvets, had found their way to America at this time. Because New England ladies found oil paints expensive to procure, they satisfied themselves by using local dyes and water colors combined with gum tragacanth. They used these colors on imported white velvets. The use of dark pigments on a white ground with water colors replacing oils, brought a notable change in technique and appearance.

Three techniques were widely used in teaching velvet painting—a popular subject in the majority of female seminaries from 1810–1840.

The first method was to find a suitable print or engraving. This was held to a well-lighted window, the velvet placed on top, and the outline traced onto the fabric. Color was then applied as individual taste prompted.

The next method which produced precise effects was employed by means of stencils, called theorems. After the print was selected, it was necessary to prepare papers to produce the theorems. These were called horn papers and were produced by coating both sides of drawing paper with linseed oil, drying it thoroughly, then recoating it with spirits of turpentine or fir balsam, and again letting it dry two days to a week or more. The design was then traced onto a white paper with a soft lead pencil. Next, all areas which did not touch one another in the design were marked with a number one. Another set of areas were marked number two and so on until the complete design was reduced to numbered areas. A sheet of horn paper was then laid on the sketch and all the number one areas were traced and cut out, then the number twos and so on. The velvet or velveteen was fixed in place by stitching onto a heavy paper or tacking onto a board. The theorems were placed one at a time on top the fabric and weighted or tacked into position. Paint was then applied to the openings in the stencil.

The third technique evolved from the other two. Theorems would be assembled individually to suit the whim of the creator. One stencil would be used repeatedly, as for instance, an individual grape or leaf. Freehand was employed for finishing vines, grasses, and background effects.

Beyond the 1820s and into the 1840s factories were well along in production and were hiring women as decorators of furniture (Hitchcock) and tinwares (Butler). Most of the designers were pupils from young ladies finishing schools, who were familiar with stenciling.

Painting on velvet was taught and practiced throughout the country. Instructions and models were given in such publications as *Art Recreations*, *Grahams'*, and *Godey's Ladies Books* which had wide circulation. Today we

(Please Turn the Page)

Poonah—A delicately stencilled piece on fine silk, watercolored in shades of blue, green and brown; ca. 1820. Collection Mr. & Mrs. James Frey, Smoketown, Pa. (Photo by Barry Thumas.)

Still Lifes—Oil on velvet, using the method of freely moving stencils in overlapping positions while composing the painting. Recent renditions made by David Ellinger, Pottstown, Pa.

A basic diagram of a theorem composition from the 1885 edition of **The Young Ladies Journal**. Each number represents a different stencil which, together, produced a finished piece. (Photo by Barry Thumas.)

Theorem on Paper—The Moss rose was a very popular subject as it gave artists the opportunity to display delicate pen or brush work along the leaves and stems. Author's collection.

Floral Spray—Watercolor and gum tragacanth on white cotton velveteen painted by Mrs. Ruth Hersh, 1969. Mrs. Hersh demonstrated Theorem painting at Old Sturbridge Village for a number of years. (Photo by Barry Thumas.)

Mourning Picture—In memorium themes became fashionable in the early 19th century and prevailed through the Victorian era of sentiment and romanticism. This piece is worked in somber tones on velvet. Collection Mr. & Mrs. C. R. Jones, Cooperstown, N. Y.

may still find examples of this school-girl artcraft at house sales and in antique shops. This type of painting wasn't restricted to velvet, but is found on silk, satin, muslin, paper, and wood.

Through the years names originally given the specific arts and crafts were loosely applied to others. "Poonah," which originated from Poona, Bombay, where it was supposed multiple stencils were first used, came to embrace any type of painting on silk.

"Oriental Tinting," which were Chinese paintings on dark velvets, came to mean the application of transparent colors to the reverse side of glass with a surrounding field of lamp black. Tinfoil was applied as a backing.

"Theorem" is the pure multiple stencil. It is accomplished systematically by following the rules step by step until the finished piece results.

With the modern trend of finding pleasure in reviving the old arts and crafts, this old art is taking new life. Two people stand out in the field of modern Theorem, and their delightful paintings are still to be had—David Ellinger of Pennsylvania, who was greatly active in helping to reproduce the folk art of Pennsylvania in *The Index of American Design,* and Ruth Hersh, one of the original craftspeople demonstrating and relating the history of Velvet Painting at Old Sturbridge Village, Mass.

Poonah is defined on the title page of this 1885 London edition of **The Young Ladies Journal** as painting executed on any surface, textile, paper or wood. Collection Penna. Farm Museum of Landis Valley. (Photo by Barry Thumas.)

Painting on Velvet—Romantic landscape painted in shades of blue and brown; ca. 1840. Possibly painted by a school girl. A naive attempt at sponging; large empty spaces between painted areas suggest a beginner. It is interesting in that only two colors were used. Author's Collection. (Photo by Barry Thumas.)

Feather Flowers

By LILIAN BAKER CARLISLE

VISITORS to the Exhibition at New York's Crystal Palace in 1853 marvelled at the magnificent bouquet of feather flowers located west of the center transcept. One of the popular home encyclopedias in 1857 published the directions from which this particular bouquet was made and mentioned that the art of making feather flowers, although a very easy and inexpensive accomplishment, was but little pursued. Many persons, they pointed out, were under the impression that these pretty ornaments for the mantelpiece or chiffonier could be made only from the expensive plumage of exotic birds. Not so, they said.

Materials required included some good white goose or swan's feathers; a little fine wire in different sizes; skeins of fine floss silk; some good cotton wool or wadding; reel of No. 4 Moravian cotton; skein of India silk; pair of small sharp scissors; a few sheets of colored silk paper; some water colors; starch and gum for the pastes; and the dyes. For these last two items, they gave the recipes.

The first step in forming the flowers was to procure two good specimens of each variety to be included in the arrangement. From one of the blossoms, the petals were carefully pulled off one by one, and used as patterns from which tissue paper outlines were cut. The tissue patterns were then placed on the feathers and similar feather petals were cut out, taking care to leave the shaft of the feather half an inch longer than the petal for binding petals together after finishing.

Feathers were first freed from down, soaked in hot water and, if necessary, washed in soapy water. After rinsing, draining, and separating, they were put into the dyes. Clear, cold water rinses set the colors, and the feathers were then laid out before a good fire on trays over which cloths had been spread. As they began to dry and unfold, each feather was drawn gently between thumb and forefinger until it regained its proper shape.

Yellow dye was made with tumeric and boiling water; soda added to the mixture gave an orange hue. Blue dye contained oil of vitriol and indigo. The green color was obtained by mixing the indigo liquid with tumeric. Lilac

459
Ladies'
Crafts

Wreath of feather flowers, in Fenimore House, Cooperstown, New York, has centers of bittersweet. Curled feather petals were made by drawing feather across the edge of a penknife with sharp quick motion. (Photo LeBel's Studio.)

was derived from cudbear and boiling water; cream of tartar turned the shade to amethyst. Red was the most expensive color of all; prepared cochineal and muriate of tin were added to the boiling water in which cream of tartar had been dissolved.

The stem and pistil were first fabricated from a piece of wire about six inches long. A small wad of cotton wool laid across the top of the wire was wound round with the wire and moulded between thumb and forefinger until the correct size and shape for the flower being copied. One could cover this with pasted-on velvet of the proper color, but a more realistic effect was gained with tinted or painted pastes.

Common white starch was the base of the paste. This was mixed with gum water until it was as thick as treacle, and if kept from the air, could be made up in advance and bottled. It was then tinted as needed.

The stamens, made of stiffened small feathers, fine India silk, or manilla grass, were arranged around the pistil. The farina used to stiffen them was made from ground rice, colored with tumeric for yellow, or if some other color was needed, a starch of ground rice, water and dye was mixed up, dried before the fire, and when quite hard, pounded into a fine powder. The powder was then mixed with more of the ground rice to make the farina, or could be mixed with the pastes to color them.

Then, around the pistil and stamens of the bloom, the feather petals were arranged, one at a time, and as nearly like the natural flower as possible. These could be shaped with thumb and forefinger at this point, if care was taken not to break the web. The petals were bound together with the Moravian sewing cotton after the stems were cut even. Narrow green paper or silken strips about one-quarter inch wide were wrapped about the stems and the blosom was complete.

Foliage was made from dyed green feathers, cut like those of the blossom, but serrated at edges with small sharp scissors.

When all blooms and foliage had been completed, the lady artist grouped her flowers to suit her fancy. They could be preserved as a bouquet under a glass globe or, what was even more popular, arranged in wreath form, sewed to a black velvet background and mounted inside a boxed-in type of glass-covered picture frame.

Made in New Hampshire in 1883, of live goose feathers, this wreath of all white flowers, green foliage, is at the Brick Store Museum, Kennebunk, a gift from Mr. Harry C. Parker, in whose family it has been all these years.

Crystallized "Coral" and Alum Baskets

by Lilian Baker Carlisle

Waxen basket filled with wax flowers. Basket was formed, over inverted mixing bowl, of serpentine twisted wire, wound with cotton and covered with lemon-yellow wax. Princess Pine ground moss fills basket and foot, and is arranged loosely at base. A penny toy bird whistle was probably used to make mold for the hollow-cast bird perched at handle cross-over. Bird is of yellow wax painted with green and red on wings and tail. Found in Burlington, Vermont; probably dates 1860-65.

Author's collection. Photo by Horace Eldred

IN THE MID-1800s, the revolutionary new style of serving dinners *a la Russe,* with all food being dished up from the sideboard, brought about the innovation of placing the dessert permanently on the table, before the company was seated. The guests were thus enabled to look with pleasurable anticipation on the culinary delicacies before them in this elegant, artistic display of ornamental confectionary or gorgeous fruit which formed the chief element of the Fashionable Dessert.

To compose or dress the large baskets with a variety of confections and fruits was a new skill which had to be learned by the ladies of the 19th century. To teach them how to "dish up dessert stands," the retired maitre d' hotel to her Majesty, Queen Victoria, published in 1862 his *Practical Treatise on the Art of Confectionary in all its Branches.*

M. Francatelli pointed out that fruits possessed in themselves an all-powerful attraction to the admiring gaze of all who beheld them, and that when they were tastefully grouped in graceful pyramids upon rich services in old Sevres, Dresden, or Chelsea china, their beauty was further enhanced. He preferred pure white

Dresden for the container, for, he said, the absence of colors on the basket, tazza, or comportier afforded a neutral ground which displayed to greater advantage the richness and beauty of the fruits.

It was all very well for M. Francatelli to give his instructions for dressing, garnishing, and dishing up combinations of cherries, plums, pears, peaches, grapes, apricots, apples, oranges, currants, pineapples, and medlars, but for the majority of families, a fruit pyramid containing all these varieties was far too expensive a luxury. Unless one was fortunate enough to possess a hothouse, where would one find this variety of fruits all ripened at the same season of the year?

The mid-19th century ladies solved both these problems by making artificial fruits in wax, and after they finished the fruits, they even made the baskets in which to arrange their counterfeit harvest. The same women's magazines and home encyclopedias which furnished the instructions for forming the fruit, also gave directions for making pastel colored waxen comportiers, imitation coral baskets, and crystallized alum containers.

One started with a wire basket or wicker frame of any desired shape. Dried raisin stems or particles of irregular bent wire were fastened to the frame, or the surface was roughened by wrapping with worsted thread strings. Knots were spaced irregularly about one inch apart all over the frame, and some of the ends of the twine were left dangling.

A half-pound of beeswax was melted in a shallow pan and the frame rolled in the wax until it was coated all over. The wax could be tinted in pastel colors, or if one fancied a red "coral" basket, Japanese vermilion was stirred into the wax until the perfect shade was reached. The coral baskets could also be coated with melted red sealing wax instead of the tinted beeswax.

Frequently the coral baskets were fitted with a hanger and planted with delicate green vines. The effect of the bright red coralized basket glowing through the drooping greenery was much admired.

Another type of container, but far less durable, was the crystallized alum basket. A metallic frame — for crystals adhered most readily to metals — was produced by weaving wire in and out like basketwork. A rough surface was produced by winding the strands with worsted or thread. Pure rain water (in quantity twice as much as would be necessary for the depth of the basket, including the handle) was gently heated and alum added until there was a saturated solution, and no more of the alum would dissolve.

The solution was tested by placing a drop on a piece of glass. If the globule crystallized, the solution was sufficiently strong. The liquor was poured into a stone or glass vessel and allowed to cool somewhat. When nearly cold, the basket, hanging from a small stick laid across the jar, was immersed in the solution where it remained for 24 hours.

Temperature of the solution was very important. If it was too chilled, the crystals would be large, and if too warm, the crystals would be small and insignificant. A temperature of about 95 degrees was best. As the solution cooled, the alum became incrusted on the basket, but the slightest motion during this time inhibited the formation of the crystals. In summer, a cool, still place in the cellar was an ideal spot for the crystallization.

It was a simple matter to color the crystals by adding various dyeing agents during the boiling of the alum solution. Bright yellow crystals were produced by adding gamboge or saffron; purple, by adding logwood. They could also be made red, white, or blue, according as one used bichromate of potash, alum, or nitrate of copper. Sulphate of copper corroded iron wire and destroyed it. Exceedingly beautiful crystals, however, were produced by this agent.

Other Crystallized Ornaments

Crystallized chimney ornaments were also popular in the 1860s. A crooked twig of white or black thorn was selected; loose wool or cotton was wound round the branch and tied on with worsted. This was suspended in a basin or deep jar and allowed to stand in the alum solution for 12 hours. Although more difficult, by following the same directions, one could crystallize flowers such as the moss rose, hyacinth, pinks, ranuculus, garden daisies, and a host of others. Holly berries, fruit of the sloe bush, and grasses such as bearded wheat could be crystallized.

The alum crystals frequently chipped off after the articles were finished, and great care was required to preserve them. If one was lucky enough to succeed in making a perfect basket or chimney ornament, it was well worth taking the extra precaution of covering it with a glass bell, and subsequently moving it about as little as possible.

Note to modern lady alum-crystallizers: Ordinary dyes such as Tintex or Rit may be substituted for coloring the alum crystals.

Shell Work

by LILIAN BAKER CARLISLE

A VISITOR to a museum, on viewing an example of shell work such as the one pictured, cannot help but esteem the form, shape, and color of the delicate shells making up the flower forms; admiration for the patient work of the artist who fashioned it becomes boundless.

In mid-19th century, many shell flower, animal, and bird pictures were brought home from the Mediterranean by the clipper ship sailors. Their wives and sweethearts found these pictures pretty and pleasing, and some were inspired to try their hand at fashioning a like creation.

First the shells were sorted as to size and color. Naturally the rice shells and others of small size were preferred as they allowed for finer work. If enough shells of the same color for the petals were not available, they were tinged with water color. A design or paper pattern was made for the entire picture and then individual flower patterns were cut from a piece of thick pasteboard.

Thin round shells, those most resembling petals, were selected in varying sizes and the smallest ones were dipped into a mixture of two parts of white wax and one part of glue, mixed and warmed. Only the lower ends were coated. The shells were then set close together on the pasteboard pattern in a circular design for the center; for a rose, similarly shaped shells were then arranged in the surrounding circles with the larger ones on the outside. Roses were perhaps the most difficult to make, but dahlias and zinnias were also a challenge. The tiny forget-me-nots were easier to make and were arranged loosely in bunches. Fuchsia blooms in purest white contrasted with the delicate colorings of the other flowers.

Sprays of orange blossoms were made by filing down the conical end of a delicate rice shell. The opposite end was cleaned out with a pin, and a silver wire was passed through the filed end, brought down and twisted for the stalk. Often a guitar string was used for the wire. Fifteen to twenty pairs on one branch, neatly covered with white or green silk floss, made a charming ornament for the hair, a suitable gift for a bride.

After the shell work was finished, each shell was varnished with the lightest possible coat of copal varnish. If it was a wreath the artist was making, it was then assembled and mounted in a shadow box frame.

The shells the ladies used could be ordered by mail from Godey's, or from such fancy repositories, such as Tilton's in Boston and Mrs. Hollingsworth of Philadelphia. But as one contemporary home encyclopedia pointed out, "In almost every family, enough shells, small and appropriate, can be found to make some ornamental article. Sea captains bring home valuable collections; and who among our readers has not some friends or acquaintances who 'go down to the sea in ships'?"

Shell flower wreath pictured, made by Mrs. Alfred Harris, Rutland, Vermont, ca. 1875. Shells tinted with water color; flower centers of strawflowers or bristles tipped with color; buds and calyx covered with green silk chiffon; cloth leaves. **Courtesy Sheldon Museum, Middlebury, Vermont.**

WAX FLOWERS

by LILIAN BAKER CARLISLE

Wax flowers in bouquet of mixed varieties paired with the magnolias shown on cover. According to family tradition, vases were of porcelain, surfaced over with wax and decorated with leaves and flowers by Melissa. Glittering particles on this vase are of "diamond dust"; a box containing more of these tiny flakes of mica, identified in Melissa's hand as "white frosting," was found among her wax flower implements and bottles of dry colors.

A HOME encyclopedia, *Inquire Within, or Over 3,700 Facts for the People,* published in 1856, introduced its section on making wax flowers thusly:

"There is no art more easily acquired nor more encouraging in its immediate results than that of modeling flowers and fruit in wax. We do not mean that it is easy to attain the highest perfection in this art, but that compared with other pursuits of a similar nature, the difficulties to be surmounted are comparatively few . . . rewards of perseverance come very speedily and are surprisingly agreeable. The art, however, is attended by this drawback — that the materials required are somewhat expensive. They will cost from $5 to $10, and no progress can be made without this outlay at the starting. The materials may be obtained at most fancy repositories in large towns . . . ."

For ladies living in rural communities or away from "fancy repositories," the ladies' magazines of the era published directions and listed mail order sources for supplies.

Godey's, the first of the ladies' periodicals to publish instructions in wax work, printed three lessons in 1856. Charles Pepper wrote the 12-part series presented in the 1860 *Peterson's Magazines,* and Emma Newton, in 1868, wrote the wax flower directions for *Ladies' Friend.* Of all parlor crafts enjoyed by the ladies during the latter half of the 19th century, wax flower modeling and skeletonizing leaves were by far the most popular.

When articles were purchased through *Godey's* mail order department, the fashion editress noted, in a special column each month, the articles shipped. Thus we know that in 1859, molding pins were sent to R. J. D., wax sheets to C. M., and in July of 1861, articles for making flowers went to E. K. F.

Peterson's Magazine during the 1860s recommended Mrs. Hollingsworth of Philadelphia who dealt in "materials for potichomanie, paper flowers, wax flowers, and all sorts of fancy work." Even as late as 1872, the column, "Our Post Office" in *Leslie's Lady Journal* was advertising

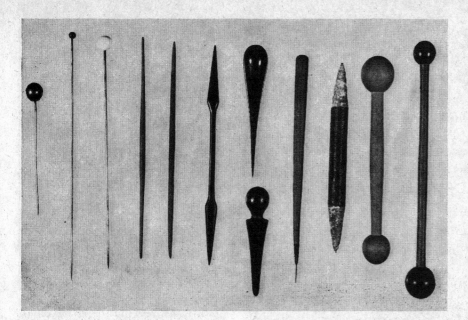

wax was bleached white. It was then tinted. Chrome yellow, Prussian blue, cobalt or French ultramarine, carmine, Chinese vermillion, and permanent white provided practically every tint required. The color was added to the melted wax which was then poured into tin cake or bread pans to harden.

**463
Ladies'
Crafts**

One method of sheeting was to shave sheets of varying thickness from the block with a carpenter's or cooper's spoke-shave. Another was to hold the block in the hands and force it along the greased surface of a carpenter's plane. Another method was to lift the block from its mold, and put several layers of writing paper beneath it in the bottom of the pan, raising the block slightly above the edge of the pan. The projecting wax was then trimmed off in a sheet with a knife.

Should only one or two sheets of a certain shade be desired, a small quantity of wax was melted over hot water; fir balsam, sweet oil, and spirits of turpentine were added. Then a glass bottle was plunged into the mixture. When the bottle was withdrawn, a coating of wax clung to it. After it cooled, the hardened wax was slit vertically and peeled off, giving a perfect wax sheet.

Another method of sheeting involved the use of a shallow dipping ladle, of hardwood or tin. The wax was melted slowly in an earthen vessel and fir balsam stirred into it. The ladle was wet in a basin of warm soapsuds, then rubbed over with soap. It was dipped with a quick motion into the hot wax, then plunged into the basin of warm soapsuds. A sheet of thin, semi-transparent, flexible wax floated off the ladle.

that all materials for making wax flowers could be procured through their purchasing agency.

Professors who could teach the art of wax work were in demand, and several of them wrote informative books on the subject. Each treatise, naturally, recommended the particular brand of paints and materials sold by the instructor. One gentleman from abroad, Professor George Worgan, settled in Brooklyn, and his book, *The Art of Modeling Flowers in Wax*, published in 1869, advised his readers that he gave lessons at a pupil's residence, if in New York City or Brooklyn. His wax sheets and colors were distributed by agents located throughout the states.

In the 1850s and '60s, Messrs. J. E. Tilton & Company of Boston were probably the largest and best known vendors of artists' supplies and materials. Their products were advertised in all the ladies' magazines, and in 1859, they published their own encyclopedia of ornamental parlor crafts, *Art Recreations.* Here 19 pages were devoted to wax work. Ten years later, the material was expanded into a 116-page volume, *Wax Flowers, How to Make Them, with New Methods of Sheeting Wax, Modelling Fruit, &c.*

Wax flowers were modelled in several different ways. The individual petals could be cut from wax sheets and assembled on stems, or petals of wax could be scraped with a sharp penknife from a painted lump of wax —a practice frequently used for pinks and other flowers which displayed quilled petals with jagged edges.

Bell flowers—tobacco, honeysuckle, and poppy—could be formed by bending the thin sheet of wax over a hardwood molding stick, turned by a skilled workman in shapes imitating the natural flower. For a convolvulus, lily of the valley, lilac, and jonquii cup, a shaped molding stick could be plunged into slightly warmed wax, then into soapsuds. the waxen coat was slipped from the molding stick while still warm, and was mounted later.

To Sheet Wax

Tinted wax sheets could be bought, but they could also be made at home. Before sheeting, beeswax had first to be bleached. This was done by melting the wax and allowing a thin stream to flow into cold water, where it formed thin wavy ribbons. These were exposed to sunlight, then remelted, and the process repeated until the

Modeling Wax Flowers

After the sheets had been assembled, the wax worker was ready to model her flowers. She needed sharp scissors, curling pins with bead and wooden heads in varying sizes, turned wooden bell flower molds, colors in powder, round stiff bristle brushes, called scrubs or theorem brushes, fine camel's hair brushes for lines and spots, and thin flexible wire in different sizes.

The best guide to the construction of a flower was to take two examples, as nearly alike as possible, and carefully pick one of them to pieces, laying the petals down in the order in which they were taken from the flower. Paper patterns were then cut from these petals and numbered from the center of the flower so the relative position could be remembered. If many of the same type flowers were to be made, the pattern was cut from a very thin type of tin called tagplate, readily cut with scissors, but more durable than paper. Patterns were laid with the grain on the dull side of the wax, and the various parts cut out with scissors rendered loose in the rivet.

Art supply stores sold tin cutters in graduated sizes, shaped like the petals of the various flowers. These diminished labor, but a bunch of flowers with petals all exactly alike tended to look extremely stiff, however well they were arranged.

Stems for the blossoms were of wire of suitable thickness, covered with silk and overlaid with wax.

The leaves were shaped of warmed sheets of green wax pressed into plaster-of-Paris molds, or of thin sheets of wax pressed on top of embossed cloth specimens purchasable at stores. Stamens and threadlike parts were made with white, yellow, or green sewing cotton, starched and dipped in melted wax. Bristles dyed in the proper color, or tiny slips of colored wax could be substituted for the cotton. Hairy or mealy leaves and stalks were imitated by dusting on hair powder or flock. Succulent stems, buds, and other accessories to the flowers were modelled by hand or cast in molds made of plaster-of-Paris.

Water colors in cakes were used to give transparent and bright colors over the basic tinted wax and to add ornamental markings, such as streaks on painted tulips.

Sometimes dry colors were rubbed on the flower petals with the fingers to give a different tint in a specific part of the flower. For instance, if the blossom was blue with a white center, the petals would be cut from the white wax and the blue color stroked on when the petals were united. Occasionally petals showed one color outside, another on the inside, as in the Madonna lily whose petals are green and white. To achieve this effect, a piece of thin white muslin was spread between two sheets of wax, one of green and one of white, and the petal cut through the whole; the cloth interlining kept the colors from showing through.

The perfect flower which had not been picked apart was the guide for constructing the wax blossom, and it was quite an art to curl and shape the petals according to nature. The wax worker placed the wax petal in the palm of her left hand, and with the aid of a curling pin, pressed it into the proper contour. Each petal was molded in this manner. The individual petals were then pressed together to assemble the flower; the wax was adhesive enough to hold them in place.

Beginners were cautioned to start with single and simple flowers — the primrose, pansy, snowdrop, crocus, and violet—then progress to the tulip, hyacinth, narcissus, pink, jessamine, daisy, forget-me-not, coreopsis, and cyclamen. The rose, dahlia, camellia, carnation, ranuculus, anemone, and gardenia were also judged fairly easy of execution. Compound flowers, such as the chrysanthemum, China aster, and other quilled flowers were not difficult, but were tedious to make. The aster, for instance, contained more than a hundred individual petals.

When all the flowers were finished,

Tinned implements: ladles used to sheet wax. Commercial tin shapes for cutting flower petal forms from wax sheets. Partitioned tin box held paintbrushes.

they were grouped in a bouquet. Professor Worgan warned against the "vulgar practice of arranging them in the formal manner some florists adopt, namely, placing one large flower in the center of the group and a row of flowers round in red, white, or blue." He was sure such a "barbarous and repulsive custom," never originated in Paris, "where flowers are one of the necessities of life," nor in London, "where they are used more in garden or hothouse decorations that agrements for the drawing room."

It was difficult, though, to avoid a stiff, awkward bouquet, even with truly elegant representations of individual flowers. Likely a great many of the young ladies of a century ago ended up with just such results as Professor Worgan deplored.

Assortment of copper leaves, used to make plaster-of-Paris molds for wax foliage; durable and easier to use than natural leaves which sometimes stuck to the plaster. These were purchased individually, and were not inexpensive; original price tag on small grape leaf read 50¢.

Plaster-of-Paris molds, made by Melissa Wood, for wax leaves; elongated molds were used for magnolia leaves.

Dried Seaweed and Moss Arrangements

by LILIAN BAKER CARLISLE

"THE SEA SHORE is an inexhaustible source of pleasure and instruction." wrote Mme. Urbino in the book *Art Recreations,* published in 1859, "and to one who has a taste for the beautiful or who loves to search out the wonders of the ocean and trace in them the footprints of the Creator, new avenues are constantly being opened for the acquisition of knowledge and the means of rational and elevating pleasures."

A 19th-century vacation at a seaside family hotel or boarding house was hardly considered complete unless the lady visitor took home with her a little dried arrangement of seaweeds or mosses as a memento of her holiday.

Specimens for these arrangements were gathered when the tide was out, for naturally more varieties were exposed on the beaches at this time. The days preceeding the autumnal equinox were most auspicious, and if one could time her visit to coincide with the termination of a good nor'easter, so much the better. Godey's *Lady Book* of 1866 gave quite specific directions for the collecting of the specimens:

"Go to the shore at low tide, after a blow from the sea. Best time is after the moon falls, for the tides are lowest then. Examine narrowly everything on the sand and rocks, and take up with your stick (which you had better have stout enough to steady your steps in passing over slimy rocks) everything you see that looks nearest like NOTHING. Then fish all you can of the same sort from the waves. Pick for the bright colors, but do not always reject

Shadow box frame 1½" deep contains basket arrangement of sea mosses highlighted with scallop, helix, and cockle shells along with tiny coral branches and other zoophytes. Overall measurements 13¼ x 15¼". Ca. 1865. *Courtesy Sheldon Museum, Middlebury, Vt. Photo by Horace Eldred, Burlington, Vt.*

dull ones. They often change to bright or at least deep hues after pressing."

After gathering, the mosses and weeds were soaked in fresh water to extract the salt before they were laid out to dry. If the collector preferred to wait until returning home to prepare her specimens, she dried them in the open air and tied them loosely in strong brown paper. Where the final arrangement was one of mosses, no further treatment of the specimens was required before mounting.

If the arrangement combined pressed seaweeds along with the mosses, the dried weeds were soaked in fresh rain water again until they expanded to the size when first gathered. A piece of stiff cardboard or bristol board was cut in the approximate size of the specimen and its surface well oiled. Then, holding the cardboard under water, the specimen was floated onto the paper, and with a sharp needle, pin or small camel's hair brush, all the minute thread-like fibers were separated. The board was then carefully lifted up, tilted to a slanting position, and the excess water drained off.

The specimen was now positioned in the press between sheets of blotting paper covered with muslin or linen, having a care not to disturb the little branches. Papers and cloths were changed every other day and in about two weeks the specimen was ready for mounting. A tasteful arrangement in bouquet or wreath form was prepared and ends of specimens secured to the mounting paper with gum arabic. The coarser kinds of algae were brushed over with spirits of turpentine in which a little gum mastic had been dissolved.

Sometimes, as in the illustration shown, a tiny basket was cut through the middle and sewed to the mounting paper. This was filled with various kinds of mosses or combinations of seaweeds and mosses. These little framed arrangements made charming gifts, and Mme. Urbino mentioned, "A lady of our acquaintance who has been in the habit of spending much time in collecting seaweeds, tells us that she filled no less than forty little baskets with moss in one season, for presents to friends. We are so happy to have one of them hanging in our parlor which does great credit to the artist, so beautiful are the combination of colors and the delicacy and taste displayed in the arrangement."

Part of a collection of dried and pressed seaweeds or algae made (probably) by Miss L. F. Ford of Tenafly, N.J. Miniature size of specimens may be gauged by fact that most of them are mounted on back of engraved calling cards. Some of the cards are dated; the earliest July 25, 1878, the latest July 1905. There was sufficient glutinous material in the sea mosses to cause them to adhere to the paper during the pressing operation without the use of any other glue or paste. *Author's collection. Gift of Mrs. Alice Dibble, Shoreham, Vt. Photo by Horace Eldred, Burlington, Vt.*

Panel 11 x 12", shows intricate landscape within a shield, surrounded by border of scrolls and stylized blossoms.

The Art of Pyrography

Illustrations from the collection of Mrs. Betty Lewis, Thurmont, Md., unless otherwise noted.

by BETTYE LAWSON McCURLEY

IN THE OCTOBER, 1891, issue of *Art Interchange,* a monthly "illustrated guide for amateurs and students with hints on artistic decoration," in the Household Trade Notes column appeared the following notice:

"MISS OSGOOD, of the Osgood Art School [Broadway & 14th St., N.Y.] announces classes in Burnt Wood (or as it is sometimes called 'Poker Decoration'). This pastime has had a great vogue in England and it is likely to be popular here. Some charming and ambitious examples of it were shown at an art studio exhibition a year ago."

Miss Osgood's enterprise heralded the revival and refinement of hot poker decoration, a studio art form recognized fifty years earlier (see SW, jan '56). As the technique of the medium spread from the studio into the home in the two decades from 1890 to 1910, individuals of creative bent welcomed pyrography as a parlor pastime and produced hundreds of useful and ornamental pieces of burntwood.

The popularization of woodburning was made possible by the invention of the platinum-pointed burner, a hollow shell made of a platinum alloy employing iridium for added strength. By pumping gas through a rubber hose to the heated point with a rubber squeeze-bulb, the artist could easily burn designs into soft wood.

Inside the lid of a Flemish Art Pyrographic Outfit, preserved as part of the collection of Mrs. Betty Lewis, Thurmont, Maryland, the directions for its use are printed:

"Fill square bottle half full of BENZINE and add our NON-EXPLOSIVE ABSORBENT until surplus liquid is absorbed, (be sure to use 65% BENZINE only), then insert the metal cork union firmly into bottle and attach rubber tubing from hand bulb to one side, and rubber tubing from handle to the other. Screw platinum point to the handle. Fill the alcohol lamp, and light. Hold the platinum point in the flame of the alcohol lamp until thoroughly heated, letting the heat extend well up to the point, then press the hand bulb slowly. When the point becomes red, remove from the flame, using great care to continue the operation of the bulb, pumping same no harder than necessary to keep the point red." (Use of the Non-Explosive Absorbent was an imperative injunction, to prevent fire or explosion in the event the bottle was overturned or broken.)

After burning the outlines of his design, often also shading the background with his platinum burner, the pyrographic artist might fill in between the lines with any of a wide selection of shades of oil or water colors, especially made to dry rapidly and mat, or his choice of oil stains in a variety of wood tones. He might highlight his work further with touches of gold enamel before applying a final finish of clear lacquer, white shellac, French varnish or wax.

Manufacturers offered all materials required, as well as kits ranging in completeness from simple beginners' to professional. For the professional artist or avid amateur, foot treadles were available for pumping the gas instead of the more arduous hand bulb. Should the artist feel restricted by commercially-stamped designs, he could revert to earlier practice and execute original designs upon plain panels of three-ply basswood available from the same source.

As the practitioners of the art increased in numbers, several manufacturers vied in offering ready-stamped articles of basswood or other soft woods for burning. The most familiar name today among these is, perhaps, the Flemish Art Company. Because Flemish seems to have marked more pieces with a stencil than other factories, the name Flemish Art is often used generically in ads and queries referring to burntwood objects, and may well become a permanent addition to the vocabulary of antiques. Other names are less often seen on pyrographic items; most can be identified only by a study of manufacturers' catalogs.

Outstanding among manufacturers was the firm of Thayer & Chandler, 160 - 164 W. Jackson Blvd., Chicago, who obtained copyright permission from *Collier's* to reproduce Charles Dana Gibson's popular pen-and-ink drawings. The same company produced a line of Sunbonnet Babies — Overall Boys wall plaques, after Bertha May Corbett's famous primer illustrations. A Thayer & Chandler catalog, complete with several pages illustrated in full color, is a handsome and valuable research aid for anyone who wishes to learn more about the subject.

The 1907 -8 catalog of F. F. Frick & Co., Buffalo, N.Y., is fairly typical in offering a choice of more than 700 items in half a hundred categories for woodburning, plus several

Box with hinged lid, brass fittings, 22 x 5½ x 4½". On base is burned the name "Ellen."

Left: Candleholder, saucer type, with original design of scrolls and arabesques. Signed on base with burner "G. M. Flickinger Oct. 06. H B G." Metal candle cup. Signatures and inscriptions are not uncommon: **Center:** Inkstand with two glass wells, grooved pen rack in front, hinged lid. Floral design is repeated on top of lid. Flemish Art Co. **Right:** A delicate ring tree with a leaf design against a darkened, closely burned background. Appears to be an original design.

Top: Needlework box, 9 x 5½ x 4½", design of poinsettias and holly, evidently never finished, as inside lid has not been burnt and only top lid was painted red and green. **Bottom:** Hand mirror, 7" long overall, cherry decoration, beveled glass.

Left to right: Egg-shaped Easter greeting placque, 4 x 6", decorated with newly hatched chick and border of rabbits. Toy shovel, hand carved and burnt with original portrait of an Indian, bright colors added; 10" long. Boy's tie rack, "over the fence for a tie score," was only partially painted. (Author's collection.)

Left: Case for spectacles, decorated with green holly leaves and red berries, and burned outline of a pair of "Granny" glasses. Inside is padded and lined with yellow silk damask. Finish imitates the graining used on furniture and woodwork of the period. Bottom bears original paper label, "Warranted Pyrography." **Center:** Thread or twine holder, only 3" diameter, of very thin wood; hole at center of lid allows passage of string. **Right:** A candy box, one of three in the Lewis collection. This one is stenciled on the base, "A. H. Balliet, Allentown, Pa. Pyrographic Boxes and Novelties"; the other two were commercially used by confectioners, as one bears as part of the side design the words, "Headley's Chocolates, Baltimore, Md." and the second, "Modern Candy Mfg. Co., St. Louis, U.S.A."

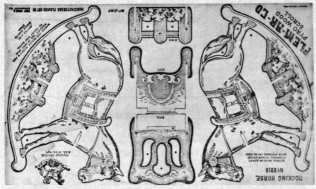

Unworked and uncut toy rocking horse, 22 x 12", by Flemish Art Co. Printed instructions suggest painting, burning, or a combination of both. After cutting with jigsaw and assembly, finished toy would be 10" high. $1.45, crayoned on the piece, may be original retail price. (Author's collection.)

An "Amateur Pyrographic Outfit," from an illustration in Thayer & Chandler's Catalog No. 57, ca. 1904.

pages of leather goods to which the same decorative technique might be applied. For the home there were center tables, chairs, magazine stands, shelves, hat racks, fireplace screens, umbrella racks, tabourettes, and a 15-inch clock (movement included). Boxes of all sizes, to hold everything from pins to shirtwaists, survive in great numbers; small household accessories such as napkin rings, candlesticks, string holders, inkstands, and frames for pictures and mirrors are found less often today.

Scores of ornamental wall plaques and panels pictured in the catalog show a range of designs from mottos and verses to the pin-up girls of the day. For personal adornment the mail-order customer might select handmade holly wood brooches and hatpins, also buttons in several sizes, hand-turned with a choice of eye or stud back. Senders of greeting cards in that heyday of the postcard might choose comic or view cards in either basswood or leather; for special holiday observance there were egg-shaped Easter greetings and Valentine hearts.

To judge from the profusion of offerings in the Frick catalog, the most popular subject for woodburning was the outline of a beautiful girl, not in this case a Gibson girl because a competitor held the copyright, but one of her equally enticing uncopyrighted cousins. Girls were portrayed fullface, in profile, half- or full-length, alone or with a handsome swain; girls drooped languidly, or posed busily spinning; girls were depicted on horseback, golfing, or swinging a tennis racquet.

In addition, native types, particularly Oriental, Dutch and American Indian, were common subjects, also horses, dogs, children, and still life arrangements of fruits and flowers. Landscapes, perhaps because they required more skill and time to execute well, are observed less often. The art nouveau influence is prevalent in stylized flowers and foliage and in the typical gracefully flowing tresses and scarves of the ladies.

Today's collector in search of a collection requiring a modest outlay can still assemble a grouping of woodburnt articles to suit his taste and pocketbook. Prices of the more usual small pieces hover in the under $10 bracket, although signed Gibson Girls and larger or uncommon items will run slightly higher; a hutch table or blanket chest can be expected to carry a price of $100 or over.

If you are not impelled to collect woodburning in general, you may prefer a topical collection, such as boxes or tie-racks. Collectors in other popular fields, like buttons, hatpins or clocks, will want to seek out the pyrographic examples within their own specialties. And if you approach pyrography as a decorator rather than as a collector, you may add a touch of whimsy, the warm tones and texture of wood, and the appeal of a handcraft grown sophisticated — from hot fireplace poker to assembly-line mass production — to your interior scheme by including here and there an accent piece of pyrographic art.

Profile of Indian maiden and border are given 3-D effect against closely burned background. Simulated jewels are multicolored glass beads. Flemish Art Co. 17" diameter.

On a 13-inch panel, a bowl of flowers in sculptured effect, surrounded by conventional border. Center of each yellow daisy is an inset faceted red glass "jewel"; bowl-vase is a soft red color. Flemish Art Co. (Author's collection.)

Bottom of salad bowl, 12½" diameter, 3½" deep. Has been closely burned to suggest parquetry design. Interior is embellished with three large clusters of fruit against the same pattern of close burning to create a very dark surface.

LIGHTING

Ever since man first discovered fire, there have been attempts to increase the illumination cast by this element. In Colonial times Betty lamps and candles were all that could be found in American homes. After the discovery of burning fluids, like kerosene, lamps became more elaborate than ever. While greater illumination was of prime concern to lamp manufacturers, competition was so great that they had to offer the American public lamps that were a decorative attribute to the home as well as a lighting device. Perhaps the most fabulous era for lamps was the art nouveau period, when colorful leaded and painted glass shades enjoyed a great popularity. While Tiffany lamps are in the realm of the rare and expensive, lamps made by Handel and others are still modestly priced and within the reach of the collector of average means.

VEGETABLE OIL
& WHALE OIL LIGHTING

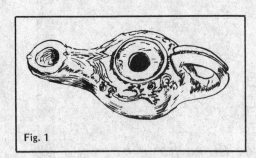

Fig. 1

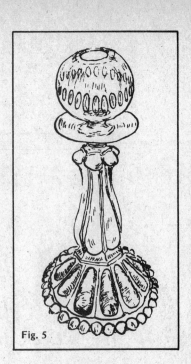

Fig. 5

Fig. 2

by WILLIAM PALEY

*Sketches by the author
of lamps in his collection.*

Fig. 3

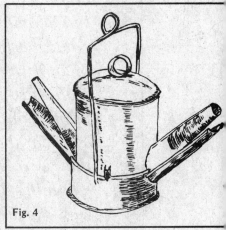

Fig. 4

DURING THE 2000 years of recorded history prior to 1850, lighting developed very slowly. Animal and vegetable oils, depending on their availability, were used as burning fluids.

In Mediterranean areas where native olive oil was used in perfumes for anointing the wealthy after their baths, a lower quality olive oil was used in lamps. In American seaboard areas, whale oil, rendered from the blubber of various kinds of whale, and the finer sperm oil, obtained from the

head cavity of the sperm whale, were discovered as early as 1712 and reached the height of popularity as lamp oils just before 1850. They were also used to oil woolen and vegetable fibres for processing and as a lubricant.

It is difficult, and often impossible, to date lighting devices made prior to 1850. The order in which the illustrations here are numbered will serve as a rough gauge to their chronology.

The terra cotta *(Fig. 1)* and sterling silver *(Fig. 2)* lamps from Greece may

be centuries apart, or may have been used at the same time. It is almost certain that both burned olive oil.

The single burners work well with most refined oils. The author has even used corn oil in the lantern of *Fig. 3* with success. This small tin and glass device has a removable container for the oil.

Fig. 4 shows a double kyal or Cape Cod spout lamp. This early heavy tin lamp has wick tubes almost half an inch diameter at the top and drip

Fig. 9

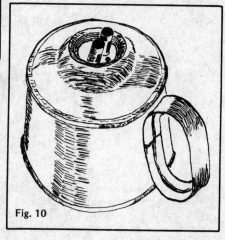
Fig. 10

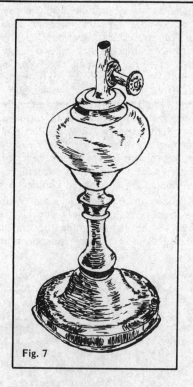
Skirt detail showing peg.

Fig. 6

Fig. 8

Fig. 7

Fig. 11

catching troughs to drain the un-burned oil into the lower pan.

The early pressed and blown glass lamp shown in *Fig. 5* is an early 19th century piece. It was used with a drop burner which pre-dates the idea of screwing the burner to the font for safety.

The single burner tin petticoat lamp in *Fig. 6* was aptly named. The skirt allowed the lamp to stand on a table or shelf, while concealing the peg which enabled it to be used in any candlesocket for greater height.

Figs. 7 and *8* show two brass whale oil lamps of French origin with patented wick-raising wheels. *Fig. 8* is a chamber piece with blown glass globe and handle for convenience in lighting the way to bed. *Fig. 9* is also a brass chamber lamp, complete with its original whale oil double burner.

Burners with two short wick tubes have a doubtful attribution to Benjamin Franklin. The early accepted principle that two adjacent wicks produce more than twice as much light as two separate wicks is valid. Wicks burning close together draw more air, thus producing more heat, hence greater light. The double burner wick tubes in the tin lamp of *Fig. 10* are inexplicably slanted toward the handle. Perhaps this would produce better draught. The slit visible in the wick tubes of both *Fig. 10* and *Fig. 11* allow the user to adjust the height of the wick with a pointed needle called a pickwick.

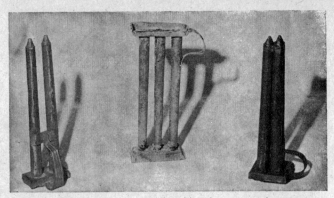

Right: Tin molds with 2, 3 or 4 tubes were used by American housewives in the early 19th century. Left: A rare 12 tube copper candlemold; early 19th century. Tin candlemold with an unusual arrangement of its 6 tubes; early 19th century. Authors' collection.

CANDLEMOLDS and CANDLEMAKING

by DONALD R. and CAROL M. RAYCRAFT

IN HIS definitive study on early lighting devices, Arthur Hayward (3) comments, "candlemolds a few years ago were very plentiful and lightly valued, but the demands of collectors have become so insistent lately as to practically sweep the market here."

Mr. Hayward's statement is familiar to collectors of early lighting, primitives, and country antiques and accessories. The difficulty in acquiring candlemolds is further emphasized when one considers that Hayward's comment was made over 40 years ago. His book, *Colonial Lighting,* was first published in 1923 and a second edition was issued in 1927.

Erwin Christensen (1) writes that "candlemolds tell at a glance how

candles were made. It (the candlemold) is purely utilitarian yet extremely attractive." Candlemolds vary greatly in size and shape, ranging from single tube molds to molds containing as many as nine dozen or more tubes. The most common candlemolds contain 4, 6, 8, or 12 tubes. Candlemolds are usually constructed of tin. However, early pine framed pewter molds containing from two to three dozen tubes are available. Candlemolds made of copper are scarce, though much later than the framed pewter molds.

Among the most sought after candlemolds are molds with an odd number of tubes or those with an unusual arrangement of tubes within the mold. Most candlemolds are rectangular in shape. Among collectors the most sought after mold is the rare round candlemold. This mold has the tubes within it arranged in a circular fashion rather than in a rectangular or square pattern. The authors recently witnessed a round 12-tube mold sell for $180 at an auction.

Candles were considered a great luxury in colonial America. A prime request when the colonies were being supplied with British goods was for tallow and candles. The major difficulty in making candles in colonial America was finding a substitute for beef tallow. Cattle were not plentiful in the colonies until the late seventeenth century. Among the several substitutes for the scarce tallow were wax from the honey combs of wild bees and spermaceti.

Spermaceti is a waxy substance ob-

tained from the head of the sperm whale. It was found in a thick, oily form. Whale fat and blubber also were a source for spermaceti. The spermaceti emerges as a mass of flaky white crystals. As much as 12 to 15 pounds of spermaceti could be gathered from a single sperm whale. Mary Earle Gould (2) writes that "a candle made from spermaceti wax gave as much light as three tallow candles and a flame four times as large." The mid-eighteenth century found a number of Eastern coastal cities with street lights illuminated by spermaceti candles.

Tallow made from fat found near the kidneys of cattle was considered to be of the highest grade for use in making candles. Tallow makers used

A rectangular 36 tube tin mold used in the 19th century by itinerant chandlers or candlemakers who traveled the rural areas selling their wares. Collection Mr. & Mrs. John Curry.

Square 48 tube tin mold of the early 19th century. Some molds were made with as many as 120 tubes. Authors' collection.

a number of processes to obtain this substance. One common manner was to cut suet (hard, light fat found around the loin and kidney areas of cattle) into small pieces and heat it in large iron pots until the fat melted. It was then dried and the residue pressed until all the tallow was extracted from the tissue.

The most sought after substance for making candles undoubtedly was the bayberry or candleberry. Bayberry candles emit a fragrant aroma when lit, and burn quite slowly with little smoke. Miss Gould reported that bayberry picking reached such heights that laws were passed prohibiting the picking of the berries before a set date.

In his work, *The Ballad of William Sycamore*, Stephen Vincent Benet touched upon his dying character's lasting memory of early frontier living:

"And some remember a white starched lap,
And a ewer with silver handles,
But I remember a coonskin cap,
And the smell of bayberry candles."

The berry is found growing in clusters on the stem of the bayberry shrub (*Myrica pennslyvanica*) which grows along the Atlantic coast and as far west as Louisiana. The berries were carefully picked, slowly boiled, and skimmed repeatedly until the wax took on a light green color. Bayberry candles were used only on special occasions and were expensive when purchased from a traveling candlemaker or chandler. The cost and relative scarcity of bayberry candles was due to the great amount of berries

needed to make a single candle. A bushel of berries produces only four or five pounds of bayberry wax. Scientists today make use of the bark of the bayberry root in making a drug that shrinks tissue.

The productivity of the housewife-candlemaker was highly dependent upon the weather conditions outside her door. The months of September, October, and early November were considered the best time for molding candles. The fall months were advantageous for reasons other than the weather. Normally, cattle were butchered at this time and the tallow was readily available. A single candlemaking day could produce enough candles to light many a dank, dark winter's evening. It was possible for a housewife to make as many as four to five hundred candles in a day if she possessed a number of large molds.

The wicks used in making early candles were usually made from loosely spun cotton. Four to eight strands of the spun cotton were twisted together into a single wick. The greatest difficulty in molding candles was keeping the wicks taut within the tubes of the candlemold.

After the tallow was poured into the molds it took from a quarter to three-quarters of an hour to harden. When the candles were ready to be taken from the individual tubes the mold was dipped into a tub of hot water. The hot water loosened the tallow on the inside of each tube and the candles emerged from the mold unscathed.

After the candles were removed they were stored in the cellar of the home for from three days to a week. The candles were then stored in wooden, and later tin, candle boxes. An early prestige symbol for housewives of this period was candles that were pure white.

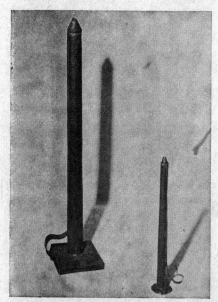

Left: Tin candlemold used to make large altar candles for churches; height 21". Right: Early 19th century single tube tin mold with fluted base; height 9½". Molds with 1, 2 or 3 tubes are more difficult to find. Authors' collection.

Bibliography

1. Christensen, Erwin. *The Index of American Design.* New York: MacMillan Company, 1950, p. 92.
2. Gould, Mary Earle. *Antique Tin and Tole Ware.* Rutland, Vermont: Charles E. Tuttle Company, 1958, p. 104.
3. Hayward, Arthur. *Colonial Lighting.* New York: Dover Publications, 1923 (revised 1962), p. 78.
4. Coffin, Margaret. *History and Folklore of American Country Tinware, 1700-1900.* Camden, N. J.: Thomas Nelson & Sons, 1968.

Ham Lanterns and Lamps

WHEN an auctioneer at a sale holds up an old lantern and says, "This is a Ham," he is praising, not condemning. The C. T. Ham Lantern Works, established at Rochester, New York, in the 1850s, produced such excellent lanterns and carried on so extensive a business that by 1890 their factory measured 60 by 150 feet, and was five stories high. Their products were lanterns—station, bridge, dash, pole, switch, caboose, hand and signal lanterns, hand lamps, fireman's lanterns—street lamps and flood lights. All were oil burners, some made for lard oil, some for kerosene. They were bought by railroads, lake shipping lines, fire departments, town and city departments, farmers, and artisans, and may be found today in almost any geographical location in the country. The firm also made street and park lamps and lanterns to order, and constructed special building lamps and lanterns from architect's blue prints.

Shown at the right, are ten examples as the Ham Company illustrated them in 1890: 1. Tubular side reflector lamp with 5" silvered reflector. 2. Triangular frame lamp for ship and shore use. 3. Guarded lamp, corrugated glass reflector. 4. Tubular frame bridge or signal lamp. 5. Conductor's brass lantern. 6. Wire bottom conductor's lantern, brass. 7. Railroad utility lantern. 8. Square tubular frame lamp for brilliant illumination on ship or shore. 9. Lard oil lamp with large fuel tank. 10. Pair of ship's lanterns; while shown small in the picture, they are actually the same size as the railroad lanterns.

For Oil.   For Candle.

For Kerosene.

The wire frame hinged-top lantern pictured above, which may or may not be a Ham, is of interest because the attachments for adjusting it to oil, kerosene, and candle are shown. The No. O tubular globe it used was available in clear, red, or green. It was pictured in the first issue of *The Illuminator*, Spring 1880, New York,

(Please turn the page)

The Ups and Downs Of Early Lighting

by EDWIN C. WHITTEMORE

IN THE earlier types of lighting devices, it is noticeable that a high percentage are of a sort where the position of the light can be raised and lowered in relation to the person using it.

Lighting collectors are often crudely awakened, and even disappointed, the first time they actually test an early lighting device. Observed in a dark room, the light is amazingly insignificant; it can be compared to that of a wooden kitchen match or a small candle. This slight amount of illumination given off by rush lights, Betty lamps, grease lamps, etc., probably explains the great attention given to the adjustability of the light to a desired level. The user wanted it placed where it would do him the most good!

What to Look For

An interesting approach to the study of early lighting is to examine the many types in terms of classifying them according to the methods of this up-and-down adjustment. There are eight easily recognizable types, and a lighting collection that included at least one of each would be outstanding.

In simple terms, these are the eight classifications:

1. Dependence on what the lighting fixture rests upon. *Example:* a tin Ipswich Betty Lamp with its weighted cone base.

2. Dependence upon the point from which the fixture is suspended. *Example:* wrought iron loom light with vertical bar to hang down from nail or peg at variable heights.

3. Dependence on varying the height of the suspending unit. *Example:* the trammel-type fixture with paired members that can shorten or lengthen the vertical height.

4. Dependence on spiral-cut or screw-type central unit around which the candle or lamp carrier rests. *Example:* the sought-after revolving candlestand with crossbar.

5. Dependence on friction wedging. *Example:* a candle-carrying crossbar held to any position on a vertical shaft by a wedge.

6. Dependence on the spring tension of metals. *Example:* a hog-scraper iron candlestick. The movable platform holding up the candle stays where it is put by tension between it and the wall of the tube.

7. Dependence on spaced notches or holes in the vertical member. *Example:* a slot-type vertical candlestand.

8. Dependence on turnscrew wedging. *Example:* a crossbar candlestand where the bar rests on a separate turnscrew, fitting into the vertical member.

Left to right: iron hog-scraper candlestick (#6); table or miniature revolving candlestand (#4); wood-based candlestand of the 17th century with spiral-cut iron top section (also #4).

"a quarterly journal [actually a 4-page 9½ x 12" flyer] devoted to the diffusion of light." Selected lanterns and street lamps were illustrated without manufacturer's identification, but with the assurance that all goods shown could be "obtained of any Hardware, House Furnishing, or Crockery Dealer."

Fascinating Accessories For Candlelight

by LOUISE K. LANTZ

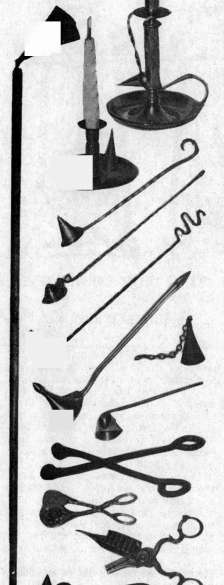

Royal Worcester porcelain candle cones, 1848, with nightingale's heads, represent Jenny Lind; are listed as "Diffidence" and "Confidence." N. Y. Historical Society.

CANDLELIGHT to us is romantic and mood-making. We find its warmth and glow cozy and charming. However, to the early American, candlelight was a much more serious matter. Daylight and candlelight were his main sources of light to work, eat, and live by. Keeping the candle burning brightly and evenly was a time-consuming daily task; extinguishing it with the least odor and mess was an accomplishment.

One addition to the refinement of candlelight was the snuffer. The snuffer is a metal scissorlike gadget for trimming the burnt wick of the candle and catching this burnt end in the boxlike part of the snuffer. The snuffer derived its name from the word "snuff," which meant "the charred portion on the end of the burned candlewick." Trimming the burnt end helped assure a bright, smokeless, even flame. When a candle was carefully snuffed, it aided in reducing the unpleasant odor which often lingered in the air from the homemade tallow candles. A skillful person could snuff a candle while it was burning and not extinguish the flame. A real accomplishment! Snuffers were indeed a neat improvement over pinching off this charred tip with the fingernails or a clumsy knife.

The first snuffers were like small scissors and the cut snuff fell where it would. A later ingenious improvement added a boxlike attachment to one blade to catch the cut charred wick. This made for a much neater job. Some snuffers have a pick or spike on one blade tip to uncurl the wick or pick it out of the melted wax to facilitate cutting it off. Snuffers were occasionally attached to floor candlestands by means of a special hook for their placement. Some snuffers were raised on little feet to facilitate picking them up. Special snuffers were made for chan-

deliers and hurricane light globes.

Snuffers were made of brass, iron, silver, and even gold. They have been in use in Europe, at least since the 15th century, and in this country from its very beginning, brought by the early settlers from Europe. Snuffers were sometimes called candleshears because of their obvious similarity to scissors. Other names for snuffers are snit, snytel, snoffer, snuffing iron, and wick trimmer, an apt description of its duty. Snuffers were commonly used in the seventeenth and eighteenth centuries and persisted into the mid-nineteenth.

Trays for Snuffers

Snuffers were sometimes paired with a matching flat tray or an upright stand, enabling them to be carried neatly about the house. At first these trays were designed in the outline of the snuffer. Later they were made more comely in appearance and a handle was added. Snuffer holders or stands made like pockets into which the snuffers fit are called snuffer cases. A snuffer tray was also called a snuffer dish, snuffer boat, snuffer pan, or snuffer slice. These snuffer trays were usually made of the same metal as the snuffer or of japanned metal or tin. Rare snuffer trays of pressed glass exist.

Gradual improvements in the candlewick eventually outmoded the need for snuffers. The improved candlewick, invented about 1840, was consumed completely by the flame and did away with the necessity of wick trimming or snuffing.

Another refinement for candlelight was the invention of the attractive and practical candle extinguisher. No longer did one have to blow out the candle, often scattering dust and melted wax about, or to put out the flame messily with the moistened fingertips. The new candle extinguishers or candle cones were in the shape of a cone or a miniature pointed dunce cap. They were made of pewter, silver, tin, sheet iron, copper, brass,

—Photos by Willafred Studios

ILLUSTRATIONS

At left: Long handled chandelier and sconce extinguisher, possibly from a church, wood handle, tin cone.

Top to bottom: Brass chambersticks with extinguisher which hooks on candle; swirl stem of extinguisher matches swirl pattern of candlestick stem. Copper chamberstick with candle thimble which has hook to fit into slot on candlestick stem. Brass "dunce cap" extinguisher. Brass "hat" extinguisher. Wrought iron extinguisher, hand wrought. Large pewter extinguisher. Tin candle cone with chain for hanging. Sterling silver extinguisher for candelabra. Wrought iron hand-forged douter. Small fancy silver douter. Steel three-legged snuffer. Short stem wrought iron extinguisher.

or, more rarely, china. The material of which they were made often depended upon the wealth of the owner and the section in which he lived. The more expensive ones were sometimes made of porcelain or pottery in the interesting shapes of human figures. These are quite rare now. Royal Worcester made them in the shapes of heads of old women wearing nightcaps. Another English potter made one in the shape of a dog's head with a nightcap. Some of these pottery ones had handles; others were cones. The metal candle cones often had short handles, not much more than a brief curled stem. More elegant ones had longer handles, perhaps twirled and ending in a curlicue for hanging. Some had straight long stems fancily engraved. There were even special ones with extra long handles, sometimes of wood, for extinguishing high chandeliers, and other specialized ones for dousing the candles protected by glass hurricane globes, candles on beams, and candles in sconces. The cones on these were often attached in such a manner that they swiveled, and their mobility made them very versatile. Some candleholders came equipped with their own matching candle cones, especially the finer brass, bronze, and silver ones. The saucer-type chamberstick such as the silver ones made in Sheffield occasionally had a special little notch into which the hooked short stem of the candle cone would be inserted to prevent its being misplaced.

Other names for candle cones are dowse and candle dowse, and candle thimble for the handleless ones. Candle cones are probably very old, dating from the seventeenth century. They are a simple yet competent device for extinguishing a candle flame.

What Are Douters?

Douters are quite rare now and are probably even older than the conical extinguisher. It is possible that they date from the early sixteenth century. Douters are believed to have derived their odd name from the words "do out" in the old time expression of "do out the candles." Douters are scissorlike or tong-shaped devices which have a heavy disc on each blade between which the candle flame is extinguished. They are sometimes confused with snuffers because of their similarity in appearance. They were used most prevalently between 1680 and 1780 and were often rather crudely made of brass or wrought iron. Occasionally more elegant ones were designed in finer brass and silver. They literally squeezed out the candle flame. Many people considered the conical extinguisher more effective than the douter in retarding the spread of the objectionable odor of the extinguished candle. Candle cones are also sometimes called douters for they perform the same task of extinguishing the flame. A most picturesque name also used for douters is outquenchers.

Edwards' Parlor Lamp Stove

FOR LIGHTING - FOR HEATING - FOR COOKING

by BISSELL BROOKE

A UNIQUE invention introduced at the World's Columbian Exposition in Chicago, in 1893, was the Edwards' Parlor Lamp Stove. In the gaslight era, at the first exposition illuminated by electricity, this novel device revealed new potentials in the old-fashioned kerosene lamp.

American housewives, usually so eager to accept inventions for the home, steadfastly refused to be "shed" of their ornate, colorful kerosene lamps. The coal oil lamp remained so popular that many shops in the 1890s were regularly advertising new lamps, both foreign and domestic, "below cost." Designs and decorations changed so frequently that hundreds of them have never been catalogued, but are recorded only in contemporary advertisements, or sales folders.

Recently an original 1893 folder of the Edwards' Parlor Lamp Stove turned up after sixty years in storage. Illustrations from it, shown above, explain some baffling odd parts found by collectors, like two gleaming silvery grooved rods, stashed in a smoke house, and an impressive "genuine silver crown of an Oriental potentate," in an antiques shop.

The first illustration shows the complete device, 34 inches high, with a highly polished nickel plate tripod stand topped by a portable piano-reading lamp of nickel, with fabric fringed shade, and a capacity of 300 candlepower. The second portrays the device supplying heat for a room or office, with the lamp providing heat to the tubular circulating radiator that was mistaken for an Oriental crown. The folder explains: "The secret of the great heating power of this stove is *circulation;* no device ever produced has anything like its circulating power; so great is it, that all the air in the room passes through the tubes and is heated in the *Radiator* in a few minutes, so that the temperature is kept even and at any degree desired."

The third illustration shows how the lamp was converted into a cookstove by removing the radiator lid, thereby giving burner space, 13 inches in circumference, for kettle, saucepan, or spider. The folder claimed it would "cook faster than any ordinary wood or coal stove, and unlike oil stoves, it *does not produce an odor nor soot the kettles* . . . it will boil water in fifteen minutes."

Stressing the economy of the device, the folder continued: "The thousands of people who do *Light House-Keeping* can now be supplied with a 'long felt want' without feeling that all their spare money is going into the coffers of the coal barons and rich gas companies, as a few cents a day will make all your *Light* and fuel for both *Heating* and *Cooking*. . . ."

Besides the large "Parlor" size illustrated, priced to dealers at $12 each, there was a smaller size, "The Student Lamp," for use in smaller rooms, at $6 each to dealers. Edwards' Parlor Lamp Stove Co., 9 & 11 N. Canal St., Chicago, was the manufacturer.

Fostoria Lamps

No. 179 Flat Hand.

No. 179 Footed Hand. Height, 6½ in.

No. 179 Sewing. Height, 9 in.

No. 179 D. Height, 11 in.

by

SUSAN B. HOWARD

The "Vesper" lamp by Fostoria. Right, the 11 inch high reading lamp; center, the "sewing" model; left, the "footed hand" and "flat hand" models. There were intermediate sizes of the same design. This lamp was manufactured in clear crystal, brilliant all-over red glass, and all-over green glass. When sold with a decorated chimney, the chimney was decorated with a banding of the same color with an opaque stripe. Prices were ridiculously low at the time they were manufactured because the lamps were machine made throughout. The "sewing" model, in color, sold for $4.65 per dozen, wholesale.

THE Fostoria Glass Company of Moundsville, W. Va., has weathered many business recessions and depressions and survived each. They have been one of the few really resourceful glass companies in America, and were among the first to use natural gas for fuel.

Fostoria developed a new technique for making kerosene lamps of glass—back in the days when kerosene was this nation's number one lighting source. The burner collars on these lamps were not fastened to the glass with cement; they were literally fused to the glass by shrinkage. They were on to stay and there was not the faintest leakage or osmosis of kerosene.

These glass lamps were the strongest and safest made. The stands, fonts and chimneys, globes and shades were of glass. The bodies were of "pressed and blown" glass, sometimes colored all over and sometimes parti-colored with analine dyes. The basic pattern of these lamps were the *Sunbeam*, the *Vesper* (see illustrations) and the *Renown*.

Fostoria oil lamps are relatively easy to find these days, and very often they have been electrified and shaded for immediate use in the home.

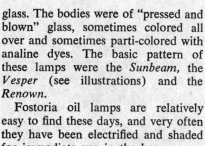

No. 181 Flat Hand.

No. 181 Footed Hand. Height, 6½ in.

No. 181 D. Height, 11 in.

The "Sunbeam" lamp by Fostoria. Pressed and blown in one piece and "superior to the all pressed lamps," said the maker. Decorated with looped panels, these were made in clear crystal, with alternating red and yellow panels, or with green and red panels. Same sizes and prices as the "Vesper" model. Colored panel models were fitted with color banded chimneys.

Sunbeam O Lamp.

Miniature Lamps

THE HISTORY of miniature lamps repeats that of lamps in larger size, and was similarly directed by the illuminant in popular use. As early as the 1820s, miniature glass lamps were being made at Sandwich for use with whale oil. Camphene and other burning fluids, composed of varying mixtures of turpentine, alcohol, and such, were known in the 1830s, but not until the 1850s did they begin to edge out the increasingly costly whale oil. Miniature lamps made for use with burning fluids were equipped with characteristic wick-holders of pewter. Like those which burned whale oil, they had no chimneys.

In the mid-1850s, just prior to the discovery of kerosene, when shale oil was being experimented with, lamp chimneys of glass were found to increase light and reduce smoking and odor. The first petroleum well was drilled in Titusville, Pennsylvania, in 1858; and with kerosene came the Golden Age of the miniature lamp, beginning in the 1870s, swelling through the 1880s, and declining by the end of the century when electricity took over.

Contrary to the intriguing thought that miniature lamps were made as "courting" lamps for lovers, it would seem they were actually developed as a utilitarian night light to replace candles; though they gave scarcely more light, they were somewhat safer. The many early examples with handles suggest their use as a means of lighting the way to bed.

Miniature lamps were made in metals as well as glass: pewter, brass, britannia. In design they followed the larger lamps of each period. Those before mid-century were small, growing slightly larger in the 1850s and appearing then in colored and opaque glass as well as clear.

With the years, they continued to grow in size and elaboration of design. As refinements were made in glass and in lamp designs, the miniatures became fancier, too, closing the century in a blaze of Art Glass, bird, animal, and other figure bases, and tiny Gone-with-the-wind replicas. Small size Rochester burners carried the miniature lamp for a short space in the 20th century.

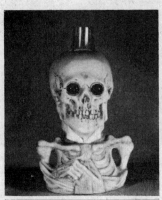

Top: Skeleton lamp; white bisque, blue and orchid trim; green glass eyes. Ht. 5½". Nutmeg burner. Possibly German. **Above:** Bulldog lamp; camphor glass, gold decoration; ht. 8". Hornet burner. **Below:** Tiffany oil lamp, signed L.C.T. on base and shade; chimney not signed. Ht. 12¾". Nutmeg burner; shade holder marked "The Twilight."

Top: Miniature hanging hall lamp; brass fixtures; pink satin glass shade; 20" to top of chain. **Bottom:** Brass hanging lamp; ribbed pink cased glass shade; cut crystal prisms; 22½" from top of chain. Nutmeg burner. Recently reproduced in the Lancaster, Pa. area, with milk glass shade and base.

Milk glass Gone-with-the-wind; painted pink, blue and green; praying child on shade, angel on base; ht. 9".

Milk glass; painted decoration of angels in deep pink and white on painted pale pink ground; ht. 7¾". Hornet burner.

Milk glass; embossed roses and scrolls painted orange; ht. 10½". Hornet burner.

Plume & Atwood

From Left: Acorn No. 733, Horner No. 633, and Nutmeg No. 1516, burners for miniature lamps from an original Plume & Atwood catalog, ca. 1906.

THE PLUME & Atwood Manufacturing Company of Waterbury and Thomaston, Connecticut, was founded in 1869. The company was composed of two branches, a brass strip mill located in Thomaston, and a fabricating plant in Waterbury where they manufactured brass lamp fixtures. It was here that the "Acorn," "Nutmeg," and "Hornet" burners for miniature lamps were made. Some burners are marked "P & A Mfg. Co.," and a few of the Nutmeg size burners bear the patent date of February 27, 1877.

Though they advertised all kinds of lamps for sale, Plume & Atwood made only the brass handles, collars, and burners; they purchased the glass bases and shades from various sources in America and abroad. The burners and collars were attached to the glass bases with plaster-of-Paris, not beeswax as some people have thought.

Conversely, some glass manufacturers purchased brass lamp fixtures from Plume & Atwood for their own wares; the Consolidated Lamp & Glass Company of Pittsburgh, Pennsylvania, offered miniature lamps equipped with Plume & Atwood burners in the trade magazine, *China, Glass and Lamps,* in 1894.

The fabricating division of Plume & Atwood Manufacturing Company was sold to Landers, Frary & Clark, and is now operating as the Dorset Division of the J. B. Williams Company, Incorporated. Miniature lamps with Plume & Atwood fixtures were being offered to the trade by their successors as late as 1920, and probably sold by them until 1921-22. Many of the burners originally made by Plume & Atwood are still being manufactured by the Dorset Division and have the initials "P & A" on the bottom.

Top: Elephant lamp, porcelain base, ivory color; matching glass shade, with brown and gold trim; ht. 9¾". Nutmeg burner. **Center:** Columbus lamp, satin-finished milk glass; ht. 10"; made by Consolidated Lamp and Glass Co., Pittsburgh, Pa., ca. 1894. **Bottom:** Bisque House lamp, embossed green trim, multi-color flowers; ht. 7½". Possibly German.

AMERICAN ART NOUVEAU LAMPS

by
Albert Christian Revi

EVEN in their day, Tiffany lamps were very expensive, and very few families could afford to grace their home with such opulent lighting fixtures. Fortunately there were firms in America manufacturing less expensive lamps in the Art Nouveau style. Their combined output was enormous, and these are the lamps collectors of modest means can find without too much difficulty.

In Meriden, Conn., Bradley & Hubbard, The Charles Parker Company, P. J. Handel & Company, Miller Brothers and others, were producing decorative lighting fixtures using Leaded Art Glass, Bent Glass, and painted glass shades.

Bradley & Hubbard were one of the largest manufacturers of fancy metalwares in America. They produced all of the metal parts for their lamps, but the glass parts and shades were purchased from various sources in and around Meriden.

The Charles Parker Company offered Art Nouveau table, boudoir, and desk lamps in their 1921–22 catalog. The shades used on these lamps were described as "Leaded Art Glass Overlaid Shades" (a combination of leaded glass with overlaid pierced metal frames), and "Overlaid Art Glass Shades" (panels of flat or bent colored glass with pierced metal overlaid frames). Parker's lamps were made in the following finishes: "Assyrian"—a combination of brown and green similar to an old Verde finish, but with more life; "Flemish"—old brass relieved with dark oxidation; "Pompeian"—a Verde finish; "Nubian"—a combination of light bronze and green simulating an antiqued effect; "Babylonian"—an old brass finish with relief in brown producing a gold effect; "Bazantine" (sic)—a Verde finish relieved with antique copper; "Persian"—golden brown with black relief designs producing an antique effect.

Glass shades, chipped on the outer surface and painted with colorful designs on the inside, were a specialty at P. J. Handel & Company. Mr. Handel

(Please turn the page)

Above: "Electric Portable" (table lamp) with "Leaded Art Glass Overlaid" shade and "Nubian" finished metal base; height, 21¾"; The Charles Parker Co.; ca. 1920. **Center:** Floor lamp with Leaded Art Glass shade and "Russian Bronze" base; height, 57"; Bradley & Hubbard; ca. 1915. **Right:** Table lamp with "Leaded Art Glass Overlaid" shade and "Flemish" finished metal base; height, 21¼"; The Charles Parker Co.; ca. 1920.

Above and left: Flower pots, illuminated inside the base and overhead, patented by Carl V. Helmschmied, April 14, 1908. From an original Helmschmied catalog.

Right: "Aquarium" table lamp; hand painted shade with "Verde" bronze base; Handel & Company; ca. 1920.

Left to right: "Hollyhock" table lamp; Bent Glass shade with "Old Copper" base; height, 20"; Bradley & Hubbard; ca. 1915. Table lamp with Leaded Art Glass shade and "Romanesque" metal base; height, 31"; Bradley & Hubbard; ca. 1915. "English Gothic" reading lamp; "Colonial Brass" with green and opal agate glass inserts in shade; height, 24"; Bradley & Hubbard; ca. 1915. "Pond Lily" lamp; green and opal Bent Glass shade with "Russian Bronze" base; height, 25"; Bradley & Hubbard; ca. 1915.

HANDEL Lamps

Advertisement for Handel table lamp; hand painted shade (No. 6852) with bronzed tripod stem and foot. These were usually 30" tall.

Above: "Egyptian" table lamp. Leaded Art Glass shade with bronze base; height, 30"; signed "Handel" on shade and base; ca. 1915. Author's collection.

Below and right: An assortment of table desk, and floor lamps from a brochure issued by Handel & Company; all of the lamps have hand painted glass shades; ca. 1915.

patented several decorating techniques, designs for lamps, and various kinds of metal fixtures for lamps. His patented design for a Pond Lily lamp is beautiful, but it wasn't the only lamp of this design produced in America. Similar lamps were made by Tiffany. The Albert Sechrist Manufacturing Company of Denver, Colo., Bradley & Hubbard, and others.

Miller Brothers produced lamps that were similar in design to those made by other Meriden, Conn., firms. For the most part they consisted of fancy metal bases with combination colored glass and pierced metal shades. Leaded Art Glass shades and Bent Glass shades were also made by this company, but—like Bradley & Hubbard—they purchased their glass shades and glass parts from an outside source.

In 1908, Carl V. Helmschmied of Meriden, Conn., patented an unusual combination lamp and flower receptacle. These illuminated Bent Glass flower pots were originally made by the Helmschmied Manufacturing Company; later, when he was in business for himself, Helmschmied continued to make these fixtures.

Hanging dome of Leaded Art Glass; diameter, 24"; H. J. Peters Co.; ca. 1910.

THE U. S. Art Bent Glass Co., Inc. of Hartford, Conn., manufactured very handsome Art Nouveau style shades for lamps and ceiling fixtures. Leaded Art Glass Shades, Bent Glass shades, and combination Leaded Art Glass and Bent Glass shades — some with long beaded

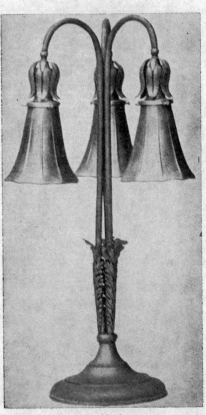

Moran & Hastings' table lamp, with "Verde Antique" finish and "iridescent glass shades," resembles Tiffany's "Pond Lily Shower Lamps"; ca. 1915; height, 24".

Hanging dome of Bent Glass with beaded fringe; diameter, 24"; H. J. Peters Co.; ca 1910.

fringe about the rim—were shown in color and black and white illustrations in their 1910 catalog.

On May 12, 1903, Alfred H. Freeman of Mt. Vernon, N. Y., patented a means for producing cameo relief designs on Art Glass windows and lamp shades. The relief designs were fashioned separately and attached to the surface of the glass where spaces of suitable size were etched or cut out. (See *Nineteenth Century Glass— Revised Edition,* by A. C. Revi.) Mr. Freeman worked on Art Glass windows and shades in New York City between 1892 and 1901; in 1899 he was employed by Louis C. Tiffany. From 1902 to 1919, Freeman owned and operated his own Art Glass business in Mt. Vernon, N. Y.

Four firms in Chicago, Ill., were producing Art Nouveau lamps and ceiling lights in the first quarter of the 20th century. R. Williamson & Company, established in 1885, offered some beautiful lighting fixtures to the

Hanging dome of brass with inserts of colored glass; diameter, 18"; Cincinnati Artistic Wrought Iron Works; ca. 1915.

trade in their 1917 catalog. The Moran & Hastings Manufacturing Company produced a comprehensive line of decorative lighting fixtures with Leaded Art Glass and Bent Glass shades. Their metal bases were advertised in a variety of finishes— "Rich Gilt," "Polished Brass," "Lemon Brass," "Black Iron," "Polished Nickel," "Polished Blue Steel," and "Statuary Bronze." The H. J. Peters Company was selling Bent Glass lamp shades and Leaded Art Glass windows in 1914. One of their catalogs contained several pages of full-color illustrations of iridescent glass shades, and color charts showing the various hues available in agate-like glass for windows and lamp shades. In December 1907, the Clinton Glass Company, 171 West 21 Street, Chicago, Illinois, advertised a new line of "Art Lamps" for home use in McClure's Magazine—a trade journal. These lamps consisted of Leaded Art Glass shades and metal bases *a la*

Table lamp with Bent Glass and pierced metal shade, "Verde Antique" tree trunk base; height, 23"; Moran & Hastings; ca. 1915. (Note resemblance to Tiffany's "Rustic" bases.)

Leaded Art Glass hanging dome; diam., 24"; The U.S. Art Bent Glass Co., Inc.; ca. 1915.

Table lamp of wrought iron with inserts of colored glass in shade; height, 25"; Cincinnati Artistic Wrought Iron Works; ca. 1915.

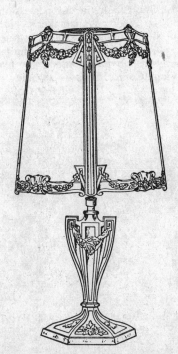

Leaded Art Glass and panelled hanging shade; diameter, 20"; Moran & Hastings; ca. 1915.

Tiffany. For ten years prior to 1907, the firm had created Leaded Art Glass windows for homes, churches and public buildings, and had just turned their attention to the manufacture of lighting fixtures for the home.

The Frankel Light Company of Cleveland, Ohio, manufactured lamps of every description. Many of their designs were similar to lamps produced by P. J. Handel & Company and William R. Noe & Sons of New York City. Frankel's cast metal openwork shades with art glass inserts were offered in finishes called "Roman Bronze," "Oxidized Copper," "Butler Silver," "White Enamel," and "Polished Nickel."

Table lamp with leaded Art Glass shade decorated about the rim with pink roses in full relief; shade marked "Pat. May 12, 1903" (Alfred H. Freeman, patentee); Bradley & Hubbard metal base. Height, 25 inches. Author's Collection.

Several American Art Nouveau glass manufacturers could have supplied this type of iridescent glass shade illustrated in Moran & Hastings' 1915 catalog.

Ceiling fixture of copper inlaid opal glass; R. Williamson & Co.; ca. 1920.

In Cincinnati, Ohio, the Cincinnati Artistic Wrought Iron Works, suppliers of artistic metal goods of every description, made lamps combining fancy wrought iron frames and bases with inserts of colored glass.

The Albert Sechrist Manufacturing Company, Denver, Colo., made "Water Lily" table lamps, ceiling and wall fixtures not unlike those made by P. J. Handel & Company. Their 1910, 1912, and 1914 catalogs were filled to overflowing with illustrations of Leaded Art Glass and Bent Glass lamp shades.

Many of the manufacturers mentioned in this article supplied fine department stores and specialty shops from coast to coast with beautiful lamps. One catalog in our possession, issued by John Wanamaker's New York store, about 1910, illustrates more than 40 Art Nouveau lamps; some were obviously made by two Meriden, Conn., firms — Bradley & Hubbard and P. J. Handel & Co.

"Water Lily" shade of green and white Bent Glass; diameter, approximately 10"; The Albert Sechrist Manufacturing Co.; ca. 1915.

Oil lamps with metal bases and Leaded Art Glass and Bent Glass shades (some with fringe). From a catalog issued by John Wanamaker, New York City; ca. 1910; height of center lamp, 18".

Ceiling fixture of Bent Glass and pierced metal; diameter, 17"; Frankel Light Co.; ca. 1920.

METALWARES AND TOOLS

Anything made of copper, brass, tin or iron appeals to an ever-increasing number of collectors. Some are attracted by the warm glow of polished copper or brass; others find the simple decorated or undecorated tinwares irresistable; still others find the heft and solidity of iron-wares most satisfying. Tools of all kinds, especially if their use is known to the collector, are bringing higher prices every day. Here, there is a trend towards specialization. There are collectors who acquire only sharp-edged tools, like axes, spokeshaves, planes and the like. Still others collect only measuring devices, or agricultural implements.

Early American Brass and Copper

... and its makers

by HENRY J. KAUFFMAN

THE quantities of copper and brass wares found in antiques shops in this country focus attention on the fact that though pieces may look alike they are not always equal in value. All copper teakettles, for example, appear essentially the same wherever they were made. While there is little difference in the value of imported English and Scandinavian kettles, the average American copper teakettle is worth a great deal more than either. This conclusion applies in a general way to all antiques, but it is recognized more acutely in the field of copper and brass because of the difficulty in determining the place of origin.

The historical perspective of coppersmithing in America might start as early as 1738 when Peacock Rigger advertised in the *Pennsylvania Gazette* that he was located in Philadelphia, "in Market Street, near the Sign of the Indian King," where he made and sold all kinds of copper work.

In the *Pennsylvania Journal* of September 4, 1766, Benjamin Harbeson announced he had removed his shop to the corner of Laetitia Court. He listed himself ready to serve on reasonable terms in such copper work as "stills, brewing coppers, sugar boilers, copper fish kettles, teakettles, boilers, soap coppers, brass and copper washing kettles, stew pans, frying pans, capuchin plate warmers, brass and copper scales, warming pans, chafing dishes, chocolate pots, copper ships' stoves, silversmith's boilers, brass and iron candlesticks, brass cocks of all sorts," and various items of London pewter, bell metal, and tin.

This imposing list of objects made by one man before the American Revolution indicates that there was a sizeable production of these objects at that time. Not all coppersmiths who worked at the trade until about 1850 made as wide a range of objects as Mr. Harbeson. However, styles changed very little as long as these objects were made by hand. The function of stills, for example, changed little throughout the period; hence the shapes remained much the same. The same is true of skillets, stewpans, warming pans, and the like.

It is important to note that many of the objects named in early advertisements in America have never been found or identified with a maker. The writer has never seen, definitely attributed to an American maker, brewing coppers, sugar boilers, soap boilers, washing coppers, copper ships' stoves and other of the items enumerated. Objects he has seen that have been positively identified as American products include one or two each of warming pans, liquid measures, stew pans, skillets, half-bushel measures, many copper kettles, and hundreds of copper teakettles.

A number of large copper kettles for making apple butter were made by the Schaum family in Lancaster, Pennsylvania. However, this particular use has never been found listed among products made by an 18th or early 19th century coppersmith. Kettles for making apple butter were not lined with tin as most other vessels were. Schaum kettles, made until 1926, were widely distributed through the country by Sears, Roebuck & Company.

The scarcity of stills, signed or unsigned, is curious, considering how many were made and how widely they were used. Of the half dozen the writer has seen, only three were marked.

It must be obvious to the reader that this perspective on early coppersmithing is focusing directly toward Pennsylvania. Though coppersmiths were working all over the Colonies, more signed pieces have been found by Pennsylvania craftsmen than the rest of the country put together. It may be that more Pennsylvania craftsmen signed their products, but it is the writer's opinion that the bulk of 18th century coppersmithing, and a great deal in the 19th century, was done in the Keystone State. A small number of New York coppersmiths signed their work, and there are scattered examples from New England and the South, but the main route for signed pieces seems to be from Philadelphia to Pittsburgh. Perhaps John Getz of Lancaster signed more pieces of copper ware than any other American coppersmith.

In identifying objects of copper and brass, a connoisseur may know styles well enough to attribute unmarked objects to American craftsmen or to European sources. For instance, teakettles with a hinged lid on the spout are regarded as foreign; no American examples are

FRANCIS SANDERSON,
COPPERSMITH from LANCASTER, living in GAY-STREET, BALTIMORE-TOWN, a few Doors above Mr. *Andrew Steiger's*,

MAKES and sells all sorts of COPPER-WORK, viz. stills of all sizes, fish and wash kettles, copper and brass, brewing-kettles, saucepans, coffee and chocolate pots, stew-pans, and Dutch ovens. He sells any of the above articles as cheap as can be imported from *England*, and carries on his Business in *Lancaster* as usual. He likewise carries on the TIN-BUSINESS in all its branches. Country shop-keepers may be supplied, either by wholesale or retail, and all orders sent from the country shall be carefully executed.

Advertisement from the *Maryland Journal and Baltimore Advertiser,* August 20, 1773. Sanderson worked in Lancaster, Pa. before the Revolution, later in Baltimore. At least one signed piece is known; others may exist in the Pennsylvania-Maryland region.

Typical Pennsylvania teakettle, signed by W. Heiss, 123 North Third St. Philadelphia, in rare 6½" diameter size. Most are 8 to 10" in diameter; a few are 12".

known. This need not mean that one signed by an American craftsman may not be found tomorrow. Such an exception will not greatly change the conclusion, for principles are not established on one or two exceptions.

The only sure method of identifying an American object of copper or brass is by finding a *bona fide* name of an American craftsman on it. A name alone is not proof of American production as a number of European craftsmen placed their names on their products. In the columns below are listed some of the craftsmen known to have worked in sheet copper and brass in America, with an identifying date. Any of their names *might* be found on an early brass or copper piece.

Copper frying pan made in Philadelphia, though maker's name cannot be distinguished. Possibly made by Bentley, a Philadelphia craftsman who made interesting forms and signed many pieces.

Some American Coppersmiths from Contemporary Records

Apple, Jacob	Philadelphia	1852
Apple, Philip	Philadelphia	1811
Attlee, William	Lancaster, Pa.	1790
Babb, John	Reading, Pa.	1806
Babb, Mathias	Reading, Pa.	1796
Bailey, William	Maryland & Pa.	1770 -1800
Beader, Henry	Harrisburg, Pa.	1820 -1826
Benson, John	New York	1841
Bentley, David	Philadelphia	1842 -1852
Bigger, Peacock	Philadelphia and Annapolis	1740 -1750
Bintzel, Daniel	Philadelphia	1842
Bintzel, William	Philadelphia	1852
Blanc, Victor	Philadelphia	1811
Bratzman, Andreas	Reading, Pa.	1813
Brotherton, E.	Lancaster, Pa.	1806
Brown, Thomas	Philadelphia	1852
Bruce, John	Baltimore	1850
Buchanan, James	Pittsburgh	1818
Buckhard, Peter	New York	1841
Carpenter, Alfred	Boston	1848
Carter, John	Boston	1848
Chessen, George	Philadelphia	1811
Clark, Forbes	Harrisburg, Pa.	1814
Clemm & Bailey	Baltimore	1784
Coltman, J. W.	Boston	1848
Cook, John	Philadelphia	1811
Cropley, John	Philadelphia	1852
Cunningham, Wm.	New York	1841
Darby, William	New York	1841
Davis & Wiley	Pittsburgh	1837
Deich, John	Philadelphia	1840
Delaney, John	Carlisle, Pa.	1792
Dickey, Isaiah & Co.	Pittsburgh	1837
	Maryland & Pa.	1770 -1800
Diller, Samuel	Lancaster, Pa.	1869
Dusenbury, Thomas	New York	1841
Dverter, Wm.	Lancaster, Pa.	1869
Eicholtz, Jacob	Lancaster, Pa.	1810
Eisenhut. John	Philadelphia	1811

Eisenhut, John D.	Philadelphia	1852
Fisher, Charles	York, Pa.	1832
Foos, Jacob	Lancaster, Pa.	1869
Forrest, Jacob	Lancaster, Pa.	1869
Gallagher, P.	Boston	1848
Getz, John	Lancaster, Pa.	1817 -1835
Gould, Joseph	Boston	1848
Graff, Joseph	Philadelphia	1852
Grauel, Daniel	Philadelphia	1811
Grimes, James	Pittsburgh	1837
Haldane, James	Philadelphia	1765
Hammett & Hiles	Philadelphia	1840
Hannah & Launy	New York	1841
Harberger, Henry	Philadelphia	1811
Harbeson, Benjamin	Philadelphia	1790
Harbeson, Joseph	Philadelphia	1766
Harbeson, Joseph	Pittsburgh	1807
Harley, Francis	Philadelphia	1840
Hasler, John	New York	1841
Heiss, Goddard	Philadelphia	1852
Heiss, Wm. Jr.	Philadelphia	1852
Heller, Henry	Philadelphia	1840
Hemmenway, B.	Boston	1848
Hill and Chamberlin	Boston	1848
Howard & Rodgers	Pittsburgh	1837
Hunneman & Co.	Boston	1848
Hutton, William	Philadelphia	1840
Jewell, Charles	New York	1841
Keefer, J & F.	Pittsburgh	1837
Kidd, John	Reading, Pa.	1790 -1800
Knox, Edward	New York	1841
Kower, John	Kutztown, Pa.	1841
Leacock, William	Philadelphia	1840
Lee, William	Philadelphia	1852
LeFrentz, George	York, Pa.	1783
Lightbody, Collin	New York	1841
Lindsay, David	Carlisle, Pa.	1792
Lock & Cordwell	Boston	1848
Loring, A. B.	Boston	1848
Loring, John G.	Boston	1848

Lyne, John	Harrisburg, Pa.	1811
Lyne, Robert	Philadelphia	1800
McBride, John	York, Co. Pa.	1783
McCauley, John	Philadelphia	1800
McCoy, Neil	York, Pa.	1784
Megee, George	Philadelphia	1840 -1852
Meredith, John	Philadelphia	1840
Miller, F.	Chambersburg, Pa.	1800
Miller, Jacob	Harrisburg, Pa.	1820
Minshall, Thomas	Middletown, Pa.	1802
Morrison, John	Philadelphia	1790
Noble, James	Philadelphia	1840
Oat, George	Philadelphia	1852
Oat, Israel	Philadelphia	1852
Oat, Jesse	Philadelphia	1811
Oat, Joseph	Philadelphia	1840
Oat, Joseph & Son	Philadelphia	1852
O'Bryon, Benjamin	Philadelphia	1840
Orr, Robert	Philadelphia	1800
Peters & Co.	Philadelphia	1811
Pier, Benjamin	New York	1841
Potter, James	Philadelphia	1790
Raborg, Christopher	Baltimore	1785
Read, W.	Philadelphia	1840
Reed, Robert	Lancaster, Pa.	1795
Reigart, Henry	Lancaster, Pa.	1803
Rink, Miller H.	Philadelphia	1840
Roberts & Son	Philadelphia	1840
Roberts, Israel	Philadelphia	1811 -1852
Roberts, James	Philadelphia	1852
Rulon, Jane	Philadelphia	1852
Schaum, Benjamin	Lancaster, Pa.	1790
Schaum, Peter	Lancaster, Pa.	1790
Schoenfelder	Reading, Pa.	1803
Seffron, George	York, Pa.	1789
Shenfelder, Asop	Reading, Pa.	1838
Shuler, George	Middletown, Pa.	1803
Simons, John	Philadelphia	1852
Stafford, Spencer	Albany, N. Y.	1794
Steele, George	Hartford, Conn.	1790
Stoehr, Daniel	Hanover, Pa.	1787 -1863
Strickler, Issac	Philadelphia	1811
Sweet, William	New York	1841
Thayer, Cornelius	Litchfield	1785
Thompson, John	Harrisburg, Pa.	1814
Tophan, Reuben	Philadelphia	1800
Town, John	Pittsburgh	1813
Trueman, Thomas	Philadelphia	1790
Tryon, George	Philadelphia	1811
Upperman, John	Lancaster, Pa.	1811
Varley, Abram	Marietta, Pa.	1814
Waters & Milk	Boston	1848
Weitzel, George	Lancaster, Pa.	1830
West, Jacob	Philadelphia	1840
Whitaker, Robert	Philadelphia	1811
Williamson, Isaac	New York	1841
Winter, Jonathan	York Co. Pa.	1788
Witherle, Joshua & Co.	Boston	1789
Witman, John	Kutztown, Pa.	1804
Wright, John	New York	1841
Yeates, Edmund	Philadelphia	1811
Youse, George	Harrisburg, Pa.	1807 -1814

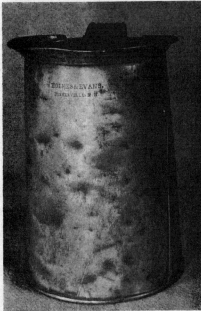

Copper measure by Holmes & Evans, Fisherville, N. H. Measures of copper are common, but signed ones are very rare. The sets were used for selling liquor to the retail trade at distilleries.

Unusually attractive brass warming pan with maker's intaglio stamp under group of holes near top showing initial "C" and a possible, though indistinct "A P." Surprisingly few warming pans, either of brass or copper, were signed, though almost every coppersmith of the 18th century mentioned them in his advertising. It is Mr. Kauffman's opinion that those which do exist with name of craftsman engraved on the lids are imported. Of the 3 marked pans in his own collection, none can positively be attributed to an American craftsman. One has an intaglio stamp with initials "I W" on the hinge, which might be interpreted as Joshua Witherle, a coppersmith in Boston in 1789. However, attribution of this type is precarious.

THE CHARM OF CAST IRON

by HENRY J. KAUFFMAN

A cast iron five-plate jamb stove, fired from the kitchen room was used to heat the Miksch Tobacco Shop. This stove, dated 1760, was cast in Pennsylvania by a local furnace and has the low German Biblical quotation: "Las Dich Nicht Gelyssten Deines Neststen Gut" (Thou shalt not covet thy neighbor's goods).

THE COLLECTING cognoscenti, whose specialty has been the artifacts of the 17th and 18th centuries are now turning to those of more recent origin. The products of Paul Revere, Henry Will, and Thomas Savery seem to have vanished, and what was once regarded as nondescript is now moving slowly to the center of the stage.

The logical solution for the embryonic collector is to begin acquiring commodities which have been back stage or are just emerging from the wings to show up in recent antiques shows and prestigious shops. Objects made of cast iron fit into this category; some early trivets and Hessian soldier and andirons are now regarded as good company for objects made of silver, pewter, or blown glass.

A limitation inherent in objects made of cast iron is that the material itself cannot claim an ancient heritage. None was found in the tomb of King Tutankhamen, nor did the Greeks use it in building the Parthenon. Cast iron is an invention of the late Middle Ages and a virtual newcomer among the substances of which important objects are made. If a blob of cast iron did appear in a bloomery before that time, it was thrown away because technicians did not know what to do with it.

By American standards, however, it is old, almost as old as the earliest settlements, for in the 1640s a furnace was built at Saugus, Massachusetts. It has recently been rebuilt so that anyone who visits it may see how metal was cast "in the good old days." Incidentally, Saugus was the first capitalistic venture in the New World, a fact which has little relevance to its production of artifacts. Up to now, only one product remains which can be attributed to it with any degree of confidence, but as objects of cast iron become increasingly sought after, others may be found.

Throughout the 18th and 19th centuries, many furnaces were operating along the eastern seacoast, producing pigs of iron as well as numerous finished objects such as cannons, cannon balls, skillets, griddles, trivets, kettles, firebacks, stove parts, and mortars and pestles. Over the years, most of these products had been relegated to scrap heaps or the bottoms of wells. Some of them have been rescued and given places of prominence in private collections and museums. Unfortunately, only a few of these fascinating objects can be identified as the products of a particular furnace or foundry since the name of the facility which produced them was rarely imprinted by

Trivet of cast iron marked on the back "W. B. Rimby, Baltimore, 1843." Notice the use of Pennsylvania German decorative motifs. Osburn Collection.

Unmarked mortar and pestle. Many of these were made in America in the 19th century. Only a few bear the imprint of the maker. Kauffman Collection.

Tulips decorate this cast iron trivet. Marked on the back "W. B. R. 1843." The flat surfaces on the designs were created by wear, probably sliding of a flat-iron across its surface for many years.

Heart-shaped waffle iron thought to be 18th century and of Pennsylvania origin.

Waffle iron of cast iron decorated with Pennsylvania German motifs. Kauffman Collection.

the pattern maker or foundryman.

Possibly the most desirable products of the furnace in the collector's view are firebacks and stove plates. To make these, patterns of wood were pressed in a bed of sand in front of a furnace; after the furnace was tapped, the cavity was filled with molten iron. In this way the details of the pattern were dramatically duplicated.

A fireback was a single sheet of iron placed against the back wall of the fireplace to promote the reflection of heat into the room, a function for which a masonry wall was quite ineffective. Before the 1760s, when stove pipe came into common use in America, a Pennsylvania stove consisted of five plates, the open end being inserted into the rear wall of a fireplace in the adjoining room. The wood was fed into the stove through the fireplace, and both the stove and the fireplace used a common chimney for the disposal of smoke. Many of the side plates of the stoves were decorated with designs with Biblical themes. An authorative book, describing these stove plates in great detail, was published in 1914 by their most avid collector, Henry Mercer. It is aptly called *The Bible In Iron.*

Several furnaces were famous because they produced military "materiel" for the American Revolution, but such products are a bit clumsy to collect, and few of them have survived. A cannon which was rejected because of imperfections lies on the casting bed at Cornwall Furnace, near Lebanon, Pennsylvania. Such identification is unusual. In general the lack of identifying marks has caused a certain apathy among collectors regarding the owning of such objects.

A number of so-called gypsy kettles survive, ranging in size from quite small to very large, which bear the names of the furnaces where they were cast. Although the large kettles cannot be regarded as household collectibles, the small ones fit well into this category; a perfect example might be regarded by some collectors as an object of considerable charm. In addition, a number of signed teakettles survive; these are attractive, particularly if they are suspended with a tilting device, which permits the pouring of hot water from the kettle without removing it from the fireplace.

A profusion of trivets has survived; however, most of them might be regarded as "late," and few of the earliest examples are signed. W. B. Rimby, a foundryman working in Baltimore in the 1840s, made several attractive models, some of which are signed and dated. Doubtless other signed examples survive; however, those by Rimby are particularly pleasing. His use of Pennsylvania folk art motifs suggests that many of them were made for merchants or peddlers operating in Pennsylvania.

Frying pans, andirons, mortars and pestles, and similar objects frequently bear the imprint of their makers. Some of the cast iron balusters and porch posts used in the South were made in the North and shipped to such ports as Charleston and New Orleans. When the gold rush was at its height, entire houses of cast iron were shipped to California where they were assembled in a few days; they proved to be completely adequate for miners who were "in a hurry."

Finally, in the middle of the 19th century, entire buildings were constructed of cast iron, some of them being many stories high. The most famous structure was the Crystal Palace in London which housed the great British Trade Exhibition of 1851. A few buildings in America employed a facade of cast iron. A number of them survive in the Front and Arch Street area in Philadelphia. Though one can collect such items only photographically, they remain an interesting facet of American industry and architecture and are well worth preserving as typical of an era when America was solidly built.

Friends of Cast-Iron Architecture

The Friends of Cast-Iron Architecture are seeking new members who want to see that cast-iron buildings are recognized and appreciated. Honorary co-chairmen of the group are Henry-Russell Hitchcock and Sir Nikolaus Pevsner. Dues for becoming a Friend are $2.00. Write: Mrs. Margot Gayle, Chairman, Friends of Cast-Iron Architecture, 44 West 9th Street, Room 20, New York, N.Y. 10011.

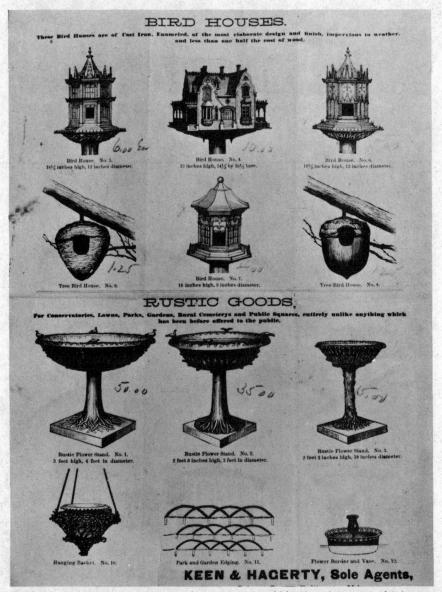

Bird houses and "Rustic" goods made of cast iron were sold by Keen & Hagerty of Baltimore, Md., in the late 19th century.

COLLECTING CAST IRON COMFORT

by FLORENCE THOMPSON HOWE

Cast-iron comfort with an old wood-burning Victorian stove of elegant design.

OLD STOVES, in today's electrically operated space-age, are fast becoming as obsolete as the horse and buggy or the milkman. Should world conditions create an oil shortage, as was the case in the second World War in the early 1940s, these old wood-burning stoves could become the pot of gold at the end of the heatless householder's rainbow.

Hopefully, no such situation will arise. But these antique heat makers still have a place, even in the normal programs of the "affluent society." There's cast iron comfort for you in the old wood-burning stove in a hunting cabin or a fishing shack; in a guest cottage or studio at your summer place; or even in the ell of a remodelled farmhouse in a cold climate. Installed as stand-by equipment, they do a job for you in remote areas where electricity suffers frequent "outages" from storms. They'll keep your water pipes from freezing or, used as auxiliary heat, cut your operating cost on your main heating system in extreme weather.

But where could you buy a stove today? Not at a city hardware store. At the antique dealer's, the second-hand shop, or the country auction, perhaps. So it's good to know something about these old stoves before you buy.

Philadelphia pattern stoves were introduced in New England in the early 1800s, some of them are dated "1774." Stumble onto one of these and you really have a collector's item. They were box stoves with an oven over the fire. The only boiler hose was in the bottom of the oven. Castings weighed from 700 to 800 pounds and appeared to have been made by pouring the metal into an open flat mold. There was no rim on the pipe-hole by which to secure the pipe, but a wrought-iron rim of a half-inch thickness with a flange for support was fitted to the hole to form the union between the stove and the pipe.

A Philip Willcox stove is worth picking up, too. Philip Willcox was a stove-maker and an early merchant (1823) in Springfield, Massachusetts.

In 1827, Philip Wilcox advertised stoves, stove pipes, and iron hollow ware.

Wood-burning stove with hearth and brass finials on top made by Philip Wilcox. First quarter 19th century.

Wood-burner with Gothic facade and dainty cabriole legs made in Troy, N. Y.

Wood-burning stove of sheet metal bears manufacturer's identification "Reeves/Dover/Copper Alloy."

He thought well of his merchandise, for in one of his advertisements he says:

PHILIP WILLCOX

Respectfully informs his friends and the public that he has just received from New York an assortment of E. Hoyt's highly approved patent COOKING STOVES. The above mentioned stoves are so constructed as to convey the steam arising from the boilers (which is admitted to be almost the only objection to cooking stoves) directly into the pipe without the least inconvenience to the cooking; also the extreme heat that arises directly from the fire passes off, which renders it equally as pleasant and as healthy as an open Franklin; with the addition of his patent oven. They are considered by those who have had them in use, superior to any stoves offered to the public.

Willcox also advertised in 1826, stove-pipes, live geese feathers, and fan and side lights, probably for the old front door, "filled to any pattern." He announced, too, that "PEDLARS will be accommodated with a good assortment, and at low prices." And believe it or not, he said he had "a bathing-tub to let."

Styles and decorative design in 19th century stoves usually related to the furniture of the period. Delicate Victorian filigree often reflected a mighty hot fire. There were some of the New York-born "parlor" stoves that were positively Gothic in feeling. Others, notably those made by the Shakers in Connecticut, were chaste and simple, with ornamentation reduced to the least common denominator. These little Shaker stoves, low-slung, long and narrow, with duck feet, would not be out of tune with contemporary decor.

The Franklin stoves used often today in lieu of fire-place heating, carry much of fireplace charm, but throw out more heat because not so much is lost up the chimney. Franklin himself said of his device: "My common room, I know, is made twice as warm as it used to be with a quarter of the wood I formerly consumed there." (This he wrote in 1744!)

Antiques dealers report that there is still much interest in these old stoves. Prices vary, of course, with their age, condition, and desirability either for functional use or decorative antiques. One of the most delightful of the later stoves is an early model of the Florence oilstove, a rococo little number topped with a slide-out plate and grill. Called "Florence Favorite," and dated "1871," it is only 18 inches high. It is not a wood-burner, but it throws out a lot of heat on a gallon of oil! A forerunner, doubtless, of our present-day portable, though much more engaging in appearance, it is really a desirable old stove. It was made by the Florence Mfg. Co. of Florence, Massachusetts, almost a hundred years ago.

Early oilstove (1871) made by Florence Manufacturing Co., Florence, Mass.; height 18 inches.

The "Economy" wood and coal heating and cooking stove manufactured by Comstock, Castle & Co., Quincy, Ill., ca. 1880.

"The Ivy," manufactured by The Richmond Stove Co., Norwich, Conn., 1882. Decorated with Low's Art Tiles, bronze and nickel trimmings.

Universal Base Burner No. 50, manufactured by Co-Operative Stove Works, Troy, N. Y., 1883.

An Introduction to the...
TIN PEDDLER

by
MARGARET MATTISON COFFIN

Low oval caddy, probably used for tea or spices. Decoration typical of Pennsylvania wares. Collection Mrs. Emily Heath.

Tin PEDDLERS grew popular in the mid-eighteenth century after New England tinsmiths began making more tinware than they could sell at home. Rural communities are filled with stories about these itinerants. Some tales are true; many have been embroidered.

Most states enacted laws controlling the licensing of peddlers. In Vermont, Vilas Noyes of Burlington was issued a license on March 28, 1845, granting him the privilege of being a "PEDLER (sic) within this State for one year from the date hereof, for the purpose of pedling (sic) goods, wares and merchandise (except jewelry) of the growth and manufacture of the United States, and he has paid therefor the sum of Fifteen dollars." In 1840 the state of New York amended its yearly fee for peddling: If the peddler traveled "On Foot," $20; if he used one horse, or if he used a boat or boats, $30; if he used a vehicle drawn by more than one horse his annual license fee was $50.

Peddlers seldom received cash for their goods; usually they traded for whatever the farmer had on hand— food and farm products, including cow

hides and horns, old silver and rubber, old wrought and cast iron, wool and woolen stockings, furs and pelts, and the like. Morillo Noyes of Burlington, Vt., was one who left printed lists along his route, giving the prices he would allow for various items. On his "List of Barter" dated November 25, 1854, were more than 90 items from apples and eggs to mustard seed. He noted, in handwriting at the bottom, "Woodchucks, Weasels, and Squirrels worthless." However, in the wanted list he was allowing 2¢ for a house cat and kittens. A prime mink brought $1.

Connecticut became notorious as the breeding place for these early door-to-door salesmen who might specialize in such notions as needles, thread, and jackknives, or sell just tinware. As time went on, they were apt to carry a conglomeration of necessities—tinware and indigo, textiles and brooms, clocks and knocked-down chairs. Legend even has them carrying wooden nutmegs and handcarved hams.

Many peddlers started their routes on "shank's mare"—they walked. One peddler, Mike Beason from Turkey Valley, Pa., pulled a two-wheeled cart.

Red coffee pot from Pennsylvania has symmetrical design. Hershey Estates Museum, Hershey, Penna.

Decorated tin tray found in Maine. Scratched on back "Mary Ellen B . . . (illegible), Brookfield, 1845." Author's collection.

Oval box has design typical of many New York State pieces. Author's collection.

Some peddlers rode horseback, their goods in saddlebags or tin trunks. When roads improved in the 1800s, most of them graduated to horse-drawn carts somewhat similar to stagecoaches although more box-like. Cart wheels were high and iron-rimmed. (Sometimes runners replaced these wheels although peddling in wintertime was rare.)

These tin carts, divided into compartments of assorted sizes, sported racks on top from which pots and pans rattled. At the back, a sharp stake held sheepskins and other bartered pelts. Here the scales to weigh barter usually hung, and the tailgate was often piled high with bartered rags and old metal. Usually there was a drawer beneath the peddler's seat to hold personal belongings. Most carts were gaily painted in red, green, and yellow or in elegant black and gold. Elaborate printing on the side of the cart announced the peddler's name and his hometown. A few master peddlers had fleets of carts as fancy as circus wagons; matched horses towed these traveling country stores from town to town.

A peddler did not lead an easy life. Frequently he had to prove his independence—he was his own doctor, cook, and mechanic. Although many peddlers were welcome visitors—often they traveled the same routes for years—sometimes it was difficult to find a place to stay at night. A peddler whose route went through Charlton, N. Y., nickamed the present Maple Avenue "Featherbed Lane" because, although he was frequently invited to "stay the night" along this road, he swore that every bed had a feather tick, and he was allergic to feathers!

In contrast, Milo Wells, a New England peddler known to have a fondness for rum, experienced difficulty in finding a place to stay at night. Finally,. one evening, he pounded on the door of a darkened farmhouse. The farmer stuck his night-capped head out of an upstairs window and called, "Why in tunket are y' a-tryin' t' peddle tinware in the middle of the night?" The peddler explained that he'd de-

Deed box with fine brush strokes and typical symmetry of design. Author's collection.

cided to work all night since he hadn't been able to find a place to sleep. As he'd anticipated· he was invited in—the farmer wanted to return to bed.

The diary of William Holbrook, a peddler who worked out of Burlington, Vt., mentions a time his horse fell through the ice on Lake Champlain; the horse was lost and the tin cart damaged. Holbrook walked for miles. (An occasional walk may have been a relief: A tin cart had no springs; the chassis rested on leather straps which, of course, did not give; and the best roads were corduroy roads where logs lay side by side to give a solid base.) Ruts and holes in dirt roads caused many broken wheels, a plague to all travelers.

Inns which welcomed peddlers—

some didn't—left much to be desired. Holbrook wrote about a stay at Waterloo, N. Y., where he was "drove out of bed by an army of bedbugs." In Fort Covington, also in northern New York, he commented: "Oh the musketoes — enough to kill body and soul. No sleep nor rest on the bed, then under it, then on the piazzo."

Peddling, despite its objectionable features, was an occupation which appealed to many adventurous young men who wanted to see the world and earn a living while doing so. A Maine gentleman wrote in the early 1800s that more of his state's young men were being graduated from her tin carts than from her favorite college,

Large tin teapot. Courtesy The Farmer's Museum, Cooperstown, N. Y.

Early tin colander, probably the work of Shaker tinsmiths. Author's collection.

Covered sugar bowl with painted decoration of autumn leaves. Hershey Estates Museum, Hershey, Penna.

Tray with crystalized tin in center. Similar decoration found today in Connecticut, New York and Pennsylvania. Author's collection.

spot. Here a peddler was murdered and robbed, and today, supposedly, this place is haunted. Pedlar's Bridge (New Rochelle, N. Y.) was also the site of murder. On No Head Hill in Washington County, N. Y., a peddler was decapitated by robbers, and we're told that his ghost wanders disconsolately still, searching for its head. Near Bellows Falls, Vt., Horse Heaven Hill has another story to tell: A peddler, his cart out of control, shouted, "Go to heaven!" to his horse, and rode his cart over an embankment.

A peddler ghost returns to Dresden on Lake Champlain each year on the anniversary of his murder to float across the lake and back, moaning with a loon-like cry. Another peddler ghost in Fishkill in the Catskills used to haunt the cellar of an old inn, holding a faint light and peeking timidly through the high windows.

Still another phantom drives his tin cart at night along an old road; folks can hear horse hooves hit the ruts, wheels creak, and tinware rattle until the cart reaches the exact place where a peddler was once ambushed, robbed, and killed.

But the life of the peddler couldn't have been *too* bad, after all—many of them return to their peddling, even as ghosts.

Bowdoin. "And," said he, "it is believed and judged a far less proportion of all the pedlars (sic) have been failures in life than of the college graduates."

Many peddlers eventually settled down in country stores; some, like Isaac Gimbel, Nathan Strauss and David May, originated department stores which are prominent today.

There were several peddlers who were characters — like Cling Clang, who vaulted through Maine and Nova Scotia using long, brass-tipped poles, carrying his ware in a sack slung over his shoulder. Cling Clang never mixed his foods; he'd drink a cup of tea, then suck a teaspoonful of sugar. He wore clothes made from gunny sacks, went barefoot except in mid-winter, and hated to hear a rooster crow.

Sidney Thomas, of Herkimer County in New York, who had lost a foot in an accident was both tinsmith and peddler: he moved by cart along his route, and when he needed to walk, traveled on a tin foot he had manufactured for himself.

Peddler Briggs, another New Yorker, had lost both legs just below the hips. He wore short, heavy leather breeches and swung along using hands for feet and arms for legs.

Near Norton, Vt., Blind Cripton peddled for years. The voices of neighborhood children were his landmarks. He was a beloved visitor who enjoyed philosophizing with his friends, discussing religion, history, or medicine.

Place names remind old timers of legendary peddlers, frequently ones who were murdered by thieves. Spook Hollow near Milton, N. Y., is such a

Tin teakettle. Courtesy The Farmer's Museum, Cooperstown, N. Y.

Peddler's cart with side raised to show compartments. Courtesy The Farmer's Museum, Cooperstown, N. Y.

ODDITIES IN EARLY AMERICAN TINWARE

by CARROLL HOPF

THE COLLECTOR of antiques has a wide choice from which to make his personal concentration. If, for example, he elects Folk Art as his interest, he may generalize and collect objects in such diverse media as iron, wood, pottery, or glass, or he may specialize in some particular category. The photographs here represent a specialization of artifacts fashioned from tinplate.

Tinwares are made of thin iron sheets coated with tin. The tin retarded rust and provided a bright, easy-to-clean, sanitary surface. By present day standards, the tinplate objects pictured here can be classified as oddities, or at least in the realm of the unusual, when compared to the ordinary everyday utensils fashioned in tin over the years —the pails, dippers, measures, and canisters that were made in abundance.

All of these examples are products of local tinsmiths who, along with various other craftsmen, once formed an important segment of our rural society. In addition to being unusual in form, each piece reflects a high degree of skill and expertise of craftsmanship on the part of its maker.

Good tinware of high quality may still be found on today's antique market. Approximately half of the items illustrated were purchased within the past four years.

This particular form of ear trumpet is advertised as the "Miss Greene Hearing Horn" in the 1901 Sears, Roebuck & Co. catalog. "Its peculiar formation is especially adapted to gather in sounds and convey them audibly and distinctly to the ear." It has a black japanned finish and measures 18¼" in length. **Collection of Miss M. Carrie.** (Photo by Poist)

Below: Upon several occasions tinplate containers similar to the illustrated examples have been referred to in contemporary writings as "measures." Certainly they may have served this purpose; however, their cylindrical form and side-mounted strap handles at the top are derivative of the drinking mug form used in the latter 18th and early 19th centuries. It may well be that they were used as drinking vessels. Respectively they measure 6" and 9⅝" high by 4" and 5" diameter. Both probably date before mid-19th century. **Penna. Farm Museum Coll.**

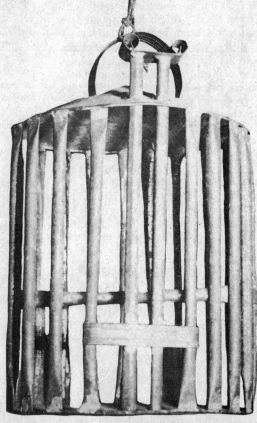

Of early 19th century origin, this bird cage may well have housed a quail, cardinal, robin, or any other bird small enough to fit in it. Completely made by hand, it has a sliding up and down door, two bars of which extend through the top of the cage. It is 13" high; 9" in diameter. It was discovered in central New York state. **Author's Collection.**

Above: Tin Horns are generally common items. The majority are straight forms measuring anywhere from 12" to over 4 ft. in length. They were used frequently by coach and stage drivers, peddlers, and on the farm to hail the men in from the fields. This example is unusual for its rectangular form. It emits a powerful one-note tone. Probably dating mid-19th century, it measures 23" overall length. **Penna. Farm Museum Coll.**

Below: Possibly tin handle table forks and knives were common at one time. However, the fork shown here is the only example the author has seen. The shaft of the fork is skillfully fitted into the hollow tin handle. This example probably dates from the first half of the 19th century; it measures 7 1/8" in length. **Penna. Farm Museum Coll.**

The tin shaving mug is probably contemporary with pottery and porcelain examples which also bear an appendage to the side. It is interesting to note the variance in the appendages. Many are in circular shallow bowl form added at the top of the mug; in this form the lather was raised from soap. The other type of appendage, as shown here, was fitted onto the side and extends the height of the mug. This probably served as a storage receptacle for the shaving brush. Measuring 4 1/4" high and 3 1/4" diameter, this example dates from the last half of the 19th century. **Penna. Farm Museum Coll.**

"Mr. & Mrs. D. W. Van Auken, From Reform School" is inscribed on the crest rail of this delightful tin chair. A decorative twisted banding is applied to the top of the crest rail, center splat, and around the seat skirt. The chair has never been painted. Probably dating from the last quarter of the 19th century, it has an overall height of 35". **William Penn Memorial Museum Collection, Harrisburg, Pa.** (Photo by Karl G. Rath)

That our ancestors were a thrifty and saving lot is well attested by this pitcher, mended with a tin handle. The humble repair is ably done and expresses someone's skill as a worker of tinplate. The pitcher is an earthenware type quite common during the middle decades of the 19th century. It is banded in blue and white slip and of English origin; 8" high, 6" diameter. **Penna. Farm Museum Coll.**

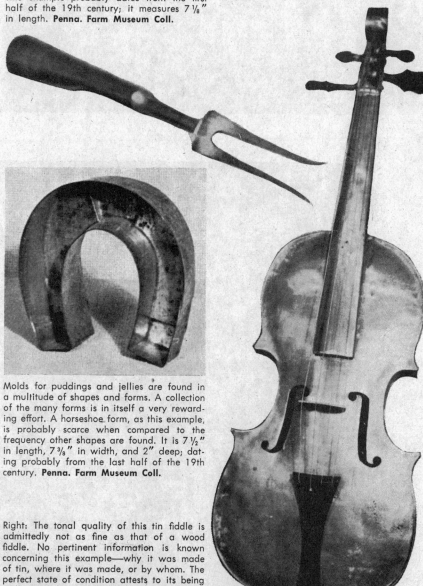

Molds for puddings and jellies are found in a multitude of shapes and forms. A collection of the many forms is in itself a very rewarding effort. A horseshoe form, as this example, is probably scarce when compared to the frequency other shapes are found. It is 7 1/2" in length, 7 3/8" in width, and 2" deep; dating probably from the last half of the 19th century. **Penna. Farm Museum Coll.**

Right: The tonal quality of this tin fiddle is admittedly not as fine as that of a wood fiddle. No pertinent information is known concerning this example—why it was made of tin, where it was made, or by whom. The perfect state of condition attests to its being well cared for through the years. Its length is 22". **Penna. Farm Museum Coll.**

LEFT:
Resting on the shaving horse, or schnitzelbank, at the Pennsylvania Farm Museum, Landis Valley, Lancaster, Pa. is a buck saw to the **right**, a chamfer knife at **left**; floor plane and frame saw are in background.

BELOW:
Collection of woodworking tools, also at the Pennsylvania Farm Museum. Shown above a carpenter's bench are, **at left**, an assortment of broad and hewing axes; **in center**, various types of post hole or mortising axes; **at right**, adzes.

EARLY TOOLS
for Building Houses

by PHYLLIS T. BALLINGER

MOST important of the pioneer's tools was his axe. With it, he felled the trees to clear his land for planting and to provide lumber for the buildings he would erect. There are many types and many sizes of axes, as the novice collector will discover. The broadaxe with its flaring blade is the most distinctive. Some were designed for specific jobs, like one with a very short blade used in making the mortise for fence poles.

The better axes were made by folding the iron around the handle pattern and inserting a steel edge between the two halves, hammering it in. Sometimes two separate pieces of iron were used instead of one folded piece. The steel blade could be honed to hair-splitting sharpness.

Important in the early community was the blacksmith who fashioned the tools and kept them in repair. By the color of the iron and the length of the spark, he knew when they were properly forged to withstand the grueling treatment they would have to take. Regional characteristics which bespoke the blacksmith's heritage, be he German or English, are discernible in tools produced in different areas.

Frequently the farmsteader gave his livestock precedence over his family and erected his barn before he built his house. For all his buildings, he had to square the logs to get beams, corner posts, and rafters. Tools had to be flexible in their use, and in squaring his logs he probably used the same axe with which he had felled his trees. Likely he used an adze to smooth off some of the roughness.

The adze, which has a three or four inch blade positioned along the same line as the handle, was forged in a similar fashion as the axe. Those with steel cutting edges were the most desirable. Close inspection of the head frequently reveals where it was hammer-welded. Adze markings are what we look for in early construction to determine its hand-made quality.

To get planks, before saw mills were readily available, the builder suspended his squared logs over a pit or on trestles where they were sawn lengthwise by two men handling a long saw. Some such saw blades were single; others were supported by a frame. Those in a frame are considered earlier in style.

Making Shingles

To make his shingles, he used a froe, a cutting tool with a blade at right angles to a short handle, the blade varying in length from six to 13 inches. He took blocks of wood, 14 inches or so long, and using a wooden mallet to strike the froe at the proper angle, he could split off a number of shingles, or "shakes," in quick succession. When he had split or "rived" a sufficient quantity, he would shave the edges with a drawknife so they would fit snugly, slightly overlapping, on the roof.

A shaving horse, called a schnitzel-bank in areas settled by Germans, was a help in shaving shingles. The worker sat astride the bench; the wood was held in a vise-like clamp, with his foot applying pressure on the supporting piece. Both his hands were free to draw the knife.

With the structure framed in and the roof in place, the builder faced the interior work. The inside finish required many more tools than the framework, and finishing tools offer a wide field for collecting. Most frequently found are planes. It would not be uncommon for a professional builder to have had a hundred or more planes, each making a distinctive cut. Many of them bear initials of the craftsman and the year in which they were made. After 1800, tools stamped with the name of the manufacturing company are found.

The professional housewright or joiner used many tools besides those mentioned here. He needed a "dog" to keep his logs from rolling when he worked with heavy rough timber before it was dressed. He needed a chalkline and scribes to mark where he would make his cuts, a square and a level and a plumbline to keep him accurate. Augers, braces and bits, and other drilling tools were important; hammers, indispensable.

Craftsmen were careful about their tools. If they made them themselves, which they frequently did during their apprenticeship, their tools were often artfully fashioned with decorative touches. Proportions were good, and everything about them had the appearance of artistry and careful craftsmanship.

Starting with a few basic tools used by the pioneer and progressing to the more advanced tools which enabled the master builder to construct handsome Georgian edifices with finely carved woodwork and handsome detail, we have an infinite range of collectibles.

The old patina on tools is a mark of integrity and should be retained. To preserve iron tools, aluminum oxide cloth is frequently used to take away the heavy rust accumulated over years of non-use. A little stove black serves where touching up is desired, and a rub of wax protects the metal from further oxidation. To revive wooden surfaces of tools, boiled linseed oil thinned with turpentine is favored.

Tools Used By Early American Farmers

by PHYLLIS T. BALLINGER

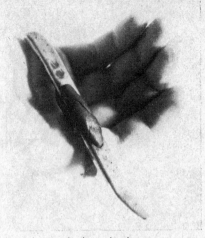

A steel corn shucker, also known as a corn pick. The leather loop held the tool in the palm of the farmer's hand, and he used the tip to rip the husk from the corn as he removed the ear from the stalk. Author's collection.

An assortment of tools used by 19th century farmers. Left to right: Two types of portable grist mills; a corn sheller; a bag holder; a portable mill for pulverizing sugar; a hay hook to lift hay into the mow; a seed potato cutter; and a grinding stone. Hanging on the uprights are bag wagons to move large sacks of produce, and a wheel barrow made from a single piece of wood. The cross piece on the ground, which resemble ladders, were used to support hay when stacked in wagons. Hanging on the rear wall are a plow, harrows, spacers, and planters. The Conestoga wagon was an important vehicle used to transport farm produce to nearby towns and cities. Courtesy Pennsylvania Historical & Museum Commission, Harrisburg, Pa.

ALTHOUGH AN industrial giant and tops in the field of technology, our nation is rightfully proud of its agrarian heritage. Farms throughout the United States, many of them owned by the fourth and fifth generation of farmers, have fed and helped sustain the world's population. The tools once used to plow the fields and cultivate the land have been dwarfed by today's mechanized equipment, but collectors are taking an increased interest in them.

The farmer who had only man power, or that supplied by the horse or ox, had to clear his land with crude equipment. He was lucky if he could harness his horse to a huge chain with a mammoth hook to pull boulders and tree stumps, with roots attached, from his field. After clearing most of the

obstacles he pushed and guided his plow while his horse in front of him pulled. Many old plows are made entirely of wood except for the iron clod breaker. Well proportioned to stand the stress, they echo the rugged character of the early American farmer.

Rollers were used to firm the earth; or to crush large clods of soil in preparation for planting. The early rollers were frequently cross sections of logs with a channel hollowed out of the middle so that it could be fastened with pins to a rope and drawn by a horse or ox. Harrows that smooth the fields in preparation for planting, or "drags" as the handmade types were frequently called, can be found in several shapes, the "A" harrow being the most common. These

were particularly useful on ground that was being planted for the first time or to help cover seeds sown on light soil. One of the harrows in the Pennsylvania Farm Museum is made entirely of wood; even the cross members and teeth were lashed into place with sturdy vines.

Going back to time immemorial, farmers sowed their seed by throwing it out with their hands; this was called broadcasting. Forerunners of modern planters permitted the farmer to place his seeds in rows or furrows so that none might be cast on rocky or barren areas. There is an infinite variety of early planters; farmers called them "grain drills." Some would automatically space the seed while others were used in conjunction with a marker.

Cultivators gradually replaced hoes

to loosen the soil during the growing period. Sickles were used for reaping, as were scythes. A little later, cradle scythes were used. These consisted of a broad blade with three or more wooden fingers the same length as the blade which gathered the grain in bunches as it was cut. Flails used to thresh the grain were made from two pieces of wood held together with a leather thong. The staff or handle was made of oak; the break or club of hickory. Manipulating it to separate the chaff from the grain was a tricky job which required a certain knack and an experienced flick of the wrist if it was to be done safely. When Cyrus H. McCormick patented his reaper in 1834 and upset conservative farmers, the balance of labor was tipped and the mechanical age was introduced to the farm.

Among the collectibles depicting our farm heritage are wooden hay forks, made of birch and hickory and steamed into their graceful curved shape; wooden grain shovels smoothed to a satin finish with the abrasive wear of many harvestings. Open or pierced shovels used for harvesting root crops such as potatoes are interesting.

A collector might find the large grinders the farmer used to sharpen his tools unwieldly in his game room but the smaller whetstones in their horn holders have a unique charm. Some are initialed and dated and they are, of course, more desirable. Choppers to harvest and cut pumpkin and squash for barnyard feeding of livestock are also of interest. Hand forged with wooden handles, they can

be found in almost as many shapes as the smaller hand chopper the farmers' wives used in their kitchens.

The gracefully curved cornshucker with its leather finger grip and padding to protect the farmer's hand as he pulled the corn from the stalk is another device often overlooked. One might not associate this homey tool with the praxitelean curve known to

students of art, but there it is, beautiful and useful.

Collectors of tools are impressed with their esthetics, their fineness of line and beauty. The patina of age enhances the integrity of their design. No wonder the tools of the farmer along with those of the tradesman are taking a prominent place in today's collections!

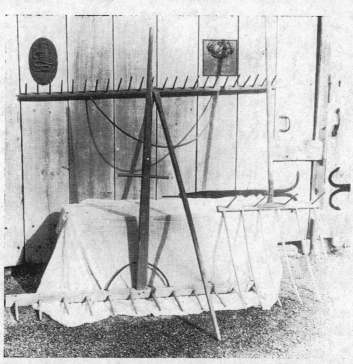

Two wooden rakes and a hay fork used in the 19th century. After the farmer had cut and sheaved his grain he would use these huge rakes, which were also called bull rakes or hay drags, to gather that which was left behind. To the long shaft he would harness his horse and comb the field for loose grain. The hay fork at the right has dowels spaced across the transverse bar to stack the hay. Collection Pennsylvania Farm Museum.

Early 19th century plow with cast iron moldboard. These varied considerably in design, and the use of iron in their construction was at first resisted by some farmers who thought iron "poisoned the soil and encouraged the growth of weeds." The fence pole vice, seen behind the plow, was used to hold the rail while its ends were shaped to fit the holes in the vertical posts. Collection Pennsylvania Farm Museum.

A pumpkin cutter, also used to cut roots, turnips, and squash for feeding livestock. Made of wrought iron and stamped with the maker's name, "J. Knoll," it has a wooden handle with a foot tread allowing the farmer to exert added pressure for chopping. Blacksmiths often made these implements to their own design and they can be found in a variety of forms. Collection Pennsylvania Farm Museum.

EARLY AMERICAN BORING TOOLS

by HALLOCK S. MARSH

Above—Left to right: Early spiral bit, before advent of screwpoint (18"); pod bit with spike point (12"); small gouge bit, or reamer—possibly used by clockmakers (3¼"); early spiral bit (6¼"); countersink (4¾"); spoon bit (8"); nose bit with spike point (6½"); early spiral screw bit—no routing blades below the spiral (9"); gimlets from other illustration repeated for scale (3½" and 7½"). Notches in shanks indicate manufacture between 1800 and 1850, for use with Marple's patent bitstock catch. (Author's collection.)

Below—Left to right: Taper auger (24"); nose auger, side view (20"); nose auger, front view (25"); early spiral screw auger (16½"); bell-hanger's gimlet (3½"); taper gimlet, or reamer (7½"). (Author's collection.)

O**NE OF THE INITIAL STEPS** towards civilized living must have been the boring or burning through of holes, in hides or wood to permit lashing them together, and in stone or wood to make containers for grain and liquids. Even the wheel could not have been invented if someone hadn't bored or burned a hole through its center to accommodate an axle.

Several excellent reference works on early tools and their uses only hint at the order of appearance in the evolution of boring tools. All of the types of early boring tools mentioned in this article—with the exception of the nose auger—have been found in Roman ruins. The gouge and spoon auger were depicted in ancient Egyptian tomb paintings.

Boring tools are generally classified as to size and function. Large augers, usually fitted with a wooden crossbar handle turned by two hands, or by two men, were used for boring large holes; smaller bits were used in bit-braces, or bitstocks, for boring smaller holes. Gimlets or "wimbles" were employed for boring very small holes. These smaller tools were often needed to start holes for larger tools.

The method for casting steel was invented in England in 1740, and was a closely guarded commercial secret for several years; the process was not known in this country until 1832. Prior to that date, perhaps as early as 1728, crude, hand wrought tools were produced from types of steel known, at various stages of refinement, as "blister steel" (crude steel with hard and soft areas throughout the metal), "tilted steel" (blister steel that was refined somewhat by being hammered under "tilt hammers"), and "shear steel" (layers of tilted steel welded together and thinned down under tilt hammers to make it more uniformly hard and suitable for the manufacture of shears).

Before the advent of the spiral screw auger, about five major types of boring tools were used: (a) the gouge auger, (b) the spoon auger, (c) the nose auger, (d) the pod auger, and (e) the taper auger.

Possibly the simple gouge auger was the earliest boring tool. Its form was a half cylinder with a bottom edge curved and sharpened so that it cut out a core of wood—but it pro-vided no means for discharging waste.

The spoon auger was similar in form, except that its cutting edge was cupped so that it could be used to scrape out the shavings from the hole. Both of these augers were down-cutting tools.

The taper auger, usually equipped with a spike point to start the hole, may have been the first side-cutting borer. It was used for reaming, or enlarging the sides of a small hole already started with a gimlet or a bit.

The pod auger, a somewhat more sophisticated side-cutting tool with a sharpened part-spiral edge, resembles a half pea pod, twisted, and was probably a refined version of some cruder tool.

About 1770, Phineas Cooke improved the side-cutting pod auger by adding more twists to the pod; this innovation made for a truer spiral, which bored in a straight line and removed wood shavings more efficiently. In 1809, Ezra L'Hommedieu introduced a double-podded spiral with down-cutting routing edges on the bottom of the spirals, just above the screw point, which pulled the routers into the wood. In 1885, Russell Jennings improved on L'Hommedieu's idea by adding spurs below the outer edges of the routers, causing the waste cut by the routers to discharge cleanly and without splintering the wood.

All of these improvements were reasonably catenate steps in the evolution of boring tools, but the nose auger remained somewhere off to one side. Since it survived intact, what did it do so efficiently to obviate any change or improvement in its form? Limited tests with a couple of large nose augers in the writer's collection —even allowing for their dulled and rusted condition—indicated that they were relatively inefficient in boring either with the grain or across the grain of the wood. On the other hand, experiments with a similar, but smaller nose bit having an elongated piercing spike, proved it was reasonably successful in piercing a hole across the grain of the wood—but it did splinter the wood slightly. Nevertheless, these tools must have been useful to early American craftsmen, or they would not have gone to the trouble and expense of having them hand-forged. The thought of their be-

ing used for some special function is tantalizing, but no evidence to support such a notion has been discovered as yet.

Equally unclear is the historical background of the nose auger. Mercer mentions nose augers as a Colonial tool "of unknown antiquity . . . now almost obsolete" and further states that Diderot's illustrations of tools did not show them. Nose augers do appear in at least a few 19th century tool catalogs and manuals. Goodman's study of English and European tools does not list nose augers, although some illustrations in 19th century catalogs appear to show this type of boring tool.

PAPER ANTIQUES

Those ephemeral pieces of paper called Valentines, are just one of a number of paper antiques being collected these days. The saccharine sweet poetry found on very early examples emits a fragrance of nostalgia too strong to ignore. But even the mundane general store ledger can be a wonderful source of entertainment and history. Colorful invitations, stationary, and post cards are among the many bits and pieces of paper antiques being eagerly sought out by a special breed of collectors. Here's one field of collecting that can cost a little or a lot of money. Among the more expensive items in this area of collecting are letters and documents written by famous personalities in American history.

1820. Double-fold paper, 7½x9"; figure, rose spray in ochre, green, magenta; 8-stanza poem begins on front.

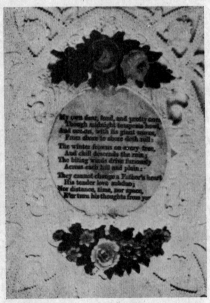

Ca. 1850. Affectionate verse, father to child, printed on white satin; superinposed embossed frame, die-cuts, 2x3¾".

Ca. 1860. Embossed paper fold, cupid and mirror frame, gold; green spray printed; flowers, pink die-cuts; pencilled sentiment inside. 4x5½".

An Ex-School Teacher Collects . . .

Valentines and Valentine Lore

WHEN Miss Ruth Walker of Brooklyn, N. Y., retired from public school teaching, she turned to collecting, she says, to continue her education. Her first interest was in foreign dolls, with research focused on customs and costumes. She rediscovered history and fashion design as she dressed some twenty Queen of England dolls in authentic styles of their times. From dolls, she moved to Christmas cards. Valentines were an inevitable "next". Her valentine collection centers on types, not numbers, and her delight is finding—and sharing—early references to the . . .

THE VALENTINE STORY

THE CUSTOM of sending love tokens on February 14, the feast day of St. Valentine, martyred in the 3rd century in Rome, according to *Webster's New International Dictionary*, has "no actual connection with the saint, whose name was probably introduced by some mistake." Certainly scholars for centuries have sought without success to find the link. Yet, however, dim and debated its origin, St. Valentine's Day was recognized and celebrated in very early England.

When Hugh Bourne, an English theologian (1772–1852) wrote: "There is a rural tradition that on this day every bird chooses its mate . . . so can man, in this season, do the same," he was only citing Chaucer who had made a similar observation some four hundred years earlier.

Francis Douce (1757–1834), an English antiquarian, sought a source of valentine customs in the Roman Lupercalia, a feast to Pan and Juno, where "amidst various ceremonies the names of young women were put into a box from which they were drawn by young men. A most sensuous affair followed."

Bourne described the more restrained drawing for valentines among 13th century English gentry: "On the eve before Valentine Day, the names of a select number of one sex are, with an equal number of the other sex, put in a vessel and after that everyone draws a name which for the present is called their Valentine and is looked upon as a good omen for their being man and wife after a while."

"Looking for a Valentine" is mentioned in several early works. Charles, Duke of Orleans, in 1415, in an amorous poem of many verses, now in the British Museum, wrote: "Oh, thou bright morning star/ 'Tis I that come so far/ My Valentine to seek."

And mad Ophelia, in Shakespeare's *Hamlet*, written in 1600, sings: "Good morrow! Tis St. Valentine Day/ All in the morning betime/ And I a maid at your window/ To be your Valentine."

Samuel Pepys in his famous diary set forth more intimate details of St. Valentine observances. He enter-ed for February 14, 1660: "My wife, hearing Mr. Moore's voice in my dressing chamber, got himself ready, came down and challenged him for her Valentine." On February 14, 1661: "I took Mrs. Martha for my Valentine which I did only for complacency [she was the daughter of his friend Sir Wm. Batten] and Sir Wm. go in the same manner to my wife so we were very merry." On February 18: "In the afternoon my wife and I and Mrs. Martha, my Valentine, to the Exchange and there upon a payre of embroidered and six payre of plain gloves, I laid out 40 shillings upon her." And on the 22nd: "Mr. Batten sent yesterday to my wife a half dozen pair of gloves, a pair of silk stockings and garters for her valentine."

Two hundred years later, in a United States of which Pepys had never dreamed, commercial valentines were "big business." *Harper's Weekly* stated that over three million valentines, both sentimental and comic, at prices from 3 cents to $30, were sold in 1857.

—RUTH N. WALKER

Ca. 1880. Ornate lacy pattern, hinged to embossed gold background; outlines, dots, etc., light blue; applied die-cuts; 5-stanza poem inside; 4½x7".

WHAT TO DO WITH A GENERAL STORE LEDGER

by MARJORIE CONGRAM

Moore and Bellis's
Day Book, 603 pages,
10x14 inches in size.

GENERAL STORE LEDGERS of the 19th century still turn up at auctions and antiques shops. What do you do with them? An old ledger is one antique that can't be made into a lamp. The ledgers and day-books vary from short to long, the writing from neat to almost illegible. Some books have pieces of their paper clipped out; some have notes and memos written 30 years after the last bookkeeping entries. Our forebears wasted not; what was finished as a ledger was still useful as a child's copy book.

What you do with an old ledger is learn how to read and appreciate it. The hundreds of pages of handwritten entries do not give up their stories at a glance. But time and thought spent in reading a ledger yield a wealth of interesting data. Discovered is a profile of the community, a picture of the times and the people who lived in them. The "Day-Book" of Moore and Bellis of Stockton, Hunterton County, New Jersey, dated spring 1888, is a case in point.

Begin at the beginning. How big is it? Substantial 10 by 14 inches, with 600 numbered pages bound in heavy cloth covered boards. The first page is dated Thursday, March 1, 1888. Was this opening day for the store? This day 93 transactions and $84.47 gross sales are listed. The largest transaction totals $8.34; the smallest, 2 cents for a cake of yeast. Most transactions are for less than a dollar.

How many people came into the store each day? Transactions are easier to count than people. Some people had several transactions in the same day. Moore and Bellis appear to have been favored with a steady business. For instance 59 transactions are entered for Thursday, April 5; 65 for Friday, 86 for Saturday, 62 for Monday, 68 for Tuesday, and 89 for Wednesday. Wednesday and Saturday, apparently, were the big shopping days.

Who were the people who came into the store? Everybody came to Moore and Bellis's, it seems. The regular accounts are numbered 1 to 115. Thirty-seven others are given the numbers 380 to 395. In some cases, several people shared the same number. Eight other people have accounts numbered 470 to 477. What do these special numbers mean, perhaps business and charity accounts? Purchases under these accounts indicate nothing unusual—a cake of soap, a paper of tobacco, a pair of shoes.

Most of the names in the accounts sound English, Scotch or Welsh. Ten different Smiths are listed. Old Hunterton County names such as Apgar, Dilts (five accounts), Dalrymple, and Holcombe appear. Irish names are few—Meakim, Farlee, Moonan. Latin names are fewer still—Bonelli, Solvio, Napoli, Benzo. Angle Anopolis is perhaps the solitary Greek name.

Who is missing from this list of accounts? Women! Assuming that the account name represents head of household, and that all members of a household bought under the one account, female heads of households are extremely rare. Ellie Pittman, No. 98, and Mrs. Amy Heath, No. 3, are alone.

What could you buy at Moore and Bellis's store in spring, 1888? A variety of goods were available—food, clothing, dry goods, household hardware, patent medicines, coal oil. You could buy food staples such as flour, sugar, lard, salt, and molasses by the pound, sack, gallon, or barrel. You could buy some foods in cans, too, if you could stand the expense—cans of corn, peas, beans, and tomatoes at two for a quarter, condensed milk at 18 cents, a can of salmon for 22 cents. You could get fresh meat, fresh vegetables and fish occasionally, too. Whiskey is conspicuous by its absence.

You would find the dry goods department sufficiently stocked. Ready-made men's clothing was on hand: soft hats $1 and stiff hats $2, overalls 50 cents, slippers 90 cents, shirts 50 cents and 85 cents (a choice), gum shoes for 40 cents, among other things. Women's notions were available—hairpins for a nickel, corsets for 50 cents, a bustle for 19 cents. You could buy many kinds of cloth by the yard—shirting, calico, selicia, muslin, plaid, flannel, chintz, crash, scrim, cambric, drilling, cassmire and oil cloth. Many are priced at "1-" or 12½ cents (one shilling?).

You would find a few household essentials in their hardware department such as coal oil lamp parts, window panes at 10 cents each, dinner pails, washboards, tin cups and basins.

In fact, Moore and Bellis catered to the health and comfort of their customers. They sold a lot of tobacco, by plug, paper, and cigar. "Pills" were sold at 10 cents a dozen, castor oil, epsom salts, and paregoric were 10 cents a bottle. Worm syrup, cattle powder and blue vitriol cost a little more. You could buy cabbage and tomato plants for 10 cents a dozen, too. Ten cents would also buy a pound of crackers, a can of lime, a pound of lard, two loaves of bread, a pint of onion sets, or a stick of stove polish.

Who were the big spenders in the store's ledger? In Moore and Bellis's Day-Book, six people achieved more than 50 transactions a month. Big spenders? Not exactly—mostly they bought a paper of tobacco or a loaf of bread in a transaction. More than seven items in an order are rare. On March 3, 1888, for instance Jordan Harris bought flour, sugar, a chicken, lard, butter, baking powder, a cake of yeast, a cabbage, pies, and two-for-a-nickel cigars. This unusually large order taking up 11 hand-written lines in the Day-Book totaled $2.42. A $3 dollar order was a special event.

Do the storekeepers take produce in trade from their customers? Store ledgers of an earlier age show barter in all

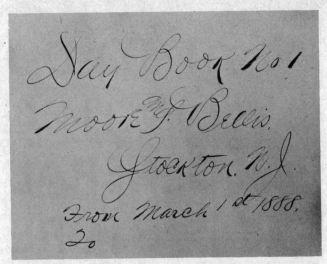

Title page from Moore & Bellis's Day Book No. 1, from March 1, 1888 to —.

kinds of farm produce and in labor. Stockton in 1888, with a spokes works, saw mill, several stone quarries, and a paper mill had a money rather than a barter economy. Still, Moore and Bellis bought customers' eggs at 15 cents a dozen, butter at 26 cents a pound, rhubarb at a penny a stalk, and shad from the Delaware River, three for a dollar.

Take a close look at the buying patterns of the customers. Do their purchases reveal their characters? Take Frank Williamson, account No. 16. Frank liked to visit the store. Almost every day he stopped to buy two-for-a-nickel cigars. Did he also stay to "chew the fat" around the cracker barrel? He visited the store 42 times in April, sometimes four times in a day. His april purchases total $12.12. Was Frank a lonely bachelor? He bought cigars, bread, butter, and eggs. His most expensive purchase was a bottle of sarsaparilla for a dollar. This root extract was deemed to be a tonic and blood purifier. Was Frank then a sick old bachelor? He was not given to fripperies in his purchases. Bread, butter, eggs, and cigars were his staff of life. He is not what one would call a literary man, judging by his purchases. On April 12 he bought one sheet of paper and one envelope for a cent each. Cigars are Frank's thing—in April he bought 42 cigars at a cost of $1.25, but he bought them mainly a nickel's worth at a time.

The lone female account of any importance, Mrs. Amy Heath, is less revealing in her purchases. Still, she was a frequent customer, with 38 transactions totaling $40 in March. Did Mrs. Heath run a boarding house? That month she bought 98 loaves of bread, 40 pounds of fish, and 15 dozen eggs.

Scan, browse, and read through the whole book for unusual items and peculiarities. Peculiar from today's point of view is that country store customers used the place as a small loan agency—cash advances of 30 cents and 50 cents are listed. An item of merchandise on the horizon of the future, apparently, was the turkish towel. Only one sale of a turkish towel is listed in the 600 pages of Moore and Bellis, and at 44 cents, it was an expensive item. Shirt wadding for a nickel is listed several times—what is shirt wadding? What kind of cloth is selica? How odd that the 12½ cent shilling unit should be carried so long in the storekeeper's arithmetic.

Another small curiosity in the Moore and Bellis Day-Book is "Account No. 397, Stockton Lucrative Society." It purchased a gallon of oil and one galvanized pail, total cost 55 cents. And the seven item order of proprietor Bellis is typical and because of that, singular;

A page of entries indicating that Moore and Bellis on occasion took goods in trade—"By Susan Sherman 2¼ doz. eggs—.40."

May 21, 1888:

10 yd muslin	.80
1 7/12 doz hoocks (sic) & eyes	.10
1 doz oranges	.18
25 lbs oats	.34
1 bustle	.19
1 sack salt	.03
cash	5.00
	$6.64

Such is the overall view of one general store ledger. It ends on May 22, covering two months and 22 days of trade. Presumably many other day books followed. One cannot help being impressed with the enormous labor involved in this system of bookkeeping. A handwritten entry in the day book was necessary for even small sums. Some customers flitted in and out, buying an item at a time, and each time the account number, name, item, quantity, unit price, and

Stockton, N.J., is a narrow T-shaped village. The "cross bar" is its main road, running between the bluffs and the Delaware River and Delaware Canal. The stem is the street which ends in a bridge crossing the river (above).

A typical page of entries in the Moore & Bellis Day Book. Unusual is the size of J. H. Bond's order, some sixteen items.

total price had to be written out. At the end of the day, the day book entries had to be copied into the books of individual accounts, plus any other ledgers, such as sales, the storekeeper thought fit to keep.

If you care to look up the locality of your country store ledger, you can check county history books and talk to people presently living in the area. Moore and Bellis's store, I'm told, operated under various proprietors until the 1930s. Its building stood next to its spiritual successor, Errico's Quality Market, serving Stockton today.

1

2

An Invitation to Mardi Gras

3

by JESS GREGG

RAIN WAS NEARLY ALWAYS predicted, but nothing ever dampened the glitter of the Rex Ball, a climax of the Mardi Gras week of parties and parades in old New Orleans. Weeks in advance, black boys in neat alpaca jackets delivered the invitations by hand. A white vellum sheath protected a more ornate envelope which reflected the theme of that year's celebration: Babylon, Neptune's Treasure, Versailles. This in turn contained the invitation itself—and such an invitation! Intricately printed in far-away Paris, multicolored and gilded, it was a paper fold-out more ingenious than a valentine, to be opened up and opened up, flap after flap, surprise after surprise.

Even present day invitations are collectors' items, not easy to come by; but their acquisition was infinitely more difficult in the days of their currency. The social pressure to receive this entree to the grand masque became so intense that a black market in invitations was inevitable, and theft not an unthinkable solution. At last, each guest of Rex, King of Carnival, was checked against a strict list at the outer door, and again at the inner, before being allowed to enter the vast ballroom. Anyone found guilty of giving his invitation to another, or

worse, selling it, forfeited all hope of ever again being invited to the festivity.

The first of these great Rex Ball masquerades was given in 1872 because a city council of carpetbaggers, too busy with politics to play host, all but ignored the Mardi Gras visit of Grand Duke Alexis of Russia. A group of indignant Louisiana aristocrats and officials—possibly the already established Mystic Crewe of Comus—quickly instigated Rex as King of the parade, with a coronation ball afterwards, extravagant enough that a Grand Duke might comfortably preside. Although His Highness was notably late to this festivity in his honor, and chose to remain among the revelers rather than mount the throne, the ball was an enormous success, and was repeated the following year. Indeed, it has become an annual event, continuing right into our own time.

Today, the costumes are as dazzling as ever, and the gaity as extravagant. However, the intricate, hand-delivered invitations are no more. Their expense had begun to weigh heavily by 1914 and, imperceptibly dimming the Crescent, they were replaced after the First World War by mere formal, engraved cards.

4

Key to Illustrations

1. A crown in gold and crimson makes a fitting envelope for an invitation to the Rex Ball of 1884.

2. The world opens up, petal by petal, each side of which (3 & 4) reveals Neptune's riches, for the Mardi Gras Ball of 1889.

5. A superb blue and gold medallion gradually discloses the phases of the moon (6) before opening on Jupiter's Festival (7) on this Rex invitation of 1883.

8. Nebuchadnezzar's Book, engraved with scenes of a coronation, is the circular outcome of (9) an electric blue Babylonian quiver of gold arrows, for 1884.

509
Paper
Antiques

10. The orange and blue silk Pavilion can be drawn back, fold by fold, to show scenes of feudal gallantry (see 11, and cover). This invitation to the Masque of 1885 was printed by F. Appel, 12 rue du Delta, Paris, France.

12. The russet and gilt Babylonian volume makes a curious envelope for the invitation of 1883, which featured Greek gods at play.

13. Printed entirely in blue, the Watteau sedan chair (1887) gradually unfolds a scene of strolling players (14) and at last, in six colors, the glorification of Rex (15).

1

510
Paper
Antiques

2

3

4

HISTORY ON

by F. M. GOSLING

MARCH 1, 1907, WAS an important date for many commercial photographers then in business throughout the United States. That was the date when a change in postal regulations allowed a written message to be placed on the back of a picture postcard, and a one-cent stamp was all the postage required for mailing. Up to this time the back of the picture postcard was reserved for name and address only; any message had to be written on the other side over the picture or in the margin around it.

Photographic supply houses began at once to supply postcard size sensitized paper with divided backs, the left portion headed "Correspondence Here," and the right side, "Name and Address Here." This enabled photographers to take postcard size photographs of interesting and unusual events, make contact prints from the negatives, and place the cards on sale, practically overnight. Often these photos were of local interest only, and sales distribution was limited, usually in the photographer's studio or a local drug store or two.

Pictures of wider interest were generally handled by postcard companies in the larger cities and were produced on printing presses: often the actual work was done in Germany. Most of these were processed in color or hand-colored and were turned out by the hundreds. The local photographer producing his own cards, did have one advantage; if a particular photo was sold out, he could quickly come up with an additional supply.

The collector whose hobby is photography and who likes to do copying and enlargement work will find that some of these postcard photographs make excellent enlargements.

For those whose interest lies in the early days of this century, the postcards pictured here serve as examples of what can be found in old albums or other accumulations of cards. Among the many other subjects that can turn up are parades, fires, train wrecks, shipwrecks, Mexican border incidents, interiors and exteriors of old business places.

The following captions are given in order from top to bottom the left hand page and similarly on the right hand page, though the pictured cards are not themselves numbered. While all of them offer opportunities for research, a fascinating and informative endeavor, only *Card No. 1* has been carefully identified.

A POST CARD

5

6

Card No. 1 presents a disaster. As the destruction appears to be all on the ground, a good guess would be a flood. "Bisbee Commercial Co." on one of the awnings, suggests Bisbee, Arizona. Information from Mary L. Hose, the librarian at Bisbee, states that a flood in the summer of 1908 brought down thousands of tons of earth from the hillside, but that their big flood occurred in 1890.

A more careful look at the photo reveals a sign outside the Orpheum Theatre; "Every Night the Latest Moving Pictures." Since the first motion picture was in 1896, the photo has to be of the 1908 Bisbee flood. Further proof — the postcard has a divided back.

Card No. 2, postmarked Dec. 17, 1907, was photographed in Goldfield, Nevada, showing two men and their pack burros about to start on a prospecting trip. Welch & Tune were the photographers. They were also on hand at the Goldfield depot on December 7, 1907, to record on postcards the arrival of troops by train, called to quell labor trouble at the mines. The following day, they photographed the soldiers' camp on Combination Hill.

Card No. 3 bears the caption "First Train on WP Ry from Oroville to Salt Lake, Hogan Photo, Oroville, Cal." The Depot, under construction, is at the right of the locomotive.

Card No. 4, from Portland, Oregon, bears the written message that this is " the new Police auto with two of the second night relief men in it." License plates are for 1912.

Card No. 5 shows a jerkline team hauling sacks of grain in the San Joaquin valley of California. Seen quite clearly is the single line used to control the team and, on the lead team, a set of team bells fastened to the hames. This particular set has five bells; often there are seven.

Card No. 6, written in Tanana, Alaska, on Sept. 22, 1913, was mailed at Eagle, Alaska, On Oct. 2. Sign in front reads: "Str. Yukon will make direct connections at Dawson for the Sushana Strike. Will sail 7 p.m."

Card No. 7, perhaps taken for advertising purposes, shows early disc phonographs with record cabinets. The card was unmailed and there is no indication of when or where this shop operated.

Card No. 8, is a photo taken in September 1918 of the members of a Red Cross Canteen Unit at Omaha, Nebraska, during World War I. This card was never mailed; it was probably kept as a souvenir. On the back someone carefully identified all the ladies by name.

7

8

Starch books from the author's collection; kitchen match, lower left, indicates size. Illustrations of school recitations, little girls in long stockings and sunbonnets, and grocery interiors are typical of the series. "The Fairies" is Vol. 1; "The Trials of Mrs. Graycoat," Vol. 2.

The Starch Books

by CLAIRE T. McCLELLAN

DO you remember the "Starch Books"? Chances are you do, if you were a child at the turn of the century or in the early years of the 1900s. For a generation these unprepossessing little booklets were saved by mothers, and loved, read, traded, collected, and prized by children throughout most of America.

They were issued by the Faultless Starch Company of Kansas City, Missouri, and given as a premium with their product, which had wide distribution, though not on the Atlantic seaboard. Records of the firm were destroyed in the floods of 1903 and 1951, and Mr. Gordon T. Beaham, the present head of the company founded by his grandfather in 1887, does not know the exact date of their appearance. He thinks, however, it was around 1895, and the illustrations would seem to confirm this.

There are 36 numbered booklets in the series, each 15 pages in length, and 3 by 5 inches in size. They vary in color, and it is evident they were not all issued at one time, as the cover format varies.

The first twelve are labeled "Faultless Starch Books"; the next six are headed "Jokes and Conundrums Series"; and the rest, "Faultless Starch Library," in several type-forms. The first part of each is an illustrated story in prose or rhyme, followed by a section of riddles, jokes, games, useful facts, hints on manners, and such. The firm's product is extolled in glowing terms in every story, with appealing frankness.

Mr. Beaham does not remember that the booklets were ever put inside the packages, though Mr. T. E. Caulfield, of the Waco, Texas, *News-Tribune,* thinks otherwise. He gives some pros and cons on the matter in his column "Reading for Fun," and cites the fact that they always smelled "starchy." Later they were attached with rubber bands by the grocer, and one booklet came with each package of starch. What a thrill to get one that no one else in the neighborhood had seen, and be first with the riddles! What child today could guess "What is worse than raining cats and dogs?" when the answer is "Hailing streetcars"!

D. Arthur Brown wrote the stories, but there is no record of the illustrators; there appear to have been several. They were published by the firm of Brown's brother, the Charles E. Brown Publishing Company of Kansas City, and many of them were written for children in the Brown families. They have the illusive ingredient that makes stories successful with children, whether they tell a familiar tale with a new twist, like "Red Riding Hood," in which the wolf is so taken with Grandma's starched apron that he stays for tea, or an original one, such as "A Trip to the Moon," in which moonbeams and elves anticipate space capsules. Several have the "rags to riches" theme, like "Prink and Prank," in which a little country boy becomes President.

Until about 1930, the booklets were now and then reprinted. The facsimile of the package on the back cover indicates the later ones, as it includes the Good Housekeeping seal. Few of these later ones were issued. Gentlemen were no longer judged by the board-like quality of their collars and cuffs, nor ladies by the stiffness of their petticoats. Children had more distractions, and were perhaps finding stories involving coal-bins and gaslights, difficult to understand.

So the Starch Books faded from the American scene. But many still survive, and they should be hunted out and preserved. Aside from being one of the most successful commercials ever devised, they are an authentic, if humble, addition to Americana—and they're fun!

PEWTER

Why do so many people collect pewter? Henry J. Kauffman submits that some people collect pewter for its historical appeal, representing as it does a phase of American life. Everything from spoons to handsomely proportioned tankards were in daily use by Americans between 1750 and 1850. Now these objects are difficult to find, and expensive to acquire. The 20th century revival of interest in pewter was the reason silver manufacturers turned to this medium for a wide variety of household goods—candlesticks, center bowls, coffee and tea sets, and flatware designs reminiscent of Colonial times.

Bowl with wriggle engraving, English or Continental, late 17th century. Attached handles show rough finish inside where molten metal was held in place with burlap pad. Though sometimes attributed to Penna., there is no evidence such pieces were made there.

Because Pewter Seems To Have Been Made
For The Modest Home With Modest Furnishings
May Be The Real Reason . . .

Why So Many People Collect Pewter

by HENRY J. KAUFFMAN

Pewter in appealing shapes from Lady Hilda Liddell's collection, sold at Parke-Bernet Galleries, 1958: Charles II charger by Wm. Green, London, ca. 1680, broad border bears 7 touches, 24″ dia.; William and Mary charger, English, late 17th century, plain with molded rim, touch mark underfoot, 20½″ dia.; 18th century pieces: pestle-shaped flagon, hinged cover, dual acorn thumbpiece, French, 11″ high; wine can, screw cover, loop handle, tall arched spout, spout cover bears touches, 11″ high; George III tappit hen, incurvate neck, semi-dome hinged cover, scroll thumbpiece and handle. *Photo by Taylor & Dull.*

THOSE engaged in the selling or collecting of antiques are aware of the enduring importance of pewter. Its continuous and steady popularity seems all the more remarkable in that none of its qualities appear to offer competition to other more colorful and intrinsically valuable collectibles.

As a composition of tin, lead, antimony, and copper, it can boast no inherent rare metal. It really can't be called beautiful for its texture is dull, unless it is regularly polished. Except for a very few early pieces, which usually gravitate to museums, the simple forms are rarely enhanced with surface decoration. Few pieces have been so well preserved that they can be used for eating or drinking. The unknown quantity of lead which early pieces contain makes for a low melting point and eliminates its use on a stove; the late pewter and coffee pots with copper bottoms are rare, and usually unattractive in form.

Yet pewter has a mysterious and potent attraction, not only for those who collect pewter exclusively, but for the Mr. and Mrs. John Does of America, who probably own individually less than a dozen pieces, and who purchase by far the greatest mass of pewter sold today.

What is this powerful attraction?

Some people collect pewter for its historic appeal, as representative of a phase of American life. In the evolution of household utensils, pewter followed utensils of

Pewter coffee pot with floral finial has a copper bottom. Manufactured rather than fabricated by hand, it is the work of one of the Boardmans of the 1830-1850 period.

The face of this Swedish plate is not unlike plates of other nations, but the piece is unusual because marked pewter from Sweden is rare. The maker was Sven Roos, of Gotheborg. Name and city easily read, other marks are obscure.

This porringer, a very simple one-piece form, was made in Pennsylvania, and is generally called a Westtown type as such porringers are thought to have been made in that area. Some are marked with an S.P. and are attributed to Simon or Samuel Pennock, but there is no documentary evidence for this attribution. Thomas Melville of Newport, Rhode Island, made a porringer very similar to this, but with a solid handle.

wood, and was superseded by china, glass, and pottery. From 1750 to 1850, almost every cupboard in America displayed at least a few pieces of pewter, and there was likely a pewter snuff box in the parlor and a pewter funnel in the cellar.

For others, purchase is inspired by the decorative quality of the simple forms of early pewter, an outgrowth of a casting process which required costly molds and careful skimming after the forms were made.

Some buy pewter as an investment, others buy it to use. One of the great museums of America serves lunch on old pewter plates, and many people think tea brews best in a pewter teapot. Water pitchers are particularly attractive in use, and basins are widely employed for fruit and flower arrangements. Candlesticks, continuing their original function, are especially appropriate in Early American settings.

The first step in pewter collecting is usually the acquisition of a few plates, teapots, and basins, followed by that of such rarer pieces as beakers, mugs, candlesticks, flagons, and tankards. As his discrimination develops, the collector will find he can often barter an average piece for a rarity by adding some cash. When he has acquired a Queen Anne teapot or a tankard with a crenate lip, he has arrived at the top.

Some collectors hunt pewter from a specific area, such as Pennsylvania or New York. Others collect the work of certain makers, while still others are partial to particular forms, as porringers or tankards.

To the writer the most attractive quality of pewter is the warm, soft, unobtrusive quality of the metal which complements so ideally a simple pine mantel or an old walnut table. There is nothing quite like it—no similar objects are available in silver, brass, or copper. It is not too new and shiny, or too old and grimy—it is "just right".

The straight side tankard with crenate lip is American, bearing the mark of Henry Will, who worked in New York City from 1761 to 1793, except for an 8-year stay in Albany from 1775 to 1783. He made a large variety of forms including an oval plate, the only one known by an American maker. The tulip shaped tankard is English, marked on the inside of the bottom, as is the American piece. The mark, an hour glass with the initials C. E. on the sides, is not listed by Cotterell in his "Old Pewter, Its Makers and Marks", but the cipher W R, stamped on the outside, identifies it definitely as English.

There is little difference in style between English pewter and American, and though there are certain subtle means of distinguishing one from the other, the most satisfactory is by the marks of the makers. Comparative values of American and foreign pewter are now well established; the English tankard is worth on today's market about $75, the American, $1,000.

The enviable selection of early pewter displayed in this open cupboard includes a wide variety of hollow forms — tankards, mugs, communion vessels, beakers, and a rare drahm bottle.

Pennsylvania pewter of the 18th century was simple and graceful in form with little superficial ornamentation; the three pieces shown are typical. Around the top the tankard has a beaded edge, a characteristic of Philadelphia pewter; the sugar bowl, a simple band. The drahm bottle has a concave band between the flat side and the curved edge.

The tulip shaped tankard was made by William Will of Philadelphia, who worked from 1764 to 1798, except for a term of Revolutionary War service. His early lamb and dove mark shows English influence; later he conformed to the American pattern with his famous eagle mark. This tankard has a simple W W mark. His pewter is of highest quality, and is currently considered the most desirable of all American pewter.

Johann Christopher Heyne of Lancaster, Penna., who worked from 1754 to 1780, made the drahm bottle. His work is unique because it shows a Germanic influence not found in the products of any other American maker, though this influence is not seen in the piece pictured. His chalices and flagons are dramatically large. The mark on his drahm bottles is on top of lid.

The sugar bowl, though attributed to Heyne, is unmarked. Resembling in form the glass sugar bowls of Stiegel, these pewter sugar bowls are very rare and much sought.

Pewter Ice Cream Molds

by DUNCAN B. WOLCOTT

QUITE POSSIBLY the first ice cream served in the White House, by Dolly Madison in 1809, was molded in fancy shapes. Certainly pewter ice cream molds were then available, for they had been listed ten years earlier in the 1799 inventory of William Will, Philadelphia pewterer (1742-1798), along with plates, dishes, teapots, and such utilitarian pieces. Presumably other pewterers of the period made them, too.

However, it was not until the mid-19th century, after ice cream factories appeared, that molded ice cream was commercially packed. One of the earliest large-scale makers of pewter ice cream molds was Schall & Co., of New York City, established in 1854.

For almost three-quarters of a century, individual ice cream in all sorts of intriguing shapes added the crowning touch to all proper family celebrations, children's parties, and formal dinners alike. Then as labor costs rose and the packing of these individual novelties became unprofitable, ice cream companies began to discontinue them, and to scrap their molds. Only a few companies make them up today. Though molds are still produced for special occasions, they must be specially ordered and custom built, and are expensive.

Despite the numbers that have been scrapped over the years, there are still enough old pewter ice cream molds around to keep a collector happy and enthused. Nor is it likely such molds will ever be reproduced to confuse him. Today's high cost of tin and lead, as well as labor, would make the price prohibitive.

In the Wolcott collection at the present time, there are 984 different designs of pewter ice cream molds;

186 of them, one of a kind. The most desirable, from a collector's point of view, are those depicting eagles, of which there are several designs. The most common molds are of flowers, fruits, and holiday motifs, but there are also some very unlikely subjects for ice cream sculpture.

Among the most improbable are molds depicting an asparagus spear, cauliflower, horse's hoof, beehive, salt cellar, pork chop, fan in hand, mouse, suckling pig, barrel, watering can, wall-type telephone, piece of pie, celery stalk, cigar, bird's nest, engraved teapot, the Perisphere and

〰〰〰〰〰〰〰〰

About Ice Cream

In the 1st century A.D., the Roman Emperor Nero was fond of a sort of sherbet made of snow flavored with honey and fruit juices, and employed runners to bring back snow from nearby mountains. Ice cream, made with milk, as we know it, was not introduced to the Western world until the 13th century, when Marco Polo brought back the remarkable recipe from China. It became an extravagance, reserved for royalty in the English court of Charles I, King from 1625 to 1640. In early America, ice cream was made commercially by a Mr. Hall of 76 Chatham Street (now Park Row), New York, who advertised it, June 8, 1786. George Washington's Expense Ledger under date of May 17, 1784, recorded the purchase of a "cream machine for ice," and in 1809, Dolly Madison, wife of President James Madison, served it at the White House, for the first time. Jacob Fussel of Baltimore, Maryland was the country's first ice cream wholesaler. A milk dealer, he took this means of using up his surplus cream He started manufacturing ice cream in 1851, and charged 60¢ a quart for it.

Trylon of New York's 1939 World's Fair, battleship Monitor, potato, Knight Templar in full regalia, Plymouth Rock, and George Washington as a boy chopping the cherry tree.

Ninety-nine percent of the molds in this collection were made in the United States. Of the four or five American companies making molds, the two leading were Eppelsheimer & Co., who marked their pieces, "E & Co. N. Y.," and Schall & Co., who marked theirs, "S & Co." The oldest are by Schall.

One mold in the collection is marked "J. Ernst, N. York." This is in the form of a pair of lovebirds, and is obviously quite early; it was recently found in Portland, Oregon. Search of New York City Directories at the Cleveland Public Library, revealed that a listing for Jacob Ernst, moldmaker, 146 Forsythe, appeared first in 1858. The Directory for 1872 lists him at 146 Fourth Avenue. Quite likely he worked later than that date.

Other molds were made in France. Some are identified by such French registry marks as "S.G.D.G." (sans garantie du gouvernment) and "Brevete" (patent). The "CC" mark (easily mistaken for "GG") is also French, and the molds it is found on are usually quite old. This mark was used by M. Cadot et Cie, of Paris, a company founded in 1826, specializing in tin and pewter molds. In 1904, when "Successors" was being used with the company name, the firm was located at 88 rue St. Martin, and the mark pictured an old type hand crank freezer with the words "Marque Deposee."

Positive identification of this long-puzzling "CC" mark came about in this fashion. An old catalog of ice cream molds, purchased from an antiques dealer in New Hampshire,

Personages: Washington, Admiral Dewey, Teddy Roosevelt, Napoleon, Miss Columbia, Uncle Sam.

Civil War items: drum, cannon, knapsack, sailor, soldier.

quoted prices on pewter molds at $9 a dozen, and said, on the back cover, "Our molds are superior to the celebrated CC molds of Paris." A visit to the Cleveland Public Library located a Paris City Directory for 1904—and the information.

A large 3-pint mold of a dog, recently found in Milford, Pa., bears the CC mark, the same design of the old hand-crank ice cream freezer, but the words, "Marque Fabrique," instead of "Deposee."

Another mold, a little over a pint in size, of a sheaf of wheat, which had been purchased in England, was found near Hartville, Ohio. However, the touchmark on the inner surface of its round bottom cover indicates it was made by a French, or possibly a Swiss, pewterer.

Mold Numbers

Practically all molds carry a mold number. Sometimes different numbers appear on identical molds, indicating that they were manufactured by different companies. While many molds will also bear a date, this is not necessarily the date of manufacture. "Des. cop'd. 1888," for example, merely indicates when the mold was designed and first made. Favored designs were often in production for many years.

Most of the molds in the collection are about the same size, running 6 to 8 to the quart, with an average weight of 14.6 oz. There are some bite-size fruits and flowers (three to a mold) that were used to make up fruit and flower baskets. Today, collectors are using these small molds to make up individual butter servings. There are also some large individual molds that run to three pints or half-a-gallon. These are mostly large baskets, Santas, rabbits, logs, turkeys, horses, sail boats, love doves, pumpkins, and melons.

These molds are actually pewter, but not the exact metal used in early pewter dishes; the ratio of tin to lead in the content was varied somewhat depending on the use to which the piece was to be put. Pewterers in Old Sturbridge Village, Massachusetts, are making spoons from original molds and using a metal made up of 83% tin and 17% other metal, mainly lead. At Fr. Krauss Son, Milford, Pa., one of the few concerns still making

molds, moldmaker Walter Perry uses 61% tin and 39% lead for his ice cream molds.

At one time the Health Department of the City of New York banned the use of lead in ice cream molds on the chance it might produce lead poisoning — actually the danger was slight — and all early molds in the New York area were scrapped. Later, molds began to appear bearing the words, "99% pure tin."

Even very old molds will look new and shiny on the inside and a cloudy pewter color on the outside. This is because the molds have been kept closed for many years; the inside is protected, but the outside loses its brightness from exposure to air and oxidation.

In determining the value of pewter ice cream molds, a collector will consider rarity, appearance, and utility. Rarity alone does not necessarily make a mold desirable. Some of the least often found molds are not of much value *except* as rarities — the horse's hoof, for example, the cauliflower, or the pork chop.

Appearance is especially important as regards the looks of the mold when it is closed. Does it tell anything? In some molds, much of the detail is on the inside. Plymouth Rock, for one, looks like a rock when closed, nothing more.

The utility value depends on how the mold is to be used by the owner. If he plans it as an ash tray, will it lie flat? Sometimes the hinge will interfere. If he wants it for decoration or as a conversation piece, it should to a certain extent tell its own story. Many of today's collectors of pewter ice cream molds are actually using them to make up their own fancy individual ice cream desserts.

Molds are often displayed as pairs or in multiples — George and Martha Washington; Lady Golfer and Gentleman Golfer; perhaps a variety of Masonic emblems, or Civil War rarities, a row of Christmas candles on a mantel; Thanksgiving and Christmas displays in season. One of the pleasures in any collection, large or small, is being able to use it in some fashion.

Unusuals: hen on nest, crown, beehive, fire engine.

Sports: lady bicyclist, 1896; baseball player, man golfer, lady golfer.

Pewter of

by LOUISE K. LANTZ   Illustrations courtesy E.P. Hogan,

No. 523
Porringer

No. 505 Bowl
Made in four sizes

518
Pewter

No. 546
Tobacco Jar

No. 561
Ash Tray

INSICO
PEWTER

No. 0540
Syrup and Plate

"PEWTER IS BACK!" was the excited cry of interior decorators as American pewterware experienced a vibrant rebirth during the turbulent years of the 1920s.

The cast pewter in everyday use in the 17th and 18th centuries evolved to the spun pewter called "Britannia" of the early 19th century. After 1840 silverplated articles made by the newly developed process of electroplating almost completely replaced pewterware in American homes. The soft, muted gleam of pewter was overshadowed by the harsh, bright shine of inexpensive electroplated silverware. Pewterware became "old-fashioned" and "dull" and as such was relegated to the attic or banished to the rag-bone man. It virtually disappeared under the pressure of machine-age-made glass, pottery, and silverplate.

In the 1920s a resurgence of interest in American craftsmanship, a sudden longing for the simple beauty of hand-made articles, a yearning for simpler days, and a nostalgic yen for the secure home life of pre-World War I years combined to revive an interest in pewterware of simple lines, quaint charm, and mellow lustre. It met a demand for

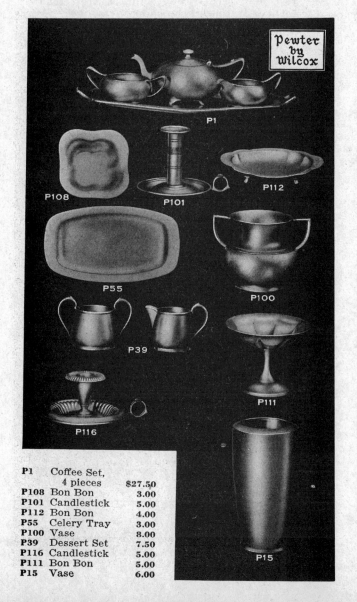

Pewter by Wilcox

P1	Coffee Set,	
	4 pieces	$27.50
P108	Bon Bon	3.00
P101	Candlestick	5.00
P112	Bon Bon	4.00
P55	Celery Tray	3.00
P100	Vase	8.00
P39	Dessert Set	7.50
P116	Candlestick	5.00
P111	Bon Bon	5.00
P15	Vase	6.00

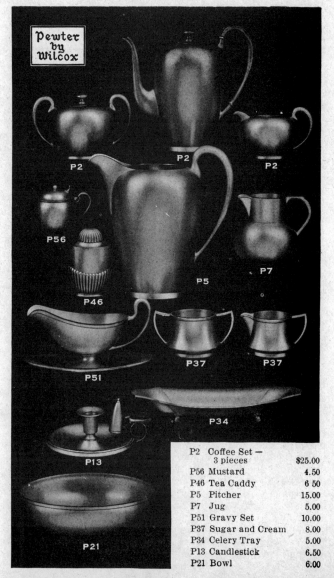

Pewter by Wilcox

P2	Coffee Set —	
	3 pieces	$25.00
P56	Mustard	4.50
P46	Tea Caddy	6.50
P5	Pitcher	15.00
P7	Jug	5.00
P51	Gravy Set	10.00
P37	Sugar and Cream	8.00
P34	Celery Tray	5.00
P13	Candlestick	6.50
P21	Bowl	6.00

the 1920's

Librarian, the International Silver Company Historical Collection.

beauty and stability coupled with inexpensiveness and durability.

The restoration of Colonial Williamsburg in Virginia, in which John D. Rockefeller, Jr. became interested in 1925, evoked even more enthusiasm for early American craftsmanship. The pewterer, along with the tinsmith, the silversmith, and the blacksmith, was an honored and essential craftsman of his day. The skills and talents of these various craftsmen were zealously studied and appreciated.

Not all the new pieces of pewterware were reproductions. Some were faithful copies of early American pieces or replicas of old Tudor English antiques. Others were made in the "modern" style, simple in design and devoid of decoration. These featured utter simplicity, swooping curves, and flashing planes, characteristics of the design trends of the times.

Subsidiaries of the well known International Silver Company made all three designs of pewter during this era. They manufactured early American reproductions, copies of old English masterpieces, and originals in the "Modern Man-

No. 549
Compote

No. 532
Goblet

No. 531
Guernsey Jug

**519
Pewter**

No. 550 Bowl
Made in three sizes

84	Coffee Set, 4 pcs.,	$31.00
80	Three-in-One Tea Set	10.00
37	Bowl	15.00
25	Bowl	7.00
32	Vegetable Dish	12.00
27	Bowl	5.00
57	Bread and Butter Plate	3.75
62	Candlestick	8.00
63	Vase	7.50

P54	Muffineer	$6.00
P4	Sugar and Cream with Tray	13.50
P9	Syrup with Plate	7.50
P44	Biscuit Tray	5.00
P43	Tea Set, 4 pcs.	50.50
P23	Hot Milk Jug	7.50
P45	Roll Tray	8.00
P67	Candlestick	4.00
P66	Candlestick	11.00
P68	Vase	7.50

ner." Several of their designs illustrate this article.

The true reason for the renewed interest in delightful pewter during the 1920s, whether in modern or reproduced designs, is the abiding charm inherent in the smokey metal itself. Its haunting, deep, shadowy glow, like the twilight dimness of candlelight and the luminous flickering of a fire on the hearth has a tranquilizing and fantasizing quality. It evokes thoughts of peace and plenty, serenity and security.

Pewter has been called "the poor man's silver"; it might more aptly be called "the metal of peace."

Trademarks found on pewter made by The International Silver Company and its subsidiaries. "INSICO PEWTER" identifies pieces made by The Derby Silver Co.; "Pewter by Wilcox" was made by the Wilcox Silver Plate Co.

520 Pewter

549	Compote	$10.00	505 Bowl, 7 inch	$6.00	550 Bowl, 6 inch	$7.50	0540 Syrup and Plate	$11.50
532	Goblet	5.00	526 Salt and Pepper, pr.,	5.00	531 Guernsey Jug	7.50	545 Tobacco Jar	7.50
555	Plate	7.00	546 Tobacco Jar	9.50	524 Water Set	8.50	561 Ash Tray	6.00
539	Vase	7.50	558 Ash Tray	3.75	571 Electric Lamp	12.50	556 Ash Tray	2.50
529	Salt and Pepper, pr.,	4.00	535 Candlestick	4.50	508 Tea Set, 4 pieces	27.50	523 Porringer	3.50

POLITICAL ANTIQUES

*Search around in old bureau drawers and trunks long
stored in the attic and, somewhere among the hodge podge
of items, you'll find at least one campaign button or
souvenir. Here's an area of collecting that would seem
limitless in scope. Of course, the earlier items are oftentime
the most valuable; but later things, produced in smaller
quantities, will bring extremely high prices. Do you
remember Landon's sunflower campaign button? Or the
subsequent Roosevelt buttons with his various running
mates' faces and names on them? Don't throw them away.
Instead save them as an investment that cost you little
or nothing to acquire.*

Aluminum token with cartoon-like portrait of Bryan. Legend reads, "In God We Trust For The Other 47 Cents." Diameter 3½ inches.

One of the many varieties of crudely made white metal Bryan Dollars resembling a real silver dollar, and dated 1896. Diameter 3⅜ inches.

"One Bryan Dollar" made of nickel plated steel with sharply milled edge. This is one of the plainer tokens, but the obverse bears the legend "Free Trade—Free Silver—16 to 1—1896—Free Hell." Diameter 1½ inches.

BRYAN'S MONEY

by ELMER A. PIERCY

Illustrations from the author's collection.

Above and below: Cast iron "Pie Plate" dollar, holed so that it could be worn about the neck. Legend on obverse reads: "Sixteen to One/1897." Legend on reverse reads: "In Bryan Free Coinage We Trust/One Dollar." Diameter 6 inches; weight, one pound.

REFERRING TO his Republican opponents in his acceptance speech at the Chicago convention where he was chosen as the Democratic presidential candidate, in 1896, William Jennings Bryan said, "You shall not press down upon the brow of labor this crown of thorns; you shall not crucify mankind upon a cross of gold."

Bryan, the so-called "Silver Candidate," was referring to his party's proposal for a bimetal monetary standard wherein the value of silver would be tied to the value of gold at a fixed ratio of sixteen ounces of silver to one ounce of gold. Had Bryan been the winner, the price of silver would have been increased by forty-seven cents an ounce, making the existing dollar worth but fifty-three cents.

The "For Gold Only" advocates, headed by the Republican presidential candidate William McKinley, could not miss this opportunity to ridicule an idea which they considered financially unsound. They campaigned vigorously, with no holds barred, and forecast that a period of depression and famine would overtake the whole country should Bryan and his advocates win the election and make bimetallism the law of the land.

During the 1896 campaign several tokens bearing derogatory legends were issued which have since become known as "Bryan's Money." The Republicans came forth with a series of tokens made in various sizes, from that of the present day quarter to what was then called a "Pie Plate" measuring six inches in diameter. These tokens were made of lead, pewter, type metal, aluminum, brass, bronze, white metal and iron. They all purported to show the size of our currency should the bimetallists win the election. Most certainly these tokens had a very important effect on the outcome of the election that year. Many golden-tongued Republican orators, while berating bimetallism, would hold up one of these "Bryan Dollars" and shout, "Is this what you want for money?"

Although Bryan made other attempts to win the presidency, in 1900 and 1908, he failed to change the minds of the people concerning bimetallism.

Some years after these bitter campaigns, Mr. Farran Zerbe collected all the various types of Bryan Money that he could find and cataloged them for the *Numismatist* magazine's July 1926 issue. Zerbe listed 141 types, and described others that he had heard of but had not actually seen. Zerbe's personal collection eventually reached 181 types and varieties, and there are still more being discovered in attics, grandmother's sewing basket, coin shops, antiques stores, and other places.

Mr. Zerbe separated the pieces he located into categories. The first consisted of the silver items put out by reputable firms and simply showing the size of the silver dollar as it then existed and the size it would have to be if the sixteen-to-one ratio advocated by Bryan were established. These tokens were struck in coin silver and are beautifully made.

The next classification included those with derogatory legends purportedly showing the size of a nickel or dime if Bryan's silver policy became the monetary standard in this country. Some of the legends cast or stamped on these tokens read, "In God We Trust, In Bryan We Bust," "Free Silver, 53% Purchasing Power," "Teno Cento," "Bryan's Idea of Coinage," "From Silver Mines of Bunko States," "Free Silver, Free Hell." And there were many, many more equally as vitriolic.

The classification of the so-called "dollars" listed by Mr. Zerbe seemed most interesting to collectors of that day (1926). There were a great many types cast, stamped, or made by hand.

Above and below: Type metal token closely resembling a real silver dollar of the period. Legends read "Bryan's Money/1898" (obverse) and "Bryan's Idea of Coinage/Aber 16 to 1 Nit" (reverse). "Aber," in German, means, "but"; the word "Nit" was commonly used during this campaign to indicate "no" or "not." Diameter 3½ inches.

Political cartoon, published July 7, 1896, depicts a Bryan Dollar and declares "When Silver Is King—The Dollar Of The Future—(will be the) Size Of Life." From **Life**, copyright 1896 by Mitchell & Miller. Size 5 x 7".

"If Bryan Should Be Able To Open The Pandora Box Of 1896." All sorts of dire predictions were made in this cartoon published in the **San Francisco Chronicle**, September 25, 1896; signed by the artist Newberry. Size 7 x 8".

Ferrotype Campaign Tokens of 1860

by S. W. FREEMAN

REPUBLICAN CANDIDATES

Abraham Lincoln (Illinois)—Hannibal Hamlin (Maine)

Condensed Platform—"Three Strings in their Bow"

1. Opposition to slavery in the territories, but leaving out the issue of the Fugitive Slave Law and abolition in the District of Columbia. Pronounced slavery an evil, but denied an intent to intervene in states where it existed.

2. Proposed a protective tariff for American industry.

3. Advocated a homestead law.

States voting: Me., N. H., Vt., Mass., R. I., Conn., N. Y., Pa., Ohio, Mich., Ind., Ill., Wis., Minn., Iowa, Ore., Calif., and all except 3 votes of N. J.

Electoral votes—180. Popular votes—1,866,452

NORTHERN DEMOCRATS

Stephen A. Douglas (Illinois)—Herschel V. Johnson (Georgia)

Condensed Platform

"Slavery in the territories to be determined by the courts."

States voting: Missouri, with 9 votes, and 3 of N. J.

Electoral votes—12. Popular votes—1,376,957

SOUTHERN DEMOCRATS

John C. Breckinridge (Kentucky)—Joseph Lane (Oregon)

Condensed Platform

Based on the Davis resolution in the Senate: "No power could exclude slavery in the territories"—and that Congress must protect it.

States voting: Md., N. C., S. C., Ga., Fla., Ala., Miss., La., Ark., Texas.

Electoral votes—72. Popular votes—849,781

FOUR political parties were afield during the Presidential campaign of 1860, and none of the various names given that turbulent campaign suited it better than "The Campaign of Party Strife." Here the last truly national party, Democratic, was split asunder by party issues and sectional principles. The Republican Party came into prominence. The Constitutional Union party entered the field, formulated principally of hangers-on of the Whig party, clinging to the Clay-Webster principles of compromise. Remnant Whigs and Know-Nothings joined forces with the party whose platform pleased them most or offended them least.

In one respect, at least, the political parties of 1860 were in accord. Each used tokens with metallic, minted borders, in the center of which was impressed a miniature ferrotype portrait of a Presidential candidate, while on the reverse was a similar portrait of the Vice-Presidential running-mate. All of these seen are pierced at the top for suspension. They were handed out by members of political clubs or other boosters to further the popularity of the candidates of their choice. Thus began the popular campaign devices which evolved into celluloid pins and buttons and their modern variations.

Ferrotypes, often referred to as tintypes, came into being through the evolution of photographic processes. In 1839 Louis Jacques Mandé Daguerre, of France, had introduced the daguerreotype, which enjoyed the height of its popularity in America in the late 1840s.

An Englishman, Fox Talbot, is said to have begun work on a similar process in 1834, and to have claimed priority over Daguerre. His process, known as colotype, never achieved the popularity of the daguerreotype.

Another Englishman, Scott Archer, is credited with the improved wet collodian process of photography which he introduced in 1851. This new technique rapidly displaced and made obsolete both colotypes and daguerreotypes in their original form. Most of the great photographs made during the Civil War were by this wet collodian process.

Ferrotypes are photographic images taken on thin iron or tin plates by collodian process. Not only were they less expensive than daguerreotypes, which were taken on silver-coated copper plates, but the collodian process made the images less susceptible to abrasions.

Mr. Freeman has been a collector and student of coins since 1919, specializing in early American coinage. He is associated with The Numismatist, holds life membership in the A.N.A., is past president of the Arkansas Numismatic Society. Tokens pictured, (1/3 larger than actual) are from his collection.

CONSTITUTIONAL UNION

John Bell (Tennessee)—Edward Everett (Massachusetts)

Condensed Platform

Clinging to the Clay-Webster Compromise: "The Constitution, the Union, and the enforcement of the laws". (Said Horace Greely, "Means anything in general and nothing in particular.")

States voting: Va., Ky., Tenn.

Electoral votes—39. Popular votes—588,879

Gold finished Garfield fobs. Left to right: Mechanical hand; non-mechanical; mechanical hand and tail; height 1 ⅝".

The GARFIELD and HANCOCK *"Devil Dolls"*

by MARIE CURIAL MENEFEE

Illustrations from the author's collection.

Gold finished Hancock fobs. Left to right: Mechanical hand; non-mechanical; mechanical hand and tail; height 1 ⅝".

ABOUT 1879, the author's father, Edward L. Curial, a jeweler living in Anoka, Minn., designed and patented a mechanical watch fob publicizing the presidential campaign being waged that year between James Abram Garfield and General Winfield Scott Hancock, a Civil War hero. Mr. Curial was a first class artist and engraver, consequently he designed

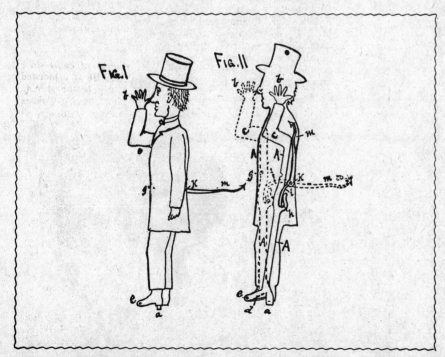

The working mechanism of E. L. Curial's watch fob was clearly defined in drawings (above) which accompanied his patent (No. 231,408), dated August 24, 1880.

and cut the dies for these mechanical campaign souvenirs himself. The dies were sent to a manufacturer in New York City with an initial order for 500 fobs to be finished in gold wash and nickel-plate. Curial hoped to test the market for his fobs with this small order before going into large-scale production.

The Hancock fob depicted the general in full uniform with his name across the band of his high hat; Garfield was shown in his characteristic "hands in pocket" pose; his name also was across the band of his hat. Some of the fobs were made without moving parts, some were made with a moving hand, and some were made with both moving hand and a pointed tail. Pressing down the foot of the figure on a hard surface activated the moving parts hidden between the front and back facings of the fob causing them to pop out in a most undignified gesture. A few non-mechanical pins were also produced.

The manufacturer of the watch fobs

recommended to Mr. Curial that he employ street hawkers to sell these campaign trinkets so they could be demonstrated. Curial, following this advice, sent a selection of gold and nickel finished fobs to "sidewalk merchants" in various parts of the country—a hundred fobs went to a man in Philadelphia. Within a few days Mr. Curial was inundated with requests from his outlets for more fobs; many of the salesmen reported that they were literally mobbed by crowds of people wanting to buy one of his "devil dolls."

Curial sent an urgent request for more fobs to the New York manufacturer, but unfortunately the supplier's employees were out on strike at that time and he could not fill the order. By the time the strike was settled the campaign was over, and Mr. Garfield had won the election. Since only 500 of Curial's "devil doll" fobs were made, it's quite obvious that these campaign novelties are relatively rare.

A few years later, during the Blaine-Cleveland presidential campaign of 1883, similar mechanical fobs were produced — but not by Mr. Curial. Apparently his patented idea had been adopted and used by someone else.

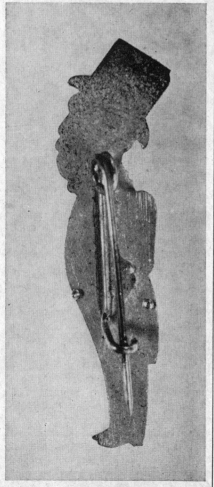

Back view of nickel-plated non-mechanical Garfield pin; length 1 5/8".

Parade Torches

TIME was when political campaigns meant parades. Hundreds of partisan marching clubs in towns and cities across the nation spent deliriously on bands, uniforms, and torches. G. W. Simons & Co., Boston, Massachusetts, established prior to 1835, claimed themselves, in 1877, the "Largest Dealers in Campaign, Band and Military Equipment in the United States." Such a business span, for one company alone, indicates the age and variety of torches to be found by today's collectors.

Torches shown here are from the Simons 1877 catalog. Below, the Non-Consumable Wick Hurricane Torch, producing a flame which "could not be extinguished by high winds," cost $18 a hundred; the poles on which they were carried sold separately at $1.50 a hundred. The Shaler Flash Torch, beneath it, "a brilliant burner, capable of producing a flash nearly 3 feet high", came packed in boxes of 50, with wicks and handles; cost $30 a hundred. Other popular numbers were swinging-frame torches, double or single, similar to the band lamp above, but used on poles.

President Coolidge Memorabilia

by BARBARA B. CHIOLINO

Souvenir post card entitled "At Plymouth, Vt., Aug. 19—1924." Left to right, it pictures Harvey Firestone, Pres. Coolidge, Henry Ford, Thomas A. Edison, Russell Firestone (standing), Mrs. Coolidge, and Col. John Coolidge.

ONE HUNDRED YEARS AGO, July 4, 1872, Calvin Coolidge, our 30th president, was born in Plymouth, Vermont, more specifically, in Plymouth Notch, one small hamlet in that country town. He came from a pioneering and farming background, and his steady rise from obscurity to the foremost political office still challenges the imagination.

Many people make a "pilgrimage" to this little place in the Green Mountains, which, fortunately, because of concerned Government agencies and the Calvin Coolidge Memorial Foundation, will be appropriately preserved as a memorial area and as a museum. Several buildings in the area will be open to the public this summer. A reception center to aid visitors will also be ready for the centenary of the birth.

The collectors of Coolidge memorabilia should perhaps first of all, look for books, particularly those by President Coolidge himself. In his *Autobiography* (to be republished this year), and in his collections of speeches, such as *The Price of Freedom* and *Have Faith in Massachusetts,* will be found what Coolidge really said. The Fuess biography, *Calvin Coolidge, the Man From Vermont,* and that by William Allen White, entitled *A Puritan in Babylon,* are among others. And there appear from time to time fascinating new studies, such as *Meet Calvin Coolidge,* edited by Lathem (1960) and *The Talkative President* (1964), which is off-the-record press conferences edited by Quint and Ferrell. He seems to be an enigma still to many. (Or might he be a source where we can find the old virtues of simplicity, economy, integrity?)

There are other books and unnumerable pamphlets, old and new. Over and over is told the story of how Calvin's father, Colonel John, swore him into office at 2:47 a.m., August 3, 1923. Vice-president at that time, Calvin was on vacation in Vermont when President Harding died. He asked his father if he were still a Notary Public and as such to swear him into office so the country would not be without a president. (Townspeople relished the story that Calvin, upon being asked how he knew his father *could* swear him in, replied that he did not know he *couldn't!*)

The kerosene lamp by which the ceremony took place was a drape pattern (probably one of the Lincoln drape patterns). It is pictured here. Since that time, it has been called Coolidge drape, and is to be found in antiques shops in clear glass and sometimes in cobalt blue in a variety of sizes and shapes.

Other paper items are photographs, postcards, magazine and newspaper articles pertaining to Coolidge. Also to be collected are souvenir chinaware and campaign items.

Other Coolidge memorabilia may concern Plymouth, Vermont, history. Of interest are the handmade farming tools (like the sap bucket we see Coolidge presenting to Henry Ford in the postcard photograph pictured here). Pioneering, homespun items that portray the life of such a town enter into the picture.

One of the earlier Coolidges made ladder-back chairs. (A particular kind of finial is said to distinguish these and they *are* scarce.)

Plymouth was an iron-mining center at one time and

Souvenir chinaware: plate and teapot in blue and white Staffordshire-type pottery, showing Coolidge birthplace (also came in tea tiles, pitchers, bowls, sugar and cream sets, and in pink as well as blue); small pitcher is German fine porcelain, hand painted; redware bust of Coolidge bank with slogan "Save as Coolidge Does"; brown calendar tile for 1925, made by Wedgwood for Jones, McDuffee & Stratton of Boston, shows Coolidge Homestead. Much of this souvenir china was made to order for Miss Ruth Aldrich who had a gift shop in Plymouth.

Some Coolidge campaign items: two medals from the Republican Convention of 1924; sheet music "Keep Cool with Coolidge," put out by the Home Town Coolidge Club; a beanie from the Harding-Coolidge campaign; and various campaign buttons. Not shown, but nice to find, is a cardboard fan with the "Keep Cool With Coolidge" slogan.

Two views of a small box stove made in Plymouth, Vt., 1839.

here was located the Tyson Furnace, making stoves like the one pictured and other items. These, too, are scarce.

Gold was mined in the 1850s onward, and there is extant a map of Plymouth showing extensive gold claims. There are also rare advertisements of the Rooks Mining Company, which sold stock in the venture. In my own collection is an assayer's cup said to be from the gold mines. Many stories are told of the Plymouth gold rush. Some sold their wedding rings to buy claims. (It is doubtful that any of Calvin Coolidge's immediate family did.) One man became the sole owner of the mine and was at the end, a hermit, mentally unbalanced and never to give up his dream of gold in Plymouth. He died just before Coolidge became President.

Souvenir post card of "The Lamp That Lit The Path To The White House."

PRESIDENTIAL CAMPAIGN PIPES
from the collection of Peter Shurke

Theodore Roosevelt Rough Rider pipe made for the 1904 Presidential campaign. The briarwood bowl has been expertly carved into a full-relief portrait head of Teddy Roosevelt wearing his famous Rough Rider hat, decorated with crossed cavalry swords; crossed swords and the letters "U.S.V." appear on the high uniform collar. A silver band joins the wooden portion of the pipe to a black composition stem. The maker's mark, the initials "W.D.C." within a triangle, appears on the briarwood portion of the stem. Length 6 inches.

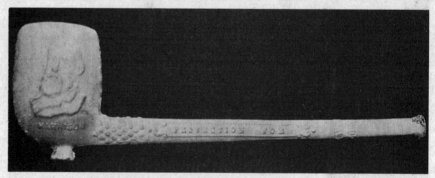

Harrison clay pipe made for the presidential campaign of 1888. One side of the bowl bears a portrait of Benjamin Harrison; the opposite side is decorated with an eagle with spread wings holding a shield and arrows. The inscription "Protection for American Labor" appears in raised letters along both sides of the stem. Several years ago a box of these clay pipes was found in an old pipe and tobacco shop in Amsterdam, Holland; presumably they had been stored on a shelf in a back room since 1888. Length 5½ inches.

The Lincoln Emancipation pipe, made entirely of clay decorated with colored enamels, represents a portrait head of our martyred President wearing a green laurel wreath. Mr. Lincoln has white eyes with black pupils and brows, red lips, and is wearing a blue band about his neck. Reclining against the back of Lincoln's head is a negro child holding a black chain. The name "Lincoln" appears in raised letters along the other side of the stem, directly opposite the feet of the child. This extremely rare pipe was made as a souvenir of the presidential campaign of 1864. Length 5½ inches.

PRIMITIVES

The prerequisite of a primitive is that it be entirely hand made from materials that are readily available to the maker. Consequently a wide variety of items qualify as primitives—everything from a hand made cheese box to a carved wooden spoon. The most desirable primitives are those that have some added embellishment or decoration—either carved, wrought or applied. Useful objects made of discarded pieces also fall into the category of primitives. Many things considered folk art are primitives, too. Drawing the line between primitives and folk art is difficult, but keep in mind that some of these things can, and do, fall into both categories.

GRATERS and STRAINERS

Practical Primitives Made of

Pierced Tinware

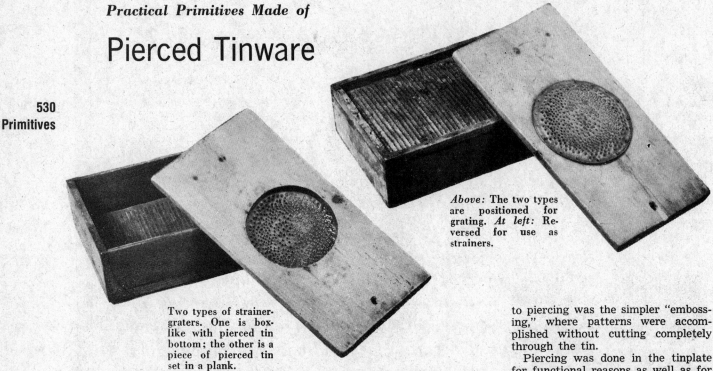

Above: The two types are positioned for grating. *At left:* Reversed for use as strainers.

Two types of strainer-graters. One is box-like with pierced tin bottom; the other is a piece of pierced tin set in a plank.

by EDWIN C. WHITTEMORE

TWO OR three hundred years ago, household utensils in most of America were made of iron, pewter, or earthenware. Iron was heavy and brittle, and it rusted. Pewter was heavy and dentable, and it melted. Earthenware was bulky and heavy, and it broke. They were not ideal materials for items to be given hard use, in contact with cold liquids and hot fires.

It is easy to see why "tinware" was accepted so quickly, and became popular so very fast. Actually, the term "tinware" is a misnomer, for tinware, as we know it, is actually sheet iron on which layers of tin have been deposited. Often 85 percent of the total content is iron.

Tinware was developed in Germany in the 1500s, moved quickly to the British Isles where there were both rolling mills and a supply of tin ore. In England, tinplate, and tinware items made from it, were produced in the early 1600s. In the early 1700s, the American colonies started importing both finished tinware items and the rolled tinplate sheets from which to fabricate household utensils.

Tinware actually did not need much of a push for housewives accepted it willingly. It was shiny and sparkling, the "poor man's silver." It was light; it stood heat; it could easily be fashioned into many types of items. It was relatively inexpensive; it did not crack or melt; it resisted rust, and could easily be mended by soldering.

The special category of "pierced tin" housewares is one of the most interesting in the tinware field. Immediately we think of pie safes with pierced tin panels, foot warmers, lanterns, graters, colanders, and related items.

Usually the tinplate was pierced before the item was assembled. A sheet of tinplate of the required size was cut from a flat sheet and placed, still flat, on a suitable surface, such as a sheet of lead, a pine plank, or even hard wet sand, packed solid. Then, with a hammer and nail, or better, a hammer and sharp edged chisel, the worker pierced the sheet in various designs, simple or intricate.

If a nail was being used and hit-or-miss designs employed, the result was most varied. With a more skillful artisan, using a sharp chisel, the result could be quite delightful. Most often the piercings were slots or dots, but with special cutters, other design elements were incorporated, such as stars, half moons, and crosses. Related to piercing was the simpler "embossing," where patterns were accomplished without cutting completely through the tin.

Piercing was done in the tinplate for functional reasons as well as for design. In lighting devices such as lanterns, it let oxygen in, heat and smoke out. In graters, the rough side became the work side, the rough edges of the pierced holes doing the grating. As a strainer, the smooth side was a practical workable surface which provided drainage.

We show here two examples of an ingenious household device depending on pierced tinplate—the combination grater-strainer. Both sides of the tinplate are functional in the same piece. In the boxlike example, a sheet of pierced tinplate covers one whole side. Placed with the rough side up, it serves as an excellent grater for cabbage, carrots, and potatoes when they are being grated to make coleslaw, to color butter, and in making starch. Turned to the other side, it becomes an excellent strainer or colander of good capacity for washing vegetables and such.

The other example, made from a plank, is identical in function, but with smaller capacity, and probably represents a huried improvisation.

These combination grater-strainers are very collectible. They may be used for their original purpose, or simply hung on the wall for decorative effect. They may be wired with a low-wattage bulb to give a soft and patterned light in a special location, such as a hall or infant's room. They represent an interesting group of the "practical primitives" which are becoming more and more popular with collectors.

Carved Horse Blanket Pins

AS far as presently determined, Roger Williams I, a race horse owned by Huxhum P. Kent about 1836, was operating on the tracks near Providence, Rhode Island.

Then, as now, a horse was covered, after a race, with a light wool blanket pinned together under his throat, sometimes a second pin at his chest, and walked slowly until he "cooled out."

Someone, perhaps his caretaker, carved for this special horse a wealth of wooden blanket pins and a pincushion, horseshoe-shaped, to hold them. The horseshoe, 14¼ × 12½ inches, was carved of one piece of walnut with nailheads and calks plugged in. The cushion center was stuffed with straw. Of seventy or more original pins, forty-eight remain. (See this month's cover.)

The pins are from four to five inches long. Tops shown here are actual size. A few were fancifully carved in stylized design; most relate to horse and stable, showing farrier's tools, harness parts, horse furnishings, and a miscellany of stable appointments. Unique examples of true art in wood carving, they offer help today in identifying and dating actual horse items of the early nineteenth century.

ILLUSTRATIONS

Above—left to right, all actual size: anvil; shoeing hammer; heavy hammer; nippers, above; hoof knife, below. *Left— reading down, left to right:* foot tub; feed box; mane comb; curry comb; hoof rasp; unidentified, above, perhaps a rein ring; tail comb, below; sickle; sprinkler can; corn broom. *Center:* hand bellows; bale of hay; bottle and sponge; carriage jack. *Right—reading down:* horse collar; snaffle bit; leg pad; stirrup; unidentified; lady's side-laced boot. The "K" was probably for H. P. Kent who owned the horse for which these blanket pins were made.

-- Of Tankards, Toddy Spoons, and Swizzle Sticks

by MARY EARLE GOULD

(Illustrations from the author's collection.)

Tankard of Pennsylvania origin; slide lock holds cover on; 2" pewter tip on spout. Initials of the owner, "S. L. S.," and date, "1855," were painted on the sides.

Tin tankard with glass window on side for measuring contents.

Three fine wooden tankards, staved and hooped. The handles were made in one piece with a stave.

IN 17TH CENTURY England, water as a drinkable was under suspicion; ale or beer was the everyday drink. Coming to the New World, the Pilgrims and other of our earliest settlers continued this English practice. Though the Pilgrims were forced to drink water, once the store of ale brought over on the Mayflower was exhausted and no other ship had come in, they were always leery of it.

But shortly after the settlers, fruit trees arrived, and in a few years apple orchards were producing fruit for cider. By 1700, New Englanders had abandoned beer and ale for cider. It became the common drink, served at every meal, to every person, including small children. President John Adams, though favoring temperance, is said to have taken a large tankard of hard cider the first thing each morning.

Some drinking tankards had been brought from the home country, but many were made here to meet the needs of the growing population. These early tankards were of wood. The cooper made his share of them, though the handy man at home often made his own. As with all hand-made woodenware, each piece was slightly different from all others.

Such tankards were staved, hooped, and tapered toward the top. The handle was cut in one piece with the stave. At the top, the cover was set in and pegged. An extension on the cover allowed the cover to be lifted by the pressure of the thumb. Hoops made of withes, the bark removed, were set in groups of three at top, bottom, and middle.

You have heard the expression, "Go whistle for it." In England, tankards were sometimes made with a whistle at the top of the handle. When a man wanted another drink, he whistled for it.

The first tankard I found for my collection was a fine one. In the middle of the cover a cork was plugged. Removal of the cork disclosed a round hole, charred where a toddy iron, heated in the embers, had been inserted into the drink to warm it.

While this example is an excellent and unusual find, two others that came to my collection are more rare. One is of

tin, painted green with a narrow glass window down one side the length of the tankard. Through it could be seen the amount in the tankard—how much was served, how much was drunk, and when it was time to ask for more.

The second, of Pennsylvania origin, was quite different. Of wood, with a 2-inch pewter tip on the spout, it bore, in yellow paint, the large initials of the owner, "S.L.S.," and the date, "1855." The cover was fastened by a lock, a strip of wood running through a hole. This one was stolen from me, but its photograph is shown here.

As time went on, drinks became more varied. Perry was made from pears, peachy from peaches, metheglin from honey, yeast, and water. In Virginia, the honey-locust tree furnished locust beans for making metheglin. Such names as whistle-nelly, shug, and grog appeared in old diaries and in the account books of country stores.

Then came rum's turn. Long before the Revolution it was consumed in immense quantities. We are told, "It appeared at weddings, funerals, christenings, all public meetings and private feasts." Old store ledgers which carried Town accounts revealed that the Town Fathers in providing for destitute widows counted rum among the necessities.

The various tools used in making drinks form a collection in themselves. Toddy spoons and stirrers are pic-

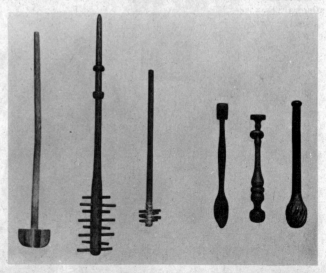

Left to right: Three swizzle sticks; third from the left has bamboo sticks tied on with a cord. Three toddy stirrers; the first one has a masher on one end and a spoon on the other.

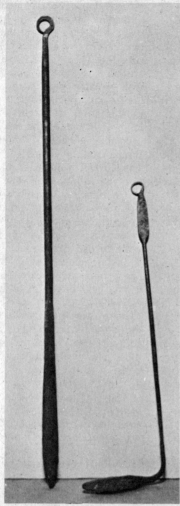

Two toddy irons; the one on the right has been bent and flattened.

Two wooden tankards; the one on the right has a hole in the lid for inserting a toddy stick.

Swizzle was a mixture of hard liquors with sugar and bitters added, then iced. It required a special stirrer—a swizzle stick. This was longer than the toddy stirrer and had either cross arms or a winged head. In use, the swizzle stick was held between the palms of the hands and twirled, thus stirring the drink by means of the head or cross arms. Sometimes the cross sticks were made of bamboo, tied on with a coarse cord, or perhaps the cross arms were set in. There were many variations.

A collection of wooden tankards and mixing tools speak eloquently of olden times when days were cold, snow was deep, and the open fire was the magnet about which men gathered, tankards in hand, to conduct their businesses or enjoy friendships.

tured here in various shapes and sizes. Toddy, a concoction of spirits, hot water, sugar and lemon, had to be mixed, crushed, and heated. The toddy iron was the heating element. Thrust into the fire until it was red hot, it was then plunged into the drink, making it sizzle and raising its temperature.

Flip, too, had to be stirred. This was made of any liquor, often sherry, mixed with eggs, sugar and spices. Spoons and stirrers were carved from a stick of wood, often by artistic as well as skillful hands.

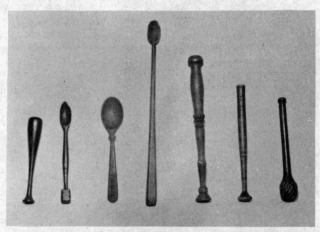

A row of wooden toddy stirrers and spoons.

THOSE OLD PANTRY BOXES

by MARY EARLE GOULD

IN THE EARLY DAYS of this country's settlement, household utensils and implements came into being as the need presented itself. They were made of wood since that material was over-abundant, at hand to be used. Some villages had their coopers, but it was usually the handy man of the house who fashioned in his spare time the spoons and graters and the many pantry boxes his good wife considered necessary. She needed pill boxes, spice boxes, meal boxes, butter boxes, cheese boxes, and large-size herb boxes. Occasionally some considerate husband made his wife a pie box.

The boxes were made from whatever wood was handy—pine, birch, oak, ash, beech, chestnut, fruitwood. In general they were all fashioned in the same way. The worker cut his strip of wood, thinned it, and made a pointed lap. Then he steamed it or soaked it to make it pliable. He readied his tops and bottoms, round or oval, from a pattern of the desired size. Then he lapped the side strip around the bottom and fastened it with wooden pegs such as cobblers used—tiny pointed pegs cut from slender strips of birch, a short inch long. He fastened the lap with whatever nails he had; they might be hand-forged iron, or copper, or even tacks. The cover, made to fit the box, was fastened with one lap. The more artistic the maker, the more artistic the laps. Some were true creations.

There were molds on which to shape the boxes which the cooper came to use. Some molds had a strip down one side into which to pound the nails; some had an extension by which it was held in a vise or between the worker's knees.

Boxes were often made to nest one inside the other, each box for a different purpose. Pill boxes, spice boxes, those for meals, butter, cheese, and herbs was the order in which most nests were arranged.

The tiny pill boxes, some round, some oval, varied in size from two to three inches. The wood used for them was pine, thinned on the grindstone before cutting. Laps were held with a tack, but covers and bottoms were held in by pressure—no tacks were possible. Because of their fragility, few pill boxes are found today. Eye-stones and sealing wafers, as well as medicinal tablets, were frequently kept in such boxes.

Next in size came the spice boxes. Though woodenware was the cooper's business, it was ofen the man of the house, working out in the ell or in a small shop in his yard, who fashioned these pantry necessaries. Spice boxes and those which held soda were not large enough to have a decorative lap and usually were finished with just one point. Seven spices were most commonly used—mace, cinnamon, clove, ginger, pepper, allspice, and nutmeg; their distinctive odors still

A nest of odd round boxes.

A nest of Shaker oval boxes.

Odd boxes peculiarly put together with wire fastenings and slipped in notches. Decorated box at the right is dated 1767.

cling to the boxes which held them long ago. Cinnamon was the strongest scent of all; clove turned the wood dark, its oil penetrating the wood.

The next size, the meal box, was large enough for more decoration than the smaller boxes enjoyed. Various woods were used for them—maple, sometimes curly or bird's-eye, birch, fruit, or ash. They were made up round or oval. Often they fitted into the nests, but the most beauiful of all, with ornamental laps, were those made up as individual boxes.

The herb boxes, largest of all with the exception of the butter and cheese boxes, are the most scarce for today's finding. Herbs were commonly planted and gathered in full bloom. Tied in bunches, they were hung to dry. Some stalks were put away in boxes while others were crushed for use. Some of the oval herb boxes were as much as 20 inches long.

Sometimes large boxes, both round and oval, were used as catch-alls, not classified for any particular use, while others, like the pie box were made for a specific purpose. The pie box is round and has an inside rack on three short legs so that the pie within rested on the rack and could be easily handled.

There is a difference between a butter box and a cheese box though they are both round and about the same size. Butter boxes were staved and hooped, for butter was moist and the staves had to give. Odorless white pine was used for the tops, bottoms, and staves. Hoops were ash or hickory that would bend. Sometimes the staves were dowelled, two pegs and holes for each stave. Such construction demanded a great deal of work and was infrequently used.

Cheese boxes are round lapped boxes to hold the round head of cheese. They came in sizes from one foot to two or more, depending on whether the cheese was made to be used by a family, a hostelry, or a store where cheese was cut off as desired. The cheese box, like the butter box, had a pine top and bottom, but the body wood varied; usually it was made of ash or oak, quartered or plain, nailed with copper nails. Since cheese was wrapped in cloth, it did not come in contact with the nails, but the tops and bottoms were pegged with wooden pegs as other boxes were. The thin gauze cloth used to wrap the cheese before it was put into the press or cupboard for ripening, attained the permanent name of "cheesecloth."

The Shakers followed a different pattern in their boxes. They called the laps "fingers," and each box had a set number of fingers according to its size. Their boxes were oval in shape and fastened—laps, tops, and bottoms —with copper nails or tacks. I have never seen nor heard of a round box made by Shakers or any with a pointed lap. Sometimes boxes with crudely fashioned fingers instead of the one lap, put together with handmade nails and crude workmanship, will show up but these were not Shaker-made. The Shakers always used copper nails and were meticulous in their work.

Shaker boxes were usually made in sets or nests, most often 12 to a nest, from tiny ovals to large herb boxes. Edward Andrews' book, *Shaker Industries,* tells of their work, and gives lists of contemporary prices.

Pantry boxes were often painted, since paint served as a protection to the wood. It also introduced a bright touch into a somber kitchen. Grays, greens, blues, yellows and a few shades of red were the colors employed. Paint was made from the clay in the soil. Gray clay, mixed with skim milk, whey, or white of eggs, was used when making a color dyed with barks, berries, stalks, and the indigo plant. When no red clay was available, yellow clay turned to red when baked or heated. Different veins of red clay produced different shades of red.

The Indians used all of these clays mixed with the whites of wild turkey eggs to paint their tepees, totem poles, and bodies. They even painted tiny flowers on their splint baskets, using a frayed hickory twig for a brush. The colonist evidently learned from them how to make the paint for their pantry boxes and other items.

Early nails were cut, shaped, and pounded out on an anvil. (Often you can see this being done nowadays by a blacksmith in some recreated village.) Some men made their own nails at home in the same way. The early boxes were made with handmade nails. In later boxes where machine nails are used, the wood will be different and the hand work is lacking.

Cheese boxes, one painted gray and one green, with large handmade nails.

The largest cheese box, over 20" in diameter.

Pie box with three-legged rack.

Nutmegs preserved in a jar of alcohol for over 100 years. Small spice box and nutmeg grater.

Two butter boxes (one painted green) with laps.

A large herb box painted red. Small pill boxes and a calico lined box for jewelry.

Variety of burl bowls, collected 30 years ago when such pieces were more plentiful than they are today.

Refinishing Burl Bowls

by
IOLA A. SMITH

A BURL is a malformation—a hard woody growth — which protrudes from the trunk or branches of a tree. It is caused by some type of injury, usually associated with adventitious buds. It is a very dense piece of wood with an irregular, mottled grain. English cabinetmakers have used it for veneer and inlay since the 16th century, and colonial cabinetmakers in America also used it.

But its popular use was for the bowls every early housewife needed, and for which it was admirably suited by the nature of its flattened hemispherical shape. Burls form on many trees, but those provided by the maple and ash, being less porous, were best for bowls; a few were walnut.

The burl bowls made by the Indians in America were laboriously gouged out by hand. Their usual tool was a sharpened flint, somewhat like an axe or adze, but they also used implements fashioned of stone, shell, or beaver teeth. The procedure was to air dry the burl after it was taken from the tree, then burn the flat side until the wood was charred and softened for gouging. A characteristic of Indian work is the visible mark of their tools, and their most common bowls were deep oval with handle holes.

The colonists made most of their bowls on a lathe, using a chisel-like tool to hollow out the wood as it was rotated. Often they contrived a bevelled edge, using hand tools.

Burl bowls were made round, oval, or boat-shaped, in a variety of sizes. The handles might protrude, be under-cut, or open cut. The last, in good condition, are hardest to find today; too often the open-cut handles have broken off with use. Other items were made of burl, too—mortars and pestles, butter paddles, dishes, even herb grinders.

The pictures shown here were taken some thirty years ago of examples owned by Mr. H. M. Wiltsie, then of Kenmore, N. Y. His collection included a wide variety of sizes, from a chopping bowl 24 inches across and 8 inches deep to a little salt dish, 4 inches wide. Some of his bowls had rounded bottoms and sides, others were flat-bottomed with sides flaring or perpendicular.

What has since become of the collection, or its owner, the author has been unable to discover, but Mr. Wiltsie's notes on refinishing his bowls, given her so long ago and carefully saved, deserve recall.

His method was similar to that used to finish colonial furniture. He sanded by hand and used boiled linseed oil finish—a process tedious but intensely satisfying. For sanding he used seven grades of sandpaper followed by four of steel wool, a rubdown with pumice stone, and a final polishing with rottenstone. Then he applied the boiled linseed oil, letting it stand till the wood had absorbed all it could before he wiped it off. Finally, with the palm of his hand, he rubbed in pumice stone to preserve the wood as well as give it a polish. This finish does not spot with water.

When he wanted to bring out the grain still more, he used soot instead of pumice stone for the last rubdown. His directions: moisten hands in boiled linseed oil, then dip them in a dish of soot. Rub well into the bowl and wipe off the excess. The soot darkens and brings out the grain—a dirty job but the results are worth it.

If he considered a little wax would bring out the grain even further, he rubbed in a combination of canuba wax, beeswax, and turpentine, mixed to a creamy paste. (He found floor wax too yellow and discolored the wood, while beeswax by itself gave a pleasant finish, but white spotted with water.)

The distressed burl bowl, softened by dry rot, he preserved with a coat of thin colorless varnish, shellac, or linseed oil. Cracks or wormholes he patched with plastic wood before the polishing process.

Refinished round burl bowl shows the irregular, mottled grain.

Large burl bowl is 24" across, 8" deep; small one, 4" across, 1½" deep.

QUILTS

Nothing links the antique with family traditions like a quilt. For more than two hundred years the women of America have been making quilts for their families and friends. At first, scraps of colorful fabric were sewed together in a variety of patterns simulating stars, flowers, trailing vines, trees, log cabins, a flight of birds, or just a hodge podge of color, or appliqued in various patterns on a background of plain or colored fabric. In every case, the stitching was ever important and always a part of the overall design. Many antique quilts are signed and dated, making them more valuable to the collector. Most quilts are large enough for a double bed; still others are much larger; and some are quite small being meant for a baby's crib covering. If the designs you see on the following pages do not bear the name you know them by, this is not unusual at all. Some quilt designs are known by as many as four or five names depending on what part of the country they are found.

STITCHING
American History

by ANOMA HOFFMEISTER
Chairman of the Museum Committee,
Chase County (Nebraska)
Historical Society Museum

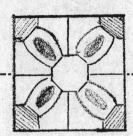

"Job's Tears."

ALTHOUGH women were not permitted to vote in the early years of our republic, they were very much aware of national events and named many of their quilt patterns for them. The *Pine Tree,* one of the oldest quilt patterns used in the United States, was developed during the Revolutionary War period. It honored the colonists' Pine Tree flag, which centered a pine

The "Pine Tree" pattern.

tree above the legend "An Appeal to Heaven." When one of our ships flying the Pine Tree flag was captured by the British, English newspapers made great sport of the "Appeal to Heaven" motto. The Pine Tree quilt was stitched into being in all 13 original states.

The eagle, after it was adopted by Congress in 1782 for the Great Seal of the United States, was a motif ladies worked in applique on quilts, and in quilting designs. One of the more elaborate eagle quilts depicts George Washington doffing his hat to Miss Liberty beneath the spreading wings of our national bird. The eagle motif in quiltmaking was again popular in the North for a short time during the Civil War period. Made with four spread-winged eagles in the cen-

The "Union Quilt."

ter, it was called the *Union Quilt.*

Dolly Madison acted as hostess at the White House during her husband's term of office, and again for President Thomas Jefferson, who was a widower. She was the first "First Lady" of our country to be honored with a quilt pattern; it was called the *Dolly Madison Star.* President Cleveland was mar-

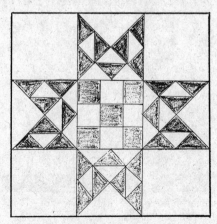

The "Dolly Madison Star" pattern.

ried while in the White House, and the ladies of our country designed a quilting block which they called *Mrs.*

"Mrs. Cleveland's Choice."

Cleveland's Choice.

The western migration during the 1860s, suggested wagons rolling; a quilt pattern made up of stylized versions of wagon wheels and chains was known as *The Road to California.*

"The Road to California" pattern.

Stephen A. Douglas must have fascinated the ladies of his time with his spirited debates with Abraham Lincoln, for they devised a most intricate pattern in his honor called *The Little Giant.*

Around 1800, there was a quilt pat-

"The Little Giant" pattern.

Crazy Patch Quilts

by EMMA STILES

tern, without intervening blocks, which was called "Job's Tears." Events in history caused the ladies to change its name often. In the early 1800s, it was known as *The Slave Chain,* at the time Missouri was asking for admission to the Union and the question of its being a "slave" or "free" state was paramount. By 1840, when our nation was concerned with the annexation of Texas to the Union, the quilt name was changed to *Texas Tears.* When the prairie states were being settled after the Civil War, it became *The Rocky Road to Kansas;* and still later, the *Endless Chain* pattern.

When William Henry Harrison was running for President, he was portrayed as a battle-scarred hero. One of his most important battles was the conquest of the great Indian chief Tecumseh at Tippecanoe in 1811. John Tyler was Harrison's running mate and the catch slogan under which they campaigned provided the ladies with still another name for a quilting pattern—*Tippecanoe and Tyler, Too.*

If American women of our time were to design quilting patterns, what would they choose to honor? Perhaps our historic space ventures would suggest the *Gemini II;* and it wouldn't be a bad idea to revive our great American symbol—the eagle.

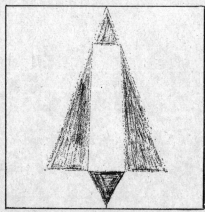

"Gemini II"; an original design suggested by the author for modern quiltmaking.

THE CRAZY patchwork quilts of the Victorian era are among the most picturesque examples of American folk art. Some were so elaborate that they took years to complete, and it is not surprising that many of them, handed down as heirlooms, occupy honored places in present day homes and museums. But the crazy quilt in America—"crazy" because it had no fixed design—did not begin with the Victorian version.

The first crazy quilts were born of necessity. In colonial days, cloth was a prized commodity; every scrap was treasured and eventually put to use. As soon as raw materials were available—the harvest reaped and the sheep shorn — colonists began to spin their hemp and wool into thread and weave it into cloth. The garments they fashioned from the cloth they made were worn until they were beyond mending. Children's clothes were eked out of grown-ups' discards; the scraps were used in quilts.

Those early quilts were strictly utilitarian, created for a basic need—warmth. They not only provided covers for the bed, but were also hung at windows and doors to keep out the winter's blast. These quilts had no planned design; there was little choice of materials. Scraps at hand, large and small, were fitted together like a picture puzzle. The size of the finished product depended on the number of pieces available. Woolen plaids, linsey-woolsey, red woolen underwear, and shoddy were combined in hit-or-miss fashion. Warmth was essential; appearance didn't matter.

Prior to 1750, beds and bedding were considered important house furnishings. Bedding was left in wills, passed down in families, listed in sheriffs' sales, and advertised for sale in early newspapers. Up to that time, almost all quilts were pieced in the "make-do" hit-or-miss manner.

As cloth steadily became more abundant and women had more time to think of "pretties," pieced quilts became more elaborate and developed in set patterns and designs. The early crazy quilt was relegated to the humblest households or forgotten altogether.

Then in the 1870s, the crazy quilt was resurrected. In an elaborated form it began to show up in the parlor as a "slumber robe" or couch throw. It was now sheet size, about 90 to 108 inches, and though still fashioned of scraps, the bits and pieces were of silk, velvet, brocade, plush, and satin as well as wool, cotton, and linen. The patches were neatly joined and the seams hidden beneath a plethora of fancy embroidery stitching.

Soon a more complicated type of crazy quilt was introduced, made in a patch or block form, and called the "crazy patch quilt." This differed from the earlier hit-or-miss variety by being made up in large blocks of small patches, each large block fitting in a given area an equal number of times.

Each finished block was hand-sewn to a backing of coarsely woven material. When all the blocks were positioned, their edges were united in an overall effect by fancy stitchery in variously colored threads. Chain stitch, bead stitch, buttonhole stitch, herringbone stitch, and all kinds of fagotting were popular, and a great variety of fancy stitches might be used on the same quilt. Sometimes a border of rich plain colored material was added to the finished quilt.

Each large block was treated decoratively, and often with great ingenuity and imagination. Some blocks were made up of hit-or-miss patches, or in patches planned to produce a design. Sometimes the blocks were embroidered, like a picture; the small patches in the block were delicately embroidered with flowers, bugs, spiders, and the like. Outlined birds, animals, flowers, people, and names made splashy blocks, especially if the outlined object was filled in with satin stitch.

Other decorative motifs used in the large blocks were hand paintings or india ink drawings on silk or satin,

Cigar advertisement woven on cloth makes a colorful center for this block.

Beadwork of this lyre-centered block is definitely unusual.

"Washday Monday" is outlined for the central patch within a block.

Printed satin portrait center; a type of print sometimes used on candy box tops.

advertisements or pictures printed on satin, woven silk badges, especially those of historical significance. Sometimes the design in the material itself was accentuated with outline stitch.

The more elaborately the blocks were embroidered or painted, the more prized was the quilt in its own day—and even more in ours.

Illustrations of blocks from various crazy quilts, photographed by the author, give an idea of the many different treatments imaginative makers gave their own quilts. Each one is an original!

A CRAZY QUILT

They do not make them anymore
For quilts are cheaper at the store
Than woman's labor, though a wife
Men think the cheapest thing in
   life.
But now and then a quilt is spread
Upon a quaint old walnut bed,
A crazy quilt of those old days
That I am old enough to praise.

Some woman sewed these points
   and squares
Into a pattern like life's cares.
Here is a velvet that was strong,
The poplin that she wore so long,
A fragment from her daughter's
   dress,
Like her, a vanished loveliness;
Old patches of such things as these,
Old garments and old memories.

And what is life? A crazy quilt;
Sorrow and joy, and grace and
   guilt,
With here and there a square of
   blue
For some old happiness we knew;
And so the hand of time will take
The fragments of our life and
   make,
One of life's remnants, as they fall,
A thing of beauty, after all.
          Douglas Malloch

Four blocks make up this circular center for a handsome silk, satin, and velvet crazy quilt. Corner blocks repeat the single fan-shaped pattern. Complete quilt contains 36 blocks, 9 by 9", and uses a total of 100 patches in a riot of color.

Block using woven silk badge of the Jewelers Legion for Garfield, 1880.

Delicately hand-painted flower on silk comprises one large block.

Rose printed on the material is embellished with outline stitch.

Hand-drawn "winter girl," filled in with embroidery, is part of a block.

Hawaiian Quilts

by MARCIA RAY

Vase of Dahlias, bright pink on white.

THE patchwork quilt, along with the use of needle and thread, was introduced to Hawaii by American mission ladies even before they were settled ashore. On March 31, 1820, the brig *Thaddeus,* with its first American mission complement, 162 days out of Boston, dropped anchor at Kohala, Hawaii. A few royal passengers were picked up and on April 3rd, still aboard ship, sailing along Hawaii's west coast toward Kailua, the American Board of Missions held its first sewing circle. Lucy Thurston's voluminous journal detailed the event. Eleven women attended: Kalakua, mother of the young king Liholiho I; Mamahana, her sister; two wives of chief Kalanimoko, and seven New England matrons, wives of the first missionaries. The four women of rank were furnished with calico patchwork to sew, "a new employment for them."

Before this introduction to the needle, the simple Hawaiian garments had been tied, not sewn; tapas were used for coverlets.

Like all Polynesians, the Hawaiians were fastidious about their beds and bedding. The bed consisted of a pile of coarse mats spread on a stone floor; additional layers of finer woven mats served as mattress. The higher the rank of its user, the higher both bed and mattress. Tapa is a pounded fabric made from the wet inner bark of the mulberry plant. Its white surface can be decorated with hand-stamped designs, and the Hawaiians had early developed dyes in many colors. Bed tapas were made up of four large sheets of white, topped by a stamped tapa, all fastened together at the foot. They were washed with a damp cloth and sunned frequently. When not in use, they were rolled, with a sprinkling of fragrant sandal-

Aloha, red on white.

The Hawaiian quilt, or *kapa,* developed from the missionaries' patchwork quilt by the Hawaiians themselves as an expression of their own creative talents, is quite different from its pieced ancestor. Fashioned of two whole pieces of material, it is appliqued in a free-style Island motif usually in one color on white, the exact repetition of the motif being achieved by a peculiar folding and cutting. The quilting, done freehand, "follows the pattern," giving it a grace and rhythm characteristically Hawaiian.

wood in the roll, and kept across the rafters of the house.

The patchwork quilt was an intriguing innovation. Mission barrels from Boston almost always contained patch pieces which were distributed among Hawaiian women or used at mission sewing classes. Occasionally

American Eagle and Buffalo, red on white, designed by William Malina after going to Niagara Falls.

Breadfruit, bright pink on white.

Pu Kukui (Chandelier) Kahului, marine blue on white.

Kaiulani's Comb and Kahili (royal standard), lavender on white.

finished quilts were received. The pupils of Miss E. Dewey's School in Blanford, Mass., made and sent one to Kaahumanu in 1822, "which was very acceptable to this honored female ruler." The "friendship blocks," sent to Mrs. Laura Fish Judd in 1830 "from the East," each with a Bible quotation and the name of the donor in outline stitch, were an inspiration.

But patchwork quilts were impractical for Hawaiian handwork. There were no Hawaiian scrapbags; *holokus,* or Mother Hubbards, were made full and straight from a single width of material with hardly a smidgeon of cloth left over. Calico and sheeting could be purchased but it seemed silly to cut up new material just to sew it together again.

Yet eager for cloth quilts, the Hawaiians adapted to material at hand. Accustomed to making their own tapa designs on individual wood blocks, they worked out quilt patterns of their own, appliqueing them to large seam-

less sheets. By a certain folding of the material and cutting freehand one motif 8-fold, the entire border, sometimes the entire pattern, was produced at one time with exact repetition of the motif.

The cut-out pattern was basted on a large seamless sheet and appliqued. A second sheet was used for the backing, with a padding of wool or cotton batting between back and front. The quilting, done free hand, followed the pattern, inner spaces being filled with graceful scrolls. Seldom were more than two colors used. Red and yellow, the royal colors, used on white were *kapa* favorites. Blue, orange, purple, and green on white were also much used.

Designs might be naturalistic, associated with some place, or of a historical theme, but always with Hawaiian significance. Baskets of flowers, ferns, fig and pumpkin leaves, turtles, octopi, and the crescent moon were old-time themes. The breadfruit was perhaps the most popular of all.

The originator of a design named it and that design and that name were held inseparable. Only good friends exchanged patterns; designers were chary of their patterns until their work was finished and acknowledged. Often a pattern was dedicated—like a book —to a person as a mark of respect.

Almost every museum in the Islands today, large or small, shows examples of old Hawaiian quilts, from the Bernice P. Bishop Museum in Honolulu to the Hulihee Palace at Kalui, Kona, on Hawaii and the Hale Hoikeike at Wailuku on Maui. Old Island families treasure quilts made by their grandmothers and great grandmothers.

Happily, new quilts are still being made, utilizing the old patterns and the old methods. A few are completely hand-stitched; more, these days, are stitched by machine. The ladies of various church and civic societies all over the Islands make quilts for fund-raising, offering them at bazaars, festivals, and the like. Some are completely finished; others are cut and basted ready for sewing by the purchaser.

At the Mauna Kea Beach Hotel on Kauai, Laurance Rockefeller's most elegant and luxurious hotel, new Hawaiian quilts in a wide range of authentic designs and colors have been framed and hung as corridor decoration.

Hawaiian Quilts, by Stella M. Jones, published by the Honolulu Academy of Arts, 1930, gives their history. *Your Hawaiian Quilt,* by Mrs. Helen Inns, put out by the Hawaii Home Demonstration Council, Honolulu (1957), tells how to make one.

Lilla Hoku, Star Lily, green on white.

American Crib Quilts

Rising Sun and Easter Lilies Pieced Work Crib Coverlet 45x40½". This coverlet features an elaborated rising sun motif and eight diagonally placed squares containing pieced work Easter lily flowers with applique stems and leaves. Great ingenuity in designing and developing this quilt was displayed by the needleworker, for she has utilized many small remnants of material to form her controlled result, and has even home-dyed some of the calicos where she needed certain colors. Offset blocks separating the lily motifs are of blue plaid calico sprigged with darker blue sprays. Lily flowers are red with green or blue bracts and stems; connecting background pieces are yellow calico. Rising sun shows pieced red calico center, diamonds and points, separated by yellow printed calico points and triangles. Quilting stitches follow design motifs; medium heavy fill; backing is blue and white mosaic printed calico turned to face and hemmed down. Second quarter 19th century.

by LILIAN BAKER CARLISLE

QUILTMAKING IN AMERICA may be said to have started with the era preceeding the Revolutionary War and to have ended with the decade following the Civil War. Few examples of the quiltmaker's art prior to 1776 exist and consequently their history is too fragmentary to be other than suggested. In the years immediately after the close of the Civil War in 1865,

machines supplanted hand labor and it became cheaper to purchase the finished product than to produce it with home labor, especially where the raw materials had to be bought, instead of being home grown.

Olden times have a way of telescoping into a period known as "The Past," but even as early as a hundred years ago, in December 1872, *Harper's Weekly* commented on the dying out of the antiquated craft of quiltmaking:

There was a time when American housewives prided themselves on their neat and often elaborate patchwork

quilts; and merry indeed were the quilting bees when the women, young and old, married and single, used to gather at some neighbor's house to take a hand in the work. What a hum of voices, what cheery laughter, what playing of needles, made the afternoon pass swiftly, while the work progressed as if invisible hands assisted. How pleasant it was when evening came, and needles and thimbles and chalk and line and scissors were laid aside, and the cheerful hostess invited her friends into the clean, tidy kitchen to tea. What abundance crowned the

Twelve Flowers Applique Crib Coverlet 39x30". An even dozen white muslin blocks display applied flowers fashioned of 8 calico petals. The 4 smaller petals are made of pinky red calico printed in white; larger petals are of navy blue dotted print. A red muslin binding separates blocks from border which features an orderly undulating green vine interspersed with green and pink leaves. Quilting stitches are crossed double diagonal lines; medium cotton fill; white cotton backing. Bound all around with pieced pink and blue calico. Circa 1850.

Civil War Pieced Work Crib Coverlet 43½x36". Small triangles, measuring 1x1x1½", 1,344 of them, in a variety of calicos are pieced together to make this coverlet. Border is red, white and blue

muslin stripes with flags in lower corners. Each flag shows 7 red stripes, 6 white stripes and 6 white stars in the blue canton. These 6 stars represent the original southern states which in December 1860 and January 1861 voted to form their own government: South Carolina, Mississippi, Florida, Alabama, Georgia, and Louisiana. The date "1862" has been embroidered in red on the right flag. Quilting is in crossed diagonal stitches; bound around 4 sides with white muslin; backing is coarse hand-woven linen. Dated 1862.

Spread Eagle Applique Crib Coverlet 46x46". Design features 4 corner eagles appliqued to white muslin, green wings, red heads and tails, orange bodies and talons; also centered 8-petal flower, orange, green and red. Quilting in this coverlet is outstanding and shows hand-drawn tulip and leaf designs in center section, and interlacing curves around the border. Thin cotton fill shows many cotton seeds. Face of quilt has been turned over white cotton backing and hemmed. Circa 1860.

Sunburst Pieced Work Crib Coverlet 40x38". Nine sunburst motifs of red and white muslin make up this quilt. Centered sun is red; it is surrounded with 14 sharp white points, which are fitted between 14 diamonds. Additional white triangular pieces with curved bases fill in spaces between the diamond points. The completed sun motifs are laid into squares of white calico printed with tiny black dots and dashes. Candy-stripe set separating the motifs is of alternating red and white diamonds. Binding is red muslin. Sunburst motifs are quilted with nine double parallel

lines of stitching; remainder of quilt shows crossed diagonal quilting. Backing is of grey calico printed with white and tan flowers; medium heavy cotton fill. Mid-19th century.

Christmas Wreath Applique Coverlet 42½x34". Fourteen Christmas trees formed of red and green calico, some ornamented with Christmas ball ornaments in yellow calico, frame and wreath of alternating red and green petals tied with a red Christmas bow. The center flower vase is of yellow calico; tulips and roses are in a variety of colored calicos. Quilting stitches outline the appliqued motifs. Some of the flowers are

lightly stuffed with cotton and further embellished with embroidery stitches. Binding of red calico; light cotton fill; backing is white muslin. Circa 1860.

board! The steaming teapot, hot "riz" bisquit, smoking from the oven, cream toast, three or four varieties of homemade cake and preserves of every description—"sweetmeats" as they were generally termed. Besides the men folks of the household, the minister usually was the only representative of the masculine sex; the husbands, brothers and lovers came later in the evening when all kinds of merry, harmless games were in order. There are few parts of the country where this custom still lingers, cheap manufacturers having superseded the

necessity of this branch of domestic industry.

Perhaps the art of quilting did die out for a century, but today a whole new generation of young women have taken up quilt making as a hobby. At county and state agricultural fairs, displays of quilts in the Arts & Crafts exhibits have increased with each passing year, and quilt kits are for sale at every hobby shop, as well as from mail order, discount and department stores. Creative needleworkers who are intimidated by the sheer enormity of completing a full-sized quilt, but who

would like the same creative satisfaction of actually designing and making a quilt of their own might be interested in undertaking a small-size crib quilt. The modus operandi for all quilts is the same, regardless of proportions.

Illustrated are some lovingly worked crib coverlets of the 1800s, from the collection of Mr. Ross Trump, Medina, Ohio. May they prove an inspiration to quilt makers of today.

SEWING ANTIQUES

Mrs. Connie Stuart, secretary to Mrs. Richard Nixon, is an avid thimble collector. And even Queen Victoria collected sewing implements like needle cases, thimbles and pincushions. Pincushions in the form of fruits and vegetables make a most pleasing centerpiece piled high in a handsome burl bowl. Very early sewing machines are usually kept intact, but much later trestle models have been dismantled and the various parts put to other uses—the metal bases for table legs, drawers for planters, and tops for mirror frames.

Thimbles to collect *by MARILYN ESTES SMITH*

EVER SINCE THE first woman tried to push the first bone splinter through two layers of animal hide in order to fashion a garment, some sort of device has been used as a "pusher" or "thimble." Stone age woman probably used a handy rock. As sewing became a more exact art, thimbles were carved of stone, ivory, or bone. Eskimos used thick pieces of leather shaped to fit the finger.

The word *thimble* evolved from *thumbell* or *thumbstall,* so called because it was originally worn on the thumb, working its way through such variations as thumble, thymel, thummie, and thumbell before it settled down to thimble.

Thimbles have been made from almost all durable substances such as silver, gold, brass, iron, wood, rubber, alabaster, and whale's teeth. The most common collectible thimble is made of silver as these were manufactured in huge quantities in the 18th, 19th, and early 20th centuries by all silversmiths.

The first task given apprentice silversmiths was the designing of thimbles; they were relatively easy to make and used a comparatively small amount of silver.

For American use, the first thimbles were English-made, and then only for the wealthy. However, by 1766 the *New York Weekly Post* was advertising thimbles and scissors made by Thomas Brown, cutler. The *New York Gazette* ran an ad the same year for steel thimbles made by Benjamin Halstead.

In 1794 Mr. Halstead placed the following ad in the *Diary or Evening Register:*

Thimble Manufactory—Benjamin Halstead respectfully informs his Friends and the Public in general, that he still continues carrying on the gold and silversmith business at No. 67 Broad St.; he has brought the manufactory of gold silver and pinchbeck thimbles with steel tops to great perfection and thinks he could make a sufficient quantity to supply the United States citizens, consider your interest, and encourage American manufactures.

Those imported are of the slightest kind. I will engage that one of mine will do more service than three of them, and I know by experience that imported ones of the quality of mine cost 18 s. per doz. and could not be sold by 25 per cent as low as mine. Every dealer in this article will soon find the advantage of keeping Halstead's thimbles and have the satisfaction of knowing that he does his customers justice. Silver and steel bodkins, tooth and ear picks by the dozen or single.

In 1824 James Peters advertised thimbles in the *Philadelphia Directory.* David Platt started a thimble manufacturing business in New York in 1824 which continued until 1900. To confuse the issue, George Pratt was also a New York silversmith, making thimbles in business with Ezra Prime from 1825 to 1895; indeed, there were 8 Platts and 17 Pratts all in the silversmithing business during the 18th and 19th centuries.

Paul Revere, silversmith, is known to have made a gold thimble for his wife. After his death she used it to pay rent on a house, but the thimble then disappeared. Jabez Gorham (1792-1869), whose descendants have also been silversmiths, was first apprenticed to Nehemiah Dodge in Providence, R.I., as a boy, making thimbles.

The true craftsmanship of silversmithing began to die about 1840 with the advent of stamping machines. Thimbles could be turned out so quickly on machines there was no point in doing hard work. One way to tell a truly old thimble is that the hand done decoration will not be perfectly symmetrical.

Thimbles were so commonly used they were standard stock for the early house-to-house peddlar. Indeed, by 1850 they were sold in such quantities that Ketcham and McDougall of New York opened the Thimble House. This store sold nothing but thimbles and small sewing accessories.

Today there are no factories solely devoted to the making of thimbles. In 1963 Gabler Bros. of Schondorf, Germany, closed their doors after making thimbles for 140 years.

It is hard for the modern woman to realize the importance of thimbles in earlier days. Well before the age of six, little girls were expected to have learned

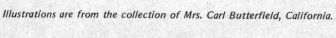

Illustrations are from the collection of Mrs. Carl Butterfield, California.

to sew. Every girl made a sampler in the process of learning the various stitches. Sewing was almost the only recreation acceptable for women, who took great pride in their ability to embroider as well as "sew a fine seam" when clothing for the family had to be fashioned by hand.

McGuffey's Second Reader published in 1836 used the following story about thimbles to point a moral to their little readers:

A Place For Everything

Mary: I wish you would lend me your thimble. I can never find my own.

Sarah: Why is it, Mary, you can never find it. I have a place

**547
Sewing
Antiques**

Fig. 1: A heavy American sterling silver thimble made by Ketcham & McDougall, ca. 1895. **Fig. 2:** Handcarved dark brown bog oak thimble from Ireland. **Fig. 3:** English sterling silver thimble, ca. 1880; this design is still being made, creating a problem for the serious collector. **Fig. 4:** Political souvenir of the Coolidge-Dawes campaign; made of aluminum with blue painted band. **Fig. 5:** Nixon thimble, sought by collectors of political memorabilia as well as thimble collectors. **Fig. 6:** Handcarved Eskimo ivory thimble. This is a type of scrimshaw, but not the exquisite, delicate work done by whalers. **Fig. 7:** English mother-of-pearl thimble with solid gold bands, ca. 1825. **Fig. 8:** English sterling silver filigree thimble, 18th century. Contains space for engraved name or date. **Fig. 9:** A French "fable" thimble, one of a set of 6 fables portrayed on silver thimbles. This one tells the story of a milkmaid, who spilled her milk. **Fig. 10:** Solid gold thimble given to Mrs. Butterfield as she entered college, in 1915. **Fig. 11:** Austrian petit point thimble. These are still being made, usually in a gold wash. **Fig. 12:** Solid gold thimble, ca. 1895. **Fig. 13:** Black Hills thimble handwrought of green, white, and yellow gold. **Fig. 14:** Danish sterling silver thimble with carnelian top. **Fig. 15:** Handmade padded silk Korean thimble. **Fig. 16:** Chinese handcarved ivory thimble. Age unknown, but believed to be extremely old. **Fig. 17:** Sterling silver English thimble, early 18th century; rounded top and asymmetrical pin pricks attest to age. This thimble was designed for use with extremely fine needle as the pin pricks are so small they will not hold a larger needle.

Tiny brass tape measure holder, about 1½" tall; little tailor wears a miniature thimble for a hat; very early Victorian.

An authentic reproduction of the hide thimble and ivory needle.

Carved celluloid tape measure case, ca. 1900.

Left: Sterling silver thimble case to be hung on a chatelaine at the waist (1890). Right: Sterling thread box is of the same age.

Handcrafted walnut sewing bird with home-spun covered pincushion on top, ca. 1850. Cloth was pinned on to be held taut for long seams.

for everything and I put everything in its place when I have done using it.

Mary: *I am ashamed. Before tonight I will have a place for everything. You have taught me a lesson.*

A tiny thimble, engraved "For a good girl," was made in quantity; it may be found in many collections so apparently most little girls were like Sarah, keeping their valuables in safe places.

A beautiful gold thimble, engraved "Esther Willit," was found in the garden of the ruins of the Thomas Willit home in Riverside, R.I. It is known that silversmiths made an ecclesiastical cup engraved "Capt. Willit's donation to ye Ch. of Rehoboth, 1674." It has been conjectured that Capt. Willit had the thimble made for his daughter for her fifteenth birthday. Elaborate thimbles were traditionally given to 15-year old girls to recognize their maturity and as a tribute to their accomplishments as needlewomen.

Another traditional thimble was the silver and gold "wedding band" thimble. The rather tall thimble has a silver top ending in a gold band at the base. It was given to a young woman on the occasion of her betrothal by her fiance. At the time of the marriage, the gold band was cut off to serve as a wedding ring. These are occasionally found, making one speculate as to why they are still intact.

Scrimshaw thimbles were prized New England gifts in the heyday of whaling ships. On the long arduous trips, seamen had little to do but think of home. When a whale was killed, its teeth were distributed among the men, who then carved them into useful objects with meticulous care. Thimbles and other sewing aids were popular items. After the thimble or other item was complete, it was often delicately

A group of patented thimbles with thread cutters or needle threaders soldered to the side.

carved or embossed with a fine-pointed instrument. The design was rubbed with lamp black to make it stand out against the delicate pale ivory, making a beautiful gift.

Thimble collectors also look for the ornate thimble cases which were made to hold fine thimbles. These cases are of many designs and many materials. Some are carved to look like little baskets, nuts, or fruit. Some look like little caskets, or are round to be hung by a ribbon—there are almost as many designs as there are cases. Some cases are really tiny sewing kits including a winding or two of thread and a couple of needles with the thimble being the screw on top of the case. In World War I, tiny tin sewing kits painted olive drab were used by the American doughboys.

Along with thimble and thimble case collecting is the accompanying hobby of acquiring other sewing aids. Etuis, which are fitted sewing boxes, usually elaborate and quite expensive, are prized items. Fancy scissors, measuring tapes in elegant cases, and even thread boxes may be found. It was common to wear a chatelaine at the waist from which hung a thimble case, a thread case, small scissors, and a small pin cushion to hold needles and pins.

Thimble, thread, and needle cases. The one in the center (ca. 1870) is lavender with the ivory thimble painted lavender to match; the thimble has screw threads carved to fit the top of the case.

Souvenir thimbles of plastic or other inexpensive materials account for many thousands of those made. They have commemorated centennials, coronations, dedications, expositions, and other important events. In the day when travel was a rare occurrence, many women bought thimbles to remember the occasion. They were imprinted with place names and sometimes dates.

Thimbles have long been an important part of political memorabilia. Political advertising on thimbles was even done by President Nixon when he was running for Congress, years ago.

As the number of thimble collectors has increased, so have the prices. When a collector finds a bargain

A set of brass childhood thimbles belonging to Meta Mason of Aberdeen, So. Dakota. The smallest was given to Meta when she was three years old, the largest, of sterling silver, is engraved with her name and the date 1885, when she was eleven years old.

Turkish thimble of sterling silver. The ring goes over the little finger to prevent loss.

Steel Chinese tailor's thimble from San Francisco. It is made like the sterling silver strip thimble (foreground) from Formosa. This thimble was given to Mrs. Butterfield by the daughter of one of Chiang Kai-sheck's generals.

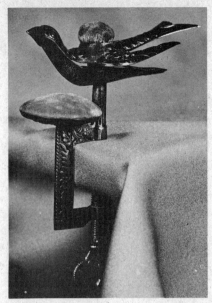

American sterling silver sewing bird dated Feb. 15, 1893. Has two small plush pincushions, one turquoise, the other mustard.

hidden in a jar of nondescript buttons or in the drawer of an old treadle sewing machine, it is cause for jubilation. Mrs. Connie Stuart, secretary to Mrs. Richard Nixon, is an avid thimble collector as are many other women who happened on this fascinating collectible. The increasing rarity of thimbles makes the search that much more intriguing.

So many different materials were used in the designing and decorating of thimbles that a brief glossary of descriptive terms may be helpful:

Carnelian: Chalcedony, a deep red stone which takes a high polish. Used as a decorative thimble top.
Chasing: Cutting into metal to make design.
Damascene: A method of decorating with wavy markings; in-

Sewing aid, handcarved of South American tagua nuts called "vegetable ivory." These soft nuts were carved by sailors on the long trip around Cape Horn. With age they became very hard, turning to a soft caramel color. This piece was made of 4 nuts screwed together on a post also made of tagua nut.

laying with a contrasting metal as silver on gold.
Delft: Blue and white earthenware made in Holland.
Dresden: Fine china ware made in the early 18th century.
Embossing: Design raised in relief.
Enamel: A glossy, colored opaque substance fused to metal with heat.
Engraving: Similar to chasing; cutting into metal to create a design.
Filigree: Lacelike wire ornamentation fastened to metal so it stands out in relief:
Niello: An alloy of sulfur and silver making a deep black color used for inlay.

This primitive handcarved walnut thimble holder was given by an ardent suitor to his intended almost one hundred years ago. In spite of his fine workmanship, she married someone else.

Petit point: An elaborate design stitched into fine canvas and stretched tightly over a metal-based thimble.
Pinchbeck: An alloy of copper and zinc made to look like gold, invented in 1795.
Porcelain: White, translucent earthenware with a transparent glaze. Chelsea, Royal Worcester or Derby: flowers and leaf designs in gold and various colors used as decoration.
Scrimshaw: Carved ivory with design cut in with sharp instrument.
Venetian: Ornamental glass coming from Murano near Venice, decorated with flowers and leaves.

Sewing Machines

Unusual Styles of the 1850's

by GRACE ROGERS COOPER

THERE were many patentees and many manufacturers who, in the mid-1850s and 1860s, attempted to produce a sewing machine that would circumvent both the patents held by the Sewing Machine Combination and the high cost of manufacturing a complicated machine. These machines, quite simple mechanically, were usually turned by hand and formed a chainstitch with one or sometimes two threads. As early as the mid-1850s these machines had highly ornamental frames.

In the September 29, 1960, issue of Scientific American, among other manufacturers, are listed two sewing machine names that are synonymous with these interesting ornate types. They are "Robertson's," manufactured in New York City, and "Clark's," manufactured in Bridgeport, Connecticut.

Thomas J. W. Robertson had one earlier two-thread inter-locked stitch machine to his credit when, in 1855, he applied for a patent covering the use of a looper to direct the needle thread. The required patent model that he submitted to show his im-

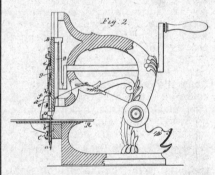

Above: illustration in patent specification, No. 13064, granted T. J. W. Robertson, June 12, 1855. Thread spool is held in horizontal position, attached perpendicularly to main supporting frame at lower right; makes a single-thread chain stitch.

provement was a small hand-turned machine with a frame cast in the shape of a dolphin. The inventor did not mention the design in the patent claims.

Another dolphin machine was used by Robertson for a second patent in the same year, figure 1, and another early in 1857, figure 2, obviously in-

Left: patent model submitted by David W. Clark; he received Pat. No. 19732, March 23, 1858. Machine makes a double-loop stitch, uses 2 needles and 2 threads; both threads taken from spools; second spool is placed under the cloth plate. Dolphin castings of Clark machines can be distinguished from Robertsons by the "ring" on the tail. Diminutive size of machine is indicated by comparative size of modern spool of thread.

dicating that the machine was being manufactured.

Late in 1857, David W. Clark of Bridgeport forwarded two applications to the Patent Office, both accompanied by small dolphin machines as the patent models. The first patent, granted to Clark on January 12, 1858, states that "the fame of the machine . . . may be made in any desired ornamental form . . . ." But the second one submitted, and also another patent granted to Clark in 1858 using a dolphin machine, do not mention the style of the frame, *figure 3.*

The dolphin design is believed to have been originated by Robertson. Since the design was not patented, it could be copied by anyone. The dolphin machines made by Clark differ not only in the stitching mechanism but also in a single design feature, that of a ring around the dolphin's tail. There are three Clark-dolphin machines in the Smithsonian Museum collection, but we are not aware of any Robertson-dolphin machines in either a museum or private collection.

Another design originated by Robertson, but also used by Clark, is of two cherubs with a dragonfly. Robertson's machine was filed on August 6, 1857; the patent was issued on October 20, 1857 and no mention is made in the specifications of the particular design, *figure 4.* The Clark machine was filed on October 23, 1857, and issued on January 5, 1858. In the specifications Clark states ". . . the frame, which may be wrought in the ornamental form shown, or made in any style to suit the manufacturer." Only the model submitted with the

Clark patent, and now in the Museum collection is known to have survived to preserve this design in three-dimensional form.

Robertson continued to invent and to receive patents, but he did not submit any more ornately designed frames. In a patent issued to him on October 25, 1859, he states ". . . the frame of the machine, which may be made in any fanciful or convenient form," but he did not offer an inspiration and submitted his invention on a very plain frame.

Clark, on the other hand, produced an additional interesting design; this time one believed to have been originated by him. The frame appeared to be made up of boughs and leaves; we termed it "Foliage." The design was first used on a patent model submitted on February 11, 1858. And although Clark used the same design on several additional patent models, *figure 6,* he never referred to the casting of the frame in the specifications. It is most likely that this machine is the style of the machine referred to as "Clark's" in the 1860 issue of *Scientific American.*

It is believed that the machine was not manufactured long after that date as it had been all but forgotten by 1908. In that year the *Sewing Machine Times* ran a series of contests in which they published illustrations of early machines, requesting identifications. The "Foliage" machine was pictured in two issues and not a single identification was received. Finally the periodical had to identify it for the readers with the following information:

"This is one of the several models made in the late fifties, the invention by David W. Clark, of Bridgeport, Connecticut . . . All of the models were distinguished by fanciful designs in the castings. Some of his devices would now be styled freaks, though not out of line with numerous experiments of those days."

Three of these "Foliage" machines are in the museum collection.

These machines, all quite small, as can be determined by the comparative size of the spools of thread, used full-size needles and were not toys or miniature models. Their appearance was quite attractive as they were cast in brass. Traces of gilt indicate that some of the machines were originally gilt on brass. The charm and interest of the unusual designs of these and many other delightful machines of the 1850-1870 period indicate that the early sewing machine was not only an important invention but also an attractive consumer product.

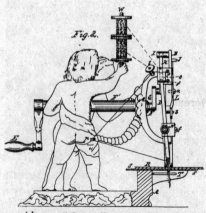

Above: "cherub" machine illustration in patent specifications, No. 18470, granted T. J. W. Robertson, October 20, 1857. Machine uses 2 threads, taken directly from the spools, and 2 needles to form the double back stitch.

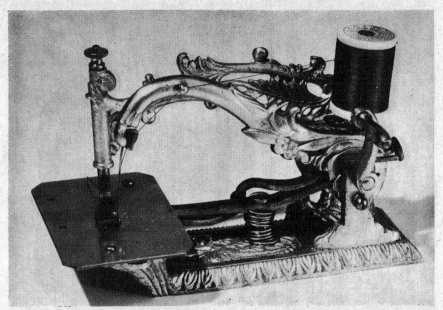

Above: patent model submitted by David W. Clark; he received Pat. No. 21322, August 31, 1858. Machine makes single-thread chain stitch. Clark's invention here was another change related to feeding mechanism.

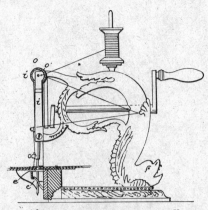

Above: "dolphin" machine illustration in the patent specifications, No. 16609, granted T. J. W. Robertson, February 10, 1857. Thread spool is placed on the top, vertically, in the more usual manner; machine makes a single-thread chain stitch.

FLORENCE SEWING MACHINE

The Florence Sewing Machine was first manufactured about 1860, based on the patents of Leander W. Langdon. While his first patent was obtained in 1855, it was his patent of March 20, 1860, which was the immediate forerunner of the commercial Florence machines. The name was derived from the city of manufacture, Florence, Massachusetts.

Langdon's patent of July 14, 1863—always stamped "July 18, 1863" was incorporated into the machines after that date. Patent dates and serial number are found on the plate on top of the round stitching area. Because of this location they are frequently either illegible or worn away completely. There was so little change in the style of the machine over the period of its manufacture that it is very difficult to tell, without the serial number, whether a machine was made in the 1860s or 1870s.

The Howe royalty records of 1860 listed the Florence Sewing Machine as one of the companies that took out a license. In 1865, the machine won a silver medal at the Tenth Exhibition of the Boston, Massachusetts, Charitable Mechanics Association.

By 1870, over 100,000 Florence machines had been manufactured. About 1880 the company changed the name of the machine to Crown. Improvements led to the name New Crown by 1885.

About this time the right to use the name "Florence" for a sewing machine was purchased by a mid-western firm for an entirely different machine. In August 1885, the then-termed Florence Machine Company (Florence, Massachusetts) began advertising Lamp Stoves, and in November of that year, heating stoves. Shortly afterwards the company discontinued the manufacture of sewing machines.

Sewing

in the

days of

Victoria

by
MARGARET LOVELL RENWICK

VICTORIAN interest in needlework was shown by the number of workboxes on display at London's Great Exhibition of 1851, where the one illustrated here was bought. Stoutly made of pearwood, it is covered in crimson leatherette, lined with apple green paper, and brass-bound, with brass ornaments, feet, and handles. It has a flap-pocket inside the lid, a drawer, and a tray spaced for pincushion, emery-cushion, scissors, bodkin, tweezers, crochet hook, yard measure neatly coiled, and two flannel-leaved needlebooks in apple green silk. According to family tradition, pinheads once lettered the matching silk pincushion with V and A, in honor of Queen Victoria and Albert, the Prince Consort. Still un-blurred on the flap-pocket is the black and white print of Britannia, on a rocky seat beneath a British oak, the cliffs of Dover rising behind her and, crouching at her sandalled foot, a British lion.

The three pairs of handmade early Victorian scissors are interesting as examples of the lost craft of scissor-filing. The smallest was meant for cutting hairs in the art, lost also, of hair-embroidery.

"Thimble egg" is the usual name in antiques shops for the little brass screw-top case, fitted centrally with a tiny hollow tube over which hangs a thimble; round the tube turns a spool, carrying two half-inch reels for black and white thread; inside are needles and pins. To its original nineteenth century owner, it was a "lady's companion."

SKETCHES BY
EDITH LOVELL ANDREWS

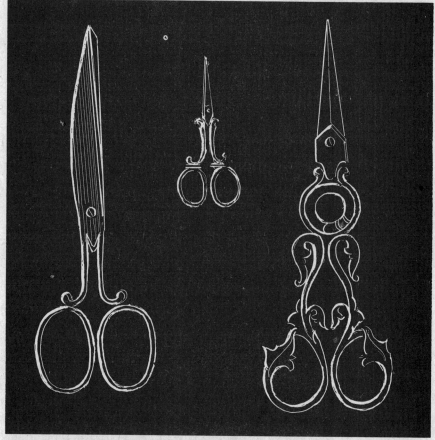

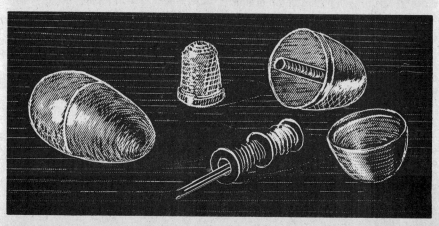

PINS and PINCUSHIONS

by EDWIN C. WHITTEMORE

Few pincushions are dated; these are particularly desirable and of more value. *From left:* very early pinball to hang from the belt, dated 1786; cushion dated 1836; sofa made of horn, with dainty cut-out back, bearing 1847 date; cushion dated 1869.

FEW OBJECTS of everyday life are as important yet as unobtrusive as the common pin. This was, of course, even more true in the days before the introduction of magical adhesives, zippers, and other closures that modern methods and materials have made possible. Before the invention of the pin, closures on clothing, draperies, and various ornamentations were ingeniously taken care of by ribbons, loops and loop-holes, laces with pearls and tags, clasps,

hooks, eyes, and skewers. Actually a common pin is a diminutive skewer and descended from it.

The first recorded mention of pins in England was in 1483; sixty years later their use was so widespread it required regulation by the government. Egyptian ladies used seven- or eight-inch pins of bronze or even silver and gold. Roman pins were of various lengths, from 1½ to 8 inches, usually of bronze, and the heads were not only round but square, and per-

forated and ornamented. Primitive man, then and even recently, used thorns as pins.

Over the centuries the ever-increasing production of finer fabrics stimulated by the invention of automatic looms, the development of urban standards of living resulting in more complicated clothing, and finally the patenting of Elias Howe's sewing machine in 1846—all contributed to an ever greater use of the common pin in its simplified form, much as we know it today.

A staggering thing about the history of pins is the enormous quantity that were used and, therefore, the enormous problems of manufacturing them in the pre-industrial era when the work was done by hand. It is interesting to review briefly that hand process.

How They Were Made

Brass wire was drawn down to pin diameter and cut into lengths equal to the combined lengths of six pins. Then boys, sitting between paired coarse and fine grindstones, sharpened the ends of the six-pin length wire. As soon as the two extreme ends were sharpened, these ends were cut off pin length, and the new ends sharpened. This process was repeated until all were sharp.

In the meantime, other wire had been spun into a continuous series of rings by holding it against a rapidly revolving vertical shaft. Later the shaft was removed, the rings cut off in pairs and heated almost red hot in a furnace.

Pincushions in shapes of fruit and vegetables were common, simple in construction, often very colorful, frequently life-size. *Above, left to right:* Pumpkin, strawberry, pear. *Below:* carrot, apple.

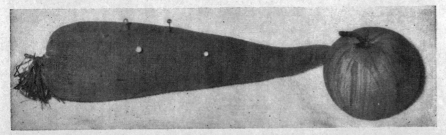

Pincushions in shape of living things, chiefly pets and familiar animals, had wide vogue a hundred years ago. Shown here: frog, child, bird, pig, dog, cat, monkey, turtle. Incorporation of pincushion into heavier metal "body" gave it a steadier base.

Almost any object around the farm and home inspired a pincushion replica. *Top row, from left:* footstool, cradle, cricket-type footstool, chair (or was it a sewing basket?); *below:* automobile, grindstone that turns, 2-wheel cart.

Boys grasped a sharpened half-finished pin and dipped it into the pan, catching a pair of rings on the "head" end. Then a blow from a foot-controlled anvil mechanism joined the rings to the pin and made a head out of the paired rings. The pin was then tinned by immersing in a liquid tin solution, polished by tossing in bran, and finally cleaned by a crude fanning or winnowing operation.

Even in modern years of time-and-motion studies and production incentives, pin production by this hand method seems amazingly big. For example, a trained boy of 14 could sharpen about 16,000 pins an hour. This he accomplished by learning to manipulate a handful of pins at a time, rotating them within his hand as he exposed them to the sharpening grindstones.

Industrial advances brought basic changes. Wright's Pin Making Machine was introduced in 1824 and its use, plus the improvements upon it, changed procedures rapidly, and did away with hand manufacturing. Pins became as we know them now.

It is interesting to find examples of early hand-made pins, but they are not essentially collectible. Their very size makes them rather insignificant, and examples of the skewer type pins of earlier civilization are, of course, only for the advanced collector.

But with pins came pincushions, and pincushions are very collectible. In fact, to those who say that the price of antiques has killed the fun of collecting, of haunting antique shops and rummage shops and auctions and antique shows, a pincushion collection may be a very rewarding goal.

Infinite Variety

Pincushions were made in infinite variety of shape, size, material. A pincushion collection permits distinct categories within the general collection as the photographs on these pages indicate. A pincushion collection can be varied and colorful; is adaptable to cabinet shelf or elsewhere; and it has two big advantages. First, the unit cost of pincushions is not high, need not be high. Second, the collector may choose those aspects

of pincushions that appeal to him most, such as pincushions resembling animals, and ignore the rest, yet still be collecting in an area where those he wants can be found. Pincushions are collectible for both budget watcher and the well-financed, for the occasional hunter or the inveterate and continuous antiquer, and it requires no expert knowledge of anything—a boon to the beginner.

It is not practical to classify pincushions in groups by dated periods. The most satisfactory system for the average collector is to classify by type of subject or design: Fruits and Vegetables; Articles of Clothing; Shapes of Living Things; etc. A careful look at the illustrations here will make clear that a charming variety of pincushions — amusing, decorative, and attractive — are available. They represent a part of a collection of about 250. The average cost was in the $1-5 bracket, while a few, such as the dated 1786 belt pinball, would today be priced at possibly $10-15. It is an exception to the low budget principle of pincushion collecting.

Above: Example of elaborate, larger type pincushion. Good cabinet making went into this 7" long "double runner," a sled popular in the late 1800s. Lace-edged cushion extends entire length of seat area.

Left: Metals as well as cloth were used in making pincushions resembling articles of clothing. *Top row:* Lady's shoe; baby's boot; *middle:* military cap; crocheted hat; silk jockey cap; *bottom:* mitten; crazy-quilt high boot; early high shoe. Mitten and high shoe are practically flat; others are 3-dimensional.

SILVER

The possibilities of finding a marked piece of Paul Revere's silver at a bargain price is rather remote these days. But the later silver and silverplated wares are still plentiful and reasonably priced. Here's an area for collectors to invest in with almost absolute certainty of a handsome return of profits in the years ahead. The later pieces are, for the most part, quite elaborately decorated with repousse and hand chased designs. In the 1880s, tea sets consisted of several pieces—two or three pots, a covered sugar bowl, a waste bowl, and a large matching tray. Finding a complete set isn't easy, but so many sets in these designs were produced that it wouldn't be impossible to fill out a partial set. Out-of-date flatware patterns can be filled out without too much difficulty, too. There are antiques dealers all over the country who specialize in outmoded flatware patterns. For the collector with a limited amount of space there are hundreds of silver bibelots to pick and choose from at every antiques show and sale.

Engraver's tools with engraved silverplated cup.

A set of tools used in hand chasing with the chaser's hammer. Tools varied in size, b averaged about 4½" long.

Hand Chasing and other Ornamentation on Silverware

An especially fine example of raised or embossed chasing. A product of Rogers, Smith & Co., New Haven, Conn., 1887.

by E. P. HOGAN

Illustrations from the International Silver Company Historical Collection

THE INDUSTRIAL REVOLUTION in America, employing as it did the use of steam power and more sophisticated machinery, brought to an end much of the laborious handcrafting which typified the work of the early colonial silversmiths. Yet a remarkable amount of handwork was still done on the mid and late Victorian silverplate, particularly in the field of ornamentation.

Silverware catalogs of the 1860s, 1870s and 1880s describe tea sets, for example, as available in plain, engine-turned (sometimes simply called "engine"), engraved, satin-engraved, and chased.

Engine-turning was a machine process, however, and not done by hand. It used a stylus-like tool which cut lines in patterns and produced an interesting ornamentation. Although it was not a common form of decoration, it is still being used in a limited way, primarily on the backs of brushes and hand mirrors in sterling silver.

Satin-engraved was a popular decoration that survived well up into the first quarter of the 20th century. The "satin" part was achieved through the use of a circular wire brush on a lathe and imparted a frosted or satin finish to the silverplate. Into this, the design was cut or engraved by hand with sharp engraving tools. It was a highly skilled operation whereby the metal was actually cut away and removed. The contrast between the engraving and the satin background made a most attractive type of decoration. Some of the old pieces are stamped B.C. on the bottom which signified "Bright Cut" and referred to the type of engraving. Some pieces were simply engraved in the same manner, but without the satin finish.

Chasing seems to have been by far the most popular decoration. Here again was handwork requiring a long apprenticeship as well as native ability. There were two types of chasing—flat chasing and raised chasing; both were used extensively on silverplate from about 1855 through the early 1900s.

(Please turn the page)

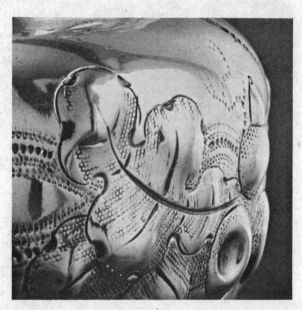

Raised chasing has been used on this "Charter Oak" coffee pot made by the Meriden Britannia Co. in 1861.

Close-up of raised chasing on "Charter Oak" coffee pot.

An example of flat chasing. Ice pitcher with porcelain lining made by the Meriden Britannia Co., 1868.

Handsome teapot with engine-turned ornamentation made by the Meriden Britannia Co. in 1867.

Satin engraved mustache cup and saucer made by the Wilcox Silver Plate Co. in 1895. Marked "B.C." for bright cut.

The chasing operation cut away no metal but, through the use of small steel tools and a hammer, incised the design into the surface of the metal. Although some of these tools were bought, many of them were handmade by the chaser himself. The ends of these tiny tools had different shapes to make a certain type of mark when struck with the hammer. There were little, chisel-like shapes which could form a line or a twig or a vine, a shape to form a small leaf with a single tap of the hammer. There were shapes for circles of various sizes, shapes to make a matt finish, and shapes for fluting. It was not uncommon for a set of chasing tools to consist of hundreds of different forms.

In flat chasing, the ornamentation is more or less all on the same plane, while in raised chasing certain portions of the pattern were "bumped" up from the inside before chasing the outside to give high relief to the finished decoration. This was sometimes called embossed. Despite all this handwork, the fine hand chasing was not excessive in price. The Meriden Britannia Co., in a catalog for 1861, offered six pieces in the Charter Oak pattern consisting of Coffee, Tea, Water, Sugar, Cream, and Slop for $33 plain and only $39 chased.

In 1886 a similar service was offered at $52 plain and $62 chased.

In order to preserve the shape of the piece and achieved sharp, clear-cut work, any hollow piece was first filled with hot pitch which hardened when cold. This was melted and cleaned out with solvents after the chasing was finished. Flat pieces were embedded in pitch.

Hand chasing is fast becoming a lost art. A shortage of interested apprentices, plus the relatively high cost of finished pieces, will probably end this beautiful type of decoration before many more years have passed.

GORHAM . . . silversmiths since 1818

JABEZ GORHAM was born in Providence, Rhode Island, in 1792. By 1818 he had finished a 7-year apprenticeship in silversmithing, worked a short time with others, and had that year opened his own shop. Jewelry was his forte, and he made beads, earrings, breast pins, finger rings, and a specially designed gold chain, known as the "Gorham chain." Most of his work he sold to travellers; occasionally he carried pieces to Boston and sold them there.

In 1831 he added silver spoons to his manufactures. These were made by Henry L. Webster, a young silver artisan from Boston, and the firm name became Gorham and Webster. Soon they were making forks, thimbles, combs, children's cups, and other small hand-crafted articles.

When Jabez' son John, at 21, joined the business in 1841, the firm was restyled Jabez Gorham and Son. Up to that time little mechanical progress had been made in sterling manufacture. John Gorham was early to recognize the advantages of machinery in working with precious metal, and with foresight, courage, and mechanical genius pioneered in its use.

Designed Own Machines

His father retired in 1847, and within the year John, now sole proprietor, purchased and installed a steam engine in his plant. He broadened the use of machinery in making flat silver, then in silver holloware. If he could not purchase machinery suitable for his purpose, he designed and built the machines he needed.

By 1861 the company had opened a New York office and was distributing extensively in America and Canada. The number of employed workers had risen from 10 or 12 in 1847 to more than 200. When silver was temporarily abandoned as a basic material during the Civil War, the company turned its facilities to the manufacture of electro-silverplated wares, made with a nickel silver base, and processed by the same methods as their sterling silver wares.

The firm was chartered by the Rhode Island Legislature as The Gorham Manufacturing Company in 1863, and organized as a corporation in 1865.

In 1868, the company abandoned the coin silver standard, (900/1000 fine silver) and adopted the sterling standard of 925/1000 fine silver. At that time, too, it began to use its now familiar trademark on its sterling articles —a lion, an anchor, and a capital "G."

A separate department for the manufacture of ecclesiastical wares was organized in 1885. Here gold, brass, bronze, stone, and wood were utilized as well as sterling. This led, quite naturally, to the execution of important commissions in statuaries and memorials, chiefly in bronze, and a substantial business in architectural bronze work.

The latter part of the 19th century was a period of national prosperity. Fine silverware was in great demand. At Gorham's, handmade, partially handmade, and hand-chased items were developed in great variety. The Chantilly and Strasbourg flatware patterns, still popular, were developed during this period. William J. Codman. a talented English artist, contributed his conception of *l'art nouveau,* a new free style of design in silver; his hand-crafted 950/1000 fine silver articles were marketed under the name "Martele."

Acquisitions

In 1905 the Gorham Manufacturing Company purchased the silverware concerns of Whiting Manufacturing Company of New York and the William B. Durgin Company of Concord, New Hampshire; in 1906, it added the William B. Kerr Company of Newark, New Jersey, and in 1913, the Mt. Vernon Company-Silversmiths, Inc. (This last concern had resulted from the merging of the Roger Williams Silver Company of Providence, the Mauser Manufacturing Company of Mt. Vernon, New York, and Hayes and McFarland of New York City.)

The company expanded its interests further in 1928 when the Alvin Silver Company was acquired, and in 1931, when the McChesney Company was purchased and its tools and dies moved to Providence. The Quaker Silver Company of North Attleboro, Massachusetts, was added in 1959, and the Friedman Silver Company of Brooklyn, New York, in 1960.

In 1941, Gorham began the manufacture of industrial products in the new world of electronics, designing and making radar and special microwave antenna, tuners, and like equipment in the war effort. Success here led to expansion in diversified fields, and the company has since acquired several firms unrelated to silver manufacture. In April 1961, the name of the Gorham Manufacturing Company was changed to Gorham Corporation. In addition to their sterling products, they now make stainless steel flatware and silverplated holloware in many new patterns.

The Small Silver Wares of Birmingham

by MARGARET HOLLAND

A COLLECTION that is capable of display in a tiny area is tailor-made for to-day's living conditions, especially when its subject is so varied that some form of specialization is necessary from the outset. Birmingham, in England, had been noted for her small silver wares, mainly buttons and buckles, long before 1773, when she was granted the right to hall mark silver in her own assay office; it was therefore natural for her craftsmen to concern themselves with the making of all little things, as they came into fashion, and to excel at them. These include many not described here, such as spectacle frames, whistles, bottle tops, sugar tongs and nutmeg graters.

Silver hair ornament by Henry Adcock, Birmingham, 1807.

Shell-shaped caddy spoon by Frances Clark, Birmingham, 1828.

Snuff boxes and vinaigrettes, however, have proved their popularity in America, and a considerable quantity by Birmingham makers appear in New York salerooms from time to time, while good examples can also be seen in the majority of the major museums in the United States. Little boxes of many sorts were made in the city, and occasionally their exact purpose is hard to determine. For instance the Birmingham Assay Office recently acquired one for their collection, by Samuel Pemberton, an important name in this field, evidently made to hold toothpicks. There are few exceptions, however, to the rule that boxes with a lift off lid were a feature of tobacco boxes, made before the Midland's city gained the right to stamp her own work with an anchor mark. Samuel Pemberton made a few "patch boxes," with detachable lids, copying a bygone fashion, as did Cocks & Bettridge, and a few such containers were also made for gaming counters.

Snuff boxes, of course, were not made exclusively in Birmingham, any more than vinaigrettes, wine labels, caddy

spoons or any other small items, but the city's craftsmen made important contributions towards their development, and concentration upon their work makes a good introduction to the subject, which had its beginnings well before Thomas Boulsover developed the idea in Birmingham, in 1750, using the Sheffield Plate he had perfected; later the silver craftsmen took them up, and produced them in quantity. The first half of the 19th century was Birmingham's greatest era, when rectangular boxes, usually measuring about 3½" x 2½" with repousse cast tops, depicting definable types of subject, could be described as average. Nevertheless, generalities only serve to highlight exceptions and in a recent New York sale a small snuff box by Joseph Taylor, 1807, was sold, lightly engraved with panels of festoons enclosing oak leaves and acorns, which measured only 2" x 1¾"; two by John Shaw, 1809 and 1811, of much the same size, were decorated with bright cut sprays, and an overall fish scale design respectively, while in London a snail by Matthew Linwood showed just how different a snuff box could be. Frances Clark specialized in the engine turned box, and many others, including the best known names, relied on moulded reeds, formal scrolls and strapwork. One, sold in New York, by Joseph Willmore,

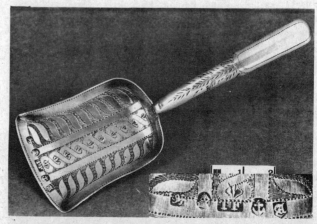

Shovel-shaped caddy spoon by Thomas Freeman, Birmingham, 1824.

1822, was engine turned, the cover centred by a gold plaque, with a chased floral rim and thumbpiece and gilt interior. This was typical only of the exceptionally fine work of Joseph Willmore.

Nevertheless, the pictorial, die-stamped lid is more interesting and gives the collector the best chance to specialize. Sporting subjects, with fishing less common, include some fine English hunting scenes, with horses and hounds, sometimes pursuing a fox; game birds, in range of aimed guns at a sportsman's shoulder, or racing, usually with horses in action. Pastoral scenes are also popular, often featuring swans, shepherds, or purely floral motifs, with suitable borders, while mythology, so popular at that time in Europe, was both common and very varied. A box by John Barber, 1826, featuring Pegasus, is remarkable for the fact that it was made in the escutcheon shape, more common in London. None of these subjects, of course, were special to Birmingham, but were well and prolifically made there. An octagonal shaped box, with a foliate border, sold in New York, by William Homes, Jr., of Boston, 1800, was a shape rarely, if ever, made in Birmingham.

Perhaps the most typical of the city were the lids depicting fine buildings, very frequently by Nathaniel Mills, who cast them strongly, in high relief. The railways, in opening up England, had created a great interest in its glories, and this was reflected in almost every art form. Battle Abbey, embossed on a snuff box by Matthew Linwood, 1810, illustrates a particular feature of this, for the

"Coral and Rattle" by Joseph Willmore, Birmingham, 1812.

Wine labels for "Brandy" and "Port" by Matthew Boulton and John Fothergill, Birmingham, 1776.

Snuff Box with cast front rim by John Lawrence & Co., Birmingham, 1822.

Abbey shown is most unlike the building that visitors see to-day, in which I spent my school-days. A devastating fire in 1931 caused enough damage to make restoration of its former outline possible, without the turrets, etc., that had been added through the years. While it is possible to date other art forms, such as Tunbridge Ware, by knowing when a building was structurally altered, the date marks on silver allow deduction in reverse, either way they add fascination.

Virtually all these types of lid also appeared on vinaigrettes, with many by Nathaniel Mills again, showing the cathedrals, castles, and stately homes of England. One example, showing Battle Abbey, which they described as "a castellated mansion," with raised floral borders, reeded sides and an engine turned base, by Nathaniel Mills, 1841, was sold in New York recently, in a sale that featured these fascinating "body fresheners."

Vinaigrettes started life in Roman times as "Pomanders," but the custom of using perfume, largely to fumigate against the effects of not washing, goes back to about 1800

B.C. From the close of the eighteenth century A.D., hundreds of makers produced thousands of vinaigrettes in Birmingham, and while those that appear for sale are more generally of basic box shape, they were made in almost any conceivable shape and form, such as acorns, strawberries, miniature guns, fish, hearts, baskets, and so forth.

These little containers, whether worn from the belt, concealed in the bosom, or held in the hand, were heavily gilt inside to prevent tarnishing from the spiced vinegars they held. They had an inner lid in the form of a hinged grille, and while at first these were plainly punched, the inventive Birmingham makers soon pierced them with all the pictorial imagination for which they were famed, dainty, light, and a never failing source of surprise as the lid was opened. Tightly fitting, with an equally well hinged lid, basic workmanship was as important as decoration, and in this medium Birmingham really outclassed London, virtually the only other source of production.

One of those sold in New York, in the form of a purse, by Matthew Linwood, 1816, had its inner lid pierced with a grape vine. The same sale produced three, shaped like a book, one, engraved with hearts, by Thropp and Taylor, 1811; a baron's coronet, unmarked; several cylindrical ex-

Silver vinaigrettes by N. Mills, Birmingham. Left to right and top to bottom: A castle, 1845; Windsor Castle, 1827; Battle Abbey, 1836; York Minister, 1833.

amples, and a plain box by John Shaw, circa 1810, its inner lid pierced with cornucopia. These are very collectible items, and there is virtually no limit to the ingenuity and form they could take in Birmingham, although London-made examples were much more staid.

Wine labels were another type of small item in which this city's craftsmen excelled. Originally known as "bottle tickets," they first appeared in about 1730, and by 1750, when a whole new class of people were drinking a large variety of wines, their use had become widespread. At first these were not hallmarked, except for maker's initials, but full marks became compulsory in an Act of 1790; this limits the possibilities of Birmingham workmanship in unmarked samples to the years 1773-90. The earliest seen personally were a set of five by Matthew Boulton and John Fothergill, 1775, sold recently at Christie, Manson and Woods, in London. As can be expected with Boulton, the workmanship is superb, the names deeply engraved within drapery festoons. Small objects were rare for these makers, but a similar pair, for brandy and port, 1776, belong to the Birmingham Assay Office.

Oval silver-gilt snuff box by Gervase Wheeler, Birmingham, 1837. The center of the cover, chased in high relief, depicts Mazeppa on his horse surrounded by wolves within a scrolled cartouche; the remainder of the box engine-turned with chased foilage thumbpiece; 3" wide. Courtesy Christies, London.

At first wine labels were entirely made by hand, many of the country's leading craftsmen taking infinite trouble over their delicate workmanship. Then, in 1784, Matthew Linwood, one of Birmingham's finest craftsmen, produced the first die stamped labels which, although generally thinner, further widened the scope of a truly versatile subject. The city's craftsmen had always been inventive, but this was an important advance, for the casts Linwood made were superbly cut, raising the standard well above any known by the old hand tooling methods. If this appears extraordinary, it must be remembered that the cutting of the pattern, in reverse, in hardened steel, was very much a skilled job, by no means to be confused with mass production. Others hurried to copy his methods, but his skill was not surpassed; nor did attempts to take casts from his labels succeed, for they lost sharpness in the process.

In 1810, the process was somewhat debased by some, who by using a mould in the production of labels, lost the sharpness, almost comparable to a Memling miniature in detail, that makes the die stamped examples so exquisite. Nevertheless, fine work was done by many craftsmen up until about 1840.

In 1860 it became compulsory for all wine bottles to bear a descriptive paper label, which killed the need for silver tickets and their genuine manufacture. Standards had, however, fallen away since 1840, even while interest was maintained for the more modest collector, not only through the mid-century work of George Unite, but the fascination of collecting strange names on these labels. The discovery that "noyeau" for instance, was a mixture of brandy, celery and prunes, adds an extra dimension, and some of the loveliest labels were made for equally strange concoctions.

When tea first arrived in England, in the late seventeenth century, it was packed in chests with some large sea shells, useful as scoops, and some blue and white porcelain containers, each capable of holding a Malay measure, called a "kati," of tea; the earliest silver tea caddies during Queen Anne's reign, copied them almost exactly. The lid of these was used as a measure, making spoons unnecessary, and the special purposed caddy spoon only came into being after the cannister changed its form, which it did many times.

Birmingham soon showed her usual inventiveness in the creation of new styles, and more enterprising versions of the old. Matthew Linwood, for instance, not only modelled fine shells in the manner of Sheffield and London, but also mounted beautiful varieties of real shells from about 1790, generally adding a plain, fiddle-pattern, silver handle. Whatever Matthew Linwood made, the likelihood was that a shell of some sort, would be featured in it, and somehow he always made them special. The shell was, however, the standard caddy spoon, and an example by Joseph Taylor, 1814, sold in New York, had the shell shaped bowl, the handle engraved with script initials and vermicelli.

Caddy spoons, unlike wine labels, soon ceased to be purely practical, for the fun of creating something really different became the prime purpose. Types showed enormous variety, and while Birmingham makers brought something different to the most ordinary spoons, they also created specialties of their own. The "Eagle's Wing," for instance, originated in Birmingham, the majority made by Joseph Willmore between 1814-17. The fine detail die stamping allowed, showed every feather appearing on the back of the bowl, continuing up the neck handle, to end in a sharp beak. It is naturally difficult to find the marks among so much plumage, and a strong glass is usually necessary.

Joseph's less famous father, Thomas Willmore, made a unique caddy spoon in the form of a harebell, in 1791. This was hand-raised, the deep bell shaped bowl embossed with a whorl of petals, joined to a small leaf by a narrow stem-like handle.

The Jockey Cap, a popular form of caddy spoon in London, also originated in Birmingham, where Joseph Taylor specialized in the plain, segmented cap, which frequently had a star motif on the crown and bright cut engraving on the peak. These prized (and most expensive) spoons are fully marked, with the strange exception of the maker's mark. Yet he found space for his initials on a filigree cap, usually left untouched. Samuel Pemberton often used filigree panels in jockey cap spoons, while die stamping allowed him, and other Birmingham makers, to simulate filigree in caddy spoons of many types, incorporating neo-classical themes in great variety, lightly balanced. Cocks and Bettridge were adept at this art.

The forms caddy spoons, like vinaigrettes, were capable of taking could fill a book, and still leave the collector the thrill of finding something altogether different. It is worth watching the sales for their appearance.

An unusual Victorian casket by Edward Smith, Birmingham, 1851; 6" wide.

Pearl-handled ELEGANCE

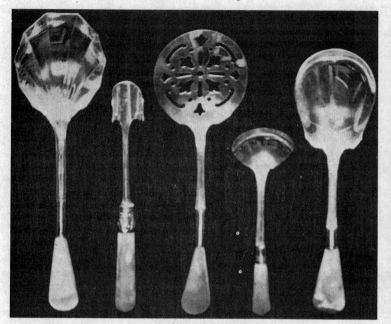

Left to right: large serving spoon, rather plain ferrule; cheese scoop; tomato server, matches serving spoon; gravy ladle, lightly pointed handle, ferrule in shape of thimble, large serving spoon. None are marked.

From left: matching knife and fork, blade marked John Primble, India Steel Works; knife, marked 1834, J. Russell & Co. 12; matching fork and knife, knife marked Landers Frary & Clark, Aetna Works; matching fork and knife, latter marked L F & C.

VICTORIAN TASTE for elegance in household decoration and appurtenances found typical expression in lovely table cutlery with handles of mother-of-pearl. This ware, largely of American make, was distributed throughout the country, and produced into the 20th century.

Following the Civil War and before World War I, Americans, in general prosperous and fond of pleasure, enjoyed entertaining — particularly home-entertaining, with dinners and luncheons as elaborate as their means permitted. Accessories to delight and impress were in demand, and pearl-handled table cutlery fitted the description perfectly.

Pearl shell is a layered, pervious material, and prolonged soaking in hot soapy water will dull its luster; this treatment also tends to weaken the binding agent joining the handles to the blades and tines. Many Victorian hostesses, unwilling to trust the delicate task to the household help and harsh soaps of the period, washed their pearl-handled tableware themselves. This, and the fact it was usually kept for "company-best," may account for the excellent condition in which most of it is found today.

History and Description

The individual pearl-handled piece, of whatever form, consists of several parts. The handle is made of a solid block of mother-of-pearl, either plain polished or carved, drilled with a hole in its lower end to receive the extension of the blade or tines made to fit into it. The joint is sealed with pitch or a special cement, and the rather unsightly juncture covered by a decorative ferrule of sterling silver. Most of these ferrules are quite ornate, and usually they are the only sterling part of the item.

Exceptions will come to light where ferrule and blade are in one piece, as in an elaborate cheese scoop with a sterling blade applied directly to the handle. If the British hallmark of this particular piece has been correctly interpreted, it originated in Birmingham, in 1881.

Pieces most often seen are knives—table, fruit, butter, fish, carving, and such—since knives alone were considered cutlery for some time. They were used with silver forks and spoons. Later pearl-handled forks were added to the line. With these pearl-handled sets the popular odd spoons of the period, or matching sets of sterling spoons, were used. The writer has yet to see a pearl-handled teaspoon made to match a knife and fork set, though serving spoons, ladles, etc. are often found.

None of the items so far encountered has carried any patent mark. It seems somewhat doubtful, in view of the number of firms making the ware, that it was patented. Nor can it be claimed as an innovation of the 19th century. In *History of the Spoon, Knife and Fork,* published by Reed and Barton in 1926, both a knife and a fork of 16th century Italian-make, with handles partly of mother-of-pearl, are shown. In the same publication, a 17th century fork with an agate handle, shaped like our modern pearl ones, is pictured. (The writer once owned an 18th century etui covered with mother-of-pearl, which included among its fittings a tiny folding fork with pearl handle. Pearl shell has always lent itself to such decorative treatment of otherwise common objects.)

The fruit knife, pictured here, with British cutlery marks on the blade, also carries the silversmith's mark in addition to the Sheffield hallmarks on the ferrule. None of the American pieces so far seen by the writer has had any marking on the ferrule other than the word *sterling*, nor has any of the silversmiths contacted claimed manufacture of these decorative bands. Their place of origin is still in question. Cutlery firms bought the ferrules and handles separately and assembled the pieces themselves.

Early 1900 catalogues of Daniel Low and Company list the pearl-handled line as "Manila Pearl." This may furnish a clue as to the source of supply of the raw material for the handles, which were made by New England pearl-works. One such firm was located in Taunton, Massachusetts, and continued in business until the 1930s, though it discontinued manufacture of the handles some years previously. Carving on these handles is sometimes reminiscent of that on buttons of the same material, and no doubt many firms manufactured both articles. Since none of the pearl handles are marked, place of origin of a particular piece is impossible to assess.

Meriden Cutlery Company

One of the earliest and most important American makers of pearl-handled cutlery was the Meriden Cutlery Company of South Meriden, Connecticut. Their knives usually carry the date 1855, the year the company was incorporated after taking over an earlier factory. Nearly all of its employees came from England and, at one time, most of the families of South Meriden were of British nationality. Quite likely some of these men had worked on pearl-handled cutlery in England. Early catalogues of the Meriden Cutlery Company list knives with handles of mother-of-pearl, as well as of various other materials, but no forks.

Landers, Frary and Clark

In 1866, the Meriden Cutlery Company was purchased by Landers, Frary and Clark. This concern built a new factory to house the cutlery division, which was named the Aetna Works. It was completed in 1867, and the event celebrated with a great ball on March 15th of that year. This factory burned to the ground in 1874, but was rebuilt at once, with improved facilities.

Over a long period of time, Landers, Frary and Clark made much pearl-handled tableware, and various marks were used. The firm name and *Aetna Works* is often seen, though sometimes an elaborate monogram of the firm's initials is the only mark. Pieces with the *Universal* mark in addition to the firm's initials can definitely be assigned a later date, as the *Universal* name was not used prior to 1897.

Meriden Britannia Company

Another important maker of pearl-handled ware was the Meriden Britannia Company. Though at one time Meriden Britannia Company shared a New York showroom with the Meriden Cutlery Company, the two firms had no other connection. The Meriden Britannia Company merged with several other concerns to form the International Silver Company in 1898; but in its history as an independent firm, its catalogues furnished a fascinating picture of American taste. Steel knives only were offered by the company until 1861, when some with ivory handles were listed.

It was in the catalogue of 1886 that the first pearl-handled pieces appeared. These were dessert knives, and were priced at $39.50 and $46 per dozen for three-inch and three and one-quarter-inch handles, respectively. From these prices one may readily see that this was a deluxe line. The last mention of pearl-handled items is in the catalogue of 1895, when both knives and forks, silver-plated, were offered. These were priced at $26.50 and $32 per dozen for dessert and medium forks, with matching knives at $30 and $37. Fruit knives were priced from $15 to $21 per dozen, and nutpicks at $16.

Why this firm discontinued the line three years before its merger with the International Silver Company is a mystery. Other concerns were making pearl-handled pieces much later.

Other Marks

Two marks frequently seen are *John Primble, India Steel Works,* and *J. Russell & Co.* The latter factory used the date 1834 on most of its products. This was the date of the company's founding not of the manufacture of the piece. Both these companies often marked their knife blades with the numeral *12,* and it has been suggested this means that the item was intended to be sold in dozen lots. A fine carving set with the J. Russell mark shows the letters *I.D.* instead of the *12.* This may refer to "Individual Design," since the set is an ornate one with carved handles; however, confirmation is needed before it can be so stated.

Recently the writer was shown a very lovely set of pearl-handled dinner knives, in a case, with ornate silver forks. The knives were marked *Haynes-Mellichamp, Atlanta Georgia.* The forks, not pearl-handled, were also marked with this name, and carried in addition a fancy hallmark and "925/1000." The Atlanta Chamber of Commerce furnished this information:

"The 1904 Atlanta City Directory lists 'Haynes-Mellichamp (E u g e n e H a y n e s, Joseph C. Mellichamp) Jewelry, Art Goods and Silverware, 37 Whitehall Street.' This listing appears in the alphabetical section and not in the list of manufacturers, so we have no assurance that the firm operated its own factory.

"The 1903 Directory lists Mr. Mellichamp as bookkeeper for Maier and Berkle, and Mr. Haynes as a salesman for the same firm. Maier and Berkle

were local jewelers. There seems to be doubt that these pieces were actually made in Atlanta." (A souvenir spoon from the Cotton States and International Exposition in Atlanta, 1895, carrying the mark of Maier and Berkle, was illustrated in SW, April '64, p. 32.)

About the time of World War I, whether from difficulty in obtaining pearl shell or because plastics were coming into general use genuine mother-of-pearl gradually gave place to synthetic materials. This simulated pearl could be molded directly onto the blades and tines without the use of binding agents, and greatly reduced manufacturing costs. With synthetics, the elegance was gone from the ware, and it eventually disappeared from the market. Silverware in matching sets became the vogue i n s t e a d . Pearl-handled cold-meat forks, tomato servers, and other serving pieces were among later articles made; none so far seen by the writer have carried any identifying marks other than the *sterling* on the ferrule.

Pearl-handled silverware can be found in many antiques shops today for little, if any, more than its original cost. While it is most at home with the Haviland and cut glass of the gaslit era, it also makes a lovely accompaniment for fine modern china and crystal. With reasonable care, it will provide its owner pleasure and service for many years.

Though widely admired, pearl-handled ware has received little attention from the researcher. Factual information seems never to have been assembled. Taking factory-marked family pieces as a basis of study, Mrs. McClellan set out to identify their makers and assess precise dates. While, in some cases, this proved impossible, many facts did come to light, and they are offered here in the hope that other collectors may add to her excellent beginnings.

Many individuals and firms were most helpful to her in her research, particularly the International Silver Company; Reed and Barton; Landers, Frary and Clark; and Daniel Low & Company; Pearl-handled pieces pictured are from the author's and other Gatesville, Texas, collections.

Railroad Silverware

564
Silver

by KATHARINE MORRISON McCLINTON

Left: Union Pacific R.R. syrup pitcher.

Right: California Zephyer teapot.

Left: Burlington Route (CB & Q R.R.) sugar bowl.

THE PLATED SILVERWARE once used in the dining cars of American Railroads has become a collector's item. Like many other articles no longer in use, it has now an antique value. Its appeal is mainly nostalgic, closely related to collecting ash trays with names of hotels or restaurants once visited, though railroad silverware offers a broader panorama.

For those who have experienced the "red carpet" treatment of the New York Central's *Twentieth Century* or crossed the continent to California on the *Santa Fe Super Chief* (still running) there are not only memories of places visited but also of a way of living no longer practiced. (The author remembers a trip from California to Chicago in a private car in 1935. Upon arrival at Chicago an actual red carpet was rolled out and handsome colored porters, standing at attention, lined the length of the car.) There were also the Union Pacific's *City of San Francisco* and the *City of Los Angeles* (still running) where the passengers used to be treated as guests, addressed by name, and given the choice of white or red wine "on the house."

Silverware from any of the above named trains would be especially collectible. But silverware from railroads that ran only one train a day for short distances, such as the old San Diego Arizona, which crossed the gorge from Yuma to San Diego, California, or from the Richmond, Fredericksburg and Potomac, or the defunct Delaware, Lackawana & Western are also considered choice. To be sure some few dining cars continue in operation but many trains now have only snack bar service. Thus there is a surplus of obsolete silver.

Railroad silver was actually "Nickel Silver," that is, an alloy of nickel, copper, and zinc. It was silver soldered.

All railroad silverware is marked with name, initials, or emblem of the railroad or special train where it was used and with the mark of the manufacturer. Most of the railroad dining car silverware was made by the Meriden Britannia Company and, after 1898, when that company became a subsidiary of the International Silver Company, by the parent firm; by R. Wallace Co.; and by the Gorham Manufacturing Company. The International Silver Company or its subsidiaries made services for the Southern Railway; Florida East Coast; Boston & Maine; Missouri Pacific; Great Northern; The Pullman Company; Delaware Lackawana & Western; Southern Pacific; New York Central; and Union Pacific.

This silver was mostly made between 1900 and the 1930s; most of that available to collectors today was made in the 20th Century.

Railroad dining car silver services usually include the following items: teapot, coffeepot, creamer, sugar bowl, bread tray, vegetable dishes, soup tureen, sauce boat, water pitcher, syrup jug, crumb tray, finger bowl, salt and pepper shakers, mustard pot, toothpick stand, large serving tray, cash tray, and butter pats. There were also such pieces as corn holders, bottle holders, casters, menu holders, flower vases, tea strainers, cocktail shakers, and wine coolers as well as holders for glass cream soups, grapefruit, orange juice, and ice cream. There were also copper-clad dishes, thermos-type coffeepots, and ice water pitchers. Flatware was made to match the services, usually in a plain old English pattern.

Railroad holloware is simple in shape and heavy. Sometimes the only ornament is a rounded band at the rim, center, and base of the piece. Other pieces are decorated with groups of bandings, and some services, such as that made for the Pullman Company by International Silver Company, have more refined shapes and bandings spaced with ribbon bow-knots. There are two sizes of trays to this set, a cash or card tray and a waiter. The teapot is especially interesting since it is made of Lenox blue china and is set in a metal frame. It is marked "Pullman" and "International Silver Co."

The service for the Great Northern Railway, made by Meriden Britannia Company, has a beaded border. The bread tray has a pierced design in its body. There is also a footed compote with pierced border and a footed cakestand with similar decoration. The crumb tray is ornamented with gadrooning and a center shell motif. In addition to the usual tea and coffeepots there is a black coffee server with straight handle. There is a small butter pat, a square serving tray, and a cash tray. Other pieces include a wine cooler and a chafing dish. All pieces are marked with the monogram of the Great Northern Railway and have the Meriden nickel silver, silver soldered mark on their bases.

One set of silverware made for the Missouri Pacific Railroad has a border of husks; flower finials top the tea and coffee pots. The holloware shapes are slightly reminiscent of Adam style, and the combination crumb tray and scraper has a handle with an Adam pattern. The oval ice bowl has handles and is the most interesting piece of the set. This service was made by the International Silver Company. Some pieces are marked "Missouri Pacific," others "Missouri Pacific Railway," and still others "Missouri Pacific Line" with the Eagle insignia on the front of such pieces as thermos coffeepots.

The Union Pacific service includes such unusual pieces as a bar jigger and cocktail strainer. There is also a teapot of Lenox china with metal frame, a flower vase, corn holders, and a menu holder in addition to the usual dinnerware and tea and syrup pots. All pieces are etched on the side with the Union Pacific *Streamline* crest and stamped "U.P.R.R." in script on the base together with the International Silver Company's mark of their Hotel Division. Silver for the *Challenger* is marked with the name on such pieces as teapots, cream and sugars.

The silverware service for the Southern Pacific Company's *Forty Niner* is ornamented with bandings crossed with leaves; the lids of teapots, coffeepots, cream and syrup pitchers have leaf-decorated finials. The teapot is of black Lenox china with a silver frame. Pieces are marked with the "SP" crest in a circle and "Southern Pacific Lines" on the under side.

There are a great number of silver articles from the Santa-Fe Railroad available. The holloware pieces are of fluted design and are marked "Santa Fe." The first pattern used on the Santa Fe *Super Chief* was of diamond-shaped design. It was marked "Super Chief" and "Santa Fe." Some of this silver was made by Harrison & Housen, England.

The silver for the Burlington Route, Chicago, Burlington and Quincy, is quite elegant with fluting and vase finials on covers of tea and coffeepots. It is marked with the raised letters "B.R." That made by the Mulholland Bros. Inc. of Aurora, Illinois, is marked "C.B. & Q., Mulholland Bros." Other pieces are marked "Burlington Route" or "Property of C.B. & Q. R.R." The silver of the *California Zephyr* has the distinctive C/Z mark.

Silver is also available from the New Haven Railroad, the Richmond, Fredericksburg & Potomac Railroad, the Florida East Coast, the Pennsylvania Railroad (marked "Pennsylvania Keystone" and the monogram "PRR"), the New York Central, the Seaboard, The Rock Island Lines, The Chicago Northwestern, and the Southern Railway. Single items of flatware are often the only pieces from such railroads as Central Vermont Railway.

Trays, cocktail shakers, and thermos bottles are in demand and such articles as coffeepots with matching cream and sugar and footed bowls are rare. Among rare and unusual articles is a large pedestal-type ice bowl which was used on the Illinois Central. It is marked with the inscription "Central Mississippi Valley Route – Illinois Central Railroad" and a diamond in circle insignia.

Some of this silverware is available in shops. One Chicago dealer specializes in railroad silver and other railroad items. Also from time to time the dining car division of railroads in Chicago sells obsolete silver at auction.

Left and Right: Dining Car services furnished the Great Northern Railroad Company by The International Silver Co., Meriden, Conn.

Myer Myers, Silversmith

1723-1795

MYER MYERS, working in New York City, was one of America's outstanding colonial silversmiths, a contemporary of Paul Revere though less well-known, and the only early American craftsman who created Judaic ritual silver.

Myer's parents had migrated from Holland to New York where Myer was born in 1723. The name of the master silversmith to whom he was apprenticed as a boy is not known, but records show that in 1746 he became a Freeman of the City of New York, privileged to engage in silversmithing as master craftsman himself.

Information on his early career is meager, but various bits pieced together indicate that his talent was not long in being recognized. Several times in 1754 his name appeared in New York newspapers, once when two large silver spoons bearing his maker's mark had been stolen from the home of a prominent citizen, again in his own extensive advertisements when he moved his shop from Meal Market (lower Wall Street) to King Street (now Pine). A daybook of a Jewish merchant in Philadelphia shows entries of several transactions to sell Myers' thimbles, rings, and earrings in that city. Fine teasets, coffee pots, canns, sugar bowls, porringers, and tankards, preserved today, speak of the many commissions he executed for New York's important families.

Myers was active in civic and religious affairs, being honored in 1786 by his election as Chairman of the Silversmith's Society, an organization created to protect the economic and social interests of its members. He also held the high office of Master of the King David Masonic Lodge in New York City, and was twice President of the Shearith Israel, the congregation he served with devotion.

During the Revolution and the occupation of New York by the British, this congregation closed its house of worship. At that time Myers and his family left New York, living first in Norwalk, Connecticut, later in Philadelphia. After the war, when the Shearith Isreal resumed its activities, Myers was one of the three men chosen to sign and present a letter to Governor George Clinton, congratulating him on his distinguished military career during the Revolution.

Of the ceremonial silver Myers made for American synagogues, the most noted are his Rimonim (Scroll ornaments). Two pair, one belonging to Shearith Isreal in New York, the other to the Touro Synagogue in Newport, Rhode Island, were made around 1765. Two more pair went to the Congregation Mikveh Isreal in Philadelphia in 1772, accompanied by the one existing letter known to have been written by Myers.

Nor was his ceremonial silver limited to Jewish pieces. The Brick Presbyterian Church in New York owns one of his baptismal bowls; the First Presbyterian Church there has three of his alms basins.

Myers died December 12, 1795, and was buried in the cemetery belonging to the synagogue he loved. The exact site of his grave is unknown.

Wedding Cup

SILVER wedding cups, in the form of a girl in wide spreading skirt, holding a bowl over her head, first appeared in Germany about 1575, and continued in fashion through the 17th century. Many were made at Nuremberg. The bowl is pivoted, so that when the figure is inverted, the skirt forms an upper cup, and the bowl a lower one. The groom was supposed to drink the contents of the larger cup, without spilling any from the smaller, which he passed to his bride. They were also known as wager-cups. The example shown here is from Brother Timothy's collection and is on display at the Christian Brothers Champagne Cellars in St. Helena, California.

Myer Myers pieces, included in a recent sale of the late Dr. Norman Treves' Collections at the Parke-Bernet Galleries in New York. Pair of silver sauce boats, 7" long, with shell-and hoof tripod feet, brought $2,800; silver porringer, monogramed S.M., $1,200.

SPOONS

While Daniel Low of Salem, Massachusetts, is credited with popularizing the souvenir spoon, he was not the first to make them. The first souvenir spoon was designed by M. W. Galt of Washington, D. C., after a ladle once owned by George Washington. From America the craze for souvenir spoons spread to Europe, and before many years had passed literally hundreds of designs for these spoons were patented or registered in America and abroad. There are so many variations on the theme, that one collector couldn't possibly acquire an example of every souvenir spoon produced over a period of about fifty or sixty years. The craze for souvenir spoons has been revived in recent years, and now there are a host of modern souvenir spoons being offered collectors.

Early American Souvenir Spoons

by DOROTHY T. RAINWATER

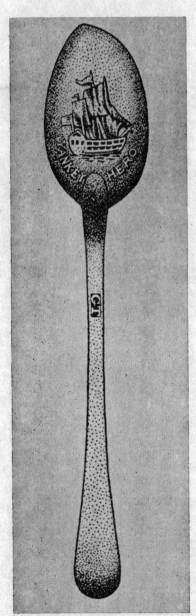

Fig. 2. "Bottom Mark" souvenir spoon of the Revolution, commemorating the privateer, *Yankee Hero*; note spelling of "Yankey" on spoon.

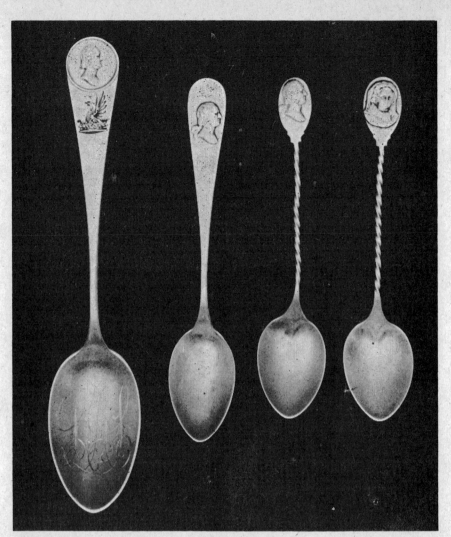

Fig. 3. Washington souvenir spoons designed and made for M. W. Galt, Washington, D. C. Teaspoon is gold-washed and has the Washington crest; the two spoons on the left are stamped "M. W. Galt Bro. & Co."; all four bear the fleur-de-lis in a shield trademark of Davis & Galt, Philadelphia.
Collection of Helen Hoegsberg, Coronado, Calif. Photo by H. Ivan Rainwater.

IT WAS Daniel Low, of Salem, Massachusetts, who popularized souvenir spoons throughout the United States till they became a national craze. Two Witch spoons, designed by his son, Seth, and patented in 1891 and 1892, were advertised in three-quarter page ads in national magazines. Popular as these spoons were, they were not the very first American souvenir spoons.

M. W. Galt, of Washington, D. C., designed spoons after the Washington ladle preserved in U. S. National Museum. Issued May 11, 1889, they bore a medallion of George Washington on either the handle or the bowl. The spoons were extremely popular; more than 10,000 a year were sold by the Galt firm (now Galt & Bros., Inc.). Similar spoons bearing a likeness of Martha Washington (Fig. 3) soon followed.

Still earlier is the souvenir spoon design (Fig. 1) by Myron H. Kinsley, of Wallingford, Connecticut, for which he received a patent on August 23, 1881. (Design No. 12, 428; application filed June 29, 1881; term of patent 7 years.) According to the specifi-

cations accompanying the design patent, "The principal feature of this design is the representation of Niagara Falls and Suspension Bridge on the surface of the handle, with the representation of the bank of the river upon each side, a diagonal ornamental band cutting off the river and bank at the front."

The earliest souvenir spoon to come to the attention of the writer commemorates the "Yankee Hero," a Newburyport, Massachusetts, privateer. (Fig. 2) The present location of this spoon is not known, but it was of sufficient interest to George P. Tilton, designer for Towle Silversmiths from the late 1890s until c. 1916, for him to illustrate it in his *The Colonial Book of Newburyport & Vicinity*, published in 1908. Mr. Tilton states, "Newburyport privateer, the Yankee Hero, reinforced by Gloucester sailors, was captured off the Cape [Ann], by a British man-of-war, disguised as a merchantman, after a hard-fought battle . . . The souvenir spoon commemorating this event . . . was probably the first of this character in America." Mr. Tilton's careful delineation of the spoon, reproduced here, shows clearly that it was worn from use.

The Yankee Hero was well known off Newburyport and numerous references to her success as a privateer are chronicled in histories of the area. John James Currier, in his *Ould Newbury: Historical & Biographical Sketches*, 1890, tells his version of her last voyage in 1776. "A . . . privateer (Yankee Hero) from Newburyport, on a cruise to the West Indies for the purpose of intercepting English ships laden with merchandise or supplies for the army . . . carried twenty guns, and was manned by one hundred and seventy men, including fifty from the first families of Newburyport. After leaving the harbor on this unfortunate voyage, the vessel, officers, and crew were never heard from again."

The maker of this spoon has not been identified with certainty, but the style of his mark very closely resembles that of George Tyler, silversmith of Boston, Massachusetts (1740–1785).

"Bottom Mark" spoons, while of comparative rarity, are known both in American and English silver. A set of six English "bottom mark" spoons with ship pattern, from the third quarter of the 18th century, is illustrated in *Antiques*, May 1946. They have the rounded drop on the back of the bowl as does the Yankee Hero spoon. More often found are designs of shells, scrolls, or flowers. The ship design on the Yankee Hero spoon could well be unique in American silver.

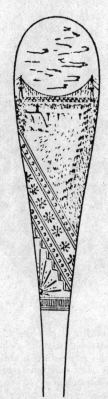

Fig. 1. Niagara Falls spoon. Design patented by Myron H. Kinsley, 8/23/1881.

Spoon Collectors' Favorite

Men at the Top

LAST Christmas, Mrs. Pearl V. Gunnerson of Winter Park, Florida, whose spoon collection, displayed in a local bank, was pictured in the July-August '62 *Spinning Wheel*, gave herself a present of three sterling souvenir spoons featuring the U. S. Navy, Merchant Marines, and Marine Corps, shown above in that order.

The Navy and Marine Corps spoons, both 5½ inches long, were made by C. M. Robbins; the Merchant Marine, 5¾ inches long, by F. A. Whitney. The bowl of the last pictures the "Monitor & Merrimac, March 9, 1862." All figures have reverse detail.

The die for the U. S. Navy spoon was later used for less expensive metals as evidenced by the picture which accompanied Isabel Schrader's article, "When Is Sterling *Not* Sterling?" in SW, September '59, reprinted September '61. The Schrader example is in bronze, and the word "Bronze" is struck, somewhat imperfectly, over the original "Sterling" mark. "Patented" appears in small letters above the other marks.

Identification of the "Gusky's 1894" plated spoon, topped with a Grand Army soldier, was a task set Mrs. Isabel Schrader of Mt. Shasta, California. A G.A.R. reunion, surely, but where? Was Gusky's a place or a person? Part of the answer came from Jerry Garret of Houston, Texas, who owns a spoon inscribed "28th Encampment, G.A.R. Pittsburgh, 1894," and one from the Columbia Exposition marked "Souvenir, Gusky's, Pittsburgh." R. D. Christie of the Historical Society of Western Pennsylvania supplied the rest.

J. M. Gusky was a retail clothier, located at 300-400 Market Street, in the '90s, a man given to unusual methods of advertising. He owned an elephant named Gusky which always headed a parade of his delivery wagons just before Christmas, delivering presents to all the orphanages in the city. Later he established a Hebrew orphanage and home. His G.A.R. spoon carried his fame far, for the Schrader example was found in Stockton, Calif.

Mustache Spoons

by Dorothy Rainwater

SOME EARLY explorers and first settlers of this country wore whiskers, being mustachioed or full-bearded. When wigs became fashionable in the latter part of the 17th century, facial foliage was no longer cultivated. During the 18th century, men were clean-shaven. None of the signers of the Declaration of Independence or of the Constitution wore any kind of facial adornment. No President of the United States before Lincoln wore either beard or mustache—and he grew *his* beard between his nomination and inauguration.

Explanations of the sudden flowering of hirsute adornments among American men are many. One is that following the war with Mexico (1846-47), men of the Army and Navy cultivated mustaches. The Gold Rush followed soon after and there was great interest in the Far West. Men found it difficult to shave in rugged surroundings, and there was the added feeling hairiness indicated virility.

With the exception of McKinley, all the presidents from Grant to Taft sported at least a flowing mustache—four of them also being bearded.

Men in all walks of life wore some form of facial hair. This vogue continued for about thirty-five years when it began to phase out. By 1885-90, only the mustache remained in popular favor. This, too, largely disappeared by World War I. Currently, beards are enjoying minor favor.

When mustaches were popular, great numbers of brushes, combs, curlers, dyes, oils, waxes and mustache cups and spoons were advertised. The difficulties of eating and drinking through a "soup strainer" can easily be imagined.

Patented Mustache Spoons

The earliest mustache spoon patent found in the U. S. Patent Office is dated March 3, 1868; it was granted to Solon Farrer of New York.

Reed & Barton, silversmiths in Taunton, Massachusetts, illustrated a plated silver mustache spoon in their now famous catalogue of 1885. This spoon, made in the *Palace* pattern, was 8¼ inches in length and was offered in four qualities, depending on the amount of silver deposited on the nickel silver base. Prices varied from $27 to $45 a dozen.

Also in 1885, the Denver Novelty Company advertised a mustache spoon shield described as "Neatness and Comfort for Moustache Wearers. The neatest Novelty of the Age. Can be immediately adjusted to any tablespoon. Try one and you will never be without it. Mailed to any address in the U. S., Canada or Europe on receipt of 25¢. . . . Trade supplied at liberal discounts. . . ."

This spoon shield is stamped, "Pat'd. 1885," and the patent is recorded in the United States Patent Office, rather unexpectedly, under Cutlery. L. B. France of Denver, Colorado, was the patentee.

The most ornate mustache spoon to come to our attention is from the collection of Mrs. Clara Price, Wildwood Inn, Breezewood, Pennsylvania. It was made to commemorate the California Midwinter International Exposition, held in San Francisco, January 27 to June 30, 1894—its purpose being the portrayal of the wealth and beauty of California. "Sunset City," as the Exposition was called by San Franciscans, was the inspiration of M. H. de Young, owner and

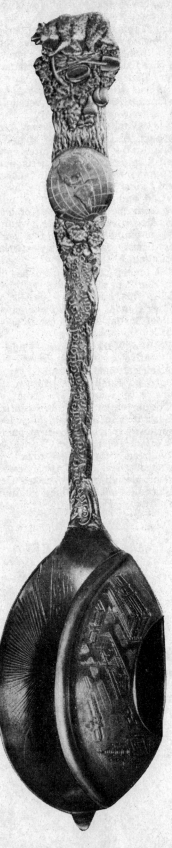

Mustache spoon made for the California Midwinter International Exposition, 1894. Several of the Exposition buildings are depicted on the mustache shield; in center is an Electric Tower, copy of the Eiffel Tower, 226 ft. high, used to light the concourse and to house bandstands and observation platforms. *Collection of Clara Price, Breezewood, Penna.*

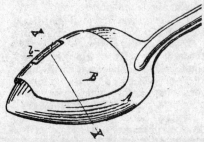

David G. Williams, Port Huron, Mich., patented this mustache spoon with side-hinged cover, July 10, 1883.

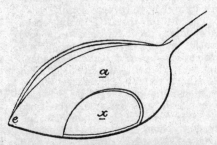

Mustache spoon patented Jan. 21, 1873, by Ellen B. A. Mitcheson, Philadelphia.

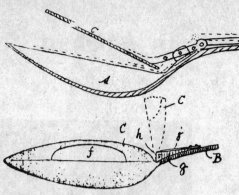

Above: Earliest mustache spoon design found in U.S. Patent Office. Patented March 3, 1868, by Solon Farrer, New York. Hinged cover lifts by a spring for cleaning.

Left: Mustache cap, patented by **Phebe C. Goodwin,** Boston, Sept. 27, 1892. It has a spring hinge so that "spoon and cap can be cleansed."

Right: Winged and inclined mustache guard featured in this spoon was patented by **Roger Williams,** Yonkers, N. Y., Sept. 11, 1877.

editor of the San Francisco *Chronicle,* and vice president of the Columbian Exposition held in Chicago in 1893.

Exhibits from the Chicago Midway, including several from foreign countries, were moved to San Francisco. At the end of the very successful Midwinter Exposition, the Fine Arts Building, some of the exhibits, and a surplus of money were turned over to Mr. de Young, who had served as Director-General, to establish the M. H. de Young Memorial Museum.

"Patented" MSC

The above mark is stamped on the back of this California souvenir spoon. Though clearly marked "Patented," neither this spoon nor the trademark could be found in the United States Patent Office. Design patents expire after a period of years and come into the public domain. It is quite probable that the word "Patented" stamped on this spoon refers to Ellen B. A. Mitcheson's patent for mustache spoons dated January 21, 1873.

The trademark was used by the Maltby, Stevens & Curtiss Company, Wallingford, Connecticut, successors to Maltby, Stevens & Company's spoon factory, Birmingham, Conn.

This company was formed about 1890 by Elizur Seneca Stevens, Chapman Maltby, and John Curtiss, who purchased the old Hall, Elton & Company plant and began the manufacture of flatware for plating. In 1896, Maltby, Stevens & Curtiss was purchased by the Watrous Manufacturing Company, one of the original companies to become part of the International Silver Company in 1898.

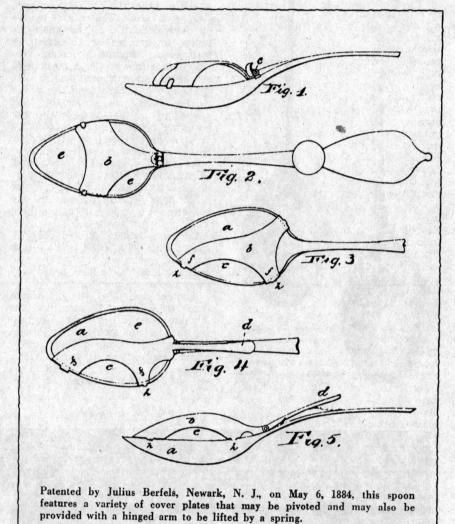

Patented by **Julius Berfels,** Newark, N. J., on May 6, 1884, this spoon features a variety of cover plates that may be pivoted and may also be provided with a hinged arm to be lifted by a spring.

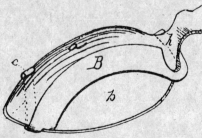

Albert Furniss, Meriden, Conn., claimed his mustache guard, patented Nov. 13, 1877, could be "carried by the traveler and attached to a cup or spoon."

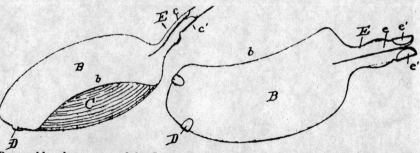

Removable plate, patented by **Lewis B. France,** Denver, Colorado, August 4, 1885, was widely advertised in magazines.

Spoons in Sets by Gorham

From the collection of Mr. and Mrs. Carl R. Almgren

by GERTRUDE SCHMIDT

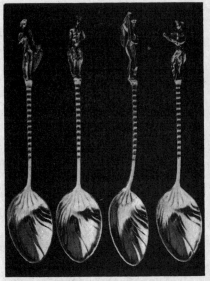

From Gorham's Apollo set, 1892

GORHAM'S Nuremburg spoons and forks, so treasured by collectors, were first made during the 1880s. Company records show their casting patterns ran from #7304 through #7315, and that the last set was made January 24, 1934. The cut-out figures on these delightful spoons, each different in the set of 12, illustrate picturesque costumes and characteristic occupations of Old Nuremburg's peasants, burghers, and nobles.

These were special order sets, the handles being cast separately, then applied to the type bowl or tine the customer requested. They could be ordered in sterling, or entirely or partly gold-washed, with a date or place name engraved in the bowl. Gorham listed them in their catalogs of the early 1890s, but did not picture all of them. Because of this, later day collectors often did not realize there were twelve in the set.

Gorham listings offered 5½-inch spoons with plain bowls, and a 5-inch size with embossed bowls. The two 4-inch spoons, shown here, prove they were also made in coffee size.

Another spoon set which Gorham made from special castings was the Alphabet set, in coffee size. According to Ann Holbrook of the Gorham Company, the first alphabet coffee spoon was made in September, 1885. This set was never a "line-item." A cut-out letter with flowers or leaves

entwined forms the finial; the handle resembles a branch; bowls are fluted and scalloped. Finials and bowls are gold-washed.

In 1892, Gorham brought out their Apollo coffee spoons, a set of 12, with full-figure cut-out finials showing men (or gods) in Greek dress, each in a different pose. Incomplete Gorham records offer no clue to the identification of the individual figures. The handles, 4 inches over-all, are horizontally ridged; bowls are swirl-fluted; the whole is gold-washed.

Nuremburg coffee spoons, 4" long, from set of 12. Shown are, tinker mending pot, maid with brush and pan.

Nine of Gorham's 26 Alphabet spoons: A,C,I,L,N,O,R,S,T; 4¾" long; made from about 1875 to 1934.

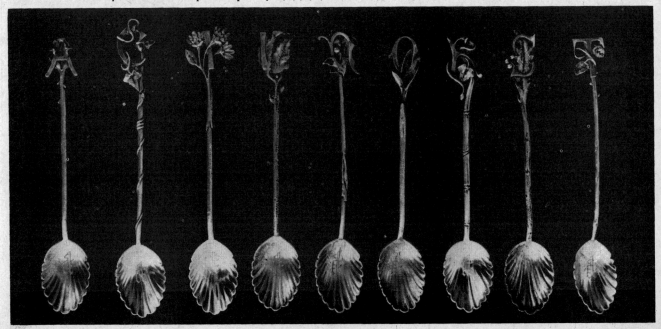

TOBACCO ANTIQUES

Modern processing and packaging has done away with a lot of the paraphernalia needed in years past to prepare a cigar, cigarette or pipe for smoking. Because of this collectors of such things are having a pleasant experience seeking out old cigar cutters, matchsafes, pipe tampers and snuff boxes. Some collect old cigar boxes, cigar bands, and matchbooks. Among the many and varied collections owned by the late Egyptian Monarch, King Farouk, was a collection of several thousand matchbooks and matchboxes, many of them from famous restaurants and spas all over the world.

Fig. 5

CIGAR SMOKERS' PARAPHERNALIA

by F. M. GOSLING

WHEN THE CIGAR SMOKER of today desires a fresh cigar he selects his favorite brand at any cigar counter, removes the protective clear plastic wrapper, places one end of the cigar in his mouth, and uses his pocket lighter or a book of paper advertising matches, often given with the purchase of the cigar, to light the other end, and he is ready to puff away.

It was not always this simple. Fifty to more than 100 years ago a good bit of paraphernalia was usually called into play before the smoker could get a cigar into operation. These articles, no longer used, are now of interest to collectors.

It long has been the custom to ship cigars to the retailer in boxes containing 25 or 50. These boxes until fairly recently were made of wood, usually cedar, and were put together with small nails. The hinged lids were nailed shut. Shown in *Fig. 1* are two styles of metal tools for prying open the lids, driving back the nails and removing them by use of the notch in the tool. These tools still can be found. They were made in a number of shapes and sizes. Some bear the name of the wholesale tobacco company.

Before manufacturers started making cigars with both ends open it was necessary to remove a bit of the sealed end in order to draw the smoke into the mouth when the other end was lighted. There were several ways of doing this. On the cigar counter usually could be found a cigar cutter. See *Fig. 2 and 3.*

Fig. 2 is made of glass with a wood base. Inside are rotating knives powered by a clock-type spring. A key is attached at the back for winding. By placing the end of the cigar in the hole on top of the machine, the knife is activated, cutting the tip off the cigar. Appearing above the hole is the printed warning: "Do Not Stick Finger Into Cutter." Approximate measurements of the machine are 7 x 8¼ in. by 5 in. high. A hinged metal door in the base is provided for removal of the cigar clippings.

Fig. 3 is all metal and has two clippers. As the cigar is pressed into the hole, the clipper arm is forced down and the blade moves forward, clipping the cigar. Springs return the arm to normal position. Measurements are 10 in. wide by about 7 in. deep and 7 in. high. Clippings can be removed from the bottom. The back plate, which is attached with bolts, carries advertising for "Tirador Spanish Made Havana Cigars." The name of the maker, or of the distributor appears as "The Brunhuff Mfg. Co., Cincinnati, O."

If a counter-type cutter was not available, the smoker had other alternatives. He could bite off the end of the cigar, cut it off with a pen knife, or use a pocket-type cutter. *Fig. 4* shows four styles of these cutters. The one at lower right can be opened and used as a pocket knife, or by pressing on the back edge of the blade it passes across the hole to cut the cigar. A ring on the end makes it suitable for attaching to the end of a watch chain and carried in a vest pocket. This type, and the one at lower left can be found nickel plated, in sterling silver, and in 14-karat gold. They come plain, etched, and engraved.

Cutter at upper left bears the wording "Black & White 5¢ Cigar, National Cigar Stands," together with an outline of the nation's capitol as a trade mark. The one at top right was made in Germany. Cutter in *Fig. 5* also is designed for attaching to a watch chain. The sides are of mother-of-pearl. The top of the cigar is inserted into the end for cutting. This, also, is of German manufacture.

Fig. 1

Fig. 2

Fig. 3

Fig. 4

Fig. 6   Fig. 7

At the cigar counter some type of lighter usually was available. *Fig. 6* shows a battery operated one manufactured by Star Electric Co., Waterloo, Ind., and first patented in 1894. It is 14 inches long and is nickel over brass. Fuel is contained in the handle at the bottom with a wick emerging from an attached 2½ inch metal tube. The lighter was suspended over the counter by an electric cord, the other end of which was attached to a dry cell battery mechanism. When the handle was grasped and pushed back on its hinge, the wick tube moved forward; causing the end of the tube to come in contact with a metal pin creating an electrical spark which lit the wick. When the handle was released the wick tube returned to its normal position, snuffing out the flame.

A wooden box, large enough to hold the battery assembly, with the lighter mechanism mounted on top of the box is another arrangement of this type of lighter.

In cities where natural gas was available, a lamp with a gas burner often was used. Mounted on the counter the lamp burned continuously during business hours. *Fig. 7* illustrates such a lamp with one glass panel removed to show the burner. Some of the lamps used on cigar counters were quite elaborate and bring fancy prices when found today in antiques shops. *Fig. 8* shows a silverplated cigar lighter made by "The Brunhoff Manufacturing Company, Cinn., O.," makers of "Advertising Specialties" according to the markings on the base. The pierced tin shade, lined with oilpaper, reads "James G. Blaine 5 Cigars." The wire wicks (one is shown in front of the lighter) were heated in the flame of the oil lamp until they were glowing red hot, then they were touched to the

end of the customer's cigar to light it.

Away from the cigar counter, matches were the usual means of lighting a cigar. Match safes were in common use for carrying matches in one's pocket. These are metal containers with hinged lids. They measure about 1½ inches wide by 2¾ inches high and can be found in great variety. Some are nickel over brass. This type was often produced for advertising purposes or as souvenirs of special events. Three of these are shown in *Fig. 9.*

Fig. 8

Fig. 9

The one at the left is engraved *St. Louis* with *1904* on the reverse side and is a souvenir of the Louisiana Purchase Exposition. The middle one bears advertising for the Napa Soda Springs in California. At the right is a souvenir of the Midwinter Fair held in Golden Gate Park, San Francisco, in 1894. Depicted is the 362 ft. Electric Tower and its 8,000 lights. The reverse side shows the Administration Building.

Others were produced in 14-karat gold, sterling silver, white metal, and silverplate. They can be found plain, etched, engraved, with applied designs, polished, hammered or set with dia-

monds, sapphires, or other stones. Some have raised ornamentation and space for a photograph, with mica cover.

Fig. 10 shows a match safe with a cigar cutter on the bottom. The entire cutter is hinged to the match container and can be opened to remove the cigar clippings. The ribbed striking edge, usually on the bottom, appears on the lid of this combination match safe and cutter.

Small cardboard or wooden boxes of matches were sold at cigar counters for one cent a box. These often were dispensed through a machine such as shown in *Fig. 11.*

Advertising signs in the cigar category are also collectible. Although they can take up a lot of space in a collection, they are colorful and interesting. *Fig. 12* shows a metal sign in red, green, gold and brown, measuring 27 x 19 inches.

Fig. 10

Fig. 11

Fig. 12

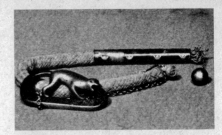

Brass (silver inlaid) tinder tube, using match tinder, has a brass monkey with tempered steel tail for a striker; piece of flint is carried separately. Silver ball attached to match extinguishes ember when pulled against the tube.

EARLY CIGARETTE LIGHTERS

by SAM COUSLEY

ALTHOUGH THE 1920s focused attention upon the many handy "name brand" cigarette lighters of the fluid and flint class—Ronson's, Zippo's, Dunhill's and others—which rapidly became "must" trinkets for the feminine purse and the male pocket, the use of these little machines was not so much an innovation as a revival in modern dress of a device in use for more than 100 years.

The swank instantaneous lighter of today is actually an improved version of firemaking equipment which is older than the Roman Empire—the tinderbox. Requisites of the venerable tinderbox were a quantity of very dry, readily combustible material—tinder—and a piece of flint with which to strike sparks into the tinder by crashing the flint with a sharp glancing blow against a piece of tempered steel.

For the steel an old file, a piece of sword, or knife blade would suffice. The tinderbox itself was merely a tight, dry container for the tinder, flint, and steel. It could be of most any material—wood, horn, metal, sometimes leather. It usually was kept in the kitchen or any other place convenient for starting the household fires.

The first pocket lighter was simply a pocket tinderbox, the need for which was recognized immediately after the tobacco smoking novelty was transported from the Americas to Europe in the 16th century. It was soon found that a most reliable kind of tinder for portable firemakers was a loosely-woven soft cotton rope, called "match," which was used to fire the "matchlock" muskets of the 15th century.

This "match," which was impregnated with saltpeter (potassium nitrate) would, when lighted by a spark, burn slowly with a glowing ember without bursting into flame. Some of the first smokers' pocket lighters, called "tinder tubes," used this type of fuel. Progress eventually replaced the striking steel and fragment of flint with a knurled wheel attached to the match tube which could be revolved against a particle of synthetic flint—a composition of cerium and iron filings—to obtain the spark. However, small pocket tinderboxes, complete with tinder, flint, and striker, continued to be used in this country until long after the Civil War.

In the 17th century mechanics adapted the firing mechanism of flintlock guns to create a pistol-like pocket piece which ignited tinder, instead of gun powder, when fired. Soon after Japan was opened to American and European trade in the 1850s, Japanese craftsmen began making tiny but precise adaptations of the flintlock

Koopman "Magic Pocket Lamp," patented 1889, believed to be the first American-made fluid and flint lighter.

mechanism for small egg-shape pocket lighters. These were among the first Japanese exports.

The first American-made fluid and flint lighter is believed to have been the Koopman Magic Pocket Lamp patented in 1889. It was an automatic instantaneous firemaker. When a knob on the side was pressed, the lid flew back and a spark ignited a wick. The fuel was alcohol. Spots of a synthetic flint composition were spaced around a paper disk which revolved against a sharp steel point to strike the spark. A packet of replaceable disks was provided with each pocket lamp sold.

Several lighters in the shape of pocket watches came out in the 1890s, and in 1907 there was patented the most interesting and ingenious lighter of all time. Working on the principle of catalysis, the lighter has a cylindrical wick wet with high grade alcohol. When a particle of sponge

Watch pocket lighter, popular in the late 1890s and early 1900s, used synthetic flint and asbestos wick on the striker. Fuel was alcohol or naphtha.

platinum (the catalyst) is introduced into the chamber containing the wick, the thin film of pure oxygen which always surrounds platinum combines with the alcohol vapor to produce a flame which lights the wick.

This type of lighter, which is still being manufactured and sold by the New Method Co., Bradford, Pa., is based upon the Dobereiner Lamp, invented by Prof. Johan W. Dobereiner, Jena University, Germany, in 1823. The Dobereiner divice generated hydrogen by means of zinc and diluted sulphuric acid, and when a stream of hydrogen issuing from a fine nozzle played upon a small piece of sponge platinum, the platinum became incandescent and the hydrogen ignited. The principle was used to some extent in the gaslight era to provide a simple automatic instantaneous method of lighting ordinary gas jets.

During the last 50 years, pocket and table lighters have been produced in hundreds of fascinating shapes. Long ago people started making collections of them. Some collections are quite impressive. For instance, Anthony Donofrio has more than 200 fantastic examples on display in his Hackensack, N.J., barbershop---a wonder and pleasure to his patrons.

OTHER COLLECTIBLE CIGARETANA

Cigarette smoking is generally believed to have been introduced to this country in the last half of the 19th century by southern Europeans who settled in New York. Until the early 1880s, the custom was mostly confined to the New York metropolitan area.

Since the 17th century, "papaletes" (paper wrapped tobacco tubes) were the poor man's cigarette in Spain. However, there was a distinctly American cigarette popular in the Southwest from before the Mexican War. This was a roll-your-own corn shuck cigarette smoked by women as well as men, according to reports of early travelers over the old Santa Fe Trail. Spanish-speaking natives of the then Mexican territory carried the "makings" in the pockets of their fancy vests so that smokes could be rolled as desired, and in their pantaloon pockets there was always a flint

Ormolu and agate purse tinderbox which once belonged to Susan B. Anthony. Top has alternating white and red agate slabs. Ca. 1840. Length 2 5/8".

Lighter which uses match cord tinder (lower end protrudes from bottom of case). A turn of the ring on side revolves small wheel of synthetic flint composition (cerium and steel filings) against a fixed steel striker. Resulting sparks fall on charred end of match tinder to ignite it. Illustration three-fourths actual size.

and steel and a roll of cotton tinder for producing the needed light.

If, as it seems possible, the present decline in cigarette smoking continues, there will likely be a corresponding interest on the part of collectors and antiques buffs in the accouterments thereof. More people than ever will be searching out "cigaretana" and here are some of the items they'll be looking for:

Cigarette Cards bearing pictures of stage folk, ball players, prize fighters, ships, birds, and animals, going back to such popular Gay '90s smokes as Sweet Caporels, Admirals, Dukes, Cameos, Conquerors, and Judges, and the colorful card albums published by some manufacturers.

Miniature rugs and blankets of cotton flannel and small colored silks, bearing pictures of presidents, zodiac signs, college emblems, emblems, various national flags and state seals; some of these woven on Jacquard looms like Stevengraphs, distributed with cigarettes in the late 1890s and early 1900s.

Cigarette boxes, the colorful cardboard type which held Turkish Trophies, Hassans, Helmars, and Egytian Deities of the early 1900s; Melachrinos, Makaroffs, Moguls, English Ovals, and London Lifes of World War I years; and the 50-pack tins and the 20-pack paper wrappers of such well-known smokes of the 1920s as Omars, Fatimas, Lucky Strikes, Camels, and Chesterfields. Nor must we forget the various denominations of *revenue stamps*.

Cigarette stompers, popular in brass and aluminum animal shapes in the 1920s and 1930s. *Cigarette holders* (some with the first cigarette filters) which appeared in many varieties in the 1930s and 1940s.

Vest pocket "roll your own" devices, which utilized grain tobacco

such as Bull Durham and Duke's Mixture, and Riz la Croix papers. These were widely advertised for smokers who preferred "homemades" to "tailormades," but did not "possess the manual dexterity to twist their own," even with two hands. Any Western cowboy, of course, could roll beautiful smokes with one hand while galloping his cayuse across the prairie.

Matchsafes, designed early in the 19th century to protect person and clothing from the dangerous consequences of carrying those first, completely unreliable, friction matches, and popular till penny pocket boxes and matchbooks reduced them to obsolescence.

Small safety match boxes, foreign and domestic, with their colorful labels, and *advertising matchbooks*.

Most treasured of all cigarette collectibles are the *pocket lighters* which have long proved practical for those who smoke and often convenient for those who do not.

Sterling silver tinderbox bearing London hallmarks. Steel attached to back edge. Holds a small quantity of tinder, some sulphur dips, and tiny agate flint. Ca. 1800.

Patented in 1907, this ingenious lighter operates in a manner that seems magic. Here, the silver case is shown closed but at the right is a lid from a similar lighter. The large cylinder is lined with a wick saturated in high grade alcohol. Suspended from a protective cage in the lid of the smaller cylinder are several platinum wires on which are strung two sponge platinum globules. When this wire is inserted into the alcohol gas-filled large cylinder, the platinum instantly heats to incandescence and the circular wick is ignited.

Snuff Boxes and Spittle Cups

by EDWIN C. WHITTEMORE

THE USE of tobacco has been so universal and has had such varied forms that objects relating to it constitute many branches of an active antique collecting category. *Spinning Wheel* explored two of these phases in an article on Tobacco Jars in June 1964 and Cuspadores in April 1965. Here we explore others.

America is responsible for tobacco. All over this country American Indians were smoking crude cigar-like rolls of it, enjoying it in rudely fashioned pipes, and "snuffing" it in dried powdery form long before Columbus and others arrived here. Though it did not grow in Europe, smoking and snuffing of other materials was known, and when celebrities like Sir Walter Raleigh brought fragrant aromatic tobacco back to England in the 1500s, it was adopted quickly and enthusiastically, so much so that various rulers forbade its use.

Banning the use of tobacco built the success of snuff, for with snuff there was no telltale smoke to give away the user. Even more responsible for the success of snuff than the possibility of its secret use was its social acceptance, almost as a cult of its own. The very act of snuffing was made a highly polished social ritual. Schools taught it. People practiced it. The opening of the snuff box after the traditional three finger taps, the removal of the snuff, its insertion into the nostrils, even the gratifying sneeze itself became a highly developed rite. No tinder box, no sputtering candle, no awkward handling of a hot coal marred its grace and elegance.

This was also true in America where it flourished, even though tobacco was opposed by the Puritans and by leaders such as William Penn. Snuff is dried powdered tobacco subjected to various processes, chiefly the incorporation of materials such as vanilla, licorice, rose, lemon, verbena, lavender oil, gentian root or tamarind for flavor and aroma. Obviously there had to be containers to carry it in.

The earliest dated snuff box bears the mark 1655. Then came the avalanche of pockets, bags, pouches, bottles, and boxes in materials that were animal, vegetable, and mineral—precious metals, horn, bone, wood, amber, ivory, tin. There were big boxes, little boxes, boxes in all shapes, realistic and otherwise, some representing hats, animals, fans, everything imaginable. There were all sorts of closures, secret compartments, inlay and embellishments, hidden romantic and erotic pictures. They were made for each day of the week, each costume, each special occasion. Consequently, this is a fertile field for the collector of antiques. It is true that there is no strict dividing line between boxes for snuff and for items such as patches, but it matters little, for boxes designed for other purposes were often used to carry snuff. The field is wide and varied. The seeking is fun.

In *Photograph 1*, there are a few typical examples of snuff items, each within the reach of the average collector. The plain small oval snuff box is the most common type, made of tin, in other words, tin-plated rolled sheet iron. It has a snap catch. Next to it is a decorated one of brass, engraved with a floral design and bearing the owner's name; it was apparently a presentation piece, and has a friction lid. The larger oval box is typical toleware or decorated tin, with a snap catch. The rectangular snuff box is unique; it is made of cow's horn, inlaid around the top with tortoiseshell, and has an interior friction closure. Also shown is a snuff mull, fashioned from a horn tip and having a lid with threaded closure. The slim little spoon is a snuff spoon of ivory with a spade and a scoop end, basically for removing a small amount of snuff from a box or bottle.

Photograph 2 shows three types of spittle cups for the ladies. The use of snuff encouraged expectoration, and while many ladies may have used the cuspadores of their coarser menfolk, a touch of daintiness was provided by furnishing the lady with a small, light, handled spittle cup. They were made of many materials, from common white ironstone to delicate flowered china. The photograph shows one of Rockingham pottery, one of Mocha pottery, the one in the center is in lovely deep blue free-blown glass. Dating such items is most difficult. A sound approximation would be early 1800s for the free-blown glass, also the Mocha, and possibly 1850 for the Rockingham.

TOYS AND GAMES

Once playthings for children, early toys are now collectors' items of great value. The simple wooden toys produced by Albert Schoenhut in the early 1900s sell for many times their original price, even when found in somewhat "used" condition. Much earlier toys, constructed of tin usually, and made mobile with simple clock works, bring even more money on today's market. The famous Buddy-L toys—tractors, trucks, trains, and other machinary in miniature—are skyrocketing in value. Old games are apt to be less expensive and have the added value of being usable and entertaining.

HUMPTY DUMPTY CIRCUS

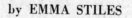

Schoenhut's Humpty Dumpty Circus Set No. 20-38 came complete with collapsible canvas tent, flags of all nations, moveable divided curtain, sawdust ring, trapeze and rings, performers and accessories.

by EMMA STILES
Illustrations from the Author's Collection.

THE HUMPTY DUMPTY Circus of performing animals and performers—the wonder toy of world-wide fame—was introduced in the early 1900s by Albert Schoenhut, perhaps the best known toy manufacturer in the United States. His circus proved one of the country's most popular toys for over a generation and remained in production into the 1930s.

The Humpty Dumpty Circus offered a variety of jointed wooden figures of circus performers and animals, as well as accessory units such as tents, sawdust ring, balancing and acrobatic equipment.

Schoenhut's animals were lifelike, painted with waterproof colors, and where hair was needed, it was true to nature. All animals balanced perfectly in a variety of positions. There were three or more figures with each set. Each figure had four to six joints connected with a rubber elastic cord which held limbs and heads in place, but allowed them to be moved to different positions, offering limitless possibilities.

The funniest toy available, Schoenhut's animals and performers with flexible joints could be put in all sorts of positions. An endless variety of tricks could be done with them. For instance, you could pose one clown kicking another; you could make the lion sit on a chair; put clowns in the middle of a somersault; balance the lady horseback rider on her galloping

Schoenhut's beautiful educated horses were found in sets #s 20-22, 20-31 and 20-38. Top to bottom: Dappled White Horse, Bay and Brown Horse.

Left and right: Giraffe and Zebra handsomely enamelled in life-like colors.

steed; make an elephant stand on his head.

The figures of performers were dressed in appropriate clothes and had slots in their hands and feet making it possible for them to stand on rungs of ladders and backs of chairs.

A booklet was included with the Circus sets which pictured a few of the thousands of tricks that could be made with the Humpty Dumpty circus toys. The booklet also showed the variety of sets available as well as individual accessories.

Listed in Schoenhut's booklet as No. 30-1 were Circus Rings—made of wood, nicely painted, 24¼ inches square, weighing 5 pounds. This splendid accessory added greatly to the enjoyment of the Humpty Dumpty toys as it helped to make them more real and circus-like.

Another fine accessory was the combination circus tent and ring No. 30-5 (Hatter), 24 x 24 x 36 inches, weighing 10½ pounds. The tent was collapsible and was decorated with flags of all nations; it had a moveable divided curtain in the back. The tent was mounted on a 2 x 3 foot wooden base containing a 2-foot sawdust ring which was equipped with a trapeze and rings. The tent could not be sold separately without the board as its peculiar construction made it incomplete without the board. It could not be used with circus rings listed as No. 30-1.

You could purchase separately an adjustable Tight-Rope with base and supports painted in gay colors, 32½ x 6 x 10 inches, weighing 2 pounds, No. 30-10 (Hurt).

The following Humpty Dumpty Circus toy animals were sold individually: elephants, donkeys, dark horses, white horses, poodles, goats, pigs, lions, tigers, leopards, hippopotamuses, gi-

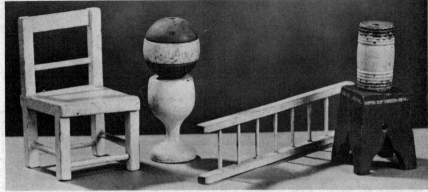

Miniature chairs, ladders, balls, barrels, and various kinds of stands were part of the Humpty Dumpty Circus equipment.

raffes, Arabian camels, zebras, buffalos, bears, alligators, and ostriches.

Max and Moritz, No. 20-22 (Huma), in the Circus contained 7 pieces. Max and Moritz, No. 26-61 (Hurry), contained 16 pieces. Max and Moritz were dressed in clothes and were 7½ inches tall. The set also contained pigs and a variety of acrobatic accessories.

Set No. 20-21 contained 22 pieces including a hobo, clowns, animals, balancing equipment and Schoenhut's beautiful educated horse.

Set No. 20-40 and Set No. 20-41 (Hanger) each had 26 pieces including a lady rider, Turk lion tamer, clowns, animals, animal cages, and balancing accessories.

Thousands of tricks could be performed with Schoenhut's acrobats and tight rope performers in Sets No. 20-50 and 20-52. Each set had 29 pieces including one tight rope with two supports, two lady acrobats, two gent acrobats, one common clown, one Chinaman, one Negro dude, one hobo, one poodle, one fancy clown, two ladders, two chairs, one

(Please Turn the Page)

Dressed clowns had slots in hands and feet making it possible to balance them on rungs of ladders and backs of chairs.

Humpty Dumpty bears, lions, tigers and elephants came in various sizes.

table, one pedestal No. 12-11, one ball, one tub, one barrel, one goblet, one bottle, one cane, one hoop, one parasol, one spinning top, one balancing rod, one flag, one booklet, one tent and ring combination.

Set No. 20-38 consisted of 33 pieces including one elephant with blanket, one donkey with blanket, one white horse, one bay horse, one poodle, one goat, two common clowns, two fancy clowns, one hobo, one Negro dude, one lady rider, one ring master, two ladders, two chairs, two tubs, one ball, three barrels, three goblets, one hoop, one flag, one whip, one cane, one platform saddle, one tent and ring combination and one booklet.

Schoenhut's Humpty Dumpty Menagerie of Wild Beasts, Set No. 20-42, contained 33 pieces. This set was almost identical to Set No. 20-45, Humpty Dumpty Menagerie, the largest complete set. This set contained 34 pieces and was packed in a wooden case, 39 x 26¼ x 6 inches, weighing 41 pounds. Included also were two flexible cages which could be formed into circles or ovals. The two could also be combined to make a single large cage for trained animal performances.

Set No. 20-45 was recommended for its educational value in teaching young children the prime characteristics of wild animals. This set included one lion, one giraffe, one buffalo, one tiger, one leopard, one zebra, one hippopotamus, one alligator, one bear, one ostrich, one monkey, one camel, one lady rider, one Turk lion tamer, one fancy clown, three tubs, two chairs, two ladders, one ball, one flag, one hoop, one whip, one goblet, one barrel, two pedestals No. 12-11, one pedestal No. 12-12, two cages, one tent and ring combination and one booklet.

A double page spread in the May 1903 issue of *Plaything* announced Humpty Dumpty's "Greatest Show on Earth" selling from $1 to $4, the price depending on the number of pieces in each set. Later, more figures were added and these more expensive sets sold well.

The Schoenhut booklet listed the following patent dates on the Humpty Dumpty Circus toys:

United States, December 2, 1902
United States, April 14, 1903
United States, May 17, 1904
United States, June 28, 1904
United States, November 28, 1905
United States, August 21, 1906
United States, January 29, 1907
British, January 12, 1903
Germany, April 12, 1903
Additional patents pending.

Here Comes the

PEEP SHOW

by FLORENCE THOMPSON HOWE

THE Peep Show, when America was young, came to 18th century village streets strapped to the back of the Peep Show man. Somewhat irregular in shape, and having a slanting top not unlike the so-called "Governor Winthrop" desk, this "fun box" was open on the side corresponding to the front of the desk it resembles. A mirror was fastened to the inside of the slanting top, and two circular "windows" with "shutters" were cut in what would correspond to the back of the desk. These round windows were fitted with magnifying glasses. The scenes our ancestors viewed with wonder, when a farm or village green was the boundary of their whole world, were usually old French prints depicting far away places. Popular views were cities on the Continent—London, Paris, Rome, and Venice—and landscapes in Italy and France.

The Peep Show man placed the pictures on the bottom of the box, and the beholder, looking through the round windows or "peep-holes," saw the picture reflected, enlarged and standing alive, much in the manner of the stereopticon views of later date. Tradition has it that the price of the entertainment was 5¢ in America, possibly a penny or half-penny in London.

The Peep Show, as an institution, dates back for centuries. Old English court records in London, and in outlying districts, too, show the Peep Show man often entangled with the law. His living, at best, was a precarious one.

One authority wrote that the English Peep Show man tramped through the country with the show on his back and a pair of trestles under his arm. He blew a trumpet or rang a bell to collect a crowd, and putting his trestles down he placed the show upon it. Those expectant ones lucky enough to have coins to spare could peep through the circular windows and behold the wonders within. As each picture was shown, the old showman described the subjects with dramatic genius such as only a Cockney could muster. It seems reasonable to assume that those venturesome vendors who braved an Atlantic crossing used much the same tactics in America.

Richardson Wright, in his *Hawkers & Walkers in Early America*, likens the Peep to the Puppet Show. One of these strange little shows was encountered by Nathaniel Hawthorne at North Adams, Massachusetts, in 1838. The picture he drew, as Mr. Wright suggested, was rather pathetic. "After supper, as the sun was setting, a man passed the door [of the tavern] with a hand organ, connected with which was a row of figures . . . all keeping time to the lively or slow tunes of the organ. The man had a pleasant but sly, dark face. He carried his whole establishment on his shoulders, it being fastened to a staff which he rested in the ground when he performed. He had come over the high solitary mountains where for miles hardly a soul could have been encountered to hear his music."

The Peep Show pictured above and left (back and front views) was found in New England, and is believed to have been used in the Massachusetts towns of Hadley, Amherst, and vicinity. The box stands about 27" high.

SAND TOYS

by CLARA NISBET

THE TERM, "Sand Toy," covers, in general, those mechanical playthings set in motion by the force of sand pouring onto a power or paddle wheel. These toys may be freestanding objects with simple mechanisms, or they may be elaborate boxed-in affairs with glass-fronted stages on which one or more figures go through prescribed motions. These mechanical toys date back, in some form, for several centuries — some authorities claim to the Middle Ages.

Nineteenth century toymakers in France and Germany produced sand toys by inexpensive methods and exported them far and wide. American toy manufacturers produced a line of their own about 1825 to compete with imported sand toys. Examples of the latter are considered very desirable collectibles today. The maker's label is often the only means of identification.

Cardboard was first employed in the manufacture of the more pretentious box-type sand toys, followed later on by those with wooden frames. A piece of glass covered one of the larger sides behind which was a stage with appropriate setting on which the figures went through their routine. The remaining space in the box concealed the mechanism, consisting of a master hopper from which sand poured through a chute onto a power or paddle wheel; this, in turn, was connected by rods and levers to the parts of the figures to be activated. The cycle completed, the sand settled in a reservoir at the base of the toy. Simplicity of the works is considered a mark of antiquity; the more complicated multiple-action sand toys were an invention of later years.

The sand toy pictured is representative of its type—an import of about 1850. The wooden box stands 14 inches high, is 11 inches wide, and 4 inches in depth. One inch of the depth is given over to the stage which has as a backdrop a hand-colored print; also hand colored are the cardboard cutouts of the man and his wheel, with signs announcing "J. G. Dunn, Cutler, any tools set & ground," and "Knives &c ground."

Directions in faded print affixed to the back of the box read: "To work the toy turn the box over so as to allow the sand to fall in the receiver, then place it on a level surface and the figure and wheel will be in motion." This accomplished, Mr. Dunn springs into action swinging his left leg back and fourth, raising and lowering his arms to apply the tool held in his hands to the wheel, which is spinning rapidly.

Sand Toy, ca. 1850, From the Author's Collection

These entertaining toys are sensitive to atmospheric changes and undue jarring, so must be protected from over-enthusiastic handling. One wonders that any of these playthings of yore have survived the ravages of use and time.

A later sand toy, developed on this same principal of sand falling from a higher to a lower level to make things move, was the Sandy Andy, patented in 1909 and manufactured by the Sand Toy Company of Pittsburgh. This was a free-standing toy with hoppers, chutes, and receiving buckets, the action being supplied by sand poured into the hopper by the child at play. The Sand Toy Company was taken over by the Wolverine Supply and Manufacturing Company, makers of lithographed-metal toys, which has continued to make Sandy Andys, with various improvements, for years. The 1909 model is pictured in *Toys in America,* by Marshall and Inez McClintock.

Illustrations from the author's collection. Photographs by Adam Kierst, South Amboy, N. J.

IRON TRACKLESS TOY TRAINS

by EMMA STILES

WIDELY SOUGHT BY COLLECTORS today are the trackless iron toy trains which first appeared in America in the late 1870s. These trackless trains were string-pulled, hand-pushed, or mechanical, the mechanical locomotives housing a strong clockwork movement.

Made of cast, as well as malleable iron—the malleable being earlier and most rare — locomotives and molded cars were cast in lengthwise sections. Molten metal was poured into sand molds, which were removed when the metal had cooled and solidified. Joining the seams, adding the axle and wheels completed the car.

The first iron trains were rather stiff in style, more or less copied from earlier tin types; many were virtually scale models. From 1880 to 1890, they grew more refined and more elaborate. They continued to flourish up to about 1930. By then, the models were generally smaller and less detailed.

Locomotives were sold individually, as were extra large freight and passenger cars, measuring more than 17 inches long, and wholesaled in 1893 at $13.50 per dozen. Locomotives and tenders were sold as a unit; but most often the complete train consisted of locomotive, tender, and one, two, or three cars. The tender, of course, always came with a complete train, but seldom was a little tag-behind caboose included. Locomotives pulling one freight car and one passenger car were called "combination trains."

Most freight cars were gondola-like; many carried a brakeman standing in each open car. Large closed freight cars were manufactured with movable side doors; these are considered rare today. Vestibule, observation, and passenger cars were also made.

The Wilkins Toy Company of Keene, N. H., in their 1911 toy catalog advertised "coal freight trains"—locomotive, tender, and one, two, or three coal cars. These were enameled, embossed, and decorated. "P.R.R." in high raised gold letters covered the entire sides of each coal car. A movement of lever to either side of the coal car opened swinging doors in the bottom, allowing the load to dump; returning lever to normal position closed the doors.

The terms of the Wilkins Toy Co. stated "All shipments F.O.B." They made no allowance for breakage, nor guaranteed delivery. Their goods were packed in regular crates or cases as specified and if ordered differently or in less quantity, a higher price would be charged for special handling. Of the 32 trains in their 1911 catalog, only two included a caboose.

Ehrich Brothers, Eighth Avenue, New York, N. Y., advertised in their 1882 winter mail order catalog a solid iron toy train—locomotive, tender, and

two freight cars, painted red and black, packed in a sliding-cover wooden box at 95 cents, but stated shipment would be made by express.

The Ives, Blakeslee and Williams Company, 294 Broadway, New York City, whose factory was in Bridgeport, Conn., displayed a most attractive line of iron toy trains in their 1893 toy catalog. Locomotives had been included in the Ives toy production since the 1870s. The Ives company was the great pioneer in the iron toy field and where it led, others followed. Competitive imitations, lacking the finer detail and castings of the Ives models, appeared a year or two after Ives introduced some new toy.

In their 1893 catalog, Ives introduced an entirely new and original steel passenger train with observation car. It was 58 inches long; the locomotive and tender were iron and japanned black; the passenger coaches were of steel and painted in brilliant colors.

In the same catalog, Ives advertised

The manufacturer(s) of these iron toy trains could not be identified, but they are typical of the types made in the late 19th century and can be found in various sizes.

their new model, the "Cannon Ball Train," the largest iron train made, with locomotive, tender, closed freight car and vestibule car. The number "189" was embossed in an oblong panel on both sides of the tender; "Union/*/Line/*" was embossed on the right front side of the freight car, and "Capacity 50,000 pounds" on the back side. The decoration was reversed on the opposite side. Printed in raised letters on the passenger car were the words, "Limited Vestibule Express." Despite its lettering, the passenger car was of the non-vestibule design. The locomotive was an extremely accurate representation of the real thing. The details on it extended to tiny bolt heads, cast on the side rods. When coupled together as a unit, this large cast iron trackless pull-train measured almost five feet long. It wholesaled at $54 per dozen. Three trains, packed for shipping in a wooden crate, 13 x 20 x 32 inches, weighed 104 pounds.

"Cannon Ball Train," the largest iron toy train made by Ives, Blakeslee and Williams Company, in 1893.

The Carpenter Line of Toys catalog, a 5x7 inch, 22-page, paper-cover pamphlet, reprinted by F. A. O. Schwarz of New York for the Antique Toy Collectors Club, carried a good selection of iron trains. Though the date of the original catalog is not given, patent dates appear under each picture. One freight train listed five patents and re-issue dates between May 4, 1880, and May 13, 1884. The name Williard & McKee, 21 Park Place, New York City, presumably the distributors, appeared on the front cover of the catalog.

There is some mystery in connection with the Carpenter toys, for no one yet has been able to pin down a

in the Carpenter catalog, not one came with a caboose.

The Hubley Manufacturing Company, Lancaster, Pa., in their 1906 catalog, advertised train "No. 60-½"—locomotive, tender, and two passenger cars, polished copper oxidized." It weighed over 12 pounds and was 43 inches long. There were 14 complete trains shown in the Hubley catalog; of these only three pulled a caboose.

The most desirable of the early iron locomotives, aside from the very large pieces, are 2-2-0 models, lettered "Big Six" or bearing the patent dates May 4, 1880, May 25, 1880, June 8, 1880, Aug. 16, 1881, or Aug. 19, 1884. Models bearing these patent dates were manufactured until about 1900 by J. & E. Stevens Co., Cromwell, Conn., as well as by others.

Of the 1915 period, the largest size cars, 15 inches or more in length, any of the model street cars, and the iron electric-type locomotive are the most desirable.

The little locomotives with the tender cast integral and only one pair of movable wheels were staple designs in virtually every line for more than 40 years and are quite common. To entice children to play with the trains, parents called, "Johnnie, come pull the puffers." The subsequent puffing noise that was heard issued not from the train but from its proud owner's pursed lips.

"Michigan Central R.R.," a scarce nickle-plated iron toy train believed to have been made by either the Kenton Hardware Company, Kenton, Ohio, or the Grey Iron Company, Reading, Pennsylvania (?), ca. 1910.

Another special train advertised by Ives that year was the celebrated White Train or Ghost Train, 41 inches long—locomotive, tender, and two white vestibule cars. It wholesaled at $21 per dozen; one dozen, packed in a crate, weighed 198 pounds.

The least expensive four-unit passenger train in the Ives 1893 catalog was called "The Hero." It was 14 inches long and sold at $4 per dozen. The least expensive four-unit freight sold at $2 a dozen; it, too, was 14 inches long. Of the 13 complete trains displayed in their 1893 catalog, not one showed a caboose.

manufacturer's name or address for them. Apparently Carpenter farmed out his work. Patent No. 227216 for a toy train was issued to Francis W. Carpenter at Rye, N. Y., on May 4, 1880, and Patent No. 298446, for a toy railroad, to Francis W. Carpenter at Harrison, N. Y., on May 13, 1884. Of the five complete trains displayed

"Baltimore & Ohio" iron toy train attributed to the Wilkins Toy Company, ca. 1900.

GAME HUNTING IS BIG

by LEE DENNIS

Flinch, first manufactured by the Flinch Card Co., Kalamazoo, Mich., after 1930 by Parker Brothers, at one time outsold all other card games.

All Parker game photos, courtesy of Parker Brothers Company. Other photos by James W. Milligan.

Old Bachelor, Forlorn & Lonely, was made by McLoughlin Bros., 1892; their *House that Jack Built* in 1887.

THE FASCINATION of old American games is luring more collectors each year. Games are big business today, but their beginnings were simple enough in the years ago when entertainment centered around the home. Like toys, the average life of a game is short, so the chances of finding old ones fairly intact are challenging.

Of the earlier manufacturers of games whose companies have persisted, two were from Massachusetts —Milton Bradley and George Parker. Milton Bradley started in 1860 in Springfield. Today the Milton Bradley trademark, "Makers of the World's Best Games," is internationally known, particularly in the field of education. The firm is especially noted for games which make learning fun. George Parker, in 1883, began the manufacture of games in Salem, in a small building next door to a paint shop. Today Salem is known as

"the game capital of the world." Parker Brothers, at their present factory, have an archives of their own old games and also of their competitors'. It is well worth a visit.

The Checkered Game of Life was the first game put out by Milton Bradley, in 1860. (See SW feb '61.) It has its counterpart today in the company's new *Game of Life.* Early Bradley games drew upon nursery rhymes and included *Old Woman in the Shoe* (1880) and *Old Mother Hubbard.*

A century ago, regular playing cards were considered by the devout to be "instruments of the devil." So, many innocuous card games were invented to overcome this stigma and prejudice. One of the many to be introduced was the game of *Authors,* brought out by the Bradley Company late in the last century. The game itself was devised in 1861 by August Smith, a teacher in a girls' school in

Salem, Massachusetts, with the aid of several of his student young ladies. When it became apparent that "puritans" were playing *Authors* without objection, other game manufacturers brought out their own version of the game.

The *Game of Mind Reading,* which appeared in 1887, actually evolved from the efforts of several guests at Milton Bradley's home. *Fortune Telling Cards,* even more successful than the mind reading game, came out in 1908, and enjoyed great popularity with its amusing fortunes.

A children's favorite, *The Toy Town Conductor's Game,* was issued in 1910. Perhaps one of the oldest and most popular of Milton Bradley's children's games was the *Uncle Wiggily* board game, adapted from Howard R. Garis's rabbit bedtime story series, which was nationally syndicated in newspapers, as well as in book covers. Mr. Garis, a newspaper man from Newark, New Jersey, thought up the game, too. First published by Bradley in 1919, it remained a best seller for the company for 40 years, and the genial rabbit and his animal friends continue to delight youngsters today.

In 1920, Milton Bradley acquired a controlling interest in McLoughlin Brothers, of Brooklyn, New York, an early game manufacturer and book publishing concern. Their older games included *Jackstraws, The House that Jack Built* (1887), *Fish Pond* (1890), *Yacht Race* (1891), and *Old Bachelor* (1892). McLoughlin Brothers moved from Brooklyn to Springfield and operated as a separate entity within the Bradley Company until 1944. In Springfield, the McLoughlin division concentrated mainly on the sale of books.

Still, the Milton Bradley Company's greatest fame lies in its contribution to the field of education. Over the years, they have produced a wealth of teaching materials and school aids for the school systems of the United States.

The games of Parker Brothers Company, on the other hand, reflect the whole American saga. They make intriguing collectibles because they mirror the American way of life over the last 80 years.

One of the first board games was their *Mansion of Happiness.* This was

(Please turn the page)

1904 saw the first edition of Parker Brothers' *Sherlock Holmes.*

Mansion of Happiness, by W. & S. B. Ives, 1840, was bought and reissued by Parker Brothers in 1885.

Bradley's early *Old Mother Hubbard.*

Innocence Abroad, by Parker Brothers (1888), "encouraged" travel.

Parker's *Grocery Store Game,* with sugar 5¢ a pound, was an improvement of their *Corner Grocery* (1897).

Uncle Wiggily, of storybook fame, 1919, is still a Bradley product.

Game of Banking, another Parker product, came out in 1883.

originally a card game devised by Miss Anne W. Abbott of Beverly, Massachusetts, about 1840, and published by W. & S. B. Ives of Salem. However, Parker Brothers bought all rights to the old Ives games and reissued *Mansion of Happiness* in 1885.

Games of transportation and travel included *Innocence Abroad* (1888), *Across the Continent* (1891), *Crossing the Ocean* (1893), and *Touring*. Occupations were incorporated into *Banking* (1883), *Corner Grocery* (1897), and *The Doctors and the Quack*. There were many of sports. *Pike's Peak or Bust* (1895), *The Battle of Manila* (1898), and *Klondike* echo events of American history.

Popular Card Games

Sherlock Holmes appeared in 1904; in 1905, Parker Brothers came out with *Pit*, which is still featured. *Rook* made its debut in 1906, and enjoyed great popularity. *Lindy*, "the new flying game," was opportunely published by Parker Brothers after Lindbergh's Atlantic flight in 1927.

In the early 1930s, Parker Brothers bought out the Flinch Card Company of Kalamazoo, Michigan. This company had manufactured only the one card game, *Flinch*, which was played with a thick deck of cards from 1 to 15. For a time, *Flinch* outsold all other card games ever published.

Parker Brothers games are known for the "excellence of their actual playing qualities." This came about because George Parker, the founder, tested each of his games by personally playing them over and over with friends. He constantly refined and improved their playing abilities. All Parker games today attest to this background of ingenuity and knowledge of what people need to be amused. Their most famous game of all time, *Monopoly*, may well be the "antique" game of tomorrow.

A beginning game collector has an enriching hunt ahead of him. At the same time, he will become intrigued with the parlor amusements of yesterday.

by EDWIN C. WHITTEMORE

CARD playing is a universal pastime, centuries old, but curiously, nobody knows who invented playing cards. Some say the 12th century Chinese Emperor Seun-Ho thought them up to keep his many wives busy and contented. Others claim a Gentleman of the Court of Charles VI of France created them to divert that mad monarch from melancholia. A Hindu legend attributes them to India. The Puritans assigned their origin to the Devil. The crews of Christopher Columbus' ships played cards during the sea voyage, and found American natives using painted sticks in a game similar to card games of the Far East.

Coincidence, the simultaneous unrelated birth and development of an idea without any mutual dependence whatsoever, probably accounts for this early global use of playing cards. It seems a more likely theory than that a Chinese or Indian creation was carried so immediately throughout the world by caravan, sea trade, or the Crusaders.

This widespread and long continued use of playing cards makes them, for collectors, a field of infinite variety. To work out a complete step-series system of categories for filing collections of playing cards would take the combined talents of a magician, computer programmer, library authority, and anthropologist, so endless are the variations. Many collectors start with cards of national origins — French, German, and the like—then move on to variations.

Here we can merely suggest some of the special categories which make for interesting study within the field—variables in special classifications to round out a collection already begun, or to start a new collection on a sound foundation.

Variations in Shape and Size. Today's standard playing card is 2¼ inches wide, 3½ inches long. For years, it was 2½ inches by 3½ inches, but was made narrower for easier handling. A vast percentage of cards are either one of these sizes. Yet now and then, other shapes and sizes have come into being.

In *Illustration A,* we see, left to right: a standard 2¼ by 3½" card; an older, 2½ by 3½" size, with a special design for the poor sighted; a round card; a narrow Chinese card; and an odd angular-cut card.

Round cards and those with different colors for different suits seem to be the variations most often attempted by card manufacturers; neither has made any permanent headway. There are, of course, miniature and jumbo-sized packs of cards, and some with curve-cut sides. Any collection of playing cards should include examples of such variations if only to prove the public's insistence on the conventional rectangular card.

Variations in Card Identification. Today's card player is well used to immediately identifying any card by the suit symbol and unit designation in the upper left hand corner of the card, as shown by the first card in *Illustration B.* This is a standard card, and a quick look at the corner shows it to be the six of Diamonds. The other cards in this group indicate that quick identification was not always possible. The second in the row is an old eight of Hearts; only by looking carefully and mentally counting the spots does one recognize it. Next is an early attempt to simplify the situation by reproducing the entire card in two corners, of benefit when cards, held in the hand, are not seen in their entirety. Though an improvement, the small card symbols are not easily recognized. The last is an early version of today's refinement with suit symbol and numerical designation.

Variations: Single or Double Header? Many steps have been taken over the years to make the handling of cards easier and identification quicker. Originally there was only one "right-side-up" to a card — for example, only one head to a Jack—and the cards had to be arranged in the hand accordingly. In *Illustration C,* two cards at left are very early, simplified "Single Headers," usable only one way up. The other two cards show two ages or steps of "Double Headers" where either end of the card may be upmost in the hand and the card is equally recognizable. The latter two also illustrate the gradual improvement in both design and reproduction through which card manufacture progressed.

(Please turn the page)

**589
Toys
Games**

ILLUSTRATION B

ILLUSTRATION A

Variations in Suit Symbols. Americans are pretty well used to the four standardized suit symbols — Spades, Clubs, Hearts, Diamonds—yet one of the greatest places for discovering variety in cards is in the matter of suit symbols. Incidentally, the suits (and there are usually four) can in most cases be traced back to symbolism for class distinctions.

In early Italian and Spanish cards, a sword took the place of the spade and represented nobility; a cup or chalice represented the clergy; money, the citizens; and clubs or sticks, the peasantry. The French used a lancehead for nobility, hearts for the clergy, clover for the husbandmen, and a diamond-shaped arrowhead for the common soldier.

590
Toys
Games

Illustration D shows four cards from an early German deck. The four suits seem to be bells, acorns, hearts, and leaves; their descendants today, respectively, would be Spades, Clubs, Hearts, and Diamonds. The illustrations on these particular cards are all in a series, apparently portraying a journey of conquest or adventure, perhaps a contemporary event of importance. The search for cards with colorful, imaginative, and different suit symbols is one of the great joys of card collecting.

Variations — Individual Examples. So endless are the variations in playing cards that about all one can do is to point out the types of differences and the divergence of the scope of card design as illustrated by specific examples.

In *Illustration E*, there are four such cards. First, the Ten of Stars might be called a Patriotic Card, or perhaps a Propaganda Card. It is of Civil War vintage, produced by somebody who felt it a healthy and pleasant habit to be thinking and talking stars instead of diamonds or hearts. This style of card has never had long life. Next is an Educational Card, a type which has been successfully used on many occasions for training purposes along with recreation. This is from a training pack designed to educate plane spotters as to the outline or silhouettes of enemy planes.

The third is a simple illustration of the color-manipulation idea which has been tried and tried, but has never been permanently successful. This example is a standard card with black

ILLUSTRATION F

ILLUSTRATION E

ILLUSTRATION C

instead of white background. The last card is an amusing specimen from a type that is thoroughly delightful, and could almost be a subject for a collection in itself. This is known as a Transformation Card. The basic idea is to incorporate the suit symbol into an illustration—not easy to do in the multiple spot cards. This one is the five of Diamonds, with the five diamonds forming the helmets of soldiers in "The Begorra Brigade."

Variations—Oddities. Examples in *Illustration F* demonstrate more rewards in seeking the unusual and varied in playing cards, irrespective of year or nationality, or any other rigid standard of classification. First is an extremely early playing card— simple, crude and charming; the design was hand drawn and hand colored on paper, then folded over the edges of a stiffer card and glued. The second is from a deck advertising cut plug tobacco, each card showing a "pin-up girl."

The center card is from an out-and-out comic pack; the poor King has an eye patch, arm bandage, foot bandage, and cane! Next is a political card, no doubt a campaign tool, showing Grover Cleveland, candidate for President. The last card is a curious mixture — a World's Fair souvenir, combining various ideas in playing card improvements, such as the actual use of the word "ten" for quick recognition of the ten spot of Clubs, plus two types of corner spots.

Risk for the excitement of risk itself, added to man's love of entertainment and competition gives us a world where countless millions of playing cards exist. So vast are their variables that collecting them may be simple and inexpensive, or life-long, and substantial.

ILLUSTRATION D

TRIVETS AND BOOTJACKS

Trivets can be plain or fancy, artistically made or primitive, have a single use or a multiple use, and can be found in a variety of metals from rich gold-colored brass to blackest iron. In almost every instance, they are still functional, and many collectors enjoy using them every day. Bootjacks, on the other hand, have long been outmoded, but their appeal to collectors is just as strong. Here's a field for collecting that offers a wide variety of forms and designs. There are bootjack and trivet collections numbering in the hundreds with not one single duplicate.

IS IT

Fig. 1

Fig. 2

A TRIVET ?

by WILLIAM PALEY

Sketches are by the author from pieces in his collection.

Fig. 3

Fig. 4

A recent letter from a knowledgeable friend chastised me for using the word "trivet" indiscriminately in referring to stands in general. He made me wonder how many people, both collectors and dealers, also are guilty of the offense, or if it can be called an offense.

Of course, by early references, he is right in stating that the object upon which a sad-iron rests is not a trivet but a "stand." There are, however, not only trivets and iron stands but also kettle stands, teapot stands, winters, quads, footmen, brackets, broilers, and rests for various specific objects.

The 11th edition of the *Encyclopaedia Britannica* (1910-1911) defined a trivet as "a small metal tripod for holding cooking vessels near a fire. The word is also applied to a round, square or oval openwork plate, usually of steel or brass, fixed to the bars of a grate by a socket for keeping hot plates, dishes, or food." Chambers's *Twentieth Century Dictionary* calls a trivet "a stool or other thing supported on three feet: a movable iron frame in a kitchen fire-grate for supporting kettles, &c."

Figures 1, 2, 3 and *4* illustrate the two types of trivet that these definitions mention. The trivets in *Fig. 1* and *Fig. 2*, of heavy and early wrought iron, were for holding cauldrons and heavy pots used for cooking and heating. *Fig. 3* shows a brass trivet, which, according to the *Oxford Universal Dictionary* definition, is late Middle English. It has an adjustable iron bracket for securing it to the top bar

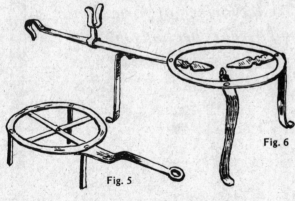

Fig. 6

Fig. 5

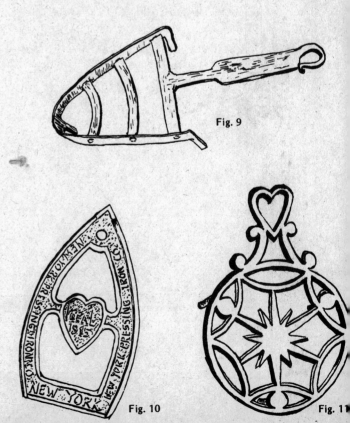

Fig. 9

Fig. 7

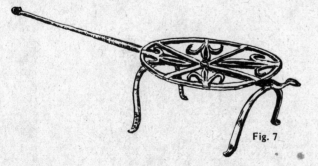

Fig. 8

Fig. 10

Fig. 11

of a grate. *Fig. 4* shows an 18th century finely wrought iron bracket trivet. It follows that a trivet may have either three legs or no legs at all.

In *Figs. 5* and *6*, we have hand-wrought iron pieces similar to those shown by Wallace Nutting in his *Furniture Treasury* (No. 4009 and No. 4010) and called 'trivets.'

Webster's *Third New International Dictionary Unabridged* gives as one of three definitions of a trivet: "a metal rack for holding meat roasting in a pan." The object in *Fig. 7* would qualify. Wallace Nutting called similar objects "Whirling Broilers." Jeanne Minhinnick, in her new book, *At Home in Upper Canada*, calls them "Gridirons."

The early steel sad-iron rest shown in *Fig. 8* and the earlier hand-wrought iron one in *Fig. 9* are called "trivets" today by most authors. Funk & Wagnall's *Standard College Dictionary* (1963) defines a trivet as "a three-legged stand for holding cooking vessels in a fireplace, a heating iron, or a hot dish on a table." The sad-iron stand in *Fig. 10*, dated 1915, made for the New York Pressing Iron Co., and the teapot stand in *Fig. 11* are, therefore, both examples of cast iron trivets.

The brass quads in *Figs. 12, 13* and *14* also qualify as trivets by this definition. The forelegs of the brass piece in *Fig. 15* are adjustable when this trivet is attached to the grate. It can also hold a kettle or teapot when standing on its own three shaped steel legs.

A winter, according to Chambers's *Twentieth Century Dictionary* is "an appliance for fixing on the front of a grate, to keep warm a teakettle or the like." A winter, then, would be a type of trivet, illustrated in *Figs. 3, 4* or *15*.

A footman is "a name given among articles of furniture to a metal stand, usually of polished steel or brass, and either oblong or oval in shape, for keeping plates and dishes hot before a dining - room fire. In the days before the general use of hot-water dishes the footman possessed definite utility; although it is still in occasional use, it is now chiefly regarded as an ornament. It is especially common in the hardware counties of England, where it is still frequently seen; the simple conventionality of its form is not inelegant." – 11th edition, *Encyclopaedia Britannica*. *Figs. 16* and *17* show decorative pieces which would satisfy this definition of a footman.

A kettle stand, either oblong, oval or round, has long legs, and usually stood beside a fireplace in either kitchen, dining room, parlor or bedroom. *Figs. 13, 14, 15* and *16* show variations.

Is applying the word "trivet" to all of these, taking the meaning of the word too loosely? Many words have altered in meaning within the past several decades. Perhaps our word "trivet" now has the broader meaning that most authors have given it, and includes not only kettle stands and fire-bar trivets, but also winters, footmen, teapot and iron stands.

(Pen and ink sketches are by the author.)

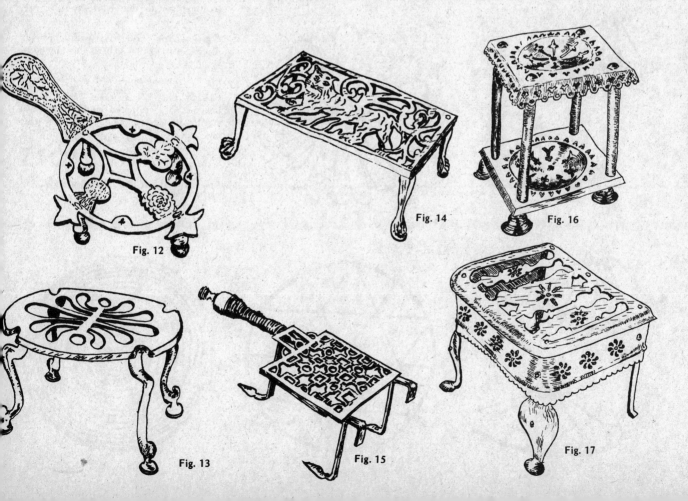

Fig. 12

Fig. 13

Fig. 14

Fig. 15

Fig. 16

Fig. 17

WIRE

by WILLIAM PALEY

Fig. 3

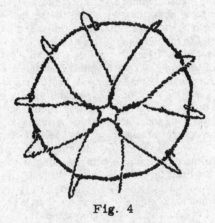

Fig. 2

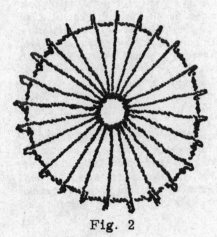

2 (a)

2 (b)

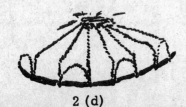

2 (c)

2 (d)

Fig. 5

Fig. 6

Fig. 7

Fig. 1

AS A NEW and rather novel collection, wire trivets offer a rewarding challenge for both the novice and advanced collector. Not only are they still reasonably priced and easily obtained, but they also are available in an interesting assortment of designs.

The production of wire goes back to at least 2000 B. C., when very fine threads were made of gold and other precious metals to be used in the fabric of cloth for the wealthy. Less malleable metals were flattened into sheets, then cut into strips which could be shaped with mallet and file into coarse "wire." In Europe during the late 13th century, there was developed a method of drawing, or pulling wire through a series of progressively smaller holes until the desired diameter was obtained—a process requiring

Key to Illustrations

Figs. 1 and 2—The 12- and 24-spoke wheel, made of twisted wire, are two of the most common patterns available. Various rim treatments of the latter are shown in (a), (b), (c) and (d).

Fig. 3—A reversible trivet with rim made of a ¼″ corrugated strip of sheet metal to support the wire.

Fig. 4—Two-strand, twisted wire trivet.

Fig. 5—This 6″ diameter trivet has a heavier wire scalloped rim. The twisted strands of each spoke separate near rim, and one strand loops down to form a leg.

Fig. 6—Rim is of heavier gauge than framework of this 9″ diameter cake stand.

Fig. 7—Spiral of wire is bound to each of eight spokes with finer wire.

Fig. 4

TRIVETS

Sketches by the author

great physical strength for its success.

The Industrial Revolution of the late 18th and early 19th centuries brought about the invention of machinery for the making of wire. Hence, although they may not be so old as some of the wrought iron trivets, those of wire have been made since early in the 19th century to replace the heavier iron ones.

Wire has been made into teapot stands, stands for use with sadirons, and stands for cooling cakes and pastries. The thickness of wire in the trivet depends on the use for which the piece was intended. Some trivets have employed two or three different grades of wire in their making.

The pieces sketched here show some of the designs obtainable, and suggests the ingenuity of their makers.

Fig. 8—The three legs of this 11¾" diameter trivet are down-turned loops of the heavier wire rim.

Figs. 9 and 10—A lacy, snowflake pattern of cut and hammered wire.

Fig. 11—8" in diameter, this trivet is both dainty and sturdy.

Fig. 12—A heavy wire spiral, confined by lugs on the two metal cross bars that support it and form legs.

Fig. 13—Metal collars hold the ends of the wires and form the legs of this 6⅞" piece.

Fig. 14—A dainty piece, welded together.

Fig. 15—Outer framework and legs are one length of wire.

Figs. 16 and 17—A single and double triangle. Joints are bound with finer wire.

(Please Turn the Page)

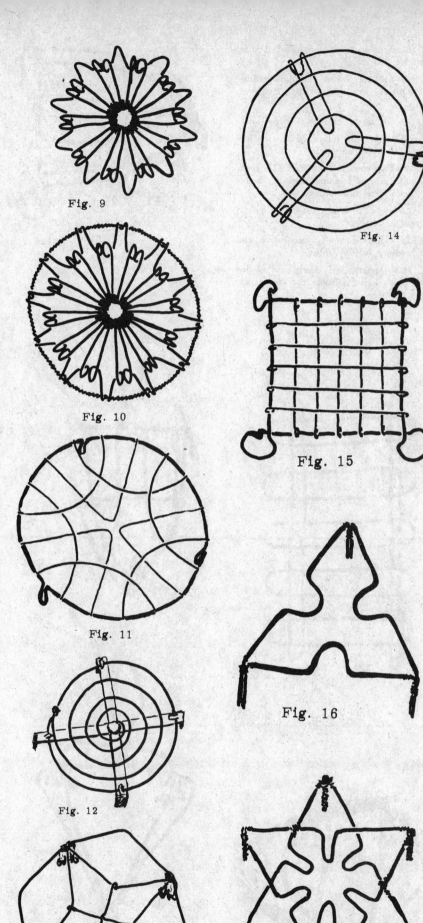

Fig. 9

Fig. 10

Fig. 11

Fig. 12

Fig. 13

Fig. 14

Fig. 15

Fig. 16

Fig. 17

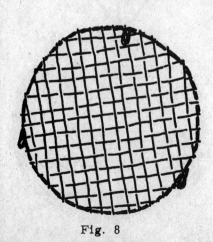

Fig. 8

Fig. 18—Nine cigar-shaped loops of wire comprise this stand.

Fig. 19—An early trivet. Bars and handle are made of cut and twisted strips of metal.

Fig. 20—A more common iron stand.

Fig. 21—A folding handle and wire bar make this trivet unusual.

Fig. 22—Two strands of twisted wire form top and handle; feet are made by bending down wire and soldering.

Fig. 23 and 24—Iron stands, with and without gallery.

Fig. 25—This unusually decorative and sturdy piece is 10½″ long.

Fig. 26—A particularly early and choice trivet with gallery, made at a forge, entirely of wire.

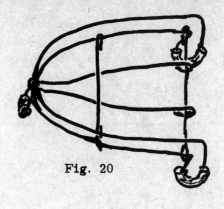

Fig. 20

Fig. 21

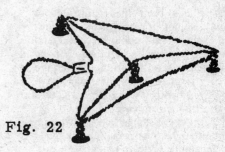

Fig. 22

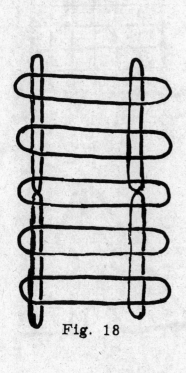

Fig. 18

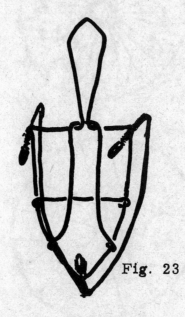

Fig. 23

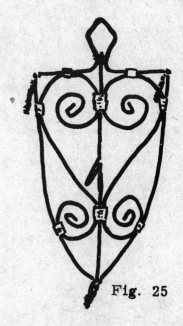

Fig. 25

Fig. 19

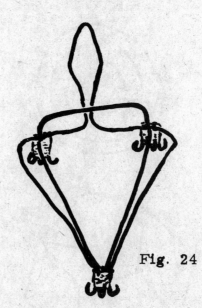

Fig. 24

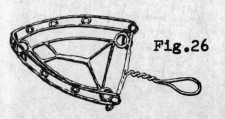

Fig. 26

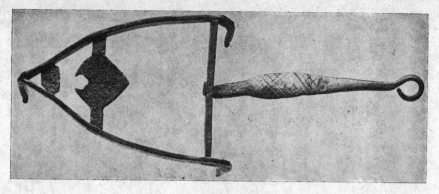

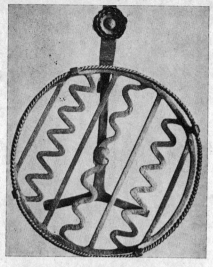

Handwrought Iron Trivets

by DICK HANKENSON

HANDWROUGHT iron trivets of the eighteenth and early nineteenth centuries — and a few were known to be in use in America as early as the seventeenth—stood in the fireplace or on the hearth to hold a pot or kettle whose contents were to be kept warm. They were of all sizes and shapes — triangular, round, rectangular, even of irregular design. They were made with high legs and short legs — the high-legged trivets were the earliest type—with handles, and without handles. Some were made at home by the man of the house; most were fashioned by the village blacksmith. Either the housewife suggested a design for her trivet, or the blacksmith followed his own ideas. No two are found exactly alike.

Many methods of decoration were used. In some cases, metal was heated in the forge, bent into shapes and twisted for artistic decoration. Trivets are found with inserts of iron, or even copper, cut in fancy shapes. Sometimes these inserts were hammered attractively.

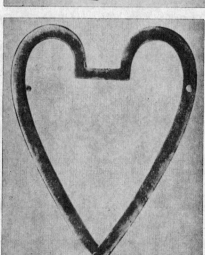

Trivet legs and feet were often very fancy. Some were twisted and flattened; more were welded to the body by the forge-welding process. In this, the metal was heated in the forge to a very high temperature; a little flux was added; and the two pieces of metal were joined by hammering them together on the anvil.

Occasionally trivets were found with the legs riveted on. Here, a hole was made in the edge of the body, the shaped leg inserted, and the protruding end pounded until it was riveted tight. This method was also used when an insert was added as part of the body.

Handles were frequently ornate, and disclosed a fine quality of workmanship. Rattail ends were made by heating the iron and drawing the metal to a point by hammer and anvil.

Wrought iron stands for smoothing irons, also called trivets, were in early use. They are most often found in triangular shape, though they were made in other shapes, too. About 1830 cast iron trivets appeared, and by 1850, the handwrought iron trivet was well on its way to oblivion.

Wrought iron trivets, pictured, from the author's collection, indicate various types and shapes that may be found, and should be cherished.

ILLUSTRATIONS

Counterclockwise from top:

Intricate detail is shown here; crossbars are mortised into body, legs bent down, rattail handle used. Design is hand-cut with cold chisel.

Rare Lazy Susan with unusual railing of twisted iron. Body is of forged pieces welded together; side supports for railing are riveted to body, bent over railing. Legs are forged and bent, welded together; short handle has applied 3-piece rosette. Large loose rivet allows turning.

The rim here is a flat iron strip; center bars and legs are each one piece, riveted to rim.

Early "Heart" design; body forged of one piece and welded at point; legs riveted to body.

Forged of round iron, three separate pieces are used, with legs bent down. All pieces forge-welded together.

Three separate pieces of square iron are forge-welded together; legs and body are formed of the same pieces.

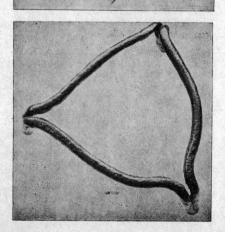

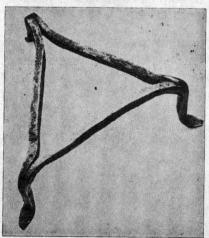

BOOTJACKS

by WILLIAM PALEY

Illustrations drawn by the author.

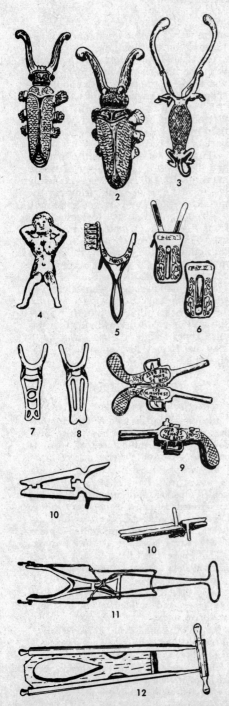

A BOOTJACK, like a footscraper, usually had its place near the service door of the house—often doing double duty as a doorstop. Its primary function was to assist in removing the high, tight boots, which were fashionable in the eighteenth and nineteenth centuries, without the inconvenience to the wearer of stooping or of soiling his hands. Not only were bootjacks made for gentlemen but for ladies as well, as evidenced by the adjustable and the double-ended types. The Industrial Revolution with its increasing emphasis on travel, and the Civil War which necessitated it, brought about the invention of the small portable and folding bootjacks.

When low-cut, laced shoes became popular late in the nineteenth century, bootjacks, like the boots for which they were designed, became obsolete. Many have survived, however, and some interesting examples can be found in cast and wrought iron, brass, and wood. The several illustrations accompanying this article show a variety of types that can be found.

Key to Illustrations

1 and 2: Two versions of the iron beetle bootjack. *3:* Of brass, with two movable mandibles which clamp over the instep of the boot as the heel is forced into place.

4: Variously known as "Naughty Nellie" or "Naughty Lady." *5:* Equipped with a stiff brush and handle for removing caked mud and cleaning boots; this piece is marked "Patd. March 3D 68." *6:* As the prongs retract, the fore-legs fold back against the body making this a very compact portable bootjack.

7: A small, lightweight iron bootjack. *8:* One like this is shown in the Bennington Historical Museum; like most iron bootjacks, it is late 19th century. *9:* A realistic pistol when closed, and a bootjack when open. *10:* Another lightweight folding piece.

11: Of cast iron and wire, this bootjack was designed for someone who could not bend or stoop. The long wire handle can be operated from a standing position, and a wire clamp holds the heel firmly in place while the boot is being removed. *12:* The loop in this oak bootjack was designed to hold down the instep of the boot as the foot was withdrawn.

13: An ingenious combination of wood and iron. As pressure is applied by the free foot, the metal prongs close tightly about the heel of the boot. *14 and 15:* Neatly made hardwood bootjacks.

16: Bootjack carved from one piece of oak. *17 and 18:* Two folding bootjacks made of walnut.

19: The opening for the heel is bound with leather to prevent scuffing the boot; a strip of rubber provides a firm grip for the free foot. *20:* A large, heavy cast iron bootjack.

21 and 22: Differ only in the design around the heel opening. *23:* A fairly common entwined scroll pattern, cast iron.

24 and 25: Variations on the same design. *26:* The fishtail design is somewhat refined in this example.

27, 28 and 29: Cast iron bootjacks marked "Downs & Co.," "Try Me," and "J. G. Scott."

30: Cast iron bootjack with shoe design in center. *31:* Two boots form the heel-grip for this cast iron bootjack. The initials "G. R." are impressed on the back. *32:* A decorative, but sturdy cast iron bootjack.

33: A rather crudely cast iron bootjack. *34:* A simple design in a cast iron bootjack. *35:* Cast iron in a plain vertical design.

36: Designed for use as a wrench or a bootjack. *37, 38, 39 and 40:* Heavy cast iron bootjacks. *41:* Cast iron with a pleasing heart design.

42: Very early cast iron bootjack with heart motifs. *43 and 44:* Two different forms with similar designs.

45 and 46: Similar forms, but different designs. *47:* An elaborate heart design.

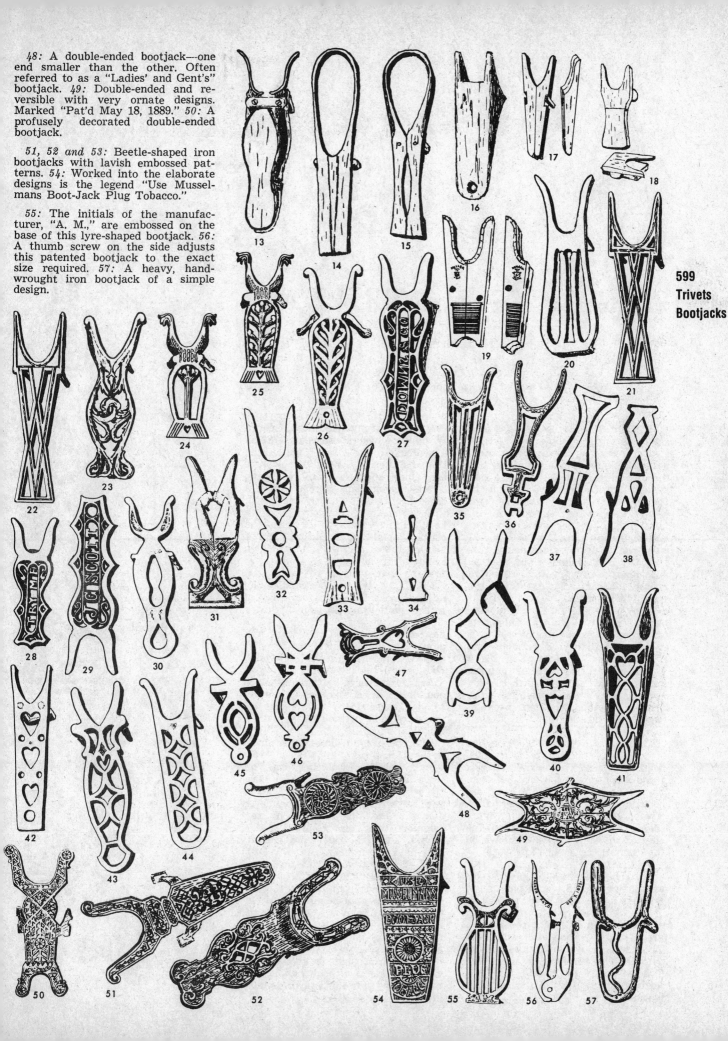

48: A double-ended bootjack—one end smaller than the other. Often referred to as a "Ladies' and Gent's" bootjack. *49:* Double-ended and reversible with very ornate designs. Marked "Pat'd May 18, 1889." *50:* A profusely decorated double-ended bootjack.

51, 52 and 53: Beetle-shaped iron bootjacks with lavish embossed patterns. *54:* Worked into the elaborate designs is the legend "Use Mussel-mans Boot-Jack Plug Tobacco."

55: The initials of the manufacturer, "A. M.," are embossed on the base of this lyre-shaped bootjack. *56:* A thumb screw on the side adjusts this patented bootjack to the exact size required. *57:* A heavy, hand-wrought iron bootjack of a simple design.

599
Trivets
Bootjacks

Fig. 2

Fig. 1

Fig. 3

Fig. 4

Fig. 5

Birds and Animals in TRIVETS

by WILLIAM PALEY

*Sketches by the author from trivets in his collection.
His "Trivets in Heart Design" appeared in SW, May '66.*

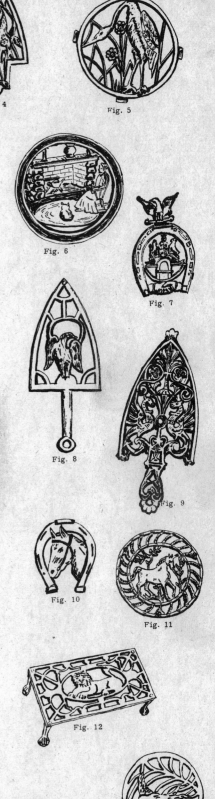

Fig. 6

Fig. 7

Fig. 8

Fig. 9

Fig. 10

Fig. 11

Fig. 12

Fig. 13

Fig. 14

SYMBOLISM, the use of signs representing something entirely different from the object shown, was, perhaps, more common among our forefathers than it is today. In our present age, however, we continue to use chemical symbols—one or two letters to represent an element. Ag, for example, denotes silver, the symbol originating from the Latin *argentum.* Our drugstores frequently display the mortar and pestle, just as such signs were used in the past to enable illiterate people to find the wares they sought.

Many objects in art were symbolic; others were used simply as elements of design. In the making of trivets, it is probable that both symbolic and representational designs were used.

Trivets featuring birds and animals are relatively scarce. Their making required greater skill than geometric designs. Whether they are representational or symbolic, they add interest to any trivet collection.

The dog, a descendant of the fox, is sometimes difficult to distinguish from the latter. The animals in *Figs. 1* and *2* are simply outlines, cut from brass. The initials "L O" of *Fig. 2* are probably those of the maker. Both trivets are of English origin. Very slight bas-relief modeling, consisting only of rounding edges, is shown on the cast iron trivet of *Fig. 3.*

The cast iron trivets of *Figs. 4, 5,* and *6* each present a complete scene, and show the full use of bas or low relief as it was used in the latter half of the 19th century when the casting of iron became an art requiring a great deal of knowledge and skill. The flowers and marsh grass in *Figs. 4* and *5* add strength to the trivet. The cat before the hearth, in *Fig. 6,* lends a homey touch of serenity and warmth.

The eagle, a favorite bird of George Washington, was approved in 1782 as a symbol on the Great Seal of the United States. A symbol of power, it has since adorned many artifacts, trivets among them. Perched above a horseshoe, it is frequently cast along with various other emblems and symbols. *Fig. 7* shows it so, with the clasped hands of friendship and a fraternal crest. In *Fig. 8,* it dominates a beautiful heavy cast iron trivet from the early 1850s.

Fig. 9, a trivet of Scandinavian origin, is of nickel-steel, an alloy of nickel and iron, probably with a small amount of chromium, which has greater strength than cast iron alone. The mythological figures portrayed, make a pleasing, although elaborate design.

Fig. 10 shows a wall plaque which could be inverted and used as a trivet for hot dishes. Many trivets like this one were made without legs, just for this dual purpose.

The horse, symbolic of faithfulness appears again in *Fig. 11,* a brass winter with legs 3¾ inches long. This piece was made in England, as were the winters in *Figs. 12* and *13,* to be used either as kettle stands or as stools before the hearth. The rectangular ones are about 6 × 10¼ inches, and are bent from weights they have had to bear.

Of all the trivets with birds and animals, the turtle, *Fig. 14,* is the only one which comprises the entire trivet rather than being just an element of its design. Its feet form the legs of the stand; its head is the handle. This pattern was made in several sizes, in brass as well as in iron. One iron turtle in the author's collection has a wooden handle, less realistic, but more practical for holding.